Exploring the World of Business

Exploring the World of Business

Kenneth Blanchard

Blanchard Training and Development

Charles Schewe

University of Massachusetts, Amherst

Robert Nelson

Blanchard Training and Development

Alexander Hiam

University of Massachusetts, Amherst

WORTH PUBLISHERS

Manufactured in the United States of America

Library of Congress Catalog Card Number: 95-61214

ISBN: 1-57259-070-X

Printing: 5 4 3 2 1

Year: 99 98 97 96

Editorial Development: Barbara Brooks

Design: Malcolm Grear Designers

Art Director: George Touloumes

Project Editor: Timothy Prairie

Production Supervisor: Barbara Anne Seixas

Layout: Heriberto Lugo

Picture Editor: June Lundborg Whitworth

Line Art: Demetrios Zangos

Composition and Separations: TSI Graphics, Inc.

Printing and Binding: Von Hoffmann Press, Inc.

Cover Illustration: Mick Wiggins

Illustration credits begin on page IC-1 and constitute a continuation of the copyright page.

WORTH PUBLISHERS

33 IRVING PLACE

NEW YORK, NY 10003

Value Packs

Blanchard et al: **Exploring the World of Business** with Babson/Brunton: Study Guide for **Exploring the World of Business**	1-57259-204-4
Blanchard et al: **Exploring the World of Business** with **Career Navigator** (Windows)	1-57259-205-2

Our Mission

Our mission in writing *Exploring the World of Business* was:

- *to provide you with a foundation in the vocabulary, concepts, and principles that guide successful businesses;*

- *to develop your critical thinking skills and improve your study skills;*

- *to assist you in choosing your major and charting your future career path;*

- *and to help you succeed in this course, in future business courses, and throughout a challenging career.*

We hope our text will engage your mind and inspire you to join in the reinvention of business now taking place.

About the Authors

Ken Blanchard

Few people have had as much influence on the world of business as Ken Blanchard with his long career as an author, management consultant, teacher, and public speaker. Ken's impact as a writer in the field of management has been especially far-reaching. *The One Minute Manager* (1982), the best-selling business book of all time, has sold over nine million copies and been translated into more than 25 languages. *Management of Organizational Behavior*, the textbook Ken co-wrote with Dr. Paul Hersey, has become a classic and is now in its sixth edition. Throughout 1995, the *Business Week* best-seller list included two of Ken's most recent books—*Raving Fans: Satisfied Customers Just Aren't Good Enough* (1992) and *Everyone's A Coach* (1995), co-written with Don Shula—nestled next to the still-influential *One Minute Manager*.

Blanchard Training and Development, Inc., a full-service management consulting and training company whose clients include some of America's most well-respected educational institutions and Fortune 500 firms, was founded in 1979. As chairman of Blanchard Training, Ken promotes his tenet that "there is no leadership style—it all depends on the situation." He has used his prominence as a speaker to make accessible a long line of leadership concepts—including situational leadership and employee empowerment—to managers around the world. Situational Leadership® II has been one of the most widely and internationally used leadership models of the last 25 years. Ken has received many awards for his business and speaking acumen, including, most recently, the 1991 Council of Peers Award of Excellence from the National Speaker's Association and the 1992 Golden Gavel Award, presented by Toastmasters International.

Ken Blanchard spent eleven years as a professor of management at Ohio University and the University of Massachusetts. He has a Ph.D. in educational administration and leadership from Cornell University, an M.A. in sociology from Colgate University, and a B.A. in government and philosophy from Cornell University. Ken is a member of the Board of Trustees at Cornell University.

Charles Schewe

Currently a professor of marketing at the University of Massachusetts at Amherst, Charles Schewe is no stranger to academic life. In the past 30 years, he has also taught at Roosevelt University, the University of Illinois–Chicago, Loyola University, and Lansing Community College, introducing over 10,000 students to the basic principles of marketing. Twice he's been presented the Distinguished Teaching Award from the School of Management at the University of Massachusetts. He has also published over 50 articles about his research in periodicals such as the *Journal of Marketing, Journal of Marketing Research, Business Horizons, Journal of Consumer Marketing*, and *American Demographics*. His most recent book is *The Portable MBA in Marketing* (1992), which he co-wrote with Alex Hiam.

Outside of the classroom, Charlie is a highly sought-after principal of LifeStage Matrix Marketing, a California research and consulting firm. He has spent the last 15 years studying the marketing management implications of our aging population, using the results of his research to advise companies on how to target the over-50 population. Among his clients are such well-known names as Spalding Sports Worldwide, IBM, RJR Nabisco, Kraft General Foods, Procter & Gamble, and Sara Lee.

Charlie received his Ph.D. in marketing from The Kellogg Graduate School of Management at Northwestern University. His undergraduate work and MBA were done at the University of Michigan. In 1979, he was a Fulbright-Hays Scholar at the University of Lund, in Sweden, where he frequently teaches and conducts research.

Robert Nelson

A prolific author in the field of management, Robert Nelson's publications include *1001 Ways to Reward Employees*, recently listed as the number two best-selling business paperback in the country by *Business Week* magazine; *Empowering Employees Through Delegation*, named one of the 30 best business books of 1994 by Soundview Executive Summaries; and *We Have to Start Meeting Like This: A Guide To Successful Business Meeting Management*, which *Fortune* magazine called one of the best books on the topic. Bob also writes a monthly column for and is a contributing editor of *Potentials in Marketing* magazine.

As a vice president of Blanchard Training and Development Inc., a leading management training and consulting company, Bob Nelson serves in the strategic planning group and manages product development, customized products assessments, and publications for the company. Previously, Bob was a management trainer for Control Data Corporation and Norwest Banks.

Bob is a Ph.D. candidate in the Executive Management program of The Peter F. Drucker Management Center at the Claremont Graduate School in Los Angeles. His concentration is in organizational design and development. He also holds a masters degree in business administration from the University of California at Berkeley with an emphasis in organizational behavior. Bob has taught introductory business courses at San Diego Mesa College, in San Diego, California, Lakewood Community College in Minnesota, and at the University of California at San Diego.

Alexander Hiam

Alexander Hiam currently heads a research and consulting firm specializing in strategy and organizational change with an emphasis on new management practices. He has helped institutions ranging from very large corporations and not-for-profits to small start-ups in the fast-paced fields of computer technology, transportation, and biotechnology.

Alex has parlayed his knowledge of the business world into twelve popular books on the art and practice of management, covering such topics as quality, marketing, negotiation, entrepreneurship, CEO decision-making, and even alternative careers for college students. He wrote two books in the popular Vest-Pocket series—*The Vest-Pocket CEO* (1990) and *The Vest-Pocket Marketer* (1991)—and co-authored the best-selling text, *The Portable MBA in Marketing* (1992). His *Closing the Quality Gap: Lessons from America's Leading Companies* (1992) was a ground-breaking study identifying the key elements of successful Total Quality Management programs at companies like 3M, Ford, Xerox, IBM, Corning, and Motorola. Alex is currently at work on a book exploring change management, a new field that studies the creation and management of major transitions in a business.

Alex is on the faculty of the marketing department at the University of Massachusetts at Amherst, and has previously taught in undergraduate and graduate business programs at Western New England College and American International College. He received his M.B.A. from the University of California at Berkeley, and his B.A. from Harvard University.

Contents in Brief

Contents

2 Launching the Business   135

3 Managing the Business 225

4 Empowering the Employee 319

Preface

Change is the only constant in business. Change, in and of itself, does not alter the essential content of this first course in business. We believe that the essence of success in business lies in developing vision and values—and embodying them in planning, managing, and decision making. Our textbook reflects this belief by presenting the best mix of traditional approaches and emerging practices. We are determined to avoid faddish trends that soon will disappear, but we embrace reliable, newer ideas that grew out of needs that traditional practices did not satisfy.

Our book is grounded in solid business principles. We designed it and its supporting materials to approach business the way you teach it. We are professors as well as practitioners: we teach students how business really works because we work in business every day.

A student's first course in business must provide a solid foundation for future course work. This task—to spark interest and involvement while developing a solid base of knowledge—requires an easy-to-use teaching tool that lays a solid conceptual foundation. Since these students soon will be at work in business, they need skills: how to find a job, work on a quality improvement team, or cope with downsizing. Indeed, since students can now expect to change careers at least four times over the course of their working lives, it's apparent that self-management and lifelong learning are keys to success. Throughout the text, as well as in the Careers Appendix, we emphasize to students the advantages of developing the skills and attitudes that will enable them to compete and succeed in a business world of constant change.

We respond to the experience of this generation of students, one for whom information and communication technologies are a given. Today's students are pragmatic when it comes to their education. Our aim is to interest and involve them all, regardless of background or gender or age. They will see themselves represented in these pages—in the examples, exercises, and illustrations.

Since we began work on this book, instructors around the country have kept reminding us:

- TO SUPPORT their goals and those of their students by presenting an involving, real-world introduction to the business process, its functions, its environment, and its concepts and vocabulary.

- TO DEVELOP students' knowledge-worker skills—in teamwork, communication, and tolerance; in problem-solving, decision-making, critical thinking, and technology—to enable them to advance in a turbulent business world, where self-management and lifelong learning are keys to success.

- TO EXPLAIN the vital roles of vision, values, and entrepreneurial capitalism in the continuing growth of the American economy and the emerging global economy.

In essence, this is our approach. As you review the sections following, which first detail this book's themes, organization, and coverage, and then its pedagogy and supporting materials; and as you review the text itself, judge for yourself whether we have achieved our mission. And because continuous improvement is the heartbeat of every business process and product, your reaction to our efforts and your suggestions for improvement are both critical and welcome. You can contact us at Worth Publishers, 33 Irving Place, New York, New York 10003; or e-mail us at econsci@worthpub.com.

Presenting the New Basics for the New Century

Our vision lies in presenting the best mix of traditional approaches and newer perspectives—to show students how businesspeople everywhere are living the practices that instructors teach in their classrooms. To survive and thrive in a changing environment that's been characterized as "permanent white water," businesses are adopting strategies that make their processes

- Quick to respond to opportunities and threats
- Flexible in organization
- Customer focused
- Continuously improving

Transforming internal business processes requires a company to rethink its operations and to focus change on five basic values:

- Employee involvement
- Competitiveness
- Customer satisfaction
- Quality
- Productivity

Introducing Students to Successful Businesses and Their Stories

Chapter by chapter, part by part, *Exploring the World of Business* introduces what's new and what's working at America's best companies. We share with students the insights we've gained from our teaching, our interactions with more than 200 companies each year, and our research on competitive businesses worldwide. Among them:

- Xerox Corporation
- Ford Motor Corporation
- IBM
- AT&T
- Bell Atlantic
- General Electric
- Fel-Pro
- Harley-Davidson
- St. Louis Bread Co.
- Union Carbide
- The Body Shop
- VeriFone
- Netscape
- Microsoft
- The Ritz Carlton
- Nike
- General Motors Saturn
- ICI Pharmaceuticals
- Seattle City Lights
- Honda Motor Corporation
- FedEx
- Semco S.A.
- Milliken
- Motorola
- Stride Rite
- Coopers & Lybrand
- Merrill Lynch
- Boston Market

Global Business Permeates the Book

Like information technology, globalization is transforming business. Our coverage begins in Chapter 1, since globalization is integral to the changing environment of business and business processes. It continues in Chapter 2, particularly in the sections on Economic Choices and Economic Exchanges. Global Business is the focus of Chapter 3, and Chapter 4 explores globalization within the context of Ethics, Law, and Government.

Each succeeding chapter expands and integrates these global themes. For example, students learn about the opportunities that global business offers to entrepreneurs and to companies of every form and size in Part 2. They see the effects of globalization on organizational structure and production processes in Part 3. In Part 4 globalization forms a backdrop for discussions of workplace diversity and unionization. Part 5 assumes a completely global environment in its coverage of marketing. Part 6 drives home the concept of global, real-time information networks. Part 7 explains how businesses react to the opportunities and threats posed by a global financial marketplace.

Helping Students Develop Their Knowledge-Worker Skills

To survive and thrive in a world where the only constant is change, it's good business to start with a plan. Our focus throughout, beginning with Chapter 1, is to help students recognize the value of taking personal responsibility. In the short term this means planning their study time and course work, and developing their budding business skills. In the long run it means planning for career self-management and lifelong learning to continually improve their performance as businesspeople. The text's examples, illustrations, and learning aids support students in three ways. First, the text's pedagogy motivates students to learn by involving them in the narrative. Second, it reinforces the content by providing learning aids that support their efforts. Third, it teaches by asking students to think critically and apply what they have learned.

Motivating Students

One Minute Manager vignettes profile real companies in the context of a dialog among two students and their mentor. Appearing at the start of each chapter, the conversational style of these discussions invites students to read on and learn more.

Doing Business boxes in each chapter explain how real businesses are applying key principles and practices introduced in the chapter.

Ethics Check boxes, beginning in Chapter 2, showcase ethical issues that businesses face and ask students to evaluate the situation and the response of the company or industry. Students are exposed to the range of ethical issues businesses regularly face.

Clear, simple *illustrations* and relevant *photographs* both reinforce and extend the concepts and examples presented in the text.

Reinforcing That Helps Students Learn to Learn

To focus on and check their progress, the *Learning Goals* that open each chapter direct students' attention to the key concepts they must master. To direct reading and provide further reinforcement, each goal appears in the text margin adjacent to key presentations. Finally, the goals form the foundation of the end-of-chapter *Reviewing* summary, grouped by the chapter's main headings, to help students organize their study.

The *Reviewing* section continues with a listing of *Key Terms*, referenced by text page number. Key-term definitions appear in the text margins where the terms are first used. Definitions reflect current usage in business, and each is clear, concise, and consistent with the text's presentation. Of course, we've included a complete alphabetical *Glossary* of key terms and their definitions at the back of the book.

To reinforce basic text principles and demonstrate students' understanding in their own words, we provide a set of *Review Questions* that cover basic concepts presented in each chapter in stepwise fashion.

To demonstrate a broader understanding of basic chapter principles, we include a *Review Case* with questions that ask students to identify how those concepts relate to a real company or industry.

Thinking Critically About and Applying the Content

The real test of knowledge is whether the student can use it to solve new problems and think through new issues. We encourage this necessary aspect of the modern workplace, both within the text and in four distinct learning aids designed to encourage critical thinking:

- Career-oriented *Skills Check* boxes, located throughout the text, encourage students to solve business problems, engage in business and career planning, and think critically about business and career issues.
- *Critical Thinking Questions* require students to apply the concepts they are currently studying and to integrate those concepts into their existing base of business knowledge.
- *Critical Thinking Cases* apply the same integrative rationale in the context of a particular company and/or industry.
- *Critical Thinking with the One Minute Manager*, at the end of each chapter, revisits the opening One Minute Manager vignette and wraps up the real business example that introduced the chapter.

Emerging Strategies and Techniques Are Integrated Throughout

PART 1: The Business World

The four chapters in Part 1 ground students in the basics—what business is and what business does. Part 1 also establishes the context of business, the external environment, from the economics of free markets to global competition to business ethics and business law. Throughout, we emphasize how businesses successfully—and unsuccessfully—respond to change, including topics such as:

- Customer focus and global competition
- The learning cycle, learning organizations, and process improvement innovations

- Benchmarking, business process reengineering, and downsizing
- Employee empowerment, teaming, and the link between knowledge work and productivity
- The advantages gained from developing transferable, all-purpose job skills in critical thinking and problem solving
- Partnering, including public service partnerships
- Trading blocs, including NAFTA, the EU, APEC, and GATT, and newly industrializing countries (NICs)
- Strategic alliances
- Ethical management, ethics statements, and the principle of doing business in good faith
- Workplace diversity

PART 2: Launching the Business

The three chapters in Part 2 explain how an organization's legal form flows from its vision and mission, and how that form may change. Students learn the role of entrepreneurship as an engine of economic growth in market economies worldwide, what it takes to be an entrepreneur, and whether entrepreneurship suits them. Finally, they learn how "fast and flexible" small businesses furnish jobs and growth to the U.S. economy, contribute economic well-being to their communities, and provide U.S. workers with the widest range of career opportunities. Terms and topics include:

- Limited liability corporations
- Skunk works
- Gazelles
- Business networks
- Networking to build business contacts
- Kitchen capital, sweat equity, business incubators, and multiple franchising

PART 3: Managing the Business

No matter what they produce or how they market their products, all businesses share a core of five functions: management, employee development, marketing, control systems, and finance. The interactions among these functions dictate every business process. The chapters in Part 3 describe how forces such as increasing competition, globalization, and emerging technologies and innovations prompt business management to move from commanding and controlling employees to coaching them and collaborating with them in support of the company's vision and mission. To make their internal organizations fast and flexible, businesses are turning to decentralized, flat designs. Flat organizations mean fewer layers of management, more teams of empowered employees, and wider delegation of decision-making. To describe how managers are embracing change, topics of special interest include:

- Mission statements and learning organizations
- Delegation, empowerment, and team-based management
- Situational leadership and management by walking around
- The high-involvement workplace and teaming: self-directed, cross-functional, project, and process improvement teams
- Open-book management
- Inverted hierarchies and refocusing from business functions to business processes
- Downsizing, outsourcing, and virtual companies
- Push versus pull processes and just-in-time systems
- Reengineering, total quality management, process improvement, and brainstorming
- Cycle times, cost of quality, and root cost analysis

PART 4: Empowering the Employee

In order to flourish as the U.S. workplace and work force change, businesses seek capable people, invest in training, and develop benefit and compensation programs that respond to employees' needs and motivations. Employing part-time, temporary, and independent contract workers is a major human resource strategy right now. Finally, as union membership in traditional industries continues to shrink, unions are expanding into "new collar" workplaces, and turning from confrontation to cooperation with management. Special-interest terms and topics include:

- Task clarity and SMART goals
- Small group incentives
- The contingent work force, from outsourcing to employee leasing
- Diversity training
- Mentoring and networking
- Flexibility in compensation, scheduling, and benefits
- Management rights clauses

PART 5: Pleasing the Customer

The business markets to its shareholders and suppliers, its creditors and its employees, as well as to the ultimate consumer. Marketing focuses the business on customer satisfaction by developing quality products, pricing them for value, placing them for convenience, promoting them energetically, and providing extraordinary customer service. While integrated marketing communications ensure that the business speaks to all its customers with one voice, interactive technologies empower consumers to control the company's message as never before. Topics at the heart of marketing today include:

- Environmental scanning and globalization
- Relationship marketing, customer service, and customer satisfaction
- Internal and external customers
- Targeting, segmentation, and repositioning strategies
- Demarketing
- Product improvement strategies
- The AIDA model
- Unsought products
- Dual distribution
- Reverse distribution channels
- Everyday low prices
- Interactive media, infomercials, and at-home shopping

PART 6: Controlling the Business

The competitive business uses information as a tool to improve the speed and quality of its decision making. Decentralized, networked businesses foster information sharing and a faster, more flexible decision-making process. For example, no longer does accounting deal solely with past performance. Rather, accounting and financial controls focus management, marketing, and finance on cutting costs and expenses, managing inventory, and increasing the company's profitability. Among the terms and topics to watch for are:

- Cyberspace: the information superhighway, including the Internet and World Wide Web, on-line services, and web browsers
- Interactive information technology: groupware, wireless communications, personal digital assistants, and television
- Tools for open-book management: activity-based costing, cost drivers, and the cost of quality
- Intellectual property as an intangible asset
- Forensic accounting

PART 7: Financing the Business

Competitive businesses know that profitability improves when management broadens the internal base for financial decision-making and forms partnerships with financial institutions and investors. Deregulation of financial markets and consolidation in the banking industry broaden the range of financing options for the business. Capital markets for debt and equity financing operate as global, electronic, real-time networks. And lastly, planning for disaster is the first step in managing the company's pure risks. Topics of particular relevance in business finance include:

- Undercapitalization, poor cash flow, and inadequate expense control as causes of business failure
- The process of open-book management
- Virtual banking
- Microenterprise lending
- Derivative securities
- The rise of managed health care: HMO, PPO, and POS plans

The Teaching and Learning Package

Our innovative, comprehensive support system builds on the same customer focus as this book. Our overall package detailed below offers quality supplements to maximize students' learning experience; it will help students master core concepts and will encourage them to apply their growing knowledge of business.

EXPLORING THE WORLD OF BUSINESS VIDEO JOURNEY

Featuring Ken Blanchard

Our coauthor Ken Blanchard, who has filmed some of the most successful business videos ever, hosts our *Exploring the World of Business Video Journey*. He introduces each of the seven text parts in four-minute segments. Ken integrates part concepts and illustrates them with vivid stories in his motivational and entertaining style.

This video package incorporates seven hours of videos into 42 segments, all introduced by Ken Blanchard. Most segments are between five and ten minutes in length. Among them are seven outstanding programs by Tom Peters, including on-location profiles of such companies as Harley Davidson, Southwest Airlines, and MCI. In addition, we present *Future Perfect*, by Stan Davis, a renowned futurist who offers a fresh perspective on the future of American business with a revolutionary method of managing. These programs are offered exclusively to users of our text by Video Publishing House, leading producer and distributor of video-based training programs in the video training market.

Other featured companies and programs include:

- NASDAQ
- World Class Quality at Playmobil with Tom Peters
- Making It! Minority Success Story of Panda Express
- Lincoln Electric—Jobs for Life
- Employee Empowerment at AT&T
- Malcolm Baldrige National Quality Award winners: FedEx, GTE, Wainwright Industries, Motorola, and Xerox

We are also offering exclusively to the college market *Inc.* magazine's acclaimed video, *How to Really Start Your Own Business*. This video is divided into ten segments of four to seven minutes each—ideal lengths for teaching.

This flexible video teaching package offers an unprecedented wealth of possibilities for students and teachers alike as you explore the world of business.

VIDEO GUIDE

Robb Bay, Community College of Southern Nevada

This indispensable resource accompanying the *Exploring the World of Business Video Journey* not only gives quick summaries of each video segment, making it easy to select videos to use in class, but also cross-references each segment with the appropriate text chapter, and provides a list of questions to stimulate class discussions.

STUDY GUIDE

Harold C. Babson, Columbus State Community College;
Murray S. Brunton, Central Ohio Technical College

By completing any chapter in the Study Guide, your students will not only know the material in the text chapter, but also understand it and be able to *apply* it to real-life situations. Each section actively engages students and challenges them to learn. From the Chapter Review, which asks students to complete fill-in statements while guiding them step-by-step through the key lessons of the text chapter, to matching and fill-in vocabulary reviews—and even in mini-cases to be analyzed—you will not find one passive section. All sections have been designed to promote learning through active involvement. The chapter sections are:

- Learning Goals
- Chapter Review
- Self-Test: Vocabulary Building, Matching, True/False, and Multiple Choice
- Concept Application
- Mini-Case

This guide offers the *Small Business Venture Program*, a truly innovative and exciting approach to the realities of small business. A series of detailed questions and answers highlight the applicability of text material to modern small business issues. In the Small Business Venture Advanced Exercise, students are taken, step-by-step, through the process of writing a business plan. They begin by developing, in writing, an idea for a marketable product or service. Then they are asked to estimate the amount of start-up capital they would need, research possible sources for that capital, and even plan the logistics of full-scale production and sale. Students will have completed a professional business plan by the end of the course.

INC. MAGAZINE READER

Inc., the preeminent publication for entrepreneurs, addresses the unique needs of growing companies. The magazine is written specifically for people starting and running small and growing businesses. If you use the magazine in your class, you can help your students really understand what running a small business is about. Through an arrangement between *Inc.* and Worth Publishers, you may order from *Inc.* a selection of the top articles of 1995 as a custom book of readings. You will be able to put together your own readings from *Inc.* using as few as 10 articles or as many as 25 from a listing of 300 articles published in 1995. Worth Publishers' representatives will provide you with ordering information and selection options for the *Inc.* 1995 Reader. We plan to continue this arrangement as an "annual edition" in future years. Information on an educational discount subscription program will also be made available.

CAREER NAVIGATOR SOFTWARE

For a limited time only, the brand-new, 1996 student edition of *Career Navigator* (Drake Beam Morin, Inc.), the best-selling career software for over ten years, is being made available to adopters of *Exploring the World of Business*. This computer program, available for Windows, guides students through exploring their interests, aptitudes, and accomplishments as they select a career path. It also shows them how to structure and write a resumé and cover letter; how to prepare for an interview, with advice on how best to answer questions they may be asked; and how to follow-up by writing a thank you letter. *Career Navigator* provides students with an invaluable tool for finding a job.

INC. BUSINESS SOFTWARE PACKAGE

Also available is the *How to Really Start Your Own Business* software package from *Inc.* Business Resources. The package consists of software for Windows, a CD-ROM, and a special, tie-in video.

LECTURE PRESENTATION SOFTWARE

The Lecture Presentation Software is a great resource for utilizing multimedia in classroom demonstrations. It provides instructors with electronic lecture outlines keyed to figures from the textbook as well as additional charts and diagrams prepared especially for this package. Created in PowerPoint, it integrates text coverage with salient information from other teaching ancillaries.

STOCK MARKET PROJECT

Kathryn W. Hegar, Mountain View College

Upon completion of this project, students will be able to describe the information in a stock quotation listing, buy and sell stocks from any major stock market exchange through a stockbroker, explain stockbroker commissions, and use financial resources to research companies for potential investment purposes. The immediate goal: get a return on a $20,000 investment in any company on the New York Stock Exchange or on the NASDAQ exchange. This game is designed to run a maximum of ten weeks.

INSTRUCTOR'S RESOURCE MANUAL

Candida A. Johnson, Holyoke Community College; Coleen C. Pantalone, Northeastern University; Joseph C. Santora, Essex County College; and Harold C. Babson, Columbus State Community College

This invaluable resource is easy to use and comprehensive in its coverage. Insightful examples, engaging class exercises, and overhead transparencies have all been integrated with complete coverage of the text material to help you enhance your class lectures. The sections have been designed to facilitate lecture preparation and introduce new approaches to teaching the material. Each chapter includes the following sections:

- Chapter Overview
- Student Learning Goals
- Lecture Outline, including boxed examples with citations, overhead transparency cross references, teaching suggestions and questions, and class discussion exercises
- Class Discussion Guide with handouts
- Answers to End-of-Chapter Questions and Cases
- Suggestions for Guest Speakers
- Review Sheet to be distributed to guide students' studying
- Additional Case: a full-length supplementary case drawn from an article in a magazine such as *Inc.* or *Fortune*, with discussion questions
- Transparency masters of text art not in acetates

The Lecture Outline details each chapter while adding many *brand new* examples (with complete citations), teaching questions, and references to charts and diagrams (in the form of overhead transparencies or transparency masters) to share with students. The Outline also includes a choice of Class Exercises to deepen comprehension of text material and involve students in class discussion. Each exercise is accompanied by a hand-out and answer sheet which can be distributed in class, as homework, or even as part of an exam.

TEST BANK

Robert Cox, Salt Lake Community College; Patricia Setlik, William Rainey Harper College; Bruce Handley, Weber State University; and Andy C. Saucedo, Doña Ana Branch Community College.

The Test Bank contains more than 2500 carefully crafted, clearly written questions. It is designed to measure students' comprehension of basic business concepts as well as their ability to apply those concepts to real-world situations. The Test Bank's coverage of the text is accurate, fair, and thorough; every key term and learning goal is addressed.

Each chapter includes 60 to 80 multiple-choice, 20 to 30 true/false, 12 to 15 fill-in-the-blank, and 5 to 6 short-answer questions. Five or more of the multiple-choice questions are based on a hypothetical case that illustrates the concepts presented in the chapter. There is at least one case per chapter. Together with each question, the Test Bank provides the text page number where the answer can be found, an objective keyed to the appropriate learning goal in the text, and the answer to the question. Both the multiple-choice and true/false questions are classified by question type: factual/definitional or conceptual. Factual/definitional questions test students' knowledge of the text material, while conceptual questions test students' ability to apply what they have learned. The multiple-choice questions are also rated for difficulty (easy, medium, or difficult).

COMPUTERIZED TEST BANK

The printed Test Bank forms the database for test-generation software available for use on Windows, IBM, and Macintosh computer systems. Instructors can edit test questions, add new questions, scramble questions, and create multiple versions of the same test.

OVERHEAD TRANSPARENCIES

Approximately 200 full-color overhead transparency acetates which are all referenced in the Lecture Outline in the Instructor's Resource Manual. Each overhead visually illustrates a key concept in the outline. Some important figures from the text are included as acetates, but most are new figures not found in the text. All text figures not used as acetates are available in the Instructor's Resource Manual as transparency masters.

Acknowledgments

We are grateful to the following colleagues who reviewed all or part of our manuscript. In the first edition you must be specially responsive and we have endeavored to listen very carefully to this group of fine business educators who labored long and hard in their reading of the many manuscript drafts. Their sharing of classroom experiences and teaching examples has contributed greatly to the user-friendliness of this text. We would especially like to single out Robb Bay, Michael Cicero, Bill Small, and Michael Padbury, who went far beyond any of our expectations to point out the realities of their classrooms to us.

The insights of all our reviewers are reflected in this completed textbook.

Hal Babson, Columbus State Community College

Robb Bay, Community College of Southern Nevada

Barbara Boyington, Brookdale Community College

Murray Brunton, Central Ohio Technical College

Bruce Charnov, Hofstra University

Michael Cicero, Highline Community College

Robert Cox, Salt Lake Community College

John Foster, Montgomery College

Chaim Ginsberg, Manhattan Community College

Donald Gordon, Illinois Central College

Robert Grau, Cuyahoga Community College

Sanford Helman, Middlesex Community College

Nathan Himelstein, Essex County College

Candida Johnson, Holyoke Community College

George Katz, St. Philips College

Roger Kaufman, Smith College

James McKenzie, Tarrant County Junior College, Northeast
Erica Michaels

Richard Morrison, Doña Ana Community College

Michael Padbury, Arapahoe Community College

Dennis Pappas, Columbus State Community College

Ginger Parker, Miami Dade Community College

Anne Potter, Holyoke Community College

Richard Randall, Nassau Community College

Richard Randolph, Johnson County Community College

Patricia Setlik, William Rainey Harper College

William Small, Spokane Community College

Darrell Thompson, Mountain View College

Judy Woo, Bellevue Community College

Larry Ziegler, University of Texas, Arlington

We would like to thank the following focus group participants who shared with us many ideas on pedagogy and on improving the introduction to business course. They also offered their perspectives on the use of videos in the classroom; many of our ideas crystallized from those discussions. In addition, we did a market research survey with over 100 respondents. Both forms of market research helped us shape the book you are now holding.

Abraham Axelrod, Queensborough Community College

Bruce Charnov, Hofstra University

Thomas Cox, Passaic County Community College

Nicholas Dietz, State University of New York at Farmingdale

Robert Fishco, Middlesex County College

Nathan Himelstein, Essex County College

Jannette Knowles, Long Island University

George Kroecker, Suffolk County Community College

Donald Mellon, Bergen Community College

James Meszaros, County College of Morris

Philip Nufrio, Essex County College

Harold Perl, County College of Morris

Richard Randall, Nassau Community College

Jack Riley, State University of New York at Farmingdale

Ben Wieder, Queensborough County College

We appreciate the detailed work of our reviewers who have shaped and strengthened the coverage of finance and economics in our textbook. These areas require the expertise of productive researchers and experienced, capable educators, especially in the fast-changing financial and economic environment of business. We would like to thank the following experts:

Bruce Charnov, Hofstra University

Harry Chevan, Cowles Business Media

Andrew John, University of Virginia

Roger Kaufman, Smith College

Jeff Madura, Florida Atlantic University

Walter Reinhart, Loyola University (Maryland)

Larry Ziegler, University of Texas, Arlington

We would also like to thank our creative, hard-working supplements authors who have prepared a marvelous array of business teaching resources from their considerable classroom experience. Some of the most caring, experienced, and resourceful business educators of the introduction to business course have contributed their teaching ideas to this instructional package. We are deeply in debt to them for providing their materials for us to share with instructors everywhere.

This book would not have been made possible without the efforts of many individuals beyond the authors. Foremost is Bob Worth, who, along with Tom Gay, had the foresight to see the possibilities, and to Mike Needham who took over the helm at Worth Publishers and followed through with our project. Special editorial assistance at the conceptual stage was ably given by Marjorie Weiser, and we hope she is satisfied with our execution. Our greatest appreciation goes to our editors Paul Shensa and Anne Vinnicombe who together managed to show the necessary patience, to prod us to work harder and longer, and to ensure that the book and all its ancillary materials came into being. We owe them immensely; their commitment to this project was unending.

Barbara Brooks made customer focus a reality in developing the text, its photo program, and the video package. As we labored through many draft chapters, Barbara was aided immensely, first by Nancy Fleming then by Betty Probert, who helped us express our thoughts and concepts with proper precision. Their contribution was immeasurable. Timothy Prairie managed the manuscript, oversaw the development of the figures, and provided countless ideas on how to improve and fine-tune numerous concepts and ideas.

Linda Gal coordinated our supplements package. She worked with the authors to create the innovative pedagogy that appears in the Study Guide, Instructor's Resource Manual, and the Overhead Transparency package. Louise Harris Berlin managed the impressive video package. Maja Lorkovic worked with the test bank authors to create a comprehensive testing program. Toni Ann Scaramuzzo coordinated the production editorial and supplements teams.

Sandy Fernandez, Julie Kerr, and Yuna Lee provided valuable editorial assistance at critical times throughout the process. Photo research was creatively managed by June Lundborg Whitworth who, along with Cindy Joyce, helped extend the important concepts with just the right photo. Our design team of George Touloumes and Demetrios Zangos crafted a beautiful and effective book. The layout and production of each page has provided an open, student-friendly design. Finally, Jonelle Calon, our marketing director, created and developed an innovative marketing campaign.

This book took form through the efforts of many supporters outside Worth Publishers, as well. Charlie and Alex would like to thank Candida Johnson, who provided wise counsel throughout the project. The research that spawned the chapters you read came from our able assistants: Jay Stohl, Hannah Gordon, Heather Miller, Pat Meny, Zhiming Xue, Anita Ash, Colin Danby, and S. Charusheela. We thank them profusely. At Blanchard Training and Development, Ken and Bob would like to thank Dana Kyle, Linda Hulce, David Witt, and Peter Economy for their encouragement and support for this book and for their research assistance.

To all these colleagues and friends, we offer heartfelt thanks.

And to the students who will explore the world of business with us, we hope this book and your course will enlarge your vision about how people and businesses should interact.

Exploring the World of Business

1 Business in a Changing Environment

It is a fascinating time to study and work in business. This chapter helps you understand how business works, how business is changing, and how those changes affect your education and career options. You will meet two students and a manager, whose story introduces and concludes each chapter and explores its key concepts. You will see how each Part of this book focuses on an important function within business. And you will learn the terms and concepts that form the necessary foundation for any study of business that you may undertake in the future. After reading this chapter, you will be able to reach the learning goals below.

Learning Goals

1. State the main objective of business and describe how success is measured.
2. List the six functions of business and describe the integrative nature of the business process.
3. Explain the influence of the natural environment on the conduct of business.
4. Discuss the relationships between the social and political/legal environments.
5. Describe how the technological and competitive environments contribute to changes in business functions.
6. State the relationship between economic and political systems and describe the economic environment created by these systems.
7. Discuss the relationship between changes in the external business environment and the adoption of new business values.
8. Discuss how the strategies of flexibility and management innovation contribute to changes in business functions.
9. Discuss how a focus on people—through the strategies of employee development and customer focus—helps transform business functions.
10. Describe business's financial strategies for improving performance and financing operations.
11. Identify the skills now required for a business career.

On a Roll

Joanna and Carlos were talking in the corridor before class. They had studied together last semester and were happy to discover they were in the same class again.

"Let's go in now," Joanna said. "It's time for class to start."

"I have to wait for my cousin," Carlos explained. "She knows the professor and is going to be a guest speaker today."

"Really? Which business does she work for?"

"She *runs* a business," Carlos boasted. "An electronics firm in the city. It's . . ."

"Look out!" Joanna pulled Carlos to the side as a woman hurtled past them on in-line skates and skidded to a stop. "That woman nearly ran into us!"

Carlos laughed, then called out, "I thought you were going to *meet* me here, not run into me!"

He introduced Joanna to his cousin, explaining that she was known as a One Minute Manager and that she often spoke to groups in the city. The name, she told Joanna, came from the idea that people often need to take a minute to think about how they do their work so they can improve their own performance.

This learning approach, first made famous in a book called *The One Minute Manager*, is especially appropriate today because of the fast rate of change in business and the resulting need for everyone to keep learning and improving their skills.

"But why did you skate here?" Joanna asked.

"I wore these to illustrate the story I'm going to tell your class today, about the company that makes them. Rollerblade, Inc., was founded by a college-age skating enthusiast. Scott Olson was only 20 when he sold his first pair of in-line skates. After five years, his sales reached $100 million a year! And the product is now so successful that dozens of other companies have jumped in with competing brands.

"Olson's success story illustrates what makes the U.S. economy tick," she went on. "Innovation and change, sometimes by people no older than you and your fellow students. Did you know that more than half a million new businesses are started in this country every year? And, of course, big companies are innovating and changing constantly, too. That makes for an incredible number of opportunities for students like you. Well, I guess we'd better go into the classroom. Come on."

"Wait!" Carlos shouted. "Too late. I wanted to warn her that the aisles in this lecture hall slope down toward the front."

The Business and Its Functions

A **business** is any organization that maintains itself by taking in resources and increasing their value for customers. For example, a grocery story purchases thousands of different food items and sells them to customers in convenient locations. An auto manufacturer turns raw materials like steel, rubber, and plastic into a car through a complex series of design and manufacturing processes. A bank handles financial transactions for its customers.

All these businesses provide customers with valuable goods or services in order to make profits for their owners. **Profit** is the difference between a firm's revenues and its costs. Revenues—the money the business takes in—must be greater than expenses over the long run for the business to maintain itself and profit its owners. And for this reason, many businesses measure their success in terms of profits.

However, many organizations exist to achieve a social goal rather than to make a profit. These businesses do not need to profit any owner and are usually referred to as not-for-profit businesses. As long as their income equals their expenses they can continue working toward their goal. Your college is a good example. It exists to educate students, not to make money. The Red Cross is another example. It exists to help civilian victims of war, famine, and natural disasters around the world. Your town's police department and the U.S. Environmental Protection Agency are also business organizations, even though they are part of government. We will learn about all the forms of business in Chapter 5. While many organizations do not work for profit, much of what we will learn about for-profit businesses applies to them as well.

 business

Any organization that maintains itself by taking in resources and increasing their value for customers.

 profit

The difference between a firm's revenues and its costs.

customers

The people or organizations that consume what businesses produce.

---

figure **1.1** **What a Business Does**

Resources
- Raw materials
- Component parts
- Services
- Labor
- Information
- Money

The Business
Value added through work

Products for Customers
- Good
- Service
- Idea

Businesses take in resources and add value to them in order to benefit their customers, as shown in Figure 1.1. **Customers** are the people or organizations that consume what businesses produce. Goya Foods, the largest Hispanic-owned business in the United States, produces canned beans, frozen meat pies, and many other foods for people to buy at grocery stores. If you use one of these products you are a Goya customer, and Goya works continually to perfect recipes its customers will enjoy. But Goya also counts grocery stores as customers, since they buy its products, too. And what grocers want is fast, responsive service, so Goya guarantees next-day delivery of orders to all supermarkets.[1]

1. State the main objective of business and describe how success is measured.

The Functions of Business

To perform its work, a business must engage in a wide range of activities. Employees are hired, materials purchased and transported, information acquired and analyzed. Every business is unique and performs its work for its customers in unique ways. But businesses have many similarities as well, because all must perform six basic functions. These functions are described below, and each one is covered in a Part of this book.

Business Formation

Every business was started by someone, who had to name it and decide upon its structure. And as a business grows, its form must constantly be monitored and updated to reflect needs and opportunities. This function, forming the business, is ongoing because businesses, like people, need to grow and change. A business is like a house that is constantly under construction. New offices may be opened in new countries or old factories at home closed down. At other times, a business will buy or merge with another in order to take on a new, more useful form. Many students will be involved in starting up or growing a business during their careers.

Uno-Dos-Tres, Delicioso

Customer focus and Spanish style are the keys to Goya Foods's growing popularity. Company president Joseph A. Unanue, at left, and his brother Frank, President of Goya de Puerto Rico, have built the company their father started more than 50 years ago into the largest Latino-owned business in the United States, with annual sales approaching $1 billion.

Management

What work should be done, when and how, and by whom? Where should people be located to do their work most efficiently? These sorts of questions are answered daily by managers, the people who supervise other people's work. **Management** means accomplishing organizational goals through people and other resources. Management is therefore responsible for all the other functions and people in the business. In addition, management is responsible for the production processes of a business, such as Toyota's factories, AT&T's telephone services, and Goya's canning plants. **Production** is the transformation of resources into goods or services that customers value. The cost and quality of such processes in large part determine how well the business meets customer needs, how much customers buy, and therefore how much profit the business

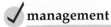 **management**

Accomplishing organizational goals through people and other resources.

 production

The transformation of resources into goods or services that customers value.

makes (or how well it accomplishes its social mission). College students who major in management may work for a business or start their own companies.

Human Resources

People, the company's human resources, are at the heart of every business, whether it's a small home-based business or a huge company operating around the world. Goya Foods employs 1,800 people, which sounds like a lot until you compare it with a *really* big company.[2] AT&T, for example, employs 274,000 people, some of whom work as far away from its New York headquarters as the People's Republic of China.[3] Many businesses have separate human resources or personnel departments that help hire and motivate employees. When you apply for a job, your first contact may be a human resources manager. Specialized courses in human resources will prepare you to work in this field.

Marketing

Marketing is the process of creating, pricing, promoting, and distributing ideas, goods, and services to create exchanges that satisfy the customer and the business. Marketing helps the business find a customer need and fill it. The goals of the marketing function are to please customers by finding out what they want and need, to help the business develop and produce it, to bring it to the attention of customers, and to make it available for purchase. Many students also take marketing courses or major in the subject. Entry-level marketing jobs in sales, advertising, customer research, and other areas of marketing are common first jobs for business graduates.

Control Systems

Many businesses use computerized systems to collect, store, and analyze information about their internal operations and the world beyond their doors. **Controlling** is the process of monitoring and evaluating activities to ensure that objectives are being achieved. Control systems enable managers to make better decisions—to set objectives, establish and implement policies, evaluate employee performance and take action to improve performance, and adjust to the changing business environment. **Accounting** is the process of collecting, summarizing, and reporting financial information for decision making. Students who train to become accountants may work within a business or in specialized accounting firms that service other businesses. Accounting, which tracks the financial life of the organization, is part of a business's larger **information systems**, which collect, process, store, and disseminate information in support of decision making, control, and analysis. Students who become experts in information management enjoy the challenge of actually improving the way the business runs.

Financial Management

Businesses raise money either by borrowing it or by attracting new owners who buy a share of the business. This money is then used to invest in new equipment, hire more employees, or obtain other resources needed to maintain and grow the business. The money businesses raise and earn must be managed day to day. **Financial management** is the function of obtaining funds, managing the day-to-day flow of funds, and committing funds for long-term expenditures. Students who go on to study finance might work in the finance department of a business or in one of the many financial service firms that help businesses and individuals manage their money, such as a bank or insurance firm.

 marketing

The process of creating, pricing, promoting, and distributing ideas, goods, and services to create exchanges that satisfy the customer and the business.

 controlling

The process of monitoring and evaluating activities to ensure that objectives are being achieved.

 accounting

The process of collecting, summarizing, and reporting financial information for decision making.

 information systems

Business systems that collect, process, store, and disseminate information in support of decision making, control, and analysis.

 financial management

The function of obtaining funds, managing the day-to-day flow of funds, and committing funds for long-term expenditures.

The Business Process

You will explore each business function—from formation to finance—in turn as you read this book. To see how the various functions work together, we next take an overview of the entire business process.

Every activity of the business touches on at least one of these six functions, and most work flows back and forth from function to function as different people contribute and different resources are used. Raw materials and information are purchased, transported to the people who need them, made into products, passed on to the people who market the products, and ultimately sold to customers. The revenue from sales flows back to finance the business, where it is used to pay operating expenses and to fund new projects. Profits are invested and saved or paid out to owners. All these activities are monitored and analyzed by control systems.

The main production process of a business is where the goods or services are actually produced. A factory or service center does much of the work needed to transform basic inputs into outputs of value to customers. But many processes are needed to support production, and all are important to the business and its customers. For example, the human resources department of a company manages the process that recruits and hires capable employees to staff the functions of the business. This process provides vital support to the factory where a product is made. The work of hiring new employees to staff a factory starts with the human resources department. Once the employees are hired, factory managers supervise their work. Two separate functions, human resources and management, thus participate in this process.

The process of developing and marketing a new product is more complex. It may start with a new product idea in the marketing department, then get passed to the control function for research into the idea's feasibility. Production managers evaluate the design and suggest ways to make it cheaper and easier to produce. The finance function gets involved in finding funding for developing the new product. Once management approval and funding are secured, the new product is finally developed and produced for customers.

The business process gives employees and managers many opportunities for improvement. Any time a step can be removed or the people from two functions can combine a step by collaborating, the business process runs a little faster and a little smoother. As Figure 1.2 illustrates, the business process crosses all business functions, touching each of them in the effort to satisfy customers and earn profits for the business. This integrated *process view* of the business is a helpful alternative to the independent *functional view*. Both views are essential to your understanding of business. Throughout this book you will explore the business process and the many ways businesses are working to improve it.

figure **1.2**
The Business Process

Resources

↓

Functions of the business process
- Formation
- Management
- Human resources
- Marketing
- Control
- Finance

↓

Products for customers

The Changing Business Environment

Everything outside a business has the power to influence it. The external business environment has six components: the natural environment, the social environment, the political/legal environment, the technological environment, the competitive environment, and the economic environment. Part 1 of this book describes the components of the business environment and explains how businesses operate within it.

The Natural Environment

Businesses use natural resources. Energy is used to power equipment, iron ore is made into the steel chassis of cars, trees are made into the paper that books are printed on. A grocery store depends on the waterfall, uranium, or coal used to generate the electricity that runs its coolers, freezers, lights, air conditioning, and cash registers—not to mention the rain, sun, and soil needed to grow the vegetables and fruit with which the grocery store's coolers are stocked. Businesses also use the natural environment in less obvious ways. They use up space in landfills when customers throw away the packaging of their products or discard products that no long work or are no longer needed. They use up the capacity of air, soil, and water to absorb contaminants when their wastes enter the environment. They affect the natural environment when they build new factories or offices, sometimes unknowingly destroying the habitats of plants and animals. Many natural resources are scarce and many others are nonrenewable, meaning they will eventually be used up.

Businesses have traditionally treated the preservation of the natural environment passively, as a secondary concern. All they had to do was comply with environmental regulations and avoid any major catastrophes that would make bad headlines. Today, businesses are taking an active approach to helping to preserve the natural environment, part of a trend toward social responsibility that we will explore in Chapter 4.

One example is the waste exchanges that businesses have formed in many parts of the United States and Canada. Waste exchanges turn one company's garbage into another company's resource. For instance, the paper one company throws away can often be recycled to make packing materials by another. Groups like the Canadian Waste Materials Exchange, the Hawaii Waste Exchange, and the Indiana Waste Exchange now recycle 6 million tons of refuse for businesses yearly. This is a sign that business is taking responsibility for its impact on the natural environment, but it is only a first step. So far, waste exchanges handle less than 10 percent of the total waste generated in the United States.[4] In your career, you will probably participate in an unprecedented effort to solve the environmental problems resulting from economic growth.

3. Explain the influence of the natural environment on the conduct of business.

Ford Recycles!

Ford Motor Company grinds up around 50 million plastic soda bottles each year to make luggage racks, door padding, and the grille opening reinforcements shown here. Ford makes brake pedal pads from recycled tires, taillight housings from old plastic bumpers, and splash shields from auto battery casings. Think about that the next time you turn in your empties.

social environment

All the people who affect the performance of a business or are affected by it.

organizational culture

The shared customs, beliefs, values, and attitudes that give a company its identity and sense of community.

The Social Environment

The **social environment** is all the people who affect the performance of a business or are affected by it. It includes a business's customers as well as its employees, the communities and countries in which it operates, and all the beliefs, customs, and laws of those people and their societies.

The Dallas Cowboys is a football team, and it is also a profitable business. Like other football franchises in the National Football League, the Cowboys used to hire African American players, but not African American managers. The National Association for the Advancement of Colored People (NAACP) complained about the hiring practices of NFL franchises, and the Cowboys were the first to respond. The team now employs three black managers and has decided to use more minority-owned suppliers. And it has a new fan—the NAACP. In Chapter 4 we will explore the legal and ethical issues behind such responses to the social environment.

The social environment is now global for many businesses. Population growth is greatest in developing countries, such as the People's Republic of China and India, which means that much future business growth will be in foreign countries, not in the United States. To take advantage of growing global markets, U.S. companies are learning new skills and becoming more knowledgeable about other countries and cultures. There will be more new customers in fast-developing countries like Mexico and Brazil than in slow-growing industrial nations like the United States, England, Germany, Japan, and France. In fact, four out of every five new jobs in the United States are generated by growth in sales to other countries.[5] Global business opportunities are explored in Chapter 2.

Within the United States, employees and customers are ethnically and culturally diverse. Each company has shared customs, beliefs, values, and attitudes, called its **organizational culture**, that give it its identity and sense of community. "Changing a culture is never easy," according to Nathaniel R. Thompkins, diversity manager for Baxter International, Inc., in Deerfield, Illinois.[6] Like the Dallas Cowboys, U.S. companies are in the process of changing their organizational cultures to accommodate diversity in healthy ways. Employees at Sears, Roebuck and Co., AT&T, Baxter International, and hundreds of other businesses around the country participate in diversity-training programs, and many local police forces now receive similar training.

Responding to the Social Environment

To accommodate its employees' family responsibilities—to their children and to their parents—The Stride Rite Corporation of Cambridge, Massachusetts, runs an intergenerational care center, where members of the community-at-large are welcome to participate as well.

The Political/Legal Environment

The Prudential Insurance Co. of America ran into legal problems when the media reported that the company had given some of its customers inaccurate information about the value of real estate in which they were investing. How did this happen? Apparently, some managers overstated the value of the properties in order to make them more attractive to investors.[7]

This sort of deception is illegal: It violates laws designed to protect consumers. But the government cannot take action unless such activities are discovered. That is why a Prudential employee reported the deception to the press. Once the truth came out, the company repaid the cheated investors and also instituted safeguards to ensure more honest practices in the future. The Prudential case is just one of thousands of examples of deceptive practices in the investment industry. Because many such problems have occurred in the past, the U.S. government regulates the sale of investments very carefully. For example, the Securities and Exchange Commission determines how companies can sell investments and what information they must give to customers.

The Prudential case illustrates the three key components of a business's political/legal environment: laws governing the conduct of the business and its employees, the ethics of the employees and their community, and the regulatory activities of national and local government. Laws set boundaries on the behavior of businesses, defining the ways they can set prices, hire and fire employees, advertise to customers, or discharge waste products into the natural environment. But these laws have no power unless they are enforced.

Businesses follow the laws of the countries in which they operate; in many instances, they do more than the laws require because of the ethics of their employees. It was a handful of unethical employees at Prudential who decided to lie to customers to make more sales and thus to profit from higher sales commissions. And it was a single ethical employee who objected to this illegal activity and worked to have it stopped and the customers repaid.

Businesses are also held to a country's laws by government regulatory organizations. In the United States, dozens of federal agencies and hundreds of state and local ones regulate every aspect of business conduct. The courts mediate legal disputes among businesses and between businesses and their customers. These regulatory activities serve to test and apply the laws, giving them authority and making it costly for businesses to violate them.

The political/legal environment has a powerful influence on the behavior of every business, and the ethical attitudes of a firm's managers and employees play a major role in determining how a business responds to its political/legal environment. The social environment interacts closely with the political/legal environment because it shapes ethical attitudes. Historically, whenever businesses in a U.S. industry have habitually behaved in ways that society views as unethical, the government has stepped in to create laws and regulatory bodies to stop them. That means trends in the political/legal environment can often be predicted by studying attitudes toward business in the social environment.

The Technological Environment

The **technological environment** is the body of scientific and practical knowledge available for product and process development. The discovery of electricity, for example, transformed not only science but all of business as well. Scientific research has spawned computers, pharmaceuticals, synthetic fabrics, refrigerators, telephones, televisions, and many other goods and services that we take for granted today. Research is now underway in government-funded laboratories, on university campuses, and in the laboratories of many businesses as well. Business owners and managers wonder what the next breakthrough will be—and whether it will make their technology obsolete.

 technological environment

The body of scientific and practical knowledge available for product and process development.

4. Discuss the relationships between the social and political/legal environments.

5. Describe how the technological and competitive environments contribute to changes in business functions.

markets

Groups of customers who want a good or service and have the ability to pay for it.

market share

The proportion of total market sales captured by any single competitor.

Staying Ahead of the Competition

Rollerblade, Inc., the pioneer and leader of the in-line skating industry, features Team Rollerblade® at special events worldwide. Team member Chris Edwards, shown here, embodies the excitement his group creates about the sport of in-line skating and Rollerblade brand skates.

Innovation is accelerating in areas ranging from biotechnology to computers, from satellites to surfactants (the chemicals that make soaps work), from composite plastics to metal alloys with new and better properties, and in production processes as well. Innovation stimulates technological advances and speeds their application to goods and services. The business world is made more competitive and challenging by the rapid pace of technology and the opportunities it provides to us all.

The Competitive Environment

Businesses must compete in order to survive and thrive. They compete for customers and also for suppliers, employees, space on store shelves, even for new ideas and technologies—anything that is in limited supply and affects the outcome of the competition. We will explore this topic in Chapter 2.

In recent years competition for customers has grown more intense as the number and quality of competitors grow in most markets. **Markets** are groups of customers who want a good or service and have the ability to pay for it. Markets are generally grouped within industries. For instance, within the auto industry are many markets, including the European market for midsized sedans, the American market for small pickup trucks, and the global market for luxury sports cars. Also within the auto industry are business-to-business markets like the market for windshields. Automakers such as Ford and Toyota and auto body repair shops are the only customers of windshield manufacturers. There are also many service markets, including those for auto loans and repairs.

Competition occurs on many levels within an industry. Suppliers of windshields compete to sell to automakers, which compete to sell cars to us. Automakers, banks, and other financial businesses compete to sell us loans when we buy cars. Dealers and independent repair shops compete to fix our cars when they break down.

Competition for customers is often measured in **market share**, the proportion of total market sales captured by any single competitor. Market share is measured by the percentage of customers, units sold, or dollar value of sales a product captures in a market. The company with the largest market share has many advantages that tend to make it more profitable than its competitors. It is able to operate on a larger scale (which often allows it to produce goods at a lower cost per unit), it has more visibility in the market, and it is known and trusted by more customers.

Rollerblade, Inc., was the first company to make and sell in-line skates, back in 1980. It was the only supplier for seven years, meaning it had a 100 percent market share. In 1987, First Team Sports, Inc., introduced the competing Ultra-Wheels brand, and then ice-skate maker Bauer and several other companies entered the market. What do you think happened to Rollerblade's market share? Yes, it fell, but not below a third, as many might guess. Because of its early leadership, it is still considered the best brand by many customers and has an estimated 37 percent share of sales. The next largest competitor is now Variflex, with a 24 percent market share, followed by Roller Derby at 10 percent, Bauer at 9.5 percent, and First Team at 9.3 percent market share. These estimates come from sales data for the leading companies, and they assume that the 20 or so smaller competitors have a combined 10 percent market share. Total industry sales are estimated at $382 million, compared with Rollerblade's $140 million in sales.[8]

As competition increases, businesses like Rollerblade, Inc., are forced to keep changing and improving in order to hold onto their market share. It is easy to imagine how different business is if you go from having very few competitors to having a great many. You cannot rest for a moment in a highly com-

doing business

And on His Farm He Had Some . . . Members?

Times have changed since Old MacDonald had a farm. The big farm next door has switched over to laser-driven robot tractors and produces 10 times as much corn as Old MacDonald did, at half the cost. One year, bad weather caught up with the old man, he fell behind on his loan payments, and the bank came in and took over the farm.

This fate or a similar one has befallen thousands of farms across America. The small family farm is now an endangered species. But Caretaker Farm in Williamstown, Massachusetts, has found a way to survive in a more competitive farming environment. Instead of selling its harvest in the fall and toughing it out the rest of the year, this farm receives monthly payments from 240 members who receive weekly crates of organic produce in exchange for their membership dues. Those who wish to can visit the farm and pick their own. All get the benefit of fresh local produce grown without any chemical sprays or powders.

The farm is doing well now, and its members are happy customers because they receive better produce at the same price as supermarket produce. While it is more expensive to grow organic food on a small-scale farm, the direct link to customers cuts out the costs of transportation, packaging, and storage, and eliminates the need for distributors and grocery stores to make a profit. In this sense the small farm is highly competitive, enabling its customers to get more for their money.

Old MacDonald's farm is buried under a new subdivision. Out by the road a new mini-mall boasts a successful McDonald's franchise. Where the land once produced hundreds of pounds of vegetables (along with all those sheep, goats, cows, and ducks), all you can get today is a burger and fries, both made from the cheapest beef and potatoes available on the world market. Caretaker Farm creates a different kind of business exchange, one closer to the old-fashioned relationship between farmer and local customers. As Sam Smith, manager of Caretaker Farm, sees it, "The farm is secured by the community, and the community is given some security by the farm. It's a mutual benefit." Old MacDonald couldn't have put it better. But if he had tried it might have gone something like this: "With a member here, a member there, here a member there a member everywhere a member . . ."

Source: Paul Karr, "The Last Best Hope for Family Farms," *Sanctuary: The Journal of the Massachusetts Audubon Society,* July/Aug. 1993, pp. 5–9.

petitive market. Increasing competition is a major concern for managers and one of the key forces driving changes in the business process. This is true even of that emblem of traditional America, the family farm, as the doing business box entitled "And on His Farm He Had Some . . . Members?" explains.

The Economic Environment

Economics is the study of how scarce resources are allocated among competing uses.[9] Businesses compete for the resources they need to operate, and through their production of goods and services they help make these resources more useful and available to their customers. Therefore, businesses are strongly affected by the economic systems in which they operate, and the study of economics is useful to anyone planning to work in business. There are local, national, and international economies. The economy of the Southwest is local, the U.S. economy is national, and the North American economy is international. We will explore economics in Chapter 2.

Economic Systems

A **market economy** is a system in which individuals and businesses make their own decisions about what to produce and consume. The market determines how much is sold at what price. In a **command economy**, the government determines both prices and quantities to be produced. There are three political systems that determine to what degree a country adopts a market or a command economy. They are capitalism, socialism, and communism. **Capitalism**

 economics

The study of how scarce resources are allocated among competing uses.

 market economy

An economic system in which individuals and businesses make their own decisions about what to produce and consume, and the market determines how much is sold at what price.

 command economy

An economic system whereby the government determines both prices and quantities to be produced.

 capitalism

A political system that encourages free markets and private ownership of money, land, equipment, and other resources businesses need.

6. State the relationship between economic and political systems and describe the economic environment created by these systems.

encourages free markets and private ownership of money, land, equipment, and other resources businesses need. Private ownership makes it possible for people to start and to operate businesses when they see opportunities. The U.S. economy is mainly capitalist: Consumers and businesses enjoy considerable freedom to make decisions about sales and purchases.

Socialism encourages government planning and ownership of vital industries along with private ownership of other businesses. Sweden is a socialist country. Socialism imposes restrictions on businesses with the goal of making them more accountable to the public than to their profit-seeking owners. It attempts to allocate scarce resources so that everyone has access to them, even people who might not be able to afford them in a capitalist economy. Socialism produces a **mixed economy**—a blend of government and private ownership of resources. The People's Republic of China calls its mixed system a socialist-market economy.

Under **communism**, almost all resources needed for business are owned by the state. There is no private property. Communism is based on the ideas of the nineteenth-century German political philosopher Karl Marx and is modeled on the commune, a collective community that, according to Marx's principle, exacts "from each according to his abilities" and gives "to each according to his needs." But on the national level communism requires a powerful central government and a rigid command economy in which individuals and businesses have few independent rights and privileges. The former Soviet Union and the countries of the old Soviet bloc were communist, but most have now adopted capitalism or socialism, with at least partial market economies. By the mid-1990s, only Cuba and North Korea remained communist.

In practice, all systems are mixed economies, but a more free market approach is increasingly common throughout the world. Economists consider the United States the classic *free market system*, even though the government does influence some prices through its regulation of industries such as cable television, its control of imports, and its price supports for farmers. In general, U.S. businesses are free to respond to customer needs by producing more of what customers demand and less of what they do not. And to compete for those customers, businesses in a free market economy must keep improving. Free market economies encourage rapid learning and change and fuel economic growth as a result. However, they also create poverty by allocating resources unevenly, a problem that governments try to solve with social welfare programs, minimum wage laws, and other such regulations.

✓ **socialism**

A political system that encourages government planning and ownership of vital industries along with private ownership of other businesses.

✓ **mixed economy**

An economic system in which there is a blend of government and private ownership of resources.

✓ **communism**

A political system in which almost all resources needed for business are owned by the state.

✓ **gross domestic product (GDP)**

The dollar value of all the goods and services a country produces within a given time period.

✓ **imports**

Goods or services brought into a country for purchase.

✓ **exports**

The opposite of imports—goods or services produced in one country and sent to customers in other countries.

Economic Growth

The **gross domestic product (GDP)** is the dollar value of all the goods and services a country produces within a given time period. When GDP grows steadily, business booms. But GDP growth in the United States and most other industrialized countries has slowed in the last two decades. During the 1960s, the economies of all noncommunist countries grew at 4.9 percent a year. This generous growth rate fell to 3.8 percent per year in the 1970s, to only 2.9 percent per year in the 1980s, and so far has been no higher during the 1990s.[10]

The slower rate of economic growth in industrialized countries after 1970 meant that many businesses had to compete harder to keep up the sales growth they had come to expect and need. If growth in their sales could not come from basic growth in the economy, then it would have to come at the expense of *other* businesses' sales. Competition for customers has increased dramatically in most U.S. industries since the 1970s as a direct result of this downturn in GDP.

Today the American car market is split among seven large automakers and at least ten smaller ones, compared to just three big automakers in 1970.[11] And life has changed in similar ways in other industries. In the 1960s, American companies dominated sales, not just in the United States but in all industrialized countries. Businesses could afford to be slow-moving and stable because the world around them was, too. To grow, all they had to do was participate in the growth of the national and world economies. Then the environment changed. Around the world, American businesses lost 16 percent of their share of world markets in the 1960s and another 23 percent in the 1970s as global competition grew tougher.[12]

   Imports are goods or services brought into a country for purchase. **Exports** are the opposite—goods or services produced in one country and sent to customers in other countries. Figure 1.3 shows the trends in U.S. imports and exports. Both have grown rapidly since 1970—a clear indicator that we now operate in a global economy. And, as evidence of the difficulty of competing globally, we can see that exports of U.S. goods have failed to grow as rapidly as imports. The exception is small business. The roughly 100,000 U.S. businesses with fewer than 500 employees ship about a quarter of all exports measured in dollar value. And their export rates are growing *twice* as fast as those of big businesses.[13]

According to a 1993 General Motors sales brochure for its Saturn automobile, "In the 1940s, four out of five cars were built in America. In 1960, only half were made here. And by 1990, less than one-fourth of the world's cars came from America."

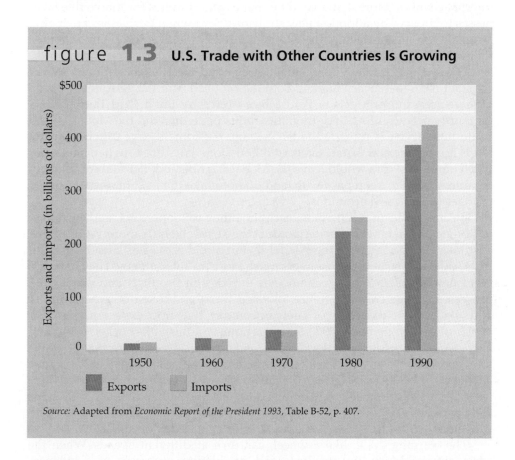

figure **1.3** **U.S. Trade with Other Countries Is Growing**

Source: Adapted from *Economic Report of the President 1993*, Table B-52, p. 407.

Putting It All Together

External business environments interact. For example, technological advances in telecommunications and shipping combine with a trend toward lower legal barriers to foreign trade; the burgeoning economic development of countries like South Korea, Mexico, and China; and growing social acceptance by Americans of foreign products. Together, these trends make competition global instead of national for most companies. Over the last two decades, business managers report that change in their business environments is accelerating. They find changes occur more often and are harder to predict.[14]

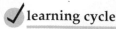 **learning cycle**

The constant improvement of products and processes to offer more value to customers.

7. Discuss the relationship between changes in the external business environment and the adoption of new business values.

table 1.1

Managers on Change

Executive's View	Percentage Agreeing
Change in my company is extremely rapid.	79
The pace of change will accelerate.	61
My company is good at coping with change.	47

Managers agree that change is rapid and accelerating, but not all are confident their companies can handle it.

Source: Data from a survey of 400 U.S. executives by the consulting firm Proudfoot Change Management. See *Business Week,* Sept. 20, 1993, p. 44.

Changes in each component of the business environment combine to make it harder to guess what the future will be like and to make the future less familiar when it does arrive. The combination makes for a turbulent environment, one in which bumps and surprises are routine. Many managers refer to this condition as "permanent white water," meaning that doing business today is like rafting down white-water rapids. Business as usual is not the answer to this new challenge. Instead, businesses are responding in new, creative ways, as we will see in the next section.

Transforming the Business Process

In a survey of 400 U.S. executives, most agreed that their companies are undergoing rapid change (see Table 1.1). However, less than half were confident that their companies could cope effectively with that change.

Changes in the external business environment require businesses to make internal changes. More than that, they create opportunities for innovative businesses to prosper by adopting new strategies. And when businesses are highly innovative, they may actually take the lead in their field, forcing competitors to follow them.

The interaction of environmental changes and business innovations creates constant change in every market. Both the Model T and the Taurus have been highly successful products of Ford Motor Company. But a Ford Taurus offers far more safety, comfort, and durability for its price than did the Model T. Ford could not survive if it made Model Ts today. Customers have different tastes, roads are bigger and faster, safety and emissions laws are tougher, and other auto companies' cars would leave the Model T far behind. Ford has changed in countless ways to keep pace with, and often to take the lead in, these ongoing changes in the world around it.

Businesses learn a little more each time they sell a product, and each time customers buy a new and better product they expect a little more. At one time, customers were content to buy Model Ts, but millions of sales later, businesses have learned how to give customers much more for their money. They have applied new ideas and new technologies to redesign products and production processes. Where customers once tolerated cars that broke down periodically and offered little in the way of safety or comfort, they now expect manufacturers to offer seven-year, 70,000-mile warranties, adjustable bucket seats, and crash-safe designs with antilock brakes and air bags. Everything that is sold is reinvented, over and over, each reinvention offering something new of value to customers. This cycle of change has always been an important aspect of business, and because of the accelerating rate of environmental change it is the most important aspect right now. We call it the **learning cycle**, the constant improvement of products and processes to offer more value to customers.

The learning cycle, like a wheel, can turn at different speeds. When the cycle moves slowly, the products and production processes of a business change slowly. Customers do not demand or receive many improvements. For many years, the U.S. Postal Service offered the same services—first-, second-, or third-class delivery of letters and packages. Mail delivery gradually moved faster as the Postal Service took advantage of highways and jet airplanes, but internal change was slow. Few new services were offered. Then, in the 1970s and 1980s, the Postal Service began to feel pressure from competing delivery services. United Parcel Service offered faster, more reliable package delivery. Federal Express pioneered overnight delivery of letters and small packages, and soon Airborne Express, Purolator, Emery Worldwide, and other businesses joined the competition, along with the new fax and e-mail technologies. The

Postal Service lost customers and money and was forced to introduce new services to stay competitive. Now post offices provide overnight or two-day delivery, just like Federal Express, and the Postal Service trains its employees to provide more helpful and polite customer service. The U.S. Postal Service was forced to change more rapidly when changes in the world around it created a more challenging and competitive business environment.

New Values and Strategies

Businesses are responding in many ways to the challenges in the environment, and behind the many responses are a new set of values and a handful of powerful strategies. Many businesses used to be motivated by values that emphasized short-term profits and the advancement of managers' interests. Now they have to be more farsighted. A business's **values** are deep-seated beliefs that are important to its survival and future direction, as one survey of senior managers indicates. The managers cited these five as their greatest concerns:[15]

- *Employee commitment.* Managers need active employee involvement now more than ever.
- *Competitiveness.* Companies need to respond to stiffer competition by becoming stronger competitors.
- *Customer satisfaction.* Businesses need to listen to and please customers better than they have in the past.
- *Quality.* Businesses need to improve the quality of their products and processes.
- *Productivity.* Companies need to learn how to do more with less.

These five values share two characteristics. First, each requires significant change in the average business. Second, each is a long-term concern. Take employee commitment, for example. Most businesses do not have the high level of employee commitment that managers say their businesses need. More than three-fourths of managers in this survey said there is room for improvement in the level of trust that exists within their organization. To increase trust and commitment over the long term, managers may have to sacrifice profits in the short term. For example, they may have to find an alternative to employee layoffs as a cure for a short-term drop in sales or profits. One of the greatest challenges for U.S. businesses is switching from short-term thinking to a long-term vision of how to change. Despite this difficulty, businesses are beginning to act on their new values. New strategies are emerging that make companies more competitive and fast-changing and that promise to change the nature of business by altering the functions of the business process. The following sections describe six new strategies illustrated in Figure 1.4.

Flexibility

Small, young businesses started by creative thinkers are doing better on average than big, mature businesses in today's turbulent environment. The small businesses have the flexibility and creativity to pursue new opportunities or avoid new problems. Small and midsized U.S. businesses grew enough between 1987 and 1993 to create almost 7 million new jobs. Compare this with the record of big businesses—those with more than 500 employees—which cut 2.5 million jobs in the same period![16] Midsized businesses did better but failed to add as many jobs as small businesses did.

Organizations of all sizes are encouraging their employees to learn and change—to develop new ideas, new products, and even new businesses. This is

✓ values

Deep-seated beliefs that are important to the survival and future direction of a business.

figure 1.4
New Business Strategies

- Flexibility in business formation
- Management innovation
- Employee development
- Increased customer focus
- Improved control systems
- Creative financial management

↓

Improved products, increased sales and profits

8. Discuss how the strategies of flexibility and management innovation contribute to changes in business functions.

all part of a larger movement to break up rigid, top-heavy structures and create looser, more flexible organizations. Of course, people already learn and change every day. But established businesses often lose the flexibility and initiative that enabled their founders to succeed. Businesses have a good chance of rekindling this flame through **entrepreneurship**, risk-taking behaviors leading to the start-up and growth of businesses. You will learn much more about entrepreneurship and the flexibility strategy in Part 2, Launching the Business.

Now midsized and big businesses are trying to regain their entrepreneurial spirit. One way they do this is by breaking their operations up into a number of smaller operating groups, each with the flexibility of a smaller business but the resources of a larger one. Midsized chemicals manufacturer Hoechst Celanese Corp. is headquartered in Somerville, New Jersey, but its vice president of quality management, Darrell Nordeen, describes it as a "federation of forty separate businesses."[17] Company headquarters provides vision and resources and reviews strategies to help these separate businesses succeed—but it does not run them. Similarly, Hoechst Celanese is owned, along with 270 other companies, by industrial giant Hoechst AG of Germany.

How much harder is it to be innovative in a big company? One study says it is 2.4 times harder—small businesses currently produce 2.4 times as many innovations as big companies on average. That is why John F. Welch, Jr., chairman of General Electric Co., says, "Size is no longer the trump card it once was in today's brutally competitive world marketplace," and it is why his goal for GE is to "get that small-company soul—and small-company speed—inside our big-company body."[18]

A rubber raft is better in white-water rapids than a river boat because it can maneuver far more quickly and flexibly. As the business environment becomes more turbulent, businesses are trying to become as flexible as rubber life rafts. They are breaking up their top-heavy structures and dividing into more and smaller parts. Better to be a flotilla of small boats, each with its own pilot, than one big, lumbering ocean liner. To unite their many more flexible parts, businesses are emphasizing a shared vision and set of values.

Business consultants Tom Peters and Robert Waterman discovered that many big companies have to isolate groups of employees from the rest of the company before they can be creative and entrepreneurial. Their landmark book, *In Search of Excellence*, reports that many companies are "proud of their 'skunk works,' bands of eight or ten zealots off in the corner, often outproducing . . . groups that numbered in the hundreds."[20] The skunk works concept is now being adopted at many big companies through the use of *venture teams*, each a small business operated by employees within a big business.[21]

Management Innovation

Managers accomplish organizational goals by means of people and other resources. When the business environment is stable, there is little need to change the way businesses are managed. But when the environment changes, management must adapt. One of the most powerful business strategies right now is **innovation**, creative change in products or business processes. While technological development is an important form of innovation, as we saw in our earlier discussions of the changing business environment, management innovation focuses on improving the quality of work processes. You will learn more about management innovation and quality improvement strategies in Part 3, Managing the Business.

For example, to its customers, Xerox is "The Document Company." But chief executive Paul Allaire recalls that competition from Japanese companies became so intense in the 1980s that his organization "had to change dramatically from top to bottom." One of the cornerstones of Xerox's successful change

---

"When we did play it safe, we usually fell behind. Ford will always be at its strongest when it is taking risks, innovating and leading the way."
Robert Rewey, Vice President,
North American Sales Operations for
Ford[19]

✔ **entrepreneurship**

Risk-taking behaviors leading to the start-up and growth of businesses.

✔ **innovation**

Creative change in products or business processes.

The Problem-Solving Process

If you go to work at a quality-conscious company like Xerox, you will become expert in using the problem-solving process. You will also find it invaluable in many other situations. In fact, formal problem solving can even help you study better.[1] Here is the process.

STEP 1. *Identify the problem.* The individual or group considers various ways of looking at the problem and chooses the one that is most helpful in solving it. This requires opening your mind (and your team's agenda) to lots of ideas, then focusing in on the most useful problem definition.

STEP 2. *Analyze the problem.* Look for causes, issues, and questions. Gather the information you need to understand the problem. Again, start by opening up to lots of potential causes. Then close in on one or a few key causes for action.

STEP 3. *List possible solutions.* Be creative. Think of lots of ideas. At Xerox, employees ask, "How could we make a change?" Then think about each option to make it as clear as possible.

STEP 4. *Select and plan one solution.* Which is the best way? Compare the options in as many ways as possible. Then focus on *how* to implement the one you chose.

STEP 5. *Implement the solution.* Follow through on your plan to solve the problem or make the change.

STEP 6. *Check the solution.* How well does it work? Identify any continuing problems and start the process again.

How many times do you stop to analyze a problem and redefine it? The problem-solving process makes us stop and think before we start working on a project—which can save a lot of wasted effort later! For instance, at Xerox a complaint from an important customer might be defined in Step 1 as a symptom of a problem in customer service. This will lead to improvements in the way *every* customer is served, rather than just a one-time fix for the customer who complained. And it will help improve quality by making a permanent change for the better instead of a one-time Band-Aid.

Xerox's approach gives problem solvers insight. It encourages us to look beneath the surface—a view that benefits everyone. For you as a student, this might mean asking in Step 1, "Have I understood the assignment correctly?" and "Is there a better way to approach it?" By using the problem-solving process you can avoid wasting time studying unimportant material or doing an assignment the hard way. On the job, it might mean asking, "Why do we do it this way? Is there a better way nobody has thought of?"

Most employees were not trained to be insightful problem solvers. In fact, Xerox and other large U.S. companies using the quality strategy recently banded together to encourage colleges to modernize their business training by teaching problem solving and other new techniques.[2] You are among the first college students to benefit from this request.

[1]David A. Garvin, "Building a Learning Organization," *Harvard Business Review,* July-Aug. 1993, p. 81.

[2]Edwin L. Artzt, chairman and CEO of Procter & Gamble, summed up the group's thinking as follows: "Our schools must help forge change. They must prepare students to be total quality practitioners and leaders in business, government, and academia as well. Business and engineering graduates must be equipped to implement quality as a business strategy." The Total Quality Forum, *Forging Strategic Links with Higher Education, A Report of Proceedings* (Cincinnati, Ohio: The Procter & Gamble Company, 1991), p. 3.

effort, he says, was a whole new approach to the "way we managed and worked." The result is that Xerox has now "involved all of our people in quality and hence in achieving our business objectives."[22] Right now, Xerox defines its main objective as "providing our customers with Document Services that enhance business productivity."[23]

Xerox employees are involved in the delivery of continually improving products and services to the company's many business customers through their participation in more than 7,000 quality improvement teams. Every team member is trained in critical thinking skills, starting with Xerox's problem-solving process. See the skills check on "The Problem-Solving Process" for Xerox's approach to training in these methods. Instead of asking their managers what to do, teams dive right in and develop solutions of their own. This means everyone is helping to improve the company. Paul Allaire and other senior managers do not have to make all the difficult decisions. In many cases, employees can identify problems and solve them on their own, which makes Xerox more innovative and flexible than ever before.

✓ **empowerment**

The transfer to employees of authority and responsibility for a task, along with the necessary resources and power to excel at the task.

✓ **total quality management (TQM)**

The continuous improvement of a business and its processes by its employees and for its customers.

Quality strategies drive down company costs at the same time that they increase customer satisfaction. Teams of employees are trained in the technical and personal skills needed to identify and eliminate the root causes of problems. Problem-solving skills are now an essential part of business training, because they give employees the ability to respond to problems by making positive changes. At companies that use quality improvement strategies—Motorola, Xerox, Corning, and AT&T—employees are expected to become expert at formal problem-solving methods.

The quality improvement strategy is radically different from traditional approaches to quality. In the past, companies hired special quality control engineers to police the work of their employees. Their job was to catch errors *after* they were made and send defective products to the rework or scrap piles. The problem with this approach is that it ignores the sources of errors, which makes it hard for employees—and the company—to learn from mistakes. The quality improvement strategy gives workers responsibility for their own errors so they can learn from them and improve the way they work.

Empowerment is the transfer to employees of authority and responsibility for a task, along with the necessary resources and power to excel at the task. For instance, at Hewlett-Packard Co.'s factory in San Jose, California, hundreds of employees work in the manufacture of computer chips. Recently, the company began to train them in statistical methods, which enables them to measure the quality of their *own* work as they do it. As a result of this training, one worker was able to determine that a layer of material her team was adding to a batch of chips was too thick—a delicate measuring job, since the layers are of microscopic thickness. Rather than calling over an inspector or supervisor, her team stopped its regular work and spent an hour tracking down the problem using formal problem-solving methods they had learned in quality training provided by the company. They found out that the "wafer," a spinning disk out of which chips are made, was moving too slowly. They fixed it and went back to production in record time. As supervisor Glenn Loriaux sums up, "Basically, it was a case where a process was out of control and she put it back in."[24] At Hewlett-Packard, Xerox, and many other companies, quality improvement is accomplished using a method first developed at Japanese companies like Sony and Toyota. **Total quality management (TQM)** is the continuous improvement of a business and its processes by its employees and for its customers. You will learn more about this management approach in Chapter 10, Producing Quality Goods and Services.

Employee Development

9. Discuss how a focus on people—through the strategies of employee development and customer focus—helps transform business functions.

Each person who works in a business helps that business succeed or fail. Changes in the ways employees are treated and managed are another set of important new business strategies detailed in Part 4, Empowering the Employee. Are employees trained and motivated to improve the business? Do they have the power to make needed changes? In traditional companies, they do not.

Norman S. Nopper is an employee development specialist at the computer company Honeywell Canada, Ltd., in Scarborough, Ontario. He explains his work with an example: "Vasso is a Greek immigrant who works as an assembler at a Honeywell, Inc., factory in Scarborough, Ontario. Just six months ago, Vasso spoke very little English. Today, she is conducting a tour of the production line for a group of senior executives from a major food processing company. They are gathering ideas for factory redesign from the Honeywell facility. Vasso is proud of how far she has come in a mere six months."[25] Vasso did not make the trip alone. Honeywell offers training in language skills, basic math,

AT&T's Human Resources

At AT&T Transmissions Systems's Merrimack Valley Works, 12,000 employees, including this production associate, make the complex equipment used to run telecommunications systems worldwide, and helped the business to win the prestigious Malcolm Baldrige National Award for Quality in 1992.

and computer literacy, along with advanced courses in subjects like teamwork and conflict resolution—all through Honeywell College, which offers degrees through after-work classes held at the factory for employees' convenience.

Why train employees? Why not just fire the ones who don't have the needed skills and hire new ones? Some companies do, but others now see their employees as the key to future success. Employees who can "grow" their careers at one business will be more enthusiastic about working for that business than will employees who continually jump from job to job. As Johnna Howell, a manager at the government-funded Lawrence Livermore National Laboratory in California, explains, "Careers are fragile. They are fragile to the organization as well as to the individual." She argues that businesses should manage their employees' careers, and in fact her organization helps all of its 8,500 employees pursue their career goals. As part of this effort, John Nuckolls, the lab's director, insists that "lifelong education must be part of the job assignment" for every employee.[26]

By learning new skills, employees can help their employers learn and develop in response to the changing environment. It sounds funny to talk about a business learning—after all, it's a thing, not a person. Yet managers are now trying to create **learning organizations**, businesses that are good at developing and using knowledge in ways that help them change for the better.[27] Learning organizations have to be especially good at five activities, each requiring active thinking and learning on the part of employees:[28]

- Problem solving
- Experimenting with new approaches
- Learning from experience
- **Benchmarking**, adapting better approaches from other businesses
- Sharing knowledge within the business

Together these activities speed up the learning cycle and create businesses that learn and improve rapidly.

 learning organizations

Businesses that are good at developing and using knowledge in ways that help them change for the better.

 benchmarking

Adapting better approaches from other businesses.

Customer Focus

Customers are the lifeblood of any business—without them there would be no sales, no learning cycle, no profits. Businesses are learning how to listen more attentively to the voice of the customer. They are asking customers more questions. And they are developing new ways to make sure the customer's answers are always heard as products are developed, produced, and marketed. Businesses are finding that it costs far less to keep one customer happy than to lose customer after customer and have to replace them. The customer focus strategy begins with marketing, and you will learn how marketing is changing as you study Part 5, Pleasing the Customer.

Computer maker IBM is working hard to bring its customers into clearer focus. Senior executive Steven Schwartz explains: "Competition had become tougher than ever. We were heavy with resources, with structure, and not responsive enough to customer needs. We decided the way to get straight answers was from the source—the customer."[29] The result was an overhaul of IBM's management methods and extensive retraining for all its employees. When Louis Gerstner took over as top executive at IBM, taking on the job of turning the troubled company around, he started by listening to customers. He talked to thousands of customers and showed videotapes of his customer meetings to other IBM executives. He told his top 24 managers to, as he put it, "bear hug" five customers and report on their findings. Each manager told his employees to bear hug more customers, and so on, until everyone was talking to customers.[30]

Four Steps to Customer Focus

Catalog merchant Lands' End keeps customers in focus—even though they aren't in sight—by following a simple set of rules that protect their customers' interests at each step in the business process.

The problem of customer focus is different, but just as challenging, for service businesses. Most services require direct contact between an employee and a customer—the bank teller cashes a check, the waiter serves your food, the checkout clerk bags your groceries. And if you think back, someone in one of those jobs has probably made you angry in the last month! As an executive at Marriott Hotels-Resorts admits, "The most difficult part of our business is managing employee/customer interactions."[31] His company gives employees special training, and it also surveys customer opinions to identify problems so they can be avoided in the future.

Businesses are also discovering the power of customer service that is so good it *surprises* customers—so they come back again and again, bringing their friends with them. To surprise customers with service so good that they become "raving fans," employees need to be flexible, consistent, and good at listening. These skills help them go the extra mile to make sure customers are happy.[32]

Improved Control Systems

Technology plays an ever-larger role in controlling the business process. New uses of technology, from faxes to on-line financial updates, are supposed to make companies more flexible and responsive. In practice, however, the huge volume of rapidly moving information that now flows through businesses creates its own set of problems. A recent study of how businesses use new information technologies concludes that information is not flowing freely within companies. Instead, power struggles sometimes derail managers' attempts to control the flow of information. Control of information has always been a source of power for managers, but in new business structures the power of information must be shared more broadly.[33] A business can learn and change rapidly only if it develops new, more open ways of sharing and using all available information, as you will learn in Part 6, Controlling the Business Process.

Many businesses are improving their performance by using information creatively. Federal Express, United Parcel Service, and large trucking companies like Yellow Freight Systems and Consolidated Freightways now track each individual shipment wherever it goes. Bar codes, satellites, and computers combine to tell every customer where his or her packages are, anywhere in the country or the world, at any moment. These information tools also tell the business how it is performing by supplying details about sales volume and employee efficiency.

Accounting focuses both on reporting financial information about *past* operations and on projecting *future* performance. More and more businesses are using accounting controls to estimate what the future holds. For example, by determining the cost of business processes, accounting reveals the potential financial impact of decisions; assigns costs to business activities, or *cost drivers*, rather than to departments; and identifies areas where the business can boost its profits by making improvements in the quality of its products.

Thomas J. Malone, the president of textile maker Milliken & Co., uses control systems to push his company to adopt such quality improvement and employee development strategies. Milliken has been very successful as a result. At Milliken, he explains, "We measure everything. I'm telling you that if you went to the bathroom one extra time, it would show up on a Milliken chart."[34] That information might not be of much use in improving the company, but Milliken tracks a great deal of other information as well, including data on customers, suppliers, environmental safety, manufacturing processes, and the quality of the products and services provided by more than 400 competitors.[35]

Creative Financial Management

10. Describe business's financial strategies for improving performance and financing operations.

Businesses spend money on materials, equipment, and employees in order to run their business processes. Ideally, sales to customers generate enough cash to pay the costs of doing business and to make profits for the company's owners or for investment in business improvements. But relying on sales revenues alone is risky. In reality, firms often look to outside sources for cash to finance their operations. You will learn how businesses manage their finances and about the financial services industry in Part 7, Financing the Business.

Changes in the business environment have a dramatic impact on how businesses manage their money. For example, until the 1980s, the U.S. banking industry was strictly regulated by the federal government. Today, the businesses that provide financial services, such as banking, investing, and fund raising, are less strongly regulated, and there is more competition and faster change in the financial services industry, too. As a result, businesses can pick and choose among more competing financial services than ever before.

The national barriers that used to limit the flow of money are also coming down. The European Union is working to replace many national currencies with a single one. Legal and technological barriers to foreign investment are falling as business goes global. Investment managers can work around the clock, following the sun from major financial centers in London to New York, all the way to Tokyo and Hong Kong, buying and selling through a global computer network.

Raising money to run the business is one side of the financial management coin. The flip side involves saving money. Today, financial managers are especially concerned with cost savings. How do you drive business costs down? Strategies focus on helping companies increase the value of their products while holding the line on costs. Business process **reengineering**, the clean-slate design of a process, cuts costs by simplifying processes. Reengineering efforts at chemical maker Union Carbide have saved more than $400 million in just three years. One team of employees that handles maintenance at a Union Carbide plant in Taft, Louisiana, redesigned its work process and saved the company $20 million.[36] The secret to reengineering's success is its radical approach to changing the business. How radical? The main tool needed for reengineering is a blank piece of paper, which is the most radical thing possible in an established business. Reengineering asks about the best way to do something right now and is willing to consider the answer, even if it completely departs from tradition.

Reengineering takes an offensive approach to dealing with growing cost pressures. The alternative is a defensive approach called **downsizing**—eliminating jobs to cut costs and make the business smaller. Two hundred thousand unionized workers lost their jobs from downsizing at General Motors alone over the last 10 years.[37] Job cuts have dominated the headlines for years, and a majority of managers in surveys of large American companies say they expect periodic job cuts to continue through the 1990s.[38] The impact on employees is great. Military aircraft manufacturer McDonnell Douglas Corp. employed more than 7,000 people in the mid-1980s. Cuts brought the total down to 5,200 by 1993, and the current target is just 4,500.[39] Business giant Procter & Gamble Co., the maker of Tide, Ivory, Pampers, and thousands of other consumer products, is in the process of closing 30 plants and eliminating 13,000 positions.[40] Cuts like these may save costs, but they come at a high price. Businesses are often left with a work force in which not only morale but also accumulated knowledge and skills are diminished.

Nevertheless, downsizings are sometimes necessary as businesses find it harder to make a profit in the current business environment. For many busi-

reengineering

The clean-slate design of a process that cuts costs by simplifying business processes.

downsizing

Eliminating jobs to cut costs and make the business smaller.

doing business

Business Failures Climb in the United States

Defensive approaches to cost control are unfortunately far more common than reengineering. Financial retreat goes by many names—downsizing, rightsizing, virtual manufacturing, and strategic withdrawal, to name a few. You need not memorize them, because fancy terms cannot disguise the fact that many businesses are retreating from their own communities and customers. And for some, retreat is too little, too late. For many years, businesses failed at a rate of 10,000 to 15,000 a year. That is a large number of business deaths, but the real shocker is that the number began to grow rapidly in the 1980s, as the business environment became more turbulent. There are now close to 75,000 failures a year.

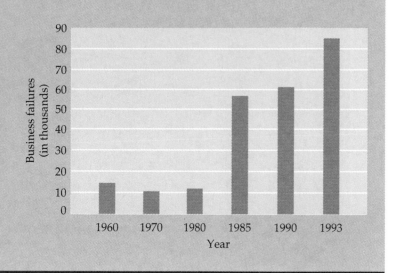

Source: Economic Report of the President 1994, Table B-95, p. 378

nesses, downsizing is the last alternative before business failure. The number of failures has increased dramatically in recent years, as the doing business box entitled, "Business Failures Climb in the United States" reveals.

The Changing Job Market

What does the new business environment mean for college students—for your own education and career choices? We will explore these questions in an appendix on careers, but some points deserve our attention here as well. A fast-changing business environment creates fast-growth careers at the same time that it turns other careers into dead ends. The conventional wisdom holds that the wisest course is to pick a field that is on the upswing. Figure 1.5 on page 26 shows the fastest growing jobs in the 1990s in terms of number of employees needed.

The conventional wisdom is right—to a degree. Better to train for a growth job in health care, computing, or marketing than in a field that is not in demand. However, in a turbulent environment you cannot count on stability—especially in growth projections. Today's hot careers may soon be dead ends, replaced by tomorrow's hot careers. The average business student's career will last more than four decades, and likely none of the fast-growth careers in Figure 1.5 will still be growing fast in 40 years. This means success will come from considering first what you want to do and what you are good at, and then developing a set of all-purpose job skills that you can transfer to the next growth area and the one after that.

Your knowledge of how business works; your thinking, communication, and problem-solving skills; your ability to master new technologies; your mastery of teamwork all carry over from job to job. Any job can give you an opportunity to build your skills and experience. The important thing is to keep learning and developing new skills through your work, whatever it may be. Your career will be strongly affected by the fast pace of change in business. Your success will depend upon your understanding of and preparation for change.

11. Identify the skills now required for a business career.

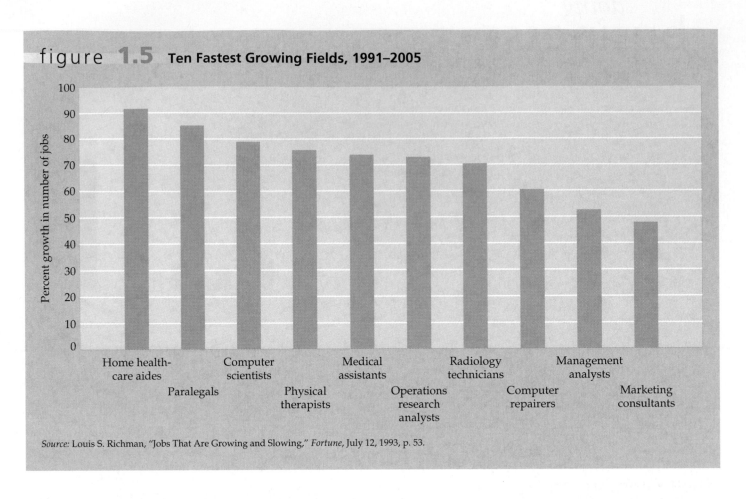

figure **1.5**   **Ten Fastest Growing Fields, 1991–2005**

Source: Louis S. Richman, "Jobs That Are Growing and Slowing," *Fortune*, July 12, 1993, p. 53.

New Skills Needed

The active participation of employees adds new responsibilities and opportunities to jobs at all levels. For starters, employees need new skills. The employee training budgets of U.S. businesses show the kinds of skills companies stress. The most common type of employee training is, and always has been, **employee orientation**, training that brings new employees up to speed on how the business and its industry work. Nine out of ten large and midsized businesses provide new-employee orientation, and your general knowledge of business, gained from this course, will help you start building this essential foundation in advance.

Beyond employee orientation, several new kinds of training are increasingly common. Six out of ten large and midsized businesses now train employees in *quality improvement*. Three-fourths provide training in *leadership skills*. More participative approaches to business require managers and supervisors to make the shift from giving orders to coaching teams of employees, and some employee teams are now expected to manage themselves. Seven out of ten large and midsized companies now provide employee training in *teamwork* because new approaches to business require more cooperation and less personal competition. We emphasize these topics in this text because your knowledge of them will prepare you for the new priorities in the job market.

Also new is the emphasis on *problem-solving skills* and *creativity*—two-thirds of midsized and large companies now train employees in problem solving and well over one-third stress creativity. They recognize that these thinking skills are important for employees at all levels of business. Critical thinking exercises in the text and at the end of each chapter will help you develop these skills.

✓ **employee orientation**

Training that brings new employees up to speed on how the business and its industry work.

Finally, more than half of these businesses are now giving employees training in how to deal with *change*—the underlying theme of this book. You are the first generation of business students to receive training in how to cope with and lead change in business, and this book is one of the first to offer this training.

In sum, your career begins here. This text offers you a solid orientation in the traditional world of business, and it introduces you to new skills in quality improvement, leadership, teamwork, problem solving, creativity, and how to deal with change. Learning these skills as you study business will enable you to apply them in future jobs as *you* help businesses speed up their learning cycles and improve their basic business processes.

Reviewing *Business in a Changing Environment*

The Business and Its Functions

1. **State the main objective of business and describe how success is measured**. The objective of all businesses is to take in resources and increase their value for customers. Businesses measure their success in terms of profits or accomplishment of social goals. For-profit businesses thus seek to obtain revenues that exceed expenses; organizations with a social goal need only be sure that income equals expenses.

2. **List the six functions of business and describe the integrative nature of the business process**. All business activities fall within one or more of six broad functions. The first step is formation, and the form may be altered as needs and the environment change. Once the business is formed, the management function is responsible for all the other functions: human resources, whereby employees are hired and motivated; marketing, the processes through which the business finds and fills customer needs; control systems, which monitor and evaluate all business functions; and financial management, which controls the flow of funds in and out of the business. These functions do not operate in a vacuum. Work flows between functions and each function may affect several others.

The Changing Business Environment

3. **Explain the influence of the natural environment on the conduct of business**. Businesses are influenced not only by internal factors but also by external environmental factors. The natural environment is becoming an increasingly important factor. In deciding how to use and disperse limited natural resources, businesses are required by law and by ethical considerations to preserve and protect the natural environment. This may require changes in processes and procedures.

4. **Discuss the relationships between the social and political/legal environments**. The social and political/legal environments interact because the ethical attitudes of the social environment determine whether and when government will create laws and regulatory bodies to alter or stop a disapproved behavior. The increasingly global nature of business means that companies must consider ethnically and culturally diverse groups of employees and customers in making operating and sales decisions. Business behavior is also bound by laws regarding pricing, hiring and firing of employees, and advertising to customers. These laws are enforced in large part by government regulatory agencies.

5. **Describe how the technological and competitive environments contribute to changes in business functions**. In some cases, innovations developed by businesses in their research departments spawn change; in other cases, innovation by competitors or government-funded laboratories lead to change. As competition—for suppliers, for financing, and for customers—increases, businesses are forced to change and improve to hold on to and/or increase their market share.

6. **State the relationship between economic and political systems and describe the economic environment created by these systems**. A country's political system—capitalism, socialism, or communism—determines the degree to which it adopts a market or command economy. While a free market economy encourages change and fuels economic growth, some government regulation is necessary to compensate for the unequal distribution of limited resources that results when the main goal of businesses is to earn a profit. Socialism and communism attempt to allocate scarce resources so that everyone has access to them. However, while socialism allows some private business ownership, communism does not, requiring a strong central government and a rigid command economy. Today, all systems are actually mixed economies, although the free market approach of capitalism is becoming increasingly common throughout the world.

Transforming the Business Process

7. **Discuss the relationship between changes in the external business environment and the adoption of new business values**. Changes in the external business environment—

involving customer tastes, new laws and regulations, and improved technology, for example—require businesses to rethink their products and processes and to make internal changes so that they can offer new or improved value to customers and maintain their market share. The pace of this learning cycle depends on the extent of changes in the external environment. In responding to the external environment and in order to ensure their survival, businesses act on the basis of five values: employee commitment, competitiveness, customer satisfaction, quality, and productivity. These values share two characteristics: Each requires significant change and each is a long-term concern.

8. **Discuss how the strategies of flexibility and management innovation contribute to changes in business functions**. In order to meet the challenges of a constantly changing external environment, businesses must be flexible and innovative. Managers of large and midsized companies need to adopt the entrepreneurial spirit of smaller companies to gain the flexibility and creativity to pursue new opportunities or avoid new problems. Innovation involves changes in products, in the quality of work processes, and in the empowering of employees.

9. **Discuss how a focus on people—through the strategies of employee development and customer focus—helps transform business functions**. In changing the way employees are treated and managed, management empowers employees to help the business learn and develop in response to the changing environment. Increased concern for customers' needs begins with marketing and extends through management to the employees on the frontlines, who provide service to customers.

10. **Describe business's financial strategies for improving performance and financing operations**. Rapid technological improvements in methods of tracking and controlling finances can be used to help a business learn and change rapidly by enabling more open ways of sharing and using all available information. Through accounting, this information can be used to project into the future and to adopt quality improvement and employee development strategies. Financial management must also be creative in locating outside sources for cash to finance the business's operations and in increasing the value of its products while holding the line on costs, perhaps through business process reengineering or downsizing.

11. **Identify the skills now required for a business career**. In choosing a career, students should consider what they want to do and what they are good at, then develop all-purpose job skills that can be transferred from one growth area to another. The new skills needed involve quality improvement, leadership, teamwork, problem solving and creativity, and how to deal with change.

Key Terms

business **5**	social environment **10**	socialism **14**	innovation **18**
profit **5**	organizational culture **10**	mixed economy **14**	empowerment **20**
customers **5**	technological environment	communism **14**	total quality management
management **6**	**11**	gross domestic product	(TQM) **20**
production **6**	markets **12**	(GDP) **14**	learning organizations **21**
marketing **7**	market share **12**	imports **15**	benchmarking **21**
controlling **7**	economics **13**	exports **15**	reengineering **24**
accounting **7**	market economy **13**	learning cycle **16**	downsizing **24**
information systems **7**	command economy **13**	values **17**	employee orientation **26**
financial management **7**	capitalism **13**	entrepreneurship **18**	

● Review Questions

1. In terms of overall goals, how are for-profit and social-oriented businesses similar and different?

2. How do the six functions of a business work together as an ever-changing business process?

3. How would the six external environments of business influence a paper manufacturer, for example?

4. Why do economists say that most countries have mixed economies?

5. In response to the changing external environment, businesses are concerned about five values. What are they and what characteristics do they share?

6. What six strategies are businesses employing in order to satisfy their values?

7. How does the quality improvement strategy differ from traditional approaches?

8. How do the five activities of learning organizations speed up the learning cycle?

9. How does the business process reengineering approach improve on downsizing as a means of dealing with growing cost pressures?

10. If you decided that you wanted a career in home health-care assistance, the fastest growing field, what types of skills would you need to develop?

• Critical Thinking Questions

1. Why are companies like Xerox teaching employees teamwork and problem-solving skills?

2. Do you think businesses should downsize at the same time that they use employee development strategies?

3. Why do you think small businesses are hiring while big businesses are laying off employees?

4. Why do you think the proportions of temporary and part-time workers are increasing in the United States?

5. Social scientists predict that two consumer groups—minorities and retirees—will increase in size and spending power in the 1990s. What changes might your school want to make to attract customers from either group?

PRACTICE CASE   *S.C. Johnson Wax*[41]

In this book we will help you use what you learn through cases. Each chapter features a Review Case and a Critical Thinking Case that challenge you to think about current business issues. For practice, analyze the following case. First read the case, then use the concepts you learned in Chapter 1 to answer the questions.

S.C. Johnson Wax, a well-known producer of household cleansers such as Windex, Glade, and Pledge, has recently enjoyed a dollar sales growth rate of 12 percent per year. Over the years, the company has grown by buying similar companies overseas and by expanding its product lines in the United States. Of late, competition has increased because the company's market share growth challenges its major competitors. For example, Johnson Wax now sells products that compete directly with the products of giant companies such as Procter & Gamble and Clorox.

To compete with them, Johnson Wax is focusing on its employees. As noted in *Fortune* magazine, Johnson Wax has a reputation for being "a paternalistic company with a tradition of lifetime employment and check-your-brains-at-the-door assembly lines." But now the company is changing that

by introducing work teams and giving them considerable freedom. Johnson Wax has become more customer focused, too, and it has increased innovation through research and product development. One new product, Plug-Ins, brought a spark of entrepreneurial spirit into the market in 1994. These air fresheners plug into electrical outlets and emit longer-lasting fragrances than competing products. The new strategies are summed up by Johnson Wax Chief Executive William George: "We're more focused. We're using our resources where they have a better chance of success."

Now, read the questions and use concepts from the chapter to answer them.

1. Why did Johnson Wax need to become more customer focused?

2. What other business strategies could the company have used? How?

3. Is Johnson Wax implementing an employee development strategy? How?

4. Based on what the case tells you about Johnson Wax's strategies, do you think the company is likely to downsize in the future? Why or why not?

REVIEW CASE   *Can You Save Goodyear?*[42]

Stanley Gault built Rubbermaid into a profitable, fast-moving innovator. Then he took charge of Goodyear Tire & Rubber, with the difficult task of reversing the fortunes of this large, traditional U.S. manufacturer. Goodyear's turnaround in the early 1990s is a well-known example of implementing new strategies effectively in an old company.

The company used to have the largest market share of U.S. tire sales, but foreign competitors that had made innovations in technology and quality were able to capture much of Goodyear's market. When Gault arrived, sales were down and the company was losing money instead of making a profit. Within 18 months, Gault turned losses into profits and began making radical changes in the company's organizational culture. He brought a new focus on profits, innovative ideas, quality, and customer service. And he made another major change by including every employee in the effort to turn the company around. Gault says, "I explained the objectives to all our people. I wanted everyone in the organization to know why these were our objectives, what they meant to each individual position, and how everyone fit into the picture—with no one excluded."

These were the big changes, but one little change was also important. According to Gault, "We discontinued use of the word 'employee,' and we instituted the word 'associate' because that was a leveling action. Regardless of your station in the organization, you are an associate. It is particularly important to women and minorities because they feel that the word 'employee' means you work for someone. Well, we don't work for each other, we work *with* each other."

1. Why do you think Goodyear ran into trouble initially?
2. Which of the business strategies discussed in the chapter does Goodyear's new emphasis on profits, innovative ideas, quality, and customer service represent?
3. Is Goodyear implementing an employee development strategy? How?
4. If you were Gault, which strategy would you emphasize most strongly?
5. In Gault's first year with Goodyear he paid off $1.7 million in business loans, cut costs, and increased market share. The combination turned the company's losses into profits. Which of the business strategies did Gault decide was most important to pursue first? Why?
6. Based on what the case tells you about Gault's attitude toward employees, do you think Goodyear downsized by eliminating jobs in Gault's first year there?
7. If you were Gault, what strategy would you emphasize now that Goodyear is profitable again?

CRITICAL THINKING CASE   *What Are They Doing to Your Career?*[43]

The challenges of the changing business environment have a dramatic impact on employees and their careers. A recent poll of top managers at the 1,000 largest industrial and service businesses in America pointed to a number of trends that will make a big difference to anyone working in business. The survey revealed that . . . Wait a minute! Now that you have studied recent changes in the business environment and their impact on companies and careers, you should be able to *guess* how the top executives at the largest U.S. companies answered the first three of the following questions! Give the answer you think was most common, and explain *why*.

1. Do you expect the number of regular, full-time employees at your company to increase, decrease, or remain about the same in the next three years?

2. Do you expect wages and salaries paid at your company to grow, stay the same, or shrink over the next three years?
3. Which of the following management skills are most important for new employees at your firm: leadership, production management, marketing, finance, people management, or accounting?
4. Which of the skills from the list in the previous question do you think managers ranked as *least* important?
5. If you asked top managers from small, entrepreneurial companies the same questions, what answers do you think they would give? If they differ, explain why.

Critical Thinking with the ONE MINUTE MANAGER [44]

"I'm amazed that Scott Olson was able to build such a huge company—didn't you say Rollerblade, Inc., currently sells more than half of all the in-line skates sold in the United States?" Carlos asked as the students left the building with the One Minute Manager.

"Yes," Joanna added, "and that graph you put up showed that industry sales have grown from a few thousand dollars in 1980 to more than $380 million in 1995. It's amazing to think that one entrepreneur can single-handedly create a major new industry in just 15 years."

"He can't—at least not by himself," answered the One Minute Manager. "Olson's idea certainly spawned an industry, but he needed lots of help and expertise from others, too. For instance, in order to expand Rollerblade, Inc., Olson had to bring in investors. And in 1985, he and the investors disagreed about how to manage the company. Do you know where Olson is today? He left Rollerblade, Inc. In fact, he is now one of their competitors, running a new company called Innovative Sport Systems that makes high-performance in-line skates."

"Wow, I guess even successful entrepreneurs are not immune to change in the business environment," Carlos commented with a shake of his head. "Is Olson's new company the biggest competitor for Rollerblade, Inc.?"

"No, it only sells about 3 percent of all in-line skates. The biggest competitor is Variflex, with about a fourth of the market. But the biggest long-term threat might be Bauer. It's a leader in the hockey skate market, but it entered the in-line skate market late and has about 10 percent of it so far."

1. What sports do in-line skates compete with indirectly? How might the growth in sales of roller skates affect sales of ice skates? Bicycles? Skateboards? Running shoes? Surfboards?

2. Can you think of reasons why this new sport might help other types of products increase their sales? For example, what impact does this new product have on sales of knee pads?

3. Bauer, a leading maker of ice skates, did not enter the in-line skate market until the early 1990s. If you ran Bauer, would you have entered the in-line skate market as soon as you learned about Rollerblade, Inc., and its products back in the early 1980s? Consider the pros and cons of entering a new but related market.

4. Now assume that this new market would have been profitable for Bauer in the 1980s. What internal factors might have kept Bauer from entering despite the opportunity it represented? Why don't companies always pursue new opportunities when they first see them?

2 Business and Economics

Business operates in an economic environment, as you learned in Chapter 1. *Economic systems*, such as capitalism, dictate how a society allocates scarce resources among competing uses. But all of us produce, consume, and exchange goods and services in the economy. So economics, at its root, studies everyday life. You might think that millions of Americans, each making countless economic decisions each day, would be a recipe for complete confusion. Yet somehow our economic system combines all those decisions into a vibrant economy in which businesses can thrive and people can pursue happiness and material well-being. After reading this chapter, you will be able to reach the learning goals below.

Learning Goals

1. State the basic premise underlying economic decision making and identify the four factors of production.
2. Discuss how demand and supply, in relation to equilibrium price, determine the exchange of goods and services.
3. Identify the four degrees of competition and describe how each exists in a free market economy.
4. Describe the circular flow of economic activity and explain how the categories of gross domestic product (GDP) relate to that flow.
5. Explain the effect of inflation on GDP and describe how inflation is measured.
6. Discuss the causes of economic fluctuations in the business cycle.
7. Identify the types of unemployment.
8. Identify and describe the sources of economic growth.
9. Describe the ways in which government can help create a secure and stable business environment.
10. Describe government's role in correcting market failures and protecting the disadvantaged.

This Is Cotton Country

"Thanks for breakfast," the One Minute Manager said contentedly as the waiter cleared their plates.

"Don't mention it," Carlos replied. "We want to repay you in a small way for the time you're giving us."

"I've been admiring your T-shirts," the One Minute Manager said with a smile. "Are Ralph Lauren and Tommy Hilfiger related?"

"Only by entrepreneurship," Joanna quipped. "Ralph Lauren has his label on everything from clothing to cologne to sheets and towels. And Tommy Hilfiger started out in around 1970 with $150 selling bell-bottom jeans to his friends in high school. Now his clothing business is worth millions, and he's the fashion choice of lots of big-name music stars."[1]

"Everybody I know likes his clothing because it's so comfortable," Carlos added.

"He knows his cotton, that's for sure," the One Minute Manager observed. "An article I read in the *Wall Street Journal*[2] described how the popularity of cotton clothing coupled with crop failures in cotton-producing countries like China and Pakistan has driven up the price of cotton and encouraged farmers all over the South to begin planting it again."

"I thought the boll weevil pretty much wiped out cotton farming in the South," Carlos said.

"You're right," she replied. "But low prices also played a major part. So many countries produced so much cotton that American farmers simply couldn't make a living growing it. They turned to other crops like peanuts and tobacco. But when China's cotton crops began failing in the early 1990s, prices rose 40 percent, to roughly a dollar a pound in mid-1995. That's the first 'dollar cotton' U.S. farmers have seen since the Civil War."

"But what will happen when foreign production picks up again?" Joanna asked.

"Time will tell," replied the One Minute Manager. "What if styles change and the demand for cotton drops? It's all a matter of supply and demand—basic economics."

Economic Choices

We continually confront economic choices because we cannot have everything we want. And we can't have everything we want because resources are limited. **Resources** are the inputs used to produce goods and services. For example, construction of a new house requires materials such as timber, brick, and metal; tools such as drills, saws, bulldozers, and cranes; and people—their time and their skills. These resources have many different potential uses. The timber could have been used to make paper. The tools could have been used to build a school. The construction workers could have spent their time repairing a road, or playing with their children. Our world is one in which we must constantly decide how to make the best use of our limited resources.

Economists recognize that every decision involves trade-offs. If you buy a cup of coffee for 70 cents, you are giving up other things that you could have bought with the money. Because your income is limited, whenever you choose to consume one thing, you are giving up other things. If you choose to consume coffee, you may be giving up donuts. Time, too, is a limited resource. If you choose to consume some of your time at the movies, you're giving up study time. Economists call the value of these sacrificed possibilities their **opportunity cost**. The opportunity cost of a cup of coffee is the donuts or the newspaper or anything else on which you might have spent your 70 cents.

Factors of Production

Economists often classify the limited resources that we can use to produce goods and services into four **factors of production**: land, capital, labor, and entrepreneurship.

- **Land**, as the word is used by economists, refers to all nonhuman natural resources—timber; fresh water; mineral deposits such as copper, oil, and uranium; and agricultural products such as cotton and grain. Some countries are endowed with many such natural resources; other countries have only a few. An abundance of resources is no guarantee of economic success, however, for land must be combined with other factors of production to produce goods and services.

- **Capital** is any form of wealth used to produce more wealth. Capital goods are valuable because they can be used to produce other goods and services. An automobile factory and the machines within it constitute economic capital. An 18-wheeler that transports goods from a warehouse to a store is a type of capital. An office building is capital, as are all the fixtures within it—desks, chairs, carpets, lights, personal computers. And farming equipment is also capital.

- **Labor** is the time and effort expended by individuals to produce goods and services. It's simplest just to think of labor as hours of work, even though this does not take into account the fact that different people have different skills and abilities.

- *Entrepreneurship*, as you learned in Chapter 1, is risk-taking behaviors leading to the start-up and growth of businesses. It is the factor of production that organizes land, labor, and capital into a business. Ralph Lauren and Tommy Hilfiger are entrepreneurs in the fashion industry. Entrepreneurs assume many of the risks of operating a business—they enjoy the rewards of success or suffer the losses from failure. We will discuss the special role of entrepreneurship later in this chapter and in Chapter 6.

1. State the basic premise underlying economic decision making and identify the four factors of production.

Businesspeople often use the word capital *to refer to money or other financial resources used to start up or operate a business. But to an economist, capital refers only to goods that can be used to help produce other goods and services.*

 resources

The inputs used to produce goods and services.

 opportunity cost

The value of sacrificed possibilities.

 factors of production

The four classes of limited resources: land, capital, labor, and entrepreneurship.

 land

All nonhuman natural resources.

 capital

Any form of wealth used to produce more wealth.

 labor

The time and effort expended by individuals to produce goods and services.

The Big Economic Questions

Economics studies production, consumption, and exchange in a world of limited resources that have competing uses. Because these topics are so basic to the functioning of the world we live in, economics helps us think about some fundamental questions concerning our society.

- *What should we produce?* With the resources at our disposal we could produce *consumer* products (food, clothing, haircuts) to satisfy our wants today. Or we could produce *capital* goods (engines, airplanes, factories) that will help us have more goods tomorrow. We could devote our resources to national defense, or we could devote our resources to public education. Economics helps us understand how we can choose among the different potential uses of our resources.

- *How should we produce?* We can produce many different products with the same resources. We can also produce the same products in different ways using different resources. For example, we could farm cotton using many farm workers and little machinery or few workers and a lot of machinery. Economics helps us to understand how to organize and use our resources in the most efficient ways to produce what we want.

How Should We Produce?

Auto factories represent economic capital, even when they are idle, as Chrysler Corp.'s South plant in St. Louis was for three years in the early 1990s. When sales improved, Chrysler chose to expand production capacity by redesigning its old factories rather than building new ones at far greater expense. The reengineered plant, featuring a state-of-the-art assembly line and a totally self-directed work force, has dramatically improved productivity and quality control.

- *For whom should we produce?* Who gets the benefit of production? Who does well in our economy and who does not? Does our society distribute goods and services relatively equally or relatively unequally? Economics helps us to understand how economic systems like capitalism and socialism distribute goods and services among all the members of a society.

Economic Exchanges

An economic system provides the environment in which people and businesses exchange goods and services. As you learned in Chapter 1, individual decisions about how much to buy and sell determine the allocation of limited resources in a free market economy. Every transaction, every exchange, brings benefits to the participants. The freedom to buy and sell things keeps our market economy functioning and underpins our economic well-being.

Did you buy a cup of coffee this morning? If so, you handed 70 cents or so to the counterperson and got a cup of coffee in return. You participated in this exchange voluntarily—nobody made you buy the coffee—because it was worth it to you to give up 70 cents to get a cup. Likewise, nobody forced the coffee shop to sell you coffee. For the shop, it was worth it to give you the coffee and get 70 cents in exchange.

The simple fact is that the seller of coffee and you, the buyer of coffee, both gained because you both *chose* to take part in this exchange. You got a cup of coffee, which was worth more to you than the 70 cents you gave up. The coffee shop got 70 cents, which was worth more to it than the cup of coffee it gave up. Everybody's happy. Who says economics is a dismal science?

Buying a cup of coffee is an example of perhaps the most important single idea in economics: Trade makes people better off. In a free market, there are lots of chances for mutually beneficial trade. This is why economists generally like free market economies, and this is why economists usually support free trade among nations. Just as your trading money for coffee benefits both you and the seller of coffee, so U.S. trade with other countries benefits both us and other countries. The reason is the same in both cases. Nobody forces us to buy products produced in other countries, and nobody forces foreigners to buy our products. You will learn more about international trade in Chapter 3.

Demand: The Willingness to Buy

Many factors influence your willingness to buy a cup of coffee in the morning, or your willingness to buy a car or health insurance or any other product. One of the most important is the *price* you have to pay. At a price of 70 cents, you are willing to buy one cup of coffee. If the price of a cup of coffee were $1, you might decide not to buy any at all. If the price were 30 cents, you might decide to buy two cups. Generally, when the price of a good or service is lower, we expect that people will be willing to buy more of it. Remember that the opportunity cost of a cup of coffee is the other goods and services you could have bought instead. If the price is lower, the opportunity cost is lower, and you will therefore be willing to buy more. Economists call your willingness to buy a good or service **demand**.

Economists picture the entire range of quantities consumers will demand at different prices as a **demand curve**, shown in Figure 2.1 (page 38). For example, we obtain the demand curve for cups of coffee on a typical day in your town by adding up the quantity demanded by all potential buyers. The demand curve might look like Figure 2.1(a): At a price of $1 per cup, only 20 cups would be demanded. At a price of 70 cents per cup, 80 cups would be demanded. And at a price of 30 cents per cup, the quantity demanded would be 160 cups.

Of course, your demand for coffee doesn't depend only on its price. It also depends on your income, on how much you like coffee relative to tea, on the price of donuts, on the price of a cup of tea, and on other factors too numerous to mention. A change in any one of these might change the quantity you demand. For example, if you got a pay raise, you might be willing to buy two

2. Discuss how demand and supply, in relation to equilibrium price, determine the exchange of goods and services.

 demand

The willingness to buy a good or service.

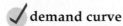 **demand curve**

The entire range of quantities consumers will demand at different prices.

cups of coffee at 70 cents a cup. If everyone's income were higher, we would expect to see an increase in demand for coffee at all prices. Changes of this sort cause the entire demand curve to move to the right, as in Figure 2.1(b). If the price of a cup of tea fell substantially, people might decide to drink tea instead of coffee. The demand curve for coffee would then move to the left, as in Figure 2.1(c).

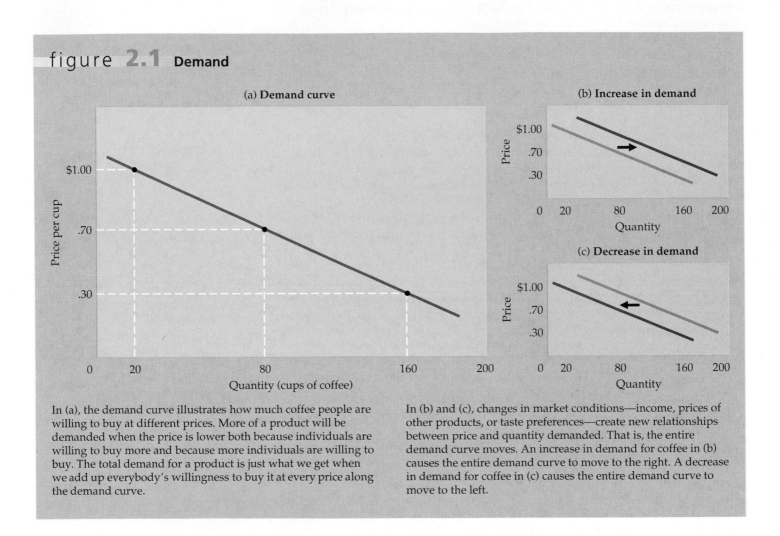

figure 2.1   Demand

(a) Demand curve

(b) Increase in demand

(c) Decrease in demand

In (a), the demand curve illustrates how much coffee people are willing to buy at different prices. More of a product will be demanded when the price is lower both because individuals are willing to buy more and because more individuals are willing to buy. The total demand for a product is just what we get when we add up everybody's willingness to buy it at every price along the demand curve.

In (b) and (c), changes in market conditions—income, prices of other products, or taste preferences—create new relationships between price and quantity demanded. That is, the entire demand curve moves. An increase in demand for coffee in (b) causes the entire demand curve to move to the right. A decrease in demand for coffee in (c) causes the entire demand curve to move to the left.

Supply: The Willingness to Sell

Demand is the willingness to buy a good or service. Now let's think about the other side of the exchange, **supply**, which is the willingness to sell a good or service.

   If the price of a product is high, sellers are likely to be willing to supply a lot of it. If the price is low, on the other hand, sellers may not think it's worth their while to sell. So, if the price of coffee goes up, we would expect coffee producers to be willing to sell more. Just as with demand, we would find both that individual suppliers were willing to sell more and that more suppliers were interested in selling. Notice that, at a higher price, demanders are willing to buy less but suppliers are willing to sell more, independent of demand.

   We could figure out the quantity of coffee supplied to the market at any given price by adding up the entire range of quantities sellers will supply at

 supply

The willingness to sell a good or service.

figure **2.2** Supply

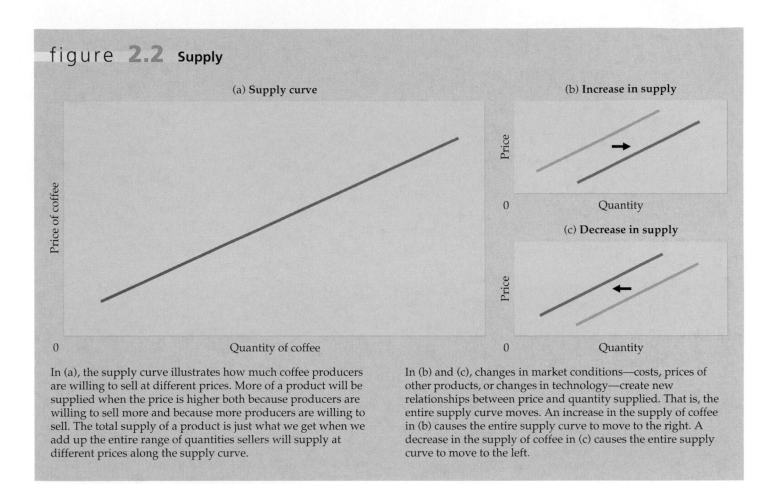

(a) Supply curve

(b) Increase in supply

(c) Decrease in supply

In (a), the supply curve illustrates how much coffee producers are willing to sell at different prices. More of a product will be supplied when the price is higher both because producers are willing to sell more and because more producers are willing to sell. The total supply of a product is just what we get when we add up the entire range of quantities sellers will supply at different prices along the supply curve.

In (b) and (c), changes in market conditions—costs, prices of other products, or changes in technology—create new relationships between price and quantity supplied. That is, the entire supply curve moves. An increase in the supply of coffee in (b) causes the entire supply curve to move to the right. A decrease in the supply of coffee in (c) causes the entire supply curve to move to the left.

different prices. If we graph this **supply curve** for all possible prices of coffee, we get a picture such as Figure 2.2(a).

Many factors other than price affect the willingness to sell coffee. For example, a bad harvest might mean that coffee producers would supply fewer coffee beans to the market at every price. If the cost of hiring workers to harvest coffee beans were to fall, on the other hand, suppliers might be willing to supply more to the market at every price. Think about what would happen to the supply curve in each of these two cases. If suppliers were willing to sell more coffee at every price, then the supply curve would shift to the right, as in Figure 2.2(b). If suppliers were willing to sell less coffee at every price, then the supply curve would shift to the left, as in Figure 2.2(c).

Determining the Price

For any product, there is one price at which the quantity supplied and the quantity demanded are exactly equal. This is the **equilibrium price**. Figure 2.3 (page 40) shows how the demand and supply for cotton T-shirts together determine the price of T-shirts.

The equilibrium price is the price at which a good or service will usually be sold. Why? Suppose that the equilibrium price of T-shirts is $10, but they are being offered for sale at $12. Suppliers will want to sell more T-shirts than demanders are willing to buy. Nobody can force people to buy more T-shirts than they want. So suppliers are going to be disappointed because they are not going to be able to sell as many T-shirts as they would like.

supply curve

The entire range of quantities sellers will supply at different prices.

equilibrium price

The one price at which the quantity supplied and the quantity demanded are exactly equal.

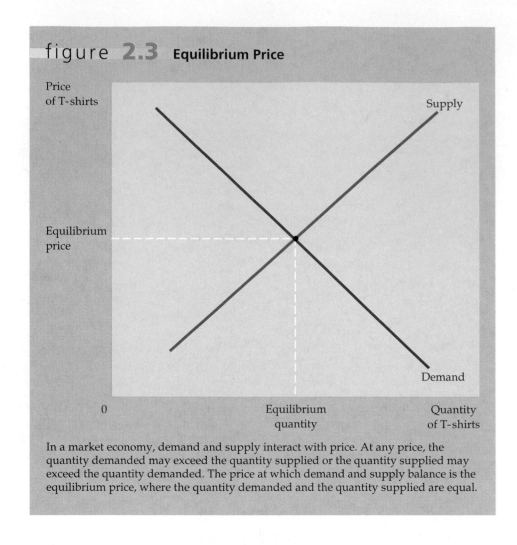

figure **2.3**   **Equilibrium Price**

In a market economy, demand and supply interact with price. At any price, the quantity demanded may exceed the quantity supplied or the quantity supplied may exceed the quantity demanded. The price at which demand and supply balance is the equilibrium price, where the quantity demanded and the quantity supplied are equal.

How will suppliers and demanders respond to this situation? Smart buyers might offer to buy T-shirts at a lower price. Suppliers, meanwhile, are likely to reduce the price to try to get rid of their unsold T-shirts. If the actual price is above the equilibrium price, the actual price will fall. Similarly, if the actual price is below the equilibrium price, buyers will be disappointed because they will want to buy more T-shirts than suppliers are willing to sell. Suppliers are likely to respond by raising their prices, and demanders are likely to offer a higher price.

And so, whenever a product is being bought and sold at some price other than its equilibrium price, market forces tend to move the price toward equilibrium. Only when T-shirts are trading at their equilibrium price will there be no reason for the price to change. This interaction of supply and demand to create equilibrium is the single most important tool used by economists. To learn more about using supply and demand, see the skills check entitled "Using Supply and Demand."

The Magic of Free Markets

Think for a moment more about the supply and demand picture in Figure 2.3. Why is it that more of a product will be bought and sold at the equilibrium price than at any other price? First, if the prices were higher, buyers (demanders) would be willing to buy less. If the price were lower, sellers (suppliers) would be willing to supply less. And remember, people aren't forced to buy or sell.

skills check

Using Supply and Demand

Suppose someone told you that frosts in Brazil had ruined much of the coffee crop. What would you expect to happen to the price of coffee beans and to the quantity of coffee beans bought and sold? To answer this question, you first need to draw a supply and demand picture like that in (a). Then ask yourself: What effect does the bad weather have on the supply and demand curves? If frosts have damaged the coffee crop, suppliers will be willing to sell less coffee at any given price. So the supply curve will shift to the left. The bad weather won't affect the demand for coffee—you're just as likely to drink coffee when it's cold in Brazil as when it's warm there. So you would get a picture like that in (b).

Now you can see that the equilibrium price of coffee beans will rise and that fewer beans will be bought and sold. That's important news if you're a coffee producer in Brazil, a coffee producer in Mexico, a supermarket manager in Chicago, or even if you're just someone who likes to drink coffee. The conclusion we just drew from our supply and demand picture also describes exactly what happened in the summer of 1994. Frosts in Brazil destroyed between one-third and one-half of the Brazilian coffee crop. As a result, the price of coffee beans rose from 48 cents a pound in 1993 to $2.74 a pound in July 1994.[*]

Work out the following examples for yourself. In each case, think about what happens to the demand curve and the supply curve, and draw the supply and demand picture.

1. What will happen to the price of sodas in a heat wave? Draw the picture. What happens to the number of sodas bought and sold?

2. What happens to the price of snowblowers in summer? In winter?

3. Suppose medical researchers announce that hot fudge sundaes help prevent heart attacks. What will happen to the price of sundaes? Draw the picture. Will more or fewer be sold?

4. Suppose a hurricane destroys thousands of buildings in Miami. What will happen to the price of houses there? To the price of lumber and other building materials? To the wages of construction workers in Miami?

[*]*The Economist,* July 16, 1994, p. 70.

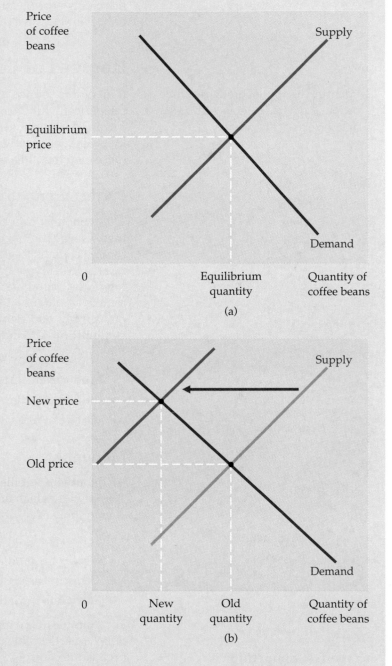

Now remember also that sellers and buyers choose to take part in exchanges because those exchanges make them better off. If they weren't going to gain, they wouldn't be willing to participate. So there is benefit obtained from each exchange. At the equilibrium price, therefore, the maximum possible number of mutually beneficial exchanges occurs, and *all the possible gains from exchange will be exhausted.* This makes free markets more efficient than other economic systems.

Besides being efficient, market systems help direct society's resources to produce the goods that society desires. Suppose people become more health conscious, and so want to eat more fish and less beef. The increased demand for fish will raise the price of fish, so suppliers will be willing to sell a greater quantity. The decreased demand for beef will lower the price of beef, so suppliers will be willing to sell a smaller quantity. The higher price of fish and the lower price of beef will cause producers to shift resources away from the production of beef and toward the production of fish.

Degrees of Competition

3. Identify the four degrees of competition and describe how each exists in a free market economy.

If all of this sounds too good to be true, that's because it is. Economists picture the perfectly functioning markets of their supply and demand curve as an ideal free market, not a description of reality. Some markets do operate close to this ideal. Others operate with no competition at all. Most markets operate between these extremes. In a market economy four degrees of competition exist.

Perfect Competition

The economist's ideal market applies well to the market for cotton. First of all, there are large numbers of buyers and sellers. Second, all cotton is pretty much the same. It is a *homogeneous* good. If you're a cotton farmer, you're not going to be able to sell your cotton at a price higher than equilibrium, the price prevailing in the cotton market. If you tried to sell cotton at a higher price, your customers would buy their cotton elsewhere. The market for cotton works just like our supply and demand picture, a situation economists describe as **perfect competition**. The industry conditions for this ideal are as follows:

- There are many sellers.
- Products are virtually identical.
- Individual sellers have no influence on price.
- Firms can freely enter into and exit from the industry.

Monopoly

At the other extreme from perfect competition is the **monopoly**, an industry condition in which one firm sells a unique product and there is no competition. A monopoly exists if the following conditions prevail:

- There is only one firm in the industry.
- The firm is producing a good for which no good substitutes exist.
- The firm has great control over price.
- Entry into the industry is difficult or impossible.

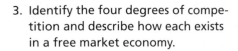

perfect competition

An industry condition in which there are many sellers, the products are virtually identical, individual sellers have no influence on price, and firms can freely enter into and exit from the industry.

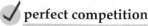

monopoly

An industry condition in which one firm sells a unique product and there is no competition.

For example, there may be only one supplier of cable television in your area, in which case the cable company has a monopoly. Or a firm may have a monopoly because it controls an important patent. Business rivals complain that computer software giant Microsoft Corp. holds a virtual monopoly on the software that runs personal computers.[3]

A company with a monopoly realizes that it can keep prices high by making less of its product available. Economists say that it has *market power* (such a company is described in the ethics check entitled "Diamonds Are a Monopoly's Best Friend"). As a result, it will charge a price higher than the one it would charger under perfect competition, and fewer products will be sold. The company makes extra profits, but consumers lose out—and they lose more than the company with the monopoly gains, so society as a whole loses. That is why the government seeks to regulate monopolies such as those of many electric utility companies.

ethics check

Diamonds Are a Monopoly's Best Friend

Gem-quality diamonds are prized for their beauty and rarity. And they are rare—and expensive—because the total supply of gem-quality stones is controlled by one supplier, the DeBeers Company of South Africa. By tightly controlling the quantity of diamonds it releases for sale on world markets, DeBeers keeps the price of diamonds artificially high.

In fact, if all the gem-quality diamonds available from the DeBeers mines in Zimbabwe and South Africa were released for sale, the vast increase in supply would cause a plunge in diamond prices worldwide. That's exactly what happened to the price of amethysts in the 1800s. At that time, amethysts were very highly prized. But when abundant deposits of the gems were found in Brazil, suppliers flooded the market and the price of amethysts dropped for good.

Business ethics is a topic we consider in detail in Chapter 4. For now, take a minute to think about both sides of this issue. How would you view the DeBeers monopoly if you:

1. Owned stock in the company?

2. Operated a local jewelry store?

3. Wanted to buy an engagement ring?

Monopolistic Competition

Most U.S. industries lie between the extremes of perfect competition and monopoly. Firms may have a monopoly over their own product, perhaps because they own a brand name such as Snapple, but many close substitutes, such as Lipton, Fruitopia, or Arizona, can still exist. Economists call this level of competition **monopolistic competition**, an industry condition in which sellers differentiate their products on the basis of price and quality and so have some influence over price.

Consider restaurant meals, for example. A meal at McDonald's is different from a meal at Red Lobster, and both are different from a meal at a fancy French restaurant. So each restaurant has a monopoly: If you really want a McDonald's hamburger, you won't be able to buy one at Pizza Hut. Still, if you think the prices at the French restaurant are too high, you can go to the Thai restaurant next door. All these restaurants produce meals, but each meal is different.

Monopolistic competitors emphasize differences in product quality and price by advertising. Once a product is successful, competitors are quick to jump into the market. Other examples of differentiated products are cotton T-shirts and dental services. Monopolistic competition is characterized by these conditions:

- There are large numbers of sellers.

- Products are differentiated.

- Sellers have some control over price.

- Entry and exit are relatively easy, and success invites new competitors.

✓ **monopolistic competition**

An industry condition in which sellers differentiate their products on the basis of price and quality and so have some influence over price.

oligopoly

An industry condition in which a few firms, each large enough to influence pricing, sell similar or differentiated products.

microeconomics

Study of the economic activity of individual buyers and sellers.

macroeconomics

Study of the workings of an economy as a whole.

Monopolistic competitors possess some market power—they can raise their prices a little bit without losing all their sales. As a consequence, they will set their prices higher than they would under perfect competition.

Oligopoly

Finally, there is the **oligopoly**, an industry condition in which a few firms, each large enough to influence pricing, sell similar or differentiated products. An example is the automobile industry. Another is the cement industry. These two industries are different—automobiles are differentiated products, whereas cement is not. The key feature of an oligopoly is the small number of firms, not what they produce. Specifically, an oligopoly is characterized by the following:

- There are a small number of large firms.
- Products may be differentiated or similar.
- Firms have control over price but must consider how competitors will react to price changes.
- Entry and exit are limited.

Table 2.1 summarizes the four degrees of competition that exist in a market economy.

table **2.1**   Degrees of Competition

Level of Competition	Number of Sellers	Products Are	Market Power?	Easy to Enter?	Basis of Competition	Examples
Perfect competition	Many	Homogeneous	No	Yes	Price only	Cotton, wheat
Monopoly	One	Unique	Yes	No	Market demand; government regulation	Electric company, water company
Monopolistic competition	Many	Differentiated	Yes	Yes	Price, quality	Auto repair shops, credit cards
Oligopoly	Few	Homogeneous or differentiated	Some	Limited	Actions of competitors	Breakfast cereals, copper pipe

The Economic System as a Whole

So far, we have been studying the economic activity of individual buyers and sellers. This is **microeconomics**. In this section, we explore **macroeconomics**, the workings of an economy as a whole.

The performance of an entire economy depends upon all the individual exchanges that take place within it. Billions of transactions take place in the United States every day. Did you buy coffee and donuts this morning? If so, you didn't just engage in a microeconomic exchange; in a tiny way, you influenced the economy's macroeconomic performance. So, too, did the people who bought and sold bus rides, apples, haircuts, televisions, insurance, and every other good or service you can think of.

The Circular Flow

So far, we've talked about producers making supply decisions and consumers making demand decisions. But it's important to realize that although businesses *supply* products, such as cups of coffee or copper pipe, they also *demand* labor and other inputs. Likewise, while your buying decisions may be part of the *demand* for coffee, you also make selling decisions that are part of the *supply* of labor. Perhaps you have a job now or plan to get one when you leave college. An economist would think of your work as your supply of labor to the labor market, where businesses are the demanders.

To make sense of all the exchanges in an economy, we adopt a macro perspective. We ignore individual exchanges in order to focus on the overall level of activity in the economy. One way to do this is to pretend that there is only one good produced in the economy. Let's call it pizza.

In our pizza economy there are households and firms. Firms hire workers from the households and employ them to produce pizza. Households spend the wages they get from working to buy pizza. So firms buy labor and sell pizza, while households buy pizza and sell labor. In Figure 2.4, we see that pizza flows from the firms to the households, and dollars flow from the households to the firms in exchange. Likewise, labor hours flow from households to the firms, and dollars flow from firms to households in exchange. The constant interactions among buyers and sellers in an economy are called the **circular flow**.

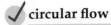
circular flow

The constant interactions among buyers and sellers in an economy.

4. Describe the circular flow of economic activity and explain how the categories of gross domestic product (GDP) relate to that flow.

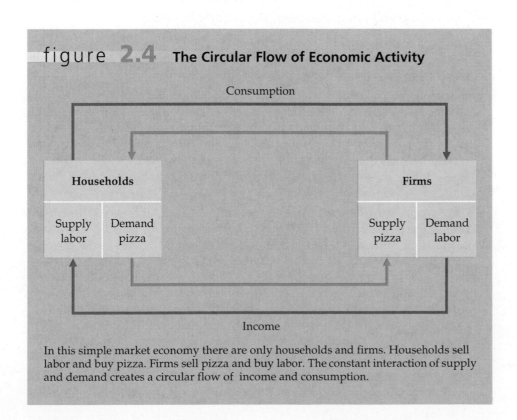

figure 2.4   **The Circular Flow of Economic Activity**

Consumption

Households
Supply labor | Demand pizza

Firms
Supply pizza | Demand labor

Income

In this simple market economy there are only households and firms. Households sell labor and buy pizza. Firms sell pizza and buy labor. The constant interaction of supply and demand creates a circular flow of income and consumption.

Gross Domestic Product

As you learned in Chapter 1, the *gross domestic product* measures the dollar value of all the goods and services a country produces in a given time period. Suppose that there are 10 households in our pizza economy, each with one worker, and suppose each worker can produce 20 pizzas a week. We could count up the total number of pizzas produced in a week by everyone and find that our economy produces 200 pizzas a week. This is a measure of the *total output* of the economy. If the price of a pizza is $5, then gross domestic product per week is $200 \times \$5 = \$1,000$.

Because households bought 200 pizzas from firms over the course of the week, $1,000 flowed from the households to the firms as income. Where did the households get that money? They received it as wages from the firms. So $1,000 also flowed from the firms to the households as income. Where did the firms get the money? They got it from the households as payment for the pizzas they sold. This is the circular flow of income: In our economy, $1,000 flows from the firms to the workers and back to the firms each week.

Gross domestic product measures the dollar value of the total final output of the economy. Notice that it also measures *total income* in the economy. What is more, it measures *total spending* in the economy. This remarkable fact that

$$\text{Total income} = \text{Total output} = \text{Total spending}$$

is true not just in our simple pizza economy but also in real, complicated macroeconomies like that of the United States.

The Uses of GDP

In our pizza economy, there is just one good—pizza. There's really only one use for pizza: You eat it. There are millions of different goods and services produced in the U.S. economy, however, with many different uses. Each represents a flow of dollars through the economy. Government statisticians divide total GDP into four broad categories, based on its different uses.

Another component of investment is changes in inventories. If an auto dealer buys a car from the manufacturer but doesn't sell it, then the number of cars on the dealer's lot goes up by one. That is, the dealer's inventory has increased. The value of that car is counted in GDP as part of investment.

- *Consumption* is purchases by individuals for their own needs. Examples are food, clothing, and pizza. Figure 2.4 shows an economy in which the only use for GDP is consumption.

- *Investment* refers primarily to purchases by businesses of new capital (machines, factories, etc.). Also included are purchases of *new* houses by individuals. Notice that there are now two uses of household income: It can be spent on consumption, or it can be saved. Household saving makes investment funds available to firms for purchases of new factories and machines. These funds flow from households into financial markets and from financial markets to firms.

- *Government spending* is purchases by federal, state, and local governments of things like new aircraft carriers, roads, or the services of teachers and social workers. Some funds flow from households and businesses to the government as taxes—personal and corporate income taxes, sales taxes, and so on. Businesses and households therefore have less income to divide between consumption and investment. And there are now three uses of GDP: consumption, investment, and government purchases. If government spending exceeds the amount it takes in in taxes, the government must borrow in the financial markets to make up the shortfall. As with taxes, the more the government borrows, the fewer are the funds available to firms for investment.

- *Net exports* are purchases by foreigners of U.S. goods (*exports*), minus goods bought from foreigners (*imports*). If U.S. consumers buy German automobiles or Brazilian coffee, their purchases contribute to German or Brazilian GDP, not to U.S. GDP. That is, U.S. spending on import goods flows to foreign economies, not to U.S. firms. But spending by foreigners on U.S. exports leads to a flow of dollars into U.S. firms as well. And trade with other countries opens our economy to foreign investment, as we will see in Chapter 3.

The circular flow of all four uses of GDP—consumption, investment, government spending, and net exports—is shown in Figure 2.5. Consumption is the largest component: About two-thirds of U.S. GDP goes to consumption. Government spending accounts for about one-fifth of GDP, and investment accounts for about 15 percent. Exports and imports roughly cancel out. In recent years, net exports have been −1 to −2 percent of GDP. The minus sign reflects the fact that the United States typically imports more than it exports (see Table 2.2 on the facing page).[4]

figure 2.5   The Uses of GDP in the Circular Flow

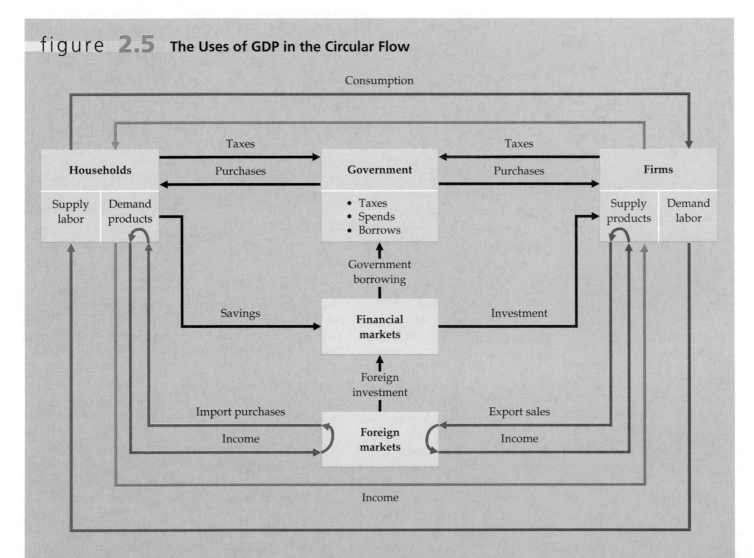

In the circular flow diagram in Figure 2.4, the economy consists only of households and firms, and consumption is the only use of income, or GDP. In the U.S. economy there are households, firms, financial markets, government, and foreign markets. And there are four uses of GDP: consumption, investment, government spending on purchases, and net exports (exports - imports). The lines indicate the flow of dollars in the economy.

Inflation

The circular flow describes demand and supply in the macroeconomy. What about prices? The prices of goods and services are constantly changing. We learned earlier in this chapter that the price of a product will change if there are shifts in the demand curve or supply curve for that product. But, on average, prices increase more than they decrease, going up a few percent each year. This increase in the overall price level is called **inflation**.

GDP and Inflation

5. Explain the effect of inflation on GDP and describe how inflation is measured.

Let's begin by thinking about inflation in our pizza economy. Remember that our economy had 10 workers, each producing 20 pizzas a week, and that each pizza sold for $5. GDP was equal to $10 \times 20 \times \$5 = \$1,000$.

Now suppose that the price of a pizza were to double, from $5 per pizza to $10 per pizza. Then our GDP would double also, from $1,000 to $2,000. If we look just at GDP we might think that the size of the economy has doubled and that we are all much richer. But the number of pizzas we are producing is the same. The apparent growth is an illusion brought about by inflation. The income of each household has doubled, but so has the price of the pizzas they buy, so they are no better or worse off than they were before.

As this example shows, it is very important to correct for inflation when we are trying to figure out whether growth in GDP reflects growing living standards (more pizza per household), or whether it just reflects higher prices. In our pizza economy, **nominal GDP**, that is, GDP measured in today's dollars, unadjusted for inflation, rose from $1,000 to $2,000. But inflation-adjusted GDP, or **real GDP**, was unchanged. Figure 2.6 shows the difference between real GDP and nominal GDP for the U.S. economy from 1990 through 1994. You can see the effect of inflation during this period. While nominal GDP rose in all five years, real GDP actually declined from 1990 to 1991.

Measuring Inflation

Government statisticians try to come up with measures of overall inflation in the economy. One such measure, the **consumer price index (CPI),** is calculated by comparing how the cost of a typical *basket of goods* that a household might buy changes from month to month or year to year. If the basket of products cost $1,000 last year and $1,050 this year, the inflation rate is 5 percent [(1,050 − 1,000) ÷ 1,000 = 0.05].

Two factors make coming up with reliable measures of inflation a difficult task. First, the products that people purchase change over time: Twenty years ago, very few people were buying personal computers, for example. Second, the quality of goods changes over time: The $2,000 you spend on a new personal computer today buys you much more computing power than $2,000 bought you five years ago. While the price of a state-of-the-art IBM PC or Apple Macintosh hasn't changed much over the last few years, the price of *computing power* has dropped dramatically.[5] But even our best measures of inflation do not properly account for these changes.

All well-informed, effective businesspeople are careful to distinguish between economic statistics that are in *real* terms (adjusted for inflation) and those that are in *nominal* terms (today's dollars). Whenever you see or hear economic figures being quoted, consider whether or not those figures have been corrected for inflation. What you will soon learn is that information can be very misleading when it does not distinguish properly between nominal figures and real figures.

inflation

Increase in the overall price level.

nominal GDP

GDP measured in today's dollars, unadjusted for inflation.

real GDP

Inflation-adjusted GDP.

consumer price index (CPI)

A measure of inflation calculated by comparing how the cost of a typical basket of goods that a household might buy changes from month to month or year to year.

In recent years, Americans have enjoyed relatively low inflation rates. From 1989 to the middle of 1991, for example, the CPI inflation rate averaged about 5 percent per year. From 1991 to mid-1995, the inflation rate was even lower—about 3 percent per year on average. Inflation of 3 percent means that a kitchen table that cost $100 this year will cost $103 next year. Even such relatively low inflation rates can accumulate rapidly, however. After 25 years of 3 percent inflation, that $100 table would cost well over $200. Not so very long ago, at the end of the 1970s, Americans experienced inflation of over 10 percent per year. Inflation at that rate will cause prices to double after a period of only seven years.

There are actually many measures of inflation. They differ according to the kinds of products included in the market basket. The CPI is the most important measure because it best captures the price changes faced by consumers.

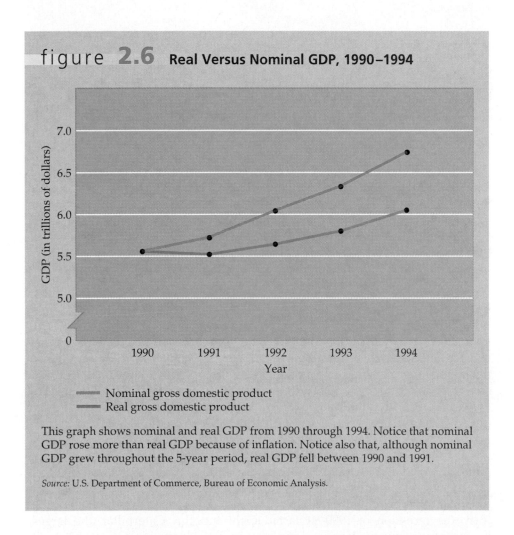

figure **2.6** **Real Versus Nominal GDP, 1990–1994**

── Nominal gross domestic product
── Real gross domestic product

This graph shows nominal and real GDP from 1990 through 1994. Notice that nominal GDP rose more than real GDP because of inflation. Notice also that, although nominal GDP grew throughout the 5-year period, real GDP fell between 1990 and 1991.

Source: U.S. Department of Commerce, Bureau of Economic Analysis.

The Costs of Inflation

Is inflation a bad thing? We can return to our pizza economy to think about this question. Imagine that the price of pizza has doubled (100 percent inflation). If you lived in that economy and looked just at the price of pizza, you'd be pretty upset. But remember that workers' wages have also doubled, so your household has twice as much income as before. Provided your dollar income rises in line with inflation, you're no worse off than you were before.

An Economic Crisis: Hyperinflation

As these grocery shoppers in Brazil know all too well, inflation can get out of control, with prices doubling every month or even every day. In 1990, Brazil's inflation rate was 1,795 percent! An economy suffering such runaway inflation, or hyperinflation, is in danger of collapse. Nobody wants to hold cash because it loses its value so quickly. But cash allows exchanges to take place easily in a market economy, so hyperinflation can cause the collapse of much economic activity. Ukraine, Israel, and Bolivia have also experienced hyperinflations.

Still, most people dislike inflation because it distorts the value of money. One group that is hit hard by rising inflation is retired people who live on fixed incomes that don't change in line with inflation. And because our tax system does not take proper account of inflation, homeowners who sell face an unfair tax burden if the value of their house has increased because of inflation. Inflation is not easy to predict in the real world, so consumers and businesses have to make decisions in an uncertain environment.

The Business Cycle

Even after we correct for the fact that some growth in nominal GDP is due only to inflation, we discover that, on average, real GDP increases over time. Sometimes economic growth is rapid, and sometimes it is slow. Occasionally, growth stalls completely, and the economy actually produces less one year than it did the year before. Recall the blip in Figure 2.6. Prolonged downturns in economic activity are called **recessions**. The pattern of overall, up-and-down fluctuations in economic growth over time is called the **business cycle**.

Recessions cause widespread unemployment and business failures. In the granddaddy of all recessions, the Great Depression of the 1930s, real GDP fell by almost a third and one-quarter of U.S. workers were unemployed. Millions lost their jobs and homes. The Great Depression lasted several years. By contrast, the recession of 1990–91 lasted eight months. Caterpillar, the largest heavy construction equipment manufacturer in the United States, lost $404 million in 1991 as a result of that recession. The three biggest U.S. automakers, General Motors, Ford, and Chrysler, lost a combined total of $7.5 billion that year.[6] While overall corporate profits were climbing in the mid-1990s, economists feared that some weak industries, such as retailing and aerospace, could be devastated by the next recession.

To guard against fluctuations in the business cycle, U.S. firms are applying the strategies you learned about in Chapter 1. Their goal is to make their companies recession-proof. They are adopting more flexible forms of doing business, innovating in the areas of management and employee empowerment, focusing on their customers, and improving their control systems and financial management.

 recessions

Prolonged downturns in economic activity.

 business cycle

Pattern of overall, up-and-down fluctuations in economic growth over time.

Explaining the Business Cycle

Periodic downturns in economic activity are inevitable, as are periodic upswings. As you might expect, a lot of effort goes into trying to explain, anticipate, and control the business cycle. Among the causes of business cycle fluctuations are changes in spending by businesses, consumers, and government and changes in the supply of the factors of production.

Changes in Consumption Spending Our discussion of the circular flow taught us that consumption spending is the major source of demand for the goods and services produced by firms. But if your company is downsizing and you are nervous that you might lose your job, you probably will buy no more than you need, diverting your extra money to savings or to paying off bills. If you feel secure about your future, however, you're more likely to buy that new car or washing machine. So one source of business cycle fluctuation is *consumer confidence*. When consumer confidence goes up, consumption spending goes up and real GDP increases. If consumer confidence goes down, real GDP falls.

Consumption spending is affected not only by beliefs about the future but also by changes in government policy. For example, if the government cuts income taxes, consumers may use that extra money on consumption goods.

Changes in Investment Spending Like consumption spending, investment spending also depends a lot on what people expect is going to happen in the future. Buying new capital equipment is a risky bet on the future. A new machine may have a useful life of 10 or 20 years, over which time business managers hope that it earns the firm enough profit to justify its price. But suppose that next year the market dries up or prices are undercut by a more efficient competitor or new technology makes it possible to manufacture the product at half the cost. That expensive machine may suddenly have no more than scrap value. When businesspeople are optimistic about the future, spending on new capital increases and real GDP increases. When there is pessimism, orders for new capital goods may dry up and real GDP may fall.

Changes in interest rates can also cause changes in investment spending. If interest rates go down, it is cheaper for firms to borrow money to buy new machinery. So investment spending goes up and real GDP rises. Changes in taxation also matter. If the government cuts business tax rates, for example, firms will increase their investment spending and real GDP will rise.

Changes in Government Spending If the government spends more on national defense or schools or roads and bridges, then real GDP will increase. If the government cuts back on its spending, real GDP will fall.

Government cutbacks in defense spending after the Cold War ended crippled firms like McDonnell Douglas, Lockheed, and other defense contractors. To survive, firms like these have diversified into other businesses. One success story is Sonalyst Labs in Waterford, Connecticut. Once a leading supplier of sonar devices to the U.S. Navy, the company has applied its knowledge of acoustics to other industries. Sonalyst now boasts a media division that supplies special audio effects to major studios for use in feature films.

Changes in Supply New technology may make firms more productive, and when they produce more, real GDP rises. Improvements in information technology are a significant source of technological advance today. Conversely, an increase in the price of oil may raise energy costs and so cause firms to scale back their production. Changes in the price of oil had a big effect on macroeconomic performance in the 1970s and 1980s.

Just as government agencies monitor inflation by using statistics like the CPI, they monitor the business cycle by evaluating statistics called *economic indica-*

6. Discuss the causes of economic fluctuations in the business cycle.

doing business

Economic Indicators

If you knew when the economy would grow or shrink, and by how much, you could make better business decisions. Managers would know when to invest in increased production and when to scale back. Employees would know when to switch jobs. Economists try to predict economic growth by analyzing 11 separate statistics that tend to go up or down six months to a year before a corresponding change in GDP. Among these leading economic indicators are:

- First-time claims for unemployment insurance weekly.
- Manufacturers' new orders for consumer goods and materials.
- Contracts and orders for new capital (factories and equipment).
- Index of building permits for new, private housing units.
- Index of 500 common stock prices.
- Index of consumer expectations.

Forecasting economic performance is, not surprisingly, very difficult. The leading indicators essentially pick the brains of different people in the economy who have a lot of incentive to make good predictions. Dealers on the stock market have an incentive to try to forecast economic performance, for example, and their knowledge is partly summarized in stock prices. Construction companies do their best to forecast housing demand. Their knowledge is summarized in the index of building permits.

Business Week magazine makes it easy to make your own economic forecast by printing the weekly and year-to-date changes in its own list of leading indicators. The *Business Week* indicators are similar to the U.S. government's list but easier to obtain on a weekly basis. The "*Business Week* Index" appears at the end of each issue.

Making good economic forecasts is tricky, however, because many unpredictable events affect economic performance. To take an example, Iraq's invasion of Kuwait in 1990 pushed up oil prices and made consumers nervous, both of which probably contributed to the eight-month recession that followed shortly afterwards. Neither businesspeople nor policymakers could have predicted those happenings.

tors, which tend to anticipate, or lead, the direction of the business cycle—to rise or fall ahead of the economy at large. See the doing business box entitled "Economic Indicators."

Unemployment

7. Identify the types of unemployment.

The number of people who apply for unemployment insurance each week is one economic indicator. At any time in the economy, some people are out of work and are looking for a job. These people are unemployed. People who have jobs are employed. The **labor force** consists of everyone who is either employed or unemployed. Not everyone is in the labor force: Full-time students are not, nor are homemakers, nor are people who don't have jobs but are not seeking work. The **unemployment rate** is the percentage of the labor force that is unemployed. When the economy is booming, the unemployment rate may be 5 percent or lower. During recessions, the unemployment rate may rise to 10 percent or higher.

People may be unemployed because they have quit one job and are looking for another, or because they are just entering the labor force, looking for that first job. Economists refer to joblessness related to the normal workings of the labor market as **frictional unemployment**. Frictional unemployment is not a problem; it is a sign of a healthy economy. In a well-functioning economy, we expect to see movement of workers among jobs. Workers are looking for the right job for them; firms are looking for the right workers to fill vacancies. Getting a good match between workers and jobs involves time and possibly some trial and error. Frictional unemployment is a sign that resources are moving to where they are most productive. Those who are frictionally unemployed usually find jobs within a month or so.

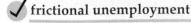

labor force

Everyone who is either employed or unemployed.

unemployment rate

Percentage of the labor force that is unemployed.

frictional unemployment

Joblessness related to the normal workings of the labor market.

Structural unemployment is joblessness that results from the permanent displacement of workers due to changes in technology or long-term shifts in the demand for certain products. When automobiles took over from horses, the demand for horseshoes fell, and blacksmiths were structurally unemployed. When General Motors closed down plants in Flint, Michigan, automobile workers in that area were structurally unemployed. Workers who are structurally unemployed may remain unemployed for long periods of time—several months, or even years. Structurally unemployed workers often find that there is little work available where they are living and there is less demand for their particular skills. Society can alleviate the problems of structural unemployment by helping such workers retrain and relocate.

Business cycle fluctuations also affect the unemployment rate. When the economy is on the upswing, firms hire extra workers and the unemployment rate goes down. When the economy goes into recession, firms produce fewer goods and services, and so lay off some of their workers. Unemployment goes up. Economists call this **cyclical unemployment.** In order to eliminate cyclical unemployment, we would need to eliminate the business cycle.

Seasonal unemployment results from the seasonal demand that characterizes some industries, such as agriculture, tourism, or retailing. Workers in these industries are forced to search for alternative employment during the seasons when the demand for products in their industry is low.

Why Economies Grow

After you strip away the effects of unemployment and inflation, after you back up far enough to see beyond the peaks and valleys of the business cycle, you find that almost all economies have a long-term upward growth trend. Although GDP growth in the United States has been slowing down since the 1970s, on average, real GDP in the United States continues to grow by about 3 percent every year. Why?

Sources of Economic Growth

The total output—real GDP—of our economy depends upon two things:

1. The economic resources that we possess
2. The technical and entrepreneurial knowledge that allows us to turn those resources into goods and services that people want to consume

8. Identify and describe the sources of economic growth.

Land

Our stock of basic raw materials doesn't grow through time. In fact, we may be using up our natural resources. Although technological advances have given us better access to natural resources and replacements for some of them—fiber optic cables instead of copper wire, for example—growth in resources can hardly be a source of economic growth.

Labor and Productivity

One reason that economies grow is quite simple: As the population grows, more people are available to produce goods and services. Remember that labor is a factor of production: With more labor, we can produce more goods. But increased labor accounts for only about one-third of total U.S. growth each year. In our economy, though, per capita GDP, or output per person, has been rising because GDP has grown faster than the population. This increase in GDP per person reflects increased **productivity**, the total value of output per hour of labor.

 structural unemployment

Joblessness that results from the permanent displacement of workers due to changes in technology or long-term shifts in demand for certain products.

 cyclical unemployment

Joblessness due to business cycle fluctuations.

 productivity

The total value of output per hour of labor.

Capital Accumulation

But what is the source of productivity growth? We know that a percentage of GDP each year goes to purchase new capital goods—new factories, machines, houses. Some capital goods also wear out each year and must be replaced— buildings fall down, 18-wheelers go to the junkyard. The new capital that firms purchase more than compensates for the capital that wears out, however, so *accumulation of capital* is another source of economic growth.

As we accumulate capital, workers are equipped with newer and better machines, so their productivity rises. Capital growth, like labor and productivity growth, accounts for about one-third of the yearly increase in our GDP.

Many economists are concerned that we are not investing enough in our future. Americans consume about 95 percent of their current income and save about 5 percent for the future.[7] By contrast, the French, Germans, and Japanese save about 15 percent of their incomes—about three times as much as Americans.[8] Our relatively low savings rate means that there are fewer funds available for firms to borrow, so they invest less (remember the circular flow diagram). While it's nice to consume a lot today, our economic growth rate and our future standard of living will be lower as a consequence.

Technical and Entrepreneurial Knowledge

Growth in the labor force and in our stock of capital together account for economic growth of about 2 percent per year in the United States. That still leaves 1 percent per year—or about a third of total growth in GDP—unexplained. Economists know that this growth must be due to a combination of improvements in entrepreneurship, innovation, invention, and the development of new ideas, new skills, and new technologies. This aspect of economic growth is one of the most exciting areas of research in modern economics, and entrepreneurship is viewed by many as the engine of U.S. business growth, as you will learn when you read Chapter 6.

Here's an example of how entrepreneurship can contribute to economic growth. People used to consider chicken farming a perfectly competitive industry. There was little difference among chickens, after all, and sellers had no influence on price. Then Maryland-based Perdue Farms changed the level of competition in the chicken industry. By listening to his customers, Frank Perdue was able to identify some key attributes buyers perceived as important: the meat-to-bone ratio, the absence of pinfeathers, the freshness of the bird. By concentrating his efforts on improving the quality of his chickens in terms of these key attributes, Perdue was able to deliver a higher-quality product. And he used a vigorous advertising campaign to project the Perdue brand name and support a superior product image.[9] In effect, Frank Perdue innovated by using existing resources to produce a new and superior product, premium chicken, and to change the nature of his industry from pure to monopolistic competition.

An equally important source of increased productivity, and hence economic growth, is improved technology. The development of the internal combustion engine a century ago, combined with techniques of mass production dating from the beginnings of the Industrial Revolution in the eighteenth century, meant that ordinary people could afford automobiles, trucks, and tractors. The development of commercial television in the 1940s and the personal computer in the 1970s brought new categories of goods within the reach of consumers and launched a new revolution, the Information Age.

Technological advances allow manufacturers to produce goods of higher quality at lower prices. Even goods that would have been familiar to people a hundred years ago, like shirts or frying pans, can now be produced more efficiently and with greater quality. A better car design might result in a lighter

doing business

Knowledge Workers and Productivity

Farmers used to both grow crops and shoe horses. Then specialization allowed farmers to grow crops and blacksmiths to shoe horses—specialized farmers and blacksmiths were more productive than their unspecialized predecessors. In the modern factory and office, the productivity of individual workers continues to increase. Computer screens, headsets, and training make the modern telephone operator more productive than his predecessor. Statistical techniques for controlling quality, automated manufacture, and innovative engineering make the modern automobile assembler more productive than her predecessor.

At Bell Labs, hundreds of engineers work in teams to invent and design new products and processes. Their work varies from drawing blueprints to writing computer code, but regardless of the details, production goes on *inside their heads*. How can managers measure the productivity of work performed inside someone else's head? How can you increase such productivity?

At Bell Labs, the solution was to start by identifying the stars—individuals who were perceived to be highly productive. Next, researchers studied how these star performers worked. They found that high productivity in knowledge work resulted from nine work strategies:

1. *Taking initiative* to do more than the required work

2. *Networking* to share knowledge

3. *Self-management* to take charge of your own job

4. *Teamwork effectiveness* to make collaborations work

5. *Leadership* in moving toward your goals

6. *Fellowship* in which you help leaders accomplish goals

7. *Perspective* to see the big picture and alternative views

8. *Show-and-tell* in which you present your ideas well

9. *Organizational savvy* to get things done inside a complex business

Knowledge workers at Bell Labs were then trained in these nine strategies. What happened? Later surveys revealed that employees who received the training were more productive.

New skills and strategies are the productivity enhancers of brain work. They play the same role that new technologies play in a factory, allowing knowledge workers to increase their productivity. Experts predict that the United States and other industrialized nations are entering an era in which knowledge work drives economic performance. Nations that manage brain work better will experience greater economic growth and prosperity.

Source: Based on Robert Kelley and Janet Caplan, "How Bell Labs Creates Star Performers," *Harvard Business Review*, July–Aug. 1993, p. 131.

---

vehicle that uses less steel and requires less gas yet still provides the same transportation capabilities.

Sustained economic growth depends upon the continuing development of new knowledge, skills, and ideas. This observation lies behind arguments for increased investment in education, training, and research and development. But it is still up to individuals—entrepreneurs, managers, researchers, workers—to develop new and better products, and new and better ways to produce existing products. Read about nine work strategies associated with high productivity in the doing business box entitled "Knowledge Workers and Productivity."

Economic Growth and the Quality of Life

When our economy grows—when real GDP increases—we have more goods and services to go around. We can consume more; our government can spend more on education and infrastructure; we can invest more for our future prosperity. Increased GDP means increased well-being and a better quality of life.

Still, GDP alone doesn't measure society's welfare. GDP does not measure the quality of our schools or the safety of our streets or the health of our workers. If achieving a higher GDP means polluting our atmosphere, our rivers, and our oceans, we might well question the wisdom of continually striving for economic growth. And even in the richest country in the world, we have families who are homeless and children who are hungry.

Economists recognize that GDP is not a perfect measure of well-being. But most economists still believe that higher GDP is good for our society. With higher GDP, we can afford better schools, safer streets, and healthier workers. We can afford to clean up our environment—in fact, rich countries have cleaner air and water than poor countries. And with high GDP, we can better care for the worst off in our society. If we have a problem as a society, it is not that we are rich, it is that we do not always use our riches wisely.

The Role of Government

Governments play three major roles in the functioning of market economies. By creating and enforcing laws and attempting to influence the ups and downs in the business cycle, government seeks to provide a stable environment for conducting business. Government also steps in when free markets fail to provide goods and services that the society wants and needs. Finally, government intervenes to provide protection for the disadvantaged in our society.

Although there is broad agreement on these general roles, the scope of government activity in the economy is a subject of constant debate. In the 1930s, during the Great Depression, and again in the 1960s, Americans favored more government intervention. During the 1980s and 1990s, the balance has tipped in favor of less government involvement in the nation's business.

Creating a Stable Business Environment

9. Describe the ways in which government can help create a secure and stable business environment.

A primary responsibility of government is to provide an economic environment in which businesses can flourish.

Laws

The government affects the economic climate for business through the laws and regulations that it enacts. As you will learn in Chapter 4, by providing a system of laws to safeguard private property and to enforce contracts, our government makes it possible for businesses to operate in a safe and predictable environment. The economic success of many developing countries is greatly inhibited by the lack of such laws. Investors are reluctant to put their funds into an economy if they fear that the government will not uphold contracts and protect their interests.

Monetary Policy

Chapter 21 details many different measures of the money supply. Cash plus balances in checking accounts is called M1. *You will also hear or read about measures of money—*M2 *or* M3, *for example—that include other assets, such as money market accounts.*

The Federal Reserve, the central bank of the United States, controls the nation's money supply. The Federal Reserve therefore controls **monetary policy**, adjustments to the money supply aimed at influencing economic performance. There are two aspects to monetary policy:

1. In the *long run*, the Federal Reserve tries to manage the money supply to avoid inflation. The main influence on the inflation rate in the long run is simply how fast the money supply grows. If the money supply increases too fast, inflation is the result.

2. In the *short run*, the Federal Reserve may try to influence business cycle fluctuations and control GDP. The policies of the Federal Reserve have a major impact on spending in the short run through their effect on interest rates. For example, if the Federal Reserve decreases the money supply, interest rates rise. Consumers are then less likely to borrow for new cars or new houses, and firms are less likely to borrow to buy new capital goods.

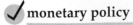

monetary policy

Adjustments to the money supply aimed at influencing economic performance.

From February 1994 to February 1995, the Federal Reserve raised interest rates seven times in an attempt to slow economic growth and the threat of rising inflation.

The Federal Reserve's task is more difficult than it sounds because it actually cannot control the money supply exactly. It can control the number of dollars in circulation, but the amount held in checking accounts depends in part on the decisions of banks and individuals.

Fiscal Policy

The taxing and spending decisions of government are its **fiscal policy**. We already know that government spending decisions can influence real GDP. Taxation by the government, which amounts to roughly one-fifth of GDP yearly, also has a substantial effect on the economy.[10] Economists recognize that the personal income tax, the corporate income tax, sales taxes, property taxes, and other forms of taxation all affect our individual economic decisions and so have an impact on the entire economy. We will study some ways that taxation affects forms of business in Chapter 5.

The government not only takes money in through taxation, it also gives money out through **transfer payments**, cash payments made by the government directly to individuals, including unemployment insurance, Social Security payments, and welfare programs. Note that there is no economic exchange here. Transfer payments are *not* purchases of goods and services by the government. They are therefore not counted as part of GDP.

Since the 1970s, the government has generally spent more than it has taken in each year. The **budget deficit** is the difference between the amount the government spends on purchases and transfer payments and the amount it receives from taxation in a given time period. Just as you must borrow if you want to spend more than you earn, so, too, must the government borrow from the public to cover its deficits. We saw this earlier in the circular flow diagram.

Because the government has been borrowing for many years, it has now built up a substantial **national debt**, the total of all budget deficits added together. Take care to distinguish between the deficit, which determines the amount the government must borrow *each year*, and the debt, which is the total of all these deficits added together. The interest payments that the government must make on its ongoing debt now contribute substantially to the yearly budget deficit. Indeed, if it were not for interest payments on the national debt, the yearly budget deficit would almost disappear.

Budget deficits are not necessarily bad. For example, if the government borrows to build a new highway, the investment will bring benefits for years to come. Still, the size of recent deficits concerns economists. If the government is borrowing funds to pay for its deficits, then those funds are not available for private businesses to borrow for investment. We have already learned that lower investment adversely affects long-term economic growth.

The budget deficit is also a tool that the government can use to try to smooth out business cycle fluctuations. Higher government spending directly increases output in the short run. Lower taxes and higher transfer payments lead to increased consumption spending, which also increases output. So if the economy is in a recession, the government can try to increase spending, or cut taxes and transfer payments, to help the economy grow again.

Although the government can in principle use taxing and spending to help the economy recover from a recession, many economists think that such policies are a bad idea. The problem is that changes in taxing and spending require budgetary changes that must be approved by the president and the Congress. By the time politicians agree on these policies, they may no longer be needed—the economy may have recovered on its own.

Fiscus is the Latin word for treasury.

A higher budget deficit results from lower taxes, higher transfer payments, or higher government spending.

 fiscal policy
The taxing and spending decisions of government.

transfer payments
Cash payments made by the government directly to individuals.

budget deficit
The difference between the amount the government spends on purchases and transfer payments and the amount it receives from taxation in a given time period.

national debt
The total of all budget deficits added together.

10. Describe government's role in correcting market failures and protecting the disadvantaged.

Correcting Market Failures

We learned earlier that a free market economy usually does an efficient job of using a society's resources to satisfy its citizens' wants and needs. But there are occasions when a free market economy may fail to allocate society's resources properly, and government action is needed.

Public Goods

Some goods will not be adequately supplied by private businesses because they cannot be bought and sold in the marketplace. Examples include national defense and clean air. These goods or services that benefit everyone in society are called **public goods**. They possess two characteristics.

1. It is difficult or impossible to exclude people from benefiting from public goods. It's easy to exclude someone from a movie theater if he or she hasn't bought a ticket. But you cannot exclude someone from the benefits of national defense.

2. One person's enjoyment of the public good does not prevent others from enjoying it also. If you're wearing a pair of shoes, your best friend can't wear them at the same time. But others can breathe the air at the same time that you are breathing it.

The provision of public goods is one of the most important functions of government. Note that government also supplies some goods that society wishes to make available to everyone, such as public education.

Market Power

We learned earlier that whenever monopoly, oligopoly, or monopolistic competition exist, firms will take advantage of their market power to keep prices above equilibrium. The result is a misallocation of resources: Prices are too high and output is too low. For this reason, the government often regulates monopolies to prevent producers with market power from keeping prices high, as we will see in Chapter 4. In a sense, these laws try to make industries with a few producers more like perfectly competitive industries.

Externalities

Businesses and individuals may take actions that either impose costs or confer benefits on society at large, without making the appropriate payment or obtaining the appropriate reward. These are **externalities**. For example, a business might pollute rivers, lakes, oceans, or the atmosphere, or it might develop a new product or technology that is imitated by others. Externalities cause misallocations of resources. Because a polluting firm does not bear the true opportunity cost of its actions, it will pollute too much. If a firm cannot reap all the benefits of a technology it develops, it will devote too few resources to research and development.

Government intervenes to deal with externalities in three ways.

1. Government passes laws and imposes regulations on businesses. Patent laws, for example, help ensure that businesses have an incentive to develop new technologies. Regulations help protect the environment and safeguard the health of consumers and workers. Laws and regulations have costs, however, including the opportunity cost of the resources devoted to regulatory agencies and the fact that cumbersome regulations may inhibit the efficient functioning of businesses.

public goods

Goods or services that benefit everyone in society.

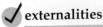
externalities

Actions by individuals or businesses that either impose costs or confer benefits on society at large.

One Role of Government

In a free market economy, externalities may cause misallocations of resources and thus discourage desirable—but expensive—activities, such as basic scientific research. Government-subsidized programs at private and public institutions help the United States maintain its leadership in many areas of science and technology.

2. Government uses taxes and subsidies to change the behavior of individuals and firms. For example, governments tax people who buy tobacco products. And the federal government subsidizes basic research and technology development in universities, private businesses, and institutions such as the Centers for Disease Control.

3. Government creates new possibilities for exchange. Clean air is something that people value. But you cannot buy and sell clean air. As a result, consumers and firms pollute the air. Consumers drive automobiles that generate air pollution; firms pump smoke and soot into the atmosphere. Since nobody owns the atmosphere, everybody abuses it. People cannot buy and sell the atmosphere, yet an understanding of supply and demand can help us deal with problems of air pollution. The Clean Air Act of 1990 established a market for *pollution permits*, which give firms the right to emit sulfur dioxide (a contributor to smog and acid rain) into the atmosphere. Why is this a good idea? Some firms can reduce their emissions cheaply while others—perhaps because they have older equipment—must incur substantial costs to reduce emissions. Firms that can reduce their emissions cheaply are able to sell their pollution permits to firms that cannot. The firms that are best at reducing pollution are the ones that do so.

Protecting the Disadvantaged

Some people are more successful than others in our economy. Success, in a free market economy, results from ability, effort—and luck. Governments use transfer payments to provide a safety net for the unlucky. Examples of transfer payments include unemployment compensation, Medicare and Medicaid payments, and Aid to Families with Dependent Children.

Governments may also pursue explicit policies of redistributing resources from the rich to the poor. For example, individuals in a democracy can decide to elect a government that taxes the well-off and makes transfers to the less well-off in order to have a more equitable society. Socialist and communist societies, in particular, emphasize such policies of redistribution.

The Economic Challenge

The same challenge faces any economy: to maintain sufficient stability and growth to allow its people an improving standard of living. How can the United States continue to maintain a vigorous economy with continuing productivity growth? Will it succeed as its businesses compete with those of other nations in global competition? Will the wealth created in its economic system reach the poor as well as the rich?

These questions are difficult—they trouble leading economists, politicians, and business managers, not just students! But it is questions like these that make studying economics exciting, and understanding economics vital, if you want to succeed in business. The answers to these questions ultimately depend on you and on everyone else who works in our economy and makes our economy work.

Reviewing *Business and Economics*

Economic Choices

1. **State the basic premise underlying economic decision making and identify the four factors of production.** With every economic decision we are choosing how best to allocate scarce resources among competing uses. Each decision involves a trade-off in which we consider the opportunity cost of selecting one resource over another. These limited resources, referred to as the factors of production, are land, capital, labor, and entrepreneurship. Economic study helps in this decision making by providing information about what to produce, how to organize and use our resources in the most efficient ways in order to produce the goods we want, and how economic systems distribute goods and services among all members of society.

Economic Exchanges

2. **Discuss how demand and supply, in relation to equilibrium price, determine the exchange of goods and services.** Consumers and sellers have opposite interests in a free market: As a group, consumers will demand more of a good or service at a lower price; sellers will supply more at a higher price. Demand and supply are also affected by factors other than price. Demand also depends on income and the perceived value of a product relative to substitute items or to other desirable items, for example. Supply may be affected by the cost of labor and environmental conditions. The equilibrium price is the price at which demand and supply are equal. If the price of an item is higher than the equilibrium price, consumers will demand less and the price will fall back toward equilibrium. If the price is below the equilibrium price, consumers will demand more and the price will rise to equilibrium. In other words, prices change if there are shifts in the demand or supply curves.

3. **Identify the four degrees of competition and describe how they operate in a free market economy.** The four degrees are perfect competition at one extreme, monopolistic competition and oligopoly in the middle, and monopoly at the other extreme of the market continuum. All four may exist within a market economy, depending on the particular industry. Perfect competition is the ideal situation, with the laws of supply and demand operating and price being set by these market forces. However, most industries in a free market economy are characterized by monopolistic competition. That is, while a firm's product may be differentiated, many close substitutes provide competition, allowing the laws of supply and demand to operate. Oligopolies exist where only a few large firms dominate an industry. A monopoly is the least satisfactory level of competition because society as a whole loses from the higher prices charged by the controlling firm.

The Economic System as a Whole

4. **Describe the circular flow of economic activity and explain how the categories of gross domestic product (GDP) relate to that flow.** In a circular flow pattern, products go from firms to households, and dollars go from households to firms; at the same time, firms receive labor hours from households, and households receive dollars from firms in exchange. GDP is a measure of the dollar value of the total final output of the economy. This output includes not only the consumption by households and the investments by firms described in the basic cycle but also investment, or saving, by households; federal, state, and local government spending, which uses funds obtained from taxes on households and firms; and net exports, which account for purchases by foreigners minus goods bought from foreigners. Consumption spending is the most important component of total spending.

5. **Explain the effect of inflation on GDP and describe how inflation is measured**. Inflation, an increase in overall or average prices, produces a corresponding increase in GDP. However, since it reflects only higher prices, it does not indicate growth—that is, higher living standards. GDP, to accurately reflect growth, must be adjusted for inflation (this is called real GDP). Unadjusted GDP (nominal GDP) does not show growth. Inflation is measured in a variety of ways. One is the consumer price index (CPI), whereby the cost of a basket of goods such as a typical household might buy is compared from one year to the next. Inflation may not be harmful, unless the individual's income does not rise in relation to price increases—for example, if the person is on a fixed income.

6. **Discuss the causes of economic fluctuations in the business cycle**. Typically, the economy fluctuates between inflationary and recessionary periods. These fluctuations are caused by four broad changes, which, in turn, occur for a variety of reasons. Changes in consumption spending may occur because of an increase or decrease in confidence about the future or because of changes in government policy. Investment spending is likewise linked to feelings about the future; it also may be affected by changes in interest rates and taxes. Changes in government spending will also affect real GDP, as will changes in supply such as those resulting from the increased productivity that occurs with new technology.

7. **Identify the types of unemployment**. Unemployment refers only to nonworking members of the labor force. Frictional unemployment is typical of a healthy economy and is a sign that resources are moving to where they are most productive. Structural unemployment, on the other hand, points to serious problems or shifts in the economy. Cyclical unemployment is an unavoidable function of business cycle fluctuations.

Why Economies Grow

8. **Identify and describe the sources of economic growth**. Growth of real GDP depends on economic resources and on technical and entrepreneurial knowledge. The major contributors to growth are labor and capital accumulation. This combination of more working-age people and new capital goods results in increased productivity, and hence higher real GDP. Technical and entrepreneurial knowledge contribute innovation, inventions, and the development of new ideas, new skills, and new and improved technologies that lead to an increase in real GDP.

The Role of Government

9. **Describe the ways in which government can help create a secure and stable business environment**. Government helps to create a secure and stable business environment through laws and regulations that safeguard property and enforce contracts, and through monetary and fiscal policy. The Federal Reserve controls monetary policy; that is, it adjusts the money supply so as to influence economic performance and control inflation. Fiscal policy relates to the government's decisions regarding taxation and spending (on transfer payments, for example). When spending is higher than taxation, a budget deficit results. While the government can use deficit spending to smooth out business cycles, continued budget deficits can add up to a serious national debt. Financing interest payments on the debt can weaken the economy by making less money available for business investment.

10. **Describe government's role in correcting market failures and protecting the disadvantaged**. Government steps in when private businesses are unable to satisfy consumer needs adequately. Some examples of government participation are supplying public goods, regulating monopolies, and dealing with externalities through laws and regulations and taxes and subsidies and by creating new possibilities for exchange. Governments protect the disadvantaged through transfer payments and by redistributing resources from the rich to the poor.

✓ Key Terms

resources **35**	equilibrium price **39**	nominal GDP **48**	structural unemployment **53**
opportunity cost **35**	perfect competition **42**	real GDP **48**	cyclical unemployment **53**
factors of production **35**	monopoly **42**	consumer price index (CPI) **48**	productivity **53**
land **35**	monopolistic competition **43**	recessions **50**	monetary policy **56**
capital **35**	oligopoly **44**	business cycle **50**	fiscal policy **57**
labor **35**	microeconomics **44**	labor force **52**	transfer payments **57**
demand **37**	macroeconomics **44**	unemployment rate **52**	budget deficit **57**
demand curve **37**	circular flow **45**	frictional unemployment **52**	national debt **57**
supply **38**	inflation **48**		public goods **58**
supply curve **39**			externalities **58**

● Review Questions

1. What factors would you consider in deciding whether to buy a car?

2. What questions does economics help society to answer?

3. How would the equilibrium price for milk be set in a free market economy?

4. How do the four degrees of competition differ in terms of the number of firms in and the products offered by an industry?

5. Assume that our economy produces only computers. Describe the circular flow of economic activity and, using any numbers you wish, show how GDP would be calculated.

6. What are the four components of gross domestic product? Give an example of how a college student with a part-time job might fit into or relate to each.

7. Inflation is considered by many to be bad. Is it really? Why or why not?

8. What changes in economic activity might lead to a recession? Why might those changes occur?

9. How, if at all, does each of the four factors of production contribute to economic growth?

10. What role does the Federal Reserve play in regulating the U.S. economy?

● Critical Thinking Questions

1. In discussing the factors of production, economists often refer to the specialized skills and knowledge of, say, medical doctors, plumbers, managers, and chefs as human capital rather than simply as labor. Why do you suppose they use the term *human capital*?

2. You decide to go into business to produce a baseball cap with a unique insignia. What degree of competition would you expect to encounter? Why? Why would other levels of competition be unlikely?

3. Does the airline industry qualify as an oligopoly? Defend your answer.

4. During the 1990s, Americans have increased their savings rate from an average of 3 percent of annual income to over 5 percent. How might this increased savings rate affect U.S. macroeconomic growth at the end of the decade?

5. Few, if any, U.S. companies make televisions, cameras, or CD players today. Instead, we import these products from Europe and Asia. Why?

6. Our society spends over $1 trillion each year on health care, about 15 percent of the U.S. GDP. In your opinion, should health care be a public good? Defend your answer.

REVIEW CASE   *If Robin Hood Went to Congress*

In 1990, Congress was hard at work on a national budget to help the United States cut costs and raise tax revenues. When economic growth slows, businesses and individuals make less money and therefore pay less in taxes—which means the government takes in less money to pay for its billions of dollars in programs too. Weak economic growth and a huge federal deficit made the 1990 budget an especially tough one to write. And the Bush administration had promised not to raise taxes. So where would the extra money the government needed come from? Somebody suggested a "luxury tax," an extra sales tax on expensive luxury items like personal airplanes and boats. Members of Congress went along with the tax, since it did not affect the majority of working people who would be voting for or against them in the next election. After all, most of us can't afford to buy a new airplane or boat, tax or no. And when they looked at the numbers, a luxury tax seemed likely to bring in lots of extra money for the government. A special congressional committee estimated that it would bring in $6 million in 1991 alone.

But by the end of 1991, the total money raised stood at only $53,000. What happened to the other $5,947,000 the tax was supposed to raise? The case of Beech Aircraft Corp. provides a clue.[11] Its sales were 80 planes short of what management expected in 1991. It lost $130 million in expected sales and had to cut 480 jobs that year. A customer survey revealed that most people avoided buying new planes because of the luxury tax. And similar results drove many U.S. boat builders out of business in the early 1990s. What went wrong?

1. How did the demand curve for luxury goods shift in 1991? Draw a picture to show this.

2. What factor or factors caused the demand curve to shift?

3. What impact did the luxury tax have on unemployment?

4. The luxury tax was later repealed. What do you think changed as a result of its elimination?

Will newly industrializing countries like South Korea and Singapore grow fast enough to overtake and even surpass America's standard of living? Economists are currently debating the point. If you measure standard of living by per capita gross domestic product (or income per person), the newly industrializing countries (economists call them NICs for short) are gaining rapidly. Per capita GDP is high in the United States but not growing much from year to year. Japan's per capita GDP surpassed that of the United States in the late 1980s. In South Korea, per capita GDP is less than half that of the United States. But because its GDP is growing even faster than that of Japan, South Korea's per capita GDP is up from the 1950 figure of one-tenth that of the United States. At the current rate, South Korea could pass the United States in a couple of decades. Will the NICs displace the United States and become the world's richest nations?

Let's review a few statistics before we answer that question. Some economists say capital investment is the key to future economic growth. They say that if a country invests a large share of its income in capital goods such as new factories, equipment, and technologies, business will become more productive and economic growth will increase. Right now, the United States spends about 15 percent of its GDP on capital investments, but the NICs invest much more—South Korea, for example, invests a whopping 35 percent of its GDP. That's why some economists say the U.S. government needs to encourage Americans to save money, making more investment capital available.

Other economists say the key to economic growth is a well-educated labor force. If people have a high level of skill and are trained in new technologies, they can work more productively. A well-educated work force can help employers take advantage of growth factors like technology and entrepreneurship. A higher percentage of students in the NICs study engineering and other technology-oriented subjects than do American students, and a common complaint of U.S. businesses is that recent graduates are less prepared for work than they used to be.

Still other economists focus on science and technology. The country that leads in technical development has an advantage in business because it can keep introducing new, more advanced products. And in recent decades, the United States has led the field in most of the sciences. But spending on research and development as a percentage of GDP is lower in the United States than in many of the NICs.

1. What factors suggest that the NICs may overtake the United States in per capita GDP?

2. Why do you think per capita GDP is used as an indication of a nation's wealth, and can you suggest any alternative measures?

3. Do you think the NICs will overtake the United States in other measures of prosperity, too? Why? If so, will they do so before or after they catch up in per capita GDP?

4. If you were president of the United States, what single policy would you make your top priority in order to foster U.S. economic growth?

5. Why do you think U.S. per capita GDP is currently among the highest in the world?

Critical Thinking with the ONE MINUTE MANAGER

"We're reporting in to let you know what we've learned about basic economics," Carlos announced as he and Joanna breezed into the One Minute Manager's office.

"I'm all ears," she replied.

Joanna took over. "It seems to me that the market for cotton is perfectly competitive. There are lots of sellers and no one has any influence on price."

"Demand and supply set the price," Carlos continued.

"From what I recall," said the One Minute Manager, "cotton farmers generally need a price of 50 to 60 cents a pound to break even. So at $1 a pound, U.S. cotton farmers should be in the money, unless demand drops at the same time supplies surge. You see, cotton is an expensive crop to grow and harvest. It requires farming expertise and lots of expensive equipment. Cotton gin prices run into the millions, so groups of farmers in a community usually band together to buy a gin. But I remember reading that each farmer has to invest around $250,000 just to switch into cotton production."[12]

"So the farmers have to invest a lot before they see any profit," Joanna observed. "And the weather has to be good, not to mention soil conditions, and they must cope with threats from crop diseases and insects. Sounds like risky business."

1. Economists fear a boom-to-bust business cycle for cotton farmers, who take on heavy debt when prices are high and lose their farms when prices fall. In fact, government subsidies keep many U.S. farmers afloat. Are government subsidies good for the economy? Why or why not?

2. Based on 1994 average crop yields, 1,000 acres planted in cotton could make a profit of $100,000 to $200,000 after all expenses. If you were a farmer, would you jump on the bandwagon and plant cotton? Explain why or why not.

3. High cotton prices drive up prices of clothing and other products made from cotton. In mid-1995, textile mills raised their prices on cotton cloth between 5 and 8 percent. What do you suppose happened to the demand for cotton? If supplies stayed high, what do you suppose happened to the price farmers got for their cotton?

3

Global Business

To succeed in business, you will have to both compete and collaborate with workers and managers in foreign lands. You may have opportunities to live and work abroad or to work for foreign companies operating within the United States. These opportunities may be the best paths to career advancement in future years. As you plan your classroom and work experiences, prepare for a global career, not just a U.S. career. This chapter explains why a global perspective is important for businesses and for business students. After reading this chapter, you will be able to reach the learning goals below.

Learning Goals

1. Discuss the reasons for the increasingly global nature of business.
2. Define the major elements of global trade and explain how global trade is measured.
3. Explain how exchange rates work, noting their significance to a country's economy.
4. Describe how countries are classified economically.
5. Discuss the issue of protectionism versus free trade.
6. Describe the role of international trade agreements and trading blocs in promoting free trade.
7. Explain the significance for global businesses of a country's political climate.
8. Identify the three most common categories of legal systems and explain their impact on the operations of a global business.
9. Describe the social/cultural factors that affect global businesses.
10. Describe several strategies for entering foreign markets.
11. Contrast global strategy and adaptation as strategies for conducting business in foreign markets.

ONE MINUTE MANAGER

L'Importanza Della Clientela e Della Qualita

Joanna and Carlos stood beside the One Minute Manager in front of a large glass-framed poster. "What do you think?" she asked the students.

"I don't know what to think," Joanna replied, "I can't read a word of it!"

"I can," Carlos said. "See, on this line it says, 'La importancia de los clientes y la calidad.'"

"Which means?" Joanna prompted.

"It's Spanish for 'The importance of customers and quality.' And I bet that's what it says in all those other languages, too. See, I think this is French here: 'L'importance des clients et de la qualité.' And this must be German, and this is Arabic, and these look like they are Japanese characters. It must say the same thing in fifteen different languages!"

"Yes, Carlos, that's right," said the One Minute Manager. "I got this poster from a friend at Bausch & Lomb's International Division, which makes and markets sunglasses and other Bausch & Lomb products in dozens of countries around the world. In recent years, the company has been working to improve its products' quality worldwide. The theme of this quality improvement effort is 'The importance of customers and quality,' but of course most of the people they work with in other countries cannot read that very easily. So they carefully translated it into every language needed to communicate with almost 4,000 employees speaking fifteen different languages around the world, as well as with people in the hundreds of thousands of stores and businesses that buy Bausch & Lomb products worldwide."

"Everything must be more difficult on a global scale," Joanna said, "especially managing a company with operations in fifteen different countries."

"That's true, but on the other hand, the opportunities are much bigger as well. Let me give you another example—one in which *everything* is done globally. The company is VeriFone, Inc., and it provides the service that retailers use to check customers' credit cards. VeriFone has to have a global computer network to do this background checking quickly, so its managers decided to organize everything else around that network, too."

"Like what?" Carlos asked.

"Everything! If you want to check in with your boss, you e-mail her. Written communication is forbidden. And your boss could just as easily be in another country as in yours. By going electronic, VeriFone is not constrained by geography. It can be a truly global company."

"But do they know how to say 'quality' in Spanish?" Joanna joked. "Even computers have trouble with language barriers, after all!"

Perspectives on Global Business

Dramatic shifts are refashioning the business world. Russia and Eastern Europe are converting government-run industries into privately run businesses. The Berlin Wall has crumbled. The People's Republic of China is edging toward participation in Western industrial traditions. The overthrow of apartheid in South Africa has reopened the gates to trade. A tentative peace exists in the Middle East. But political change is only the tip of the iceberg. National economies ebb and flow throughout the world; Japan falters while Europe gets stronger. The free trade agreement between the United States, Mexico, and Canada has opened up markets in North America and improved business. Technology transfer is opening up opportunities to rapidly improve the economic climate in less developed countries such as Taiwan, South Korea, and Singapore. As we saw with VeriFone, instant information transfer lubricates worldwide trade like never before. All these lightning-speed changes are transforming the way we conduct business and shaping the foundation on which a one-world economic and market system will be built.[1]

Business and Culture

Successful business people today understand and respect cultural differences in global markets and at home. And cultural differences—even small ones— matter, especially if you are unaware of them. In Egypt, for example, you express your appreciation for a plentiful meal by leaving some food on your plate, indicating that your host has generously provided more food than you can consume. When dining as a guest of the thrifty Belgians, however, you should clean your plate. Having a second helping compliments your Greek hosts, and finishing your tea in China signals that you would like more. But don't overeat in Colombia, where it is considered impolite; instead, graciously refuse additional helpings. Practice good table manners in the Netherlands and France; your hosts will be paying attention.

In Argentina, it is bad manners to clear your throat or blow your nose at the table. In Brazil, avoid touching your food with your fingers, and be sure to wipe your mouth before taking a drink. When dining with Muslim companions, be careful not to use your left hand for eating, touching others, giving or receiving objects, or pointing.

Such amazing diversity in the simple act of sharing food is but one example of the variety of social behaviors among cultures. Expansive gestures and animated facial expressions are characteristic of many Arabs and Latin Americans, who prefer to stand very close while conversing. Stepping back to create the three-foot distance most Americans prefer may create the impression that you are insulted by or disagree with what's been said. In Italy, your same-gender companion is likely to walk arm-in-arm with you as you stroll along, but your new Swedish friend will be physically reserved.

Why do these differences matter? Because many of us will be participating in the global marketplace, and all of us will experience diversity in the workplace. (Read the skills check on "Cultural Dos and Don'ts.") Let's begin here with a look at the forces that drive business globalization, which makes a global perspective imperative for today's business student.

Business Goes Global

Intensified competition and slow growth in domestic markets are making international markets vital for any U.S. business, large or small. Business has evolved from local to regional to national to international.[2] For example,

1. Discuss the reasons for the increasingly global nature of business.

Cultural Dos and Don'ts

To check your cultural savvy, read the following paragraphs, then fill in the table.

Hong Kong business dealings are high pressure and fast-paced. Many appointment calendars are quite full, so you will need to make good advance plans for your meeting. Sending along a detailed written agenda beforehand is a good idea. In this largely Chinese population, business relationships are formal, respectful, reserved, and task-oriented. Expect a minimum of small talk before getting under way. Your Hong Kong business partners will want to thoroughly discuss all aspects of your arrangement before concessions are introduced. Most Hong Kong businesspeople speak fluent English, but as in any bilingual situation, be careful to avoid slang and make sure you have been clear. While the fine legal points of an agreement are important here, the personal trust you are able to establish with your business partners is usually more significant.

Calling or writing your Nigerian prospect renders the matter trivial; your personal visit is the first step. Extroverted, talkative Nigerians value friendship in their business relationships, but don't be surprised by their tough negotiating abilities. Your respectful, confident, refined presentation will meet with a positive response in this country, where many businesspeople are U.S.-educated. Nigeria has several distinct cultural groups, each with different habits and characteristics. When preparing for your trip, take the time to learn about the customs and characteristics of your Nigerian counterparts.

Your Malaysian business partners will be much more interested in building a strong personal relationship than in doing business at the outset of your negotiations. Courtesy, manners, and diplomacy are important components of any negotiation. Be prepared as well to spend a great deal of time on the details of your arrangements. Malaysians reach a decision gradually and after much careful consideration, and your presentation style should reflect this tendency.

Canada is our largest trading partner. More goods are bought and sold between Canada and the United States than between any other two countries in the world. But many Americans forget that our friendly northern neighbor is a distinct cultural entity, with strong British and French influences. This European influence means many Canadians are more genteel than Americans, so be mannerly and courteous in your conversation. Their reserved manner also often means that Canadians will be more receptive to a restrained presentation than to a "hard sell." Canadians are very prompt; be prepared to meet any deadlines that are established. And when in Quebec, expect to be addressed in French and have any written material you present available in both English and French.

Be prepared for lots of traffic in Cairo, and allow plenty of time to get to your destination. Once you have arrived for your meeting, however, you should expect your counterpart to be late! As your meeting gets under way, take time for some social conversation; Egypt's rich cultural and archeological heritage is a valued topic. Your Egyptian counterpart will want to be sure that a good relationship exists before any serious negotiations proceed. A slow-paced meeting, frequent telephone interruptions, and several cups of tea are the norm. And in this deeply Muslim country, many aspects of life are believed to be in God's hands, and many business agreements are assumed to be successful *Insha'allah*, or if God wills.

Boeing Aircraft earns half its revenues outside the United States, while Procter & Gamble sells about 40 percent of its products offshore. Gillette receives 70 percent of its profits from abroad. While only about 10 percent of its total sales are made overseas, General Motors derives a whopping $14 billion in revenues from foreign markets. Federal Express, Nike, Time Warner, CNN, and Microsoft all produce and sell an increasing volume of goods and services around the world. Coca-Cola, the best-known brand name in the world, earns almost 80 percent of its profits outside America. Clearly, American companies are well-established internationally. And this global activity is not confined to the large, well-known companies. Many entrepreneurs seek sales throughout the world. Consider Montague Corp., an entrepreneurial business that designs its unique folding mountain bikes in Massachusetts, builds them in Taiwan, and sells them mostly in Europe.

In the United States, foreign companies are capturing our buying preferences. Over 70 percent of the video recorders, televisions and video cameras, footwear, and telephone instruments Americans buy come from foreign countries. Foreign brands—Panasonic, BMW, Laura Ashley, Michelin, and Nestlé—

If English is your only language and you are on your way to Mexico, courteously ask your colleagues in advance if negotiations may be conducted in English. While many Mexican businesspeople speak fluent English, they may refuse to do so for "tactical" reasons. Best to know beforehand if you will need an interpreter. Learning enough Spanish to greet your Mexican negotiation partners will be appreciated and considered respectful. And be sure to take time for some general conversation, perhaps about Mexico's natural beauty or recent accomplishments, before you get down to business.

Headed off to Brazil to negotiate a contract? Be punctual for your appointment even though your Brazilian counterpart is likely to be a few minutes late. While most Americans pride themselves on being honest, Brazilians tend to expect deception in the early stages of a negotiation when the parties do not know each other well. You may be presented with some "facts" at the outset that turn out not to be true later on. Brazilians are intense and often argue their points passionately—don't mistake their fervor for anger. With a population of more than 150 million, Brazil is a large market. Many kinds of U.S. products are highly sought after, and Brazilians are generally positive about doing business with Americans.

Expressive, energetic Israelis like a brisk pace in meetings and will bargain hard. Strongly worded positions are typical in Israeli negotiations, even when the underlying atmosphere seems friendly. Israelis are comfortable doing business with Americans, and the rapidly growing technology-based segment of their economy means there is a lot of potential business to be done. A friendly, firm, and patient approach works well in this environment.

When doing business in . . .	*Key principle for conducting business*
Hong Kong	
Nigeria	
Malaysia	
Canada	
Egypt	
Mexico	
Brazil	
Israel	

are household names. Less well-known is the foreign ownership of many U.S. companies: Pillsbury (Britain), CBS Records (Japan), Chesebrough-Pond's (the Netherlands). To meet American demand, many foreign companies have built manufacturing facilities in the United States, including Matsushita, Honda, and Germany's industrial giant Siemens. One in nine U.S. manufacturing workers now works for a foreign-owned company.

Global business means global trade. The following sections explain how trade affects the economy and why nations become trading partners.

Why Do Countries Trade?

For centuries, China's borders were closed to prevent trade and other contact with Western "barbarians," whom Chinese rulers believed would contaminate their culture. But eventually, China had to open its borders to develop economically. Countries cannot depend solely on the goods and services produced within their own boundaries for three reasons: availability of products and resources, opportunity costs, and specialization.[3] First, many goods and services

✓ **absolute advantage**

When a country can produce a good or service far more efficiently than its trading partner.

✓ **theory of comparative advantage**

A country's productivity increases when its businesses specialize in the products they can make most efficiently.

✓ **importing**

Purchasing resources, finished goods, and services from a foreign country.

✓ **exporting**

Selling resources, goods, and services to buyers in foreign countries.

✓ **countertrade**

The exchange of one good for another without using money. Also known as *barter*.

Comparative advantage doesn't just apply to trade between nations. Suppose that you're a really good manager and that you also make a great cappuccino. But you can earn much more as a manager than you can making cappuccino. You won't spend half of each day as a manager and half at the coffee shop. You will specialize in being a manager and leave the cappuccino making to others—even if they're not as good at it as you are.

simply do not exist within a given country in the quantities needed to serve its population. The United States, for example, cannot produce bananas because its climate is not suitable. And while we do produce oil within our borders, we cannot provide sufficient quantities to meet the demand of the entire U.S. population. When products or resources are limited, countries can satisfy domestic demand by trading with one another.

The second reason countries trade is *opportunity cost*, the alternatives an individual gives up by choosing to pursue one alternative. You know from economics that every decision involves trade-offs. Whenever a country decides to use its resources to produce one product, it cannot use those inputs to produce other products. The resources that U.S. businesses devote to producing oil cannot be devoted to producing copper, for example. Those products that are given up represent the opportunity cost.

It may be necessary to trade for products that cannot be produced domestically. Handcrafted rugs, for instance, are more likely to be traded by countries where labor costs are low—countries such as Pakistan, India, and the People's Republic of China. South Korea, Taiwan, Hong Kong, and Singapore have taken advantage of their low labor rates to enter many industries. Countries direct their resources toward those products they can produce most efficiently, which brings us to the third reason for trade: specialization.

A country enjoys an **absolute advantage** when it can produce a good or service far more efficiently than its trading partner. The Japanese specialize in electronics, the French excel in wine production, the Brazilians are outstanding in growing oranges. Let's say the United States is ten times more efficient than Brazil in producing computers. This means that the United States has an absolute advantage in computers. Brazil may be ten times more efficient than the United States in producing oranges; Brazil therefore has an absolute advantage in oranges. More rarely, a country may even have a monopoly on a product. South Africa, for example, holds a virtual monopoly in gem-quality diamonds—one reason these are the world's most costly jewels. This situation is rare, though.

Even if a nation has an absolute advantage in all products, it can still gain from international trade. The reason lies in the **theory of comparative advantage**. This theory holds that a country's productivity increases when its businesses specialize in the products they can make most efficiently. Countries then trade with one another to get the other products that they need and desire, and all countries win—the total supply of goods is expanded and total costs everywhere are reduced.

Consider the following example. Let's say that Peru and the United States both produce copper and wheat. In one day Peru can produce either 8 tons of wheat or 30 tons of copper with the resources it has. In that same day, the United States can produce 4 tons of wheat or 10 tons of copper. Peru thus has an absolute advantage in the production of either good. However, it has a comparative advantage in the production of copper (30:10 vs. 8:4). Therefore, Peru should specialize in the good in which it has the higher comparative advantage—copper, in this simplified example.

How Do Countries Account for Global Trade?

Trade advantages can come from valuable natural resources such as oil or diamonds, as noted earlier. They also can be acquired from specialized production skills, such as those found in Danish furniture making or Swedish glass manufacturing. The emerging global economy is fueled by improvements in information technology. Production processes that incorporate emerging technologies—computerized design, robotic assembly, and electronic information flows—increasingly hold the key to gaining a global competitive advantage. Think how the Japanese have captured the dominant world market share in many technology-driven products—televisions, cameras, sound systems, and the like—that are made by technology-driven manufacturing processes.

Imports and Exports

Importing is purchasing resources, finished goods, and services from a foreign country. The United States is the largest importer in the world, with Germany close on its heels. Imports account for about 10 percent of total purchases within the United States. That may seem a small percentage, but think of what you would miss in your daily life without imports. Coffee, tea, olive oil, and pepper are almost 100 percent imported. Americans consume imported orange juice, sugar, and even eggs because we do not produce sufficient quantities within the United States. Then there are the Italian suits, the German radios, and the Japanese microwave ovens that have worked their way into our lifestyles. We read newspapers printed on paper from abroad and use electricity generated by foreign oil.

Exporting is selling resources, goods, and services to buyers in foreign countries. Exports represent about 10 percent of U.S. gross domestic product (GDP). Exports of U.S. products, for example, reflect the wants and needs of buyers in the foreign importing countries (see Table 3.1). Most U.S. imports and exports consist of manufactured goods, since about 85 percent of services—a haircut, for example—are not exportable.[4] The United States enjoys a comparative advantage in a wide range of goods. For example, we export more wheat, soybeans, pharmaceuticals, chemicals, telecommunications equipment, computers, and medical equipment than we import. Examining the range of products a country imports and exports shows where its comparative advantage lies.

In addition to importing and exporting, where money is exchanged for resources, goods, or services, international trade can also occur through the oldest form of exchange—barter, or **countertrade**. Countertrade is the exchange of one good for another without using money. A company in Austria may barter Italian marble for Japanese computers in the same way you might swap a CD for a videotape.

2. Define the major elements of global trade and explain how global trade is measured.

Gross domestic product (GDP) is the dollar value of all the goods and services a country produces within a given time period.

table **3.1**

The Most Wanted Consumer Products in China

1970s	1980s	1990s
Watch	Color TV	VCR
Bicycle	Washing machine	Air conditioner
Sewing machine	Tape recorder	Stereo

The tastes and spending power of consumers can evolve rapidly in developing countries. In China, consumers strive for the "Three Bigs," the three most desired consumer products. The table shows how quickly the Chinese economy is developing by contrasting the Three Bigs over three decades.

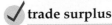

balance of trade

The relationship between a country's imports and its exports.

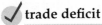

trade surplus

When a country exports more than it imports.

trade deficit

When a country imports more than it exports; a negative balance of trade.

balance of payments

The total flow of money into and out of a country during a specified period of time.

The Balance of Trade

The relationship between a country's imports and its exports is its **balance of trade**. If a country exports more than it imports, it enjoys a **trade surplus**; it brings in more money than it spends. Similarly, a country that imports more than it exports has a negative balance of trade, or a **trade deficit** (see Figure 3.1). Like budget deficits, which we examined in Chapter 2, trade deficits are not necessarily bad for a country's economy.

The United States has enjoyed a trade surplus in only three years of the last 25. The U.S. trade deficit hit an all-time high of $170 billion in 1994. The 1994 deficit was 2.5 percent of GDP, compared to 3.5 percent in 1987, when the deficit was $160 billion. So while the deficit was larger, its impact on our economy was less than in 1987. Imported oil and petroleum products account for the lion's share of the trade deficit, but Americans are increasingly buying such foreign goods as computers, machine tools, and steel—goods that are likely to yield productivity gains for the U.S. economy. And the balance of trade reveals an imbalance between goods and services. U.S. services (such as management consulting) enjoy a trade surplus, while a trade deficit continues for U.S. goods.

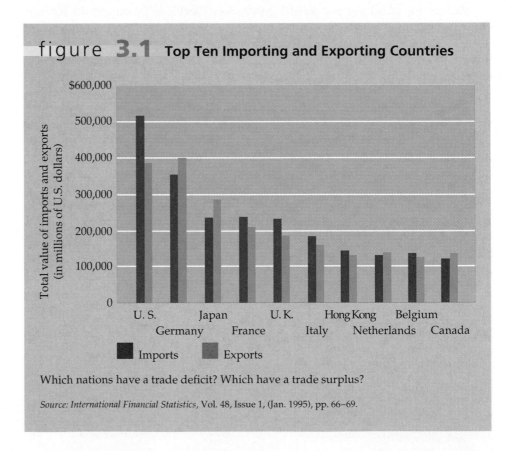

figure **3.1** **Top Ten Importing and Exporting Countries**

Which nations have a trade deficit? Which have a trade surplus?

Source: International Financial Statistics, Vol. 48, Issue 1, (Jan. 1995), pp. 66–69.

The Balance of Payments

The total flow of money into and out of a country during a specified period of time (quarterly, say, or annually) is an important economic indicator called the **balance of payments**. On the positive side of that flow are the following:

- Exports
- Money spent by foreign tourists
- Payments individuals receive in interest on investments made abroad

- New foreign investment in the country
- Money domestic firms receive from sources outside the country for insurance, transportation, and other services
- All payments to the country from foreign governments

The negative side—the money moving out of the country—includes:

- Imports
- Money spent by tourists outside the country
- Investments in the real estate of other countries
- Aid payments to foreign governments

As these lists show, the balance of trade is only one component of the balance of payments, which encompasses the total flow of money into and out of a country during any period. In the 1980s, foreign investment, another balance of payments item, caused heated debate in the United States, with investors from Japan, Germany, Great Britain, and other countries buying up everything from cattle ranches in Montana to movie studios in Hollywood to Rockefeller Center in New York City. Many Americans worried that much of the country would soon be owned by foreign investors.

On the positive side of all this, however, foreign investment brought a tremendous surge of capital into the United States, contributing to years of robust economic performance and unprecedented job creation. When the dollar weakened against the yen in the 1990s, the value of Japanese investments in the United States declined sharply. Mitsubishi Corporation saw its investment in Rockefeller Center drop by half and declared it bankrupt. Matsushita searched for a buyer to take entertainment conglomerate MCA off its hands.

Exchange Rates

After lots of scrimping and saving, you are taking your first European vacation to London, Paris, and Rome. Armed with maps, a guide to famous castles and nightclubs, and a Eurail Pass, you set out to experience the history and beauty of Europe. As you move from country to country, you find you must exchange your U.S. dollars for British pounds, French francs, and Italian lira.

In London, you exchange $100 for £65 in spending money (every dollar exchanges for about £0.65). After a few days, you see a beautiful handknit sweater selling for £65. You decide you must have it, and you return to the exchange service and present another $100. This time, however, they give you only £62. Puzzled, you ask for the missing £3, explaining that just a few days ago you exchanged $100 for £65. The staffperson tells you crisply that the "rate has just changed," and she adds something about the dollar "falling." While you're not certain what all this means, you do quickly figure out that your £65 sweater will now cost about $106, even though the price tag in British pounds is still the same. You take a deep breath and hand over another $6.

In Rome you are planning to sample every restaurant in town, so you immediately exchange $100 for about 170,000 Italian lira. As in London, your initial $100 runs out and a few days later you return to the exchange service, presenting another $100. But now you get 194,000 lira. With each restaurant visit costing about 24,000 lira, you can now splurge on eight meals instead of the seven your first $100 bought. The price of the meals hasn't changed, but your U.S. dollar buys more lira, and you experience what feels like a small windfall (nicely making up for the shrinking value of your dollar in the United Kingdom!).

3. Explain how exchange rates work, noting their significance to a country's economy.

What's the Exchange Rate?

Before you decide to sample the food in this Paris bistro, you'll translate both the menu and the prices to estimate how much each item costs in U.S. dollars. See something you'd like? Check your supply of francs, and *bon appetit*!

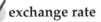

exchange rate

The price of one currency in terms of another currency.

World Bank

An entity created by Western governments to administer long-term loans to countries for economic development.

International Monetary Fund (IMF)

Western governments created this fund both to administer short-term loans to help countries establish international trade and to oversee the orderly exchange of currencies.

This fantasy vacation in Europe illustrates something that businesses, financial institutions, investors, and governments deal with daily: foreign currency exchange rates. The **exchange rate** is the price of one currency, say a U.S. dollar, in terms of another currency, say, a Japanese yen. It is a kind of translating device that allows currencies from many different countries to be compared. In 1986, for example, a U.S. dollar bought 200.87 Japanese yen, 0.69 British pounds, and 7.55 French francs. More recently, a U.S. dollar bought only 83.50 Japanese yen, 0.62 British pounds, and 4.84 French francs. The U.S. dollar had *lost value* in relation to the pound, yen, and franc because each dollar purchased less of those currencies than it had before. But, at the same time, the U.S. dollar had *gained value* with respect to the Italian lira, with each U.S. dollar purchasing more lira than it did before.

As these examples show, currency values "rise" or "fall" in relation to other currencies. As the dollar falls in value against the yen, which it has done over the last several years, Japanese products become more expensive for American citizens. If the exchange rate of $1 to 200 yen changes over a few years to $1 to 100 yen, what is the cost in dollars of a Japanese product priced at 5,000 yen at each rate? If the exchange rate is $1:200 yen, the cost in dollars is $25. When the exchange rate is $1:100 yen, the cost of that same 5,000-yen product is $50. As we saw in the fantasy vacation, the price of the product hasn't changed, but the value of the money in your hand has suddenly increased or decreased in terms of its buying power in the other currency.

Fluctuations in the exchange rate affect the level of demand for a country's products. When dollars have less buying power in foreign countries, items produced in those countries become more expensive for Americans—we pay more dollars to get them. But at the same time, U.S. products become less expensive overseas. This means that U.S. imports decrease and U.S. exports increase. And when that happens, the balance of trade swings in favor of the United States.

At the individual company level, a weakening U.S. currency makes American companies more price competitive in the world marketplace. As the U.S. dollar weakened into the mid-1990s, a farmer told the *Wall Street Journal*, "We know the dollar has been low against the yen which normally makes our grain cheaper." A cheaper dollar also makes foreign investment in the United States more attractive. At the same time, it makes it more expensive for U.S. citizens and firms to buy into foreign companies, to build plants abroad, and even to travel.[5]

When the U.S. dollar fell sharply against many currencies around the world in the mid-1990s, opportunities opened up for many U.S. companies. Food and beverage companies slashed prices and boosted promotional spending abroad to seize market share. U.S. automobile manufacturers benefited because American cars were cheaper than Japanese and German cars. Some U.S. companies invested in foreign companies: AFLAC Inc., a Georgia-based insurance company that derives 80 percent of its revenues from Japan, reinvested its profits in Japan to capitalize on the strong yen. But other U.S. companies found the declining dollar less advantageous. The price of oil, a major cost to Federal Express's international business, rose when the dollar fell. That meant that each of FedEx's dollars bought less oil. In response, FedEx now buys fuel in French francs at its Paris hub to keep costs and revenues in balance.

At the end of the Second World War, the Western Allied governments focused on ensuring economic stability for the free world. They created two programs to help reach that end. The first is the **World Bank**, which administers long-term loans to countries for economic development. The second is the **International Monetary Fund (IMF)**, which administers short-term loans to help countries establish international trade and oversees the orderly exchange of currencies. Over 150 countries now are members of the IMF. Exchange rates initially were fixed in terms of the U.S. dollar because of its strength. In 1973, the fixed exchange rate system was altered to create an open market, or a **floating exchange rate system**, in which the values of all currencies are determined by the forces of supply and demand. Today, exchange rates float against one another based on buyers' and sellers' beliefs about the economic strengths and weaknesses of a country's economy.

A country may decide to intervene to improve its exchange rate. **Devaluation** occurs when a government actually lowers the rate of exchange for its currency relative to foreign currencies. In this case, foreigners receive more of the currency for each unit of their own currency. This increases exports and reduces imports.

Factors That Shape Global Business Conduct

Global businesses must understand not only the laws of their own country, but also those of the host countries in which they are doing business and any international regulations that govern their business. But the political-legal environment is only one factor that global businesses must contend with. Two other environments—the economic and the social/cultural—are also critical to the success of an international business. We begin by looking at the impact of the economic environment.

The Economic Environment

Countries frequently are classified into two main economic categories based on GDP per capita (that is, per person), or *GDP divided by the number of people in the country*. **Developed countries** are those in which per capita GDP is relatively high, over $10,000 per year. The U.S. falls into this group of 34 countries, along with Australia, Bermuda, Canada, Denmark, France, Portugal, Sweden, Switzerland, Turkey, and the United Kingdom. **Developing countries** are those in which per capita GDP is relatively low, less than $10,000 per year and typically below $5,000. Living standards in developing countries often are low, population growth high, and advanced technology unavailable to the vast majority of citizens. Bolivia, Chile, Côte d'Ivoire, Egypt, Iran, Greenland, Oman, Thailand, and Vietnam are among the 175 developing countries.

Newly industrializing countries, or **NICs**, are developing countries that are undergoing rapid economic growth. NIC populations have made the shift from agricultural work to factory work, high technology is available, and per capita GDP is rising rapidly as a result. Mexico and the so-called Four Tigers of Asia—Hong Kong, South Korea, Singapore, and Taiwan—qualify as newly industrializing countries.

The remaining, least developed countries have no significant economic growth. Per capita GDP typically is less than $500. In these countries, workers farm or fish using traditional methods and sometimes work in low-technology factories to assemble simple products for export. Often they can find no paying work at all. Afghanistan, Bangladesh, Cape Verde, Chad, Haiti, Laos, Mozambique, Nepal, Sierra Leone, and Uganda are among this large group of nations.

The economic gap between the poorest and richest nations is widening because economic growth is offset by rapid population growth. The world population stands at over 5.5 billion people today, and 4.3 billion of them—more than three-quarters—live in developing countries. By current estimates, world population will rise to 7 billion persons by the year 2010, and the bulk of

---

✓ **floating exchange rate system**

A system of exchange in which the values of all currencies are determined by the forces of supply and demand.

✓ **devaluation**

Occurs when a government actually lowers the rate of exchange for its currency relative to foreign currencies.

✓ **developed countries**

The 34 countries in which per capita GDP is relatively high, over $10,000 per year.

✓ **developing countries**

The 175 countries in which per capita GDP is relatively low, less than $10,000 per year and typically below $5,000.

✓ **newly industrializing countries (NICs)**

Developing countries that are undergoing rapid economic growth.

4. Describe how countries are classified economically.

doing business

Job Migration

Experts predict that within a generation, 60 percent of the world's population will live in cities. This compares with 35 percent today. Migration to cities is motivated by the quest for improved employment, educational opportunities, and social services. This population shift will create both a diversified labor force in cities and greater unemployment, since the vast majority of new workers will be unskilled.

The growth of labor markets in developing countries fuels job exporting, the transfer of labor-intensive jobs from high-wage, developed countries to low-wage countries. It is behind much of the loss of manufacturing jobs in the United States and other developed countries. But the story is more complex than that. Jobs actually migrate around the world, chasing appropriate labor markets. Labor-intensive, low-skill jobs such as sewing sneakers and soccer balls are the first to migrate to countries whose economies are beginning to develop. The countries with the lowest per capita incomes are the cheapest places to make such products. In 1992, for instance, hourly wage rates in manufacturing were $16.90 in Japan, and $15.45 in the United States, but $1.80 in Hungary and $0.50 in China.[1] However, as these countries begin to industrialize, wage rates go up, and the technical sophistication of their labor force and businesses increases. The lower-wage jobs migrate away from them in search of cheaper work forces, and new, light manufacturing jobs migrate to them from other, more developed countries.[2] This phenomenon is termed *job migration*, the continuous movement of work around the changing world labor market.

Matsushita is a Japanese-based global manufacturer of electronics and appliances. It has over 150 plants in 38 countries, many of which produce the company's goods at lower cost than Japan itself can. Electronic components, televisions, air conditioners, and VCRs are being made abroad and imported back to Japan. This creates problems for Matsushita's 250,000 Japanese employees who find themselves being displaced by workers in Latin America, Asia, and Africa.

[1] Tim Lang and Colin Hines, "GATT: The Pitfalls Amid the Promise," *New York Times*, April 17, 1994, p. F13.
[2] William B. Johnston, "Global Work Force 2000: The New World Labor Market," *Harvard Business Review*, Vol. 69, No. 2 (March-April 1991), p. 115.

population growth will continue to occur in the least developed countries. Birth rates in countries such as Germany, England, and the United States approach "replacement rates," so that the total population size (excluding any increases due to immigration) does not grow much. In contrast, women in Kenya give birth to eight children on average.

In Africa, 40 percent of the population is under the age of 14. With meager incomes, people spend most of their money on food: 38 percent compared to 10 percent in the United States. Like Africa, Latin America's population is skewed toward the young. While many are better educated than their parents, many are very poor as well. And South Americans also spend a disproportionate amount of their income on food.

All these facts underline the great diversity of business and living conditions around the world. And they demonstrate that conditions are changing rapidly as well. By the year 2025, it is predicted that 80 percent of the world's population will be concentrated in developing countries. (Can you think why?) Consumers in both Eastern and Western Europe are highly educated, with a literacy rate of 95 percent, but many consumption differences exist between the two populations, since Eastern Europe has little income for imports. The gap between Eastern and Western Europe will close over the coming years, feeding the already strong demand for all forms of Western goods.

The greatest business opportunities will exist in countries whose GDP per capita is growing as wages increase. People in these economies will have greater spending power in the future. The highest economic growth rates are occurring in Asia, and high population growth is occurring throughout most of Asia, Africa, and Latin America. (See the doing business box "Job Migration" to learn how the global labor market is changing.) Rapid increases in GDP in countries like China and South Korea mean demand for all kinds of products—diapers, computers, washing machines—should grow for many years.

Protectionism Versus Free Trade

Chapter 2 describes how economic systems produce and distribute wealth. In reality, 200-odd national economies rub shoulders with one another around the globe, and where they touch, friendship or animosity shapes economic behavior. Politics affects economic conditions as governments set policies designed to regulate international business in their favor. Japan, for instance, restricts foreign access to its automobile market in order to protect Japanese manufacturers. Countries differ in the extent to which they encourage other countries to participate in their domestic markets. Attitudes toward foreign goods can be viewed as a continuum running from protectionism to free trade.

Protectionism is the attempt to protect domestic industries from foreign competition through the erection of legal barriers to trade. **Free trade** is an open situation in which no such barriers to trade exist and countries can trade freely. Protectionist barriers can take a variety of forms. The most common are tariffs and quotas.

A **tariff** is a tax on imported goods. Until early in this century, the U.S. government used *revenue tariffs* as a major source of funds. During the Great Depression, many ailing countries imposed *protective tariffs*, which raise the retail price of imports, to give their domestic industries pricing advantages and make them more competitive. But the effect of these protective measures was to stifle world trade and actually make the economic downturn worse.

Although tariffs have generally lost their prominence as a protectionist measure, the United States threatened Japanese luxury car makers with 100 percent tariffs in 1995 in order to persuade the Japanese government to open its markets to U.S. autos. Critics argued that such an extreme protective tariff would only wound U.S. dealers who sold cars such as the Infiniti and the Lexus. Still, tariffs are no longer the major bottleneck to global trade that they once were—another reason for the emergence of a global economy.

A **quota** is a specific limit on the number of items of a particular kind that may be imported. More extreme is an **embargo**, which totally bans imports in designated categories. The United States, for example, maintains an embargo against Cuba, one of the last communist countries in the world. In 1994, the United States lifted its trade embargo against Vietnam and allowed American companies to do business there for the first time since before the start of the

protectionism

The attempt to protect domestic industries from foreign competition through the erection of legal barriers to trade.

free trade

An open situation in which no barriers to trade exist and countries can trade freely.

tariff

A tax on imported goods.

quota

A specific limit on the number of items of a particular kind that may be imported.

embargo

A total ban on imports in designated categories.

5. Discuss the issue of protectionism versus free trade.

A Protectionist Reaction

Faced with the prospect of decreasing farm subsidies and increasing competition from imports, these French farmers protested their government's trade policy by tossing sacks of grain into the Seine River late in 1993.

doing business

Getting Down to Business in Vietnam

The two leaders sat face to face across the negotiating table, each eager to open economic relations. On one side, Vietnamese Prime Minister Vo Van Kiet knew that World Bank loans to his country would give him the spending power to build the electrical networks and highways needed to modernize Vietnam's economy. On the other, the president and chief executive officer of General Electric Co., John Trani, knew his company would soon be granted legal access to the Vietnamese market. After this meeting in 1994, Trani predicted that Vietnam will become one of GE's biggest customers within a decade.

The legacy of the Vietnam War has held U.S. companies back, allowing European and Japanese rivals to enter Vietnam first. In 1994 the thirty-year U.S. embargo against Vietnam was lifted. Trading began again, and U.S. companies are now eager to do business in Vietnam. Caterpillar is competing to supply manufacturing equipment, and construction company Morrison Knudsen is competing to sell engineering and project management for a $2 billion highway project. Mobil has joined three Japanese partners to begin drilling for oil off Vietnam's shores. GE of course plans to electrify Vietnam, Coca-Cola has its own plans to conquer Vietnam's consumer market, and Citibank is opening branch offices in Hanoi and other Vietnamese cities.

And Mars, Inc., entered the Vietnamese market only to discover it was already there—in the form of counterfeit versions of its candy bars made by local companies![1]

Why trade with Vietnam? The Vietnamese economy is growing, and while per capita GDP is still low, spending power is increasing rapidly. The prospect of 75 million new consumers makes U.S. company managers eager to learn a new language. Also encouraging to U.S. businesses is the fact that Vietnamese consumers have watched advertisements for U.S. products for many years—they see them on satellite television broadcasts from nearby countries—and this creates latent demand for Coke, candy bars, and many other brand-name products. Vietnam is an emerging market, and growth is found in emerging markets. The "Hanoi Hilton" prison in which U.S. fighter pilots were held during the war is now being converted to a shopping center, and U.S. companies are eager to land space in it.[2]

[1] Joyce Barnathan, Alex McKinnon, and Doug Harbrecht, "Destination, Vietnam," *Business Week*, Feb. 14, 1994, pp. 26–27.
[2] Mark Wilson, "U.S. Goods Find Open Market in Vietnam," *U.S.A. Today*, July 14, 1994, p. 6B.

Vietnam War (see the doing business box "Getting Down to Business in Vietnam"). In July 1995, the U.S. government resumed full diplomatic relations with Vietnam.

A country's economic status is a good measure of whether its political climate favors protectionism or free trade. Proponents of protectionism argue that keeping other countries' products out of domestic markets helps protect infant industries. They say it also maintains the country's standard of living by holding up wage rates, maintaining employment, protecting national defense, and preventing the country's wealth from flowing across its borders. Most economists would agree only in part. They would support the argument that protectionism helps infant industries, protects national defense, and aids in industrializing developing countries.

Critics of protectionism champion free trade, with no restrictions on global trade. They argue that protectionism is a costly way of saving jobs and that wages are artificially propped up for protected industries. Jobs saved may even result in jobs lost in other industries. For example, when the importation of shoes is restricted, domestic shoe producers' jobs are saved. But jobs are lost in warehouses that would have held inventories of imported shoes. And because the domestic workers' wages are protected, consumers ultimately pay higher prices for the shoes they purchase.

Trade barriers can limit consumer choice as well as elevate consumer prices. And, perhaps most damaging, barriers can artificially isolate firms in protected industries. Tariffs are difficult to undo once they've been enacted. Isolated from world markets and world competitors, protected firms tend to learn and change more slowly, becoming less competitive over time.

International Trade Agreements

Governments also affect their economies through the agreements they reach with one another. Perhaps the most important international trade pact is the **General Agreement on Tariffs and Trade (GATT)**, which binds 124 of the world's trading nations to mutual agreements that set limits on both tariff and nontariff barriers. Established in 1948 under United Nations auspices, GATT now governs about 95 percent of world trade. In each decade since GATT was created, special sessions (called "rounds") have been convened to discuss current problems in international trade.

Begun in 1986, the Uruguay Round of trade talks successfully concluded with the signing of a new GATT agreement in 1994. It increases free trade throughout the world by reducing protectionist barriers and addresses issues of consumer price increases caused by agricultural subsidies, restrictions on internationally traded services, and the erection of nontariff barriers. The Uruguay Round has expanded the limits of free trade by extending GATT's authority to new areas: agriculture, textiles, services, and international investment (see Table 3.2). It strengthens restrictions on counterfeiters who pirate patented products and provides for stronger reinforcement of antidumping laws.

 General Agreement on Tariffs and Trade (GATT)

The trade pact that binds 124 of the world's trading nations to mutual agreements that set limits on both tariff and nontariff barriers.

6. Describe the role of international trade agreements and trading blocs in promoting free trade.

t a b l e **3.2** Who Gets What from GATT's Uruguay Round

Agriculture	Farm subsidies decrease in Europe, creating more opportunities for the United States to export wheat and corn. However, a loss of subsidies to the fruit and peanut industries in the United States will reduce their exports.
Automotive products	The Japanese auto industry may find restrictions lifted on cars, since GATT dictates that *only one* industry can be protected in each country by "voluntary" restraints limiting imports. U.S. automakers fear that that industry may not be the auto industry.
Entertainment, pharmaceuticals, and software	France voted not to ease access to its market for U.S. entertainment companies. Increased worldwide protection will come for patents, copyrights, and trademarks.
Financial, legal, and accounting services	For the first time, trade in services will come under GATT rules. U.S. service industries benefit significantly.
Textiles and apparel	Quotas limiting imports from developing countries will be phased out over 10 years, causing a loss of jobs in the United States. However, strict quotas add approximately $15 billion a year to the price of clothing, which is a boon for U.S. retailers.

Trading Rights Versus Human Rights

One multinational trading agreement called most favored nation (MFN) status gives special treatment to a trading partner, or a set of trading partners, in connection with specific products. The United States, for example, gives developing nations limited tariff-free access to certain markets. The People's Republic of China has MFN status with the United States. American companies generally favor this status, but deplore Chinese treatment of political prisoners, many of whom are held in Chinese prisons as forced laborers and tortured for actions considered legal and admirable in the United States.

Some believe that eliminating China's MFN status might curb these objectionable practices. But that could come at a price. China would probably respond by reducing U.S. exports to its vast market. Most U.S. exports are low-tech products like tennis shoes, toys, and small appliances. Since China has the world's fastest growing economy and its 1.2 billion people have expanding per capita income, many American companies want to keep trade routes open to capture global revenues. Others argue that trade should first be used as a lever to push China toward improving human rights.

What do you think? Should the United States require human rights reform as a condition of open trade with China?

Source: Robert Keatley, "U.S. Firms, Anticipating Huge Market, Worry China May Lose Its MFN Status," *Wall Street Journal*, May 14, 1993.

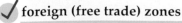

dumping

Occurs when a company sells goods abroad below cost or at a lower price than it charges in its protected home market.

foreign (free trade) zones

A form of trading agreement in which a foreign company is allowed to import goods free of tax if it creates domestic jobs in the import zone.

Dumping occurs when a company sells goods abroad below cost or at a lower price than it charges in its protected home market. Antidumping laws impose extra import taxes on companies that employ dumping. Antidumping laws are the most frequently invoked of GATT member nations' foreign trade laws. And the United States leads all other countries in using these laws to restrict dumping. In theory, antidumping laws promote free trade. But in reality, countries often use these laws to protect domestic industries from foreign competition.

Recent dumping charges have focused on commodities like steel, manganese, and silicon. Russia has sold silicon in the United States at prices lower than Western levels. Chinese manganese has been dumped in the United States at prices below the average cost of U.S. production. Mexico has complained of U.S. dumping of steel, and European countries have complained that the Czech Republic and Hungary have exported structural beams at prices 40 to 50 percent lower than the going rates.

The U.S. Fresh Garlic Producers Association complained that imports of Chinese fresh garlic surged from 3 million pounds in 1991 to over 54 million pounds in 1993 because of undercut prices. Imported garlic sold for as little as 28 cents a pound, while U.S. growers said it cost them 50 cents to produce a pound of garlic that went for 70 to 80 cents a pound. They charged that Chinese garlic is cheap because China relies on cheap prison labor for harvesting. See the ethics check entitled "Trading Rights Versus Human Rights."

Generally, the recent GATT agreement will benefit Americans enormously. European governments have decreased agricultural subsidies and widened markets for U.S. farmers. Asian countries have cut tariffs to open the door for U.S. meat exports. Tariffs on American heavy construction equipment and specialty steel have dropped by 40 percent. And the Uruguay Round created a World Trade Organization to enforce the agreement by assessing penalties against member nations.

Foreign, or **free trade, zones** are a form of trading agreement in which a foreign company is allowed to import goods free of tax if it creates domestic jobs in the import zone. But this approach to increasing trade can backfire, as it has in the United States, where Japanese manufacturers import component parts from Japan, citing quality concerns with American parts. In the early 1990s, more than 80 percent of all Japanese imports were purchased by Japanese subsidiaries operating in the United States.[6] Meanwhile, Japan resists opening up its markets to U.S. products. Thus, foreign trade zones have widened the U.S. trade deficit with Japan.

Mexican-U.S. economic cooperation has spawned the **maquiladora**, a form of free trade zone that allows U.S. companies to ship their raw materials and parts from the United States to Mexico for processing by low-wage Mexican workers. The parts return to the United States as finished products or as partially finished parts, but the United States charges duty on only the non-U.S. portion of the product. In this way, Mexico "exports" its cheap labor without losing laborers and U.S. businesses gain the benefits of low wages without actually moving south. Some 2,200 *maquiladoras* exist; Sony, GE, Johnson & Johnson, and Germany's Siemens use them. Zenith Electronics assembles its entire production of 3 million television sets in Mexico. And since the company pays its 17,000 workers in pesos rather than dollars, it gained millions of dollars in savings when the peso was devalued in late 1994.

Trading Blocs

Free trade is at the core of **trading blocs**, countries that band together as one market of regional trading partners and that apply the same rules and regulations to trade among themselves as to trade with nations outside the bloc. One widely known trading bloc is the **common market**, a form of economic cooperation among several nations, such as is found in the European Union, formerly called the European Community (EC). Formed in 1957 by six Western European countries, the European Union has expanded to embrace most of Western Europe, including:

Belgium	Italy
Denmark	Luxembourg
Finland	The Netherlands
France	Portugal
Germany	Spain
Greece	Sweden
Ireland	The United Kingdom

In a sweeping program begun in 1992, the European Union is eliminating much of the red tape, regulations, and fiscal restrictions that grew up over the decades to protect member nations. In the European Union, 320 million consumers are unified into one market regulated by a common set of trade laws. In effect, people, products, and services are able to move across national borders with the same ease that they move across state borders in the United States.

Observers expect that protectionist regulations will eventually be imposed to favor member nations and insulate the European Union from outsiders, especially Japan and the United States. However, foreign companies already firmly entrenched in the European Union before 1992 should continue to do well. With Europe economically united, vast markets are opening up to global businesses. Transportation is quicker and cheaper without the border stops, fewer product changes are needed to meet national product specifications, and advertising can be standardized across nations.

In 1993, the **North American Free Trade Agreement (NAFTA)** pushed open more doors for free trade. Trade barriers between the United States, Canada, and Mexico came tumbling down, creating a market of 366 million people. Approval of NAFTA in the United States was a long and hard battle.

 maquiladora

A form of free trade zone that allows U.S. companies to ship their raw materials and parts from the United States to Mexico for processing by low-wage Mexican workers.

 trading blocs

Countries that band together as one market of regional trading partners and that apply the same rules and regulations to trade among themselves as to trade with nations outside the bloc.

 common market

A form of economic cooperation among several nations, such as is found in the European Union.

 North American Free Trade Agreement (NAFTA)

A 1993 agreement that extended the U.S.–Canadian treaty to include Mexico, creating a market of 366 million people.

Proponents pointed to the increased market for U.S. industries, while critics warned of the jobs that would be lost as companies headed south to take advantage of cheaper labor. To date, NAFTA has proven a success (see Figure 3.2). In the first year, U.S. trade with Canada and Mexico expanded at about twice the rate of trade with non-NAFTA countries. U.S. exports to Mexico grew by 22 percent in NAFTA's first year,[7] while exports to Canada grew at a rate of 13 percent.[8] Before NAFTA's approval, critics forecasted doom for U.S. autoworkers, predicting that automakers would invest in Mexico to take advantage of low labor rates. But U.S. exports of cars to Mexico increased by 500 percent in the first eight months. And Mexican companies have begun moving into the United States to build plants, strike deals, and garner increased sales in the massive American market. As the president of a ceramic bathroom tile manufacturer building a factory in Texas told the *Wall Street Journal*, "This is where the market is."[9]

The European Union and NAFTA are highly visible trading blocs to U.S. observers, but blocs are also forming in other regions. Many Latin American countries are banding together to enhance their economic status. Brazil, Argentina, Uruguay, and Paraguay are members of Mercosur, a free trade bloc with 200 million consumers and a GDP of $550 billion. In fact, Mercosur goes beyond internal free trade and attempts to improve trade between its members and nations outside the group by standardizing tariffs at 14 percent, down from as much as 35 percent. Another trading bloc, the Andean Pact, comprises Venezuela, Colombia, Ecuador, and Peru. Future mergers among trading blocs are expected. As a Latin American Hewlett-Packard Co. executive said, "Before we have a hemispheric trade agreement, we're going to see some of these trade blocs get together."[10]

Others already are. NAFTA partners Canada, Mexico, and the United States also participate in the Asia-Pacific Economic Cooperation group (APEC). This diverse, loosely knit agglomeration of 18 nations ranges from Singapore and China to Australia and New Zealand to Chile. At their 1994 summit, APEC members reached agreement on ending all regional trade barriers within 25 years. Asian members such as Indonesia and many of its neighbors are joining the worldwide push for open markets by cutting tariffs, breaking up monopolies, and opening key markets to foreigners.

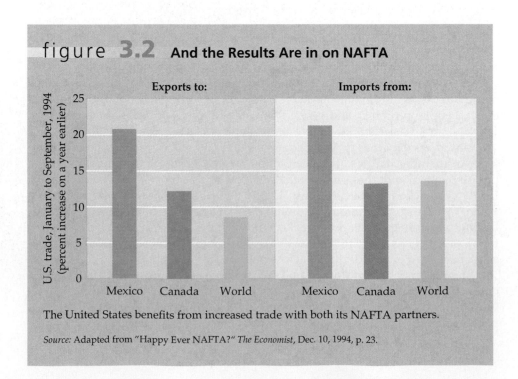

figure **3.2**   **And the Results Are in on NAFTA**

The United States benefits from increased trade with both its NAFTA partners.

Source: Adapted from "Happy Ever NAFTA?" *The Economist,* Dec. 10, 1994, p. 23.

Jumbo Trading Bloc

Late in 1994, at the APEC summit in Bogor, Indonesia, Japanese Prime Minister Tomiichi Morayama, South Korean President Kim Young-sam, and U.S. President Bill Clinton, shown here, joined all attending delegates in wearing batik print shirts at the request of their host, President Suharto. Turning the Pacific into a mammoth free trade zone by 2020 is a goal of APEC, which has a total GDP of $13 trillion and encompasses 40 percent of all global trade.

The Political/Legal Environment

An integral part of global success is understanding the host country's political environment and its laws. The host country's government can and does dictate the opportunities for foreign business activity. It can encourage and support that activity or discourage and ban it, often in a seemingly whimsical way. Global businesses must understand not only the political climate, but also a three-part legal context: their own country's laws, the laws of the host countries in which they are doing business, and international regulations.

Political Climate

Businesses prefer political environments in host countries that are stable and friendly. But as we saw in Chapter 2, especially among developing countries, governments are not always able to ensure a stable business environment. Governments change, new political parties form, and power struggles create stress. When Deng Xiaping, the Chinese leader, neared death in the mid-1990s, a power struggle among those who would be his successor created widespread concern among foreign businesses regarding the stability of that nation's economic and political systems. All governments enact laws to protect their political and economic interests domestically and internationally. When political philosophies change—sometimes dramatically and overnight—countries will often change their attitude and policies toward foreign business. In such cases, newly enacted laws, codes, and restrictions can shape a global firm's success or failure.

In South Korea, for example, political promises suggest a more open Korean market for foreign business. Yet consumer goods companies find doing business there very difficult. South Korea's nationalistic politics create a protectionist environment that hinders successful business performance by foreign companies. South Korea's consumer products industry is dominated by four multibillion-dollar giants: Daewoo, Goldstar, Hyundai, and Samsung. These companies are subsidized by the government, which therefore has a stake in their success. Hence, the South Korean government strictly enforces restrictions on imported electronic equipment, televisions, and radios, and often demands from foreign companies what would be classified as proprietary information. Korean firms that stock American goods are frequently harassed by extra audits and special regulation.

7. Explain the significance for global businesses of a country's political climate.

U.S. Laws

A company that does business abroad is not exempt from the laws of its home country. U.S. laws that affect global business cover business practices relating to competition, national security, and ethics. For example, U.S. firms and their foreign subsidiaries are prohibited from making sales that would damage U.S. national security.

Some laws protect the rights of foreign companies to compete within the United States; others govern the actions of U.S. firms doing business in foreign markets. For example, the **Foreign Corrupt Practices Act** forbids American companies from paying bribes to foreign officials, political candidates, or government parties. Officials and companies may be liable if they had "reason to know" that a bribe was involved. Bribery, however, is a way of life in many countries. Hence, the law is controversial, since adherence to it may restrict U.S. companies from competing effectively abroad.

Host Country Laws

8. Identify the three most common categories of legal systems and explain their impact on the operations of a global business.

All countries have legal systems, the majority of which can be classified into three categories: common law, code law, and theocratic systems.[11] Under a common law system, laws of custom and precedent are interpreted within a court system. The United States, Canada, and the United Kingdom have common law systems. Code law systems, operating in over 70 countries, provide all inclusive written rules meant to eliminate the need for interpretation. In Singapore, for example, chewing gum under any circumstances is illegal. In theocratic systems, religious laws govern the legal system. Consider Muslim law, which is followed in some way in 27 countries. It is based on the teachings of the Koran, which governs all parts of life, including legal behavior.

In global business, host country laws govern the establishment of firms; taxation; pricing; environmental, health, and safety standards; minimum wages; and trademarks. No firm can function effectively without understanding the legal system of the country in which it is doing business.

One area that has been a source of conflict between foreign businesses and host countries has been the protection of **intellectual property**, which is intangible personal property such as ideas, patents, brand names, trademarks, and copyrights. The way countries protect intellectual property varies enormously and often is very involved. In some countries, protection is obtained simply by *using* the intellectual property—labeling your product with a brand name makes that brand yours to use exclusively. In others, businesses can protect ideas, names, and the like even though they are *not used*. Companies can therefore prevent competitors from using their intellectual property, such as a brand name, merely by registering it in the country. In still other countries, such as Korea and Taiwan, intellectual property can be used by anyone; no protection exists.

Some Chinese companies have become master pirates, openly flaunting their infringement of American brands and products. Piracy is the unauthorized use or reproduction of copyrighted or patented material. Chinese firms counterfeit sunglasses that look like Bausch & Lomb's and call them "Ran Bans." Counterfeiters produce beaming-red toothpaste packages marked "Cologate." Kellogg's corn flakes are pirated with a look-alike box of Kongalu Corn Strips sporting the slogan, "the trustworthy sign of quality which is famous around the world." Microsoft estimates it loses $30 million annually at the hands of software pirates. Said a leading Chinese lawyer, "It's only beginning to dawn on people [in China] that copyrights and trademarks are property."[12] For example, Table 3.3 shows the dimensions of this problem in Hong Kong.

 Foreign Corrupt Practices Act

A law that forbids American companies from paying bribes to foreign officials, political candidates, or government parties.

intellectual property

Intangible personal property such as ideas, patents, brand names, trademarks, and copyrights.

piracy

The unauthorized use or reproduction of copyrighted or patented material.

table 3.3   Breaking the Price Barrier in Hong Kong

Software	Boston-area price (manufacturer's version)	Hong Kong price (pirated version)
Microsoft Word	$319 (disk)	$18.18
Aladdin, Disney's Activity Center	$27.32 (CD)	$15.58
The Way Things Work	$50 (CD)	$16.23
Super Mario Land for Super Nintendo	$29.99	$15.58
Mortal Kombat II for Super Nintendo	$69.99	$22.07
The Bible	$40 (CD)	$16.88

Source: Charles A. Radin, "Pssst, Want Some Software CHEAP?" *Boston Globe*, Feb. 28, 1995, p. 57.

International Regulation

In the United States, federal laws override state and local laws. Yet no international legal body exists to override the legal systems of individual nations. However, the United States and many other countries have treaties and agreements with other nations that determine how international business will be conducted. These treaties govern the flow of finished products, raw materials, workers and managers, and capital. Such treaties tend to focus on the following issues:

- The right of individuals to enter a country
- The movement of goods across national borders
- The entry of ships and cargoes
- The movement of capital
- The acquisition of property
- The protection of persons and property engaged in international trade.[13]

As more trading blocs are formed, these treaties appear to be gaining in strength.

Social/Cultural Forces

Once you've read lots of books on your host country's economic and legal systems, surely you're ready to do business there, right? Not quite. If you don't have some understanding of the country's culture, you may defeat your own best efforts. Consider a company selling baby food in Sweden. Sweden has a 99 percent literacy rate, so the company can safely advertise its product in various magazines and newspapers, perhaps including information about the product's nutritional content. But in Yemen, the literacy rate is about 30 percent. Here, an approach based on visual media such as picture posters would be more appropriate. Even then, cultural problems can occur. One company, hoping to market baby food in central Africa, put a picture of a cute baby from a local tribe on the jar. But local consumers had little experience with the culture of packaging and came to believe that the picture on the package

9. Describe the social/cultural factors that affect global businesses.

represented its contents. They concluded that the baby food jars contained processed baby!

The social and cultural environment affects businesses in many ways.[14] The people of a culture play many roles—as customers, employees, political administrators, competitors, and sources of financial resources. Differences in their behavior can be traced to a number of cultural elements: language, values, religion, superstition, and social organization.

Language

An understanding of the local language can make or break a firm doing business in a host country. Consider the following. A soft drink company's marketing slogan was "Come Alive," but the translation used in a sales campaign in Germany meant "Come Alive Out of the Grave." A U.S. airline pitched its waiting areas as "Rendezvous Lounges," but in the version used in Brazil these became "Rooms for Lovemaking." A German exporter of chocolates introduced its candy into the United States under the name "Zit." Such stories are amusing, but they emphasize how easily companies can make mistakes when moving from one language to another.

Acquiring language expertise in a foreign country is not easy. There are approximately 3,000 languages and 10,000 different dialects spoken in the world today. In India alone there are 15 major languages, and the most prominent of them, Hindi, is spoken by only 28 percent of the population. Fortunately for U.S. firms, English, Spanish, or French is spoken in most countries. And English is the dominant language of international business.

Communication has more dimensions than just words. International businesspeople also communicate through their understanding of time and space.[15] In India "time is a river," while in the United States "time is money." The meaning of deadlines and delivery times also varies widely. In Portugal and Brazil, it is not uncommon for a businessperson to come to a meeting an hour or two later than the appointed time. In those countries, time means approximate time. But in Sweden, appointments are kept—to the minute. As noted early in the chapter, personal space is also viewed differently in different nations. American businesspeople sometimes feel uncomfortable when negotiating with people from the Middle East, who tend to stand closer to others than is generally acceptable in the United States. Space also symbolizes the different relationships between workers. In the United States, the organization's president is located in the highest office, often on the top floor. In Japan, where communication among workers is prized, work is done in large open areas.

Values, Religion, and Superstition

People of different countries differ in their values and in their attitudes toward work, success, clothing, food, music, sex, social status, honesty, human rights, and much else.[16] Differences in values can affect just about any business. In countries such as Taiwan and Japan, the work ethic is very strong, and that ethic is acted out daily in factories and offices. Workers in the communist bloc countries, who grew up with the assumption that government will provide for everyone's minimum needs, may not respond to purely individualistic financial incentives, as U.S. workers do.

Beliefs about the supernatural play an important role in the values of all cultures. Those who conduct business internationally should be aware that the Western distinction between superstition and religious belief is not universal. In some cultures, ghosts, palm reading, the phases of the moon, soothsayers, and demons are a part of life. In Thailand, for example, the location of buildings is often determined by astrologers. Thais also believe that all the wood in a building should come from the same forest so that individual boards will not "argue" with one another. In Malaysia, production runs in a plant can be halted while a goat is sacrificed and its blood sprinkled on the factory floor to drive away evil spirits. In Buddhist, Hindu, and Moslem cultures, many events are simply considered "acts of God." Plant workers may therefore be less motivated than in the United States, for instance, to take accident prevention measures on the factory floor, since accidents are fated and cannot be avoided.

Social Organization

Members of the middle and upper classes are more likely than members of the lower classes to use imported products. This makes countries with large lower-class populations, such as Chile, less attractive to international businesses than countries where the middle and upper classes are larger, such as Sweden, Britain, and Germany.

Around the globe, the middle class is growing explosively, as diagrammed in Figure 3.3. In Mexico City, cars now line up around the block to get into the parking lot of a local Sam's Club, opened by Wal-Mart stores in 1991. The U.S. Department of Commerce names the following as the world's ten biggest emerging markets: the People's Republic of China, Indonesia, India, South Korea, Turkey, Mexico, Brazil, South Africa, Argentina, and Poland.[17] These countries are expected to provide 20 percent of the world's GDP by the year 2010 because of the growth of their middle classes. As income grows, the opportunities to sell diapers and detergent, automobiles and microwave ovens, soar. But middle-class life is not all the same worldwide.

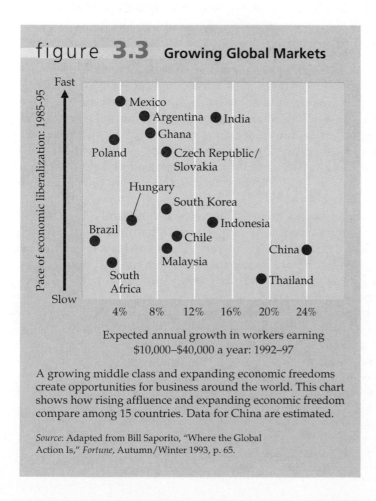

figure **3.3** **Growing Global Markets**

Expected annual growth in workers earning
$10,000–$40,000 a year: 1992–97

A growing middle class and expanding economic freedoms create opportunities for business around the world. This chart shows how rising affluence and expanding economic freedom compare among 15 countries. Data for China are estimated.

Source: Adapted from Bill Saporito, "Where the Global Action Is," *Fortune*, Autumn/Winter 1993, p. 65.

In the United States, we spend almost half our incomes on rent, transportation, health care, and education. The Chinese spend only about 5 percent in these categories because they are so highly subsidized by the government. Hence, the $1,837 average household income in the major cities of the People's Republic of China provides strong purchasing power. In Shanghai, 85 percent of households now have washing machines and 93 percent own color televisions, compared to 72 and 81 percent, respectively, in 1991.[18]

The Practice of Global Business

International business is the norm today, and firms can become involved in a variety of ways. Monitoring change and adjusting to it are the keys to success. This section explores the various ways companies operate internationally.

Approaches to Global Business

10. Describe several strategies for entering foreign markets.

There are numerous ways for businesses to gain access to new markets and do business in foreign countries. Many firms become global businesses rather casually, neither actively seeking international trade nor being particularly attuned to the needs of foreign markets. For example, a small German toy manufacturer might sell its products at the 400-year-old Nuremberg Christmas market, where a French buyer places a one-time order. The German toy company will not systematically examine international opportunities before filling the order, but the transaction may launch the firm into the global marketplace. Not all businesses, however, become global businesses quite so casually.

Direct and Indirect Exporting

The easiest way to get into international markets is through exporting, which we discussed earlier in this chapter. The most common form of exporting among companies entering international markets is **indirect export**. The company contracts with host country nationals who provide various services plus international selling expertise. Little investment is needed. Most indirect exporting is done through domestic-based export merchants who buy the domestic products and sell them abroad, and through domestic-based export agents who never actually own the goods but merely seek out foreign buyers and receive a commission on their sales.

When the company's foreign business has grown sufficiently large, it will likely shift to **direct export**, creating its own export department or division to conduct business directly with foreign buyers. The firm may hire overseas agents or contract with one or more import houses within the host country. Still another alternative is to set up a *sales office* on foreign soil staffed with salespeople from the parent or host country.

Mead Corp.'s coated-board division is a successful direct exporter. The company built a $500 million plant in Alabama to double its production of coated paperboard used in packaging. Most of the added capacity is earmarked for Asian countries. To ensure that it meets the local needs of Japanese customers, Mead signed an agreement with Seibu Saison Group, a $20 billion retailer. Seibu Saison functions as Mead's representative, and the deal ensures that Mead knows what its ultimate customers want and can tailor its boxes to their specific products.

✓ **indirect export**

The most common form of exporting among companies entering international markets; the company contracts with host country nationals who provide various services plus international selling expertise.

✓ **direct export**

A form of exporting used by companies that have grown sufficiently large, in which the company creates its own export department or division to conduct business directly with foreign buyers.

Licensing and Franchising

Businesses can join together with a foreign partner in licensing. **Licensing** allows the partner in the host country (the licensee) to produce some good or service by bearing the costs of production and paying some fee or royalty to the business granting the license. The license may cover production processes, brand name, patent, or some other valued asset. Spalding Sports Worldwide, the American athletic goods manufacturer, now generates more sales revenue from licensing than from the direct production of goods. However, this strategy is rather risky because the licensor has less control over the licensee and over product quality than it does with its own manufacturing. Sometimes the licensor finds when the contract ends that the arrangement has created a direct competitor.

Holiday Inns, McDonald's, Avis, and Kentucky Fried Chicken have all expanded into foreign countries, as they have throughout the United States, via franchising. As in licensing, the franchise agreement spells out the specific rights and responsibilities of each party. But, as you will see in Chapter 7, franchising involves an investment on the part of the individual buying the franchise. To maintain control of quality, the franchisor usually sets restrictions on such factors as location and merchandise programs.

Production Contracting

Many Japanese companies have entered U.S. markets through **production contracting**—agreements with a local producer in the foreign country to make the product. Generally the contracting company retains the selling functions, often through its foreign sales branches. While not ensuring good control over production, contracting does provide quicker access to foreign markets than does setting up one's own manufacturing facilities. Sapporo Breweries Ltd. contracted with southern California's Hansen Foods Inc. to bottle soft drinks for sale here. And Kirin Brewery Co. of Japan has an agreement with Molson Breweries of Canada to bottle Japanese beer for sale in the United States.

✔ **licensing**

An arrangement that allows the partner in the host country (the licensee) to produce some good or service by bearing the costs of production and paying some fee or royalty to the business granting the license.

✔ **production contracting**

An agreement with a local producer in a foreign country to make a product.

Growing a Global Market

At a technology fair in Delhi, India, the representative of a Japanese company holds the crowd's attention. India now has a middle class of more than 200 million—that's larger than the comparable market in Great Britain and France combined. The Indian government has liberalized its economic policies, and Indian firms are pursuing joint ventures in computer hardware and software development with high-tech American companies such as Hewlett Packard.

Joint Ventures

Joint ventures arise when domestic and foreign companies join together in a partnership in which they share ownership and control—and risk. Three options exist. The domestic company may buy a share in the existing operation of the foreign company. The foreign investor may buy an interest in the local company. Or the two partners may form a completely new company. The joint venture is particularly effective when one of the parties needs the financial, production, labor, or marketing expertise of the other partner. And some governments demand joint ventures, often making foreign ownership of less than 50 percent a condition of entry. In the late 1970s, the Indian government demanded that IBM and Coca-Cola reduce their stake in their Indian subsidiaries to 40 percent. In response, both stopped doing business there. India's policies have eased somewhat since then, and IBM has joined in a 50–50 venture with India's Tata group to produce computer hardware and develop software. Joint ventures are often most helpful in gaining trust in the host country.

In 1977, 3M paired with South Korea's Doosan Food Co. of Seoul to manufacture its products there. By the mid-1990s, the partnership had led to two major manufacturing plants on Korean soil, employing 500. And more importantly for 3M, it now sells Scotch tape, Post-it notes, and Scotchguard throughout South Korea. Helping to develop the Korean economy and working closely with nationals created the mutual respect Koreans demand as a prerequisite to doing business.

Strategic Alliances

In the quest for greater worldwide market share, **strategic alliances**—agreements between organizations that may or may not involve ownership—have become increasingly popular. Strategic alliances do not require the formation of a new, independent business. Alliance members share business risk and often provide outside firms with fast entry into a country's market.

The leather processing subsidiary of India's Tata group has joined with France's TFR to challenge Italian dominance in upscale leather goods. America's Caterpillar has teamed up with Japan's Mitsubishi to manufacture enormous earthmoving equipment. Some strategic alliances seek world dominance. Philips, the Dutch electronics conglomerate, has joined up with many partners to grab the lion's share of the worldwide optical disc market. Sometimes strategic alliances produce industries not otherwise feasible, as was the case when South Korea's Jindo Corp. coupled with Siberian sable ranchers. The combination of Jindo's designers and stitchers with the isolated pelt producers created a huge new fur business.

Foreign Ownership

When the foreign country can offer sufficient expertise or a large market, companies will often start a *wholly owned foreign subsidiary*. Here the company owns and runs the entire operation on foreign soil, sometimes even building its own production plants. This strategy has the advantage of maintaining control, creating jobs in the foreign country (which enhances the company's image politically and culturally), and building relationships with the government and with local residents, suppliers, and retailers. Of course, it also exposes the domestic company to greater risk from unstable foreign governments, changing markets, and even local government takeover. Foreign ownership has been a recent trend among U.S. companies seeking to gain stronger foreign footholds, increase global market share, and develop a better competitive position.

✓ **joint ventures**

Arrangements in which domestic and foreign companies join together in a partnership in which they share ownership, control, and risk.

✓ **strategic alliances**

Agreements between organizations that may or may not involve ownership.

✓ **multinational corporation (MNC)**

A corporation based in one country (called the parent country) that produces goods and/or services in one or more host countries.

✓ **global strategy**

"Selling the same product, the same way, everywhere"; based on the assumption that consumers around the world are growing more and more similar.

Multinational Corporations

Complete globalization is the aim of a **multinational corporation (MNC)**, which is based in one country (called the parent country) and which produces goods and/or services in one or more host countries. MNCs do not distinguish between domestic and foreign business. They make all business decisions within a global framework, viewing the world as a set of alternative markets, sources of supply, and locations for production and distribution facilities. MNCs focus on standardized products that can be altered to meet the unique demands of different countries. IBM follows this strategy, adjusting its products to match local markets. Its keyboards, for example, can all be modified for different languages. In Europe alone there is a need for 20 such keyboards. Leading MNCs are shown in Table 3.4.

table 3.4 Leading Multinational Corporations by Sales Volume

1993 Rank	Company	Parent Country	Sales (in millions of dollars)	Profits (Losses) (in millions of dollars)	Employees
1	General Motors	United States	$133,621.9	$2,465.8	710,800
2	Ford Motor	United States	108,521.0	2,529.0	322,200
3	Exxon	United States	97,825.0	5,280.0	91,000
4	Royal Dutch/Shell Group	Britain/Netherlands	95,134.4	4,505.2	117,000
5	Toyota Motor	Japan	85,283.2	1,473.9	109,279
6	Hitachi	Japan	68,581.8	605.0	330,637
7	International Business Machines	United States	62,716.0	(8,101.0)	267,196
8	Matsushita Electric Industrial	Japan	61,384.5	227.0	254,059
9	General Electric	United States	60,823.0	4,315.0	222,000
10	Daimler-Benz	Germany	59,102.0	364.0	366,736
11	Mobil	United States	56,576.0	2,084.0	61,900
12	Nissan Motor	Japan	53,759.8	(805.5)	143,310
13	British Petroleum	Britain	52,485.4	923.6	72,600
14	Samsung	South Korea	51,345.2	519.7	191,303
15	Philip Morris	United States	50,621.0	3,091.0	173,000

Source: "Guide to the Global 500," Fortune, July 25, 1994, p. 143.

Standardization and Adaptation Strategies

The degree to which a product should be adapted to local cultural and business conditions is an important international strategic decision. One popular, though controversial,[19] strategy is referred to as the **global strategy**, or "selling the same product, the same way, everywhere."[20] The global strategy is based on the assumption that consumers around the world are growing more and more alike. Its champions know that a standardized product, brand name, and advertising program can achieve enormous economies by not changing from nation to nation.

11. Contrast global strategy and adaptation as strategies for conducting business in foreign markets.

Coca-Cola, Kodak, Perrier, and Exxon embrace the global strategy and believe modern technology has created common wants and needs among people around the world. Global travel and communication have exposed more and more people to goods and services from other cultures. Consumers throughout the world desire products that they have heard about, seen, or even occasionally used. While differences exist in consumer preferences, shopping behavior, cultural institutions, and promotional media, those who support the global strategy believe cross-cultural consumer preferences and practices can and will become more alike. They therefore think that the general strategy of offering high-quality, lower-priced products will prevail in any global market.

Most companies cannot follow a cost-effective global strategy. Income levels in some nations for example, demand *adaptation*. Stripped down, cheaper versions of products generally sell better in developing countries. Singer sewing machines sold in Africa are hand-powered. In Latin America, where shopping is a daily routine, small packages are preferred for products such as detergent. The large, economy size just doesn't sell well. Different consumer preferences often dictate adaptation. Nestlé blends dozens of versions of Nescafé for markets around the globe. Even Campbell Soup uses various recipes for its mainstay tomato soup. There is Italian tomato soup, English tomato soup, and so on. Companies choose either a global or an adaptation strategy depending on which approach offers the best balance between costs and revenues. But recognizing the best strategy is not always easy.

Global Strategy

In its "United Colors of Benetton" advertising campaign, the Italian clothier pursues a global strategy as well as a strong political ideology. Benetton runs 150 stores in the United States alone, but U.S. sales represent only about 5 percent of the company's yearly sales of $2 billion worldwide.

Australian media mogul Rupert Murdoch, who launched the Fox TV network in America, initially beamed his Star TV satellite network into Asia with a "one-size-fits-all" approach of offering English-language programming to a population making up two-thirds of the earth's population. But losses resulted. So the strategy was altered, for example, by customizing music programming to local tastes. Syrupy love ballads were broadcast to Taiwan. Fast-action music videos were beamed to Indian viewers. Said Star TV's station manager, "The idea that there is a pan-Asian taste in music is a myth."[21] Sports programs were also tailored to local interests. Chinese viewers were provided with more gymnastics, soccer, and track, while in India, where the British influence remains strong, Star broadcast more cricket matches. Movies were made in Mandarin for Hong Kong and in Hindi for India. Eventually, digital technology will allow Star TV and other broadcasters to offer dozens of more customized channels throughout Asia.

Within the European Union, elimination of trade and monetary barriers will present greater opportunities for companies to use a global strategy successfully. Many companies are treating Europe as one market. Satellite television transmissions to all of Europe provide a medium for global advertising campaigns. With increased travel among European countries, companies are striving to offer standard brands, retail locations, and even shelf space so that customers will know where to buy their products all over the continent.

Reviewing *Global Business*

Perspectives on Global Business

1. **Discuss the reasons for the increasingly global nature of business**. Changes in politics, economics, and technology have opened up previously unknown international trade opportunities. Countries trade for three reasons: some resources, products, and services are not available within their geographic boundaries; the opportunity cost of producing a product prevents use of resources for alternative products; and specialization gives countries a comparative advantage in producing items that they can make most efficiently.

2. **Define the major elements of global trade and explain how global trade is measured**. The major elements of global trade are imports, exports, and countertraded items. Global trade is measured in terms of balance of trade and balance of payments. The difference between a country's imports and exports is its balance of trade; the flow of money into and out of a country over a specified period of time is its balance of payments. Imports and exports are just two factors in the balance of payments; others include money spent by tourists, interest earned on foreign investments, and foreign government payments on the positive side, and money spent by tourists abroad and aid to foreign governments on the negative side.

3. **Explain how exchange rates work, noting their significance to a country's economy**. The exchange rate is the price of one currency in terms of another currency. Currency values rise and fall in relation to other currencies according to a floating exchange rate system. These fluctuations affect demand for a country's products. For example, when U.S. dollars have less buying power, decreasing demand causes a decrease in imports and an increase in exports, swinging the balance of trade in favor of the United States and making American companies more price-competitive in the world marketplace. When a country wants to improve its exchange rate, it can devalue its currency, which increases exports and reduces imports.

Factors That Shape Global Business Conduct

4. **Describe how countries are classified economically**. Countries are classified economically according to GDP per capita. In developed countries, per capita GDP is over $10,000 per year; in developing countries, it is below $10,000, typically below $5,000. Within the latter category are newly industrializing countries (NICs), which are undergoing rapid economic growth. In the poorest countries, rapid population growth is offsetting any economic growth. In NICs, where GDP per capita is growing as wages increase, enormous business opportunities will be available in the years to come. In addition, their increasing GDP will increase the demand for Western goods.

5. **Discuss the issue of protectionism versus free trade**. Protectionism, the erection of barriers to trade in an attempt to protect domestic industries from foreign competition, involves the use of tariffs, quotas, and embargoes. Proponents of protectionist economic policies believe that they help infant industries, maintain the country's standard of living, protect national defense, and help industrialize underdeveloped countries. With free trade there are no restrictions on international trade. Supporters of free trade argue that the cost of saving jobs under protectionist policies is extremely high, that other jobs are sacrificed for those saved jobs, and that consumers pay higher prices under protectionism. Further, protectionism limits consumer choice and isolates protected industries, making them less competitive.

6. **Describe the role of international trade agreements and trading blocs in promoting free trade**. International trade agreements provide specific mechanisms for encouraging free trade and eliminating protectionist policies. The General Agreement on Tariffs and Trade (GATT), for example, limits the use of both tariff and nontariff barriers to trade in 124 countries. Under the most favored nation approach, special trade benefits are provided for specific trading partners. With foreign, or free trade, zones, companies are allowed to import goods tax-free if they create domestic jobs in the import zone.

Like international trade agreements, trading blocs open vast markets to global businesses. A widely known trading bloc is the common market. Two well-known examples of common markets are the European Union and the trading group established among Mexico, Canada, and the United States by the North American Free Trade Agreement (NAFTA).

7. **Explain the significance for global businesses of a country's political climate.** To be successful, global businesses must be aware of a host country's political climate and be alert to possible changes. When political philosophies change, countries can change their attitudes and policies toward foreign businesses and, of course, these changes may result in changes in the host country's relevant laws.

8. **Identify the three most common categories of legal systems and explain their impact on the operations of a global business.** The three categories are common law, code law, and theocratic systems. The United States, having a common law system, operates with formal, written laws, which are interpreted within a court system. Code law systems have all-inclusive written laws, for which no interpretation is necessary. In theocratic systems, religious beliefs govern the legal system. A business cannot operate outside its borders if it does not understand the laws of its host country. While no legal body overrides the legal system within a country, the United States and other countries have treaties and agreements regarding the conduct of international business.

9. **Describe the social/cultural factors that affect global businesses.** Cultural factors are language, values, religion, and ethics. Language includes not only words, but also time and space. Values refers to attitudes toward work, which set the stage for ethics regarding the conduct of business (exploitation of workers, harming natural resources, and such). Westerners should be aware that in many countries superstition is part of religious belief

and often plays a major role in the conduct of business. The social makeup of a country is also important; countries with large middle- and upper-class populations are more likely than those with a large lower class to use imported products, an important factor in establishing worldwide markets.

The Practice of Global Business

10. **Describe several strategies for entering foreign markets.** The easiest way for a company to reach international markets is through exporting. Alternatively, companies may license their production processes, brand names, patents, or other valued assets to companies in a host country, or they may franchise their businesses to investors in the host country. With production contracting—another route to foreign markets—the company retains sales rights but arranges for foreign production. In joint ventures, domestic and foreign companies form a partnership in which they share ownership and control as well as risk; strategic alliances are similar to joint ventures except that they may or may not involve ownership. Another option is to create a wholly owned foreign subsidiary. Multinational corporations are based in one country, called the parent country, and produce goods and/or services in one or more countries, called host countries.

11. **Contrast global strategy and adaptation as strategies for conducting business in foreign markets.** The strategy applied depends on the product or service in relation to the needs and wants of consumers in the foreign markets. With a global strategy, a company sells the same product, the same way, everywhere, because it assumes that consumers around the world have the same wants and needs. This strategy provides the company with economies of scale in production and marketing. A more viable alternative for most global businesses is adaptation, which provides different products and strategies for differing foreign markets.

Key Terms

absolute advantage **70**
theory of comparative advantage **70**
importing **71**
exporting **71**
countertrade **71**
balance of trade **72**
trade surplus **72**
trade deficit **72**
balance of payments **72**
exchange rate **74**
World Bank **74**

International Monetary Fund (IMF) **74**
floating exchange rate system **75**
devaluation **75**
developed countries **75**
developing countries **75**
newly industrializing countries (NICs) **75**
protectionism **77**
free trade **77**
tariff **77**
quota **77**

embargo **77**
General Agreement on Tariffs and Trade (GATT) **79**
dumping **80**
foreign (free trade) zones **80**
maquiladora **81**
trading blocs **81**
common market **81**
North American Free Trade Agreement (NAFTA) **81**

Foreign Corrupt Practices Act **84**
intellectual property **84**
piracy **84**
indirect export **88**
direct export **88**
licensing **89**
production contracting **89**
joint ventures **90**
strategic alliances **90**
multinational corporation (MNC) **91**
global strategy **91**

• Review Questions

1. For what three reasons do countries trade with one another?
2. What does the theory of comparative advantage hold?
3. What is the balance of trade?
4. What is the balance of payments?
5. What is the exchange rate and how does it influence trade among countries?
6. What are the respective advantages and disadvantages of protectionism and free trade?
7. What role do trade agreements play in global business?
8. What are the various kinds of laws that global businesses must understand?
9. What is the impact of culture on global companies?
10. What are nine approaches to global business? Give an example of each.
11. What are the differences between the global strategy and the adaptation strategy?

• Critical Thinking Questions

1. Most of the world's population lives in developing nations, as noted in the chapter. The majority of people in those countries do not have much income. Should a multinational corporation be interested in the large, relatively poor majority in those nations? Why or why not?

2. Cummins manufactures its aircraft engines in the United States, where labor rates average $15.45 per hour, and exports them to its aircraft assembly plant in Mexico, where the average labor rate is $4.50 per hour. Is this a good or a bad business practice? Explain your answer.

3. As a top executive at the Caterpillar Co. (a leading manufacturer of earthmoving equipment), you have been asked to develop a corporate statement on the role of the U.S. government in international trade. What will you focus on and why?

4. Kmart and other American discount retailers have opened stores in England and various other countries in the European Union. From your reading of the global business environment, what advice would you offer these companies as they enter these new international markets?

5. Think of two foreign-based companies (e.g., The Body Shop and Sony) that sell products in the United States. Why do you think they have been successful?

REVIEW CASE   *Walt Disney Company*[22]

Under the leadership of Michael Eisner, the Walt Disney Company increased its revenues from $1.5 to $8.5 billion between 1984 and 1993. Three major categories of products account for Disney's sales: filmed entertainment, consumer products such as Mickey Mouse T-shirts and Dopey coffee mugs, and theme parks. Its formula for success is to create new animated characters through its filmed entertainment division and then generate new products from these characters. The recent successes of the movies *Aladdin*, *The Little Mermaid*, *The Lion King*, and *Pocahontas* reflect this strategy. Eisner's formula for the future is to expand these categories overseas.

Disney movies and home videos are booming worldwide. In 1985, filmed entertainment represented 10 percent of Disney's income. In 1993, it accounted for 36 percent. Disney Studios produces filmed entertainment through three companies. Walt Disney Pictures produces cartoon-type movies and family entertainment. Both Touchstone Pictures and Hollywood Pictures produce more adult-oriented films such as *Pretty Woman* and *Sister Act*. The company is making a push internationally with its filmed entertainment. Disney's hugely successful *The Lion King* has now been translated into 25 languages. The company also develops partnerships with local foreign broadcasters to develop Disney Clubs and broadcast Disney films in their countries.

Disney's consumer products division also is going gangbusters. Expansion into Asia, South America, the Middle East, and Europe has been most successful. Disney licenses its name for foreign products and has opened retail stores on foreign soil. In 1994 alone, Disney opened 100 stores in France, Spain, Japan, Singapore, Canada, England, Germany, and the United States. Disney's store on Paris's fashionable Champs-Elysées is its premier retailer. The division also publishes books, records, and products such as Mickey Mouse watches, Goofy hats, and Little Mermaid jewelry.

Disney's success with theme parks, DisneyLand and

DisneyWorld, was to be duplicated in Europe with Euro Disney. But that park has been most troublesome; Euro Disney suffered an almost $1 billion loss in its first year. And profits are not expected until late in the 1990s. Eisner points to the European recession and poor targeting of European tastes as the culprits.

When Euro Disney prohibited the sale of all forms of alcohol and served up European food instead of American-style fast-food in quick eateries, European tourists were not impressed. "We know that Americans don't want us to open a French restaurant in New York or Los Angeles that serves a double-patty cheeseburger, and that the French don't want us to come over there and do crêpes, and the Germans don't want us to serve knackwurst and sauerkraut. They want us

to do what we do," Eisner said. So the complexion of Euro Disney is changing to include beer and wine, fast-food franchises, and American-style promotional discounts intended to lure tourists to Disney hotels. Eisner believes in the potential of Disney theme parks and is looking for locations for new parks in Asia, South America, Australia, and Europe.

1. What business environments are influencing Walt Disney Company in its foreign expansion?

2. Which global approaches do you find Disney taking?

3. Do you believe Disney can use a global strategy? Why or why not?

CRITICAL THINKING CASE   *Weber-Stephen Products Co.* [23]

In 1958, George Stephen bought the design rights from Weber Brothers for a charcoal grill and formed Weber-Stephen Products Co., based outside Chicago. The distinct grill with its spherical shape was fashioned from a design for marine buoys. While most competitors did not provide a top for their grills, this one had a lid that eliminated flying ashes and periodic flame flareups. By 1994, 16 million American households owned a Weber charcoal grill.

With their durable components, Weber grills did not wear out and replacement sales were low. As more and more grills were sold, it became difficult for Weber-Stephen to grow. To increase sales, the company added gas grills to its charcoal product line. But the design mirrored the kettle shape of the charcoal grill and was not met with consumer enthusiasm. By 1985, when a new rectangular model was finally being sold, Weber-Stephen's competitors—Char-Broil, Thermos, and Sunbeam—had grabbed leadership in the market.

Weber-Stephen tried other approaches to increase company sales during the 1970s and 1980s. Bird feeders were sold along with the charcoal grills. So were mailboxes. Tablecloths, sail covers, and electronic bug zappers were marketed. None was a hit. Along the way, the company began to explore foreign markets for its grills.

Many countries throughout the world began to come out of recession by the mid-1990s. Incomes and leisure time were increasing. And the rising middle class found barbecuing an enjoyable leisure-time activity. But manufacturing the heavy grills in Illinois and transporting them around the world is costly. Moreover, foreign competition is fiercely aggressive. In countries like the People's Republic of China and Taiwan, businesses regularly ignore patent protection, and cheaply made copies of the Weber charcoal grill are easily produced. Distribution costs abroad are also much lower, and these foreign competitors offer buyers outside the U.S. a dramatic price advantage.

1. Which of the environments addressed in this chapter will be important to the success or failure of Weber-Stephen's international strategy? Discuss how you would advise the company to meet these environmental challenges.

2. Which of the eight approaches to global business would you recommend for Weber-Stephen? Why?

3. Do you think a global strategy or adaptation would be more appropriate? Explain your reasoning.

Critical Thinking with the ONE MINUTE MANAGER

"VeriFone's technology helps it operate in Europe, Asia, and South America as well as in North America. And its network helps it operate in a decentralized manner, with 25 local offices taking care of customers all around the world. That way, nobody at San Francisco headquarters has to know the local culture and language of Bangalore, India, for example. Local staff handle these customers."

"Are more companies adopting VeriFone's strategy?" Joanna asked the One Minute Manager.

"Yes, for two key reasons. First is the advantage of a local presence that I already described. And second, there are productivity gains to be made. VeriFone does its work around the clock, since there is always an office where the sun is shining. It will sometimes pass a key project from time zone to time zone, handing the work along electronically from team to team around the world. Now that's what I call going global!"

1. What kinds of culturally based human resources problems might occur across the various countries by doing business VeriFone's way?

2. What precautionary strategies should VeriFone employ to ensure that there would be no loss of productivity should the computer system transmitting information between countries fail?

3. Exactly what internal accommodations would VeriFone need to make to facilitate employee communication across different countries with their respective languages?

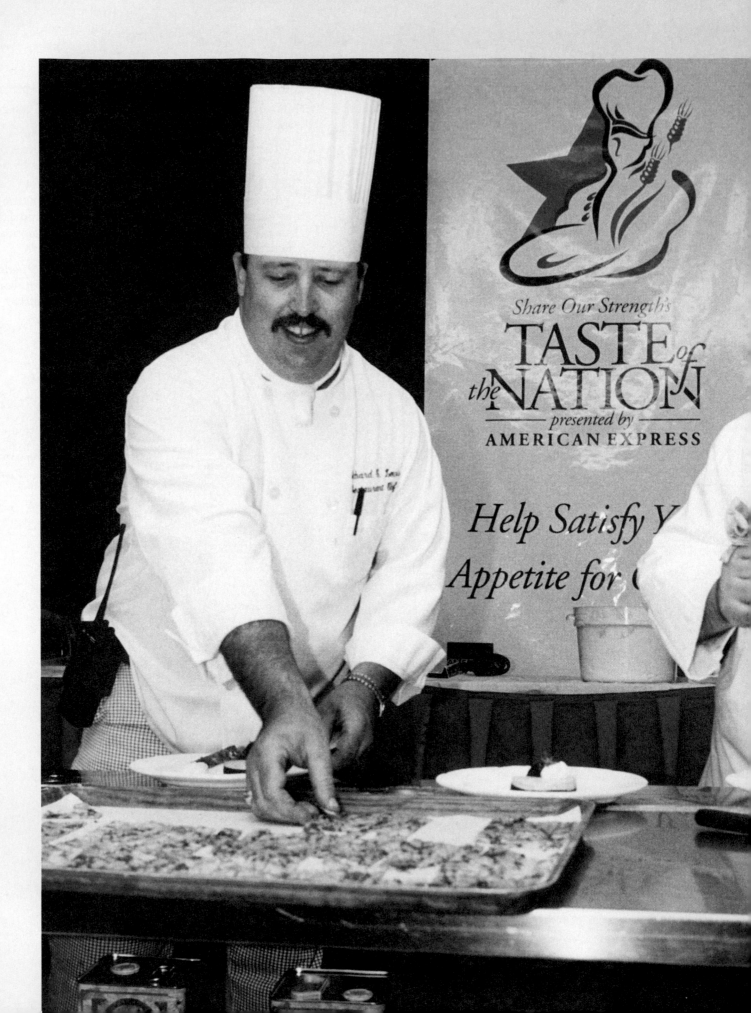

4

Ethics, Law, and Government

Major changes in the business environment have forced a shift toward innovative business strategies. One of the areas in which businesses now innovate is their role in society. In this chapter, we examine business laws, business ethics, and the concept of social responsibility in business to see why ethical decision making as well as legal compliance are necessary for success in a challenging business environment. After reading this chapter, you will be able to reach the learning goals below.

Learning Goals

1. Discuss the relationship between business ethics and law and broadly describe government's role in business conduct.

2. Describe how businesses might apply ethical management to meeting their social responsibilities.

3. Identify and describe the three types of U.S. law.

4. Briefly review the laws that have been passed to protect free market competition.

5. Describe how government regulations and consumer protection groups support the four basic rights of consumers.

6. Identify and describe the laws that prohibit discrimination in the workplace and protect the natural environment.

7. Discuss how contract and tort law and ethical considerations contribute to fair interbusiness conduct.

8. Identify the laws designed to protect employee diversity, health, and safety.

9. List the three questions that can help focus attention on ethical business conduct.

10. Describe the content and purpose of an ethics statement and list four management techniques for reinforcing ethical behavior.

11. Discuss ways of encouraging socially responsible behavior in a business.

An Ethical Dilemma

"Our chapter assignment is ethics in business, but I'm not sure how relevant that topic is to daily work at a company like yours," Joanna said to the One Minute Manager. "I mean, I assume you don't break any laws, and tough moral and ethical issues seem more likely to come up in a religious gathering or philosophy course than at work."

"At first thought," the One Minute Manager replied, "ethics does seem very far from the daily work of people in businesses, doesn't it? Sure, sometimes companies get caught giving bribes, or somebody steals something. Legal compliance is always an issue. But in fact there are *many* more common and subtle ethical issues. Nobody bribes or steals around here, but I can't think of a single day when I don't deal with some kind of ethical decision."

"I had no idea ethics was so important in business. Can you give us some examples?"

"No."

"No?" Carlos and Joanna looked at the One Minute Manager in surprise.

"Well, I'd rather not, because I think you will get more out of a story a friend of mine wrote up about *his* experiences with business ethics. It describes an ethical problem he ran into as a young sales manager." She pushed toward them a small book with some pages marked with a yellow highlighter. Here is the first section they read:

Being a division sales manager of a large high-tech company in a very competitive industry can have its difficult moments. This definitely was one of them. Sales had been down for almost six months and my boss was putting pressure on me to get my division's numbers up. I'd been involved for a month in a search for a topflight, experienced sales representative to add to my sales force, and three days ago I had interviewed a very likely prospect.

He had an outstanding sales record and knew our industry backward and forward. Most intriguingly, he had just quit a top job with our major competitor. I'd just about made up my mind to hire him . . . when he smiled, reached into his attaché case, and pulled out a . . . computer disc and held it up as if it were a priceless gem. . . .

Still smiling, his voice oozing with self-assurance, he proceeded to explain that the disc contained a wealth of confidential information about our competitor, his former employer— including . . . cost data on a major defense-contract bid for which our company was also competing. He promised me that, if I hired him, he would give me this disc and more of the same.

After he left my office, I had two immediate responses . . . [First] I knew that what he proposed was wrong and because of that he wasn't the kind of person I wanted on my team. . . . [Second] I realized that this person was offering us a virtual gold mine. If I hired him, I could, most likely, bring in not only the giant defense contract but several other huge accounts. . . . It was one of those once-in-a-lifetime opportunities. And I certainly could use such an opportunity now.[1]

Business Ethics, Business Law, and Social Responsibility

Businesses and their employees often face tough decisions such as the one described in this chapter's opening story. Decisions that affect others may have legal ramifications; they typically have ethical ramifications as well. What is legal, and, even harder, what is right? As an employee of a business or as an independent entrepreneur, you will face these two questions many times in the course of your career.

Businesses have to compete in innovative ways to survive in today's highly competitive markets. **Business ethics**, the application of moral principles to business decision making, is a vital part of this activity. A company's ethics helps define its relationships with its employees, its customers, its investors, and the society at large.

Ethics is the code of moral principles that embody a culture's standards of good and bad behavior. Societies develop laws partly to express these standards of behavior and partly to enforce them. Laws can never address all the possible ways in which individuals behave and all the choices they can make. And because personal judgment is always involved, ethical issues will always be a part of daily life and business life. But laws can help ensure that certain minimum standards of ethical conduct are met.

Business law—laws that set enforceable standards of business conduct—both influences and regulates business activity. In the United States, such laws are created at the local, state, and federal levels, and regulatory bodies exist at all levels to clarify and enforce them. At the local level, for example, a town's building inspector regulates new construction, making sure builders comply with state and local building codes.

Governments intervene in business in three ways. First, in their *regulatory role*, they influence and control the behavior of business through the creation and enforcement of laws—the primary focus of the next main section of the chapter. Second, in their *economic role*, governments help and support businesses by acting as major customers of business, by encouraging marketplace competition and trade relations with the global economy, and by monitoring economic stability and the business cycle. Third, in their role as *service provider*, governments treat businesses as *their* customers by supplying public goods, and they transfer payments by collecting taxes and spending them in the private sector.

Government regulations combine with the ethics of the societies in which a business operates to form a legal and ethical environment for the business. When businesses and their employees plan or act, they need to learn and think about the legal and ethical issues that constrain their actions. And, to be competitive, they try to turn these constraints into opportunities—finding ways to operate that are good for society and for the business.

1. Discuss the relationship between business ethics and law and broadly describe government's role in business conduct.

Law and Ethics

Some people who study business ethics take the position that appropriate professional conduct consists of minimal conformity to ethical behavior, as set by laws. However, a society's ethics generally sets different and higher standards for behavior than those outlined in its laws. To see the difference, ask some of your friends if it is unethical to park for an hour and a quarter at a one-hour parking meter. This behavior is against the law, but as it does not do any harm most people do not consider it wrong. In this case, ethical standards are lower than legal standards. To see how ethical standards are often *higher*, imagine that

 business ethics

The application of moral principles to business decision making.

 business law

Laws that set enforceable standards of business conduct.

you are one member of an office team and you just opened a New Year's gift box from a company that is thanking your firm for the past year's business. The box is full of your favorite chocolates. Should you take it home and not tell your associates about it, or should you share it with your teammates? There are no pressing legal issues here, yet when you pose the problem to friends you probably will find that they say it is clearly wrong to take a company gift home for personal consumption. As these two situations indicate, ethical behavior—by a person or a business—requires compliance with both ethics *and* the law. Figure 4.1 illustrates the relationship between law and ethics by showing them as a matrix. Simple legal compliance will not ensure ethical behavior any more than ethics alone will guarantee legal behavior. You need to understand business law and ethics—both dimensions of the grid.

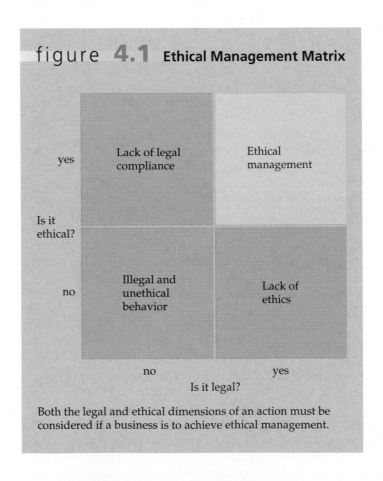

figure **4.1**   **Ethical Management Matrix**

Both the legal and ethical dimensions of an action must be considered if a business is to achieve ethical management.

To use ethical principles as an innovative strategy means going beyond minimal acceptable standards of conduct. This strategy is called **ethical management**, strong commitment to aligning the interests of the business with those of its stakeholders. **Stakeholders** are all the people affected by an action of the business—from its board of directors and stockholders, to its managers and employees, to its suppliers, distributors, and customers. Underlying the relationship between a business and its stakeholders is the concept of **good faith**—a set of assumptions about the mutual duties and responsibilities of both parties, going beyond the legal restraints of business law. At a minimum, ethical behavior in this context means making a positive effort to honor those duties and responsibilities. Reebok strives for the commitment and vision of ethical management through its annual human rights award. Its president explains the company's vision: "Our hope is to bring to market the missing consciousness, the indignation that can once and for all make it simply unacceptable to mistreat human beings. We want to ignite people's outrage."[2]

ethical management

A strong commitment to aligning the interests of a business with those of its stakeholders.

stakeholders

All the people affected by an action of a business.

good faith

A set of assumptions about the mutual duties and responsibilities of both a business and its stakeholders.

Social Responsibility and Business

Businesses are part of society, and business practices have social consequences. Businesses' social impact is especially important in the following areas: environmental issues, employee treatment, plant closings, political contributions, and the effect of products and ads on people's behavior.

The physical environment in which we live has been drastically damaged, due in part to business. The overuse of raw materials used for production has depleted natural resources. During the physical process of transforming these materials into products for sale, harmful by-products have been introduced into the environment. And the disposal of products that are no longer usable is an increasing problem as landfills and dumps close across the country.

Each business can respond by ensuring that its own products and practices do not further damage the environment. Texas Instruments has started recycling laser-printer cartridges and polystyrene and polyurethane packaging materials, in addition to recycling paper, cans, and bottles.[3] Bio Gro Systems makes sludge from waste generated in New York City, treats the material to destroy harmful bacteria and odors, and sends it to agriculturists across the country as a nutrient-rich alternative to chemical fertilizers.[4]

The work conditions, salaries, and benefits a business offers its employees also have a social impact. And when a company closes a plant, it affects not only the employees it fires but also the communities in which they live. In many areas, large plants provide the single largest source of employment. When the plant closes, the loss of jobs means high unemployment, lost state and local taxes—not only from the corporation but from the newly jobless workers—and a loss for local business as workers no longer have the incomes to demand local business services and products. The movie *Roger and Me* chronicles the social and economic devastation wreaked by the closing of a General Motors plant in Flint, Michigan.

Sometimes, changes in the economy make plant closings an unavoidable necessity. But the concept of ethical management suggests that businesses should not use their impact on the local economy in unfair ways. Particularly problematic in plant closings is "whipsawing," a bidding war set in motion by

2. Describe how businesses might apply ethical management to meeting their social responsibilities.

Social Responsibility as Practiced at Patagonia, Inc.

Outdoor clothing maker Patagonia, Inc., of Bozeman, Montana, invented synchilla fleece fabric, a popular choice in brisk climates. Synchilla, which is made from recycled plastic soda bottles, is part of Patagonia's commitment to environmental preservation. The company also pays a voluntary "earth tax" of at least 1 percent of sales in donations to environmental groups. Its mission statement: "To deliver innovative, high-quality products and services to our customers on time; share the company's success with its employees; honor our obligations to each other, to the natural environment, and to society; and to achieve a sufficient profit to pursue these objectives." The success of synchilla offers proof for the adage that businesses can "do well by doing good."

What do you think? How far should business go in trying to bend politics in its favor?

a company that owns plants in two or more communities and plans to close one of them. Using the threat of plant closure, the company plays off members of the communities against each other, weakening labor unions at the plants involved and negotiating away benefits from communities desperate to retain their plants. The "Plant Closing Bill" (the *Worker Adjustment and Retraining Notification Act* of 1988) requires firms in the United States to give workers 60 days notice in case of plant closings or mass layoffs to help them and their communities make adequate preparations. But ethical management may require far greater efforts to protect communities and society at large.

Businesses sometimes will engage in bribery or excessive gift giving, or will contribute excessively to political campaigns to promote the passage of laws favorable to them. The cost of such practices is paid by society at large. Businesses do, of course, have the right to help finance political campaigns, but their managers need to define the limits of such contributions. There is a fine line between supporting a cause and distorting the political process, and business ethics faces some of its most difficult tests in this area.

Businesses also exert an influence through advertising, which can affect the way people act. Burger King found an ethical way to advertise on Channel One, an advertiser-sponsored program for high school students. Mindful that commercials could detract from the program's educational purpose, the company designed its advertisements to encourage students to stay in school.[5] In fact, almost every action a business takes has some impact on society—whether it is a toy company making water pistols or a movie studio consistently casting actors of only one gender or from one ethnic group as heroes in its films.

Such widespread and perplexing problems can be resolved, however, if they are recognized as ethical issues. By making stakeholder impact an item on the firm's agenda, the ethical manager can make steady progress on tough issues that arise in the area of **social responsibility**—the balance a business strikes among its commitments to its own goals, to its stakeholders, and to society at large.

You will run into three different concepts of social responsibility in the business world. Some people argue that the key social responsibility of a business is to its *owners*, and that being socially responsible therefore requires the firm to maximize profits. Some managers cite this argument to justify practices such as plant closings or lax environmental standards, which may save the owners money. A more common view is that social responsibility should extend to the *stakeholders*—including the firm's customers, employees, suppliers, and distributors. Finally there is the view that social responsibility extends to *all of society*, including the general public, public interest groups, and even the natural environment on which society depends. This third view is now becoming dominant, whereas the responsibility to maximize profits was the dominant view throughout much of U.S. history. Social responsibility advocate Robert Haas, chief executive of Levi Strauss & Co., says businesses should be "capable of both reaping profits and making the world a better place to live."[6] Figure 4.2 illustrates these three competing views of social responsibility.

The Social Audit

Some businesses perform a periodic **social audit**, a critical analysis of the business's impact on society, as a way to track and manage social responsibility. This analysis can be extended to legal compliance as well, allowing the business to plot its position on the Ethical Management Matrix in Figure 4.1. Firms that ask for key stakeholders' views on the organization's legal and ethical behavior sometimes find that stakeholder ratings are lower than those of managers. Large gaps are red flags, indicating that the firm needs to direct its attention to its image in the community.

 social responsibility

The balance a business strikes among its commitments to its own goals, to its stakeholders, and to society at large.

social audit

Critical analysis of a business's impact on society.

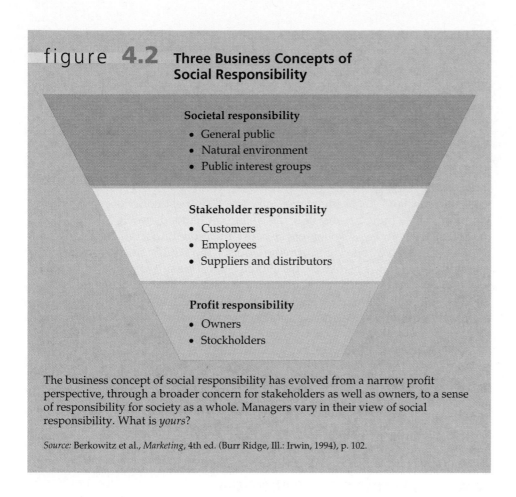

figure **4.2** **Three Business Concepts of Social Responsibility**

Societal responsibility
- General public
- Natural environment
- Public interest groups

Stakeholder responsibility
- Customers
- Employees
- Suppliers and distributors

Profit responsibility
- Owners
- Stockholders

The business concept of social responsibility has evolved from a narrow profit perspective, through a broader concern for stakeholders as well as owners, to a sense of responsibility for society as a whole. Managers vary in their view of social responsibility. What is *yours*?

Source: Berkowitz et al., *Marketing*, 4th ed. (Burr Ridge, Ill.: Irwin, 1994), p. 102.

Business Law and Government Regulation

Laws addressing the conduct of business relate to nearly every business activity, from the hiring and paying of employees, to their safety on the job, to the safety of products advertised and sold to consumers, to the use of the natural resources needed to create products and services, to the disposal of unwanted by-products. These laws attempt to capture our society's notions about the fair treatment of individuals, the right of employees not to be injured by their work, the right of consumers to receive safe and pure products, and the responsibility of all of us to conserve and protect the natural world.

Role of Government

In the United States, laws are built on the foundation provided by the Constitution and the Bill of Rights. These documents focus on individual rights and responsibilities. Business law extends many of these rights and responsibilities to businesses as well. Businesses may own private property in the same manner that individuals can, and businesses can be held legally liable, or responsible, for their actions—just as individuals are.

Laws built upon these constitutional foundations must be consistent with them. Laws are created in three different ways, and there are therefore three types of laws:

Chapter 5 details the legal forms of business.

3. Identify and describe the three types of U.S. law.

✓ **statutory law**

Laws created by a legislative body.

✓ **administrative law**

Rules and regulations created by administrative authority.

✓ **common law**

Legal interpretations of the law based on past court decisions.

✓ **price fixing**

Any effort to set high prices by collaborating with other sellers.

✓ **bid rigging**

Collusion between one bidder and the buyer in order to gain a contract.

✓ **deregulation**

The process of removing restrictions on business competition.

4. Briefly review the laws that have been passed to protect free market competition.

Is this price fixing?

Following is part of a taped conversation between Robert Crandall, then president of American Airlines, and Howard Putnam, at the time president of Braniff Airlines.

Putnam: Do you have a suggestion for me?

Crandall: Yes, raise your fares 20 percent. I'll raise mine the next morning.

Putnam: Robert, we . . .

Crandall: You'll make more money and I will, too.

Putnam: We can't talk about pricing.

Crandall: Oh, Howard, we can talk about anything we want to.[7]

If you think this is price fixing, you're right, and so was Putnam. The U.S. Justice Department filed suit and forced Crandall to stop talking about prices with competitors.

- **Statutory law**—laws created by a legislative body. These are formed in the U.S. Congress or in state legislatures when bills (proposed laws) are voted into law.

- **Administrative law**—rules and regulations created by administrative authority. This authority is held by the president of the United States and by various federal agencies and commissions. Administrative authority is also held at the state and local levels by a great many regulatory bodies, ranging from town councils to state environmental agencies. Many administrative laws are designed to interpret and enforce statutory laws, and statutory laws determine the degree and nature of administrative authority.

- **Common law**—legal interpretations based on past court decisions. Common law is built up through the decisions handed down in courtrooms across the country. The higher the court, the more impact its decisions have on common law. The U.S. Supreme Court is the highest level at which common law can be created in the United States. Businesses and individuals who believe there are good arguments in favor of their interpretation of common law sometimes appeal unfavorable decisions from one court to another until they reach the Supreme Court. Because common law is based on the interpretation of past judicial opinions, it can be more difficult to interpret than are administrative and statutory laws.

In practice, any area of business law is a *combination* of all three types of laws. Businesses rely on legal experts and the advice of regulatory agencies to help them interpret the huge number of laws and so determine what is legal in any specific situation. The following sections examine some of the most important laws affecting business.

Laws Governing Competition

Many U.S. laws attempt to regulate markets to encourage free market competition. The general focus of this set of laws is preventing businesses from gaining monopoly powers. The laws do so by encouraging competition and the innovations and lower prices that competition stimulates. For example, **price fixing**, any effort to set high prices by collaborating with other sellers, is illegal in the United States and many other developed countries. Another illegal practice that interferes with free market competition is **bid rigging**—collusion between one bidder and the buyer in order to gain a contract.

Government regulation of business competition began with the passage in 1887 of the *Interstate Commerce Act*, whose purpose was to create the Interstate Commerce Commission (ICC) in order to regulate the powerful railroad companies that threatened to gain monopoly power. The ICC still exists today and has broad power over interstate transportation. However, beginning in 1978, government **deregulation**, the process of removing restrictions on business competition, eliminated ICC control over prices charged for interstate transportation. Figure 4.3 shows the scope of deregulation efforts since 1968. Why were these industries deregulated? Because competition had grown in many industries, and Congress believed fair competition was now possible. And, as they predicted, prices for trucking and air transportation did fall after deregulation.

The *Sherman Antitrust Act* of 1890 targeted trusts, a form of business ownership that was used at the time to gain control over multiple competitors in an industry and thereby achieve monopoly power. The act is still important today because it outlawed any strategies a business or individual might use to restrain trade or commerce, in other words, to gain monopoly power in a market. And it was reinforced in 1914 by the *Clayton Antitrust Act*, which added specific definitions of illegal trade behavior to the general constraints of the Sherman Antitrust Act. The Clayton Act specified two business practices that

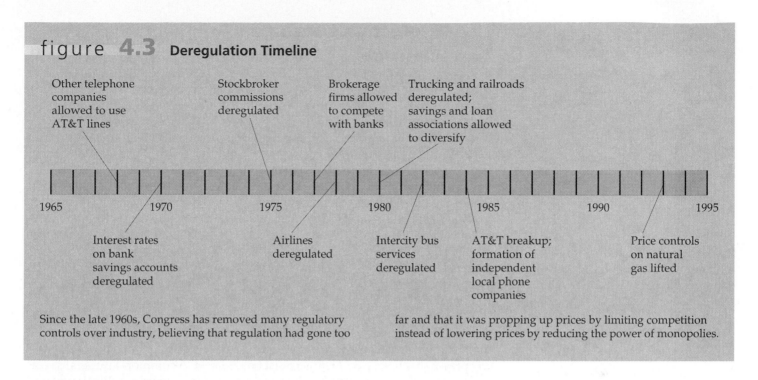

figure **4.3** **Deregulation Timeline**

Other telephone companies allowed to use AT&T lines

Stockbroker commissions deregulated

Brokerage firms allowed to compete with banks

Trucking and railroads deregulated; savings and loan associations allowed to diversify

1965   1970   1975   1980   1985   1990   1995

Interest rates on bank savings accounts deregulated

Airlines deregulated

Intercity bus services deregulated

AT&T breakup; formation of independent local phone companies

Price controls on natural gas lifted

Since the late 1960s, Congress has removed many regulatory controls over industry, believing that regulation had gone too far and that it was propping up prices by limiting competition instead of lowering prices by reducing the power of monopolies.

are illegal. The first is **tying contracts**, which force buyers to purchase unwanted products in order to purchase the products they do desire. The second, an **interlocking directorate**, is a situation in which the same people sit on the boards of directors of two competing firms and are thereby able to use the combined resources and power of both to compete.

The protection of free market competition seems to require periodic intervention by the government—much as a referee must sometimes step in to keep competition fair in a game of soccer or basketball. Antitrust law was extended with the *Federal Trade Commission Act* of 1914, which created a government commission with the power to investigate and take legal action against companies suspected of unfair trade practices. The Federal Trade Commission (FTC) is still quite active today. For example, the FTC constantly watches and often takes action against Microsoft, because its 70 percent-plus share of the market for computer operating system software is large enough to create the potential for monopoly powers. In 1936, Congress passed the *Robinson-Patman Act* to protect small stores from the giant chains that emerged after the Great Depression of the 1930s. And in 1938, Congress added the *Wheeler-Lea Amendment* to the law that originally established the Federal Trade Commission. This amendment gave the FTC more power to regulate business practices, including unfair competition. It also gave the FTC power to regulate against false advertising of consumer products.

Several more antitrust laws have been passed, including the *Celler-Kefauver Amendment*, which strengthened the Clayton Act in 1950; the *Antitrust Procedures and Penalties Act* of 1974, which raised the fines for violations of the Sherman Act; and the *Antitrust Improvements Act* of 1976, which required companies to notify the FTC if they planned to merge and thereby create an opportunity for unfair competition. The FTC disallows some proposed mergers every year, either preventing them completely or requiring the companies to sell off a part of their business in order to avoid becoming too large and powerful in their market.

The most recent antitrust law is the *Anti-Trust Amendments Act* of 1990, which raised fines for antitrust activities to a top limit of $10 million. Businesses with large market shares pay careful attention to the laws in this area in order to avoid fines and other penalties imposed by the FTC.

✔ **tying contracts**

A business practice that forces buyers to purchase unwanted products in order to purchase the products they do desire.

✔ **interlocking directorate**

A situation in which the same people sit on the boards of directors of two competing firms.

consumerism

The promotion of buyers' interests.

implied warranty

The expectation that products are fit for normal use even if no written guarantee is provided.

express warranty

A formal written promise of performance.

5. Describe how government regulations and consumer protection groups support the four basic rights of consumers.

Laws Protecting Consumers

A generation ago, a rising tide of consumer activism prompted President John F. Kennedy to present to Congress a four-point consumer bill of rights, outlining the consumer's rights to safety, to information, to choice, and to be heard. Since the 1960s, consumer activists from Ralph Nader to the American Association of Retired Persons (AARP) have championed **consumerism**, the promotion of buyers' interests. This growing social movement has contributed to an expanded view of the social responsibility of business and to a wealth of consumer legislation supporting the four basic rights of consumers.

When businesses agree to sell consumers a specific quality of goods or services for a specified price, consumers expect to receive the promised product, and they expect that the product will not have any unexpected or hidden harmful effects. If the product is sent out without care for safety, the firm may lose money due to litigation by angry customers. For example, in the 1970s, A.H. Robins Company sold the Dalkon Shield™, an intrauterine contraceptive device, without doing adequate safety tests first. Many women experienced medical problems, and the firm lost a large amount of money in later lawsuits.

Many laws protect consumers. Merchants or businesses selling products to consumers are legally constrained by **implied warranty**, the expectation that their products are fit for normal use even if no written guarantee is provided. A CD player that breaks on first use must be replaced. A common-law legal precedent for implied warranties has been established by a bizarre collection of bad products: exploding light bulbs, burning pajamas, breakable high heels, and prematurely exploding shotgun shells.[8] The law also requires businesses to make good on any **express warranty**, a formal written promise of performance.

In addition to laws that define consumer rights in terms of warranties, many government agency regulations offer additional consumer protection. An early law regulating food products was the *Pure Food and Drug Act* of 1906.

Before the FDA

This Chicago meat-packing plant was typical of food-processing standards in 1905, the year before Congress passed the Pure Food and Drug Act. In this era before consumerism, unsanitary conditions in food handling and processing were common, and product testing was unheard of.

The U.S. Food and Drug Administration (FDA) now regulates the safety of the food and medicine we consume. The FDA is specifically charged with:

1. Setting standards for and inspecting, testing, and licensing the manufacture of biological products.
2. Setting standards for and testing, monitoring the quality of, and approving for release all drugs for human use.
3. Developing and enforcing regulations regarding the composition, quality, nutritional value, and safety of foods, food additives, dyes, and cosmetics and inspecting processing and manufacturing plants.
4. Setting safety standards limiting radiation exposure.
5. Developing policy for and evaluating the safety, efficacy, and labeling of all medical devices.
6. Evaluating the safety of veterinary preparations.

Consumer protection groups and government regulations work to keep firms from hiding vital information from consumers about possible harm caused by their products and from withholding safer techniques or products from the market to maintain their profits. A sampling of major consumer protection laws appears in Table 4.1. Why do consumers need all this protection?

table 4.1 Consumer Protection Laws and Agencies

Federal Laws

Year	Act	Impact
1906	Pure Food and Drug	Regulated safety of food products.
1936	Robinson-Patman	Reduced price discrimination.
1937	Fair Packaging and Labeling	Required consumer product labels to include information on the product and manufacturer.
1968	Truth in Lending	Forced lenders to disclose terms of loans when marketing them.
1970	Fair Credit Reporting	Limited information contained in credit reports and gives consumers access to such reports.
1972	Consumer Product Safety	Set safety standards for many products.
1975	Consumer Goods Pricing	Stopped some unfair pricing agreements between stores and producers of products.
1990	Nutrition Labeling and Education	Standardized food labels and made them clearer to consumers.

Federal Regulatory Agencies

Name	Activities
Consumer Products Safety Commission	Enforces product safety laws.
Environmental Protection Agency	Creates, communicates, and enforces regulations concerning environmental impact.
Federal Trade Commission	Regulates unfair business practices and deceptive advertising.
Food and Drug Administration	Regulates safety of foods, drugs, and cosmetics.
Securities and Exchange Commission	Regulates buying and selling of shares in publicly owned businesses.

Consider the recall and seizing of the products of a California-based baby formula manufacturer in 1995, and the arrest of its managers. The company had been selling fake powdered baby formula, using the well-known Similac brand's packaging to disguise its product. FDA investigators discovered the fraud, quickly removed all of the fake product, and performed laboratory tests to make sure there was no health risk to babies who had consumed it. Fortunately, there was nothing poisonous in the formula, but it lacked proper nutrients and caused allergic reactions in some babies. Without the FDA, this fraud might never have been discovered.[9]

Contrast this example with the conduct of Switzerland's Nestlé Corporation, which sold powdered baby formula to mothers in developing countries in Africa and Asia, even though these mothers were ill equipped to use the product. Many children became sick from contaminated water used to prepare the formula; others suffered from malnutrition when their mothers ran out of money to buy more formula but were no longer able to produce breast milk. While legal, Nestlé's action was unethical. Eventually concerned consumers in the United States and Europe organized a boycott of all Nestlé products. In response, the World Health Organization (WHO) set limits on the use and marketing of Nestlé's formula and all such products. Nestlé's behavior was intended to make money for the company, but the boycott is estimated to have cost it over $40 million in lost revenues.[10]

Until WHO stepped in, Nestlé could claim that it had violated no rules. There are far fewer consumer protection laws in many other countries than there are in the United States. Developing countries generally have the fewest of these laws, but the trend is toward more consumer protection worldwide. In China, where advertising is a new phenomenon, many ads were at first deceptive and inaccurate. For example, many consumers were deceived by ads guaranteeing the effectiveness of love potions.[11] In 1992, the Chinese government imposed rules to prevent false advertising of scientific and medical products.

Some business practices are clearly illegal, such as false advertising and refusing to honor warranties. But there are also many practices that are legal but unethical. For example, Thorn EMI PLC's subsidiary, Rent-A-Center, used high-pressure tactics to encourage poor customers to rent more goods than they could afford at very high prices. According to Angela Adams, a mother receiving welfare benefits, salespeople pushed her to rent items at a total cost of about $325 a month, despite their knowledge of her meager income. Rent-A-Center's sales and service manual from February 1993 taught employees to try hard to close sales quickly and often. Further, it taught employees to convince buyers to rent a more expensive version of the item they needed.[12]

Laws Prohibiting Discrimination

6. Identify and describe the laws that prohibit discrimination in the workplace and protect the natural environment.

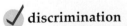

discrimination

The unequal treatment of an individual based on group affiliation.

Workplaces are growing ever more diverse, and businesses must ensure that they are fostering diversity, not contributing to **discrimination**—unequal treatment based on group affiliation. Such discrimination can occur in relation to a business's customers and other external contacts or in relation to its employees, a topic we deal with in more detail later in this chapter. The *Civil Rights Act* of 1964 prohibits discrimination on the basis of race, gender, religion, color, or national origin. Congress has extended and reinforced the 1964 act with other laws. Some extend protection to additional groups, as does the *Americans with Disabilities Act* of 1990, which ensures access to services and facilities and participation in economic activity, including the workplace. Under this act, denial of physical access is a form of discrimination; many organizations are therefore altering entryways and restrooms and providing special parking facilities. Congress has also passed laws clarifying the meaning of discrimination where it was not explicit, as in the *Age Discrimination in Employment Act* of 1967 and the *Equal Pay Act* of 1963, which attempted to outlaw the practice of paying men higher wages than were paid to women doing the same job. The Civil Rights Act of 1991 and other laws have further defined illegal practices. A variety of cases reaching the courts have also clarified the meaning, extent, and scope of these laws.

Although discrimination that excludes people from markets because of race, gender, age, sexual orientation, or some other characteristic is clearly unethical and usually illegal, such discrimination unfortunately still takes place. For example, lawsuits by angry customers revealed that Denny's restaurant chain engaged in a systematic policy of discouraging African Americans from eating at its restaurants. Some Denny's locked their doors when they saw these customers approaching.[13]

It is the responsibility of an ethical manager or employee to ensure that no customer is discriminated against. If managers and employees do not supervise this area, the courts will. Later in this chapter, in the section on the laws that protect employees, we look further into laws prohibiting discrimination. We also discuss the Equal Employment Opportunity Commission, which helps guarantee rights in the workplace.

Laws Protecting the Natural Environment

The *National Environmental Policy Act* of 1969 was the first law to address the harmful impact of business activities on human health and the natural environment. This law represents a turning point in business regulation. In effect, it requires businesses to address the potential harm that a legitimate and necessary business activity may cause to both people and the environment. The National Environmental Policy Act created two federal agencies with complementary roles. The first, the Council on Environmental Quality (CEQ), focuses on environmental impact issues and national policy development. It administers the process by which businesses file environmental impact statements, and it develops and recommends to the president policies regarding the protection and improvement of the quality of the environment. The scope of the Environmental Protection Agency (EPA), the second agency created by the act, is broader, and the EPA also has authority to implement and enforce laws addressing various kinds of pollution control. The EPA implements legislation regarding air quality, water quality, solid waste, pesticides, toxic substances, drinking water, radiation, and noise. For each pollutant, the EPA develops:

1. National programs and technical policies.
2. National emission standards and effluent (liquid waste) guidelines.
3. Rules and procedures to guide industry reporting, registration, and certification programs.
4. Air standards.

Additionally, the EPA keeps a watchful eye on industry waste discharge and disposal, radioactivity in the environment, new nuclear facility proposals, new chemicals and new chemical uses, and pesticide residues in foodstuffs (see the doing business box entitled "Government's Role in the Florida Nursery Business" on the next page).

Government's Role in the Florida Nursery Business

Nurseries that raised landscape plants in Florida were devastated by Hurricane Andrew in 1992, and many received federal disaster relief funds to help them rebuild. Now some nursery owners have turned to the government for help with an even worse problem: Their plants are dying and nursery workers are getting sick. The reason? The growers believe that Benlate, an agricultural chemical made by U.S. chemical company DuPont, is to blame. DuPont's scientists say the evidence is not clear, but the company has paid out millions of dollars already to settle lawsuits by growers. Now the state government is involved in the Benlate controversy because the Florida Health and Rehabilitation Services Department receives dozens of complaints from nursery owners. And it has called in the help of federal agencies, including the Environmental Protection Agency and the National Institute for Occupational Safety and Health. Whatever happens to Florida's nurseries, you can be sure that government will play a large role.

Source: "A Blight That's Eating Away at DuPont," *Business Week*, Oct. 5, 1992, p. 46.

Contract Law

7. Discuss how contract and tort law and ethical considerations contribute to fair interbusiness conduct.

Both consumers and businesses are protected by **contract law**, the body of laws that defines the rights and obligations of parties engaged in business relationships. The purpose of this set of laws is to provide stability and predictability, thereby making business interactions easier and less risky.[14] A valid contract must satisfy six basic requirements:

1. It must involve an *agreement* between parties to specific terms.
2. It must involve a *consideration*, an exchange of something of value.
3. Both parties must have the *capacity* to enter into the agreement. Hence, minors and the intoxicated or mentally incompetent may not be able to enter into contracts.
4. The purpose of the contract must be to accomplish something that is *legal*.
5. The parties must give their *genuine assent*, or agreement, to the contract, with neither being forced to do so.
6. The contract must take the legally required *form*, in many cases in writing.

Contracts that fail to meet these requirements are considered void in a court of law. For example, let's say a classmate proposes the following deal to you. Your classmate has an opportunity to buy some brand-new computers that have been seized from illegal importers and are being auctioned, but he needs to raise $500 today. He already has customers who will buy the computers for $10,000, and he offers a written contract guaranteeing you payment of $1,000 tomorrow, or 20 percent interest *per month* if he fails to pay you back by then. His deal seems too good to be true—even if it falls through, the interest rate in your contract is so favorable you may be tempted to lend him the money. *Don't!* In truth, your contract *is* too good to be true, because it violates state **usury laws**, which regulate the maximum rate of interest on loans. That means the contract is void, because it fails the fourth requirement—legality. While the maximum allowable interest varies from state to state, nowhere is it as high as the rate in your contract. You will never see a dime of your money again, because your so-called friend is running a common con, one that takes advantage of people's lack of knowledge of business laws.[15]

 contract law

The body of laws that defines the rights and obligations of parties engaged in business relationships.

 usury laws

Laws regulating the maximum rate of interest on loans.

Ethics may require choices that go beyond the scope of contract law. In dealing with vendors and suppliers, it is best to treat them *fairly*. Why? Let's look at an example. A Mars, Inc., purchasing agent was able to negotiate a very low price on the cacao beans used in chocolate candy because the supplier was desperate for the order. There was nothing illegal about this hard-nosed negotiating. But Mars management decided that the supplier should get a higher price for the beans, explaining that the company did not want to take unfair advantage of its supplier's bad times. This decision ensured that in the future it would have a loyal supplier, one who might not take advantage of any hardships that Mars faced.[16]

tort law

The body of laws governing civil wrongs arising from causes other than a breach of contract.

Tort Law

But what about business relationships not covered by a contract? If they involve criminal activities, like robbery or bribery, they are covered by criminal law. But sometimes people are hurt by noncriminal, or civil, actions of businesses. Imagine, for example, that a new factory is built and that its smokestacks emit a foul odor, which causes residential property values to fall in the area. Such cases are subject to **tort law**, the body of laws governing civil wrongs arising from causes other than a breach of contract. Fraud, trespass, product liability, and other improper business practices are treated under tort law. Because these practices are noncriminal, penalties may include fines and compensation to victims but will not include jail terms. Slander and libel—spoken and written defamation of character—are also torts.

Johnson & Johnson produces surgical equipment that must meet many legal consumer protection standards in order to be sold in the United States. Nevertheless, the company knows that patients may sue J & J under tort law if the equipment is a factor in unsuccessful surgeries. J & J tries to safeguard against such an event by offering special training to help surgeons improve their skills with the new equipment. In so doing, the company believes it prevents accidents that might result in legal problems.[17]

The Uniform Commercial Code

During the rapid industrial expansion of the mid- and late 1800s, the number and complexity of agreements between businesses grew at a rapid pace. By this time many states had enacted laws to address business transactions, but businesses often operated across state lines. Variations in state laws created difficulties in resolving disputes or enforcing written agreements between companies. The legal profession (which bore the brunt of the difficulties in its role as the representative of disputing clients) finally came together in the late 1800s to develop a uniform code of regulations and specifications for the various kinds of contractual agreements businesses enter into. Once this code was complete, the legal profession worked to encourage state legislatures to adopt it. The *Uniform Commercial Code* (UCC) is the most important of the codes developed. It helps to specify what constitutes an enforceable, legal contract and how the rights and responsibilities of each party can be enforced by law and the courts.

Laws Protecting Employees

To produce goods or services, most business owners need employees. In developed countries such as the United States, most individuals depend on some business for their employment and livelihood. This necessary and fragile alliance has been the focal point of a large number of laws governing the balance of power between employers and employees. In this context, two sets of laws

8. Identify the laws designed to protect employee diversity, health, and safety.

Equal Pay for Equal Work

At Seattle City Lights, a Washington electric company, employees are paid for the worth of their work, period. Thus, female and male line workers receive the same wages.

workplace diversity

Ethnic and cultural differences among workers.

sex discrimination

The unequal treatment of individuals because of their gender.

glass ceiling

The limit on the job level to which a woman will be promoted.

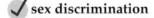

sexual harassment

Inappropriate sexual advances that create a hostile environment or harmful stress.

have been written. The first set relates to **workplace diversity**—ethnic and cultural differences among workers—and employees' right not to have those differences used against them in ways that restrict their access to a job or their ability to perform well on the job. The second set of issues focuses on the health and safety of workers.

Workplace Diversity

One key law in this area is the Civil Rights Act of 1964, discussed earlier in this chapter. This broad act is divided into several sections, which are called titles. *Title VII*, which deals with employment issues, is intended to protect employees from discrimination by employers. Title VII acknowledges the need for a business to hire the best possible people for a given job. It also promotes fairness by requiring that businesses consider only *objective, job-related criteria* in hiring, training, paying, retaining, and promoting employees. This law, which applies to every business with 15 or more employees, prohibits discrimination in employment-related decisions on the basis of gender, race, color, national origin, or religion.

Sex discrimination is the unequal treatment of individuals because of their gender. Women now make up about 47 percent of the work force, and they are demanding that their gender not be used to restrict their advancement. Nevertheless, more than three decades after the passage of the Equal Pay Act in 1963, women are still often paid less than men who do the same job. In fact, women who work for wages make only 70 cents for every dollar earned by a man working for wages. Women of color make even less—64 percent if they are African American and 55 percent if they are Hispanic.[18] Another consequence of sex discrimination in the workplace is showing up as the **glass ceiling**, a limit on the job level to which a woman will be promoted.

Sexual harassment—inappropriate sexual advances that create a hostile environment or harmful stress—reportedly is widespread in the workplace. In one study, 42 percent of female government employees and 15 percent of male employees said they had experienced sexual harassment on the job.[19]

Homosexuals are not identified as a group protected from discrimination under Title VII of the Civil Rights Act of 1964, but some states and local governments have passed laws protecting them from employment-related discrimination. Some cases based on those laws are now being heard in the courts. Furthermore, since laws against sexual harassment do not specify gender, it is possible for same-sex harassment to be reported and tried under those laws.

The Civil Rights Act of 1964 also created the Equal Employment Opportunity Commission (EEOC), the federal agency charged with the implementation and enforcement of Title VII (and, subsequently, of other civil rights acts as well). The EEOC is responsible for the following:

1. Issuing employment discrimination guidelines that explain to employers the meaning of discriminatory conduct and that describe nondiscriminatory practices in selecting, hiring, and managing a work force.

2. Monitoring the compliance of businesses under the jurisdiction of the EEOC by requiring and reviewing reports on hiring and management practices.

3. Investigating charges of discrimination, including reviewing the employer's actions with particular people or groups; deciding whether discriminatory acts have occurred; and making these findings public.

4. Bringing to court any case in which the EEOC decides a discriminatory act has occurred.

Most states and cities have legislation that parallels federal legislation on civil rights issues. Such legislation can expand the protection established by federal law but cannot reduce that protection.

Employee Health and Safety

A second group of employer-related laws address the health and safety of workers. The initial impetus for their creation was actually the cost of injuries to businesses and to society. During the nineteenth century, the rapid industrialization of the American economy, coupled with the introduction of heavy machinery in production operations, greatly increased the number of significant injuries on the job. With more people working for wages, serious injuries accompanied by lengthy recovery periods could impoverish entire families. *Workers' Compensation* laws, which provide a continuing, though decreased, income for an injured or disabled worker, originated in Wisconsin in 1911 as a response by the state's government to companies that simply fired workers injured on the job with no compensation. Such compensation is now mandatory in 47 states and voluntary in New Jersey, South Carolina, and Texas.

Workers' Compensation laws made businesses responsible for such compensation as a normal cost of doing business. Insurance companies began to provide insurance coverage for business to meet the expense of compensating injured or disabled workers. As the hazards of the industrialization and mechanization of work increased, and as insurance premiums rose, business finally had an economic incentive to try to reduce the risk of injury to workers. But this incentive left it to the individual business owner to decide if the costs of reducing the risk of injury were worth the possible savings in compensation costs and insurance premiums.

Although labor groups had a long history of campaigning for better workplace safety, the seriousness of unsafe work sites drew national attention in 1968 when a coal mine explosion killed 78 workers in Farmington, West Virginia. This tragedy helped to reveal the extent of preventable danger some workers faced; at the same time, it focused public attention on the ravages of black lung disease among mine workers. In 1969 the federal government entered the arena of workplace safety with the *Coal Mine Health and Safety Act*. In response to mounting public pressure for an effective national system of regulation to cover all industries, Congress passed the *Occupational Health and Safety Act* in 1970. The act's stated goal was to ensure, as far as possible, that working conditions for all Americans were healthful and safe. Congress simultaneously created the Occupational Safety and Health Administration (OSHA) to enforce this act. OSHA's duties are to:

We discuss unions and labor laws in detail in Chapter 13.

- Develop and enforce mandatory job safety and health standards.
- Maintain a reporting and recordkeeping system to monitor job-related illness and injury.
- Establish training programs for occupational safety personnel.
- Develop, analyze, evaluate, and improve state occupational safety and health programs.
- Provide for research in workplace safety and health and develop responses to health and safety problems.
- Establish rights and responsibilities for both employers and employees for workplace safety and health.
- Encourage the reduction of workplace hazards with improved or new health and safety programs.

OSHA inspectors conduct "walkaround" surveys of a worksite to examine practices visually. Workplaces found to be out of compliance are given a chance to correct the problem and are later reinspected. Businesses that commit serious violations of safety and health requirements may be cited, fined, or both, depending on the seriousness of the violation and whether it is chronic.

Many of the terrible conditions that prevailed in factories and sweatshops have been eliminated in the United States, though some employers do still break the law and expose workers to hazardous work conditions. But many factory jobs have been exported to other countries, where some U.S. firms are recreating a harmful work environment. In Mexico's enterprise zones, young women labor long hours for low pay in hazardous conditions, only a few miles beyond the reach of Mexican labor laws.[20] And companies that design and market goods produced abroad face questions that were resolved generations ago in the United States.

Nike's annual revenue from the sale of sports shoes alone is $2 billion. Nike handles the design and marketing of the shoes but does not produce them directly. It contracts abroad, mostly in Asia, for their actual production. Many of Nike's contractors are in Indonesia. The factories employ mostly girls and young women, who get an entry-level salary of $1.80 a day for sewing the shoes. Basic workers' rights and protections are nearly nonexistent for these employees, who are often forced to do mandatory overtime work. It costs Nike about $17.50 to produce the shoes, which usually sell for between $45 and $80. Nike claims that it does not know much about either the production processes or conditions under which its shoes are made. But as a *New York Times* article asks, "If Nike, which profits from these shoes, does not take responsibility for the people who make the shoes, who does?"[21] We saw earlier that Nike's competitor, Reebok, emphasizes human rights as a business value. It, too, does business in Indonesia. Do you think its business ethics lead it to treat foreign workers better than Nike does? We will discuss Reebok's policy later in the chapter, after you have had a chance to form your own opinion.

Do you believe U.S. firms should observe U.S. labor laws when they employ foreign workers or use foreign suppliers?

Intellectual Property Laws

This chapter's opening story presented a sales manager with an interesting problem: Should he hire a salesman from a competing company who offers to bring information about that company with him? This information may be protected by intellectual property laws, which—as you may recall from Chapter 3—address trademarks, copyrights, and patents.

Trademarks are words, symbols, and designs that identify a product or business. If registered with the U.S. Patent and Trademark Office, trademarks can be legally owned and protected in the United States and in the many foreign countries that have intellectual property treaties with the United States. The Nike name and curving line symbol are trademarks.

Copyrights are rights to written work, art, or software. To protect their rights in the United States, authors or other legal owners of such work must register it with the U.S. Copyright Office. This textbook is copyrighted by the publisher and may not be copied without permission.

Patents are exclusive rights to make, use, and sell new inventions for 17 years. Inventors or their employers must prove to the U.S. Patent and Trademark Office and to comparable agencies in other countries that their inventions are genuine, novel, useful, and not obvious, given the technology of the time.[22] If they do so, they receive protection from competitors who might otherwise copy their invention. Xerox patented the plain-paper copier and dominated the photocopier market until its patents expired in the early 1980s.

✓ trademarks

Words, symbols, and designs that identify a product or business.

✓ copyrights

Rights to written work, art, or software.

✓ patents

Exclusive rights to make, use, and sell new inventions for 17 years.

These three types of intellectual property encourage innovation by helping people and businesses profit from their original ideas and inventions. But what about **trade secrets**, information that a business wants to keep secret but that is not protected by intellectual property laws? This is just one area where you will face difficult decisions, and the answers won't necessarily come from other people. You can expect to work with many people who have not studied business law and ethics and who will not recognize the ethical and legal sides of issues. Even those who do may give you conflicting advice, as the sales manager in our chapter opening vignette discovers. The story continues like this:

> I realized that I was caught somewhere between the two reactions of rage and temptation and I decided to go to talk to one of our senior managers about the situation. He had been a mentor to me ever since I'd joined the company. After I had told him the whole story, his reply was short and to the point, and it surprised me. What he said was, "Hire this guy before someone else does. I know it's a risk, but everyone in our industry tries to get reliable data on competitors any way they can. We stand to lose a real *competitive edge* if you don't strike while the iron's hot." The way he said "competitive edge" was, I knew, a mimic of my boss, who was always hitting us with those words and in that tone.
>
> As I left his office, he patted my shoulder and winked as he assured me he knew I'd do the sensible thing.
>
> As I wandered down the hall toward my office, I ran into my top assistant, a sharp, aggressive business graduate. She said, "You look troubled. Anything wrong?"
>
> I quickly motioned her to follow me to my office. Once inside, I shut the door and spilled out the whole story, again. Her response was the exact opposite of my mentor's. She looked me straight in the eye and said, "Listen, think about what you're contemplating here. Not only is what this guy is doing wrong, but if you hire him, you would be supporting that kind of behavior. Besides, there's no telling when he might start stealing from *us* and selling to the highest bidder." I nodded; I'd thought of this myself. "And," she went on, "if the story ever gets out that you hired him knowing he had stolen confidential information, the whole thing could blow up in your face and give our company a bad name."
>
> After she'd left, I sat there realizing that my two associates, rather than helping me, had made my decision more difficult. I wondered what I should do. Hire him or say, "Thanks, but no thanks." Or maybe hire him but tell him not to bring stolen information. "But could I trust him to be honest once he started working here?" I wondered. "Then again, maybe I should turn him in—call his former boss."[23]

One adviser says do it—you won't get caught. The other says no, it's illegal and you could get in trouble. Is it illegal? Would you get caught? We'll return to this question later in the chapter.

Various tort laws protect trade secrets, and sometimes employees sign contracts in which they promise not to disclose company information. In such cases, using information such as that offered by the salesman in his job interview would be illegal, even though the information is not copyrighted or patented. Most likely, the issue would be settled in court. That is just what is happening in the case of two Dallas telecommunications equipment makers, DSC Communications and DGI Technologies. Each is suing the other over a dispute arising from DGI's claim that its products were DSC-approved (DSC's

 trade secrets

Information that a business wants to keep secret but that is not protected by intellectual property laws.

name is trademarked). On the other side, DSC claims that DGI stole copies of secret papers from its dumpster and accuses DGI of industrial espionage, trespassing, and misappropriation of trade secrets.[24] As this example indicates, intellectual property is a frequently debated legal concept, one that keeps many lawyers gainfully employed!

Business Ethics

The previous section described a broad range of legal issues, any of which might crop up on the job. There are also many cases in which the law does not determine your actions, but ethical considerations ought to. An example is the situation described in the ethics check entitled "New and Improved . . . It Even Resists Fingerprints!" Nike and Reebok face legal constraints over how they treat U.S. workers, but the same issues abroad are ethical rather than legal. Whenever stakeholders are affected by a decision or action, businesses and their employees must consider the ethical as well as the legal dimensions.

Recognizing ethical problems, or ethical dilemmas, is a first step toward responding to them. But knowing right from wrong is often easier than knowing how to *do* the right thing. This section discusses three useful questions that can guide ethical decision making.

The Ethics Check

Reebok's president says his firm hopes to make it "unacceptable to mistreat human beings." Reebok obviously knows what is right and wrong when it comes to employee treatment. Yet, as you may have guessed, it has not been able to translate its business ethics into enlightened policies. The company produces almost a third of its shoes in Indonesia. The workers making these shoes receive the country's minimum wage of $1.80 a day. The problem is that about $3.30 a day is needed to satisfy an individual's basic needs in Indonesia. According to a United Nations study, 88 percent of Indonesian women earning the minimum wage are malnourished.[25] The government deliberately sets the minimum wage too low in order to attract companies like Reebok and Nike. And when given the option of underpaying workers, it is hard for these companies to stick to their ethics and do what they know is right.

One reason companies fail to do the right thing when faced with such dilemmas is that their employees may not stop to think about the ethical dimensions of certain decisions. The local managers in Indonesia may not realize that Reebok's vision of human rights is one that applies to *their* business decisions. To make sure ethics are considered in every decision, you can use the three questions of the Ethics Check.[26] None of these questions is adequate by itself, but together they may help you see issues in a new light.

9. List the three questions that can help focus attention on ethical business conduct.

Is It Legal?

At first glance, this question seems to be asking "Can I get away with it?", which most of us would not consider a terribly ethical approach. But "Is it legal?" can actually be seen as two questions. First, is the action clearly and undeniably illegal? If so, it ought to be avoided as a matter of good judgment, if not good citizenship. Thus, this question can at least dispose of some unethical choices.

But the law does not always draw a clear line. Many legal actions just skirt the law, and this is the second part of this two-part question: Is it just barely legal and therefore questionable? Sometimes firms are in only partial compli-

New and Improved . . . It Even Resists Fingerprints!

Millions of guns are in the hands of U.S. citizens, some of them legally registered and many not. Some illegal guns are turned in to police departments in exchange for amnesty and cash—local police increasingly use such tactics to try to limit the number of guns reaching the hands of criminals. In general, the manufacturers are not held legally liable when one of their guns is used in a crime. But victims or their relatives often argue that the manufacturers are ethically responsible for illegal uses of their weapons, and ought to be held liable as well. For example, lawyers representing the victims of a 1993 attack in a San Francisco office building argued in court that the manufacturer of the weapon used should be held liable for the eight dead and six wounded. The gun, a TEC-DC9 automatic pistol, was manufactured by U.S. gun maker Navegar, Inc., and lawyers argued that Navegar encouraged its use by "madmen to kill as many people as possible" because they advertised it as being "as tough as your toughest customer" and "resistant to fingerprints." (*Note*: This case is heading for trial. Watch for it to see how a court rules on these issues.)

1. What view of social responsibility do you think the manufacturer takes?

2. What view do you think the victims and their lawyers take?

3. Imagine you were just offered a high-paying job as assistant marketing manager at Navegar with responsibility for its automatic pistols. Develop the pro and con arguments on accepting the job. Do you think you could perform it in an ethical manner?

Source: "Lawyers for Shooting Victims Seek to Sue a Gun Manufacturer," *New York Times*, Feb. 19, 1995, p. 37.

---

ance with applicable regulations or deliberately look for ways to circumvent legal restrictions. Here, you should think carefully about which side of the law you are on. The law represents the accumulation of thousands of years of effort to resolve disputes and right wrongs. At the very least, you should carefully try to understand the legal issues involved and reflect on the spirit and intent of the law. Reebok's decision to pay Indonesian workers minimum wage does comply with that country's laws. But will it pass the next test?

Is It Fair?

Since ethical lapses almost always involve being unfair to one or more stakeholders, your perception that something is unfair may be an indicator that some serious ethical problem lurks below the surface. A good example is in dealings with customers. Superficially, the firm and its customers might seem to have opposite interests—the firm wants to be paid a high price and the customer wants to pay a low price. This may encourage a firm to use deceptive selling practices, such as lowering the quality of the product (and hence its costs) without telling the customer. Any such moves that seem unfair are certainly unethical. For instance, downsizing, or reducing the amount of product in a package, is unfair if it seems likely that the customer won't notice. Have you ever wondered why some candy bars come in very large wrappers? Years ago, the candy bars filled those packages, but the manufacturers downsized them so many times that the products are now half air. The net effect is that consumers pay more for less, but they may not notice because the process was so gradual.

Any time you find yourself thinking of a situation as a **zero-sum game**—a situation in which there can be only one winner because what one wins another loses—take extra time to be sure your actions are fair. In such situations, strong temptations exist for unethical behavior. To make sure you consider the fair-

 zero-sum game

A situation in which there can be only one winner because what one wins another loses.

table 4.2 Stakeholder Checklist: Should Indonesian Workers Producing Goods for a U.S. Company Be Paid More Than Minimum Wage?

Stakeholders	Impact
Internal	
• Owners	Short-term profit loss?
• U.S. purchasing department	Inconvenience of having to audit Indonesian subcontractors' work forces
External	
• U.S. employees	Consistent example of ethical management
• Indonesian subcontractors	Higher labor costs, but more committed and happy employees
• Indonesian workers	Better wages and living standards
Society	
• U.S. public	Little impact
• Indonesian public	Positive impact on development of labor practices

ness of an action for everyone affected, you can write a list of the stakeholders and their stakes. Table 4.2 shows a stakeholder checklist, filled in for the example of whether to pay Indonesian employees above minimum wage.

How Do I Feel About It?

This third question rounds out your Ethics Check. Think about the contemplated action. Are you the kind of person who does this sort of thing? Would you like to be known as someone who does? How will it make you feel about yourself? This sounds like a vague criterion, but there's a lot to be said for trusting your instincts. For instance, most unethical actions would never have been taken if the decision maker had first asked, "Would I feel good about this if my family learned about it on the local news?"

Let's see how these three questions help our sales manager, whom we left on the horns of a dilemma, considering the views of one associate who said he ought to hire the new salesman and the other who said not to. Since then, he has talked to a friend who works at another company; here is the advice he got:

"If someone in your company were to come to you with such a dilemma, what would you suggest?", I asked my friend.

"I'd give that person the *Ethics Check*," she said. "You see, many people think nowadays that there is a big gray area between right and wrong, and they use that gray area as an excuse not to worry about being ethical. But we've come to realize that a lot of the grayness can be taken out of ethical dilemmas if one takes the time to sort out the situation. It is easy to charge ahead without thinking and then rationalize your behavior after the fact. But the truth is, *there is no right way to do a wrong thing!*"

The Ethics Check helps the sales manager to think the dilemma through and avoid doing the wrong thing, even for the right reasons. His friend asks him each of the questions in turn:

"The first question is straightforward: *Is it legal?*"

"I have no trouble answering that one," I said. "My answer has to be a resounding 'No' when it comes to this sales representative. He is stealing proprietary information."

My friend nodded. "Our company feels that if you give a 'no' answer to that first question, then you don't even have to consider the next two. However, I'm not sure it's always that simple, so I tell people they should answer all the questions before deciding. The second question is, *Is it balanced?* By that we mean is the decision going to favor one party or the other unfairly?"

"You mean," I said, "is there going to be a big winner or loser in the long run?"

She nodded. "Our feeling is that lopsided, win-lose decisions invariably end up as lose-lose situations. Everyone cannot win equally in every situation all the time, but we want to avoid major imbalances over the course of relationships."

"But we are talking about one of our major competitors here," I objected.

"Right," said my friend, "And when it becomes clear what happened, your competitor will look for ways to get even. They'll be asking themselves what top people they can pirate from you or what information they can get from your company to use against you. And while you are playing one-upsmanship with each other," she added, "another competitor may very well pass you both by. Or even worse, you may both give your industry a bad name. There's no peace of mind in being Number One in a troubled industry. If customers begin to mistrust people in your company, everyone's business is affected."

"When I ask myself if it's fair to hire this sales representative—with his confidential information—the answer is clearly 'No!' Even though I already have two nos, what's the last question on this Ethics Check?"

"The last question is, *How will it make me feel about myself?* This question focuses on your own standards of morality. John Wooden, the legendary UCLA basketball coach, said that there is no pillow as soft as a clear conscience."

"That certainly hits home with me," I said. "Ever since I was confronted with this ethical issue, I haven't been able to sleep."

"What has kept you awake is the realization that you were seriously considering doing something you knew was wrong because it might help your career in the short run. Isn't that the issue?"

"That's definitely it," I agreed. "And that hasn't made me feel very good about myself. I can see how this Ethics Check of yours can help someone decide what is right."[27]

The manager in this story uses the Ethics Check to identify the best course of action. But he faces pressures at work to take a different course. Such conflicts can make it hard to do the right thing, even when you know what is best. In the next section we will explore ways of helping employees do what is right.

Helping Employees Do the Right Thing

How can an organization encourage its people to develop the ethical power to do what's right even when the pressures of the job may pull the other way? A

table 4.3   The Five Principles of Ethical Power

Principle	Personal statement
1. Purpose	I see myself as being an ethically sound person. I let my conscience be my guide. No matter what happens, I am always able to face the mirror, look myself straight in the eye, and feel good about myself.
2. Pride	I feel good about myself. I don't need the acceptance of other people to feel important. My self-esteem keeps my ego and my desire to be accepted from influencing my decisions.
3. Patience	I believe that things will eventually work out well. I don't need everything to happen right now. I am at peace with what comes my way.
4. Persistence	I stick to my purpose, especially when it seems inconvenient to do so! My behavior is consistent with my intentions. As Sir Winston Churchill said, "Never! Never! Never! Never give up!"
5. Perspective	I reflect carefully about decisions, taking the time I need to see things more clearly before acting.

Source: K. Blanchard and N.V. Peale, *The Power of Ethical Management* (New York: William Morrow, 1988), p. 125.

first step is to prepare an **ethics statement**, a written outline of the business's ethical principles. Such statements may be stand-alone documents, or they may be part of the mission statement of the business. Ethics statements are most effective when they translate powerful personal principles into norms for the entire organization.

Table 4.3 presents five principles that can be adapted to the company level and used as a template for ethics statements. For example, statements under "Purpose" and "Pride" can serve as a reminder of what the organization stands for and become a basis for other decisions. Statements under "Patience" and "Persistence" could be specific reminders to employees that the most worthwhile results are usually long-term rather than temporary. Finally, "Perspective" might emphasize the importance of making decisions carefully and resisting pressures that can produce hasty choices. Confronting ethical dilemmas can be very stressful, and it's worth making the effort to reflect carefully on the impact of a particular decision on other important areas.

The five principles of ethical power provide a useful framework for analyzing companies. Note that even if a company did not use the five principles in drafting its ethics statement, it might still display all five ethical traits in its behavior. Levi Strauss & Co. does. The following list identifies aspects of the company's behavior that exemplify the five principles.[28]

10. Describe the content and purpose of an ethics statement and list four management techniques for reinforcing ethical behavior.

✔ **ethics statement**

A written outline of the ethical principles of a business.

- Purpose: At Levi Strauss & Co., employees know that the company aspires to diversity, ethical management, and employee empowerment.
- Pride: This is expressed in Levi's mission to "provide greater recognition for individuals and teams that contribute to our success."
- Patience: Levi's chief executive, Robert Haas, says his ethical approach to management is "more efficient in the long run."
- Persistence: At Levi's this meant cracking down on use of child labor by Bangladeshi contractors in 1992. The contractors fired anyone under 14— and Levi's paid for these children to go to school, then guaranteed them jobs upon graduation!
- Perspective: Perspective is helpful to Levi's Haas in dealing with dilemmas such as whether to spend money on educating child laborers in Bangladesh—something other companies (including Nike and Reebok) might not be willing to spend money on. As Haas says, "In today's world, a TV exposé on working conditions can undo years of effort to build brand loyalty. Why squander your investment when, with commitment, reputational problems can be avoided?"

For the organization, ethical behavior must flow from the *top down*. Lower-level employees will find it very hard to act ethically if they are under counter-pressures from those higher up. It is up to management to articulate an ethical vision as part of the firm's goals and to work in a way that avoids pressure to cut corners for short-term advantage.

A second example of the influence of an ethics statement is Johnson & Johnson. The company's statement of purpose says:

> We believe our first responsibility is to the doctors, nurses and patients, to the mothers and fathers and all others who use our products and services. In meeting their needs, everything must be of high quality. We constantly strive to reduce our costs in order to maintain reasonable prices. Customers' orders must be serviced promptly and accurately. Our suppliers and distributors must have an opportunity to make a fair profit.

For Johnson & Johnson, this ethics statement is more than a piece of paper. In 1981 and 1984, some containers of its Tylenol pain reliever were poisoned (by criminals outside the company). Even though it was not at fault, Johnson & Johnson did not hesitate to order costly recalls of all Tylenol on the market; at further expense it then created innovative tamper-proof forms of the product. Having developed an organizational culture that stressed customer service and the importance of maintaining the customer's trust, Johnson & Johnson had no trouble reaching the right decision. At the time of the tampering scares, many observers thought that the brand, in which Johnson & Johnson had invested enormous resources, was doomed. But the prompt recall, followed by the introduction of tamper-proof "caplets," protected the company's brand equity and market position.[29]

One of the conclusions that emerges most strongly from reviewing the different responses of firms to ethical dilemmas is that *ethical behavior is learned by doing*. Elaborate ethics codes are of little use without an organizational culture guided by ethical values. A management that is not accustomed to using ethical guidelines on a regular basis will have considerable difficulty responding ethically to a dilemma such as the one Johnson & Johnson faced. A lot of organizational culture is established by past history—who did what, and what happened. If ethical considerations were routinely sidelined in the events that employees remember and in the "war stories" they tell others, then ethical standards would enjoy little authority.[30]

Organizational Culture

The Body Shop is a company that wears its ethics on its packaging, and most of its packaging is recyclable or refillable. The company also campaigns against animal testing of products. What do you think? Should businesses promote their beliefs along with their products? Would you seek out such a company as an employer?

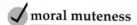

moral muteness

The reluctance to discuss ethical questions with others.

Talking About Ethics

Research on corporate decision making has found that in many cases managers suffer from **moral muteness**, a reluctance to discuss ethical questions with others. In a workplace environment where ethics is seldom discussed, people who do bring up ethical objections may be seen as preachy, self-righteous, even disloyal. As a result, ethical considerations may be completely suppressed in discussion. What you don't talk about, you tend not to think about, and decision making suffers as a result.[31] It is one reason why firms do not always do what is right, even when they know what is right.

If ethical considerations are not explicitly valued and promoted within a firm, they are likely to be downgraded and avoided. Eleven percent of America's largest firms were convicted of breaking the law between 1970 and 1980.[32] An employee at National Semiconductor described how the company started breaking government rules on the testing of semiconductors, for which it was fined $1.75 million in 1984. As demand for semiconductors grew between 1979 and 1981, managers faced intense pressure to take shortcuts in meeting contract schedules. The company slowly began to omit required tests on the products and then falsified records to cover the omissions. Over time, more than 100 employees participated in this falsification.[33] They knew it was unethical and probably illegal as well. They knew they would have felt bad to see their actions described in the local paper. But they did not have the ethical power to prevent or curtail the falsifications. Each felt isolated and fearful of losing his or her job. But they never got together and talked the problem through! Had 100 employees walked into the boss's office together to complain, the story might have had a very different ending.

Research has suggested five ways that businesses can help their employees overcome moral muteness:[34]

1. *Clarify employees' responsibilities to stakeholders.* A business that considers the health and safety of customers to be more important than the next quarter's earnings should say so! While no statement of purpose or ethics does any good unless it is put into effect, a clear ethics statement at least provides a foundation for ethical management.

2. *Don't punish employees for expressing moral views.* Employees who expect to be ostracized or ridiculed for raising ethical considerations will not raise them.

3. *Encourage people to resolve problems through collaboration.* Frank discussions are unlikely when problems are discussed only in hierarchical settings in which employees are afraid of upsetting their superiors. Collaborative groups make participants feel more comfortable with each other and offer participants the opportunity to build common values by discussing issues that arise in the workplace.

4. *Eliminate all abuses of ethical standards.* As stated earlier, people learn by doing and observing what others do. Employees will not raise ethical concerns if they know their company has a history of overlooking and tolerating ethical abuses. The inconsistency between Reebok's Human Rights Award and its wage policies in Indonesia, for example, may have caused Reebok employees to doubt the company's dedication to human rights.

5. *Encourage discussion of ethical questions.* Senior managers can set an example by putting moral and ethical issues on the table and encouraging employee input on them. Such actions not only raise ethical standards but also reduce other employees' reluctance to raise ethical questions.

"The figures for the last quarter are in. We made significant gains in the fifteen-to-twenty-six-year-old age group, but we lost our immortal souls."

Managing Ethics

Effective ethical management must be more than a standard that is consulted from time to time. Firms need to institute ongoing programs that help employees know what the right choice is and develop the personal power to *do* the right thing. Here are some specific management techniques organizations can use to reinforce ethical behavior.

1. Don't Reward Unethical Behavior

   Competition can create opportunities for unethical behavior, and businesses must watch carefully to ensure that they are not rewarding such behavior. One of the biggest problems that a manager faces is how to set incentives and standards for subordinates. The easiest way is to use quantitative standards: the number of units produced or sold during some period of time. Such standards permit simple comparisons, but, if blindly applied, they encourage ethical corner cutting and the neglect of quality. A salesperson under pressure to achieve a certain number of sales may use deceptive sales tactics that undermine long-term sales in order to produce the desired short-term result.

   Different divisions of a large firm often find themselves in direct competition with one another, and midlevel managers may be driven to do things that artificially inflate profits or sales. Here again, leadership really has to come from the top, which is where the standards by which people are judged originate. For example, Boeing Company maintained very high ethical standards under the leadership of William Allen. When T.A. Wilson took over from Allen, a collapse in the airplane market led him to cut employees and focus heavily on financial performance. Boeing found that as ethics took a backseat, standards within the company deteriorated, and employees were caught making bribes to foreign customers in 1974 and indulging in bid rigging in 1984. Wilson and his successor had to institute programs to ensure that such ethical lapses did not recur.[35]

2. Create Departments of Ethics and Law

Ethics and law should be built into routine decision making. Large firms have legal experts on staff to help them identify and resolve legal issues; ethical issues should receive equal consideration. Some of the important functions of a law and ethics office include keeping track of discussions of ethical issues and standards outside the firm, alerting managers to specific concerns, overseeing employee training programs, and playing a policing role. For example, FMC Corporation, a large provider of distribution services, has an ethics hotline operated by such an office, where employees can call anonymously to report any possible legal and ethical violations without fear of retaliation.[36] A law and ethics office can also conduct "exit interviews" with people leaving the firm. Departing employees often have less at stake and so are more willing to report any ethical lapses or legal problems they are aware of.

3. Provide Legal and Ethics Training

Although some ethical issues are straightforward, others are dilemmas that even knowledgeable employees have difficulty resolving. For example, if you can't accept personal gifts from a supplier, can you accept lunch or an expensive dinner? The clarification and discussion that occur during legal and ethics training can help employees clarify such issues. Many firms undertake training for employees focusing on very specific problems like racism or sexism. Training does not, of course, substitute for ethical management actively carried out from the top down, on a day-to-day basis.

Training in teamwork and cooperation can also reinforce ethical behavior. This finding is consistent with our understanding that ethical management helps the business innovate and profit by creating a favorable climate for employees and other stakeholders. At General Electric Plastics Group, team-building exercises have a direct tie-in to business ethics. The business uses community projects like the conversion of a warehouse to a homeless shelter as a way to train its employee teams. Employees love these projects, and managers find they meet training and social responsibility goals at the same time.[37]

The Future of Management

Atlas Headwear, Inc., of Phoenix, Arizona, makes military and sports hats—and makes a practice of promoting from within the company, where 94 percent of employees are Asian Americans or Latinos. The senior management team includes minorities and women—including president Michele Luna, shown here with two members of her team. Atlas's emphasis on diversity at the top contrasts sharply with the picture at the largest U.S. corporations, according to a 1995 report by the Federal Glass Ceiling Commission, which states that 97 percent of corporate senior managers are white and at least 95 percent are male. The bipartisan commission, which was created by the Civil Rights Act of 1991, also reports that women and minority men will comprise 62 percent of the U.S. work force by 2005.

4. Provide Ethical Leadership

An ethics statement is an opportunity for the managers of a business to put forward their own vision of ethics and how they want employees to carry it out. For ethics statements to be useful guides for managers and employees, however, they have to be clear and concrete. Ideally, they should include a description of the company's purpose and beliefs; a description of the company's main stakeholders; a description of the company's obligations to each group of stakeholders; examples of behavior toward stakeholders that meets the company's mission and values; and a description of sanctions the company will impose on those who behave unethically toward stakeholders.[38] And senior managers have to "walk their talk" by exemplifying the beliefs of the ethics statement in their own behavior.

If a business's ethical code is to be effective, managers must involve employees and incorporate their concerns and perspectives. Employees will ultimately have to practice the code as they make day-to-day decisions, so their participation is crucial. When Security Pacific Bank decided to create a corporate vision, it had 70 senior managers create a draft statement after discussing at length the core values they envisioned for the company and the specific issues they and their staff encountered. Employees reviewed the draft, which was then revised to incorporate their concerns. This participation ensured that the code was clear and workable and that it included the ethical issues employees face in their daily activities within the firm.[39]

Doing Well by Doing Good

Is it possible to resolve difficult ethical dilemmas responsibly without hurting one or another stakeholder? Can win-win solutions really work in the real world? The case of Reebok might suggest that the answer is no. The head of Reebok's Indonesian operation points out that "cutting costs is part of our business." And the head of one of the factories making shoes for Reebok in Indonesia observes, "Even if all the Reebok producers got together and went to Reebok and said, 'Give me $13 for these so we can pay workers more,' it wouldn't work! I think they would say, 'We'll go to China and pay $8.' But I wouldn't even risk asking, for fear of what would happen." It sounds hopeless for the Indonesian worker.

But there *are* other approaches. Gillette also manufactures in Indonesia, and its workers receive three to four times the minimum wage of Reebok's workers, plus U.S.-style benefits. Gillette's values have translated into ethical management at the local level. The manager of Gillette's Indonesian subsidiary does not suffer from moral muteness when he says, "The job of a good company is to help raise the living standard where you operate. You do that by looking after your people."[40]

Accountability, honesty, and trust within a firm make the organization far more effective and form an essential basis for good management. Fair treatment and respect for differences often unleash employees' energy and creative capacities, to the benefit of the firm. Up-front dealings with customers not only build reputation and loyalty but also promote the dialogue with customers that can translate into improved products. At least that's how firms like Levi Strauss & Co. see it. Robert Haas of Levi's calls this strategy "responsible commercial success."[41] Leadership on social issues opens doors to new markets and new ways of doing business, improves morale within the organization, and enhances the firm's image.

11. Discuss ways of encouraging socially responsible behavior in a business.

Many managers argue that social responsibility is more profitable than a narrow focus on profit responsibility. How can this be true?

Public-Service Partnerships

You will learn more about not-for-profits in Chapter 5.

Another way businesses show leadership on social issues is through **public-service partnerships**, collaborations between a business and a not-for-profit organization that help each party achieve its goals. Not-for-profits include a great variety of charitable, educational, cultural, and public interest organizations.

At first glance, the differences between businesses that have to earn a profit and not-for-profits that place their "cause" first might seem too great to permit any useful collaboration. But each has something the other needs. Not-for-profits are generally short of resources—money, facilities, volunteers—but they have a relatively high public profile and enjoy considerable goodwill. Businesses often have resources, but they have trouble building an image and developing consumer loyalty. By aligning their long-term interests, each benefits. Public-service partnerships take many forms, including:

- Establishing simple sponsorships, in which a firm provides money in exchange for publicity.
- Creating product and promotional tie-ins, in which some percentage of a consumer's purchase of a product goes to a charitable purpose.
- Giving employees paid release time to volunteer, or donating use of a firm's facilities (e.g., phones, office space).[42]

Some of the most innovative partnerships have helped firms develop new consumer products. The fabric producer F. Schumacher & Co. entered into a relationship with the National Trust for Historic Preservation and received permission to use fabric patterns from furniture in buildings owned by the trust. Schumacher got the chance to develop and market a set of distinctive products, and the trust received royalty income from sales. Other companies have collaborated to conserve natural resources. A corporation that owned a large parcel of land on the edge of a city in the South knew that residents valued the open space. To develop the property and generate revenues without jeopardizing the land valued by residents, the firm hired a not-for-profit organization to help develop a mixed-use community that retained many open spaces and park areas and that did not mar the beauty of the natural surroundings.[43]

An Ethical Work Environment

In your career, you will benefit by making sure you work for organizations that practice ethical management. They will offer more secure, supportive, and successful work environments, ones in which you can learn and grow to your full potential! They will be far less likely to mislead you about the potential of your job, to discriminate against you, or to pressure you to do things you do not think are safe, healthy, or ethical for you or others. And in the long run they are more likely to grow and prosper, allowing you and other stakeholders to do so as well.

public-service partnerships

Collaborations between a business and a not-for-profit organization that help each party achieve its goals.

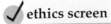

ethics screen

An evaluation of a business by potential employees, customers, communities, or other stakeholders to make sure it meets ethical criteria.

How can prospective employees know whether to trust a business or not? The best way is to perform a careful **ethics screen**, an evaluation of a business by potential employees, customers, communities, or other stakeholders to make sure it meets ethical criteria. Businesses routinely do background checks on potential employees to see whether they are trustworthy. But most legal and ethical problems have their roots within the business process itself, not the individual employees. We urge job applicants to screen businesses as carefully as businesses screen their applicants. Ethical management can be identified by screening (see the skills check "Job Seeker's Ethics Screen") and should be as important to a job applicant as salary, location, and other traditional priorities.

skills check

Job Seeker's Ethics Screen

Instructions: Answer the following questions by checking "yes" or "no." You can use the ethics screen to assess your current employer and to make sure a prospective employer is ethical.

1. Does the business have an ethics statement?
   ☐ YES ☐ NO

2. Has it lost any major lawsuits for illegal employee, competitive marketing, environmental, or community practices? (Ask, and check in an index of newspaper articles.)
   ☐ YES ☐ NO

3. Is your future boss willing to discuss ethics openly with you?
   ☐ YES ☐ NO

4. Do employees of the firm know what the ethics of the business are? Can they easily describe and apply the ethics code or principles?
   ☐ YES ☐ NO

5. Are all ads, brochures, and public statements honest and consistent with the code of ethics—including the job ad?
   ☐ YES ☐ NO

6. Does the business contribute to the community and society through beneficial projects that receive a significant share of money, attention, and other resources?
   ☐ YES ☐ NO

7. Does it value its employees' contributions highly? (Look for suggestion programs, employee awards, generous benefits, recent strike breaking or downsizings, and improvement goals driven by employee attitude surveys.)
   ☐ YES ☐ NO

8. Does it work to improve the environment? (Look for recycling programs and innovations to reduce waste and use sustainable resources.)
   ☐ YES ☐ NO

9. Are its products and services healthy for customers and society?
   ☐ YES ☐ NO

10. Does it apply lower standards of employee care in foreign countries?
    ☐ YES ☐ NO

Each "yes" answer counts as one point. Subtract one point for each "no" answer. The highest possible score is 10, and anything lower than an 8 may indicate trouble.

Copyright © Alexander Hiam & Associates, 1994

Reviewing *Ethics, Law, and Government*

Business Ethics, Business Law, and Social Responsibility

1. **Discuss the relationship between business ethics and law and broadly describe government's role in business conduct**. While business laws attempt to embody the ethics of our society, they may not go far enough. Business ethics applies moral principles to business decision making. Governments intervene in business in three ways: Through their regulatory role, they create and enforce laws; economically, they act as major customers and they monitor the economic environment; and as service providers, they collect the taxes that are used to supply public goods and transfer payments.

2. **Describe how businesses might apply ethical management to meeting their social responsibilities**. With regard to social issues, ethical management means that businesses should not limit themselves to "the letter of the law." Businesses should be responsible for and con-

tribute to environmental protection, better treatment of employees, community concern and involvement, and, most obviously, the manufacture of safe products. To do this, a business must strike a balance among its commitments to its goals, its stakeholders, and society at large.

Business Law and Government Regulation

3. **Identify and describe the three types of U.S. law**. U.S. laws, based on the Constitution and the Bill of Rights, are categorized according to the way they are created. Statutory laws are created by legislative bodies, administrative laws are created by the president and various federal agencies and commissions, and common law is based on legal interpretations of past court decisions.

4. **Briefly review the laws that have been passed to protect free market competition**. Since 1887, with the passage of the Interstate Commerce Act, government has enacted legislation to prevent the growth of monopolies and

other business activities that inhibit free market competition. Other laws include the Sherman Antitrust Act of 1890, the Clayton Antitrust and Federal Trade Commission Acts of 1914, the Robinson-Patman Act of 1936, and most recently, the Anti-Trust Amendments Act of 1990.

5. **Describe how government regulations and consumer protection groups support the four basic rights of consumers.** The consumer's four basic rights—to safety, to information, to choice, and to be heard—are protected by extensive legislation enforced by federal regulatory agencies, including, for example, laws requiring businesses to make good on either implied or express warranties. Consumer groups monitor and work with government agencies to ensure that consumers' rights are protected and that businesses are adhering to the law.

6. **Identify and describe the laws that prohibit discrimination in the workplace and protect the natural environment.** Discrimination against employees and consumers is prohibited by the Civil Rights Act of 1964. The strength of this act has since been bolstered by the Age Discrimination in Employment Act of 1967, the Americans with Disabilities Act of 1990, and the Civil Rights Act of 1991. With the passage in 1969 of the National Environmental Policy Act, the government began taking steps to protect the environment. This law established the Council on Environmental Quality and the Environmental Protection Agency to ensure enforcement of its mandates.

7. **Discuss how contract and tort law and ethical considerations contribute to fair interbusiness conduct.** Contract law defines the requirements of a valid contract, with the Uniform Commercial Code helping to define an enforceable legal contract across state lines. To regulate noncontractual business conduct, tort law deals with civil wrongs arising from fraud, trespass, product liability, and other improper business practices. Ethical considerations take up the slack left by contract and tort law, directing businesses to treat vendors and suppliers fairly, not only because it is right but also because it is good business.

8. **Identify the laws designed to protect employee diversity, health, and safety.** Employee concerns about discrimination—ethnic and sex discrimination, as well as sexual harassment—are addressed in the Equal Pay Act of 1963 and the Civil Rights Act of 1964, which established the Equal Employment Opportunity Commission. Since homosexuals are not identified in the Civil Rights Act, some state and local governments have passed additional laws to protect them. Workers' health and safety are protected by state Workers' Compensation laws, as well as by the Occupational Health and Safety Act of 1970.

Business Ethics

9. **List the three questions that can help focus attention on ethical business conduct.** The three questions are: Is it legal? Is it fair? How do I feel about it? The first question refers to more than a literal interpretation of the law; rather, it goes to the spirit of the law. The second question forces the decision maker to consider the needs of the stakeholders and to avoid zero-sum situations. The third focuses on the individual's personal morality.

10. **Describe the content and purpose of an ethics statement and list four management techniques for reinforcing ethical behavior.** An ethics statement identifies the business's ethical principles in terms of purpose, pride, patience, persistence, and perspective. It serves as a template for employee behavior and should be advocated foremost by top management as a model for employees at all levels. Four techniques for reinforcing ethical behavior are: Don't reward unethical behavior, create departments of ethics and law, provide legal and ethics training, and provide ethical leadership.

Doing Well by Doing Good

11. **Discuss ways of encouraging socially responsible behavior in a business.** Socially responsible behavior flows from leaders who encourage accountability, honesty, and trust; fair treatment and respect for differences; and up-front dealings with customers. Similarly, public-service partnerships enable businesses to benefit stakeholders and society at large while still making a profit.

✓ Key Terms

business ethics **101**	price fixing **106**	discrimination **110**	copyrights **116**
business law **101**	bid rigging **106**	contract law **112**	patents **116**
ethical management **102**	deregulation **106**	usury laws **112**	trade secrets **117**
stakeholders **102**	tying contracts **107**	tort law **113**	zero-sum game **119**
good faith **102**	interlocking directorate **107**	workplace diversity **114**	ethics statement **122**
social responsibility **104**	consumerism **108**	sex discrimination **114**	moral muteness **124**
social audit **104**	implied warranty **108**	glass ceiling **114**	public-service partnerships **128**
statutory law **106**	express warranty **108**	sexual harassment **114**	ethics screen **128**
administrative law **106**		trademarks **116**	
common law **106**			

• Review Questions

1. Employees of any business must make many decisions and take many actions during the average work week. What portion of these decisions and actions—most, some, or only a few—are likely to have a legal dimension, requiring some knowledge of business law?

2. What portion of a typical business employee's actions and decisions are likely to have an ethical dimension?

3. How is common law created?

4. Why does the U.S. government pass laws such as the Sherman Antitrust Act and the Robinson-Patman Act?

5. If a business developed a vaccine that promised to prevent infection by the AIDS virus, what regulatory agency would it have to deal with before it could sell the product in the United States?

6. If the business decided to market its vaccine abroad, in developing countries that lacked regulation of medications, would it be free to pursue profitable sales without considering issues that concern the FDA in the United States (such as side effects and effectiveness)? Explain.

7. Imagine that an employee of one company, while visiting a friend at another company, secretly pockets information about that company's new product plans, which she later gives to her company's product development department. What legal issues are involved? What kind of law? What sort of punishment, if any, might a court impose on her should she be convicted of breaking a law?

8. What are the two fundamental problems of business ethics?

9. Imagine a situation in which your boss suggests that you fire a third of the employees in your department as an easy way to make this year's profits look better. Using the Ethics Check, answer each question and then decide whether you would do it or would object and suggest alternative approaches.

10. Many state and community colleges are downsizing right now because legislatures are calling for cuts in state funding for higher education. Imagine you are a legislator deciding how to vote on a bill that would require a 10 percent cut in the budget for *your* school. To help you decide, you make a list of the stakeholders. Who are they?

• Critical Thinking Questions

1. Managers at Scott Paper Co. fired a third of the company's employees in order to boost profits for its owners. They argued that management has "only one constituency: the shareholders." What view of social responsibility do these managers hold? Do you agree with them? What view would you take in their position?

2. Companies that downsize often find themselves unable to employ all their people profitably because they have fallen into a bad position in their markets. Past strategies did not anticipate all the changes that would occur and so failed to prepare the companies for today's situation. For example, IBM had to cut many jobs because it failed to shift its emphasis soon enough from large, expensive computers to inexpensive portable ones. When looked at in this way, does strategy have an ethical dimension? What responsibilities, to what stakeholders, do you think senior managers have when they make decisions affecting the future direction of their business?

3. Does economics have anything to do with law and ethics? You might not think so at first, but recall that many U.S. laws exist to encourage competition in the economy. Current debate in Washington, D.C., often revolves around this relationship between ethical management on the one hand, and the economic system on the other. Specifically, some politicians believe that regulations to protect consumers, employees, and the environment are bad for the economy because they interfere with the freedom of markets. They believe an economy free of business laws will take care of such problems by itself. Others argue that these regulations were created in the first place because the unhindered operation of the market led to unfair and unethical business practices. Which side do you agree with? Why?

4. Congratulations! You have just been invited to Russia to give advice to policymakers struggling to develop a successful market economy. They tell you that, so far, economic freedom has created a terrible wave of crime and that most businesses now hire armed guards to protect their employees—or to steal from other businesses. They ask you for ideas about how to improve the behavior of businesses and their employees in Russia. Got any?

5. Employees over 40 sometimes feel they are denied access to new jobs or promotions because of their age. Explore the legal and ethical issues in age discrimination. What, if anything, should a company's ethics statement say about the topic?

REVIEW CASE *Butler v. Acme Markets, Inc.* [44]

This lawsuit reached the New Jersey Court of Appeals, which decided in favor of the plaintiff, Helen Butler, and awarded her $3,600 for personal injuries sustained as the result of a criminal attack in an Acme Markets parking lot. It was evening and Butler had been shopping. She rested her grocery bags on the bumper of her car and got out the keys to the trunk. Suddenly a man ran up, hit her, grabbed her purse, and ran away. Butler felt the supermarket had a responsibility to provide a safe parking lot for its customers. The first judge to hear the case said the supermarket was not responsible for her safety, but the appeals court disagreed. There were two reasons for its conclusion:

- In *Brody v. Albert Lifson & Sons*, the New Jersey Court of Appeals had ruled that the business operator has a responsibility to exercise reasonable care to see that customers entering its premises to conduct business have a reasonably safe place in which to do so. And in *Picco v. Fords Diner Inc.*, the same court extended the business proprietor's duty of care to parking lots provided for customer use.

- Acme Markets knew about the risk of criminal attacks on customers but did not take adequate steps to prevent them. There were police records of four previous attacks in the parking lot in recent months. And while the supermarket did employ security guards, the guard on duty that night was assigned to look for shoplifters inside the store and was not patroling the parking lot.

The court concluded that reasonable security measures taken by the supermarket probably would have prevented the attack on its customer, and that there was a resulting legal obligation for it to take those measures.

The court decision addressed an ambiguous area of the law. How far are businesses required to go to protect their customers? For instance, are colleges responsible for protecting their students against rape and other violent crimes? There have been many cases involving such issues, and the outcomes vary depending upon the circumstances, the court, and that famous concern of legal philosophers: what the judge had for breakfast!

1. Which of the three types of laws was or were most important in the judge's decision?
2. Was the grocery store management's behavior in this case consistent with ethical management as defined in the chapter?
3. List the stakeholders who have an interest in the safety of this company's parking lots and the impact that increased lighting and patrols might have on each.
4. Apply the term "implied warranty" to this case. Do customers have expectations about the safety of shopping services provided by stores that might be called an implied warranty?
5. Does the company's responsibility to make a profit include extra spending to make its parking lots safe?
6. Does the company's social responsibility include extra spending to make its parking lots safe?
7. Apply the Ethics Check to the question of whether it is OK for management to ignore the safety of company parking lots. Is it legal? Is it fair? How would you, as a manager, feel about it?
8. If the company had had an ethics statement, do you think it would have taken a different position—one that would have kept it out of court? Discuss.
9. Can you think of any organizations with which a grocery store could form a public-service partnership to help keep its neighborhood safe?

CRITICAL THINKING CASE *Whistle Blowing at Prudential*

Whistle blowers are people who "blow the whistle" to summon the police or other authorities when their employer does something illegal. Now that companies often have training programs in ethics and the law, many employees have strong opinions about what their employers should and should not do. But what happens when some of the people you work with seem to be doing something wrong, and the company lets them get away with it? This creates a dilemma for an ethical employee. Should he or she blow the whistle by complaining to the media or the appropriate governmental authority? Because this often leads to trouble for fellow employees, there may be strong peer pressure not to "snitch." And some companies, fearing negative publicity, try to cover up a problem by firing the whistle blower instead of the people who did wrong. Here is the story of one such whistle blower.

Mark Jorgensen, a manager of real estate funds for the Prudential Insurance Co. of America, discovered fraud in the appraisal of some real estate properties. Managers were raising their value as a way of getting more money from investors. After finding out that his superiors were involved, Jorgensen reported the fraud to the company's legal department. Instead of helping him, the legal department's investigation cleared his superiors. Jorgensen was first pressured to cover up the fraud, then was accused of wrongdoing, and finally was transferred out of the department. After much harassment, he sued Prudential and was promptly fired. But publicity about the lawsuit brought pressure on the company to conduct a second investigation using outside lawyers. They eventually discovered the fraud, and Prudential publicly admitted that Jorgensen had been right all along. Prudential had to compensate him for his loss of employment and also to repay the investors who had been cheated.[45]

1. What was the impact on stakeholders of the fraud at Prudential? Identify the stakeholders, then define the impact, positive and/or negative, on each.

2. If you were in charge of Prudential, what management steps might you take to prevent practices such as the fraud in this case?

3. If you were in charge of Prudential, what might you do to make it easier and less risky for employees to blow the whistle in cases such as this one?

4. What, if any, legal issues do you think might be relevant in the Prudential case?

5. Some people believe there should be federal legislation that prevents whistle blowers from being fired. Do you think such a law would improve the behavior of businesses? Explain your view.

6. If you were advising a friend or family member about the consequences of whistle blowing, what would you tell them to expect?

Critical Thinking with the ONE MINUTE MANAGER

"I think the sales manager's choice is obvious," Carlos argued as he and Joanna discussed the story with the One Minute Manager. "Hiring the competitor's salesman would mean failing the first of the Ethics Check questions—I'm sure it's illegal to use secret information about a competitor's bid on a defense contract. The courts would probably consider it a trade secret. And I'm sure he would never be able to trust that guy, anyway. I would just tell him to go to . . ."

"Not so fast!" Joanna broke in. "What about his boss? The boss implied that this kind of thing was to be expected and that it is necessary for the company right now. I'm sure the sales manager will be in trouble with his boss if he does not hire that salesman. He'll probably be looking for a job next month if he turns this chance down. And I wouldn't take it for granted that the law is clear—there's often a gray area in cases like this. It would be nice to imagine that every sales manager would do the right thing in this situation, but in reality, many of them would probably bow to the pressure and hire the dishonest salesman."

"What do you think?" Carlos asked, appealing to the One Minute Manager.

"I think you're both right. I agree with Carlos that the right decision is fairly clear—not to hire the salesman. But I also agree with Joanna that many employees would end up making the wrong decision anyway, for the simple reason that the company does not encourage ethical decision making in a situation such as this. The pressure is certainly strong for the sales manager to do the wrong thing instead of the right thing, which leads me to think that we can learn the most from this story by answering some simple questions."

1. What advice does the salesman get that might help him do the right thing despite the pressures to the contrary?

2. What steps should this company take to make decisions like the one the sales manager faces easier for employees to make?

3. In this story, there is a clear trade-off in the short term between company profits and individual ethics. Is the situation also a zero-sum game in the *long* term? Explain from both the sales manager's and the company's viewpoints.

5

The Forms of Business

We used to think of businesses as growing gradually from new to old and small to large, just like people. But in today's turbulent business environment, the shape and size a business takes must change often. Its all-important legal form—how it is defined and run in the eyes of the law—may also change as it grows, downsizes, or combines with or separates from other businesses. This means the form the business takes is an important concern, something that can either help it succeed or stand in the way of success. After reading this chapter you will be able to reach the learning goals below.

Learning Goals

1. Describe the advantages and disadvantages of a sole proprietorship.
2. Identify the different forms of partnerships and explain how a partnership is formed.
3. Describe the advantages and disadvantages of a partnership.
4. Briefly review the history of the corporate form of business.
5. Explain how a corporation is formed and describe the four major types of corporations.
6. Describe the advantages and disadvantages of corporations.
7. Explain how the S and limited liability corporations enable small businesses to adopt the corporate form of business.
8. Distinguish between the owners and managers of a corporation.
9. List the five factors to be considered in deciding on the best business form.
10. Explain how a business's strategic form relates to its purpose and actions.
11. Identify the most important forms of business innovations and adaptations, and give an example of each.
12. Differentiate among acquisitions, mergers, and divestitures, and explain the significance of privatization.

At Starbucks, Form Is as Fluid as Coffee

"How do you go from being a single coffee shop in Seattle to a chain of six stores?" the One Minute Manager asked the students. On her desk she rested a coffee cup from the new Starbucks across the street.

"You would need to rent more store space, hire more workers, and buy more equipment and supplies," Carlos thought out loud.

"And it would take money," Joanna added. "You'd have to save it up from your profits or find someone to lend it to you."

"Starbucks Coffee did all those things back in the early 1980s," the One Minute Manager explained. "The company went from a single store at Pike's Place Market in Seattle in 1971 to a chain of six stores by 1987. That business expansion required money. To raise it, Starbucks changed its legal form."

"So businesses have to change their form in order to grow?" Joanna asked.

"Often, they do. It depends on the company's goals. Starbucks went on to add over 300 new stores by 1995. Starbucks outlets from Los Angeles to New York and Dallas to Minneapolis all offer the company's premium coffee. Running a single store is a lot different from running hundreds. To maintain control over the quality of its coffee beans, for example, Starbucks formed closer relationships with coffee producers all over the world and expanded its roasting capabilities in the United States.

"Starbucks also expanded its business scope. The company licensed stores at airports, entered joint ventures with other companies such as PepsiCo, even developed a European-made line of home espresso machines, and this business growth required raising money again. So in 1992 Starbucks changed its legal business form again, this time to become a public corporation. This change in form allows Starbucks to raise money by selling shares of company ownership to the general public. You could buy shares of Starbucks stock now if you wanted to."

"Does changing legal form concern only new or rapidly growing businesses?" asked Joanna.

"Not at all. Even established businesses change their form depending on their goals," the One Minute Manager continued, reaching for the buzzing telephone.

The call seemed important. Carlos and Joanna realized that their time was up, and waved their thanks as they left the One Minute Manager's office.

Legal Forms of Business

Every business was started by someone, who had to name it and decide on its structure. Finding the "right" structure for a business is no easy task, in part because businesses must be fluid enough to respond quickly to new needs and opportunities, growing and shrinking as necessary to remain successful. In this chapter, we begin with a general look at the legal forms a business can take. Then, in Chapters 6 and 7, we look more closely at two special kinds of businesses, the entrepreneurial business and the small business. We begin here with the three standard legal forms of business: *sole proprietorships*, *partnerships*, and *corporations*.

Sole Proprietorships

A **sole proprietorship** is a business with only one owner, who bears full responsibility for its legal obligations and its compliance with the law. The owner of the business usually adopts a business name, signified by the initials *d.b.a.* (doing business as). Thus, Tom Jones may be d.b.a. Tom Jones Appliance Repair. All he must do is publish his d.b.a. in the local newspaper. The law makes no distinction between Tom Jones the man and the business known as Tom Jones Appliance Repair. Everything the business has—capital, stock in trade, money, and debts—is the owner's. And everything the owner has—home, automobile, sailboat, savings account, and vacation cottage—is inseparable from the business. And that brings us to the next topic: the advantages and disadvantages of this form of business.

1. Describe the advantages and disadvantages of a sole proprietorship.

Advantages of Sole Proprietorships

Sole proprietorships have definite advantages that make them best for many small and new businesses. These advantages include pride of ownership, ease of start-up, and flexibility.

Pride of Ownership

A business is far more than a job to its owner. For example, Beverly Antiques gives its owner, Beverly James, access to the excitement of antique shows and the camaraderie of other dealers and allows her to spend time working with the valuable antique furniture she loves.

Ease of Start-up

There is little legal hassle involved in starting up a sole proprietorship—just ensuring that you don't take on a business name already in use, that you have all the licenses you need for the specific type of business you do, and that you meet any national, state, or local codes. Closing the business is easy, too, should that become necessary.

Flexibility

The owner can run the business as he or she sees fit, without having to consult anyone else (within the constraints of ethics and the law). For example, as long as Beverly James keeps accurate records, she can borrow any furniture from her antique business and keep it in her living room for her own personal use instead of selling it. In doing so, she is just taking money out of one pocket and

 sole proprietorship

A business with only one owner, who bears full responsibility for its legal obligations and its compliance with the law.

A Sole Proprietorship

Bill Griffin, d.b.a. Griffin/Ace Hardware, of Santa Ana, California, says that strategies such as extending store hours, creating a 40-hour training program for employees, and expanding his plumbing department to stock hard-to-find fixtures and fittings help him compete with a nearby Home Depot superstore. While the top 25 home-center chains accounted for one third of hardware sales in 1993, most of the 22,000 hardware dealers in the United States are both independent and affiliated with a purchasing collective, such as Ace and True Value, to keep prices low. Mom-and-pop hardware stores like Bill Griffin's also offer customers the advantages of convenience and personal service.

putting it in another. But if she worked for a business with multiple owners, her actions would be both unethical and illegal.

A sole proprietor may also keep any profits the business earns. Again, Beverly James does not need to consult with anyone else if she decides to sell all her inventory from her antiques business and open a country inn. Of course, she must pay taxes on the proceeds of the sale, as on any income, but even here she has some flexibility. She may, for example, decide to plow some of her profits into her new business or to protect a portion of her income from taxation by setting up a retirement fund.

Disadvantages of Sole Proprietorships

Okay, that's the good news. The bad news, as we hinted earlier, is that the owner is solely responsible for everything that goes wrong. If your business gets into debt, you pay. In fact, you may find yourself selling everything you own to pay the individuals to whom the business owes money. In legal terms, this personal responsibility for the debts and actions of the business is termed **unlimited liability**. Because of it, a sole proprietorship can be ruinous to your financial health. Of course, sole proprietors do attempt to shield themselves as much as possible, hiring lawyers to draw up special forms of trusts and buying insurance, much as physicians buy malpractice insurance. Nevertheless, sole proprietors are very exposed. If Beverly James borrows money from a bank to buy antiques and finds she cannot repay the loan through profits from her business, she is still personally responsible for paying back the loan.

Knowing this, banks and other lenders will lend a sole proprietor money only if they are satisfied that the owner's personal wealth more than covers the loan. As most sole proprietors are not rich, the amount they can borrow is small. Even if a sole proprietor has sufficient means to warrant a loan, banks worry that the owner might suddenly quit, die, or run into trouble in what may be a first business venture. A single-owned business seldom outlasts its owner or its owner's interest in its existence, which also contributes to lenders' fears.

Additional disadvantages of this form of business include few fringe benefits, such as group health insurance or paid vacations and sick days. Sole proprietorships also require an enormous time commitment on the part of their owners. Most sole proprietors operate the business themselves, which may translate into overwork, few days off, long hours, and isolation.

unlimited liability

Personal responsibility for the debts and actions of a business.

To most people starting businesses, the benefits of a sole proprietorship, especially its relative simplicity and flexibility, outweigh its disadvantages. Any business designed to *stay* small should be a sole proprietorship. Independent consultants, writers, craftspeople, antique dealers, hair salon owners, shop owners, and sales representatives are all typically sole proprietorships. In fact, the majority of U.S. businesses are sole proprietorships. But for some purposes, a partnership or corporation may be a better legal form.

Partnerships

Partnerships are businesses owned by two or more people under the terms of a written partnership agreement. A partnership resembles a sole proprietorship in most ways, except that it has multiple owners. The law, as set out in the Uniform Partnership Act, defines a partnership as two or more people who voluntarily agree to operate a business as co-owners and are "jointly and severally liable" for everything the business does. This means that if one partner dumps the company's toxic waste in a local forest or runs up huge debts with wholesalers, the other partner cannot say, "It wasn't me!" In the law's eyes, it was. And, as with sole proprietorships, liability is unlimited—the partners are each personally liable for all debts of the business. Before examining the advantages and disadvantages of partnerships, let's look first at forms of partnerships.

Forms of Partnerships

Legal variations on the partnership have been developed in order to alter the sharing of liability. A **general partnership** is a partnership in which co-owners are jointly and separately liable for everything the business does. The general partnership is distinct from two other common forms, limited and master limited partnerships.

In **limited partnerships**, each partner's liability is limited to his or her share in the partnership. Generally, the conditions of limited partnership require that limited partners take no active part in running the business—they just invest money in it.

Master limited partnerships (MLPs) are an arrangement in which one business controls another business from a distance through contractual obligation, not ownership. The controlling corporation may enter into the master limited partnership if it does not want its competitors to know it owns another company. Because the MLP is not owned by the corporation, only controlled by it, its profits are taxed to the partners, not to the corporation. And because it is a separate business, the MLP can be used to raise money from investors for any new project that the company wants to keep separate from its other activities. This is now common in biotechnology, where companies need to raise millions of dollars to develop each new project and product. A separate MLP for each one allows investors to pick the project they like instead of having to invest in the entire company.

Partnership Agreements

Partnerships, like sole proprietorships, can be easily formed. Minimally, you must register the business at the local town hall and take out the necessary licenses. Strictly speaking, no legal document need bind the partners. A simple handshake may be enough, and it often is when the partners know each other well and when the partnership involves little money and is meant to achieve a limited purpose within a short period of time.

2. Identify the different forms of partnerships and explain how a partnership is formed.

 partnership

A business owned by two or more people under the terms of a written partnership agreement.

 general partnership

A business partnership in which co-owners are jointly and separately liable for everything the business does.

 limited partnership

A business in which each partner's liability is limited to his or her share in the partnership.

 master limited partnership (MLP)

An arrangement in which one business controls another business from a distance through contractual obligation, not ownership.

Writing Your Articles of Partnership

Let's imagine you decide to start selling caps and T-shirts at a table in the student center on your campus, and you want to join forces with a friend to share the cost and time requirements. A simple partnership is probably the best form of business to start with, so you decide to draw up an agreement with your friend. What should be covered? Here is a checklist of the major topics included in most articles of partnership:

- Name of partnership
- Purpose of partnership
- Domicile (the mailing address and place of business)
- Partners (who they are; the roles they will play)
- Contributions of partners (both at start-up and during future operations)
- Draws (share of earnings) or salaries of partners
- Rights of continuing partner (what will happen if one partner graduates or leaves campus, for example?)

- Wind-up (how you can end the business)
- Handling of business expenses (will you establish a joint business checking account, for example?)
- Method of accounting and recordkeeping
- Authority of each partner to conduct business (what decisions can each of you make on your own?)
- Settlement of disputes
- Modifying partnership

This may take a lot more thought and planning than you expected! Better get started right away.

Source: Donald Kuratko and Richard Hodgetts, *Entrepreneurship: A Contemporary Approach*, 3d ed. (Fort Worth: Dryden Press, 1995), p. 350.

But as we have seen, there are many forms of partnerships, and they are formed for a variety of reasons. In most cases, partners are bound by a written **partnership agreement**, a legal document setting out the nature of the business and each partner's rights, duties, and responsibilities. These agreements spell out such matters as who gets what, where, when, and how. They state in detail what can happen in the event of irreparable disagreement between the partners or the death, bankruptcy, or retirement of one of them. For instance, they define how the money and valuables will be shared if the business closes for any reason. And they specify how the business's taxes will be paid—something that is often of great importance to the partners.

Generally, partners can come to whatever agreement they think best. They can divide up the business's income any way they like and can contribute property, goods, or special services to the company instead of cash. Whatever their understanding is, however, the terms of it must be written into the partnership agreement. For a sample list of topics covered in most partnership agreements, see the skills check "Writing Your Articles of Partnership."

Advantages of Partnerships

Successful partnerships offer many of the advantages of sole proprietorships with the added benefit of more flexibility. Like proprietorships, partnerships can be very easy to set up. And they allow people to combine forces and do things they could not do on their own. For instance, partnerships are often formed to bring people with money together with people who have a good idea for a new product but cannot afford to make and sell it. Partnerships also offer the advantage of sharing the work and worry with another person.

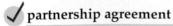
partnership agreement

Legal document setting out the nature of the business and each partner's rights, duties, and responsibilities.

Disadvantages of Partnerships

In a partnership, each partner is responsible not only for his or her own actions but for those of the other partner or partners as well. This unlimited liability is a disadvantage. Let's look at an illustrative case. John Smith and Bill Brown go into partnership together. Brown, behind Smith's back, borrows a huge sum in the partnership's name and disappears. It's a big country. Smith can't turn to his creditors and say, "Hey, that was Bill. I didn't know anything about it!" He must pay back the debt just as though he had borrowed the money himself.

Because of the dangers inherent in unlimited liability, many people who used partnerships in the past, such as doctors, lawyers, and accountants, use them no longer. Now they favor *professional corporations (PCs)* and *service corporations (SCs)*, which are special forms of corporations that offer the tax benefits of partnerships without the full liability.

Partnerships may be between individuals or businesses (the general and limited partnership forms usually involve larger businesses). When individuals form a partnership, personality differences can lead to problems. Disagreements arise in every partnership, and these differences are the cause of the eventual downfall of a majority of them. Two- or three-person partnerships therefore are shorter lived even than sole proprietorships. A good partnership agreement anticipates arguments between partners and prolongs the life of the partnership by helping partners cope with inevitable problems.

Despite the risks involved, many entrepreneurs still enter into partnerships. They are the first choice of start-ups founded by friends and couples, for example, because partnerships offer the flexibility and low start-up costs of sole proprietorships, but they make them available to groups of two or more. For instance, a husband who is a lawyer and a wife who is an accountant would be likely to use a partnership agreement for a business serving the needs of other small business owners in their town. The arrangement would allow them to share clients and ideas, and also to share the profits.

3. Describe the advantages and disadvantages of a partnership.

Corporations

Corporations have been around for a long time. As early as 1600, Queen Elizabeth I granted a group of investors the right to be "one body corporate" in order to trade in India. Similar corporations were formed in the following years for investment in the British colony that would later become the United States. Among those early U.S. corporations were the Virginia Company, the Massachusetts Company, and William Penn's Free Society of Traders in Pennsylvania. Unlike modern corporations such as General Motors and Apple Computer, these early corporations did not compete in free markets. Rather, they were licensed monopolies, with the sole right to trade in a given colony. Nevertheless, they were formed for at least two reasons that are also the foundation of today's large corporations: the need for large amounts of investment and the need to limit an investor's loss to the money he or she has put into the corporation.

The change to competitive business corporations came in around 1811, when New York State adopted a general act of incorporation. By this law, all a businessperson needed for incorporation was a summary description of his intentions. This allowed many corporations to form and compete for business. By the 1850s, other states had followed New York's example. Now, some 150 years later, most midsized and large businesses are corporations.

Today, a **corporation** is a business that has legal rights, privileges, and liabilities separate from those of its owners, the shareholders. As a separate legal entity, a corporation can own property, buy and sell, hire and fire, and do any-

4. Briefly review the history of the corporate form of business.

 corporation

A business that has legal rights, privileges, and liabilities separate from those of its owners, the shareholders.

thing else a human being can lawfully do in business. It can outlive its founders and managers. It can even "marry" other businesses and give birth to spin-offs, as we will see in the final section of this chapter.

A Corporation

Microsoft Corp. is a major player in the information industry, but it's not a giant, Microsoft earned $5 billion in revenues in 1994, less than one tenth the revenues of IBM. Shown here is Microsoft's corporate headquarters in France; international sales accounted for 40 percent of their 1994 revenues.

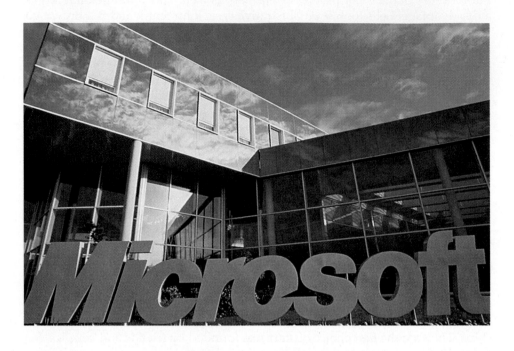

Creating a Corporation

5. Explain how a corporation is formed and describe the four major types of corporations.

Corporations are regulated by the states, and proper forms must be filed with the office of the secretary of state in the state in which the new corporation will be based. Corporations are created, or chartered, by filing **articles of incorporation**, a document describing the organization and naming it. The articles must explain who owns and runs the new company and state its purpose. A new corporation must also submit its **corporate by-laws**, a document defining the procedures for distributing ownership, appointing directors, and running the company.

Types of Corporations

Corporations take many legal forms, but the most important categories are government-owned, private, not-for-profit, and mixed. As their name implies, **government-owned corporations** are owned and usually operated by a government for the benefit of society. They usually perform some specific function, such as providing energy, public transport, or telecommunications. Government-owned corporations are more common in communist and socialist economies than in market economies. In the People's Republic of China, for example, all farms and factories were owned by the government until very recently, and some still are. A further use of government-owned corporations is for political ends. When the oil companies of many nations boycotted South Africa to protest its policy of apartheid, the South African government decided to form a government-owned corporation, SASOL, to produce its own oil from shale. Private companies would not take on such a job because it is not an economical way to produce oil.

Should public schools in the United States be run by private corporations, instead of by government-owned corporations or other public groups? This

✓ articles of incorporation

Document describing the organization and naming it.

✓ corporate by-laws

Document defining the procedures for distributing ownership, appointing directors, and running the company.

✓ government-owned corporation

Organization owned and usually operated by a government for the benefit of society.

idea seems strange to many people, who worry that privately owned corporations will put profits before the needs of students. Yet private businesses have recently been hired to run schools in Minneapolis, Miami, Baltimore, and Hartford. The businesses won the contracts by convincing officials that they could bring superior management skills to the job of administering school districts.[1] This idea of privatizing public forms of business is under consideration in other areas as well. For example, Republican legislators want private for-profit corporations to take over the public Corporation for Public Broadcasting, which supplies programs to local public television and radio stations in the United States. Telecommunications giant Bell Atlantic has already expressed interest in considering this possibility.[2]

Private corporations are owned by private individuals or other private corporations, not by governments. U.S. businesses with "Corp." or "Inc." after their name are most likely to be private corporations. Making money for its owners is generally a key part of the mission of a private corporation.

A **not-for-profit corporation** is a private organization with a public interest goal rather than a profit-making goal. Typical examples include the Salvation Army, Oxfam, and many hospitals, colleges, and libraries. Not-for-profit corporations cannot raise capital from investors who want a return on their investment. Instead, individuals, businesses, and sometimes governments that support the corporation's mission donate money to finance its activities. The Corporation for Public Broadcasting, for example, receives 14 percent of its broadcasting budget from the U.S. government; the remainder comes from private and corporate contributions.

The U.S. government encourages not-for-profits and their work by allowing them to operate without paying taxes and by allowing tax-deductible charitable donations. The law does not prevent these corporations from pursuing some lucrative activities. For example, the National Geographic Society makes money from its magazine, *National Geographic*, which it uses to fund research, exploration, and teaching.

Mixed corporations are established and regulated by a government, but they sell stock to private investors. Mixed corporations are rare in the United States because corporations have more freedom to compete if they are not partially owned by the government. But sometimes the government forms a mixed corporation to fill a gap that private corporations cannot appropriately fill. For example, in 1987 Congress created the Malcolm Baldrige National Quality Award, to be given annually to businesses making the greatest improvements in management. Because Congress wanted private corporations to fund and help run the foundation that administers the award, it formed a mixed corporation. The Foundation for the Malcolm Baldrige National Quality Award receives donations from many private corporations, hires staff and judges, writes the award applications and instructions, and so on. Unlike private or not-for-profit corporations, the foundation is regulated by the government to ensure that applications for the award are judged fairly and impartially.

The Center for Manufacturing Sciences is another mixed corporation set up by the federal government. Its goal is to encourage the formation of learning centers in this country. The center itself is set up as a mixed corporation, and the individual learning centers it spawns are not-for-profit corporations. It illustrates the fact that organizations may be made up of multiple businesses, each with a different form to suit its function. The federal government backed this effort in order to help educate the business community about technological developments in the area of manufacturing.

The majority of corporations are for-profits. Now let's examine some of the advantages and disadvantages of the corporate form for companies that define profit as one of their goals.

Cotton Incorporated

Some corporations exist to promote an idea, organization, or industry. Cotton Incorporated works on behalf of U.S. Cotton farmers, for example. The familiar Cotton Seal is Cotton Incorporated's registered trademark for products made of 100 percent U.S. Cotton.

Ask your instructor how your college is organized. Chances are good that it is either a not-for-profit or a public corporation owned by the state you live in.

 private corporation

Corporation owned by private individuals or other private corporations.

 not-for-profit corporation

Private organization with a public interest rather than a profit-making goal.

 mixed corporation

Corporation that is established and regulated by a government but that sells stock to private investors.

6. Describe the advantages and
disadvantages of corporations.

Advantages of Corporations

The reason so many mid- and large-sized companies incorporate is obvious when one examines the five advantages corporations have over other legal forms of business. Those advantages are ease of raising capital, limits on liability, transferability of shares, duration, and control.

Ease of Raising Capital

Capital is any form of wealth used to produce more wealth. Corporations can raise capital by selling shares of ownership to private investors or to the public. This is a very important advantage, especially in industries that require substantial funds for purchasing goods and supplies.

The process of offering shares to the public is called **going public**. Corporations whose stock is traded on the open market are known as **publicly traded companies**. The U.S. government regulates the public sale of stocks through the Securities and Exchange Commission (SEC). The SEC oversees such sales in an effort to prevent dishonest managers from selling shares of companies without disclosing negative information about those companies. Most governments force corporations selling stock to the public to disclose business information of a most detailed kind. In theory, if investors know what the corporation owns and does, who runs it, and so forth, they can spot problems and avoid bad investments. The decision to go public requires a lot of thought, and not all companies are comfortable with it. For the story of one that chose to remain private, see the doing business box entitled "When Whales Grow Up."

Limits on Liability

If a sole proprietor like Beverly James runs over a pedestrian while delivering products by van, she will be held legally responsible. Few investors would be interested in buying shares if they were liable for all of a company's debts or actions in the same way that a sole proprietor or partner is liable. **Limited liability** protects owners by limiting their legal responsibility to the value of the stock they hold. Hundreds of investors may own small shares in a single corporation, and they do not have sufficient power or knowledge to be active in the management of the business. Corporations also protect employees and owners from personal liability—to a degree. A court of law may still hold the owner-operator of a small corporation personally liable, as it may likewise hold the directors who have ultimate control over larger corporations.

Transferability of Shares

The fact that stock can be sold or transferred means that it can be converted into cash relatively easily, which makes stock an attractive investment. Unlike buildings and partnerships, shares are readily bought and sold. Stockholders dissatisfied with a company's performance can sell their stock whenever they please, as long as a buyer can be found.

Duration of Organization

Unlike a real person, a legal person doesn't die. Directors may die or be replaced, employees may be hired and fired, property may be bought and sold, but throughout these changes the corporation's life continues. This duration does not necessarily translate into stability. In fact, as we saw in Chapter 1, many businesses do die every year, and corporations are among them. Baring Bank had to close down in 1995 when one of its traders lost hundreds of millions of dollars in bad trades out of this British corporation's Singapore offices.

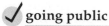 **capital**

Any form of wealth used to produce more wealth.

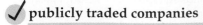 **going public**

Process of offering shares to the public.

publicly traded companies

Companies whose stock is traded on the open market.

 **limited liability**

Limitation of owners' legal responsibility to the value of the stock they hold.

doing business

When Whales Grow Up

When Brad Armstrong and Blake Miller founded Blue Whale Moving Co. in Austin, Texas, in 1989, they must have known what happens to whales when they grow up. They get big. Really big.

By 1995, the business had organized as a privately owned corporation with 68 employees and more than $2 million in revenues. Its owners were interested in going national and growing even more, but they debated the form the business should take as it continued to grow. At first, they thought a transition to a publicly traded corporation would make the most sense. Underwriters, the investment banks that take companies public by selling their stock in compliance with Securities and Exchange Commission regulations, assured the managers of Blue Whale Moving Co. that they could raise tens of millions of dollars to fund a rapid expansion.

But as Blue Whale managers explored this option, they decided to back away from it. As Armstrong explained, "It got pretty scary looking at how much ownership we would have to give up. It's still too much our child to run the risk of losing it." Further, he and Miller were worried that public owners would require more rapid expansion than they thought was wise.

Instead, Armstrong and Miller decided to stay private and to sell franchises in order to expand gradually to 100 locations around the United States. "Franchising gave us the local ownership we felt we needed to maintain our high standard of service," Miller explains. "It will allow us to grow more slowly and spend more time training, and we like that." Which goes to show that there is more than one way to raise a whale. The combination of private ownership and franchise-based expansion proved to be the best form for Blue Whale's current vision and strategies.

Source: Roberta Maynard, "Are You Ready to Go Public?" *Nation's Business,* Jan. 1995, pp. 31, 32.

A corporation that consistently spends more than it earns will be unable to pay its bills. If the corporation ceases to be a moneymaker, its assets will probably be liquidated and after its debts are paid, the proceeds, if any, will be distributed to shareholders in proportion to their holdings.

Control of the Company

In theory, the stockholders who own the company control its management. In reality, the small stockholder does not have much say in anything. Only someone who owns at least 5 percent of a company can hope to influence its managers in major decisions. Stockholders exercise their control indirectly, through an elected board of directors that has the power to set or change the company's vision and mission and to hire and fire the senior managers. This control, combined with limited liability, reduces the risks of ownership.

Disadvantages of Corporations

Corporations also have disadvantages. Founding a corporation is more expensive and complicated than setting up a sole proprietorship or partnership. And because the law requires corporations to file many forms and reports each year to keep government agencies and shareholders informed, far more paperwork is involved in starting up and running a corporation. One consequence of this required filing is that corporations are vulnerable to industrial espionage because the forms and reports, which contain details of their operations, become public information that is available to competitors.

The private corporation must pay taxes on its profits. After paying taxes, it can either reinvest the profits to grow, or it can give them to the owners in the form of dividends. **Dividends** are payments made to stockholders from a corporation's profits. When an owner receives dividends, he or she has to pay per-

dividends

Payments made to stockholders from a corporation's profits.

S corporation

Special type of corporation that enables owners to pay taxes like partners but to have limited liability like shareholders.

limited liability corporation (LLC)

A privately owned for-profit that combines lower C corporation tax rates with the simple structure of an S corporation.

7. Explain how the S and limited liability corporations enable small businesses to adopt the corporate form of business.

sonal income tax on them as well. In other words, stockholders are taxed twice on the same earnings—once as owners of the corporation and again as receivers of dividends.

A final disadvantage is that ownership by numerous distant shareholders means that a corporation's owners do not have the long-term commitment to the company's goals that a sole proprietor or partner might have. When profits dwindle, stockholders head for the nearest exit or attempt to change the company's goals.

Small Corporations

Double taxation can be a hardship for small corporations run by their owners. To make it easier for owners of small businesses to take advantage of the corporate form, the government created a special type of corporation, called an **S corporation**, which enables owners to pay taxes like partners but to have limited liability like shareholders. Unlike other private corporations, the S corporation is not taxed; the partners pay taxes on their share of the corporation's earnings when they file their personal income tax returns with the Internal Revenue Service. S corporations get their name from Subchapter S, the law that established them; the S stands for "small," which is defined as a company with 35 or fewer owners, who must be U.S. citizens. Regular corporations are termed *C corporations*, to differentiate them from S corporations. Figure 5.1 compares S and C corporations.

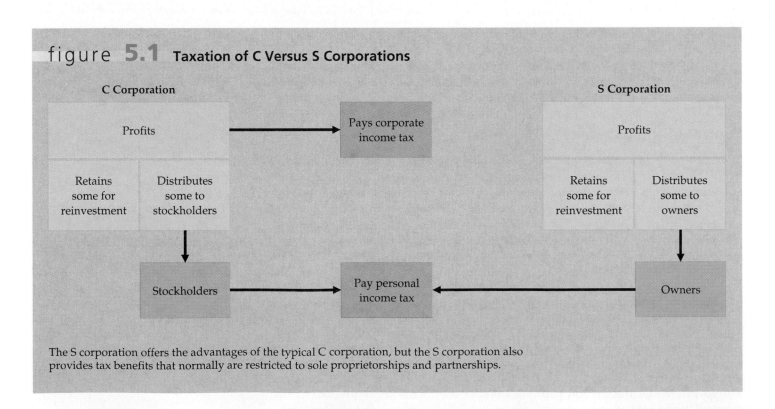

figure **5.1**   **Taxation of C Versus S Corporations**

The S corporation offers the advantages of the typical C corporation, but the S corporation also provides tax benefits that normally are restricted to sole proprietorships and partnerships.

A new legal form for small corporations that is now emerging is the **limited liability corporation (LLC)**, a privately owned for-profit that combines lower C corporation tax rates with the simple structure of an S corporation. Some states are passing laws permitting the limited liability corporation; New York, for example, permitted the form for the first time in 1994.[3] The idea is that real estate, high-technology, and other high-growth businesses will do better if they are formed as limited liability corporations rather than as sole proprietorships or partnerships, and so be encouraged to locate in the states that permit them. The form offers the limited liability of a corporation and is as easy to set up and run as an S corporation, but it pays taxes at lower corporate rates instead of at individual rates. The impact in New York is about a $35 million decrease in taxes collected from such businesses each year—and a corresponding savings for their owners.[4]

LLCs are also increasingly popular in Wyoming, where Robert Shriner, for example, established one to raise money from investment partners to buy a new building for his Cheyenne-based printing company. Traditionally, real estate investors formed general partnerships or standard corporations, but now they favor LLCs because of the protection from liability they provide.[5] Table 5.1 compares forms of business on liability, limits on structure, and taxation.

 board of directors

Elected governing body of a corporation that protects the stockholders' interests by setting policy and selecting top management.

 chief executive officer (CEO)

The person hired by the board of directors who is responsible for all of a company's operations and management decisions.

---

t a b l e 5.1 How Forms of Business Compare on Liability, Limits on Structure, and Taxation

Business Advantage	Sole Proprietorship	Partnership		Corporation		
		General Partnership	Limited Partnership	C Corporation	S Corporation	Limited Liability Corporation
Limited liability?	No	No	Only limited partners	Yes	Yes	Yes
Partners restricted?	Yes	No	No	No	Yes	No
Profits double-taxed?	No	No	No	Yes, if distributed	No	No

Who Runs the Corporation?

A small corporation may be run by its owner or owners, but larger corporations are formally governed by a board elected or appointed to represent the owners. Managers are in turn hired by these directors.

The Board of Directors and Management

Stockholders own the corporation, but they delegate their managerial rights to a board of directors, which they elect. The **board of directors** sits at the peak of the corporate pyramid, and its job is to protect stockholders' interests. It selects the corporation's top management and sets the organization's broadest policies, including its dividend policy.

The board of directors appoints the corporation's officers, who are the legal representatives of the corporation. They typically include a treasurer, secretary, and chair of the board of directors. The board also hires a **chief executive officer (CEO)**, the person responsible for all operations and management decisions in the company. The CEO, in turn, delegates responsibility to other managers and employees. CEOs often sit on the board as directors and sometimes even as chairs of the board; boards of directors and CEOs may share much of the power

8. Distinguish between the owners and managers of a corporation.

Chapter 8 discusses the role of management in detail.

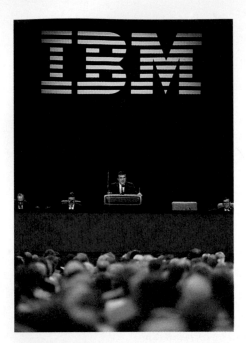

Stockholders Own the Corporation

All share owners are welcome at IBM stockholders' meetings, but those with the most shares cast the most votes.

institutional investors

Public and private organizations that buy stock on behalf of large institutions.

subsidiary company

A company whose stock is wholly or partly owned by another corporation.

holding company

A company that owns most or all of a subsidiary's stock but takes no part in its management.

parent company

A company that holds most or all of a subsidiary's stock and also takes a direct role in managing the subsidiary.

and responsibility for directing the company. In practice, major decisions concerning the corporation are made by a vote of the full board of directors or by special committees empowered by the board.

The board of directors leaves most day-to-day management decisions to the CEO and other senior managers, but it must generally approve any large expenditures or important changes in strategy or form. Board members take an active interest in any issues of importance to the long-term survival and success of the corporation. A recent survey indicates that directors are greatly concerned with ensuring that stockholders make good money from their investments. They are also interested in the development of the next generation of senior managers, in the selection of strategies, and in the company's competitiveness and the quality of its products and services.[6]

Institutional Investors

In theory, stockholders have the last word in running the corporation they own, but in practice—especially in very large corporations—stockholders usually accept the management's say on long- and short-term policy. Stockholder meetings are *not* based on "one person, one vote"; rather, the rule is usually one unit of stock, one vote. This means that investors who hold large blocks of shares have more say in running the company than those with only a few shares. Very often those investors are **institutional investors**—a broad spectrum of public and private organizations that buy stock on behalf of large institutions such as universities, pension funds, insurance companies, and a host of charitable and research foundations. Institutional investors are increasingly important; they already own more than half the stock of the leading U.S. corporations. According to the American Bar Association, they have recently become so active that they can now exert a strong influence on managers.[7] For example, when institutional investors disapprove of how a company is managed, they can fire senior managers or influence their policies through the threat of dismissal. Chief executive officers at IBM and American Express were booted out by their boards when the companies failed to perform well. As the power of institutional investors increases, managers are losing some of their traditional independence and are being held more accountable to shareholders. Figure 5.2 summarizes the decision-making structure in large corporations.

Corporate Owners

As we noted earlier, corporations can be parents, and when they are, the "child" is called a **subsidiary company**—a company whose stock is wholly or partly owned by another corporation. The corporate owner is generally either a holding company or a parent company. The difference is simply in the extent and nature of the control. A **holding company** owns most or all of the subsidiary's stock but takes no part in its management. Holding companies often are investment firms that buy stocks for income returns and future growth. In contrast, a **parent company** holds most or all of the subsidiary's stock, but it also takes a direct role in managing the subsidiary.

Large corporations create many subsidiaries corresponding to the many different business activities they wish to pursue. Each has its own articles of incorporation, specifying how it will be owned and run and for what purpose. For example, you may see the Consolidated Freightways name on trucks all across the United States, but Consolidated Freightways in fact owns no trucks directly. Instead, this parent company—headquartered in Palo Alto, California—has a long-haul trucking subsidiary in nearby Menlo Park. The parent company also owns regional trucking subsidiaries around the country and an-

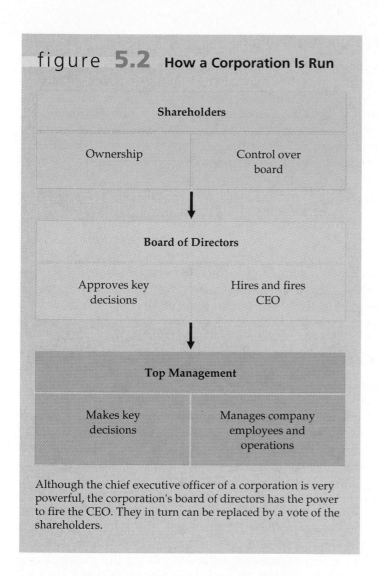

figure **5.2**   **How a Corporation Is Run**

Although the chief executive officer of a corporation is very powerful, the corporation's board of directors has the power to fire the CEO. They in turn can be replaced by a vote of the shareholders.

other subsidiary that specializes in air freight. In all, the parent company is owner or part owner of more than 30 subsidiaries. As might be expected, the form of such a company is extremely complex.

Choosing the Best Business Form

Let's say you have a great idea and want to start your own business. You have read enough to have a general understanding of the legal forms of business. How do you decide which one is best for you? According to the J.K. Lasser Tax Institute, five key factors can help in determining which legal form makes the most sense for a start-up venture.[8]

9. List the five factors to be considered in deciding on the best business form.

Personal Liability

Sole proprietorships are exposed to the greatest risk of liability in the event of litigation. Defective products or poorly rendered services result in thousands of lawsuits every year. Corporations offer owners the greatest protection against personal liability. And the new limited liability corporation combines this protection with the single taxation of a sole proprietorship or partnership.

draw

Distribution of business earnings to an owner.

Keeping the Business Competitive

Jim Koch, founder of the Boston Beer Company, incorporated his family's generations-old brewing business. Along with the change in business form, Koch emphasized premium quality and global markets. One result: The company's Samuel Adams lager is the only U.S. beer imported by Germany, the world's toughest beer market.

Drawing Profits from the Business

It is especially easy for owners of sole proprietorships and partnerships to take draws against the firm's earnings. A **draw** is a distribution of business earnings to an owner. In a corporation, shareholders receive dividends at the discretion of the board of directors. In many companies most of the profits are reinvested, so dividends alone will not make shareholders wealthy. The other way that owners of a corporation can tap into corporate profits is to sell off shares of stock if they have become more valuable since they were purchased.

Amount of Taxes Paid

In a sole proprietorship or partnership, the business's income is generally treated as personal income to the owners. As we pointed out earlier, however, a form of double taxation exists for C corporations, though not for S corporations. The IRS treats the S corporation's income like that of a sole proprietorship or partnership. C corporations, however, pay taxes on their earnings, and the stockholders pay capital gains taxes when they sell shares of stock and pay personal income tax on their dividends.

Availability of Capital

If you do not need to raise very much money, a sole proprietorship may be the way to go. If you cannot go it alone, then consider joining with other individuals in a partnership. If you require large amounts of capital at start-up, it may be wise to incorporate and sell shares of stock to raise funds. But note that most new businesses do not have enough customers and revenues to look like good investments to the public. New businesses are hard to take public.

Management Style

The more owners a business has, the less control any one owner will have. If you want total control of all aspects of your business, you may want to consider a sole proprietorship. Partnerships dilute authority among the partners, and decisions must necessarily be reached by consensus. Ownership of a corporation may be spread among thousands of shareholders. Even the founder of a corporation can be ousted by the board of directors or shareholders, and this happens fairly frequently when there is a difference of opinion about how to run the business.

Questions about the best business form are asked periodically in any business—and the answers may change as the business changes. As a result, the company's legal form may be altered to keep the business competitive. Additionally, there are other ways to define, and alter, the form of a business—ways that are less important legally but equally important competitively. We look at form from another perspective in the following section.

Keeping the Form of the Business Competitive

Businesses change constantly, adjusting to different circumstances, conditions, and demands, and their form must change along with them. Businesses usually start small. As they grow, they may go from sole proprietorship to partnership, or from partnership to corporation. They may develop extended networks of

Family Limited Partnerships

One of the newest and fastest growing variations on the partnership form is the family limited partnership. It is generally used to put a family-owned business into a partnership in which the parent who founded and manages the business is the general partner, and the founder's children become owners as limited partners. This arrangement transfers ownership to the next generation less expensively than would be the case if a corporation or sole proprietorship were left to them in a parent's will. The advantage stems from the way the Internal Revenue Service (IRS) taxes the children. If the children inherit the business outright, the IRS imposes estate taxes based on a fair market valuation of the family business: the figure it would sell for. But if individual children own minority shares as limited partners, the IRS reasons that no one child could easily sell his or her minority share (assuming the family business is privately held, not publicly traded). Using this reasoning, an individual's share of the business is worth something less than it would be if that person could sell his or her share at market value. The IRS has typically allowed a discount of about 30 percent, meaning the heirs save 30 percent on taxes when they inherit the family business at the death of the founding parent.

So far, nothing about this arrangement raises ethical questions. But some people are beginning to view family limited partnerships as a tax loophole for all sorts of other uses. Partnerships are being formed to obtain tax discounts on family possessions like a fancy summer house or even the financial savings of a wealthy family member. And some of these partnerships claim discounts as high as 60 percent, double the typical savings. So far, the IRS has not targeted these partnerships for audits, so no one is really sure where the legal boundaries lie. But it is clear that the more extreme forms of partnership violate the spirit of this law, even if they do not always bring the IRS down on the necks of the partners.

What do you think? Should families push this new form of partnership to its limits in order to minimize inheritance taxes? Or is there an ethical argument against trying to take advantage of loopholes in the law? And what about the legal side—do you think the IRS might change its attitude and start policing family limited partnerships more aggressively?

Source: Mary Rowland, "Keeping It in the Family," *Nation's Business*, Jan. 1995, pp. 563–564.

collaborating companies, suppliers, and distributors. They may seek financing for expansion through a sale of stock to the public, becoming corporations in the process. They may also buy other companies, spin off units, combine forces with other companies, and so on.

Sometimes these changes are driven by increasing size, but often businesses grow in ways other than size. They may need to become more expert in a certain area or to move their operations into a new market. Whatever the cause, form must change often. The most common methods for changing the form of a business fall into two broad categories: external and internal reorganization. Internal reorganization is covered in depth in Chapter 9, Organizational Design.

Strategic form is the external organization, or form, needed to implement a strategy successfully. It is related to an organization's competitive needs—the advantages and disadvantages of being big or small, located in the United States or abroad, and other similar matters.

The organization's *social form* is a reflection of its role in society. A business formed, run, and owned by minority managers plays an important role in the social and economic elimination of oppression, for example. As we shall see in Chapter 7, federal, state, and local governments sometimes offer special encouragement in the form of loans, contracts, or other privileges to businesses that play an important social role, such as family-owned businesses. The ethics check entitled "Family Limited Partnerships" outlines an ethical question that arises in one such situation.

Let's examine the relationship between strategy and form in detail, and then we'll look at the ways form can be changed.

Strategic Form: Purpose and Actions

10. Explain how a business's strategic form relates to its purpose and actions.

What purpose does a business have? In other words, why does it exist? Some businesses exist to make a monetary profit for their owners. Others—not-for-profits, like the Salvation Army—exist to help the homeless, to protect the environment, or for some similar reason.

Businesses define their purpose through a *vision*, or view of why they exist, and a *mission*, or statement of how they will pursue that vision. Mission flows from vision, and together they give the business its purpose. The purpose is translated into specific actions through a set of *strategies*, or general guidelines for accomplishing a mission. Strategies are typically written down in a plan every six months to a year, as it can take that long to accomplish them.

At Maytag, the vision is described as "switching from a defensive to an offensive position." Instead of waiting for customers to complain, for example, the company should improve so fast that customers praise it. That's offensive instead of defensive. But it can be hard to see what specific actions are needed to turn a vision into reality. So Maytag also has a mission statement containing six simple principles (see Figure 5.3). These principles provide clear pointers on how to achieve the company's vision. And every year, its employees break into groups to develop specific strategies that work toward and support the principles and vision. These strategies guide employees in their efforts to improve quality, increase customer satisfaction, and undertake other offensive efforts to improve their company. The strategies also shape the form of the business.

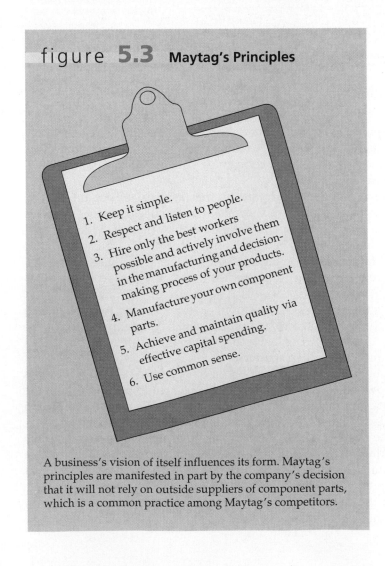

figure **5.3**   **Maytag's Principles**

1. Keep it simple.
2. Respect and listen to people.
3. Hire only the best workers possible and actively involve them in the manufacturing and decision-making process of your products.
4. Manufacture your own component parts.
5. Achieve and maintain quality via effective capital spending.
6. Use common sense.

A business's vision of itself influences its form. Maytag's principles are manifested in part by the company's decision that it will not rely on outside suppliers of component parts, which is a common practice among Maytag's competitors.

For instance, let's say Maytag wants to start making a particular component part, instead of buying it from another company, so that it can have more control over its quality. This strategy might require a new factory, a new building, more employees, new equipment, and so forth. How should these additions be made? Will the company have to grow? Will it need to raise money from investors through a limited partnership? Or should it buy out a manufacturer of the part or close one of its own U.S. factories? These are *form* decisions, and they have to be answered to implement the strategy.

The specific actions a business takes on a daily or weekly basis are designed to accomplish its strategies. They range from developing a new product or service to selling it, and from hiring employees to paying bills. These are called *tactics*, detailed descriptions of actions needed to implement strategies. The terms may become clearer if you think of their military origins: Strategy is the overall battle plan; tactics are the detailed movements of troops and supplies needed to implement that plan.

What does a business's form have to do with its vision, mission, strategies, and tactics? Form has to be consistent with all of these so that the business can accomplish them in the most efficient manner possible, as shown in Figure 5.4. For example, an organization like the Salvation Army, whose vision is to benefit society, should have a legal form appropriate to this purpose—the not-for-profit corporation.

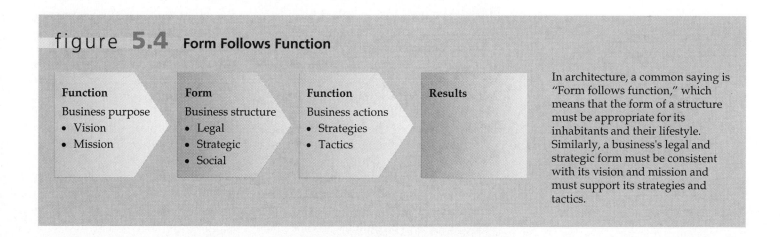

figure **5.4**   **Form Follows Function**

Function	Form	Function	Results
Business purpose	Business structure	Business actions	
• Vision	• Legal	• Strategies	
• Mission	• Strategic	• Tactics	
	• Social		

In architecture, a common saying is "Form follows function," which means that the form of a structure must be appropriate for its inhabitants and their lifestyle. Similarly, a business's legal and strategic form must be consistent with its vision and mission and must support its strategies and tactics.

Form should be consistent with a company's actions as well as its purpose. A for-profit business that intends to sell clothing by catalog, for instance, must buy clothes, photograph them, design and print a catalog, and mail the catalog to appropriate consumers. Then the catalog business must respond to telephone and mail requests for its products by verifying its customers' credit card information and finding and shipping the items ordered. These key actions demand certain facilities and capabilities. The business may wish to buy or rent facilities in which its products are warehoused and from which they are shipped, for example. At any one time there will be better and worse ways to organize and shape the business to do these jobs. The form the business takes makes a big difference in how well it can accomplish its function.

One strategic form, the so-called gazelle, emerged as the most successful type of business in the 1990s. **Gazelles** are fast-growing businesses that consistently increase their sales by 15 percent or more a year. They are too small to be on the list of the 500 biggest companies—they average only 60 employees, compared with tens of thousands at many big companies. They are young and usu-

 gazelle

A fast-growing business that consistently increases its sales by 15 percent or more a year.

ally are formed by experienced employees from larger organizations who have all the connections and know-how needed to make their ideas bear fruit in a hurry. And they focus on a specific opportunity of which other businesses have failed to take full advantage. Gazelles make up only 4 percent of U.S. businesses, but they create 70 percent of all the new jobs in the U.S. economy. Compare this to the big businesses, which have cut 4.4 million jobs since 1980![9] Less is now more when it comes to strategic form, and many big businesses are frantically trying to scale down or break up into smaller units in order to achieve the success of the gazelles.

When you realize that form is essential to function, you can see that the form a business takes makes a big difference in whether it is successful. A small business cannot successfully implement a strategy that requires millions of dollars and thousands of people—not unless it expands first or joins forces with a big business.

Innovations and Adaptations

11. Identify the most important forms of business innovations and adaptations, and give an example of each.

The strategic needs of businesses are sometimes best met by adapting conventional legal forms in innovative ways. Here we examine some of the most important adaptations of the conventional forms of business.

Networks

Business networks are linked businesses that cooperate to achieve a common purpose. They are increasing in popularity because networks of smaller businesses are more flexible and fast-moving than a single, large business. The networking idea originated in Japan, where groups of businesses operate in close-knit family groups called *keiretsus*. For instance, Toyota is part of a *keiretsu* that includes banks from which it can borrow money, suppliers from which it can buy parts, and even insurance companies from which employees can get health insurance. The many businesses in this network favor other members over outsiders, helping each other out and making all of them more competitive as a result.

Computer technology makes it possible to build business networks among far-flung companies. Jim Manzi, chief executive of U.S. software maker Lotus Development Corp., says American and European companies are now forming what he calls "computer *keiretsus*." They use computer networks, electronic mail, databases, and portable computers to communicate across company and national boundaries. For instance, Compaq Computer networks with the dozens of distributors that sell its products through a single software program that they all use in common. As a result, everyone at each of the companies can communicate quickly and easily via computer.[10] New technologies make it possible to build networks that bind many businesses together into a shared form and purpose.

Strategic Alliances

Another innovation in form is also spreading from Japan. Toshiba Corp. was one of the first companies to make heavy use of the strategic alliance, which, as you may recall from Chapter 3, is an agreement between organizations that may or may not involve ownership. These long-term collaborations with another company to implement a shared strategy are based on relationships that are fewer and tighter than in a *keiretsu* or other network. Toshiba has long-term relationships with Motorola, Apple Computer, Sun Microsystems, and General Electric in the United States; with Olivetti and Rhone-Poulenc in Europe; and with many Japanese businesses as well. Toshiba's president speaks regularly by

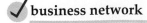

business network

Linked businesses that cooperate to achieve a common purpose.

telephone with GE's president and with the officers of the other companies. Teams of employees from the companies collaborate on jointly funded projects. Strategic alliances are in essence partnerships between pairs of companies that can accomplish more by joining forces than either could accomplish on its own. They are not, however, legal partnerships.

Customer-Owned Businesses (Cooperatives)

A **cooperative**, or customer-owned business, is a business owned by a group of individuals working toward some common economic goal. The goal may be to purchase products for the use of the members or to market the products produced by the cooperative. Although the co-op members elect a board of directors from among themselves, the board rarely plays an active management role. Instead, much like any other board of directors, it usually appoints managers who run the business.

Of the many co-ops in this country, farmers' cooperatives are among the most important. Here a number of small farmers join together to become more competitive while preserving their independence. Many of these cooperatives—such as Sunkist, Associated Mills, and Ocean Spray—have become household names. Customer-owned power companies are another common form of U.S. co-op. They supply 10 percent of the country's power to 25 million customers and earn $20 billion yearly. Northern Virginia Power, for example, supplies energy to some 70,000 consumer members over 3,700 miles of power lines.

Student cooperatives can be found on almost every college campus. (The oldest is the Harvard Coop, founded in the 1880s.) Robert Cox, executive director of North American Students of Cooperation, says student co-ops have low failure rates: "Once the student co-ops get big enough to hire a full-time staff person to provide continuity, they tend to be incredibly resilient."[11]

Employee-Owned Businesses

The employee-owned business does not have separate, independent investors as owners. This means its board and senior managers represent employees, not independent stockholders. And it means the board's usual focus on profits for stockholders is replaced by concern for the employees. Employee ownership therefore is far more likely to create the kind of work environment that employees prefer and in which they are most productive.

Employee-owned businesses may be organized as private corporations that happen to be owned by the employees. This is often the case with small businesses in which the founders are the owners and also the main employees. For instance, many small retail stores are owned and run by one individual.

However, these conventional private corporations do not always create the kind of work environment that benefits all employees equally. The owner-manager of a small business often puts his or her own interests above those of other employees. An alternative approach has therefore been developed to ensure long-term trust and commitment between employees and the business. *Collective ownership* is defined as equal ownership of the business and equal say in decision making by all employees, with no ownership or say by anyone else. Collective businesses may be incorporated as for-profits or as not-for-profits, or they may be set up using partnership agreements. They are run according to a set of principles and guidelines that generally give current employees equal control over decisions and equal claim on the profits. Typically, all important decisions are made by consensus at weekly meetings of employees. And employees decide whom to hire, when to add new equipment or products, and what strategies to pursue.

 cooperative

Business owned by a group of individuals working toward some common economic goal.

Employee Ownership

In 1994, United Airlines became the largest employee-owned company on Earth. Its 55,000 employee-owners launched an advertising campaign to let air travellers know that United's management is always within easy reach of the customer.

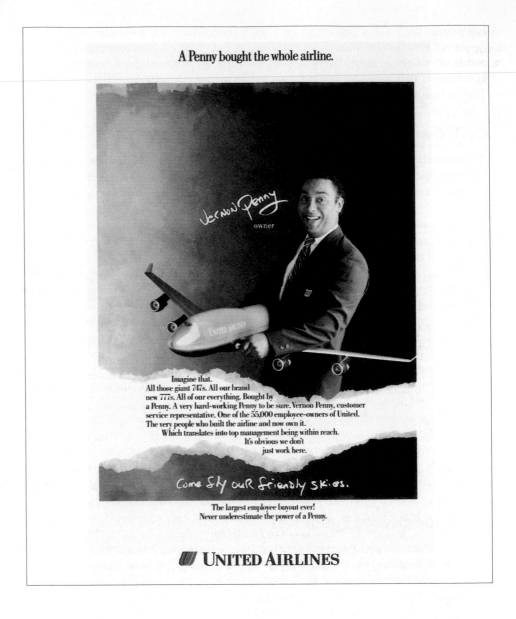

In practice, employee ownership is implemented in varying degrees and does not always go as far as full collective ownership. In the current era of downsizings and employee cutbacks, employees' needs are more likely to be in conflict with shareholders' needs than in the past. As a result, many employees are pushing their employers to adopt employee ownership and to give them at least partial control over the governance of the business.

Many of IBM's plants have been shut down and their employees laid off in a series of cost-cutting efforts designed to help keep the price of the company's stock as high as possible. But while these cutbacks may benefit stockholders, they do not benefit the employees. When IBM announced that its Brooklyn, New York, subsidiary, Advanced Technical Solutions, Inc. (ATS), would have to be shut down, the employees got together and bought the company for $6.5 million, making it one of the largest employee-owned corporations in the country. As the new president of the company said, "What we have been able to accomplish is unprecedented. This was possible because IBM was willing to negotiate and public officials were concerned with fostering job and business development among minorities."[12] Apart from being owned by its employees, ATS operates like any other business. To succeed in the tough computer market, it has slashed wages and benefits 15 to 20 percent from the top down. However, ATS employees get stock equaling 10 percent of their annual salaries and wages for the first five years of operation. In the president's words, "The more we sweat, the more we get."[13]

Collective Copies, of Amherst, Massachusetts, is a classic collective in which each worker in the company is also an owner, and each owner is a worker.[14] The by-laws that govern membership in Collective Copies specify that a worker must stay for at least four months before he or she gets an invitation to join. If a worker leaves, the process starts all over with someone new. Collective ownership suffers from many of the disadvantages of partnerships, in that much depends on the owners getting along together. Collective Copies, however, shows that businesses of this kind can endure. Established more than 10 years ago, the photocopy shop has expanded steadily and now earns over $600,000 in annual sales. Its employees take home more of its earnings, have more say in its management, and as a result are more committed and motivated than employees at its more conventional competitors.

In the coming years, we can expect to see many more experiments in employee ownership. Right now it is making inroads in steel and airlines, two industries in which overcapacity and fierce global competition are making conventional forms of business unprofitable for many companies. Algoma, one of Canada's largest steel mills, switched over to employee ownership and is now recovering from a brush with death.[15] And, while they are generally too small to make business headlines, collectives like Collective Copies are also growing in number.

Changing Form Through Acquisitions, Mergers, Divestitures, and Privatization

The most dramatic changes in form often are the ones that result from the purchase of one business by another, the merging of two businesses, or the sale of a business to new owners. This section examines the legal and practical mechanisms by which major changes in ownership are adopted by, or forced upon, a business.

12. Differentiate among acquisitions, mergers, and divestitures, and explain the significance of privatization.

Acquisitions

Acquisition is the outright purchase of one corporation by another corporation, either in whole or in part. Chemicals maker Hoechst AG of Germany bought U.S. chemicals maker Celanese Corp., then combined Celanese with Hoechst's own U.S. subsidiary. The result was Hoechst Celanese Corp., now a leading U.S. chemicals company with more than a dozen of its own subsidiaries—including some formed from other companies that *it* bought.

In some acquisitions, the whole company is purchased; in others, only part of the company is purchased. When a business considers the purchase of a failed company, it will usually stipulate that the purchase is made on the condition that the buyer will not be responsible for the seller's debts.

Mergers

In a **merger**, two corporations combine to become one company. An example is the merger of Switzerland's two major chemical giants, Ciba and Geigy, into one gigantic corporation, Ciba-Geigy, which has 70,000 employees in Switzerland and abroad. Another merger, even more international in character, was that of Sweden's ASEA Svetsmekano AB and Switzerland's huge electro-mechanical manufacturing company, Brown-Boveri-Baden AG, into ABB Asea

 acquisition

The outright purchase of one corporation by another corporation, either in whole or in part.

 merger

The combining of two corporations into one company.

Brown Boveri Ltd., which has branches worldwide. Mergers tend to be good for business, but bad for names!

Mergers can take place not only between for-profit private corporations but also between not-for-profit corporations, such as hospitals and nursing homes. Recently, Peter Bent-Brigham Hospital of Boston merged with Boston's Women's Hospital, itself the result of a previous merger. These were friendly mergers, meaning that each institution agreed that the merger would be to their mutual benefit. As we shall see shortly, mergers can also be hostile, with one company forcing the merger by buying up the stock of the other company.

As shown in Figure 5.5, mergers generally take place to accomplish one of three objectives: vertical integration, horizontal integration, or conglomeration. Companies integrate or merge vertically by joining with other companies involved in different parts of their production, distribution, or marketing processes. They integrate horizontally when two companies selling similar products or services merge, as in the Ciba-Geigy case mentioned earlier.

figure **5.5** **Three Types of Mergers**

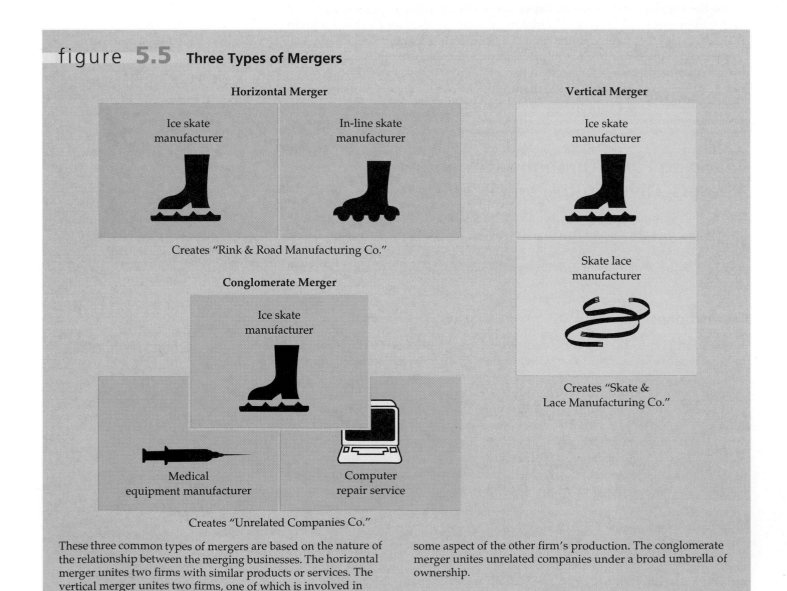

These three common types of mergers are based on the nature of the relationship between the merging businesses. The horizontal merger unites two firms with similar products or services. The vertical merger unites two firms, one of which is involved in some aspect of the other firm's production. The conglomerate merger unites unrelated companies under a broad umbrella of ownership.

Conglomerate mergers, sometimes called "mergers for growth," unite a number of unrelated companies and combine them into one big company. Conglomerate mergers enjoyed a boom in the 1960s; most of them were friendly and accomplished by simple exchanges of stock. The conglomerate bubble burst with the stock market collapse of 1970 and the recession that followed. Nowadays very few conglomerate mergers occur.

In the 1980s mergers called *hostile takeovers*—the business equivalent of war—became popular. The rooms where these were planned were often called "command centers" or "war rooms." The takeovers were accomplished by one company or wealthy individual offering shareholders so much money that they all sold their shares. The new owner would then break up the company and re-form it into many smaller businesses, each of which could then be sold to other investors. The trick was for the new owner to make more money selling parts of the company than it had spent to acquire the whole company.

Hostile takeovers are made possible by the ability of corporations or wealthy individuals to borrow large amounts of money. Without this debt as a lever, most businesses would not be able to afford to buy other businesses.

Divestitures

Divestiture is the process of selling a subsidiary or other unit. Divestitures have little of the high drama of mergers; in fact, they often follow mergers. The large debt required to acquire other companies sometimes forces businesses to sell off their strongest (and therefore most valuable) subsidiaries in order to raise cash and make loan payments. In addition, many businesses now use divestiture to get out of mature or overly competitive markets so they can focus on the fastest growing parts of their business.

Privatization

The collapse of communism in Eastern Europe and the poor performance of state-run enterprises in the West have focused attention on **privatization**—selling government-owned businesses to private owners. Privatization gives entrepreneurs opportunities and tends to improve the entire business environment. Countries launching privatization programs usually find that the performance of the remaining government-owned businesses improves along with that of the private sector.

However, privatization often proves to be far from simple. Most state-run businesses in the former Soviet Union, for example, are inefficient and run down. The equipment is largely obsolete, and the businesses often suffer from pollution problems, inept management, and a demoralized work force. Some critics of current methods of privatization argue that they do not go far enough because the result is often mixed corporations instead of private corporations. A large proportion of the industries of Eastern Europe, for instance, are only partially privatized. The government not only retains a substantial stake but imposes such heavy bureaucratic barriers that privatization produces neither greater productivity nor greater competitiveness.

In addition, privatizing monopolies without adding new competitors achieves little more than a formal change of ownership. For instance, New Zealand privatized the postal system but left its monopoly intact. Finally, privatization may reduce competition instead of increasing it as intended. When Britain privatized British Airways, the company bought out Caledonian Airways, reducing the number of both domestic and international airlines.[16]

 divestiture

The process of selling a subsidiary or other unit.

 privatization

Selling government-owned businesses to private owners.

As we stated in Chapter 1, the form that a business will take is one of the key considerations when starting a new business or applying entrepreneurial vision to turn an old business around. In the next chapter, we see how entrepreneurs form and grow their businesses. Many new businesses remain small, never needing the larger and more complex corporate forms we reviewed in this chapter. But right now, these small businesses are of particular importance to the U.S. economy, so Chapter 7 ends Part 2 by focusing on the unique aspects of the small form of business.

Reviewing *The Forms of Business*

Sole Proprietorships

1. **Describe the advantages and disadvantages of a sole proprietorship**. Sole proprietorships have the advantages of pride of ownership, ease of start-up, and flexibility. The disadvantages include unlimited liability, few fringe benefits, and an enormous time commitment.

Partnerships

2. **Identify the different forms of partnerships and explain how a partnership is formed**. In a general partnership, the owners are jointly and separately liable. In limited partnerships, liability is limited to the person's share in the partnership. Master limited partnerships are used by corporations that wish to keep a particular project separate from the main business. Most often, a partnership is legalized through a written agreement, spelling out the partners' responsibilities, rights, and duties, as well as any procedures for the dissolution of the partnership.

3. **Describe the advantages and disadvantages of a partnership**. Partnerships have the same advantages as sole proprietorships plus some others. Two or more partners can share the burden and have greater operating flexibility. Partnerships also have the same disadvantages as sole proprietorships. However, unlimited liability is an even greater disadvantage for partners, because each partner is responsible for the debts of the other partners. Another disadvantage is the potential for differences of opinion that hinder operation.

Corporations

4. **Briefly review the history of the corporate form of business**. The corporate form of business has existed since 1600, when Queen Elizabeth I granted investors the right to trade in India. The corporations first established in the United States differ from today's corporations in that they were licensed monopolies. As in current corporations, however, the incentives for their creation were the need for large amounts of capital and limited liability. Today's corporate form dates back to 1811, when New York adopted a general act of incorporation.

5. **Explain how a corporation is formed and describe the four major types of corporations**. Corporations are created (chartered) by filing with the state government articles of incorporation describing and naming the organization and by-laws defining company operating procedures. There are four major categories of corporations: government-owned, private, mixed, and not-for-profit. As their name implies, government-owned corporations are owned by the government; private corporations are owned by individuals or other corporations; mixed corporations are owned and regulated by the government but invested in by individuals. Unlike other corporations, not-for-profit corporations have as their goal serving the public rather than making a profit.

6. **Describe the advantages and disadvantages of corporations**. The advantages of the corporate form are ease of raising capital, limited liability for investors, ease of transfer of ownership, duration, and control. The disadvantages include the expense and complexity of setup, vulnerability to industrial espionage, double taxation of stockholders, and lack of long-term commitment of stockholders to the company's goals.

7. **Explain how the S and limited liability corporations enable small businesses to adopt the corporate form of business**. To help small businesses offset the corporate disadvantage of double taxation, the government created the S corporation. Owners have the benefits of a corporation but pay taxes only on their share of earnings. Like S corporations, limited liability corporations are easy to set up, owners have limited liability, and profits are taxed at a lower rate. Unlike S corporations, they are not restricted to 35 or fewer owners, and their owners need not be U.S. citizens.

8. **Distinguish between the owners and managers of a corporation**. Although a small corporation may be managed by its owners, in most cases owners are represented by an elected board of directors. The board hires a chief executive officer, who is charged with the actual management of the company's operations. While the CEO, with subordinate managers and employees, makes daily operating decisions, the board of directors makes major

policy, strategy, and financial decisions related to the long-term survival and success of the corporation.

9. **List the five factors to be considered in deciding on the best business form**. The five factors are amount of personal liability, ease of drawing profits from the business, amount of taxes to be paid, amount of capital needed, and amount of control desired. As a business grows, its needs and goals may change and with them so may its legal form.

Keeping the Form of the Business Competitive

10. **Explain how a business's strategic form relates to its purpose and actions**. A business's strategic form, or external organization, must be consistent with its actions as well as its purpose in order to accomplish its strategies and implement its tactics in the most efficient manner. Businesses review their mission (purpose) every six months or year to ensure that their legal form is the best one for accomplishing that purpose.

11. **Identify the most important forms of business innovations and adaptations, and give an example of each**. The four major categories of business innovations and adaptations are business networks, strategic alliances, cooperatives, and employee-owned businesses. An example of a business network is Toyota's *keiretsu*, which includes Toyota, a bank, suppliers, and insurance companies. A strategic alliance might be a jointly funded project between Apple Computer and IBM. Cooperatives are formed by farmers, students, and others seeking a competitive advantage; an example is Sunkist. Employee-owned businesses focus on the needs of employees—for example, United Airlines.

12. **Differentiate among acquisitions, mergers, and divestitures, and explain the significance of privatization**. With an acquisition, one company is absorbed by another; in a merger, on the other hand, both companies are absorbed into a new company. Mergers may be horizontal, vertical, or conglomerate. Following a merger, the new company may sell one of its subsidiaries or units—a process known as divestiture. Privatization of government-owned businesses is designed to increase productivity and competitiveness.

Key Terms

sole proprietorship **139**	corporate by-laws **144**	limited liability **146**	holding company **150**
unlimited liability **140**	government-owned	dividends **147**	parent company **150**
partnership **141**	corporation **144**	S corporation **148**	draw **152**
general partnership **141**	private corporation **145**	limited liability corpora-	gazelle **155**
limited partnership **141**	not-for-profit corporation	tion (LLC) **148**	business network **156**
master limited partnership	**145**	board of directors **149**	cooperative **157**
(MLP) **141**	mixed corporation **145**	chief executive officer	acquisition **159**
partnership agreement **142**	capital **146**	(CEO) **149**	merger **159**
corporation **143**	going public **146**	institutional investors **150**	divestiture **161**
articles of incorporation	publicly traded companies	subsidiary company **150**	privatization **161**
144	**146**		

• Review Questions

1. In starting your own for-profit business, what legal forms are available to you?

2. What are the main disadvantages of partnerships versus sole proprietorships?

3. What advantages does a partnership offer over a sole proprietorship?

4. If you wanted to start a business whose mission is to serve the community, what legal form would be most appropriate?

5. Can private citizens invest in a mixed corporation that combines government and private ownership? Give an example of a mixed corporation.

6. If the founder and largest shareholder of an S corpora-

tion runs over someone while driving the company car, will the corporate form protect the shareholder from personal liability?

7. If your grandmother buys one share of stock in a big corporation that is later sued for selling a dangerous product, will the corporate form protect her from personal liability?

8. What are three disadvantages of corporations over sole proprietorships?

9. What are three important innovations in strategic form? Explain how they differ.

10. What is privatization? Why does it occur?

• Critical Thinking Questions

1. You have a great idea for a new software package and you want to hit the ground running by raising lots of capital and hiring skilled employees for your new company. What factors will you consider? List the pros and cons of various legal forms and pick the best one for your start-up.

2. Should corporations be given many of the rights and obligations of individual people? Discuss.

3. What does it mean when we say a business must fit form to function? Discuss.

4. Collaborative forms of business such as business networks blur the boundaries between individual businesses. Why are they typical of new strategic forms?

5. What are the three most important points made in this chapter? Pick them, list them, and explain why you chose them.

REVIEW CASE   *Who's Changing What?*[17]

It is easy to assume that businesses are fairly stable and do not change their form often, if ever. But interviews with the chief executive officers of 373 leading businesses in North America and Europe show that business form is changing very rapidly at present. The study, by researchers at the Conference Board, a not-for-profit research organization, discovered that many businesses are changing in their business form and that the most common change involves the creation of new business relationships with other companies.

Strategic alliances are increasingly common—most companies in the study are using them. The alliances can take many forms. Many companies form tactical alliances, which are usually informal. In these informal alliances, companies collaborate without a formal, legal agreement and pursue tactical instead of strategic goals. For example, suppliers to a large automobile manufacturer may collaborate to help develop a new car, and they expect to sell parts to the manufacturer when the new car is finally produced. If these informal alliances work, they often lead to more formal arrangements.

The most common form of building long-term strategic alliances is an acquisition: 31 percent of the CEOs surveyed said their firms were involved in acquisitions of other companies. In these acquisitions, the bigger company often buys only a portion of the smaller one, allowing it some indepen-

dence but ensuring close ties as well. The second most common form for alliances was the joint venture, in which two firms pool resources to create a third firm that they own jointly; 29 percent said they use joint ventures. For example, chemical company DuPont and pharmaceutical company Merck created a joint venture called DuPont Merck Pharmaceutical Company to apply some of DuPont's technology to the drug business.

1. Aside from acquisitions and joint ventures, what other legal forms might a company use to create a strategic alliance?

2. Why do you think the Conference Board interviewed CEOs rather than business owners?

3. If the owners of two small sole proprietorships wanted to create a formal strategic alliance, what forms would make the most sense for them to consider?

4. If a privately owned U.S. corporation wanted to form a strategic alliance with a state-owned corporation in the People's Republic of China in order to start and co-own a new manufacturing business in China, what form would the new business most likely take?

CRITICAL THINKING CASE *Spruce Falls Rises*[18]

The Spruce Falls Paper Mill in Kapuskasing, Ontario, supplied some pretty hefty customers. Both the New York Times and Kimberly-Clark Corporation, which manufactures Kleenex tissues and Huggies diapers, bought substantial amounts of paper from Spruce Falls. The two companies were also the mill's owners, with 49 and 51 percent ownership, respectively.

When these two owners realized that the mill was no longer profitable because of its remote location, outdated technology, and high labor costs, they decided to sell it. When they were unable to find interested buyers, they decided to close it down. That's when the employees got together and decided to purchase the mill themselves.

Assisted by another local employee-owned paper and wood company, Tembec Inc., the employees bought a majority share of the Spruce Falls Paper Mill. Under the terms of the deal, the plant was modernized and the employees agreed to give up some of their benefits for a 52 percent share in the company and a program that enabled them to share in the mill's profits. Most of the remaining shares went to Tembec in exchange for helping finance the deal. Today, the 32 million shares of stock in the company sell at nearly $5 each (up from $1 at the time of the buyout). With newsprint costs rising, Spruce Falls should continue to prosper.

1. Who wins in this situation? Investors? Workers? The community? Sellers? All? None? Explain.

2. This buyout saved employees from unemployment and kept the major employer in a small town open. But when corporate owners decide that a plant is no longer profitable, they usually simply close it down and transfer production to a low-wage market overseas. In your opinion, why aren't employee buyouts more common? Can you think of any ways of encouraging this form of business?

3. If you had been an employee at the mill, would you have participated in the buyout? What would have encouraged you (or discouraged you) in this situation?

Critical Thinking with the ONE MINUTE MANAGER [19]

"Do large corporations ever do business with sole proprietors?" Carlos asked.

"Of course," replied the One Minute Manager. "And the new limited liability corporation is often chosen as the form for such collaborations because of its flexibility."

"But why do big businesses need the help of individual entrepreneurs?" Joanna interjected.

"Let me tell you a story that answers your question," the One Minute Manager said. "In Romania, Coca-Cola helped revitalize a failing economy by providing people with the opportunity to work for and with Coca-Cola. When it arrived in 1990, the company needed to work with Romanian community businesses that would help further the production and sales of Coke products."

"What kinds of businesses?" Carlos asked.

"Well, some Romanians went into business as distributors, some as label printers, and some as local advertising agents. More than 20,000 small businesses arose in what economists now call a 'Coke economy.'"

"Did any of these businesses form partnerships with Coca-Cola?" asked Joanna.

"Yes, actually, some did. Coke brought its technology to local plastics manufacturers, which worked as partners with the company in the production of returnable bottles. So you see, sometimes even the smallest and the largest businesses join forces to produce a product."

1. Can you think of another type of company in Romania that would benefit from a partnership with Coca-Cola? How might each partner benefit?

2. Choosing only from the forms of business described in this chapter, which forms do you think would be appropriate for Romanian start-ups mentioned in this case? How did you arrive at this answer?

3. Again using only the forms described in this chapter, what (if any) changes in form would you recommend for the Romanian start-ups as they grow? List and discuss several alternatives.

6 Entrepreneurship and Planning a Business

In this chapter we explore entrepreneurship—a topic we touched on briefly in Chapters 1 and 2. Entrepreneurial behavior, the behavior associated with innovations and the successful start-up of new businesses, is a vital source of growth in an economy. We outline the six steps in the entrepreneurship process, and then take a close look at the planning process. We conclude by examining some of the ways large corporations attempt to harness the spirit of entrepreneurship within their own established organizations.

No matter what work you choose, you are far more likely to play the role of entrepreneur than are the previous graduates of your college. Don't make the mistake of thinking that entrepreneurial skills are valuable only to small businesses or that only other people—those with special talents, advanced degrees, or some magical combination of age, experience, and riches—can start their own business. The entrepreneur we describe may well be you. After reading this chapter, you will be able to reach the learning goals below.

Learning Goals

1. Identify the six steps of the entrepreneurship process.
2. State the four basic personal characteristics of an entrepreneur.
3. Define *precipitating event* and explain how such an event might lead to a new business.
4. List and describe seven sources of innovation in business.
5. Describe the three-step process for building an entrepreneurial network.
6. Discuss the five primary reasons for preparing a business plan.
7. List the six factors that minimize risk for new ventures.
8. Describe the seven topics covered by a business plan.
9. Identify the five potential sources of capital for a new business.
10. Explain how intrapreneurship differs from entrepreneurship.

The Search for Champions

"I just read that entrepreneurship is the behavior associated with starting and growing a new business. That must be pretty far from what businesspeople do in an established company like this one," Carlos suggested.

The One Minute Manager shook her head and smiled. "Entrepreneurship is often thought of as common only in small businesses. But a small business that is stable and growing slowly is not entrepreneurial. Nor, of course, is a big business that is growing slowly. But when either one begins to innovate, to search for new ways of adding value for its customers, then you have real entrepreneurship."

"This company sure looks like a stable, growing business when you walk into the reception area downstairs," Joanna said. "How do you keep the entrepreneurial spirit alive?"

"You're right, Joanna. As we get bigger, it's harder to think and act like entrepreneurs. At one time, a few people owned and ran this business, and when they had a good idea, they just went for it. Now you have to run your idea by your boss or talk your team into supporting it. But it's also true that we now have more resources when we want to pursue a new idea. We often fund new ventures out of the company's own bank account, for instance; that means we don't have to convince a bank or an investor that our idea will pay off."

"Is entrepreneurship something you all do in your daily work, then?" Carlos asked.

"Yes and no. Look at my IN box," the One Minute Manager answered, waving at the pile of papers on her desk. "I don't know what's in that pile yet, but I do know it *won't* be lots of neat new ideas to grow our business. The daily details of managing a business get in the way of being an entrepreneur. That's why we started a special program a few years ago, modeled on a program called Champion, which Bell Atlantic uses. Bell Atlantic employees submit new ideas that might produce revenues for the company, and the best ideas are turned into projects for the company's New Business Development Group. The employee who suggested the idea gets a six-month break to pursue the project, and he or she becomes a "champion," an internal entrepreneur with the company's official support. Not only that, champions can choose to invest up to 10 percent of their salaries in the project; then, if the project makes money for the company, champions receive 5 percent of the revenues. A champion can get very rich through Bell Atlantic's program."[1]

Entrepreneurship

All businesses, no matter how large they may be now, owe their existence to individuals who had the vision to found them and the courage to risk failure. **Entrepreneurship** is the term used to describe the risk-taking behavior associated with the start-up and growth of a business. Some economists argue that the high level of entrepreneurial activity in the United States explains its rise to global economic importance over the last century. And, if the United States is to remain a major player in the world economy and maintain its technological leadership, it must support entrepreneurship and allow it to bloom.

There is a little bit of the entrepreneur in each of us. In fact, chances are very good that some of you reading this chapter will come up with a good idea, do some careful planning, follow it up with a lot of hard work and perseverance, and launch your own business. More than half a million new businesses are started in the United States every year.[2] Although many of them fail within their first few years, more than three-fourths survive at least until their third anniversary.[3] Some of these entrepreneurs—like Bill Gates, who designed the operating system for IBM's personal computer and launched a multibillion-dollar software empire of his own—become world famous. Others, like the local mom-and-pop grocery store owners, become famous in their own neighborhoods. But all of them help write the pages of American business history.

Entrepreneurial behavior is not limited to the formation of new businesses. **Intrapreneurship** is behavior associated with the start-up and growth of new products, systems, and processes within an existing business. Innovations in the laboratories of 3M, on the production lines of Toyota, and within the quality improvement teams at Xerox all produced growth and change in these mature businesses, and all are examples of successful intrapreneurship.

This chapter focuses on the importance of entrepreneurship to the American economy and on how and why businesses are formed. It focuses on the six basic steps of the entrepreneurship process: imagination, formation, networking, analyzing risk, writing a business plan, and implementation. As Table 6.1 indicates, they occur in three stages, and they are the steps entrepreneurs take when starting a successful business.

✓ entrepreneurship

Risk-taking behavior associated with the start-up and growth of a business.

✓ intrapreneurship

Behavior associated with the start-up and growth of new products, systems, and processes within an existing business.

1. Identify the six steps of the entrepreneurship process.

table 6.1 The Six Steps of the Entrepreneurship Process

Stage	Steps	Actions
Conception	1. Imagination	Generate and screen innovative ideas.
	2. Formation	Select a legal form appropriate for the idea.
	3. Networking	Build contacts and convert them to business relationships to gain access to needed resources.
Planning	4. Analyzing risk	Understand risks and try to minimize them.
	5. Writing a business plan	Write plan: describe business environment, legal form, management and organization, employees, marketing, control systems, and finances. Outline strategy for success.
Implementation	6. Implementing the plan	Do it! Apply your knowledge to the successful creation and management of the new venture.

Source: Based on Alexander Hiam and Karen Olander, *The Prentice-Hall Handbook of Entrepreneurship and Small Business Management*, Part 1 (Englewood Cliffs, N.J.: Prentice-Hall, in press).

✓ **precipitating event**

A change in the environment that spurs an individual to take action.

In this chapter, you will learn about how entrepreneurs find their ideas and about how newly formed businesses network with other organizations to help ensure their ultimate success. You will come to appreciate the importance of analyzing the potential risk of a venture. You will also learn how to write a business plan, and you will see how a plan is implemented. Finally, you will look over the shoulders of large businesses as they try to regain some of the excitement and creativity they had when they first began.

What Makes an Entrepreneur Tick?

2. State the four basic personal characteristics of an entrepreneur.

Many colleges and universities now offer courses in entrepreneurship because research shows that entrepreneurial skills can be learned. Although some people may be better suited than others to be entrepreneurs, all of us can nurture the traits that characterize entrepreneurial behavior.[4] Entrepreneurs are

1. Creative innovators
2. Moderate risk takers
3. Independent
4. Determined to achieve success

3. Define *precipitating event* and explain how such an event might lead to a new business.

In addition, previous experience in managing a business often helps. A person who has these characteristics may not be motivated to use them to launch a business until a precipitating event occurs. A **precipitating event** is a change in the environment that spurs an individual to take action. Such events can take various forms. They may be part of an individual's personal life, such as a change in health status, family makeup, or financial status. They may be technological innovations that enable a new type of work or work in a new location. Or else they may be job-related events beyond the individual's control—layoffs, mergers, changes in corporate management, market changes, or even a sudden entrepreneurial opportunity. Michael Kittredge, founder of Yankee Candle International in Massachusetts, originally saw candle making as a hobby. He explains, "The original concept wasn't to be a businessman. It was to be an English teacher and make an extra $50 on the side." However, growing demand for his candles precipitated Kittredge's switch to full-time candle making.[5]

You might want to try rating your own entrepreneurial capacity and characteristics by completing the exercise in the skills check entitled "Evaluating Your Readiness for Entrepreneurship."

Conception: Finding a Need and Filling It

Entrepreneurship and its close relative intrapreneurship bring growth not only for the individual but for the entire economy. Growth translates into jobs, which are created as the demand for new products increases and additional employees and materials are needed to satisfy that demand. A *Fortune* magazine survey showed that, from mid-1992 to mid-1993, America's 100 fastest-growing companies sold approximately $40 billion worth of goods and services. As a result of these sales, these 100 firms earned almost $3 billion and hired tens of thousands of new employees.[6]

Let's take a closer look at one entrepreneur in action—Masayoshi Son, a University of California, Berkeley, graduate who, at the age of 22, started Softbank Corporation of Tokyo, a personal computer (PC) software distribution company.

Evaluating Your Readiness for Entrepreneurship

Are you ready to be an entrepreneur? You can gauge your interest and ability to be an entrepreneur by rating yourself on the four basic personal characteristics discussed in this chapter, as well as some additional ones that studies of entrepreneurship indicate may increase your chances of success. Circle the number on the scale of 1 (definitely not me) to 5 (definitely me) that best describes your position on each of the following characteristics.

To arrive at your score, add all your individual ratings and divide that total by 15: ____. A score below 4 indicates you may not have the personal characteristics that most studies associate with high levels of entrepreneurship.

Source: Based on literature reviewed in Donald Kuratko and Richard Hodgetts, *Entrepreneurship: A Contemporary Approach,* 3d ed. (Orlando, Fla.: Dryden Press, 1995), pp. 40–43.

Basic characteristics	*Scale*				
Creative, innovative	1	2	3	4	5
Moderate risk taker	1	2	3	4	5
Independent	1	2	3	4	5
Determined to achieve success	1	2	3	4	5
Additional characteristics					
Good health	1	2	3	4	5
Realistic attitude	1	2	3	4	5
Superior conceptual ability	1	2	3	4	5
Self-confident	1	2	3	4	5
Tendency to control or direct others	1	2	3	4	5
Attracted to challenges	1	2	3	4	5
Emotionally stable	1	2	3	4	5
Self-controlled	1	2	3	4	5
Tendency to take the initiative	1	2	3	4	5
Balanced	1	2	3	4	5
Self-reliant	1	2	3	4	5

"I wanted to start my own company when I came back to Japan," Son says. "I thought of 40 different businesses I could start. It was like thinking of an invention." He developed 25 success measures. One was that he should fall in love with the business and believe that love would last for at least 50 years. Another was that the business would be unique. Still another was that he would be number one in Japan in that particular business within 10 years. "I had all those measurements, about 25 in all, and 40 new ideas," Son says. "I took a big sheet of paper and I drew a matrix and put down scores and comments for each. Then I picked the best one, which turned out to be the personal computer software business."[7] That was how Softbank was born. (The matrix Son used to gauge his interest was similar to the sample screening matrix illustrated in Figure 6.1 on the next page.)

When Masayoshi Son first started his company, he had only two part-time workers. Every morning, he would stand on two apple boxes and address his two employees: "You guys have to listen to me because I am the president of this company. In five years, I'm going to have $75 million in sales. In five years, I will be supplying 1,000 dealer outlets, and we'll be number one in PC software distribution." According to Son, Softbank's first two employees thought

figure 6.1 Sample Screening Matrix

This screening matrix shows how three alternative business ideas measure up on a series of factors an entrepreneur is using to make a decision about starting a business. The matrix can be adapted to reflect the traits the individual considers important. The numbers in the boxes are the entrepreneur's judgment of how well each business idea meets the requirements listed for each item. (Zero equals not at all; 10 equals ideal.) The score in the last column is the average of all factors in that row for the business idea.

Business Idea	Decision factors					Average score
	Interesting?	Customers?	Little competition?	Do I know how?	Steady work?	
Ski sharpening service	7	5	7	8	1	5
Pizza delivery service	8	9	2	7	9	7
Computer repair service	2	4	3	0	6	3

Final Ratings

Business idea	Average score	Comments
Pizza delivery service (highest score) 8 + 9 + 2 + 7 + 9 = 35 ÷ 5 = 7	7	Lots of hungry customers. Necessary to buy truck.
Ski sharpening service	5	Already have the equipment necessary to open. Business is seasonal.
Computer repair service	3	Highly competitive. Don't know the first thing about computers.

he was crazy and quit.[8] But Masayoshi Son *wasn't* crazy, despite what his employees thought. A year and a half after commencing business, Softbank was supplying software to 200 dealers. By 1993, just 10 years later, that figure had increased to 15,000. During this period, Softbank grew to 570 employees, with annual sales of $354 million.

Son's business was exceptionally successful, but it began as every business does—with an idea. Sometimes that idea is part of a more idealistic vision, as was the case when Anita Roddick founded The Body Shop, a natural cosmetics, skin, and hair products company. Roddick's initial idea was simple: Offer a line of 25 naturally based skin and hair products bottled in five different sizes of containers. Says Roddick, "I didn't know anything about the cosmetics industry when I opened my first shop."[9] But she did know about environmental issues, and she was determined to offer natural products through a business that helped the environment instead of hurting it. This unique vision is now embodied in more than 1,000 Body Shop outlets in 45 countries worldwide. And the firm's environmental policy still expresses that vision (see Figure 6.2). Where do new ideas like Roddick's and Son's come from? Let's find out.

figure **6.2** **The Body Shop's Statement of Its Relationship to the Environment**

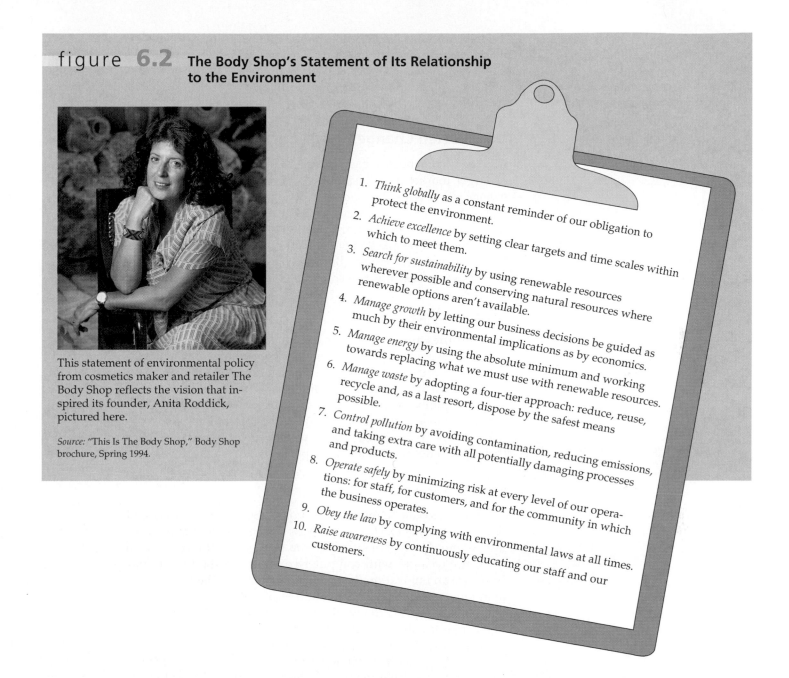

This statement of environmental policy from cosmetics maker and retailer The Body Shop reflects the vision that inspired its founder, Anita Roddick, pictured here.

Source: "This Is The Body Shop," Body Shop brochure, Spring 1994.

1. *Think globally* as a constant reminder of our obligation to protect the environment.
2. *Achieve excellence* by setting clear targets and time scales within which to meet them.
3. *Search for sustainability* by using renewable resources wherever possible and conserving natural resources where renewable options aren't available.
4. *Manage growth* by letting our business decisions be guided as much by their environmental implications as by economics.
5. *Manage energy* by using the absolute minimum and working towards replacing what we must use with renewable resources.
6. *Manage waste* by adopting a four-tier approach: reduce, reuse, recycle and, as a last resort, dispose by the safest means possible.
7. *Control pollution* by avoiding contamination, reducing emissions, and taking extra care with all potentially damaging processes and products.
8. *Operate safely* by minimizing risk at every level of our operations: for staff, for customers, and for the community in which the business operates.
9. *Obey the law* by complying with environmental laws at all times.
10. *Raise awareness* by continuously educating our staff and our customers.

Imagination: The Search for New Ideas

Entrepreneurship depends on the creative development of new and better ideas—a process that involves **innovation**, or creative change in products or processes. There are two ways to answer the question of where new ideas come from. First, one can think of innovation as just another creative task, involving the application of the techniques of creativity to developing good entrepreneurial ideas.

Alternatively, we can examine the elements that inspired other people who were successful innovators. Business professor Peter Drucker, who has studied entrepreneurs and intrapreneurs for this purpose, says that people mistakenly assume that most new ideas are the result of high-tech laboratory research. In fact, his research turned up seven sources of successful innovations in business; of these seven, technological breakthroughs were the *least* common. Drucker's

 innovation

A creative change in products or processes.

seven sources are unexpected changes, incongruities, process need, changes in market structure, demographics, perception, and new knowledge and technology.[10] We discuss each of these in detail, in order of their importance to entrepreneurs, beginning with the most common sources of new ideas: unexpected changes in the market and incongruities.

4. List and describe seven sources of innovation in business.

Unexpected Changes

Unexpected changes in basic business conditions may offer the chance of a new or larger market. Long-established businesses often fail to benefit from such events, either ignoring them or viewing them as irritating problems. Only the truly entrepreneurial business sees them as an opportunity. For example, it took manufacturers of suntan lotion a long time to see an opportunity in their problem—that people do not deliberately attempt to tan as much now that they know it causes skin cancer. But in the last decade, these companies have introduced sunscreens and their sales are going up again.

Incongruities

Incongruities are surprising events that clash with assumptions about a business and its environment. Incongruities generally indicate that some important change has occurred without anyone's noticing it. For example, Nike marketers were startled when sales of running shoes began to fall in the mid-1980s. Until then, the number of runners had grown rapidly every year. When Nike investigated the cause of this incongruous event, it found that the baby-boomers—the many people born in the 1950s—were switching to sports that were easier on their aging knees and shins. In response, Nike quickly developed cross-trainers.

Process Need

Every process can be improved—if only slightly. A **process need** is a weakness or bottleneck that exists in a business system and that may present an opportunity for innovation. For example, you may have noticed that your mail often arrives in envelopes with computer bar codes in the lower right corner. These codes are an innovation that grew in response to the U.S. Postal Service's need to automate the sorting and handling of millions of pieces of mail each year. Manual sorting was the weak point, causing delays and errors in the system. The bar codes allow computers to sort mountains of mail at a fraction of the time and cost of their human counterparts. But not all such innovations replace human beings with machines. The reengineering and quality improvement teams that now drive change in many companies attempt to come up with innovations that improve the existing work process. People who work *within* the process are often in the best position to suggest innovations.

Changes in Market Structure

Changes in market structure occur when an industry that has been stable for years suddenly undergoes a fundamental shift. Innovators can profit by leading such changes or riding their crests. Perhaps you remember receiving your first digital watch. Digital watches swept the market in the late 1970s. For centuries before that time, Swiss watchmakers had the watch market locked up. Even most American watches proudly claimed to have "Swiss-made" movements, which employed gears and a mainspring to make the hands move. Although Swiss scientists had developed a design for a new, electronic digital watch, the Swiss watch industry ignored the innovation, assuming that watch movements would always be mechanical. No Swiss maker even bothered to patent the new technology. The innovation did not escape the attention of

 incongruities

Surprising events that clash with assumptions about a business and its environment.

 process need

A weakness or bottleneck that exists in a business system and that may present an opportunity for innovation.

Japanese electronics companies, however. By the early 1980s, their new digital watches had captured most of the worldwide market. In the process, they cut costs and improved reliability so much that many Swiss manufacturers were driven out of business. Digital watches were also available in many more places, rather than in just the few jewelry or upscale department stores that had been the main outlets for Swiss watches.

These structural changes in the manufacture and distribution of watches opened the door to many new, entrepreneurial competitors that had been locked out when Swiss watches dominated the market. Swatch, for example, developed and introduced the first line of colorful, high-quality watches and distributed them through clothing stores.

Demographics

Demographics is the statistical study of the characteristics of a population, such as age, gender, marital status, income, and education. Entrepreneurs who keep close track of rapid changes in demographics can respond to opportunities for innovation quickly because such changes are relatively easy to predict and track. Strangely enough, few businesses make full use of available demographic data. The aging of the North American, European, and Japanese populations, for example, is clear in any demographic forecast, but most businesses continue to focus their products and services on the youth culture, as Nike must have regretted doing when sales of its running shoes stopped growing.

Perception

Customer perception of products and social trends can also create opportunities for innovation. The brief "yuppie" (young urban professional) phenome-

✓ **demographics**

The statistical study of the characteristics of a population, such as age, gender, marital status, income, and education.

Can you think of any new opportunities for entrepreneurs in services for older Americans?

6.0, 6.0, 6.0, 6.0, 6.0! If I had to rate milk as an after-sports drink, it would definitely get the gold. Besides being a better source of potassium than the leading sports drink, it has more vitamins and minerals per ounce. And how do I like it? On ice, of course.

MILK
What a surprise!™

Changing Customer Perceptions

The market for milk is a lot like the market for cotton: undifferentiated product, many producers with no market power, in other words, a perfectly competitive industry. Yet milk producers know they face competition from all other beverages. And so, like Cotton Incorporated, the dairy industry's National Fluid Milk Processor Promotion Board works to boost milk sales, sometimes by exposing consumers to a fresh perspective. This campaign, called "Milk, What a Surprise!", features celebrities, including Kristi Yamaguchi, sporting milk mustaches. The message? Milk is a terrific sports drink.

non of the 1980s was one such trend. This group of wage earners had substantial amounts of disposable income and a growing desire to purchase items that displayed the status that accompanied this newfound wealth. The firms that satisfied this desire—BMW, Rolex, Armani, and a host of new firms that targeted these young people—advertised their products as high-status luxury items for the successful. These companies discovered that customer perception of a product was indeed the key to gaining this group's business.

Unlike demographic changes, changes in customer perceptions of products can be difficult to predict or track. Nevertheless, companies that can successfully innovate to identify with new perceptions may have little or no competition in the initial stages of their business.

New Knowledge and Technology

Innovations based on new knowledge are unpredictable, expensive, and particularly hard to control—but they are very exciting. Some firms, such as Hewlett-Packard and Intel, have done a superb job of successfully introducing technological innovations. And biotechnology start-up Genentech became a multimillion-dollar company in the 1980s by betting on the right technology.

Formation: Choosing the "Right" Legal Form

You may recall from Chapter 5 that a company's corporate by-laws define the procedures for distributing ownership, appointing directors, and running the company.

Forming the business means choosing a legal form: sole proprietorship, some form of partnership, or some form of corporation—C corporation, S corporation, or the new limited liability corporation—as discussed in Chapter 5. The entrepreneur must select the most appropriate form and file the required papers with state and local agencies. In addition, the entrepreneur must decide how the business will be governed and by whom. For example, the entrepreneur may write a set of by-laws that empower five associates to be directors of the new corporation.

Networking: Building Business Contacts

Let's say you have decided on a legal form for the business. Your next step would be getting a business loan, right? Wrong. Money is the first thing entrepreneurs tend to think of when they are trying to get started, but money tends to flow to the business later on *from other resources*. Chasing the money first is putting the cart before the horse. Your first job is networking.[11] **Networking** is the informal process in which people who share an interest provide advice, information, and resources to one another. Let's stop and consider this point for a minute.

To be successful, every new business needs both economic and noneconomic resources—including ideas, funding, facilities, and technical expertise. Networking can take many forms. Contacts with potential customers can produce orders. Good relationships with bank personnel may translate into a loan to fill orders. Friendships with people at supplier businesses can help you get permission to pay for your supplies 30 or 60 days after receiving them, instead of upon receipt, as is usual for new businesses. This extra time can allow you to raise the money to pay for the supplies through your own sales, instead of borrowing it from a bank. Similarly, personal contacts may lead you to low-cost rental space, better ideas and advice, and many other benefits. All these resources help to make the business valuable enough that people may wish to invest money in it.

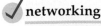

networking

The informal process in which people who share an interest provide advice, information, and resources to one another.

Groups like a local chamber of commerce or an association of women in business can provide a place to network with other entrepreneurs and managers in your area. Some entrepreneurs tap into the networks of other local businesses—for example, by asking a successful store owner for the name of a banker he or she recommends.

Every business—whether it uses the contacts to sell products, arrange financing, or obtain advice on handling a difficult issue—relies on networking to a surprisingly large extent. For example, Masayoshi Son of Softbank discovered the importance of his personal network of contacts when he tried to obtain his first bank loan for his company. The context was hardly favorable—a four-month-old company with $10,000 in revenues wanting to borrow $750,000. Son explains:

> The people at the Dai-ichi Kangyo Bank just started laughing. We can't give you a loan, they said. Do you have anything that can convince us? I said, no, I don't have anything. But if you really think about business in the future, what we're doing might interest you. Then they asked me, is there anyone you can use as a reference?[12]

Fortunately, Masayoshi Son had a good relationship with a senior manager at Sharp. While a student at Berkeley, Son had built and patented a pocket language translator; Sharp had purchased the rights to Son's invention, which the company later introduced as the Sharp Wizard. (Son eventually made $1 million from the sale to Sharp, but that's another story!) The branch manager of the bank agreed to call the executive at Sharp, who said, "Mr. Son has good business potential, so please give him this loan." This recommendation convinced the branch manager. Son's new business got its loan because of Son's network, and the rest is history.

But we don't all have friends in high places. How can other entrepreneurs develop networks? Recent research by business school professors has identified a three-step process (illustrated in Figure 6.3) by which entrepreneurs build relationships with other organizations to get their businesses engaged in the economy.[13]

Step 1. Build a Personal Network

Focus on essential contacts. At this initial stage of network development, you consider every relationship you have and assess its potential benefit to your new business. Let's say you graduate and decide to open a gourmet pizza-by-the-slice restaurant near campus. First you consider every potential source of advice and support—friends, relatives, customers, business associates, former classmates, and so on. Then you narrow down this initial list, focusing on contacts that meet the most critical resource needs of your organization. For example, a roommate who now works for a local real estate brokerage may help you find a good storefront, and a friendly professor may be able to help you pick up catering jobs for special events on campus.

Step 2. Convert Key Relationships into Business Contacts

In this second stage, you focus on the informal, social relationships you identified in the first stage and work on transforming them into formal business relationships. An old family friend may be a source of capital with which to buy your pizza ovens. Younger siblings or college friends may have the potential to become trustworthy employees. As you hire employees, sign contracts, and arrange investments, relationships continue to solidify throughout this second stage of network development.

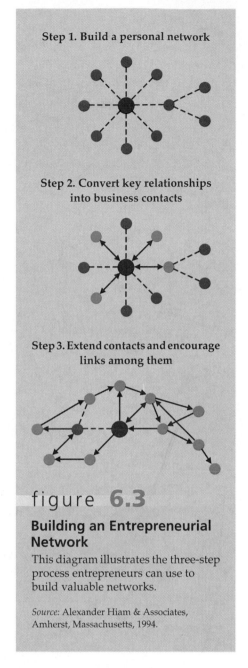

Step 1. Build a personal network

Step 2. Convert key relationships into business contacts

Step 3. Extend contacts and encourage links among them

figure **6.3**

Building an Entrepreneurial Network

This diagram illustrates the three-step process entrepreneurs can use to build valuable networks.

Source: Alexander Hiam & Associates, Amherst, Massachusetts, 1994.

5. Describe the three-step process for building an entrepreneurial network.

Step 3. Extend Contacts and Encourage Links Among Them

Next you attempt to create many interdependent links among the individuals in the relationships you developed in the second stage. A professor in your current network may lead you to other professors and administrators who use catering services. College friends who now work for you may extend the network into their old dorms or clubs, producing new customers. As you can see, the members of your network are becoming more closely knit and interdependent, and the business no longer relies solely on you for sales. Eventually, the network you build may become more important than the personal relationships that drew the participants into the network in the first phase.

Organizations devoted to fostering informal business networks are often listed in the business activities section of any local business newspaper. Among them are local chambers of commerce, associations of business owners, and groups such as ReferNet and ReferOne America. Your school may also have an organization that helps budding entrepreneurs develop links to people and organizations in the business world.

A hidden advantage of the corporation as a form of business is its built-in networking resource, namely its board of directors. The directors oversee the firm's operations and, if it is public, they look out for the public owners' interests. If the corporation is small and private, the board usually has strong ties to the owner—perhaps as relatives or key employees. But a recent study by the accounting firm Coopers & Lybrand revealed that small companies have more luck obtaining financing if they appoint outside directors.[14] This is because outside directors do *not* have strong ties to the business or its owner. They typically manage other, noncompeting businesses—supplier or customer businesses, or, if the entrepreneur is lucky enough, a business in the banking industry. An outside director gives the business credibility, making it easier to network. And, of course, the outside director also gives the business access to his or her business network.

Planning

Informal networks ensure access to all the resources the new business needs, but this access alone cannot guarantee success. Research indicates there is a strong correlation between business planning and improved sales and profits.[15] Planning helps an owner to get a new business up and running, and it helps established businesses to stay on course. Two essential planning activities are analyzing risk and preparing a business plan.

A **business plan** is a written document that analyzes and describes all the important issues involved in the start-up and ongoing operations of a business. The plan contains an analysis of the market the business will enter, a strategy for success in that market, and a set of well-defined financial objectives and forecasts. Business plans are developed for five primary reasons:

1. To figure out the best way to manage the business
2. To identify and minimize risks that might cause the business to fail
3. To project financial operations so the entrepreneur can take maximum advantage of financial resources
4. To attract investors by showing them that the business represents a good financial opportunity
5. To establish the vision and values that will guide the business and to show how they will be translated into an effective and ethical organization

6. Discuss the five primary reasons for preparing a business plan.

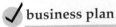

business plan

A written document that analyzes and describes all the important issues involved in the start-up and ongoing operations of a business.

Many entrepreneurs write plans solely for the purpose of attracting **investors**—people or organizations that exchange money for a share in the future income of the business. Investors look for businesses with a low chance of failure, since failure would mean the loss of the money they invested. They also look for a good chance of successful growth, which could mean higher profits for them. Investors that like your business may help finance it through debt or equity capital. **Debt capital**, funds raised by borrowing, must be repaid. **Equity capital**, funds raised by selling shares of ownership in a business, actually transfers to the investor part ownership of the company and its future profits.

Other aspects of equity capital are covered in Chapter 20.

Investors are certainly important, and attracting them is a valid reason for writing a business plan. But a business plan has other equally important uses. Business planning improves the performance of entrepreneurial and small businesses by emphasizing long-range thinking. It also lessens the focus on day-to-day details and helps to identify and evaluate business alternatives.

Analyzing Risk

Business plans often attempt to describe the risks associated with the business, and, once the business is operating, its managers need to work on keeping risk down to a level they find comfortable. *Risk* is the chance of a loss. It varies tremendously, according to the business type, location, available financial resources, market, quality of management, and (most important to us right now) *how well the entrepreneur understands and manages the risks*. A three-year nationwide study commissioned by American Express and the National Federation of Independent Business (NFIB) Foundations indicates that 77 percent of new ventures are still in business three years after their founding.[16] According to the vice president of small-business services at American Express, "This study helps debunk the myth that most new businesses fail." Although it still indicates a significant level of risk, that risk can be minimized by careful analysis and planning.

Part 7 covers business risks in greater detail.

The American Express/NFIB study pinpointed six factors that minimize risk and maximize chances of success for new ventures:

7. List the six factors that minimize risk for new ventures.

- *Self-confidence.* Businesses whose owners strongly believed they would succeed (rating themselves 9 or higher on a 10-point scale) were more likely to be in business after three years than were those with lower expectations (6 or below). If you decide the risks are high for a pizza business, heed your analysis and wait until the odds improve.

- *Business size.* Larger businesses fared better than smaller businesses. Firms with an initial investment of more than $50,000 were more likely to survive their first three years than were businesses with initial investments of less than $20,000. And firms starting out with six or more employees were more likely to make it than those with one or two employees. A new pizza business with enough capital to hire full-time employees has a better chance of providing the consistent quality and service needed to succeed in this competitive business.

- *Quality orientation versus price orientation.* A business strategy of providing better customer service was a better ticket to three-year survival than was a strategy based on low prices. This means your business should pride itself on serving *good* food quickly and politely, not on having the lowest prices in town.

- *Hard work (but not too hard).* At the end of three years, entrepreneurs working between 60 and 69 hours a week were more likely to be in business than those who worked either more or fewer hours. If you try to run a pizza place all by yourself, your chance of failure may be higher than if you get some help and some rest.

 investors

People or organizations that exchange money for a share in the future income of the business.

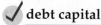 **debt capital**

Funds raised by borrowing.

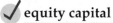 **equity capital**

Funds raised by selling shares of ownership in a business.

- *Devotion*. Entrepreneurs who gave full-time attention to their new enterprise were more likely to celebrate the end of their third year of business than were those who held another job. *Moral*: Don't try to run that pizza business at night after you finish work at a full-time day job.

- *Product knowledge*. Entrepreneurs who provided goods or services they knew well from previous jobs had a better chance of surviving than those who had no previous experience with their products. The best way to prepare for starting up a new pizza business is to spend a few months working at a successful one.

Most experts tell entrepreneurs that "ineffective management accounts for 90 to 95 percent of all business failures," as a handbook published by the Greater San Diego Chamber of Commerce puts it.[17] If you have never hired employees, done basic accounting, or designed an advertisement, you will have to learn these skills as you go—which could increase your risk of failure. Entrepreneurs do not actually have to be experienced managers, but they do need *some* relevant background knowledge. And the four core personal characteristics mentioned earlier in this chapter—being a creative innovator, a moderate risk taker, independent, and determined to achieve success—are as important as relevant management skills. Add up all these factors and you have a new venture in which the risk of failure is minimized.

If entrepreneurs combine the six factors for minimizing business risk with good management and an entrepreneurial personality, they can reduce the chance of failure to less than 20 percent in their first three years. And if you compare this to the chance of being downsized out of a job with an established company, it does not sound any riskier than working for someone else. Figure 6.4 presents a risk scorecard that assesses risk from several perspectives.

Writing a Business Plan

8. Describe the seven topics covered by a business plan.

The business plan should address seven topics: the business environment, the form of the business, management and organization, employees, marketing, control systems, and finances. These seven topics correspond to the seven main parts of this textbook, so as you study for this course you will learn the basic information needed to write a sound business plan. Here are the main questions and issues a plan needs to address in each of these seven areas.

Business Environment

What changes and trends in the environment create an opportunity for the new business, and how will the environment change over the coming years? The analysis should look at each of the elements of the business environment, which, as noted in Chapter 1, are the natural, social, political/legal, technological, competitive, and economic environments. And the analysis should look at these environments from two angles: as *opportunities* and as *threats*.

Opportunities are exemplified by Drucker's seven sources of innovation, discussed earlier in this chapter: aspects of the external environment that create a customer need you think you can fill. For example, in analyzing the environment around campus, a young entrepreneur might learn that (1) a local pizza place is closing because the owner is retiring, (2) a new shuttle-bus service is starting up, making downtown stores more accessible to on-campus students, and (3) the social trend in the nation and in the area is toward more nutritious foods like pizza and away from high-fat, high-cholesterol burgers and fries. This information about the business environment points out an opportunity for a pizza business located downtown near the campus shuttle-bus stop. Threats

figure 6.4 Risk Scorecard for a Small Business

If an entrepreneur has to do difficult things to make a business succeed, the chance of failure increases. Tasks can be more difficult if the entrepreneur is new to the industry. They can also be more difficult if the new product or service requires a high level of innovation or faces stiff competition. This is a simple version of a "risk scorecard" that an expert might use to assess these types of risks.

Directions: Use this scorecard to estimate the risk of failure for a business. Compute individual scores by choosing the statement that most closely applies to the business. Positive numbers represent advantages. Negative numbers, such as –1, represent drawbacks. To arrive at a total score, sum all five individual scores. A total score of zero or below indicates the business has a high risk of failure.

Product/Market

Established product	+1
New product	–2
Established market	+1
New market	–3
Score _____	

Management

Has run identical firm	+2
No industry experience	–1
Score _____	

Technical

Design stage	–3
Prototype stage	–2
Initial production run	+1
Score _____	

Competition

Patented	+1
Secret recipe	+1
No copyright/patent	–2
Unique efficiency	+1
Proprietary process	+1
Score _____	

Financial

Realistic projections	+1
Unrealistic projection	–1
Deep pocket backers	+2
Score _____	

Total Score _____

Source: Adapted from James Theroux, "How to Assess Risk or Is It Really That Risky?" *Working Paper*, University of Massachusetts School of Management, 1993.

can be of many kinds. If the university is considering a ban on late-night food deliveries to dorms, this could be a threat to the pizza business.

Form of the Business

What legal and strategic forms make the most sense for the new business? The entrepreneur might choose to avoid the double taxation of a regular corporation but have the partial protection from liability that the corporate form provides. Perhaps her library research revealed a number of cases in which restaurant customers sued the owners for damages when they slipped and hurt themselves on spilled food, for example. Furthermore, she may decide that one of her best bets for financing is selling shares to a wealthy aunt from Hong Kong—so the S corporation restrictions on foreign ownership make that option undesirable. Her solution is to form a limited liability corporation for her new pizza business.

Management and Organization

How will people and other key resources be organized and managed to ensure effective production and delivery of the business's products or services? The business plan must address all three aspects of the management and organization of the new business—management, internal organization, and production. It should specify what the management tasks are—in the case of a pizza business, who will do the hiring, who will purchase supplies, and who will supervise day and evening shifts? The plan should also show how the business will be organized. For example, will the entrepreneur hire a manager to supervise employees on one of the two shifts? And it should describe the production processes. What kinds of ovens will be used? How will the pizzas be assembled? What recipes will be followed?

Management, internal organization, and production are covered in Part 3.

Employees

What "people" roles are the key to the success of the business, and how will the necessary people be found, hired, and motivated? This part of the business plan focuses on issues such as employee motivation, human resources management, and employee-management relations. For our pizza entrepreneur, key issues are the types of skills needed in the business and the salaries required by employees who possess those skills. This section of the plan should end with a list of the positions that need to be filled and the payroll costs for those positions.

You will learn more about employee motivation, human resources management, and employee-management relations in Part 4.

Marketing

The analysis of the business environment should already point toward a specific group of customers and an opportunity to meet their needs. (A business plan should always start by identifying the customer need the new business will address.) The marketing section of the plan now takes a systematic approach to the problem of developing a product for the targeted customer and to the pricing, promotion, and distribution of the product. It also develops a goal for how you want the customer to think about the product. The marketing section always includes a projection, or estimate, of expected sales, by month, over the first few years. For our entrepreneur, the marketing section would identify the targeted customers, asking, for example, which group of people in the area eat the most pizza. And it would specify business location, the menu of product offerings, typical prices, and the types of advertising and other promotions needed to make the business a success.

We discuss these marketing tasks in Part 5.

Control Systems

Information is at the heart of controlling the business, as you learned in Chapter 1. Control systems enable the business owner to monitor and evaluate the company's performance and to make better decisions. What information is vital to the success of the business, and how will the business obtain, organize, and use this information? This section of the plan covers two important points: the information systems and technologies the business will use and the standard accounting and financial controls it will put in place.

The business plan for the pizza parlor would probably specify that a computerized cash register will be used to track sales by type of product and that some specific software program will be used to record and analyze all business costs. The plan would also identify the accountant or other person who will prepare the company's financial statements, which the entrepreneur and the investors will use to track the business's performance and to avoid financial problems. For small businesses, a sudden cash shortage can be a major prob-

doing business

Executive Summary: Noelle & Eliot's Pizza Delivery

We plan to open a pizza delivery business serving students in dormitories and apartments in the State University main campus area. Our projections indicate that we can capture 20 percent of the town's pizza market of $3.5 million in annual sales, giving us an estimated $700,000 in revenues by our second year.

We will attract college students by offering a wider variety of pizza toppings than those offered by competitors, by distributing fliers to all dormitory rooms and student apartment buildings, by sponsoring university teams and musical events, and by offering fast delivery 24 hours a day.

We anticipate that our expenses will be low because we will not offer any walk-in retail service; we therefore will not need to rent an expensive retail restaurant site. We plan to lease pizza ovens and delivery vans and to hire teams of two to handle deliveries in areas where parking is forbidden or by permit only.

We estimate monthly operating expenses will total $35,000, including our own salaries. This will give us a gross profit of approximately $23,000 per month. We wish to borrow $50,000 from a local bank or private investor in order to cover one-time costs associated with start-up.

---

lem, so this section of the plan often includes information about how the business will manage its checking account and pay its bills.

Part 6 covers information systems and accounting and financial control issues in detail.

Finances

What funding is needed to start and run the business, who is expected to provide it, and how will they be repaid through growth and profits? These financial issues are addressed both verbally and in the form of mathematical calculations in the final section of the business plan. The financial analysis usually starts with an estimate of expenses by month, which is then subtracted from the projected monthly revenues (described in the marketing section of the business plan). The result, an estimate of monthly profit or loss, gives the entrepreneur a rough idea of how much start-up money is needed. For instance, if $10,000 is needed to fix up the pizza kitchen before the business can open, the entrepreneur will have to raise at least $10,000 to cover the first month's loss.

Part 7 contains a detailed discussion of how a financial analysis is performed and where debt or equity funds can be raised.

Executive Summary and Plan Format

A business plan can be many pages long, and although the details are important, not everyone will want to wade through all of them. After completing the seven sections of the plan, the entrepreneur should prepare a clear, simple, one-page executive summary. The summary is placed at the front of the printed or bound plan to give potential lenders and investors, outside directors, and other interested parties a concise view of the proposed business (see the doing business box entitled "Executive Summary: Noelle & Eliot's Pizza Delivery").

As mentioned earlier, the business plan serves potential investors by explaining how the business is expected to work, whether the entrepreneurs seem to have a good idea, and whether they know how to execute their idea. Investors can check information on potential customers and the business environment to make sure they agree there really is an opportunity. And they can look at the financial projections to find out how much they would have to contribute and how much they could expect to earn if the business succeeds.

Investors examine all this information to assess their risk and compare it to their potential reward. Although investors always look for great new ideas that have the potential to grow into large and profitable businesses, such ventures

start-up financing

Funds to develop a product and conduct beginning marketing efforts.

undercapitalization

Lack of sufficient funds to meet the day-to-day expenses of a business.

kitchen capital

Personal savings used to finance a start-up business.

may also carry the greatest risk of failure. Investments, especially large ones, are carefully evaluated, with lots of research and analysis; investors turn down many of the business plans they review.

How much detail should your business plan present? The answer depends on the level of investment you are seeking. Short business plans—10 to 15 pages in length—have become increasingly acceptable in the U.S. financial and investment community.[18] In fact, unless you are seeking a *very* large amount of financing, there is little reason to consider the more traditional length of 40 to 50 pages. According to Bill Holt, vice president of Wachovia Bank of North Carolina, "We are looking for a good, concise summary, not a thesis. In fact, we prefer to see the facts presented one by one rather than in a paragraph format. We are making a factual decision so we want facts, not fluff."[19]

Implementation

Okay. You've got a great idea for a business. You've drafted a business plan and the numbers are exciting. All indications are that you are sitting on a potential gold mine. What next?

Implementing the Plan

In the immortal words of Nike, Just do it! But how? The long answer is that you must create the right form for your business, manage the business, empower your employees, identify and serve your customers, capture the power of information, and manage your finances well in order to make the business work. Those are the subjects of this and the following sections of this textbook—a very long answer, indeed! But the point is that implementation draws on the same core skills needed in any business, whether entrepreneurial or not.

The short answer is that your first concern is likely to be money. Yes, now it's time to think about it. You can't do much without funding. You may need **start-up financing**—funds to develop a product and conduct beginning marketing efforts. Depending on how your business fares during the crucial first months, you may also need additional financing. Your probable first step toward implementation will therefore be to raise capital.

Raising Capital

9. Identify the five potential sources of capital for a new business.

One of the key reasons new ventures fail is **undercapitalization**, the lack of sufficient funds to meet the day-to-day expenses of a business. This means you must choose your source of financing carefully so that you will have sufficient capital available to tide you through the critical first years of business. The sources most often used are personal savings, investment by family or friends, partnerships, loans from financial institutions, and venture capital investment.

Personal Savings Personal savings are the easiest form of financing to tap into. Personal savings used to finance a start-up business are also known as **kitchen capital**. The terms are easy, there are no application forms to fill out, and there are no investors to impress (besides yourself, of course). For a look at one entrepreneur who used $1,500 in personal savings to launch a business that is now worth millions, see the doing business box entitled "Capitalizing on a Fresh Perspective."

There is a downside to using kitchen capital, however. Many of us don't have the quantities of cash required to start up a business and keep it running long enough to become self-sufficient. This is especially true when businesses require substantial investments in facilities, inventory, or equipment. If your

doing business

Capitalizing on a Fresh Perspective

At the age of 26, Victoria Bondoc withdrew $1,500 from her personal savings to start up Gemini Industries, Inc. The year was 1986. By 1995, her Burlington, Massachusetts, consulting company was earning $5 million in yearly revenue and employed 110 people in six offices situated in Massachusetts, New York, Virginia, and the Philippines, her parents' native land. But Gemini's growth curve did not shoot straight up. Bondoc's story is a lesson in capitalizing on what makes you unique.

Though legally blind since birth, Bondoc holds degrees from the Massachusetts Institute of Technology in mathematics and from Boston University in computer science. After working for two major consulting firms in Boston, mainly on jobs for the military, Bondoc decided that the rigors of a daily commute by public transit combined with a ponderous, bureaucratic work pace were not for her, and she founded Gemini. The company designs computerized information and facilities management systems.

Bondoc used the network of work contacts she had developed to land Gemini's first contract, a small assignment from the U.S. Navy. Most of Gemini's early contracts were piecework—small parts of larger projects—which was all that military customers were willing to entrust to a young woman with no military background. Although Gemini built a strong track record of success and received larger projects as a result, Bondoc suffered a setback in 1991, losing a major contract to a competing firm. Gemini went into a tailspin. Morale sank as rumors spread about the lost client's negative attitudes toward Bondoc as an outsider—a physically challenged, minority woman with no direct military experience. Key staff abandoned Gemini to work for competitors, and revenue fell by one-third in 1992.

With the help of her remaining employees and clients, Bondoc turned the negative perceptions into strengths. Gemini became known as the "expert beginner"—the company that brings a fresh perspective to problem solving and to designing technology to meet the unique needs of its clients. Bondoc turned the adversity of being labeled an outsider into a positive selling point. In 1994, Gemini's clients ranged from government agencies, including the Air Force and the Department of Transportation, to technology giants Unisys Corporation and Digital Equipment Corporation, to a music industry promoter who stages performances by the artist formerly known as Prince.

Bondoc is at home in a world of rapid technological change. She says that a business's success is determined by its attitude toward change. Gemini's unique strength, says Bondoc, lies in helping its clients "maximize their ability to initiate change, adapt to change, use change to their advantage, and work within the continuing chaos that characterizes the world." And she should know.

Source: Based on Harriet Webster, "The 'Expert Beginner,'" *Nation's Business,* Jan. 1995, p 16.

"kitchen" falls short of your needs, you will have to attract outside investors—and for many people, that means calling on relatives.

Investment by Family or Friends Perhaps your parents have a little extra money they would be willing to invest in your idea. Or maybe you have a rich uncle who might be interested in sharing your risks and your profits. A key benefit of such arrangements is the relative ease of obtaining the financing and the flexible terms you can arrange for paying back the investor. The investment can be treated as a loan, with monthly payments of principal and interest. Alternatively, it can be repaid through distributions of a fixed percentage of company earnings or a share in its ownership. But consider this option carefully. There is a risk that you will lose the money your relatives lend you. If that happens, it may cause them financial hardship and you a great deal of emotional stress.

Partnerships Another fund-raising option is to invite a friend or business associate to join you in a partnership. Recall from Chapter 5 that each partner in the partnership invests in the venture, and each generally draws out money in direct proportion to his or her investment. Since any number of partners can be brought into a partnership, the overall amount of funds raised can be quite high. The downside is that the amount of control and the value of the ownership stake of each partner are diluted as new partners are brought in.

Kitchen Capital

Bitten by the entrepreneurial bug early—at 14—Stephanie Karp started out in 1985 with $200 worth of hair accessories. What started out as a selling job became a full-fledged wholesaling business before Karp graduated from high school. In 1994, Jolie and Co. (the company is named for Karp's French poodle) grossed $54,000 in revenues. Though tempted by college, and later by job offers, Karp knew, finally, that she simply wanted to continue building her own business. She says, "It's something that I've worked very hard at. I guess I wasn't ready to let go."

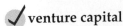 **loan guarantee**

Another party's promise of full repayment of a loan if the borrower defaults.

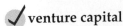 **venture capital**

Financing offered to high-risk ventures, usually in exchange for a substantial equity or ownership stake.

Loans from Financial Institutions When starting a new venture, many entrepreneurs immediately think of obtaining a loan to finance their start-up. Loans from banks, savings and loans, thrifts, and similar financial institutions have financed countless new businesses. Despite the fact that increased pressure from regulatory agencies has recently made it more difficult for entrepreneurs to obtain loans from financial institutions, loans still form the fiscal backbone of many new ventures.

Besides making direct loans to businesspeople, many financial institutions participate in loan guarantee programs, which are sponsored by the Small Business Administration (SBA) and other governmental and private sources. (The SBA is the federal agency that promotes and protects the interests of American small businesses. You will learn more about this agency in Chapter 7.) A **loan guarantee** is another party's promise of full repayment of a loan if the borrower defaults. To get a sense of the impact of these programs, consider the fact that in 1992, one SBA program provided guarantees on about 22,500 loans with a total value of more than $5.5 billion.[20] Without SBA loan guarantees and the security they provide to lenders, the vast majority of these loans would not have been approved.

Venture Capital Investment Many new ventures are particularly risky. However, these high-risk enterprises also offer the possibility of tremendous rewards if the product or service succeeds. For businesses in this category, the financing source of choice is **venture capital**: financing offered to high-risk ventures, usually in exchange for a substantial equity or ownership stake. In 1993, venture capital investment in such businesses totaled $4.2 billion, almost half of it in firms in Massachusetts and California.[21]

Preparing for Opening Day

Once you have secured the funds necessary to develop your product and conduct beginning marketing efforts, your next steps will be to organize and staff the business, and then to commence operations. If you have done your homework and developed a business plan, you have already identified and described many of the steps required to get your business off the ground. The story of the rise of the Saint Louis Bread Co. illustrates how one team of entrepreneurs got their new venture up and running.[22]

After 17 years of selling retail women's apparel, Linda and Ken Rosenthal knew they wanted to start a chain of stores, which they decided would be bakery/cafes that would sell the bread they would bake. During 1986 and 1987, Ken made six visits to bakeries in San Francisco to research their techniques. It cost thousands of hours of Ken's time and $50,000 in cash to learn the secrets of baking. Ken and Linda spent an additional $350,000 to open their first store: $100,000 of it came from a second mortgage on their home, $125,000 from the Small Business Administration, and $125,000 from personal savings. Saint Louis Bread Co. opened for business in October 1987.

From October 1987 to January 1989 the new owners made lots of mistakes, but they learned from them. As Ken Rosenthal commented, "We didn't know what we didn't know." Although the operation was far from perfect, total sales for the first nine months came to $245,600—not too much less than their initial investment. It was clear that the Rosenthals had come up with a winning idea.

In January 1989, the Rosenthals opened a second store, followed by a third, fourth, and fifth store in late 1989 and early 1990. During this expansion, the Rosenthals concentrated on stabilizing their group of products and making their operations more efficient. Working with vendors such as Stern Fixture Co., Saint Louis Bread was able to design more efficient sandwich-production stations. According to Mal Dardick, chairman of Stern, "We helped them think about better layouts for mass production."

Starting in late 1989, the Rosenthals developed their management team, bringing in partners to provide expertise in the areas of purchasing, regulatory compliance, real estate, and management. In exchange for a small amount of cash and a large commitment of **sweat equity**, or uncompensated labor that increases the value of a business, each new partner received a 17 percent stake in the business. In 1990, Saint Louis Bread began a new strategy of introducing a new product every 90 days as a means of stimulating sales. At the same time, it stepped up its community involvement efforts—introducing Operation: Dough-Nation in 1992 to collect customer cash donations to buy food for people in need and to match these contributions with donations of fresh bread.

By mid-1992, however, it was becoming clear that something was going wrong. Although the company had opened ten stores, with seven more slated to open by the end of the year, profits were abysmal. In 1991, Saint Louis Bread Co. had only a 1.7 percent profit margin on sales of $5.8 million. This is low, compared with companies like Au Bon Pain, a publicly traded chain of cafes that bakes bread and pastries. Au Bon Pain's profit margin at the time was 5.5 percent. The writing was on the wall—it was time to stop expanding and start planning. Or as Ken Rosenthal stated, "Each time you decide to grow again, you realize you're starting at the bottom of another ladder."

In 1992, the partners hired a team of consultants to lead the management of Saint Louis Bread through an extensive program of planning. The result was a carefully designed business plan that included a calendar of actions that would be necessary if the company was to meet its goals. This planning focused management's attentions on a coherent program of operations and growth.

Apparently the plan paid off (see Figure 6.5). In November 1993, the Rosenthals sold Saint Louis Bread Co. to Au Bon Pain. This pattern—called *cashing out*—is quite common: The entrepreneur builds a successful business until it catches the eye of an industry leader, which buys a major interest in it. If the Rosenthals are like many entrepreneurs, their name may crop up again, attached to another start-up venture. (Donuts, anyone?)

 **sweat equity**

Uncompensated labor that increases the value of a business.

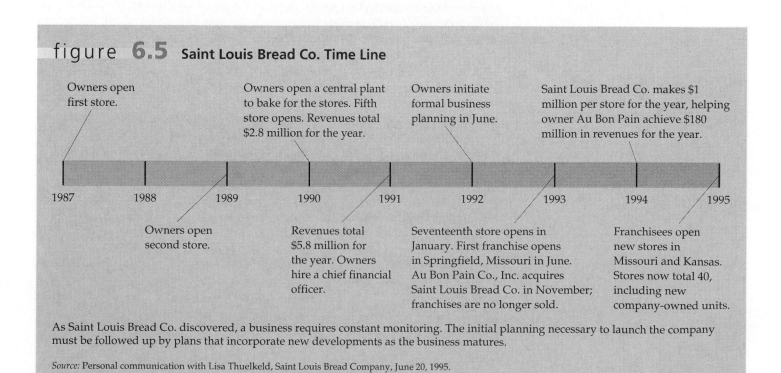

figure **6.5** **Saint Louis Bread Co. Time Line**

Owners open first store.

Owners open a central plant to bake for the stores. Fifth store opens. Revenues total $2.8 million for the year.

Owners initiate formal business planning in June.

Saint Louis Bread Co. makes $1 million per store for the year, helping owner Au Bon Pain achieve $180 million in revenues for the year.

1987   1988   1989   1990   1991   1992   1993   1994   1995

Owners open second store.

Revenues total $5.8 million for the year. Owners hire a chief financial officer.

Seventeenth store opens in January. First franchise opens in Springfield, Missouri in June. Au Bon Pain Co., Inc. acquires Saint Louis Bread Co. in November; franchises are no longer sold.

Franchisees open new stores in Missouri and Kansas. Stores now total 40, including new company-owned units.

As Saint Louis Bread Co. discovered, a business requires constant monitoring. The initial planning necessary to launch the company must be followed up by plans that incorporate new developments as the business matures.

Source: Personal communication with Lisa Thuelkeld, Saint Louis Bread Company, June 20, 1995.

✓ skunk works

Independent intrapreneurial unit that
develops new products within an existing business.

10. Explain how intrapreneurship
differs from entrepreneurship.

*Total quality management was defined in
Chapter 1 as a management approach to
long-term success through customer satisfaction based on all members of an organization participating in improving its
processes, products, and culture.*

Intrapreneurship in Traditional Businesses

Regardless of how innovative they may originally have been, many mature
businesses lose their ability to take risks. Layers of red tape and bureaucracy
often suffocate the imagination and drive that created great new products. This
happened, for example, to the American automobile industry, which for
decades was at the cutting edge of innovation, setting the standard by which all
other automobiles were judged. Things changed in the early 1970s, when the
industry forgot how to build exciting, quality products. Instead, it found itself
watching from the sidelines as Americans flocked to buy imported cars from
Honda, BMW, and Toyota. These Japanese and German car manufacturers
were marketing innovative products with quality second to none.

What is the cure for companies that forget how to act like entrepreneurs?
For the vast majority of businesses, intrapreneurship—defined earlier as behavior associated with the start-up and growth of new products, systems, and
processes *within* an existing business—is the answer. Intrapreneurship is distinguished from entrepreneurship by the environment in which it occurs. Entrepreneurship takes place beyond the framework of an established business. But
intrapreneurs work within an established business, which gives them more job
security and easier access to financing and other resources. These are the benefits of the intrapreneurial environment, but there is a trade-off. The intrapreneur lacks two key advantages of entrepreneurship: a high personal ownership
stake and the freedom to pursue business ideas without getting approval from
an employer.

Some companies encourage innovation by setting up a **skunk works**, an
independent intrapreneurial unit that develops new products within an existing business.[23] Bell Atlantic's program, mentioned in this chapter's opening example, set up this kind of environment. General Motors launched Saturn Corp.
when it realized that it had forgotten how to act like an entrepreneur and experienced tough competition from Japanese and European car manufacturers.
GM's new subsidiary created a more competitive car, and it used innovative
total quality management processes to design and manufacture it.

Although a subsidiary of General Motors, Saturn is structured to be an independent, self-supporting business. The idea was to assemble GM's best and

Intrapreneurship

The continuing success of GM's Saturn
Corp. demonstrates both the benefits of an
intrapreneurial environment and the growing importance of entrepreneurial behavior
in all forms of business.

brightest employees and allow them to start their own business—as though they were entrepreneurs. Saturn employees would design and manufacture cars using the most modern facilities and equipment available within a company that employed the most progressive methods of personnel management and labor relations. The plan worked. The Saturn automobile has been a big hit with American car buyers, who consistently rate it very high in quality and a great value.

Encouraging Intrapreneurial Behavior

Intrapreneurship doesn't just happen. An organization that wants to encourage intrapreneurial behavior among its employees has to provide an environment in which the characteristics described early in this chapter—creativity, moderate risk-taking, independence, and determination to achieve success—can flourish. Five factors seem to be particularly important in fostering intrapreneurship: support for employees who take risks, freedom to make mistakes, rewards for intrapreneurial behavior, time to think creatively, and encouragement for exploring new possibilities.[24]

Support for Employees Who Take Risks

The organization must clearly show its support of employees who behave intrapreneurially. Formal recognition of employee innovation and rapid adoption of employee initiatives are two easy ways to support intrapreneurial employees. Bell Atlantic does both for its champions.

Freedom to Make Mistakes

Employees must be trained in their jobs and then be allowed to determine exactly how they will perform them. Managers can stifle creativity if they criticize employees who make an honest mistake while testing an innovation. Often freedom can be achieved only by moving the intrapreneurs to a special skunkworks site where they are isolated from the rest of the company, as Bell Atlantic did. GM's Saturn group also is separate from the rest of GM.

Rewards for Intrapreneurial Behavior

Employees who behave intrapreneurially should receive rewards and recognition. All employees who exhibit intrapreneurial behavior should receive reinforcement in the form of job challenges, promotions, and increased responsibilities. Profit-sharing provides a big reward for successful champions at Bell Atlantic.

Time to Think Creatively

Every organization should ensure that its employees are not so overwhelmed with work that they don't have time to think. Employees who are too busy fighting fires will never have time to think about new ways of doing the job better.

Encouragement for Exploration

Intrapreneurial organizations encourage their employees to look beyond the narrow constraints of their own job descriptions and to consider organization-wide improvements. Standards of performance should not be so rigid that they discourage employees from exploring innovations. 3M's organizational culture favors innovation; as a result, employees feel free to explore.

Despite the increasing interest in intrapreneurship, a majority of entrepreneurs still find independence the best option. They may not be able to gain access to a corporate intrapreneurship program or may not be willing to give up control of their idea. These entrepreneurs start their own businesses—usually small businesses, at least in the beginning. In Chapter 7 we examine the characteristics of entrepreneurial small businesses as well as other types of small businesses and franchises.

Reviewing *Entrepreneurship and Planning a Business*

Entrepreneurship

1. **Identify the six steps of the entrepreneurship process.** Entrepreneurship is risk-taking behavior associated with the start-up and growth of a business. The six steps in the entrepreneurship process are imagination, formation, networking, analyzing risk, writing a business plan, and implementing the plan.

2. **State the four basic personal characteristics of an entrepreneur.** Research indicates that entrepreneurial skills can be learned, and many colleges and universities now offer courses to teach them. But four basic personal traits seem to characterize entrepreneurs: They are creative innovators, moderate risk takers, independent, and determined to achieve success. Previous managerial experience is a valuable background for an entrepreneur.

3. **Define *precipitating event* and explain how such an event might lead to a new business.** A precipitating event is a change in the environment that spurs an individual to take action. Such events may take the form of technological advances, changes in the individual's personal or physical well-being, social or family events, job- or market-related events, or simply a sudden entrepreneurial opportunity.

Conception: Finding a Need and Filling It

4. **List and describe seven sources of innovation in business.** Every new business starts with an innovation, a creative change in products or processes. An innovation may be the product of unexpected changes in basic business conditions or incongruities (strange events that clash with our assumptions about a business and its environment). The need to improve a process in the business system also may generate a new idea. A change in market structure may produce a profit for innovators who lead such changes or ride their crests. Other sources of innovation include changes in demographics—the aging of the U.S. population, for example—changes in customer perception of products and social trends, and new knowledge and technology.

5. **Describe the three-step process for building an entrepreneurial network.** Networking is the first task an entrepreneur must tend to after conceiving the idea for the business, because networking can lead to many financial and nonfinancial resources. The first step in the networking process is building a personal network of friends, relatives, customers, business associates, classmates, and other people who can provide advice and support to help launch the new business. The second step is converting these relationships into business contacts. In the third step, the entrepreneur extends and networks these contacts, creating further links among them to build a strong support for the new business.

Planning

6. **Discuss the five primary reasons for preparing a business plan.** A business plan analyzes and describes all the important issues involved in the start-up and ongoing operations of a business. A sound business plan will help an entrepreneur focus on his or her goals. Thus the five reasons are to determine the best way to manage the business, to identify and minimize risks that might cause the business to fail, to project financial operations so the entrepreneur can take maximum advantage of financial resources, to attract investors by showing that the business is a good financial opportunity, and to establish the vision and values that will guide the business and show how they will be translated into an effective and ethical organization.

7. **List the six factors that minimize risk for new ventures.** Research reveals that six factors minimize risk while maximizing chances of success. They are high self-confidence; larger business size, as defined by initial investments above $50,000 and six or more employees; a focus on quality rather than low price; a willingness to work hard, but not to overwork; devotion of full-time energy to the new venture, rather than working another job simultaneously; and knowledge of the product being produced. These six factors, combined with good management and an entrepreneurial personality, can reduce a new business's risk of failure to less than 20 percent in its first three years.

8. **Describe the seven topics covered by a business plan.** A business plan should describe and analyze seven areas of concern. It should analyze the current and future environment for opportunities and threats; describe the legal form of the business; define how the business will be

managed and organized and how production will proceed; describe employee skills and salaries, setting forth a plan for finding, hiring, and motivating employees; project sales based on a marketing plan that describes pricing, promoting, and distributing the product; describe the control systems and technologies and how information will be obtained and used; and analyze projected revenues and expenses to determine funding (who will provide it and how it will be repaid). The level of detail varies, but plans frequently run about ten to fifteen pages in length and should always begin with a one-page executive summary.

Implementation

9. **Identify the five potential sources of capital for a new business**. Businesses may need start-up financing to develop a product and conduct beginning marketing efforts, or additional financing to keep the business on course during its first critical months. Undercapitalization is one of the key reasons businesses fail. Personal savings (kitchen capital) are the most available form of financing, although they are rarely adequate. Other relatively easy sources of funds are investments by family and friends. Forming a partnership may provide relatively large amounts of capital but it can dilute control. Alternatively, or additionally, the entrepreneur may try to obtain a loan from a financial institution, which may be guaranteed by the SBA or other agency. Venture capital may be an option, particularly if the owner is willing to give up a substantial share of ownership in exchange for funding for a high-risk product.

Intrapreneurship in Traditional Businesses

10. **Explain how intrapreneurship differs from entrepreneurship**. Red tape and bureaucracy can threaten to suffocate the innovative spirit of an established business. In such cases, intrapreneurship—behavior associated with the start-up and growth of new products, systems, and processes *within* an existing business—may be the answer. Some large companies create skunk works—independent intrapreneurial units operating within the larger company. Even so, intrapreneurship differs from entrepreneurship. Entrepreneurs face a risky future because they operate beyond the framework of an established business. Intrapreneurs operate from an established base, which gives them more job security and easier access to financing and other resources. Intrapreneurs do not, however, receive the rewards of operating their own businesses—their personal stake in the business is lower and they usually cannot pursue business ideas without their employer's approval.

 Key Terms

entrepreneurship **169**	process need **174**	debt capital **179**	loan guarantee **186**
intrapreneurship **169**	demographics **175**	equity capital **179**	venture capital **186**
precipitating event **170**	networking **176**	start-up financing **184**	sweat equity **187**
innovation **173**	business plan **178**	undercapitalization **184**	skunk works **188**
incongruities **174**	investors **179**	kitchen capital **184**	

● Review Questions

1. What is entrepreneurship and why is it so important to the economy?

2. What are the six steps in the entrepreneurship process?

3. What four personal traits characterize entrepreneurs? Can these traits be learned?

4. What are the seven sources of innovation, according to Peter Drucker?

5. Why is networking an important activity for an entrepreneur launching a new business?

6. How does preparing a business plan help an entrepreneur launch a successful business? Give five reasons for developing a business plan.

7. How risky are new business ventures? What factors can minimize risk and increase the chances that a business will succeed?

8. What topics should a business plan address, and how long should a plan be?

9. What are the major sources of business capital, and what is *undercapitalization*?

10. Does intrapreneurship have advantages and disadvantages compared with entrepreneurship? If so, what are they?

• Critical Thinking Questions

1. If you were the president of the United States, what steps would you take to support entrepreneurship?

2. If you believed you had a great business idea, what steps would you take to make it a reality? Which step would be most difficult for you?

3. Who would be on your first list of contacts if you were developing a network for a new business? Explain why you chose those people.

4. What steps would you take to ensure that your new venture was not undercapitalized?

5. Do you possess the four personal traits that characterize entrepreneurs? Describe how your personal characteristics match the four basic traits or differ from them, and explain how that might affect your future as an entrepreneur or intrapreneur.

REVIEW CASE *La Palapa*[25]

In February 1993, John Kopecky changed his life. After years of working his way up the corporate ladder, he decided he had finally had enough. As the manager of software development for a growing defense contractor, Kopecky was by all measures a success. His salary was almost $70,000, he owned three homes, and he even had time to play lead guitar in a blues-rock band. Despite all this, Kopecky was dissatisfied—he wanted to start his own business and be his own boss.

Pooling the money from his retirement plan with some additional funds invested by his sister and brother-in-law, Kopecky came up with $30,000 in start-up capital. He moved to Phoenix, Arizona, and prepared to make his dream real by opening La Palapa, a Mexican restaurant. La Palapa would be different from most Mexican restaurants in Phoenix, which were either fast-food chains or formal dining rooms in which waiters served U.S. versions of Mexican food rather than the real thing. Kopecky's idea was a restaurant that would serve *authentic* Mexican food, packaged for home consumption. Only a small counter and three barstools would be available for customers who preferred eating in the restaurant.

Without too much difficulty, Kopecky found a location in a shopping center near the Arizona State University campus. He bought used stoves, fixtures, and other equipment for far less than they would have cost new. And he used his fix-up skills to build the counters and paint the walls. After spending $20,000 in start-up capital, Kopecky was ready to open the doors of La Palapa.

Only time would tell whether the new venture would be a success. Kopecky knew it would take a lot of hard work and a measure of luck to ensure La Palapa's survival beyond the critical first three years. At the end of each day, however, he was satisfied, knowing he had no one to answer to but himself and knowing he had given his best that day.

1. Does Kopecky exhibit any of the four personal characteristics common to entrepreneurs? If so, which one or ones?

2. Kopecky did not write a business plan for La Palapa. How might that hurt his chances of surviving his first three years? Should he write one now?

3. Could Kopecky's previous experience help him to make La Palapa a success?

4. Assuming La Palapa is undercapitalized, what other sources of financing should Kopecky consider, and why?

5. If Kopecky decides to begin networking to help La Palapa succeed, whom should he include on his list of contacts?

CRITICAL THINKING CASE   *The Telephone Doctor*[26]

Was it good timing, hard work, or just plain luck? Nancy Friedman is not quite sure why her business—The Telephone Doctor, as it came to be called—is such a success. What she does remember is that her idea of conducting seminars to train people in courteous telephone manners came shortly after a rude telephone encounter with her insurance agent's office.

Friedman's experience as a telephone representative caused her to realize that her understanding of telephone manners could be a salable product. She also had acted on stage, so she was not afraid to speak in front of a large group of trainees. And she was willing to work hard to make her business a success.

Her first seminar generated a profit of just 38 cents. Nevertheless, Friedman believed in her idea. She knew many people in the local business community, and through personal contacts she found an association of local businesses willing to sponsor seminars for its members.

During the early days, Friedman traveled extensively, giving seminars all over the United States. As her business grew, she spread her message by using other forms of com-munication—instructional videos and audiotapes—which were promptly snapped up by corporations eager to please their customers. Friedman now also runs a school for receptionists and is writing a book on telephone tips. The company has annual sales of $2 million, more than 20 employees, and clients around the globe.

1. Which of Drucker's seven sources of innovation most closely matches the ideas that launched Nancy Friedman's business?

2. Which factors from the American Express/NFIB study of risks would have predicted that Friedman's business would be successful? Which would have predicted that the business was risky?

3. If you were hired to help Friedman come up with another breakthrough innovation, what would you recommend for her business?

4. Should Friedman create a skunk works to develop the idea you suggested in question 3? Why or why not?

Critical Thinking with the ONE MINUTE MANAGER

"The Bell Atlantic Champion Program sounds like a great concept. Do you have champions here?" Carlos asked the One Minute Manager.

"Yes, Carlos, but our approach is a little different. See this pin I'm wearing on my lapel?" She leaned forward to display a small brass pin in the shape of a skunk. "Here we call our champions 'skunks,' and the way we treat them seems pretty shabby, though it really isn't. If employees choose to develop their ideas, we force them out of this nice new office building and make them set up an office in our skunk works, an old warehouse we don't use any more. We give them separate quarters to protect both them from us and us from them. When the skunks are focusing on building their own new products or businesses, they need to be free-wheeling and completely unconcerned about everybody else's projects or problems. Nobody can be an entrepreneur for long when the people around them are *not*. And other employees find entrepreneurs difficult to work with. They don't understand their total commitment and passion for their project. If you come in here on a Sunday morning at 9:00 a.m., the office will be completely empty, but there will be people crawling all over the skunk works offices!"

"Were you ever a skunk? Is that why you wear that pin?" Joanna asked.

"Yes, I spent a year and a half developing a new product line that nobody else thought was worthwhile. When I came back, the company gave me this pin. I'm not sure whether it was intended to reward me or to warn others, but I like to wear it anyway! And I certainly hope you both have a chance to do something similar at some point."

1. Why might it be necessary to protect intrapreneurs from their own companies?

2. Why might it be necessary to protect the rest of the company from a skunk works?

3. Intrapreneurs often return to more traditional jobs after the product they championed has been introduced. Why might an intrapreneur be willing to do this? (*Hint*: Consider the personal characteristics of entrepreneurs and how a new product project might change after the product is introduced.)

7 Small Business and Franchising

In this chapter we explore the critically important role that small businesses play in the American business environment. As technology continues to put low-cost information-processing tools into the hands of small businesses and as small-business owners become more competitive, the advantages of scale or size advantages that in the past gave large businesses a significant cost advantage over smaller companies are dwindling. In addition, given the current economic climate, you are far more likely to work in one or more small businesses than were students in previous generations. After reading this chapter, you will be able to reach the learning goals below.

Learning Goals

1. Define small business, as specified by the SBA.
2. List and describe the advantages and disadvantages of a small business.
3. Describe the two general types of small businesses and give an example of each.
4. Discuss the role of small businesses in job creation, noting in particular their significance for women and minorities.
5. Broadly describe the federal government's contribution in promoting small businesses and give some examples.
6. Describe the development of enterprise zones and business incubators as sources of state and local assistance to small businesses.
7. Explain how small businesses help themselves to maintain their competitive edge.
8. Identify the three major forms of franchising and describe the advantages of franchising in general.
9. Discuss the risks involved in buying a franchise.
10. Describe the best strategy for finding a job with a small business.
11. Outline the four factors that suggest future success for a small business.

Think Small

"As eager young business students, I expect you are thinking pretty big: a good job with a well-known company, a rapid rise to the top, big responsibilities, big salary. Right?"

The students nodded as they settled into the One Minute Manager's office for another discussion session.

"And enthusiasm and confidence are important—don't get me wrong. It's just that so many students today are focused on the traditional ideal of an entry-level job with one of the few hundred largest companies in the country. I have to warn you that most of the companies whose names you know are not likely to hire you in the current economy. Did you know that General Motors hasn't hired a single new employee over the last *decade*? That's why I tell students to think *small*, not big."

"Are you trying to discourage us?" Joanna asked. "I thought the job prospects for business majors were pretty good."

"They are—that's not the point. The point is that many of the jobs are with smaller companies, ones you may never have heard of, ones that are unlikely to come to your campus to interview prospective employees. And, in many cases, they are less likely to offer you a huge starting salary and lots of responsibility. But on the other hand, small-business jobs may give you more opportunity for career growth, because small businesses often grow faster than their larger counterparts. Here, where did I put that . . . "

The One Minute Manager propped her reading glasses on her nose, picked up a photocopied article, and read: "'Career growth in smaller firms comes through the company's growth, says Michael Wellman, vice president of the recruiting firm of Korn Ferry.' Recruiters are businesses that help companies find employees," she explained. "And this article goes on to say that, because small businesses have the growth to offer a good career path, they 'often have an advantage over their larger counterparts in hiring.' Which means," the One Minute Manager summed up, "that people often find the job openings in small business *more appealing* than those in big business."[1]

The Importance of Small Business

What exactly is a small business? It's obvious that the family-owned pizza place near your campus is a small business, but what about the farmer who produces $495 million worth of tomatoes a year and sells them to the manufacturer of the sauce used in the pizza parlor? Is that farm a small business? Or how about the cookie manufacturer who employs 700 employees and supplies your school's cafeteria—is her firm a small business? How about a bank with $95 million in annual receipts—is it a small business? The answer depends on your definition of small business.

The **Small Business Administration (SBA)** was established under the Small Business Act of 1953 to foster the development of small businesses. The act defines a **small business** as a business that meets three requirements:

- It is independently owned and operated.
- It is not dominant in its field of operation.
- It meets SBA standards for number of employees and income.[2]

By this definition, Domino's Pizza is not a small business, because it is dominant in its field. The locally owned pizza parlor, however, qualifies nicely. Surprisingly enough, however, so does each of the other businesses mentioned earlier. They may seem like fairly large businesses, but they qualify by SBA guidelines.

SBA-defined small businesses generally have fewer than 500 employees, but size standards vary.[3] Here are some examples of SBA size standards for five specific categories of business:

- *Agriculture*—An agricultural business is considered small if its annual revenues do not exceed $500,000 to $7 million, depending on the particular animal or crop raised.
- *Construction*—To be considered a small business, a contractor's average annual sales cannot have exceeded $17 million ($7 million for specialty contractors) in the preceding three years.
- *Manufacturing*—Any manufacturer with 500 or fewer employees in the preceding four calendar quarters is considered a small business. A manufacturer employing between 500 and 1,500 people may or may not be a small business, depending on the industry.
- *Services and Stores*—A business in this category is considered small if its annual revenues do not exceed $2.5 to $13.5 million, again depending on the nature of the business.
- *Wholesaling*—A wholesaler, one that buys products to sell to stores, is a small business if it employs no more than 100 people.[4]

According to the Small Business Administration, 99 percent of U.S. businesses qualify as small businesses under SBA size standards.[5] Note that so-called midsize and big businesses do *not* have a formal definition, since no laws or government programs target them.

What Makes Small Businesses Competitive?

Small businesses are capable of providing superior service or products. One such business, Superior Tomato and Avocado Co., Inc., a small business supplying grocery stores in San Antonio, Texas, was ranked number one in *Hispanic Business* magazine's 1993 list of the 100 fastest growing Hispanic firms.

 Small Business Administration (SBA)

Agency established under the Small Business Act of 1953 to foster the development of small businesses.

small business

A business that is independently owned and operated, is not dominant in its field of operation, and meets SBA standards for number of employees and income.

1. Define small business, as specified by the SBA.

2. List and describe the advantages and disadvantages of a small business.

Bertha Caballero, president of Superior Tomato and Avocado, says Superior's success is the result of a lot of hard work and long hours. And in addition to hard work, Caballero has discovered that success depends on more than simply offering a quality product at a reasonable price. To capture and retain customers, the employees and management of Superior Tomato and Avocado do things for their customers that their competitors don't. For example, Superior services small mom-and-pop customers as well as major accounts such as wholesalers, supermarket chains, and large hotels and restaurants.[6] Caballero's hard work pays off for her customers, who value the personal service and superior products she offers. And it pays off for Caballero, who enjoys the challenges and rewards of running her own business. Not all small businesses succeed, of course—their failure rate is higher than that of big businesses. But small businesses are essential to innovation and economic growth in the United States and in many European countries.

Despite the tremendous attention the media give to large consumer goods firms such as PepsiCo, Procter & Gamble, Philip Morris, Nike, and General Mills, the Fortune 500 top U.S. firms now employ only about 11 percent of the overall American work force. In contrast, small businesses employ 57 percent of the work force. (The remainder of the work force is employed in government, in not-for-profit organizations, or in the few midsize businesses that fall between small and large, or is unemployed.) Figure 7.1 illustrates the decline in the Fortune 500's share of the American work force since the 1950s. As these statistics show, more and more people are joining Bertha Caballero in the small-business sector of our economy. Small businesses also create many new jobs—a topic we examine later in this chapter.

Small businesses are a significant force not only in domestic markets but also in U.S. exports to foreign countries. According to government trade statis-

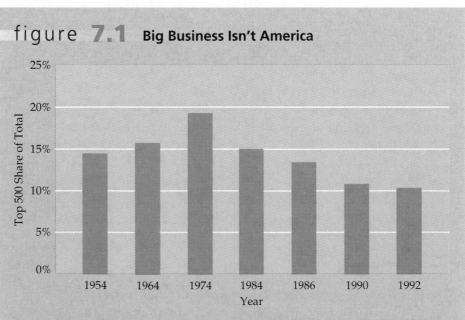

figure **7.1** **Big Business Isn't America**

Top 500 Share of Total (y-axis)

Year (x-axis): 1954, 1964, 1974, 1984, 1986, 1990, 1992

The 500 biggest U.S. firms employed one-fifth of all U.S. business employees in the mid-1970s, when most of today's college students were born. Now that share is closer to one-tenth.

Source: David Hale, "Small Business Tax Plan's Victim," *Wall Street Journal*, July 30, 1993.

tics, small businesses with 500 or fewer employees generated $69.1 billion, or 29 percent, of the $241.2 billion worth of goods and services exported in 1987. Even more impressive, small businesses constitute more than 80 percent of the total number of exporting firms.[7]

As these statistics show, small businesses are surprisingly competitive in both domestic and global markets. Let's look at five characteristics that are common to successful small businesses and that help explain their economic strength.

Personal Service

Customers get the direct benefit of owners' expertise and attention. Chemical Finishing Inc., a Massachusetts supplier of products used to coat and polish metals, is a small business that sells to other small and midsize businesses. One of the company's goals is to retain 100 percent of its customers, and it rarely loses one of them. Chemical Finishing has no marketing department—its owners and top managers all work directly with customers to help them make better products. In a bigger company, top managers could not provide such personal service to each customer.[8]

Narrow Focus

Small businesses tend to specialize in a narrow range of products or services, which often leads to high-quality products directly targeted at specific customer needs. When you do only one thing, it is easier to do it well. And focusing on one set of customer needs encourages innovation for those customers.

Adaptability

Since small businesses typically are not saddled with the multiple layers of bureaucracy commonly found in large businesses, they can respond to market changes more quickly. Of course, their size can give them flexibility, but flexibility can also be limited by a lack of financial resources. Sometimes big companies beat small ones into a new market by buying up another small business already in that market.

Innovativeness

According to one study, small businesses produce more than twice as many innovations per employee as do large businesses. Recall from Chapter 1 that big businesses are attempting to find ways to "get that small-company soul—and small-company speed—inside [a] big-company body," as General Electric Co.'s chairman John F. Welch, Jr., expressed it.[9] Big business needs to learn how to innovate by studying small businesses that do it well.

Less Organizational Fat

Small businesses tend to be lean, with few layers of management, which can translate into more efficiency and higher productivity. That means they can sometimes do the same job for less money, compared with a larger competitor.

The characteristics that help small businesses compete with large ones also enable them to serve their customers well and to benefit the economy as a result. That is why many people want to work for or own a small business. When asked in a survey what "dream job" they would like to have for one year, 38 percent of the men and 47 percent of the women questioned gave "head of own business" as their preference. High-paying jobs such as professional athlete and president of a large corporation didn't even come close.[10]

The Challenges of Small Business

Owning or running a small business may be many people's dream job, but in reality that dream sometimes becomes a nightmare. Small businesses can be difficult to manage for several reasons.

High Stress

An owner-manager feels personally responsible for the business's problems, which can lead to stress symptoms such as anxiety, ulcers, high blood pressure, and insomnia. Small-business managers need to learn how to manage high job stress, and learning to delegate work to others is an important first step in this process.[11]

Family–Business Conflict

Many small businesses employ multiple family members who do not always agree on business strategy. Even when this is not the case, a sole proprietor may feel torn between the demands of work and the needs of his or her spouse or children—many divorces each year are attributed to this problem. John Ward of the Georgia-based Family Business Consulting Group, Inc., says small-business managers have to learn to be "hard on issues, soft on people" to minimize conflict between family and business.[12]

Risk of Failure

Every year, more than 80,000 U.S. businesses fail, closing their doors and leaving their employees and owners without work or pay. Of these, at least three-fourths are small businesses.[13] While these failures represent fewer than 2 percent of all small businesses, they affect hundreds of thousands of people. And failure rates are much higher for new businesses. Estimates vary, but approximately one-quarter of small businesses fail in their first three years, and more than half may fail before their sixth birthday.[14] That means the risk of failure can be very high in younger small businesses, threatening employees and owners with sudden disaster.

Life-style Business or Growth Business?

3. Describe the two general types of small businesses and give an example of each.

There are two general types of small businesses: life-style businesses and growth businesses. Each type offers benefits to its owners and employees, but those benefits differ.

Life-style Businesses: Built for Comfort

The **life-style business** is a small business that supports its owners and tends to be stable in size. One currently popular life-style business is the small home-town microbrewery. Instead of measuring their output in millions of barrels of beer as do the big breweries, microbreweries measure their output in hundreds of barrels. For the big breweries' reaction to this current trend, see the doing business box "If You Can't Beat Them, Join Them." The local pizza shop is another life-style business, and it typically supports a single family. It is unlikely to add new locations or take other actions that expose it to high risk. It does not need to grow rapidly for its owners to maintain their life-style.

While many small businesses can potentially grow into large businesses, not every business owner wants to expand his or her venture into a multibillion-dollar transnational empire. As businesses grow, so does the need to create

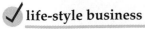

life-style business

A small business that supports its owners and tends to be stable in size.

doing business

If You Can't Beat Them, Join Them

The proliferation of microbreweries has not gone unnoticed by megabrewers such as Anheuser-Busch, Coors, and Miller. Indeed, with declining sales of such mainline brands as Budweiser (down 9 percent from 1990 through 1993) and Miller Lite (down 16 percent from 1990 through 1993), the big breweries are scrambling to capture the special aura of their smaller competitors. And why not? The market for microbrewed beers is currently growing at a whopping 50 percent per year.

So, can an old dog really learn new tricks? The answer is yes, and no. While pouring more money into the marketing of their ebbing flagship brands, megabrewers are applying several different strategies to meet the microbrewery challenge. Miller's response to the microbrewery challenge was to create its own virtual microbrewery—the Plank Road Brewery. While the name conjures up a rustic vision of a small-time brewer hidden away on some dusty back road, make no mistake that Plank Road's product—Icehouse beer—is a mass-produced commodity. Indeed, Miller produces Icehouse beer in the same megabreweries,

and in the same type of huge stainless steel tank, it uses to produce its more familiar products Miller Lite and Miller Genuine Draft.

Industry giant Anheuser-Busch has taken a different tack in competing against the upstart microbreweries. Instead of creating a new, microbrewlike product, Anheuser-Busch has seen its vision of the future of the industry and has invested in the Redhook Ale Brewery, a Seattle microbrewery. While Anheuser-Busch sold 90 million barrels of beer last year, Redhook sold only 76,000.

For its investment, Anheuser-Busch gets an upscale, niche brand to sell. As a part of the deal, Anheuser-Busch will distribute Redhook's products nationwide, giving it in only a few months market exposure that would have taken many years to develop, while catapulting Redhook virtually overnight from small-business, cult status into the big time.

Source: Patricia Sellers, "A Whole New Game in Beer," *Fortune,* Sept. 19, 1994.

---

a bureaucracy to deal with that growth. For life-style businesses, small is best, as Terrylynn Pearson decided when she left a high-paying public relations job and started up her own firm, Pearson PR, in 1991. Instead of scrambling for every client she could get, Pearson settled on five, turning down all other potential clients who requested her assistance.

Pearson is happy doing what she does best—providing quality service to her clients—without having to assume the extra headaches of hiring employees, issuing paychecks, developing personnel policies and procedures, and paying for employee health care and other benefits. "I don't want to take that on," she explains. "I have a manageable number of accounts. I'm making six figures. I've fallen in love with working on my own." And, as Pearson is quick to point out, running a home-based business such as hers has other benefits: "I don't have to be dressed for success."[15]

Life-style businesses offer a supportive environment for owners and employees, unless they run into direct competition from more aggressive competitors. When they do, the party is over and the owners must either close down the business or adopt a more aggressive style. Toy stores used to be a great life-style business, but now the market share of the five biggest national chains just keeps growing—from 42 percent in 1990 to an estimated 55 percent in 1996. Many small competitors have been forced out of business by Toys 'R' Us, Wal-Mart Stores, Inc., and other big competitors.[16]

Growth Businesses: Built for Speed

A **growth business** is a small business that is managed for rapid growth and that may take high risks to achieve that growth. If successful, a growth business may become a gazelle, one of the few companies that consistently increases its revenues by more than 20 percent each year. Eventually, such a business may become a big business.

 growth business

A small business that is managed for rapid growth and that may take high risks to achieve that growth.

Horizons Technology, Inc., a Southern California commercial software developer and government research and development firm, is a growth business well on its way to becoming a large business. Already a major player in the delivery of computerized information systems to the federal government, Horizons has long had the goal of becoming a dominant player in the world of commercial software development. With the acquisition of new digital video software and new software for computer network management, Horizons Technology may well meet its goal. Overall revenues have climbed steadily in the past decade—from $7 million in 1984 to $56 million, eight times that figure, in 1994. Although Horizons Technology is still a small business, its management plans to outgrow the small-business label by the year 2000 and to continue its growth beyond the $100 million per year mark.

Goya Foods, another small business that took the high-growth path, is now the nation's largest privately owned food company specializing in Hispanic products. Joseph A. Unanue's father founded Goya Foods over 50 years ago. Now, Unanue presides over a food empire that offers 800 different products, including coffee, rice, beans, orange juice, and ice cream. The secret of Goya's success was taking simple grocery products and marketing them with an ethnic spin that appealed to the burgeoning Hispanic market. With the continuing growth of the Hispanic population in the United States and the growing enthusiasm for Goya's products among *all* consumers, company executives predict that annual sales will surpass $1 billion by the year 2000.[17] Goya is no longer a small business by formal government standards; it is midsize and on its way to true big-business status.

Small Businesses Are Job Factories

There are more than 30,000 small businesses listed in the Manhattan Yellow Pages. If only 1 percent of these 30,000 Manhattan-area small businesses were hiring full-time positions at any given time, a student wishing to work in New York would have 3,000 or more job openings to apply for!

Small businesses have consistently led the way in the generation of new jobs, and their ability to create jobs is very important during recessions. During the period from 1977 to 1987, small businesses were responsible for 11.3 million jobs, or 68 percent of the 16.5 million net new jobs created in the United States. As small-business job opportunities have increased, large-business opportunities have decreased. Between 1988 and 1990, for example, large businesses registered significant job losses, and small businesses accounted for *all* new jobs in the American economy.[18] A significant layoff for a small business in financial trouble might be five or ten employees. When a large business gets into financial trouble, however, a layoff can be in the tens of thousands. On July 27, 1993, for example, IBM announced that 35,000 jobs would be eliminated as part of a corporate reorganization and restructuring.[19]

Job creation is most notable in the nation's smallest firms, those with fewer than 20 employees. From 1988 to 1990, firms with fewer than 20 employees created approximately 4 million new jobs. This extraordinary performance is in sharp contrast with the loss of more than 500,000 jobs in large businesses and the loss of 850,000 jobs in firms with 20 to 499 employees during the same period.[20] If the nation's smallest businesses had not contributed these jobs, the recession that gripped the United States in the early 1990s might well have continued its downward spiral into depression. Instead, its impact was moderated and, at the time of this writing, the U.S. economy was able to make good progress toward recovery.

The economic impact of small businesses has not always received the attention it deserves. Until 1979, economists tended to concentrate on the activity of large businesses. In 1979, when David Birch published the results of a study of all U.S. firms and their employment statistics, the illusion of large-business dominance of the American economy was finally shattered. Economists generally agree that one of the key measures of economic growth is new job creation. And since, as Birch showed, businesses with 100 or fewer employees were responsible for the vast majority—81 percent—of new jobs during the period 1969 through 1976, it was necessary to conclude that small businesses must be directly responsible for the major part of American economic growth.[21] Although economists at first doubted Birch's conclusions, his findings were ultimately confirmed independently by a wide variety of economists worldwide. However, debate can be expected to continue on this important issue.

Small businesses' total contribution of new jobs varies from period to period, in a movement that seems to be a cycle. Every other year, the Small Business Administration tracks the contributions of small businesses and large businesses to new job creation. These data indicate that small businesses of 100 employees or fewer dominate the creation of new jobs in two situations: during periods of economic recession and during the first two years immediately following a recession. In periods of rapid economic expansion, large businesses lead small businesses in the creation of new jobs.[22] Figure 7.2 on the next page illustrates small firms' share of new jobs created in the United States since 1969. Three factors help small firms create job opportunities.

1. *Faster Growth*—Small businesses often grow at a much faster rate than do large, more established businesses. This is especially true during and just following a recession. Faster growth means more new jobs and more promotion opportunities for employees.

2. *More Choices*—Since more than 99 percent of American businesses are small businesses, it makes sense that the majority of job opportunities can be found in these organizations. Take a look at your local Yellow Pages. How many listings are there for Fortune 500 businesses? How many listings can you find for small businesses? Convinced?

4. Discuss the role of small businesses in job creation, noting in particular their significance for women and minorities.

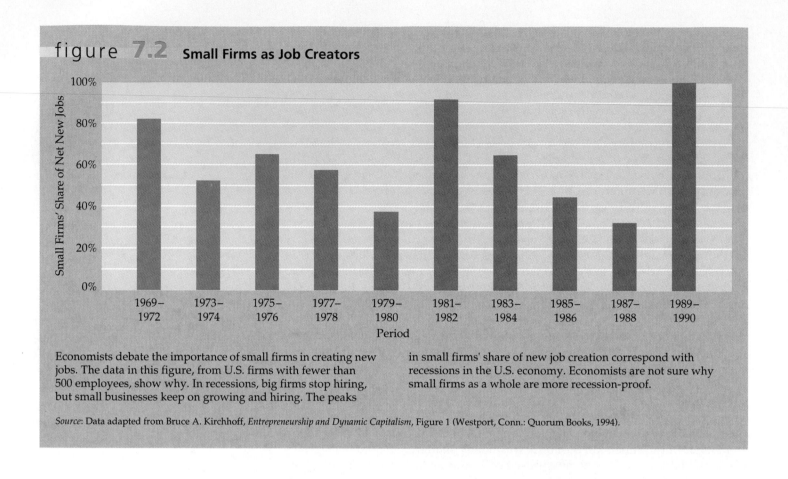

figure **7.2** **Small Firms as Job Creators**

Economists debate the importance of small firms in creating new jobs. The data in this figure, from U.S. firms with fewer than 500 employees, show why. In recessions, big firms stop hiring, but small businesses keep on growing and hiring. The peaks in small firms' share of new job creation correspond with recessions in the U.S. economy. Economists are not sure why small firms as a whole are more recession-proof.

Source: Data adapted from Bruce A. Kirchhoff, *Entrepreneurship and Dynamic Capitalism*, Figure 1 (Westport, Conn.: Quorum Books, 1994).

3. *Accessible Jobs*—Smaller businesses are often more sympathetic to ethnic minorities, women, and older workers.

Minorities and Women in Small Business

Small businesses excel in diversity—both in the products and services they provide and in the opportunities for ownership and employment they offer to all segments of the population. Small businesses carry the faces of Americans of every ethnic group, age, gender, disability, religious belief, political persuasion, sexual orientation, and geographic region. For these Americans, small business holds the promise of true growth—both financial and personal.

Between 1982 and 1987, the number of businesses owned by women increased almost 60 percent, from 2.6 million to 4.1 million. During this same period, sales by women-owned businesses tripled—from $98.3 billion in 1982 to $278.1 billion in 1987. Similar growth occurred in the number of firms owned by African Americans: an increase of 38 percent from 308,000 in 1982 to 424,000 in 1987. During this period, sales by African-American firms more than doubled—from $9.6 billion in 1982 to $19.8 billion in 1987. Hispanic-owned firms have shown even more dramatic gains. Between 1982 and 1987, their number almost doubled—from 233,975 to 422,373—and total sales more than doubled, from $11.8 billion in 1982 to $24.7 billion in 1987.[23]

Let's take a closer look at the remarkable gains being made by Hispanic-owned firms. A survey of the 100 fastest growing Hispanic firms showed average compounded sales growth over a five-year period of 68 percent a year. The net sales increase during this period was from $262 million in 1988 to more than $1.5 billion in 1992. Employment at these 100 firms quintupled—from 4,000 in 1988 to more than 20,000 in 1992. And, while the Forbes Sales 500 grew at an average annual compound rate of 4.9 percent from 1988 to 1992, the Hispanic Business 100 grew 14 times as fast during the same period.[24]

It is interesting to note that minority-owned firms tend to hire more minority workers than do their nonminority-owned counterparts. A survey conducted by the Joint Center for Political and Economic Studies found that 96 percent of African American–owned firms located in minority communities were staffed with 50 percent or more minority employees. Among white-owned firms, only 38 percent had 50 percent or more minority employees. And while 33 percent of white-owned firms in minority communities had no minority employees at all, fewer than 2 percent of African American–owned firms had no minority employees.[25]

Clearly, small businesses create employment opportunities for community members. Consider the story of Food From the 'Hood, America's first student-run natural food and salad dressing company.

Run by 39 predominantly Hispanic and African-American students at Crenshaw High School in the riot-torn South-Central district of Los Angeles, Food From the 'Hood was created to establish a student scholarship fund (see the photo on page 134). Biology teacher Tammy Bird convinced the students to convert a vacant lot adjacent to the school into a lush urban garden. The venture garnered the support of many different sponsors and advisers. Rebuild L.A., a group formed to help Los Angeles recover from the 1992 riots, provided a $50,000 grant, and Melinda McCullen, a full-time public relations executive, left her job to work full time for Food From the 'Hood. As 16-year-old Ben Osborne, commenting on the venture's first commercial product, a salad dressing named Straight Out 'the Garden, says, "It tastes good and it's for a good cause. If it's successful, it'll pay for a lot of scholarships."

Straight Out 'the Garden now sells for $2.59 for a 12-ounce bottle and can be found in over 2,000 southern California grocery stores and supermarkets. All proceeds, currently projected at $100,000 per year, are placed in the scholarship fund. Individual scholarships can total up to $15,000 a year for qualifying students. Says McCullen, "People said it couldn't be done. We just planted the seeds in their minds and the students took it from there." Adds Osborne, "It's our way of fighting stereotypes about South-Central and inner-city neighborhoods. It proves you can do anything you set your mind to."[26]

Small businesses offer opportunities for people of all ages to participate in all sorts of projects and assignments that might not be possible in larger organizations. Often this is a function of necessity. For example, very few large businesses would entrust their strategic plans to a relatively inexperienced 29-year-old. But Pyrocap International Corporation didn't hesitate to do so. Of course, the 29-year-old was Theodore Adams III, the company's president, who founded Pyrocap while pursuing his M.B.A. degree. As a result of the international marketing plan he wrote for the venture's fire suppression products, his firm was listed on the American Stock Exchange's January 1994 register of emerging young companies. Since the company's founding, Pyrocap has made a large sale to a Japanese customer, and Pyrocap products have found their way into the inventories of the Washington, D.C., Philadelphia, and Oakland, California, fire departments as well as those of the U.S. Army. Says Adams, "I'm one of those people too hard-headed to realize they can't do something"[27]

The federal government sponsors several programs that assist women and minorities in starting their own businesses. These programs are just one of the many forms of assistance the government provides to small businesses.

Growth Business

Lids, the business built on baseball caps, grew from a leased vendor cart in a Massachusetts mall to 15 stores in two years. Partners Benjamin Fischman (center) and Douglass Karp (right), along with CEO Nancy Kuchinsky (left) aim to expand to 300 stores nationwide by 1999. The Boston venture capitalists who invested in Lids in 1992 were sold by the young entrepreneurs' focused concept and their product and market knowledge. Fischman and Karp know the market and the customers, what they want, and what they like to wear. And their timing is good. In 1993, baseball caps accounted for about 80 percent of the $1.25 billion headwear industry.

5. Broadly describe the federal government's contribution in promoting small businesses and give some examples.

Building Small-Business Performance

Small businesses receive special aid and assistance from the government because of their importance in job formation, export growth, and overall economic health. Many government programs target small businesses and minority businesses (many of which are small). After reviewing government assistance to small businesses, we look at some new ways in which small businesses are learning to help themselves to improve productivity and achieve growth or other goals. New management strategies such as those described in Chapter 1 were originated by big businesses, but they are now being adapted to small businesses as well.

Government Assistance to Small Business

The federal government has taken an active role in promoting the formation of new businesses, and since the downturn of the late 1980s and early 1990s, state and local governments have also offered support. Why should government at any level support small businesses? The answer is really quite simple. National, regional, and local economic conditions are directly related to the health of business. If you are laid off because a business goes under, both your income and your tax contribution will stop. If you are unable to find another job, you may even become a consumer of government benefits, such as unemployment compensation, food stamps, Aid to Families with Dependent Children, and so on. It is in everyone's interest to lend small businesses a helping hand if the cost to other sectors of society is not too great. And since small businesses are frequently owned by people who traditionally have been excluded from any substantial participation in business, many believe that this is one area in which government can play a role in evening the score. A final reason government assists small businesses is that it is in the nation's interest to remain globally competitive by fostering new businesses and new ideas.

Federal Programs

The federal government offers the widest variety of government assistance, including advice, counseling, contracts, loans, and other forms of aid. Since Congress created it in 1953, the Small Business Administration's assistance to small businesses has exceeded 9 million individual acts. The SBA now has 110 offices nationwide, and Congress has authorized annual loan guarantees to small businesses in the amount of $4 billion.[28] Originally, the SBA provided management and technical assistance mostly through its own employees. Over the years, however, it has entered into numerous partnerships to provide a wider range of service.

The SBA programs we consider in this chapter are the Small Business Development Centers, the Service Corps of Retired Executives, the Small Business Institutes, the Minority Business Development Agency, and the Minority Small Business and Capital Ownership Development Program. Most of these programs provide funding and management assistance. In addition to the programs discussed here, the federal government provides direct support to women-owned small businesses by ensuring that every SBA office has a designated Women's Business Ownership Representative. Every local SBA office also has a designated Veterans Affairs Officer to assist veterans in starting their own small businesses.

Management and Counseling Assistance The federal government provides a variety of services designed to help small businesses improve their management practices by giving them information and other forms of support.

- Established by Congress in 1980, the **Small Business Development Centers (SBDCs)** are one-stop centers where entrepreneurs can receive written information, counseling, and business training classes and workshops at a reasonable cost. The SBA provides up to 50 percent of the funding for the SBDCs; the balance comes from private, state, or local sources.[29]

- The **Service Corps of Retired Executives (SCORE)** is a volunteer organization staffed by active and retired business executives who provide counseling, training, and workshops. SCORE was founded in 1964, and since then its approximately 13,000 volunteers have assisted more than 2.5 million aspiring small-business owners.[30] The SBA and SCORE recently teamed up to establish *business information centers* in Atlanta, Boston, Chicago, Denver, Houston, Los Angeles, New York City, St. Louis, Seattle, and Washington, D.C. These centers contain a wide variety of useful business resources, such as business book libraries, video libraries, on-line research services, and computer services.

- **Small Business Institutes (SBIs)** are school-based programs that provide specialized help to small businesses in the areas of accounting, marketing, and business plan preparation. SBIs are staffed by undergraduate and graduate business students. With SBIs at over 500 colleges and universities nationwide, it is possible that there is one at your school. Volunteering at an SBI can provide you with valuable work-related experience that would be difficult to obtain elsewhere while you are in college.

- The **Minority Business Development Agency (MBDA)** is a U.S. Department of Commerce agency responsible for developing legislation and programs that assist the development of minority-owned businesses. The MBDA has established a national network of Minority and Indian Business Development Centers, organizations that provide direct assistance to small-business owners in areas with large concentrations of minority or Native American residents.

Financial Assistance The SBA also provides support to entrepreneurs through a comprehensive program of financial assistance that includes loan guarantees, direct loans, micro-loans, and a variety of other loan programs. Small businesses can receive financial aid from one or more programs simultaneously, although each borrower is limited to a maximum of $750,000 in SBA loan guarantees.

- *Loan guarantees* are the primary form of financial assistance from the SBA; they represent well over 90 percent of the agency's total funds committed to financial support. There are many different programs under the umbrella of SBA loan guarantees, each with specific features and economic goals. In all of them, however, commercial lenders make the actual loan and the SBA guarantees its repayment if the small business goes bankrupt or, for some other reason, cannot meet its loan obligations. This arrangement is similar to the federal government's guarantee to repay certain student loans if the borrower defaults.

- Unlike the loan guarantee programs, *direct loans* from the SBA are made with the SBA's own funds, not those of commercial lenders. Direct loans are an increasingly rare form of SBA financial assistance. They are currently limited to a maximum of $150,000, and they are available only to veterans or others with disabilities, residents of economically distressed areas, and a few additional targeted groups.

- In 1992, the SBA initiated an innovative micro-loan program in conjunction with 45 not-for-profit organizations in 30 states. A **micro-loan** is a direct loan from the SBA, limited to $25,000 or less, made to women, minority,

Small Business Development Centers (SBDCs)

One-stop centers where entrepreneurs can receive written information, counseling, and business training classes and workshops at a reasonable cost.

Service Corps of Retired Executives (SCORE)

Volunteer organization staffed by active and retired business executives who provide counseling, training, and workshops.

Small Business Institutes (SBIs)

School-based programs that provide specialized help to small businesses in the areas of accounting, marketing, and business plan preparation.

Minority Business Development Agency (MBDA)

U.S. Department of Commerce agency responsible for developing legislation and programs that assist the development of minority-owned businesses.

micro-loan

A direct loan from the SBA, limited to $25,000 or less, made to women, minority, and low-income entrepreneurs in economically distressed areas.

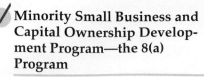

Minority Small Business and Capital Ownership Development Program—the 8(a) Program

A contracting set-aside program for minority-owned small businesses.

table 7.1

8(a) Program Participants

Category	Percentage
African American	48.5%
All Spanish speaking	24.1
Asian American	16.8
Native American	6.5
Puerto Rican	2.7
Eskimo/Aleut	0.2
Undetermined	0.1
Other	1.1
Total	100.0%

Source: Small Business Participation in SBA's 8(a) Business Development Program (Washington, D.C.: GAO, 1991).

and low-income entrepreneurs in economically distressed areas. The intent of micro-loans is to help small—often home-based—businesses get off the ground in communities that are traditionally ignored by commercial lenders. In the words of SBA spokesperson Mike Stamler, loan recipients are "people who don't have much of a chance at banks because of who they are and how much they're seeking." The intent of these loans is to brighten the economic outlook of disadvantaged areas by generating jobs and improving the stability of local business enterprises.[31]

- In fiscal year 1991, the federal government procured more than $200 billion worth of goods and services through purchase orders, contracts, and other agreements.[32] The federal government uses the tremendous leverage of these outlays to help direct funds to small, minority, and other disadvantaged businesses. For example, all purchases of $25,000 or less are specifically set aside for small-business enterprises, which compete to win the contracts. *Minority-supplier development programs* are special arrangements that assist these small firms to compete against larger, more well-established businesses. Such assistance might include granting special expedited payment terms, splitting large orders into smaller orders for which small firms can effectively bid, and providing advice on how a firm can cut through bureaucratic red tape.

- One federal contracting program that has had a significant and positive effect on the development of minority-owned start-ups is the SBA's **Minority Small Business and Capital Ownership Development Program—the 8(a) Program**—a contracting set-aside program for minority-owned small businesses. Every federal agency establishes a goal for participation and then contracts with the SBA to provide support for specific programs. The SBA then subcontracts the work to a selected certified 8(a) firm. Besides providing contracting opportunities to 8(a) program participants, the SBA also provides technical, managerial, and financial assistance to these firms. Table 7.1 shows the ethnic background of participants in the 8(a) Program; Table 7.2 lists a series of contacts for all federal programs.

table 7.2   Contacts for Federal Programs

Small Business Administration (SBA)
General Information   *(800) 827-5722*
Ask for
- The Small Business Development Center nearest you (there are 500 nationwide).
- The nearest bank participating in the SBA's guaranteed loan program.
- The nearest regional SBA office participating in the Women's Prequalification Pilot Loan Program (if your business is majority owned by women).

Federal Trade Commission (FTC)   *(202) 326-3128*
Ask for information about the FTC Franchise and Business Opportunity Disclosure Rule if you are considering a franchise.

Federal Information Center   *(800) 347-1997*
Call for information and referrals to any U.S. federal government services.

Source: Alexander Hiam and Karen Olander, *The Prentice-Hall Handbook of Entrepreneurship and Small Business Management* (Englewood Cliffs, N.J.: Prentice-Hall), in press for 1996.

State and Local Programs

State and local governments' support of small-business owners is not nearly as active and comprehensive as is that of the federal government, but they have recently offered more forms of assistance. One that has made a big difference is the development of enterprise zones. An **enterprise zone** is a district, typically in an economically depressed area, in which state or local government-sponsored incentives are offered to businesses that locate there. Incentives may include streamlined licensing, issuance of building permits and other regulatory approvals, and tax breaks.

Roland Christensen's company, Applied Composite, which manufactures artificial limbs, is located in the Sanpete County enterprise zone in Utah. Christensen has directly benefited from the tax credits he receives against his state corporate income tax bill. Applied Composite has more than doubled its work force since its founding in 1985, and it receives a state tax credit of from $700 to $1,000 for every new employee it hires.[33]

In addition to enterprise zones, state and local governments have sponsored initiatives such as the Massachusetts Centers for Excellence and various business incubators. A **business incubator** is a facility that provides entrepreneurs and small businesses with low-cost access to office space and equipment, legal and accounting advice, and training in how to run a business.

One example of a successful business training program is the Roads to Self Employment (ROSE) entrepreneurial workshop sponsored by the San Diego Housing Commission.[34] The ROSE workshop, which targets public housing residents, includes:

- A 12-week, 60-hour confidence-building and business development training session
- One-on-one business counseling
- The pairing of workshop attendees with established businesspeople who agree to act as mentors for a one-year period
- Monthly discussion groups to provide business support and assistance
- A micro-loan fund to assist workshop attendees

Businesses that have resulted from the ROSE workshop include a hair-braiding salon, a personal shopping service, a professional and technical writing service, a residential AIDS shelter, and a caterer of Caribbean food.

How Small Businesses Help Themselves

The United States Chamber of Commerce is a national not-for-profit organization dedicated to supporting small businesses. Each year, after reviewing thousands of applications, it presents this country's top-performing small businesses with a Blue Chip Enterprise Award. The finalists, as you might imagine, are exceptional organizations, but so was one that did *not* win, though it received an honorary mention. Fred and Richard Tedesco, who own and run a small spring manufacturing company, explained that "preparing this application has been another valuable self-appraisal, which we've learned every management needs to undertake regularly."[35]

The point this father-son management team makes is a vital one: *Small businesses must examine their own performance regularly* in order to keep growing and improving. This is essential in both life-style and growth businesses. For the life-style business, growth may mean growing in understanding and sophistication instead of in sales. But because growth and change happen in the environment *surrounding* every small business, they must also take place *within* every small business.

6. Describe the development of enterprise zones and business incubators as sources of state and local assistance to small businesses.

 enterprise zone

A district, typically in an economically depressed area, in which state or local government-sponsored incentives are offered to businesses that locate there.

 business incubator

Facility that provides entrepreneurs and small businesses with low-cost access to office space and equipment, legal and accounting advice, and training in how to run a business.

doing business

The Virtual Enterprise

The Information Revolution has spawned a new breed of small business—one that combines the adaptability and responsiveness of a small business with the depth of experience and talent base of the large business. This new breed of small business—the virtual enterprise—is becoming more and more common. A virtual enterprise is a business that appears from the outside to be large but is actually quite small—perhaps with only one or two permanent employees.

Armed with a vast array of digital, microprocessor-based technology such as laptop computers, modems, fax machines, cellular phones, and voice pagers, a small-business owner can do anything his or her large business counterpart can do—perhaps even better. A virtual enterprise can exist anywhere—in a coffee house, an airliner seat, or a spare bedroom. While the virtual enterprise may employ only a few people and maintain no fixed office space, it can draw on a vast pool of resources necessary to complete specific projects and tasks.

KnowledgeNet, incorporated in 1993, is one of the first of this new breed of small business. KnowledgeNet, with only a few full-time employees, is a consortium of more than 150 individual consultants and professional services firms—all of which are small businesses in their own right. The direction of the firm is provided by its founder, D.L. Boone. By bidding on and winning federal government contracts—pulling together proposal teams of member firms and individuals tailored to the specific project—KnowledgeNet is able to make a profit. Most important, with the large pool of talent available within the organization, the owners and associates of KnowledgeNet can carry on business as though they were a much larger firm. In this case, the whole is definitely greater than the individual pieces.

Source: Internet Promotional E-Mail, KnowledgeNet/D.L. Boone & Company (Sept. 16, 1994).

---

7. Explain how small businesses help themselves to maintain their competitive edge.

It is difficult for small-business owners and employees to stop working long enough to appraise their performance and improve it. Small businesses do not have the extra money a big business has to hire specialists in performance improvement. There is no planning department, there are no quality improvement engineers on staff, and few consulting firms are interested in working for the small fees a small business can afford to pay. Some small businesses have been very innovative in coping with limitations such as these. For an example, see the doing business box "The Virtual Enterprise." In many cases, however, small-business owners and their employees are relatively isolated, and they must be able to examine and improve their own work.

The small-business owner or employee needs to understand fundamental business concepts, from economics to finance and from management to accounting. These concepts are just as vital in the small business as they are in the large business—perhaps even more so, since small-business owners and employees often wear many hats. And because small businesses must keep improving, their owners and employees need a firm grasp of all the strategies used to boost performance. As we learned in Chapter 1, these include flexibility, customer focus, innovative management, and employee development. Each is a source of improvements for small businesses, as the winners of the Blue Chip Enterprise Award demonstrate each year. Figure 7.3 shows how small businesses can improve with information technology.

Improving Quality

Many businesses consider the Malcolm Baldrige National Quality Award to be the epitome of quality achievement. Established in 1989, the Baldrige award is bestowed only on firms with a truly superlative record of quality improvement. In 1991, only three were awarded, all of them to small or midsize companies. Small-business participation in the Baldrige competition has dramatically increased in recent years. In 1988, 18 percent of the applicant pool consisted of small businesses; by 1992, that figure had risen to 48 percent.[36]

Quality not only makes customers happy but costs less in the long run. It used to take computer-component manufacturer Iomega 28 days to build a Bernoulli disk drive. By implementing quality initiatives, Iomega's management was able to reduce the production cycle to 1.5 days. The resulting decrease in purchased parts, work in progress, and unsold inventories of product allowed Iomega to save $6 million a year. Arden Sims, chief executive officer of Globe Metallurgical, Inc., a Baldrige winner in the small-business category, estimates that the company's investments in quality have returned $40 for every dollar it spent.[37]

While many small businesses are voluntarily implementing quality programs, others are joining the parade only reluctantly. In an effort to improve the quality of their own products, large businesses are increasingly pressuring their suppliers to implement quality programs. For example, Motorola set a 1994 deadline for its (generally small) vendors to implement quality initiatives—or risk being dropped. Since large businesses rely on small businesses for more than 50 percent of their finished products, it is clear that quality improvements at small businesses are vital to the health of the entire economy.[38]

Improving Productivity

Productivity, or the lack of it, is an issue in businesses of any size. The effects of productivity loss are particularly destructive in small firms because they have far fewer employees to shoulder the extra burden. If, for example, alcoholism causes one employee in a 5,000-person organization to be substantially unpro-

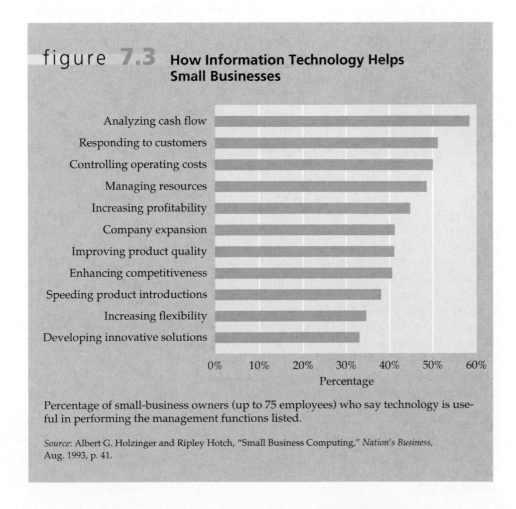

figure **7.3** **How Information Technology Helps Small Businesses**

Percentage of small-business owners (up to 75 employees) who say technology is useful in performing the management functions listed.

Source: Albert G. Holzinger and Ripley Hotch, "Small Business Computing," *Nation's Business*, Aug. 1993, p. 41.

ductive, the overall loss to the firm is relatively minor. If one employee is similarly unproductive in a three-person firm, however, the effect on the business can be devastating.

Small businesses have traditionally paid little attention to productivity, focusing instead on simply staying in business. But market conditions are now forcing them to change their ways. Consider the case of Mid-South Industries, which Jerry Weaver built into a $110 million business. The company specializes in the manufacture of a wide variety of products, working under contract with other firms, including Xerox Corp. Mid-South built its success on a firm foundation: Provide a good product at a good price, and treat customers like friends.

When the Xerox auditors came to visit, Mid-South was in for a shock. To help cut its production costs, Xerox had developed efficiency standards for its suppliers. Companies that could not meet those standards were dropped. Not only did Mid-South fail Xerox's test, it didn't even come close. According to Weaver, "They took me behind the woodshed over quality problems and a high cost structure." Knowing that Mid-South could not afford to lose the Xerox account, Weaver got serious about improving productivity at the company. In a two-year period, he invested $1 million in efficiency training for his employees and $400,000 in automation and robotics upgrades. As a result, product defects were virtually banished and operating costs were trimmed to the tune of 5 percent per year.[39]

Nationwide, the attitudes of small-business owners have dramatically shifted. Quality and efficiency are "in." Shoddy products, indifferent service, and waste are "out." In a 1993 survey of 100 small and midsize firms conducted by management consultants Arthur Anderson & Company with National Small Business United, 68 percent of respondents reported that they had improved their company's productivity in the previous 12 months. This is more than double the number reporting productivity gains a year earlier.[40]

Franchising

Arturo Torres sold his 236 Pizza Hut and Taco Bell franchises to PepsiCo in 1992 for cash and stock worth approximately $100 million. In 1965, when he was washing dishes at an Amarillo, Texas, pizza parlor, Torres had no idea that one day he would own and operate his own restaurants. Eventually, he worked his way into a position helping his boss open new franchise units. Torres got so good at opening new stores that he struck out on his own in 1972, buying franchises and running them himself. Now, three decades later, Torres's net worth is estimated at more than $130 million. Torres's story illustrates the potential that franchising offers to small-business owners.

Franchising is an agreement in which one business grants another business the right to distribute its products or services. The terms of the agreement are spelled out in a signed, legal franchise contract, which formally states the obligations of the two parties. The company granting the license to use its knowledge and identity is called the **franchisor**. The individual buying the license is the **franchisee**. A franchise is not a separate legal form of business; the franchisee must set up the business as a sole proprietorship, partnership, or corporation. Most franchises are corporations. The mother-and-son team of Jim and Georgia Young formed a partnership to go into the specialty coffee business. Then their business negotiated a franchise contract with Gloria Jean's Gourmet Coffee Franchises, purchasing three store sites in Milwaukee-area malls. As Jim Young explains, "A franchisor like Gloria Jean's, which has 196 stores nationwide, has a lot of pull with the landlords. We get better spaces, better locations, better rent."[41]

 franchising

An agreement in which one business grants another business the right to distribute its products or services.

 franchisor

A company that grants others a license to use its knowledge and identity.

franchisee

An individual who buys a license to operate a franchise.

Franchise Foundation
Stop for gas on your way to the drive-thru? In the United States, three franchises in ten are automobile-related businesses, and two in ten are food related.

Advantages of Franchises

Franchising allows many businesses to share in and benefit from the operating knowledge and reputation of the franchisor. Over the last several decades, franchising has become a major force in small business in the United States, with the number of franchises now exceeding 600,000. Franchises ring up a third of all retail sales in the United States and may account for half of them by the end of this century.[42] The number of franchises grew most rapidly in the 1980s but is now slowing down.[43] In the United States, the most popular franchises are gasoline service stations—there are 107,000 of them. But restaurant franchises are gaining (103,000). Automobile-related franchises follow, with 43,000 auto and truck product and service franchises and 27,000 auto and truck dealers. Then come the 26,000 food retailers, such as the Gloria Jean's coffee bean stores.[44]

Franchises are also contributing to the growth of small-business exports and overseas operations. Fruit juice franchise Orange Julius has outlets in Canada and Asia, and Baskin-Robbins stores span 47 countries.[45] In all, U.S. franchises now have approximately a half-million foreign locations.[46]

Franchises fall into three major categories:

- A *product franchise* allows you to distribute goods carrying the franchisor's trademark, such as a certain brand of tire or swimming pool.

- A *manufacturing franchise* allows you to manufacture and sell the franchisor's product under its trademark. The most common examples are soft drink bottlers that manufacture and distribute such popular brands as Coca-Cola and 7-Up.

- A *business-format franchise* allows you to open a retail store, such as a fast-food restaurant, using the franchisor's business format and sales lines.

The last category is what most of us think of as franchises. In addition to fast-food chains such as McDonald's, Burger King, Pizza Hut, Subway, and Kentucky Fried Chicken, business-format franchises include automobile dealerships; servicing and repair shops such as AAMCO Transmission and Midas Muffler; and dispatch and parcel services such as Mail Boxes Etc. Your local McDonald's, for example, is run by a local businessperson who pays for the

8. Identify the three major forms of franchising and describe the advantages of franchising in general.

right to operate under the McDonald's name and agrees to comply with its policies and rules. The local McDonald's is probably incorporated—a privately owned corporation.

When you buy a franchise you buy the right to use the products, trademarks, and business methods the franchisor developed, usually within a defined area. Note that what you are purchasing is not a business—you will have to buy your own building, hire your own staff, and so on. What you are buying is *a way of conducting business*—one that hopefully will succeed because of the experience the franchisor has built up over time.

Because franchises are small businesses operating under the umbrella of a large business, they offer much of the independence and opportunity of a small business, but the support from the franchisor helps to free the franchisee from many of the inevitable risks of starting a business from scratch. Some of the services franchisors may supply are help in choosing a location; designing and outfitting space in line with the franchisor's image; help with negotiating leases and setting up accounts with local utilities; training for the owner and/or key staff; supplying advertising and public relations services; and offering bulk buying from trusted suppliers. Some franchisors—about one-fourth—also offer financing in the form of direct loans or help in obtaining bank loans to pay for franchise fees and other start-up costs.[47] Such financing usually covers less than half of the costs, which range from less than $10,000 to more than $500,000. These figures include a one-time franchise fee, start-up costs for the business, and the first year of royalty payments to the franchisor, which may be anywhere between 2 percent and 15 percent of sales.[48]

Franchisors zealously protect their trademarks and the image and recognition that go with them, for these may be the only part of a franchise that has real value. In exchange for permission to distribute the product or service and to use a trademarked name (like McDonald's), you as the franchisee must agree to certain conditions. First among them, of course, is the financial agreement, because franchisors, like other businesses, want to make a profit. They do so from initial fees paid by new franchisees and from regular payments required thereafter to retain the franchise—usually between 2 percent and 15 percent of sales. In addition, by selling franchises, franchisors can expand their businesses without risking their own capital.

Franchise Frontier

Find a need and fill it is good advice when starting a business. Enterprising transportation services relieve scheduling pressures from working parents by providing the shuttle service to and from soccer practice or dance class. Drivers escort children door to door for an average prepaid price of $5 one way. Many local, independent services exist, as do national franchises. The largest franchisor, Kids Kab, operates in a dozen states.

As a franchisee, you must conduct your business as the franchisor specifies. Your franchise contract usually will specify the following:[49]

- Services provided by the franchisor
- Location and design of store
- Cost (up-front fee plus percentage of sales)
- Any training the franchisor will provide for the franchisee and employees
- Use of trademark and identity
- Performance and quality standards
- Advertising requirements
- Requirements for purchasing supplies and raw materials
- Territory in which the franchisee has an exclusive right to operate

For example, to ensure that a franchise's french fries conform to McDonald's specifications, a McDonald's contract may state that the franchisee will buy potatoes from McDonald's or from an approved supplier.

Just how expensive is it to buy a franchise? The answer to this question varies widely, depending on the particular franchise. The franchise route can be one of the most expensive ways of going into business, sometimes as much as 25 percent higher than going it alone. The price of entry generally depends on how well established and successful the franchisor is; on the degree of management, training, and services the franchisor provides; and on the terms of the specific franchise agreement. Table 7.3 specifies the initial investment cost of a wide variety of franchises. In some cases, smaller, less well-known franchises sell for only a few thousand dollars, whereas the fees for large, well-established franchises may measure in the hundreds of thousands of dollars. Usually—though not always—risk and initial fees are inversely related.

table 7.3 Costs of Starting a "Top 10" Franchise*

Franchise (type)	Franchise Fee (in thousands of dollars)	Start-Up Costs (in thousands of dollars, unless otherwise noted)	Royalty Rate (% sales, unless stated as flat payment)
1. Subway (submarine sandwiches)	$10	$43–84.5	8%
2. McDonald's (hamburgers)	45	400–535	12.5%+
3. Burger King Corp. (hamburgers)	40	73–511	3.5%
4. Hardee's (hamburgers)	15	497.2–722.8	3.5–4%
5. 7-Eleven Convenience Stores (convenience stores)	varies	12.5+	varies
6. Dunkin' Donuts (food/quick service)	40	181.6–255.1	4.9%
7. Mail Boxes Etc. (service business)	24.95	68.5–112.4	5%
8. Choice Hotels International (hotels)	15–40	1.5 million to 4 million dollars	3–5%
9. Snap-On Inc. (hardware)	3	79.33–162	$50/mo.
10. Dairy Queen (soft serve ice cream)	30	370–715	4%

*Ranked by *Entrepreneur* magazine based on franchisee value.
Source: Data derived from "The Franchise 500," *Entrepreneur*, Jan. 1995, pp. 135–237.

9. Discuss the risks involved in buying a franchise.

Franchising and Risk: Let the Buyer Beware

A recent study of more than 7,000 small businesses that opened their doors for business in the mid-1980s showed that, overall, franchises are riskier than independent small businesses. According to the study, by the early 1990s, 28 percent of the independent small businesses had failed, compared with 35 percent of the franchises.[50] These figures contradict the franchise industry's claim that franchises have very low failure rates. The difference of opinion is the result of different methods of measurement. Well-established franchises, such as those in the top 10 (see Table 7.3), have failure rates well under 10 percent per year. However, if figures for the many smaller and newer franchises are included, the rates are far higher. Franchisees have to be careful to choose a low-risk franchise.

Not all franchises are profitable. Anyone entering into a franchise agreement should check out the franchisor thoroughly, beginning with the company's business reputation and background. How long has it been selling franchises? How many franchises does the company own, compared with the number owned by franchisees? How many franchises has the franchisor terminated, and for what reasons? How many other franchises operate within the same area? Are others now planned for that area, or could they be in the future? All claims of profits and management assistance that the franchisor makes should be verified with banks, suppliers, and other franchisees. Organizations such as the Better Business Bureau, local chambers of commerce, the Federal Trade Commission, and sources such as the annual review of 500 franchises published annually in *Entrepreneur* magazine offer invaluable assistance and information.

Although many states have laws governing franchises, lawsuits are expensive and loopholes allow franchisors to juggle the system in their favor. Given the present patchwork of laws and the tendency of the courts to stick to the letter of a contract, buying a franchise should be a matter of caveat emptor—let the buyer beware.

In its annual study of business-format franchises, consulting firm Ernst & Young asks questions about the following topics:

- Financial performance
- Growth and management
- Corporate stability
- Franchisor attitude and service
- Franchisee relationship with franchisor

Heading a recent Ernst & Young list of the 100 best franchises are retail food franchise Sonic Drive-Ins, real estate franchise Coldwell Banker, and travel franchise CleanNet USA, along with Travel Network, Merry Maids, Interim Services, and the Krystal Co. These companies have a "solid financial base, sound investment potential, measured growth that indicates long-term stability, and a strong, complementary relationship with their franchisees," according to a report on the study.[51] Interestingly, none of the best-known fast-food franchises made the Ernst & Young list, although they dominate *Entrepreneur* magazine's annual review discussed earlier. The desirability of any franchise depends on how you analyze it and on what you are looking for—there is no one answer as to which is the best opportunity for a small-business owner.

An interesting new concept is **multiple franchising**, an arrangement whereby a franchisee combines several franchises to reduce risk. For example, one franchisor makes multiple franchising easy by offering a four-concept franchise: I Can't Believe It's Yogurt, Boxies Cafe, Java Coast Fine Coffees, and Crumbles Bakery.[52] Innovations such as this are currently rare, but their potential to reduce risk suggests that their popularity may increase in the future.

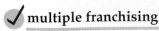

multiple franchising

An arrangement whereby a franchisee combines several franchises to reduce risk.

Finding a Job in Small Business

Where do you as a future employee fit into the picture we described in this chapter? Finding a job in small business is different from a big business–oriented job search. You must contact many more small businesses to find good openings. And you must be careful to select a small business that is successful enough to give you a secure environment for your work and career.

10. Describe the best strategy for finding a job with a small business.

New Life for Your Job Search

This is the reality of the job search today: The large companies that can afford to recruit on campus, that take out the largest ads in the newspaper's classified job listings, and that have the best reputation as employers offer only a fraction of the job openings for which business majors can apply. Traditionally, students have been taught how to find jobs in big businesses. Now they need to have two job strategies: one for big and one for small businesses. So, how do you go about finding a job with a small company—one of thousands in your area, and probably one that you have not heard of?

1. *Write a resumé.* The resumé is the standard ticket for admission into the job market, regardless of the size of the business. It is not a guarantee that you will get a job, but it is a rare company that will seriously consider you for employment without one. There are many books available to guide you through the right way to construct your resumé. If you have any friends or relatives in the business world, ask them to review and comment on your draft.

2. *Work part time or volunteer to gain experience.* If you had to choose between two candidates with new degrees—one with business experience and one with none—which one would you select? Experience is very important to employers—*especially* to small-business employers who expect you to hit the ground running. Working part time or volunteering in a business environment will give you an advantage over inexperienced applicants. And note that *functional experience,* experience in a business function or process, is more important than *industry experience,* experience in a specific industry, when it comes to qualifying for small-business jobs. Small businesses are so varied that their managers usually do not expect you to know the details of their business—you can gain industry experience on the job. But they do need to know that you have a general knowledge of how to do important jobs, whether it be in sales, service, accounting, or manufacturing.

3. *Broaden your search.* Targeting only a few firms may be effective with large businesses that employ thousands of people, but it won't work with small businesses that have fewer job openings. Job opportunities in small business are generally spread across a much larger area. You may need to consider opportunities on a state, regional, national, or even international basis. And even within your hometown, be sure to check out a large number of businesses and industries.

4. *Research the opportunities, using as many resources as possible.* Many firms have job lines or computerized job bulletin boards. Check listings in the local business newspaper. Visit your school's career placement center, and see what your alumni association offers in career networking opportunities. Many of these offices can give you phone numbers of graduates who have experience in small businesses and are willing to answer your questions.

5. *Go to the opportunity.* Don't expect employers to seek you out—you are a salesperson, and the product you are selling is yourself. Plan to visit poten-

tial employers to drop off your resumé and to ask about their future staffing needs. Visit business incubators and franchises. In these visits, persistence, good listening skills, and a polite approach are essential.

Finding a job may be the toughest job you will ever have, as anyone who has been the victim of a layoff can tell you. If you take the time now to gain the skills and experience you need to be attractive to large and small businesses, you will be far ahead of other applicants who bypass such preparations.

Signs of Success in a Small-Business Employer

11. Outline the four factors that suggest future success for a small business.

There are four signs of success[53] that small-business employees need to see—and small-business owners need to adopt—to minimize the risk of failure. As a prospective employee, you are within your rights to ask about these factors in a job interview.

1. *A business plan.* As noted in Chapter 6, a business plan is a necessary first step for any business, and it should be rewritten periodically to guide growth and development. The business plan precisely states the goals and direction of the business and exactly how it plans to make money. If you were considering a job at a restaurant, for instance, it would be important for you to see that the business has a clear idea of what kind of food it wants to serve, who its customers are, and who the competition is. If the plans are not clear or cannot be stated by the owners, working at this business may be risky.

2. *Good accounting and record keeping.* This area is vital; disorganization often leads to disaster! Be sure that the business you are thinking of joining has well-organized accounting and recordkeeping practices in place. This includes paying payroll and income taxes in a timely manner and keeping track of all money that comes into the business as well as all money that is spent. Is the office well organized? Are papers filed and easily accessible? An employee who cannot find a vital piece of paper at a critical moment can cost a business time, money, and even a client.

3. *Delegation.* Part of good management is the ability to assign important tasks to others. Find out if employees feel supported and motivated or are operating in fear of their manager. Also, check to see if there are written employee policies and operating procedures. Written policies provide workers with a list of their rights and benefits. Operating procedures are guidelines that all workers follow in performing the tasks needed to run the business. Imagine being left in charge of a restaurant on your first day of work with no directions. How would you know what quantities of food should be prepared, where ingredients were kept, or what to charge customers for their meals?

4. *Evaluating and acting on customer feedback.* Find out if the business has a way of measuring customer satisfaction, such as through a suggestion box, mail-in postcard, or posted phone number. See if the business knows its customers well. Who buys its product? Are customers repeat buyers or new business? This information is important because knowing and listening to customers means being better able to satisfy their needs. Imagine that the restaurant where you're considering a job makes relatively simple dishes, that its customers have been suggesting that it add a few hot and spicy items, and that management has ignored those suggestions. What would happen? The clientele would eventually seek out another eatery to satisfy its spicy tastes, and the restaurant would lose customers.

The *Prentice-Hall Small Business Survival Guide: A Blueprint for Success* states that "sales-oriented companies try to fit their customers to their products; mar-

Fit the Product to the Customer

In 1992, Thomas A. McCrary, Jr. founded USA Printing and Advertising to provide creative, printing, and voice mail services to small, mail-order businesses. When customers kept asking McCrary where they could test their ads, he launched *USAdvertiser,* a monthly newspaper aimed at home-based businesses. In 1995, *USAdvertiser* boasted 230 advertisers and accounted for half of McCrary's gross revenue.

Finding "Immortal" Employers

You will probably interview with small businesses many times in your working life. In recessions they may be the only ones creating new jobs, and even in economic growth periods they will contribute one-third to one-half of new jobs. (Of course, turnover of employees in old jobs also creates some hiring opportunities.) The text reviewed some of the fundamentals of sound small-business management, and you should look for these in any small business before taking a job there. Here are four questions you can ask in an interview to make sure a small business covers all the bases:

1. Do you do business planning?
2. Do you use standard bookkeeping and accounting practices?
3. Does senior management delegate any key responsibilities to employees?
4. Do you gather reliable information about customer satisfaction and complaints?

An employer who can at least say "sort of" to all of these is on fairly solid ground. But what if you want to know more—what if you want to find one of those few small businesses that will go on for decades, growing and prospering, perhaps to become the next Hewlett-Packard Co. or 3M Corporation? These "immortal" companies provide incredible job growth opportunities for employees who get in on the ground floor. A study of such companies produces a second, more difficult list of screening questions you can also ask:

1. Is there a powerful, consistent core ideology? (A strong vision, like 3M's dedication to innovation or department store Nordstrom's dedication to customer service, correlates with long-term success.)
2. Is the corporate culture strong? (A "cultlike" corporate culture based on the core values is also related to long-term success. For example, everyone at rock-and-asphalt supplier Granite Rock of Watsonville, California, is fanatical about quality and service.)
3. Do you hire managers from within the company? ("Home-grown" management also seems to be characteristic of long-lived success cases.)
4. Do you innovate and change often in the pursuit of progress? (Although their ideologies are constant, companies characterized by long-term success are more open to innovation and change than are most companies. Companies that are not afraid of innovation can increase quality and introduce new and better services and products.)

Sources: Robert J. Cooke, "Famous Last Words: 24 Quick and Easy Ways to Kill Your Business," *Entrepreneur,* June 1994; James C. Collins, "Building Companies to Last," *Inc. Special Issue: The State of Small Business,* 1995, pp. 83–88.

---

ket-oriented companies try to fit their products to their customers." It also notes that:

- One customer in four is dissatisfied with the service provided in the typical commercial transaction.
- The dissatisfied customer, on average, will complain to 12 other people about the company that provided the poor service.
- Only 5 percent of dissatisfied customers complain to the company that offered the product or service. The vast "silent majority" would rather switch than fight. They take their business elsewhere rather than risk an unpleasant confrontation. Lost customers are a major but difficult-to-measure risk for small businesses.[54]

A business's chances of success are greater if it evaluates and responds to customer feedback. The skills check "Finding 'Immortal' Employers" suggests some specific questions you might ask in a small-business job interview.

In your search, you may also wish to target small businesses in high-growth industries. Ask yourself what changes in the business environment are creating opportunities for small business. One study suggests that health concerns, fresh-water shortages, new technologies, and the loss of ozone may create a strange assortment of new high-growth franchises in the next century, as Table 7.4 shows. Perhaps you will own and run an electric-car recharging center 20 years from now!

table 7.4

Tomorrow's Top Franchise Categories

1. Macrobiotic fast-food
2. Electric-car recharging centers
3. "Virtual reality" photography
4. Automatic voice translation
5. Vintage clothing stores
6. Sunblock salons
7. Carpal tunnel care (for repetitive motion disorders)
8. Satellite advertising
9. Aromatherapy
10. Desalination centers

Source: Erika Kotite, "2044: A Franchising Odyssey," *Entrepreneur,* Sept. 1994, pp. 152, 155.

Reviewing   *Small Business and Franchising*

The Importance of Small Business

1. **Define small business, as specified by the SBA**. Most people limit their definition of a small business to "the store on main street"—the local pizza parlor, card store, and so on. The requirements set forth by the SBA, however, extend that definition to include businesses with as many as 500 employees, depending on the type of business. The SBA also requires that the business be independently owned and operated, that it not dominate its field of operation, and that it generate income no larger than that specified for its category.

2. **List and describe the advantages and disadvantages of a small business**. The advantages of a small business include the ability to provide personal service to customers, a focus on a narrow range of products, the ability to adapt quickly to market changes, a tendency to be more innovative than large businesses, and greater efficiency and productivity, which results from few layers of management. Disadvantages include the stress of being personally responsible for all problems, conflicts with family members who are also employees or who resent the excessive time devoted to work, and, of course, the high risk of failure.

3. **Describe the two general types of small businesses and give an example of each**. A small business may be a life-style or a growth business. Life-style businesses support their owners and tend to be stable in size—for example, the local pizza parlor, gift shop, or dress store. Growth businesses, on the other hand, are designed for rapid growth, with the owners taking risks to achieve their goals. Examples include software developers and food producers.

4. **Discuss the role of small businesses in job creation, noting in particular their significance for women and minorities**. Under SBA size standards, small businesses account for 99 percent of U.S. business. Naturally, they therefore generate the majority of jobs. The factors that help small firms create job opportunities are faster growth rates, more choices—they offer many different types of work—and greater accessibility for ethnic minorities, women, and older workers. More significantly, between 1982 and 1987, for example, small-business ownership by women and minorities increased substantially—60 percent for women, 38 percent for African Americans, and 100 percent for Hispanic Americans.

Building Small-Business Performance

5. **Broadly describe the federal government's contribution in promoting small businesses and give some examples**. The federal government assists small businesses by providing advice, counseling, contracts, loans, and other forms of aid. Although the SBA provides extensive financial assistance *directly* through loans, loan guarantees, microloans, and contracts with small businesses, it provides most of its management and technical assistance indirectly through partnerships in programs such as the Small Business Development Centers, the Service Corps of Retired Executives, and the Minority Business Development Agency. With the 8(a) Program, the SBA subcontracts work to selected, certified minority firms.

6. **Describe the development of enterprise zones and business incubators as sources of state and local assistance to small businesses**. State and local governments have recently increased their role in helping small businesses. Enterprise zones are designed to attract businesses to economically depressed areas. Another form of local aid comes through business incubators, facilities that provide low-cost office space and equipment, legal and accounting advice, and training on how to run a business.

7. **Explain how small businesses help themselves to maintain their competitive edge**. To maintain their competitive edge, small-business owners must examine their performance regularly. Because they do not have access to on-staff experts, the owner(s) must understand fundamental business concepts related to all areas. The most important areas requiring constant improvement are quality and productivity. Small businesses that have flexibility, a customer focus, innovative management, and employee development generally succeed in improving their operations.

Franchising

8. **Identify the three major forms of franchising and describe the advantages of franchising in general**. Franchising, whereby a person or business buys *a way of conducting business*, may involve distributing a product carrying the franchisor's trademark, manufacturing and selling a product under its trademark, or using the franchisor's business format. Franchises offer much of the same independence and opportunity of a small business plus the advantage of freeing the franchisee from many of the risks associated with starting a new business. The franchisor provides advice and technical and financial help in setting up the business; in return, the franchisor expects the franchisee to adhere to certain rules of conduct, as spelled out in a contract.

9. **Discuss the risks involved in buying a franchise**. Before buying a franchise, a potential franchisee must carefully research the financial performance, growth and management, corporate stability, attitude and service, and prior relationships with franchisees of any franchisor under consideration. Because the laws governing franchises provide inadequate protection to franchisees, some fran-

chisors take advantage of the system; the franchisee may be taking risks that are the same as or greater than those of starting a business from scratch.

Finding a Job in Small Business

10. **Describe the best strategy for finding a job with a small business**. Finding a job with a small business involves many of the same steps as finding a job with a large business—writing a resumé and having some prior experience. However, for a small business, you should emphasize functional experience over industry experience; you should broaden your search, using as many resources as are available to you; and you should go to a large number of potential employers (they won't come to you).

11. **Outline the four factors that suggest future success for a small business**. Before accepting a job with a small business, a prospective employee should check that the company has a sound business plan that is periodically revised; good accounting and recordkeeping; good management, including the ability to delegate tasks and the application of written policies and procedures; and an interest in listening to and acting on customer feedback.

 ## Key Terms

Small Business Administration (SBA) **197**	Service Corps of Retired Executives (SCORE) **207**	micro-loan **207**	business incubator **209**
small business **197**	Small Business Institutes (SBIs) **207**	Minority Small Business and Capital Ownership Development Program— the 8(a) Program **208**	franchising **212**
life-style business **200**			franchisor **212**
growth business **201**	Minority Business Development Agency (MBDA) **207**		franchisee **212**
Small Business Development Centers (SBDCs) **207**		enterprise zone **209**	multiple franchising **216**

● Review Questions

1. What is a small business?

2. What five characteristics are common to most small businesses?

3. How does a life-style business differ from a growth business?

4. Under what conditions are small businesses most important to U.S. job growth?

5. What characteristics of small businesses help to create job opportunities for women and minorities?

6. What two forms of assistance does the U.S. Small Business Administration offer? Give specific examples of each.

7. What factors make it difficult for small-business managers to improve the quality of their performance and products?

8. What are the advantages and disadvantages of opening a franchise compared with starting a business from scratch?

9. What are the three major forms of franchises, and how do they differ?

10. Why are you more likely to work for a small business than for a large corporation?

● Critical Thinking Questions

1. Small businesses have been shown to produce twice the number of innovations per employee as their large business counterparts. What might be some of the reasons for this?

2. Small businesses don't produce the majority of new jobs in all economic conditions. Why do large businesses sometimes outpace small businesses, and vice versa?

3. Imagine that you work for a restaurant that has lost 10 percent of its business in the last 12 months. Your boss has asked you to find out why business has dropped off. What inexpensive ways will you suggest for getting customer comments on the restaurant, its staff, and the food it serves?

4. Do you believe the current emphasis on quality improvement will last, or do you think it will be a short-lived fad? Explain your answer.

5. How should the search for a job in small business differ from a search for a job in a large corporation?

REVIEW CASE   *Icon Acoustics, Inc.*

When Dave Fokos first sketched out the vision of his new business, everything seemed perfect. First, he would be able to pursue his dream of designing and producing the best stereo speakers on the market. Second, based on his modest financial projections, he was sitting on a potential gold mine. With projected total profits rising from $2,000 on $303,000 in sales in the first year of business to $1 million on $3.3 million of sales by the fifth year of business, how could he go wrong? Finally, Fokos would have the clout to form an enlightened company that would provide a quality work environment and subsidized educational opportunities for its workers.

Icon speakers are targeted to the high-end stereo consumer. At $795 per pair for the basic Lumens model and $1,795 per pair for the top-of-the-line Parsecs, these speakers are definitely not affordable to the average stereo buyer. But by selling his speakers direct to buyers, bypassing the standard audio dealer distribution channel, Fokos would enable his customers to avoid paying steep dealer markups and so get a top-quality product for less money.

Unfortunately, the business that seemed perfect on paper turned out to be less than perfect in reality. Icon's troubles began shortly after it opened for business. Dave Fokos had to delve into his own personal savings to pay the rent when an anticipated stock offering to raise $100,000 was delayed three months. Then the prototype speakers fell several months behind schedule and the cabinets were of poor quality—necessitating a search for a new cabinetmaker. Next, just as Icon's products were receiving their first favorable reviews in audio magazines and orders were starting to pick up, the German manufacturer of a key speaker component mixed up the order, causing a severe shortage of the part. Finally, Fokos's bank failed, denying Icon customers the option of charging their purchases.

Icon survived these early tribulations, and now investors are nervously optimistic about the company's prospects. Dave Fokos, still the only employee of Icon Acoustics, is convinced there is a market for his speakers, and he will continue to pursue it until he gets it right.

1. Why is a small business the most appropriate size for Icon Acoustics?

2. What four advantages might a small business like Icon Acoustics offer over its large-business competitors?

3. Dave Fokos did not draft a business plan. In what ways would a business plan have benefited his company's growth and progress?

4. When Icon Acoustics opened for business, Dave Fokos was less than 30 years old. Do you think a large business would have offered him the same level of responsibility as he has with Icon? Why or why not?

5. Can you suggest any government services that might be of help to Fokos?

6. Is Icon Acoustics too small to implement quality improvements? Support your answer with some points discussed in this chapter.

7. If Dave Fokos had opened a franchise instead of starting his own business, how might his risks and potential rewards have differed from those described in this case?

8. Would you take a job with a company like Icon Acoustics? Explain your answer.

CRITICAL THINKING CASE   *FROYD, Inc.*[55]

FROYD is a product in search of a market. Conceived by Carolyne Greene, a New York jewelry designer, FROYD is a yellow doll with a big, funny-looking nose. The doll comes with a message to the kids that buy it: You can make your dreams come true if you work at them. FROYD's initials stand for "For Reality of Your Dreams."

The plan was to create a highly popular character that could be licensed to manufacturers for a hefty profit. Projections called for the sale of 60,000 FROYDs, for a pretax loss of $330,000 in the first year of business, growing to sales of 3 million dolls in the third year of business, resulting in a pretax profit of $20.3 million. The majority of this profit was expected to come from accessories and licensing.

Investing $700,000 of their own money, Carolyne Greene

and her husband Jeffrey raised an additional $600,000 by giving up 26 percent of the company to private investors. This money was plowed into product development, advertising, test marketing, and production. Soon, 20,000 FROYDs were created to distribute to the test market—New York City, Boston, and Philadelphia.

The Greenes spent $100,000 to produce a series of television commercials, and four weeks of television advertising in the test market cost another $190,000. On the eve of the test, the Greenes became even more optimistic—sales were now expected to approach 6 million in the first year, with resultant profits of up to $34.5 million. The Greenes seemed to be riding on the crest of a smashing marketing success.

Then, a funny thing happened. Of the 6,300 dolls initially shipped to stores for test marketing, only 1,500 sold. The Toys 'R' Us chain decided against ordering any more FROYDs. Despite this setback, the Greenes are undaunted. They continue to pump money into their product, hoping to make it a success—regardless of the market's cold response.

1. Despite relatively healthy financing, FROYD, Inc., employed only two people. What are some of the company's disadvantages compared with its larger competitors?

2. The Greenes and others have invested well over a million dollars in bringing the FROYD concept to market. What steps would you have taken to ensure the success of the doll before you spent money on product manufacture and test marketing?

3. The FROYD test marketing flopped. Would you recommend that the product be redesigned at this point, or would you continue to promote the original product as is—hoping that it will eventually catch on? Why?

4. The Greenes approached a major network with the idea of spinning off a FROYD television show. What other approaches would you suggest to help the Greenes develop a market for their product?

5. If success continued to elude the FROYD venture, at what point would you pull the plug and let the product die a natural death? Would you continue to seek private investment funds even if it appeared the product would not be a success? Is there an ethical issue to consider in seeking such funds?

Critical Thinking with the ONE MINUTE MANAGER

"I have a friend from high school who works in a small business," Carlos said. "He's been doing lubes and oil changes for two years and he still earns close to minimum wage. What is *his* career path?"

"Is the business growing or innovating in any way?"

"Fred's Auto Service is not exactly a world-class innovator," Carlos explained. "I think it would be a big innovation if they just painted their building and repaired their sign!"

"Well, we all know small businesses that don't offer much opportunity for growth, and if you work for one of them your career path probably requires a job search as soon as possible. But if a small business innovates and grows, it can provide a wonderful work environment."

Joanna asked, "Isn't innovation too expensive and complex for the average small business?"

"You might think so, and so do some small-business managers. But if you ask somebody like Mark Sebell, a consultant with the Boston-based Creative Realities consulting firm, you'd be surprised at the answer. His firm specializes in teaching small businesses how to harness the power of innovation by encouraging creative forms of participation by employees, and by tapping into the needs and ideas of customers. They say *any* business can innovate, regardless of its size. Last year, they came in here and helped us become better innovators."

"Wait a minute," Carlos asked, "Why did you hire a small-business consultant? Isn't this a large business?"

"No," the One Minute Manager answered with a laugh. "We may seem big to you, but I doubt anybody beyond our industry has ever heard of us, even though we sell millions of dollars worth of products, employ hundreds of people, and work in a big office building. But we have competitors that are more than 10 times our size. As you'll see when you study the topic in school, there are lots of businesses like us that are dwarfed by their competitors and have to think small in order to survive! Take Maxis, for example, a successful computer game developer. (SimCity is one of their products.) In 1990, the company employed 20 people and was making millions of dollars. But its market share began to fall, and its owners realized they needed a new direction. So they hired a professional sales manager to take over marketing and also stepped up the company's new product development. Now Maxis sells its games in all the major computer stores, and its growth is healthy."[56]

1. The One Minute Manager is talking about growth businesses. But do you think innovation is important for life-style businesses, too? Support your answer by discussing some issues covered in this chapter.

2. Maxis grew in the 1990s by improving its sales and marketing, an important strategy for many types of small business. How might a franchise arrangement help a small business implement this strategy? Can you think of a relevant example? (*Hint*: Think about TV ads for fast-food franchise products.)

3. Can you think of any ways to find out how innovative a small business is? To make it more innovative?

PART 3

Managing the Business

Production
540

Min. Requirement
46

Efficiency
92 70

8

The Role of Management

Studies of entrepreneurial businesses indicate that the prior management experience of the founders helps determine the success of a new business venture: The more the founder knows about management, the more likely the new business is to thrive.[1] And the need for management expertise is multiplied in larger organizations, where the greater number of people and tasks can create chaos unless sound management practices prevail. In this chapter, we examine the role of management and its contribution to a business's success. After reading this chapter, you will be able to reach the learning goals below.

Learning Goals

1. Describe command-and-control management and identify types of situations in which it is appropriate.
2. List the four functions of management and explain how they relate to different approaches to management.
3. Identify and describe the three levels of planning, noting the importance of contingency planning.
4. List the four steps in organizing a business.
5. Describe the different levels of the management hierarchy and explain how they relate to one another.
6. Explain the operation of team-based organizations.
7. Contrast transactional and transformational approaches to leading.
8. Describe the basic styles of leading and explain how the four styles of situational leadership are variously applied.
9. Discuss the control process and its relationship to the planning process.
10. Describe the complementary roles of the technical and conceptual skills needed by managers.
11. Discuss the components of human relations skills and describe the characteristics of an effective learning organization.

The One Minute Coach

*"If you really want to understand management, talk to a drama coach,"
the One Minute Manager said to Carlos and Joanna. "I learned more
from helping coach the actors in my son's school play last year than I
have from most management training workshops I've been to."*

*"How does being a drama coach relate to managing a business?" Carlos
asked, looking up in surprise.*

"A lot of managers think coaches are the best role models. Coaches train, direct, and support talented people and help them to do their best work. And drama coaches know that *it's the actor who must play the role*. The coach cannot stop the play and tell an actor to try something different. The coach has to focus on helping the players learn their parts themselves. In business, managers often forget that their role is to bring out the best in their employees and co-workers. They sometimes act as though they should do all the important work themselves instead of letting the employee be the star."

Joanna nodded. "I know that's how my supervisor acted at my summer job. It left us feeling that he didn't trust us."

"Businesses are learning to trust their employees," the One Minute Manager continued, "and that's why many are refocusing their priorities on training—and on something else that every good coach already does."

"What's that?" Carlos asked.

"Inspiring their teams to do their best. Providing leadership and a vision of success is a big part of the coach's job, and also of the good manager's job. The best managers are the ones who can inspire outstanding performance in their employees."

"And I always thought that the best managers were the ones that made all the decisions themselves and then told their employees what to do," Carlos said.

The One Minute Manager laughed. "No, now more than ever, the best managers rely on their employees to make a lot of decisions, and they spend a lot of time interacting with employees. Take, for example, Jack Welch, the CEO of General Electric. He defines a good manager as a business leader who creates a vision, articulates the vision, passionately owns the vision, and relentlessly drives it to completion. Welch says that 'above all else, good leaders are open. They go up, down and around their organization to reach people. They don't stick to the established channels. They're informal. They're straight with people. . . . Real communication takes countless hours of eyeball to eyeball, back and forth.' "[2]

Joanna looked a little concerned. "That sounds as though he would always be looking over your shoulder, giving you orders. I'm not sure I'd like that."

"Not at all, Joanna. In fact, good managers understand that their employees know a lot about the company's products and the customers who buy them. Employees will put that knowledge to work for the company if they feel trusted, valued, and supported."

The Manager's Challenge

Management is accomplishing organizational goals through people and other resources. The goal might be for the organization to grow at a rate of 10 percent per year, to achieve a 45 percent market share for its most profitable product, to open 15 overseas outlets in the next 24 months, or to increase the diversity of its work force. Effective management enables an organization to achieve its goals so long as they reflect a reasonable understanding of the organization's current situation and the resources available.

Managers are everywhere—almost all organizations have more than one. Some supervise other managers, while others supervise hands-on workers. The people who schedule performances and hire and fire the clowns in the Ringling Bros. circus are managers. So is the chief information officer of VeriFone, Inc., who lives and works in Santa Fe, New Mexico, and uses entirely electronic means to communicate with other employees who work for this California-based company. And so is Deborah S. Kent, who manages a Ford Motor Co. plant in Lake Avon, Ohio. The first woman to manage a Ford plant, she is responsible for the work of more than 3,700 employees and 420 robots as they make 56 vans an hour on an assembly line almost 20 miles long.[3]

In all these cases, the manager's job is to achieve the goals of the organization. This creates what is known as the "manager's challenge," the responsibility for achieving something through other people's work. A simple way to look at the manager's challenge is to see the manager's job as making things happen rather than doing them directly.

Managers are particularly challenged by today's competitive business environment. Customers and stockholders expect improved product and service quality, faster development and delivery, and rapid technological advances. As we have seen earlier in this text, competition comes not only from other U.S. companies but also from companies based abroad. The roles of managers and their skills are evolving to keep pace with all these challenges. As we will see later in this chapter, it is increasingly important for managers to build a learning organization and become lifelong learners themselves, always building their management skills. We will also see how managers create a supportive work environment that enables employees to bring their best ideas and initiative to the workplace every day. But first we will explore the traditional methods and functions of management, which provide the foundation for current managerial innovations.

Command-and-Control Management

The classical approach to management is called **command-and-control management**—management exercised through a chain of command. Command-and-control management is based on the following rules:[4]

- There should be a clear and unbroken line of communication from the top to the bottom of every organization.
- Each person should receive orders from only one boss.
- Each task or project should be managed by only one person.

For most of this century, command and control was viewed as the ideal form of management. Managers were paid to be in charge, to issue orders, and to control what happened within their area in order to produce certain results.

 management

Accomplishing organizational goals through people and other resources.

command-and-control management

Management exercised through a chain of command.

1. Describe command-and-control management and identify types of situations in which it is appropriate.

Compliant subordinates did what they were told, held in check by the fear of punishment or dismissal. A manager who could deliver the goods—regardless of how employees were treated in the process—got nice bonuses and was eventually promoted.

In some contexts, this traditional style is still the preferred way of managing. It is still the norm in the military, where combat situations require people to perform tightly controlled tasks that are often unpleasant and dangerous—and thus might not be done at all without the discipline of military command and control. In businesses, crises often demand command-and-control management. For example, even in companies where many decisions are made by employee teams instead of by managers, there is still one person in charge of managing the evacuation of the building in the event of fire. Emergencies are not the best time for group discussions! Similarly, when a company's survival is threatened by a financial crisis, its board of directors usually appoints a tough new executive and gives him or her absolute authority to make emergency cuts in spending and jobs in order to turn the business around.

Applying Command-and-Control Management

At Domino's Pizza, where a uniform product and guaranteed delivery in 30 minutes are keys to customer satisfaction and profitability, the command-and-control management approach gets the job done.

Command and control is also appropriate where technical knowledge or access to timely information makes one or a few individuals best suited to make decisions, as in an air traffic control center, or when a sequence of precise tasks must be performed, as in a surgical procedure. Complex and delicate manufacturing processes are generally controlled tightly as well—although as we will learn when we study production, some factories now expect employees to manage many of the controls their managers used to oversee. But in most businesses and other organizations, new approaches to management now supplement or replace command and control. Whether traditional or innovative, however, all managers must perform four basic functions in order to get results from their people.

The Four Functions of Management

Bruce Gordon joined telecommunications company Bell Atlantic right out of college, rising through the ranks to manage the company's marketing program. To improve customer service, he set a goal for the customer service reps who worked for him: Answer 90 percent of customer calls within 20 seconds, instead of the meager 70 percent they were answering when he took over. (Why within 20 seconds? That's how long most people will wait before hanging up.)[5] To accomplish this goal, which came to be known as the 90/20 goal, Gordon faced the classic manager's challenge: He could not answer all those calls himself, so he had to improve the performance of his employees. But they felt they were doing as well as they could, given the resources available to them. Gordon met the challenge through the four functions of management: planning, organizing, leading, and controlling.[6]

Planning is the process of defining goals and the strategies and tactics for reaching them. Gordon's plan was to achieve the 90/20 goal by, first, forming a team of troubleshooters to find out what the problems were. Their conclusion? Employees were wasting too much time in meetings and training sessions, or just goofing off. So the next step in Gordon's plan was to form corrective action teams to propose ways to solve this problem.

Organizing is the process of arranging employees and material resources to carry out plans. Gordon decided that he did not have sufficient resources to hire enough new employees and install adequate phone lines to achieve his goal at the current work level. So he organized teams to come up with ways to solve the problem by improving the performance of the existing work force. And when his teams developed a tight schedule for employee breaks, meetings, and training sessions, Gordon used this schedule to better organize employees' time.

Leading is a process that involves both directing and motivating employees to accomplish tasks. Gordon led employees toward his goal by making it the focus of their work. He also motivated them to improve their performance by announcing that all jobs were "up for grabs." Employees had to reapply and compete for their jobs. When the dust settled, 20 percent of them were gone. In addition, Gordon worked to open the lines of communication with remaining employees—he supervises 9,000—by moving to an office on the employees' floor instead of staying in the distant executive suite.

Controlling is the process of monitoring and evaluating activities to ensure that objectives are being achieved. Bell Atlantic now tracks the performance of each service representative. According to Gordon, "A good number of people felt we had compromised their freedom by managing their adherence to a schedule, but they reached the '90/20' goal in two months, and no one has looked back."[7]

Gordon relied on the authority of command-and-control management to plan, organize, lead, and control the improvement of Bell Atlantic's customer service. These four functions of management are important to all managers, and later in this chapter we examine them in greater detail. But Gordon also used a new management tool—employee teams—to identify and solve problems. Even though he used a traditional approach, he combined it with some new management methods.

The management process that Bruce Gordon and managers like him use is illustrated in Figure 8.1. Managers plan, organize, lead, and control company resources—including human resources—to accomplish the goals of the business. In practice, managers use a wide variety of tools and techniques, taken

2. List the four functions of management and explain how they relate to different approaches to management.

Because the traditional approach is so directive, some people call this management function directing *instead of leading.*

 planning

The process of defining goals and the strategies and tactics for reaching them.

 organizing

The process of arranging employees and material resources to carry out plans.

 leading

The process that involves both directing and motivating employees to accomplish tasks.

 controlling

The process of monitoring and evaluating activities to ensure that objectives are being achieved.

figure 8.1 The Management Process

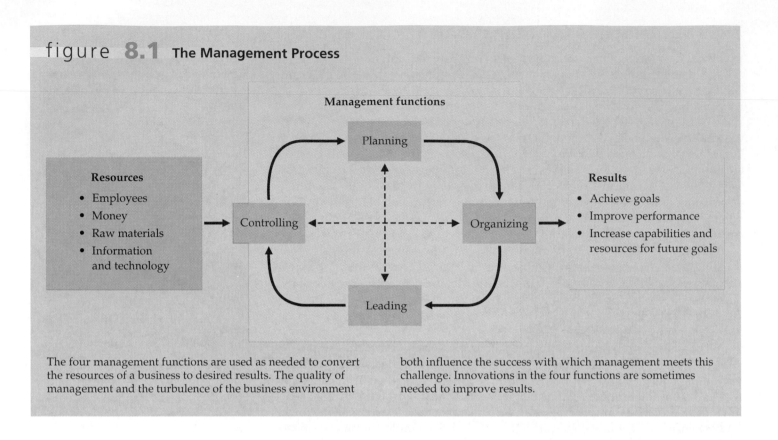

Management functions

Planning

Resources
- Employees
- Money
- Raw materials
- Information and technology

Controlling

Organizing

Results
- Achieve goals
- Improve performance
- Increase capabilities and resources for future goals

Leading

The four management functions are used as needed to convert the resources of a business to desired results. The quality of management and the turbulence of the business environment both influence the success with which management meets this challenge. Innovations in the four functions are sometimes needed to improve results.

from all four functions, to accomplish any single goal. Management is, therefore, a flexible process—the only hard-and-fast requirement is that it produce the needed results.

Alternatives to Command and Control

Why do we need alternatives to the traditional methods of management? Because, as we saw in the opening chapters of this book, businesses face new and difficult challenges that call for innovation in all things—including management. Command-and-control management is limited in its ability to bring about quality improvements, for example. But traditional management methods worked well for many companies for many decades and are therefore difficult for some managers to abandon.

The need for management alternatives is underscored by the ongoing research of Tom Peters, one of America's best-known business consultants and authors. His popular book, *In Search of Excellence* (coauthored with Robert Waterman), reported on the management practices of those American companies that achieved consistently superior performance from 1961 through 1980. They included giants like IBM, General Motors, computer makers Digital Equipment Corp. and Data General, Eastman Kodak, and Delta Airlines. Although these large organizations had superior management practices in these earlier decades, all of them suffered performance problems in the 1980s or 1990s. In a more recent book, Peters concluded that long-term excellent performance is no longer likely to result from any single management system. In his words, "There are no excellent companies."[8] What Peters meant, of course, is that management practices must continue to adapt to the needs of the organization, even in the best companies.

Delegation and Empowerment

The primary goal of managers remains seeing that the work gets done. Managers continue to play traditional roles in many organizations. In many others, however, managers see themselves as coaches, counselors, team leaders, and colleagues in a more supportive work environment that enables each employee to feel valued and to be more productive. These new-style managers believe their main job is encouraging, developing, and supporting their employees rather than dictating how and when they perform tasks. These organizations have shifted power downward to frontline employees who are closer to customers and better able to respond to their needs.

DuPont takes this approach in its "Adopt a Customer" program, which encourages hands-on factory workers to visit a customer once each month, to learn the customer's needs, and to be that customer's representative on the factory floor. Then, if quality or delivery problems arise, workers are more likely to see them from the customer's point of view and to help make decisions that support customer needs as well as those of the organization.[9]

The shifting approach to management is best illustrated by the shift from delegation to empowerment at many businesses. **Delegation** is the assignment of a manager's responsibility and authority for a task to an employee. To get anything done, managers have to delegate work to employees, a process we analyze in Chapter 9. Delegation is a common practice among managers. But what happens if the employee lacks the knowledge needed to succeed? Or the business does not have the equipment or technology needed to do the task? Or the employees need to achieve high levels of teamwork and creativity to succeed? Then delegation must be coupled with **empowerment**, the transfer to employees of authority and responsibility for a task, along with the necessary resources and power to excel at the task.

Note the difference between delegation and empowerment. In delegating, a manager is more like a dictator. Employees passively receive orders. In empowerment, the manager brings employees actively into the process by transferring decision making to them. Empowerment makes employees active participants in the business process. Recall from Chapter 1 that empowerment is a vital part of quality improvement strategies in business and often results in special training for employee teams. As a result, empowerment typically makes it possible for managers to delegate broader tasks and responsibilities to employees.

delegation

The assignment of a manager's responsibility and authority for a task to employees.

empowerment

The transfer to employees of authority and responsibility for a task, along with the necessary resources and power to excel at the task.

Planning

Recall that *planning* is the process of defining goals and the strategies and tactics for reaching them. Plans can be simple and brief: Your plan for preparing dinner tonight might be as simple as popping a frozen dinner into the microwave. But most businesses have more complex goals and tasks, requiring many more steps over a longer period of time. Their plans are more elaborate as a result. Managers spend much of their time developing plans, and in a growing number of companies, many other employees participate in planning as well. For example, at chemicals manufacturer Hoechst Celanese, dozens of U.S. subsidiaries each submit an annual business plan to Charles Langston, vice president of strategic resources management at the company's Somerville, New Jersey, headquarters office. He and his staff help the subsidiary managers, if needed, in the weeks before they submit their plans. Then Langston evaluates each plan to decide whether it will be approved and funded by headquarters.[10]

mission statement

A written description of the goals the business should accomplish through its planning and management.

 strategic plans

Plans that describe broad objectives and general methods for achieving them.

3. Identify and describe the three levels of planning, noting the importance of contingency planning.

The Hierarchy of Plans

Planning is typically performed in a hierarchical (top-down) sequence, reflecting the typical hierarchical structure found in most businesses.

The Mission Statement

Senior managers and the board of directors develop broad goals for the business. These are stated in a written **mission statement**, a description of the goals the business should accomplish through its planning and management. Missions provide focus by stating the ultimate purpose of all activities, and they are often inspiring as well. Part of Federal Express Corp.'s mission statement promises that service "will produce outstanding financial returns by providing totally reliable, competitively superior global air-ground transportation of high-priority goods and documents that require rapid, time-certain delivery."[11] To see how seriously the world's largest clothing manufacturer takes its mission statement, read the ethics check "Vision and Values Drive Levi Strauss."

Strategic Plans

Senior managers and managers who work for them typically collaborate to develop **strategic plans**, plans that describe broad objectives and general methods for achieving them. For example, one of Federal Express's (FedEx) key strategic plans for achieving its mission of totally reliable transportation is "Get closer to our customers."[12]

Strategic plans answer three important questions:

1. *Where do we want to go?* Planners set their objectives—to increase sales by 50 percent in the Midwest, to produce better-quality products than those of competitors, or to improve the speed of delivery services.

2. *What is our current situation?* Planners examine the company's strengths and weaknesses, and they look for opportunities and threats in the business environment. See Figure 8.2 for an example of this so-called SWOT analysis.

figure **8.2**   SWOT Analysis for FedEx

	Positive	Negative
Internal	Strengths • Largest market share • Most reliable service • Strong TQM initiative	Weaknesses • Company relies solely on package delivery market • Efforts to enter fax market failed
External	Opportunities • Growth in overseas markets • Trend toward decentralized management may require more communications in businesses	Threats • Direct competition is increasingly strong • Fax and e-mail also compete with overnight letters

Planners assess their business's situation as a first step in strategic planning, and the SWOT analysis is often used for this purpose.

ethics check

Vision and Values Drive Levi Strauss

San Francisco–based Levi Strauss & Co., with retail sales in excess of $6 billion, is the world's largest clothing manufacturer. Since the privately held company was founded more than 140 years ago, Levi's has sold more than 2.5 billion pairs of jeans. Robert Haas, chief executive officer and great-great-grand-nephew of Levi Strauss, the founder of the company, is determined to ensure that the corporate vision and values that Strauss helped define are taken seriously by all employees.

In the late 1980s, Robert Haas took charge of developing the Levi Strauss *Aspirations Statement*—a document that defines the shared values guiding both worker and corporate decision making. And, like other progressive companies such as Ben & Jerry's and The Body Shop, Levi's has adopted a written proclamation of the company's values in a wide variety of areas. One policy, the "Terms of Engagement," spells out minimum standards that foreign contractors must meet in the areas of environmental quality and employee safety and health. Moreover, rather than adopting the policy and filing it away, Levi's takes this document very seriously.

Soon after the Terms of Engagement policy was adopted, Levi Strauss reviewed the practices of more than 600 foreign contractors and suspended 30 that didn't meet the company's minimum standards. In 1993, citing "pervasive violations of basic human rights," Levi's took the extraordinary step of forgo-ing investment in the People's Republic of China and gradually phasing out its Chinese clothing manufacturing contracts.

Says Haas, "Companies have to wake up to the fact that they are more than a product on a shelf. They're behavior as well." As long as Levi Strauss's great-great-grandnephew is in charge, vision and values will drive Levi's behavior.

1. What style of leadership does Haas seem to prefer? How can you tell?

2. Why should companies like Levi's explicitly establish and communicate their values?

3. Is it important to include the input of all employees when defining a company's vision and values?

4. Imagine that you are a middle manager at Levi's. You just learned that a retail chain that carries your clothing has been cited by government inspectors on numerous occasions for safety violations. Knowing what you know about Robert Haas, what actions would you recommend?

Source: Based on Jim Impoco, "Working for Mr. Clean Jeans," *U.S. News & World Report,* Aug. 2, 1993, p. 49.

---

3. *How do we get there from here?* Planners define the general approach the organization will take to put its strategies in action. Strategic plans do not spell out all the details, but they do give guidance to planners at the operational level.

Operational Plans

The third step in the planning hierarchy is to create **operational plans**, plans that give the details needed to carry out strategic plans in daily work. Operational plans say who does what, how, when, and where in order to convert the organization's mission and strategies into concrete actions that can be carried out by individual employees. This step is also called *implementation*.

Federal Express's strategic plan of getting closer to its customers gave birth to an operational plan of giving customers access to the company's computer tracking network so that they could trace the progress of their own packages. Middle- and lower-level managers and, increasingly, teams of employees collaborate to develop detailed operational plans. To implement strategies, planners must develop appropriate **tactics**, detailed descriptions of the actions employees will need to take to carry out strategic plans. Since operational plans describe the tactics to be used, in some businesses, operational plans are actually called tactical plans.

 operational plans

Plans that give the details needed to carry out strategic plans in daily work.

 tactics

Detailed descriptions of the actions employees will need to take to carry out strategic plans.

contingency planning

The process of preparing alternatives in case of a change in the situation or a problem with the plans.

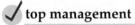
staffing

The hiring, development, and assignment of people to activities and positions.

top management

The employees who have the most power and responsibility in the organization.

4. List the four steps in organizing a business.

Contingency Planning

What if something goes wrong? Perhaps the situation changes, or the planners' information and assumptions were flawed. Or maybe frontline employees discover that the pace or volume of the operational plan is unrealistic. One way companies try to minimize such problems is by planning more frequently, and for that reason *planning cycles* are often shorter than they used to be. Five- or ten-year strategic plans are giving way to annual plans, and in fast-moving industries like computing, semiannual or quarterly strategic plans are the norm.

Another alternative is **contingency planning**, the process of preparing alternatives in case of a change in the situation or a problem with the plans. Charles Langston of Hoechst Celanese prefers this approach: "I wouldn't say the strategies have to be done more often, but the strategies have to have contingency plans based on different types of competitor responses and different economic assumptions. Today's faster rate of change has been incorporated into strategy so that strategies are no longer linear plans, they have strategic options built into them."[13] This approach is sometimes termed *informed opportunism* because it gives businesses the flexibility to act on opportunities as they arise, combined with the advantage of the focus provided by the general strategic direction of the plans.[14] For plans to become actions, however, managers must organize the work of others, the topic we turn to next.

Organizing

We defined *organizing* as the process of arranging employees and material resources to carry out plans. To meet the management challenge, managers must organize the work of others. This involves four basic organizational steps:

1. Identify the activities and resources needed to accomplish goals and implement plans.

2. Group related activities in a useful manner (form should follow function, as we learned in Chapter 5).

3. Decide which individuals or teams will perform the activities identified in steps 1 and 2. At this point, **staffing**—the hiring, development, and assignment of people to activities and positions—takes place. Some activities may not be assigned to employees. An increasing number of businesses are subcontracting to outside firms some of the work that employees have traditionally performed.

4. Create the structures people need to perform those activities well. This final step is the main focus of Chapter 9. As you will see, it concerns the location of authority, responsibility, and accountability for work.

These four organizing steps sound simple, but through them managers exert a powerful influence over business performance. Many a business has failed because its organization was too rigid to permit needed change. Daniel Duncan, president of consulting firm Management Structures and Systems, Inc., of Louisville, Kentucky, explains the current organizational challenge: "Instead of creating an elaborate series of interlocking units held together by a formalized chain of command—the essence of traditional organizational structure—businesses of the 1990s would be far better off letting their shapes and configurations be dictated by the work they do and the complex world they face."[15] Teamwork helps meet this challenge in traditional command-and-control structures. And in Chapter 9 and other upcoming chapters, we explore subcontracting, downsizing, and other strategies by which managers are making their organizations simpler and smaller in order to become more flexible and innovative. However, even the newer, more flexible organization relies to some extent on a hierarchical approach to management.

The Management Hierarchy

As Figure 8.3 indicates, managers typically constitute a hierarchy within an organization, occupying top, middle, and supervisory levels. In management hierarchies, the reporting relationships define each manager's level. For example, if you have to report what you do to your boss, who in turn reports to the company president, then you are two levels below the top employee in the company.

The number of management levels varies, depending on the organization's size and approach. In companies with thousands of employees, five to seven management levels are common, and some have more than a dozen. For example, Deborah Kent, the Ford plant manager we met earlier, has area managers beneath her, such as the body and assembly operations manager for Econoline vans. These area managers may have assistant managers reporting to them, who in turn manage supervisors and foremen, who perform routine management of factory workers. That is an average of four layers of management. And other layers extend upward in Ford's corporate management hierarchy. Kent reports to Ford's vehicle operations manager, who reports to another manager at Ford Motor Co. North America, who reports to a senior manager at Ford Motor Co.'s Dearborn, Michigan, headquarters, who in turn reports to Ford's president, chairman, and CEO, Alexander Trotman.[16] Contrast all these layers with the one to three management levels usually found in small businesses. In some cases, a single manager or management team performs all management activities, as is the case in a sole proprietorship.

Top Management

At the peak of the management pyramid is **top management**, the employees who have the most power and responsibility in the organization. In any company, relatively few people are top managers—usually fewer than 2 percent of all employees. Typical titles include president, chief executive officer (CEO), chief financial officer (CFO), and various vice presidents. Vice presidents report to the company's president or chief executive officer; a vice president is typically the top manager of a division, department, or function. Top management's tasks include setting long-term goals, establishing policies and standards, determining long-term financing needs and the sources for those funds, and setting strategies for entering or exiting markets.

The motto on President Harry S Truman's desk said "the buck stops here," and that's almost true of top managers—but not quite. Although top management is the highest level of employees, even it reports to a higher level. As you may recall from Chapter 5, the president of a corporation typically reports to the owners or their board of directors.

Top managers typically earn the highest salaries in any organization, but they may also work the longest hours. It is difficult to assess the value of top managers' contributions to a company. Some people believe top management is overpaid in the United States, where the top executive often receives 40 times the compensation of the typical nonmanagement employee. For example, the median total compensation for a CEO in 1993 was $770,000, while the mean earnings of a production worker during that same year were only $19,500.[17]

5. Describe the different levels of the management hierarchy and explain how they relate to one another.

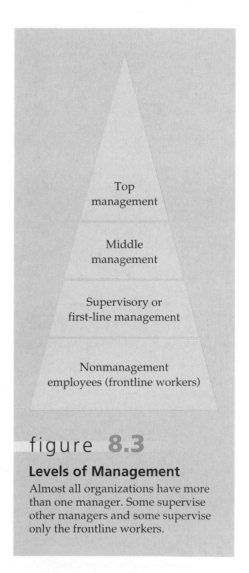

figure **8.3**

Levels of Management
Almost all organizations have more than one manager. Some supervise other managers and some supervise only the frontline workers.

Next time you visit your campus bookstore, ask a cashier whom he or she reports to, whom that person reports to, and so on. Two to three layers of management are common in such stores.

This wage gap between top management and low-level employees can be a bargaining issue for employees and a policy decision for directors. It is smaller in many Japanese companies than in similar U.S. companies, and some companies do try to narrow the gap. Ben & Jerry's Homemade, Inc., used to permit a maximum top salary of only seven times the lowest worker's salary, but the company had to abandon this restriction when it hired a new president in 1995—it could not find a qualified candidate to work at that pay level.

Middle Management

Middle management consists of the managers who report directly to top management and are responsible for the organization's short-term goals. Middle managers usually account for fewer than 5 percent of an organization's total number of employees. Middle managers must help to develop and then implement the detailed plans by which the business will attempt to meet goals set by top management. Middle managers direct the day-to-day activities of their subordinates and help them make good use of equipment, supplies, and other resources.

There may be many layers within the middle management level. Typical middle management positions include division or department heads, bank branch managers, supermarket managers, and principals and deans. Typical activities of this level of management include budgeting, hiring, and handling problems that cannot be solved at a lower level. Middle managers decide how many people or teams to assign to a project in order to complete it quickly and efficiently. They authorize specific expenditures required to meet organizational objectives, and they provide training and other support to their workers. Deborah Kent is a middle manager at Ford, responsible for making sure her plant meets budget, quality, and production goals set by the managers above her. And she relies on the middle managers directly below her to help achieve these goals in each area of the plant.

A major trend in business today is to reduce or eliminate levels of middle management in order to cut the cost of doing business, shorten the time required for making decisions, and decrease the distance between managers and customers. For example, Citicorp halved the number of layers of management at its Diner's Club unit, compressing eight levels into four. And a General Electric Medical Systems factory in Michigan now operates with only two layers of management.[18]

Computers help take the place of some of these missing managers. One small instance of this trend can be seen in retail checkout lines. Cashiers, who have been trained to understand the conditions under which the store accepts checks, now routinely approve customers' checks without calling a store manager. Computer systems that give knowledgeable employees the information they need to make fast decisions save time and produce more satisfied customers in the process.

Supervisory Management

Supervisory management, or **first-line management**, comprises the managers who give daily direction and assistance to nonmanagement employees. Typical positions in this category include manufacturing plant foremen, warehouse supervisors, bank teller supervisors, and construction managers. All of these people are responsible for daily operations, and all report to middle managers. For example, a shift manager in a supermarket is responsible for scheduling employees' time, resolving work-flow problems, coordinating the repair of equipment, directing inventory taking, and resolving employee complaints. The shift manager then reports to the store manager.

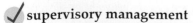 **middle management**

The managers who report directly to top management and are responsible for the organization's short-term goals.

supervisory management

The managers who give daily direction and assistance to nonmanagement employees. (Also known as *first-line management*.)

The supervisory management level typically has more managers than any higher level but still comprises only a fraction of the organization's total work force—usually no more than 10 percent. As is the case with middle managers, many businesses are attempting to reduce the number of supervisory managers and shift some of their responsibilities to frontline employees through empowerment. Computer technology and the rise of teamwork help make this shift practical. One force behind this trend is the realization that the traditional pyramid shape can create an organization in which nothing happens without time-consuming conferences with those at the top of the hierarchy. Chapter 9 examines this problem in depth.

The Management Hierarchy and Its Role in Planning

We saw earlier that planning is usually performed in a hierarchical sequence. The hierarchy of plans corresponds to the management hierarchy, as Figure 8.4 shows. Top managers develop the mission and oversee its translation into strategic and operational plans. Middle managers take on most of the responsibility for converting the mission into strategic plans. Supervisory management often works out the tactical details of the operational plan. This correspondence is not ironclad; in businesses where top managers are highly authoritative and controlling, most plans are written by top managers. And in businesses where frontline employees participate in management decisions, for example, through their work teams, they may have a voice in deciding an organization's mission, strategy, and tactics.

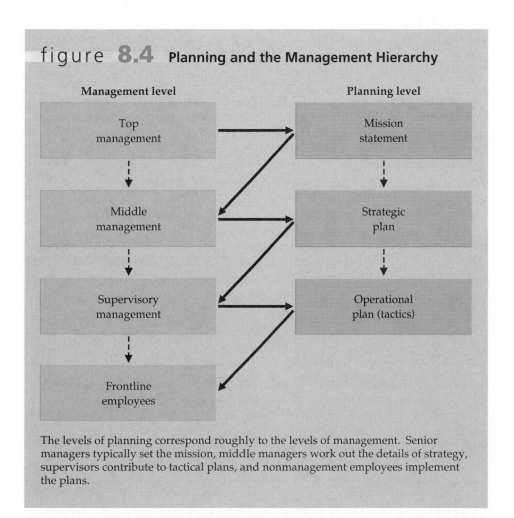

figure **8.4** **Planning and the Management Hierarchy**

The levels of planning correspond roughly to the levels of management. Senior managers typically set the mission, middle managers work out the details of strategy, supervisors contribute to tactical plans, and nonmanagement employees implement the plans.

6. Explain the operation of team-based organizations.

Team-Based Management

Many managerial responsibilities are now becoming part of the job of **work teams**, project-oriented groups of employees. As we have already noted, team-based organizations are more flexible than hierarchical organizations—many teams exist only as long as their project lasts. And teams also gain flexibility by combining people from different areas of the business or people with complementary skills and abilities. Groups of employees can make effective decisions when they are empowered to do so.

For example, a new General Electric factory that makes surge protectors for power stations employs 15 salaried "advisers" and 172 hourly workers—about half the number of managers a conventional GE plant would have. The workers are organized into work teams that are assigned specific factory tasks. Team meetings are run by hourly workers—each team selects its own leaders—while an adviser sits in the back of the room and speaks up only if the team needs help. And at Semco S.A., a small manufacturing firm that produces industrial equipment in Brazil, employees actually vote on certain management decisions.[19] Generally, employees who are granted a greater voice in the assignment of tasks and duties are more satisfied with their jobs and their employers than are those employees who have no control over the scope and timing of their duties. In other words, involvement equals commitment. Team-based management is discussed further in Chapter 9.

Leading

7. Contrast transactional and transformational approaches to leading.

We defined *leading* as the process of directing and motivating employees to accomplish tasks. In command-and-control management, leading is accomplished largely by telling employees what to do—and what will happen to them if they don't! The secretary, bookkeeper, and factory worker in a traditional business know they must come to work on time and do what their managers say must be done—at least they must meet certain minimum standards if they wish to keep their jobs. And managers need not worry too much about motivating their employees in this traditional system because the management hierarchy gives them enough power to ensure minimum performance from most employees.

But what if the minimum is not good enough? It rarely is in today's competitive business environment. Good managers need to help employees not just to *do* their jobs, but to do their jobs well. When it comes to leading, the manager's challenge demands more than any single approach can deliver, so it is not surprising that alternative approaches have emerged. We will examine both traditional, directive approaches and newer, motivation-oriented alternatives to leading.

Transactional Leaders

The traditional approach to leading produces the best performance when managers are **transactional leaders**, leaders who define what employees must do to achieve work goals and then help them do it.[20] Breaking work down into narrow tasks related to broader performance goals helps both manager and employee. The manager who says, "Pick up all the garbage in New York City, and do it on time!" is not much help to the employees who are given this difficult job. But when managers say, "Pick up the garbage better by figuring out how to keep our garbage trucks from breaking down all the time," then the employees can focus their efforts in a useful way, and both they and their managers will be more pleased with the results.

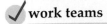
work teams

Project-oriented groups of employees.

transactional leaders

Leaders who define what employees must do to achieve work goals and then help them do it.

This is just what happened at New York City's Department of Sanitation, where deputy sanitation commissioner Roger Liwer recalls that "we had the worst-run fleet [of trucks] in the city, poor productivity, and constant grievances from workers." And garbage often piled up because more than half the trucks were broken down on the average day. But a change in management style seems to have solved these problems. Managers now encourage employees' innovations by offering prizes for their ideas and allowing teams to work on key problems. Mechanics invented a device that automatically turns trucks off when oil levels drop too low, for example—and now drivers don't burn up the engines by running their trucks without oil. Now, on the average day only 16 percent of the department's 6,200 trucks are out of commission, and workers are happier and more productive, too. As one employee puts it, "Morale around here used to be bottom, bottom, bottom." But now, "The lines of communication are open. Everyone is comfortable."[21]

Transactional leaders can structure employees' work by helping them set specific goals or objectives that relate to desired results. This style of leadership produces a hierarchy of objectives in which the top-level goals of the mission statement are broken down into lower-level goals, all the way down to specific objectives for individual employees. The result is a chain in which lower-level goals form links that, taken together, lead to the accomplishment of higher-level goals.[22] In one method, *management by objectives* (MBO), the manager helps employees set objectives and develop action plans, then evaluates their performance against the plans.

A related goal-setting technique is One-Minute Management, originally introduced in the book *The One Minute Manager* in 1982. It uses one-minute goal setting, in which managers sit down with employees to develop a list of specific work goals or objectives. It is important for the employee to agree on the merit of these goals. The employee then describes each goal briefly and clearly on paper. The written goals provide guidance for employees in daily work— they are expected to take a minute every day to reread them and see whether their actions are helping them achieve their goals. Managers can also use the goals as a yardstick to evaluate each employee's progress.[23] You will learn more about MBO, One-Minute Management, and other goal-setting techniques in Chapter 11.

Transformational Leaders

Transactional leadership emphasizes the *directing* part of leading, but leading also requires managers to *motivate* employees. **Transformational leaders** inspire employees to change in pursuit of a compelling vision of the future.[24] The transformational, even revolutionary, nature of leading is expressed in the often-quoted insight that managers produce order, while leaders create change. Managers who are able to excite and inspire employees so that they perform far better than usual exhibit true **leadership**—the ability to inspire others to achieve exceptional performance.

Managers typically are most in need of leadership qualities when a major change is required. People don't like to change. Unless their manager presents a compelling vision of where they need to go, they often won't follow. Lawrence A. Bossidy is the chairman and CEO of the aerospace, auto, and chemical giant, AlliedSignal, headquartered in Morristown, New Jersey. Bossidy, who led the company through a major turnaround, believes in the "burning platform" theory of change: "When roustabouts are standing on the offshore oil rig and the foreman yells, 'Jump into the water,' not only won't they jump but they also won't feel too friendly toward the foreman. There may be sharks in the water. They'll jump only when they themselves see the flames shooting up from the platform."[25]

 transformational leaders

Leaders who inspire employees to change in pursuit of a compelling vision of the future.

 leadership

The ability to inspire others to achieve exceptional performance.

table 8.1 Transactional Versus Transformational Leaders

Approaches to leading vary from transactional, which focuses on making operations run smoothly, to transformational, which focuses on changing existing operations. Managers need to adopt the approach most appropriate to their specific situation.

Transactional Leaders	Transformational Leaders
Command	Inspire
Delegate	Empower
Execute plans	Communicate a vision
Lead incremental improvements	Lead big changes

Bossidy contends that leadership must be inspirational to fire up employees who would not otherwise make the leap to new strategies and processes. He believes leaders must communicate a compelling vision—that the changing world has indeed set the oil platform on fire—in order to inspire employees to commit to the necessary change. Bossidy's approach to leading is quite different from the transactional leader's approach: he is a transformational leader. Table 8.1 summarizes the contrasts between the two approaches to leading.

Styles of Leading

8. Describe the basic styles of leading and explain how the four styles of situational leadership are variously applied.

Some managers approach leading in the spirit of command-and-control management. They use their authority to make a decision and announce it. If they are inspiring leaders, their employees may be motivated to implement the decision well—leadership ability makes some command-and-control managers more effective than others. Such an **autocratic leader** adopts a style based largely on the use of authority. Extreme autocratic leaders just tell subordinates what to do—period. A less autocratic leader will explain why and answer questions in an effort to sell his or her decision to employees.

The opposite of an autocratic leader is a **democratic leader**, one whose style is based on empowerment and employee participation. This style, taken

EXECUTIVE SOFTBALL LEAGUE

SOMEBODY PICK THAT UP!

Drawing by C. Barsotti; © 1995 *The New Yorker Magazine, Inc.*

doing business

Managing the Miami Dolphins on the Run

Don Shula, coach of the Miami Dolphins, doesn't believe in holding to a game plan that isn't working. He values the ability to adapt, to deviate from a predetermined plan when circumstances change. He calls this skill being *audible-ready*.

The key to being adaptable is to be well prepared in the first place. "Audibles," or verbal commands on the playing field, are well thought out and choreographed ahead of time. They are contingency plans that can be used on command at the last moment in place of the official play. The team is audible-ready, for example, if players can switch plans instantly on command from quarterback Dan Marino.

Coach Shula knows that an inflexible, fixed game plan can be deadly to organizations today. He is always asking, "What if . . . ?" so that when a change happens, neither he nor his players are caught flat-footed. When the Dolphins were en route to their perfect season, they had the services of a fine punter named Larry Seiple. Shula told Seiple he was free to run any time from punt formation—as long as he made the first down.

In the AFC championship game against Pittsburgh, Shula was surprised when Seiple faked a punt on fourth down and ran for 37 yards to set up the Dolphins' first score. As he watched Seiple take off and start to run the ball, Shula started yelling, "No! No! No!" Then when he saw Seiple in the clear, he changed it to "Go! Go! Go!" That was a real audible!

Just as Dan Marino's on-field audibles have turned crisis situations into game-winning touchdowns, effective managers need to be ready to change their game plan when the circumstances demand it. Managers who are prepared with a variety of options for executing quick, on-target decisions in the face of unexpected change or challenge are more likely to reach their organization's goals.

Source: Ken Blanchard and Don Shula, *Everyone's a Coach* (New York: Harper Business, 1995).

---

to its extreme, gives employees full authority to make their own decisions within reasonable limits set by general policies or guidelines. In a less extreme approach, the democratic leader may describe a problem to employees and ask for solutions but retain the authority of final approval.[26] Some managers exhibit a third style, that of the *free-rein leader*, who abdicates responsibility and hands over the reins to employees, thus offering no leadership at all.

The choice of style should depend on the organization. A hierarchical structure calls for an autocratic leader; the empowered organization demands a more participatory style. But a shift in style is difficult for many managers. In a book entitled *Memoirs of a Recovering Autocrat*, experienced bank manager Richard Hallstein writes, "Hi. My name is Dick. I'm a recovering autocrat. My life has been one long attempt to gain control of all that is around me." He argues that while "participative management is increasingly required in our changing world, the transition is very painful and difficult for most managers."[27]

Cathleen Black, publisher of *USA Today*, is the opposite—a democratic leader by nature. She prefers a cooperative style of management in which employees participate in many of her decisions. "I believe in strength with a cooperative management style," Black says. "A powerful boss isn't necessarily a tough boss."[28] Black's style is more typical of women than of men. According to one study, "women managers . . . have demonstrated that using the command-and-control style of managing others, a style generally associated with men in large, traditional organizations, is not the only way to succeed."[29]

In practice, most managers combine aspects of different styles of leading. Don Shula, coach of the Miami Dolphins football team, for example, acts at times as an autocratic leader and at times as a democratic leader. But Shula has won more games than any other coach, perhaps because his players and coaches consider him such a great leader.[30] For a close-up look at Shula's style at work, see the doing business box entitled "Managing the Miami Dolphins on the Run."

 autocratic leader

A leader who adopts a style based largely on the use of authority.

 democratic leader

A leader whose style is based on empowerment and employee participation.

situational leadership

An approach that varies the level of direction and support to suit the follower's developmental level.

Situational Leadership

The switch from autocratic to democratic style reflects changes in organizational structure, as we just saw. Similarly, we have learned that a shift from the transactional to the transformational approach is needed when the business environment becomes turbulent. There is also a third factor driving changes in management style: the people being led.

Managers who learn to adapt their leadership style to each employee's situation are practicing **situational leadership**—an approach that varies the level of direction and support to suit the follower's developmental level. Developmental level has two dimensions: an employee's *willingness* to do something and his or her *ability* to do it.[31] Experienced, motivated employees score high on both dimensions—they are both willing and able to work. They are best led with a minimum of direction and help, and participation and empowerment are the best ways to manage them. But unwilling employees with limited ability need a different style of leadership. They will succeed only if they are told exactly what to do and how to do it. In this situation, goal setting by an autocratic leader will be more successful.

As Figure 8.5(a) indicates, four styles of situational leadership are possible. (Note that *directing, coaching, supporting,* and *delegating* are specialized terms used in a very limited way here.)

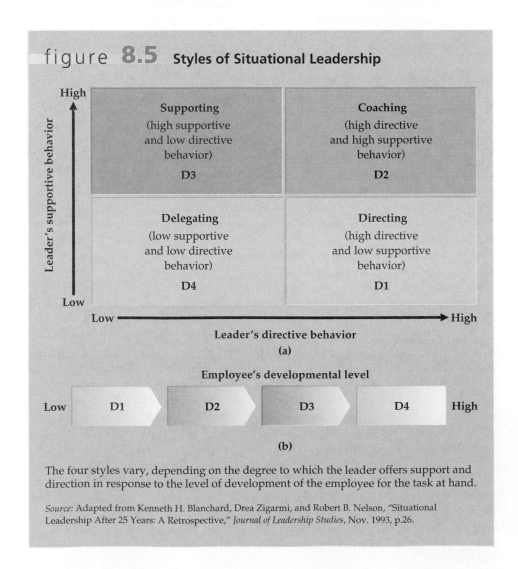

figure **8.5** **Styles of Situational Leadership**

The four styles vary, depending on the degree to which the leader offers support and direction in response to the level of development of the employee for the task at hand.

Source: Adapted from Kenneth H. Blanchard, Drea Zigarmi, and Robert B. Nelson, "Situational Leadership After 25 Years: A Retrospective," *Journal of Leadership Studies,* Nov. 1993, p.26.

- *Directing* (high directive/low supportive) The leader tells the subordinate what tasks to do and how, when, and where to do them. This is especially important when employees are new to a job or task and need ample direction and guidance in order to perform well.

- *Coaching* (high directive/high supportive) The leader still provides a great deal of direction but also considers employees' feelings about a decision and encourages their ideas and suggestions. This is important because an employee who has been working on a new job or task for a while typically becomes frustrated when problems arise.

- *Supporting* (high supportive/low directive) The leader's role is to provide employees with recognition and support, to listen to them actively, and to facilitate their problem solving and decision making. This style is important once an employee has demonstrated an ability to perform a task but still lacks confidence that he or she can consistently perform as expected.

- *Delegating* (low supportive/low directive) Employees are given greater freedom and independence because they have demonstrated the competence, confidence, and commitment to accomplish tasks on their own.

Deciding when to use each style of situational leadership depends primarily on the developmental level of the worker doing the task and on the degree of difficulty of the task itself. Situational leaders adapt their style to accommodate the worker and the task. There are four developmental levels, labeled D1 through D4 in Figure 8.5(b). Workers undertaking a new task about which they have little prior knowledge or experience—those at the point labeled D1 on the employee development scale in Figure 8.5(b)—are at a low developmental level for the task. These *enthusiastic beginners* are ready to learn, and managers should use a directing style to show them how to perform the task at hand.

As workers gain competence and begin to learn a task—point D2—they may find it more difficult than they expected and perhaps lose interest, which decreases their commitment. These *disillusioned learners* respond best to a coaching style of management, which encourages them to continue building their skills and increases their commitment.

As workers' competence continues to improve, they may go through a stage of self-doubt, questioning whether they can perform the task on their own even though their boss says they can. Workers with alternating feelings of competence and self-doubt are classified as *cautious contributors*—developmental level D3. Such subordinates need a supporting style of management, which requires listening to and encouraging them but not providing much direction, since these workers have already demonstrated competence in the task.

At the highest level of development—D4—employees usually demonstrate high levels of both competence and commitment. They are classified as *peak performers*. Managers should delegate as much responsibility as possible to such workers—giving them increased autonomy to do the job in which they've demonstrated both competence and commitment.

Controlling

We defined *controlling* as the process of monitoring and evaluating activities to ensure that objectives are being achieved. Managers have to create formal and informal measures of performance and make sure that someone tracks these measures.

Think about a simple business such as a privately owned stationery store. Its managers must create a system to track inventory and place reorders so that

9. Discuss the control process and its relationship to the planning process.

they do not run out of any of the thousands of products you expect to find on their shelves. They must track and control their cash to make sure they have enough money to pay for these reorders, as well as enough to pay the rent and the salaries and payroll taxes of their employees. They must also plan and track staffing to make sure clerks and supervisors are there during each day's store hours. And they need to record the purchases of customers who buy on credit, send them monthly bills, and terminate their credit if the bills aren't paid.

At A.J. Hastings, a family-owned stationery store in Amherst, Massachusetts, these control needs are met by a computer system connected to the cash registers; a full-time middle manager who helps with accounting, ordering, and billing; and a monthly inventory count by employees. Without these systems, Hastings would soon spin out of control, regardless of the quality of its plans, organization, and leadership. Control systems are the nervous system of business, providing the feedback managers and other employees need through information systems and accounting, which are covered in Part 6.

The Control Process

The control process is driven by the planning process. Plans set out the goals, strategies, and tactics of the business. Managers use controls to make sure tactics are followed in daily operations, strategies are pursued, and objectives are accomplished.

The control process consists of these five main activities:

1. Create standards and measures based on plans.
2. Measure performance. (Measures need to be specific and easy to communicate to employees.[32])
3. Determine whether performance matches standards.
4. If yes, decide when next to measure performance.
5. If no, correct performance, then check standards and measures again.

When controls indicate that everything is on target, managers do not need to interfere with employee performance. They can just do nothing, but as step 4 indicates, they would be wise to think about when to measure performance in the future. For example, less frequent checks or fewer reports may be possible, which would save time and money.

If performance does not measure up, it must be corrected. How? It should depend on the situation, as our study of leadership taught us. In some cases, managers fix the problem themselves. In other situations, employees can make big contributions. For example, in **open-book management**, companies empower employees to help control the company's finances. They train employees to create budgets, then give them authority and responsibility to control the approved budgets. Mid-States Technical Staffing Services, an engineering service firm in Davenport, Iowa, cut expenses by 15 percent over a three-year period thanks to open-book management. You'll learn more about it in Chapter 20.[33] Figure 8.6 charts the five main activities of the control process. But notice in particular the box, "If corrections don't work. . . ." Sometimes, repeated corrections and revisions *still* fail to improve performance. In such cases, a mediocre manager may be overwhelmed, and employees get the blame. Good managers react differently. They know they must reexamine their contributions to employee performance: plans, organization, and leadership. Any of the other three functions of management may need to be adjusted in order to control business performance.

✓ **open-book management**

A strategy that empowers employees to help control the company's finances.

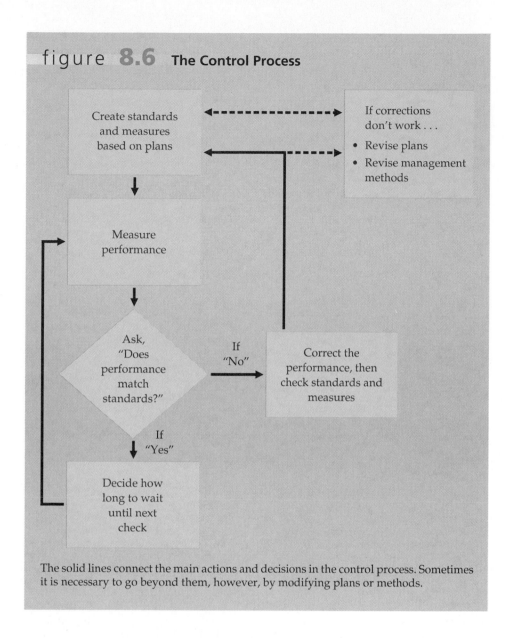

figure 8.6 **The Control Process**

The solid lines connect the main actions and decisions in the control process. Sometimes it is necessary to go beyond them, however, by modifying plans or methods.

Management Skills

Deborah Kent, the Ford plant manager we met earlier, encounters a wide variety of challenges in a typical workday. To meet them, she must use a wide range of management skills. Here is a description of her work in the words of a reporter who visited her plant. "On a recent day, which began at 7:30 a.m. with a review of the night shift's production report and was followed by a walk through the assembly plant, Kent manages to carry on two to three conversations at once—one on the telephone, another with a visitor, a third with her secretary—without losing her train of thought."[34] Her morning routine challenges her technical knowledge—most of us wouldn't be able to make heads or tails of that production report. It also requires a high level of communication and thinking skills, including decisions about how to manage her time in light of the many competing demands on it.

10. Describe the complementary roles of the technical and conceptual skills needed by managers.

Managers need to develop a set of complementary skills to succeed. These skills fall into three basic categories: technical skills, conceptual skills, and human relations skills.[35] Figure 8.7 shows which skill is key at each management level. The following sections detail the skills themselves. At the end of this overview is a self-assessment skills check entitled "Evaluating Your Management Skills" (page 252).

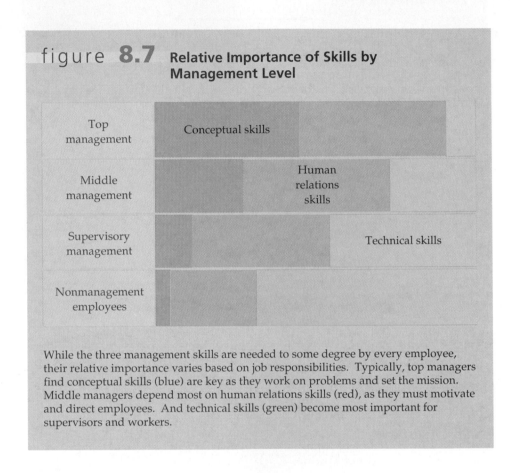

figure **8.7** **Relative Importance of Skills by Management Level**

While the three management skills are needed to some degree by every employee, their relative importance varies based on job responsibilities. Typically, top managers find conceptual skills (blue) are key as they work on problems and set the mission. Middle managers depend most on human relations skills (red), as they must motivate and direct employees. And technical skills (green) become most important for supervisors and workers.

Technical Skills

Every industry uses specialized skills—knowledge, language, tools, and techniques specific to an occupation or profession like accounting, computer software development, nuclear physics, or plumbing. In the context of management, **technical skills** enable the manager to understand and use the specialized aspects of a job or function. Some management positions require a high level of technical skills. A shift manager at a factory must understand the equipment, and a financial vice president must know how to invest the firm's money. In other cases, a manager may not need detailed technical knowledge—a printing company manager, for example, may be more concerned with scheduling problems than with the fine points of printing press operation.

Supervisory managers generally work closer to technological processes and equipment, and technical skills may therefore be more important for them than are other skills. Nevertheless, employees at every level are now expected to keep up with general technological advances—from using such office technologies as voice mail, fax machines, and word processing and spreadsheet software to clearing jams in laser printers. As James Baughman, director of cor-

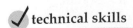
technical skills

The ability to understand and use the specialized aspects of a job or function.

porate management development for General Electric, points out, "All other things being equal, the leader who is multilingual, multicultural, and fluent enough in information technology to maintain a proprietary edge will come out ahead."[36]

✓ **conceptual skills**

The ability to perform complex, abstract thinking tasks.

Conceptual Skills

A manager without conceptual skills would look only at the trees and never see the forest. **Conceptual skills** enable the manager to perform complex, abstract thinking tasks. They include the ability to consider the organization and its functions as a whole and to understand the way the parts relate to one another. Conceptual skills include analytical and quantitative skills (math reasoning in general); problem solving; creativity; time management (efficient, productive use of the day); decision making; learning; and systems thinking—the ability to see how complex systems like a business or an economy work.

Systems thinking may be the most difficult conceptual skill for managers to master. Yet it is vital when analyzing changes in the business environment and developing responses to them. The business environment is, after all, a complex system in which a single change can have far-reaching effects. William O'Brien, a former CEO of the large Hanover Insurance Co. and now an expert on organizational learning at the Massachusetts Institute of Technology, explains the conceptual challenge faced by managers in his industry: "In the insurance industry, we have extensive information, large computers. . . . We're good at the type of problem which lends itself to scientific solution. [But] we are absolutely illiterate in subjects that require us to understand systems and interrelationships."[37]

Managers need conceptual skills to grasp ideas readily and foresee how innovations can benefit the organization. Managers draw on these skills when they prepare strategic plans, make decisions based on analyses of limited information, and monitor controls, such as schedules and budgets. As Figure 8.7 indicates, conceptual skills have traditionally been most important for higher-level managers. But in the future, whatever your role in an organization, you can expect to draw heavily on your conceptual skills. They are increasingly important throughout the organization, as workers are being tapped to provide information, recommend solutions to problems, and make decisions relating to their work teams.

Problem Solving and Decision Making

Problem solving and decision making are closely related conceptual skills. Problems call for decisions, just as opportunities do. Both require the use of a general decision-making process and the application of information-gathering, analytical and creative thinking, and planning skills. The process that Xerox trains its employees to use is a good example, as we first learned in Chapter 1. It is illustrated in Figure 8.8.

Deborah Kent faced a problem when she learned one morning that the Ford assembly line making Mercury Villagers had run out of alternator belts. The production manager wanted to know if they should keep making the cars and add the missing part later. But Kent felt this would clash with her plant's goal of producing perfect cars. She explains her analysis as follows: "I can't tell the staff one day that quality is our No. 1 priority, then say don't worry about that part, just keep building these cars and we'll put the part on later." She also identified a leadership issue in her analysis of the problem. "When you have to make a pivotal decision," she explains, "that's when the organization looks to see what kind of a leader they got. Does she walk like she talks?"[38]

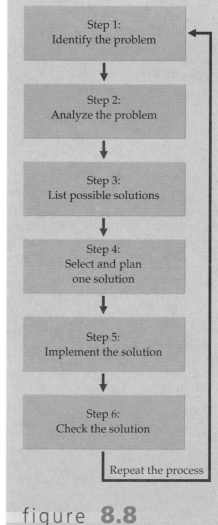

figure **8.8**

Steps in the Problem-Solving Process

As we learned in Chapter 1, employees at Xerox and many other companies now receive training in problem solving using this method or one like it. Problem solving is an increasingly important conceptual skill for managers and employees.

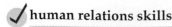

human relations skills

The ability to communicate with, motivate, and work together with others.

11. Discuss the components of human relations skills and describe the characteristics of an effective learning organization.

So Kent came up with a creative alternative. She stopped the production line, sent everyone to lunch early, and had the part flown in by helicopter while they were eating. The result: a classic win-win solution in which quality and leadership were not compromised, and the production schedule was met.

Human Relations Skills

John D. Rockefeller, one of the most successful managers in the history of American business, once remarked, "I will pay more for the ability to deal with people than for any other ability under the sun."[39] **Human relations skills**— the ability to communicate with, motivate, and work together with others—are perhaps the most valuable tools in any manager's kit. They include the ability to communicate both face to face and in groups, to negotiate, and to coach employees and lead them.

A survey of managers conducted by the American Management Association confirms Rockefeller's observation about the value of human relations skills. Respondents rated the ability to get along with others as the single most important management characteristic—surpassing intelligence, decisiveness, knowledge, or job skills. And another survey shows that employees agree. The Families and Work Institute reports that, in rating the attractiveness of jobs, workers rank open communication in the workplace at the top of their list of priorities, followed closely by senior management and supervisor quality.[40] Let's look more closely at some of the components of good human relations skills.

Communicating Effectively

Advanced communications technology has changed the way businesses operate and the way managers and their employees communicate. Managers and employees often start the workday by checking their electronic mail—messages that have sometimes traveled halfway around the globe. Deborah Kent knew that a production line was out of a part because the warning came in on her pager. And perhaps you recall from the discussion in Chapter 3 that VeriFone, Inc., runs its credit card verification business by means of a global computer network that passes projects from site to site around the world. VeriFone need never close down. VeriFone also has a rule that forbids written communication between its employees—everyone must use the computer network. In this high-tech environment, information technology skills are critical to good communications.

Not all organizations operate like VeriFone. Much business communication still takes the form of memos and team meetings. And most still takes place in traditional settings. But whatever the form communications take—whether face to face, written, or electronic—it is essential both to state your ideas clearly and to understand the message sent by co-workers and clients.

Sending Messages: Be Specific Communication depends on clear messages, and that means they should be specific. Through clear and specific communications, such as the following, managers can translate higher-level goals and objectives into the business routine:

- Please include the cost of materials in your proposal.
- Please see that our telephone customers are never on hold for longer than 15 seconds without an explanation for the delay.
- I was pleased to see that you went to the customer's office to help with the installation of the new workstations.

Specific statements are especially important when managers are giving corrective feedback. Employees need to know exactly what to change and why. Being specific makes the difference between leaving people feeling punished and leaving them feeling encouraged to change what is wrong. You might think this simple rule would be obvious to managers, but many companies have to provide special training in communication to help managers develop such skills.

Receiving Messages: Listen Carefully Good listening skills strengthen the relationship between managers and employees by creating mutual respect. People often focus more on what they themselves are saying than on what the other person is saying. One way to be sure you understand is to repeat the other person's statement in somewhat different words: "John, I think you are saying that you don't agree with the proposed plan for three reasons. . . ." Effective listening can help you gather information not only on the dry facts of a situation but also on what employees think and feel about the way a task is progressing, the problems they anticipate, and any additional resources they might require.

Building Self-esteem

An important part of human relations skills is building employee self-esteem. As *The One Minute Manager* points out, "People who feel good about themselves produce good results."[41] This means that managers must display genuine respect for and interest in the people they supervise, even when giving directions or making corrections, because the way employees feel about themselves is reflected in the work they produce. Chapter 11 focuses on various methods managers use to motivate employees.

Bruce Gordon, the Bell Atlantic Corp. marketing manager we met at the beginning of this chapter, illustrates the trend toward greater employee–manager communication that is typical of companies today. Recall that he decided to locate his office on the floor where many of his employees work, instead of in the executive suite. The reason? "Information gets filtered when you're up there, and you cut yourself off."[42]

Management by Walking Around

Tom Chappell, co-founder with wife Kate of Tom's of Maine—an all-natural, personal care products company—says he found profitability an easier goal to achieve than the right management approach. Between 1981 and 1985, Tom's grew by 25 percent per year on average, to reach $5 million in sales. But the bigger the company grew, the tougher Chappell found it to nurture the values he finds as important an ingredient in business as profitability. Chappell, shown with the manager of his Kennebunk, Maine, outlet store, took time off and wrote a book about his management principles. A quote: "The success of the company lies in its capacity to become a new kind of company . . . to manage by values, to care about people and the environment, and still to run up and down the court with the big boys and make money."

Evaluating Your Management Skills

Technical, conceptual, and human relations skills are important in management. You can acquire many skills through coursework and work experience, including part-time and summer jobs or internships. To evaluate your current set of management skills, use the following charts. Then plan your future courses and work experiences to fill gaps and build strengths. Track your progress and update your plans every semester.

Evaluating Your Technical Management Skills

Technical Skills	Weak	Fair	Good	Excellent
Information technology	☐	☐	☐	☐
Manufacturing	☐	☐	☐	☐
Marketing	☐	☐	☐	☐
Accounting	☐	☐	☐	☐
Finance	☐	☐	☐	☐
Office and audiovideo equipment	☐	☐	☐	☐
Law	☐	☐	☐	☐
Project management	☐	☐	☐	☐
Industry-specific knowledge (e.g., autos, chemicals, banking, restaurants, nursing)	☐	☐	☐	☐

Evaluating Your Conceptual Management Skills

Conceptual Skills	Weak	Fair	Good	Excellent
Analytical	☐	☐	☐	☐
Quantitative	☐	☐	☐	☐
Problem solving	☐	☐	☐	☐
Creativity	☐	☐	☐	☐
Time management	☐	☐	☐	☐
Decision making	☐	☐	☐	☐
Learning	☐	☐	☐	☐
Systems thinking	☐	☐	☐	☐

Evaluating Your Human Relations Management Skills

Human Relations Skills	Weak	Fair	Good	Excellent
Spoken messages	☐	☐	☐	☐
Written messages	☐	☐	☐	☐
Computer communications	☐	☐	☐	☐
Foreign language	☐	☐	☐	☐
Familiarity with other cultures	☐	☐	☐	☐
Listening	☐	☐	☐	☐
Leadership	☐	☐	☐	☐
Conflict resolution	☐	☐	☐	☐
Teamwork	☐	☐	☐	☐

Increased accessibility to management is essential in organizations that are moving away from traditional command-and-control structures because new approaches depend on more and better communication with employees. Some managers increase their accessibility by practicing a technique called **management by walking around**, making themselves available where the work gets done and keeping the lines of communication open to employees and customers.

Ricardo Semler, CEO of Semco S.A., the Brazilian equipment manufacturer, strongly supports this technique, which he calls "management by wandering around." He notes that "Semco is designed to allow people to mingle. Our offices don't have walls."[43]

management by walking around

A technique for promoting accessibility in which managers make themselves available where the work gets done and keep the lines of communication open to employees and customers.

Learning and the Learning Organization

In Chapter 1 we saw how important the learning cycle is to success in a competitive business environment. And we learned that managers are working to increase flexibility, improve productivity, and boost innovation by developing their employees' capabilities. At British giant ICI's Pharmaceuticals subsidiary, this effort takes place within a structured performance management system, a process designed to improve the communication of objectives and the development of employees' abilities to meet those objectives. One result of ICI Pharmaceuticals's system is closer relationships between frontline staff members and their managers.[44] This close relationship is essential to the coaching role many managers now play as empowerment increases the learning required of each employee.

Management expert Bob Waterman (co-author with Tom Peters of *In Search of Excellence*) defines *coaching* as "helping individuals develop," which is clearly how firms like ICI define the management challenge today.[45] Human development may seem more appropriate to a school, international aid group, or not-for-profit organization like the Girl Scouts whose mission is "to help girls reach their potential."[46] But helping employees reach *their* potential is increasingly applicable to for-profit businesses like ICI as well. It is certainly consistent with the shift to empowerment that characterizes the management style emerging at many companies.

One way managers encourage their own employees' development is by creating a learning organization. You may recall from Chapter 1 that **learning organizations** are businesses that are good at developing and using knowledge in ways that help them change for the better. Organizational learning encourages individuals to gain new insights and knowledge and to modify their behavior, actions, and perspective to stay in tune with the world around them. Organizational learning also encourages groups of individuals to enhance and build collectively on their shared knowledge and insights. There are many ways to build a learning organization, but the most effective learning environments are characterized by openness, recall, and objectivity.[47]

- *Openness* An effective learning organization must have an environment that encourages questions and comments. In a truly open environment, individuals can express concerns without fear of retribution, hidden agendas do not exist, and people say the same kind of things at work that they say after work.

- *Recall* The ability to recall what you already know so that you can build on it is harder for an organization than for an individual. When addressing a new issue, managers consult with their co-workers and review what is already known, going back to the records of previous decisions before they proceed. Clear documentation and communication of issues that have been resolved are critical to the learning organization.

- *Objectivity* An objective approach involves seeking the best answer to a problem or question based on sound logic and available data. This can be achieved when a manager systematically asks a set series of questions: What do we know about this situation from past experience? What is the ideal solution to the problem at hand? What forces are keeping the ideal solution from being implemented? What is likely to go wrong when implementing our ideal solution? How could we make it work? Such questions allow employees to focus better on the overall solution to a problem.

An organizational interest in learning will not in itself create a learning organization. Managers must coach and support learning in the workplace so that it ultimately becomes a way of life. Honda is a good example of a company that practices what it preaches. Its employees are encouraged to speak frankly to one another—across all levels of the organization. Information about performance, sales, customer satisfaction, internal operations, and competitors is circulated widely and quickly, and preexisting biases about possible courses of action tend to be absent, especially among managers. An overall level of trust,

✓ **learning organizations**

Businesses that are good at developing and using knowledge in ways that help them change for the better.

respect, and closeness prevails throughout the organization. According to Pat Sparks, a member of the purchasing department at the company's Marysville, Ohio, factory, "The Honda philosophy is a way of life. It's characterized by closeness, communication, and frankness at all levels. Honda employs thinking people, creative people. We want people to sound off."[48]

Innovative managers are bringing the skills of the learning organization into the workplace, coaching their workers and committing resources to training and development. And innovative managers are implementing the role of management in new and creative ways: empowering instead of delegating, leading instead of directing, communicating instead of commanding, and replacing rigid management structures with flexible teams, a topic we turn to in Chapter 9.

Reviewing *The Role of Management*

The Manager's Challenge

1. **Describe command-and-control management and identify types of situations in which it is appropriate**. Command-and-control management is a traditional management style in which lines of authority are exercised through a clear and unbroken chain of command. Because the managers issue orders and control all activities, this management style is appropriate in the military, in emergency situations, and in industries where technology or procedures require centralized control.

2. **List the four functions of management and explain how they relate to different approaches to management**. The four functions of management are planning, organizing, leading, and controlling. Together, they form the sequence of events that enable management to accomplish the goals of the organization. In command-and-control management, the functions are performed by managers who direct employees to follow *their* strategies in order to reach *their* goals. In contrast, the challenges of doing business prompt many managers to be more flexible, to both delegate and empower, allowing employees to participate in the decision-making process.

Planning

3. **Identify and describe the three levels of planning, noting the importance of contingency planning**. Planning is typically performed in a hierarchical sequence corresponding to the levels of management. At the highest level, senior managers and the board of directors prepare a mission statement, setting forth the organization's broad goals. At the next level, managers develop strategic plans that define specific objectives, provide a SWOT analysis, and identify a general approach for accomplishing strategies. At the lowest level are operational plans that specify the tactics needed to carry out the strategic plans. To guard against problems occurring as a result of internal or external changes, plans may be reviewed and revised frequently or contingency plans may be prepared as part of the original strategic plan.

Organizing

4. **List the four steps in organizing a business**. Once plans are made, employees and material resources must be organized to carry out those plans. This means that management must identify the activities and resources, group related activities, assign individuals or teams to activities, and create the structures needed to perform the activities well. Today, business organizations must be flexible enough to respond to changes in the environment.

5. **Describe the different levels of the management hierarchy and explain how they relate to one another**. Planning and organizing are performed by management, hierarchically organized to define reporting relationships. Top management—CEOs and presidents, for example—creates the organization's goals and policies and deals with all issues related to the organization's survival. Middle management—division heads and branch managers, for example—helps to develop and implement the detailed plans for achieving long-term goals. Depending on the size of the business, there may be several levels of middle management. At the lowest level are supervisory, or first-line, managers—foremen and supervisors, for example—who are responsible for daily activities.

6. **Explain the operation of team-based organizations**. The use of work teams provides flexibility in an organization. These teams may exist only to perform a particular project, or they may be longer term to perform a particular group of functions. Combining people from different areas or with complementary skills, teams can make more effective decisions if they are given adequate information, training, and support.

Leading

7. **Contrast transactional and transformational approaches to leading.** Transactional leaders help employees set specific goals that, taken together, enable the company to reach the goals set forth in the mission statement. These leaders emphasize the directive aspect of leading. Transformational leaders, on the other hand, focus on the motivational aspect of true leadership. The ability to inspire employees is particularly useful when a major change is required.

8. **Describe the basic styles of leading and explain how the four styles of situational leadership are variously applied.** Whereas autocratic leaders apply the spirit of command-and-control management by focusing on the use of authority to lead, democratic leaders emphasize empowerment and employee participation. The style of leading used depends on the organizational structure: autocratic for the hierarchical and democratic for the empowered organization. As the need for flexibility in organizational structures increases, managers must consider alternative styles. Situational leadership—in which degree of direction and support is related to employees' developmental level and the difficulty of the task itself—is now more appropriate. Situational leadership evolves through four levels: directing, coaching, supporting, and delegating, with each level representing a decreasing amount of direction as employees' confidence and abilities increase.

Controlling

9. **Discuss the control process and its relationship to the planning process.** Planning and controlling are intertwined. Whether the goals set forth in plans are being accomplished can only be determined if the control function is fully operational. Controlling involves the setting of standards for performance based on the prepared plans. Performance is then measured against these standards at specified intervals. These checks tell management when performance does not satisfy standards. Management can then correct performance or revise the standards.

Management Skills

10. **Describe the complementary roles of the technical and conceptual skills needed by managers.** The degree of technical and conceptual skills required of managers depends on the organization of the business and on the manager's relationship to the technological processes. Traditionally, the conceptual skills of analytical thinking, problem solving, creativity, time management, decision making, learning, and systems thinking belonged to higher-level managers. Today, as decision making is filtering down to the lowest levels of the organization through work teams, conceptual skills are being required of all employees. Conversely, technical skills, which were traditionally more important at the lower levels, are becoming increasingly vital for managers at all levels.

11. **Discuss the components of human relations skills and describe the characteristics of an effective learning organization.** Human relations skills involve both effective communication—being clear and specific and listening carefully—and building employee self-esteem. The better employees feel about themselves and the more they feel a part of the process, the more productive they will be. One way to improve productivity, and to achieve flexibility and boost innovation, is to make a business into a learning organization, characterized by openness, recall, and objectivity.

✓ Key Terms

management **229**
command-and-control management **229**
planning **231**
organizing **231**
leading **231**
controlling **231**
delegation **233**
empowerment **233**
mission statement **234**

strategic plans **234**
operational plans **235**
tactics **235**
contingency planning **236**
staffing **236**
top management **237**
middle management **238**
supervisory management (first-line management) **238**

work teams **240**
transactional leaders **240**
transformational leaders **241**
leadership **241**
autocratic leader **242**
democratic leader **242**
situational leadership **244**
open-book management **246**

technical skills **248**
conceptual skills **249**
human relations skills **250**
management by walking around **252**
learning organizations **253**

• Review Questions

1. What are the advantages and disadvantages of a command-and-control style of management?

2. What are the four functions of management? Who is responsible for seeing that these activities are carried out?

3. What is a strategic plan and who creates it for an organization?

4. What are the three main levels of the management hierarchy? What types of activities characterize each level?

5. What advantages does team management offer?

6. How do transactional and transformational leading differ? State at least three differences.

7. Is an autocratic leader more effective than a democratic leader? Explain why or why not.

8. Drawing on what you have learned about situational leadership, how would you manage a new employee who is eager but inexperienced?

9. What are the three primary management skills? Are they equally important at all levels of management? Explain your answer.

10. What three characteristics are important for a learning organization?

• Critical Thinking Questions

1. How can a manager's actions inside the business affect its ability to compete in its markets? Give an example.

2. What three things could a manager do to encourage greater initiative on the part of employees?

3. If you were asked to manage a group research project for a class, how would you use the four functions of management to succeed?

4. Why do managers plan for contingencies? Why don't they simply wait to see whether a change in plans is necessary?

5. What management problems are likely to occur as an organization moves toward more team-based management? What opportunities will likely arise?

REVIEW CASE *A Changing Picture at Kodak*

Managers are especially concerned with cost savings today. Strategies focus on increasing the value of products while holding the line on costs. In Chapter 1 you learned about two strategies that focus on cost cutting, reengineering and downsizing. Business process reengineering, or clean-slate design, cuts costs by simplifying processes. It's an offensive approach to cost cutting. The alternative, defensive approach is downsizing, eliminating jobs to cut costs and make a business smaller.

Many companies reengineer their organizations to maintain or improve their competitiveness in rapidly changing markets. For example, Eastman Kodak Co. targeted many of its units for improvement. At its black-and-white film manufacturing unit, a reengineering focus helped Kodak cut response time in half, come in 15 percent under budget, and improve morale in the process.[49]

Competitive pressures also forced Kodak to cut the management team in its apparatus division by 30 percent and its layers of management from seven to three. The division's vice president and general manager, Frank Zaffino, believes the cuts improved efficiency and Kodak's profitability. Productivity in the division jumped 25 percent to over 95 percent of orders being handled within five days.

These changes came at a cost, however. As a result of downsizing, first-line supervisors were suddenly made responsible for setting goals and strategy for their products instead of merely carrying out orders. Some couldn't make the transition effectively, even with training. Zaffino says, "They were used to being star technicians, not communicators or leaders."

Zaffino adjusted to change as well. When only three people reported directly to him, he claims he could "second-guess them a lot and end-run them for information." Now he oversees twice as many managers and must trust them to perform and make decisions. "I can no longer outmanage them on details," he says.[50]

1. Why do you think the reengineering focus in Kodak's black-and-white unit raised morale?

2. Why might the downsizing focus in the apparatus division make for a tough transition?

3. How could Zaffino use work teams to improve morale in his division?

CRITICAL THINKING CASE *Communicating Hard Facts*[51]

Imagine that you recently accepted a job as manager of the art department of a small publishing company that produces coffee-table books with a large number of illustrations and photographs. When the president of the company interviewed you, he said that the company had lost market share and would be making some changes to increase its profits in the near future. On the day you started work, you had 10 people reporting to you: an assistant manager, who also hired freelance designers and researchers; six artist/designers, who did the bulk of the design work; two researchers, who worked with the artist/designers; and an administrative assistant whom you shared with the assistant manager. You have made it a practice to personally approve all book designs, give directions to all freelancers, and approve all decisions made in your department. To do this, you are working about 60 hours a week, and you still take work home with you.

Last month you learned that the changes the president referred to included some heavy cuts in the work force. Your department lost three positions: the assistant manager, one of the artist/designers, and one of the researchers. The work load remains the same. Money is tight, and no overtime pay is allowed, although your freelance budget has been increased by 20 percent. A notice to all departments states that no department will be allowed to hire additional employees for at least 18 months.

Your department is in a crisis. Schedules are slipping, which will affect company profits for the year unless you can repair the damage quickly. In addition, top management and the employees who report to you are both demanding that you communicate their problems to each other. You have made two decisions about what to do next: (1) form a troubleshooting committee to suggest solutions to the new work situation and (2) improve communication so that top management and your employees will begin to appreciate one another's positions.

1. What skills will you look for in appointing someone to head the new committee?

2. What management style will work best in this situation? Is your practice of approving all decisions appropriate?

3. What will you say to top management and to your employees to try to convince both to be more understanding of one another's positions?

4. Could open-book management be of any use to you?

5. How can you use the increased freelance budget to help the people who report to you?

Critical Thinking with the ONE MINUTE MANAGER

"So you both can see that management is much, much more than just telling people what to do," said the One Minute Manager. "The best managers inspire outstanding performance in their employees by inviting them to participate in the decision-making process. Now more than ever, managers rely on their employees to make decisions that directly affect customers. After all, many frontline employees spend more time with customers than their managers do."

"Is that why you said managers should act like drama coaches and let their employees be the stars?" Joanna asked.

"Exactly." The One Minute Manager beamed. "Jack Welch, CEO of General Electric, knows the value of having managers create a supportive work environment and not just tell people what to do. He recently said he hoped his company would be remembered as a place where people had the freedom to be creative, a place that brought out the best in everybody. His exact words were 'An open, fair place where people have a sense that what they do matters, and where the sense of accomplishment is rewarded in both the pocketbook and the soul. That will be our report card.'"[52]

1. The skills used to manage employees are not all that different from the skills we use to gain the cooperation of classmates, friends, and relatives. What style do you use when you are in charge of a group or team? Are you autocratic? Democratic? Or do you tend toward a free-rein style? What would happen if you changed your style?

2. It seems natural that, as employees rise higher in an organization, they should know more about what the customer wants. Why is this often not the case? What are the benefits to an organization of pushing the decision-making process farther down the hierarchy? Can you think of any obstacles to giving frontline employees more authority?

3. For many new managers, the shift to using a new mix of skills that focus primarily on human relations is too much of a challenge. Instead, they continue to concentrate on their expertise in technical areas. Why would this be a liability for new managers and for their employees? How could a new manager plan a successful transition to using the new mix of skills? How can employees help the new manager succeed?

CHAPTER

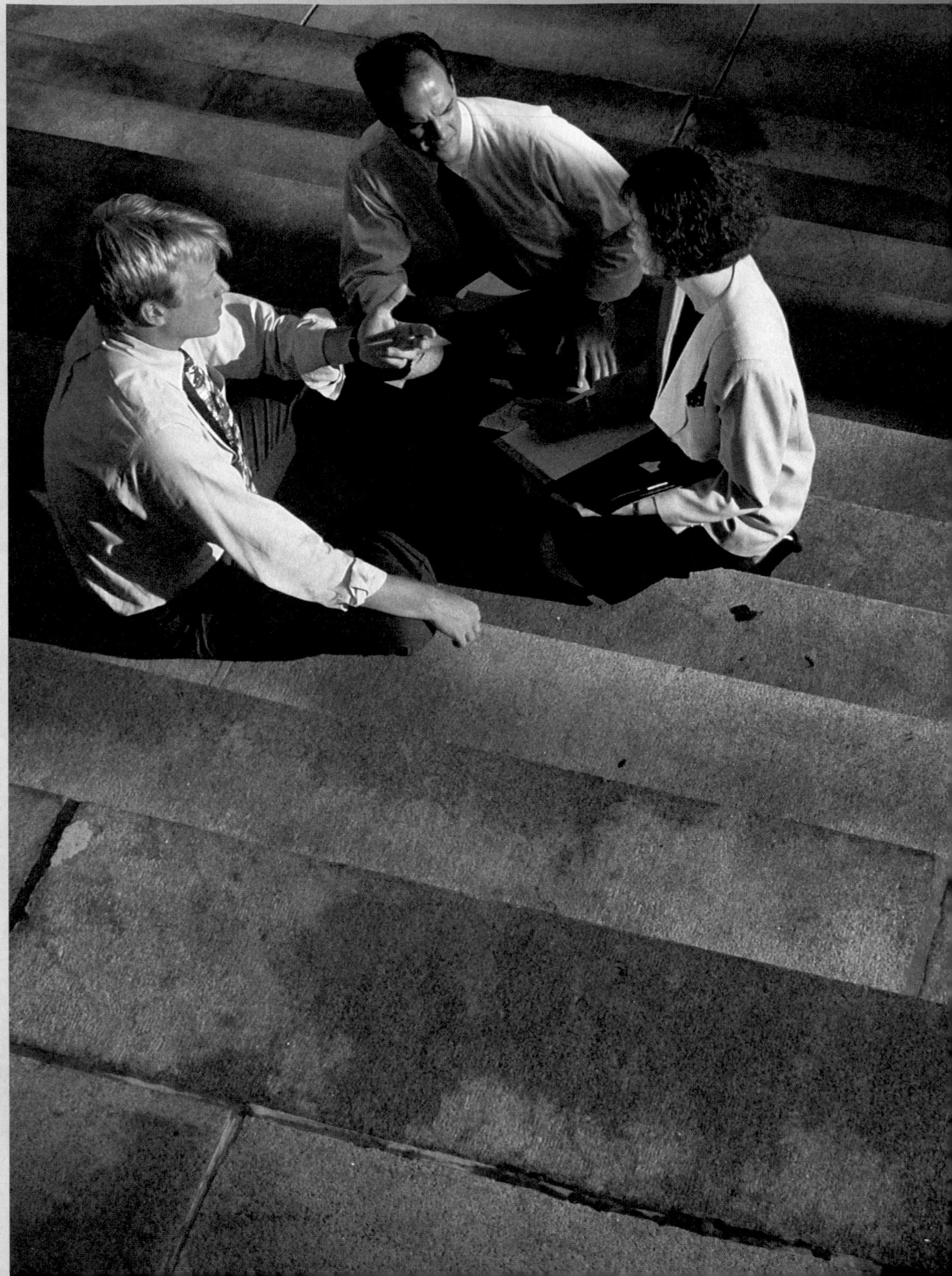

9 Organizational Design

An essential question all businesses face is how best to organize their resources to achieve their goals. This chapter explores the issues that owners and managers must consider as they design their organizational structures. We discuss the basic elements of organizational design as well as the key decisions that affect design. We consider the pros and cons of focusing organizations around particular aspects of the business, such as function or geography, and then examine important trends in the evolution of organizational structures. After reading this chapter, you will be able to reach the learning goals below.

Learning Goals

1. Distinguish between a company's formal and informal organizations and explain why organizational designs vary.
2. Explain the relationship between delegation and the three elements of task assignment.
3. Differentiate line from line-and-staff organizations and identify the advantages and disadvantages of each.
4. Describe the advantages and disadvantages of matrix organizations compared with more traditional organizational designs.
5. Discuss the three factors considered in determining an organization's structure.
6. Identify and describe the five primary areas of focus for departmentalization.
7. Identify reasons for a business to reorganize and restructure.
8. Discuss the benefits of downsizing and explain how it relates to the use of teams.
9. Identify and describe the different types of teams.
10. Describe the relative advantages of organizing by process.
11. Discuss the role of a company's informal structure and use of outsourcing in improved efficiency.

Building New Relationships

"I just don't understand it," said Carlos to the One Minute Manager. "I don't understand how companies decide who makes decisions and how to divide up the work."

The One Minute Manager looked up from the weekly financial reports. "Carlos, both of those functions are part of organizational design, which is one of the most important tasks facing management. The formal organization provides a structure to a business and its employees, just as your skeleton provides support for the muscles and organs of your body. But unlike your body, the ideal organizational structure is constantly changing in response to the organization's goals, its environment, and the needs of its customers. The structure really helps the organization get its work done."

"How does an organization's structure help it to do its work?" Carlos asked.

"In many ways. A company might organize around its customers by locating field offices near them. Or it might organize for maximum efficiency by streamlining its structure to support key processes."

"So structure is the set of formal relationships in an organization?" Joanna ventured.

"Yes, partly—but every organization also has a set of informal day-to-day relationships, and those are important, too."

"You mean like the people you play volleyball with at lunch?"

"Yes, and the people who gather around the water cooler and swap office stories. A lot of business takes place in those informal settings. Some companies have even designed their work environments to support this kind of interchange. The new 3M Corporation building in Austin, Texas, for example, is arranged to increase the number of informal contacts among employees from all parts of the organization."

Eyes twinkling, Joanna asked, "Did they put in a new volleyball court for the employees, too?"

"I don't know if they went that far, Joanna, but they did install coffee machines, couches, and blackboards next to the restrooms to encourage employees to stop and talk.[1] 3M has discovered that some of its best employee ideas come from informal meetings. So you see, the most important meetings don't necessarily take place in conference rooms."

Designing Organizations

When a business has only one employee, that person—often the owner—decides what needs doing and then does it. However, as soon as a business employs two or more people, tasks need to be divided among workers in some logical and efficient way. This process of organizing employees and their work is known as **organizational design**. As we learned in Chapter 8, organizing is one of the four basic functions of management. In this chapter we focus on **formal organization**—the official structure of reporting relationships developed by management to achieve the organization's goals. This formal organization defines who is responsible for which tasks, and who reports to whom.

1. Distinguish between a company's formal and informal organizations and explain why organizational designs vary.

Organizational Design

What's going on here? Is this a faculty advisor's office? A group of students working on a team project perhaps? Nope. This is a staff meeting in an art director's office at Microsoft Corp., where the formal organization operates in a most informal way.

Of course, all organizations also have an **informal organization**—an unofficial network of personal relationships and interactions among employees. As 3M Corp. and many other businesses have discovered, the informal organization exerts a great deal of power within any company; we'll explore this later. Let's begin by examining the elements that make up a formal organizational design.

Design Elements in Organizing

Dividing large, complex tasks into smaller, distinct tasks that are assigned to specialized workers is known as **division of labor**. Specialization permits employees to concentrate their efforts on and develop expertise in some aspect of the organization's work. The management of the University of California, San Diego (UCSD) Medical Center, for example, has structured the center as a series of organizational units, among them adolescent medicine, the cancer center, family medicine, the kidney transplant center, physical therapy, and the stroke center. UCSD Medical Center chose its organizational design to reflect the specialization of its employees and to deliver efficient and effective health care to its customers.

Organizational designs vary because there is no one "best" design for all purposes. Each organization must tailor its design to fit its short-term and long-

 organizational design

The process of organizing employees and their work.

 formal organization

The official structure of reporting relationships developed by management to achieve the organization's goals.

 informal organization

An unofficial network of personal relationships and interactions among employees.

 division of labor

Dividing large, complex tasks into smaller, distinct tasks that are assigned to specialized workers.

term goals. The ideal design encompasses the tasks that must be performed to reach those goals, the assignment of those tasks to the organization's personnel, and the coordination of work and resources within the organization as a whole. Even within a specific industry, organizational design varies from one business to the next. Another health care facility, for example, might find UCSD's design inappropriate for its size, complexity, or even the personalities of its top managers. Designs also vary over time within the same business. If UCSD's goals, plans, or customers change, the center may have to modify its structure to meet its changing needs. At UCSD Medical Center, as in other businesses, it is management's job to constantly monitor changing economic conditions, customer needs, technology, and a host of other factors to ensure that the organization's design remains the right choice for achieving its goals.

As businesses create formal organizational designs, one of their first acts is to delegate responsibility, authority, and accountability for completion of tasks to employees. Let's examine these three essential elements of delegation in more detail.

Responsibility, Authority, Accountability, and Their Delegation

2. Explain the relationship between delegation and the three elements of task assignment.

In Chapter 8, we discussed the contrast between *delegating* work to employees and *empowering* them to achieve tasks and goals. **Responsibility** is an employee's obligation to perform an assigned task. An example of the assignment of responsibility can be found in a typical Starbucks coffee store. Named for the coffee-loving first mate in the classic novel *Moby Dick*, Starbucks Corp., based in Seattle, Washington, has ridden the crest of the nationwide boom in coffee consumption. Since 1987, Starbucks has grown from 11 stores employing fewer than 100 in the Pacific Northwest to a nationwide chain of 480 stores with annual sales of $285 million in fiscal 1994.[2] Worldwide sales are expected to climb to $1 billion by the year 2000.[3] In a Starbucks store, the manager assigns responsibility for different tasks to different employees, making one employee responsible for preparing coffee drinks and another responsible for taking orders and running the cash register. To maximize organizational flexibility, employees are cross-trained to perform all the tasks necessary to run the store. Each person is encouraged to identify a need, such as answering questions regarding the difference between different types of coffee beans, and to take personal responsibility for helping the customer.[4]

Recall from Chapter 8 that delegation is the assignment of a manager's responsibility and authority for a task to an employee, and empowerment is the transfer to an employee of authority and responsibility for a task, along with the necessary resources and power to excel at the task.

Responsibility for a task is meaningless unless authority to complete the task is also conferred. **Authority** is the power to take the actions and make the decisions necessary to fulfill one's responsibility. Inadequate authority can prevent employees from fulfilling their responsibilities. In the case of Starbucks, an employee responsible for preparing coffee drinks must also be able to remove coffee supplies from the stock room and discard coffee drinks that do not conform to quality standards. Otherwise, delays may result and the consequence could be dissatisfied customers not likely to return.

The third element in delegation is **accountability**—being answerable for the actions taken to complete a task. The Starbucks employee with the responsibility and authority to prepare coffee drinks may choose to read a newspaper instead of serving customers promptly. The store manager will undoubtedly hold him accountable for his actions—perhaps by reprimanding him or, if this is a repeat performance, by firing him. Remember that even though accountability can be delegated to employees, the manager always retains ultimate responsibility for any task that he or she assigns.

Effective delegation benefits employees, managers, and the organization. It benefits employees by increasing their involvement in projects, by enabling them to develop new skills, and by enhancing their promotion potential. Dele-

responsibility

An employee's obligation to perform an assigned task.

authority

The power to take the actions and make the decisions necessary to fulfill one's responsibility.

accountability

Being answerable for the actions taken to complete a task.

gation benefits managers by enabling them accomplish much more, by allowing more cost-effective use of their time, and by increasing *their* promotion potential. For the organization, effective delegation promotes cost-effectiveness, higher-quality products, and increased flexibility.[5]

✓ **chain of command**

The line of reporting relationships that describes the flow of responsibility, authority, and accountability from the top of an organization to the bottom.

table 9.1 Likely Outcomes When Essential Elements Are Missing from Delegated Tasks

Delegated Elements	Likely Outcome
Authority and accountability, no responsibility.	Work expectations are not clearly communicated; employee becomes frustrated.
Responsibility and accountability, no authority	Employee is unable to complete delegated work due to lack of power or resources and becomes frustrated.
Responsibility and authority, no accountability	There is no consequence for either positive or negative performance; employee performance becomes random over time.

Source: Robert B. Nelson, *Empowering Employees Through Delegation* (New York: Richard D. Irwin Publishers, 1994), pp. 108–112.

Managers must delegate all three elements—authority, responsibility, and accountability—if employees are to complete tasks successfully. Withholding one or more of them will cause confusion and frustration between managers and workers. In the words of John Nevin, former CEO of Firestone Tire and Rubber, "If you want to drive a person crazy, the easiest way to do it is to give him a deep sense of responsibility and no authority. And the definition of terror is to give someone authority and no responsibility."[6] Table 9.1 illustrates the likely outcomes when these key elements are missing from delegation.

The **chain of command** is the line of reporting relationships that describes the flow of responsibility, authority, and accountability from the top of an organization to the bottom. The formal chain of command is a logical, organized way to focus everyone's individual efforts toward common goals. Each person in a chain of command is accountable for the work done by employees at lower levels. Thus, the president of an organization is ultimately responsible for the total results achieved by the organization, even though he or she has delegated authority to midlevel managers for specific tasks or groups of tasks. Figure 9.1 shows a simple chain of command from the owner of a bookstore to the cashier.

The goal of a military organization such as the U.S. Army is very clear and very direct: to be prepared to fight and win a war at any time, in any place. Similarly, the Army's chain of command is very clear and very direct: Privates report to corporals, who report to sergeants, who report on up the line to the commander in chief at the top of the organization—the president of the United States. When the president gives an order, the order is passed down the chain of command from superior to subordinate. All along the way, responsibility, authority, and accountability are assigned to various individuals for some aspect of carrying out the order. When the order has been carried out, this fact is reported back up the chain of command from subordinate to superior until it reaches the commander in chief. This is command-and-control management in its purest state.

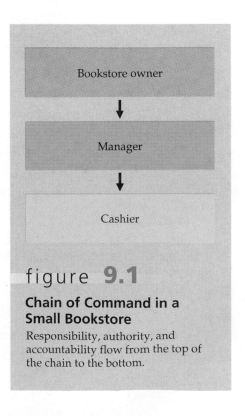

figure 9.1

Chain of Command in a Small Bookstore

Responsibility, authority, and accountability flow from the top of the chain to the bottom.

organization chart

A diagram of an organization's formal structure and reporting relationships.

Many organizations keep track of who reports to whom by issuing an **organization chart**, a diagram of the organization's formal structure and reporting relationships. It is the road map to an organization's structure. An organization chart uses boxes to show job titles and functions and lines to show reporting relationships. Solid lines indicate direct reporting relationships, such as that between a manager and subordinate.

The organization chart in Figure 9.2 shows a portion of 3M Corp. It is typical of a large manufacturing company. Top management positions, those involving the most authority and responsibility, are at the peak of the chart in the few boxes in the upper section. Middle sections show middle management. Detailed organization charts will also show frontline employees in their lower sections. Positions of approximately equal power and authority are usually shown at the same level and are linked by horizontal lines. Let's look now at some of the design alternatives that can be represented in organizational structures and the charts that portray them.

figure **9.2** **Organization Chart for Top Management at 3M Corp.**

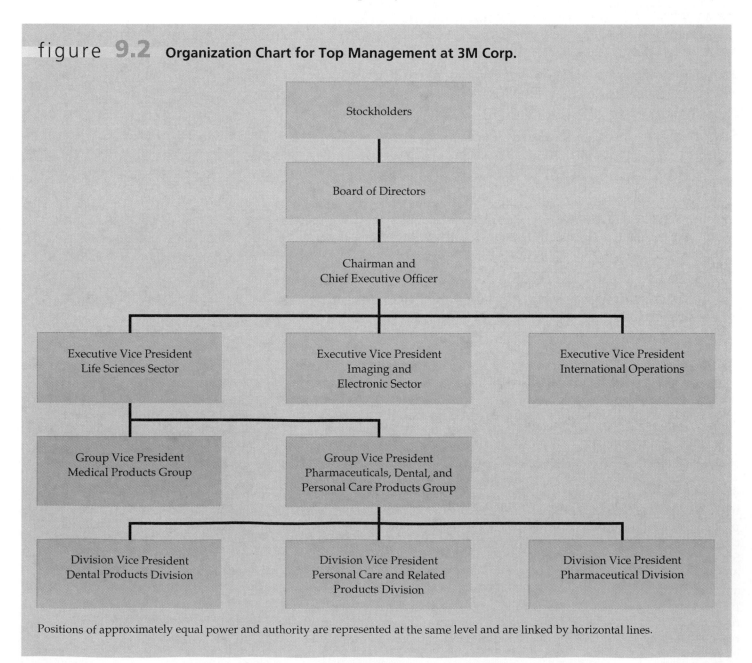

Positions of approximately equal power and authority are represented at the same level and are linked by horizontal lines.

Line Organization

In a **line organization**, responsibility, authority, and accountability flow in a direct line from the highest person to the lowest. **Line employees** are individuals who perform activities directly related to the goals of the business. The mission of Kinko's Graphics Corp., which has 650 copy centers located in all 50 states and in Canada and England, is to serve the customer from the point at which a document is created until the point it is completed.[7] In a typical Kinko's, an employee—the manager, in this example—takes a customer's order for, say, 400 enlarged copies of a series of multicolor maps, prices the job, and fills out an order specifying the type of paper, number of copies, and time by which the work must be completed. The manager then delegates the actual copying to an assistant who specializes in running the color copying machine. After copying the maps, the assistant transfers them to another employee, the finisher, who assembles and wraps the order and places it on a finished-work shelf. Finally, a cashier gives the finished job to the customer and accepts payment. Although three line employees have worked on this order, the manager is ultimately accountable to the customer for the quality of the copies. Figure 9.3 illustrates the line organization.

3. Differentiate line from line-and-staff organizations and identify the advantages and disadvantages of each.

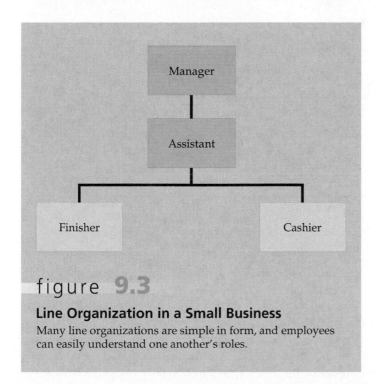

figure 9.3

Line Organization in a Small Business

Many line organizations are simple in form, and employees can easily understand one another's roles.

Line organizations offer several advantages. First, they are relatively simple, and employees can easily understand one another's roles. Second, because the chain goes from supervisor to subordinate all the way from the top of the organization to the bottom, lines of authority are very clear and communication is very direct. Finally, since decision-making authority is concentrated at the top of the organization, simple decisions can be made quickly.

The line organization also has numerous disadvantages. With decision making concentrated at the top of the organization, lower-level employees may feel left out of the process. Line organizations can be very inflexible and chains of command can be quite long, so it can take a long time for management to deal with complex issues or to respond to the changing needs of customers. Employees in line organizations tend to lack specialized knowledge, and line managers are often overburdened with administrative paperwork. The line-

 line organization

An organization in which responsibility, authority, and accountability flow in a direct line from the highest person to the lowest.

 line employees

Employees who perform activities directly related to the goals of the business.

✓ line-and-staff organization

An organization that combines the direct reporting relationships of line employees with the advisory relationships of staff employees.

✓ staff employees

Employees who advise and support the work of line employees but have no authority to assign tasks to them or to direct them.

and-staff organization described in the next section has evolved to help overcome these disadvantages.

Line-and-Staff Organization

A **line-and-staff organization** combines the direct reporting relationships of line employees with the advisory relationships of staff employees. **Staff employees** advise and support the work of line employees, helping them to accomplish the goals of the organization. Staff employees are unique because they have authority neither to assign tasks to line employees nor to direct them—the staff employee's job is to provide specialized advice and support, not to manage. Common staff positions are located in human resources, accounting, purchasing, information systems, and legal departments. Figure 9.4 illustrates the relationship of the staff legal counsel to the line organization in a portion of a typical business.

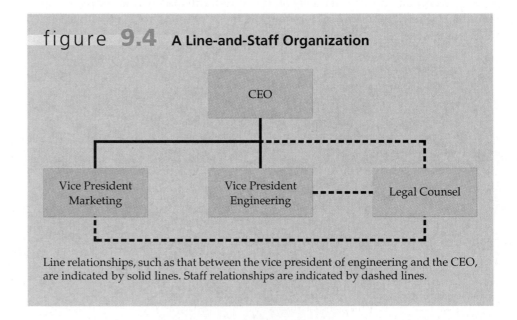

figure **9.4**   **A Line-and-Staff Organization**

Line relationships, such as that between the vice president of engineering and the CEO, are indicated by solid lines. Staff relationships are indicated by dashed lines.

As you can see from Figure 9.4, the legal counsel reports directly to the CEO and provides support to both the marketing vice president and the vice president of engineering—line employees actually responsible for producing the organization's products. Although the members of the staff organization provide advice to members of the line organization, they are not directly responsible for producing revenue.

A line-and-staff organization has several advantages over a line organization. The foremost advantage is that the organization can draw on the specialized expertise of its staff employees. Furthermore, since line and staff employees have to work closely together, cooperation and communication are encouraged within the entire organization.

There are also numerous disadvantages of the line-and-staff organization. Since staff employees are not directly involved in the production of goods or services, they represent a drain on the company's financial resources. Also, since staff employees do not report through the direct chain of command used by line employees, they can be perceived as impeding the efforts of line managers rather than supporting them. For their part, staff employees may be frustrated by their lack of authority. To counteract some of these problems, some large organizations have adopted a matrix organization.

Matrix Organization

A **matrix organization** is a hybrid structure in which line and staff employees work together as a team on specific projects. Although employees are members of teams that cut across several departments or work groups, they retain their permanent positions in the line-and-staff organization. Consequently, each employee reports to both a permanent manager and a temporary project manager.

Although matrix organizations are used primarily by large companies such as Boeing Co. and McDonnell Douglas Corp., they can also be appropriate for small businesses. Horizons Technology, Inc., an emerging multimedia computer software developer located in southern California, has incorporated the matrix organization into its standard line-and-staff organization. At any given time, Horizons Technology has numerous software development projects in the works. Some will be completed in a few weeks or months; others will continue for years. Team members on these projects report not only to their line supervisors or managers but also to the product manager directing the total development, production, and marketing of the new software product. Thus, each employee has two reporting relationships rather than the single, direct chain of command typically found in a line-and-staff structure. Figure 9.5 illustrates some of the relationships in the matrix organization at Horizons Technology.

4. Describe the advantages and disadvantages of matrix organizations compared with more traditional organizational designs.

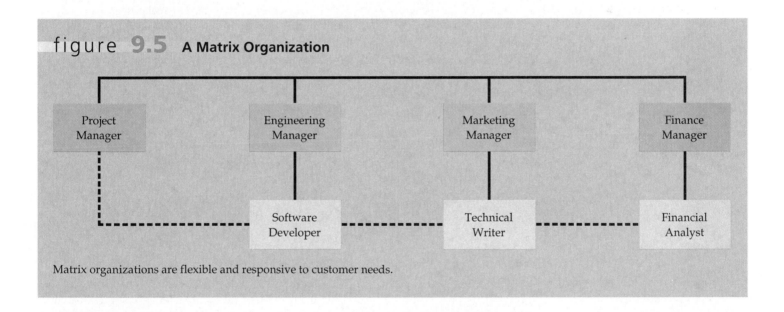

figure **9.5** **A Matrix Organization**

Matrix organizations are flexible and responsive to customer needs.

To cut costs in its European market, the Procter & Gamble Co. adapted a traditional line-and-staff structure to a matrix structure. In the past, the company had an autonomous organization set up in each country in which it did business. But this structure led to inefficiencies, such as the operation of nine separate detergent plants—one in each country. Each organization considered itself independent of the others and communication between the units was almost nonexistent. According to Stanford University business professor David Montgomery, "Country managers were barons. These folks had a lot of power and they didn't want to give it up."[8] To correct these problems, Procter & Gamble has adopted a matrix structure in which each local manager wears two hats—one for an entire category of products and one for a region. Fewer layers of management now separate the top of the pyramid from the market, communication between units has been greatly enhanced, and the company is able to respond more quickly to moves by its competitors.

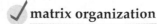 **matrix organization**

A hybrid structure in which line and staff employees work together as a team on specific projects.

Matrix organizations offer many advantages. They enable managers to be flexible and to respond quickly to changing customer needs with innovative solutions. The need for line and staff employees to work closely together breeds cooperation. Finally, since the matrix design allows employees to be reassigned from project to project quickly and easily, the business can start new projects without adding new branches to its organizational structure.

The matrix structure also has disadvantages. Employees who report to two managers can become confused about their role in the organization and the appropriate object of their loyalty. And managers may find that rewarding or disciplining an employee is more complicated when reporting relationships become blurred. In any case, managers must have highly developed interpersonal skills, since the matrix organization relies on the ability of line and staff employees to work closely together. Table 9.2 summarizes the advantages and disadvantages of the line, line-and-staff, and matrix structures.

table 9.2 **Advantages and Disadvantages of Line, Line-and-Staff, and Matrix Organizations**

	Advantages	Disadvantages
Line Organization	• Easy for employees to understand lines of authority • Direct communication • Simple decisions can be made quickly	• Lower-level employees may feel powerless • Inflexible and unresponsive to change • Complex decisions can take a long time • Managers overburdened with paperwork
Line-and-Staff Organization	• Organization benefits from the specialized expertise of staff employees • Encourages cooperation and communication	• Staff positions drain financial resources but do not produce revenue • Line managers feel their efforts are impeded • Lack of authority can lead to frustration in staff employees
Matrix Organization	• Flexible • Responsive • Encourages cooperation • Company can take on new projects without adding employees	• Reporting relationships complex and sometimes confusing • Managers must have highly developed interpersonal skills • Can be difficult to reward and discipline employees

Decisions in Organizing

5. Discuss the three factors considered in determining an organization's structure.

Several basic decisions help determine an organization's structure. They include the number of employees who will report to a manager, the extent to which decision making will be shared, and the number of reporting levels there will be between frontline employees and top management.

Span of Control: The Manager-Employee Ratio

Span of control, also known as *span of management*, describes the number of people one manager supervises directly. Managers who supervise few workers have a narrow span of control. Those who supervise many workers have a broad span of control. Early in this century, management theorists believed there was an ideal number of employees (typically thought to be from five to seven) who could most effectively be supervised by one manager. Today we know that, just as no one organizational design is best for all businesses, neither is any one span of control ideal. Even within a given organization, the span of control of different managers varies according to the nature of the work and the skill and experience of the managers and workers. For example, within the same company, managers of highly educated employees such as computer programmers are likely to have a narrower span of control than do managers of employees who perform less skilled jobs, such as data entry.

In general, workers who perform routine tasks such as typing shipping documents require very little direct supervision, which means that the manager can supervise more people. Workers with nonroutine assignments, or those learning new and unfamiliar tasks, require closer and more frequent attention because they may have questions or need training. In such situations, one manager can supervise only a few people.

Wider spans of control can translate into savings for an organization. A business that can operate with fewer managers will have a cost advantage over a competitor that employs more managers—savings that can be spent on upgrading equipment, researching a new product, expanding into a new market, or just keeping shareholders happy by generating larger profits.

Location of Decision Making: Centralized or Decentralized?

A second decision in organizational design is whether decision making should be centralized or decentralized. **Centralization** is the concentration of decision making in one primary location, typically with the owners in a smaller organization or at corporate headquarters in a larger organization.

Union Pacific Corp. (UPRR), the rail and trucking giant with annual revenues in excess of $5 billion, was once a highly centralized decision-making organization. Within the operations division, Union Pacific had nine layers of management between the operations chief and the railroaders—the frontline employees. When a railroader needed a decision on some important issue, the request had to make its way up the nine rungs of the management ladder before it arrived on the desk of the operations chief, who was the decision maker. Then, as in the U.S. Army, the decision had to make the return trip down the same chain of command. Needless to say, Union Pacific's decision-making apparatus was slow—a railroader might wait weeks or even months to get an answer.[9]

Centralization enables managers to provide clear direction, consistent implementation of company policies and operating procedures, and tight control over human and material resources. When administrative functions are centralized, operating costs are lower because many divisions share central resources instead of duplicating them in numerous places within the organization. These advantages come at a price, however: decreased independence and creativity for lower-level and frontline employees, who often feel frustrated and unwilling to assume additional responsibility.

Decentralization is the dispersal of decision making throughout the organization. When Union Pacific revised its centralized philosophy and management structure in the early 1990s, it moved more responsibility and authority to middle managers and frontline employees. The company's top managers believed that, by shifting decision-making authority closer to the places where the work is actually done, the organization could become more responsive to its customers. This belief was confirmed after Union Pacific management reorganized its operations division—in the process removing five layers of management and 800 middle managers. Decisions that once took weeks or months

 span of control

The number of people one manager supervises directly; also known as *span of management*.

 centralization

Concentration of decision making in one primary location.

decentralization

Dispersal of decision making throughout an organization.

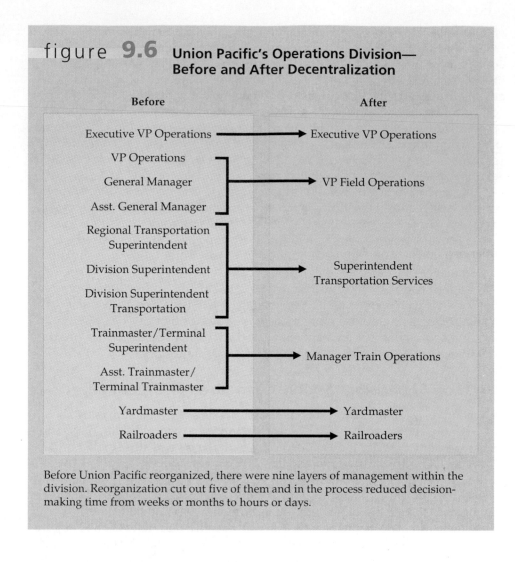

figure **9.6** Union Pacific's Operations Division—Before and After Decentralization

Before Union Pacific reorganized, there were nine layers of management within the division. Reorganization cut out five of them and in the process reduced decision-making time from weeks or months to hours or days.

were now made in hours or days.[10] Figure 9.6 illustrates the Union Pacific operations division before and after decentralization.

Advantages of decentralization include empowered workers, quick and responsive decision making, and low administrative costs. But there can be a trade-off for these advantages. Decision making that is spread out over a number of people may produce decisions of inconsistent quality. Company policies and practices may be implemented in quite different ways in various parts of the organization. In the worst case, decentralization can lead to duplicated and wasted effort, inefficiency, and communication breakdowns.

We have presented centralization and decentralization as two clearly distinct options. In practice, however, most organizations are neither completely centralized nor completely decentralized. A fully centralized organization would soon find itself paralyzed as it waited for overburdened top executives to make decisions, and a fully decentralized organization could be an unsupervised invitation to chaos. Even within the same company, it is best for some decision making to be centralized and some to be decentralized. Decisions critical to the overall success of the organization, such as planning, are usually highly centralized. Even as Union Pacific decentralized many of its operational activities, the company continued with a centralized approach to dispatch and customer service.[11] And in most organizations, routine low-level decisions, such as the timing of lunch and break schedules, are decentralized.

In general, though, U.S. businesses are moving in the direction taken by Union Pacific—greater decentralization to give more autonomy and power to employees close to the organization's customers. The current move to team-based work produces empowered, decentralized organizations in which groups of employees make many key decisions about how to improve their own work processes.

Layers of Management: Tall or Flat Organization?

Organizations with many layers of management and narrow spans of control have steep, pyramid-shaped structures and are known as **tall organizations** or *vertical organizations*. One such organization is depicted in Figure 9.7(a). An organization's height also reflects its degree of centralization. Centralized decision making can produce many layers of management as each manager or supervisor looks upward for answers, as we saw in the case of Union Pacific.

Organizations with few levels of management and wide spans of control have flatter organizational charts, like the one in Figure 9.7(b), where each director is at the same level and reports directly to the president. Such structures are known as **flat organizations** or *horizontal organizations*. In flat organizations, empowered employees act independently to solve problems and satisfy customer needs. Decision making is faster, and the organization can respond more easily to its customers and to changes in its environment. Many flat organizations have harnessed the power of technology to take the place of the many managers previously focused on communication, coordination, and decision making.

 tall organizations

Steep, pyramid-shaped organizations with many layers of management and narrow spans of control; also known as *vertical organizations*.

 flat organizations

Organizations with few layers of management and wide spans of control; also known as *horizontal organizations*.

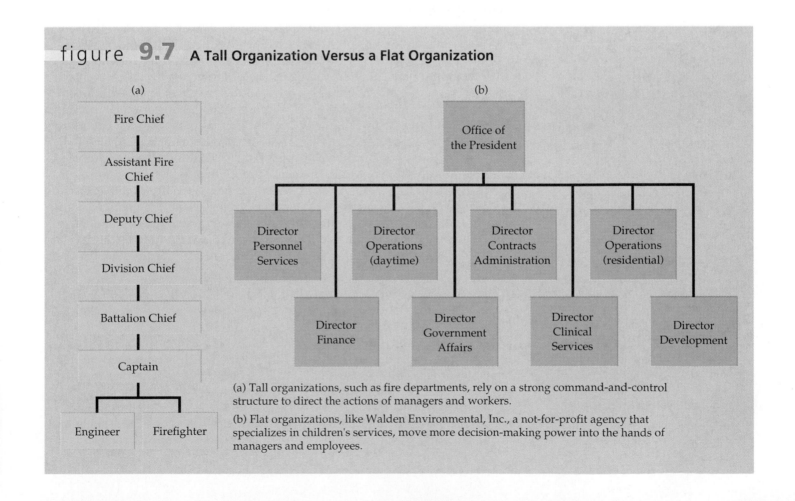

figure **9.7** **A Tall Organization Versus a Flat Organization**

(a) Tall organizations, such as fire departments, rely on a strong command-and-control structure to direct the actions of managers and workers.

(b) Flat organizations, like Walden Environmental, Inc., a not-for-profit agency that specializes in children's services, move more decision-making power into the hands of managers and employees.

Departmentalization: Choosing a Focus

6. Identify and describe the five primary areas of focus for departmentalization.

We have looked at the basic elements that affect organizational design: authority, responsibility, accountability, and delegation. We have also considered some of the decisions management makes in designing an organizational structure: line, line-and-staff, or matrix structures; span of control; degree of centralization; and the number of layers of management. A final ingredient in the design of the organization is **departmentalization**, the organization of work groups or activities into subunits within the company.

Most organizations departmentalize by focusing on one of five primary areas:

- Product—the goods or services the company produces
- Function—the specialized, related activities of different workers
- Geography—the company's regional offices and facilities
- Customer—groups of customers who share particular characteristics
- Process—the logical flow of work

A company may align its entire organization around one area of focus—geography, for example—or it may organize different parts of the organization around different areas of focus, as 3M Corp. has done. In the sections that follow, we use selected parts of 3M's organization chart plus other company examples to illustrate the five areas of departmentalization.

Organizing by Product

Most companies provide one good or service in their first years of operation. As companies grow and develop multiple product lines and services, they may choose to form subunits by **organizing by product**—grouping work tasks around specific products or product lines. General Mills, Inc., for example, is organized into many different subunits, each built around a specific product such as Cheerios. Each subunit is led by a product manager, who is responsible for capturing as much market share as possible for that particular product. From the photo on the front of the box to the coupons in the Sunday papers, the Cheerios group's plans and activities focus on that one cereal.

The 3M Corp. organization chart in Figure 9.8(a) illustrates the company's Pharmaceuticals, Dental, and Personal Care Group, which is organized by product. The major benefit of departmentalization by product is that each subunit within the organization dedicates its attention to the unique needs of its own product. However, this strength can become a weakness if taken too far. The disadvantages of organizing by product are that territoriality can develop within each product group and communication and coordination between groups may be poor.

✓ **departmentalization**

The organization of work groups or activities into subunits within a company.

✓ **organizing by product**

Grouping work tasks around specific products or product lines.

✓ **organizing by function**

Grouping employees by the specialized, related tasks they perform.

Organizing by Function

Organizing by function groups employees by the specialized, related tasks they perform. Figure. 9.8(b) illustrates 3M's staff, which is organized by function. (Note that each vice president is at the same level.) Some typical business subunits organized by function are production, research and development, finance, marketing, personnel, and sales. Each of these functions is quite different from the others, and each requires workers with specialized skills and qualifications. A hospital organized by function has separate departments for

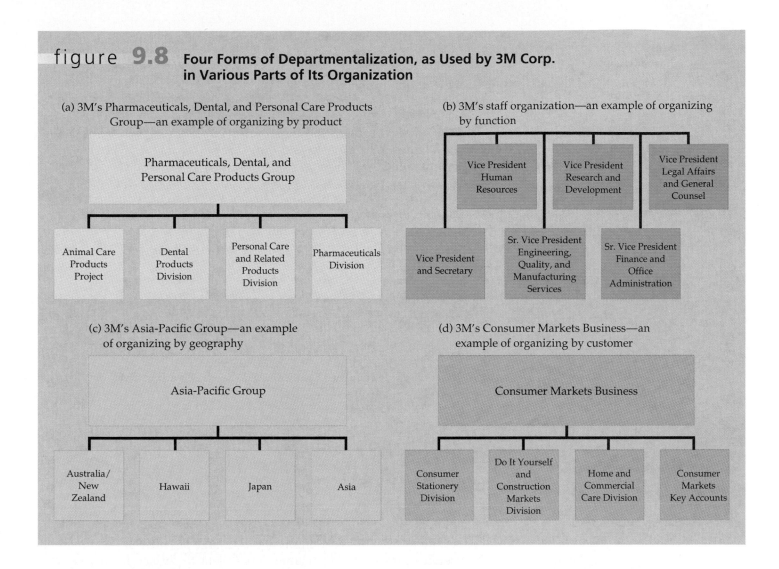

figure **9.8** **Four Forms of Departmentalization, as Used by 3M Corp. in Various Parts of Its Organization**

(a) 3M's Pharmaceuticals, Dental, and Personal Care Products Group—an example of organizing by product

(b) 3M's staff organization—an example of organizing by function

(c) 3M's Asia-Pacific Group—an example of organizing by geography

(d) 3M's Consumer Markets Business—an example of organizing by customer

administration, radiology, surgery, obstetrics, emergency care, and so forth. An automobile manufacturer organized by function has departments for sales, marketing, manufacturing, administration, and so on. Organizing by function has traditionally been the most frequently used basis for departmentalization in business.

One major advantage of organizing by function is the extent to which specialized knowledge develops within the organization as people with similar skills work together. Another advantage is the ease of communication within each department. Like organizing by product, however, organizing by function has the potential to create barriers between departments, with a corresponding breakdown in communication and coordination. In addition, subunits may lose their ability to focus mutually on the overall goals of the entire organization.

Organizing by Geography

Another alternative for companies that do business nationally or globally is **organizing by geography**—forming subunits focused on regional offices and facilities. Large airlines organize by geography. While most of them have a fixed location for their corporate headquarters, most also operate numerous satellite

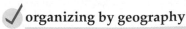 **organizing by geography**

Forming subunits focused on regional offices and facilities.

offices and facilities. They do so because their operations, equipment, and personnel are located at the various airports that the airline services. The National Football League is also organized by geography. Franchises for teams are awarded to owners in specific cities.

Organizing by geography helps a company respond quickly to the needs and habits of particular customers. Employees provide a local presence for the company, even if its corporate headquarters is hundreds or even thousands of miles away, without the expense and time delays that might otherwise be incurred by travel and long-distance communication. For example, a sales representative located in Boston, Massachusetts, can respond to customers in the northeastern United States more easily than if he or she were located at company headquarters in Los Angeles, California.

A major disadvantage of organizing by geography is that field offices can be expensive to maintain. Business units located at a distance from headquarters may also feel neglected and isolated from the action at the home office. In extreme situations, such feelings can lead to rebellion against the authority represented by the home office.

Information technology has made organization by geography less important than it once was. Conducting business at a distance is now faster and easier than ever, thanks to computers and fax machines. There is still a need, however, for face-to-face interaction with customers—wherever they are. Figure 9.8(c) shows the organization of the Asia-Pacific group of 3M Corp., which is organized by geography.

Organizing by Customer

Sometimes as a company grows and diversifies it loses contact with an important element of the business—its customers. To ensure that customer needs are being met, many companies turn to **organizing by customer**—forming subunits focused on customers who share particular characteristics.

For example, U.S. West Communications, a large provider of telecommunications services, maintains a separate department to service its government customers most effectively.[12] Like many other organizations, U.S. West does this because government rules for purchasing products are much more specialized and restrictive than those set by most commercial firms. Figure 9.8(d) illustrates 3M's Consumer Markets Business, which is also organized by customer.

Organizing by Process

For some companies, **organizing by process**—grouping employees by the logical flow of work—is the most efficient way to departmentalize. As we will see in Chapter 10, this is often the case in a production function, where one group of tasks follows another in a logical process flow. A guitar manufacturer, for example, might have one group of employees who cut, shape, and glue the wood together. Another group might apply the lacquer, and still another group might polish the guitar and install the hardware. Such a sequence of tasks allows departments to specialize and hence be more efficient in their operations.

Organizing by process is more difficult to represent in an organization chart than are other organizational designs. In part, that is because organization charts cannot easily show how processes operate, though they may demonstrate who has authority and responsibility for managing them. For this reason, the boxes on the organization chart are sometimes referred to as "black boxes," a topic you will hear more about in Chapter 10, Producing Quality Goods and Services.

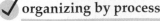 **organizing by customer**

Forming subunits focused on customers who share particular characteristics.

organizing by process

Grouping employees by the logical flow of work.

Trends in Organizational Design

Because organizational design must be tailored to a specific business at a specific time, one company's perfect structure could well paralyze another firm, or even the same firm at another time. Companies hobbled by organizational structures rooted too firmly in the past may be unable to see major shifts in market direction or product acceptance. Companies restructure for many reasons, in both good times and bad. These reorganizations may or may not involve changes in the size of the work force. Catalysts for reorganization include:

- Changes in company leadership
- Changes in organizational goals
- Corporate mergers
- Changes in the regional, national, or global economy
- Improved access to existing technology
- Technological breakthroughs
- New laws or social movements
- Changes in sources of supply
- Demographic changes in the customer base
- The need to improve responsiveness to customers

Many businesses are fine-tuning their organizations for one or more of these reasons. In this section we look at five major trends currently affecting U.S. businesses: downsizing, teaming, focusing on process, moving toward a more informal organizational culture, and outsourcing.

Downsizing: From Tall to Flat Organizations

Downsizing, as you may recall from Chapter 1, is eliminating jobs to cut costs and make the business smaller. It is an extreme measure, and most organizations think carefully before closing plants or laying off employees. Downsizing is often a response to forces beyond the control of management, such as a recession that slows sales and reduces profits. However, increased competition can also motivate a business to downsize in order to operate more efficiently.

Downsizing frequently removes middle management levels. More and more organizations are requiring managers to be doers—not just thinkers. As management consultant Peter Block asserts, "No one should be allowed to make a living simply planning, watching, controlling, or evaluating the actions of others."[13] Many companies are finding that the payoff for cutting unnecessary layers of management is increased productivity and creativity. Says Richard McCloskey, CEO of System Connection Inc., a cable and modem manufacturer in Provo, Utah, "We've tried to avoid having a lot of people reporting to other people and have tried to keep decision making within the groups. People make decisions themselves, for instance, about returns or swap-outs with customers. What you get is a lot more creativity."[14] Flatter organizations have fewer employees. By removing layers of management and empowering employees to handle problems directly, organizations can be more responsive to customer needs.

Lexmark International Inc., formerly a unit of IBM, cut management positions by 60 percent, simplified procedures, and flattened its hierarchy.[15] For Lexmark, these actions paid off to the tune of a pretax profit of $100 million on $2 billion in sales in its first year as an independent company. Union Pacific Corp. cut out five layers of management and, in the process, empowered frontline employees to make decisions on the spot, instead of waiting weeks for a response to wind its way through the dense bureaucracy of the old organization.[16]

7. Identify reasons for a business to reorganize and restructure.

8. Discuss the benefits of downsizing and explain how it relates to the use of teams.

Advances in information technology have allowed many companies to eliminate entire layers of management and in the process be more responsive to customers and, hence, more competitive. Says General Electric Lighting's John Opie, "There are just two people between me and a salesman—information technology replaced the rest." Frederick Kovac, vice president for planning at the Goodyear Tire & Rubber Co., voiced similar sentiments: "It used to be, if you wanted information, you had to go up, over, and down through the organization. Now you just tap into the computerized data bank. Everybody can know as much about the company as the chairman of the board. That's what broke down the hierarchy."[17]

Teaming: From Matrix to Teams

9. Identify and describe the different types of teams.

You may recall from the earlier discussion in this chapter that a matrix organization provides the benefits of flexibility, improved employee cooperation, and the ability to take on new projects without adding to the organization's structure. However, many organizations have evolved to team-based structures that create even more flexibility and employee involvement than does the traditional matrix organization.

In many cases, companies' shift to fewer layers of management has corresponded with an increased use of teams. Teams can take over many of the tasks traditionally performed by supervisors, such as setting goals and measuring the quality of work produced. Titeflex, a Massachusetts manufacturer of fluid and gas hoses, slashed layers of management and created employee teams. The reorganization reduced the time between receiving an order and manufacturing and shipping the product from an average of ten weeks to less than one week. Before the reorganization, only 23 percent of the orders at Titeflex's Industrial Products Division went out on time. After the reorganization, on-time performance climbed to 90 percent.[18]

Throughout this text, we have noted that *work teams*—groups of two or more employees working together to accomplish a common goal—are increasingly popular. Teams offer flexibility. They can be assembled quickly when needed and can be dispersed just as quickly after the work is done. Teams are of several types: self-directed work teams, cross-functional teams, project teams (or task forces), and committees.

Self-directed work teams are groups of employees responsible for managing their own activities. Team members plan their own work, assign tasks cooperatively, solve problems that arise, make decisions without consulting with supervisors. According to Marvin Weisbord, an expert on organizational development, the advantage of teams is that "the people who do the work [have] in their hands the means to change to suit the customer."[19] The ability of teams to be self-managed also frees up managers to focus on work that only they can do.

Members of self-directed work teams have the incentive and the authority to be responsive to anyone who benefits from their work—the customer or some other individual or group within the organization. At Ortho (makers of garden and lawn care products), for example, an increased focus on teams has helped to increase sales by 50 percent in each of two recent years with only a 15 percent increase in workers and an 8 percent decrease in employee turnover.[20]

Self-directed work teams are a major component of the *high-involvement workplace,* in which employees are central to all aspects of the operation, including decision making. At the Levi Strauss Associates Inc. sewing plant in Murphy, North Carolina, team workers are trained to do 36 tasks instead of one or two, and they are given responsibility for running the plant—from organizing supplies to setting production goals to making personnel policy.[21]

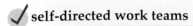
self-directed work teams

Groups of employees responsible for managing their own activities.

Cross-functional teams draw together personnel from different functional areas of the organization to improve operations and communication. They differ from self-directed work teams in that they do not manage themselves and their recommendations to management are advisory in nature. At General Electric Co.'s capacitor and power protection operations in Bayamon, Puerto Rico, hourly workers meet weekly in teams of 10 or so. Each team includes members from every area of the plant and "owns" (is responsible for) part of the plant's operations—such as assembly and shipping and receiving.[22] At Edy's Grand Ice Cream, cross-functional teams include four or five people who actually make the ice cream, plus a packaging operator, an engineer, a shipper, a maintenance person, and so on. Each team is responsible for everything from quality and sanitation checks, meeting individual business goals, and internal scheduling and discipline to training and career development for all its members.[23]

Cross-functional Team

In 1992, AT&T Global Information Solutions adopted a customer-focused business model that mandates no more than three management levels between its CEO and its customers. That didn't leave much room for the unit's sales managers, who found their authority and responsibility greatly reduced. Former regional sales manager David Scott—the man in the middle of this photo—is now a team leader. He directs and advises the 25 members of his cross-functional team, and finds that he relies more on his leadership and negotiating skills than on traditional management skills. Now, Scott says, "I'm dealing with people who have strong opinions and who are strong in skills that I don't have. You have to give them a lot of freedom. My job is to clear their path and remove obstacles."

A **project team** or *task force* is a group formed to deal with a specific product, project, problem, issue, or task. Such a group is usually temporary, working until the specific project is completed or until the problem is resolved. A task force might identify the cause of a persistent quality problem and resolve it. Procter & Gamble and many other companies use project teams to develop products and bring them to market as efficiently as possible. At Oryx Energy Co., management organized middle managers and lower-level staffers into 26 teams that were asked to come up with solutions to problems they were having. According to James McCormick, the company's president, the use of teams enabled Oryx to cut out three levels of management, reduce field offices from 14 to 4, and eliminate some 300 jobs.[24]

A **committee** is a group to which decision-making power is delegated for specific purposes. Committee members often represent all areas of the organization. For example, an operations committee, which sets and reviews policies, may have as its members the top managers from each of the departments in the

 cross-functional teams

Teams that draw together personnel from different functional areas of an organization to improve operations and communication.

 project team

A group, usually temporary, formed to deal with a specific product, project, problem, issue, or task; also known as a *task force*.

 committee

A group to which decision-making power is delegated for specific purposes.

organizational culture
The shared customs, beliefs, values, and attitudes that give a company its identity and sense of community.

Information technology is the subject of Chapter 18.

10. Describe the relative advantages of organizing by process.

11. Discuss the role of a company's informal structure and use of outsourcing in improved efficiency.

organization. Temporary committees may share some of the characteristics of task forces. Long-term, "standing" committees often deal with quality-of-work issues, social responsibility issues, and employee benefits issues.

Advances in information technology have also contributed to the growth of teams. Companies increasingly expect their employees to use computer-based information technology on the job in the form of electronic mail, customer and financial databases, and decision support software. Some managers who were formerly responsible for the distribution of information on paper have even found themselves replaced by computers.

In many businesses, teams may even consist of people at various locations who meet and collaborate with the aid of e-mail, voice mail, and video and conference calling. 3M encourages such collaboration through its Technical Forum, which sponsors worldwide networks and meetings of established groups of employees who share similar technical interests. At these meetings, 3M employees participate in seminars with scientists and researchers from outside the organization. According to a long-held company maxim, "Products belong to divisions, but technology belongs to the company."[25]

In addition, 3M created the Technical Council to discuss new technologies and ways to improve their transfer from unit to unit, across departmental lines. The company also sponsors an annual technology fair so that 3M researchers can present their research to each other and develop their informal networks.[26]

Refocusing: From Function to Process

Many companies in recent years have changed the focus of departmentaliztion within their organizations. The tendency has been to switch from organizing by function—such as marketing, manufacturing, and finance—to organizing by process. Most companies have five to seven essential, or core, processes, such as production, research, sales, invoicing, fulfillment, and customer service. In the past, dozens of departments, divisions, and functional groups might have cut across each of these core processes, with no one owning the whole process. As a result, if work was not completed on schedule, within budget, or free of defects, few people felt responsible. A process-based organizational structure can help eliminate inefficiencies in the process and make all employees feel a sense of ownership in a company's products. This pride often translates into better products at a lower production cost. People feel responsible.

Kao Corp., Japan's leading soap and detergent manufacturer, reoriented its organization from a functional to a process focus. After only seven years, it became Japan's second largest manufacturer of cosmetics. Kao's product development takes place in cross-functional meetings attended by representatives from research, marketing, management, and production. These meetings allow the organization to respond quickly to changes in its environment. Yoshio Maruta, chairman of Kao Corp., encourages his employees to cross traditional organizational lines to get their work done. Says Maruta, "If anything goes wrong in one department, those in other parts of the organization should sense the problem and provide help without being asked."[27]

Culture: From Formal to Informal

Organizational culture consists of the shared customs, beliefs, values, and attitudes that give a company its identity and sense of community. Although organization charts do not represent these elements directly, they do offer clues to what a company considers important. For example, if the company's chief executive officer has a special interest in quality control, the chart may show a

ethics
check

Should Ethics Be a Part of Organizational Design?

Most large firms have experts on staff to help managers identify and resolve legal issues. A separate ethics officer, or ombudsman, could likewise serve as counsel on ethical issues as they arise. This may seem like a strange approach, since we suggested in Chapter 4 that ethics should be built into routine decision making, not pushed off into an obscure corner of the corporate hierarchy.

Nonetheless, an ethics office could serve important functions. The office could track discussion of ethical issues and standards outside the firm and alert managers to specific concerns that directly affect the company, such as questionable business practices. An ethics office could also offer special training in ethical issues, or play a troubleshooting role, running an ethics hotline and serving as a corporate buffer if charges of unethical conduct are made by employees or stakeholders outside the firm. The ethics office might also conduct interviews when employees leave the company. Departing employees often have less at stake and are therefore more willing to report ethical lapses within the company.

What's your opinion? Should companies build an ethics office into their organizational design? To whom should the ethics officer report?

quality control officer or group reporting directly to the CEO. (See also the ethics check entitled "Should Ethics Be a Part of Organizational Design?") Paula Cholmondeley, of Owens-Corning Fiberglass Corp., described a culture change that occurred in that company:

> We just finished totally redesigning our planning process. With a new CEO, we needed to create a culture change within our company. Before the change, our culture was very top-down. Top management would tell the operating line areas what they ought to be doing. Now, top management only sets some very broad parameters. For example, an overarching goal for our organization is to grow from $3 billion to $5 billion. Top management also defined the three key values that everybody had to address in their plans: customer satisfaction, shareholder value, and individual dignity.[28]

An organization is no better and no worse than the people who work for it. Good managers realize how important their employees are and do not see them as tools to be used and discarded when a job is done. Bucking the common business philosophy that "the customer always comes first," Starbucks Corp. has turned this maxim on its head. According to Howard Schultz, chairman and CEO of Starbucks, "Our people come first, then customers, then shareholders. It may sound out of order, but we can't exceed the expectations of our customers unless we exceed it for our employees first."[29]

An important part of a company's culture is its informal organization, the unofficial network of personal relationships among employees. Such relationships develop gradually over time, as 3M recognized when it designed informal meeting areas into the plan for its office building in Austin, Texas. Employees meet and form relationships in training sessions, company social functions, organized sports events, carpools, and even outside the workplace in such places as community schools.

These relationships build bridges between individuals and networks within the organization. If they are based on good feelings—friendship and trust, for instance—workers will seek out opportunities to interact. When distrust and dislike are common, individuals will interact only when they must. These positive or negative informal relationships can have a tremendous influence on worker performance.[30]

In the best situations, informal interactions among employees can be a rich resource for both the company and the employee. A manager in the production area, for example, may share both lunch and a product problem regarding customer specifications with her counterpart in sales. The result is frequently faster, better problem solving than the formal organization can provide. For example, using formal channels, the production manager might have to report the problem a long way up the ladder to higher management, which would then delegate responsibility for devising a solution to subordinates in the sales area. Figure 9.9 shows an informal network within a more formal organizational structure.

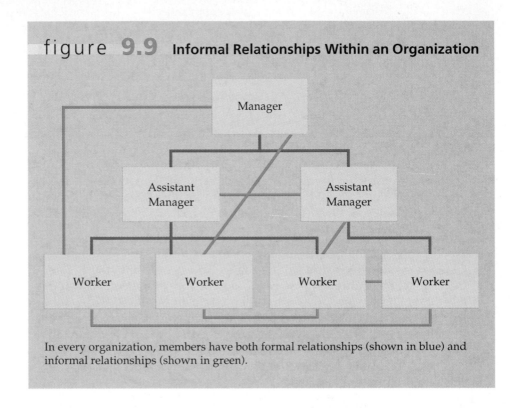

figure **9.9** **Informal Relationships Within an Organization**

In every organization, members have both formal relationships (shown in blue) and informal relationships (shown in green).

The informal organization also has an underground news service—the **grapevine**, an unofficial and informal communication network that exists in virtually all organizations. Because its members trust each other, the grapevine tends to be better—or at least faster—at communicating information than the formal structure.

In many cases the grapevine bypasses senior managers, who may not share the same views and personal objectives as the rest of the employees. In at least one case, however, senior managers used the grapevine to circulate news of their own choosing. When the trend toward greater informality in the workplace finally reached IBM corporate headquarters in Armonk, New York, the new, relaxed dress code was announced not in a company memo but through the unofficial grapevine.

 grapevine

An unofficial and informal communication network that exists in virtually all organizations.

outsourcing

Contracting with outside organizations for one or more business services.

Outsourcing: From Doing It All to Doing What You Do Best

Contracting with outside organizations for one or more business services is known as **outsourcing**. Neodata, the world's largest provider of direct marketing services, outsources most of its technology operations to Electronic Data

doing business

Providing Temporary Solutions

With the trends toward downsizing and outsourcing, temporary placement services have experienced a business boom. One company, Freelance Access, places high-tech graphic arts professionals in temporary, part-time, and permanent positions in companies of all sizes. In just three years, from 1991 to 1994, the Boston-based agency grew from a one-person shop with a pool of 60 graphic designers on call and $60,000 in revenues to a company with 1,000 freelancers, 168 clients, $1.2 million in revenues, and a branch office in Manhattan.

Companies such as Freelance Access find the demand for their services is growing as corporations and advertising agencies downsize or delay permanent hiring. Says Barbara Black, president of Createmps, a 10-year-old privately held company located in Boston and Los Angeles, "The advertising industry has changed dramatically. After the [1990–1991] recession, a lot of people opened their own small agencies or became inde-

pendent contractors. Now companies are hiring them back as freelancers."

Even hiring for the freelance agency has entered the electronic age. All Freelance Access applicants complete a 45-minute, computerized questionnaire that pinpoints their technical skill level. After the electronic interview, freelancers complete at least one of six examinations that test their knowledge of specific software packages. Next comes a half-hour to 45-minute face-to-face interview and portfolio review. Later, applicants can scan their work into a special Freelance Access system that displays and describes their work to clients. The work can be grouped by level of technical proficiency for easy sorting by customer need.

Source: Based on Natalie Engler, "Getting Graphic in the Temp Business," *Boston Sunday Globe*, Nov. 20, 1994, pp. A1, A5.

Systems Corp. (EDS)—so much that one EDS employee has the title "vice president of information technology, Neodata."[31] Organizations offering such services are very flexible and well suited to high-technology businesses faced with constant change, as the doing business box entitled "Providing Temporary Solutions" shows.

An organization that carries outsourcing to its extreme is the **virtual company**, which contracts with other businesses to perform such core functions as manufacturing and marketing. A virtual company, which can remain small and flexible, is in effect the coordinator of a loose confederation of different companies. The only people who have to be inside its walls are the experts who understand the technical aspects of the product. For example, a virtual company specializing in manufacturing might buy all its supplies from other companies and then hire still another company to assemble the product. The efforts of the virtual company's own employees could then focus on selling and distributing the product. If the technology changed, the virtual company could readily adapt by contracting with a new vendor rather than replacing its own expensive equipment and training its own workers to use it.

The companies that hold contracts for external, noncore activities are sometimes referred to as *modular corporations*.[32] Together, virtual companies and modular corporations form loose networks of companies that cooperate to achieve their goals. Such networks can be found in California's Silicon Valley, where a complex collection of companies supply one another with key ingredients used in the production of computer chips. One such company, Palo Alto–based Visioneer, designs and sells advanced scanners used to convert all the paper in the workplace into computer files. The actual products are made by other companies; Visioneer has no factories.[33] As the company's president commented, "Many of us like to think we work for Silicon Valley, Inc."[34]

Technology already allows more traditionally structured organizations to enjoy some of the advantages of virtual companies. Product distribution is one example, as you will learn in Chapter 16. Wal-Mart stores and Procter & Gam-

 virtual company

Company that contracts with other businesses to perform such core functions as manufacturing and marketing.

Honing Your Skills for New Career Paths

Sooner or later, you as a worker will encounter some of the organizational changes you have read about in this chapter. Your work experience will be much more comfortable if you remember these three pointers:

1. *Be positive and flexible*. When an organization changes its structure, you will be able to adapt more easily if you maintain a positive attitude and remain flexible. Focus on positive outcomes, not on temporary negative aspects of the change.

2. *Develop broad general skills*. These include communication, organization, and the ability to complete assignments. Such skills can enhance your value in any organization because they can be applied in many areas and to many tasks.

3. *Concentrate on working cooperatively within a group*. Many companies are adopting team structures, and they value employees who can function effectively as team members. Basic group interaction skills, such as knowing how to conduct yourself in a meeting, will be increasingly important as teamwork becomes a part of most jobs. With the right skills and attitudes, anyone can become a valuable employee in any type of workplace structure.

ble are linked by a computer system that interweaves their order-and-fulfillment process. As a result, the "bells of Wal-Mart's cash registers, in effect, ring in P&G warehouses," telling them to ship a new box of Tide to replace the one a customer has just bought.[35]

Small businesses have become big players by establishing relationships with large companies such as Wal-Mart. Cedar Works, Inc., of Peebles, Ohio, was registering sales of $2 million a year before Wal-Mart picked up its bird feeder product line in 1990. Sales have since risen to $15 million, and Cedar Works has increased its work force from 20 to 250 employees. Company president Jim Obenshain observed, "It's made us successful beyond our imagination."[36]

Robert Reich, secretary of labor in the Clinton administration and a Harvard economist, foresees a time when the boundaries between all organizations become so fluid that corporations will evolve into temporary arrangements among smaller bands of entrepreneurs: "Every big company will be a confederation of small ones. All small organizations will be constantly in the process of linking up into big ones."[37]

No doubt about it, the trends we've explored in this section—downsizing, teaming, focus on process, informal culture, and outsourcing—will affect your working life. See the skills check entitled "Honing Your Skills for New Career Paths" for advice that will serve you well in any organization.

Reviewing *Organizational Design*

Designing Organizations

1. **Distinguish between a company's formal and informal organizations and explain why organizational designs vary**. A company's formal organization is its official structure of reporting and functional relationships. Its informal organization describes unofficial relationships. The formal design, which is based on the idea of division of labor, varies in relation to the needs of the organization, which are defined by its short- and long-term goals. Because each organization is unique and conditions change, designs vary by industry, within industries, and from one time to another.

2. **Explain the relationship between delegation and the three elements of task assignment**. A first step in organizational design involves the delegation of tasks and goals to employees. In delegating tasks, effective managers must ensure that employees have responsibility, authority, *and* accountability for their completion. Responsibil-

ity without authority, for example, results in employee confusion and frustration and probably less-than-satisfactory performance. Although employees are accountable for their actions, managers retain ultimate responsibility. The flow of these delegation elements through an organization is defined by an organization chart.

3. **Differentiate line from line-and-staff organizations and identify the advantages and disadvantages of each**. In a line organization, reporting relationships flow directly from top to bottom, with decision making concentrated at the top. In a line-and-staff organization, staff employees with specialized knowledge advise and support line employees, those whose tasks relate directly to the organization's goals. While line organizations provide clear lines of authority, they leave lower-level employees out of the decision-making process, they are inflexible and make decisions regarding complex issues more difficult, and they do not encourage specialization of knowledge. A line-and-staff organization provides specialized expertise to line employees and encourages companywide cooperation and communication. However, lack of authority can lead to frustration in staff employees, and line managers may feel that their efforts are impeded.

4. **Describe the advantages and disadvantages of matrix organizations compared with more traditional organizational designs**. Matrix organizations are intended to eliminate the problems inherent in line and line-and-staff organizations by having line and staff employees work together on specific projects, while retaining their line reporting relationships. The result is increased flexibility, more cooperation, and the ability to start new projects without adding to the organizational structure. However, blurred reporting relationships may cause some confusion, split loyalties, and complicate the rewarding or disciplining of employees.

5. **Discuss the three factors considered in determining an organization's structure**. In creating an organization's structure, management must decide on a manager-employee ratio, the location of decision making, and the number of layers of management. The manager-employee ratio, or span of control, depends on the nature of the business, as well as the amount of supervision required for the task being performed. Decision making may be centralized or decentralized, or a combination of these within the same firm. Where clear direction, consistent implementation of policies and procedures, and tight control over resources are needed, centralized decision making is appropriate. Decentralization enables employees' empowerment, quick and responsive decision making, and low administrative costs. A company's span of control and location of decision making determine whether its structure is tall (vertical) or flat (horizontal). Flat organizations have more empowered employees and faster decision making.

Departmentalization: Choosing a Focus

6. **Identify and describe the five primary areas of focus for departmentalization**. Companies may departmentalize their entire organization according to product, function, geography, customer, or process, or they may organize different parts of the company around different areas, depending on which is most efficient for their type of business. For example, as companies grow and develop multiple products and services, grouping work tasks around individual products makes most sense. Organizing by function, the most common organizational form, encourages the development of specialized knowledge. Organizing by geography allows a company to take advantage of the efficiencies associated with travel and communication within a specific area, although improved technology makes this an increasingly less attractive alternative. Organizing by customer is useful for companies that have grown so large and so diversified that they have lost contact with specific customers' needs. Organizing by process encourages flexibility and efficiency.

Trends in Organizational Design

7. **Identify reasons for a business to reorganize and restructure**. Companies reorganize and restructure to gain efficiency and improve customer service and competitiveness. Specific internal events requiring restructuring include changes in the organization's leadership, goals, sources of supply, or a merger with another company. External factors include changes in economic conditions, new laws or social movements, and technological breakthroughs.

8. **Discuss the benefits of downsizing and explain how it relates to the use of teams**. Although downsizing creates hardships for laid-off employees, it allows companies to increase efficiency, productivity, and creativity, and of course to cut costs. In many cases, downsizing means reducing the number of management levels accompanied by a shift to an increase in the use of teams. Because teams take over an entire task, including decision making, they assume responsibility for many of the tasks traditionally performed by supervisors and middle managers.

9. **Identify and describe the different types of teams**. Work teams, which offer flexibility in terms of membership and size, may be self-directed, cross-functional, or project teams or committees, according to their permanence and function. While self-directed teams have complete responsibility and authority for completing all aspects of their operation, cross-functional teams are strictly advisory, composed of employees from different departments and providing advice in improving operations and communication. Project teams are temporary task forces set up to solve particular problems or complete a particular project. Committees are established for

specific purposes, either temporarily, to review a situation and decide on a course of action, or permanently, to deal with ongoing issues, such as employee benefits.

10. **Describe the relative advantages of organizing by process.** Organizing by process rather than by function eliminates inefficiencies and increases employees' feelings of responsibility and sense of ownership in a company's products. Reducing the number of divisions in a company from many functions to a relatively few core processes results in more focused, more responsive, and more flexible performance, and usually in cost reductions.

11. **Discuss the role of a company's informal culture and use of outsourcing in improved efficiency.** The informal relationships among employees provide a major resource for the company and employees alike, improving communications among divisions and often leading to improved operations. Outsourcing is the ultimate division of labor and improves efficiency and flexibility. At the extreme, virtual companies contract with other companies to perform core functions. Noncore functions may be performed by modular corporations. Together, these confederations of companies form loose networks that cooperate to achieve their goals.

 Key Terms

organizational design **261**	line-and-staff organization **266**	organizing by product **272**	project team **277**
formal organization **261**	staff employees **266**	organizing by function **272**	committee **277**
informal organization **261**	matrix organization **267**	organizing by geography **273**	organizational culture **278**
division of labor **261**	span of control **268**	organizing by customer **274**	grapevine **280**
responsibility **262**	centralization **269**	organizing by process **274**	outsourcing **280**
authority **262**	decentralization **269**	self-directed work teams **276**	virtual company **281**
accountability **262**	tall organizations **271**	cross-functional teams **277**	
chain of command **263**	flat organizations **271**		
organization chart **264**	departmentalization **272**		
line organization **265**			
line employees **265**			

● **Review Questions**

1. The manager of production at Compsicon gives employees in the disk division full production responsibility but no authority for making decisions, nor are they accountable for their actions. Why is this *not* proper delegation?

2. At Alpha Company, reporting responsibility is in a direct line from top to bottom. At Beta Company, employees involved directly in production are provided advice and support by accountants and others. What type of organizational design is employed by each company? What are the advantages and disadvantages of each type?

3. What are the advantages and disadvantages of a matrix organization?

4. What characteristics differentiate horizontal from vertical organizations?

5. Why do organizations departmentalize by product? Why might organizing by function or process be more efficient than product departmentalization?

6. Why might a company be forced to downsize? What does this mean in terms of organizational structure?

7. Waldo, who works for a printer, belongs to a work team assigned to four-color brochures. His friend Elena is part of a team responsible for checking printing quality throughout the plant. What type of team does each belong to? Describe how the two types of teams differ.

8. What is a company's informal organization? How is it useful?

9. A company that manufactures brooms and other small, household items has a large payroll to meet every week. How would it benefit from outsourcing?

10. What is a virtual company and what advantages does it offer over a traditional company?

• Critical Thinking Questions

1. You work in a small restaurant as one of three people waiting on tables, and the owner has asked you to be sure his customers are happy with the service during his two-week vacation. He has not, however, given you authority over the other two waiters. What is the danger in this situation? Can the restaurant's informal organization help you? Explain why or why not.

2. As the manager of a large hotel, you are trying to think of ways to provide better service to your guests. What kinds of decisions could you delegate to your employees to help make your hotel excel at customer service? Give some examples for the following employees: desk clerk, housekeeper, limousine driver, and room service phone clerk.

3. Many companies today are trying to change from a functional organization to a process organization. How would an organization chart look before and after such a change? Draw a simplified organization chart showing each structure. Base your drawing on a company you have worked for or an organization with which you are familiar, such as your college.

4. If you were assigned the responsibility of establishing a team to improve the quality of your company's highest income-producing product line, what qualities would you look for in team members? What parts of the company would you want to have represented on the team? Explain your choices.

5. Many college students have established virtual companies in their dorm rooms using a computer and a telephone line. What kind of business could you start, using your special skills and resources? Explain how you would network your business with other firms to complement your skills and talents and compensate for your weak areas. (*Hint*: To refresh yourself on networking, see Chapter 6.)

REVIEW CASE *Making Teams Work at GM's Saturn Corp.*[38]

Research suggested to General Motors Corp. management that employees are most productive when they feel they are a part of the decision-making process. This idea gave birth to the company's revolutionary approach to management at its Saturn plant.

"The primary goal is to create a culture in which employees accept ownership for the direct labor functions they perform," says R. Timothy Epps, vice president of people systems at Saturn. United Auto Workers vice president Joseph Rypkowski agrees: "We're trying to get more involvement in decision-making and ownership for activities that traditionally have been performed by management or resource-type people." With both sides cooperating, many decisions are now made by the people who produce the product.

The Saturn mission statement makes it clear to employees that they are to be involved in decision making in the areas that affect them. These decisions are reached by a "70 percent comfortable" rule of consensus; that is, each team member must feel at least 70 percent comfortable with every one of the team's decisions.

For example, assembly workers have responsibility for devising quality control procedures, building their own budgets, parts handling, and to some degree, ordering their own materials. Team members even hire new team members and teach each other new tasks. In the case of budgeting, for example, team members are trained to determine the number of products to be produced and to estimate the costs of scrap metal and other material, as well as indirect costs. They de-

velop income estimates and estimate the amount of time each person will spend annually in training, on vacation, and so on. These data become the basis for Saturn operating budgets. And when the time comes to put what has been learned into practice, experienced team leaders are there to help as needed.

There are varieties of teams. If work functions are complex, requiring a lot of skills, smaller teams (of 6 to 12 members) are more effective. If the work is relatively simple and repetitive, teams are sufficiently large so members have something meaningful to manage. If the work involves a lot of technology, people who operate equipment might be teamed with those who maintain—and even design—the equipment.

The ultimate goal is to have semiautonomous, self-directed work teams in which decisions are made by consensus. Currently, there are approximately 150 work teams of varying sizes at Saturn, each a critical link in the company's decision-making process.

1. Is the organizational structure at Saturn centralized or decentralized? How do you know?

2. How does Saturn's structure help to encourage greater involvement and communication among employees?

3. How does the team approach contribute to developing a high-quality product at Saturn?

4. List three ways teams can make a company more competitive. Do you think there are any disadvantages or problems in the way Saturn uses teams?

CRITICAL THINKING CASE *Growing Small at Xerox Corp.*

Paul Allaire outlined a bold vision for Xerox: "We intend to create a company that combines the best of both worlds . . . speed, flexibility, accountability and creativity that come from being part of a small, highly focused organization . . . economies of scale, the access to resources and the strategic vision that a large corporation can provide."[39] The former head of Rank Xerox, the company's London-based subsidiary, and now CEO of the entire organization, Allaire has successfully restructured operations, cutting staff 40 percent and reducing costs by $200 million.

Allaire first sought to replace the company's traditional functional departments with groups of relatively independent business units, each typically consisting of one or more self-directed teams. The business units were then to be arranged into "networked," "clustered," or "horizontal" organizations. He aimed for an organizational structure that would be responsive to fast-changing technology and constantly shifting markets.

As Allaire said at the time, "I have to change the company substantially to be more market driven. If we do what's right for the customer, our market share and our return on assets will take care of themselves."[40] In an initial effort to speed up customer delivery dates, a team was formed using people pulled out of their regular jobs in such functions as distribution, accounting, and sales. The team found that a major bottleneck in the delivery process was paperwork that did not correspond to the item being delivered. So the team developed a system that tracks every copier through the distribution process and makes sure that it and the accompanying paperwork match.

Changing the process helped Xerox increase customer satisfaction from 70 percent to 90 percent, as measured by a company survey. "You can't get people to focus on only the bottom line," says Allaire. "You have to give them an objective like 'satisfy the customer' that everyone can relate to. It's the only way to break down those barriers and get people from different functions working together."[41]

Soon after Xerox revamped its distribution system, it tackled inventory by forming an informal coordinating group made up of people from accounting, sales, distribution, and administration that cut across management levels. The team found that no one was coordinating the flow of copiers through the manufacturing process, into the warehouse, and out the door. At every stage, each department was ordering extra inventory out of the fear of being caught short. The coordinating team took a look at the whole chain of events and put in place new procedures to ensure that everyone along the line could always get as many copiers as needed. The result was a reduction in inventory costs of $200 million a year.[42] To further reduce expenses, Xerox plans to cut 10,000 more jobs by the end of 1996. This represents approximately 10 percent of its work force of just under 100,000 employees.[43]

1. Allaire's philosophy makes the customer the focus of the organization. Do you agree with his point of view? Can this be a win-win situation both for Xerox customers and Xerox employees? Why or why not?

2. If you were the CEO of Xerox, how would you communicate your customer service philosophy to employees throughout the organization? What measures would you take to ensure that each employee was personally working toward this corporate goal?

3. Suppose you have been called upon as a consultant to advise a service organization—a carpet-cleaning company. The company has a tall structure and a narrow span of control, and upper management grants very little authority to frontline employees. Customer complaints are increasing because work crews are showing up hours later than their scheduled start times. How could you apply Allaire's approach to change the organizational structure? Explain what changes you would suggest and how they could help the company.

Critical Thinking with the ONE MINUTE MANAGER

"Wow!" Carlos exclaimed.

"What now, Carlos?" asked the One Minute Manager.

"I didn't realize that organizing a company was so complicated. No wonder managers get paid the big bucks!"

"Well," said the One Minute Manager, "there's a lot more to running a company than designing its organization. Besides, although there are lots of different things to consider in designing an organization, smart managers keep their organizations as simple and efficient as possible."

"How do they do that?" Carlos asked.

"Let's consider 3M again, but this time let's think about its formal organization. Although 3M is a huge corporation, its management has divided the company into several smaller groups, which they call *sectors*. The sectors comprise specific collections of related products.[44] This facilitates communication and allows resources to be shared easily within a group."

"So," Carlos asked tentatively, "bigger isn't necessarily better?"

"That's right, Carlos. In the case of an organization's structure, smaller is often better. It is the challenge of the manager to get the work of the organization done while keeping things as simple as possible."

"I see. I guess that makes everyone's job easier."

"Right again, Carlos. The less the organization gets in the way of its employees, the better job they can do. Now, I have some work to do—don't let the door hit you on the way out!"

1. Every business has a formal and an informal organization. Pick a business that you are familiar with and describe its formal and informal organizations. Who is in each organization and how do the two organizations differ from one another?

2. Some businesses, fast-food restaurants for example, depend on strong central control from corporate headquarters to ensure the consistency of image and products offered to the buying public. Discuss the ways that centralization can stifle the creativity and initiative of front-line employees and managers.

3. The use of employee teams in American companies is on the rise. It is clear that teams benefit the organizations that employ them. What direct benefits do employees who participate in teams receive for their efforts? Do these benefits also benefit the organization? How?

10 Producing Quality Goods and Services

In this chapter, we look closely at the way businesses produce goods and services. We begin by examining some of the decisions businesses make about production. We then explore several different kinds of production processes and some of the activities that transform resources into goods and services. We conclude with a close look at some of the ways businesses are controlling production-related expenses in today's turbulent business environment. You will see how important it is for every employee to participate in managing and improving the production processes of the business in which he or she works. After reading this chapter, you will be able to reach the learning goals below.

Learning Goals

1. Describe the four components of the production process.
2. Identify the five main criteria used to select production sites.
3. List the steps in production planning and control.
4. Identify the foundation activity in production scheduling and give two examples of scheduling techniques that are based on it.
5. Explain the difference between push and pull processes and their importance in inventory control.
6. Distinguish between hard and soft manufacturing.
7. Define cost of quality and explain how businesses are managing this cost.
8. Compare reengineering and total quality management as improvement processes.
9. Identify two analytical approaches used in process improvement.

A Visit to the Factory

Donning safety goggles, Joanna and Carlos followed the One Minute Manager into the brightly lit building where conveyor belts connected large workstations, each with its own computer terminal. At some stations, employees deftly manipulated work; at others, machines seemed to perform tasks automatically. Reaching a small conference room, the threesome stepped inside and closed the glass door, shutting out the loud hum of the machinery.

"Well, what do you think? Does the production line look the way you expected?" the One Minute Manager asked.

"Not really," Joanna answered. "I envisioned hundreds of people working on a long line, but there can't be more than 20 people out there."

"And it's very neat," Carlos added. "I expected stacks of parts piled under benches and on shelves along the walls."

"Both of you would have been right in my generation. But factories have changed enormously in the last decade. For example, it's very expensive to store large numbers of parts when they aren't being used—they break, they get lost, and they become outdated. Now we buy only what we can use in a day. Each morning, our suppliers tap into our computer network, check our production plans for the day, and then deliver exactly what we need."

"It sounds like a great system," Carlos added, "but what happens if the power fails, or a part is defective and you can't use it? Don't you stock extras just in case?"

"We can't control everything, of course, but we didn't under the old system either. This approach works—we used to measure defects in parts per thousand, but now we measure them in parts per *million*. We work with our suppliers to help them make sure we receive perfect parts. Some bigger companies even run training sessions for their suppliers. Ford, General Motors, and Chrysler formed the not-for-profit American Supplier Institute to train U.S. auto suppliers and other U.S. businesses in new management methods. And some producers hold annual quality contests to reward excellent suppliers with recognition and prizes."

"Eliminating defects must be difficult," Joanna observed. "How can companies make sure their employees' work is always perfect?"

"These are big topics, and you'll learn more about them in your course. But I can give you a clue—see those flip charts covered with diagrams and lists over in the corner? Teams of our employees spend time in this room every day, and they analyze their own work processes to find ways of improving them. Making people responsible for their own work pays off in better quality. Our suppliers use the same approach."

"That's the biggest difference from my expectations," Carlos concluded. "The fact that every employee is involved in thinking about and improving the production process explains all the other differences, doesn't it?"

Production: From Resources to Goods and Services

Movie producer Alfred Hitchcock, creator of such hair-raising classics as *Psycho* and *The Birds*, was once detained by airport customs officials as he entered France. Looking suspiciously at the passport that described Hitchcock's occupation as "producer," the agent demanded, "What do you produce?" Hitchcock smoothly answered, "Gooseflesh."[1]

In a sense, we are all producers, for this is the simplest way to describe work. You may recall from Chapter 1 that **production** is the transformation of resources into goods and services that have value to customers. In businesses, this transformation takes the form of production processes, which have four components[2]:

1. *Inputs*—the four factors of production we mentioned in Chapter 2: land, capital, labor, and entrepreneurship. Land here means all nonhuman natural resources. To design comfortable and durable footwear, for example, Nike must have access to leather, rubber, cotton, and other raw materials to construct tops, soles, and laces. Some of the parts of the shoes will be manufactured by subcontractors—Nike's suppliers. The company must also have access to capital—buildings, transportation vehicles, office equipment, machinery, and financial resources to pay for raw materials and labor. Labor will be needed not only to construct the shoes but also to design them, to research customer reaction to the designs, to advertise them, and so on. And, of course, the company needs the creativity and entrepreneurial spirit that gives birth to ideas for a unique shoe style customers will want to buy.

2. *Activities that add value*—for Nike, these activities include engineering activities in various U.S. locations, assembly-line activities in dozens of foreign countries, and many other activities.

3. *Outputs*—finished goods, services, or ideas. Nike sells shoes, which are goods. But many production processes produce services. For example, USAir's production process orchestrates people, planes, fuel, water, food, and maintenance expertise to produce rapid long-distance transportation.

4. *The option of being repeated*—Nike's production processes can continue to turn out a successful line of shoes as long as customers are willing to buy them. Figure 10.1 shows the first three components, but you should remember that the fourth is always an option.

✓ **production**

The transformation of resources into goods and services that have value to customers.

1. Describe the four components of the production process.

figure **10.1**   **The Production Process**

Inputs	Activities that add value	Outputs
• Raw materials	• Design	Finished goods and services
• Component parts	• Manufacturing	
• Human skills and expertise	• Service agreements	
	• Warranties	

The production process has three components—inputs, activities that add value, and outputs—and the option of being repeated.

production and operations management

The coordination of an organization's resources and activities to produce finished goods or services.

As you can see, production processes cover a lot of territory. Before examining them in further depth, however, let's stop for an overview of production and operations management.

Production and Operations Management

Production and operations management is the coordination of an organization's resources and activities to produce finished goods or services. In the past, many people used a more restricted term, *production management*. *Operations* has been incorporated into that term to emphasize that production processes also apply to services.

Managers of production processes are accountable both to senior managers of the business and to its customers. Their title may be *factory manager, operations manager*, or *production manager*, but whatever the title, their job includes helping to select production sites, planning and controlling production processes, scheduling to match output to demand, materials management, and overseeing automated production processes.

Site Selection

2. Identify the five main criteria used to select production sites.

With rare exceptions, production facilities are expensive and permanent and cannot easily be moved. As a result, site selection is an important decision that can increase or decrease costs and affect the future profits of a business. In general, production sites are chosen on the basis of five main criteria: labor issues, government receptiveness, conditions of infrastructure, proximity to suppliers, and convenience for customers. Let's look at each briefly.

Site Selection

Bill Gates was attending Harvard University near Boston when he launched Microsoft Corp. Rather than setting up shop there or in California's Silicon Valley, however, he decided that there's no place like home. So he returned to the Seattle, Washington, area to build Microsoft's headquarters on the beautiful campus outside these windows. Like a magnet, Microsoft's presence has attracted an abundant, talented pool of skilled labor, both from the Pacific Northwest and from outside the region.

Labor Issues

Companies that produce services rather than goods are particularly dependent on the location of skilled labor. A company may want to go to where the most productive or technically skilled workers can easily be found. Certain regions of the United States are known for their skilled labor pools. Silicon Valley in California and the Route 128 area around Boston, for example, contain large numbers of computer programmers and technicians. Michigan has a reputation as the home of many skilled auto workers.

In this age of global competition, businesses may even choose to locate production facilities outside the United States, in countries where skilled labor costs less. Many software companies now do some of their programming in India, where highly trained programmers will work for lower wages than those expected by their U.S. counterparts.

Companies may also choose to avoid areas for labor-related reasons, such as high union activity and the higher wage and benefits packages sometimes associated with union labor.

Government Receptiveness

Government receptiveness influences site selection because many towns, states, and even foreign countries offer tax breaks or favorable regulatory environments to attract business. Competition among states has become intense. In 1993, the U.S. National Governors Association recommended that states focus their spending on improving infrastructures to attract business, rather than on offering direct incentives in the form of corporate tax credits, loans, or other such concessions. Shortly after the recommendations were announced, however, Alabama offered incentives worth $253 million to Mercedes-Benz to locate a plant there.[3] Alabama is not alone in trying to convince businesses to locate within its borders. California, Illinois, Louisiana, Minnesota, Nebraska, New York, Ohio, and many other states have offered similar incentives at various times.

Condition of Infrastructure

Infrastructure, from roads and rails to electricity and water systems, can be a critical factor in site selection. General Motors and other automobile manufacturers must carefully place their production facilities near the railroads they rely on to transport parts and finished cars.

Proximity to Suppliers

Production facilities must be convenient to suppliers. The Weyerhaeuser Company, like many other businesses, must consider both suppliers and infrastructure when it chooses locations. To avoid costly transportation expenses, Weyerhaeuser facilities must be near forests—the source of the logs that are a necessary input in its production processes—and also near major highways, so that trucks can transport finished goods from the company's lumber mills to customers.

Convenience for Customers

Many services must be produced where they are consumed, so some businesses place multiple production facilities within easy reach of their customer markets. McDonald's might be able to cook burgers for less in a single, huge factory, but they would hardly be hot by the time they reached consumers. Patagonia has located its customer service center in Bozeman, Montana, home

capacity
The quantity of goods or services a business can produce under normal working conditions.

to many of the people who use Patagonia products for outdoor recreation. According to Yvon Chouinard, chair of Patagonia, "We need to seek out and hire 'dirt bags'; these are the passionate outdoor people who are our core customers." Chouinard believes these employees understand the company's products and can offer useful information to like-minded customers.[4]

Production Planning and Control

3. List the steps in production planning and control.

In the planning stage, it is necessary to analyze the business plan and long-range production plans of the company and then to create a working plan that specifies how these will be carried out. Production control involves determining whether current performance meets the standards set out in the plans. Production management activities focus on the planning and control process illustrated in Figure 10.2.

Production Planning

Production planning flows downward from the organization's overall business plan and ends with a set of specific working plans that state who will do what, when, and where.

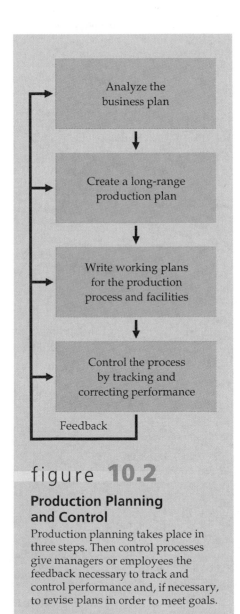

figure 10.2

Production Planning and Control

Production planning takes place in three steps. Then control processes give managers or employees the feedback necessary to track and control performance and, if necessary, to revise plans in order to meet goals.

Analyzing the Business Plan Before making more specific plans, the production manager analyzes the organization's overall business plan. For instance, assume a company's business plan calls for it to start selling its products in two additional foreign markets within the next 12 months. To ensure that the business will have an adequate supply of products to reach this goal, the production manager will create a long-range production plan to increase output.

Creating a Long-Range Production Plan Increasing output means increasing **capacity**, the quantity of goods or services a business can produce under normal working conditions. Capacity places a practical limit on sales, since obviously a business cannot sell what it cannot produce. If a business plans to expand and increase sales, the production manager must add more capacity, in one or more of three ways:

1. *Increase the efficiency of current production processes by running them faster or by reducing mistakes.* If a production process can be run twice as fast, capacity will double even though no new equipment or building has been added. Similarly, if fewer products have to be reworked or thrown away, capacity will increase.

2. *Increase the size or number of production processes.* The company can buy new, bigger equipment, hire more people, or construct new buildings in order to increase production capacity. This is an expensive approach, which will be used only if the production manager is sure the planned growth will really occur. The Big Three automobile manufacturers—Chrysler, Ford, and GM—are using a variation on this option by redesigning and refurbishing factories they closed during the recent recession. Although still expensive, this option saves on building-construction expenses.[5]

3. *Subcontract to other companies to use their production processes.* This option carries lower risk than the other two, since it adds capacity by renting instead of buying it. But costs per unit produced are usually higher when capacity is rented than when it is purchased.

Whichever option is chosen, the long-range plan must be converted to a working plan.

Developing Working Plans Working plans for running the production process specify who does what, when, and where. Working plans generally take two forms: a master production plan and a facilities plan. The *master production schedule* lists products, the facilities where they will be made, and when they will be made.

The *facilities plan* specifies the location and layout of facilities that will be needed. In some cases, the product is so large that a **fixed layout** is necessary—a plan in which all equipment and workers are brought together at one stationary location. Although facilities layouts have traditionally been described as product layout, assembly-line layout, and process layout, many observers now believe a more useful contrast is assembly line versus cell, as shown in Figure 10.3. In an **assembly line**, the product flows through a sequence of workstations where employees perform specialized tasks. The arrangement may be a straight line, a circle, or a series of parallel lines that provide different paths for multiple versions of the product.

An increasingly common alternative to assembly lines is the **cell layout**, in which small teams of workers make entire components, functioning as a subprocess within a larger production process. According to a recent survey, more than half of all U.S. factories are currently experimenting with cell manufacturing.[6] At Harley-Davidson's U.S. factories, workers in stations along a long production line used to take a full week to produce cylinder heads for motorcycle motors. After the switch to a cell layout, workers can now make an entire cylinder head in less than three hours. As an additional benefit, Harley-Davidson's production process uses one-third less floor space since it was switched to cell manufacturing.[7]

In addition to layouts, working plans also include a *detailed schedule* that specifies exactly what various employees and suppliers will need to do to meet the master production schedule. These schedules state what parts to order, when parts will be needed, and how many people will need to work on each production shift. They may also include directions for improving the production process—for example, by specifying that employees will form improvement teams, receive training in analyzing production processes, and come up

fixed layout

Work layout in which all equipment and workers are brought together at one stationary location.

assembly line

Work layout in which the product flows through a sequence of workstations where employees perform specialized tasks.

cell layout

Work layout in which small teams of workers make entire components, functioning as a subprocess in a larger production process.

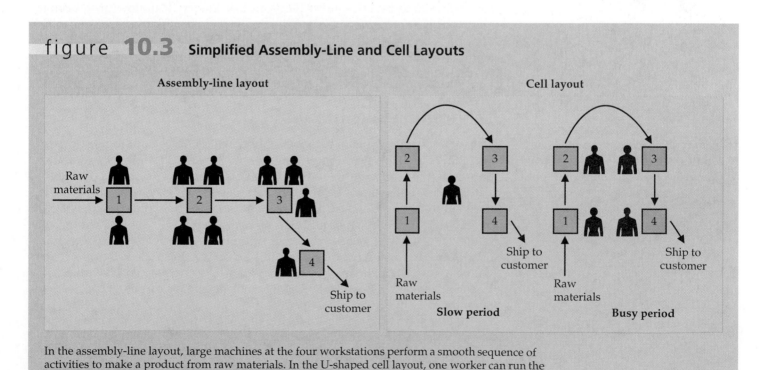

figure **10.3**   **Simplified Assembly-Line and Cell Layouts**

In the assembly-line layout, large machines at the four workstations perform a smooth sequence of activities to make a product from raw materials. In the U-shaped cell layout, one worker can run the machines at all four workstations during slow periods. More workers can be added during busy times.

✓ production control

Five-step subprocess of planning, routing, scheduling, dispatching, and follow-up.

✓ production planning

Estimating materials and resources that will be needed and stating where and when they will be used.

✓ routing

Deciding what value-adding activities should take place, where, and when.

✓ scheduling

Preparing a detailed timetable for labor, materials, and production activities.

✓ dispatching

Sending people, materials, and equipment to where they are needed.

✓ follow-up

Activities by managers or employees to compare actual work performed with plans and schedules for that work.

4. Identify the foundation activity in production scheduling and give two examples of scheduling techniques that are based on it.

with improvements in the way they do their work. You will learn more about these topics later in this chapter.

Production Control

Through production controls, managers try to determine whether current performance will allow the organization to meet its planned goals. Production managers observe their production processes, talk regularly with the people working on them, and gather and analyze many measures of performance. They make sure that the right number of products are produced and delivered to customers and that quality and design targets are met for each product. They also track efforts to improve the production process, monitoring progress and identifying areas in which employees may need help.

Production control is a five-step subprocess of planning, routing, scheduling, dispatching, and follow-up. Each is a necessary part of the control of producing complex goods or services.

1. **Production planning**: Estimating materials and resources that will be needed and stating where and when they will be used.
2. **Routing**: Deciding what value-adding activities should take place, where, and when.
3. **Scheduling**: Preparing a detailed timetable for labor, materials, and production activities.
4. **Dispatching**: Sending people, materials, and equipment to where they are needed.
5. **Follow-up**: Activities by managers or employees to compare actual work performed with plans and schedules for that work.

Follow-up is most effective when detailed plans exist and when careful analysis has been performed to indicate the best routes and schedules. With these preparations, managers or production employees know exactly what *should* happen, minute by minute, so they can ask intelligent follow-up questions. Note that we say managers *or* production employees. That's because production control was traditionally the job of managers, but employee empowerment and total quality management are changing that by giving production employees the skills and responsibilities to control and improve their own processes.

Scheduling Techniques

Scheduling is the timing of activities, and time is so important to most production processes that scheduling techniques have received a great deal of attention, both in research journals and in business practice.

All scheduling efforts begin with a detailed list of tasks, which provides the foundation for future schedules. Listing each task required to produce a good or service is no easy task itself! What tasks are required to make even the simplest product—say, the desk you are working on? A carpenter would probably list dozens, but we may be able to think of only a few. Scheduling must start with careful observations of the work that will be performed or with discussions with experts—the people who, like our imaginary carpenter, do the work or study it.

Let's say we studied desk making and listed these tasks: purchase wood, season wood to dry it, cut tops, cut legs, cut braces, sand, drill screw holes, glue and screw, wipe off dust, seal with polyurethane, dry. That's 11 tasks—but we forgot to include purchasing other materials (screws, sandpaper, and sealer)—12 tasks to schedule! You may be able to think of more, but let's assume our list is complete and we are ready to write a production schedule.

Gantt Charts

The most common scheduling technique is the Gantt chart, named for its inventor, Henry L. Gantt. A **Gantt chart** is a bar chart that shows both *when* tasks take place and *how long* they should take. Figure 10.4 is a Gantt chart showing the tasks required to make desks. Note that it arranges tasks according to when they must be started. An experienced production manager could tell by looking at this chart that buying wood is the key to successful production. This step has to happen five weeks before construction starts, or the wood will warp and quality will be poor. If the manager forgets to order enough wood, the process will be delayed far longer than if he or she forgets to schedule the cutting of enough desk legs and more have to be cut.

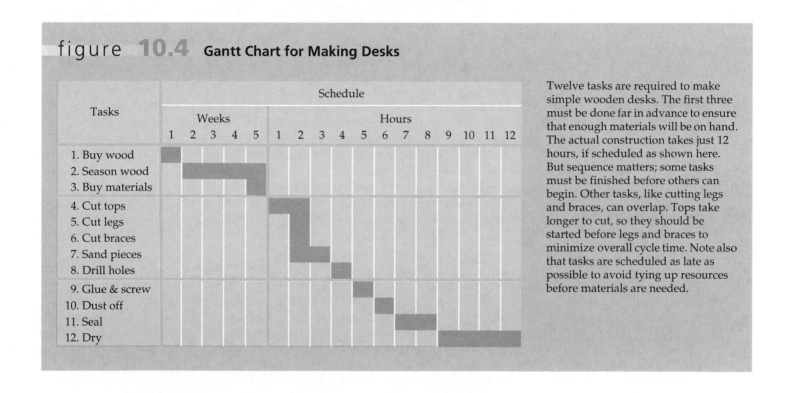

figure **10.4** **Gantt Chart for Making Desks**

Twelve tasks are required to make simple wooden desks. The first three must be done far in advance to ensure that enough materials will be on hand. The actual construction takes just 12 hours, if scheduled as shown here. But sequence matters; some tasks must be finished before others can begin. Other tasks, like cutting legs and braces, can overlap. Tops take longer to cut, so they should be started before legs and braces to minimize overall cycle time. Note also that tasks are scheduled as late as possible to avoid tying up resources before materials are needed.

Critical Path Method and PERT

Another scheduling technique is often used for complex processes with many more steps than the desk-making process above. The **critical path method (CPM)** highlights the sequence of tasks that will determine the minimum time in which a project can be completed. Production managers sometimes use CPM charts to find the critical path in a process. Each task appears as an arrow, labeled with its name and the time required to complete it. Each arrow leads into other tasks that depend on its completion. In a complex process, the arrows form an intricate maze. By summing the times along each possible path through this maze, a manager can find the *critical path*—the one sequence of tasks that takes the most time to complete in a given project. Any delay on this critical path will delay the project's end date: a one-day delay will cause the project to run late by one day, and so on.

You can see the importance of finding the critical path if you imagine that you are a builder and must commit to a time when the owners can move into their new house. Although building a house is a complex process made up of

 Gantt chart

Bar chart that shows both *when* tasks take place and *how long* they should take.

 critical path method (CPM)

Scheduling technique that highlights the sequence of tasks that will determine the minimum time in which a project can be completed.

hundreds of individual types of tasks, the critical path usually follows this sequence: excavate foundation; pour foundation; frame house; run wiring, plumbing, and heating; hang and tape sheet rock. These tasks are on the critical path because most other tasks depend upon their completion. The owners cannot move in until the floors and walls are finished and the bathroom works, but these depend on the completion of the critical path tasks. You cannot trim and paint until sheetrock is up, you cannot put up sheetrock until wires and pipes are run through the studs of the frame, and you cannot frame until the foundation is ready.

A more elaborate adaptation of the CPM technique uses a range of four estimates for each task's time. **PERT**, short for **program evaluation and review technique**, is a scheduling technique that arrives at a statistical average time for each task in a production process. It then identifies the critical path using statistics rather than by eye.

Materials Management

An essential part of production planning and control is **materials management**, the planning and organization of the flow of materials needed to support the production process. Every business that buys raw materials or assembled parts for use in its production process must decide how much to order and when to order. If the business maintains inventories of parts, how big should they be and where should they be located? If the business chooses to have suppliers deliver parts as needed, which suppliers should be included in the planning? How many or how much of each part or raw material should the purchasing department buy, and when and where should they be delivered? Such questions are so important that larger businesses usually have a materials manager or purchasing manager whose job it is to deal just with the issues of materials management.

Materials management includes **inventory control**, a system for determining the amount of inventory a business will have on hand and for tracking and maintaining that inventory. **Inventories** are stores of raw materials, partially made products, or finished products. Traditionally, production processes have used inventories to protect against uncertainties, but inventories are expensive. Monthly inventories of U.S. durable goods manufacturers are worth about $250 billion on average, and nondurable goods inventories total about $100 billion. Together, these two figures equal 80 percent of U.S. gross domestic product for a typical month![8] Inventories not only tie up money, but they also require the company to spend time on inventory management and overproduction. And in a fast-changing business environment, inventories may go out of date before they are used.

Traditional inventory practices used in U.S. business are an example of a **push process**, which produces goods in quantities estimated in management plans. (Services cannot be stored.) Push processes tend to create one-way planning and communication from the company to the customer. Half-gallon containers of chocolate ice cream, which are stored in your local supermarket's freezer, were produced in a push process, based on someone's estimate that you would buy them. Push lines work well when identical products must be made over and over, like those half-gallons of chocolate ice cream. But given this process, you're out of luck if your fantasy ice cream is some exotic combination of flavors that wasn't included in the estimate.

In contrast, a **pull process** produces goods and services only when a company receives a customer's order. Pull processes work best when flexibility is needed. The ice cream cone you receive after placing your order for a double-

5. Explain the difference between push and pull processes and their importance in inventory control.

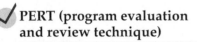 **PERT (program evaluation and review technique)**

Scheduling technique that arrives at a statistical average time for each task in a production process.

✓ **materials management**

The planning and organization of the flow of materials needed to support the production process.

✓ **inventory control**

System of determining the amount of inventory a business will have on hand and for tracking and maintaining that inventory.

✓ **inventories**

Stores of raw materials, partially made products, or finished products.

✓ **push process**

Production process that produces goods in quantities estimated in management plans.

✓ **pull process**

Production process that produces goods and services only when a company receives a customer's order.

skills check

Push Versus Pull Exercise

Supplies needed: 2 copies of this textbook, 2 pens, 2 packs of index cards. General Directions: Form the class into two long lines. Each line is to perform a production job: supplying the instructor with answers to tough questions about material in this chapter. The instructor plays the role of customer. The person closest to the instructor plays the role of salesperson. At the far end of each line sits a student with a copy of this textbook, a pen, and a pile of index cards. Students who are between the two ends of each line have the job of passing answers as quickly as possible.

Each line must follow a different set of rules, as outlined below. Each has 10 minutes, strictly measured, to meet and develop a strategy.

Line 1

Line 1 is a traditional *push process*. In this line, the student with the textbook plays the role of a traditional manager. He or she must try to anticipate what questions the instructor might ask and must prepare ready-to-use answers for those questions. Line 1 should use the 10-minute strategy session to decide what answers to produce and hold in inventory. Students may not communicate with anyone but the persons standing to their right and left in the line. To stand a chance of winning, the push process team will have to generate a lot of answers, write them on cards, pass them to the front, and hold them in inventory. The instructor will direct questions to the "salesperson"—the first student in line. Line 1 members cannot communicate these questions to the student with the textbook. The salesperson can offer the instructor an appropriate answer only if it happens to be in inventory. However, if the salesperson has the right answer, he or she can give it to the instructor very quickly.

Line 2

Line 2 is a *pull process*. Again the instructor poses questions to the "salesperson" at the end of the line. But in Line 2, members can communicate and discuss ideas, although only with each person next to them. The person at the far end of this line receives the question, looks up the answer in the textbook, writes it on a card, and then passes the card back down to the instructor. Line 2 should use the 10-minute strategy session to decide how best to help the student with the book look up answers and how to check their quality and rework them if necessary.

Line 1, the push line, has an advantage when standard, repetitive types of questions are asked because these are easy to plan for. Line 2, which is more flexible than Line 1 and better able to respond to customer needs, has an advantage if the instructor asks tough, varied questions. And because Line 2 has no inventory of cards, it will have no wasted inventory.

Teams should compete for 30 minutes. At the end of that time, the team with the higher score wins. Answers are scored as follows:

- Right answers: 4 points each.
- Unused inventory answers: Subtract 1 point for each.
- Wrong answers (defects): Subtract 6 points for each.

---

scoop butterscotch ripple rolled in coconut is produced by a pull process. Your demand "pulls" this product from its producer. The skills check entitled "Push Versus Pull Exercise" describes a class project designed to let you experience some of the advantages and disadvantages of these two processes. Your instructor will explain the exercise in detail before it begins.

The first large producers to adopt pull processes were Japanese auto and electronics makers in the 1970s and 1980s. Toyota pioneered one such system, the *kanban* system, which uses cards to signal that a part is needed. (*Kanban* is the Japanese word for card.) The cards flow from the far end of the production line, where employees receive a daily order for the exact number of cars the factory must manufacture to fill customer orders it has already received.

Empowerment is a central requirement in *kanban* or other pull systems because pull processes depend on well-trained employees with the knowledge and power to improve their own work. In Toyota's *kanban* system, each employee has the skill and responsibility to identify any flaw or problem, and the authority to shut down the entire production line until it is fixed.

✓ **automation**

Performing mechanical operations with little or no direct human involvement.

✓ **just-in-time (JIT) system**

Method of inventory control that ensures parts are delivered or assembled only as they are needed.

✓ **computer-aided design (CAD)**

The use of computers to help people design better products.

✓ **computer-aided manufacturing (CAM)**

The use of computers to control machines that produce goods.

✓ **robotics**

The use of computer-controlled machines to perform repetitive production tasks.

Automation of Production Processes

Automation is performing mechanical operations with little or no direct human involvement. Automation has been so important in improving the quality and efficiency of production processes in most industries that managing machines and computers is now a central part of every production manager's job.

Although Toyota's *kanban* system operates manually inside Toyota plants, the connection to outside suppliers is automated. The daily production plan is transmitted electronically to suppliers, who then use it to determine the number and types of parts they must deliver each day. This producer-supplier arrangement is an example of a **just-in-time (JIT) system**, a method of inventory control that ensures that parts are delivered or assembled only as they are needed. Businesses that use *kanban* or other pull systems must work with suppliers to improve the speed and accuracy of delivery of raw materials or parts, as well as to improve the quality of those inputs.

Another form of automation, **computer-aided design (CAD)**, uses computers to help people design better products. In combination with other computer graphics techniques, CAD allows designers to sit at a computer terminal and explore design options to see how they will affect the overall structure of a product. In many cases, CAD can also shorten the time required for the design phase and allow designers to pinpoint problems before they occur in the real product.

The factory described in the doing business box entitled "Spalding's Production Line Produces Satisfied Customers" has based its new production line on **computer-aided manufacturing (CAM)**, the use of computers to control machines that produce goods. Several years ago, this internationally known sporting goods supplier completely redesigned its golf ball production process in Chicopee, Massachusetts. It added automated handling and production equipment, trained employees in process control and machine maintenance, and cut the time of production from weeks to hours. These improvements made it unnecessary to move production overseas, and the millions of dollars of new equipment hum and whir in the same huge factory Spalding has occupied for decades in this small town in the western part of the state. Many of the people now working on the production line are second- and third-generation Spalding employees.

But there are differences between the work methods of earlier and present generations in this Spalding facility. It used to take hundreds of people weeks to make the million balls that the automated factory now can make in one day. Those earlier generations used to wind the cores of golf balls from rubber strands and add the many coats of covering and paint by hand. Now computers control the machines that form and move golf balls and that are the real stars of the production process. The current generation of employees plays a supporting role by programming computers and setting up and maintaining the machines they run. Some of those machines are robots, for Spalding's design also incorporates **robotics**—the use of computer-controlled machines to perform repetitive production tasks. Robots turn the golf balls while they are painted and coated.

Robots play an important role in production processes in many factories. At Nypro Inc., a plastics manufacturer that turns out diskettes for Verbatim and disposable contact lenses for Johnson & Johnson, robots are an accepted part of production processes. Nypro president Gordon B. Lankton states, "We have robots on every machine now. We had none 15 years ago. Lots of people think of robots as devices to minimize labor, which, of course, they do. But that's not the main reason. The main reason is quality."[9]

Automobile manufacturers also use robotics for a variety of tasks. At Toyota's factories, for example, robots weld pieces and bolt parts to car frames

doing business

Spalding's Production Line Produces Satisfied Customers

Spalding Sports Worldwide's factories make more golf balls than any other company in the world, providing them by the containerload to dozens of foreign countries and by the truckload to golf courses, stores, and specialty customers across the United States.

Consider this computer-aided manufacturing process. In a hangar-sized warehouse, huge machines whir and click, first heating and mixing rubber compounds into palm-sized plugs, then trucking them by the cartload to molding machines, where people pop them into half-circle molds and pull levers to drop the other set of half circles on them with great pressure and heat. After a sudden sizzle and steaming, dozens of blue, hard balls fall out of the presses.

Next, people trim away extra rubber and pop the balls into hoppers leading to miles of tubing suspended from the ceilings. A forced air vacuum sucks balls through the tubes and past Y-shaped intersections, where a computerized controller splits the flow, sending them to a production line. Next, each ball drops into a coating machine that molds special white plastics into delicate aerodynamic outside coatings, using one of dozens of proprietary patterns of dimples.

As all this happens, red electronic eyes scan each ball, hundreds a minute, watching for defective balls, which are pushed into a hopper beneath the machine. Every half hour, an employee comes by, grabs a ball from the machine's conveyor belt, weighs and measures it, examines it for imperfections under an ultraviolet light, and chops it in half to make sure its blue core is centered and properly formed. The employee then carefully records the data on a chart next to the machine and, if necessary,

makes minor adjustments or even shuts the machine down and calls for expert help from a mechanic.

If no adjustments are needed, each ball rides back into the vacuum tubes and to a spray-painting machine, which sprays metered bursts of paint, coating the ball evenly while it is turned delicately in the robot grip of pinpoint metal holders. After more automated measures and manual checks, the balls move on to drying racks in a giant walk-in oven. Then the process repeats: more coats of paint, more tubes, more machines, more measures and checks, more moves to programmed destinations. Balls will emerge so hard and shiny that they can survive 100-mile-per-hour impacts with metal objects without cracking or denting.

Finally, an employee adds the customer's company logo and hand packs the balls into custom-designed cases. With other cases of identical balls, they leave the building, bound by overnight air freight for the desk of the customer, a sales manager, who will award the golf balls to top-performing salespeople at the annual sales meeting.

But one vital step remains. As the rush order arrives on the customer's desk, a Spalding salesperson will call and ask if it meets the company's requirements. Is the number right, the logo perfect, the custom display case satisfactory? If not, Spalding will start the process anew and make another set and ship them overnight. After all, the purpose of this production process is to produce satisfied customers, not just golf balls.

Source: Personal tour of the Spalding factory in Chicopee, Massachusetts, made by Alexander Hiam in 1994.

---

without any apparent human involvement. The computers controlling the machines follow detailed operating programs, and they modify the machines' actions in response to feedback from laser sensors aimed at the work. The human involvement is indirect: People designed the machines and the car and ordered the parts; they also control and maintain the equipment.

CAD/CAM systems coordinate computer-aided design and computer-aided manufacturing to design and produce a product. This coordination allows the computerized design plans to be read and built by CAM systems. CAD/CAM is increasingly popular in business.

Taking automation a step further, **computer-integrated manufacturing (CIM)** uses a central computer to drive robots and control and coordinate the flow of materials and supplies in a production process. In CIM systems, the central computer performs many tasks that traditionally were part of the production manager's job.

There are many computer-based methods available for planning and managing the flow of materials in a production process (the third step of the pro-

 computer-integrated manufacturing (CIM)

System that uses a central computer to drive robots and control and coordinate the flow of materials and supplies in a production process.

Production Automation

Far and away the fastest-growing segment of the assembly-line labor force is the robot. While most of us think of robots as replacements for human workers—and they are—the fact is that in many industries, quality demands the consistent precision and uniformity that robotic assembly offers.

duction planning and control process). The most commonly used method is **material requirements planning (MRP)**, which uses computerized records based on bills of materials to keep track of what is bought and where it is delivered. A **bill of materials** lists all parts and materials that are to be made or purchased. MRP is effective in keeping production accurate and timely and in reducing the stockpiling of materials.

A method of integrating production planning with broader information systems within the company has become popular in recent years. **Manufacturing resource planning (MRP II)** adds computerized information from all aspects of the company and its production processes to give an even clearer picture of what is happening as materials flow into and through the production process.

✓ **material requirements planning (MRP)**

System that uses computerized records based on bills of materials to keep track of what is bought and where it is delivered.

✓ **bill of materials**

List of all parts and materials that are to be made or purchased.

✓ **manufacturing resource planning (MRP II)**

Computerized system that integrates information from all aspects of the company and its production processes to provide a clear picture of materials flow into and through the production process.

✓ **analytic process**

Production process that breaks down incoming materials into separate products.

✓ **synthetic process**

Production process that combines materials into a single product.

Production Design Alternatives

The following section describes three choices production facilities make in determining the design of their manufacturing processes: analytic versus synthetic, hard versus soft, and continuous versus intermittent. Each choice affects the type, size, and schedule of the production process and, as we shall see, each has built-in advantages and disadvantages.

Analytic Versus Synthetic Processes

An **analytic process** breaks down incoming materials into separate products. During mining, iron ore is broken down to separate the useful metal from other materials it occurs with in nature. An airline's luggage sorting service is also an analytic process, breaking down luggage according to its destination tags before loading it on the right planes.

In contrast, a **synthetic process** combines materials into a single product. To make steel, iron is combined with other materials at high temperature, then rolled or cast into shape. To make chocolate-chip cookies, flour, shortening, sugar, and other ingredients are combined.

Hard Versus Soft Manufacturing

Mass production is manufacturing large quantities of identical products by using standardized parts, an assembly-line layout, and the repetition of specialized tasks. Engineers sometimes call mass production *hard manufacturing* because, like a hard object, the shape of the process cannot be changed without difficulty.

Henry Ford pioneered mass production by standardizing the design and parts of the first Ford automobiles and assigning each employee to one specialized operation in their assembly. Mass production usually entails high **setup costs**, the time and money invested in setting up a production process to make a specific product. However, mass production also allows economies of scale and a high degree of control over the consistency of the process. If you want to make one product in large quantities, this is the cheapest way to do it.

Traditional mass production, like that used in many automobile plants, has built-in advantages and disadvantages. The primary advantages are standardized products and a short **cycle time**—the time required to complete a process once. The cost of these advantages is inflexibility. Traditional auto plants use huge machines to press and shape the metal body parts of cars. To change these machines over to a new design means rebuilding machines and retraining employees, which can take weeks or even months. The inflexibility of mass production helped spur the invention of flexible manufacturing.

Flexible manufacturing systems (FMS) are automated systems designed to be easily modified to produce varied quantities of multiple products. *Soft manufacturing* is another term for this process, as is *agile production*. Computer controls automatically make many of the setup adjustments necessary for new product designs fed into the system.

Like traditional mass productions, flexible manufacturing also typically uses an assembly line, but the structure of employee work and the design of machines differ in the two processes. In FMS, machines and lines are designed to permit rapid setup for new products, and employees are cross-trained to do multiple jobs and make multiple products. One of the biggest contributors to flexible manufacturing is cell manufacturing, discussed earlier in this chapter. Employees usually work on cross-functional teams, with responsibility for larger tasks. This increased responsibility gives them a greater sense of ownership of their work and of the products they create. Note that this points to one advantage of the human component of manufacturing: People are more flexible than machines.

Auto manufacturers have not yet perfected flexible manufacturing for whole-car manufacture because of the number of complex processes involved in making an automobile. Many other industries, however, are already using it. The Spalding golf ball described earlier is one of hundreds of customized ball designs the factory produces every year, along with dozens of different mass products, all made on the same flexible production lines.

And, although whole cars are not yet assembled by flexible manufacturing processes, many automobile components already are. For instance, within one day of receiving an order, Ford Motor Company's electronic components plant in Lansdale, Pennsylvania, can ship any of the engine controllers Ford uses—even if the plant was not set up to make the part when the order came in. This flexibility is the result of a modern design—the plant is only a few years old—and the extensive use of computers. Instead of rebuilding machines, plant managers set up production runs by typing commands into their computer terminals. The goal, according to Ford engineer Richard Chow-Wah, is to become an "agile" manufacturer.[10]

6. Distinguish between hard and soft manufacturing.

 mass production

Manufacturing large quantities of identical products by using standardized parts, an assembly-line layout, and the repetition of specialized tasks; also called *hard manufacturing*.

 setup costs

The time and money invested in setting up a production process to make a specific product.

 cycle time

The time required to complete a process once.

 flexible manufacturing systems (FMS)

Automated systems designed to be easily modified to produce varied quantities of multiple products; also called *soft manufacturing* or *agile production*.

The auto industry is currently working on the "three-day car." The goal, according to an industry expert at the Association for Manufacturing Excellence, is to "deliver a car with customer features very quickly—within three days after ordering." Right now the normal turnaround time in the fastest auto manufacturing processes (such as Toyota's) is 10 days. Once three days becomes standard, car plants will truly be flexible and customers will be able to shop for their car by sitting in a simulator and trying out hundreds of options to design a car uniquely matched to their needs, taste, and budget.[11]

As processes are improved, flexible lines are becoming as efficient as mass production lines. Ford's flexible Lansdale plant can assemble 124,000 engine controllers a day, even though each has 400 to 500 parts.[12] One key to both flexibility and efficiency is low setup cost. A flexible line, making many different products in small and large quantities, would be very costly to run if setup costs were high. Imagine stopping the process after each product is made to reconfigure all the machines, redesign the process itself, and retrain employees. Costs would be counted in millions of dollars and weeks of time and would have to be recovered through higher product prices.

Continuous Versus Intermittent Processes

A **continuous process** has high setup costs and long start times that make it most efficient when run constantly. A nuclear power plant, for example, is efficient only when run constantly. Shutdowns are very costly and may be very dangerous as well. Steel mills also employ a continuous production process in melting, forming, and rolling large amounts of steel. When a steel mill shuts down for redesign or repair, plant managers start checking their watches nervously. Large steel mills are so costly to build and the setup costs are so high that they are efficient only if run near full capacity almost all the time.

Other processes can also be continuous. The vats that melt and mix ingredients to form Spalding's golf ball cores are best kept hot and running for lengthy periods, even though the rest of the production process is more flexible. Many catalog companies run their 800-number order centers continuously. And a hospital's nursing services are necessarily continuous—patients need round-the-clock care and attention. Many, but by no means all, mass production processes are most efficient when operated continuously.

In contrast, low setup costs and short start times allow an **intermittent process** to be shut down and restarted often and to run efficiently for short periods of time. Intermittent production operates in *batches*—short or long runs of similar products—and it can handle many batches of varying sizes.

Services cannot be stored, and most service production must be intermittent. For instance, it takes just the turn of a key for an employee to bring the checkout terminal on line and to start ringing up your goods. Since people are more flexible than machines, store employees can play a sales and service role when they are not working at checkout terminals. They may also count and restock inventory, clean up, and help with ordering, accounting, or marketing chores.

The combination of just-in-time delivery of parts by suppliers, a pull production process, and the flexibility to set up for new products on demand moves a producer much closer to its customers. As Dudley Wass, the manager of Ford's Lansdale electronic components plant, explained, "Our model is the cheetah. We want to be able to stop on a dime, direct all our energy toward a goal, turn quickly, and accelerate rapidly." But according to Wass, "If you have eight days of [inventory], that means it is going to take eight days to make a change." By cutting the time between receiving an order and shipping the finished product from eight days to one, the Lansdale plant can now make changes in a single day.[13]

 continuous process

Production process with high setup costs and long start times that make it most efficient when run constantly.

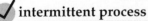 **intermittent process**

Production process with low setup costs and short start times that allow it to be shut down and restarted often and run efficiently for short periods of time.

cost of quality

Sum of costs incurred as a result of defects and errors in a process.

reengineering

The clean-slate redesign of a process that cuts costs by simplifying business processes.

Improving Production Processes

The challenges of global competitiveness have caused many U.S. businesses to carefully examine their production processes. In any business, these core areas are where the major value is added and where good management can most effectively lower costs.

A primary focus of efforts to improve production processes is lowering the **cost of quality**, the sum of costs incurred as a result of defects and errors in a process. Many experts believe *cost of quality* fails to describe the problem and that *cost of poor quality* or *costs related to quality* would be better labels. So far, however, the traditional term remains.[14]

Intel Corp. had a painful lesson in computing the cost of quality when it began marketing its Pentel microprocessor computer chip in 1994. This tiny chip, which is the brain in many personal computers, was installed in approximately 4 million machines before a mathematician-user discovered it produced an error in the tenth place following the decimal point. (Chips are expected to perform correctly to the nineteenth place after the decimal point.) Although most personal computer users would not be affected by the error, Intel finally offered a free replacement to any user who requested it. The extensive costs the company incurred in damage control were part of Intel's cost of quality.[15]

By some estimates, the cost of quality ranges from one-quarter to one-half of the total costs of production processes in a typical business.[16] It therefore is not difficult to understand why companies are looking for ways to eliminate wasteful errors and activities and to improve the quality of their products. A recent survey of 160 mid-size and large companies in North America and Europe found that three-fourths were making changes in their production processes.[17] Half of those companies said they were making major changes that would lead to dramatic redesign of their production and support processes.

Radical changes such as these are called *continuous improvement processes*. The two most common and important such processes are reengineering and total quality management. Though their goals are similar, their approaches differ.

Reengineering

Reengineering is the clean-slate redesign of a process that cuts costs by simplifying business processes.[18] In other words, instead of reworking existing production processes, the reengineering team members begin with a clean blackboard, on which they draw what they think is the best possible new design. The new version may be very different from the old process, and it may require significant changes in who works on the process and what they do. Reengineering teams follow a seven-step method, illustrated in Figure 10.5.

In reengineering, employees who work on a process—the process "owners"—form teams. To improve productivity, they map and study the process, listing specific activities and looking for those that add value to the product and those that are simply wasted time, effort, or money. The skills check "Can You Identify Waste?" (on page 306) lets you try your hand at a reengineering exercise that resembles those some employees are now asked to undertake.

Reengineering tends to generate very radical changes. In some companies, it is used to redesign processes so that they can operate with more automation and far fewer people. This approach couples redesign with downsizing of the work force. Siemens Nixdorf, the German manufacturer of personal computers and other high-tech products, engaged in a reengineering effort designed to cut and reorganize many positions to make the large company flat and flexible. According to its chief executive, "We have to reengineer more or less the whole company. In this kind of environment, the only constant is change."[19]

7. Define cost of quality and explain how businesses are managing this cost.

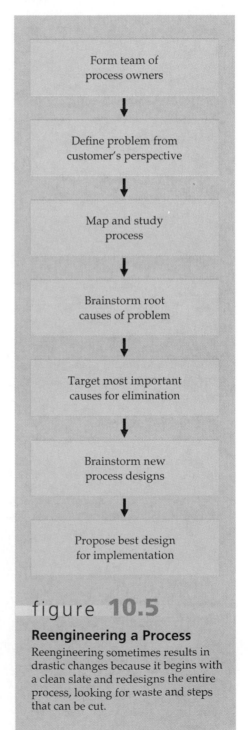

figure **10.5**

Reengineering a Process
Reengineering sometimes results in drastic changes because it begins with a clean slate and redesigns the entire process, looking for waste and steps that can be cut.

skills check

Can You Identify Waste?

In reengineering, employees identify and eliminate waste to improve productivity. This exercise lets you try your hand at a task you may someday be asked to perform as part of your job.

Identify each of the following activities as either *work*—adding value for the customer by moving a process forward—or *waste*—not adding value for the customer and not moving a process forward. (Your instructor has the correct answers if you wish to check your work.) Identify each activity by checking either *Work* or *Waste*.

Searching for information	Work ☐	Waste ☐
Assembling two components	Work ☐	Waste ☐
Repeating a step in a process	Work ☐	Waste ☐
Transporting materials	Work ☐	Waste ☐
Inspecting a part for defects	Work ☐	Waste ☐
Entering the same data a second time	Work ☐	Waste ☐

Waiting for a meeting to begin	Work ☐	Waste ☐
Looking up a customer's past order history while the customer waits on hold	Work ☐	Waste ☐
Walking to a service van to get a part	Work ☐	Waste ☐
Waiting for a machine to warm up	Work ☐	Waste ☐
Storing raw materials in a warehouse before production	Work ☐	Waste ☐
Reworking a product to correct a problem	Work ☐	Waste ☐
Calling a customer back to clarify information	Work ☐	Waste ☐

Source: Based on Jerry Harbour, *The Process Reengineering Workbook* (White Pains, N.Y.: Quality Resources, 1994), p. 12.

8. Compare reengineering and total quality management as improvement processes.

Such radical changes often generate resistance, which is focused at *stress points*—points of conflict with stakeholders inside the organization. CSC Index, a consulting firm that does a lot of reengineering projects with companies worldwide, has identified 20 separate stress points that typically arise as businesses try to implement a reengineering process. For instance, middle managers at the business typically fight over who has control of the reengineering team and its project.[20] Many businesses do overcome all this stress, however, and implement important improvements to major production and support processes. Because of its more radical nature, reengineering is done infrequently; constant reengineering would tear a company apart.

Total Quality Management

Total quality management (TQM) is the continuous improvement of a business and its processes by its employees and for its customers.[21] TQM can be done constantly, producing an ongoing stream of improvements as teams of employees watch for ways to cut costs and improve the quality of processes and products.

TQM requires new ways of working—empowering employees, forming problem-solving and improvement teams, and training teams in process management methods. And it requires managers to lead in a different way, by encouraging and helping teams of employees make improvements, instead of the traditional command-and-control style discussed in Chapter 8. These changes are so broad that they have already been described in earlier chapters, and they will pop up again in later chapters.

TQM's management style is exemplified by the criteria of the Malcolm Baldrige National Quality Award, an annual contest run by the National Institute of Standards and Technology (NIST) of the U.S. Department of Commerce in collaboration with a not-for-profit foundation of U.S. companies. The Baldrige Award was started in 1987 and is open to three categories of U.S. com-

✔ **total quality management (TQM)**

The continuous improvement of a business and its processes by its employees and for its customers.

Producing Quality Services
At the Ritz-Carlton hotel in Boston, a member of the banquets staff puts the finishing touches on a table for a special dinner. In 1992, the Ritz-Carlton Hotel Company received the Malcolm Baldrige National Quality Award in the service category. As growth in the service sector of the U.S. economy outpaces growth in the manufacturing sector, service companies like Ritz-Carlton employ all the tools of TQM to improve processes and profits.

panies: manufacturing companies, service companies, and small businesses. In addition, NIST proposes adding two new categories, health care organizations and educational institutions.

To give you a sense of how broad TQM's changes are, look at the seven categories used by the judges to evaluate applicants:

1. Leadership
2. Information and analysis
3. Strategic planning
4. Human resource development and management
5. Process management
6. Business results
7. Customer focus and satisfaction

The most obvious and far-reaching change TQM brings is in how errors and problems are diagnosed. TQM shifts blame from the person to the process. Once this shift is made, managers stop firing people when an error occurs and start encouraging employees to identify causes and redesign the process. This shift appeared in many Japanese companies during the 1960s and 1970s and in many U.S. and European companies during the 1970s and 1980s.

Masao Nemoto, a director of Toyota and one of the early innovators of TQM, explained his views like this: "I believe that people are not gods and they are bound to make mistakes no matter how hard they try. There is no benefit in assessing responsibility for committing errors. It is better to clarify the facts and work toward prevention of a recurrence."[22]

Lee Iacocca, a past president of Chrysler Corporation, which was nearly forced out of business by tough competition from Toyota and other Japanese car makers, described his frustrations over the practice of searching for a person to blame, rather than a process to fix: "Through all my years in the auto business I've been hearing manufacturing guys complain that the stupid designers made the car impossible to build. And the designers lament, 'Look, we gave them a perfectly good design. They're just too dumb to know how to put it together. It's their problem.' And all this within the same company: the ongoing belief that any problem is somebody else's fault."[23]

James Champy, a reengineering consultant who coauthored a best-selling book that popularized the method in 1993, describes reengineering and TQM

Many Japanese production management practices can be traced to advice given by an American, W. Edwards Deming. The Japanese government honored Deming's achievements in 1951 by naming their equivalent of the Baldrige Prize after him. Competition for the Deming Prize is fierce in Japan.

as "complementary."[24] In some cases they are, but downsizing runs counter to TQM's approach of including all employees in improvement efforts. Downsizing can poison the relationship between senior managers and other employees, leaving employees unwilling to participate in TQM-style improvement processes. The relationship between reengineering and TQM is currently a subject of lively debate among experts.

Tools for Process Improvement

9. Identify two analytical approaches used in process improvement.

Senior managers are responsible for the entire production process, but as a practical matter they cannot significantly improve that process unless employees tackle each piece of it separately.

Senior managers have traditionally attempted to improve a business by redesigning its organization, changing its focus in one of the many ways described in Chapter 9. But redesigned organization charts may not offer insights into business processes, although they show who has authority and responsibility for them. Processes are too often, in the terminology of process managers, *black boxes* whose workings are invisible to those who must manage them. When you cannot clearly see how a process works, the only changes you can make are additions or subtractions. Under these conditions, there appears to be a trade-off between costs and quality. As you subtract elements, quality tends to drop. As you add them, costs rise.

One of the greatest challenges of modern management is to let the sun shine into all the black boxes of a business. That means studying the process in detail and making fundamental improvements in its design, so that the trade-off disappears. To do this, process managers form teams of employees, called **process improvement teams** or *quality circles*, who redesign their own processes, looking for ways to save time and money. This requires employees to master process management methods and also to understand the technical aspects of their product and process. As a result, many businesses are increasing the amount of technical training they give employees.

For example, at Universal Instruments Corporation, a manufacturer of automated electronic assembly equipment used by other manufacturers, a new training program called the Applied Technology Program is now available to the company's 1,300 employees. The program's goals are to improve employee abilities in the following areas:

- Analyzing workplace problems
- Developing and applying innovative solutions
- Continuously improving work processes
- Training and working cross-functionally

Pat Wrobel, a training manager at Universal Instruments, explains that this program helps "make the worker a thinking worker, someone who can add value to the process, someone who is not simply doing something in a robotic fashion but has the ability to understand the underlying principles of what he or she is doing."[25] Two popular tools that many companies are teaching their employees are process flowcharting and root cause analysis.

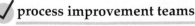
process improvement teams

Teams of employees who redesign their own processes to save time and money; also called *quality circles*.

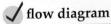
flow diagram

A process portrayed in symbols and words that map the steps and sequence of activities.

Process Flowcharting

Process flowcharting relies on a **flow diagram**, a process portrayed in symbols and words that map the steps and sequence of activities.[26] You may already be familiar with flow diagrams from computer classes.

At Dun & Bradstreet Software (DBS), one quality improvement team used process flowcharting to reveal flaws in the subprocess of receiving incoming overnight packages. This may seem to be a trivial part of a large operation, but important documents can wander through the mail rooms and corridors of a big office building for hours, days, and even weeks before reaching the addressee. (And that's assuming the sender put the correct name or department on the package!) As small and simple as this subprocess is, it can short-circuit critical business activities that depend on timely delivery of the information in the overnight package. By making the internal delivery faster and more reliable, the employee team at DBS was able to eliminate one source of delays and problems in the overall business.[27]

To see how process flowcharting works, let's say you've just decided to cut time and money spent in a routine process you know well—brushing your teeth. Brushing probably takes only a couple of minutes and only a dime's worth of toothpaste, water, and electricity for the bathroom lights. But even so, if you brush 730 times a year for 70 years, each penny you save per brushing will total $511 at the end of 70 years. Even more impressive, each 30 seconds you save will give you an extra 18 days to spend on something more interesting than brushing your teeth. If you cut time and costs even a little bit, you could afford a nice vacation. This is a process worth cutting!

So where do you begin? Can you take less time? Yes, most obviously by doing a less thorough job. What about toothpaste costs? You can cut the amount by half and save money, but again the quality of your brushing may be hurt. No point saving a few pennies and seconds if you wind up spending more in a dentist's chair! Can you save on water costs by turning the water on and off more frequently? Yes, but only by adding steps and thus adding time. If you only had a flow diagram, you could really see your options. You do—you'll find it in Figure 10.6.

figure **10.6** **A Flow Diagram Mapping a Very Simple Process—Brushing Your Teeth**

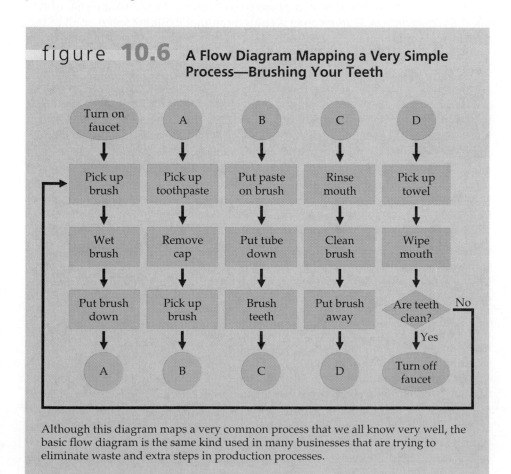

Although this diagram maps a very common process that we all know very well, the basic flow diagram is the same kind used in many businesses that are trying to eliminate waste and extra steps in production processes.

It is not uncommon for first-pass efforts at diagramming a process to miss some of the steps, and our diagram is no exception. It contains 17 steps, is incomplete, and the process itself is flawed. Can you see the problems? The diagram is incomplete because it fails to illustrate the details of rinsing your mouth and wiping up. Each is a subprocess requiring you to put other things down to pick up and fill a glass and do other things we'd rather not describe in detail in order to rinse your mouth out, and also requiring you to pick up the towel in order to use it. And you may have noticed that this process might make your roommate angry. Sure, your teeth will be clean, but what about the bathroom? You forgot to put the cap back on the toothpaste or to hang up the towel to dry.

But Figure 10.6 has another problem. The process is flawed because it is needlessly complex. We leave it to you to try some variations that will allow you to cut several steps. (Enjoy your vacation!)

Many employees are receiving training in making and using flow diagrams. After using flow diagrams to identify the weak parts of the process for handling incoming overnight mail, employees at Dun & Bradstreet Software then used the diagrams to chart an improved process that delivers packages more quickly and reliably. As you get better at this kind of analysis you will discover that most business processes are more complex and costly, and perhaps also more interesting, than the brushing example. Nevertheless, the approach is very much the same.

Root Cause Analysis

In both TQM and reengineering, root cause analysis is the first step improvement teams take in redesigning a process—otherwise, they run the risk of fixing the wrong things. A **root cause** is something that explains some or all of the variation in a particular outcome of a process.

For example, think again about Spalding's golf ball production process and consider possible causes for oversized golf balls. If a coating machine is out of adjustment and sprays coating too thickly on the cores, machine adjustment is the root cause of the oversize. Or maybe an operator accidentally ran a batch of balls through a painting machine twice, thereby doubling the thickness of the paint. Perhaps the new molds for the rubber cores of the balls are slightly larger than the old ones. Or maybe the employee measuring the diameter of the balls is not as careful as the last employee to do this job, so variation in the *measurement* creates the illusion that there is more variation in the product. And perhaps there are even multiple root causes—two, three, or more of these mistakes happening together.

Root causes are usually identified by bringing together a team of people who own the process in question—employees, managers, parts suppliers, or, in some cases, even customers. The team first maps the process, as you learned to do earlier in this chapter. Then the team examines the issues or characteristics that are causing concern. If they are worried about variation in golf ball diameter, for instance, they will study the control charts, the flowcharting map, and each step of the process. Then they use their most valuable analytic tool: they *think about* the problem. This thinking usually takes the form of brainstorming.

Brainstorming is thinking out loud to try to list as many ideas as possible without criticizing any of them. Brainstorming relies on trust among team members. Employees sitting around a conference table usually hesitate before sharing off-the-cuff ideas. What if the boss or some more experienced employee laughs, or tells them they are wrong? Minimally the speaker will be embarrassed, and in the worst case, his or her career with the company might be

✓ **root cause**

Something that explains some or all of the variation in a particular outcome of a process.

✓ **brainstorming**

Thinking out loud to try to list as many ideas as possible without criticizing any of them.

hurt. To safeguard against such worries, the team has to agree on ground rules that will allow everyone to be open and to take personal risks, free from fear of criticism and retaliation.

Once a long list of possible root causes has been written on a board or flip chart, the team analyzes the list. It is OK to criticize or improve the ideas, which now belong to the whole team, not only to the individual who first suggested them. And it is also helpful to group the ideas into general categories. Finally, the team draws a **cause-effect (CE) diagram**, an illustration of causes, effects, and their relationships. Figure 10.7 shows a hypothetical CE diagram for excessive variation in golf ball diameters. It identifies a number of major causes, and it groups other causes into these categories if they help explain the main causes. The CE diagram represents lots of ideas and possibilities, and it will lead the team to examine causes as different as machine settings and repairs, human errors, the materials used in cores, the heat of the molds used to form the cores, the time given employees to set up for producing different models, and variations in the paints and coatings obtained from suppliers. There are lots of possible root causes. The question then becomes, which should the team fix first?

 cause-effect (CE) diagram

An illustration of causes, effects, and their relationships.

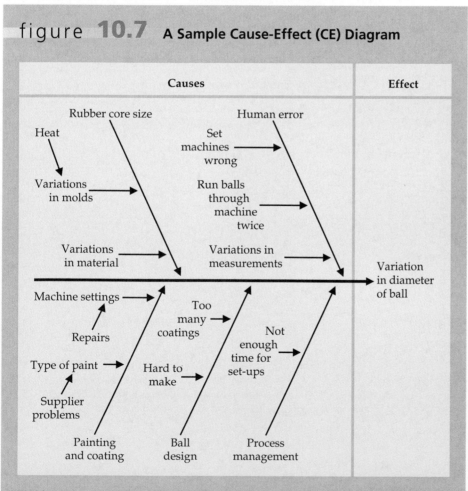

figure **10.7** **A Sample Cause-Effect (CE) Diagram**

This hypothetical CE diagram identifies a number of major causes for variations in golf ball size and groups other causes into categories that help explain the main causes. It represents lots of ideas and possibilities and will lead the team to examine many different causes, as indicated here.

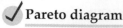 **Pareto diagram**

Bar chart ordering causes from most to least common.

Vilfredo Pareto was an Italian economist who invented the chart and the 80/20 rule. He discovered that in most countries 80 percent of the wealth is held by roughly 20 percent of the people.

To answer this question, the team applies the "80/20 rule," which states that 80 percent of the variation in any process is generally explained by 20 percent of the causes. Although not absolute, this rule is always true in a general sense. There is always a small subset of all the causes that are most important and should be eliminated first. But which are they?

The team will have to gather information to find out. They will have to look at lots of cases where balls were too large or small and track down the causes in each case. Then they will graph their data in a **Pareto diagram**, a bar chart ordering causes from most to least common. The Pareto diagram shows visually which of the causes are most common. Figure 10.8 shows a hypothetical Pareto diagram for the variation in golf ball diameters. It indicates that the most frequent causes of variation in golf ball diameter are rushed set-up (which produces incorrect machine settings), slow repairs (which allow machines to fall out of adjustment), and human errors. Any improvement team wishing to make significant gains would want to focus on process improvements that reduce or eliminate these three root causes first. Any ideas for improving the setup and repair subprocesses, and any investments in training employees or making their jobs more foolproof, will yield big improvements for the team.

The Pareto diagram is now commonly used by many businesses and for many types of processes, both manufacturing-based and service-based. Both

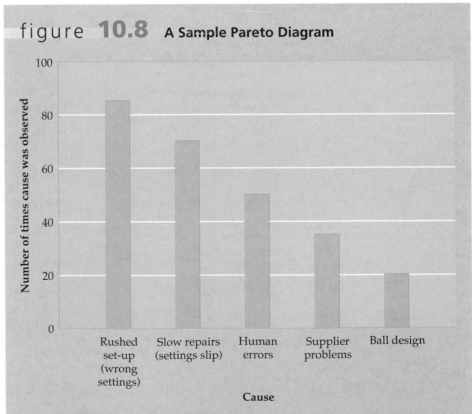

figure **10.8** **A Sample Pareto Diagram**

This hypothetical Pareto diagram graphs some possible causes for the variation in golf ball diameters. It indicates that the most frequent causes of variation in golf ball diameter are rushed set-up (which produces incorrect machine settings), slow repairs (which allow machines to fall out of adjustment), and human errors. An improvement team would focus on making improvements that would reduce or eliminate these three root causes first.

Xerox and Dun & Bradstreet Software used Pareto diagrams to improve service-based processes after analyzing the root causes of customer complaints. At DBS, the shipping and installation steps of the production process were the main causes of customer complaints, and therefore those steps became the focus of process improvement efforts. At Xerox, problems in the repair process were most often due to slow response to customer requests, and this aspect of repair service was the main focus of process improvement efforts.[28]

Throughout the business world, teams of employees are using root cause analysis and applying the CE diagram and Pareto chart to track down defects. And when the analysis is done, they come up with creative ways of modifying their processes. They flowchart their new process designs and implement the best of them. Each time this process is repeated, the teams and their organization go through another learning cycle. And if they improve their processes more quickly than competitors, they add value that makes their product more appealing to customers.

Reviewing *Producing Quality Goods and Services*

Production: From Resources to Goods and Services

1. **Describe the four components of the production process.** Production is the transformation of resources into goods or services that have value to customers. This transformation takes place through production processes, which have four components: inputs, activities that add value, outputs, and the option of being repeated. Inputs are land, capital, labor, and entrepreneurship. Outputs are finished goods, services, or ideas.

Production and Operations Management

2. **Identify the five main criteria used to select production sites.** Production site selection is based on the following criteria: (a) labor issues, such as the availability of skilled labor or a work force willing to work for wages lower than those usually offered in the United States ; (b) government receptiveness, in the form of regulations and support; (c) condition of the infrastructure—transportation, water, and power; (d) proximity of high-quality suppliers; and (e) convenience for customers.

3. **List the steps in production planning and control.** Production planning and control takes place in four basic steps. Step 1 is analyzing the overall business plan to determine what needs to be produced, how, when, and where. Step 2 is the creation of a long-range production plan, which includes decisions concerning capacity needs and how additional capacity should be added. In step 3, working plans are drawn up for the production process and production facilities. The master production schedule lists products, the facilities where they will be made, and when they will be made. The facilities plan defines the location and layout of facilities. Detailed schedules state what employees and suppliers will need to do to meet the master schedule, the parts that will be needed, and the number of workers who will be needed.

Step 4 is the subprocess of production control—the development of controls and the tracking and correction of performance. There are five steps in production control: planning, routing, scheduling, dispatching, and follow-up.

4. **Identify the foundation activity in production scheduling and give two examples of scheduling techniques that are based on it.** Production scheduling methods are based on the development of detailed, accurate lists of tasks. This provides the foundation for more sophisticated scheduling methods, such as the Gantt chart, critical path analysis using the CPM chart, and PERT, or program evaluation and review technique.

5. **Explain the difference between push and pull processes and their importance in inventory control.** A push process produces goods in quantities estimated in management plans. Inventory control systems based on push processes store up parts and raw materials, which the production line draws upon to produce the quotas established by management. The business then must try to sell the finished goods.

In contrast, a pull process starts with specific customer orders, which stimulate the production of finished products. These requests then send ripples through the production process in the form of requests for partially finished products. Each workstation or cell produces only as necessary to fulfill the request from the customer or from a workstation between it and the customer. Nothing is produced unless the customer wants it, and there is no wasted effort or inventory. This system is known as just-in-time inventory control.

Production Design Alternatives

6. **Distinguish between hard and soft manufacturing.** Hard manufacturing is another term for mass production, manufacturing large quantities of identical products by using standardized parts, an assembly-line layout, and the repetition of specialized tasks. Mass production processes often use assembly lines requiring long setup times, high setup costs, and lengthy cycle times. Hard manufacturing typically uses large inventories to protect against uncertainties. Nevertheless, it is the cheapest way to make large numbers of a single product.

Soft manufacturing is another term for flexible manufacturing systems (FMS), automated systems designed to be modified to produce varied quantities of multiple products. FMS processes can be reconfigured rapidly because of short setup and cycle times, and they often use cell layouts instead of assembly lines. They can produce a variety of products (whether goods or services) as demand dictates. Employees in FMS firms are usually cross-trained and work on cross-functional teams with responsibility for larger tasks. Soft manufacturing requires reduced inventories through just-in-time inventory management and supplier development. The shift from mass production to flexible production also depends on a shift from push to pull production methods. Soft manufacturing gives producers more flexibility in the marketplace.

Improving Production Processes

7. **Define cost of quality and explain how businesses are managing this cost.** The cost of quality is the sum of costs a business incurs as a result of defects and errors in a process. That cost may range from one-quarter to one-half of the costs of production processes in a typical business, so companies look carefully for ways to eliminate defects and errors. Most businesses are reworking their production processes to lower the cost of quality, usually through improvement processes, either by reengineering or through total quality management.

8. **Compare reengineering and total quality management as improvement processes.** Both are important methods for improving production processes. Reengineering is the clean-slate redesign of a process, and it is used to make radical improvements in production processes. It tends to produce major changes that may include heavily automated systems and downsizing of the work force. Resistance to reengineering is often very high. Ongoing reengineering would be a destructive force in a company.

TQM is a management approach to long-term success through customer satisfaction based on the participation of all members of an organization in improving the quality of processes and products. It is used to create continuous, ongoing improvements. TQM shifts blame for errors from the person to the process. Retraining employees as members of cross-functional teams is a common part of the improvement process.

9. **Identify two analytical approaches used in process improvement.** Process flowcharting reveals flaws in processes by using symbols and words in a flow diagram to portray the steps and sequence of activities in a process. Root cause analysis is the first step in both reengineering and total quality management. Root causes explain variations in process outcomes. By identifying root causes, employees can eliminate them through process improvements. Root causes can be identified and described using cause-effect diagrams and Pareto diagrams.

✓ Key Terms

production **291**

production and operations management **292**

capacity **294**

fixed layout **295**

assembly line **295**

cell layout **295**

production control **296**

production planning **296**

routing **296**

scheduling **296**

dispatching **296**

follow-up **296**

Gantt chart **297**

critical path method (CPM) **297**

PERT (program evaluation and review technique) **298**

materials management **298**

inventory control **298**

inventories **298**

push process **298**

pull process **298**

automation **300**

just-in-time (JIT) system **300**

computer-aided design (CAD) **300**

computer-aided manufacturing (CAM) **300**

robotics **300**

computer-integrated manufacturing (CIM) **301**

material requirements planning (MRP) **302**

bill of materials **302**

manufacturing resource planning (MRP II) **302**

analytic process **302**

synthetic process **302**

mass production **303**

setup costs **303**

cycle time **303**

flexible manufacturing systems (FMS) **303**

continuous process **304**

intermittent process **304**

cost of quality **305**

reengineering **305**

total quality management (TQM) **306**

process improvement teams **308**

flow diagram **308**

root cause **310**

brainstorming **310**

cause-effect (CE) diagram **311**

Pareto diagram **312**

• Review Questions

1. Why is *operations* an important part of managing the production process?

2. What are the advantages of a cell layout compared with a traditional assembly-line layout?

3. What are the three levels of production planning and how do they differ?

4. What are three ways of increasing capacity?

5. What are four forms of automation used in production?

6. How does an analytic process differ from a synthetic process?

7. What are the main advantages of mass production and flexible production?

8. Why is service production usually an intermittent process?

9. What is the cost of quality and why do production managers focus on it?

10. Why do employees resist reengineering more than they resist TQM?

• Critical Thinking Questions

1. When you last ate in a good restaurant, did you see any production management techniques that you have read about in this chapter? (*Hint:* Think of technology, task scheduling, recordkeeping, and other controls.)

2. Considering the same restaurant, how would you institute inventory controls? How would suppliers fit into your plans? How would you handle quality concerns?

3. Would you rather buy an automobile produced through a push system or a pull system? Why?

4. How does an organization gain by empowering employees to take ownership of the products they produce and the production processes they participate in?

5. What would a CE diagram showing the possible causes of students' poor performance on exams look like? Draw that diagram.

REVIEW CASE *Shelby Die Casting Co.*[29]

Located in Shelby, Mississippi, the Shelby Die Casting Co. is a small auto parts manufacturer that supplies alternator housings and engine covers to U.S. auto makers. Rives Neblett, a lawyer and farmer, owned the Shelby plant for seven years, watching it lose money and suffer from quality problems. He realized he would have to turn it around or close it, which would mean crippling job losses for the small town of Shelby.

In 1992 Neblett shut down his law practice and took over management of the plant, determined to turn it around. One year later, the plant was profitable again, and the defect rate had fallen from 35 percent to 8 percent. Four new strategies made the difference.

Communication between managers and employees At the Shelby plant, managers and hourly employees had never discussed production together. To change the situation, Neblett went to a bookstore in Memphis and bought all the books he could find on total quality management and teamwork. Then he asked all his plant managers to read a chapter each week to learn about empowering the employees. "TQM really means just involving people in the organization," Neblett says. "It means passing the decision-making process farther down the line."

Teamwork Teamwork was difficult at the beginning because the workers were not accustomed to talking about problems and managers were used to dominating all meetings. It took four to five weeks for the hourly workers to learn how to conduct a meeting without screaming at one another. But after the teams overcame the initial turmoil, they began to solve daily problems and make continuous improvements.

Reengineering By the end of 1992, Neblett was ready to take aggressive steps to restructure the management process and delegate daily operations to teams. In the reengineering process, the hourly workers decided how they should do their jobs and the managers played an advisory role. Two shop-floor employees were promoted to manager.

Training and education Training classes were offered

in work-related skills and in basic skills such as reading and writing. Most employees signed up. "We have one person, maybe two, out of 93 employees who are not attending a class," says personnel director Jackie Sanders.

The changes have made the Shelby plant profitable, but Neblett believes there is still much more to be done.

1. What kind of production process do you think is in place at the Shelby plant? Use relevant terms from this chapter to describe it.

2. What changes might Neblett consider next? (*Hint*: Think about what you learned about hard versus soft manufacturing.)

3. What techniques could have helped the Shelby workers to redesign their own work processes?

4. Although the case does not tell you, what specific pressures do you think Shelby's customers might have imposed on the company as it adopted TQM?

CRITICAL THINKING CASE *Aquafuture, Inc.*[30]

A year after graduating from Hampshire College, Joshua Goldman formed Aquafuture, Inc., to raise fish for consumption. The fish, a hybrid of saltwater striped bass and freshwater white bass, bring $2.25 to $3.00 per pound in restaurants from Toronto to Boston. One famous Boston eatery, Legal Sea Foods, uses 3,000 pounds of Goldman's fish per week.

The operation is enclosed in a one-acre-plus building. Fingerlings, young fish that are purchased from a southern supplier, arrive at age two months and then progress through a series of growth tanks. First is the quarantine tank, followed by the nursery tank; between the two, the bass are vaccinated. As they grow, they are moved to larger and larger tanks. The last growing tank has a flow current requiring fish to swim as they would in the ocean, which develops the texture of the fish.

A fish can be grown to market size in nine months at this innovative production facility. This is half the time it would take naturally. However, by lowering the water temperature, Goldman can slow the growing process in times of slack demand. The company's production process is efficient. It takes 30 percent less feed to raise Goldman bass than it does to raise a comparable amount of chicken. And when the tank water is recycled, the waste is filtered out and sold as fertilizer to local farmers.

1. If you were in charge of expanding Aquafuture, Inc., by adding a new facility, what questions would you ask before choosing a site? Which questions would be most important for this particular business?

2. If you were in charge of the long-range product planning and control for Aquafuture, what time limits would influence your plan? What key things would you need to measure and control?

3. Aquafuture's fish mortality rate is 15 percent, half the industry average. Sanitary conditions and shorter cycle times may explain the difference. How would you recommend that the company go about cutting the mortality rate even further?

Critical Thinking with the ONE MINUTE MANAGER [31]

Back in the One Minute Manager's office, Joanna asked, "Can the approaches you've been describing be used in small companies, or is it too expensive and technology-driven for smaller businesses to improve their production processes?"

"Bigger companies are certainly leading the efforts to reinvent production, but small companies are innovating too. My favorite example is Granite Rock company, a 1992 winner of the Malcolm Baldrige National Quality Award in the small-business category," the One Minute Manager explained.

"I bet I know what they produce," said Joanna, laughing. "Rocks!"

"Yes, they produce rock, sand, gravel, and ready-mix concrete in the San Francisco Bay area. A visit to the Arthur R. Wilson Quarry would show you that any production process can be improved, no matter how simple it might seem. At this quarry, customers pull up in trucks to buy the gravel or sand they need. But instead of having to wait for someone in a bulldozer to come over and serve them, these customers pop a magnetic card into an automated loading system and key in the amount and type of product they want. Then they drive to a centralized loading facility, where the truck is accurately filled over an electronic scale. They call the new system GraniteXpress."

"Sounds like the Jetsons meeting the Flintstones," Carlos remarked. "But how much waste could you possibly save in the operation of a simple quarry?"

"You'd be surprised. For starters, the cycle time for loading a truck dropped from 24 minutes to just 9 minutes with the new system, and that can mean a lot of savings for customers who are picking up many loads a day. Also, Granite Rock's customers are very happy with the accuracy of the process. The company's cost of resolving customer complaints is just two-tenths of 1 percent of sales revenues, compared with an average of 2 percent in its industry."

1. Is the new GraniteXpress production system push or pull oriented? How do you know?

2. How important is site selection in Granite Rock's industry? If you were building a highway far from Granite Rock's quarries, it would cost you more in time and gas to load your trucks there, but could faster cycle times help make up for an inconvenient location?

3. What type of production process is used at Granite Rock quarry? Is it analytic or synthetic? Mass or flexible? Continuous or intermittent?

CHAPTER

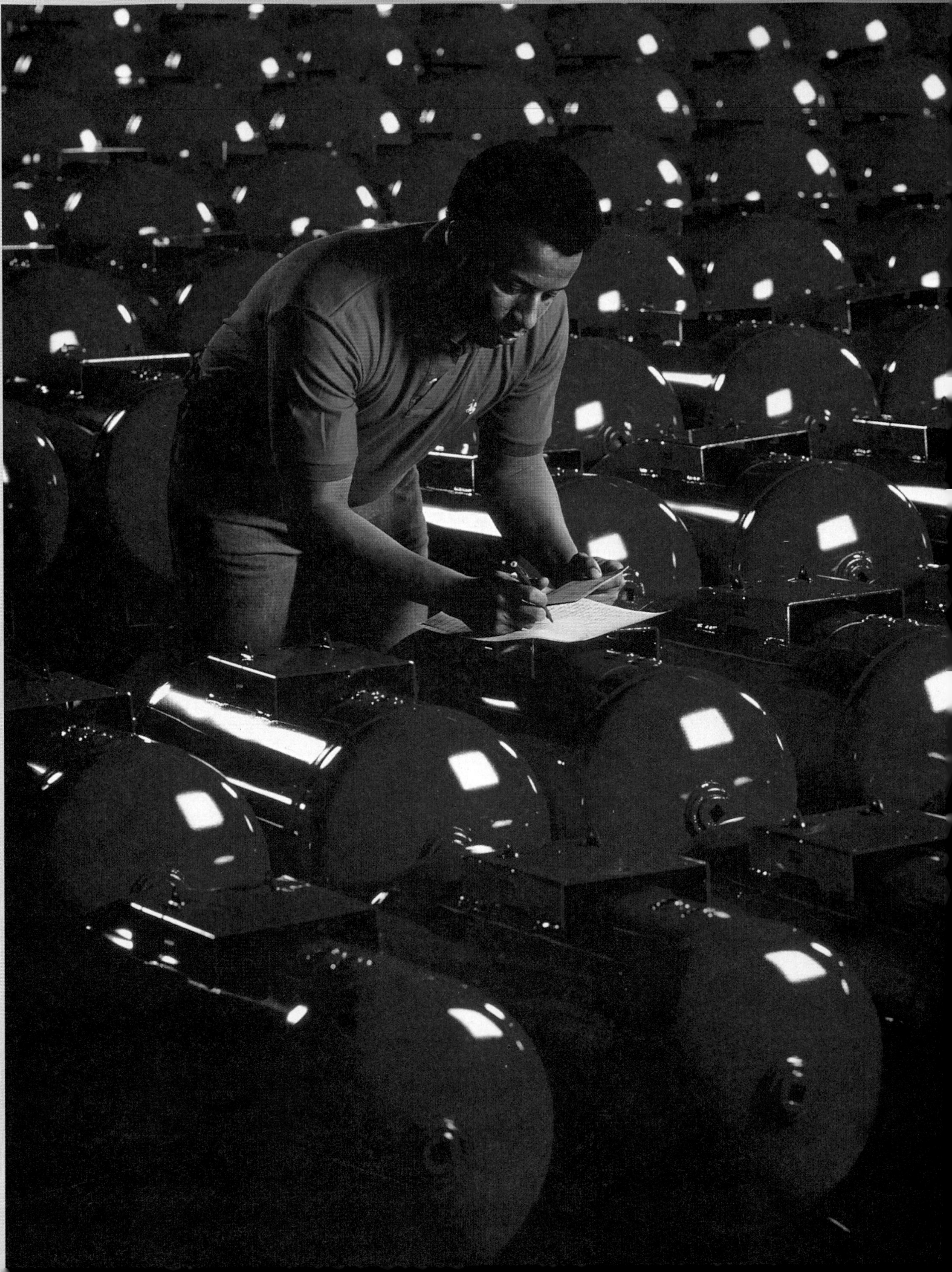

11 Motivation and Performance

A business can do its work only as well as its employees can. Motivated, high-performing employees are increasingly important to responding successfully to the challenges of today's business environment. Where companies once might have trusted employees only to carry out orders, many now value employees at all levels for their ideas and initiative. Managers are discovering that when employees are given the opportunity and power to make important contributions, they usually will. In this chapter you will discover what management theorists teach us about motivation and how these ideas can be put into practice to help employees improve their work and help businesses succeed. After reading this chapter, you will be able to reach the learning goals below.

Learning Goals

1. Name and discuss the five levels in Maslow's hierarchy of needs.
2. Explain Herzberg's theory of motivation, noting the relative importance of job enrichment and money as motivators.
3. Contrast intrinsic and extrinsic motivation and describe the use of each in optimizing worker performance.
4. Discuss the roles of task clarity and management by objectives in motivating employees.
5. Discuss Taylor's scientific management approach in terms of intrinsic motivation.
6. Describe the Hawthorne studies and explain the significance of their findings.
7. Distinguish among Theory X, Theory Y, and Theory Z management.
8. Explain why self-directed work teams help motivate employees.
9. Describe today's diverse work force.
10. List and discuss four characteristics of an effective motivation program.
11. List and describe the four steps of an effective motivation program, noting the five characteristics of effective goals.

Avoiding the Bottomless Pit

Joanna was sure this was the day that she and Carlos were scheduled to hear about employee motivation. She knocked on the half-open office door again, and peaked around the corner.

There was the One Minute Manager, settled back in her chair, staring out the window. Finally hearing Joanna and Carlos, she leaned forward and said a little sheepishly, "Guess you caught me sleeping on the job! I'm having a little trouble getting motivated today. Come in—maybe you can help inspire me." She waved at a pile of reports on the desk. "Here's the problem. I've been given a 'no-splash' task. Our company is required to file these forms with the government once a year, and this year it's my job to fill them out."

"What's a no-splash task?" asked Joanna.

"It gets its name from something that happens in adventure movies. You know how the hero sometimes drops a rock into a hole to see how long it takes to get to the bottom? And the character leans over, listening carefully, but never hears a splash? No-splash tasks are like those rocks—they seem to fall into a bottomless pit."

"I think that describes a lot of the work I've done, in school and on part-time jobs," Carlos chipped in. "Sometimes the work seems to disappear or—sometimes even worse—the back splash hits you much later when you don't expect it."

The One Minute Manager laughed. "It's hard to be motivated when you don't get any feedback. You need to know why you are doing your work and what it will accomplish, for both you and your company. And you need to know how *well* you are doing it—right away, before it's too late to improve your own performance."

"Is feedback all there is to motivation?" Joanna asked. "I thought it involved bonuses, wall plaques, trips, and extra time off."

"Sometimes it does, Joanna. Those are all ways to reward employees and to motivate them to work more effectively and efficiently. Extra time off is especially popular now that so many employees are working long hours. Perhaps it's not surprising that many people prize free time even more than additional money. Over the past 25 years, actual work time for U.S. workers has increased by 160 hours, or almost a full month out of every year.[1] The Hilton Hotels Corporation recently surveyed more than 1,000 employees and discovered that 48 percent of them would trade a day's pay for an extra day off each week. Another 17 percent were willing to trade a day's wages if they could have two days off.[2] Unfortunately, many companies can't absorb that kind of unpaid time."

"It must be really difficult to motivate employees if money is tight and time off isn't an option," Carlos observed. "What choices do companies and employees have under those conditions?"

"The answer to that question is what we're going to talk about next, Carlos."

What Motivates Workers?

A *motive* is anything that inspires action; for example, a typical motive for a worker is receiving time off the job with full pay. In business, **motivation** means inspiring people to work. Some companies find that by promising a reward of paid time off they can motivate employees to perform at their best level. But as you probably remember from earlier chapters in this text, many businesses have downsized over the past several years, putting more work into the hands of fewer employees. This means that the option of more time off, although an enticing reward, may not be something companies are in a position to offer these days.

So how can employers motivate their employees to deliver their best work? As you will see, there are several ways to answer this question. Because no single view of motivation can adequately explain every aspect of human behavior, employers draw upon a variety of theories. Each offers something of value, although none by itself provides the complete answer. We begin by looking at four theoretical frameworks: Maslow's hierarchy of needs; Herzberg's maintenance factors and motivators; intrinsic versus extrinsic motivation; and task clarity.

Maslow's Hierarchy of Needs

One of the leading motivation theories, developed by psychologist Abraham Maslow in the 1940s, is the *hierarchy of needs*, shown in Figure 11.1 (page 324). According to Maslow, these five levels of needs form a hierarchy because each level motivates our behavior until that particular need has been satisfied. At that point, the next higher level of need motivates our behavior.[3]

At the most basic level are **physiological needs**—those that stem from our biological requirements for such essentials as food and water. Once these needs are satisfied, individuals are concerned about basic **safety needs**, such as shelter, protection, and job security. When those are satisfied, higher-level **social needs** such as belonging to a group and being well-regarded by co-workers take over. **Self-esteem needs** come next. These include our desire to feel important, to feel that our contributions are valuable. Finally, when all our other needs are satisfied, we work to satisfy **self-actualization needs**, those that stem from our desire for a sense of purpose.

Although these five levels of needs form a hierarchy, individuals may pursue several levels simultaneously. For example, an unskilled laborer may be motivated to take a job washing dishes in exchange for a wage that allows him or her to purchase food and shelter (physiological and safety needs). The job may also allow the laborer to work with friends and to support a family (social needs). Finally, the job may provide the worker with enough independence and self-sufficiency to satisfy some self-esteem needs as well.

Social, self-esteem, and self-actualization needs vary with the individual. Consider, for example, an experienced lawyer who has a high standard of living and a secure life with friends and family (and so has satisfied his or her physiological and safety needs) and whose professional achievements have fulfilled his or her self-esteem needs. To motivate this person, a job opportunity probably will have to provide both recognition of accomplishments (to satisfy self-esteem needs) and interesting and challenging work (to satisfy self-actualization needs). The more options a person has when seeking a job, the more needs he or she will seek to fulfill through that job.

1. Name and discuss the five levels in Maslow's hierarchy of needs.

 motivation

Inspiring people to work.

 physiological needs

Needs stemming from the biological requirement for such essentials as food and water.

 safety needs

The need for such things as shelter, protection, and job security.

 social needs

The need for such things as belonging to a group and being well-regarded by co-workers.

 self-esteem needs

Need for such things as feeling important and feeling that one's contributions are valuable.

 self-actualization needs

Needs that stem from our desire for a sense of purpose.

figure 11.1 Maslow's Hierarchy of Needs

Self-Actualization Needs
Promote employees to leadership positions.
Empower employees and give them the chance to solve
challenging problems and make difficult decisions.

Self-Esteem Needs
Give employees opportunities to contribute to company goals through their work.
Recognize special achievements through awards such as employee of the month.

Social Needs
Bring people together to work in groups. Sponsor social
events like company softball teams and Friday night pizza parties.

Safety Needs
Offer safety training for people who work with dangerous equipment, invest in safety
equipment to protect workers, and provide liberal disability pay when an employee is hurt.

Physiological Needs
Offer wages sufficient to pay for groceries and rent. Provide a heated or
air-conditioned work environment with drinking fountains, cafeterias, and bathrooms.

According to Maslow's theory, motivation arises from our unmet needs. As our more basic levels of needs are met at work, we are motivated by higher-level needs on the hierarchy.

Herzberg's Maintenance and Motivation Factors

2. Explain Herzberg's theory of motivation, noting the relative importance of job enrichment and money as motivators.

Maintenance factors may also be called hygiene factors. Can you think why?

 maintenance factors

Characteristics of a work environment that, when deficient, cause employee dissatisfaction.

 motivators

Characteristics of work that make individuals try to excel.

Frederick Herzberg, a management professor, proposed another important theory of motivation, which he based on surveys and interviews with thousands of workers in the 1950s. Herzberg found that when people are unhappy with their jobs, it is most often due to some aspect of the work *environment* rather than to the work itself. When environmental factors such as space, lighting, job security, pay, and level of supervision are inadequate, workers become more dissatisfied. Herzberg defined these **maintenance factors** as characteristics of a work environment that, when deficient, cause employee dissatisfaction. Maintenance factors satisfy the two lowest levels of needs in Maslow's hierarchy.

Herzberg was surprised, however, to find that people who are motivated by their jobs are more concerned with the work itself than with the work environment. He called those positive aspects of the work itself **motivators**, characteristics of the work that make individuals try to excel. Motivators include the job's challenge, responsibility, and opportunity for recognition. Motivators satisfy the two upper levels of needs in Maslow's hierarchy.

Herzberg found that motivators spur people to perform better only if maintenance factors are already present in the right amount. He also found that money was a maintenance factor. A fair salary is important to workers, but most people do not work harder just to get more money. See Figure 11.2 for a range of examples of maintenance factors and motivators.

Is Herzberg right? A 1990 survey seems to support his views. Although about half the companies in the survey offered employees year-end bonuses, a share of profits, or other money incentives, the survey concluded that "much of this effort seems misdirected."[4] As Herzberg might have predicted, many of the programs that used money alone as a reward failed to improve performance significantly. But as we'll see later in this chapter, financial incentives can have a greater effect when they are part of a larger motivation package.

Consistent with Herzberg's theory, recognition and achievement are powerful motivators even when no money is attached to them. For example, entrepreneur John Brady motivates the employees in his design consulting business by giving them a jar of marbles once a year. Employees receive 12 marbles, one for each month, and each employee's marbles are a different color. Employees give the marbles to one another to recognize helpfulness or special accomplishments. Brady believes the marbles work better than bonuses or profit-sharing approaches that "cost me a lot of money" without improving employees' work. And Brady says the employees take the program seriously and "love showing off their marbles."[5] Herzberg's theory explains this easily. The marbles represent achievement and recognition, the two factors Herzberg found to have the greatest impact on motivation.

Job Enrichment as a Motivator

Herzberg's research led him to conclude that jobs are more motivating when they are enriched. **Job enrichment** refers to the addition of such motivators as responsibility, scope, and challenge.[6] Work enriched in this way becomes more interesting to those who perform it, and employees are therefore motivated to

✓ job enrichment

The addition of such motivators as responsibility, scope, and challenge.

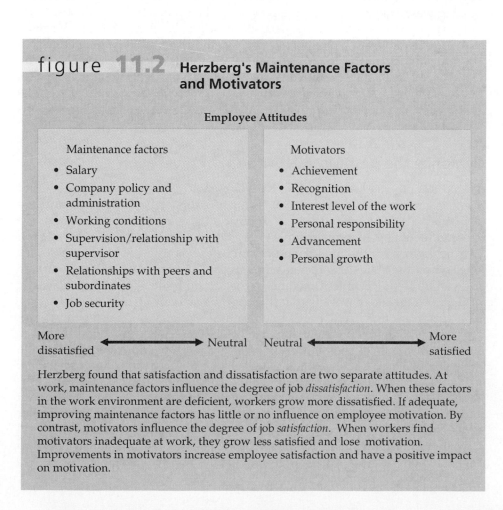

figure **11.2** **Herzberg's Maintenance Factors and Motivators**

Employee Attitudes

Maintenance factors	Motivators
• Salary	• Achievement
• Company policy and administration	• Recognition
• Working conditions	• Interest level of the work
• Supervision/relationship with supervisor	• Personal responsibility
• Relationships with peers and subordinates	• Advancement
• Job security	• Personal growth

More dissatisfied ←——————→ Neutral   Neutral ←——————→ More satisfied

Herzberg found that satisfaction and dissatisfaction are two separate attitudes. At work, maintenance factors influence the degree of job *dissatisfaction*. When these factors in the work environment are deficient, workers grow more dissatisfied. If adequate, improving maintenance factors has little or no influence on employee motivation. By contrast, motivators influence the degree of job *satisfaction*. When workers find motivators inadequate at work, they grow less satisfied and lose motivation. Improvements in motivators increase employee satisfaction and have a positive impact on motivation.

table 11.1 Empowerment Through Job Enrichment

Job Enrichment Method	Motivators Used
Remove supervisor's controls over work	Responsibility and personal achievement
Hold worker responsible for own work	Responsibility and recognition
Give worker a complete job, not a cog-in-the-machine task	Responsibility, achievement, and recognition
Give worker more freedom, authority, and autonomy	Responsibility, achievement, and recognition
Give reports on work to workers, not to their supervisors	Recognition and advancement
Give workers new, more challenging jobs	Growth and advancement
Encourage workers to become experts in certain tasks	Responsibility, growth, and advancement

work harder and better. Ideas for job enrichment that Herzberg suggested years ago are only now becoming popular as businesses attempt to empower their employees. Some of his suggestions are displayed in Table 11.1. Note that in order to be motivating, such changes need to increase the worker's opportunities for growth and learning. Changes that merely add responsibility or work without increasing the employee's chance for growth are experienced not as motivating but as burdensome.

Job enrichment can motivate employees at any level of the organization. For example, the Ritz-Carlton Hotel Co. enriched the work of front-desk clerks in a big way: They were given the power to take up to $2,000 off a guest's bill! Sima Howe, a front-desk clerk at a Ritz-Carlton hotel in McLean, Virginia, waived the full cost of one guest's bill when he complained. This cost Ritz-Carlton $405.25 but probably ensured the customer's repeat business. Howe explains, "When a guest complains, we call that an opportunity to make things better for them."[7] Since it began enriching its employees' jobs in this way, the hotel chain's service has improved dramatically. In 1992, it won the prestigious Malcolm Baldrige National Award for Quality.

Is Money the Best Motivator?

Would people work if they didn't need money? The work of Maslow and Herzberg indicates that money alone is not as strong a motivator as many people believe. Almost every study of motivation points to other factors that are more influential in inspiring people to perform better. Most people will tell you that they work for the money, and of course this is true—to a degree. But for most employees, their pay remains the same no matter how hard they work on a given day. And people sometimes refuse to do a well-paid job, whereas at other times they may work harder than they have to for no money at all.

Now you might say, "That's fine for most workers, but I personally work for money." But if you examine your motives closely you may find that your drive to earn money is more closely linked to your desire for recognition of a job well done than to the money itself. Consider this situation: Suppose you get a raise—a good raise that exceeds your expectations and pleases you enormously. Then a co-worker—someone who is the first person out the door at lunchtime and the last person back, someone consistently slow to volunteer and in general just plain lazy—tells you that he got the same raise. What would that do to your motivation? It probably would dash it pretty thoroughly to find that your boss does not notice any difference between your hard work and your co-worker's poor performance.

Money seems to motivate best when it is given in recognition for a job well done, as when wage and salary increases are expressed as merit raises. One kind of financial incentive that seems particularly successful is **small-group incentives (SGIs)**, which link pay to accomplishment of an independent work group's objectives. One study of SGIs found no reported failures in the 22 plans surveyed. All were rated as successful or partially successful by the employees' managers.[8] The success of SGIs may seem to contradict Herzberg's claim that money is not a prime motivator, but another motivator is also at work in the SGIs: Group members earn recognition and a sense of achievement *along with* their bonuses. This suggests that motivation is enhanced when several motivators are aligned to influence employees. A financial bonus for harder work may not motivate by itself, but it can increase the effectiveness of a motivation program that includes rewards such as achievement and recognition.

Although most of us do work for money, and depend upon it to fulfill our basic needs, people actually work for many other reasons as well. The need to belong, the desire to grow and succeed, the ambition to advance to a higher-status position, and the challenge of the work itself may all at times be more important than money in determining how well we perform on the job. Indeed, people's reasons for working change often over the course of their careers, and even from one day to the next. As a student, for example, you spend rather than earn money in order to accomplish a difficult learning job. And that brings us to our next topic—the power of self-imposed rewards.

Intrinsic Motivation Versus Extrinsic Motivation

Imagine you are doing a really good job at something you like to do. It's fun to get it just right. But suddenly someone comes along and tells you to do the job in a different way. Will you still enjoy your work? Probably not. Will you lose your motivation? Probably.

There is no substitute for the motivation that comes from loving your work and wanting to do a good job. This is **intrinsic motivation**, motivation arising from forces within the individual. Examples of intrinsic motivation include the pride of doing a job well, the fulfillment of belonging to a team that is accomplishing an important task, or the satisfaction of bringing personal performance up to a higher level.

 small-group incentives (SGIs)

Incentives that link pay to accomplishment of an independent work group's objectives.

 intrinsic motivation

Motivation arising from forces within the individual.

3. Contrast intrinsic and extrinsic motivation and describe the use of each in optimizing worker performance.

Job Enrichment and Motivation

These team members produce magnesium alloy wheels, which are used on high-performance automobiles. If you asked each worker what motivates him or her on the job, you'd likely get five different answers. But it's likely as well that you could relate each answer to the characteristics of the work itself—to what Herzberg called "motivators."

Paying the Price at Sears

In the summer of 1992, the California Department of Consumer Affairs, in conjunction with the Bureau of Automotive Repair, charged Sears, Roebuck and Co. with overcharging and overselling customers in its automotive repair shops in California.

Many believe the practices were a consequence of an incentive program that pressured employees to reach revenue goals set by the company. Some employees apparently recommended repairs and replacement of parts that were not actually broken, worn out, or defective.

Without claiming any liability or intentional wrongdoing, Sears reached a settlement with the state of California "for less than $15 million." But the real damage was done in the eyes of its customers. "It was a very costly situation for us," says James Thornton, the new vice president of Sears Automotive. "There is a great loss when your value, trust and credibility is challenged."[1]

As a result of the allegations, Sears made major changes. Sears Automotive eliminated its incentive compensation program for automotive service advisers and replaced it with a non-commission program designed to achieve and recognize higher customer-satisfaction levels. The company eliminated more than 10,000 full- and part-time jobs and closed a dozen freestanding Auto Centers. It also started an industrywide Maintenance Awareness Program to help establish uniform standards and practices for the automotive repair industry.

"We were very much numbers focused," said Roger Sommers, sales manager for a Sears Auto Center in Oxnard, California, "but that's clearly not the focus of our business anymore." The company's present goal is to "satisfy each customer that walks through the door," he added. To do that, associates must walk a fine line between strongly advising that they purchase parts and services and merely suggesting that they do so, according to Sommers.[2]

[1] Larry Aylward, "Thornton Driving Sears Auto Comeback," *Aftermarket Business*, Vol. 103, No. 10 (Oct. 1, 1993), p. 2.
[2] Larry Aylward, "It Was an Opportunity for Everyone to Pull Together," *Aftermarket Business*, Vol. 103, No. 11 (Nov. 1, 1993), p. 3.

In contrast, **extrinsic motivation** derives its power from external forces. Some examples are praise from one's boss, cash bonuses, award certificates, and formal recognition at a meeting or in a newsletter. Extrinsic motivators need not be rewards, of course. Both sticks and carrots can be used to motivate a donkey. Examples of negative extrinsic motivators (sticks) are reprimands from a boss, documentation of poor performance, reductions in pay, or other punishments.

Increasingly in business, sticks are being replaced by carrots. Moreover, research shows that employees are more creative and quality-conscious when they are motivated by intrinsic factors. In contrast, extrinsic motivators such as production quotas often make the goal seem more important than the means of reaching it.[9] Sometimes an extrinsic motivator can lead to unintended consequences, as was the case when Sears, Roebuck and Co. set revenue goals for its automotive repair shops in California. The ethics check "Paying the Price at Sears" describes the investigation into unethical charging practices that followed. In general, a company gets what it rewards—whether it wants it or not.

The personal satisfaction we feel when we excel in our work is highly motivating, as any of the more than 100 contestants in the Hotel Olympics can testify. Pitting chefs, bartenders, and waitresses against one another, the Olympics determines who cooks the best dish, mixes the best drink, or sprints 800 feet the fastest while carrying a tray of champagne glasses. Waitress Tina Kruczek, like many contenders, practiced her one-handed, over-the-head tray carrying for weeks in preparation. And Larry Nadon, a waiter at the Hotel Pierre in Manhattan, says, "I've been running back and forth in the dining room with all the other waiters gathered around cheering me on."[10] If that had been part of his job description, Nadon might well have felt demeaned and probably would have refused to do it!

extrinsic motivation

Motivation that derives its power from forces outside the individual.

Businesses attempt to tap intrinsic motivation by hiring people who seem to be really interested in a job and by making jobs more interesting for the people who hold them. How can a job be made more interesting? Maslow's hierarchy and Herzberg's model both help answer this question. A job is more interesting and rewarding when it meets people's needs—and these differ from person to person and over time, as Maslow observed. While Maslow's theory suggests an individualized approach, Herzberg's suggests that some intrinsic motivators may be universal. Some of the top motivators that he cites—opportunity for achievement, job challenge, and responsibility—tap into almost everyone's intrinsic desire to achieve, overcome challenges, and earn a position of trust. The power of intrinsic motivation helps explain why Herzberg's motivators motivate.

Perhaps the easiest way to find out what people's intrinsic motivators are is to ask which aspects of their work they like the most. Those are the aspects that have intrinsic motivating power. Additional motivators will be effective only if they support or enhance intrinsic ones; if they compete or interfere, they surely will fail. For example, as we saw earlier, many workers now hunger for time away from the job. An employee who is intrinsically motivated to decrease hours spent in the workplace is unlikely to welcome an offer of overtime pay for additional hours on the job. The ultimate case of conflicting motivation occurs, of course, when employees simply do not like their jobs. No amount of money or recognition is likely to counter an employee's strong desire not to work.

Task Clarity: The Power of Seeing Results

Herzberg was surprised to find that money did not rank high on most employees' lists of motivators. Some Harvard Business School researchers were equally surprised when they investigated the motivation of successful sales forces. Salespeople who achieve high levels of sales are usually given large *commissions*—payments based on a percentage of their sales. Commissions are generally considered a major motivator for salespeople because—unlike the salaried factory workers Herzberg studied—their pay varies dramatically with their performance. And the Harvard research did show that money was a motivator in the case of salespeople who earned commissions. However, the research identified another factor that was even more important: the extent to which the salespeople could see the results of their efforts.

This surprise factor, called **task clarity**, is the strength, speed, and accuracy of feedback on one's work.[11] The One Minute Manager was talking about a task clarity problem when she described "no-splash jobs" at the beginning of this chapter. When feedback is strong, fast, and accurate, workers can see the impact of their effort clearly, and this motivates them to make an even greater effort. For instance, if an individual salesperson's efforts help increase the total sales of the entire sales department, then the clarity of the selling task will be high, and all salespeople will be motivated to work toward even better results. But if there is no positive feedback, salespeople will become discouraged, and no offer of reward will be likely to motivate them. The moral: Even people producing good work will become discouraged if their manager fails to acknowledge that work.

Task clarity is often low for long, complex jobs involving many steps and many people, such as the sale of a companywide computer network or the design of a new automobile model. In such cases, the impact of any one individual's contribution to the result may be obscured. Even here, however, task clarity can be increased by giving people more accurate and rapid feedback about the progress of the job and the impact of their work on it.

task clarity

The strength, speed, and accuracy of feedback on one's work.

Empowerment will probably fail if managers delegate responsibility for work that a subordinate dislikes or has trouble doing.

4. Discuss the roles of task clarity and management by objectives in motivating employees.

doing business

At SRC, It's How You Play the Game That Counts!

Springfield Remanufacturing Center Corp. (SRC), once a dying division of International Harvester, became one of America's most competitive small companies primarily by increasing the involvement and commitment of its employees. The company specializes in remanufacturing diesel engines and engine components for truck, agricultural, and construction equipment dealers. When International Harvester ran into difficult economic times, it sold the company to itself—management, workers, and some investors. To survive, "Jack" Stack, SRC's president, had to act fast.

He decided to share with employees what he calls the Great Game of Business. As with most games, however, he didn't think people would want to play unless they understood it. "That means, first, they must understand the rules; second, they must receive enough information to let them follow the action; and third, they must have the opportunity to win or lose," Stack explains.

What Stack did was explain to the employees all the details of running the company, making it obvious what everyone must do to succeed. Everyone was given access to the company's monthly financial report, a weighty tome often running to 90 pages. In small-group sessions, managers reviewed the figures with employees, encouraging questions and providing answers. In addition, the daily printouts from the cost accounting department, which detailed the progress of every job in each supervisor's area, were explained and discussed. The financial statements became a means of involving employees in important aspects of the company's operations. The bottom-line numbers showed them how their jobs contributed to the overall results on the reports.

As employee interest mounted, Stack started offering courses on all aspects of the business, including production scheduling, purchasing, accounting, plant audit, standard cost, industrial engineering, inspection, and warehousing. The sessions lasted one or two hours and were taught by supervisors and some outside instructors.

Soon almost all the employees were working together toward the company's goals. "Their scope was no longer one of emotional protection of fiefdoms—it became one of logic and sequence," Stack says. "To me, giving ownership to the people who do the work has always seemed like the simplest way to run a business.

Sources: "The Turnaround," *Inc.*, Aug. 1986, pp. 42–48; "Motivation and the Bottom Line," *Human Capital*, July 1990, pp. 19–26.

Management by Objectives: Making Goals Explicit

Task clarity is affected by the goals that a manager assigns and an employee adopts. Many job descriptions express goals in only the vaguest and most general way. If goals are made more explicit, employees can understand more clearly the tasks involved in their jobs and how they will be evaluated. A commonly used motivation method, **management by objectives (MBO)**, depends on the link between goals and motivation. In MBO, employees and their managers collaborate on a series of short-term objectives. The manager explains what factors will be used to evaluate employee performance and when periodic reviews of progress toward the goals will take place.

Made popular in the 1950s, MBO continues to be used at many companies. Others reject the MBO approach as too formal and slow-moving, but its focus on participatory goal setting is still important. Empowered employees often set their own goals, which gives them control over an important contributor to task clarity. To see how one company president showed employees how their jobs contributed to the company's overall success, see the doing business box entitled "At SRC, It's How You Play the Game That Counts!"

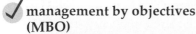 **management by objectives (MBO)**

Method for motivating employees through participation in goal setting, notification of factors that will be used in evaluating performance, and notification of when periodic reviews of progress toward the goals will occur.

One Minute Management: Goal Setting and Feedback on Performance

In *The One Minute Manager*, Ken Blanchard and Spencer Johnson outline a three-part approach to motivation that combines clear goal setting with feedback on performance.[12]

One Minute Goals This concept is based on the idea that good performance begins with a clear statement of goals that establish a model for expected behavior. First, the manager and the employee agree on the employee's goals. The employee then writes each goal—ideally, no more than three to five—on a sheet of paper or an index card. Manager and employee identify the employee's present level of performance toward each goal and the desired future level of performance, then set a deadline for reaching the new level. At this point, managers tell employees that they will provide *feedback*—that they will let the employees know how they are doing in their progress toward their goals.

One Minute Praisings Acknowledging employees' behavior only when they make mistakes is an ineffective way to motivate. Instead, one minute managers try to catch employees doing something right. That means watching for opportunities to praise employees' progress immediately or to redirect them toward the desired goal. Each small success offers an opportunity to motivate the employee toward a goal and to encourage the repetition of desirable behavior as a part of success for the whole organization and everyone who works there.

One Minute Reprimands You learned in Chapter 9 that an important part of delegation is assigning accountability for a task. Managers must hold employees accountable when they perform poorly or fail to progress toward their goals. One minute reprimands, like one minute praisings, should be immediate and specific. Managers communicate their displeasure with the employee's *behavior*, explaining that they think highly of the person but not of the performance in this instance. The intent is to motivate, not demean, the employee. For new employees, redirection—reviewing goals, trying to find out what went wrong, and helping employees get back on track—is preferable to a reprimand.

These four motivation frameworks—the hierarchy of needs, maintenance factors versus motivators, intrinsic versus extrinsic motivation, and task clarity—offer useful perspectives on motivation in the workplace. We turn next to approaches managers have used over the years in their efforts to increase motivation and boost productivity. The sometimes surprising results of these efforts were important in shaping current ideas and methods for employee motivation.

Management Approaches to Increasing Productivity

In this section we shift our attention to how managers increase the motivation, and consequently the productivity, of workers. Over time, a wide range of techniques has been tried with varying degrees of success. Under some circumstances, an authoritarian, command-and-control management style is effective; at other times a more collaborative, team approach works best. Combinations that lie between these extremes can also prove productive.

Scientific Management: Increasing Job Efficiency

In the early 1900s Frederick Taylor, an engineer and consultant, developed a way to increase the efficiency of a job's design, which he found led to an increase in productivity. He took an engineer's perspective, focusing on the actual movements workers performed on the job, such as the range of their hand motions, the movement of their bodies, and the repetition of their movements. From extensive studies of time and motion, Taylor was able to reduce repetitive or unnecessary movement and improve productivity. For example, by analyzing shovel size and shape in relation to the amount of coal a worker moved,

5. Discuss Taylor's scientific management approach in terms of intrinsic motivation.

Taylor could determine the type of shovel that would enable the worker to move the maximum amount of coal in a given period of time.[13]

Taylor's work produced specifications on the most productive way to do many jobs. His success attracted considerable attention and shaped American managers' approaches to employee motivation for many decades. Many managers viewed their job as ensuring that workers met strict performance criteria to optimize productivity. The approach, which came to be known as **scientific management**, involved developing and enforcing prescribed methods of working to increase efficiency. Strictly applied, scientific management structured every aspect of a job, substituting close supervision for a worker's own intrinsic motivation.

But scientific management imposed from above emphasizes efficiency at the expense of the worker's motivation. Unlike machines, people need both efficient methods and the *desire* to be efficient. Some managers today are applying a modified version of scientific management by asking employees to figure out ways to improve their own working methods. For example, Foxboro Co., a Foxborough, Massachusetts, firm that manufactures electronic industrial control systems, recently downsized and now relies heavily on a teamwork approach that delegates a great deal of responsibility and authority to employees. One team cut the number of steps involved in manufacturing an electronic part for the company's Intelligent Automation system from 63 to 40, thereby saving more than $500 on each unit. Another team cut assembly time on another part from one hour to about 90 seconds. "These are the things that used to be reserved for engineers to do," commented Henry B. Metcalf, Foxboro's vice president for manufacturing.[14]

When a company empowers workers to apply scientific management to their own jobs, it harnesses the power of intrinsic motivation to pull the wagon of efficiency. The new approach starts by linking increased efficiency to improved productivity, then adds employee participation to *implement* the improvements. It is, actually, closer to how Taylor first envisioned scientific management than it is to the dictatorial command-and-control approach that grew out of his work and was used by many businesses until very recently.

Scientific management is still practiced successfully in the efforts of many companies to improve or streamline processes. At United Parcel Service, for example, over 1,000 industrial engineers used time studies to improve the performance of various tasks. UPS drivers were instructed to walk up to a door at the rate of three feet per second and then knock instead of wasting time looking for a doorbell. And cutting away the sides of a delivery truck to study a driver at work resulted in changes in package-loading techniques that increased efficiency by 30 percent.[15] These scientific management techniques—while effective—are used within a larger context of employee development. A recently revised vision for UPS emphasized the ongoing development of its people as crucial to the long-term success of the company. Employees are now encouraged to think about their careers in the context of upcoming business needs.[16]

Scientific Management

Time and motion studies helped UPS streamline its processes and increase worker efficiency. But UPS also learned that employee motivation—the desire to be efficient—is critical to implementing scientific management techniques.

You will recall from Chapter 8 that command-and-control management is management through a chain of command that represents lines of authority within an organization.

6. Describe the Hawthorne studies and explain the significance of their findings.

The Hawthorne Studies: People Are Part of the Job

Spurred by Taylor's work, other management theorists attempted to discover the work situation that would best encourage workers to do their best. In 1924, Elton Mayo and other researchers at the Harvard Graduate School of Business tried to find the working conditions that would result in the maximum output at Western Electric's Hawthorne plant, which produced telephone equipment, in Cicero, Illinois. Their findings made business history.

The researchers thought brighter lighting in the work area might boost productivity. To test this hypothesis, they used an experimental group of employees, who worked under varied lighting conditions for prolonged periods, and a control group, who worked under the plant's usual conditions. As Mayo increased the lighting for the test group, its output went up, just as he had expected. But, to the researchers' surprise, output also increased in the control group, where no changes had been made!

Perplexed by the findings, Mayo measured other factors that might be responsible for the control group's increased productivity. At first, he could find no explanation. He then continued to improve the working conditions of the experimental group, giving its members added rest periods, free lunches, and shorter work weeks. With each change, the group responded with an increase in production. And again the control group, whose working conditions had not been changed, increased its production as well. Finally, Mayo returned in stages to the original working conditions. Much to his surprise, production continued to increase to all-time highs with each change.[17]

Baffled, the researchers asked the workers themselves why their productivity had improved. In both the experimental and the control groups, they said the study itself had made them feel important and had increased their motivation. What the researchers learned is known today as the **Hawthorne effect**: Employees' productivity increases when special attention makes them believe that their work is considered important. The concept of empowerment makes use of the Hawthorne effect. Empowered employees know that managers consider their ideas and initiative vital to the company's success, and this motivates them to do their best.

Mayo's research also showed that when groups of workers feel good about their managers, they are motivated, but when they do not, their level of productivity remains steady or decreases. The latter typically happens when managers supervise workers closely, giving them no control over their own work. Mayo's findings encouraged management to involve workers in planning, organizing, and controlling their own environment—the foundation of present trends toward empowerment.

Theory X and Theory Y: Task or People Orientation?

Psychologist Douglas McGregor's theory, which was popular with managers in the 1960s, holds that most managers make one of two basic assumptions about human nature, described as Theory X and Theory Y. How managers motivate their subordinates varies depending on which one they believe.

Theory X managers assume that people dislike working, work only because they must, and need constant supervision and persuasion. Theory X managers believe that employees are not interested in assuming responsibility and need to be directed. The result is a task-oriented style in which management focuses on getting workers to complete assigned tasks.

Theory Y managers assume that people do like to work and will excel if given the right opportunity. They do not believe employees are lazy or unreliable; rather, they expect employees to be self-directed and creative and to do whatever is necessary to get the job done. From the perspective of a Theory Y manager, the business's goals are best achieved by granting workers more independence. The result is a people-oriented style in which management focuses on worker autonomy and empowerment, assuming a high level of trust between manager and subordinate.

The assumptions of both Theory X and Theory Y can be useful, depending upon the situation. If employees are inexperienced, it is usually more effective to treat them in the task-oriented style of Theory X until they have learned the job. Workers with relatively little education who do simple, repetitive tasks may also respond best to a Theory X approach. In contrast, workers who per-

✓ scientific management
A management approach that involves developing and enforcing prescribed methods of working to increase efficiency.

✓ Hawthorne effect
Increases in employees' productivity when special attention makes them believe that their work is considered important.

✓ Theory X
Managerial assumption that people dislike working, work only because they must, and need constant supervision and persuasion.

✓ Theory Y
Managerial assumption that people like to work and will excel if given the right opportunity.

7. Distinguish among Theory X, Theory Y, and Theory Z management.

Theory Z

Managerial emphasis on employee involvement in all aspects of the job, including decision making.

form complex tasks involving interaction with others respond best to a Theory Y approach, as do better-educated employees. And individuals who have completed their training and display the potential for self-motivation are also best managed according to Theory Y.

Theory X is like Taylor's scientific management in its emphasis on the task. Theory Y often creates a Hawthorne effect: Employees reward management with improved quality and productivity. Notice, too, that Theory X managers think people are concerned only with satisfying their physiological and safety needs—the lower levels on Maslow's hierarchy. They therefore assume that employees will be motivated only by more money or greater job security. Theory Y managers think people are also motivated by higher-order needs, such as self-esteem and self-actualization. This is why they give workers greater freedom.

Theory Z: Participative Management

Business professor William Ouchi has added another alternative to McGregor's Theory X and Theory Y. Ouchi's early work, which contrasted the management characteristics of Japanese and American companies, led him to propose Theory Z management in the 1980s. **Theory Z** managers emphasize employee involvement in all aspects of the job. Theory Z takes the assumptions of Theory Y one step further by empowering employees to participate in important business decisions. Theory Z builds on Theory Y, just as Theory Y built on the Hawthorne effect.

In another echo of the Hawthorne effect, the involvement of employees in decision making seems to produce high motivation. Managers who use Theory Z may, for example, bring workers together in teams, as the Foxboro Co. did, each team having sufficient expertise and independence to redesign an entire work process. Table 11.2 contrasts the viewpoints held by Theories X, Y, and Z managers.

table 11.2　Theories X, Y, and Z

Theory X Managers Believe	Theory Y Managers Believe	Theory Z Managers Believe
1. Most people do not like to work.	1. Work is as natural to people as play if the conditions are favorable.	1. Work is done best when people are involved in all aspects of the job.
2. Most people lack ambition—they have little desire for responsibility and prefer to be directed.	2. People can be self-directed and creative at work if properly motivated.	2. Decision making works best when it involves everyone who will be affected by the decision.
3. Most people have little capacity for creativity in solving organizational problems.	3. Most people can solve business problems creatively.	3. Trust among all managers and workers is essential in order to maximize productivity.
4. Most people must be closely controlled and pushed to do their work.	4. Motivation occurs at the social, self-esteem, and self-actualization levels, as well as at the physiological and safety levels.	4. Employee involvement, closeness, and cooperation produce the highest level of organizational productivity.

The trend in management throughout this century has been from the tight control of scientific management to the opposite approach of worker empowerment. Each of the management methods reviewed above represents a step on that journey. Managers today are trying out new ways of empowering workers to take more initiative and responsibility than ever before.

Motivating Through Teamwork

Throughout this text, we have stressed that teamwork is an important part of doing business in the 1990s. Organizational design based on teamwork can motivate employees by giving them the freedom and responsibility to act on their own in the best interests of the organization.

8. Explain why self-directed work teams help motivate employees.

Ralph Stayer, CEO of Johnsonville Foods, a Wisconsin-based sausage manufacturer, built an organization of self-directed work teams by pushing decision making and responsibility down the hierarchy. The process started, explains Stayer, when a survey of employees "told me that people saw nothing for themselves at Johnsonville. It was a job, a means to an end that lay outside the company. I wanted them to commit themselves to a company goal, but they saw little to commit to."[18]

You may recall from Chapter 9 that a self-directed work team is a group of employees responsible for managing their own activities.

Stayer set up teams in which workers had control over their own work. They could make major decisions: whom to hire and fire and what salaries they themselves should receive. As the work groups gained the power to affect the company's performance, their members realized that they could benefit personally when the company did better. If they boosted sales and profits, they could afford to pay themselves more. If they increased productivity, they could reduce their overtime and have more leisure time while increasing profitability. They demanded more and better information about the company's finances. And they began to improve product quality to increase customer satisfaction, using customer surveys to help them make better decisions.

In giving employees the opportunity to contribute ideas and improvements, self-directed work groups motivate by meeting the self-esteem and self-actualization levels of Maslow's hierarchy of needs. This new employee role leads to a new role for managers, who now coordinate and support the employee teams. At Johnsonville Foods, this is reflected in the managers' title of "coordinator"; they provide the training, coordination, information, and support that enable teams to make decisions themselves.

Cross-functional teams are another alternative that many companies are trying. Cross-functional teams are not self-managed; they work for a team leader. Nonetheless, the work arrangement enables all team members to make important contributions. At Chrysler Corp. such teams create new car designs.[19] At Black and Decker, people from many different departments were formed into 39 teams and told to come up with ideas for improvements. Of the 200 ideas submitted by the teams, 59 were implemented, saving the company some $3 million, giving employees a heightened sense of involvement, and improving lines of communication throughout the company.[20]

Cross-functional teams, discussed in Chapter 9, draw together personnel from different functional areas of the organization to improve operations and communication.

Motivating Today's Work Force

The motivation theories we have been discussing in this chapter are the building blocks from which managers create motivation programs within their own organizations. Once managers understand what motivates people in the workplace, they can tailor these various approaches to suit their own employees, goals, and environments. Before reviewing the characteristics of an effective motivation program, let's look at the characteristics of today's work force.

Motivating a Diverse Work Force

9. Describe today's diverse work force.

The challenge of motivating workers is changing as the work force itself changes. Today's workers reflect a wide range of diversity—in nationality, age, customs, and values—and this trend will continue as the overall proportion of majority workers (those labeled as white) continues to shrink. Figure 11.3 reveals how the ethnic makeup of the U.S. work force will change by the year 2000.

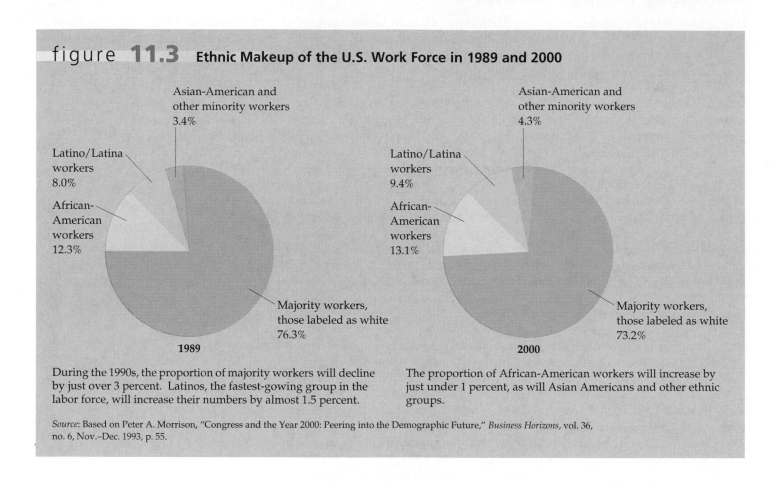

figure **11.3**   **Ethnic Makeup of the U.S. Work Force in 1989 and 2000**

Asian-American and other minority workers 3.4%

Latino/Latina workers 8.0%

African-American workers 12.3%

Majority workers, those labeled as white 76.3%

1989

Asian-American and other minority workers 4.3%

Latino/Latina workers 9.4%

African-American workers 13.1%

Majority workers, those labeled as white 73.2%

2000

During the 1990s, the proportion of majority workers will decline by just over 3 percent. Latinos, the fastest-gowing group in the labor force, will increase their numbers by almost 1.5 percent.

The proportion of African-American workers will increase by just under 1 percent, as will Asian Americans and other ethnic groups.

Source: Based on Peter A. Morrison, "Congress and the Year 2000: Peering into the Demographic Future," *Business Horizons*, vol. 36, no. 6, Nov.–Dec. 1993, p. 55.

- During the remainder of this century, three out of every five new entrants to the labor force will be members of an ethnic minority, as shown in Figure 11.4. By the end of the decade, Latinos are projected to comprise 30 percent of all new workers; African Americans, 18 percent; and Asian Americans and other minorities, 12 percent.[21]

- Between 1960 and 1990, the major change in the makeup of the U.S. work force was the proportion of women who went to work outside the home. In 1960, one-third of the labor force was women. By 1990, their numbers had grown to nearly half the labor force. Today, nearly 75 percent of women in their early forties are in the work force, and some 70 percent of women in their early twenties work outside the home. By the year 2000, women will comprise roughly 63 percent of all new workers.[22]

- As the baby-boom generation matures, the number of workers between the ages of 35 and 54 will increase to almost half the work force, up from 40 percent in 1988. But the number of workers under 35 will decline, creating a shortage of entry-level workers during the late 1990s.[23]

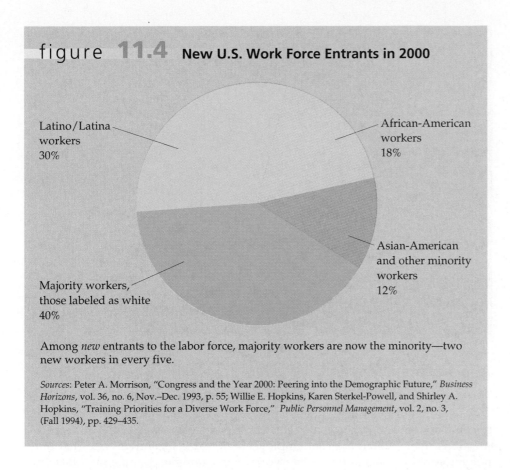

figure **11.4** **New U.S. Work Force Entrants in 2000**

Latino/Latina workers 30%

African-American workers 18%

Majority workers, those labeled as white 40%

Asian-American and other minority workers 12%

Among *new* entrants to the labor force, majority workers are now the minority—two new workers in every five.

Sources: Peter A. Morrison, "Congress and the Year 2000: Peering into the Demographic Future," *Business Horizons*, vol. 36, no. 6, Nov.–Dec. 1993, p. 55; Willie E. Hopkins, Karen Sterkel-Powell, and Shirley A. Hopkins, "Training Priorities for a Diverse Work Force," *Public Personnel Management*, vol. 2, no. 3, (Fall 1994), pp. 429–435.

As a group, workers in their twenties, widely identified as members of Generation X, embody values that reflect in many ways the best ideas we have studied in this text. They value honesty and ethical behavior in their employer, empowerment at work, and a balance between their work and personal lives. While to some this reflects a lack of respect for authority or a "slacker"attitude, most younger workers don't fit that stereotype. They are on the lookout for jobs and careers that combine creativity, flexibility, and autonomy. They want to know how they are performing at work and to contribute to the overall goals of the business.[24]

Increased labor force diversity can be a tremendous strength for organizations. Workers of different ages and from different backgrounds bring diverse perspectives to the workplace, and this diversity can result in better decision making. To successfully motivate a diverse work force, owners and managers who are sensitive to individual differences are developing motivation programs based both on the goals of the organization and on the characteristics of its employees.

Characteristics of a Well-Designed Motivation Program

A well-designed, effective program for motivating workers must be meaningful in terms of each employee's needs. It must also ensure that employees' work makes a splash that earns accurate and timely feedback from management. Let's look at some of the characteristics of such programs.

10. List and discuss four characteristics of an effective motivation program.

TQM and Motivation

George Westinghouse Vocational-Technical High School in Brooklyn, New York, is one of a growing number of U.S. schools that are employing total quality management principles to achieve educational reform. Boosted by the inception in 1996 of the Malcolm Baldrige National Award for Quality in Education, and with help from corporations such as Ricoh, IBM, and Xerox, these schools are getting results. Participants use TQM principles to improve attendance and parental involvement and to support learning techniques that stress constant improvement and better results, from higher test scores to lower dropout rates. These students are not just practicing their soldering techniques, they're perfecting them.

Appropriate Rewards

Since, as Maslow showed, motivation varies from person to person, the best way to motivate a varied work force may be through individual agreements between manager and subordinate. This can be difficult in large, traditional organizations, which often offer all employees the same incentive—one that may not be equally motivating to everyone. For example, companies often announce a prize, such as a luxury trip, to the individual or group that improves performance the most over the course of a year. For workers who have no interest in travel, or are taking care of children or aging parents, such a trip will have no motivational effect. Truly motivating rewards are best defined by each employee and his or her manager. A merit raise or promotion, more free time, or additional responsibility may be much more motivating to many individuals. A self-directed work team may even be empowered to set its own goals and the rewards for achieving them.

Advance Negotiation

Employees should be informed about and should agree in advance to the rewards they will receive for meeting goals. Manager and employee might agree, for example, that the project team will be given two days off if the project comes in a full week ahead of schedule. This takes the mystery—and the possibility of disappointment—out of the motivation system. When task and reward clarity are high, employees have clear goals to aim for and are motivated by the prospect of receiving a specific reward for their efforts.

Fairness

Motivation efforts must be fair to all workers. For instance, new employees should not be expected to produce as much or as well as more experienced employees. Good performance should always be rewarded, and poor performance should never be rewarded. If workers are not penalized for poor performance, more productive employees will be discouraged and reduce their level of performance. Fairness also manifests itself in strong antidiscriminatory policies, turning legal requirements into company policy. Electronics company EDS has actively recruited minorities and women by asking them, "Do you value working with a company that rewards on the basis of performance?"[25]

Supportive Concern

A company that shows concern for its employees' satisfaction and development takes the first step toward a relationship of mutual loyalty. Managers can show employees they care by:

- Assisting them in any way necessary to be successful in their jobs.
- Providing specific and positive feedback as soon as possible when they do something right.
- Helping them to "win,"—to reach their goals as well as the company's.
- Showing an interest in their personal lives and being responsive to personal problems, for example, by allowing time off for family emergencies.

Provisions for day-care, family health insurance, flexible work schedules, and maternity and paternity leaves all signal that a company cares. Many managers worry about the high cost of such programs, but motivation theory suggests that they are good investments that more than pay for themselves through greater employee loyalty and motivation. Two recent studies, at pharmaceutical company Johnson & Johnson and at auto-parts maker Fel-Pro, seem to confirm this. Both showed increases in worker productivity when family-oriented benefits were provided.[26] People work harder for a company that shows its appreciation of their work by working harder for them.

Designing a Motivation Program

Motivating employees is a process that evolves as managers and workers learn and develop within their organization's distinctive setting. As Figure 11.5 illustrates, motivation programs move through four steps: setting goals, establishing performance standards, providing feedback, and rewarding desired results.

11. List and describe the four steps of an effective motivation program, noting the five characteristics of effective goals.

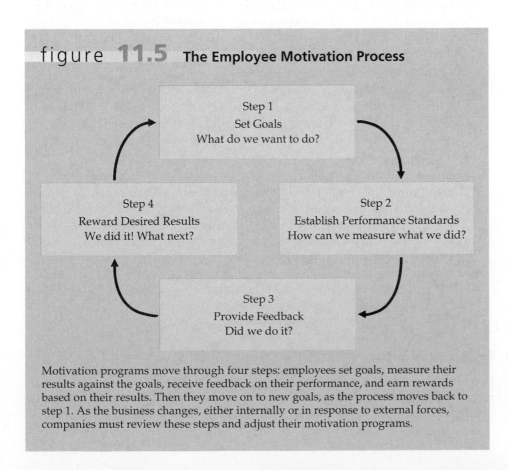

figure 11.5 The Employee Motivation Process

Step 1
Set Goals
What do we want to do?

Step 2
Establish Performance Standards
How can we measure what we did?

Step 3
Provide Feedback
Did we do it?

Step 4
Reward Desired Results
We did it! What next?

Motivation programs move through four steps: employees set goals, measure their results against the goals, receive feedback on their performance, and earn rewards based on their results. Then they move on to new goals, as the process moves back to step 1. As the business changes, either internally or in response to external forces, companies must review these steps and adjust their motivation programs.

As the business grows or shrinks, or as the business climate changes, companies review the process, adjusting their motivation program as necessary.

Step 1: Set Goals

Good performance starts by setting clear goals and objectives that are relevant to the business's strategies. Employees need to know exactly what the employer expects from them. The SMART approach to goal setting meets all the criteria for good program design. SMART is an acronym formed from the first letter of the five characteristics of effective goals: **SMART goals** are specific, motivational, attainable, relevant, and trackable. When employees are asked to accomplish goals that fit this description, their task clarity will be high and it will be easier to motivate them.

- *Specific.* A goal is a target. The more specific it is, the greater the likelihood of attaining it. A 12 percent increase in unit production will be discussed much more often and achieved much more easily than a more abstract goal, such as "working faster."
- *Motivational.* The goal needs to be exciting. Few people will be motivated by a plan to cut office phone bills by 2 percent. In contrast, Motorola did set a goal people could get excited about: cutting manufacturing errors to fewer than one in a million, which saved millions of dollars and allowed the company to grow rapidly by gaining market share. That's the kind of goal everyone can appreciate.[27]
- *Attainable.* Moderately difficult yet attainable goals are the most motivating. Goals that are too easy will bore workers; those that are too difficult will frustrate them. The best goals are those that workers will "stretch" to achieve because they make the work more interesting. For example, training a new employee might be a good "stretch" goal for a new manager, but it would be too easy for a manager who has already trained dozens of employees. Motorola's quality goal is so ambitious that it may sound too difficult. However, the company has a successful system for improving quality, and it is giving every employee the tools and training needed to make the goal attainable.
- *Relevant.* Goals need to be relevant to employees and their work. For example, a project deadline will become a significant target date if employees know the project is important to the organization or if they have to learn new skills to meet it. We are motivated to accomplish goals that are important to us.
- *Trackable.* It should be clear when a goal is reached, or when steps are being taken to reach it. A job or activity that cannot be measured probably cannot be accomplished. For example, a worker who is responsible for assembling 20 cordless telephones per hour on a production line has a clear, measurable goal. Even service goals, such as being friendly to customers, can be measured. For example, in one bank, customers identified "friendly" tellers as those who (1) smiled and made direct eye contact, (2) used the customer's name, and (3) spoke of a nonbusiness topic, such as the weather. This bank was able to track friendliness by measuring the frequency with which customers mentioned these three behaviors.

Step 2: Establish Performance Standards

Performance standards are formal descriptions of expected levels of performance. Managers cannot expect employees to know what good performance is unless someone tells them clearly, *before* an attempt is made to monitor them.

Task Clarity and Goal Setting

Workplace safety is a fundamental goal for any business. When goals and performance toward those goals are on prominent display, as they are at this oil refinery, employees are better motivated to achieve desired results.

 **SMART goals**

Goals that are specific, motivational, attainable, relevant, and trackable.

 performance standards

Formal descriptions of expected levels of performance.

Managers usually set performance standards, although empowered employees may set their own.

The Good Samaritan Hospital in Cincinnati, Ohio, initiated standards for customer service for all its workers. One of them is a satisfaction guarantee that patients will get a response within 30 minutes of telephoning a hotline.[28] This goal, which represents a performance standard for employees, has become a marketing tool for the hospital.

Step 3: Provide Feedback on Performance

No employee enjoys a "no-splash" work environment. An employee in such a situation is like an Olympic contender ignorant of his or her own speed records. Feedback is a motivator, and weak or inaccurate feedback reduces task clarity and hurts motivation. To encourage progress toward a goal, feedback should be:

- *Frequent.* Employees should receive feedback as often as possible. Increasing the amount of feedback can by itself improve performance. Salespeople are often highly motivated because information regarding sales is organized, tracked, and communicated to them quickly. Most people don't get enough feedback on the job.

- *Immediate.* To reinforce good behavior or change counterproductive behavior, prompt feedback is more effective than a delayed response. Prompt feedback is more useful because the employee receives it when his or her memory is still fresh. It also shows that the manager is tuned in to the individual's performance and is interested in trying to improve it.

- *Specific.* Feedback should be specific and directly relevant to the employee's work; this shows that the manager has been paying attention. Employees will lose motivation if their efforts and achievements are ignored. Similarly, good performers will be discouraged if their accomplishments are valued no more highly than those of poor performers.

Feedback can be positive or negative. **Positive feedback**, a response that encourages a desired behavior, is the most motivating. When a person does a job well and positive feedback follows, he or she will want to do the job well again. That is why it is so important to "catch people doing something right!"

Negative feedback, a response that discourages an unwanted behavior, is less effective than positive feedback but is sometimes necessary. Negative feedback should always focus on the performance of a task, not on the individual. Personal criticism discourages employees and reduces motivation; it may produce defensiveness or even hostility.

Step 4: Reward Desired Results

When workers meet set goals, rewards strengthen their motivation to continue the good work. The most effective rewards are tailored to people's needs. Consider these examples:

- When managers at One Valley Bank NA in Charleston, West Virginia, designed a new program to measure and reward productivity, they established performance standards and goals for each employee individually. Employees received regular reports of their progress on their goals, and those who exceeded them were rewarded with a share of the money that the new program saved the bank.

- In an effort to fight chronic absenteeism, New York Life Insurance Company holds a lottery each quarter, open only to employees who have

 positive feedback

A response that encourages a desired behavior.

 negative feedback

A response that discourages an unwanted behavior.

worked every day during that period. The first 10 names drawn earn a $2,000 bond, the next 20 earn a $100 bond, and 70 more receive one extra paid vacation day. A special lottery is also held for employees with perfect attendance records for the entire year. Prizes are two $1,000 bonds and 10 more paid days off. *Result*: The company estimates that absenteeism is 21 percent lower than it was in the year before the lottery started.[29]

- At Pegasus Personal Fitness Centers in Dallas, new physical fitness trainers are asked to list rewards, ranging in value from $25 to $200, that they would like to receive for reaching weekly and monthly goals. Employees have received concert tickets, limousine rentals, and extra half-day vacations. *Result*: Sales have more than doubled in six years.[30]

- At Delta Business Systems in Orlando, Florida, a wide range of nonsales employees are offered cash incentives for a variety of productivity improvements. For example, secretaries and administrative assistants compete monthly for a $50 award for Most Valuable Associate; dispatchers can earn up to $40 a month by scheduling preventive maintenance calls; and workers in the company's four warehouses can divide up to $400 every two months if they function smoothly as a team. *Result*: One team saved the company $10,000 within six months.[31]

- The Walt Disney Company has designed numerous programs to build a sense of camaraderie and identification with the organization, including peer recognition programs. During the Christmas holiday, the famous theme parks stay open one night just for employees and their families. On these occasions, managers dress in costumes and operate the parks for the employees. *Result*: These practices and the emphasis on employee motivation have made customer service the cornerstone of Disney's success.[32]

- Quill Corp. in Lincolnshire, Illinois, estimates its health care costs for a six-month period and places the money in a pool. Any money remaining at the end of the period is divided equally among participating employees. *Result*: Health care costs for the company declined approximately 35 percent in each of the first two years of the program.[33]

Does the fact that most of these successful programs use cash awards mean that the ideas in this chapter are wrong? No. In each program, the cash reward is a symbol representing other, more potent rewards. At the Pegasus fitness centers, for example, employees are given the power to design their own rewards, which allows them to be individualized and negotiated in advance. And New York Life Insurance Co.'s prizes are for achieving goals that meet the SMART criteria by being specific, motivational, attainable, relevant, and trackable. Each of these programs works because it was well designed. You can evaluate your own understanding of management, organizational design, and motivation by completing the skills check entitled "Putting It All Together."

You will learn more about employee benefits such as flexible time and family leave in Chapter 12.

Other examples suggest that motivation programs need not depend on cash rewards. For example, at Johnson & Johnson, absenteeism fell 50 percent among employees taking advantage of the company's flexible time and family-leave programs—a bigger improvement than in any of the programs discussed above, and one not dependent on any cash or other tangible award.[34] Johnson & Johnson also offers financial help (up to $2,000) for employees who adopt children and a referral service for employees seeking child care or elder care.[35]

As companies continue to devise ways to empower employees and develop innovative motivation programs, they are likely to move away from traditional cash awards and toward incentives that tap into the intrinsic motivation of their employees. Nonmonetary incentives will be especially powerful as an increasing number of workers search for a balance between their work and personal lives. Rewards will be more effective if they appeal to

Putting It All Together

In Chapters 8, 9, and 11 you have read about various management techniques, organizational designs, and motivation programs. Now it's your turn to apply your knowledge about how to achieve goals through the hands-on efforts of others. Using what you have learned so far, suggest a management style, organizational design, and motivation program for the following two groups. Be specific in your recommendations.

- Group 1: The 100 employees who answer the phones and take catalog orders in a mail-order, retail clothing business. The owners of the business want to increase sales by 15 percent over the next year.

- Group 2: A process improvement team of 15 faculty members, administrative staff, and students in charge of improving the class registration process at your college. The team's task is to consider the current registration process, to speed it up by eliminating all unnecessary steps, and to satisfy the customers—the students—by making the process more user friendly.

Group 1

Organizational Design (*Hint*: Consider possible benefits from working in teams rather than independently.)

Management Style (*Hint*: How can managers encourage workers' ideas about increasing sales?)

Motivation Program (*Hint*: Consider appropriate goals, a system to measure performance, and rewards for results.)

Group 2

Organizational Design (*Hint*: Consider how each step in the registration process can focus on the needs of students—the customers.)

Management Style (*Hint*: Consider benefits from asking versus telling workers involved in registration what to do.)

Motivation Program (*Hint*: Consider appropriate goals, a system to measure performance, and rewards for results.)

the varied needs of the increasingly diverse work force. The organization will need to ensure that it has adequate systems to support the new work force, from hiring and orientation to ongoing training and development. These systems are the focus of the next chapter.

Reviewing *Motivation and Performance*

What Motivates Workers?

1. **Name and discuss the five levels in Maslow's hierarchy of needs**. Starting at the lowest level, the needs are physiological, safety, social, self-esteem, and self-actualization needs. The first two levels refer to the basic needs for food, shelter, and job security and are related to adequate wages. The last three vary with the individual and relate to the need to feel part of a group, to be recognized for accomplishments, and to have interesting and challenging work. While people are not motivated to fulfill the higher-level needs until the lower-level needs are satisfied, they may continue pursuing several needs simultaneously.

2. **Explain Herzberg's theory of motivation, noting the relative importance of job enrichment and money as motivators**. According to Herzberg, unhappy workers are most concerned about maintenance factors, characteristics of the work environment—for example, space, lighting,

and pay. Those who are happy with their work focus on motivators, characteristics of the work itself—for example, responsibility, challenge, and opportunity for recognition, referred to as job enrichment. Although research indicates that money is not as strong a motivator as many people believe, it is useful when seen as recognition for a job well done, for example, through small-group incentives (SGIs).

3. **Contrast intrinsic and extrinsic motivation and describe the use of each in optimizing worker performance**. With intrinsic motivation, the person does a job for the sheer joy of doing it. Extrinsic motivation involves external rewards—praise or a cash bonus, for example—for a job well done. Research has found that people are more strongly motivated by internal rewards, that is, when a job fulfills their personal needs. However, extrinsic motivators will be effective if they support or enhance intrinsic motivators.

4. **Discuss the roles of task clarity and management by objectives in motivating employees.** Employees are best motivated when their goals are stated explicitly (management by objective) and when they are given strong, fast, and accurate feedback regarding their performance in meeting those goals (task clarity). Frequently, employees work with the manager in setting short-term goals that are reviewed at various points along the way to the final goal. Although the MBO approach is now considered too formal and slow-moving for some companies, the idea of participatory goal setting is still useful, as in the process of one minute management.

Management Approaches to Increasing Productivity

5. **Discuss Taylor's scientific management approach in terms of intrinsic motivation.** Based on extensive time-and-motion studies, Frederick Taylor developed specifications for improving job productivity. This scientific management approach structured every aspect of a job, thus substituting close supervision for a worker's intrinsic motivation. A variation of this approach, which has proved successful, empowers workers to apply scientific management to their own jobs—improving their own work methods, then implementing the improvements. This method thus engages workers' intrinsic motivation.

6. **Describe the Hawthorne studies and explain the significance of their findings.** In the Hawthorne studies, an experimental group worked under varied lighting conditions for prolonged periods, while a control group worked under the usual lighting conditions. The surprising findings were that employee productivity increases simply if the workers feel that managers consider their work important, even if working conditions are not improved. The concept of empowerment takes advantage of the Hawthorne effect by returning to workers their intrinsic motivation to perform well.

7. **Distinguish among Theory X, Theory Y, and Theory Z management.** Theory X and Theory Y managers differ in their view of employee motivation. Theory X managers, using a task-oriented style, believe that people work only because they must and do not want any responsibility, and therefore must be directed. Theory Y managers, building on the Hawthorne effect, assume that people like to work and can be self-directed and will succeed if given the opportunity. Although Theory Y is most appropriate for workers who perform complex tasks and must interact with others, Theory X may be useful for new workers and for those performing simple, repetitive tasks. Theory Z managers extend the concept of Theory Y management to include employee participation in the making of important decisions, often beyond the scope of their immediate responsibility.

8. **Explain why self-directed work teams help motivate employees.** Self-directed work teams have the freedom and responsibility to act on their own in the best interests of the organization. These teams might, for example, be in control of hiring, firing, and salaries. Being a member of a self-directing team that contributes to company profitability enhances an employee's intrinsic motivation, in particular, fulfilling his or her needs for self-esteem and self-actualization, as described by Maslow.

Motivating Today's Work Force

9. **Describe today's diverse work force.** America's strength has always been its diversity. Today, three in five new workers are members of ethnic minorities, whose representation in the U.S. labor force will grow to more than one-quarter of the total by the year 2000. The proportion of women in the work force continues to grow, as does the proportion of workers in midlife. The proportion of workers under 35, however, is shrinking. Among workers in their twenties, autonomy, empowerment, and flexibility at work are highly valued.

10. **List and discuss four characteristics of an effective motivation program.** One characteristic of an effective motivation program is to offer rewards appropriate to the needs of the employees. Because employees' needs vary, a self-directed work team may be empowered to set its own goals and rewards for achieving those goals. Another characteristic is to negotiate the rewards in advance so that employees have clear goals and specific, desirable rewards. Furthermore, motivation efforts must be fair to all workers—reward should be based on performance, taking into account experience and making sure that workers are not discriminated against because of minority status or gender. Finally, employers should show concern for employees by supporting them in reaching their goals, by providing feedback, and by showing an interest in their personal lives.

11. **List and describe the four steps of an effective motivation program, noting the five characteristics of effective goals.** The first step in a motivation program is to set goals that are specific, motivational, attainable, relevant, and trackable (SMART). The second step is for managers or empowered employees to set performance standards. In the third step, employees receive frequent, immediate, and specific feedback on their performance. Weak or inaccurate feedback reduces the clarity of performance standards and hurts motivation. Positive feedback is most motivating, although negative feedback is sometimes necessary. The final step is to provide rewards for meeting goals. To motivate workers, these rewards must be tailored to the workers' specific needs.

✓ Key Terms

motivation **323**	maintenance factors **324**	task clarity **329**	Theory Z **334**
physiological needs **323**	motivators **324**	management by objectives	SMART goals **340**
safety needs **323**	job enrichment **325**	(MBO) **330**	performance standards **340**
social needs **323**	small-group incentives	scientific management **332**	positive feedback **341**
self-esteem needs **323**	(SGIs) **327**	Hawthorne effect **333**	negative feedback **341**
self-actualization needs	intrinsic motivation **327**	Theory X **333**	
323	extrinsic motivation **328**	Theory Y **333**	

● Review Questions

1. Why do Maslow's five levels of needs form a hierarchy?

2. According to Herzberg, will good working conditions motivate you to work harder? Why or why not?

3. How does an intrinsic motivator differ from an extrinsic motivator? Describe one intrinsic motivator and one extrinsic motivator that influenced you to take this course.

4. What are the three characteristics of task clarity?

5. How did scientific management reinforce command-and-control management?

6. What was so surprising about the findings in the Hawthorne studies?

7. Think of the last time you worked for someone else. Was that person a Theory X or Theory Y manager? Cite specific examples to support your answer.

8. What two approaches to motivation does one minute management combine? What are its three steps?

9. How does empowerment help to motivate employees?

10. What are the four steps in a successful motivation program?

11. What are the characteristics of effective feedback?

12. Under what conditions are cash rewards most effective?

● Critical Thinking Questions

1. Assume that you have been working for two years to pay for a new car. You are about to make your last payment. Will you be motivated to continue working after the car loan has been paid off? Explain your answer in terms of (a) Maslow's hierarchy of needs and (b) intrinsic and extrinsic motivation.

2. If the instructor in this course wanted to ensure that the final exam had all the characteristics of task clarity, what would he or she be sure to explain during the last lecture before the exam?

3. In a company that has recently downsized and is unable to reward employees either with free time or money,

which style of management would be most effective, Theory X, Theory Y, or Theory Z? Why?

4. How do the five components of SMART goals tap into employees' intrinsic motivation? Using the examples described in this chapter, show how SMART goals can build on an employee's intrinsic motivation.

5. Why are individual agreements between a manager and an employee especially effective in motivating a diverse work force? Give two examples of tailoring a motivator to the characteristics of an employee.

REVIEW CASE *Jelly Bean Motivation*

Scott Meyers, a management consultant, says that recognition or rewards that are given to all employees regardless of how well they do their jobs are worthless. He calls such meaningless rewards "jelly bean" motivation. Jelly bean motivation occurs when someone gets something for nothing. Such recognition can even demotivate employees, especially those who are doing a good job. For example, an aircraft manufacturer in southern California decided one year to give a turkey to every employee for Christmas to improve employee motivation. The next year the company had to repeat the benefit because employees had come to expect it. But this time, employees complained that some people were getting bigger turkeys than others. So the president asked the supplier if he could get turkeys in one size. The supplier said no, that wasn't possible because turkeys don't all come in the same size. So the president sent out a memo stating that the size of the turkey had nothing to do with an employee's performance. Still the program got more and more complicated. Coupons were issued, and a full-time turkey administrator had to be hired to handle the program. Although costly, complex, and ongoing, the program never seemed to improve employee motivation.

1. What levels in the hierarchy of needs were affected by the turkey giveaway program?

2. Does jelly bean motivation use maintenance factors or motivators?

3. Do you think the turkey program could have created a Hawthorne effect? If so, in which year might it have been strongest?

4. How would you use the turkey program to empower employees?

CRITICAL THINKING CASE *Odetics Combines Creative Motivation and Fun*[36]

Having fun at work is an everyday event at Odetics, Inc., a high-technology company located—coincidentally—across the street from Disneyland in Anaheim, California. This manufacturer of spaceborne tape recorders, time-lapse video recorders, and courtroom audio recorders actually has a Fun Committee that periodically dreams up theme parties, runs a repertory theater, and maintains a relaxation room called the Odetics Oasis.

The company does a lot to maintain a motivating environment. Keith Brush, Odetics's personnel manager, summarizes the company's philosophy regarding motivation: "To get the most bang for your buck in terms of motivation you make it so comfortable that they [the employees] *want* to contribute. They don't do it for pins."

Although still relatively small, with only 450 employees, the company has developed a unique work environment since it started up in 1969. This is particularly impressive when you consider the nature of the company's business, which is for the most part focused on meeting project deadlines in the development of new products. When work teams are successful in meeting their deadlines, all members of the group are equally rewarded with large bonuses. There are also awards for Outstanding Associate (the company uses the word "associate" rather than "employee" to underscore the sense of community in the organization). And associates are encouraged to make suggestions that could improve on any aspect of the business. Promising suggestions are financially rewarded, and the suggester is often given the chance to implement the idea.

Besides creating a more enjoyable workplace, the company has succeeded in creating a more productive environment. And employees, who are given a great deal of personal freedom, love working there. In fact, the company has the lowest employee turnover of any electronics firm in California's Orange County, in an industry in which job hopping is a way of life.

1. Management at Odetics does a variety of things to cultivate a motivated work force. How do those mentioned fit into Maslow's hierarchy of needs?

2. Are these incentives primarily maintenance factors or motivators according to Herzberg's theory?

3. When Odetics faced a business decline due to a recession in the video recorder business, it did not lay off employees but rather transferred some to other divisions and did not fill positions that become vacant. Make an argument against such a policy.

4. Now argue in favor of the policy based on what you know about motivation.

5. Joel Slutzky, Odetics's chairman, teaches a course for interested employees on how to start your own business. He isn't scared that employees will leave en masse, although some have (and now do business with Odetics). Says Slutzky, "Not many decide to leave Odetics, but if they do, we want them to succeed." Classify Slutzky according to the management styles discussed in this chapter. Is he more of a Theory X, Y, or Z manager? Why does he teach the course?

Critical Thinking with the ONE MINUTE MANAGER

"You know, motivation is less of a mystery than I thought it was," Joanna observed, looking up from her text.

"Yes," said the One Minute Manager. "The topic can be overwhelming, especially for new managers trying to put it into practice. At first it seems difficult even to imagine that employees can be motivated in a systematic way. Everyone is so different and doing such different things. But once you understand the subject, it can be a rather simple and straightforward endeavor."

"I wouldn't go so far as to say it's simple," Carlos chimed in. "After all, there are lots of managers who don't seem to value or appreciate their workers, and many employees feel undervalued or underappreciated in companies everywhere."

"That may be so, but companies and managers who want to make a difference can do so by putting in a little effort, time, and thoughtfulness. For example, the Hyatt Corporation hosts monthly talks between its general managers and randomly selected groups of hotel staffers so they can keep in touch. It also periodically sends all its executives out to its hotels to provide guest services firsthand as a way of developing empathy with employees.[37] Whether you're Hilton Hotels, as we described earlier, or the Hyatt Corporation, motivation is a commonsense notion that can easily become common practice in every organization today."

1. Think about the kinds of things that motivate you. Do you think that the same kinds of things would motivate your employees, too? Why or why not?

2. Research shows that money is not as strong a motivator as most people believe. For example, recognition for a job well done is a much stronger motivator. What would you do to reward an employee for doing a particularly good job at some task?

3. You might someday be a manager. Do you think that you will be a Theory X, Y, or Z manager? Why?

12 Human Resource Management

In this chapter you will learn what human resource management is and how it attempts to match the needs of the organization with the talents of individuals who work for, or want to work for, the organization. We will examine how recent trends affect the way businesses manage their human resources, and how those trends affect employees' careers. We will look at the human resource processes for finding, hiring, training, and compensating employees.

The material in this chapter will help you in two different ways. By understanding the employer's perspective on human resource management, you may learn to be a more valuable employee. And by understanding the hiring process, you may learn to be a more successful job candidate. After reading this chapter, you will be able to reach the learning goals below.

Learning Goals

1. Explain the functions of human resource management in relation to the changing work force.
2. Identify and describe the components of human resource planning.
3. Identify the various sources of job applicants.
4. Describe methods of screening and testing potential employees and identify two alternative hiring procedures.
5. Describe the three forms of employee training and explain how employee performance is evaluated.
6. Discuss various paths in career development.
7. Identify the two forms of compensation available to employees today and describe the types of cash compensation.
8. Differentiate between fixed and flexible benefits.
9. Discuss the use of flexible work schedules and leaves to increase employee satisfaction.
10. Outline the various ways in which employees can change status in an organization.

Changing Needs for Changing Times

"I really need your advice," Joanna said as she walked into the One Minute Manager's office. "At least my best friend Emily does. She just finished her B.A. with a specialty in advertising. She's been offered work with a really good advertising agency, but she wouldn't be a regular employee. They want her to freelance on a big project they're doing. Should she accept their offer or continue looking for something on staff?"

"Emily has to decide for herself whether this is a good opportunity, Joanna. But I can tell you this much: Workers who are not full-time employees are now so common that they have a special name—the "contingency work force." According to a recent article in *Fortune* magazine, more than 40 percent of the CEOs at Fortune 500 companies use contingent workers, and the same number believe they'll be using more of them in the future.[1] It's a good way for the business to cut costs because it pays workers only when it needs them, and it doesn't have to pay for benefits, which can be very costly. Using contingent workers also helps a business to be flexible—it can grow and shrink quickly, without hiring or firing in-house staff."

"I can see why the company likes the arrangement," Carlos observed, "but why should Emily be interested in it?"

"Many contingent workers like the freedom and independence of hiring on for only one project. That way, they can try out the company without making a long-term commitment. If Emily and the agency like each other, the arrangement might become a permanent one. But even if it doesn't, temporary work can be a great way to gain experience or just have some income while looking for a permanent job."

"That sounds like a good deal for both parties," Joanna said.

"It can be," the One Minute Manager replied, "but only if both parties understand the ground rules. The company has to realize that Emily won't be as committed as she would be if she were a full-time employee. And Emily has to understand that the company's commitment is also limited, and she probably won't get paid sick days, vacation time, or health insurance. Contingent workers also have to pay their own Social Security taxes and file quarterly income taxes. Many people don't like those conditions."

"I'll be sure to tell her," Joanna promised. "My guess is that she'll take it, though, because she looked a long time before finding this opportunity. Thanks for the advice!"

Managing Human Resources in Today's Business Environment

Throughout this text, we have looked at many different businesses as they pare down layers of management, outsource, hire part-time workers, and introduce new technology to increase productivity and reduce labor costs. All these strategies help businesses to compete by cutting costs and permitting flexibility, so that they can respond rapidly to customers' changing needs. But necessary as these strategies are, they can bump headfirst into another important organizational need—finding, hiring, training, and motivating employees who can function as empowered members of work teams, pursuing organizational goals at a level of high productivity.[2] Add to this the dynamics of an increasingly diverse work force, as described in Chapter 11, and managing human resources becomes a constant challenge.

Human resource management is the process of ensuring that a business has an adequate supply of skilled, trained, and motivated employees to meet the organization's objectives. In this chapter, you will see how human resource managers work with other managers to research and forecast employment needs. You will learn how they help develop programs for hiring, training, evaluating, compensating employees—and, when necessary, for laying off employees or firing them. In some businesses, human resource managers have become adept at tailoring their techniques to the needs of the **contingent work force**—part-time, temporary, and self-employed workers who do not conform to the traditional model of the 9-to-5, full-time employee. You will also see how human resource managers must stay in touch with legal and ethical issues to ensure that the businesses they work in treat employees in acceptable ways. First, though, we review some of the trends that have made human resource management so challenging in the current business scene.

The Changing Work Force

In 1987, the Hudson Institute prepared a report, *Workforce 2000*, for the U.S. Department of Labor.[3] It has been nearly a decade since that report, but its predictions have held up well. Here are some of the predicted changes and some current findings:[4]

- *Labor shortages will occur.* Growth in the labor force will fall sharply, from 2.9 percent to 1 percent per year as fewer new job entrants join the work force.

- *Jobs will require developed skills.* Half of all jobs will be service, technical, or managerial positions that require college degrees. At the same time that the number of eligible skilled workers is expected to diminish, employers will increasingly demand more highly skilled and trained employees.[5]

- *Most available workers will be unskilled.* Each year, 700,000 students drop out of high school, and an equal number are functionally illiterate. In Los Angeles, for example, nearly 4 out of 10 students quit school, and in Chicago the dropout rate is 46 percent. As Michael Godfrey, the head of the Los Angeles dropout prevention program says, "You wind up having an unskilled labor force. That forces businesses to leave L.A."[6]

- *The work force will mature.* Nearly half of all employees will be at least 40 years of age. Almost 44 million Americans will be over age 60, and more than half of all families will be two-*pension* households—both members will have retired.

 human resource management

Ensuring that a business has an adequate supply of skilled, trained, and motivated employees to meet the organization's objectives.

 contingent work force

Part-time, temporary, and self-employed workers who do not conform to the traditional model of the 9-to-5, full-time employee.

1. Explain the functions of human resource management in relation to the changing work force.

- *Many more women will work outside the home.* More than 60 percent of all working-age women will have jobs. Women now represent 47 percent of the work force, and women with children under age 6 represent the fastest growing segment of the work force. According to a report by the Federal Glass Ceiling Commission, created by the Civil Rights Act of 1991, 57 percent of the work force are women or minorities or both. However, white males still hold 97 percent of top management jobs.[7]

- *Minority and immigrant workers will be a larger portion of the work force.* Six in 10 workers will be members of minority groups or immigrants. Nearly two-thirds of working-age immigrants will join the work force, many of them better educated than new work force entrants born in the United States.

- *The percentage of workers in the contingent work force will increase.* Part-time, temporary, and self-employed workers now represent more than 25 percent of the civilian work force. This share is expected to increase to 33 percent by 2000. In a survey of 266 young professionals earning an average of $37,500, 38 percent say their most important personal concern is marrying and having a family. And 50 percent say their favorite activity is spending time with family and friends. A decade ago, surveys showed most young professionals' top priority was work, not family.[8]

Contingent Work Force

Placing "just-in-time workers" like these stock clerks is a growing business for employment agencies around the country. In fact, many agencies are actually taking the place of traditional employers by training their job candidates in business skills, placing them in jobs, and offering them benefits such as health insurance.

At the time of this writing, the future of affirmative action programs is uncertain as politicians and elected officials pare back government spending and programs. But one thing is sure: Diversity is a permanent part of today's work force and of the management and ownership of small businesses, as we saw in Chapters 6 and 7. These changes reflect the growing diversity of the country as a whole, and smart businesses will be sure that their work forces understand and offer service to the many diverse groups that represent the current flavors in the melting pot of America.

The Need for Increased Productivity

Companies—including those that are successful—are seeking to reduce their costs in order to compete more effectively, and labor costs are one of the largest fixed expenses in a company's budget. As you saw in Chapter 10, many companies are improving production processes and retraining employees using total quality management practices. Other companies find it necessary to reduce the number of permanent, full-time employees. Downsizing to eliminate employees—even entire layers of management—requires that the remaining employees become more knowledgeable, productive, and empowered. Advances in technology also allow businesses to operate with fewer, more specialized employees.

Strategies of Flexibility

Business strategies that increase an organization's flexibility enable it to respond rapidly to changes in the environment. As we saw in Chapter 9, one such strategy is *outsourcing*, contracting with outside organizations for one or more business services. A growing number of businesses outsource marketing analysis, accounting, manufacturing, and other functions. Data services firms such as Ceridian Corp., headquartered in Minneapolis, Minnesota, and Automatic Data Processing, Inc. (ADP), of Roseland, New Jersey, specialize in processing payroll for other companies. The popularity of ADP's payroll processing services is evident: Each year the company distributes paychecks to some 16 million workers and issues more than 30 million W-2 forms.[9]

Another trend in the ongoing quest of American business for greater flexibility is the use of more part-time employees. The use of part-time employees makes it much easier for a company to schedule workers around peak periods of demand, and it creates a larger employment pool upon which to draw. For example, Federal Express Corp. accommodates wide daily swings in work volume at its Memphis, Tennessee, branch by using only part-time employees below the level of supervisor. And at Novations, Inc., a management-skills assessment company located in Provo, Utah, almost all test scoring is done by part-time subcontractors, at times including up to 40 or 50 subcontractors, depending on the company's needs. Novations has found that this flexible, part-time work force is even faster and more economical than automated computer scoring.[10]

Some companies consider **employee leasing**—purchasing the long-term services of a worker from another company—to be a good option. Texas Instruments Inc. leases about 15 percent of its employees, and nationally the number of leased employees is now more than a million.[11] Besides saving money that would otherwise be paid in benefits, leasing allows a business to avoid the commitment of time, paperwork, and expenses associated with recruiting and maintaining regular employees. In many cases, firms that lease employees to other firms recruit and screen the workers, administer payroll and other compensation, and conduct formal performance appraisals. Freed of these administrative tasks, a company can reduce its overhead and concentrate on the tasks that will bring it more business.

Although these trends affect all companies to some degree, most human resource managers perform the traditional functions of planning for the future labor needs of the business, hiring new employees, training and developing employees, determining equitable compensation and benefits, and reassigning and terminating employees. Let's turn now to the first of these, human resource planning.

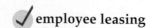

employee leasing

Purchasing the long-term services of a worker from another company.

Human Resource Planning

2. Identify and describe the components of human resource planning.

Recall from Chapter 8 that planning is one of the four functions of management.

Human resource management—like all management—begins with planning. Managers in various departments work with human resources to anticipate specific staffing needs, which then become a detailed plan. This planning process, depicted in Figure 12.1, consists of research, forecasting, and job analysis, which includes drafting job descriptions and job specifications.

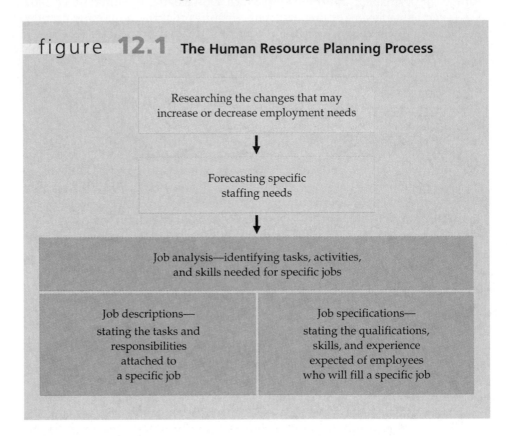

figure **12.1**   **The Human Resource Planning Process**

Researching the changes that may increase or decrease employment needs

↓

Forecasting specific staffing needs

↓

Job analysis—identifying tasks, activities, and skills needed for specific jobs

Job descriptions—stating the tasks and responsibilities attached to a specific job

Job specifications—stating the qualifications, skills, and experience expected of employees who will fill a specific job

Research

Human resource managers collect information on upcoming changes that could affect the business's labor needs. Such changes might include the business's growth plans, new products and services, or developing problems. For example, Pratt & Whitney, a manufacturer of aircraft engines, recently decided to move its operations from East Hartford, Connecticut, to Georgia to reduce its operating expenses.[12] A move of this type requires that human resource managers work with other managers to develop plans for transporting personnel who plan to move along with the company and for recruiting, hiring, and training workers at the new location.

Research indicating dramatic economic or market changes permits human resources to make creative plans to head off trouble. Alpine Banks of Colorado suffered dramatic customer losses during the recession of the early 1990s. With the closing of two of the area's largest employers, customers moved out of the area and revenues dropped dramatically. Additionally, Colorado passed legislation allowing national bank corporations to purchase Colorado banks—increasing competitive pressures on small, locally owned banks.

Alpine Banks's management had observed, however, that a large Latino community had grown up around the area's ski resorts during the preceding decade. With this knowledge in hand, the bank made a concerted effort to attract Latino depositors by hiring bilingual employees. The human resource department of Alpine Banks placed Spanish-language help-wanted ads in the local newspapers, and it asked its Latino employees for referrals of potential employees. Ultimately, the bank hired 25 bilingual workers and was able to sign up hundreds of new depositors as a result.[13]

Forecasting

Forecasting takes a close look not only at a company's labor needs but also at sources of labor supply. Highly skilled technology workers, such as computer programmers and laboratory researchers, often cluster around regions where their skills are in high demand, such as northern California's Silicon Valley. Other regions of the country have different kinds of high-skilled, specialized work forces. For example, Michigan has an extensive pool of machine operators and New York City is world famous for its financial specialists. But even within such areas, labor supply and demand change constantly, and businesses must deal with these frequent and hard-to-predict developments.

In many areas there is a serious mismatch between labor and jobs. Much of the world's labor, skilled and unskilled, is found in developing countries. At the same time, most of the growth in the need for labor is generated in the cities of the industrialized world. This mismatch is triggering massive relocations. In some cases, people follow jobs. The greatest relocation involves young, well-educated workers flocking to the cities of the developed world.[14] But employers are also migrating. Jobs with a high labor content, such as clothing and footwear manufacture, are relocating to less-developed nations as manufacturers contract work out to low-cost labor markets.[15]

Job Analysis

The human resource department prepares job analyses of individual positions throughout the company. A **job analysis** is a general overview of all aspects of a particular job. This information is gathered from those within the organization who understand the tasks involved in each position and the degree of authority, responsibility, and accountability the worker has for accomplishing those tasks. For example, a job analysis of an administrative assistant position would specify the technical and social skills the prospective employee should possess, such as word processing skills, attention to detail, a pleasant manner, and the ability to work under pressure. It would also describe the administrative assistant's responsibility for accomplishing certain tasks and the authority delegated for doing those tasks. It would probably also list the other people within the company with whom the administrative assistant would interact. Many firms develop these documents for all company positions and maintain them on file, whether the position is to be filled immediately or not.

Once the job analysis is completed, a job description and job specification are developed from it. These two tools are used to locate appropriate job candidates and subsequently to judge their performance on the job.

Job Descriptions

The basic output of any job analysis is a **job description**—a statement of the tasks and responsibilities of a particular job. In the case of an administrative assistant, the job description might list such responsibilities as drafting correspondence, typing reports, maintaining a database, routing interoffice mail, and answering department phones. Notice that these are all statements about job tasks, not about the skills of the person who will perform them.

 job analysis

A general overview of all aspects of a particular job.

 job description

A statement of the tasks and responsibilities of a particular job.

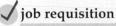

job specification

A statement of the qualifications, skills, and previous experience a person needs to perform a given job.

job requisition

A request for hiring submitted to the human resource department.

Job Specifications

A **job specification** is a statement of the qualifications, skills, and previous experience a person needs to perform a given job. Whereas the job description focuses on tasks and responsibilities, the job specification focuses on the skills and abilities of the person who will perform those tasks. A job specification for an administrative assistant might include familiarity with the WordPerfect software package, the ability to type at a minimum speed of 40 words per minute, and possession of a high school diploma and one year's work experience in an office. Figure 12.2 contains a sample job description and job specification.

The job specification helps employers decide how well a candidate's qualifications measure up to the minimum needs of a position. This is far easier to do for some requirements than for others. For example, one can easily determine whether a person has graduated from college; it is far more difficult to figure out whether a candidate has leadership qualities or the ability to work effectively as a team member.

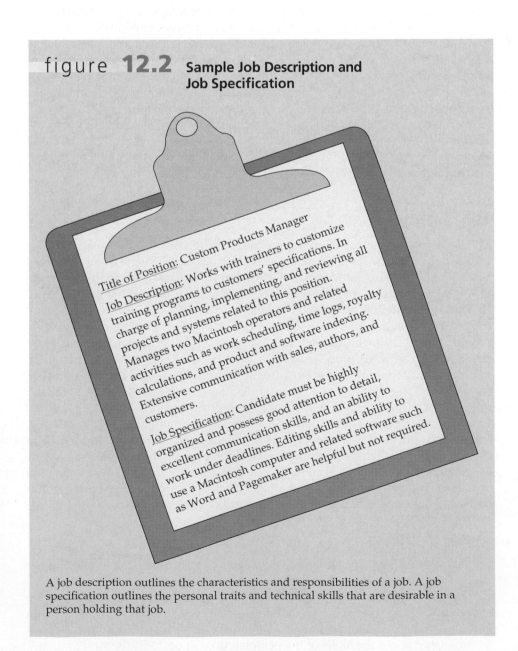

figure **12.2** **Sample Job Description and Job Specification**

Title of Position: Custom Products Manager

Job Description: Works with trainers to customize training programs to customers' specifications. In charge of planning, implementing, and reviewing all projects and systems related to this position. Manages two Macintosh operators and related activities such as work scheduling, time logs, royalty calculations, and product and software indexing. Extensive communication with sales, authors, and customers.

Job Specification: Candidate must be highly organized and possess good attention to detail, excellent communication skills, and an ability to work under deadlines. Editing skills and ability to use a Macintosh computer and related software such as Word and Pagemaker are helpful but not required.

A job description outlines the characteristics and responsibilities of a job. A job specification outlines the personal traits and technical skills that are desirable in a person holding that job.

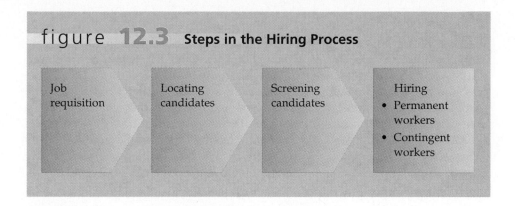

figure **12.3** **Steps in the Hiring Process**

| Job requisition | Locating candidates | Screening candidates | Hiring
• Permanent workers
• Contingent workers |

The Hiring Process

The hiring process begins when an employment need is identified, perhaps because an employee has left the company or a new contract creates a need for more employees. For instance, Eagle Bronze, Inc., a metal-casting company located in Lander, Wyoming, identified a need for trainees when demand for its products suddenly surged.[16]

The first step in finding a new employee is taken when a department manager or line supervisor submits to the human resource department a **job requisition**—a request for hiring—ideally, one based on a job specification developed in the planning process. The human resource department then begins work to locate a small number of qualified candidates. In most companies, the human resource staff screens candidates and provides information about applicants—such as test scores, resumés, and applications—to the manager who will do the actual hiring. Figure 12.3 outlines the steps in the hiring process.

Sources of Job Applicants

Sources of job applicants are almost as varied as types of applicants. To some extent, the kind of position being filled determines where a request for applicants will be placed. Managers may seek applicants with little or no experience for an *entry-level* position, such as receptionist or mailroom clerk. The pool of applicants who could fill these jobs is very large. Other openings, such as mechanic or financial systems analyst, may be limited to applicants who have many years of experience and can perform well with minimal training. Suitable applicants for such openings may be hard to find and will tend to command higher salaries. In most cases, however, employers look inside the company before moving to outside resources. Table 12.1 lists typical sources of new employees.

table **12.1** **Sources of New Employees**

Internal	External
Job postings	Local newspaper ads
Employee referrals	Campus recruitment
Walk-in applications	Private employment agencies
	Public employment agencies
	Professional associations
	Professional journals

3. Identify the various sources of job applicants.

Internal Sources

The first place most companies look for qualified applicants is inside the organization. Company employees have well-known work habits and performance records, and they are already familiar with many of the people, products, policies, and procedures of the organization. In addition, hiring from within is a tremendous morale booster for employees, who see that they can move up in their companies. Atlas Headwear, Inc., a Phoenix manufacturer of military and sports hats, has a firm policy of promoting from within. With a predominantly Asian-American and Latino work force, in which 80 percent of workers are women, Atlas Headwear's management team is a microcosm of diversity.[17]

Job Postings   A **job posting** is a notice advertising available positions within an organization. Job postings are displayed in public places, such as department bulletin boards and company newsletters, where all employees have access to them. Sun Microsystems, Inc., of Mountain View, California, publishes a weekly listing of all openings along with the job description and specifications for each position. The company encourages all employees who feel they are qualified to apply for openings that interest them.

At the former Pacific Northwest Bell, now a part of US West, Inc., based in Englewood, Colorado, a computerized job-skills bank is used to help match employer needs with employee skills and interests. Any employee may choose to fill out a detailed profile of his or her skills, experience, and job preferences, including relocation preferences. The company's computerized personnel database adds existing information about the employee to that profile, including job history and training. Once a week, the human resource staff checks current job openings against the database. When a potential match appears, the human resource department notifies the employee and asks whether he or she is interested in the available opening.[18]

Employee Referrals   Another valuable source of new hires is the **employee referral**, a current employee's recommendation of friends or acquaintances. Referrals have a high probability of success, perhaps because they already know something about the job and the company from the employee who refers them. Many employers pay a "finder's fee" to employees if their candidate is hired.

GB Tech, Inc., of Houston, Texas, used employee referrals to quickly recruit a work force of highly skilled workers. The company, which supplies information systems support to the federal government, had no real track record of performance. It wanted a pool of seasoned retirees who would lend credibility and strong staff credentials to the fledgling operation. According to Gale Burkett, GB Tech's chair and chief executive officer, "We were concerned about whether we would be accepted because we were still a fairly new company."[19]

The company started its recruiting effort by placing ads for candidates. Once a few applicants were hired, they were asked to contribute the names of other skilled workers who might want to work for the firm. Eventually, GB Tech hired 10 formerly retired workers and placed 70 others on a list of available candidates. Partly as a result of GB Tech's use of employee referrals and the success of its new workers in identifying and winning new business opportunities, employment has grown since 1990 from 14 to 415 workers.

External Sources

If internal sources fail to produce an appropriate candidate, the company will broaden its search by advertising in local newspapers, distributing job specifications to various employment agencies, or recruiting on college campuses. Government regulations may require public advertising if the firm receives taxpayer money, for example, in the form of a grant to a university or a contract with a defense contractor.

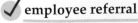 **job posting**

A notice advertising available positions within an organization.

employee referral

A current employee's recommendation of friends or acquaintances.

Employment agencies are especially helpful in locating hard-to-find applicants with advanced or specialized skills. Private agencies charge a fee for successful placements. Some charge the company for their services; others charge the job applicant. It is in the applicant's best interest to read the agency's contract closely and to be sure the responsibilities and obligations of both parties are clearly stated and understood. Important points are who pays the fee, how much will be paid, and whether the agency has an exclusive right to represent the applicant. Such issues can become major problems if applicant and agency disagree at some later time.

Federal job services and state employment development departments also operate employment agencies, but their services are free. Eagle Bronze, mentioned earlier in this section, knew that its remote location would make it more difficult to find qualified job candidates. To overcome that challenge, the company's human resource department consulted with the Wyoming Department of Employment, which identified potential job candidates at the local Wind River Indian Reservation.[20] Federal and state services are easily found in the government listings of the local phone directory.

Many large corporations and educational institutions also operate free *job lines*. These prerecorded telephone announcements list openings, brief job descriptions, and application information. Job lines may be listed in local phone books, or applicants can call the human resource department of particular organizations for their numbers.

Although numbers are down from the 1980s, many large employers recruit on college campuses. Microsoft Corp., for example, visits 137 campuses, some up to four times a year. In a recent year it reviewed more than 120,000 resumés, held face-to-face interviews with 7,400 students, and hired 2,000 of them.[21] At Howard University, the historically African-American college in Washington, D.C., approximately 400 companies recruit employees through the placement office. Senior executives of Mobil Corp. and Ford Motor Co. make regular visits to the campus.[22]

Screening Candidates

Job applicants usually submit a resumé and cover letter to introduce themselves to a firm that has a job vacancy. A **resumé** is a brief summary of an applicant's relevant experience, ideally one or two pages in length. The cover letter highlights experience that particularly qualifies the applicant for the job and provides information on contacting him or her.

Individuals selected from the pool of applicants are usually called for an interview and tests, which in large firms are administered by the human resource department. There they are required to complete the company's own application form, which asks standard questions that enable the human resource employees to determine the candidate's experience level. The form also requests salary history, references, and other necessary information that will help in evaluating the candidate.

Employers almost always seek additional information through employment interviews, which are personal meetings with the candidate. Candidates may be interviewed by several individuals in the organization, including a manager, a human resource specialist, and potential co-workers, all of whom question the applicant about his or her skills and experience and answer any questions about the position and company. The most promising applicants may be asked to return for a second or even a third interview. For a look at some questions frequently raised in interviews, see the skills check entitled "Careful What You Say—Your Job May Depend on It" on page 360.

4. Describe methods of screening and testing potential employees and identify two alternative hiring procedures.

 resumé

A brief summary of an applicant's relevant experience, ideally one or two pages in length.

skills check

Careful What You Say—
Your Job May Depend on It

While a resumé gives a potential employer a glimpse of your experience and qualifications for a position, the interview is where a potential employer really gets to know you. The more prepared you are for an interview, the more confident you will be and the better impression you will make on your interviewer. The following questions and statements often appear on interview forms.

- Why should I hire you?
- Describe your educational background.
- What was your favorite course in school? Why?
- Describe the previous jobs you have had, beginning with the most recent.
- Why did you leave your last job?
- Most jobs have positive and negative qualities. What were some of the negative qualities of your last job?

- Describe something you did that was not normally part of your job.
- Do you like working with figures?
- What do you see yourself doing in five years?
- What starting salary do you expect?
- When can you start?

By practicing your answers to these questions, you can raise your chances of being one of those selected for the final cut. But remember that you are also interviewing the employer. Take time before your interview to think about what you want to know about the job, the company, and the people you would work with. Then concentrate on phrasing your questions gracefully and tactfully.

Source: Robert B. Nelson, *The Job Hunt* (Berkeley, Calif.: Ten Speed Press, 1986), pp. 45–46.

Employment Testing

A specified skill level is an essential requirement for some jobs. In such cases, the human resource department (in larger firms) or the department with the job opening administers skills tests, which can sometimes be elaborate. For instance, Toyota Motor Corp. observes candidates for auto assembly jobs on a simulated production line before making the final selection. Other firms test candidates on their ability to use computers for word processing, data organizing, or financial recordkeeping.

Many businesses give applicants more general tests, some of which attempt to obtain a psychological profile. Although the ability of such tests to predict performance in a particular job has been questioned, their use reflects the desire of human resource managers to reduce the risk of hiring the wrong person. Travel agency Rosenbluth International, with 27 offices scattered throughout the Middle Atlantic states, uses psychological tests to screen out "freeloaders, political animals, and egotists," according to Rosenbluth's chief executive.[23]

Questions of fairness in employment testing have recently been a source of significant controversy, much of it centering on charges of cultural bias in favor of white American males. Those who question the validity of employment testing argue that the tests measure education, culture, and achievements, rather than aptitudes. These critics question whether test items accurately reflect the abilities of African Americans, Latinos, women, and others whose traditions differ from those of traditional white male-dominated culture. As researchers investigate such inquiries, many companies continue to rely on employment tests for help in making hiring decisions.

Hiring Employees

The applicant who makes a good impression, is eager to have the job, and seems qualified and likely to fit in with the existing staff will probably receive an offer—*if* his or her references check out. The hiring firm will ask the candidate's referees—former supervisors or other individuals who can attest to the applicant's skills and aptitude—for assessments of his or her performance and character. A bad assessment at this point can derail the chances of a candidate who is strong in all other areas, and a good reference can improve the chances of a candidate who previously did not seem so strong. Reference checks are also used to verify information on the application form.

If all goes well, an oral and then a written job offer will follow. That offer may specify that a medical exam is required. It typically specifies a **probation period**—an initial trial period, often of three to six months, in which newly hired employees may be terminated if their job performance is unsatisfactory.

Throughout the hiring process, many decisions—where to recruit, what to look for in potential employees, even how to describe the job—are strongly influenced by government regulations. Table 12.2 lists the legislation that has had the most profound effect on human resource management—especially on the hiring process. Note especially the restrictions designed to prevent discrimination in hiring. Each year, many candidates file lawsuits to overturn job actions based on discriminatory practices related to gender, race, disability, age, weight, and other personal characteristics.

 probation period

An initial trial period, often of three to six months, in which newly hired employees may be terminated if their job performance is unsatisfactory.

Chapter 4 discusses laws that relate to employment practices.

table **12.2** **Legislation Affecting Human Resources**

Law	Year	Effect
Equal Pay Act of 1963	1963	Grants men and women the right to earn equal pay for equal work.
Title VII of the Civil Rights Act of 1964	1964	Prohibits discrimination in employment on the basis of national origin, race, color, sex, pregnancy, and religion.
Age Discrimination in Employment Act (ADEA)	1967	Prohibits job-related age-based discrimination against people of age 40 and over.
Vietnam Era Veterans Readjustment Assistance Act	1974	Requires companies that sell goods and services to the federal government to make special efforts to employ Vietnam War veterans.
Employee Retirement Income Security Act of 1974 (ERISA)	1974	Regulates the operation of employee benefit plans.
Immigration Reform and Control Act of 1986.	1986	Prohibits the hiring of illegal aliens and requires employers to verify that employees can legally work in the United States.
Americans with Disabilities Act (ADA)	1990	Prohibits employment discrimination against qualified people who have disabilities. Employers are required to make reasonable accommodations to help people with disabilities to do their jobs.
Civil Rights Act of 1991	1991	Grants the victims of intentional discrimination the right to jury trials; created the Glass Ceiling Commission, which reports on the representation of women and minorities in the nation's work force.

Source: Practical Guidelines for Lawful Supervision (Walnut Creek, Calif.: Borgman Associates, 1992), pp. 3–6.

Hiring Contingent Workers

The process described so far is, with some variation, standard in most companies. But a new hiring process is beginning to compete with it, one that starts with a call to a temporary employment agency for the contingent worker described earlier in this chapter. This new entry path lets managers and fellow employees get to know the temporary worker. If the person has the right skills and gets along well in the company, a formal hiring process can be started to bring the worker in as a full-time employee. This new approach is highly flexible because the business does not commit to hiring anyone.

Robert Snelling, Jr., chairman of the 275-office Snelling Personnel Services, explains that, "from standing in for people out sick or on vacation, or helping out during peak and seasonal work periods, [the use of contingent workers has] become a way of running a business in a businesslike fashion."[24] In the past, temporary employees typically filled routine, easy-to-learn jobs like typing, but now highly skilled temporary employees fill many professional jobs, too. On an average workday, more than 1.5 million people work as temporaries in U.S. businesses. In the average year, 6 to 7 million people will take on at least one temporary job. Many remain in the contingent work force, but a majority of them eventually become full-time employees.[25]

Training and Developing Employees

In the early 1990s, President Bill Clinton expressed a hope that American businesses would increase spending on employee training to 1.5 percent of the combined cost of employees' salaries and benefits. Motorola, Inc., is way ahead of this target, spending more than 4 percent of payroll, or $150 million in 1995, to educate its 132,000 employees. Companywide, Motorola offers 600 different courses to its workers at 14 different locations worldwide.[26] "Motorola University," the company's Schaumberg, Illinois, training facility—and the heart and soul of Motorola's training program—is as large as most of the schools attended by the readers of this textbook! The average 36 hours a year of training that Motorola provides each employee has helped it cut costs by more than half a billion dollars a year. Over the course of three years, the company reported $30 in productivity gains for every $1 spent on training.[27]

The importance of training to productivity and competitiveness led the MIT Commission on Industrial Productivity—a team of prominent Massachusetts Institute of Technology (MIT) economists, scientists, and engineers chartered in the late 1980s—to conclude that increased worker training was essential to continued growth of the U.S. economy. Unfortunately, the commission also concluded that "there seems to be a systematic undervaluation in this country of how much difference it can make when people are well educated and when their skills are continuously developed and challenged. This translates into a pattern of training for work that turns out badly educated workers with skills that are narrow and hence vulnerable to rapid obsolescence."[28] To overcome this problem, businesses like Motorola, Inc., Corning Inc., and Federal Express Corp. invest in three key areas: employee training, employee performance evaluation, and career development.

5. Describe the three forms of employee training and explain how employee performance is evaluated.

Employee Training

Employers conduct all sorts of training activities to improve their employees' knowledge and skills so that they may better do their jobs. For example, at Motorola University, factory workers can enroll in a 12-hour program that includes

Training and Developing Employees
In the fast-growing travel services industry, ongoing classroom training and periodic retraining are necessities for maintaining competence on the job. Here a teacher assists a travel agent during a training class.

training in basic math skills such as fractions and graphs. And senior managers have the opportunity to participate in a computer-based strategic game that simulates numerous real-life problems, including factories that burn down and customers who go bankrupt.[29]

Training is especially necessary for the newly hired. Managers often hire inexperienced employees because they are easier to find, have an unbiased perspective, and can be paid less than more experienced candidates. But, these employees lack some of the skills they need to do their jobs. In addition, as managers come to trust their workers and to delegate more tasks, authority, and responsibility to them, training needs increase. As a training manager at Motorola explained, "Ten years ago, we hired people to perform set tasks and didn't ask them to do a lot of thinking. If a machine went down, workers raised their hands, and a trouble-shooter came to fix it. . . . Today, we expect them to begin any trouble-shooting themselves."[30]

As businesses hire more temporary or contract workers instead of permanent ones, training becomes a critical issue. A steady supply of new employees means an ongoing program of training to maintain a constant level of competency on the job. Of course, old hands also benefit from training, which can help motivate employees by giving them new skills in problem solving, teamwork, and quality improvement. But whether directed at full-time employees or contingent workers, training usually takes one of three forms: employee orientation, on-the-job or classroom training, or retraining.

Employee Orientation

Nine out of ten mid- to large-size companies have their new employees spend part or all of their first day on the job in **employee orientation**, training that brings new employees up to speed on how the business and its industry work. The orientation teaches new employees about the company and its products, policies, and procedures, and it introduces them to their co-workers and supervisors. A good orientation program covers five basic areas:[31]

1. The function of the organization and the new employee's specific department, providing the big picture of how his or her job supports the organization's overall objectives

2. The employee's specific role in the business process and how his or her job relates to other jobs in the company and serves the customer

 employee orientation

Training that brings new employees up to speed on how the business and its industry work.

3. The resources available to support the employee, including what supervisors and co-workers are like, how to contact the supervisor, whom to speak to about particular problems, and what manuals or team leaders to consult; many companies appoint a specific sponsor for a new employee.

4. The employee's rights, such as the right to file a complaint or to spend a specific period of time becoming familiar with a job before performing it without close supervision; training also focuses on employee responsibilities, such as satisfying customers, contributing to teams, and searching for new and better ways of working.

5. The specific activities involved in the employee's job and any training and development that the company offers to help employees improve their skills, qualify for promotions, or change careers

Chapter 1 discussed six important new business strategies: flexibility in business formation, management innovation, employee development, increased customer focus, improved control systems, and creative financial management.

A good orientation program promotes positive work values and gives employees an understanding of how their work fits into the business process. Particularly in businesses that use new strategies such as those outlined in Chapter 1, orientation introduces new employees to special aspects of this strategy as it applies to their work. For example, employees may receive special training in problem solving as a part of a team, or in enforcing the company's ethical practices in contacts with customers and suppliers.

At Federal Express Corp., all efforts to improve customer service are based on a people-service-profit philosophy. New employees are taught that keeping the company's employees happy comes first, that this policy allows FedEx to provide superior service to its customers, and that good service allows the company to make sufficient profits to sustain itself.

At Kelly Services, Inc., a Troy, Michigan–based contractor of temporary workers, more than 600,000 workers fill temporary jobs in the offices of approximately 185,000 client companies each year.[32] Many work far from the support of supervisors at Kelly Services and so, to clearly communicate that Kelly stands behind them, the firm offers a toll-free Help number that workers can call when they need advice or are having trouble.

On-the-Job and Classroom Training

The most common form of training is **on-the-job training**, in which employees learn by doing a job or by receiving one-on-one instruction—usually from a manager or co-worker—in how to do a job. Often employees apply this learning immediately to tasks for which they are responsible.

Classroom training is more formal and is conducted by the company's training department or a training consultant. Advanced techniques such as interactive computer training and role-playing exercises are now common in the classroom training of many businesses.

In the past, most training needs were met simply through on-the-job training. Now that new skills, technologies, and strategies often have to be learned, the training process is more involved. On-the-job training is still used, but often it is complemented by other activities. Whatever form it takes, effective training follows six steps:

1. *Adequate preparation*. Employees should be told how the training is expected to affect their performance.

2. *Show and tell*. Whenever possible, effective training uses demonstrations, not just explanations. A trainer—either a supervisor or a classroom trainer—might display how a machine works while describing its use, for example. Or the trainer might show the types and formats of reports used by administrative assistants within the company.

3. *Practice*. Because most learning takes place by doing, employees should attempt to perform required tasks as soon as possible. Some tasks can be

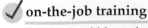

on-the-job training

Training in which employees learn by doing a job or by receiving one-on-one instruction—usually from a manager or co-worker—in how to do a job.

doing business

Washington State Ferry System Invests in Diversity Training

The face of the American workplace is changing. Since the 1960s, women and people of color have made tremendous strides in gaining acceptance by American businesses. According to some predictions, white males, formerly the majority workers in the American work force, will soon make up less than 40 percent of all U.S. workers. This is a fundamental change in the nation's socioeconomic structure, and many businesses are seeking ways to soften the transition. For some, the answer is training in diversity awareness.

Before the Washington State Ferry System instituted diversity training, there were numerous complaints by African-American workers of racial bias, and female workers complained that they were being harassed by their male co-workers. Faced with mounting lawsuits, the management of the largest ferry system in the United States committed itself to spending $1 million on an extensive training program that would reduce the number of incidents of racial bias and sexual harassment among the system's 1,500 employees. Through a series of lectures, role-playing exercises, and videos, employees were encouraged to consider the diverse perspectives of their co-workers and to be sensitive to their needs. Workers were trained to call African Americans "people of color" and to refrain from calling women "ladies" or "gals." Also banned were such words as "geriatrics" and "yuppies." According to Alice Snyder Hunter, who ran the diversity

training program along with her husband Jeffrey Hunter, "We had to start with the basics, diversity 101. We had a list of what you could and could not say, because these people did not know the basics." In addition, African-American workers reported that they were treated with increased respect and female workers said male co-workers were less likely to tell them jokes with sexual content.

The road has been a bumpy one. Resistance among employees—especially white males—has been high. Although sexually provocative calendars have disappeared from the workplace and sexist and racist jokes are no longer told openly, many employees resent being given orders on what to say or how to behave. Says Marcia Morse, one of the first women to be employed by the Washington State Ferry System, "There's a huge backlash. Tons of anger." Experts contend, however, that this kind of reaction is to be expected and that, with time, the negative attitudes can be turned around. In any case, it is in the interest of the employer to make the effort. The workplace is changing, and companies have to keep up with that change. So far, the ferry system has paid out $1 million for its diversity training program. That's a high cost, but not as high as the $1.6 million it paid out to settle lawsuits alleging bias.

Source: Timothy Egan, "Teaching Tolerance in Workplaces: A Seattle Program Illustrates Limits," *New York Times*, Oct. 8, 1993, p. A18.

---

practiced on computer-based simulators, devices that imitate the experience without the high cost of failure. This technique has been applied to a wide variety of situations, from preparing a spreadsheet to living in and operating a space shuttle.

4. *Manager observation*. Employees need to be monitored on an ongoing basis, especially after training. Training is more effective when managers take the time to observe employees and comment on their behavior.

5. *Praising progress or redirecting efforts*. Learning depends on bringing both progress and mistakes to the employee's attention. Praise does wonders for inducing repeat performances of good work. Managers should also redirect employee efforts when performance is not up to par.

6. *Integration into work routines*. New learning should be integrated into the employee's work activities. The employee's work should then be reviewed with his or her manager to make sure that what the employee learned in training is being applied correctly.

A final form of training that is occurring both on the job and in the classroom is **diversity training**—training in awareness of and respect for individual, social, and cultural differences among co-workers and customers. For the story of how one company invested in diversity training, see the doing business box "Washington State Ferry System Invests in Diversity Training."

 diversity training

Training in awareness of and respect for individual, social, and cultural differences among co-workers and customers.

performance appraisal

A periodic written evaluation of an employee's performance compared with specific goals, which are often stated in a performance plan.

 career development

The process of planning and coordinating the progress of employees through positions of increasing responsibility within an organization.

Retraining

In the past, only employees in technical jobs or jobs with frequent changes in responsibilities received retraining, but today most employees need to be retrained every year or two because of technical advances and new business strategies. Retraining provides employees with a chance to update their skills and knowledge and to remain valuable to the company.

Partly in response to the ever quickening pace of technological change and its impact on workers, Motorola plans to double its training budget to $300 million annually by the year 2000. After this plan is implemented, every worker will receive 80 to 100 hours of company-sponsored training.[33] Motorola management firmly believes that, in order to keep up with changes in technology and the marketplace, training must be an integral part of the company's strategy.

Hallmark Cards, Inc., of Kansas City, Missouri, the world's largest greeting card company, offers continuous retraining. Camera operators who once prepared color photos and illustrations using photographic printing processes have been retrained in new skills that allow them to achieve the same results using computer scanners. To keep all its workers busy, Hallmark uses workers where they are most needed. Ray Smith, age 52, is a cutting machine operator who works as a custom card imprinter, painter, or modular office assembler, according to the needs of the work load. At headquarters, manufacturing workers may work in the kitchen of the company cafeteria during slack times, but they still earn factory wages. As Hallmark CEO Irv Hockaday observed, "Through all kinds of economic cycles and market cycles, we have found ways to keep people; often by retraining them."[34] Retraining is a good way for businesses to invest in employee development and at the same time use their employees' new skills to increase company flexibility.

Evaluating Employee Performance

Direct evaluation of employees is the responsibility of their managers, not of the human resource department. But human resource managers design the evaluation process, including the evaluation forms and schedules.

One of the most frequently used tools is the **performance appraisal**, a periodic written evaluation of an employee's performance compared with specific goals, which are often stated in a performance plan. Many companies conduct performance appraisals annually. Human resource departments typically keep these appraisals in employee files for future review in case of promotions, dismissals, or other purposes. Some companies conduct performance appraisals by having mangers and their employees complete identical forms outlining the responsibilities of the position and evaluating how they were handled. This is followed by a conference in which the two discuss any differences of opinion.

A relatively new form of appraisal reverses the usual procedure by having employees evaluate their manager's performance. According to one survey, these upward appraisals were in use at 12 percent of U.S. businesses in 1993.[35] Federal Express uses this method in its annual leadership survey. Employees rate the extent to which they agree or disagree with such statements as "I feel free to tell my manager what I think," "My manager helps us find ways to do our job better," and "My manager lets me do my job without interfering." FedEx managers who receive low scores have to improve by their next performance appraisal.[36]

Career Development

6. Discuss various paths in career development.

Career development is the process of planning and coordinating the progress of employees through positions of increasing responsibility within an organization. The burden of career planning and development has traditionally fallen on the employee. F. Wade Bates, director of human resources at Nabisco Foods, observed in 1992 that "the company can't be the only one responsible for career planning. . . . An individual has to take charge of his own career."[37] This attitude is changing. Many businesses are finding that establishing a learning organization requires nurturing employee expertise. In such businesses, the human resource department helps employees grow and take on jobs of greater responsibility and higher pay within the company.

Part of career development is specifying a **career path**, a succession of jobs that employees may hold as they move upward through an organization to positions of increasing responsibility and pay. The career of Lee Iacocca, who retired a few years ago as president and chief executive officer of Chrysler Corp., illustrates such an upward path through an organization.

After graduating from college, Iacocca signed on as an engineering trainee with Ford Motor Company in 1946. After a few years he left engineering for sales and, in 1953, became assistant sales manager for the Philadelphia district. In 1956, Iacocca was promoted to sales manager for the Washington, D.C., district and in 1960 became vice president and general manager of Ford Motor Co. In this position, he developed the popular Mustang and Cougar models. Ten years later, Iacocca became the president of Ford, a position he held until Henry Ford II fired him in 1978. Iacocca then moved to Chrysler, where he was credited with saving the company from financial disaster.[38]

Many companies define standard paths by which an employee can rise within the organization, such as from administrative assistant to coordinator to office manager to department supervisor to manager to associate director and finally to director. Alternatively, career paths can be unique to the individual, as was the case with Lee Iacocca, whose path reflected both Ford Motor Company's needs and Iacocca's particular abilities. For many employees, career development includes company-sponsored programs such as job rotation, succession planning, and mentoring. Other employees contribute to their own futures through networking.

Job Rotation

Job rotation is the practice of moving employees through a series of jobs for set periods of time to give them an understanding of a variety of business functions. U.S. firms are increasingly using job rotation, and businesses in Japan and Germany have had it in place for many years. By rotating jobs, employees acquire broad experience and abilities that enable them to deal flexibly with varied production tasks, unpredictable problems, and changing technologies.[39]

Part of Ford Motor Company's ambitious plans for what it calls Ford 2000—a corporate restructuring aimed at making it the world's leading auto manufacturer—includes job rotations for managers. And in Japan, many manufacturing firms place every new employee on a production line job for some period of time. The underlying philosophy is that all employees need to understand right at the outset that production is the stage at which value is truly added to the company's products. Also, Japanese managers tend to believe that problem solving is the most important part of any job. Hence, solving increasingly difficult problems is the most meaningful career path at many companies, even if the employee's job title does not change.[40]

Succession Planning

Succession planning is a formal evaluation to determine which employees within an organization are capable of future moves into key positions. If planning fails to identify such people, the company can select a few individuals and prepare them through special training, job rotation, and other techniques.

career path

A succession of jobs that employees hold as they move upward through an organization to positions of increasing responsibility and pay.

job rotation

The practice of moving employees through a series of jobs for set periods of time to give them an understanding of a variety of business functions.

succession planning

A formal evaluation to determine which individuals within an organization are capable of future moves into key positions.

At General Electric Co., where a highly developed system of management development and evaluation is in place, succession planning is serious business. Members of the company's board of directors review extensive files on up to 15 key executives twice a year. Based on these reviews, the directors make recommendations for each executive's continued development and progress in the organization. At the same time, the board of directors becomes familiar with the best and the brightest within the corporation—the men and women who may one day succeed GE's CEO, John Welch. The practice was tested recently when Welch underwent triple-bypass heart surgery. Although rumors about who would lead the company in Welch's place were rampant in the media, investor confidence in GE's system of succession planning was reflected in the price of its stock, which actually increased in value the day after Wall Street learned of Welch's heart ailment.[41]

Mentoring

Mentoring is an informal relationship in which a more experienced employee guides and sponsors a less experienced employee in a similar work role. Although mentoring relationships may develop spontaneously between employees on the job, many companies set up formal mentoring programs.

Networking

Many employees agree with the director of human resources at Nabisco that an individual has to take charge of his or her own career. These employees often manage their own career paths in part through *networking*, the informal process in which people linked by a common interest provide advice, information, and resources to one another. The networking process for individual employees is similar to the networking process described for entrepreneurs in Chapter 6. Possible network contacts includes co-workers, managers, relatives, family friends, and acquaintances. Networking ranges from telephone conversations to chats during informal get-togethers after work or during training sessions or professional conferences. Letters are a very common and effective form of networking communications. Networking is an excellent way to learn about the availability of other types of jobs and the qualifications necessary to be considered for such opportunities.

Compensation and Benefits

You may recall from Chapter 11 that money is not always the main reason people work. Without fair payment, however, most employees would have little reason to work. **Compensation** is the payment employees receive for their work. Compensation takes two forms:

- **Pay**—cash compensation in the form of wages, salary, or incentive bonuses
- **Benefits**—noncash compensation, such as health insurance, paid vacations, or retirement plans, which employees select or receive by virtue of being members of the organization

The sum of the pay and benefits of all the organization's employees is the total labor cost of the employer. For example, a 23-person organization that each year averages $20,000 per employee in pay and $6,000 per employee in benefits will have a total annual labor cost of $598,000. With this kind of money at stake, it is small wonder that determining how much employees will be paid is such an important process.

Career Development

Face it: You are responsible for your career. Take advantage of every opportunity for training, networking, and mentoring. Don't hesitate to ask more experienced workers for help. Most people are flattered, and will be more than willing to share their knowledge with you.

7. Identify the two forms of compensation available to employees today and describe the types of cash compensation.

Wages and Salary

Wages are pay provided to hourly employees. **Salary** is pay provided to professional employees in weekly, monthly, or yearly amounts.

How does an employer calculate the value of an employee's work? Training and experience play a large part in determining compensation, as do a number of other factors. At the organization level, experts in human resources look at economic and employment trends for similar employees in the geographic area in which the business operates. These specialists try to determine the availability of similarly trained workers as well as the state of the national and local job markets and the economy. The condition of the company's own business also plays a role.

At the individual level, each employee's qualifications and experience help determine the value of his or her work. One trend is to pay for newly acquired skills. For example, at Johnsonville Foods, employees can earn an hourly increase when they learn a new job skill such as accounting, regardless of whether they need the skill in their current job. A similar pay-for-skills plan is in place at Corning Inc., where, according to a senior vice president and corporate director for quality, "If you went to work for some of our high-performance factories, you'd find your pay level depends on what skill level you reach. We're paying for what you know, not what you do."[42] By rewarding employees who learn new skills, Corning is investing in its future growth by enhancing the potential of its employees. And, as we have seen, companies review employee performance records regularly to determine whether past performance deserves to be rewarded and, if so, to what extent.

Sometimes companies try to avoid the appearance of unfairness by giving everyone wage increases or cuts of the same percentage amount. Although this may sound fair, in reality it often is not. If everyone receives a 3 percent raise, for example, a top manager making $100,000 will receive only $3,000 extra, which he or she may find demoralizing after a full year of high-stress performance. Meanwhile, the lowest-paid employee will receive only $450 on an annual wage of $15,000, which may not even cover the year's increase in basic living expenses. Neither will be satisfied, and both may feel punished rather than rewarded for their year's work.

A fairer, although more difficult, means of allocating compensation is through **pay for performance**, linking pay increases directly to an employee's level of performance. At the Yoplait Yogurt unit of General Mills, Inc., a team of managers on a pay-for-performance plan set its own goals, which were even higher than those set by the parent company. The group surpassed its goal of increasing operating earnings by 100 percent and collected bonuses of $30,000 to $50,000 each, about 50 percent of their salaries.[43]

Even with pay for performance, however, stresses can develop, especially if wage increases are limited and high rewards are given only to upper management. Andrew Romegialli, an executive with the International Association of Machinists, the union that represents employees at Pratt & Whitney in East Hartford, Connecticut, expressed these sentiments: "Pratt is making profits. They are giving big raises to top executives. If there is money for that, there is money for us, too."[44] The situation at Pratt & Whitney is not unique. In 1994, earnings of Standard & Poor's top 500 firms rose 40 percent. However, during the same period, wages increased by an average of only 2.9 percent.[45] Although most workers have resigned themselves to this state of affairs, few like it.

Another compensation issue is **comparable worth**, the payment of equal compensation to women and men in different positions that require similar levels of education, training, and skill. According to recent statistics, women still earn only 70 cents for every dollar earned by men in comparable jobs.[46] A different but related compensation issue is *equal pay*, which addresses the differ-

---

✓ **mentoring**

An informal relationship in which a more experienced employee guides and sponsors a less experienced employee in a similar work role.

✓ **compensation**

The payment—pay and benefits—that employees receive for their work.

✓ **pay**

Cash compensation in the form of wages, salary, or incentive bonuses.

✓ **benefits**

Noncash compensation, such as health insurance, paid vacations, or retirement plans, which employees select or receive by virtue of being members of the organization.

✓ **wages**

Pay provided to hourly employees.

✓ **salary**

Pay provided to professional employees in weekly, monthly, or yearly amounts.

✓ **pay for performance**

Linking pay increases directly to an employee's level of performance.

✓ **comparable worth**

The payment of equal compensation to women and men in different positions that require similar levels of education, training, and skill.

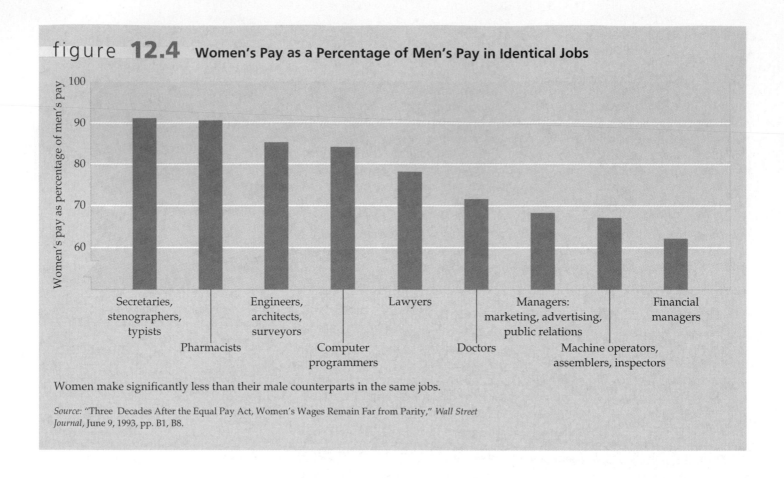

figure **12.4** **Women's Pay as a Percentage of Men's Pay in Identical Jobs**

Women make significantly less than their male counterparts in the same jobs.

Source: "Three Decades After the Equal Pay Act, Women's Wages Remain Far from Parity," *Wall Street Journal*, June 9, 1993, pp. B1, B8.

ence in pay between men and women doing the same work. Figure 12.4 shows women's pay as a percentage of men's pay in identical positions.

Commissions, Bonuses, and Profit Sharing

 commission

Pay based on a percentage of the money an employee brings into a business.

 bonus

A cash payment that rewards employees for achieving an organizational goal.

 gain sharing

The granting of periodic (quarterly, semiannual, or annual) bonuses to employees based on organizational performance, not individual performance.

 profit sharing

An incentive system that gives some or all employees a percentage of the profits earned by a business.

A **commission** is pay based on a percentage of the money an employee brings into a business. Salespeople are typically paid in whole or in part by commission. A salesperson who works on straight commission receives a commission on each sale—perhaps 4 percent of the selling price of a television, for example—but no base pay. The more typical arrangement is for an employee to receive a draw—a small base salary as well as commissions, which still form the largest part of the salesperson's compensation.

A **bonus** is a cash payment that rewards employees for achieving an organizational goal—exceeding a sales quota, achieving a quality improvement target, or developing a new product. At Cooper Tire & Rubber Co., all employees can receive bonuses. Executive bonuses are tied to financial performance benchmarks and contribute up to 30 percent of these employees' total compensation. Hourly workers get paid extra for producing over their goal, and salaried employees can earn bonuses of up to 7.5 percent of their base pay.[47]

Gain sharing is the granting of periodic (quarterly, semiannual, or annual) bonuses to employees based on organizational performance, not individual performance. Gain sharing plans are usually based on either cost savings or profit sharing. **Profit sharing** is an incentive system that gives some or all employees a percentage of the profits earned by a business. This gives employees a stake in the financial success of the company, motivating them to keep costs low and increase productivity. A similar program that attempts to motivate employees to maintain high levels of performance is the **employee stock option plan**, which allows employees to buy company stock at discounted prices.

Benefits

In the 35-year period from 1955 through 1990, the cost of employee benefits rose from 17 percent of payroll to approximately 38 percent of payroll.[48] As large as this number is, it continues to increase. Many organizations see the high cost of employee benefits as an incentive to downsize, outsource, or use temporary workers. Many employees, however, would willingly change jobs for better health coverage, retirement benefits, or family-care provisions. Benefits can be either fixed or flexible, as we are about to see.

Fixed Benefits

Fixed benefits are benefits that all employees receive by virtue of being a member of the organization. Some fixed benefits are required by law, while others are provided to employees at the sole discretion of the employer. Although many employers have cut back on the fixed benefits they provide to employees in an effort to reduce costs, some companies—like San Francisco's Business Wire—offer quite extensive fixed benefit packages.

At Business Wire, employees receive fixed benefits equal to 37 percent of their salary. This figure climbs to 60 percent for employees who stay with the company for six years. Why are some companies so generous? It's just good business. According to Lorry Lokey, Business Wire's president and founder, "If you use benefits to build a cadre of talented people who stay with you for

 employee stock option plan

Program that attempts to motivate employees to maintain high levels of performance by allowing them to buy company stock at discounted prices.

 fixed benefits

Benefits that all employees receive by virtue of being a member of the organization.

8. Differentiate between fixed and flexible benefits.

Drawing by Leo Cullum; © 1995 The New Yorker Magazine, Inc.

"Before I forget, Detrick, here's the dental plan."

years, you'll hold on to your power. Your company's future will just get stronger and stronger."[49]

Fixed employee benefits can be categorized into six groups, although not all companies offer all of them:

1. Benefits required by law.

2. Payment for time not worked. This is by far the most expensive type of benefit to the employer, and one of the most prized by employees. At Business Wire, all new employees receive seven paid holidays, two weeks of paid vacation, and five days of paid sick leave.

3. Health and accident insurance. Business Wire pays 90 percent of each employee's medical insurance. While 98 percent of firms with 100 to 499 employees offer health insurance, only 60 percent of businesses with 25 or fewer employees do.[50]

4. Insurance and security benefits. These benefits, which include life insurance, long-term disability, and supplemental unemployment benefits, have also increased in cost in recent years.

5. Employee services. This is the newest and most rapidly expanding group of benefits, limited only by the imagination. For example, Business Wire pays its veteran employees $480 a year toward membership in a health club. And PepsiCo Inc. has hired a concierge at its Purchase, New York, headquarters to run personal errands for employees, including making restaurant reservations, purchasing theater tickets, arranging events for children, and arranging for household repairs. The company started providing this service after a recent company survey showed that employees experienced stress over having no free time to take care of such matters themselves.[51]

6. Family benefits. At General Electric Co., managers in the aerospace division were startled to learn that many employees would consider changing jobs for better family benefits.[52] They obviously were unaware of the growing importance to employees of family and quality of life issues, one of the trends discussed at the beginning of this chapter.

Flexible Benefits

In fixed plans, employees receive identical benefits whether they want them, need them, or use them. Such plans have markedly decreased recently as their cost has escalated.

In their place, many businesses are offering **flexible benefits**, also known as *cafeteria benefits*, which employees choose according to their wants and needs. This option produces a customized benefit package for each employee, and it reduces costs for employers.

Most flexible benefit plans grant employees a specific number of "flex dollars," or flexible benefit credits, to spend on company benefits each year. Employees can use these flex dollars to buy any combination of benefits, or they can apply them to an employee savings plan, a stock purchase plan, or some other financial investment. For example, an employee who is 33 years old, single, and in good health may not need the wide range of benefits that the company's fixed plan offers employees with families. Instead, this employee could select a less costly medical plan, which would allow him or her to save 135 flex dollars to buy company stock or invest in a savings plan. This sort of option appeals to young employees in today's workplace. In a recent poll conducted by Roper Starch Worldwide Inc., almost 60 percent of workers in their twenties said they or their spouse participated in some retirement-focused plan offered by their employers. About 75 percent said retirement saving is a priority in their financial planning.[53]

✓ **flexible benefits**

Benefits that employees choose according to their wants and needs; also called *cafeteria benefits*.

doing
business
AT&T's Flexible Workplace

At AT&T, employees can take advantage of many innovative programs designed to increase flexibility and productivity. Telecommuting, job sharing, flextime, and alternative work schedules cater to employees who want to spend less time at the office and more time at home. Liz Cabarle and Kathy Knight share a job in the human resource department at AT&T. Their working hours are arranged so that each works three days a week, with overlapping schedules on Wednesdays.

Why do Liz Cabarle and Kathy Knight share a job? Wouldn't it be easier—and much more lucrative—to work a full-time schedule? Perhaps, but by sharing a job, Cabarle and Knight get the best of both worlds—time to spend with friends and family, plus a career with pay and benefits. According to Cabarle, "Even though being at home is fulfilling, sometimes you need to do something else." Knight says, "It's something we put a lot of ourselves into even before we had our kids. It would be hard to give up."

Why does AT&T allow employees to share jobs? Wouldn't it be easier to have fewer employees to keep track of? People in favor of job sharing point out that the company benefits by having the unique skills and knowledge of two employees while paying for only one. Also, when one employee calls in sick, the other is available as backup. A trained, fully functional backup is much more efficient and productive than a temporary employee—someone who has to learn the ropes before being fully competent at all job tasks.

Researchers have seen measurable improvements in worker productivity as a result of flexible work programs such as those at AT&T. Kathleen Christensen, director of the Work Environments Research Group at City University of New York Graduate School, says companies "will see a bottom-line pay off. You have better, more creative, and more productive management." Companies such as AT&T are leading the way to the workplace of the future, when flexible work arrangements like the one Liz Cabarle and Kathy Knight participate in may be the norm and not the exception.

Source: Based on Sallie Han, "We Can Work It Out," (New York) *Daily News*, Jan. 6, 1995.

Scheduling and Leaves

More and more workers now define success in terms of their personal life, not their work life. In a recent Roper poll, for example, approximately 80 percent of respondents said success was having a happy family life or relationship. In last place came money, career, and power.[54] But at the same time, Americans are working longer hours than ever. According to a poll of 10,000 professionals and managers conducted by Work/Family Directions, working men average 47 hours per week on the job, and working women 44 hours per week.[55] Ronald LeMay, president of Sprint Corp.,[55] in Westwood, Kansas, believes "forty-hour workweeks are a relic of the past."[56] Benefits that grant employees free time— flexible scheduling, paid and unpaid leaves, job sharing, and work-at-home programs—carry a high value because they allow employees to balance their priorities.

9. Discuss the use of flexible work schedules and leaves to increase employee satisfaction.

Flexible Work Schedules

One of the most common ways for employees to gain flexibility in their work schedules is through **flextime**, which allows them to work during hours of their choice as long as they work their required number of hours and are present during prescribed core periods. During core hours, all employees must be present for meetings, interaction with co-workers, and so forth.

Another progressive scheduling arrangement is **job sharing**, in which two employees share a full-time job, each working part time. It takes a special relationship for such an arrangement to work well, but if it does it can provide the company with savings in equipment, space, and other resources. For a glimpse at how two employees share a job at AT&T, see the doing business box "AT&T's Flexible Workplace."

 flextime

Program that allows employees to work during hours of their choice as long as they work their required number of hours and are present during prescribed core periods.

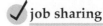 **job sharing**

Arrangement in which two employees share a full-time job, each working part time.

work-at-home programs

Benefit that allows employees to work all or some of their scheduled hours at home.

telecommuting

A form of work-at-home program in which employees communicate with the office by computer or fax machine.

leave

Time away from the job, with or without pay.

Family and Medical Leave Act

Federal law requiring firms with 50 or more employees to grant up to 12 weeks of unpaid leave following the birth or adoption of a child or the placement of a foster child, or during the serious illness of the employee or a member of his or her family.

A final, relatively new benefit is **work-at-home programs**, in which employees are allowed to work all or some of their scheduled hours at home. Employees who **telecommute** work at home and communicate with the office by computer or fax machine. Many employees report that working at home allows them to focus on a project for longer, uninterrupted periods of time. It also eliminates time wasted in commuting or socializing with co-workers. The number of people in the United States who work at home at least part time has grown by about 15 percent annually in recent years, for a total of approximately 8 million. A recent study that tracked 280 at-home workers for one year found that two-thirds of them liked it but the other third gave it up. The most common reasons for quitting were a lack of equipment and support, and problems back at the office.[57]

Leaves

Time away from the job, with or without pay, is known as **leave**. Leaves can be either short term or long term. Short-term leaves are paid periods, often of up to eight weeks at full pay. Jury leave and disability leave are examples of short-term leaves. In 1993, President Clinton signed the **Family and Medical Leave Act**, which requires firms with 50 or more employees to grant up to 12 weeks of unpaid leave following the birth or adoption of a child or the placement of a foster child in their home, or during the serious illness of the employee or members of the employee's immediate family. Although company policies vary, many disability policies include a number of weeks at full pay and some additional weeks at a portion of full pay.

Long-term leaves for periods exceeding six months are usually unpaid but may still carry continuing benefits and the guarantee of a job when the employee returns to work. Reasons for such leaves include public service activities, such as running for or holding political office or serving in the military during wartime. Some firms have even granted long-term leaves to employees who join the Peace Corps or work with a United Way agency. More common, however, are leaves to pursue additional education or training. Some employers encourage their employees to obtain advanced degrees, and they may even offer funding, in whole or in part.

While benefits cost employers a great deal of money, a well-administered benefits plan can pay for itself through increased employee productivity. One Boston University report concluded that benefits increase workers' job satisfaction and morale and also reduce carelessness, absenteeism, turnover, and tardiness.[58]

Changes in Employment Status

10. Outline the various ways in which employees can change status in an organization.

The human resource manager's work does not end with the hiring, training, periodic evaluation, and compensation of employees. Much of the human resource manager's time is also spent on maintaining appropriate staffing levels. In this section we'll look first at the many ways in which people move within an organization through reassignment and then we'll address the ways in which they separate from an organization through layoffs, terminations, and retirement.

Reassignment

During the course of their employment, employees may be reassigned to other jobs within the organization through promotion, transfer, or demotion. Although most promotions and many transfers are good news for the employee, some transfers and all demotions are bad news.

Promotion

Promotion is advancement to a position of greater responsibility and higher compensation. How does a firm decide whom to promote? Some business owners, managers, and human resource departments maintain a "promotables" list as part of their planning. Typically, such a list indicates the people who are in line for each position in the firm and an estimate of their readiness for promotion.

Many firms rely on the recommendations of managers to determine who will be promoted. For example, let's say a firm's senior accountant resigns to accept a position with another firm. Rather than recruit outside the firm, the accounting manager may select one of the company's staff accountants as a replacement. The accounting manager's hiring recommendation would be made on the basis of his or her personal knowledge of the employee's performance and personality, other managers' experience with the employee, and perhaps a series of interviews with other eligible candidates.

There are several ways for employees to prepare themselves for promotion. One is to master the skills required for a current job. Another is to seek training in skills necessary to perform higher-level tasks. Employees can also show an interest in promotion by expressing a desire to move up the career ladder. Given the option of promoting two employees, one who seems excited by the prospect of more authority and responsibility and another who seems to have little interest, most employers will choose the former.

Transfer

A **transfer** is a lateral, or sideways, move from one job to another with a similar level of authority and compensation. Some transfers are required by the organization. Ford Motor Company and many other firms now require managers and other employees to increase their flexibility by serving stints in various parts of the organization, where they can gain a larger view of the company and learn a variety of jobs and processes. Organizations also sometimes transfer troublesome employees, reassigning them to a different manager or work team where they may fit in better or be more productive.

Other transfers are initiated by employees. An employee who tires of a particular position may request a transfer into another area. Employees may also choose to transfer rather than lose their job when an organization downsizes.

Transfers that require a physical relocation to another work site can be costly to the organization and disruptive to the employee and his or her family. As a result, several companies are experimenting with alternatives to moving their employees. Ford and others use task forces or special projects instead of transfers to broaden workers' experience; Mobil Corp. moves managers within each of its three U.S. "hub" locations, where a wide range of functions and operations are clustered. And General Motors Corp. offers some managers overseas "professional development" stints lasting not more than six months, rather than the two- to three-year relocations of the past.[59]

Demotions

A **demotion** is the movement of an employee to a position of lesser responsibility, usually as a result of poor performance in a higher-level position. Demotion assumes that the person will be able to perform satisfactorily in the new position. If this does not happen, separation from the company may be required.

 promotion

Advancement to a position of greater responsibility and higher compensation.

 transfer

A lateral, or sideways, move from one job to another with a similar level of authority and compensation.

demotion

Movement of an employee to a position of lesser responsibility, usually as a result of poor performance in a higher-level position.

Should Fifty-Somethings Step Down?
Toyota Thinks So

How would you like it if you were removed or dismissed from a job because your employer decided that you were too young—or too old? If you are like most members of the American public, you probably would consider such an act patently unfair. In the United States, federal law prohibits job discrimination based on age, such as forced retirement. Other countries may view this issue from a different perspective.

In Tokyo, Japan, the Toyota Motor Corp. recently decided to enact a new policy that sets strict age limits for certain management positions: 50 years for section chiefs and 53 years for deputy general managers. Upon reaching these age limits, manages are removed from their management positions and given nonsupervisory duties at the same salary.

Why is Toyota relieving its most experienced managers of their management duties? For two reasons, according to a company spokesperson. First, Toyota believes that its management team has become stale and that the best way to pump new energy into it is to remove older employees and replace them with younger ones. Second, there are large numbers of junior managers at Toyota looking forward to promotions and career development, and older managers must make room at the top for these up-and-comers.

If a U.S. corporation like General Motors enacted make-way-for-up-and-comers policy like this, it would probably be greeted with a barrage of lawsuits alleging age discrimination. Isn't Toyota concerned about the possibility of legal action? According to a company spokesperson, management does not have to worry about such opposition because Toyota's employees accept what is best for the company.

As the American work force continues to gray and large numbers of baby-boomers continue their march upward through the organization, many U.S. companies will devote the largest percentage of their compensation costs to these older workers—increasing the pressure to cut compensation costs elsewhere in the company. Given these conditions, what options do you see for junior managers in the United States? Would you want to see Toyota's solution applied to your co-workers so that you could advance? Would you want it applied to you when you reach 50 years of age?

Source: Andrew Pollack, "Toyota Has Decided to Set Age Limits on Its Managers," *New York Times*, Oct. 25, 1994, p. 16.

Demotions usually occur because an employee has failed to perform satisfactorily in some other position, or as punishment for a serious ethical violation or infraction of company rules. In some cases, however, demotions are based on unproved assumptions about a worker's capacity. For a discussion of one company's policy of age-based demotion, see the ethics check "Should Fifty-Somethings Step Down? Toyota Thinks So."

Separation

Eventually, all employees leave their job. **Separation** is the severing of an employee's relationship with an employer. Employees may leave an organization for several reasons, including layoffs, terminations, or retirement.

Layoffs

Over the past several years, many of America's biggest businesses have laid off a large number of their employees. A **layoff** is the dismissal of an employee because of financial constraints on the firm. For example, between 1991 and 1994, IBM laid off 85,000 workers, AT&T laid off 83,500, and General Motors laid off 74,000.[60] Such large-scale layoffs are known as *downsizing*, the elimination of jobs to cut costs and make a business smaller, and they have sent shock waves throughout the country. Since the passage of the Worker Adjustment and Retraining Notification Act in 1988, employers must give at least 60 days notice of a large-scale layoff or plant closing. Many companies also extend to employees

separation

The severing of an employee's relationship with an employer through layoff, termination, or retirement.

layoff

Dismissal of an employee because of financial constraints on the firm.

the chance of returning to work if economic conditions improve. In the United States, most permanent employees who are laid off are covered by **unemployment insurance**, which pays workers who have lost their jobs a basic level of compensation for a limited time while they look for new work.

Layoffs are traumatic—not only for the workers who are laid off but also for those who are left behind, who often worry that they will be next to join the line at the unemployment office. Alternatives to layoffs include the policy of **attrition**, reducing an organization's work force through normal turnover and voluntary terminations. When employers anticipate a labor surplus, they may be able to stop hiring in time for voluntary resignations, retirements, and firings to reduce the work force to an acceptable level.

Another alternative to layoffs is to reduce the hours of all employees. About one-third of the states in the United States have "shared work" programs that allow employers to reduce workers' hours (and hence their wages) by 20 to 60 percent; the employees collect unemployment insurance for the unworked hours.[61] Shared work programs reduce layoffs and downsizings and help save employees' jobs.

A final alternative to layoffs is a voluntary early retirement program, which is part of the topic we turn to next.

Termination

Termination is a voluntary or involuntary permanent departure from a job. Most employer-employee relationships are **employment at will**, which means that either party may, in the absence of a contract, terminate the arrangement at any time and for any reason. One form of termination, **retirement**, is an employee's voluntary departure on reaching a certain age, often in combination with a requirement of having served some length of time with the company. As the average age of employees increases from year to year, retirement issues concern more and more employees. Federal legislation forbids mandatory retirement before age 70 in most private-sector jobs, but it does not prevent an organization from offering incentives to all employees who are near retirement age in return for their taking early retirement. These incentives may include a lump-sum payment, continuation of a portion of the employee's regular salary, and continued health and other retirement benefits. In some cases, the package offers greater benefits than the employee would receive by staying with the firm through normal retirement age.

Voluntary termination also occurs when employees move away, find new jobs, start their own businesses, join the military, return to school, or for a number of other reasons. In all these cases, the common factor is that the employee initiates the action, without any dismissal action on the part of the employer.

Involuntary terminations occur when employees are asked to leave the organization. As we saw earlier in the discussion of layoffs, some involuntary terminations occur through no fault of the employee. In recent years, many of the largest U.S. businesses have terminated whole work groups, departments, and even divisions in the course of mergers, reorganizations, or downsizings. Automation also frequently results in cuts in the work force.

In other cases, however, involuntary terminations happen because of an unfortunate fact of organizational life: Some people just don't work out as employers thought they would. Although there are few enforceable regulations for dealing with such employees, most organizations accept the principle of "just cause" as a basis for involuntary termination. This means that to terminate an employee, an organization must have a good reason that is related to his or her performance and behavior on the job. Generally accepted reasons include fighting or injuring others; stealing; lying (in the form of padding sales figures with dummy order forms to make a sales quota, for example); misrepre-

 unemployment insurance
Program that pays workers who have lost their jobs a basic level of compensation for a limited time while they look for new work.

 attrition
Policy of reducing an organization's work force through normal turnover and voluntary terminations.

 termination
A voluntary or involuntary permanent departure from a job.

 employment at will
An employer-employee relationship in which either party may, in the absence of a contract, terminate the arrangement at any time and for any reason.

retirement
An employee's voluntary departure from a job on reaching a certain age.

sentation (such as saying one has an M.B.A. when that is not true); and insubordination. Doing a poor job and failing to perform to the standards set for a job is, of course, a valid reason for dismissal.

An employee may be able to appeal an involuntary termination to an individual, to an appeals board within the firm, or, as you will see in Chapter 13, to a union grievance committee. If it is determined that the employee was dismissed unfairly, the decision may be reversed. The law requires businesses to have a rational and nondiscriminatory basis for terminating employees.

Companies are very careful with dismissals, since employees who feel they were wrongfully terminated may sue their former employers, either for a cash settlement or for restoration of their job. To guard against such lawsuits, businesses must have in place a formal, defensible program for evaluation and accurate and up-to-date documentation of employee performance, as discussed earlier in this chapter.

Preparing to Be a Flexible Employee

Flexibility has been forced on employee and employer alike. Most American workers—60 percent of the work force—have held their jobs for fewer than five years. Only 1 of every 4 has held his or her current job for more than four years, and 3 of every 10 have been in the same job for less than one year.[62] This means that even so-called permanent employees are not very permanent anymore. You can expect to hold many jobs in your career and to change your occupation—the work you specialize in—several times as well.

The human resource manager of the future will help employees learn new skills in order to follow flexible career paths. But at the same time, you as an employee will have to take advantage of every opportunity to build your experience and skills. Job rotation, temporary jobs and internships, training, networking, and mentoring are some of the ways in which workers can keep learning and expanding their business contacts. It is very difficult for businesses to balance their need for both flexibility and expertise in their work force. But it will be even harder for employees unless they become fast, flexible learners themselves.

Electronic Management

At St. Louis-based Edward D. Jones & Company, a financial services firm, sales administration, support, and training are completely electronic. Local investment representatives such as Andrew Boles of Madison, New Jersey, are linked to headquarters by a computer network and by the company's business television network, shown here. The video link provides product training, sales coaching, and access to upper management, and it keeps representatives nationwide in touch with the home office every day.

Reviewing *Human Resource Management*

Managing Human Resources in Today's Business Environment

1. **Explain the functions of human resource management in relation to the changing work force**. Human resource managers are charged with supplying, training, and motivating employees. Their task is becoming increasingly complicated by several trends in the composition of the work force. For example, by 2000, more skilled workers will be needed, but most available workers will be unskilled. Furthermore, the work force, with its declining growth rate, will include older adults, as well as more women and minority and immigrant workers. More important from the human resource manager's perspective is the increased use of the contingent work force. Companies must determine how to increase productivity with fewer employees and reduced costs, perhaps through part-time or leased workers.

Human Resource Planning

2. **Identify and describe the components of human resource planning**. Like all management, human resource management begins with planning, a process consisting of research, forecasting, and job analysis. Based on research regarding internal and external factors affecting the company's operations and growth, the human resource manager determines job needs and sources of labor. He or she prepares a job analysis of every position within the company, noting necessary skills and responsibilities for each. From this analysis a job description and job specification are developed in order to locate appropriate candidates and judge performance.

The Hiring Process

3. **Identify the various sources of job applicants**. When a job requisition is submitted, the human resource manager undertakes a search for applicants. The first and preferred source of applicants is the company's own employees. Other sources are employee referrals, as well as advertising in local newspapers, contacting employment agencies, and recruiting on college campuses. Many of the decisions made throughout the hiring process are strongly influenced by government regulations.

4. **Describe methods of screening and testing potential employees and identify two alternative hiring procedures**. The screening of applicants involves review of their resumés plus personal interviews with the human resource manager, the relevant job manager, and potential co-workers. In many cases, applicants are also given skills tests and tests that provide a psychological profile. If an applicant is chosen as a likely employee and if references provide positive assessments, he or she is hired for a full-time position and placed on probation. As an alternative, a company may hire a temporary worker to see how well he or she works out before making a formal commitment.

Training and Developing Employees

5. **Describe the three forms of employee training and explain how employee performance is evaluated**. Employee training—so vital to productivity and competitiveness—begins with the basic training of new employees (employee orientation). Specific skills can be taught to new employees, as well as established employees who have been promoted or transferred, through on-the-job training or classroom training. Companies are increasingly providing diversity training to increase the flexibility of their work force. Employees needing to update their skills and knowledge undergo periodic retraining. Using evaluation forms and schedules designed by the human resource manager, individual managers are responsible for periodically preparing the performance appraisals of their employees. In some cases, employees may even have the opportunity to appraise their manager's performance.

6. **Discuss various paths in career development**. Traditionally, each employee has been responsible for his or her own career development. Today, some human resource managers are helping employees to grow. Employees may take different career paths, depending on their interests and skills. The path may be based on company-sponsored programs such as job rotation, succession planning, and mentoring or on employees' own networking. Job rotation increases the flexibility of both the company and the employee. Through succession planning, the company identifies employees best suited for key positions. Both mentoring and networking most often result from the employee's own efforts to get ahead.

Compensation and Benefits

7. **Identify the two forms of compensation available to employees today and describe the types of cash compensation**. The two forms of compensation are pay and benefits. Pay may be wages for hourly work or salaries based on qualifications and experience. A fair system for allocating pay increases is pay for performance. Two important issues are comparable worth and equal pay, which ensure that both genders are treated equally and fairly. Pay is sometimes obtained through commissions (which may be all or part of a salesperson's overall pay). Bonuses, gain sharing (which is based on either cost savings or profit sharing), and employee stock option plans also motivate employees to maintain high levels of performance.

8. **Differentiate between fixed and flexible benefits**. Fixed benefits are available to all members of the organization, although not all companies offer all possible benefits. The categories of fixed benefits include benefits required by law; paid holidays, vacation, and sick leave; health and accident insurance; life insurance, long-term disabil-

ity, and supplemental unemployment benefits; employee services; and family benefits. With flexible benefits, employees are given a number of flex dollars to spend on those benefits offered by the company that best suit their needs.

9. **Discuss the use of flexible work schedules and leaves to increase employee satisfaction.** Employees increasingly want benefits that provide free time to pursue their outside interests—in family and other relationships. To provide these benefits and thus create happier, more productive workers, employers are beginning to offer such options as flextime, job sharing, work-at-home programs (sometimes using telecommuting), and leave. In fact, the Family and Medical Leave Act requires firms with 50 or more employees to provide up to 12 weeks of unpaid leave to employees with new babies or with serious illnesses—their own or their family members'. Long-term leaves—to pursue additional education or for public-service activities—are usually without pay, although the employee will retain the job until he or she returns.

Changes in Employment Status

10. **Outline the various ways in which employees can change status in an organization.** Besides hiring and training employees, the human resource manager is responsible for moving them within the organization in order to maintain appropriate staffing levels. Employees may be reassigned through a promotion to a job with more responsibility or through transfer to a job with comparable compensation but involving different skills. Transfers may result because company or employee needs change or because an employee is causing problems in his or her current job. Employees who perform poorly may be demoted and eventually terminated. Employees may leave a company because they are temporarily laid off or permanently terminated. Termination may be voluntary—as in retirement or when the employee moves, accepts another job, or starts a new company—or involuntary—as when the employee is fired for poor performance, fighting, stealing, or lying, or when a position has been eliminated.

 ## Key Terms

human resource management **351**	performance appraisal **366**	gain-sharing **370**	transfer **375**
contingent work force **351**	career development **366**	profit sharing **370**	demotion **375**
employee leasing **353**	career path **367**	employee stock option plan **371**	separation **376**
job analysis **355**	job rotation **367**	fixed benefits **371**	layoff **376**
job description **355**	succession planning **367**	flexible benefits **372**	unemployment insurance **377**
job specification **356**	mentoring **368**	flextime **373**	attrition **377**
job requisition **357**	compensation **368**	job sharing **373**	termination **377**
job posting **358**	pay **368**	work-at-home programs **374**	employment at will **377**
employee referral **358**	benefits **368**	telecommuting **374**	retirement **377**
resumé **359**	wages **369**	leave **374**	
probation period **361**	salary **369**	Family and Medical Leave Act **374**	
employee orientation **363**	pay for performance **369**	promotion **375**	
on-the-job training **364**	comparable worth **369**		
diversity training **365**	commission **370**		
	bonus **370**		

• Review Questions

1. How might human resource managers compensate for the changing makeup of the work force?

2. As human resource manager for Babble Company, a manufacturer of infants' toys, how would you plan for the company's current and future job needs?

3. Marshall Company has an opening for a systems engineer. Where would the human resource manager look for applicants?

4. Why would a company hire a permanent, full-time employee instead of obtaining temporary help? Why might a company prefer hiring temporary help?

5. How does the training of new employees differ from that of seasoned employees?

6. What options are available to employees interested in advancing through a company's hierarchy to, say, vice president of sales?

7. What types of cash compensation can employees receive for their work?

8. What is the difference between fixed and flexible benefits? What are the advantages of each?

9. Why would an employee be reassigned?

10. For what reasons would an employee leave a company?

● Critical Thinking Questions

1. If you were a member of the contingent work force, what advantages would you have over a permanent employee? What would be the disadvantages?

2. How do organizations benefit from providing initial and ongoing training and retraining for employees?

3. Considering what you learned in Chapter 11 about motivation and performance, why is it important for managers to give employees feedback about how they are doing on the job?

4. Assuming the cost of employee benefits becomes excessively high, what options do employers have?

5. How could the material you learned in this chapter help you to get a job and keep it? Give some specific examples that might help you during a job search or performance appraisal.

REVIEW CASE *Xerox Evaluates Performance Evaluations*[63]

Xerox Corp. once had a performance appraisal system that was not unlike that used by thousands of other companies in the United States. Conducted annually, the system numerically rated various aspects of each employee's responsibilities and ranked the employee's overall performance on a scale from 1 to 5. Merit increases were directly tied to the overall rating, which was communicated to employees at the performance appraisal meeting.

This type of system, implementation of which can cost a huge company like Xerox millions of dollars in employee and management time, was intended to improve communication and reward and encourage good performance. Analysis of the ratings themselves revealed that more than 95 percent of employees received either a 3 ("meets and sometimes exceeds expected level of performance") or a 4 ("consistently exceeds expected level of performance"). As a result, virtually all employees received merit increases within 1 to 2 percent of the same amount. Employees who received less than a 5 (the highest rating) felt cheated, and surveys revealed that many employees were discouraged, dissatisfied, and in many cases totally surprised by how their managers rated their work performance.

Given such a large measure of discontent among so many talented, well-trained, and valuable employees, something was clearly wrong with the entire appraisal system. Management realized that company efforts to develop a supportive team atmosphere were being undermined by an evaluation process.

Based on suggestions from employees and managers, a new process, Performance Feedback and Development, was designed. For the first time, objectives were set by both manager and employee at the beginning of each year. These were documented and approved by a second-level manager, reviewed after six months, and then used as a basis for the year-end appraisal. The emphasis of the process was on performance feedback and improvement, not on numerical rankings and a corresponding salary increase (which now takes place one to two months following the appraisal discussion). Numerical ratings were eliminated and replaced by written narratives. A survey taken during the first year of the new system showed that employees and managers liked the revised process. More than 80 percent of all employees said they better understood their work group objectives, 70 percent had met the objectives that they and their managers had set for them, and almost 85 percent considered the new appraisal process to be fair.

1. Xerox's original performance appraisal system did not clearly differentiate between the performance levels of different employees. Why would this be a problem for high-performing employees? What message does such a system send to marginal or low-performing employees?

2. How important is it for employees to perceive that they are being fairly evaluated? What should be the major objectives of any appraisal process?

3. The personal and professional development objectives set each year by managers and employees in the Performance Feedback and Development process related both to skills important in all professions—such as communication, planning, time management, and human relations—and to specialized skills and knowledge relevant to each employee's individual job. How valuable are such skills for individuals? For the organization?

CRITICAL THINKING CASE *Digital Votes for Redeployment, Not Unemployment*[64]

Like many mature companies, Digital Equipment Corp., the Massachusetts-based computer maker, was experiencing escalating costs and evaporating profits because of a glut of management employees and outdated manufacturing equipment. Although many companies in such a situation would seek to reduce costs through massive layoffs, Digital took a different approach. Management knew that the use of newer technology, combined with the same work force, could virtually double the company's output. Thus, says Frank Lanza, manager of manufacturing training, Digital in effect had an additional "5,000 people we could do something with."

Digital conducted a thorough analysis of the skills the company's employees already had and the skills they would need to install and work with an updated manufacturing system. It found that there was an excess of assemblers, product technicians, materials planners, hardware technicians, line supervisors, and managers, but that there was a clear need for more process controllers and designers, programmers, computer operators, network analysts, and multiproduct specialist.

The company set out to retrain the "excess" employees to meet the future needs of the company. For example, materials planners, who tend to be detail oriented, were trained as programmers. Supervisors who had overseen certain processes in the old system were trained to design new manufacturing processes for future products. About one hundred production supervisors were trained as salespeople. Finally, middle managers had to develop skills in project management, which Digital considered an important characteristic for managers of the future organization. All told, the company spent 9 to 12 months retraining more than 3,800 workers out of its manufacturing population of 33,500.

1. Digital's executives believe their company saved money by retraining employees instead of laying them off and hiring other people who already had the required skills. A study by the Work in America Institute, a research organization in New York, supports this conclusion. Why, then, do you think so many companies rely on downsizing and massive layoffs when times are lean?

2. Digital offered its retraining program on a voluntary basis to its manufacturing employees. An estimated 600 employees left the organization rather than learn new skills. If you had been a manager at Digital, what steps would you have taken to retain high performers who wanted to leave? Would you have tried to convince them to retrain and remain with the company? Why or why not?

3. Given the steps to effective training discussed in this chapter, describe how you might design a program to retrain the group of materials planners to become computer programmers.

Critical Thinking with the ONE MINUTE MANAGER

"There seem to be so many changes going on in business today that it must be hard to be either a manager or a person being managed," Joanna observed.

"That's true to some degree," the One Minute Manager responded. "Management can get so caught up in making changes that it forgets to consider the impact those changes have on the people in the organization. Even good changes can be stressful, and one change after another is bound to take a toll on employees."

"What can management do to make change less stressful?" asked Carlos.

"Provide lots of information and communication. Announce plans far in advance. Involve employees, especially in decisions that affect them. Those are a few of the tactics that we know can help," explained the One Minute Manager.

"But the most important thing organizations can do is to realize that management is what you do *with* people, not *to* them. We all have to remember that we're in the same boat and that if we cooperate, that boat can carry us all to our destination."

1. As a new entry in the labor market, how do you think the changes in the work force, as discussed in this chapter, will affect you?

2. The goal of many businesses today seems to be to do more with less. What assumptions must employees and managers make to turn this goal into reality?

3. Do increased outsourcing, part-time employment, and flexible working hours increase or decrease opportunities for students entering the labor market? Support your answer by discussing issues raised in this chapter.

13 Unions and Employee-Management Relations

Labor-management relations have changed drastically since the mid-1970s. Historically, U.S. labor unions have been strongest in industries such as steel, auto manufacturing, and mining, but unions grew over time with the inclusion of service industry workers. Recently, though, overall union membership has declined. Global competition, automation, increased reliance on contingent workers, and a growing white-collar work force—not a traditional union base—have been factors. But, labor unions continue to influence the way management treats its workers. As labor-management specialist John Hoerr says, "Instead of speculating whether U.S. unions will—or should—survive, it is more interesting to ask what kind of unionism makes social and economic sense, given the new realities of global competition."[1] This chapter looks at labor union development, the traditional role of unions in U.S. business, and the partnership now being forged between labor and management. After reading this chapter, you will be able to reach the learning goals below.

Learning Goals

1. Discuss the role of unions in U.S. business, focusing on their traditional relationship with management.
2. Compare the characteristics of early union members with those of today's.
3. Outline the history of unions.
4. Discuss legislation designed to regulate labor-management relations.
5. Outline the process of unionizing employees.
6. Describe the overall goal of collective bargaining and identify the three main categories of issues addressed in collective bargaining.
7. List the four steps in the collective bargaining process, noting the tactics used by labor and management to achieve an advantage.
8. Summarize the contributions of unions to all U.S. workers and discuss the future limitations and opportunities for organized labor.
9. Discuss current trends in labor practices and labor-management relations.

The New Partnership

"Did you ever belong to a union?" Joanna asked the One Minute Manager.

"No, but my father did. He worked in the coal mines—a hard and dirty job with very long hours. The work was grueling, the pay was low, and workers were easily replaced because jobs were hard to find. But he and his co-workers tried to make the most of the jobs they had through unionizing."

"Did the union really make a difference in his life?" Carlos asked.

"It really did at that point," the One Minute Manager replied. "Many people are very critical of unions now, but in those days, workers had to band together to be heard in most companies. If their numbers were large enough, they could get management to address improvements they wanted in safety, working hours, working conditions, and other areas. In many ways, the efforts of those earlier union members paved the way for many things we take for granted at work today."

"Such as?" urged Carlos.

"Such as the weekend and the eight-hour workday, paid vacations, and benefits."

"You're kidding! You mean, if it weren't for unions we wouldn't have weekends?" Carlos said, astonished.

"Some people would, of course, but many other employees might not," said the One Minute Manager. "Now the focus of union activity has shifted to other areas."

"Like a four-day workweek?" ventured Joanna.

"No," replied the One Minute Manager, "more like working with management to find ways that can help both management and employees. For example, I was just reading about an agreement the United Steelworkers of America recently negotiated with a Massachusetts manufacturer. The union employees agreed to give up strict work rules and job categories that were meant to protect jobs. In return, they received additional job security and training. Eli Mitchell, a USWA staff representative who helped negotiate the contract, summed it up this way: 'The company shared expense information with us, told us where they needed to save, and where they needed to improve, which is a new twist.'"[2]

"So the role of labor unions has really changed with the times," said Joanna.

"That's right," said the One Minute Manager. "It's an exciting time for unions, with more changes to come."

Unions and Management: Partners or Adversaries?

Although rocked not long ago by recession and economic slowdowns, the American standard of living is still one of the highest in the world. In part, we maintain this standard by taking advantage of inexpensive products readily available on the international market. These cheap goods, however, carry a hidden cost (see Chapter 4, Ethics, Law, and Government). U.S. businesses and consumers face the ethical dilemma of buying goods whose prices are low because they are produced by political prisoners (China), or by children (India, Pakistan, Korea), or by workers who do not make a living wage (as in Mexico and many developing countries), or under conditions that pollute rivers, lakes, or oceans. Ironically, the United States faced many of these problems early in the twentieth century and, thanks in part to unions, took action to improve many of these conditions.

Labor unions are organizations of workers with shared concerns, such as wages, working hours, benefits, and workplace conditions. Unions exist for the simple reason that there is greater strength in numbers—workers who act together have significantly more clout than those who bargain individually with an organization's management. **Collective bargaining** is the process by which representatives of management and labor determine wages and working conditions for employees.

The interests of owners and managers and the interests of labor need not be in conflict. Owners and managers need workers to produce goods and services, and workers need owners and managers to provide jobs. But in fact, the relationship between unions and management has traditionally been an adversarial one. As you saw in Chapter 2, labor is a factor of production. Part of an owner's interest is to reduce the cost of labor for each unit produced. At the same time, it is in the employee's interest to seek out the best exchange—in money, working conditions, and benefits—for his or her work, time, and commitment.

Although you may view unions as a peculiarly American institution, they are a common ingredient in the employee-management relationship in many countries. In fact, the United States is one of the least unionized countries in the industrialized world. Although union membership has declined in the United States over the past two decades, the union movement remains very active in much of the rest of the industrialized world. Germany, Sweden, France, and Great Britain all have long-standing union movements. Other countries, such as Spain, have only recently legalized unions. And in Israel, a union holds a central role in the country's affairs—the Israeli General Federation of Workers administers the country's health service, owns major portions of the nation's industry, and is paid dues by 80 percent of Israelis.[3] For a glimpse of the state of unions in other countries, see the doing business box "Unions Around the World" on page 388.

The traditional power relationship between unions and management in the United States tends to resemble the movement of a seesaw. Some of the conditions that throw power to the union side include a seller's market for labor, a limited number of skilled workers, and strong economic growth. Unions also tend to be strong when workers are so angry about unfair working conditions or wages that they are able to stage a united fight to improve them. Other conditions favor strong management, producing a buyer's market. Among them are an ample number of skilled workers, economic recession, competing foreign work forces, and new technology and automation. Union strength also varies according to type of business—unions have been a strong force in the steel, auto manufacturing, and mining industries, but they have traditionally played a relatively minor role among white-collar workers.

1. Discuss the role of unions in U.S. business, focusing on their traditional relationship with management.

 labor unions

Organizations of workers with shared concerns, such as wages, working hours, benefits, and workplace conditions.

 collective bargaining

The process by which representatives of management and labor determine wages and working conditions for employees.

doing business

Unions Around the World

Although union membership has declined in the United States over the past couple of decades, the union movement remains very active in much of the rest of the industrialized world. In some long-industrialized countries, such as Germany and Sweden, unions play a much more formal role in government and industry than they do in the United States. As a result, unions in those countries are much stronger and much more vital than their U.S. counterparts. In some of the newly emerging industrial nations, such as Mexico, Colombia, and Singapore, however, unions are often subject to aggressive corporate and government repression.

Mexico

Only 16 percent of the Mexican work force is unionized. Mexican unions are of two types: so-called white unions, which are controlled by business, and independent unions under the umbrella of the Authentic Labor Front. Mexican unions are often marked by corruption and violence. Although once quite influential, unions have of late given up a lot of power in the face of the government's recent probusiness policies.

Japan

Approximately one-fourth of Japanese workers are represented by LENGO, a federation of company and public-sector unions, and by two less popular federations. The Japanese union environment is generally one of cooperation between business and labor. Japanese unionism is noted for its annual process of *shunto*, or "spring wage offensive," during which workers loudly make known to management their desires for wage increases in the coming year.

Singapore

Approximately one-fourth of Singapore's workers belong to unions. Many of the leaders of Singapore's ruling party, the People's Action Party, were recruited from unions centralized under the banner of the National Trade Union Congress. The government policy of "dynamic cooperation," which places severe restrictions on workers' ability to be politically active and to strike, has resulted in strike-free relations since 1986.

Spain

In Spain, unions have been legal only since 1977. Before then, however, the Spanish Communist Party was successful at organizing militant trade unions, known as Comisiones Obreras, within the government-approved labor organizations. After legalization, the Union General de Trabajo (UGT) came to dominate the scene, benefiting from generous government funding and appointments. But a subsequent falling out between the leader of the Spanish government and the head of the UGT caused the union to lose much of its clout.

Sweden

Approximately two-thirds of Sweden's workers belong to unions. Unions played an integral role in the development of Sweden's modern economic policy, which, in fact, was devised by the Landesorganisation—the country's trade union federation. As a result, there is little of the conflict between labor and management that marks much of union activity in the rest of the world. However, recent high unemployment rates and currency devaluations have led to some labor discontent and strikes.

Poland

Poland has 2 million union members. This is far fewer than the peak of 10 million members in the early 1980s, when the trade union Solidarnosc (Solidarity), led by Lech Walensa, brought workers' issues to the forefront of Poland's political agenda. As a result of the groundswell of national support for Solidarnosc, the country's communist government was forced to make extensive concessions to workers. This change in the balance of power precipitated the fall of communism throughout Eastern Europe and in the Soviet Union.

Russia

With 50 million members, the Federation of Independent Trade Unions of Russia exercises considerable power in the Russian political scene. Founded in 1990, the union recently conducted extensive strikes to protest Russia's high unemployment and delays in the payment of wages.

Source: Ben Webb, "Striking Contrasts: The Trade Union Movement in Europe and Other Areas," *New Statesman & Society*, Sept. 2, 1994, p. S6(4).

Later in this chapter, we will examine the options that labor and management have in their relationship and how each seeks to reach its goal. First, let's look at the kind of people who join unions.

Union Members: Who Are They?

Despite the stereotype of the white male union member in a blue-collar occupation, unions represent the diverse work force described in Chapters 11 and 12. Many are women, many are people of color, many have disabilities. Union members include airline pilots, graphic artists, social workers, athletes, firefighters, opera singers, farm workers, newspaper writers, marine engineers and sailors, and people in many other occupations.

The highest concentrations of union members are in mining, construction, manufacturing, transportation, communications and public utilities, and government service. In the past, relatively few white-collar and service workers were union members, but some of the greatest successes in unionizing today have occurred in those occupations. Geography also plays a role: Union membership is more common in urban and industrial areas than in rural areas and the Sun Belt. Ethnicity also plays a role. About one of every four African Americans belongs to a union, compared with approximately one of every six white workers.

Fewer women than men belong to unions, but women make up about half of new union membership, in part because unionization is growing in occupations in which women are concentrated. Growth has been particularly notable in unions representing teachers, food service workers, and other service employees, such as nurses and health care providers. Public-sector unions have also shown dramatic growth. Before the 1960s, government employees could not bargain collectively. After the federal government and many state and local governments extended collective bargaining rights to these employees in the 1960s and 1970s, public-sector unions and employee associations became a major part of the labor movement.

Another fast-growing segment is unions of professional employees—workers such as engineers, managers, and computer programmers, whose jobs involve intellectual skills and require advanced training or education. And about 90 percent of performing artists belong to unions, as do about 60 percent of teachers and 38 percent of college professors. Unionization is also growing among physicians and nurses, as an increasingly competitive environment in the various health-related industries, along with increasing government regulation, is generating attempts to demand more work from fewer people.

In spite of these areas of growth, however, many workers see little need for labor unions. Union membership has steadily declined, from 22 million in 1975, or about 30 percent of the work force, to about 16 million, or about 16 percent of the work force, today.[4] This decrease can be traced in part to downsizing, layoffs, and consolidations in manufacturing. For example, the machinists' union once claimed 1 million members but now numbers only 827,000. Autoworker union membership peaked at 1.5 million and now stands at 1 million. Unionized steelworkers once numbered 1.4 million, but current union enrollment stands at 750,000.[5] In addition, the percentage of successful organizing votes—votes to establish new union branches in the manufacturing sector—has dropped from 54 percent two decades ago to a low of 40 percent today. Mining unions have fared even worse, winning only 32 percent of organizing votes, compared with 59 percent in 1970.[6] Table 13.1 shows the 15 largest U.S. unions, by total membership.

2. Compare the characteristics of early union members with those of today's.

The Folks Who Brought You the Weekend

The union members at this Labor Day rally in Washington, D.C., represent a heritage that dates back to colonial times. Many of the working conditions and benefits that nonunion workers take for granted today exist only because of the tradition of organized labor in the United States.

table **13.1**   The 15 Largest U.S. Unions

Union	Number of Members
American Federation of Labor & Congress of Industrial Organizations (AFL-CIO)	14 million
National Education Association (NEA)	2 million
International Brotherhood of Teamsters, Chauffeurs, Warehousemen, and Helpers of America (IBT)	1.5 million
American Federation of State, County and Municipal Employees (AFSCME)	1.2 million
United Food and Commercial Workers International Union (UFCW)	1.2 million
United Automobile, Aerospace & Agricultural Implement Workers of America, International (UAW)	1 million
Service Employees International Union (SEIU)	950,000
American Federation of Teachers (AFT)	850,000
International Association of Machinists and Aerospace Workers (IAM)	827,000
International Brotherhood of Electrical Workers (IBEW)	750,000
United Steelworkers of America (USWA)	750,000
Communications Workers of America (CWA)	700,000
Laborers' International Union of North America (LIUNA)	700,000
International Brotherhood of Carpenters and Joiners of America (IBCJA)	500,000
International Union of Operating Engineers (IUOE)	375,000

Source: "Labor Union Directory," *World Almanac and Book of Facts* (New York: Funk and Wagnalls, 1993).

No one can predict what the future holds for unions, but for now they are a significant part of the work force. That means unions and management must concentrate on finding creative new ways to work together, the topic we turn to next.

Employee-Management Options

As we have seen repeatedly in this text, the employee-management relationship in the final decade of the twentieth century offers exciting opportunities for a new kind of partnership. In some cases, that may mean employees will buy the company, as they did at Market Forge in Everett, Massachusetts, in 1994. In other cases, it means unionized employees will participate more as members of teams, working with management to ensure that they and their companies reach their goals. Unions seem comfortable supporting the participation of members in workplace decision making—a study by the General Accounting Office showed that unionized companies established more participatory programs than companies that were not unionized.[7] Shell Oil Co.

and the Energy and Chemical Workers Union, for example, have worked together to create a network of semiautonomous work teams that operate the Shell chemical plant in Sarnia, Ontario. Teams, which include union employees, hire new plant employees, train each other, and administer and settle their own work grievances.[8]

In most companies, management and employees will structure their working partnership along one of three tracks:[9]

1. The traditional adversarial relationship between labor and management, focusing on such issues as wages, benefits, and working conditions

2. Direct individual, nonunion, employee participation in such activities as teams involved in making various workplace decisions

3. Direct union involvement in decisions and administration of activities formerly considered to be management's responsibility alone

The second track produces something close to an ideal working relationship. At Ben & Jerry's Homemade, Inc., for example, owners and employees tend to work out agreements themselves, without the interventions of unions. To some extent, we have examined this option in various contexts throughout this text. In this chapter, we look more closely at the first and third options. The first represents the history of management-labor relations in this country. The third may represent its future.

The Traditional Adversarial Relationship

The traditional adversarial relationship between labor and management is still the way of doing business in some organizations. For example, recent contract talks between Local 212 of the Office and Professional Employees International Union in Buffalo, New York, and Blue Cross proved very bitter. Ultimately, the union rejected the company's final contract offer, and Blue Cross responded by refusing to permit union employees to work until a contract was signed. Union members countered by conducting a prayer service that same evening at Blue Cross headquarters. The media turned out in force to report on hundreds of workers who sang, said prayers, and chanted, "We want to work" over and over again. By the time the controversy ended, the president of Blue Cross had resigned and the union's demands had been granted.[10] The price of such confrontations, for company and employees alike, is often staggering, regardless of who walks away the "winner." To understand the background for this style of employee-management relationship, we must look at the early history of labor unions in the United States.

Craft Unions

The earliest unions in the 13 original colonies were **craft unions**, small, local organizations limited to skilled handworkers in specific trades, such as cordwainers (shoemakers), printers, and carpenters. Located in Philadelphia, New York, Boston, and other cities, the craft unions attempted to maintain, rather than improve, wages and working conditions. These early unions were so effective in representing workers' rights that Philadelphia employers turned to the courts to contain union efforts. In 1806 employers sought government assistance in resolving a dispute with the cordwainers' union. The court ruled that the cordwainers were engaged in a conspiracy in restraint of trade. This finding slowed but did not stop union growth; by the mid-1800s, U.S. courts were focusing on the legality of union objectives rather than on the unions' right to take concerted action. Since 1806, government has been closely involved with

3. Outline the history of unions.

 **craft union**

Small, local organization limited to skilled handworkers in specific trades.

employee-management relations in the United States. Table 13.2 is a timeline showing the interaction of union development and major laws supporting or limiting union activity from the early nineteenth century through today.

table 13.2 Timeline: The Emergence of Organized Labor and Laws Limiting the Power of Management and of Labor Unions in the United States

Year	Organization, Issue, or Law
1700s	Shoemakers, printers, carpenters, and other artisans form craft unions to maintain their wages and working conditions.
1806	Court decision declares Philadelphia shoemakers to be a criminal conspiracy, following precedent of British judicial system.
Mid-1800s	Courts focus on union objectives, rather than on the right to unionize, to decide whether union activity is lawful. Industrial Revolution leads to mechanization of manufacturing.
1871	Knights of Labor organizes nationally along craft lines, across craft lines, and in factories. Welcomes workers of all trades, regardless of gender or race. Favors social reform over economic action.
1886	Membership of Knights of Labor reaches 702,000.
1886	Founding of American Federation of Labor (AFL). Refocuses union movement on economic action. Most AFL members are skilled workers (craftspeople), which gives bargaining power because they are hard to replace.
1900s	Mass production techniques in manufacturing lead some union leaders to promote industrial unionism, organizing unskilled and semiskilled workers across craft lines but within the same industry—bargaining power comes from sheer numbers of workers, rather than from difficulty of replacing skilled workers.
1904	AFL membership reaches 1.4 million; AFL remains committed to craft unionism.
1914	Congress passes Clayton Antitrust Act, which helps prevent court intervention in most labor disputes.
1932	Norris-LaGuardia Anti-Injunction Act further restricts the courts' ability to intervene in most labor disputes.
1935	Individual unions within the AFL clash over issue of craft unions versus industrial unions. Eight unions, led by the United Mine Workers under John L. Lewis, break from the AFL to form the Congress of Industrial Organizations (CIO).
1935	National Labor Relations Act (NLRA), also known as the Wagner Act, passed to protect rights of workers to unionize and bargain collectively. Results in the creation of the National Labor Relations Board (NLRB), which supervises union elections and prohibits unfair practices on the part of management.
1938	Fair Labor Standards Act passed. Initially set minimum wage at 25 cents per hour for nonfarm and nonretail workers, and maximum workweek at 44 hours.
1947	Congress passes Taft-Hartley Act, limiting the power of unions. Provides for an 80-day injunction period to prevent strikes that could create a national emergency. Allows states to prohibit contracts that require an employee to join a union as a condition of employment.
1955	AFL and CIO merge, forming the AFL-CIO. Merger is in part a cooperative response to new and impending legislation limiting the power of unions.
1957	Teamsters union and its 3 million members expelled from AFL-CIO over allegations of leadership corruption.
1959	Landrum-Griffin Act ensures that union members have basic democratic rights, such as the rights to vote in union elections, to attend union meetings, and to nominate union officers.
1987	Teamsters union reinstated in the AFL-CIO.
1988	Worker Adjustment and Retraining Notification Act requires employers to provide 60-day notice of intent to close a facility or lay off large numbers of workers.

Industrial Unions and the Growth of National Organizations

Before the Civil War, much of the United States was rural, characterized by farms and small businesses. In most cases, workers and owners knew each other personally.[11] Then came the Industrial Revolution, which changed the way Americans earned their living and the way U.S. businesses produced goods for sale. Companies grew even larger, drawing thousands of workers from rural farms and small businesses to the cities, to use the new machinery that allowed more goods to be produced faster. Markets widened to serve an expanding population as immigrants arrived from Europe and settlers moved westward. Personal relationships between employer and worker deteriorated, as did working conditions and pay.

Knights of Labor

Pictured here is a group of delegates to the 1886 Knights of Labor convention. The union extended membership to all workers—and even to employers—but fell victim to internal factions and to poor public relations that same year. After the Haymarket Riot in Chicago, where a deadly bomb exploded in the midst of a group of police who were trying to break up a labor rally, public opinion turned against unions in general and the KOL in particular. Still, this early federation of craft unions is remembered as America's first national union.

This change in society and in the nature of work created fertile ground for the growth of **industrial unions**, organizations of workers in many different crafts, all working within the same industry. Some focused on economic issues alone. Others, like the Noble Order of the **Knights of Labor**, focused on political issues and action, welcoming all workers regardless of gender or race. Radical for its time, the Knights was the most successful of the political action or "uplift" unions, with a peak of 702,000 members in 1886.[12]

The AFL and the Modern Labor Movement

In 1886, the founding of an alternative to the Knights of Labor inaugurated the modern labor movement. The **American Federation of Labor (AFL)** was a national organization comprising individual craft unions focused on the economic well-being of members. A **labor federation** is a labor organization made up of a variety of individual unaffiliated local and national unions. The AFL's bargaining power stemmed from the expertise of its members, skilled workers who were harder to replace than unskilled workers. The AFL grew rapidly; by 1904, its membership had increased fivefold. By World War I, the number of members peaked at about 4 million before declining to 2.5 million at the beginning of the Great Depression in the 1930s.[13]

 industrial union

Organization of workers in many different crafts, all working within the same industry.

 Knights of Labor

Late-nineteenth-century industrial union that focused on political issues and action.

 American Federation of Labor (AFL)

National organization comprising individual craft unions focused on the economic well-being of members.

 labor federation

A labor organization made up of a variety of individual unaffiliated local and national unions.

Congress of Industrial Organizations (CIO)

Organization resulting from a split within the AFL and formed as a federation of industrial unions.

AFL-CIO

National federation of craft and industrial unions formed from the merger in 1955 of the AFL and CIO.

national union

Countrywide union organized by craft or industry.

The CIO Split and the AFL-CIO Merger

In 1935, a policy clash over craft unionism versus industrial unionism spurred eight national unions to leave the AFL and form a competing federation. These eight were led by the United Mine Workers, whose president was John L. Lewis, and the federation they formed was the **Congress of Industrial Organizations (CIO)**. The dispute centered on organizing workers in the new mass production industries, such as automobile and steel manufacturing, where thousands of semiskilled and unskilled people worked in a variety of jobs at the same plant. The rebel unions saw great potential in organizing these workers along industrial lines, with bargaining power flowing from sheer numbers of workers, rather than from difficulty in replacing skilled artisans. The traditional AFL leadership remained steadfastly committed to craft unionism.

Between 1933 and the end of World War II, union membership almost quadrupled, partly as a result of the CIO's search for members and the AFL's attempt to fight off competition from the new organization. Union organizing activities were particularly effective at the beginning of this period, when workers were looking for help to escape from the low wages and job shortages of the Depression era. By the end of this period, World War II had created a wealth of new jobs, and workers found themselves in a seller's market for labor. In the end, however, the competition for workers between the AFL and CIO proved expensive and unproductive. Under new leadership, the two organizations merged in 1955 to form the **AFL-CIO**. The merger was in part a response to impending legislation limiting the power of unions.

Today, the AFL-CIO is a voluntary federation of 94 union affiliates that represent about 13.3 million workers, or over half of all U.S. union members.[14] Its major function is to speak for the labor movement on important issues, particularly political ones. For example, it lobbies members of Congress when issues that concern its members, such as minimum wage laws, health care reform, and foreign trade, are being considered. Its other functions include chartering new national unions, helping member unions resolve disputes and coordinate activities, and providing its affiliates with organizing, legal, and research assistance.

Because of its high visibility, the AFL-CIO is sometimes thought of as the head of the labor movement. That makes it important to understand what the AFL-CIO does *not* do, as well as what it does. Most important, the AFL-CIO does not negotiate contracts collectively, nor does it set policy for the national unions within its federation. National unions do not surrender their decision-making autonomy by joining the AFL-CIO, and it is the national unions and their local affiliates that perform all collective bargaining.

Locals and Nationals: Power and Responsibility

We have noted that the AFL-CIO is a federation of member unions. Under its umbrella—and in some cases completely outside it—are the national unions. **National unions** are countrywide unions organized by craft or industry. Although most national unions belong to the AFL-CIO, some do not. The International Brotherhood of Teamsters, the largest national union in the United States, with over 1 million members, does not belong to the AFL-CIO. Most professional associations, such as the National Education Association and the American Nurses Association, are also independent.

Nationals organized by craft range in size from the 1 million-plus-member International Brotherhood of Teamsters to the 54-member Major League Umpires Association. Like the umpires, craft union members have a shared occupation or skill. For example, the American Federation of Teachers primarily represents teachers, and most members of the American Federation of Musicians are musicians. The industrial unions represent people who do many different jobs within the same or related industries, such as the United Steelworkers and the Communication Workers of America.

A number of unions combine characteristics of both craft and industrial unions. The Teamsters, for example, has a broadly defined jurisdiction that includes virtually any worker who has any contact with moving vehicles. In fact, according to a popular story justifying a Teamster attempt to organize clerical workers, "Secretaries sit on chairs with wheels, and if it has wheels it's a Teamster."

National unions may bargain with all the employers in an industry, with a group of employers, or with one major employer at a time. In industries with a nationwide product market, such as automobiles and steel, national unions do most of the bargaining. This has the effect of stabilizing wages across the product market, which is important because it prevents unionized workers in one location from undercutting the wages of workers in other regions. Some national unions delegate the bargaining function to local unions.

Local unions are small unions—often subunits of nationals—that represent workers in a limited area. That area may be a single plant, a single employer, or a single metropolitan area. For example, the Harlingen local of the Amalgamated Clothing and Textile Workers Union represents employees at the Levi Strauss Associates, Inc., plant in Harlingen, Texas, which produces Dockers brand slacks.[15] Members typically think of their local as "the union," and they expect attention and service from it, most importantly by ensuring enforcement of collective bargaining contracts. Locals elect their own presidents. Within large companies, union members are represented by a **shop steward**, a company employee and union co-worker.

Many local unions have sole responsibility for reaching contract agreements with their workers' employers, particularly in industries with a local product market, such as newspapers and construction. Even when locals are covered by a larger contract negotiated by a larger union, they negotiate local working conditions and terms. The national union often assists bargaining locals with research, legal matters, and organizing and coordinating activities with other locals. Many nationals publish newspapers and represent members on public issues. The distribution of power between locals and nationals is also influenced by tradition, the local's degree of independence, and the nature of specific issues. Large locals need little national assistance and often function almost autonomously. But a national may attempt to increase its control over

 local union

Small union—often a subunit of a national union—that represents workers in a limited area.

 shop steward

A company employee and union member who represents co-workers within large companies.

Labor Organization

At the Levi's plant in Murphy, North Carolina, workers belong to a national union, but the local union is their resource for resolving grievances and collective bargaining. Nationals may get involved in sensitive negotiations or in wider issues, such as the potential loss of jobs to overseas plants.

4. Discuss legislation designed to regulate labor-management relations.

✓ **Worker Adjustment and Retraining Notification Act**

Requires employers to give employees 60-day notice of their intent to close a facility or lay off a large number of workers.

✓ **injunction**

Court order forbidding workers to perform certain acts, like striking or boycotting.

✓ **strike**

A refusal by employees to perform their job duties until their demands have been met.

✓ **boycott**

An organized refusal to buy, sell, or use targeted goods or services.

✓ **Clayton Antitrust Act**

Passed in 1914; along with the Norris-LaGuardia Anti-Injunction Act, prevents court intervention in most labor disputes.

✓ **Norris-LaGuardia Anti-Injunction Act**

Passed in 1932; along with the Clayton Antitrust Act, prevents court intervention in most labor disputes.

✓ **National Labor Relations Act (NLRA)**

Passed in 1935; protects the rights of workers to unionize and bargain collectively; also called the *Wagner Act*.

✓ **National Labor Relations Board (NLRB)**

Administrative and enforcement agency established by the NLRA that supervises union elections and prohibits unfair management practices.

✓ **good-faith bargaining**

Management's and labor's willingness to consider alternative proposals and to compromise in order to reach a mutually acceptable agreement.

negotiations in unstable situations or when an issue seems too large for the local to handle, such as an industry's shift toward moving jobs overseas. Union action on large national issues has led to changes in legislation, as it did in this case with the passing of the **Worker Adjustment and Retraining Notification Act**, which requires employers to give employees 60-day notice of their intent to close a facility or lay off a large number of workers.

Union-Related Legislation

Extensive legislation has been written to define the respective rights of management and labor. Like the seesaw movement that characterizes union versus management power, this legislation has tended to favor first one side, then the other. (See Table 13.2, which incorporates union-development milestones and legal milestones.)

In response to early unionization attempts, employers sought help from the courts in the form of **injunctions**—court orders forbidding workers to perform certain acts, like striking or boycotting. A **strike** is a refusal by employees to perform their job duties until their demands have been met. A **boycott** is an organized refusal to buy, sell, or use targeted goods or services. In one early request for help, in 1894 the Pullman Co. asserted that unions were violating the 1890 Sherman Antitrust Act, a law that had been passed to prevent business monopolies. The courts found in management's favor, concluding that certain union actions, such as strikes, interfered with interstate commerce and thus violated the law. As a result, the striking American Railway Union was defeated by an injunction issued under the Sherman Antitrust Act.

The unions then had *their* day, turning to Congress with a request to limit the intervention by the courts in labor disputes. In response, Congress passed the 1914 **Clayton Antitrust Act** and the 1932 **Norris-LaGuardia Anti-Injunction Act**, which together prevent court intervention in most labor disputes. The Great Depression spurred the federal government, under President Franklin D. Roosevelt's leadership, to take vigorous action to reduce staggering unemployment rates and poverty. In 1935, the **National Labor Relations Act (NLRA)**, or the *Wagner Act*, was passed to protect the rights of workers to unionize and bargain collectively. The NLRA covers most private-sector businesses and some public-sector institutions such as the U.S. Postal Service and colleges and universities. The act also created the **National Labor Relations Board (NLRB)**, an administrative and enforcement agency that supervises union elections and prohibits unfair management practices. Three years later, in 1938, the Fair Labor Standards Act was passed, establishing a minimum wage of 25 cents per hour and a maximum workweek of 44 hours.

The NLRA supported the labor movement in two major ways. First, it provided for elections—rather than force—to determine if workers at a particular company wanted union representation. Second, it protected the process by which labor and management negotiated contracts by outlawing some employer practices designed to undermine unionization. Among the prohibited practices were threatening and coercing employees who tried to exercise their union rights; discriminating against employees taking part in unionizing activities; setting up employer-dominated unions; and not bargaining in good faith. **Good-faith bargaining** means that both management and labor demonstrate a willingness to consider alternative proposals and to compromise in order to reach a mutually acceptable agreement. Mostly as a result of the NLRA, unions were able to increase their membership from approximately 3.5 million in 1935 to approximately 15 million by 1947.[16]

In 1959, the Landrum-Griffin Act was passed, ensuring that union members had basic democratic rights, such as the rights to vote in union elections, to attend union meetings, and to nominate union officers.

Then the seesaw tipped again, and laws were passed protecting employers and the public from undue union pressure and unfair union practices. In 1947, a Republican-dominated Congress passed the **Taft-Hartley Act**, also known as the *Labor-Management Relations Act*, amending the NLRA and limiting the power of unions by outlawing specified practices. These practices include threatening and coercing employers, using economic pressure against employers in response to a labor dispute, pressuring employers to assign work to workers within a particular local's jurisdiction, and not bargaining in good faith. Taft-Hartley also provides for an 80-day injunction period to prevent strikes that could create a national emergency, and it allows states to prohibit contract provisions that require employees to join a union—whether they want to or not.

The Taft-Hartley Act also forbids **closed shops**, which are workplaces that require membership in a union as a condition of gaining employment. **Union shops** require union membership after some minimal probationary period. Union shops are not prohibited under Taft-Hartley, but some states have passed laws that prevent them within state boundaries. Almost half of all states have passed **right-to-work laws**, which grant employees within the state's boundaries the right to get and hold a job without belonging to a union (see Figure 13.1). In these states, the labor movement is weak and union shops are forbidden. Supporters of union shops argue that, unless union membership is required, nonunion employees unfairly receive the benefits that union members provide through their dues.

Alternatives to closed and union shops are the agency shop and the open shop. An **agency shop** requires all members of a bargaining unit—union and nonunion—to pay union dues if they receive benefits from union-negotiated contracts. In an **open shop**, employees cannot be forced to join a union or to pay union dues as a condition of getting or holding a job. For an example of an agency shop that failed because of a right-to-work law, see the ethics check entitled "Will the Redskins Pay Their Dues?" on page 398.

Taft-Hartley Act

Passed in 1947, it amends the NLRA and limits the power of unions by outlawing specified practices; also called the *Labor-Management Relations Act*.

closed shop

Workplace that requires membership in a union as a condition of gaining employment.

union shop

Workplace that requires union membership after some minimal probationary period.

right-to-work laws

State laws granting employees within the state's boundaries the right to get and hold a job without belonging to a union.

agency shop

Workplace that requires all members of a bargaining unit—union and nonunion—to pay union dues if they receive benefits from union-negotiated contracts.

open shop

Workplace where employees cannot be forced to join a union or to pay union dues as a condition of getting or holding a job.

figure 13.1 States with Right-to-Work Laws

■ States with Right-to-Work Laws

Employees in states with right-to-work laws cannot be forced to join a union or to pay dues as a condition of obtaining or holding a job.

Will the Redskins Pay Their Dues?

An organization is an *agency shop* when employees in certain job categories are required to pay dues even though they do not belong to unions. Many employees who don't want to join a union consider shops to be unfair. A few years ago, 26 members of the Washington Redskins football team refused to pay union dues to the National Football League Players Association in protest over the union's agreement to a limit on players' salaries. Union lawyers took the players to arbitration, where it was ruled that the players would have to pay the dues. At risk was the final game of the season—if the players refused to meet the arbitrator's demand, they could be suspended for the New Year's Eve game against the Minnesota Vikings.

Instead of bowing to union pressure, the players decided to stand their ground and fight. Although the Redskins play their games in Washington, D.C., they actually practice, and spend most of their working hours, in Virginia. And although Washington, D.C., does not prohibit agency shops, Virginia does, under its right-to-work law. Lawyers for the football players convinced Federal District Judge Joyce Hens Green that the team's primary workplace was in Virginia, and the judge overturned the arbitrator's ruling.

From the point of view of the disgruntled players, it was not fair for them to be forced to pay dues to a union they did not wish to join. From the union's point of view, it was not fair for some players to receive the benefits of union representation without paying for them. What do you think?

Source: Reed Larson, "Redskins Tackle the NFL's Union," *Wall Street Journal,* Jan. 11, 1994, p. A14.

How Workers Unionize

5. Outline the process of unionizing employees.

The process by which employees at a particular workplace gain union representation can begin either within the company or outside it. In an internal campaign, a group of employees, perhaps frustrated with their employer's policies, contacts an existing union for organizing assistance. This was the case at a 50-employee steel processing firm in Ohio, where employees filed a petition for a union election. Employees wanted union representation not because of wage and benefit issues, but because they were perceiving management favoritism toward certain employees and a general lack of communication.[17] In an external campaign, a union targets an employer for unionization and then attempts to convince its employees that union representation will benefit them.

In either case, union organizers, who are paid staff members of the national unions, oversee the unionizing campaign. They begin by researching the employer's employment practices, market position and profitability, and management philosophy. Another early organizing activity is the creation of workplace committees staffed by respected employees with good work records from a wide spectrum of jobs and departments within the company. Together, the union organizers and workplace committees plan the organizing campaign, using the background research and their knowledge of the employees and work environment.

Most campaigns focus on such workplace issues as wages, safety, and fair treatment. Organizers attempt to convince all employees that collective bargaining can improve any poor conditions that have been identified. They try to reassure employees who fear employer retaliation. In some campaigns, organizers make many house calls to communicate these messages in person. In other campaigns, particularly those in urban areas and those involving large numbers of people, organizers rely on mass meetings, letters, surveys, and media coverage.

When an organizing campaign begins, the employer must decide whether to oppose unionization. Some employers, particularly those with many unionized plants, do not oppose it. Levi Strauss Associates, Inc., for example, has agreed to permit the Amalgamated Clothing and Textile Workers Union—representing approximately 6,000 of its workers at 30 separate American plants—to actively recruit members in exchange for union support of improvements to its production systems.[18] At other companies, however, employers work hard to discourage employees from voting for unionization. Employers may appeal to employees' loyalty or point out potential disadvantages, such as loss of harmony within the company, the need to pay union dues, management's loss of flexibility, and the possibility of layoffs if wages rise. Management communicates its point of view through letters, payroll stuffers, bulletin board notices, films, and question-and-answer sessions with managers.

According to the National Labor Relations Act, if 30 percent of workplace employees sign authorization forms indicating a strong interest in unionizing, an election must be held, with all employees voting. This **representation election** determines whether a union will become the official representative of workers in negotiations with management and bargain with management to satisfy their demands. In the private sector, the National Labor Relations Board administers representation elections and enforces extensive rules governing what union organizers and management can and cannot do during the election process.

Voting is by secret ballot. If a majority of employees vote to approve, the union receives **certification**, or the right to act as the exclusive bargaining agent for employees for one year. If a majority of employees vote not to unionize, no other election can be held for one year. Similarly, a majority vote can result in **decertification**, or withdrawal of the union's right to represent the employees. Figure 13.2 illustrates the organizing process.

 representation election

Election to determine whether a union will become the official representative of workers in negotiations with management.

 certification

A union's right, obtained by majority vote, to act as the exclusive bargaining agent for employees for one year.

decertification

Withdrawal, by majority vote, of a union's right to represent employees.

figure **13.2** **The Process of Organizing a Union**

1. Union targets company or workers contact union for assistance

2. Campaign for employee authorization to designate union as bargaining agent

3. Union collects signed authorizations from 30 percent of employees

4. Union petitions NLRB to conduct certification election

5. Campaign for union certification

6. Certification election by secret ballot

7. Certification if more than 50 percent of employees vote in favor

As you can see from this figure, the process of unionizing a workplace is very formalized and structured.

The Collective Bargaining Process

6. Describe the overall goal of collective bargaining and identify the three main categories of issues addressed in collective bargaining.

The power of collective bargaining is the main reason employees want to be represented by unions. Collective bargaining produces contracts that outline the terms and conditions of employment and directly affect three major parties: management, bargaining unit employees, and the union as an organization. The objectives and concerns of all three determine the bargaining issues, and concerns and approaches to these issues change as the parties' needs change.

Consider these three viewpoints in relation to technological change. Management in many industries views new technology as vital to organizational profitability. The auto industry, for example, has automated assembly lines with robot welding machines and computerized process control systems. But new technology, while increasing productivity and efficiency, often also means that fewer workers are needed to do the same amount of work. For this reason, the threat of automation tends to increase employees' worries about job security. It also gives officers of the union valid reasons to be concerned, since fewer workers mean declining membership and income from dues, which can threaten the survival of the union. At the same time, however, all three parties also know that new technology will create high-paying, highly skilled jobs. These are important to union growth and, if training is included in the contract, may justify short-term job losses. In every industry and in every workplace, management, union members, and union leaders must compromise on specific issues to achieve their long-term goals. Let's look now at some of the most common issues that arise in the collective bargaining process.

Typical Bargaining Issues

Even though collective bargaining issues change with the times, they tend to fall into three main categories: economic, industry-specific, and social-cultural issues. Some typical issues are shown in Figure 13.3.

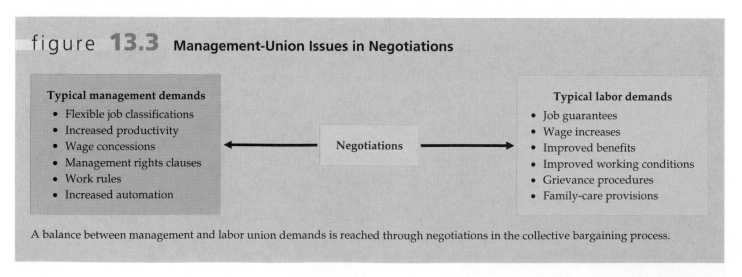

figure **13.3** **Management-Union Issues in Negotiations**

Typical management demands
- Flexible job classifications
- Increased productivity
- Wage concessions
- Management rights clauses
- Work rules
- Increased automation

Negotiations

Typical labor demands
- Job guarantees
- Wage increases
- Improved benefits
- Improved working conditions
- Grievance procedures
- Family-care provisions

A balance between management and labor union demands is reached through negotiations in the collective bargaining process.

Economic Issues

The economic package, also called the *wage and effort bargain*, outlines the work the employer expects the employees to do and the financial rewards they will receive for that work. The wage portion of the bargain outlines wages and scheduled wage increases, along with benefits such as vacations, health insurance and pension plans, and any special compensation, such as extra pay for night shift work. The effort part of the bargain specifies the work to be done and any rules or policies regarding that work, such as job classifications and scheduling.

Many contract negotiations result in some form of **wage concessions**, in which the union agrees to accept lower wages for some job categories. Along with their acceptance of a new team-based system of production, union employees at Levi Strauss's Harlingen, Texas, plant agreed to a new incentive pay scheme that resulted in a drop of the average wage from approximately $9 an hour to less than $8 an hour.[19] In the airline industry, some contracts have provided for **two-tiered wages**, that is, one wage schedule for current employees and a lower schedule for new hires. American Airlines implemented a two-tiered wage schedule for pilots and flight attendants in a successful effort to control the escalating costs of airline labor. In other contracts, the union may agree to delay or forgo promised wage or cost of living increases.

Employers may want to reduce the number of distinct job classifications to allow them greater flexibility. Workers, however, may see such a change as a job threat. In response, the union may try to obtain **job guarantees**, assurance that workers will not be laid off, and may offer in return concessions such as employee cooperation in analyzing and improving production processes.

In a time of rampant downsizing, job guarantees are becoming increasingly more valuable to workers and therefore more common in contract negotiations across the country. For example, the National Steel Corp. promised the United Steelworkers of America that, barring an economic disaster, there would be no layoffs during the life of a new labor agreement. Pacific Telesis Group made a similar guarantee to the Communication Workers of America, promising to train workers for new positions if necessary. And a unit of Tenneco Inc. agreed to protect all current workers during the life of its contract with the United Auto Workers, even if that meant replacing most workers who were retiring.[20] Thus, a common trade-off in negotiations today is reducing the number of job classifications, which is desirable for management, in return for job guarantees (such as no-layoff clauses) or related security provisions (such as supplemental unemployment benefits), which are desirable for labor.

Management rights clauses, which itemize the rights and responsibilities of management alone, are important bargaining issues for employers. Their purpose is to protect the employer's ability to effectively manage business operations. Some management rights clauses specifically outline areas over which management has full authority, such as the choice of supervisors, product lines, and marketing strategies. Other rights clauses specify that management can make decisions in any area not mentioned elsewhere in the contract.

Employer demands in contract negotiations have also focused on increasing work force adaptability and, hence, employer flexibility. Primary among these are **work rules**, the specific regulations that govern workers on the job; these can cover anything from the frequency of restroom breaks to detailed descriptions of who operates which machine.

Almost all collective bargaining contracts describe **grievance procedures**, the process for handling disputes over the interpretation of some component of the final contract. An effective grievance procedure benefits management, the union organization, and union members. Management benefits from the guaranteed freedom from strikes during the life of the contract—this is the union concession for the grievance procedure. The union benefits because the grievance procedure provides a way to question management's interpretation of the contract, which the union might otherwise have trouble disputing. Individual workers gain because they can use the grievance procedure to ensure that they are treated fairly by management. For example, an employee who is wrongly disciplined by management can use the grievance procedure to force a union-management review of the disciplinary action.

 wage concessions

Union agreement to accept lower wages for some job categories.

 two-tiered wages

Provision of one wage schedule for current employees and a lower schedule for new hires.

 job guarantees

Assurance that workers will not be laid off.

 management rights clause

Clause in union contracts itemizing the rights and responsibilities of management alone.

 work rules

Specific regulations that govern workers on the job.

 grievance procedures

The process for handling disputes over the interpretation of some component of the collective bargaining contract.

Industry-Specific Issues

A second category of issues relates to the industry or group of workers involved in the contract. For example, in industries such as petroleum refining and hospitals, mandatory overtime is common. The employer's ability to order such overtime guarantees that critical functions will be covered in case scheduled employees fail to show up for their shifts. In industries where safety is of paramount importance, such as the airline industry, strict limits are placed on the number of hours workers can be on duty. But in both cases, the issues are determined by the needs of the industry or worker.

Another issue, which we have already mentioned, is new technologies, such as computer-aided manufacturing equipment that increases productivity. Union leaders recognize that labor-saving technology may be inevitable, and perhaps even desirable, even though it leads to a loss of less-skilled jobs. One approach to dealing with lost jobs has been tried by the Ford Motor Co. and the United Auto Workers, with retraining for displaced workers and a relocation policy in which workers laid off at one plant are considered for jobs at other Ford plants.[21]

Social and Cultural Issues

New bargaining issues can follow changes in the labor market as well as changes in technology. One of every two new union members is a woman, many of whom are balancing child-care needs with job needs. As a result, family-care provisions are now common bargaining issues.

Other new issues that have become important in the last decade are diversity training in the workplace, programs for workers who abuse drugs and alcohol, workplace treatment of employees known to be HIV-positive, and limitations on smoking at work.

Steps in the Bargaining Process

7. List the four steps in the collective bargaining process, noting the tactics used by labor and management to achieve an advantage.

Contract negotiations are the most visible aspect of collective bargaining, but they are only one part of this process. Collective bargaining takes place even in early union-management discussions about where and when meetings will be held. And it continues after the contract has been signed, as both parties try to figure out how the contract applies to specific—and sometimes unexpected—work situations. In general, however, the collective bargaining process takes place in four steps: negotiations, mediation/arbitration, ratification, and contract administration, as Figure 13.4 indicates.

figure **13.4** **The Four Steps in the Collective Bargaining Process**

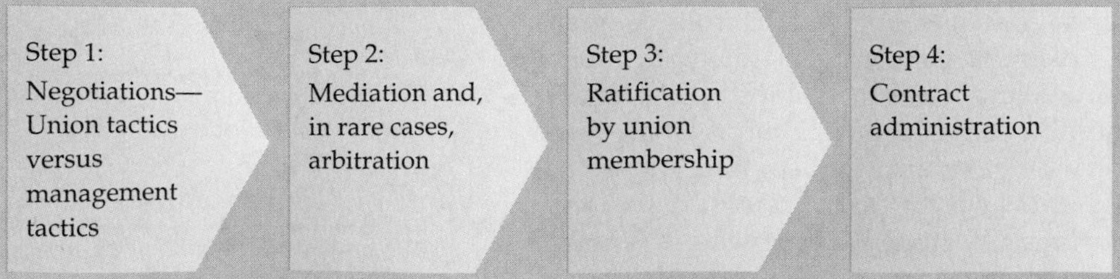

Step 1:
Negotiations—
Union tactics
versus
management
tactics

Step 2:
Mediation and,
in rare cases,
arbitration

Step 3:
Ratification
by union
membership

Step 4:
Contract
administration

The collective bargaining process is one of the most important aspects of any management–union agreement. Although the first three steps determine the terms of the contract, the fourth step provides the daily test of those terms.

Negotiations

As collective bargaining begins, both labor and management choose their bargaining objectives, set their priorities, and prepare to sit down at the bargaining table. Preparations include research, estimating the costs of various proposals, and settling on a strategy. These preparations set the stage for the actual **negotiations**, in which labor and management explore each other's positions, offer counterproposals, and bargain toward a mutually acceptable agreement.

Each party uses its bargaining power to move the other toward a compromise both sides can accept. Most negotiations end with agreement on a contract, but union and management each has an effective array of tactics to use when negotiations reach an impasse.

Union Tactics Probably the strongest union tactic is the ability to call a strike. Strikes, or the threat of strikes, have traditionally been very effective tools in labor's arsenal of negotiating techniques—particularly in the years immediately following the Great Depression. A strike, especially if supported by other unions and the public, can seriously hamper business as strikers use placards and leaflets to discourage customers and vendors from doing business with the company. When effective, a strike can lead to the resolution of difficult issues and to improved contract terms, increased organizational cohesiveness, and the knowledge that future threats of a strike will be taken seriously. But strikes carry a high cost for everyone. These costs are measured in lost wages, community damage, personal antagonism, and unpredictable outcomes.

In early 1995, 6,600 union employees called a strike at the General Motors Corp. AC Delco Systems plant in Flint, Michigan. Because this plant produced parts that other General Motors plants depended on to build automobiles, an additional 33,000 workers were directly affected by the walkout. Two days after the strike started, these 33,000 workers were told not to report to work—the production lines had been halted due to the lack of parts. The strike ended five days after it started, but the economic toll was immense—the walkout cost General Motors $90 million, plus an additional $90 million that it agreed to invest in plant improvements. In addition, nearly 40,000 workers had lost wages.[22]

President Ronald Reagan's firing of all air traffic controllers who went out on strike in 1981 brought home the fact that a strike can backfire and should be used only as a last resort. Labor's use of strike tactics has decreased in recent years, and the number of strikes involving more than 1,000 workers has fallen drastically, from 187 in 1980 to 40 in a recent year.[23] Most labor-management negotiations today end without strikes, but when strikes do occur they are usually short, typically lasting less than a week.

As the use of strikes has declined, unions have devised other ways to pressure employers without risking members' jobs. Among these new tactics are "in plant" strategies such as **work slowdowns**, or *working to rule*, in which workers perform the minimum amount of work required by job descriptions or company procedures. When union members work to rule, they strictly follow every safety and procedural rule required of them. Typically this reduces productivity but does not stop work completely. One of the most significant work slowdowns in recent years occurred at McDonnell Douglas Corporation, the airplane manufacturer. When management and the union stalled on contract negotiations, about one-third of the United Auto Workers' 10,000 members at the company's facility in Long Beach, California, started working strictly by company rules. For example, an experienced mechanic can drill precision holes using one drill bit instead of the specified four, but changing bits as required by the out-of-date rule book causes the same task to take twice as long.

Unions sometimes use the boycott instead of or in addition to striking. The United Farm Workers (UFW) used this tactic very effectively in the late 1960s.

 negotiations

Collective bargaining stage in which labor and management explore each other's positions, offer counterproposals, and bargain toward a mutually acceptable agreement.

 work slowdowns

Union pressure tactic of performing the minimum amount of work required by job descriptions or company procedures; also called *working to rule*.

Union Tactics

In 1994, workers at General Motors's Buick City plant in Flint, Michigan, exercised labor's most potent weapon, the strike, but for an unexpected reason. They wanted *less* work to do. GM had reversed almost $5 billion in losses in 1991 into almost $5 billion in profits by 1994. Yet until the Buick City workers walked out, GM had hired barely any new workers since 1986, relying instead on overtime and temporary hires, a less costly strategy than hiring, training, and extending benefits to new full-timers. While the strategy worked well for shareholders, it left GM's work force exhausted. The Buick City strike was a success, largely because the component parts made there are critical to GM's assembly lines nationwide. GM settled after only three days by promising to hire almost 800 more full-timers.

Led by Cesar Chavez, the UFW used a combination of strikes and product boycotts to force 26 growers of table grapes to accept union contracts in 1970.[24] To be truly effective, boycotts depend on the broad support of the public, and getting that support can be difficult and time-consuming.

A new twist on the boycott is the corporate campaign, a form of *secondary boycott* in which a union attempts to influence an employer by pressuring companies that supply it with goods or services. For example, union members may threaten to close their accounts at a bank that does business with their company. Like traditional boycotts, corporate campaigns have unpredictable outcomes and are usually used only when other tactics would be ineffective.

Management Tactics Management tactics have been very successful recently because conditions in the business environment have tipped the scales in management's favor, at least in relation to labor. Because so many companies have failed in industries with traditionally strong unions, unions have been unable to negotiate from a position of strength. For example, it is difficult for the United Steelworkers to bargain hard when most steel companies are either closing or cutting back severely.

Increased competition has also helped tip the scale in management's direction. A struggling company or industry is less *able* to grant concessions to unions. Many product markets have become fiercely competitive in the last decade. In some industries, such as airlines and trucking, government deregulation has spurred domestic competition, as did changes in government payments in the health care industry. Many other industries, including electrical products and clothing, face both determined domestic competition and the pressure of less expensive foreign imports.

Another factor favoring management is today's general trend toward automation, which reduces the number of workers needed and minimizes the negative impact of strikes. In many cases, management can run the new equipment themselves. As one auto industry analyst noted, "The goal of all the technology push has been to get rid of hourly workers."[25] Not all employers take this view, of course. Increased automation can lower overall costs, making the company more competitive and profitable and thus better able to pay the workers it does have. At Honda Motor Co.'s U.S. assembly plant in Marysville, Ohio, the cost of building a car is some $1,200 less than at competing U.S. car manufacturers, due in large part to Honda's automated assembly lines.

In addition to such environmental advantages, employers have specific tactics that are effective in confrontations. They may pressure union members by means of **lockouts**, closing company doors to union members and not permitting them to work. Employers may institute a lockout to pressure negotiators during a bargaining impasse or in response to a strike. Like strikes, however, lockouts carry a heavy cost. For example, USX Corp. was required to pay unemployment benefits to 22,000 union members in nine states after it locked them out and refused to extend a 40-month contract with the United Steelworkers of America.[26]

Employers faced with a strike can legally hire replacement workers, or **strikebreakers**, also known as *scabs*. This tactic, which costs union members their jobs, is emotionally explosive and often sparks violence between strikers and strikebreakers. Striker replacement usually occurs only during long strikes, when management is unable to cover essential jobs from within its own ranks.

Tough management tactics often lead unions to grant **givebacks**—concessions to management—to save jobs and help the company remain competitive. In recent years, Bethlehem Steel Co. received givebacks in the form of 8 percent pay cuts and reduced pay premiums for work on Sundays. Givebacks enabled the John Morrell meat-packing company to eliminate profit sharing and start

lockout

Management pressure tactic of closing company doors to union members and not permitting them to work.

strikebreakers

Replacement workers legally hired by employers faced with a strike; also known as *scabs*.

givebacks

Union concessions to management to save jobs and help the company remain competitive.

new employees at lower rates of pay. And they allowed the Kroger Co., National Convenience Stores, Inc., and Schnuck Markets, Inc., grocery chains to cut their top pay rates and the number of paid personal and sick days.[27]

Mediation and Arbitration

If management and labor cannot reach an agreement during negotiations, the next step is mediation and arbitration. **Mediation** is the use of neutral or third-party individuals to help resolve a bargaining impasse. Mediation is not legally binding. Mediators meet with representatives of labor and management individually to isolate the key issues and suggest ways of resolving them. They usually emphasize similarities in the two parties' proposals, develop new options, and remind everyone of the costs and unpredictable results of strikes. Mediators can also call the feuding parties back to the bargaining table (sometimes even at the private request of the parties), thereby allowing them to save face with constituents while still resuming negotiations.

Arbitration is intervention by a neutral third party whose decision *is* legally binding. Although arbitration is not a usual part of negotiations, it often is part of the contract clause covering the grievance procedure in the contract administration stage, discussed below.

In some cases, Congress mandates arbitration if national interests are threatened. Congress recently ordered an arbitration panel to review and rule on stalled negotiations between management and striking employees in the railroad industry. Railroads have been under increasing competitive pressure to reduce crew size and labor costs. With average salaries of $56,000 per year and employer benefit contributions of 40 cents for every dollar paid in wages, railroad employees make more than employees in any other American industry except for stock brokerage, investment banking, and oil. The arbitration panel imposed a mandatory new contract on labor and management in this situation.[28]

Ratification by Union Members

The final step in the negotiation process is **ratification**, a vote by a majority of union members to accept a contract. Union leaders often spend considerable effort communicating to members the underlying logic and worth of a draft contract, which may contain unpopular provisions such as wage and employment concessions. Members opposed to the contract are more likely than contract supporters to campaign for their position before the ratification vote. To avoid the contentious atmosphere that often surrounds ratification votes, Levi Strauss reached an agreement with the Amalgamated Clothing and Textile Workers Union to dispense with the traditional election altogether—instead collecting signatures on union membership cards.[29]

Contract Administration

The real test of a contract is **contract administration**—its interpretation and implementation in particular situations. Although management is the primary interpreter, unions can question its interpretation through the standardized grievance procedure outlined in the contract. Management and employee representatives meet and discuss the meaning of the contract in relation to a specific workplace issue, such as seniority, benefits, job assignment, and safety. If the two sides cannot agree, the issue will be settled by legally binding arbitration, which is also usually written into the contract. The most common grievance issues are discipline and discharge, which are also the most likely to be brought to arbitration.

 mediation

The use of neutral or third-party individuals to help resolve a bargaining impasse.

 arbitration

Intervention by a neutral third party whose decision is legally binding.

 ratification

A vote by a majority of union members to accept a contract.

contract administration

Interpretation and implementation of a contract in particular situations.

The grievance process is a cornerstone of the union movement; fear of arbitrary or unfair treatment by management is a common reason for workers' desire to join a union. Indeed, there is evidence that this fear is warranted in some cases. For example, employees at the Foxwoods casino on the Mashantucket Pequot reservation in Connecticut are not protected by state and federal labor laws, nor are they unionized. Employees accused of serious disciplinary problems appear before a panel of other employees selected at random to review these cases. The panel's recommendation is reviewed by the casino's chief executive officer, who makes the final decision. Without a grievance procedure, employees must accept the CEO's decision as final.

Assessing the Future of U.S. Unions

8. Summarize the contributions of unions to all U.S. workers and discuss the future limitations and opportunities for organized labor.

The broad impact of labor unions on the experience of all U.S. workers is expressed humorously in a popular bumper sticker that says "Support unions, the folks who brought you the weekend." Unions' impact on the nation's work force has taken two forms.

First, labor unions have tested and helped develop many of the legal protections discussed in Chapters 4 and 12. Legal rights won by unions apply to all workers, not just to union members. For example, our eight-hour workday has its origin in a contract negotiated by printers' and building trade workers' unions in the 1890s. The minimum wage and unemployment and other worker benefits, which initially were bargaining issues, are now provided to all workers by law.

Second, union-instituted bargaining and grievance procedures have set standards for all employers. For example, standards of fair workplace treatment grew out of the use of the grievance procedure by unionized workers to question disciplinary and discharge practices. As a result, it was established that discipline must be for "just cause," that the same standards must apply to all employees, and that the disciplinary measure must be suited to the infraction. Many businesses have chosen to adopt the union-won practices of other companies to keep their own employees happy and perhaps prevent calls for unionization.

Some of these rights and privileges have eroded along with the fall in union membership. Even the weekend is now under siege; the average number of hours worked by a U.S. employee has increased by 160 hours—or nearly one month—per year over the last 20 years.[30] These statistics reflect the downside of the basic business trends we have traced throughout this text:[31]

- *Increased global competition* is causing both high- and low-paying jobs to move overseas, forcing most American companies, even those in previously stable markets such as automobiles, to seek out new ways to cut costs. This competition will likely increase with the expansion of the former Soviet bloc countries and the People's Republic of China into the world economy. (See Chapter 3, Global Business.)

- *Increased technology and automation* have been boosting productivity but eroding the manufacturing job base for several decades. In the last few years, the impact of technology has moved from the factory floor to the service sector, as the jobs of "back-office" employees who process orders and track inventories have been absorbed by computer-integrated manufacturing and just-in-time inventory control methods. (See Chapter 10, Producing Quality Goods and Services.)

- *Downsizing* of major industries such as banking, construction, aerospace, and defense has affected millions of employees in previously stable and secure companies, where in the past they could expect to be employed for

Just in Time for What?

Cost-saving techniques such as downsizing, automation, and just-in-time systems have helped employers reduce their labor costs. But unions have actually used these techniques to benefit labor, for example, by employing work slowdowns and strikes to cut off supplies of materials and bring assembly lines to a halt. The success of these tactics has actually boosted interest in union organizing efforts among U.S. workers particularly hard hit by a long-term decline in real wages and standard of living.

their entire working lives. This shrinking of organizational work forces—perhaps permanently—has affected companies across the United States. The country's 500 largest manufacturers slashed nearly 4 million jobs in just over two decades. (See Chapters 8, The Role of Management, and 9, Organizational Design.)

- *Shift to a contingent work force* has led companies to rely on contract labor and on part-time and temporary workers at all levels of the organization. This trend cuts costs—especially the soaring cost of benefits—to increase profits, and it increases flexibility as well. (See Chapter 12, Human Resource Management.)

Each of these trends affects workers and their relationship to their employers. Taken together, they limit the traditional role of unions, but they also create opportunities for new partnerships between unions and management.

Challenges for Today's Labor Unions

These four trends in employee-management relations present today's unions with three major challenges: (1) the diminished effectiveness of strikes; (2) a declining membership; and (3) competition from the work forces of developing nations. Traditional attitudes and tactics are less effective today, and pressure from foreign competition is stronger than ever before.

The Ineffectiveness of Strikes

Most labor-management negotiations are concluded without a strike. There were fewer strikes and lockouts at U.S. companies in 1992 than in any of the previous 45 years.[32] The reasons for this vary and are often unique to particular industries. But a major factor has been the example of strikes that have ended disastrously.

The meat-packing industry provides a good illustration. Health-conscious Americans today eat less meat than their counterparts did a generation ago. Therefore, there is less demand, but supply is up because of new competitors, among them foreign producers. As a result, in the last decade, employment has fallen, some plants have closed, and other plants have operated with excess capacity. Many employers, including Swift, Cudahy, and Hormel Food Corp., have asked workers to accept wage cuts.

Such pressures from management make for turbulent labor relations and have led to long strikes and the hiring of strikebreakers. Local P-9 of the United Food and Commercial Workers struck against Hormel Food of Minnesota for 13 months. The strike was bitter. The company hired replacement workers, and the strikers clashed with them. National Guard troops were called in to prevent violence. Town residents found themselves pitted against one another as emotions ran high, and there were many arrests. The national union put Local P-9 in trusteeship for refusing to end the strike and negotiated the final settlement itself. The hardball tactics of the local did not pay off for its members. Unions are now hesitant to strike for fear that striking members will lose their jobs permanently.

The Decline in Union Membership

Unions have recently shown some signs of life, with membership increasing slightly in 1993—to 16.6 million members[33]—and again in 1994, when membership climbed to 16.7 million workers.[34] In the past two decades, however, overall membership has decreased steadily—from 22 million members in 1975 to 16.4 members in 1992.[35]

What caused the large decline in union membership since 1975? Some experts blame it on the overall economic shift from predominantly blue-collar employment—a traditional union stronghold—to predominantly white-collar and service employment. One problem with this explanation is that these shifts, due primarily to technological change, also occurred in most of the other Western industrialized countries, where they were sometimes accompanied by an increase, not a decrease, in union membership. It is true, however, that solidarity seems strongest when workers share a dangerous occupation, as in traditional coal mines.

Increased management opposition to unions is another explanation for declining membership. Although employers generally have never favored unionization, their efforts to discourage it were ineffective until the 1970s and 1980s. In those years, employers developed tough, sophisticated tactics to combat unionization. Some used positive policies, such as better wages and benefits, to remove the most common incentive behind organizing. Others hired consultants to run public relations campaigns discouraging employees from joining unions. Some employers also used tactics of doubtful legality. At the same time, union organizing efforts were faltering because, with declining membership, less money was available for recruiting new members. While management's use of labor relations consultants was increasing, union spending on organizing declined.

Another reason for the decline is that the image of unions has worsened among U.S. workers in general. In a recent poll, 34 to 48 percent of respondents said they believe labor unions hurt rather than help the cause of working Americans. A similar proportion believed that unions hurt the economy of the country as a whole.[36] This is largely due to the widespread impression that, in recent years, unions have been stubbornly and aggressively pitting themselves against management regardless of the costs to company or community. And, as a recent article in *The Economist* noted, "High unemployment does not help: if unions are so great, teenagers wonder, where are the jobs?"[37] A final cause of declining union membership is, of course, increasing global competition.

Competition from Work Forces in Other Countries

Competition has caused many manufacturing companies to close older, more labor-intensive plants and move their operations abroad to countries with lower wage rates and fewer union and government regulations.

In Thailand, the Philippines, and other developing countries, government leaders determined to foster economic growth have even promised foreign investors union-free shops. In China and Indonesia, unions are extensions of the government, and workers' wages and working conditions can be dictated.[38] All of these factors combine to weaken U.S. labor unions' power to bargain with management.

Already under pressure from members, national unions lobbied against the passage of the North American Free Trade Agreement (NAFTA), in part because of concern that union jobs would be lost to Mexican workers. It is not yet clear that this concern was warranted. As of this writing, there has been no large exodus of jobs across the border. Producers will, of course, always be under pressure to reduce labor costs, as we saw in Chapter 10. Low wages do not, however, always translate to lowest cost, especially if a producer's quality suffers as a result.

Opportunities for Today's Unions

Labor unions are capitalizing on the increasing frustration of U.S. workers, whose wages have fallen during two decades of corporate downsizing. For example, truckers' and dock workers' real wages declined 20 percent from 1977 to 1992. "We're walking into situations where workers are begging us to organize," says Richard Bensinger, director of the AFL-CIO's Organizing Institute, which trains workers to be organizers.[39] Frustrated workers in many industries have grown angry and are encouraged as they watch unions win some strikes they would have lost a decade ago.

Unions are also turning their attention to service workers such as nurses, waiters, and clerical workers, previously considered too difficult to organize. In fact, the fastest growing affiliate of the AFL-CIO is the Service Employees International Union (SEIU), which primarily seeks to represent the more than 20 million U.S. clerical workers. Since 1980, SEIU has increased its total membership by 400,000 members.[40]

Also being targeted are "new-collar" employees, a category of worker different from the traditional blue- or white-collar class. According to Ralph Whitehead, a University of Massachusetts at Amherst professor, these are service workers who usually have finished high school but not college.[41] Their income and status are between those of traditional blue-collar factory workers and professional white-collar employees. New-collar workers earn from $13,500 to just under $30,000 annually as insurance agents, keypunch operators, nurses, teachers, mental health aides, computer technicians, loan officers, auditors, salespeople, and clerical workers. To reach them, unions must broaden their approach to include such issues as:

- Quality-of-work concerns, including career development and professional autonomy
- Professional concerns like dealing with technological change
- Personal concerns such as pay equity, the career ladder, child care, job training, and job stress

Unions today are also advocating changes in public policy that would protect workers attempting to organize. Individual unions and the labor movement as a whole are developing new ways to organize workers and to reach those in formerly nonunionized jobs, particularly white-collar and service workers. For example, the American Federation of Teachers (AFT) hired a New York ad agency to create a direct mail campaign directed at 147,000 teachers in Texas. The mailing, which encouraged recipients to become "associate members," did not mention the word "union" even once; 20,000 teachers replied.[42]

9. Discuss current trends in labor practices and labor-management relations.

New-Collar Workers

To attract new members, such as these customer service representatives, and to broaden the base of unionized workers in the United States, unions are targeting new "customers" in traditionally nonunion, white-collar and service occupations. And women, dubbed "pink-collar workers" by the unions, represent half of all new union members.

From Confrontation to Collaboration

Earlier we noted that the management-employee relationship could follow one of three tracks, and we have devoted a considerable portion of this chapter to describing the confrontational relationship typical of the past. Many believe, however, that the future of unions in this country lies in a more collaborative working relationship with management, one that resembles a true partnership.

Increasingly, management and union leadership are finding that by cooperating with each other, everyone benefits in the long run. Some organizations are encouraging unions to help them improve the quality, productivity, and competitiveness of their business. As one executive put it, "The real question is: How do we get salaried employees to work with us to make this institution more competitive at a time of great competitive stress?" But cooperation requires mutual trust and a commitment of resources, time, and effort, and it is not found in every labor-management relationship.

An example of what management can do to cultivate this sort of cooperation occurred when Bridgestone Corp., the Japanese tire manufacturer, purchased Firestone. Bridgestone voluntarily restored more than $1 an hour that the previous owner had cut from employees' wage and benefits packages at two tire plants. It also voluntarily recognized the union at a new plant in Warren County, Tennessee, and won its help in shaping a self-directed, motivated work force.[43] For the story of another manager-owner who favors labor-management cooperation, see the doing business box entitled "Roger Penske Built His Business on Trust."

When successful, cooperation can have major benefits, as one study showed in comparing manufacturers that had ousted unions with those that had developed cooperative relations with them. The employers who had tried teamwork reported a 19 percent increase in employee productivity, whereas the combative employers reported a 15 percent decline.[44] The contrast is particularly striking in the shipping business. In Norfolk, Virginia, where the International Longshoreman's Association works closely with management, shipping traffic has increased 130 percent in the past decade. In Baltimore, Maryland, however, where relations between labor and management have been strained, shipping traffic has dropped 231 percent during the same period.[45]

The U.S. steel industry provides another example of union-management cooperation. The United Steelworkers and big steel makers such as U.S.X. and Bethlehem Steel agreed in the 1980s to form *labor-management participation teams*

doing
business
Roger Penske Built His Business on Trust

Roger Penske hates to lose. As the chairman of a transportation conglomerate that includes the engine manufacturer Detroit Diesel Corp., a truck-leasing company, and a race car team with more than 90 wins to its credit, Penske has set his sights very high. He asks, "If I'm not motivated and interested in the results, how do you expect the rest of an organization to be?" And he expects his employees to set their sights equally high.

In many cases, unions are organized in response to a lack of trust between employees and management. To Penske, however, trust is a critical element of his success as a manager. To help cement the trust of Detroit Diesel employees after he took over the organization from General Motors, Roger Penske gave the union more power, found a way to give workers a bigger share of company profits, and pledged to meet with employees several times a year to present crucial financial information and productivity measures. He also treated his employees to a free day at his Michigan International Speedway.

One reason for his employees' trust is Penske's willingness to roll up his sleeves and do whatever it takes to get the job done. In June 1994, for example, the start of a 300-mile stock-car race was jeopardized by unseasonably hot temperatures that softened the track and made it unstable. Rather than risk canceling the race, Penske worked with a crew of 12 employees until 1:30 a.m. on the morning of the race, using a push broom to work lime into the track surface to harden the soft asphalt. Their efforts paid off, and the race was run without incident.

Everyone in Penske's organization is part of his team. He knows that if he takes care of his employees and causes them to realize that they are part of a champion organization, they will do their best to make his goals a reality.

Source: David Woodruff, "Talk About Life in the Fast Lane," *Business Week,* Oct. 17, 1994, pp. 155, 158, 162, 166.

(LMPTs) to improve efficiency as well as working conditions at troubled U.S. steel mills.

Other examples of successful cooperation abound. The Clinton administration's plan to "reinvent" government included streamlining the process of dismissing federal workers so that agency managers could more easily outsource government work. Unions supported the plan, which offered a new pay system that rewarded the best workers with bigger paychecks. The agreement called for the creation of a National Partnership Council, which included the heads of federal agencies, the three biggest federal unions, and the AFL-CIO, to encourage labor-management cooperation and the development of a "high-performance workplace."[46]

A particularly impressive case of greater cooperation between management and unions took place at the Saturn Corp., which General Motors Corp. established as a completely separate company to produce a new subcompact car. According to the contract Saturn negotiated with the United Auto Workers, each employee not covered by a union contract—from the top down through the ranks—is paired with a union-represented employee, allowing Saturn's management and unions to work together on teams in every facet of the business.[47] The union helped GM design work practices that complemented new technology to produce a car that was competitive with low-priced imports. The cooperative efforts of General Motors and the United Auto Workers led management to shift production of some of its automobiles from a plant in Mexico to one in Lansing, Michigan, creating at least 800 new jobs for U.S. workers.[48]

Another cooperative effort by management occurred when nonunionized Honda North America, Inc., was recently forced by excessive inventory to trim production. Instead of laying off employees, Honda management chose to use the downtime to do additional training.[49]

Efforts to revitalize American industry continue. The stakes are high—for employers, for unions, and for union members. The dawn of the twenty-first century promises to be a demanding and exciting time for those involved in labor relations. As the AFL-CIO Committee on the Evolution of Work stated recently in a report entitled *The New American Workplace*, "the time has come for labor and management to surmount past enmities and to forge the kind of partnerships which can generate more productive, humane, and democratic systems of work organization."[50]

The World Bank, not known as a traditional supporter of unions, expressed a similar sentiment in its *World Development Report* in early July 1995, citing the role of unions in promoting stability in the work force, easing communication between management and employees, and serving to limit government intervention in the labor market. The World Bank concluded briefly that "free trade unions are a cornerstone of any effective system of industrial relations."[51]

Reviewing *Unions and Employee-Management Relations*

Unions and Management: Partners or Adversaries?

1. **Discuss the role of unions in U.S. business, focusing on their traditional relationship with management**. Although the United States is one of the least unionized countries in the industrial world, labor unions have played a major role in improving workers' wages, work hours, benefits, and workplace conditions. Traditionally, the labor-management relationship has been an adversarial one, but through collective bargaining both labor and management reach compromises that benefit both parties.

Union Members: Who Are They?

2. **Compare the characteristics of early union members with those of today's.** The highest concentration of union members has traditionally been in blue-collar occupations—mining, construction, and manufacturing, for example. Today, all occupations are represented, including white-collar and service workers. Union membership varies according to geography and type of occupation. More and more women are joining unions due to increased focus on teachers, food service workers, and other service employees. Membership in unions has, however, generally declined over the past 20 years.

Employee-Management Options

3. **Outline the history of unions**. The first unions were craft unions. With the advent of the Industrial Revolution and the shift from an agricultural to an industrial base came the growth of industrial unions, which focused on groups of workers with varied skills in particular industries rather than on members of particular trades. The modern labor movement began with the creation of the American Federation of Labor (AFL), a national federation of local and national unions of skilled workers. The development of mass production industries led dissatisfied unskilled and semiskilled workers to split from the AFL and form the Congress of Industrial Organizations (CIO). These two powerful groups eventually joined ranks, representing over half of U.S. union members. The AFL-CIO functions primarily as a political body, with contract negotiations handled by local and national unions, often with assistance from the federation. National unions are organized by craft or by industry, while local unions have a narrower focus—one plant, one employer, or one limited area.

4. **Discuss legislation designed to regulate labor-management relations**. Like the seesaw balancing of power between labor and management, legislators have seesawed between laws favoring one or the other. Early unions were confronted by legal injunctions to prevent them from striking or boycotting. Unions received support from the 1914 Clayton Antitrust Act, the 1932 Norris-LaGuardia Anti-Injunction Act, and, most importantly, the 1935 National Labor Relations Act, which protected workers' rights to unionize (or not) and to bargain collectively. On management's side was the 1947 Taft-Hartley Act, which outlawed certain union practices, such as the use of closed shops. More recently, agency and open shops have gained in popularity, and employers are required to provide 60 days' notice before closing a facility or laying off workers.

How Workers Unionize

5. **Outline the process of unionizing employees**. Interest in organizing a union to act as a bargaining agent for employees may be initiated internally, because of employee dissatisfaction, or externally, because a union has targeted a particular employer or industry. However initiated, attempts at union organization begin with a campaign launched by union organizers, who research and analyze the situation in order to collect information that will convince employees of the value of collective bargaining. Influence is exerted either through personal contact or mass advertising, depending on the size of the group. Meanwhile, employers that oppose unions express the advantages of a nonunion shop. If 30 percent of employees express an interest in unionization, a repre-

sentation election is held. If a majority of union members vote for approval, the union receives certification.

The Collective Bargaining Process

6. **Describe the overall goal of collective bargaining and identify the three main categories of issues addressed in collective bargaining.** Collective bargaining is intended to produce a contract that benefits management, bargaining unit employees, and the union as an organization. The first issue of major concern is economic—the wage and effort bargain, which usually involves such issues as wage concessions, job guarantees, work rules, and grievance procedures. Other issues are industry-specific and social-cultural.

7. **List the four steps in the collective bargaining process, noting the tactics used by labor and management to achieve an advantage.** The four steps of collective bargaining are negotiations, mediation/arbitration, ratification, and contract administration. Although most negotiations result in a mutually agreeable contract between labor and management, some reach an impasse. At such times, unions may call a strike, or threaten one; more recently, unions have tended to use work slowdowns and/or boycotts. Management tactics include lockouts and the use of strikebreakers, which may lead to union givebacks. Once a contract has been ratified by the union, its interpretation and implementation gener-

ally are done by management. Where unions dispute specific applications of the contract, they make use of grievance procedures, which are written into the contract.

Assessing the Future of U.S. Unions

8. **Summarize the contributions of unions to all U.S. workers and discuss the future limitations and opportunities for organized labor.** Unions have helped all workers by testing and developing protective legislation and by establishing bargaining and grievance procedures. Due to increased global competition, increased use of automation, the downsizing of major industries, and a shift to a contingent work force, however, unions are facing three major challenges. Strikes are less effective, membership is down, and unions' bargaining power is being eroded by competition from work forces in developing countries.

9. **Discuss current trends in labor practices and labor-management relations.** Unions today are focusing on workers frustrated by falling wages, on service workers, and on "new-collar" employees, whose concerns are broader than the traditional wages and benefits. They are also becoming advocates for public policy changes. Most important, unions are revising their approach to management from confrontation to cooperation, from the traditional adversarial track to a more participative track.

✔ Key Terms

labor unions **387**	Worker Adjustment and	Taft-Hartley Act **397**	work rules **401**
collective bargaining **387**	Retraining Notification	closed shop **397**	grievance procedures **401**
craft union **391**	Act **396**	union shop **397**	negotiations **403**
industrial union **393**	injunction **396**	right-to-work laws **397**	work slowdowns **403**
Knights of Labor **393**	strike **396**	agency shop **397**	lockout **404**
American Federation of	boycott **396**	open shop **397**	strikebreakers **404**
Labor (AFL) **393**	Clayton Antitrust Act **396**	representation election **399**	givebacks **404**
labor federation **393**	Norris-LaGuardia Anti-	certification **399**	mediation **405**
Congress of Industrial	Injunction Act **396**	decertification **399**	arbitration **405**
Organizations (CIO) **394**	National Labor Relations	wage concessions **401**	ratification **405**
AFL-CIO **394**	Act (NLRA) **396**	two-tiered wages **401**	contract administration
national union **394**	National Labor Relations	job guarantees **401**	**405**
local union **395**	Board (NLRB) **396**	management rights clause	
shop steward **395**	good-faith bargaining **396**	**401**	

● Review Questions

1. What purposes do unions serve? How would you characterize their traditional relationship with management?

2. How does early union membership differ from that of today?

3. What are the three tracks that management and labor might take in structuring their working partnership, and how do these relate to the history of unions?

4. How has the form of unionization changed since the first craft unions were established?

5. What laws protect labor unions and management? Be specific in terms of activities the laws regulate.

6. You are a union organizer for the AFL-CIO and see an opportunity to organize workers at a local company that manufactures truck parts (stacks, couplers, and mufflers, for example). What steps will you take?

7. The contract between pilots and airlines expires in five days. Through collective bargaining, union members and airline representatives are negotiating a new contract. What types of issues would be of concern to each group?

8. How does the collective bargaining process proceed? Mention union and management tactics and their relative effectiveness or ineffectiveness.

9. What four trends in labor-management relations have eroded the influence of U.S. unions? What challenges do they present to today's unions?

10. How would you characterize labor-management relations today?

• Critical Thinking Questions

1. Think of a job you hold or have held. If you were approached about joining a union, how would you decide whether to do so or not?

2. If you had a chance to give advice to the owner of a small company about how to keep a union from being organized at his firm, what would you say?

3. Think of an organization you've belonged to. How could management and workers have worked together to make the organization more successful?

4. How directly do you think workers should share in an organization's success or failure? Give examples, and support them with topics from this chapter.

5. What do you predict will be the status of labor unions in 10 years? Why?

REVIEW CASE   *Expanding Ranks at Service Employees International Union*[52]

At a time when most labor unions are facing drastic reductions in membership due to closings, downsizing, and the impact of technology, the Service Employees International Union (SEIU) has gained 400,000 members since 1980. Why? Part of the reason is job growth in the service sector, but a larger part may be aggressive organizing tactics.

Take, for example, Justice for Janitors, an SEIU organizing project begun in the late 1980s. Janitorial unions were pretty much destroyed by the growing tendency of companies to outsource janitorial services or to rely more heavily on part-time labor. The union sought to regain its strength by seeking areawide contracts with building owners regardless of the janitorial service they hired to do their cleaning. Resorting to union tactics that dated back to the 1930s, Justice for Janitors staged sit-down strikes and demonstrations to embarrass building owners and tenants. For example, demonstrators crashed an Apple Computer, Inc., shareholder meeting, shouting out questions about the company's treatment of janitors. (Apple did not directly hire these workers, but the owners of buildings they leased did.) And at the Old Ebbitt Grill in Washington, D.C., a group of janitors poured cans of ball bearings on the floor while chanting "justice for janitors." In the early 1990s, the union even organized a nationwide guerrilla assault in 30 U.S. cities, naming June 15 as Justice for Janitors Day.

In addition to these attention-getting tactics, the union often quietly seeks to collect grievances from janitors and send them to the U.S. Labor Department. The result: 40 percent of D.C. janitors are now union employees, up from zero, and 90 percent of Los Angeles janitors are now unionized, up from 30 percent. But there were costs as well. One targeted employer sued for damages in federal court, alleging that the union had violated the National Labor Relations Act, which prohibits secondary boycotts under certain conditions. (One prohibited form involves picketing companies not directly involved in a labor dispute.) The union settled with the employer and called off its boycott.

1. Janitors who belong to the SEIU receive higher wages than nonunion janitors at similar companies. What other benefits can workers get from being unionized?

2. What protections do the laws described in this chapter provide for both employers and labor unions during organizing activities?

3. What issues would you expect management to bring up the next time it negotiates a contract with the SEIU members involved in Justice for Janitors? What management tactics would be most effective?

CRITICAL THINKING CASE *The New Partnership of Management and Labor at Xerox*

The collaboration between management and labor at Xerox Corp. has become a model for other companies. In the early 1980s, Xerox was losing market share to Japanese firms and starting to close plants. Fearing increasing losses, union leaders offered to help find ways for the company to improve quality, efficiency, and competitiveness and thus help retain—or increase—business, which translates into work for union members. They recommended relaxing work rules and widening job definitions that prevented machine operators from making minor repairs on equipment. They agreed to let management hire temporary workers during peak work periods in exchange for guaranteeing union members job security for the three-year period remaining in their contract.

The union also agreed that any worker who was absent for two or more hours on four occasions (not including hospitalizations and vacations) per year could be terminated. Absenteeism fell from 8.5 to 2.5 percent as a result. Finally, the union agreed to help find additional ways to cut costs. It dropped six paid days a year, cut back on medical insurance, and established an even tougher absenteeism policy.

Later, when Xerox announced that it would close its wire harness manufacturing unit and instead buy these copier parts from Mexico, the union formed a cooperative team to identify ways to lower costs and make a competing bid. The goal was to locate $3.2 million in savings; the team found $3.5 million.

Since then, Xerox has been winning back market share in many of the markets in which it competes and hiring more employees as a result. For example, its manufacturing jobs have grown from a low of 2,600 in the early 1980s to 4,100 in the last decade. Anthony Costanza, the union's international vice president, repeated the union's commitment: "The goal of our entrepreneuring [activities] is to make the company more profitable so we can ask for more."[53]

1. Forming partnerships with management is one of the ways labor unions have managed to remain viable in recent years. What other specific issues could management and labor take action on, either at Xerox or elsewhere?

2. What methods could labor use to overcome wage differences between U.S. workers and their counterparts in Mexico or overseas? At what point are labor's interests no longer served by the kind of collaboration described in this case?

3. The collaboration at Xerox indicates some of the benefits that follow when management and labor work together. What disadvantages can result from such a partnership?

Critical Thinking with the ONE MINUTE MANAGER

"So you see," said the One Minute Manager, "in relationships like the one between Levi Strauss and the Amalgamated Clothing and Textile Workers Union, union and management are not enemies. At Levi Strauss sewing plants, workers are assigned to teams of 15 people or more. The union agreed to these teams, which significantly increase worker output, in exchange for the right to freely recruit more employees into the union.[54] Union participation in workplace decision making seems to be here to stay, as employees *and* management reap the benefits. Unions realize that they are in the same boat with management, and that they all need to work together to increase productivity and competitiveness. And management understands that it needs to share problems with employees and treat them with respect in order to gain their cooperation."

"And it's those companies—the ones in which unions and management act more as partners—that are most likely to be competitive," suggested Joanna.

"That's exactly right," agreed the One Minute Manager. "It's a new partnership for everyone involved."

1. What prevented management and labor from collaborating more in the past? What pressures could undermine this kind of cooperation now?

2. Assume that you represent management and are negotiating a new contract with union representatives. Your company wants to automate a certain process, and this will eliminate some jobs now held by union workers but create new jobs to service the new equipment. What steps will you take to gain cooperation from the union?

3. Assume that you are one of the union representatives mentioned in question 2 and that you have agreed to a rough draft of the contract. What arguments will you use when you ask union members to ratify this contract?

PART **5**

Pleasing the Customer

14

The Role of Marketing

marketing

The process of creating, pricing, promoting, and distributing ideas, goods, and services to create exchanges that satisfy the customer and the business.

Recall that in Chapter 1 we described marketing as the part of the business that focuses on understanding and meeting the needs of customers. **Marketing** is the process of creating, pricing, promoting, and distributing ideas, goods, and services to create exchanges that satisfy the customer and the business. When marketing does its job well, it brings a customer-oriented vision to the entire business process, which produces a healthy flow of sales for the organization. By continually collecting and analyzing information, marketing helps the organization learn how to manage changes to reflect new customer opportunities. After reading this chapter, you will be able to reach the learning goals below.

Learning Goals

1. Discuss the marketing goal of promoting customer satisfaction, noting the types of utility.
2. Define the marketing concept and describe how it drives the business process.
3. Describe the four Ps of the marketing mix and explain how companies enhance the mix.
4. Explain the role of environmental scanning in the marketing process.
5. Identify the forms of marketing research and list the steps in the research process.
6. List and explain the external and internal variables in the consumer decision-making process.
7. Discuss five commonly used bases for market segmentation.
8. Explain how industrial markets differ from consumer markets.
9. Explain the process of target marketing.
10. Describe how companies position their products.

A Candle in the Window

"Good morning! We're ready for the marketing tour," Joanna announced as the students filed into the One Minute Manager's office.

"The tour has already begun. Did you see the homeless man outside our building?"

"Yes," Carlos answered. "We gave him a dollar. Do you consider him an example of marketing?"

"No, but he reminded me that marketing can be used to accomplish many goals," she explained, "even to help solve the problem of homelessness. I met an interesting man the other day named Michael Richards. He runs a nonprofit business called Candle in the Window. It sells candles, of course, but it also offers a better way to help the homeless. Michael hires homeless people to make beeswax candles, which the company sells through stores and catalogs. And the employees are encouraged to use the company's facilities as they search for additional jobs. It's a stepping stone to better-paying jobs, and a way back into society."[1]

"Sounds like a great idea," Joanna commented. "But what does it have to do with marketing?"

"Here, have a look at my company's latest marketing plan," she answered, opening a thick document to its table of contents. "Notice that, after analyzing our situation, the plan specifies goals and actions for new product development, and for how our products should be distributed, priced, and promoted through marketing communications. Every marketing plan uses actions in exactly these areas to try to meet customer needs a little better, and therefore to make more sales. And Candle in the Window has innovated in each of these areas to help solve the problem of homelessness."

"Like creating a product—candles—to employ homeless people," Carlos suggested. "People are more likely to pay for a product than to give their spare change to someone on the sidewalk."

"And the business distributes this product through stores and catalogs, which makes it easier for people to buy it and help out," Joanna added.

"Yes, you're right," the One Minute Manager agreed. "And the business also uses effective communications, such as publicity and advertising, to make sure customers learn about its products. The principles of good marketing are what make that organization work, just the same as ours. Customers can't find your door unless you put a candle in the window for them!"

The Nature of Marketing

Businesses face a tough job trying to convince us consumers to buy a particular product today. We are better educated than ever before. We are much more choosy about the quality of the products we buy. We have learned how to shop aggressively and to seek out the greatest value for our dollar. And we have more products to choose from. In the mid-1980s, for example, the average supermarket carried around 15,000 products. Now the average number of products on grocery-store shelves has ballooned to more than 23,000. Finally, we consumers are becoming increasingly diverse in backgrounds, tastes, and life-styles.

Companies are also realizing that the world is changing. Not long ago, they depended on a handful of television channels and magazines to communicate with their customers. Now cable television has increased our viewing options and splintered the mass impact of television. Businesses can choose from over 11,000 magazines in which to send out their messages. And information technology is creating new ways to do business, from faxes to the Internet.

Within this clutter of information, businesses must find innovative ways to compete. And all these changes are taking place in a global marketing environment. Keep this swirling backdrop in mind as you explore now how businesses market their products.

Customer Focus

To counter encroaching competition from superstore bookseller Barnes & Noble, the owners of Harry W. Schwartz Bookshops in Milwaukee, Wisconsin, focus on what their customers want: a wide selection of titles at discount prices, a no-questions-asked policy on returns, knowledgeable employees, and conveniently located stores like this one, which invite readers to relax with a cup of freshly brewed coffee or to browse to their hearts' content.

Marketing Provides Satisfaction

At the heart of marketing is the drive to satisfy both the customer and the business. The business satisfies customers' needs and wants, and in exchange customers give the business the sales dollars it needs. Companies that are successful marketers think continually about what makes the customer pleased with a purchase; that is, they think about the customer's wants and needs.

A **need** is a feeling that something necessary to one's well-being is lacking. Chapter 11 discusses needs as levels in a hierarchy because each level motivates our behavior until those needs are satisfied. Then the next higher level of needs becomes the motivator. Some needs are physical—your needs for food and

1. Discuss the marketing goal of promoting customer satisfaction, noting the types of utility.

 need

A feeling that something necessary to one's well-being is lacking.

want

A need that has been given a form and a definition by your experience, surroundings, and personality.

form utility

The satisfaction buyers receive from a product's attributes.

time utility

The satisfaction buyers receive from being able to purchase a product when they want it.

place utility

The satisfaction buyers receive from being able to purchase a product in a convenient place.

clothing, for example. Others are social, such as the need for friendship, status, or being liked by classmates or co-workers. Still others give our lives a sense of purpose. The need for knowledge, achievement, and excitement are examples.

A **want** is a need that has been given a form and a definition by your experience, surroundings, and personality. Hunger is a need, but your desire for a burger and a shake or for an apple and a yogurt are wants. Our wants seem endless. We develop a desire for new things and feel deprived if we don't have them. We want the latest hairstyle, a just-released Janet Jackson CD, a new paint job on the car. Marketers do not create needs. They do help create wants by exposing us to new products.

Our wants and needs have little impact on our lives—as long as they are satisfied. When we lack something, we are motivated to act. And when consumers are motivated to act, marketing can influence their actions most effectively. If our actions remove the feeling that something is lacking, we feel satisfied. Marketing strives to match human needs and wants with the products that can satisfy them. The better the match, the greater the satisfaction. This is the goal of marketing—to gain a competitive advantage by providing greater satisfaction. Let's look at how marketing satisfies wants.

Utility: What Does the Product Do for Me?

Another helpful way to think about customer satisfaction is in terms of utility—how the product satisfies the customer. Figure 14.1 shows examples of five utilities. **Form utility** is the satisfaction buyers receive from a product's attributes—its shape, style, or function, for example. A coat's form utility includes both its function (it will keep you warm and dry) and its fashionable style.

But if the coat is not available when the customer wants to buy it, the coat's form utility has no value. A product must also have **time utility**—it must be available when the customer wants it—and **place utility**—it must be available where the customer wants to buy it. And even if the style is appealing and the coat is available conveniently at the right time, it may not be as useful as one you already have in your closet. To use it, you must own it. You

figure **14.1**   **How the Five Utilities Provide Satisfaction**

Ownership Utility		Form Utility
• Pay cash to own • Use credit card to buy • Rent • Lease		• Warmth • Appropriate clothing for office work • Fashionable color, material
Place Utility	**Information Utility**	**Time Utility**
• Stores in popular malls • Catalog service in customer's home • Television shopping networks	• Ask customers what they desire • Tell them about availability • Persuade customers to buy	• Available in stores from 10 a.m. to 9 p.m. • Available by phone 7 days a week, 24 hours a day

would probably buy a coat; you might rent or lease other products. **Owner-ship utility** is the satisfaction derived from possessing the legal right to use the product.

At the heart of customer satisfaction is **information utility**, the satisfaction derived from the flow of information between customers and the business. Sellers inform buyers that products are available, where to buy them, how much they cost, and how to use them. By their purchase decisions and responses to products, buyers inform sellers about how to improve all the utilities their products offer. Chapter 16 explains these information flows in detail.

To sum up, the total satisfaction a product delivers is both functional and psychological, deriving from a combination of its form, time, place, ownership and information utilities. The customer's level of satisfaction flows from the combination of these benefits. Some products offer more benefits than others—a house and a car provide much more satisfaction than a toothbrush and a tube of toothpaste—which is one reason they cost much more. And within a category of products, some brands offer greater satisfaction for roughly the same price that others charge. This extra value makes them industry leaders. Campbell's makes 80 percent of all the soup purchased today; Gillette makes over 64 percent of all the razor blades sold.[2] These two leading brands far outdistance their closest competitors because consumers derive greater satisfaction from using them than from using other brands. This is the goal of marketing—to gain a competitive advantage by providing greater satisfaction.

Mutual Satisfaction Through Exchange

Economics teaches us that trade makes people better off. In our free-market economy, the forces of supply and demand encourage mutually beneficial trade. In other words, mutual satisfaction comes about through **exchange**, a process in which buyers and sellers each benefit by trading things they value in order to satisfy their wants and needs.

For an exchange to take place each party must possess something the other desires, and each must want the other party's item more than the item they exchange for it. In short, both buyer and seller must believe that their total satisfaction will increase as a result of the exchange. But how can both parties come out ahead? Is one of them miscalculating? Not in most cases.

Economics also teaches us that it is far more efficient to trade than it is to produce everything we want and need ourselves. A clothing company, for example, can easily make a better-looking coat in less time and for less money than most of the rest of us could. We can buy the coat for *less than* we would spend to make it, but for *more than* the manufacturer will spend to make it. The exchange gives each party something of value, and both come out ahead.

The Gradual Process of Exchange

Exchange is a process in which the parties gradually move closer to the final event; communication, learning, and negotiation may take place along the way. Eventually, however, the exchange process ends in a **transaction**, an exchange of values by two or more parties. At McDonald's, for example, exchanges of Value Meals for $3.59 take place.

Your Money or Your Life: Deceptive Communications

Exchanges can't happen without communication, for each party must somehow discover that the other has something of value to exchange. This is where promotion comes into play in marketing. Promotion—through advertising,

 ownership utility

The satisfaction derived from possessing the legal right to use a product.

 information utility

The satisfaction derived from the flow of information between customers and the business.

 exchange

A process in which buyers and sellers each benefit by trading things they value in order to satisfy their wants and needs.

 transaction

An exchange of values by two or more parties.

sales, and other communication channels—helps consumers become aware that products are available for purchase.

Communications must never deceive, however. Marketers believe (and consumers expect) that both parties should enter into the exchange willingly, without force of any kind. A robbery is an exchange, but not the kind of exchange that marketing has as its goal. Nor do deceptive sales practices, like inaccurate labels or high-pressure sales pitches, lead to acceptable exchanges. They too are forms of robbery. Marketers should not push consumers into an exchange, nor should they trick them into exchanges by withholding information. Because communication is so important to the exchange process, deceptive communication is not much different from armed robbery.

The Marketing Concept

Businesses do not always think like marketers. Sometimes they are so focused on their own needs and wants that they forget to think about the customer's needs and wants. To avoid this problem, businesses try to adopt a management approach that focuses on customers and their needs.

A Customer Orientation

2. Define the marketing concept and describe how it drives the business process.

The underlying logic of our current marketing era is represented in the marketing concept. The **marketing concept** is a philosophy that views the consumer as the focal point of the business and views profits as the result of satisfying customers through high-quality goods and services. Many successful companies have stated this philosophy in their slogans:

- "Our most important package is yours" (Federal Express)
- "Your way, right away" (Burger King)
- "USAir begins with you" (USAir)
- "Nobody Else Like You Service" (Equitable Life Insurance)
- "Chosen #1 in People Pleasin'" (Holiday Inn)

The marketing concept focuses the entire business and all its employees on making and delivering what buyers want in the first place. The marketing concept recognizes that organizations are most likely to achieve their goals, including profitability, if *all* their activities are focused on satisfying the market's wants and needs. In the long run, putting the consumer's welfare and desires first leads to greater sales and profits because consumers become repeat buyers. The marketing concept leads to the conclusion that satisfying customers is the key to profitability or success for any organization.[3]

A Societal Orientation

marketing concept

A philosophy that views the consumer as the focal point of the business and views profits as the result of satisfying customers through high-quality goods and services.

Since the 1970s, business practices have come under close social scrutiny, and public interest groups have called for government regulation of many business activities. Marketing has been criticized for providing dangerous products and promoting them through misrepresentative advertising. Marketing has also been faulted for offering individual satisfaction at the expense of society as a whole. Cars without safety features or fuel-saving devices may satisfy the individual consumer's desire for lower prices and high-speed transportation. However, high rates of death and injury and poor conservation of energy resources are not in the best interests of society. Businesses must always be careful to avoid such practices as those described in the following two paragraphs.

In a recent advertising campaign of the Swedish company Volvo, commercials showed a "monster truck" running over a lineup of cars and crushing all but a Volvo station wagon. The tag line "Can You Spot the Volvo?" was used. However, investigation revealed that the advertisers had reinforced the Volvo with metal struts and weakened the other cars. Further, instead of the entire truck being driven over the station wagon for a closeup camera shot, a workman had merely rolled a truck tire over it. Embarrassingly, both television and print ads bragged, "Volvo, a car you can believe in."

Recently, flat sales in the $5 billion U.S. gun industry prodded the National Rifle Association (NRA) to target women to take up arms for personal safety. For example, in *Ladies' Home Journal*, Colt Manufacturing Co., Inc., ran an ad showing a mother putting her child to bed; two semiautomatic pistols were depicted underneath with copy that read, "Self-protection is more than your right, it's your responsibility." Critics claim that such pitches, based on fear, will only increase the amount of violence in our society. They point out that handguns are more likely to kill a family member by accident than to stop a crime.

Such practices continue in some corners of the business world, but public interest groups, government regulators, consumers, and businesses themselves are working to reduce them. The growth of environmental concerns in the 1990s has reinforced this emphasis on ethics and social impact. The growing conviction of businesses, regulators, and the consuming public is that companies should take responsibility for the effects of their products on society. Marketing's role in this is to ensure that its actions are neither deceptive nor harmful to customers and to society at large.

Beyond Business

The marketing concept is often applied by not-for-profit organizations such as hospitals, museums, zoos, trade unions, and colleges.[4] In the 1970s the armed services discovered that marketing techniques could help them gain recruits ("Be all that you can be"), and now they market as aggressively as they fight. Even religious groups use advertising: Radio ads recruit applicants to an order of Ursuline nuns by describing a nun's daily activities of community service, going to class, and meeting friends. The ad concludes: "I guess people are surprised when they find out I'm a (*pause*) nun." The order, according to marketers at Sive/Young Rubican, the ad agency it hired, had needed an image makeover.[5]

Marketing has traditionally focused on the exchange of goods and services for money. Now the role of marketing is broadening to include more than just economic exchanges. The product can be a place ("Come to Canada, the endless surprise"), an idea ("Buy American"), or a social cause ("Friends don't let friends drive drunk"). Voters can exchange their votes for a candidate's promise to enact a particular political platform. Marketing promotes energy conservation and helps prevent drug abuse. And businesses like Candle in the Window market products to raise money for charitable causes.

Marketers have recently realized that society would be better off if people bought less of some products, not more. Marketing that is used to discourage people from buying a product is called **demarketing**.[6] Campaigns by the American Cancer Society against smoking and by Mothers Against Drunk Driving (MADD) against underage drinking are classic examples of demarketing. Recent efforts by beer brewers to promote responsible drinking are an extension of the demarketing principle.

demarketing

Marketing that is used to discourage people from buying a product.

The Product Is Atlanta

Souvenirs like these commemorative T-shirts are part of marketing the 1996 Centennial Olympic Games in Atlanta, Georgia. And marketing the city of Atlanta played a key role in its selection from among a host of cities worldwide, all contending for the honor. Among the benefits to Atlanta's economy have been new jobs and increased tourism.

relationship marketing

A personalized approach to customer retention.

internal customer

A person or group within your business who uses the work you produce.

four Ps

The four elements of marketing—product, price, place, and promotion.

marketing mix

The planned use of the four Ps.

product

A good, service, or idea that is designed, produced, and offered for sale.

Building Long-Lasting Relationships

In practice, many companies translate the marketing concept into a short-sighted focus on the consumer's next purchase. The marketing concept is continuing to evolve. More and more marketers now consider customers' long-term interests, not just their immediate wants.[7] This view leads to a different kind of marketing behavior, designed to retain customers for years rather than sell the most units today. Customer retention is the result of a business's policy of establishing a long-term relationship with individual customers who repeat exchanges because they are pleased with the relationship. Raymond Zimmerman, chief executive of the catalog showroom retailer Service Merchandise, says that "the process of addressing your customers as individuals and responding to their specific needs is the strategic tool of the future."[8] This personalized approach to customer retention is called **relationship marketing**.

Marketing Begins at Home

Employees in daily contact with customers often find it easy to adopt the marketing concept in their work. But other employees who work behind the scenes—such as in manufacturing, finance, and accounting—may be less able to see the importance of the marketing concept. Their lack of regular contact with customers and, in many cases, even with marketers creates a barrier to the spread of the marketing concept within the organization. To overcome this, managers have started training employees to identify and satisfy their internal customers. An **internal customer** is a person or group within your business who uses the work you produce. For example, any employee can improve the value of his or her work by studying internal customers' needs and wants and searching for ways to give these customers greater satisfaction. When all employees satisfy their own internal customers, the benefits cascade through the company and outward to external customers as well.

Short-term tactics, such as quick sales from a price cut, cannot help a business retain customers in the face of increasingly heavy global competition. But perhaps the move toward improved quality of products and services can. Quality improvement can complement relationship marketing as businesses work to retain their customers. As Figure 14.2 shows, customers who do business with you because the quality you provide is higher will give you repeat business. Quality is therefore a long-term expression of the marketing concept.[9] At

figure **14.2** **The Quality Chain Reaction**

If you improve the quality of your product . . . → your costs fall and productivity increases because . . . → you attract and retain customers with better quality and lower prices . . . → and achieve long-term business success, which . . . → benefits your business, your customers, and the economy.

Quality improvement expert W. Edwards Deming argued that a long-term focus on improving quality for customers is beneficial to the business and the economy.

Source: Adapted from W. Edwards Deming, *Out of Crisis* (Cambridge, Mass.: MIT Center for Advanced Engineering Study, 1986).

Bell Corp., a manufacturer of aluminum containers, customers are flown in to meet the people at the company who work to satisfy their needs. Actually seeing the hourly workers, engineers, and top managers instills trust and builds a relationship worth far more than the $5,000 cost per visit.

Marketing Management

Marketing management means planning the marketing activities for an organization or product. It also means following the marketing plan through product design, pricing, distribution, and promotion. These four elements of marketing—product, price, place, and promotion—are called the **four Ps**. Marketers use the term **marketing mix** to describe the planned use of the four Ps. When the right mix is managed effectively, each element reinforces the others to produce a total effect greater than the sum of the parts.

The brand name Roach Motel, for instance, is a catchy way to describe a trap that will rid a home of unwanted insects. And the slogan "Roaches check in, but they don't check out!" is also effective. But the combination of advertising slogan, highly appropriate brand name, competitive price, and national distribution in grocery and hardware stores has a larger effect than any of these individual components could alone. Add to these four Ps a product that really catches roaches—its functional utility is high—and you ensure long-term enthusiasm for the product on the part of a majority of consumers. The purpose of Roach Motel advertising is to build a dominant position in the roach-control market by marketing a superior product.

Managing the Marketing Mix

The survival of your business will depend on your customers' perception of the value your product delivers compared to the price you charge for it. If customers in the auto industry, for example, decide that a new, lower-priced car from Japan is better than their old favorite from Detroit, they will not buy their next car from Ford, GM, or Chrysler. As thousands of customers make these decisions, the effect will be lost sales, lost jobs, and lost profits for American automakers. These problems may seem far too big for marketing to solve, but the fact is that they result from some problem in the marketing mix. Recent improvements in the standing of U.S. automakers are the result of improvements in product quality and aggressive pricing—changes in two of the four Ps.

By combining the four Ps in an appropriate marketing mix, marketers offer sufficient value to satisfy their target consumers. This task would be easier if other marketers were not also competing for those consumers. In fast-changing markets, competitors continually fine-tune the elements of their marketing mixes.

We will examine the four Ps in greater detail in the next three chapters, but now let's take a closer look at how marketing management tries to balance them to provide satisfaction.

Product

The focal point of the marketing mix is the **product**: the good, service, or idea that is designed, produced, and offered for sale. But the product, as you may remember from our earlier discussion, is more than an isolated object or service. A product is a combination of features, including its brand name, packaging, guarantees, and post-sale activities that ensure satisfaction—perhaps even its aroma (see the ethics check "The Smell of Satisfaction"). The product may

3. Describe the four Ps of the marketing mix and explain how companies enhance the mix.

A Timeless Product

Barbie: the doll of choice for countless kids of all ages, all around the world, since 1959 when Mattel introduced this original. Barbie became so popular—Mattel estimates there are more than 800 million worldwide—that playing with Barbie dolls links generations of her fans. Look for a big birthday bash when Barbie turns 40 in 1999.

The Smell of Satisfaction

Would you buy a used car from this guy? No way . . . well, maybe if he smelled a little better. One of the big three auto companies has commissioned a new cologne for its salespeople—something that makes them smell honest. (Honestly.) Smell researcher Alan Hirsch of Chicago won't say which company he's working for, but he acknowledges that he is developing an Honest Car Salesman Odor, to be sprayed on salespeople in the hope that car buyers will trust them more than they do now. Sounds ridiculous, but in fact many marketers are beginning to explore the power of scent. Because smell is more tightly linked with memory and emotions than the other senses are, it can have a surprising influence on consumer attitude. For instance, Hirsch ran an experiment in which 31 shoppers inspected Nike sneakers in two identical rooms, one of which had a special floral scent pumped in. Interviewed afterward, the shoppers in the scented room were much more interested in buying the sneakers. Several stores now use the scent regularly, but Nike was unimpressed—a spokeswoman said the company was more concerned with how "to get athletic shoes not to smell."

One of Hirsch's scents is coming on line (or on nose) at casinos around the world because it created a 45 percent increase in slot machine play when tested at the Las Vegas Hilton. You might call that one the smell of money. Elsewhere in the world of smells, English and Australian companies are now scenting their bills with androstenone, an unpleasant-smelling compound from human underarms, on the theory that customers will pay more quickly just to get the smell out of the house.

Not everyone thinks marketers should resort to nose appeal. Joan Claybrook, president of Ralph Nader's Public Citizen group, finds the use of scents "disgusting and very offensive." Like subliminal advertising, in which "Eat Popcorn" messages were rumored to flash rapidly on the screen during movies (it didn't work), aroma marketing smells like unfair salesmanship to some. If customers do not realize the scent brings out an urge to buy, perhaps it is unfair. On the other hand, marketers might argue that the pleasant smells they add are one more form of satisfaction, a valuable part of the product itself.

Sources: Alan Hirsch, speech to The Alexis Group, January 29, 1993, Denver, Colorado; N. R. Kleinfield, "The Smell of Money," *New York Times*, October 25, 1992, Styles pp. 1, 14.

---

include services such as installation, directions for use, and maintenance. As you can see, product means a lot more to a marketer than to the average customer! Consider these two examples:

- Sony learned that buyers of VCRs found the instructions for installing and programming its new products too confusing. So it began marketing a VCR with a set of synthesized vocal instructions that guided the user through the installation and operating procedures.

- Sharp Electronics discovered that over one-third of the buyers of its Half-Pint microwave oven were over 65 years old, and that these consumers found the oven's touch controls too complex. So it preprogrammed keys for heating the most common dishes.

In each of these cases, the company modified its product to provide more satisfaction to its customers. Sony and Sharp both knew that these "convenience" features are as much a part of their products as the actual products themselves.

Price

Price is what the buyer must give up to receive the product. Usually this means money, but sometimes the parties barter and exchange goods or services. In nonbusiness marketing, price can have more than one meaning: Museums ask for donations, churches pass the collection plate, and politicians seek votes. Even when a good or service is exchanged for money, companies often use price adjustments, discount coupons, rebates, and other pricing strategies. These adjustments reduce the cost to the buyer.

 price

What the buyer must give up, usually money, to receive the product.

Place

Place, or distribution as it will be called here and in Chapter 16, is the process of making the product available when and where consumers want it. Businesses have many alternative means of moving products to consumers. They can choose among different types of outlets and store locations, for example. Distribution also involves such decisions as how much inventory to have on hand, how to transport goods, and where to locate warehouses.

Distribution is usually the least visible element of the marketing mix. However, it is very important because it determines where and whether the customer can get the product. Sometimes, a distribution strategy is actually the basis for a business, as with Federal Express and United Parcel Service.

Promotion

Promotion consists of all the forms of communication organizations use to inform and persuade consumers. Advertising, personal selling, sales promotion, and public relations activities are promotional activities that marketers use to make consumers aware of a product and its unique and desirable features. Promotion can also strengthen or stimulate consumer wants. You may have experienced this yourself driving past a billboard advertising breakfast specials at a fast-food restaurant. If the thought of a quick stop for pancakes and sausage pulled you off the road, you made some marketer very happy. Sometimes we all find ourselves in unplanned exchanges.

The four Ps make a short list—until you begin to think about all the options each presents. Market management requires knowledge, skills, and creativity to produce a successful marketing mix. Some of the options marketing managers must juggle are listed in Table 14.1.

 place
The process of making the product available when and where consumers want it. Also called *distribution*.

 promotion
All the forms of communication organizations use to inform and persuade consumers.

table **14.1** Ways to Fine-tune Your Marketing Mix

Decision Area	Options
Product	Improve the quality of your product. Improve the services you offer with your product. Change the brand name. Add a warranty or guarantee, or improve the one you now offer.
Price	Change your usual asking price. Offer a discount, a reduction from the price marked on the product.
Place (distribution)	Offer your product in new stores or catalogs. Speed the shipment of your product to customers or stores. Use an 800 number to make your product available around the clock.
Promotion	Increase the money you spend on advertising. Advertise differently, on TV instead of radio, for example. Use one-on-one selling by telephoning potential customers. Encourage reporters to write or talk about your product. Hold a sweepstakes contest and package the entry forms along with your product. Integrate all communications to your customers (press coverage, ads, sales contracts, service contracts, packaging, and so on) to deliver a more consistent message. Offer free samples to encourage more customers to use your product.

customer service

Paying attention to every detail in the process of delivering satisfaction.

Delivering Extraordinary Customer Service

To compete today, a business must constantly monitor its marketing mix and change it frequently. In a growing number of cases, this means focusing on the service aspects of the product. Some products *are* services—such as your checking account or the medical exam your doctor gives you. Others—an automobile, for example—are obviously goods, not services. But in all three cases—and in lots of others—enhanced service can mean leading the competition instead of following it. You can improve a financial service such as a checking account by adding worldwide ATM service. You can improve a medical exam by making it easier to schedule an appointment or by providing a prescription more quickly. And you can offer a 50,000-mile warranty and roadside towing with the car you are selling. Improved services appeal directly to customers and send a clear signal that you have confidence in the quality of your product.

Improved customer service is one way companies are enhancing their marketing mix in an effort to develop deeply rooted relationships with their customers. They are recognizing that their mission is *to solve customers' problems*, not merely to take orders for want-satisfying goods and services. **Customer service** means paying attention to every detail in the process of delivering satisfaction. It means meeting promised delivery times, setting up toll-free customer service phone lines, extending extra credit, and providing friendly in-store assistance. In short, you must go the extra step to ensure the customer's complete satisfaction, happiness, and delight—thereby creating "raving fans" for the business.

Many companies are improving their services through different but equally demanding methods. At Dell Computer, the mail-order personal computer company, employees now memorize the Dell Vision, which states that a customer "must have a quality experience, and must be pleased, not just satisfied."[10] Marriott Corp. introduced a 15-minute delivery guarantee for room-service breakfasts; deliverers carry walkie-talkies so they can receive instructions more quickly. British Airways employs 60 highly trained "hunters" who roam London's Heathrow Airport to troubleshoot customer problems: missed connections, lost traveling companions, and hand luggage left on connecting flights. Domino's, the world's largest pizza delivery chain, pays 10,000 "mystery customers" $60 each to buy 12 pizzas throughout the year and evaluate the quality and service they receive.

Coordinating Key Marketing Functions

Managing the marketing mix is the most important, but not the only, function of marketing. The typical marketing department performs many other roles. Some key marketing functions of the modern business include the following:

- Information gathering through marketing research and environmental scanning
- Product development and improvement
- Product management, the coordination of the marketing mix for each product
- Packaging and labeling
- Sales management, the coordination of all personal selling activities
- Distribution management
- Advertising and other promotional activities
- Customer service and support

- Encouraging change within the company to enforce the overall marketing concept

The marketing manager is responsible for seeing that all functions work together to satisfy customers. But in many cases, the marketing manager is not the sole person responsible for these marketing activities. This means marketers must often coordinate their work with that of other people and groups. A special challenge exists when some marketing functions are performed *outside* the marketing department. Many companies have separate distribution, sales, and advertising departments, and some have their own customer service and product development departments. Teamwork is a key part of most marketing jobs.

Environmental Scanning

A company's decision to change the marketing mix must be based on a realistic assessment of the environment, the forces that influence the business but are beyond its control. You will recall from Chapter 1 that the business environment consists of the natural, social, political/legal, technical, competitive, and economic factors that lie outside the company and have the potential to affect it. These external forces shape the four Ps, so monitoring them is one of the most important aspects of marketing management. **Environmental scanning** is the term businesses use to describe their efforts to monitor the marketing environment and to forecast changes within it. As many businesses have found out, changes in the environment can be either opportunities or threats. For example, consumer concern for more healthful foods dampened sales of Häagen Dazs high-fat ice cream but opened the door for TCBY to score with its low-fat frozen yogurt stores. Let's take a closer look at the competitive and cultural/social environments to see how they influence marketing decisions.

4. Explain the role of environmental scanning in the marketing process.

The Competitive Environment

Marketers must constantly scan the environment for competitors that might invade their market and erode their sales. Over the last two decades, most companies have seen a steady increase in the number of competitors. Competition takes many forms, not all of them obvious. *Any* alternative satisfier of a want or need is competition. Take movies, for example. The want felt by moviegoers in the United States is the want for entertainment. Thus, Paramount must consider videos, network/cable television, basketball games, exercise salons, restaurants, and even bowling alleys to be competitors. These are *generic competitors*, or alternative kinds of products or services that can also satisfy a want or need. Within any one of these alternatives—say, videos—are *form competitors*: comedy, thriller, action, animated, and science fiction videos, among others. And within each of the forms there are *brand competitors*: Paramount, Disney, Twentieth Century Fox, and MCA-Universal.

Companies that lose sight of some of their competitors suffer from marketing myopia. *Myopia* means "short-sightedness," and marketing myopia is an inability to see your market clearly.[11] Marketing myopia is an even bigger problem in fast-changing, turbulent environments because competitors keep changing. In the early 1970s, U.S. automakers did not think the small and inexpensive Japanese and German imported cars could compete with the big, expensive U.S. cars of that era. By the time they realized their customers were buying small cars, U.S. manufacturers had already lost considerable market share.

Marketers must know not only the number and size of their competitors but also the tools they are using to compete. Some competitors offer similar products at lower prices. Others tailor the product to offer distinct advantages.

 environmental scanning

The term businesses use to describe their efforts to monitor the marketing environment and to forecast changes within it.

To compete in the women's razors and blades market, Gillette Co. introduced Sensor for Women, the first women's razor designed to reach around ankles and behind knees. Armed with a cartridge that dispenses skin moisturizer and a flat, wide-handled grip that reduces lateral movement and prevents shaving nicks, the Sensor for Women grabbed a 35.5 percent market share in its first year on the market.[12]

Cultural/Social Environment of Global Marketing

As you saw in Chapter 3, we are now members of a global market. You, too, are probably a consumer of products from many parts of the globe. Clothes are made in Asia, cookies come from England, and fruit is produced in Latin America. For many companies around the world, domestic markets have turned into global ones, so it is natural that marketing—and scanning—should go global, too. More and more foreign companies market in the United States. And many U.S. companies now earn over one-third of their total sales or profits from foreign markets—Gillette, Eastman Kodak, Coca-Cola, IBM, 3M, and Goodyear, to name a few. The market opportunities are enormous. The world outside the United States produces four times the U.S. gross domestic product. Only 3 percent of the world's population lies within U.S. borders, and the market outside those borders is growing at a rate 70 percent faster than the home market.

Consider the boon to Coca-Cola when the Berlin Wall fell. Prior to 1990, no Coke was sold in East Germany, but the demand was certainly there. East German consumers, 17 million strong, spent years watching Coca-Cola commercials on West German television. And in each of those years they had been consuming 95 bottles or cans of soft drinks per person a year—nearly as many as consumers in the West—even though the state-produced drinks tasted bitter. "There was enormous pent-up demand for the product," one Coca-Cola executive observed. Bottlers in West Berlin handed out free Cokes to the Easterners as they flooded through the opened gates of the Berlin Wall. Coke was one of the products most frequently purchased by East Germans coming across the border. By 1992, Coke was selling 180 million cases per year in this new market. Coca-Cola was reaping more profit in the new Germany than in the United States![13]

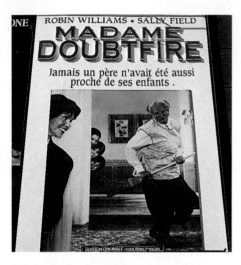

Global Marketing

Releasing their movies in foreign markets boosts American film studios' revenues. For example, "Pulp Fiction" grossed $100 million in the United States and matched that gross in foreign markets. The current feature at this Paris, France, cinema is Robin Williams as "Madame Doubtfire."

Marketing Research

5. Identify the forms of marketing research and list the steps in the research process.

Business decisions suffer if managers have to guess what customers want, what competitors offer, and how the market will respond to a new program or product. Scanning activities provide important background information about new directions and events, but they do not provide sufficient detail about customers and competitors. To fill this gap, marketers turn to **marketing research**, formal research methods that produce useful and accurate information about consumers and the marketing environment.

What additional information might you need about your customers? At Coca-Cola, marketers decided they did not know enough about customers' ideas and complaints. They needed a better way to listen to *the customer's voice*, what customers think and say about a product and the wants these reflect. To do this they installed an 800 number to receive customer feedback. When the company introduced its New Coke in 1985, calls surged from 400 to over 12,000 daily. A total of 90 percent of the callers registered a preference for the old Coke. There are many ways to tap into the customer's voice. London's Heathrow Airport provides Video Point booths so that travelers can tape their grievances as soon as they disembark. Later, customer service managers review the tapes and respond.

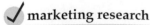

marketing research

Formal research methods that produce useful and accurate information about consumers and the marketing environment.

table **14.2** Some Examples of Secondary Sources of Information

Source	Application
Magazine and newspaper articles	Published stories can provide useful information about environmental trends, including changing market wants and needs as well as competitive activities.
Government patent filings	Patent applications can be traded to learn about new technology developed by competitors.
Competitors' annual reports	Public companies file annual reports with the Securities and Exchange Commission, a federal regulatory body. These reports can reveal details of operations and plans.
Competitors' employment ads	Classified ads in newspapers and the job bulletins distributed by companies' personnel offices reveal a great deal about their plans by showing what kind of expertise they will need and where it will be needed.
Professional associations and meetings	Trade fairs, conferences, and similar events reveal details of competitors' products and strategies through displays, speeches, and publications.
Government agencies	Under the 1966 Freedom of Information Act, many federal agencies must provide requested records to the public. Companies can, for example, obtain copies of competitors' bids, inspection reports on their products or plants, and reports filed as evidence to support advertising claims.

These approaches to gathering information are useful, but they are informal.[14] Customers are free to participate or not, which makes it difficult to control the quality of the information obtained. At Heathrow, for example, passengers are not likely to comment on *all* aspects of their trip, but rather to focus only on a few that come to mind. Most marketing information is obtained through more formal, scientific research that yields more accurate results.

Marketing research takes many forms. Sometimes it analyzes **secondary data** that have already been collected for another purpose than the one at hand. Secondary data may have their source either inside or outside the organization. For instance, a company's own sales records for the past few years can yield valuable information about its customers. Sources outside the company include U.S. census data and reports from private research companies, industry groups, or the government (see Table 14.2). Much of the work of environmental scanning focuses on tracing existing information. But when existing information is not sufficient, researchers must collect **primary data**—original information collected by a researcher for a specific purpose.

The Research Process

Research that collects original information requires careful controls. Otherwise, mistakes in how the information is gathered or analyzed can creep into the project and make the findings unreliable. The research process must be carefully planned so that it produces information directly relevant to important marketing decisions. A simple research process moves through seven steps:

 secondary data

Data used in marketing research that have already been collected for a purpose other than the one at hand.

 primary data

Original information collected by a market researcher for a specific purpose.

market

A group of people or businesses that has an interest in buying products and has the ability to pay for them.

1. Define the problem.
2. Identify the information needed, identify the sources of that information, and describe how it might affect the marketing decision.
3. If primary data are needed, prepare a research design.
4. Collect data using telephone surveys, personal interviews, or other research techniques.
5. Analyze the data to identify patterns and trends.
6. Apply the findings to the decision.
7. Check to see whether the information improved decision making.

The final step, checking to see if the information really did produce a better decision, is important because it adds a learning loop to the research process. Undertaking primary research is difficult and complicated, and the information it produces is not always as good as it should be. But the process improves continuously as long as marketers check the effects of the research on the problem's solution after each project.

Forms of Research

Marketing research takes different forms depending upon the research problem. There are many sources for secondary research, including magazine and newspaper articles, government data from the census and other sources, and the information services and publications of businesses that specialize in research. Primary research, too, can take many forms. Surveys are the most common, and they are typically performed by telephone or by mail. Discussion groups of consumers, called *focus groups*, are also used, as are in-store experiments that test consumers' reactions to a new product.

Modern marketing researchers are continually facing new challenges. Recently, technological advances have made the practice of marketing research more complex. Managers are losing confidence in the results of marketing research studies. Consumers have been over-surveyed, reducing their rates of response. And the ethics of marketing have slipped, which has undermined the credibility of study results. Some researchers misrepresent themselves to gain access to respondents, for example. Finally, marketing research itself needs to improve.

Companies have responded to the need to improve marketing research in three ways. First, more managers are learning about research, which helps them evaluate how well it is done. Second, marketing researchers are acquiring new and better methods of conducting research. Third, marketing information is increasingly treated as a valuable corporate asset.

Defining the Market

Marketing research and environmental scanning provide information vital to managing the marketing mix. No business can focus on all the needs and wants of all its individual and business customers. And in times of increasing competition, businesses must focus more narrowly to succeed. This narrow focus means that marketers must define their markets with great care.

A **market** is a group of people or businesses that has an interest in buying products and has the ability to pay for them. Selecting and defining a market is one of the most important decisions a business makes. In constantly changing environments, companies must periodically confirm that their market definition and focus are still valid. For instance, Procter & Gamble recently decided that there were so many new low-priced detergent, diaper, and coffee brands in

Who's Pushing the Grocery Cart?

Statistics from a national marketing research firm reveal that men buy a quarter of the groceries in the United States, up from 17 percent five years ago. This makes sense, considering that well over 50 percent of adult women now work outside the home. Interestingly, the percentage of groceries bought by men differs from product to product. *Can you think why?*

Product	Percentage bought by men
Bottled water	40%
Frozen foods	32
Soup	30
Cold remedies	30
Detergent	27
Baby food	24
Baking mixes	21

Source: Nielsen Homescan, reported in "Real Men Buy Paper Towels, Too," *Business Week,* November 9, 1992, p. 75.

grocery stores that it should redefine its target markets. P&G stopped serving some markets in which its brands were weak and put more resources behind its leading brands.[15]

To properly serve a market, marketers must understand as much as possible about its wants and needs. They must seek answers to many questions. Who are my customers? When will they buy? Where and how often will they buy? And the most difficult question: *Why do customers buy?* (See the skills check entitled "Who's Pushing the Grocery Cart?")

Understanding the Consumer's Purchase Decision

Our purchasing decisions are influenced by many factors, some external and others internal.[16] Let's begin by looking at some external influences. Our wants and needs are shaped by the people in our lives. The *culture* that we grow up in determines our values and feelings and the acceptable ways of conducting our lives. Our culture teaches us to share with others, take care of our children and parents, and work hard to succeed. These teachings are passed on from generation to generation. We also belong to many smaller groups called *reference groups*: friends, work colleagues, and classmates, for example. These people influence our attitudes and buying behavior, especially when it comes to products that are highly visible to others, such as clothing, golf clubs, sailboats, and wristwatches.[17] And our *families*—those we are born into and those we create through marriage—also direct our wants and needs. Today's trends of fewer children per family, more single parents, and more dual-income households all show up as wants and needs in the marketplace. For example, teenagers with working parents increasingly do the family grocery shopping and make brand choices for everyone. This explains why we see grocery products advertised during such television shows as "Beverly Hills, 90210."

Recall that *motives* also influence our buying behavior. In some cases, we seek relief from states of physiological discomfort, such as hunger and thirst. Other motives, such as the desire for prestige, belonging, pride, and recognition, are not directly linked to physical needs. In any case, it is not reality but our perception of reality that drives our behavior. *Perception* is the process by which we interpret what we see, hear, touch, taste, and smell. Businesses must work hard to ensure that the correct perceptions are created. As consumers, we

6. List and explain the external and internal variables in the consumer decision-making process.

may believe that we will live longer if we eat oat cereals, or that we will have more friends if we wear the Ralph Lauren Polo emblem on our clothes. What we perceive is what we *learn* to expect from a product, brand, store, or organization. When we compare possible purchase alternatives and judge them against our *expectations*, we form an *attitude*—a feeling of favor or disfavor—toward each choice. Marketers want us to have favorable attitudes toward their products, since these often lead to purchases.

All these external and internal factors come together in the *consumer decision-making process*, which begins with *problem recognition*, the point when you realize that you have an unsatisfied need or want. Maybe your car won't start, or you need a dress for an important date. To solve the problem, you usually first try an *internal information search*, recalling and relying on any information you already have about possible solutions. If existing information does not provide a satisfactory solution, you begin an *external information search* by consulting sources outside yourself—salespeople, friends who have had the same problem, and advertisements, for example.

Once you have acquired what you believe is sufficient information, you can make your *choice*. As Figure 14.3 shows, however, you do not stop with the purchase decision. A *postdecision evaluation* is also performed, in which you evaluate the amount of satisfaction you received from the decision. A positive experience will strengthen positive attitudes and increase the likelihood of a repeat purchase.

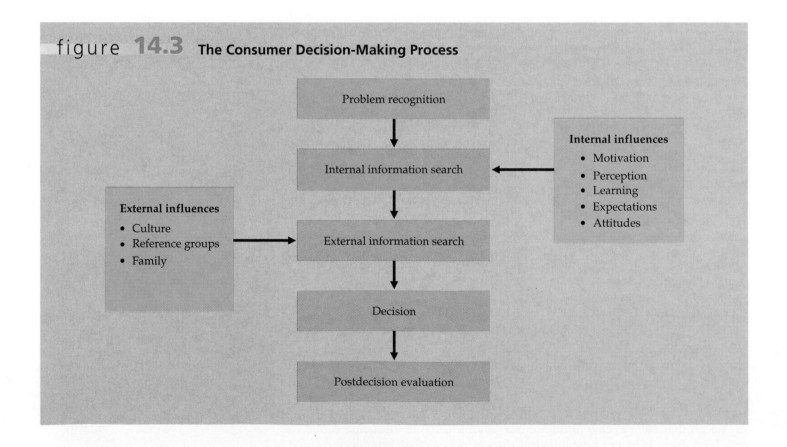

figure **14.3** **The Consumer Decision-Making Process**

Segmenting and Targeting the Market

Consumers are not identical, even within a small market. For example, in the toothpaste market everyone wants clean teeth. But some like the taste of mint and some do not. Some care most about plaque and others care most about

table **14.3**
Commonly Used Bases for Market Segmentation

Demographic characteristics
Age
Gender
Income
Occupation
Education
Family size
Religion
Race
Nationality

Geographic characteristics
Region
Climate
Population size

Behavioral characteristics
User status (nonuser/light user/heavy user)
Usage rate
Brand loyalty

Psychographic characteristics
Life-style: activities, interests, values, attitudes
Personality

Benefit characteristics
Principal benefits sought

brightness. Some want their children to avoid cavities, and others want to clean their dentures. In their effort to meet the needs of consumers, marketers divide markets into smaller segments whose members share characteristics that make their desires similar (see Table 14.3). This is **market segmentation**.[18] Separate marketing mixes, often including separate products, are developed to meet each segment's particular needs. In this way, the company is able to provide a marketing mix that "fits" a relatively uniform part of the total market. P&G offers Tide detergent for families with children who play hard outdoors. Its promotion emphasizes tough, powerful cleaning, which is just what this segment needs. In contrast, P&G's promotion of its Ivory Snow brand emphasizes skin safety and gentle washing—appropriate for families with babies in the house. And P&G has other options for other segments as well. Ariel is similar to Tide but is marketed to appeal to Hispanics. Oxydol with bleach is meant for people who wash a lot of white clothes or sheets. Dash is for those who care most about price, and Gain is for those who worry a lot about odor. A P&G spokeswoman explains the segmentation strategy for laundry detergents as follows: "*All* brands are formulated to offer good cleaning, but each offers different benefits to meet different consumer needs."[19]

7. Discuss five commonly used bases for market segmentation.

 market segmentation

Dividing markets into smaller segments whose members share characteristics that make their desires similar.

Demographic Segmentation

Demographic variables include age, gender, family size, marital status, race, religion, income, occupation, and education. Demographic variables are helpful to marketers in describing market segments because they are easy to measure and tend to be good indicators of consumer wants, needs, preferences, and product usage. Perhaps this is why demographics is the most common basis for segmentation. Consider these examples:

- Noting that the number of young adults aged 20 to 24 with skin problems now exceeds the number of teenagers with such problems, Richardson-Vicks introduced Clearasil Adult Care.

- Learning that 15 percent of cookware customers are male, San Francisco-based Williams-Sonoma, a 26-store cookware chain, purchased mailing lists from men's magazines such as *GQ* in order to boost its catalog sales.

- Coca-Cola's research found that children of working-class parents tend to gulp their drinks. The company then developed Mello Yello, a low-carbonated beverage, and called it "The World's Fastest Soft Drink."

Geographic Segmentation

Where consumers live influences many of their needs and wants. Knowing this Frito-Lay markets regional brands based on geographic preferences. Many of P&G's brands target geographic segments, too. Ariel detergent is the top-selling brand in Mexico, and it also sells well in Los Angeles, San Diego, San Francisco, Miami, and south Texas because of the large Hispanic populations in these regions. In contrast, P&G's Bold liquid detergent with fabric softener sells strongly in the Northeast, where hard tap water is a common problem. Bold is not even sold in other regions of the country.[20]

Marketers use nations, states, regions, counties, cities, and even neighborhoods as bases for segmentation. For example, New Englanders scoop up an average of 23 quarts of ice cream per person a year—more than consumers in any other region. In the sunny Southeast, the average is only 12 quarts. What you drink may also be influenced by where you live—the South, with 32 percent of the population, accounts for 48 percent of this country's tea consumption and only 21 percent of its wine consumption. People in the Northeast, with 22 percent of the population, drink 19 percent of the tea and 30 percent of the wine.

Behavioral Segmentation

Segmenting the market based on how consumers behave and think can be a powerful tool. A key behavioral segmentation is by product usage. Here marketers distinguish heavy users of a product or brand from light users and nonusers. Marketers who examine product usage rates often find the "80 to 20 principle" to be at work—20 percent of the market accounts for 80 percent of the sales. This "heavy half" is especially attractive to many marketers because identifying and measuring heavy users is often relatively easy, and they have a strong positive attitude toward the product or brand. Department stores, for example, can analyze their customers' buying behavior by scanning their charge accounts; banks can look at customer transactions and assess who is using their services.

Some marketers are more interested in nonusers than in the heavy users. Various cultural organizations seek new subscribers for lectures, concerts, and other events. The American Cancer Society continually urges people to have cancer checkups.

Psychographic Segmentation

Music is a highly segmented marketplace. For many, music and life-style interweave. Publishers of *The Source* market their magazine as "the only independent voice for the Hip-Hop Nation" as a way to target both readers and advertisers. *Source* advertisers know they are reaching target customers in their desired market segments as well.

Psychographic Segmentation

Marketers also divide the market into **psychographic segments** based on consumers' activities, values, attitudes, and interests. These combine to influence how consumers spend their time and how they feel about themselves and the world around them. In short, they describe consumers' life-styles and personalities. Many advertising campaigns reflect the results of psychographic segmentation. The macho cowboy of Marlboro cigarette ads is probably the oldest ongoing image resulting from psychographic segmentation.

Benefit Segmentation

Benefit segmentation is an increasingly popular and extremely powerful way of dividing the market by focusing on the primary benefit that the consumer is seeking. Benefit segmentation assumes that individual differences among consumers are the basic reason why different market segments exist. Buyers of Levi's jeans seek "durability"; buyers of Elmer's Glue-All want "adhesion"; and buyers of Lego Toys' building blocks are looking for "possibilities." A perceptive marketer once remarked: "Consumers do not buy three-quarter-inch drill bits, they buy three-quarter-inch holes." Benefit segmentation groups together consumers who want the same size holes.

Consumer Markets Versus Industrial Markets

A fundamental question for a company to ask when it is defining its market is whether it is servicing a consumer or an industrial market. **Consumer markets** contain the more than 260 million Americans who *ultimately* use the goods and

 psychographic segments

Division of the market based on consumers' activities, values, attitudes, and interests.

 benefit segmentation

Dividing the market by focusing on the primary benefit that the consumer is seeking.

 consumer markets

Markets that contain the more than 260 million Americans who ultimately use the goods and services produced in our economy.

✔ **industrial marketing**

Marketing that involves exchanges between the manufacturers that produce the goods and services that are sold to other firms for use in making finished products, which are then sold to the ultimate consumers.

services produced in our economy. Industrial markets include the over 8 million organizations that purchase the products and services used to make the final products that consumers buy. Although consumer markets are more visible than industrial markets, the industrial segment is far larger since it involves multiple transactions. There are more than 8 million industrial businesses in the United States, but fewer than 3 million retailers.[21] Industrial companies sell to one another in the production of finished products that, in turn, are sold to distribution companies.

Industrial marketing involves exchanges between the manufacturers that produce the goods and services that are then sold to other firms for use in making finished products; these are then sold to the ultimate consumers. For example, when Marriott Corp. purchases commercial kitchen equipment from a supplier, it uses that equipment to provide meals to its customers. Other types of industrial marketing include the purchase of industrial goods for resale to industrial buyers, governmental agencies, and not-for-profit institutions. Industrial buyers include many hospitals, universities, religious organizations, and senior-citizen centers.

How Industrial Markets Differ from Consumer Markets

8. Explain how industrial markets differ from consumer markets.

Industrial markets have characteristics that make them different from consumer markets:

- The demand for industrial goods is *derived from* the demand for consumer goods. For example, the demand for lumber depends on the demand for new houses, and much of the demand for steel is based on the demand for new automobiles.

- The demand for industrial goods is *less price-sensitive* than is the demand for consumer goods. For example, an industrywide price increase in tires will not stop automakers from putting tires on new cars—but it may stop some consumers from replacing old tires.

- Industrial purchases often involve a *long negotiating period*. A consumer product may be purchased in a matter of seconds, but months or years may elapse before a final sale is made of some types of industrial products, such as large machines for manufacturing.

- Industrial products are *purchased less frequently* and in *larger quantities* than consumer goods.

- Industrial markets used to be concentrated in *specific geographic regions*, reflecting the distribution of raw materials. Textiles, for instance, were produced throughout the South where cotton was grown, while oil production is still most intense in the Southwest because of rich oil deposits there. But globalization is broadening the focus on industrial markets. The key resources most often needed today by industry—expertise, information, technology—are more easily transferred between regions and countries.

- As a general rule, industrial buyers make *more rational purchase decisions*. They know their needs better than the consuming public does and are less swayed by the emotional components of a purchase. They look for products that will perform a specified function; they look for quality, price, and personal service and they use formal evaluation processes.

- Industrial buying is often carried out by a *buying center*, which includes all the individuals and groups participating in the industrial buying decision. The buying center for a computer system might include a purchasing agent, who processes the actual purchase; the engineering group that will use the new system; the company's computer experts, who will evaluate the alternatives; and the president, who will authorize the purchase.

Segmenting Industrial Markets

Industrial markets are segmented according to many of the same descriptive and behavioral components used to characterize consumer markets, especially demographics, usage rate, and benefits sought. For example, the specific industry, company sales volume, size of order, and number of employees are all used to divide industrial markets. Automakers segment industrial markets based on specific needs and uses, offering different products to the government (stripped-down versions), race car drivers (flashy models), and police departments (vehicles built for speed and endurance).

Selecting Target Markets

Market segmentation is like cutting up a pie. Once the pie has been cut and the marketer has targeted the piece of the market to go after, an appropriate marketing mix is developed. This process is called **target marketing**, and it usually consists of marketing directed toward those segments with the greatest potential for profit. This targeting decision must be made with great care for it is a matter of considerable importance.

Businesses that choose to target the largest segment face heavy competition. Consumers in that segment are often already very satisfied with the products and brands of competitors. A marketer's best choice may be a segment that has been neglected by the competition—one in which consumers are more likely to be dissatisfied with existing products and brands.

Dramatic changes in the marketing environment are making small, neglected segments more attractive. The last decade has been characterized by more intense price competition, increases in the number of brands and variations on existing brands, and rapid technological advances.[22] As a result, traditional boundaries between segments are blurring, and competition in major segments is becoming so intense that leaders find it hard to make a profit.[23] Marketers seek protection from these forces of change by **niche marketing**,

target marketing
Marketing that is directed toward the market segments with the greatest potential for profit.

niche marketing
Cutting up markets into smaller segments and targeting those that are least competitive.

9. Explain the process of target marketing.

which size keds® will your daughter be wearing when she notices the same thing?

Bonding with a Brand
According to the International Sports Marketing Council, women spend about $4.7 billion each year on athletic shoes, and they pay close attention to advertising messages. To connect its product with its target customers' values and core beliefs—and to promote a broader product line—Stride Rite Corp., maker of the Keds brand, launched this ad as part of a campaign called "Never Stop Growing."

doing business

Targeting the Snack Chip Consumer

The snack chip preferences of consumers are complex. Different consumers like different chips, and the chip makers are sensitive to these varied tastes. Pepsico's Frito-Lay is the most successful so far, with a 34 percent market share. The secret of Frito-Lay's success is hidden from public view in the "Potato Chip Pentagon," a well-guarded Dallas laboratory employing 500 chemists, engineers, and psychologists. Here they know which of 50 different chemical compounds make a chip that appeals to each segment of the chip market. They know that consumers like their flat chips to be 36/1000 of an inch thick; Ruffles taste best at 91/1000 of an inch. And they know the human tongue can distinguish a variation in thickness of as little as 14/1000 of an inch.

Research also focuses on the personalities of different chip buyers. Who likes Ruffles? Who likes flat chips? Tortilla chips? Its ad agency translates this research into personality profiles for each of the Frito-Lay products it advertises. Consumers of Lay's Potato Chips are "affectionate, irresistible, casual, and fun members of the family." They have pets. Ruffles eaters are "expressive, aware, confident enough to make a personal statement." Dorito Tortilla Chips chose ex-governors Ann Richards of Texas

and Mario Cuomo of New York to introduce its new bag and new shape during the 1995 Super Bowl.

The task of targeting the right group of consumers for each of Frito-Lay's 145 different brands falls to the advertisers. They must figure out how to communicate with—and appeal to—the target for each brand. Sometimes it is as simple as targeting regional preferences: Vinegar-flavored chips are a favorite in the Northeast, mesquite-flavored ones appeal to consumers in the Southwest.

The common theme in chip marketing is attention to positioning. After all, chips are a want, not a need. People do not need chips to survive. But in large part thanks to Frito-Lay's marketing, millions of people *want* them every day. In fact, Americans consume an average of more than six pounds of chips each in the course of a year, spending more than $4 billion dollars.

Sources: Based on "In the Chips," *Wall Street Journal*, March 22, 1991, p. B1; "Frito-Lay Sounds Call: Try One," *New York Times*, April 22, 1992, p. D22.

---

cutting up markets into smaller segments and targeting the least competitive of them.[24]

Another response to heightened competition is to seek new customers for old products. Women have become a major market force: 57 percent of women 16 years and older work, and 26 million households are headed by women. Marketers are now targeting them with products traditionally pitched at men—insurance, athletic equipment, beer, and cars. Toyota Motor Corp. sells close to 60 percent of its cars to women. Targeting women business travelers, Avis undertook a print advertising campaign with the tag line: "We make the road a little less lonely." Said a marketing executive at Avis, "We wanted to talk directly to women and say: 'We understand what is driving you.' But we did not want to say: 'We will only give you pastel-colored cars.'"[25]

Positioning the Product

10. Describe how companies position their products.

After a segment has been defined and targeted, companies use the tools of the marketing mix to create a core perception of their product in the mind of the consumer. Perceptions guide buying behavior. One of the main goals of marketing is to position a product or brand by communicating various messages to consumers that lead them to draw conclusions, or form perceptions, about it: Charmin is soft, Dove is for dry skin, Crest fights cavities. Ingersoll-Rand positions its door locks for consumers worried about safety; television ads pitch them as "The Doberman of Locks" (see the doing business box above). In this way, marketers establish a distinct place for a product or brand in the minds of consumers. This process of **positioning** uses the marketing mix to create a unique image of a product in the consumer's mind.[26]

 positioning

Using the marketing mix to create a unique image of a product or brand in the consumer's mind.

The shape and feel, brand name, packaging, advertisements, type of store that sells it, and even price help form the consumer's image of the product. Organizations attempt to position their products in relation to competing products and other products in the line. In some cases, products can be marketed successfully when they are positioned directly against similar products—by challenging the competition head on. The strategy is to find one or more characteristics that can be used to set the product or brand apart. Yogurt has been positioned as "healthful," diet soft drinks as "keeping America trim," and light (i.e., low-calorie) beer as "less filling." Consider the paper towel market. Most paper towels have established positions on the basis of absorbency. However, Viva, with the advertising slogan "keeps on working," pushed durability. Brawny soon followed with its positioning on the basis of strength.

When the number of competing products goes up, the consumer's mind gets crowded and it is harder to make your product stick in a distinct spot. Today, marketers struggle for a position in customers' minds, almost as if they were trying to tack notices onto an overcrowded bulletin board. Achieving a competitive position in the customer's mind takes a strong marketing vision that is implemented throughout the entire organization. In the following chapter, we will explore the most important of the four Ps, the product. We will see how businesses create and manage their products, from ideas to successful market entries.

Reviewing *The Role of Marketing*

The Nature of Marketing

1. **Discuss the marketing goal of promoting customer satisfaction, noting the types of utility.** Marketing focuses on understanding how the needs and wants of the marketplace can be satisfied. Satisfaction is provided through the five utilities—form, time, place, ownership, and information—and occurs through exchanges that are mutually satisfying to both the buyer and the seller.

2. **Define the marketing concept and describe how it drives the business process.** The marketing concept views the consumer as the focal point of the business and the source of company profitability. Thus, all business activities are centered on providing consumer satisfaction. This includes a growing emphasis on ethics and social impact, such as concern for the environment; an interest in not-for-profit organizations (hospitals and schools, for example); a concern for the consumer's long-term interests; and an extension of the concept to employees within the organization.

Marketing Management

3. **Describe the four Ps of the marketing mix and explain how companies enhance the mix.** The four Ps are product, price, place, and promotion. The product is the good, service, or idea that is designed, produced, and offered for sale; it may also include services such as installation and maintenance. The price is what the buyer must give up to receive the product. Place makes the product available when and where the customer wants it. Promotion communicates with the market to inform and persuade consumers. Today's competitive market makes it necessary for businesses constantly to monitor and perhaps change the mix. This may mean improving customer service: In product-oriented companies, this refers to better delivery, credit, and maintenance services, for example.

4. **Explain the role of environmental scanning in the marketing process.** Environmental scanning monitors the marketing environment and forecasts changes that represent opportunities or threats to the business. To maintain their advantage, marketers must scan the competitive market for generic form and brand competitors and must be aware of the tools used by competitors. Because most domestic markets have become global ones, businesses must be on the lookout for foreign competitors and for opportunities to market their product in foreign markets. Marketers must also monitor the technological, economic, political/legal, and natural environments that shape the conduct of marketing.

5. **Identify the forms of marketing research and list the steps in the research process.** Marketing research makes use of secondary data from various internal and external sources (magazines, newspapers, and so on) and primary data from surveys and focus groups. The steps in the research process are: Define the problem, identify the information needed and its sources, prepare a research design, collect data, analyze the data, apply the findings to the decision, and check the value of the information for decision making. The final step creates a learning loop to the research process.

Defining the Market

6. **List and explain the external and internal variables in the consumer decision-making process.** External variables include culture, reference groups, and families. Culture determines our values and feelings, and establishes acceptable rules of conduct. Reference groups and families direct our wants and needs, and hence our attitudes and buying behavior. Internal variables include motives, perception, and expectations. Motives involve both physical and psychological needs. Perception of a product—which may or may not agree with reality—determines our beliefs, which we compare to our expectations. This, in turn, leads to our attitude about a product.

7. **Discuss five commonly used bases for market segmentation.** Market segmentation may be based on consumer demographics, geography, behavior, psychographic factors, and benefits. Demographics, the easiest and most common method of segmentation, includes age, gender, family size, marital status, race, religion, income, occupation, and education. Benefit segmentation, an increasingly popular method, divides the market by focusing on the primary benefit the customer desires. Depending on the product, marketers will create separate market mixes for appropriate segments.

8. **Explain how industrial markets differ from consumer markets.** While industrial markets are segmented according to many of the same components used to characterize consumer markets, industrial markets differ from consumer markets in a number of ways: The demand for their product is derived from consumer demand; they are less price-sensitive; negotiating periods are longer; purchases are less frequent and in larger quantities; they are located in specific geographic regions; the decision making is more rational; and purchasing is often done through a buying center.

9. **Explain the process of target marketing.** Target marketing involves directing an appropriate marketing mix toward market segments with the greatest potential. However, targeting the largest market opens the company up to the heaviest competition. It may be beneficial, instead, for a company to target a smaller, neglected market. This is niche marketing. Target marketing may also mean finding new customers for old products.

10. **Describe how companies position their products.** Positioning uses the marketing mix to create a unique image of the product in the consumer's mind. Marketers use product features, brand name, packaging, advertisements, type of store that offers the product, and even price to position the product against the competition's products.

Key Terms

marketing **419**	transaction **423**	place **429**	market segmentation **437**
need **421**	marketing concept **424**	promotion **429**	psychographic segments **439**
want **422**	demarketing **425**	customer service **430**	
form utility **422**	relationship marketing **426**	environmental scanning **431**	benefit segmentation **439**
time utility **422**	internal customer **426**		consumer markets **439**
place utility **422**	four Ps **427**	marketing research **432**	industrial marketing **440**
ownership utility **423**	marketing mix **427**	secondary data **433**	target marketing **441**
information utility **423**	product **427**	primary data **433**	niche marketing **441**
exchange **423**	price **428**	market **434**	positioning **442**

• Review Questions

1. What are the various ways in which marketers can provide satisfaction to the market through the five utilities? Give an example of each from your own life.

2. What conditions are necessary for exchange to take place?

3. How is the marketing concept embodied in the societal orientation, relationship building, and internal customer approaches to marketing?

4. What are the four Ps? With examples, show how each can provide satisfaction.

5. What is environmental scanning? Discuss the environmental forces mentioned in the chapter that influence the decisions of marketers.

6. How do marketers obtain the information they need for marketing decisions?

7. What are the major influences on the consumer decision-making process? Give an example of each.

8. What is market segmentation and how is it accomplished? Discuss the various bases used to segment markets.

9. How does industrial marketing differ from consumer marketing?

10. How is positioning used? Give an example from your own life.

• Critical Thinking Questions

1. St. Vincent College in Latrobe, Pennsylvania, is located alongside an airport. The small liberal arts college recently began advertising in *Flying* magazine to parents who might like to jet in to visit their children. Which of the five utilities is addressed by this advertising approach?

2. How would you address the criticism that marketing makes people buy things that they don't need?

3. What major trends other than those noted in the chapter do you see developing in the social/cultural environment? Think of one type of organization that might be affected by each trend and predict how that change will influence the organization's strategy.

4. If you wanted to determine the feasibility of starting a coffee and donut shop in a corridor of your school building, what sources of information would you use?

5. In the corporate jet market, two leading companies, Gulfstream Aerospace Corp. and Avions Marcel Dassault-Breguet of France, offer top-of-the-line planes that are functionally similar. Gulfstream stresses its planes' longer range (5,000 miles versus 4,400), while Dassault emphasizes lower operating costs ($700 per hour versus $1,150 per hour for Gulfstream). How would you characterize this competition in terms of segmentation and positioning?

REVIEW CASE   *Wholesome & Healthy Foods, Inc.*[27]

Healthier diets are on the minds of 60 million Americans. Yet the huge and sophisticated marketer Archer Daniels Midland of Decatur, Illinois, has not been successful with its Harvest Burger, a mixture of soybean extract and water. With the consistency and physical appearance—but not the taste—of real hamburger, the burger has not sold well in spite of a five-year major television advertising campaign. Worthington Foods in Ohio, which has been in the meatless product business since 1939, has been equally unsuccessful with a soy-based line of products targeted at nonmeat eaters.

Paul Wenner thought he could do better. In 1984, when his restaurant failed, he started Wholesome & Healthy Foods, Inc., in Portland, Oregon, to sell the Gardenburger, a nonmeat burger made of rice, mushrooms, and vegetables. Gardenburgers contain 50 percent fewer calories and one-ninth the fat of a regular hamburger. Preparation is by frying or by toasting, as you would a slice of bread. Consumers claim the burgers aren't bad tasting, either. Gardenburgers possess a chewy consistency and a light vegetable flavor.

Wenner has done quite well. By 1994, he had 8,000 food outlets buying his product. Restaurants included the Hard Rock Cafe and Hollywood's Astroburger, where 10 percent of the 900 daily burger sales were Gardenburgers, even though they were priced a dollar higher than a regular hamburger. With success in restaurants under his belt, Wenner began to penetrate the supermarkets. Focusing on the Northwest and Southeast, Wholesome & Healthy Foods had distribution in close to 3,000 grocery stores by 1994.

Competition began to mount in 1994. Worthington Foods came out with its no-cholesterol Garden Vege-Pattie, a combination of brown rice, olives, and water chestnuts. And Minnesota's Fairmont Foods introduced entrees with no meat under the brand name Linda McCartney's Home Style Cooking (after Paul McCartney's wife, a vegetarian). Wenner's current goal is to supply McDonald's or Burger King and watch the sales roll in.

1. Describe the needs and wants that Gardenburgers are satisfying.

2. Which of the four Ps do you see being used by the companies in this case?

3. How would you segment the market if you ran Wholesome & Healthy Foods, Inc? What would be your target markets and how would you position Gardenburgers?

CRITICAL THINKING CASE *Time for a USA Swim?*

There's no brand identity in pools. We're still in that growing-up stage, like a teen-ager. If we had something called USA Swim, for example, a lot of small family competitors would be very frightened, but it would probably be very good for the industry.[28]

Rod Sterling, *president of swimming pool equipment distributor B-L Network, Inc.*

You are sitting at a large conference table, listening as the managers of a new company debate their marketing strategy. Your job, as assistant to the marketing manager, will simply be to write down the conclusions of this meeting. But you can't help wondering if they are on the right track: Will USA Swim Corp. really be able to establish itself as the McDonald's of swimming pools? Right now, the market for in-ground backyard pools has no major national competitors, but of course the burger business didn't either, before McDonald's.

Although there are 7 million in-ground pools in the United States, only 150,000 or so are purchased in a single year. These are generally made of concrete, fiberglass, or steel and aluminum, and cost on average about $25,000. In contrast, above-ground pools and spas go for an average of only $3,000. But the above-ground market is not considered important to USA Swim. Its goal is to push mid- to high-priced in-ground pools that use a special concrete liner guaranteed to last 20 years. The sales manager, a middle-aged woman who is busy arguing with the president at the other end of the table, was on the road all fall signing up distributors. You know that more than 200 independents (out of about 4,000 nationwide) have decided to join the USA Swim network, and many of them will be coming in to the company's new headquarters next month for training.

Your attention is brought back to the meeting as the room goes dark. The advertising manager stands to present the latest advertising concepts, clicking through color slides and explaining how the images would be put together in a national television commercial. Slides show a handsome, middle-aged man, the customer, dressed in casual but professional clothes. He talks earnestly to a pleasant-looking distributor. In the background you can clearly see the large USA Swim logo on the side of the distributor's van. The two men walk across an opulent backyard, pacing off the area destined for a pool. As they walk, the buyer explains his greatest fear—that the pool will begin to crack and leak after a few years, needing costly repairs. The distributor grins and explains the USA Swim guarantee. The final slide shows a technical diagram of the special patented liner that goes into all USA Swim pools. It ends with the company's new jingle: "USA. A better way to swim!"

Is this the right way to advertise the new company's product? The senior managers around the table begin to debate the question. As you listen to their arguments, you glance back through your file one more time, wondering if there is any information that might help answer the question. The market research shows that, in the target market of homeowners with a family income over $40,000 a year, 15 percent currently own a pool and another 1 percent say they intend to buy one. What about the other 84 percent? You wonder if they are important and how they can be encouraged to buy. You also note that Florida and California account for 40 percent of all in-ground pool sales, and you wonder how USA Swim's distribution and promotion ought to reflect this fact. Finally, you look at the sheet describing the buying roles played by different family members. Is it relevant that women make most of the initial calls to pool distributors? Research also shows that the whole family is involved in the purchase decision, and that women typically argue in favor of a pool while men more often raise objections to it. The decision is not a simple one for a family; it generally takes anywhere from 18 months to five years for a household to buy a new swimming pool. No wonder, you think, that 84 percent of households in the target market still have no pools!

Suddenly your thoughts are interrupted by your boss's voice. "Well, what did you think of the advertising concept? We're gridlocked on it, so you'll have to break the tie. Will it work, or not?"

1. Well, will it work or not? (Quick now, everybody's waiting.)

2. It occurs to you that the ad shows a man who evidently has already decided to buy a pool and just needs to choose the brand. What about the 84 percent who are not thinking about a purchase? You suggest to the group that the ad might convince others to buy if it also showed some of the benefits of owning a pool. Such as . . .

3. The managers' discussion has focused on pool buyers. But you think there are other people who influence sales and whose needs should be addressed by the television commercials, too. Explain your thinking to the group.

4. As you finish your comments, an idea for a different commercial comes to you—one that speaks to all the people involved in the purchase in ways that are appropriate to each of them, and one that might help USA Swim recruit new distributors as well as new pool buyers. Describe your idea briefly to the group.

Critical Thinking with the ONE MINUTE MANAGER

"You introduced us to the marketing concept by describing a not-for-profit organization that sells candles to help homeless people. I realize that marketing can be applied anywhere in theory, but in practice almost all of the marketing I see is done by for-profits. Isn't marketing really more appropriate to businesses that want to sell a product or service than to organizations that are trying to solve a problem like homelessness?"

"Marketing is a concept new to many not-for-profits, Carlos," agreed the One Minute Manager. "All across the United States, not-for-profit managers are studying marketing and trying to learn how to apply it to their businesses. I think you will see a lot more examples of marketing from such organizations in the future. And I bet you already see some. For example, have you noticed that the Veterans Administration, an agency of the U.S. government, is running radio ads right now to tell Gulf War veterans about some new health programs available to them?"

"Oh, I heard one of those on the radio this morning," Joanna said. "They gave out an 800 number for veterans to call for information. Do you consider that an example of marketing?"

"I bet you can guess my answer to that question," the One Minute Manager answered with a laugh.

Do *you* consider radio ads informing veterans of services to be a form of marketing? Explore your thoughts on the topic by answering the following questions:

1. Which of the utilities described in this chapter, if any, do health care services such as those of the Veterans Administration provide? (*Hint*: This concept may be difficult to apply to services, but *you* can do it!)

2. Do you think the concept of relationship marketing might apply to the Veterans Administration? How? (*Hint*: Do long-term relationships with customers make sense, and are the new services for Gulf War veterans an example?)

3. What is exchanged in a transaction between a Veterans Administration hospital and a patient?

4. Which of the four Ps is represented by the Veterans Administration's use of an 800 number? (*Hint*: Does it help move the product closer to the customer? Does it help communicate information about the product to the customer?)

5. Does the Veterans Administration define its target market in the same way a for-profit does? (*Hint*: Do the missions of not-for-profits and government agencies dictate who they market to?)

15 The Product and Customer Service

Organizations know that succeeding in today's competitive global marketplace means understanding what customers want and fulfilling those wants through extraordinary customer service. In this chapter, we examine the product—the first of the four Ps and the focal point of the marketing mix. You will learn how companies make their products stand out from the crowd, how new products are developed, the life cycle stages of the typical product, and strategies businesses use to manage their products. After reading this chapter, you will be able to reach the learning goals below.

Learning Goals

1. List and describe the three categories of products.
2. Describe what a business needs to understand about its product.
3. Explain the concept of customer service.
4. Describe how companies differentiate their products from those of their competitors.
5. Identify the four categories of consumer products and give an example of each.
6. Identify the three general categories of industrial products and give an example of each.
7. Discuss how businesses improve their products.
8. List and discuss the steps in the new product development process.
9. Describe the four stages of the product life cycle.
10. Describe the product strategies used by businesses to adjust to the product life cycle.

One Breakfast, Hold the Wait

"Hi, Joanna, good to see you again. How's the course coming?"

"Great, actually. We're about to study products, which should be pretty interesting."

"Say, speaking of products, I've got a great story for you. I stay at the Ritz-Carlton Hotel whenever I go to Boston, and last year I ordered breakfast from room service because I had to hurry out to a morning meeting. The hotel was wonderful, except for that breakfast. They delivered it forty minutes later, and I didn't have time to eat it. I complained to someone at the checkout desk, and on this visit I tried room service again to see if it was any better. It was. My breakfast came in twenty minutes, and there was a note with it that said, 'Sorry for the delay last year. Hope you like this service better!'"

"Wow. How did they remember?"

"It turns out they have a central computer database where they store all the information they get about repeat customers. When I checked in, they already had a file that included my past preferences and a copy of my complaint. And you know what else surprised me? When I checked out, the staff asked me if my breakfast had come quickly enough this time, then apologized again for last year's delay, and, get this—they took the cost of this year's breakfast *off my bill*. Now, that's fanatical service. And when your product is a service, that's all that counts!"

Joanna nodded her head in agreement. "It sounds like they recovered from their earlier error remarkably well," she commented. "But I wonder why room service was so late last year and whether they've been able to eliminate the problem altogether."

"As a matter of fact, Ritz-Carlton has done many things to improve its room service since my first visit. I just read about one of them in a *Success* magazine interview with the hotel's chief operating officer. One of the problems he discovered was slow elevator service in the mornings. Breakfasts were often delayed by long waits to get on an elevator. But why did the elevators take so long to come? To find out, he posted observers on each elevator, and they discovered that the elevators kept stopping for staff who were going from one floor to another, carrying towels."

"Towels?" Joanna looked at the One Minute Manager in surprise. "But why?"

"You are asking the right question, Joanna. Why did housemen, the employees who assist the maids on each floor, have to keep going to other floors to get towels? The answer is that the maids often ran out of towels. So, one of the root causes of slow room service was having too few towels on each floor. When the Ritz-Carlton bought more towels, the housemen stopped riding the elevators, and the number of room service complaints fell by 50 percent overnight."

The Product

The **product** is a good, service, or idea that is designed, produced, and offered for sale. It is the basis for any exchange. You exchange money for a new truck, baby-sitting time for a home-cooked dinner, a vote for a promise of better government. Regardless of the form of the exchange, what you are buying is *satisfaction*. Products come in a wide range. They may be pure goods (for example, roofing nails); a combination of goods and services (such as dinner at an expensive French restaurant); or a pure service (a lawyer's advice). As Table 15.1 shows, goods, services, and ideas differ in the ways they provide satisfaction.

1. List and describe the three categories of products.

table 15.1 A Comparison of Goods, Services, and Ideas as Products

Product	Characteristic	Example
Good	• Tangible • Permanent • Standardized • Not reliant on customer participation	• A fax machine • A knife sharpener • A BMW • McDonald's french fries
Service	• Intangible • Impermanent • Nonstandardized • Reliant on customer participation	• Telephone directory assistance • Snowplowing • Long-distance moving • Photo processing
Idea	• Intangible • Impermanent • Standardized • Reliant on customer participation	• "Think Before You Drink" • "Stay in School" • "Vote" • "Give Blood"

Goods

Goods are *tangible*; they can be seen, touched, or tasted. They also tend to be *permanent*; they last and can be stored, at least for a while. Goods usually come in *standard forms* or sizes; you can be fairly certain that two stores will offer the same size of roofing nails and that the nails will not rust in the rain. Finally, goods don't depend on *customer participation*—that is, they remain the same no matter who buys them. Consumers tend to prefer tangible products;[1] we like to see what we are getting for our money.

Services

Services provide satisfaction in the form of some function a seller performs directly for a buyer—mowing grass, managing investments, flying a jet plane. Services are intangible and impermanent—they do not last and cannot be stored. Every time the curtain goes down on a theatrical performance, its life as a product ends. Nor are services standardized. The quality of the service you receive in an exchange may be considerably different from the quality of the service another person receives, as many people discover when they accept a friend's recommendation for a car repair shop. Services are high in buyer participation[2]—they are much more dependent on the interaction between the seller and buyer than are goods.

 product

A good, service, or idea that is designed, produced, and offered for sale.

ethics check

Unintended Consequences?

To rejuvenate Camel cigarettes, an unfiltered brand introduced in 1913, R.J. Reynolds Tobacco Company (RJR) added filters, introduced lowered tar and nicotine Camel Lights, packaged its brands in boxes as well as soft packs, and developed a successful advertising campaign around the character Joe Camel, shown here on a billboard with his Hard Pack Band.

In 1994, *Science News* reported that Joe Camel was recognized by more than 90 percent of American 6 year olds surveyed, the same percentage who recognized Mickey Mouse. Critics say that survey results like these prove that RJR is targeting people under 21 in its cigarette advertising. The company maintains that its Camel marketing campaign is directed to adults.

What do you think? Should RJR drop the campaign? Consider both sides of this issue. Do you believe that Joe Camel's recognition by young children is an unintended consequence of a successful marketing campaign? If you worked for RJR, how would you justify the appeal of Joe Camel to people under 21? If you worked for an organization such as the American Cancer Society, marketing the idea that smoking poses health risks, how would you counter the appeal of Joe Camel?

Ideas and Other Forms of Products

Marketers also market ideas. For example, idea marketers discourage some practices, such as smoking cigarettes and killing animals for their skins, and encourage others, such as safe sex and measures for creating a cleaner environment. People, organizations, and places are marketed, too. After all, movie stars, political parties, and tourism are big business.

How an idea, organization, or place will be marketed depends on its characteristics. Take a message like "Cigarettes are bad for your health." Is this more a good or a service? It is like a service in three ways. It is intangible—you cannot touch it. It is impermanent—the message on the package of cigarettes is quickly read and then forgotten. And it certainly requires high buyer participation—you have to act on the thought for it to have any value. But like a good, it is usually marketed in a standardized form. The U.S. Surgeon General specifies that health warnings must appear in the same way on every pack of cigarettes. The ethics check entitled "Unintended Consequences?" examines the kind of marketing campaign that anti-smoking messages are meant to counter.

Might the "quit-smoking" idea sell more easily if it were not standardized? Can you think of other ways to market it?

Understanding Your Product

2. Describe what a business needs to understand about its product.

Whatever you are marketing—good, service, or idea—you have to understand what your customer expects to buy from you. Of course, you must have some ideas about this, or you wouldn't be offering the product in the first place. You can clarify those ideas by asking four questions:

- What problem does the product solve?
- What benefit does the product provide?
- Does the product satisfy physical or psychological needs and wants?
- Is the product tangible or intangible?

These four questions in turn offer useful insights for product management and improvement.

Is This Product a Good, a Service, or Both?

This mobile fitness center comes to your home for workouts. To pinpoint how this product provides satisfaction to customers, answer the four product analysis questions: What problem does the product solve? What benefit does the product provide? Does the product satisfy physical or psychological needs and wants? Is the product tangible or intangible?

What Problem Does the Product Solve?

Many products provide satisfaction by offering a solution to a problem. L'Oreal's styling mousse solves one of hairstyling's weightiest problems—how to hold hairdos firmly in place without sacrificing the hair's natural texture and color. Merrell Dow's Nicorette, a nicotine-laced chewing gum available by prescription only, satisfies the smoker's craving for nicotine, but in a nontobacco form. Quicksilver Messenger Service in Chicago solves the problem of transporting business documents between companies by means of bicycle messengers. Few marketers have understood this role of a product better than the cosmetics genius Charles Revson, founder of Revlon, who said, "In the factory we manufacture cosmetics, but in the drugstore we sell hope."

What Benefit Does the Product Provide?

Recall from Chapter 14 that one way to break markets into smaller segments is to study the benefits that particular groups of consumers are looking for. These benefits may be the most important reason a person buys your products. For instance, an individual purchasing a tennis racket may be seeking power more than anything else. To provide this benefit, the racket must offer high tension in the strings, a metal frame, and a heavy handle.

Does the Product Satisfy Physical or Psychological Needs and Wants?

Products may satisfy physical needs, psychological needs, or both. Harley-Davidson, Inc., reversed years of sales declines by packaging its motorcycles as a life-style. To attract aging baby boomers, the company started Harley Owners' Groups (HOGs), where bikers can exchange tips with other bikers. It offered magazines and clothing and even sponsored biker rallies. The company even took this concept abroad, translating its magazines into foreign languages, sponsoring rallies in Europe, and opening its own stores in Japan that sell nothing but Harley clothing and accessories. Overseas sales of Harley motorcycles now account for one-fourth of company sales. Harleys offer more than a two-wheeled vehicle—they offer the satisfaction of an alternative life-style.

Is the Product Tangible or Intangible?

Generally, goods—pillows and hand soap, for instance—are thought of as tangible. Services and ideas are considered intangible. But things usually aren't that simple; most products are both. Consider, for example, the way Shoe Carnival, Inc., sells shoes. The chain's 39 stores throughout the small towns of the Midwest display Rockport, Reebok, and Hush Puppies. That's the tangible part; the intangible part of the product is the magicians and clowns who roam balloon-filled aisles, the '50s music that pours out over the sound system, and various competitive events. For example, customers can win a T-shirt for having the most keys on their key chain, or can join in a Big Toe contest where the prize is scooping cash from a glass bowl known as the Money-Machine. Said the owner, "In some of these towns, we are the Friday night fights and the Saturday afternoon matinees. People love to buy new shoes because it makes them feel good. We are just making it fun."[3] Intangible fun and tangible shoes add up to a product that generates 64 percent more sales for the Shoe Carnival than for the average U.S. shoe store!

You can apply the four product analysis questions to a good, a service, an idea, an organization, or a place. They work for *any* product. For instance, the message that cigarettes are bad for your health helps solve the *problem* of how to warn cigarette buyers. Its *benefit* is the better health smokers can enjoy by cutting back or quitting. It provides both physical and psychological satisfaction—but only when a smoker quits. And the product, being a message, is *intangible*. In terms of marketing, the most difficult part to sell is probably the deferred, hard-to-achieve satisfaction that the idea of quitting smoking offers.

Customer Service

3. Explain the concept of customer service.

Successful companies now realize that whatever their product, they must surround it with extraordinary **customer service**—paying attention to every detail in the process of delivering satisfaction. Customer service is a companywide commitment that means more than satisfying the customer. It means pleasing and delighting the customer, often with the unexpected. A business consultant captured the essence of customer service–driven companies: "They have to make heroes and heroines out of the people who use their products."[4] Consider these examples:

- By joining Hertz's #1 Club Gold program, members can avoid airport lines. They reserve the vehicle by phone, jump on the shuttle, tell the driver their last name, and get dropped off at their car. They know it's theirs because their name is in glowing lights above it!

- Home Depot offers low, low prices for its hardware products, but service is the real difference. The company trains all salespeople in home repair techniques and encourages them to spend as much time with customers as necessary to help them solve their repair problems.

- Knowing that summer is vacation time for nearly everyone in France, Nestlé built rest stops along the main roads. At all times of day, trained hostesses offer free samples of Nestlé baby food, free diapers, and other forms of travel assistance. These areas have become social gathering spots.

To offer superior customer service, you have to analyze the entire process of buying and using a product. Customer service means treating customers with courtesy, listening intently to their desires, correctly supplying the requested product, delivering it on time, and following up to make sure the customer is satisfied. And when the customer is an intermediary or other business buyer, customer service entails knowledgeable salespeople calling with just the desired frequency, efficient and error-free handling of all orders, perfect

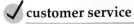

customer service

Paying attention to every detail in the process of delivering satisfaction.

doing business

Ritz-Carlton to New Employees: "We Don't Want You to Work for This Organization"

Ritz-Carlton Hotel Company probably offers the best product in its industry. It certainly offers the *most quickly improving* product, since it applies the principles of total quality management (TQM) to every aspect of hotel operation. So what might it be like to work there? If you asked its one-time dishwasher apprentice, and now president and chief operating officer, Horst Schulze, you might be startled to hear him say, "We don't want you to work for this organization." To find out why he says this, let's take a closer look at what it's like to work at one of the Ritz-Carlton hotels.

Your first seven days on the job will be devoted to training, probably conducted by senior managers, including Mr. Schulze himself. When he first meets new employees, he likes to tell them, "I'm president of this company; I'm very important. But so are you. Equally important." If you don't believe Mr. Schulze at first, you certainly will by the end of the week, when you learn that you have the authority to solve customers' problems, even if it means spending the company's money to do so. With this authority comes *responsibility*. You will learn in your training that you have just 10 minutes to call customers back after they call with a complaint, and that you must *solve* the problem, to their satisfaction, within 20 minutes. Period.

In the first three days, your training will focus only on the company's philosophy of customer service and its general principles. For instance, you will have to memorize the company's credo, which specifies that good service means achieving a high-quality relationship by ensuring that customers have a wonderful, beneficial experience at the hotel. And you'll learn the three steps of service: Greet guests warmly by name, anticipate and meet all their needs, and give them a warm farewell, also by name.

As the week wears on, you will begin to receive formal training in job-specific skills. But your training will have just begun. You will be tested on your job skills every year and must achieve and maintain certification to retain your job.

Your big day arrives. You are now a concierge, responsible for helping guests solve problems, use the hotel's services, or arrange travel plans and events. After glancing at the computer to find the name of the guest who just checked into the hotel, you walk over to give her a warm, personal greeting as she heads across the lobby. She thanks you and asks where the rest rooms are located. You smile to yourself at the thought that this is the first customer problem that you, a highly trained college graduate, are being called upon to solve. And then you . . .

What *would* you do? Politely offer directions? Wrong! Even if the doors to the bathrooms are clearly visible, you smile at the guest and say, "Right this way, Ms. Thomas," and then lead her to the entrance to the rest rooms.

Congratulations! You have just done a really good job of making that customer feel welcome and comfortable. And, as a Ritz-Carlton employee, you would be satisfied with nothing less. That's why employees submit twice as many complaints and suggestions to management as do customers. You know Mr. Schulze was right when he said, "We don't want you to work *for* this organization. We want you to be *part* of this organization."

Source: Cheri Henderson, "Putting on the Ritz," *The Quality Yearbook* (New York: McGraw-Hill, 1994).

product packaging, and always having the correct balance in the customer's account. In short, it means eliminating all problems and hassles throughout the entire process of buying and using the product.

In successful companies, every employee understands that full customer satisfaction is important, and every employee is intensely and personally interested in keeping the customer happy. All company personnel who come in contact with customers must have the authority and motivation to do anything it takes to improve customer satisfaction. The Ritz-Carlton hotel chain is one company that works hard to maintain its reputation for service and quality. This means that all employees begin their jobs by participating in a two-day orientation program followed by an additional 100 hours of customer training. They learn to warmly welcome each guest every day, saying "Good morning" or "Good afternoon," never "Hi" or "How's it going?" Expected to act as responsible professionals caring for other professionals, employees are permitted to spend up to $2,000 to resolve a guest's problem without asking for authorization! Said Ritz-Carlton's director of quality, "One of our biggest challenges

✓ **product differentiation**

Creating the perception of product superiority in the minds of consumers.

✓ **brand**

A name, term, symbol, or design (or a combination of these) that identifies a firm's goods or services and differentiates them from those of competitors.

✓ **brand name**

The words, letters, or numbers that identify a brand.

✓ **trademark**

A brand that is legally protected for exclusive use by its owner for as long as the owner uses the brand.

✓ **generic name**

The name for an entire product category.

4. Describe how companies differentiate their products from those of their competitors.

Consider the term "Internet." The Patent and Trademark Office, which grants trademarks to companies, has so far refused to grant trademarks to companies that wish to use the term "Internet" in their name. The Federal agency believes the term should be used generically, at least for now.

is to prevent any difficulties from ever reaching the customer."[5] Companies with such a focus design all their activities to ensure that the customer's experience exceeds in satisfaction any encounter he or she may have with the competition. Read the doing business box "Ritz-Carlton to New Employees" to learn about the company's training philosophy.

Differentiating the Product

Once you understand your product and have committed yourself to exceptional customer service, **product differentiation**—creating the perception of product superiority in the minds of consumers—is easier. Actual products may not differ much, or at all, but differentiation depends on the consumer's belief that they do. This perception leads to a preference for one product over another, and businesses create that perception by adjusting the marketing mix.

The main way businesses create value is by providing something that is superior—a product that is newer, better, faster, or lower in price. Differentiating on the basis of newness means offering a good, service, or idea that solves consumer problems in ways that never existed before. Think about how handy 3M's Post-it notes are. Products that outperform competitors' products differentiate on the basis of being better. For example, Callaway Golf Company improved golfers' games with its "Big Bertha" driver golf club, which has a 25 percent larger head size but weighs no more than traditionally sized drivers. Owner Ely Callaway offered his approach to differentiating: "Just make a better product and tell the truth about it."[6] Faster means bringing products to market or delivering them to customers more quickly. Some companies simply offer buyers the lowest price. Being known only for having the lowest price is not always the best approach, however, since consumers often equate low price with low quality. A better strategy is to add real and perceived value by being newer, better, or faster so that customers equate price with quality.

To work well, differentiation does not demand a whopper of a difference, but it must rest on a solid understanding of what consumers desire and value. Some organizations do institute major changes. Many hospitals, for instance, are moving from the mission of treating the sick to that of promoting "wellness" through aerobics, karate, and aquatic programs. Other companies make seemingly minor adjustments, as Coca-Cola did when it reintroduced its original glass bottle. Businesses often use brands and trademarks, packaging, labeling, and warranties to make their products stand out from the crowd.

Brands and Trademarks

A brand like Macintosh or Crayola can be a company's most valuable asset. A **brand** is a name, term, symbol, or design (or a combination of these) that identifies a firm's goods or services and differentiates them from those of competitors. A **brand name** consists of words, letters, or numbers that identify a brand—FedEx, Mercedes-Benz, ABC. To test the power of brand symbols, fill in the blanks in Table 15.2.

A **trademark** is a brand that is legally protected for exclusive use by its owner. This legal right lasts as long as the owner uses the brand. Trademarks include the name Mickey Mouse; the "nickname" Chevy; Dean Witter's slogan, "We Measure Success One Investor at a Time"; and the black and copper-top color combination of a Duracell battery.

Companies work hard to protect their brand names. It may seem a compliment when a brand name becomes so well known and so closely associated with a particular use that it becomes mistaken for a **generic name**—the name for an entire product category. Kleenex, for example, is the Kimberly-Clark

Corp. brand name for facial tissues, but over time, people have come to use it to refer to all facial tissues. The danger for a company such as Kimberly-Clark is that it can lose its legal right to exclusive use of the name. That would be a very expensive compliment!

Brands can be classified on the basis of ownership. A **national brand**, also called a manufacturer's brand, is a brand owned and marketed by its manufacturer. General Mills, Kraft General Foods, and General Electric are national brands. **Private brands** are created and owned by dealers—wholesalers or retailers. A&P's Ann Page, Montgomery Ward's Signature, and Wal-Mart's Sam's American Choice are examples. Each of those private brands is distributed and promoted more widely than many national brands.

A struggle is occurring between national brands and private brands. Throughout the 1980s, sizable promotional spending by marketers caused consumers to favor national brands for their prestige. As a result, national brands could command a higher price. But with the recession of the early 1990s, consumers abandoned national brands in droves in favor of cheaper private labels that they perceived as offering better value. Retailers began aggressively positioning their private labels as direct competitors of national brands, and more and more consumers realized that the quality of many private brands had improved significantly. In retaliation, manufacturers cut their prices to compete.[7]

A **family brand strategy**—using the same brand name for all of a company's products—can help a business expand its product line. RJR Nabisco, for instance, has complemented its LifeSavers line with LifeSavers Holes and LifeSavers Gummis. Arm & Hammer uses its name on its baking soda, heavy-duty detergent, and toothpaste. The ultimate in family branding is the *world brand*, a single brand name used throughout the world. This strategy has been successful for Sheraton hotels, Coca-Cola, and Levi's. British Airways is advertised almost identically in over 30 countries—only the language changes.

An **individual brand** is applied to only one product. It is appropriate when the firm's products vary in quality or type. Thus, Colgate-Palmolive markets Fab detergent, Baggies food and trash bags, Handiwipes, and Pritt glue sticks. Individual branding allows brands to be differentiated and targeted at particular market segments. PepsiCo's Slice can be targeted at the health-conscious segment while Diet Pepsi can be focused on the weight-conscious segment.

Branding offers marketers the opportunity to differentiate their product. A consumer who has a favorable experience with a brand is likely to repeat the purchase. In the same way, a bad experience will lead a consumer to purchase another brand. Marketers of brands work hard to ensure good quality, since estimates indicate that it costs six times more to obtain a new customer than to retain an existing one.[8]

Consumers gain from branding, too. Shopping is easier because well-known brands are easily identified and their quality is consistent from place to place. Some branding even benefits society as a whole. *Passion branding* links brands to social issues. For example, Ryka donates 7 percent of the price of its women's athletic shoes toward fighting violence against women; FTD supports the Children's Miracle Network.

Consistent quality in a brand is often difficult to achieve. Can you imagine the difficulty of keeping fresh bananas consistent in quality? But that is what Chiquita must do if it wants to maintain a following for its brand. Developing an effective brand name is also costly. It may involve extensive market testing, huge promotional expenses, and higher prices for consumers. Many businesses today are *co-branding* to share costs. General Mills markets its Betty Crocker dessert mixes by touting brand-name ingredients: Kraft caramels, Hershey's chocolate syrup, and Sunkist lemons. Kellogg's Pop-Tarts are promoted as being made with Smucker's fruit filling.

table 15.2

Demonstrate Your Product Awareness

Brand symbols offer consumers a quick way to identify companies. How many of these symbols can you match with their company?

Symbol	Company
a) Peacock	___ Kellogg's
b) Mr. Peanut	___ NBC
c) The Poppin' Fresh Doughboy	___ Pillsbury
d) Big red K	___ McDonald's
e) Golden Arches	___ Planter's

national brand

A brand owned and marketed by its manufacturer; also called a manufacturer's brand.

private brands

Brands created and owned by dealers—wholesalers or retailers.

family brand strategy

Using the same brand name for all of a company's products.

individual brand

A name applied to only one product.

✓ **packaging**

All the activities related to designing and producing a product's container or wrapper.

✓ **labeling**

Some means—packaging or a tag—for providing information about a product.

Packaging for Product Differentiation

Unique packaging gave Arizona brand iced tea a competitive advantage in the crowded beverage market. Arizona's distinctive aluminum cans, with their attractive, Southwestern motif, offer customers more for their money—16 ounces rather than 12, at about the same price in most stores. Arizona's manufacturer, Ferolito Vultaggio & Sons, a small brewing company in Brooklyn, New York, sold nearly 250 million cans in its first year on the market. At last count, Arizona customers in 40 states were downing 12 million cans each month.

Packaging

Packaging includes all the activities related to designing and producing a product's container or wrapper. Packaging, which is a big business today, not only identifies brands, it also differentiates them. Kraft General Foods' International Coffees line and Keebler's chocolate chip cookies are now encased in packaging that emits mouthwatering aromas. Packaging has always protected goods on their way to the consumer, but now businesses are attempting to protect the environment as well. The plastic packaging of compact discs, for example, was reduced to cut back on waste.

Packaging can differentiate among products by making a brand easier to use and thereby increasing consumer satisfaction. Through focus group research, BASF Wyandotte Corp., a New Jersey–based chemicals company, discovered that the standard antifreeze bottle is easy to carry out of the store but not easy to use. The firm responded with a "no-glug jug" that lets in air and allows the user to control pouring with one hand. With its angled top, the bottle can clear the engine block and other parts that otherwise make it difficult to get to the radiator cap. The new bottle, which answers specific consumer complaints, was offered exclusively to STP for the marketing of STP Antifreeze & Coolant. The packaging gave STP's product a market advantage.

Packaging can also increase product safety. We are all familiar with childproof bottles for drugs. In a similar vein, Johnson & Johnson has created value (and a competitive advantage) by designing a Tylenol bottle that is easy for older consumers with impaired grip strength to open.

Labeling

The main purpose of **labeling** is to provide information about the product. A label may be printed as part of the packaging, or it may be on a tag attached to the product. Some labels identify the quality of the product by a letter ("Grade A"), number ("No. 1"), or word ("prime" or "choice"). Other labels give instructions for the care, use, or preparation of a product ("Keep away from heat or direct sunlight"). Still others merely explain the important features or benefits of a product.

Unit pricing labels show the price per unit of standard measure (weight or volume), allowing consumers to compare the value of competing products. *Open dating labels* tell consumers the expected shelf life of the product. *Nutritional labeling* discloses the amount of nutrients and calories in processed foods. Processed foods, patent drugs, some cosmetics, textiles, and numerous other products are required by law to carry a fairly complete list of ingredients.

Under the Nutrition Labeling and Education Act of 1990, food producers must inform consumers of their products' contents in a uniform way, so that nutritional similarities between various food categories as well as within food groups can be easily compared. The hope is that this will enable consumers to plan an entire, nutritionally balanced menu. At Pillsbury, a division of British food giant Grand Metropolitan PLC, millions of dollars have been spent on re-designing more than 2,600 labels on ice cream containers and on vegetable, frozen dinner, and pizza boxes. Pillsbury rushed its redesign program to grab some product differentiation and a competitive advantage by appearing on the market way ahead of the competition.[9]

Labeling helps businesses manage their inventory. The Universal Product Code (UPC)—the bar code read by electronic scanners at the checkout counter—enables merchants to update inventory levels in their main computers automatically, so they can know what's selling and when to reorder. The scanners also print out the name of the product and its price information on your receipt. Electronic scanning greatly speeds up the checkout process and decreases the chance of error.

Warranties

The definition of customer service tells us that the job is not yet over when the product has been purchased. A **warranty** is a legal guarantee that a manufacturer's product will serve the purpose for which it is intended. Warranties provide the purchasers of a product with some psychological satisfaction by assuring them that defective products will be fixed or replaced. Even when they are not stated, however, certain rights are always guaranteed to consumers by law. In addition to these implied rights, sellers may offer express warranties that specify the exact conditions under which a manufacturer is responsible for the product's performance. Such warranties protect both the buyer and the seller.

Warranties are usually offered for high-priced or complex products, such as household appliances, electronics, and automobiles. These products are bought infrequently, and the warranty is often the factor that closes the sale. Figure 15.1 shows how warranties and other product attributes combine with customer service to differentiate the core product.

warranty

A legal guarantee that a manufacturer's product will serve the purpose for which it is intended.

Remember from Chapter 4 that implied and express warranties are consumer protections by which businesses are legally bound. An implied warranty *legally guarantees that a product is fit for normal use, even when there is no written* express warranty *offered on the product.*

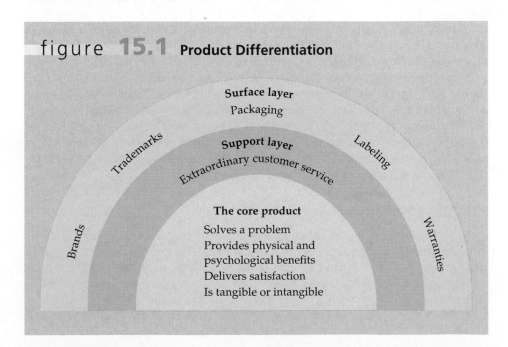
figure 15.1 **Product Differentiation**

Surface layer
Packaging

Trademarks

Support layer
Extraordinary customer service

Labeling

Brands

The core product
Solves a problem
Provides physical and psychological benefits
Delivers satisfaction
Is tangible or intangible

Warranties

Classifying Consumer Products

5. Identify the four categories of consumer products and give an example of each.

Firms classify their products by focusing—as all marketers should—on the buyer. From Chapter 14 you already know the two broadest categories: *consumer products*, destined for use by ultimate consumers, and *industrial products*, used in the production of other goods and services (see Figure 15.2). Based on shopping behavior and consumer preferences, consumer products can be classified as convenience, shopping, specialty, or unsought products.

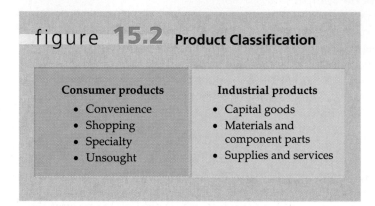

figure **15.2** **Product Classification**

Consumer products
- Convenience
- Shopping
- Specialty
- Unsought

Industrial products
- Capital goods
- Materials and component parts
- Supplies and services

Convenience Products

Convenience products are inexpensive goods and services that consumers purchase frequently and want to buy with the least possible effort. Consumers typically do not seek information about convenience products. Examples include chewing gum, milk, gasoline, banking services, and parking. Some convenience products—banking, for instance—tend to be purchased on regular shopping trips. Although some planning may be involved, banking is rather routine. Consumers may care a great deal about the brand of convenience products, but the key issue is usually whether they are available at convenient locations. Have you noticed how many bank branches and gas stations there are?

Convenience goods, services, and other product forms are often bought on impulse. The door-to-door Greenpeace solicitor who requests a donation to save dolphins from fishing nets is offering you a convenience product. Store owners who place items like candy, novelties, and magazines near the cash register are counting on sales from impulse buying. Disposable cameras are a hot new convenience product, pioneered by Fuji Film in Japan. Most sales are made to consumers who left their camera at home and have a strong desire to capture a memory on film but are unwilling to buy a costly new camera. An $8 to $10 model becomes an inexpensive option at such times. Said a consultant, "Don't think of it as a camera, think of it as convenient film."[10]

Shopping Products

A search for information by the consumer is the distinguishing feature of **shopping products**—goods and services that consumers purchase after carefully comparing price, quality, and service. Consumers may visit several stores, consult *Consumer Reports* magazine, ask friends for their opinions, or compare advertisements as they search for information about the price, quality, and features of two or more brands or substitute products. Furniture, appliances,

 convenience products

Inexpensive goods and services that consumers purchase frequently and want to buy with the least possible effort.

 shopping products

Goods and services that consumers purchase after carefully comparing price, quality, and service.

most clothing, and repair services of all kinds are examples of shopping products. Vacation spots, charitable organizations to which large sums will be donated, and political candidates to whom financial support will be given are all shopping products.

Specialty Products

Specialty products are goods or services for which there are no acceptable substitutes in the consumer's mind. Buyers have usually conducted an information search, decided on the product they want to buy, and are willing to search long and hard until they find it. Brand name is extremely important here. In fact, it may be most of what the consumer buys in a specialty product. Many people will buy only Heinz ketchup, give only to their favorite charity, allow only one dentist to work on their teeth, or vote only for their party's ticket. These people will not accept substitutes.

Of course, one person's specialty product may be another person's shopping or convenience product. Consider pantyhose. Most women treat this product as a shopping good—until they get a sudden snag just before an important meeting. At that point, pantyhose becomes a convenience product.

Unsought Products

Unsought products are goods and services, such as new products, that consumers do not know they want or need. Recent examples include antioxidant vitamins and interactive television. Hospitals, convalescent homes, and cemetery plots are other unsought products, as are little-known alternative rock bands, hidden-away vacation places (such as the Green Islands off the coast of Brazil), and emergent social causes. Consumers do not shop for such things until the need or want arises.

Classifying Industrial Products

The marketing of industrial goods and services entails a different emphasis from consumer goods. Sales calls by salespeople knowledgeable about industrial products are important—products often are expensive and may need to be customized to the particular needs of the buyer. Conveyor systems and assembly lines, for example, must be tailored to the buyer's organization. Functional satisfaction is more important than psychological satisfaction because industrial

 specialty products

Goods or services for which there are no acceptable substitutes in the consumer's mind.

 unsought products

Goods and services, such as new products, that consumers do not know they want or need.

Unsought Product, Untold Benefit

When Mothers Against Drunk Driving (MADD) began its campaign to stop motorists from drinking and driving, it created an unsought product: highway safety. MADD's marketing increased public awareness of ever-growing numbers of traffic deaths involving drunk drivers, popularized the "designated driver" by changing attitudes about personal responsibility, and encouraged stricter law enforcement. National brewers such as Coors and Anheuser Busch launched their own personal responsibility campaigns with slogans such as "Think Before You Drink." The result—fewer alcohol-related traffic deaths nationwide.

products are purchased to do a specific job. And price, while important, is less critical than the product's ability to fulfill the industrial buyer's need. Availability and delivery time are very important to ensuring that assembly of the finished product is not held up.

Industrial customers buy a huge variety of goods and services. Industrial goods can be classified in terms of how they come into the production process and how costly they are.[11] Three general categories can be differentiated: capital goods, materials and parts, and supplies and services.

Capital Goods

Capital goods are expensive, durable items used in the production of finished goods. These goods support the production of the finished product rather than becoming part of the final product. Capital goods may be either installations or equipment. *Installations* are the factories and offices that allow the industrial business to operate. They are bought infrequently, usually after a long negotiation period. Competitive bidding is common, and the seller's representatives usually work directly with the buyer.

Equipment includes both movable factory equipment and tools (forklifts, drills) and office equipment (photocopiers, desks). It has a shorter life than installations and is purchased in small quantities. Industrial purchasers look for product quality and features, availability, delivery time, price, and service in deciding which equipment to buy.

Heavy equipment includes products ranging from tractor trailers to $100 million oil-drilling rigs. Such products require large capital outlays, and the selection of a supplier may be influenced by a wide range of factors. These include strict conformance to the buyer's specifications; the supplier's service capabilities; the amount of technical assistance provided by the supplier at the time of installation; the ability of the purchased equipment to supplement or replace existing equipment; the amount of worker retraining required to use the new equipment; and the effects on production costs. Suppliers of heavy equipment must provide complete information about the equipment and satisfy numerous buyer concerns before a purchasing decision can be made.

Light equipment includes such items as forklifts and personal computers. These items generally cost less than heavy equipment and require less research on the part of the purchaser. Light equipment is often standardized and is marketed to a wide range of industries. Demand for these items is influenced by such factors as the personal preferences of those who will use them, speed of delivery, and the service capabilities of the supplier.

Materials and Parts

Materials and parts are the various goods that come together in the producer's finished product. They include raw materials, processed materials, and manufactured materials and parts. Some raw materials are cultivated on farms (grains, fruits, and vegetables); others are extracted or harvested from their natural environment (oil, lumber, and fish). Farm products are seasonal and perishable and need special marketing practices. Producers generally sell them to intermediaries, who combine them with the produce of others and then store, transport, and sell them to manufacturers. They, in turn, use the farm products in the production of food products. Naturally occurring products are limited in supply. Because of their great bulk and low unit value, transportation to the buyer becomes a major task. These products are usually marketed directly to the buyer by the seller. Because natural products are generally seen as commodities and have little differentiation, price and delivery ability are the major decision criteria.

---

6. Identify the three general categories of industrial products and give an example of each.

✔ **capital goods**

Expensive, durable items used in the production of finished goods.

Processed materials are standardized goods that can be sold to a variety of industrial customers. Examples include coal, office furniture, and packaging materials. These products are marketed in the same way as other industrial goods—that is, through sales calls and, when very large quantities or long-term contracts are involved, through competitive bidding.

Manufactured materials and parts consist of component materials (yarn, wire) and component parts (small motors, tires). Component materials are usually fed through some production process to fit the manufacturing need. For example, steel is cut and bent in the buyer's plant to meet the finished product's specifications. Price and delivery reliability are key with these usually standardized industrial products.

Component parts are incorporated directly into the finished product without any additional change in form. Tires are placed directly on the wheels of a new car, for instance. Other component parts include the microchips and circuit boards used in personal computers. These parts are generally purchased directly from the manufacturer, and orders are often placed a year or more in advance.

Demand for component parts is influenced by factors quite different from those that affect demand for heavy and light equipment. Because a component part becomes an element of the final product, demand for the final product has a major impact on demand for the component. The selection of a supplier of component parts is influenced by timeliness of delivery, availability of discounts, and the extent to which the supplier can conform to specifications and quality standards and match the technological capabilities of other suppliers.

Supplies and Services

Supplies and business services are industrial products that last a short time and enable the finished product to be developed and produced. Supplies include *operating supplies* (stationery, heating oil) and *maintenance and repair supplies* (brooms, paint). Supplies are the convenience products of industrial marketing. They are purchased with little effort and at specified times. Distributors provide these industrial products and sell them on the basis of price and service, since they are perceived to vary very little from supplier to supplier.

Business services include *maintenance and repair services* (cleaning, copier repair) and *advisory services* (professional advice). Maintenance and repair services required to keep production going are known as support services. They are generally obtained under contract with small producers, and many repair services are supplied directly by the manufacturer of the original equipment. Without sufficient support services, a business can be brought to a standstill. Advisory services vary from one buyer to another. They include legal, accounting, and tax services. They are usually bought on the basis of the seller's reputation and ability.

Improving the Product

No product is immune to change. Every successful business introduces new products and improves the old ones. Improvements tend to occur in the areas of quality, production speed, and customer service.

7. Discuss how businesses improve their products.

Quality Improvement

To improve products, businesses must improve quality. Quality improvements are possible in two areas: the design of the product itself, and the manufacturing and delivery of the product. To better serve business travelers, some hotels have added special rooms featuring free fax machines, hookups for laptop

Teaming Up to Introduce a New Product

Merry Go Round clothing stores joined forces with PhoneCard Express ™ to market fashion and phone cards. As an incentive to shop at the Merry Go Round, customers received with their purchases a free, prepaid card good for 10 minutes of long distance calls. Through this promotion, PhoneCard Express was able to introduce its prepaid phone card to potential customers in a major target market.

computers, office supplies, and voice mail. Today's products must stand on unparalleled quality. Motorola saved $1.5 billion in one year by analyzing its production processes to reduce product defects. American automakers are busy adding that "European luxury-car solidness" that gives customers a sense of confidence and security.[12]

Speeding Products to Market

Businesses also achieve product improvement by designing and producing products faster. Mattel Inc. brought its Top Speed toy cars to market in just five instead of the usual eighteen months; Hewlett-Packard brought its printer out in two years, compared to the typical four. When businesses cut the time it takes to bring a new product to market, they can beat the competition and offer improvements to their customers before their competitors do.

Customer Service

A crucial source of product improvement is customer service. Video and compact disc customers at Blockbuster Entertainment need never fear that their favorite selection will be unavailable. They just step up to a vending machine–like kiosk, select the desired title, and the recording is automatically duplicated on a blank tape or disc for immediate purchase. In the industrial sector, DuPont has an "Adopt a Customer" program. Assembly line workers visit their customers once a month and act as their representatives on the factory floor. These two examples illustrate the value of building a special customer relationship through customer service.

New Product Development

✓ **new product development**

Determining what customers want and developing a product to satisfy that want.

New product development involves determining what customers want and developing a product to satisfy that want. The product may be a wholly new product (Retin-A cream, Post-it Notes), a new brand (Arizona Iced Tea), or an improved or modified product (Fab Ultra laundry detergent, AcuVue disposable contact lenses). To succeed at new product development, a company must

Creativity Break for New Product Ideas

Product developers can easily get stuck in a rut, unable to think of good new-product ideas. The following activity gives the team or individual a "creativity break" to brainstorm silly ideas; more often than not, one of these silly ideas turns out to be a diamond in the rough that leads to a new product breakthrough!

1. Pick a common product. For example, lipstick.

2. Describe its current use or uses. How do customers use it and benefit from it?

3. Brainstorm a long list of silly alternative uses. Examples: makeup for pets, Halloween makeup for kids, writing graffiti, highlighting passages in your textbook.

4. Pick the best one and transform it into something that could really be a product. For example, a retractable pocket highlighter in a case like a lipstick.

5. Answer the three concept development questions: Who will buy the product? What is the primary benefit of the product? Under what circumstances will the product be used?

Good work. You just invented a new product!

- Listen to customers.
- Figure out what it does best.
- Understand how it devises and markets its new products.
- Chart the path of the product through the company and into the hands of the user.
- Forecast the way the competition is likely to react.[13]

Today, successful new product development rests on understanding and managing the entire business process, including how engineers make product designs into prototypes (product models), how assembly line functions are coordinated, and how marketing campaigns operate.[14] Success also requires teamwork, the blending together of all the different perspectives within a company.[15] It means speeding up the process by working on tasks simultaneously rather than one at a time. It means taking new risks and learning new ways of solving new product development and production problems.[16] (See the skills check "Creativity Break for New Product Ideas" to learn how product developers brainstorm.)

Taking those risks and winning can be highly rewarding. Just look at the success of Motorola's Micro TAC cellular phone, North Face outerwear, and the Fox TV network. And new products can be rewarding for companies, as well. Consider Apple Computer's quest for a laptop product. Its first portable Macintosh was an engineering feat and a marketing fiasco. Loaded down with options, the machine weighed in at a market-repelling 17 pounds! To improve its product, Apple sent its entire research and development team—industrial engineers, software developers, marketing managers, and designers—into the market to observe users of competitors' laptops. Said the design team head, "We looked at other notebooks and saw that they were still really desktop units, only made smaller. We asked the question, 'How do people use it?' The answers drove the product."[17] The result: a billion dollar seller, the Apple Powerbook.

Creating and bringing a successful new product to market is difficult and costly. It took Gillette 10 years and $200 million to introduce its Sensor razor. The development of General Motors' Saturn automobile cost $5 billion. The new-product graveyard is littered with expensive casualties: Ford's Edsel ($250 million), Procter & Gamble's Citrus Hill orange juice ($200 million), Steven

Jobs's NeXT computers ($200 million). Research findings on the failure rate for products vary greatly according to product category, how a new product is defined, and how product failure is defined (market share, profits). A recent study of the success rate of 11,000 consumer products introduced by 77 manufacturers found that 56 percent were still on the market after five years.[18] And the new-product failure rate for industrial products is lower than for consumer goods.[19] Giants like Ford and Procter & Gamble can absorb an occasional product failure, but a single failure can put a small firm out of business. New product development is part art, part science.

New product development is a problem-solving exercise that takes advantage of learning from earlier experiences of product development. Traditionally, new product development occurred in a sequence of steps. After designers finished their job, the engineers took over until the product was ready for manufacturing. Then it was handed over to marketing. This made for dozens or even hundreds of steps. Now these activities are usually conducted in a streamlined, overlapping process with four general steps: idea generation and screening, concept development and business analysis, product development and testing, and commercialization (see Figure 15.3). At any step, a potential product may fail to make the grade. Let's look at the specific issues and tasks involved in each of these steps.

Step 1: Idea Generation and Screening

Idea generation involves identifying problems customers are having and suggesting solutions for them. These solutions become the kernels for new products. The source of a new product idea may be a customer, a supplier, or an employee. In industrial firms, salespeople in contact with customers are well positioned to know the competition's products and what customers like and dislike. Warner Electric Brake and Clutch has its sales force report the three best ideas they hear each month. General Electric awards $2 million annually to employees with successful product ideas, and 3M gives trophies and certificates to employees with good ideas. Toyota receives 2 million ideas a year, nearly 35 per employee. In addition, a firm's scientists and technicians make discoveries that lead to new products. And of course, companies analyze competitors' products, mining them for ideas.

Consider how General Motors' Oldsmobile Division began its search for a car design to stem its flagging sales. Early in 1988, Oldsmobile held "customer clinics" with owners of European luxury cars to understand what they liked and disliked about cars like BMW and Mercedes-Benz. Performance and quality were at the top of the "likes" list. Drivers enjoyed the leather seats, wood paneling, smooth acceleration, and four-wheel disc brakes. They also loved something hard to verbalize, that European characteristic of solidness and quietness that gives drivers a sense of confidence and security.

Quickly, GM engineers investigated the cause of this "European feel," measuring vibration and chassis rigidity in the European imports. Meanwhile, designers began sketching concepts for a new car. In 1989, consumer reaction was wildly positive to a fiberglass model, and the Aurora design was born. But the manufacturing engineers had to wrestle with some knotty production problems. To iron them out, a rotating team of 50 hourly workers collaborated with the engineers to plan production over a three-year period. These assembly line workers accounted for 80 percent of the major manufacturing changes.

Once a large pool of ideas has been generated, the next step is to reduce it to a more manageable size. Three general *criteria for screening ideas* are useful:

- The idea must meet an unsatisfied want or need, making for sufficient market potential to predict profitability.

8. List and discuss the steps in the new product development process.

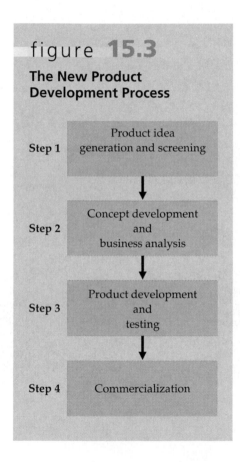

figure 15.3

The New Product Development Process

Step 1 — Product idea generation and screening

↓

Step 2 — Concept development and business analysis

↓

Step 3 — Product development and testing

↓

Step 4 — Commercialization

- It must fit into the overall direction of the business, its business strategy and mission.
- It should build on the company's distinctive resources and skills—financial, technological, managerial, and marketing.

The purpose of screening is to eliminate poor ideas as early as possible. Since new product development costs can soar at each step of the process, weeding out ideas with little or no potential can save substantial costs. This is particularly important because, as ideas get further along in the process, companies become wedded to them because of their investment.

Step 2: Concept Development and Business Analysis

Throughout the stage of idea generation and screening, product developers work only with a general product concept. In the second stage, they make that idea more specific. Many companies are creating teams of engineers, designers, and production people to provide different angles on the concept. Black & Decker calls them "fusion teams" because they make ideas come together into products. General Motors has established a Vehicle Launch Center, where its newly established project teams of marketers, accountants, and planners spend almost a year learning the process of new product development. As a GM engineer put it, "We stay on the learning curve. We take all the knowledge we gain and apply it on the next vehicle, so we never make the same mistakes twice."[20]

To understand product specifics, the project team investigates the answers to questions about sales and use such as the following:

- Who will buy the new product?
- What is the primary benefit of the new product?
- Under what circumstances will the new product be used?

After the idea becomes more formed, consumers' reactions need to be obtained. Boeing designed its 777-200 airplane by actually asking its airline customers to join the design team. Customers made over 1,000 suggestions that lowered the cost, made the plane more "passenger friendly," and reduced maintenance. Because of this extreme involvement of Boeing's customers in the development process, toilet lids no longer crash down, doors are easier to operate, and individual seats have their own video monitors.

Business analysis, also performed at this stage, is a detailed, realistic projection of maximum and minimum sales and costs and their impact on the company's financial health. Many companies require that new products show minimum sales or profit levels in the business analysis. Sometimes the rules for meeting such "by-the-numbers" criteria can be too confining. Campbell's Prego spaghetti sauce almost failed its business analysis. Corporate policy required a new product to show a profit in one year, but Prego was not expected to be profitable for three years. Some smart managers who realized that this one-year policy would hold back the development of a good product changed the rules, and Prego has become a successful product.

Step 3: Product Development and Testing

Now the new product concept becomes tangible and concrete. One or more test models, or *prototypes*, are made and tested. The project team develops brand names, packaging, and other elements of the marketing mix such as distribution, promotion, and pricing alternatives.

doing business

Ford Mustang Skunk Works

The Mustang redesign broke all the rules at Ford.

Senior managers had already analyzed the market and looked at the cost of updating the car for modern tastes and safety regulations. In 1989, they declared it not worth the investment. But a renegade product developer named John Colleti and a select group of 400 teammates—that's actually a very small number for a new car team—managed to save the car. They convinced a vice president that they could redesign it in less time, with fewer people, and for less money. Their plan was simple, but it broke all of Ford's rules for product development. Instead of building endless prototypes, the team modeled designs on computer. Instead of working in a long sequence of handoffs, everyone worked together: production specialists and financial analysts, engineers and stylists, all sharing ideas and solving problems in real time. And instead of a long, competitive bidding process, the team just picked its favorite suppliers and brought them to the table, too.

Everything went well until the chief engineer, Michael Zevalkink, took the first prototype of the convertible for a test drive in the summer of 1991. On the computer it drove like a dream. But on the track, it shimmied and shook. Would there be time to fix the problem?

Fifty members of the design team huddled together to try. Brian Skocaj, who represented supplier Augat Wiring Systems on the team, remembers, "That was a major turning point in the program. We knew immediately that we were talking about major structural revisions." But the very factors that made the team different gave it the ability to handle this challenge. Its members were used to collaborating. They were accustomed to finding ways to cut time out of the process. They were used to creative problem solving and rule breaking.

And they weren't afraid to benchmark other people's good ideas. Don't tell anybody who drives a Mustang convertible, but one of the breakthroughs was invented by Mercedes engineers! A member of the design team happened to ride in a Mercedes convertible and wondered why it had such a smooth ride. So the team bought one and took it apart. The secret? A small steel weight, positioned behind the front fender, where it damps vibrations like a finger on a tuning fork. The result? A successful new product and a whole new style of product development at Ford.

Source: Joseph White and Oscar Suris, "New Pony: How a 'Skunk Works' Kept Mustang Alive—On a Tight Budget," *Wall Street Journal*, Sept. 21, 1993, pp. A1, A12.

The development of the Boeing 777-200 used innovative approaches to development and testing. This largest of twin-engine airplanes was developed completely by computer. The project teams were multinational, with employees worldwide taking part in the process. Japanese partners linked via high-speed data communications worked on the design of the fuselage from thousands of miles away. And work continued around the clock across the different time zones. This electronic design process resulted in half the usual changes and errors expected in airplane design. Most airplane product development entails very expensive mockups to test the electrical systems. Boeing's computer-aided design system eliminated that step completely.

Prototypes that pass muster will sometimes go into test marketing, where the product is actually sold in limited, selected markets. Marketers measure consumer reactions and evaluate the probability of success in larger markets. Businesses know that test marketing can yield valuable information, but it is costly and time consuming. Under pressure to get new products on the market (for seasonal or competitive reasons, say), many companies forgo test marketing. Even when this happens, successful companies continue to consult their customers. General Motors used its "clinic" to obtain customer feedback on the Aurora throughout its development. Boeing used computers to stay in constant contact with its airline customers/product development partners. The doing business box "Ford Mustang Skunk Works" gives an example of an innovative approach to product development and testing.

Step 4: Commercialization

The biggest investment in production and marketing ocurs during commercialization, or full-scale production and distribution to the target market. BMW, the German car maker, invested $400 million to build a new plant in Spartanburg, South Carolina, so it could produce 90,000 cars annually by 1995. Mercedes-Benz built a $300 million plant in Alabama. Companies launching consumer packaged goods can spend between $20 million and $80 million on promotion in the first year.

Usually companies do not begin national or global distribution all at once. Rather, they *roll out* the new product, moving from one geographic area to another. A rollout makes it possible to spread the substantial costs of a new product launch over a longer period and to fine-tune production and marketing as the rollout progresses.

✓ product life cycle

A four-stage process that begins with new product development and ends with the removal of the product from the market.

Product Management

Product management involves monitoring the target market and adjusting the product to the changing preferences of consumers. Frito-Lay, for example, might add more nacho flavor to its nacho cheese chips if its research disclosed that consumer preference. There are so many things to manage, however, that we need a general strategy to make the right choices clearer. How does a firm select a product strategy? Its most useful tool is the **product life cycle**, a four-stage process that begins with new product development and ends with the removal of the product from the market.[21]

Product Life Cycle Stages

The length of the product life cycle varies, depending on the product. Fad products—remember Rubik's cube?—have a short life. Other products—Liquid Drano and the Grateful Dead—enjoy long product lives. As shown in Figure 15.4, the product life cycle has four stages: introduction, growth, maturity, and decline.

9. Describe the four stages of the product life cycle.

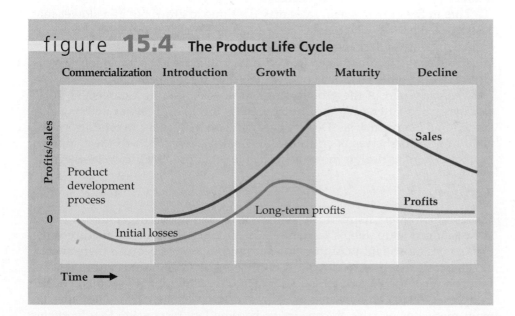

figure **15.4**   **The Product Life Cycle**

Introduction

Aside from fads and monster movie hits, most products in the introduction stage have slowly rising sales (shown in the figure as a slowly rising curve). Potential buyers generally resist change and are reluctant to buy until the risk of purchase is reduced. Product introduction is marked by high advertising costs because marketers have to get the word out. The promotion objective is to *reach and teach*—to tell as many potential buyers as possible that the product is available. This builds awareness of the entire product class (video telephones) rather than a particular brand (AT&T). The costs of making an impact are high. The major marketing objective is to develop widespread awareness and induce trials of the product. Interactive television, genetically altered tomatoes, and electric cars are all products in their introductory stages. There are few competitors, and the major problem for marketers is finding new customers.

During the introduction stage, frequent modifications to the product are often necessary to work out the bugs. These changes may range from slight adjustments in the product's style, color, or size to major overhauls. Pricing is usually either high to appeal to price insensitive buyers who want new products, or low to appeal to the mass market. And profits are nonexistent because the heavy expenses of product development and introduction exceed the low level of product sales.

Growth

Products that survive their introduction enter a stage of rapidly growing sales and profits. This rapid growth reflects the rising popularity of the product as large numbers of consumers begin to buy it. Competitors are attracted and enter the market with new product features, hoping to imitate the new product's success. The first major product adjustments occur as these competitors seek product differentiation. Cellular telephones and fax machines are currently in the growth stage.

Profits are healthiest now as heavy promotion costs are spread over a large volume of sales. Promotion emphasis switches from product acceptance to brand preference. Prices can differ in different geographic regions. Distribution becomes the critical marketing activity. Without adequate distribution and dealer support, products cannot adequately compete. Creating solid dealer relationships becomes the key to success at this stage.

Late in the growth stage, sales may continue to grow, but at a slower rate. Just about everyone who wants the product now has it. Companies introduce annual models and change styles to stimulate replacement sales, and they lower prices to capture greater sales. Product lines are cut back to lower costs. Under these conditions, some competitors leave the market.

The early part of the growth stage focuses on getting established in the market. In the latter part, the strategy shifts to building loyalty among consumers and intermediaries. Dealers become crucial because the product's availability on retail shelves is critical to new sales. To hold on to their support, promotion targets dealers more often than in other product life cycle stages.

Maturity

The product enters its maturity when sales level off. Refrigerators, running shoes, canned soup, tennis rackets—most products—are in the mature stage. Companies must fight to capture sales from competitors because there are few new customers left to recruit. Cost cutting becomes the route to profits. The number of competitors stabilizes. The market becomes highly segmented, and companies design promotional programs for each segment. Price becomes the main motivator of sales as consumers become less responsive to advertising and other forms of promotion. To urge retailers to continue pushing the products, promotion is again heavily targeted at dealers.

Many businesses with mature products seek new markets and untapped market segments, new product uses, or ways to stimulate increased use of their product by existing customers. Attention is given to improving the quality of the product, at least as far as its superficial features are concerned. But significant new features can be added as well. For example, Goodyear Tire's new product development laboratories designed the Aquatred, a tire with a deep center groove and unique tread design that pushes water out in jets from underneath. The design prevents hydroplaning on wet roads. The Aquatred became Goodyear's most successful new tire ever.

As products mature, companies must look for new products to offset their approaching decline. Most companies try to add new products regularly so that they have offerings at all stages of the product life cycle.

Decline

The sales of most products and brands eventually decline. As sales turn downward, profits usually decrease and competitors leave the industry. During decline, companies wring out whatever profits can still be made before the

table **15.3** **Characteristics of Stages in the Product Life Cycle**

	Introduction	Growth		Maturity	Decline
		Early	Late		
Strategic objective	Build awareness and induce trials	Brand loyalty, strategic positioning	Market share, strengthen distribution channels	Find new markets or new uses	Obtain all possible profits and then drop
Competitive environment	Few competitors	Heavy competition, new entries	Competitive shakeout, price competition	Market stabilizes, highly segmented	Competitors drop out
Product	Few product variations, product adjustment	Product differentiation, product adjustment	Product lines cut back, style changes	Emphasis on product quality, reducing costs	Few changes
Place	Establish distribution channels	Secure and expand distribution channels	Build dealer loyalty	Dealer loyalty imperative	Phased out
Price	Skimming or penetration pricing	Different prices for different segments	Pricing becomes a form of promotion	Pricing to meet competition and maintain volume	Stable, resistance to price cutting
Promotion	High expenditures	Build demand	Promotion to wholesalers and retailers	Promotion to wholesalers and retailers	Promotion minimized

product is dropped. At this stage, businesses do little to change the product's style, design, or other features. Prices tend to hold steady and may even rise if a loyal market segment continues to buy the product. An example is the William Marvy Company of St. Paul, Minnesota, the only remaining manufacturer of barber poles. The few people who still want barber poles really want them, and without any competitors the company can price higher than when the product was growing. In other cases, prices may decrease as the firm seeks to reduce inventories.

Distribution outlets are phased out during the decline stage as they become unprofitable. The few consumers who still want the product will seek it out, so promotional expenditures are also cut. Table 15.3 summarizes the characteristics of the four stages of the product life cycle.

Tailoring Product Strategy to Product Life Cycle Stage

10. Describe the product strategies used by businesses to adjust to the product life cycle.

Rare is the company that develops only a single product. The selection of products that a company offers to consumers is called its **product mix**. For example, Procter & Gamble's product mix includes detergents, toothpaste, bar soap, disposable diapers, and facial and toilet tissue, among others. Within the product mix are groups of products that are similar in terms of use or characteristics. These are called **product lines**. Within its detergent product line, Procter & Gamble offers Ivory Snow, Dreft, Tide, Cheer, Oxydol, Dash, Bold, Gain, Era, and Solo. Product lines must be managed with care so that viable products are kept competitive, poor products are eliminated, and new products are brought out to ensure the firm's survival and growth.

Product Assortment

Variations within a product mix are called its *assortment*. If the mix includes varied product lines—foods, household cleaners, shampoos, and other grocery products—the assortment is *wide* or *broad*. If it contains only a few, related product lines—snacks—the assortment is *narrow* or *limited*.

Throughout the product life cycle, the business can focus on changing an existing product line, on adding or deleting lines from a product mix, or on changing the features offered within a product line. Especially during the growth and maturity stages, companies strive for balance in their product mix. Thus, while sales of some products or brands are fading, sales of others are increasing. Businesses use the following product strategies to balance product life cycle stages within the product mix.

Full-Line Versus Limited-Line Strategy

Companies can employ a **full-line strategy**, offering a large number and wide assortment of product lines, or a **limited-line strategy**, offering only a limited set of products. Businesses usually introduce products as limited lines, and expand to a full-line strategy in the growth stage.

Many businesses believe that a full-line strategy gives them a competitive advantage. It's true that a full line of products enables a company to meet a wide variety of market desires. But the danger is that a company with too wide a product assortment will not be able to give each line the attention it needs. If this strategy is relied upon in place of sound managerial judgment, it can lead to poor planning, product failures, and lost profits.

Pepsi-Cola has overemphasized a full-line strategy. It has been rolling out an increasing array of beverages to target small market segments, from Crystal

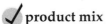

product mix

The selection of products that a company offers to consumers.

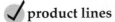

product lines

Groups of products within the product mix that are similar in terms of use or characteristics.

full-line strategy

Employed by companies offering a large number and wide assortment of product lines.

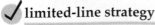

limited-line strategy

Employed by companies offering a limited set of products.

Tailoring the Product Mix

These S.C. Johnson & Son, Inc., product lines illustrate the company's focus on a narrow product assortment. Customers buy S.C. Johnson products to clean and freshen their homes, and to usher out uninvited pests. How does the S.C. Johnson product mix illustrate the limited-line, full-line, line extension, and brand extension strategies?

Pepsi to iced tea and fruit juices to sports drinks. These products take advantage of the strength of the Pepsi brand. But some believe this line-filling strategy has distracted the company from its flagship cola product lines, Pepsi and Diet Pepsi, which account for 60 percent of its profits. Said a distributor, "Last year, they put too much effort on Crystal and not enough on Pepsi. I want to see them concentrate more on regular Pepsi and Mountain Dew—the things we build our business on." The company CEO agrees: "Our people can only execute so many things. If they're building extra Crystal displays, they can't build as many Pepsi displays."[22]

Line Extension and Brand Extension

Line extensions are new variations on growing or mature products. For example, H.J. Heinz has taken one of its oldest products, vinegar, doubled its acidity, and repackaged it as a detergent called All Natural Cleaning Vinegar. A **brand extension strategy** takes the brand name from one product category and uses it in another. Usually the new category is similar to the old one,[23] as when Häagen-Dazs extended its rich ice cream to the "extra sinful" Exträas and RJR Nabisco extended its Oreo cookies to "Reduced Fat" Oreo cookies. Sometimes the brand is applied to a completely new product category, as when Stouffer extended its restaurant brand name to frozen foods and hotels.

Brand extension has two advantages. The cost of introducing the product is much lower because consumer education has already taken place. Promotional expenditures therefore produce greater consumer awareness and recognition of the whole brand, not just one product. Moreover, risk is reduced because the new product's image is already established. And should the product fail to take hold, the loss will be smaller because developmental costs were low.

Repositioning

Companies attempt to change the consumer's perception of their brand or product by using a **repositioning strategy**. Repositioning involves advertising and promotional campaigns.[24] Many businesses have repositioned their products as

line extensions

New variations on growing or mature products.

brand extension strategy

Taking the brand name from one product category and using it in another.

repositioning strategy

Attempting to change the consumer's perception of a brand or product through advertising or promotional campaigns.

✓ planned obsolescence

Intentionally forcing a product to become outdated in an attempt to increase replacement sales.

healthy, touting "no cholesterol," "low in sodium," and "high fiber" in their advertising. Other companies reposition by changing the product or packaging. To position its facial tissue as environmentally friendly, Scott Paper Co. offers tissues made from 100 percent recycled paper. 3M introduced Scotch-Brite Never Rust soap pads made from recycled plastic fiber. Companies that use repositioning strategies must be careful not to confuse the consumer about the product's position.

Planned Obsolescence

Businesses sometimes use the strategy of **planned obsolescence**, or intentionally forcing a product to become outdated. Although this sounds like a good way to lose money, it actually increases replacement sales in the maturity stage of the product life cycle.

Planned obsolescence can take a number of forms. Some products, such as batteries, pantyhose, and razor blades, are actually built to last only a limited time. Technological improvements can eliminate the demand for other products. For instance, when compact discs became available, phonograph records became obsolete. A planned obsolescence strategy may be applied if technological improvements are available but are not introduced until the demand for existing products declines and inventories are depleted. Gillette followed this strategy when it held back on the introduction of Teflon-coated razor blades until consumers' interest in chromium blades had peaked. Style changes, too, can cause obsolescence. A changed physical appearance makes existing versions appear out-of-date. This type of obsolescence strategy is most obvious in the garment and automobile industries.

What's your opinion of planned obsolescence? Is it unethical?

Planned obsolescence, especially style obsolescence, is strongly criticized for encouraging the purchase of products that may not really be needed and for creating the impression that businesses are taking advantage of consumers. Marketers counter this criticism with the argument that people desire change.

Reviewing *The Product and Customer Service*

The Product

1. **List and describe the three categories of products.** The three categories are goods, services, and ideas. Goods are tangible and permanent, they come in standard forms, and they do not depend on customer participation. Services, on the other hand, are intangible and impermanent, are not standardized, and depend on customer participation. Like services, ideas (also people, places, and organizations) are intangible and impermanent, and they depend on customer participation. Like goods, they are standardized.

2. **Describe what a business needs to understand about its product.** To successfully market a product, a business must understand the customer's expectations. This includes understanding what problem the product solves, its specific benefits, which customer needs or wants it satisfies, and whether a tangible product involves intangible elements (such as service). Knowing this information is useful for product management and improvement.

3. **Explain the concept of customer service.** Customer service is a companywide commitment to pleasing the customer by delivering the unexpected. Superior customer service means eliminating all problems and inconveniences for the customer throughout the entire buying and consuming process.

4. **Describe how companies differentiate their products from those of their competitors.** Most obviously, differentiation results when the product is superior—newer, better, faster, or lower in price. Businesses also differentiate their products through a brand name or trademark that becomes synonymous with quality and sometimes with the product itself; through packaging, by making the product stand out; through helpful labeling; and through warranties, which offer consumers confidence in a product.

5. **Identify the four categories of consumer products and give an example of each.** Consumer products are classified as convenience, shopping, specialty, and unsought goods and services. Convenience products, those purchased most frequently, include bread, milk, and banking. Shopping products, purchased less frequently and involving comparison shopping, include appliances, cars, roofing, and plumbing. A specialty product, which depends on brand identification and has no substitute, might be Philadelphia brand cream cheese, Hanes pantyhose, Midas mufflers, and the doctor who saw you through the measles. Unsought products and services, new or unfamiliar items, include interactive TV, hospitals, and emerging social causes, such as those trying to protect the environment.

6. **Identify the three general categories of industrial products and give an example of each.** Industrial products, which require a different type of marketing from consumer products, are capital goods, materials and parts, and supplies and services. Capital goods require large cash outlays and include installations, such as a manufacturing plant, and equipment, such as a printing press or a desktop computer. Materials and parts become part of the final product; for example, a car requires tires, steel, wire, a motor, etc. Supplies, the convenience products of industrial markets, include the operating, maintenance, and repair products required to keep production going—for example, stationery, pens and pencils, heating oil, and paint. Services include computer repairs and tax and legal advice.

7. **Discuss how businesses improve their products.** To maintain or increase their market share, businesses must continually improve their products, which means improving quality. Businesses can improve the quality of the product itself, they can shorten the time it takes to get the product to market, and/or they can improve their service to customers.

New Product Development

8. **List and discuss the steps in the new product development process.** In the first step, ideas generated from various sources are screened and only those that meet company criteria—meeting a customer's unsatisfied want or need, or fitting the business's overall strategy, for example—are pursued. In the second step, the concept development and business analysis stage, an idea is refined into a more specific concept, and sales, costs, and profits are projected. In the third step, the product development and testing stage, a concrete, tangible model—a prototype—is produced. Test marketing may be conducted. In the final step, commercialization, the new product is put into full-scale production and distribution to a target market.

Product Management

9. **Describe the four stages of the product life cycle.** In the introduction stage, the business is building awareness of the product (making advertising costs high), so sales rise slowly because of limited market acceptance. The growth stage is marked by rapidly growing sales as market demand increases. Gaining distribution and cementing dealer relationships is critical. Sales begin to slow late in the growth stage, resulting in price decreases and cutbacks in product lines. In the maturity stage, sales stabilize and price becomes the main motivator of consumer sales. Businesses seek new markets and new products for growth. In the decline stage, product sales decrease, profits usually drop, and competitors leave the market.

10. **Describe the product strategies used by businesses to adjust to the product life cycle.** Businesses usually begin with a limited-line strategy, but switch to a full-line strategy to give themselves a competitive advantage—for example, during the growth stage, a company may introduce a product to compensate for the declining sales of another. In building a full line of products, the business may use line or brand extension strategies. To meet changing consumer concerns, the business may reposition its product—advertising low fat content, for example. A final strategy that is part of early development is planned obsolescence, in which products are manufactured to wear out quickly or to become outdated due to changing styles or fashions.

✓ Key Terms

product **451**	private brands **457**	specialty products **461**	full-line strategy **472**
customer service **454**	family brand strategy **457**	unsought products **461**	limited-line strategy **472**
product differentiation **456**	individual brand **457**	capital goods **462**	line extensions **473**
brand **456**	packaging **458**	new product development **464**	brand extension strategy **473**
brand name **456**	labeling **458**	product life cycle **469**	repositioning strategy **473**
trademark **456**	warranty **459**	product mix **472**	planned obsolescence **474**
generic name **456**	convenience products **460**	product lines **472**	
national brand **457**	shopping products **460**		

• Review Questions

1. What are the characteristics that distinguish goods, services, and ideas from one another?

2. What are the four questions that help marketers clarify what the customer expects from the product? Give an example of each.

3. What is customer service? Be comprehensive and provide an example of good customer service from your own life.

4. How do companies achieve product differentiation?

5. What are the advantages and disadvantages of branding?

6. How can packaging, labeling, and warranties differentiate a product?

7. What are the four ways of classifying consumer products? Give an example of each.

8. What are three categories of industrial products?

9. What are the four steps involved in the new product development process? Describe each one.

10. What are the characteristics of the four stages of the product life cycle? Give examples of products in each stage.

11. What is the difference between line extension and brand extension? Give an example of each.

• Critical Thinking Questions

1. Think of your favorite restaurant. What are some of the benefits offered by the restaurant that influence you to go there?

2. Natural Pak Produce has begun selling TomAhtoes brand tomatoes. The company wants to price its produce higher than other tomatoes. What strategies would you suggest to help Natural Pak Produce?

3. Can you think of three ways to elicit new product ideas from consumers?

4. At what stage of the product life cycle are Thermos bottles? Which product management strategies would you recommend to improve their sales?

REVIEW CASE *Carnival Cruise Lines*[25]

The $7 billion cruise industry is growing at a rate of 5 percent a year. It is the darling of the travel industry, with 90 percent occupancy rates (compared to 60 percent for hotels) throughout the recession of the late 1980s and early 1990s. Yet only 7 percent of Americans have ever been on a cruise. Bob Dickinson, Carnival Cruise Lines president, wants to grab more of this tempting potential market.

For 20 years the company built a brand identity with the American public. But now that name is taking on a broader meaning with Carnival Air Lines, planes owned by the company's chairman, and a line of clothing, swimwear, and accessories. For a while the name also belonged to a line of hotels that did not prove profitable. Analysts believe the idea of "cruise-and-stay" did not fit with the firm's advertising message that "the real fun's on board." Indeed, 80 percent of passengers' time is spent on board and only 20 percent is used for onshore excursions. But Dickinson is not satisfied that hotels don't belong among the company's products. He is considering purchasing a casino in New Orleans, to be served by Carnival Air Lines.

The president is also building a larger fleet of ships. Over a three-year period, the company will spend over $1.3 billion on new cruise ships. These additions will include a 95,000 ton vessel that will be the largest cruise ship in the world. But the ships are only the tip of the product iceberg. Carnival uses the ships as platforms for entertainment, including singles cocktail parties, Las Vegas–style shows, and poolside pillow-fight tournaments.

Dickinson recalled how he began as president: "I knew nothing about the cruise business so I reasoned we were in the vacation business. What do people want on a vacation?—the most common adjective is fun." So while competing cruise lines promoted the sheer size of their ships, the capabilities of their captains, and the ports their vessels visited, Dickinson ballyhooed the fun people had aboard his ships. And Kathy Lee Gifford has been the spokesperson designated to get the message out since 1983—and with her image of the good mother, the perky and nonthreatening girl next door, she is likely to hold that berth for some time into the future.

1. How would you characterize the product offered by Carnival Cruise Lines?

2. What type of brand strategy is being used?

3. What type of consumer product is a cruise ship?

4. What product strategy or strategies are being used by Dickinson?

CRITICAL THINKING CASE *Procter & Gamble*[26]

Procter & Gamble faces some stiff and unusual competition these days, competition from private labels rather than old-line aggressors like Lever Brothers and Colgate-Palmolive. Throughout the 1980s, P&G inched up the prices on its leading brands of Tide (detergent), Crest (toothpaste), Vicks (cough syrup), and Pampers (disposable diapers). Consumers faced with recession began to shun these well-advertised brands in favor of store brands that cost them a lot less. P&G estimated that its leaders cost the average family an average of $725 per year—and the consumer simply rebelled. To counter this slide, P&G switched its pricing away from normally high prices punctuated by periodic price slashes to even pricing, which it called Everyday Low Prices. But that was just the beginning of a major restructuring at Procter & Gamble.

CEO Edwin Artzt created a shift in the company's brand strategies as well. In the past, every new technological leap forward resulted in a new, stand-alone brand. Each new product had to fight for P&G resources to establish a new market presence and increase its market share. Shunning the old approach, Artzt began to use each of the megabrands (such as Tide) as the core brand and to provide additional products *around* that brand name (Tide with Bleach, for example). Under the old approach, Tide with Bleach would have been given an entirely new and different brand name.

Introducing a new brand takes time, money, and lots of effort. When P&G designed a new disposable diaper shape, it created the brand Luvs. Instead of associating the new design with its leading brand, Pampers, P&G chose to start fresh but in so doing lost ground to Kimberly-Clark's Kimbies. And diapers were not the only goof at P&G. Ivory soap, the company's original product, was considered merely a soap, rather than a soap with a strong identity as a pure cleaning product. Improvements such as soap with cold cream were assigned new brand names when they should have been linked to purity by the Ivory brand name. Finally, Spic and Span had languished for 45 years until finally, in 1993, the company extended the line with new products such as Spic and Span bathroom spray cleaner in an attempt to add new growth. Crest with Tartar Control and Crest with Baking Soda reflect similar strategies.

1. How would you describe the brand and product strategies at P&G, in the past and now?

2. At what stages of the product life cycle are the various products in the case?

3. What advice would you give to CEO Artzt about providing customer service with the company's product lines?

Critical Thinking with the ONE MINUTE MANAGER

"Did you know that the Ritz-Carlton Hotel Company has won two major quality awards in recent years?" the One Minute Manager asked the students.

"I heard they won the Malcolm Baldrige National Quality Award."

"Their service must be great," Joanna commented. "Wish I could afford to stay in one of their hotels!"

"Well, they are expensive, but they are perceived as a good value by the business and vacation travelers who make up their target market. And recently, the company adopted what it calls a value strategy in which vacationers are offered a package that includes amenities such as a full breakfast for two, a bottle of champagne, flowers, and complementary use of the hotel's fitness center. You might say they are modifying their core product to attract more value-conscious consumers.[27]

1. What is Ritz-Carlton's core product?

2. Does the new value marketing strategy alter this core product, or does it just support the core product by modifying the customer services that surround it? (*Hint*: See Figure 15.1.)

3. What aspect of Ritz-Carlton's product is affected by winning quality awards?

4. How does Ritz-Carlton distinguish its product from those of other hotels?

5. The chapter taught us that a product can satisfy its customers in many ways. Is this true of Ritz-Carlton's product? Explain.

16 Distribution: Time and Place

Place—or distribution, as it is more commonly called—is the second of the four Ps in the marketing mix. An old saying tells us that if you build a better mousetrap, the world will beat a path to your door. But it is not that simple these days. Businesses must move the mousetrap—and any other product, whether good, service, or idea—so that consumers will have access to it when and where they want it. We begin by examining distribution channels, the chains of businesses and individuals that move products from producers to consumers. Then, after considering the reasons why producers choose one channel over another, we explore the variety of options producers have as they make these decisions. As we look at these topics, we will also point out ways that the revolution in information technology is changing traditional distribution strategies. After reading this chapter, you will be able to reach the learning goals below.

Learning Goals

1. Identify the major marketing intermediaries and describe their roles in the distribution process.
2. Differentiate between channel of distribution and physical distribution and describe the four distribution channels for consumer goods.
3. Describe industrial and service channels of distribution.
4. Explain the effect of global and dual markets on distribution channels.
5. Discuss the criteria used by businesses in selecting a distribution channel.
6. Differentiate between the three levels of distribution strategies.
7. Describe the sources of channel conflict and cooperation.
8. Discuss the relationship between customer service and the tasks of physical distribution.
9. Identify the categories of wholesalers and discuss the factors affecting the future of wholesaling.
10. Describe the categories of retailers and discuss the future of retailing.

Where and When

"Want me to show you the distribution department?"

Carlos and Joanna nodded as the One Minute Manager rose from her desk. They had just explained that they were studying how products are moved from producers to consumers. They both stood and prepared to follow her out of the office. But she stopped at the window beside her desk.

"OK, let's go," Carlos said, waiting for her to lead the way.

"Go where?" the One Minute Manager asked.

"To the distribution department," Carlos prompted.

"Oh, no . . . I mean that I'll *show* it to you, not take you there." The One Minute Manager smiled. "You see, distribution isn't really handled here at all. Distribution is what happens when products *leave* our company. That's our distribution department, out there." She gestured toward the window, indicating the city below them and the rolling hills at the horizon.

Joanna and Carlos stared out the window, then laughed. "Well, how about a story then?" Carlos suggested.

"Sure," she agreed. "I know a great one. I bought a new GE dishwasher from a store near my house recently, and they showed me how GE is changing the distribution process." She sat down and continued. "General Electric used to offer stores special prices if they bought and stocked lots of GE's dishwashers—that's called loading the trade. Producers want retailers to hold a large inventory of appliances so a store's customers will have many appliances to choose from, and it makes retailers committed to selling a company's products when they own so many. Also, loading allows less store space for competitors' products. But holding lots of inventory is very costly for retailers, so they resist loading. General Electric turned this approach to distribution upside down with its Direct Connect program. Under this new plan, retailers no longer hold large inventories. Participating stores receive a computer program that allows instant access to GE's on-line order processing system, 24 hours a day. They can check for model availability and place an order for next-day delivery. Deliveries are made from 10 General Electric warehouses, and 90 percent of dealers in the United States can obtain goods within 24 hours. Retailers in the Direct Connect program receive GE's lowest prices, delivery priority over other stores, and 90 days of interest-free credit from GE for their customers."

"Sounds great for stores, but what's in it for GE?" Joanna asked.

"In return, retailers must agree to sell nine major GE product categories and guarantee that 50 percent of their sales will be from General Electric products. And they must pay GE via electronic funds transfer on the twenty-fifth of the month after a purchase. So both General Electric and its retailers win with this innovative partnership program."[1]

How Business Creates Availability

In Chapter 14 we saw that businesses provide satisfaction through five utilities. This chapter discusses how companies ensure that the right product is in the right place at the right time, focusing on the place, time, and information utilities.

The first job of distribution is to determine the pathway that the product will take to get to the customer. Then the organization must figure out how it will physically move the product along that pathway. How will it protect, package, load, unload, sort, repackage, and reload products as they move toward the consumer?

Marketing Intermediaries

Marketing intermediaries, sometimes called *middlemen*, are businesses that help move products from producers to consumers. These retailers and wholesalers are at the heart of the distribution process. **Retailers** sell products directly to consumers—almost $2.1 trillion worth of goods and services each year.[2] **Wholesalers** sell products to retailers, to manufacturers (who use the goods to make other products), to the government, and to large institutions that purchase in quantity. In moving products from the producer to the consumer, *merchant wholesalers* take title (ownership) to the products they distribute. Grocery and hardware stores are examples. **Agents** bring buyers and sellers together and assist in making the exchange, but they never own the product.

 marketing intermediaries

Businesses that help move products from producers to consumers; sometimes called *middlemen*.

 retailers

Businesses that sell products directly to consumers.

 wholesalers

Businesses that sell products to retailers, to manufacturers, to the government, and to large institutions that purchase in quantity.

 agents

People who bring buyers and sellers together and assist in making the exchange but never own the product.

1. Identify the major marketing intermediaries and describe their roles in the distribution process.

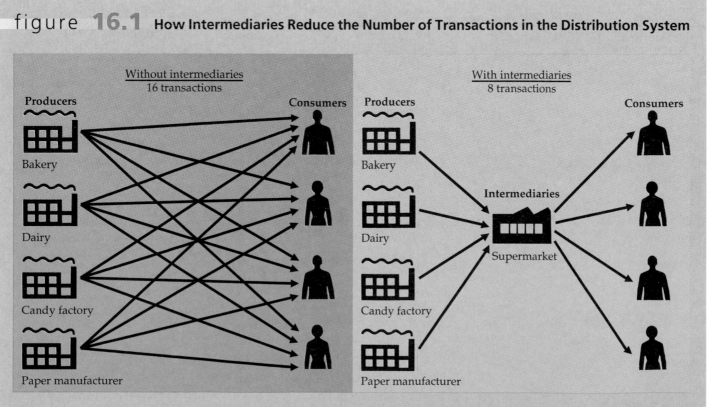

figure **16.1** **How Intermediaries Reduce the Number of Transactions in the Distribution System**

Without intermediaries
16 transactions

Producers — Consumers

Bakery
Dairy
Candy factory
Paper manufacturer

With intermediaries
8 transactions

Producers — Consumers

Bakery
Dairy
Intermediaries
Supermarket
Candy factory
Paper manufacturer

The addition of a supermarket intermediary eliminates half the transactions involved in moving products into the hands of buyers.

Are intermediaries really necessary? Don't they drive up the cost of products to us consumers? Wouldn't we, as consumers, save a bundle if we could cut out these middlemen and buy directly from producers? The answer is no, because intermediaries reduce the number of transactions required to distribute products. This sounds unlikely, but consider the situation illustrated in Figure 16.1, which shows four manufacturers and four consumers. If each consumer buys directly from each of the four producers, 16 transactions are required. When one intermediary is added, say a supermarket, only eight transactions take place. And since each transaction costs money, the cost of distribution is also reduced.

Wholesalers and retailers exist because they perform special services such as those shown in Table 16.1. The need for these services would not disappear if the intermediaries did not exist. The responsibility would fall back on the man-

table 16.1 Services Intermediaries Provide

Information Gathering
Although this process tends to be informal, intermediaries can provide useful information on consumers' wants and needs, new product ideas, and proper positioning.

Buying
Intermediaries act for the customers they serve, buying from a broad range of suppliers.

Selling
Intermediaries sell products for the manufacturers from which they buy.

Price setting
Wholesalers and retailers price the product at various points in the distribution system.

Storage
Goods are stored by intermediaries prior to sale.

Bulk breaking
A basic principle of distribution is to ship in bulk, or large quantities, which is far more economical than small shipments. The intermediary then divides up the shipments and distributes them to other middlemen.

Promotion
Intermediaries put together creative promotional programs and place advertising.

Transportation
Intermediaries often move products from one location to another.

Financing
Some intermediaries offer credit; others may help producers with financing.

Risk bearing
When intermediaries take title to the products they sell, they take on the risks of damage, deterioration, obsolescence, and the like.

Management services
Wholesalers may help their retail customers with such projects as improving accounting techniques, improving in-store promotional displays, controlling inventory, and enhancing advertising and sales training.

ufacturer. But the manufacturer is a production specialist. These important distribution functions can be carried out more efficiently and effectively by the distribution specialists—the intermediaries. Without them, the added cost to the consumer as a result of markups would disappear. But in their place would be the even greater costs of storage, transportation, buyer-seller contact, and the like. So, through the services they provide, intermediaries actually hold down the cost of products to consumers.

Because they are located closer to consumers, intermediaries can also assess the needs and wants of a particular market more accurately than manufacturers can. Intermediaries, especially retailers, actually talk and work with the buyers of products, and they feel the pulse of the market and know what those buyers want. This knowledge is fed back to the producer so that the appropriate assortment of products can be manufactured.

In the magazine industry, hundreds of millions of dollars worth of magazines are returned unsold each year and must be shredded. Without this cost, the industry could more than double its profits. Wholesalers provide detailed information on returns and sellouts by area and by type of magazine in an effort to reduce this loss. This information helps publishers regulate the number of magazines shipped and helps wholesalers and retailers select the proper combination of magazines for each area served.

Distribution Channels

A **distribution channel** is a chain of organizations that moves products from producers to consumers and industrial users. It includes all the marketing intermediaries that move raw materials into factories and finished goods into the hands of the ultimate consumers. Some channels are short, such as the direct channel between you and the farmer when you buy fresh corn directly from a roadside farm stand. Other channels are long and complex, like the one that results in the cans of corn chowder being available in the soup section of your local supermarket.

A distribution channel is supported by **physical distribution**, the activities that serve to transport and store products during their journey through a distribution channel. Physical distribution is summed up in the Coca-Cola Co. motto, "Our policy is to put Coke within an arm's length of desire," and in United Parcel Service's ad line, "Moving at the Speed of Business." Physical distribution today focuses on those activities that provide goods when buyers desire them, such as those involved in General Electric's Direct Connect program described in the opening vignette.

Distribution Channels for Consumer Goods

Products can travel through a number of alternative channels on their way to the final user. And depending on the marketer's objectives, different routes offer different advantages. The four main channels for distributing consumer products are shown in Figure 16.2.

Channel 1 The direct channel is the shortest and often the quickest way to distribute consumer products. For example, sales representatives from magazine distributors come to our doors and present their goods, and we stop at roadside fruit stands and buy fruit from growers. Manufacturers' mail-order catalogs and telephone sales of financial services are also examples of short, or "direct," channels that employ no intermediaries. As more intermediaries are added, channels become longer, or more "indirect."

2. Differentiate between channel of distribution and physical distribution and describe the four distribution channels for consumer goods.

 distribution channel

A chain of organizations that moves products from producers to consumers and industrial users; includes all the marketing intermediaries that move raw materials into factories and finished goods into the hands of the ultimate consumers.

 physical distribution

The activities that serve to transport and store products during their journey through a distribution channel.

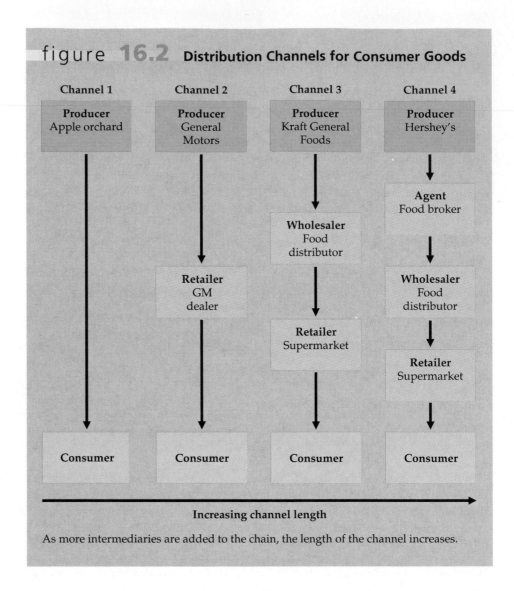

figure **16.2**   **Distribution Channels for Consumer Goods**

Channel 1	Channel 2	Channel 3	Channel 4
Producer Apple orchard	**Producer** General Motors	**Producer** Kraft General Foods	**Producer** Hershey's
			Agent Food broker
		Wholesaler Food distributor	
	Retailer GM dealer		**Wholesaler** Food distributor
		Retailer Supermarket	
			Retailer Supermarket
Consumer	Consumer	Consumer	Consumer

Increasing channel length →

As more intermediaries are added to the chain, the length of the channel increases.

Channel 2   The producer to retailer to consumer channel may be the most visible to us as consumers. We buy many different products through this kind of channel—automobiles, paint, gasoline, and clothing, for instance. Many manufacturers have special outlets that sell directly to consumers. Some own their own retail stores; Sherwin-Williams paints and Ralph Lauren merchandise are examples.

Channel 3   The third type of channel adds a wholesaler between producer and retailer; it is used to distribute such products as drugs, lumber, hardware, and food items. Products that have a large market need such a channel, since manufacturers often do not have a large enough sales force to reach the mass market effectively. Wholesalers provide a large web of contacts that otherwise would be beyond the reach of most manufacturers.

Channel 4   The longest of the frequently used distribution channels involves agents. Since agents provide another layer of intermediaries, they provide an even more extensive network of contacts. Candy is distributed to wholesalers through agents. Here a long channel makes sense, since candy is an impulse item with many potential buyers.

As explained in Chapter 14, throughout the distribution channel, a variety of exchanges take place—payment for the product, transfer of ownership, and, as we saw earlier, exchanges of information. These exchanges flow both forward and backward. Recycling is an example of a backward channel flow. In **reverse channels**, intermediaries such as soft drink distributors and redemption centers move products back through the channel. These intermediaries facilitate the movement of empty bottles and cans, used products, and many kinds of reusable trash back to where they can be refashioned into useful products. For example, in one weekend, Nike collected 1,100 pairs of used sneakers in Fort Myers, Florida. The rubber was ground up and used as a cushion in running tracks. And as we saw in Chapter 4, outdoor clothing maker Patagonia, Inc., manufactures Synchilla fleece from recycled plastic soda bottles.

Distribution Channels for Industrial Products

Figure 16.3 shows two types of distribution channels for industrial products. The channel without intermediaries is used most frequently. Because industrial markets usually require precise information from company salespeople, a short, direct channel is most appropriate. Many metal manufacturers, conveyor belt producers, and makers of construction equipment use this channel. Industrial buyers use their purchases as materials in the production of other products, usually finished products targeted for consumers.

Industrial distributors are the counterparts of wholesalers. They take title to products and perform the same functions wholesalers do for consumer products. There are more than 12,000 industrial distributors in the United States.[3] Industrial distributors act as the sales force for the many small manufacturers that serve industrial markets. This channel is found where markets are composed of small manufacturers or widely scattered industrial market segments.

Distribution Channels for Consumer Services

Services, like goods, employ channels of distribution. Universities transmit televised lectures into the homes of students. These telecourses are an alternative to the familiar on-campus distribution system. Hospitals provide mobile units to serve people in their market areas. Some even provide helicopter service for critical care emergencies. Channels of distribution for services tend to be short and direct. Aided by new technology, the banking industry provides an example.

Meridian Bancorp in Reading, Pennsylvania, offers a variety of direct distribution technologies—not only the usual telephone, television, ATM, and personal service at branches but also high-tech, two-way video remote terminals for customers who wish to talk to a bank employee but do not want to travel to the bank. Meridian lets customers tell bankers how and where they want to bank.[4]

Some service distribution channels do employ intermediaries. Hospitals gain patients through referrals by contracting with doctors who act as retailers. Insurance agents and travel agents also act as intermediaries in their respective industries. Film producers such as Walt Disney and Viacom's Paramount employ their own television networks as well as cable channels like Showtime and the Movie Channel to distribute their programming.

Distribution applies to all sorts of services. Aspiring entertainers know how important it is to be in the right place at the right time. Appearing on "Saturday Night Live" helped to propel Billy Crystal, Steve Martin, Dana Carvey, and Chris Farley to stardom. Political candidates understand the importance of properly scheduling their movement along the campaign trail. Doctors, HMOs,

reverse channels

Channels in which intermediaries such as soft drink distributors and redemption centers move products back through the channel.

3. Describe industrial and service channels of distribution.

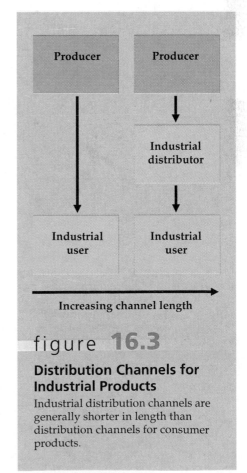

figure **16.3**

Distribution Channels for Industrial Products

Industrial distribution channels are generally shorter in length than distribution channels for consumer products.

and even hospitals are opening low-cost "urgent care centers" (referred to as "Doc-in-a-Box" or "7-Eleven Medicine" by critics and rivals) at easy-to-reach locations such as shopping malls. Dean Junior College in Massachusetts offers its "Choo-Choo U," where commuters take college courses while traveling on the Massachusetts Bay Transportation Authority. Pictures printed on milk cartons gain the greatest exposure in the effort to locate missing children.

Global Distribution Channels

4. Explain the effect of global and dual markets on distribution channels.

Distribution becomes more complex when business is conducted across national boundaries. The distance the product must travel is greater. And the means of communication between channel members are different, as are cultural values and practices. Here the channel has two components: the one between nations and the one within the target nation. Within foreign countries, distribution channels tend to be longer than in the United States. In the United States, a typical domestic channel for a small manufacturer of consumer goods is from manufacturer to wholesaler to retailer. In Turkey, Egypt, and Italy, however, the government has limited the growth of large wholesalers. Hence global companies must contact many distributors to obtain distribution.

In Japan, a strong cultural and economic value is protecting the network of small neighborhood stores. Two and sometimes three levels of wholesalers supply these shops. Those wholesalers, in turn, are linked to producers and to Japan's giant trading companies through a set of still larger distributors. Twenty percent of all Japanese workers hold jobs in distribution. Everything the Japanese consumer desires makes its way through a maze of as many as six intermediaries, causing Japanese products to be the most costly in the world. However, these lengthy channels are being challenged as Japan's slowing economy changes consumers' priorities from quality to lower price. Discounters and wholesale membership clubs are emerging that bypass the traditionally expensive distribution labyrinth to offer substantial price cuts. For instance, Kou's, a wholesale club, buys Spalding Magna Plus golf balls directly from the U.S. manufacturer and sells them for $26.80 a dozen. Elsewhere in Japan this package would cost $72.[5]

American Retailer, Japanese Customer

Specialty retailer Toys 'R' Us opened its first store in Japan in 1992. Its wide merchandise selection and low prices lure Japanese consumers away from traditional retailers, whose high prices are a result of Japan's complex distribution system. Japanese discount stores also pose serious competition to traditional Japanese retailing.

Dual Distribution

Businesses sometimes use more than one distribution channel, or **dual distrib-ution**. Appliance manufacturers sell their goods through two very different channels. To reach the housing and mobile-home market, they submit competitive bids to meet builders' specifications. To reach the consumer market, they sell through retail outlets. Computer manufacturers use retailers to sell to home users, while a direct channel is used for industrial customers. In addition to its regular retail outlets, IBM markets to home computer customers via its catalog, IBM PC Direct. Powerful retailers are also forcing dual distribution. Wal-Mart refuses to buy from agents; instead it demands a direct channel from its manufacturers/suppliers. Procter & Gamble has a sales branch near Wal-Mart's headquarters dedicated to serving only Wal-Mart. And Black & Decker has special sales divisions to serve big retailers like Home Depot.

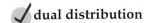

dual distribution

When businesses use more than one distribution channel.

Matching Distribution Channels to Marketing Objectives

How do businesses choose among alternative distribution channels? In the case of most new products, producers use channels that have been successful for similar products. If there is sufficient consumer demand and room on the channel member's shelf, the new product can take its place beside those of competitors. Sometimes companies branch out from the traditional outlets for a particular product. The classic example of this is when Hanes took its L'eggs pantyhose to the supermarket and drugstore instead of to the usual specialty and department stores, revolutionizing the distribution of hosiery.

Determining the Distribution Strategy

Channel strategy must be based on an assessment of the producer's and channel members' goals, resources, and understanding of the market. All distribution strategies, however, are guided by two overall criteria: market coverage and channel control.

5. Discuss the criteria used by businesses in selecting a distribution channel.

Market Coverage Strategies

We have seen how intermediaries can decrease the number of transactions necessary to reach a market. Recall from Figure 16.1 the four direct contacts one producer can make with consumers. Now if the producer instead contacts four *retailers* and each makes four contacts with ultimate consumers, the total number of contacts increases to sixteen. The longer the channel of distribution, the greater the market coverage. If the potential market for a product is very large, a long distribution channel with many intermediaries forms a wide web of customer contacts.

Let's look at two products to see how market coverage strategies work. Everyone who shaves is a potential buyer of Gillette Sensor razor blades. In the United States alone, that's a lot of people. Gillette uses a *long* channel to ensure that its product is available whenever and wherever it is wanted. Contrast this situation with the market for Mack trucks. The total market for heavy trucks is only about 300,000 customers. About 10 percent of them buy 90 percent of all the big rigs sold. In this case, Mack trucks benefits from concentrating on a *short* distribution channel.

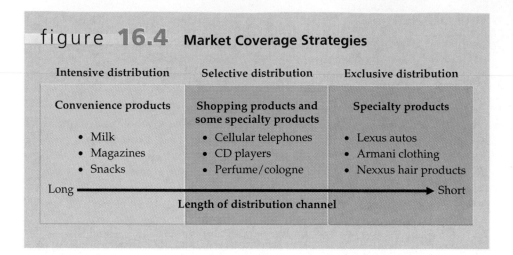

figure **16.4**   **Market Coverage Strategies**

6. Differentiate between the three levels of distribution strategies.

The number of intermediaries used to cover a market is expressed as the *intensity of distribution*. As Figure 16.4 shows, there are three strategies:

- **Intensive distribution** achieves wide market coverage, giving products the greatest exposure. At its extreme, intensive distribution ensures that the product is carried at every available outlet where buyers might shop for it. Intensive distribution is necessary for frequently purchased convenience items like milk, magazines, snacks, and razor blades. Manufacturers consider intensive distribution highly desirable, but retailers don't always agree. Such wide market coverage means that retailers have to compete with one another for customers.

- **Selective distribution** gives a limited set of retailers the right to sell a product in a given geographic area. Shopping products, such as cellular phones and CD players, and some specialty products such as Seiko watches, Reebok jogging shoes, and perfumes and colognes—products characterized by a high degree of brand awareness and brand loyalty—are candidates for selective distribution. Manufacturers gain because channel members tend to be loyal and cooperative. Retailers gain because they are guaranteed some sales and less competition from other retailers than would be the case with intensive distribution. As a result, they are usually willing to promote the manufacturer's product aggressively, provide service, and hold more stock in inventory, thereby increasing product flow through the channel.

- **Exclusive distribution** means that only one retailer has the right to represent the manufacturer in each geographic territory. Retailers are generally tied to the manufacturer by policies that guide their advertising, pricing, and sales promotion. They often are expected to carry no competing lines. In return, the retailer is guaranteed all sales of the product in a given territory. Exclusive distribution is generally employed with specialty goods, for which the manufacturer wants to ensure the proper image. We learned in the last chapter that buyers will seek out the outlet that carries specialty products, such as Lexus cars or Armani clothing. Nexxus Products Co. distributes its hair-care products exclusively through hairstyling salons. It uses intermediaries to reach the salons. Each distributor has an exclusive territory, and over half carry only Nexxus products. To support its distributors, Nexxus keeps them stocked with free samples and large amounts of sales literature. It also holds annual meetings of its distributors in beautiful Santa Barbara, California, where the company is headquartered.

✓ **intensive distribution**

A strategy used to achieve wide market coverage, giving products the greatest exposure.

✓ **selective distribution**

A strategy that gives a limited set of retailers the right to sell a product in a given geographic area.

✓ **exclusive distribution**

A strategy in which only one retailer has the right to represent the manufacturer in each geographic territory.

Market coverage is not the only factor in choosing a distribution channel. Channel control is also very important.

Channel Control

What most manufacturers want from marketing intermediaries is aggressive selling and promotion to move the product through the distribution system. They also may want to guarantee that the product will not be resold to other intermediaries whose image does not match the manufacturer's goals. Such control is important, for example, to designers of exclusive apparel and limited-edition art objects. If intermediaries in the channel take legal ownership of products, they can do almost anything they want with it.

Until recently, brand-name manufacturers were powerful enough to control the distribution of their products. This power is now ebbing away as retail giants like Wal-Mart, Home Depot, and Toys 'R' Us increasingly determine what products will be distributed and how. Big retailers seek to lower their own costs by reducing their inventory, slashing delivery time from suppliers, and demanding defect-free products. As one industry representative said, "Most suppliers would just do absolutely anything to sell Wal-Mart."[6] Manufacturers must promote their brand names to reduce the risk that the big retailer will replace them with lower-cost alternatives. Totes Inc. was selling 1.5 million pairs of socks with anti-slip rubber treads to Kmart Corp. and Wal-Mart. Suddenly the discounters replaced them with an unbranded identical product priced 25 percent below Totes's retail price!

Sources of Channel Conflict

The distribution channel links resource suppliers, producers, intermediaries, and consumers through the exchange process. In reality, however, most channel members operate independently. Each has its own goals—profits, sales volume, image, and so on—and the goals of one channel member may not be those of another. Furthermore, because each channel member may deal with many others, it may be difficult or impossible to satisfy everyone involved. To serve the diverse needs of retailers, for example, a food wholesaler may carry canned peas produced by Del Monte, Green Giant, and Stokely Van Camp. Each of these manufacturers would prefer to control the wholesaler, to have it carry only its brand and thereby increase its market coverage. The wholesaler cannot completely satisfy both the retailers and the manufacturers. As a result, conflict rather than cooperation arises among channel members. This conflict may be horizontal or vertical.

Horizontal conflict occurs between channel members at the same level— between two or more wholesalers or two or more retailers. At either level, conflict may be between intermediaries of the same type (two competing supermarkets) or of different types (a department store and a discount store). Many retailers today carry an increasingly vast array of products. The average supermarket now stocks 23,000 different products, compared with 15,000 in 1985![7] As retailers add product lines formerly carried by other types of retailers, competition for customers becomes intense. Specialty paint stores, for instance, now have to compete with lumberyards, hardware stores, discount stores, and department stores.

Vertical conflict arises between channel members at different levels in the distribution system—between producer and wholesaler, for example, or between manufacturer and retailer. When channel members do not perform their expected functions and do not behave in expected ways, conflict arises.

Until recently, manufacturers periodically offered lower prices to coax retailers to increase their inventories and provide a quick infusion of sales to the producers. (See the One Minute Manager at the beginning of this chapter.) But high inventories cause retailers' carrying costs to surge, resulting in higher prices and fewer fresh products for consumers. Because of loading, the average

7. Describe the sources of channel conflict and cooperation.

grocery product takes 84 days to move from factory to consumer.[8] In the early 1990s, Procter & Gamble began eliminating the short-term price promotions that encourage loading. Instead, it offered stable prices to smooth out the flow of goods in the distribution system. This stability allowed factories to run on normal shifts, products to move as needed by retailers, and inventories throughout the system to be trimmed. Moreover, consumers got fresher groceries (by 25 days on average) at a 6 percent lower price.[9]

Sources of Channel Cooperation

One source of cooperation within a distribution channel is the power of one channel member to influence the behavior of others. That power may be derived from superior financial strength, possession of a prestige brand, the ability to withdraw an important product, or a tradition of superior customer service. It also can come from access to a market, as we saw in the power shift to giant retailers like Wal-Mart and Toys 'R' Us. Channel power results in control and thus fosters cooperation. The channel member with the power influences the behavior of others and becomes the **channel captain**.

Knowledge is power within distribution channels. The channel member that understands the customer's wants and buying behavior at the greatest level of detail has an advantage over other members.[10] Wal-Mart operates a private satellite-communications system that daily collects and compiles data on daily sales of products in each of its stores. This information is then converted into purchase orders placed electronically with 4,000 vendors each day. Wal-Mart replenishes its stock twice weekly, compared with the industry average of once every two weeks. Suppliers, however, must institute costly new operating procedures to meet Wal-Mart's tough requirements.[11] Kraft General Foods studies scanner data gathered from its supermarket customers and supplies an inventory of its products designed for *individual stores*. Channel members at any point in the distribution system can hold the power position, and the choice of channel captain may be a reflection of information management.

A second approach to resolving channel conflict is the integration of channel members into a **vertical marketing system (VMS)**—planned partnerships between businesses and their suppliers to build mutually beneficial, cooperative relationships with their customers.[12] There are three types of vertical marketing systems: corporate, administered, and contractual.

- In a *corporate VMS*, the business gains channel control by owning both production and distribution operations. The business can own part or all of the channel. Many such systems are owned by the producer. Revco, the nation's largest discount drugstore chain, for example, has expanded into the production of drugs and related items. Coca-Cola Co. operates on the corporate VMS structure. While its main business is producing and selling concentrate and syrup to bottlers, the company also provides support—particularly advertising—to help independent bottlers move Coke. Bottlers actually produce the soft drinks, distribute them to retail and fountain outlets, and handle local promotion. In the 1980s, Coca-Cola agreed to sell concentrate and syrup to these independent bottlers at fixed prices. But as sugar prices surged and Coca-Cola began losing profits, it began buying stakes in bottlers and created Coca-Cola Enterprises Inc. (CCE), a separate company made up of these "owned" partners. By the mid-1990s, CCE was the largest of the approximately 2,500 ownerships in the bottling system.

- In an *administered VMS*, cooperation results primarily from the power of the channel captain, which usually has the most resources to invest in channel management and performs marketing functions that win the loyalty of other channel members. Cost reduction is usually the main goal,

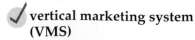

channel captain

The distribution channel member with the power to influence the behavior of others.

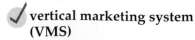

vertical marketing system (VMS)

Planned partnerships between businesses and their suppliers to build mutually beneficial, cooperative relationships with their customers.

and many companies are going to great lengths to achieve it. Bailey Controls, an Ohio-based maker of control systems for large factories, teams up with its suppliers and acts as if they were company divisions. For example, it sends six-month forecasts of materials needed to Montreal-based Future Electronics. Bailey holds only a small inventory of Future's products at its plant, and when stock gets low, an employee passes a scanner over the product code. An order is then instantaneously placed electronically for immediate delivery from Future. Another supplier, Arrow Electronics, actually operates a warehouse on Bailey's premises and stocks items in accord with its twice monthly forecasts. Through such partnering, Bailey Controls shifts inventory costs and management to the distributor, who, in turn, is assured of much greater volume. "It's like a marriage," a purchasing agent told *Fortune* magazine. "It's like committing to one relationship. . . . "[13]

- A *contractual VMS* offers a middle ground between the costly corporate system and the less controllable administered system. In these systems, channel members enter into a legal agreement that specifies each party's rights and responsibilities. This is the fastest-growing type of VMS. The most prevalent type of contractual VMS is the franchise system, which is exemplified by Subway (fast-food), TCBY (frozen yogurt), and Jazzercise (fitness centers).

The advantages and disadvantages associated with franchising were discussed in Chapter 7.

Physical Distribution

The strategic considerations of channel selection—coverage and control—establish the overall plan for getting products into the hands of consumers. (See the skills check "How to Analyze a Distribution Channel.") The goal of physical distribution, the activities that serve to transport and store products during their journey through the distribution channel, is to provide customer service: delivery of the right product to the right place at the right time, all at the lowest cost. This is a critical competitive arena right now.

The economic impact of all this is enormous. Physical distribution, also known as *logistics*, is the largest component of marketing costs. About 20 cents out of every dollar you spend goes to pay for physical distribution. That amounts to about 16 percent of GDP.[14] However, the cost of logistics varies dramatically from one industry to another. In the food industry, for example, it accounts for about one-third of each consumer dollar spent. In the textile and wood industries, it amounts to only about one-sixth of the price of goods.

Physical distribution is not confined to the movement of products from manufacturers to consumers. It also includes the movement of raw materials—ore, oil, and farm products—to manufacturers and producers. This set of relations is often called the *supply chain*. Creating and managing personal relationships with intermediaries creates a strong competitive advantage for companies striving to be leaders in their industries. As a consultant told *Fortune*, "As the economy changes, as competition becomes more global, it's no longer company versus company, but supply chain versus supply chain."[15]

8. Discuss the relationship between customer service and the tasks of physical distribution.

Customer Service Goals

Customer service in logistics means buyers purchase the product when they want it. To gain a competitive advantage, many companies strive to provide a service level slightly better than the competition. Superior customer service comes from logistics that surpass customers' desires, that are perhaps beyond their dreams. It means providing customers with availability and speed, as well as accuracy and reliability.

How to Analyze a Distribution Channel

How is a product or service distributed? Here is a simple set of questions that you can use to describe a real-life distribution channel accurately. Ben & Jerry's ice cream is our example. You should try to work through your own example, too. Pick a product you use routinely, like a CD or your favorite magazine, and analyze its distribution channels by answering all six questions. Make a diagram of the channel. Can you think of a distribution opportunity that the current channels do not take advantage of?

1. **Who are the targeted customers?** Ben & Jerry's targets ice cream lovers who are willing and able to pay a little extra for superior taste and pure ingredients.

2. **When and where do these customers buy the product?** Customers buy Ben & Jerry's while shopping at the grocery store.

3. **Who produces the product?** Ben & Jerry's ice cream is made at Ben & Jerry's factory in Vermont, and some is also made under contract at other factories around the country.

4. **Who helps to move the product from producer to consumer?** There may be no intermediaries to help out, but often there are. Who and how many? Example: A food distribution company sells Ben & Jerry's to supermarkets. It takes possession, and it provides warehousing, transportation, order taking, and sales services. To find out who the intermediaries are and what they do, you often have to ask the retailer or producer for information:

Are there . . .	And what do they do?	
	Do they take possession?	What services do they perform?
Retail stores:		
Distributors:		
Other intermediaries:		

5. **Is there another way to answer questions 1 through 4?** There may be a second distribution channel, in which case you need to do a separate analysis of it. (Example: Ben & Jerry's is also sold through convenience stores like 7-Eleven. These stores differ in the kind of distributor they use, and their convenient locations and long shopping hours encourage spur-of-the-moment purchases.)

6. **Are any customer needs NOT fully met by the existing channel(s)?** Is there a place and time when potential customers might want to buy the product, but cannot? If so, this represents a distribution opportunity you or another marketer can fill! (Example: It is not easy for most college students to buy Ben & Jerry's ice cream on campus late at night, when they might want it for a study break. Can you think of a way to meet this distribution opportunity? Would it require a new distribution channel?)

- Products must be *available* when the customer wants them. Unavailable goods cause delays for the buyer and often result in lost sales as buyers find alternative suppliers.
- Purchased goods must be *sped* to the buyer.
- The correct items and quantities ordered must be *accurately* shipped.
- Customers further expect *reliable* delivery without in-transit damage to goods.

But these customer service goals do not come without costs. To the buyer, the ultimate in delivery would be getting exactly what you want exactly when and where you want it, every time. But a supplier would find the costs of offering this service level prohibitive. Companies compromise by trading off service level for cost savings. For example, a supplier that desires to provide fast delivery service to customers but must minimize transportation costs might use second-day air service to hold down costs while still providing an acceptable level of service.

Physical Distribution Tasks

Exceptional customer service results from coordinating a set of six interacting physical distribution tasks. Their execution is so important to a business that many companies have designated a *physical distribution manager* to oversee their implementation. Sears, Roebuck & Company hired the commanding general for logistics in the Persian Gulf War to be its distribution manager. Sears reasoned that the experience of managing the deployment of 40,000 men and women to supply troops with everything from candy to tanks could only help in smoothing the flow of goods to its 800 department stores.

The tasks that control the flow of goods through the distribution system include:

- Forecasting demand
- Order processing
- Inventory control
- Warehousing
- Materials handling
- Transportation

Some of these activities take place continuously while others, such as order processing and transporting products, happen only when an order is placed. Information technology affects the way many physical distribution tasks are accomplished.

Forecasting Demand   Inaccurate estimates of the demand for a product will have a domino effect throughout the distribution channel. By forecasting demand, a business estimates the number of products it will need to supply its customers. Once again, computers and information technology have improved companies' ability to predict demand.

Like Bailey Controls, many companies work with other channel members to ensure that items will be available when needed. Sears and Levi Strauss, for example, are linked so that scanner data on daily sales of Levi products at Sears are transmitted electronically to Levi Strauss. Sears's product needs are forecast and orders placed daily. Forecasting and ordering are accomplished at the same time.[16]

Order Processing   Order processing encompasses all the procedures that enable orders to be received and shipped. The needs of each channel member echo throughout the distribution channel. Thus, the retailer orders its inventory from the wholesaler, which, in turn, orders replacement products from the distributor or manufacturer, and so on. How well products flow from one member to the next depends on how accurately and quickly orders are processed at each step. Order processing involves many clerical procedures—checking customer credit, recording purchase orders, checking product availability, reducing inventory records, setting delivery dates, invoicing customers, and so on. At any point, mistakes and delays can create a roadblock, either to the flow of goods or to the flow of information. Increasingly, order processing is an electronic process, as General Electric's Direct Connect program and Levi Strauss's link to Sears illustrate.

Inventory Control   Inventory control involves maintaining an adequate assortment of products to meet customer demand. Major decisions include when to reorder and how much to buy. In the ideal situation, sales could be perfectly predicted and products produced and delivered just in time to meet buyers' desires. In reality, however, most businesses still hold inventory to supply orders. Companies that stock too few items risk losing sales by not being able to supply an order. But holding inventory is expensive. It involves the costs of storage space, product handling, insurance, and taxes, as well as the costs associated with inventorying products that become obsolete. Companies that stock excess inventory incur significant extra costs. Inventory management is a juggling act in which the costs of holding inventory are balanced against the cost of lost sales.

Today, companies are placing increasing reliance on computerized *just-in-time inventory control*, detailed in Chapter 10. Goods slated for use in production are delivered in the smallest quantities and as close as possible to the time

 order processing

All the procedures that enable orders to be received and shipped.

 inventory control

Maintaining an adequate assortment of products to meet customer demand.

doing business

Removing Distribution Bottlenecks

Saratoga Spring Water has to travel a long distance from its origins in a spring in upstate New York to the shelves of stores around the country. And the tightest bottleneck in this journey used to occur in the warehouses and trucks of distributors, the businesses that sell the water to stores.

Each distributor handles as many as 100 other beverages, many of them made by Saratoga's competitors. Traditionally, these distributors offered the best access to stores. They visited retailers to make sales and keep their products stocked on store shelves. But distributors were not giving Saratoga Spring Water the kind of attention it needed. Saratoga's managers could not fix the problem, since they had little control over the distributors, which are independent businesses. What to do? As company president Robin Prever saw it, "the only alternative was starting our own."[1]

Now Saratoga Spring Water Co. runs its own distribution system. It rents warehouse space, hires truck drivers and salespeople, and gets its bottled water to stores without the help of the independent distributors. Nor is it the only company to eliminate these distribution bottlenecks. Take Miller Brewing Company. You've heard of cold beer, but you might not have heard about the Miller freeze out. Like all brewers, Miller used many independent distributors to reach retail stores. There are about 3,000 of these small distributors in the United States, selling mostly to neighborhood mom-and-pop stores, which are disappearing at a rapid rate.[2] But most beer is now sold at a discount in large stores that are easily reached by just a few big, regional distributors. So Miller is saying goodby to many of its small distributors, instead using its own sales force to visit stores and channeling all its business through a few large, efficient regional distributors.[3]

If you like spring water or cold beer, you benefit. The easier and cheaper the journey to your local store, the more likely you are to find what you want, when and where you want it, at a price you can afford. Both consumers and bottlers benefit when bottlenecks are removed from everything but the bottles.

[1] Gerry Khermouch and Betsy Spethmann, "New Agers Cut Out Middlemen," *Brandweek*, Nov. 15, 1993.
[2] Marj Charlier, "Existing Distributors Are Being Squeezed by Brewers, Retailers," *Wall Street Journal*, Nov. 22, 1993, p. A1.
[3] Gerry Khermouch, "Miller: Wholesale Change Ahead," *Brandweek*, Nov. 15, 1993.

they will be used, thereby saving on inventory costs. Suppliers must serve the needs of customers by reducing the time that elapses between placing an order and receiving it. JIT systems allow companies to monitor their inventory constantly and transmit purchase orders instantaneously. Of course, JIT inventory control can be risky. Suppliers can face work stoppages due to strikes, trucks can break down, and snowstorms can grind distribution to a halt.

Warehousing Channel members store inventory in warehouses for extended periods of time. **Private warehouses** are storage facilities owned and controlled exclusively by the manufacturers and intermediaries that use them. **Public warehouses** are owned by private companies that rent space to others as needed. Since public warehouses do not require a large investment on the part of each business, inventories can be expanded or contracted as the need arises.[17] This is particularly helpful for a firm that markets products for which demand fluctuates widely—snow shovels, for example. Public warehousing benefits companies that distribute their own products. See the doing business box "Removing Distribution Bottlenecks."

Warehouse automation is another means of furthering wholesaling efficiency. Fleming Co., a wholesale food merchant, has built computerized warehouses where items on order from supermarkets are categorized (breakfast cereals, canned vegetables, etc.) and bar coded. A system of laser scanners directs the assembling of the order and the movement of products to specific loading docks for shipment to retailers.

Companies are now focusing more on moving goods than on storing them. **Distribution centers**—streamlined storage facilities geared to turning orders into quickly delivered products—are replacing warehouses. These modern, single-story structures make moving goods easier and faster.

✓ **private warehouses**

Storage facilities owned and controlled exclusively by the manufacturers and intermediaries that use them.

✓ **public warehouses**

Storage facilities owned by private companies that rent space to others as needed.

✓ **distribution centers**

Streamlined storage facilities geared to turning orders into quickly delivered products.

Materials Handling **Materials handling** applies to all the activities involved in a company's warehouses and distribution centers. Materials handling tasks include receiving goods into the storage facility; identifying, sorting, and labeling them; temporarily storing them; and pulling them out of storage for shipment. The risk of damage increases each time goods are handled. To lower this risk, companies are turning to **containerization**, packing smaller packages into large, standardized, easy-to-handle containers for shipping.

Materials handling, like other areas of distribution, is in a period of rapid change. Computer-readable bar codes on inventoried goods, automated equipment, and computerized inventory control systems enable suppliers to react more quickly to customers' needs. At Bergen Brunswig Drug Co.'s California distribution center, for example, an automated item-picking system allows 10 percent of its 29,000 products to be retrieved from inventory without being touched by human hands. This system focuses on products that represent 50 percent of Bergen Brunswig's sales volume. Retailers place orders from handheld electronic devices. Bar codes on purchase orders are optically scanned, and the information dictates which stored products are to be retrieved. Small boxes of products drop out of storage and onto a high-speed conveyor belt, sending them to be delivered. The director of warehouse automation commented on the added productivity, "The time to process an order is 3½ to 5 hours, compared to 6 to 9 hours in one of our manual facilities."[18]

Transportation Physical distribution is all about moving products. *Transportation* decisions are made from among five alternatives: railroad, truck, pipeline, waterway, and airplane. Companies base their choice of transport on six characteristics:

- Speed (door-to-door delivery time)
- Availability (number of geographic locations served)
- Dependability (ability to be on time)
- Capability (ability to carry various products)
- Frequency (number of scheduled shipments per day)
- Cost (cost per ton-mile)

Carrying about 38 percent of the nation's volume of goods,[19] *railroads* remain the dominant mode of transportation. They are especially suitable for long-distance shipments of heavy goods such as coal, sand, and lumber. While their use is limited by the location of tracks, railroads have reduced this disadvantage by offering **piggyback service**: Loaded trucks are taken directly onto railroad flatcars. Combining truck and water transportation is called *fishyback*. Railroad usage has decreased over the past several decades, but low operating costs have partly offset the decline as energy costs have risen.

Trucks carry only about 26 percent of all freight between cities, but they are clearly the dominant mode of transportation within cities. Sophisticated equipment and expansion of the highway system have brought great flexibility to truck transport. Truck shipments require less handling than railroad shipments, so less protective packaging is needed. And trucks offer greater flexibility because they can go directly to the buyer's destination, avoiding the extra handling required when shipping by rail. While truck rates are not as low as railroad rates, trucks generally provide low-cost, fast, dependable, and flexible transportation.

Such products as crude oil, natural gas, and gasoline are often transported by *pipeline*. Today, approximately 200,000 miles of pipeline in the United States account for 20 percent of domestic freight volume. Pipelines are the most dependable mode of transportation, and with high fixed costs (for installation) but very low variable costs (for maintenance and labor), they are also the most inexpensive. Once installed, pipelines require little maintenance and few

 materials handling

All the activities involved in a company's warehouses and distribution centers.

 containerization

Packing smaller packages into large, standardized, easy-to-handle containers for shipping.

 piggyback service

Transportation service in which loaded trucks are taken directly onto railroad flatcars.

employees to keep them running, and there is little risk of damage to products transported in this way. Still, they are slow. Liquids move through pipelines at only 3 to 4 miles per hour. Their routes are inflexible and they are subject to strict government regulation.

Historically, the first important means of transportation was by water—one reason large commercial cities are located near major *waterways*. Waterways carry 16 percent of U.S. freight volume, especially large, bulky items of low value, such as cement, sand, gravel, steel, grain, and lumber. This mode of transportation is very slow and not very flexible. The destination must be near a waterway, or ground transportation must be added to the distribution system. And some water routes are subject to freezing during the winter and flooding at other times of the year. During the summer of 1993, Mother Nature dealt an economic blow to the upper Midwest as extraordinary rainfall swelled the Mississippi River and its tributaries and caused the worst flooding in the Mississippi River Valley in almost three decades. During the two months that the Mississippi was closed to commercial traffic, thousands of barges were idled at an estimated cost to the barge industry of $3 million per day.[20]

Airplanes, the fastest and most expensive means of transportation, are used primarily to ship products with high unit value and low bulk. Airplanes account for only 0.4 percent of domestic freight movement. Variable costs (fuel, maintenance, and labor) are extremely high, and not all destinations have airports or the means to handle air shipments. Even so, improved technology is expected to make air transport more important in the future.

Table 16.2 compares these transportation alternatives and rates them according to the criteria businesses use in choosing how to distribute products.

table **16.2**   **Comparison of Transportation Alternatives**

Characteristics	Airplanes	Pipelines	Waterways	Trucks	Railroads
Speed of delivery	**Best** 5	2	**Worst** 1	4	3
Availability— number of locations served	3	**Worst** 1	2	**Best** 5	4
On-time dependability	3	**Best** 5	**Worst** 1	4	2
Capability of carrying various products	2	**Worst** 1	**Best** 5	3	4
Frequency of shipments	3	**Best** 5	**Worst** 1	4	2
Cost per ton-mile	**Worst** 1	4	**Best** 5	2	3

Scale of 1 to 5   1 = worst, 5 = best

The Changing Nature of Wholesaling and Retailing

In Chapter 1 we saw how the environment influences business conduct. Distribution is a business activity that is also affected by outside sources.

Wholesaling

Wholesalers link the manufacturer and the retailer in the distribution chain. Broadly speaking, any transaction between one producer or intermediary and another is a wholesaling transaction. Thus, when a restaurant manager runs down the street and buys napkins from another retailer, that exchange technically is a wholesaling transaction.

In 1993, there were 280,000 firms employing 6 million persons in the wholesaling industry.[21] The number of wholesaling companies is down from 364,000 in 1987. Many small companies and only a few very large wholesalers make up the wholesaling industry. There are three types of wholesalers: merchant wholesalers, agents and brokers, and manufacturers' sales branches.

9. Identify the categories of wholesalers and discuss the factors affecting the future of wholesaling.

Merchant Wholesalers

Merchant wholesalers are intermediaries who take ownership to the products they sell and account for 60 percent of wholesaling sales.[22] Merchant wholesalers are independently owned businesses, which may be called jobbers or distributors, and are classified into two broad categories: full-service and limited-service.

A *full-service wholesaler* is a wholesaler that performs a full range of services to meet customers' needs. These services may include pickup and delivery of goods, warehousing, promotional assistance, and even help with accounting procedures. They may carry a wide variety of product lines, just one or two product lines, or specialty products rarely found elsewhere. Being full-service means going above and beyond the call of duty to meet special customer needs. Consider the full-service wholesalers called **rack jobbers**, which assume complete responsibility for a particular section of a retail store. Their services usually include delivery of goods to the retailer's site as well as setting up and maintaining displays and inventory. Products are sold on consignment so that the retailer is billed only for the amount of goods actually sold.

With over $2.5 billion in sales, Sysco Corp. is the largest single-line, full-service wholesaler in the U.S. food industry. It supplies more than 8,000 different lines of food and cooking supplies to hospitals, universities, and restaurants. Sysco provides credit for its customers, storage of products, planning support, and technical assistance such as kitchen equipment installation and repair.

A **limited-service wholesaler**, as the name suggests, performs a limited number of services for the businesses it serves. These wholesalers represent only a small portion of the wholesaling industry. *Cash and carry wholesalers*, for example, sell to small retailers on a cash-only basis and do not provide delivery. *Truck wholesalers* specialize in selling and delivery services. They are usually small operators that deliver frequently required perishable goods such as groceries, meats, and dairy products.

A *producer cooperative* is a member-owned wholesale operation that assembles farm products to sell in local markets. At year end, the profits from the cooperative are divided among the members. *Drop shippers* are limited-service wholesalers that sell goods but do not stock, handle, or deliver them. Drop shippers act as intermediaries between the manufacturer and the customer and

 merchant wholesalers

Intermediaries who take ownership to the products they sell and account for 60 percent of wholesaling sales.

 rack jobbers

Full-service wholesalers that assume complete responsibility for a particular section of a retail store.

 limited-service wholesaler

A wholesaler who performs a limited number of services for the businesses it serves.

manufacturer's agent

An independent sales representative who works for several manufacturers of related but noncompeting product lines.

assume total responsibility for the products they sell. These wholesalers tend to sell bulk items such as railcar loads of coal, lumber, chemicals, and so forth.

Agents and Brokers

Agents and brokers make up the second major category of wholesaling intermediaries. Their primary function is to bring together buyers and sellers and help them make exchanges. These intermediaries do not take title to the products they exchange. Ownership usually brings with it control. An intermediary who owns goods can establish the terms of sale. Agents and brokers provide fewer services than other wholesalers and usually work on a commission basis.

One example of an agent is the **manufacturer's agent**, an independent sales representative who works for several manufacturers of related but noncompeting product lines. These agents are usually very knowledgeable about products sold and have an extensive understanding of the needs of the customers they serve. Other agent intermediaries actually take possession of the goods sold and have wide control over price and other terms of sale. *Brokers* are intermediaries who do not handle the goods, and once they have located a buyer, they let the buyers and sellers negotiate the terms of sale. Their primary function is to supply market information and establish contacts to facilitate sales for clients. Most of the approximately 1,500 independent food brokers in the United States work regionally for a small group of food producers, such as RJR Nabisco or Heinz. They work with only a few of the producer's products and receive a small commission. The largest food broker, Daymon Associates, Inc., of New York City, has 1,700 salespeople serving about 65 major supermarket chains and reaping $175 million in gross commissions from about 1,000 manufacturers. Its specialty is moving the private-label products that are so in demand with today's value-minded grocery shoppers. Daymon is so aggressive in serving its clients that it arranges for newly marketed manufacturers' brands to be torn apart and imitative private-label "knockoffs" designed for its client manufacturers. It even provides state-of-the-art label design for its producers.

Which Is the Better Value?

Expert grocery shoppers save big by buying store brands and private-label products. A growing number of value-conscious consumers contend that private-label quality is comparable to manufacturers' brands, and the value is unbeatable.

Manufacturers' Sales Branches and Offices

These wholesaling establishments are owned and operated by manufacturers but are separate from the manufacturers' factories. As producers grow in size, they often start their own wholesale operations similar to a full-service wholesaler. They establish sales branches and offices to improve selling, inventory control, and product promotion. Manufacturers gain stricter control with their own sales branches. There are two types of this form of intermediary. *Manufacturers' sales branches* are company-owned wholesaling middlemen that carry inventory, while *manufacturers' sales offices* do not. Their relative success is due to the fact that they are usually set up in the manufacturer's best markets.

The Future of Wholesaling

In the struggle for channel power, wholesalers have not held their ground. Large-volume retailers like Wal-Mart, Kmart, and Price-Costco increasingly focus on holding down costs. This adds pressure to eliminate wholesaling intermediaries. As we have seen, Wal-Mart and Sears already have policies of buying directly from manufacturers. The growth in retail private brands, the increasing size of both manufacturer and retailer operations, and a lack of innovation in the way wholesalers conduct business have all put the squeeze on wholesaling. And foreign wholesaling firms, observing the opportunities that U.S. wholesalers are missing, are making inroads into the American market.

But don't count out wholesalers quite yet. Wholesaling intermediaries have longtime relationships with retailers that cannot easily be replaced. They are true specialists in the activities of distribution. They offer availability of stock closer to the retailer than do manufacturers, a benefit of special interest to small retailers. Their proximity to the marketplace makes a wealth of information available to them, which puts them in a prime position to spot new trends and determine their magnitude and direction.

Do small businesses have the same opportunities to build relationships with wholesalers as large volume retailers?

The survivors in the wholesaling industry will make greater use of new management techniques to reduce costs, they will make their operations more efficient, and they will create still deeper relationships with their retail customers and suppliers by incorporating value-added services desired by other channel members, as Daymon Associates does. At the top of the list will be greater use of new technologies; the future will find wholesalers as much in the business of information flow as in the business of goods flow.

Retailing

Because retailers sell goods and services to ultimate consumers, they are in the best possible position to understand their customers' specific wants and needs. This information drives the entire distribution and production system. Orders placed by retailers have a reverse domino effect all through the distribution channel, since consumers dictate supply throughout the distribution system.

Types of Retail Stores

We usually think of retailers as store owners, but not all retailing requires a store. Teachers, lawyers, consultants, doctors, and masseuses are retailers of services. Newspapers are retailed in boxes on street corners, as is shoe shining. The Mary Kay cosmetics representative who comes to the door is a retailer, and so are those kiosks and carts you see in airports and shopping malls. Anyone who sells goods and services directly to ultimate consumers is in the business of retailing.

10. Describe the categories of retailers and discuss the future of retailing.

scrambled merchandising

A strategy of carrying a nontraditional mix of product lines.

convenience stores

Retail establishments located near the residences or workplaces of their target customers; they carry a wide assortment of products and emphasize location, parking, easy movement within the store, long hours, and quick checkout service.

specialty stores

Full-service stores offering variety in a single merchandise category.

department stores

Retail stores that carry a wide variety of product lines divided into departments to facilitate merchandising.

supermarkets

Large self-service stores that carry a full line of food products and some nonfood products.

Retail categories sometimes overlap, particularly as companies practice **scrambled merchandising**, a strategy of carrying a nontraditional mix of product lines. Today's supermarkets, for example, carry kitchen utensils, books, prescription drugs, flowers, salad bars, dry cleaning services, film processing, and banking; some even offer sit-down restaurants, while others are adding optical departments and family dentistry. This trend parallels the tendency for retail stores to become bigger and more diverse. Let's take a look at the key types of retail stores.

Convenience stores are located near the residences or workplaces of their target customers. They carry a wide assortment of products and emphasize location, parking, easy movement within the store, long hours, and quick checkout service. Such stores stock an average of 3,000 fast-moving items—milk, bread, ice cream, newspapers, soft drinks, and snacks. Convenience stores are adding freshly prepared food, more health and beauty aids, and even gasoline to attract more customers. And many are offering banking services and videocassette rentals. Southland's 7-Eleven and Dairy Mart are examples.

Specialty stores are full-service stores offering variety in a single merchandise category, such as sporting goods, electronics, or toys. They are retail outlets like The Gap and Radio Shack for which customers develop a strong preference based on the assortment of products offered, the quality of service, or the store's reputation. Specialty stores must continuously strive to hold their customer's loyalty. Some specialty stores, such as Toys 'R' Us, Home Depot, and Circuit City, sell so much volume in one product line that they have become known as *"category killers."*

Department stores carry a wide variety of product lines divided into departments to facilitate merchandising. Marshall Field, Macy's, Bloomingdale's, and J.C. Penney are examples. These retailing institutions typically include departments for cosmetics, clothing, appliances, and housewares. Some also offer service departments such as travel assistance, insurance, tax preparation, and even banking and financial services.

Supermarkets are large self-service stores that carry a full line of food products and some nonfood products. Supermarkets frequently compete head on with rival chains. Chicagoland's Jewel Tea has long squared off against rival Dominick's; on the West Coast, Safeway jousts with Ralph's Market and Lucky

Category Killer

High-volume specialty retailers like East Coast electronics chain Nobody Beats the Wiz Total Entertainment Centers blitz their competition with everyday low prices, convenient locations, weekly full-color shopping circulars, easy credit, and toll-free ordering 24 hours a day.

Stores. Now they also have to compete with other types of retailers trying to bag a share of the shopper's grocery budget—food *warehouse clubs* such as Price-Costco, discounters turned food retailers like Wal-Mart Stores, and deep-discount drugstores like Drug Emporium as well as specialty chains like pet supply superstore Petco.

Discount stores are self-service general merchandise stores that combine low price with high volume. Kmart, Wal-Mart, and Target are examples. Today's discounters offer credit, have plenty of salesclerks, are located in attractive buildings in good locations, advertise in the mass media, and carry many different lines of products. *Superstores* operate like discounters but combine general merchandise with food products. Retailing today is witnessing some significant alterations. *Factory outlets* are discount stores owned and operated by manufacturers, such as Dansk or J. Crew, who sell slightly damaged or surplus merchandise. *Off-price stores* offer brand-name merchandise at prices significantly lower than regular department stores. T.J. Maxx and Filene's Basement are examples.

Retailing Today and Tomorrow

Retailing is fashioned by the business environment, and the marketplace is full of changes. Americans continue to love to shop, but not the same way as in earlier years. At the front of shoppers' minds is buying "value," which means "more for less." Americans are increasingly unwilling to pay full price, and retailers must be constantly on the lookout for cost reductions.

Consumers are in constant pursuit of convenience and efficiency as well as value. Hence we are increasingly shopping by catalog and computer, television and telephone. In 1992, American consumers bought $42 billion in merchandise by check or credit card—all from home! In 1993, 3.5 million consumers were buyers of computer services, up from 610,000 in 1987. The number of catalog shoppers has doubled in a decade. Consumers frequently go to stores to shop for *information*, to determine product or brand features, and then go home to buy via telephone, fax machine, or computer. Interactive television opens up still another convenient way for consumers to bypass the retail store. "The power of television is about to transform retailing forever," says a top retail executive.[23] Consumers with a computer and modem will be able to access on-line services and shop for the best product at the best price. Color catalogs are currently available on-line. The handwriting is on the wall for many retailers. Those that will survive must adapt to *just-in-time retailing*, which reduces the length of time, the quantity of inventory, and the number of intermediaries between the product and the consumer.

CUC International, a shopping club, provides a glimpse of this approach. It offers consumers deeply discounted prices on 250,000 branded products—luggage, appliances, even theater tickets. Membership costs $59 for telephone users, $49 for computer users. Members browse through catalogs and visit stores to determine what they want to buy. Then they place an order to CUC, which passes the order on to the manufacturer, who ships the product direct. Salespeople, parking lots, inventory, and store costs are eliminated; CUC's expenses are mostly for telephone and computer use. Hence, markups are just about half those of discount chains. The company is adding interactive video, which will enable members to compare every brand of a product via their television screen and then place their orders.

As competition between forms of retailing and between individual retailers continues to intensify, the competitive edge will increasingly come from continual improvements in the use of electronic data processing and computers. Registers at checkout points will generate more and more information on store sales by product size, vendor, price, and department. Inventory monitoring

 discount stores

Self-service general merchandise stores that combine low price with high volume.

High-Class Discounters

At factory outlet malls, such as this one in San Marcos, Texas, specialty manufacturers discount their own merchandise, from clothing to crystal. Shoppers come for the brand names and tolerate irregulars and seconds in exchange for low prices.

with automatic electronic reordering, individual store to home office computer linkage of daily sales data, and electronic dispensing of coupons and discounts will become standard retailing procedures to reduce costs and increase productivity. Some retailers are helping customers shop via in-store computers. Electronistore, an on-site computer-based shopper assistant, allows customers to locate merchandise, learn product colors and other features, and compare prices. It not only increases the convenience of shopping but also provides retailers with valuable information on browsing behavior.

Retailing Goes Global

Concerned about slowing economic growth in America and peaking domestic demand, mail-order companies like L.L. Bean, Lands' End, and South Dakota's golf equipment catalog retailer, Austad's, are seeking sales overseas. L.L. Bean, a symbol of Americana, added a special international department to serve non-U.S. outdoor enthusiasts, while Lands' End created a special catalog for the British market. And Austad's receives fax orders from all over: Saudi Arabia, South Africa, Sweden, and golf-crazy Japan. See the doing business box "Exporting a Revolution."

American retailers, especially discounters, are seeking an international presence. "American retailing is the best and most competitive in the world. We have an automatic advantage over any local retailer," a Kmart executive remarked.[24] Price-Costco, Staples, T.J. Maxx, and Pier 1 imports have all started stores in England. Kmart is forging ahead into Eastern Europe, while Toys 'R' Us has expanded into Japan and Australia. The surging global desire for American products is a powerful magnet for American retailers. But the size and diversity of the U.S. market is also a draw for foreign retailers. IKEA and Benetton are very successful. Twenty percent of food retailing in the United States is done by foreign companies, such as Loblaw, ALDI, and Food Lion.[25]

The Future of Retailing

By early 1995, home shopping was a $220 billion industry that Yankelovich Partners, Inc., estimates will grow by 20 percent each year. As consumers' desire to shop at home grows, retailers like Tower Records are going on line with eShop Technology, which allows them to create, merchandise, and control electronic stores, or eShops. Most customers pay no fee for this service. They simply order on-line, and products are shipped directly to their homes. For retailers, electronic shopping eliminates many of the operating costs that shrink profits, and allows them to target customers efficiently.

doing business

Exporting a Revolution

A spokesman for Harrod's, the prestigious English department store, says, "Napoleon once called England a nation of shopkeepers. And though he meant it as an insult, we're proud to be a nation of shopkeepers because we're very good at it." But a representative of American discounter Price-Costco disagrees. He says, "Any idiot can make money selling at a high price."[1] Who is right?

Price-Costco's first British stores opened in late 1993, and it plans to open stores throughout England and the rest of Europe in the coming years. But how can a U.S. retailer overcome the traditional barriers to entering European markets? The Price-Costco representative thinks he has the answer: "Our prices will be 30 percent lower."[2]

In recent years, big U.S. retailers have taken the United Kingdom by storm. Toys 'R' Us now opens more stores overseas every year than it does in the United States, and its English operations are its most profitable.[3] And the push is on in Japan as well. Traditional Japanese department stores still dominate the market, with their bowing elevator ladies and elaborate service. But their high prices and complex distribution channels keep them closed to U.S.-made goods; fewer than 5 percent of department store products in Japan are imports. However, Japanese versions of U.S. discount stores began to appear a few years ago and now compete strongly with the traditional retailers. These discounters mimic the Price-Costco approach—shelves of products in a warehouselike space with some cash registers by the door. But their low prices are attracting Japanese consumers.

And they are providing a beachhead for American products; a quarter or more of what they sell is imported.[4]

The big U.S. retailers and their discount concept represent a new phase in distribution. They work directly with manufacturers to buy large quantities at very low prices, then pass those low prices on to customers. Gone are the many small businesses that used to run distribution like a bucket brigade, each spilling a little of the consumer's money as it handled the bucket. In the process of expanding overseas, these U.S. retailers are forcing the foreign markets they penetrate into a new phase, too. Even before Price-Costco opened its first British store, for example, the local chains began cutting their prices in anticipation.[5] And to keep prices competitive with Price-Costco, they have had to adopt many of Price-Costco's practices. This means that local distribution channels are being forced to change to enable local retailers to compete.

Britain and Japan are *both* nations of shopkeepers—that much is true. But by the time they finish consuming the new distribution concepts the United States is exporting, they will become nations of discounters as well!

[1] Kevin Helliker, "U.S. Discount Retailers Are Targeting Europe and Its Fat Margins," *Wall Street Journal*, Sept. 20, 1993, p. A1.
[2] Helliker, "U.S. Discount Retailers."
[3] Helliker, "U.S. Discount Retailers."
[4] "What? Everyday Bargains? This Can't Be Japan," *Business Week*, Sept. 6, 1993, p. 41.
[5] "Shop Till You Drop Hits Europe," *Business Week*, Nov. 29, 1993, p. 58.

Nonstore Retailers

In-home retailing includes all sales transactions that occur in the home setting. Door-to-door and party-plan selling are the most visible. Avon, Amway, and World Book Encyclopedia are retailed by door-to-door salespeople, while Tupperware and Mary Kay Cosmetics are sold via sponsoring in-home parties where products are sampled. *Direct marketing,* another form of in-home retailing, refers to solicitations for an immediate response from buyers. It is done through telephone selling (*telemarketing*), direct mail, and newspaper, television, and radio ads. A major form of direct marketing, mail-order catalogs—L.L. Bean, Spiegel, and Horchow, for instance—allow mail or toll-free telephone purchasing.

MNI Interactive, a San Francisco entertainment business, allows customers to hear clips of new record albums over the telephone for a monthly membership fee. Members punch out the artist's name on a touch-tone telephone to hear the release. Then by pressing zero they can purchase CDs for delivery by mail. Through the use of membership codes, the telephone system detects shoppers' musical favorites and makes suggestions for previewing lesser-known recording artists.

Vending machine retailing allows customers to buy products from conveniently located machines. The products retailed this way are small, routinely purchased, standardized items such as chewing gum, soft drinks, coffee, candy, and personal hygiene products. Vending machines, open 24 hours a day, can expand a marketer's distribution to locations that might otherwise not be used—rest rooms, libraries, and hospitals, for example. Some vendors have been using *debit cards* in places like college campuses and office buildings where there is much repeat purchasing. Customers inventory their money by buying a card for, say, $10. The card has a magnetic strip that deducts the cost of each purchase from the cost of the card.

Vending machine retailing is taking full advantage of technological advances. New vending machines built around computers are tiny, self-contained businesses of their own. World TravelFile has become an automated travel agent, with vending machines that show videos of possible destinations and then allow customers to buy rail and excursion trips with credit cards—right on the spot. American Greetings has placed 2,400 personalized greeting card machines in gift stores, drugstores, and supermarkets. Customers can create the message and choose from 1,000 different designs, and watch as the card is printed in four-color before their eyes.

A new form of retailers is the *video shopping networks*. Cable television networks display products on screen and customers call in their purchases by toll-free telephone number. QVC (Quality, Value, Convenience) and the Home Shopping Network are examples. The emphasis to date has been on bargain and closeout merchandise, jewelry, and household goods. But greater assortments can be expected as more home customers become comfortable with shopping via television.

On-line computer services offer another dimension to in-home retailing. A two-way interactive computer system allows shoppers to preview products on their computer screens and make purchases electronically. IBM/Sears Roebuck's Prodigy is an example. Interactive computer on-line retailers also sell information. Prodigy, for instance, has added Internet to its product line. Here, researchers, students, and "techies" can buy access to databases and discuss topics via electronic bulletin boards through the worldwide web of 45,000 networks that exist in cyberspace. And the information highway with its interactive network will increase the retailing of entertainment and information

table 16.3 Consumer Goods Retailers

Retail stores		Nonstore retailers	Electronic retailers
Convenience stores • 7-Eleven • Dairy Mart	Supermarkets • Stop & Shop • Ralph's	In-home retailing • Amway • Tupperware	Video shopping • QVC • Home Shopping Network
Specialty stores • The Gap • Victoria's Secret *Category killers* • Toys 'R' Us • Home Depot	Discounters *Superstores* • Thrifty Acres *Warehouse clubs* • Sam's Clubs *Factory Outlets* • Calvin Klein Outlet	Direct marketing *Telemarketing* *Mail-order catalogs* • L.L. Bean • J. Crew • Williams Sonoma	On-line services • Prodigy • America On-line
Department stores • J.C. Penney • Bloomingdale's	*Off-price stores* • Filene's Basement	Vending machines	

product lines. The possibilities and the impact of these technologies on retailing are staggering.

Retailing consumer goods takes many forms, as summarized in Table 16.3, and these forms are always changing. The "wheel of retailing" theory offers an explanation for how and why this happens.

The Wheel of Retailing

The world of retailing never stops spinning. Innovations are driven by changes in the business environment. Figure 16.5 shows the **wheel of retailing**, a cycle in which new forms of retailers replace established retailers that have become high-cost competitors. For example, 100 years ago department stores were a retail innovation based on low cost and high volume. The first department stores were simple and spartan. They outcompeted general stores and other small retailers. Their success was built on limited services, low costs, and lower prices than the competition. But over time department stores expanded their services, offering an improved shopping atmosphere, free home delivery, and credit. These upgrades pushed up their expenses. And in came the low-cost, low-price retailer: discounters like Korvettes and W.T. Grant (both now out of business). Today's discounters, such as Kmart and Wal-Mart, have added services to become more appealing. And what do we see? In comes the new wave of discounters: the factory outlet malls, the warehouse stores, and the off-price retailers. Today, warehouse clubs are facing increasing pressure to expand services and merchandise lines in order to compete for a broader base of customers. Sam's Clubs, Wal-Mart's warehouse divisions, have begun to add "extras" such as in-store bakeries and optical departments.

wheel of retailing

A cycle in which new forms of retailers replace established retailers that have become high-cost competitors.

Can a new wave be far behind? Will it be at-home shopping?

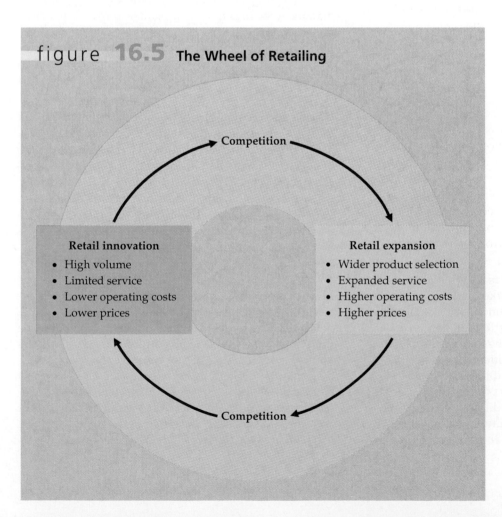

figure **16.5** **The Wheel of Retailing**

Competition

Retail innovation
- High volume
- Limited service
- Lower operating costs
- Lower prices

Retail expansion
- Wider product selection
- Expanded service
- Higher operating costs
- Higher prices

Competition

Reviewing *Distribution: Time and Place*

How Business Creates Availability

1. **Identify the major marketing intermediaries and describe their roles in the distribution process.** Marketing intermediaries are wholesalers—including merchant wholesalers, who take title to the product, and agents, who do not—and retailers. These distributors add value by providing time, place, and information utility. They reduce the number of transactions needed to distribute products, which saves consumers money, and they provide services that would otherwise have to be performed by the producer. They also are located closer to customers and know better what customers want.

2. **Differentiate between channel of distribution and physical distribution and describe the four distribution channels for consumer goods.** A channel of distribution is the route a product takes to reach the consumer, and physical distribution is the means by which it travels that route. The direct channel—from producer to consumer—is the shortest and often the quickest route. Door-to-door sales and mail-order catalogs are examples. The channel that includes a retailer between producer and consumer is the most familiar; products sold in this way include automobiles and clothing. In the third type of channel, the chain is extended to include a wholesaler between producer and retailer. Drugs, food items, and hardware are sold through this channel. The final type of channel adds an agent between producer and wholesaler. Candy is sold in this way. Today, there are also reverse channels for recycling of products.

3. **Describe industrial and service channels of distribution.** Industrial products pass through fairly short channels of distribution because more precise information is needed from the manufacturer's salespeople. If an intermediary is needed—by a small manufacturer, for example—industrial distributors act as wholesalers. Like industrial products, services usually involve direct channels—from hospital mobile unit to patient, for example—although sometimes an intermediary—a doctor referral, for instance—is involved.

4. **Explain the effect of global and dual markets on distribution channels.** A business's total market may complicate its channels of distribution. A business with a global market has longer channels of distribution, since each nation has its own channels. Global businesses must also take into account communication differences, as well as differences in the cultural values and practices of the receiving nation. A business selling its product to two very different markets must work in two different channels of distribution. Appliance manufacturers, for example, market separately to home builders and to consumers.

Matching Distribution Channels to Marketing Objectives

5. **Discuss the criteria used by businesses in selecting a distribution channel.** Businesses select a distribution channel on the basis of how much market coverage and control they desire. If the potential market is large, they seek a longer channel of distribution, which provides a larger number of contacts and hence greater market coverage. However, the longer the channel, the less control the business has; the shorter the channel, the less coverage and the greater the control.

6. **Differentiate between the three levels of distribution strategies.** Businesses may employ intensive distribution strategies for the widest exposure for convenience products such as milk and bread, selective distribution for shopping and some specialty products that are characterized by a high degree of brand awareness and loyalty, or exclusive distribution for specialty products that carry a certain image.

7. **Describe the sources of channel conflict and cooperation.** Channel conflict may be horizontal or vertical. Horizontal conflict occurs between channel members at the same level—two or more wholesalers, for example. Vertical conflict spans different levels—for example, when a manufacturer tries to force a retailer to maintain a large inventory of its product. Channel cooperation may occur in one of two situations: when a powerful channel captain influences the behavior of others or when a VMS (corporate, administered, or contractual) is established between businesses and their suppliers.

8. **Discuss the relationship between customer service and the tasks of physical distribution.** Customer service—providing customers with product availability, speed, and accuracy and reliability of product delivery—underlies all aspects of physical distribution. It is assured when the six interacting tasks of physical distribution are well coordinated. These tasks are forecasting demand, order processing, inventory control, warehousing, materials handling, and transportation.

The Changing Nature of Wholesaling and Retailing

9. **Identify the categories of wholesalers and discuss the factors affecting the future of wholesaling.** Merchant wholesalers take ownership of the product. They may be full-service wholesalers, who perform a range of services to meet customers' needs (for example, rack jobbers) or they may be limited-service wholesalers, such as cash and carry wholesalers, truck wholesalers, producer cooperatives, or drop shippers. Agents and brokers do not own the product; they simply bring buyers and sellers together and help them make exchanges. Manufacturers'

sales branches and offices are established by large producers who want stricter control over the sale of their product. The future of wholesaling is dim due to the growth of large retailers, the increasing number of retail private brands, and improved technology designed to reduce costs. However, wholesalers do offer special services that cannot easily be replaced; those who reduce costs, make their operations more efficient, and incorporate value-added services will survive.

10. **Describe the categories of retailers and discuss the future of retailing.** Anyone who sells goods or services directly to ultimate consumers is a retailer. This includes teachers, lawyers, consultants, and doctors, as well as store owners. There are several types of stores, including convenience stores such as 7-Eleven, specialty stores such as Home Depot, department stores such as Macy's and J.C. Penney, supermarkets such as Safeway, and discount stores such as Kmart. In order to survive in today's market, retailers must satisfy consumers' changing needs. Besides lower prices, consumers want convenience in shopping, which may involve computer, television, or mail. U.S. retailers are also going global to acquire sales growth.

✓ Key Terms

marketing intermediaries 481	intensive distribution 488	public warehouses 494	manufacturer's agent 498
retailers 481	selective distribution 488	distribution centers 494	scrambled merchandising 500
wholesalers 481	exclusive distribution 488	materials handling 495	convenience stores 500
agents 481	channel captain 490	containerization 495	specialty stores 500
distribution channel 483	vertical marketing system (VMS) 490	piggyback service 495	department stores 500
physical distribution 483	order processing 493	merchant wholesalers 497	supermarkets 500
reverse channels 485	inventory control 493	rack jobbers 497	discount stores 501
dual distribution 487	private warehouses 494	limited-service wholesaler 497	wheel of retailing 505

● Review Questions

1. What are the different types of marketing intermediaries?
2. Why do we need intermediaries to distribute products?
3. What is the main difference between distribution channels and physical distribution?
4. How do the distribution channels for consumer goods, industrial products, and consumer services differ?
5. How do global distribution channels differ from U.S. channels?
6. What two criteria guide the choice of a long or a short channel of distribution? Explain each.
7. Why does conflict arise within a distribution system?
8. How do businesses establish channel cooperation?
9. What are the six tasks of physical distribution?
10. What are the objectives of physical distribution and how do channel members reach them?
11. What factors will decide the future of wholesaling?
12. What are the major trends in retailing today?
13. What is the wheel of retailing and where on the wheel would you place the three types of retailers doing business today?

• Critical Thinking Questions

1. Distributing products through an inappropriate store can detract from their appeal. Selling Polo clothing in Wal-Mart would hurt the manufacturer. Why, then, do we see some of the same brands at Kmart as at small specialty stores?

2. In the chapter, we saw that Nexxus Products Co. sells hair conditioners and shampoos through hairstyling salons. What distribution channel does Nexxus use? From what you have learned about market coverage and channel control, do you think Nexxus is using the most appropriate channel?

3. Metamucil is the best-selling laxative in drugstores, but in food stores it is far behind its competitors. What will be necessary to improve sales of Metamucil in food stores?

4. Hardee's Food Systems has 4,000 fast-food outlets. All but 350 serve Coca-Cola while the others offer Pepsi-Cola. Hardee's franchise agreement does not restrict the choice of soft drink supplier. Coca-Cola offered a promotion to Hardee franchisees in which plush stuffed animal versions of its popular computer-animated Cola Bears were sold as premiums. However, those Hardee franchisees serving Pepsi-Cola were excluded from the campaign. What kind of channel conflict was involved in this situation?

5. How does just-in-time inventory control influence the physical distribution tasks of forecasting demand, order processing, inventory control, warehousing, materials handling, and transportation? Think of some industries in which the use of just-in-time is appropriate.

6. In the retailing of personal computers, chains like ComputerLand and the Computer Store have taken over the business from independents. Why do you think this happened? Today, mail-order retailing from manufacturers is beginning to take business away from the chains. Why do you think this is happening?

REVIEW CASE *Brooklyn Brewery*[26]

Stephen Hindy was editor of a Long Island (New York) newspaper. Thomas Potter, his neighbor, was a banker in Manhattan. Hindy brewed his own beer as a hobby. Potter liked what he tasted and was persuaded by Hindy to accompany him to a microbrewery convention in Portland, Oregon. (Microbreweries are small-scale regional beer producers.) The next thing they knew, they were in business together.

Potter's bank background and close ties to investors helped him raise the money to start the business. Hindy researched beer recipes, including those of the more than 40 breweries that had existed in Brooklyn before Prohibition. In the end, he chose a dry but fragrant recipe from a 1903 Brooklyn brew. The pair christened their concoction Brooklyn Lager and contracted with F.X. Matt Brewing Co. of Utica, New York, to produce it. Matt Brewing had already distinguished itself by supplying highly successful micro brands such as Samuel Adams and New Amsterdam. In 1988, trucks carrying the first bottles of Brooklyn Lager rolled down the highway toward Brooklyn.

Sales in the first year were $404,000; in the second, they reached $725,000. Yet losses in those first two years hit $400,000. Hindy returned to the newspaper to supplement his income while Potter worked on raising still more capital. But neither considered abandoning their new business. The root problem, as they saw it, was distribution.

Brooklyn Lager was distributed in eight states. Outside Brooklyn, beer distributors were used. These wholesalers moved hundreds of thousands of cases of beer for name-brand suppliers such as Anheuser-Busch and Miller Brewing. Brooklyn Lager amounted to only a few hundred cases of sales, and so their commitment to it was minimal. Further, because Brooklyn Brewery was such a small-volume operation, the distributors charged high prices for their service. In Brooklyn, where Brooklyn Brewery controlled the distribution, profit margins were 40 percent. When distributors were used, margins slipped to 20 percent.

1. What channel of distribution is most appropriate for Brooklyn Lager?

2. Which intensity of distribution is most appropriate for Brooklyn Brewing?

3. What type of conflict has arisen in the channel of distribution?

4. How might that conflict be eliminated?

5. The operations of Brooklyn Brewery include various physical distribution tasks. Which are important? How do you think Brooklyn Brewery might employ each to distribute its beer?

CRITICAL THINKING CASE *GUM Department Store* [27]

GUM (*Glavni Univermag Moskvi*) is a department store located in Moscow's Red Square that opened before the turn of this century. Its 1,000 stores—on three levels were a tribute to the pitfalls of Soviet central planning. Until recently, communist bureaucrats determined merchandise, worker pay, and store hours. Although its architecture is glorious, GUM is perhaps even better known for its discourteous salesclerks, long lines, and rock-bottom prices. But the turn of political events in Russia is changing that.

In 1993, under the management of Chairman Yuri Solomatin, GUM became a private company, selling public stock to raise money for renovations. Those improvements to the facilities that have been completed seem to be working very well. Over 30 Western companies have rented alcoves and operate side by side with traditional Soviet stores. Among those retailing in GUM are Benetton, Arrow Shirts, Samsonite luggage, and Estee Lauder cosmetics.

Shoppers can still purchase from retailers left over from the previous era. In these stores, goods are badly displayed on shelves five feet away. Shoppers wait on one line to be shown the goods, on another to pay a clerk doing calculations on an abacus, and on still another to receive their goods. Russian plastic cups are priced cheap at 4 cents each; German pots and pans are priced high at $303.

In the Western stores, shopping is in sharp contrast. Customers enter easily and quickly, browse to their hearts' content, and pay for their purchases as they leave. Salesclerks, trained by their employers, are more courteous than before, though still not quite up to Western standards. Paid about $60 per month, they tend to stand and watch rather than offer assistance to shoppers.

All stores, including the Western shops, are operated by GUM personnel. Western shops are run as GUM departments but provide all their own renovations, employee training, equipment, and, of course, merchandise. Employees are paid in Western currencies. Markups are small, just 10 to 25 percent. Russians believe that high markups result in profits, which are difficult to accept in a culture where profit has been considered an evil for three generations.

Western stores are doing quite well at GUM. Karstadt, a German department store, has expanded three times to meet demand. And Botany 500, which sells American menswear, including $50 shirts, racked up $1 million in sales in its first year.

1. What are the physical distribution tasks necessary to support sales of Western merchandise in GUM for a company such as Levi's? What difficulties in physical distribution can you envision arising that would not arise at home?

2. From what you learned in this chapter about retailing trends, what advice would you give to Mr. Solomatin that might improve his operation?

3. If you were an American retailer, would you open a store in GUM? Why or why not?

Critical Thinking with the ONE MINUTE MANAGER

"You've learned a lot of technical concepts and terms now, but can you apply them to real-world distribution channels?"

"Of course we can! Once you know a term, you can use it," Joanna responded to the One Minute Manager's question.

"Yes, but there are multiple levels of understanding. For instance, you may *recognize* terms like just-in-time inventory control or exclusive distribution, but can you *use* them to explain the many changes occurring in distribution channels today?"

"Just try us!" said Carlos.

"OK, remember the story I told you about Direct Connect? It's GE's new system that links participating appliance stores to a computerized 24-hour order processing system, and within one day fills orders to stores out of regional warehouses."

"I remember."

"Well, that story epitomized the many important changes in distribution today. Let's see if you can apply to it the concepts and terms contained in the chapter." The One Minute Manager then proceeded to ask them the following questions.

1. Is Direct Connect an example of just-in-time inventory control? Why?

2. Would Direct Connect help a retailer that wanted to adopt a just-in-time *retailing* strategy?

3. If you were in charge of the Direct Connect program for GE, would you want to offer it on an exclusive distribution basis or not? Why?

4. If you were a retailer of GE appliances, would you favor exclusive distribution or not? How might your view differ from GE's?

5. If the Direct Connect program is such a good idea, why didn't GE offer it a decade ago? What factors have changed to make it easier to do, and also to make loading the trade a less successful alternative for GE? What has been the impact of those factors?

It's for you! Sprint's low, flat rates for small businesses.

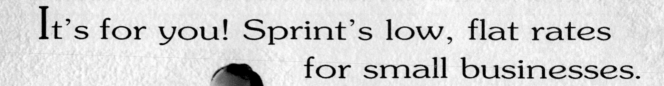

Thanks to Sprint Business, now the world is flat.

Introducing low, flat rates on your long distance services. That includes all your state-to-state calls, as well as Sprint 800 service, fax, cellular long distance and calling cards.

You pay the same low rate whenever you call.

Day or night. Weekdays or weekends. On the road, or at the office. Even if you spend as little as $50 a month.

Your long distance costs are simple to understand.

Our low, flat rates end the confusion of calculating your cost per minute. And it's easy to sign up. Just call now. We'll help your business do more business.

Sprint®
Business

1·800·827·3700

17

Price and Promotion

price

What the buyer gives up—usually money—to receive the product.

promotion

Any attempt by a seller to influence a buying decision.

In a competitive business environment, pricing and promotion together influence the customer's buying decision by communicating the *value* of a product compared with its competitors. The **price** is what the buyer gives up—usually money—to receive the product. Price generally represents the buyer's perception of the product's worth. Organizations use **promotion**, any attempt by a seller to influence a buying decision, to inform and persuade customers. Business decisions about price and promotion are therefore powerful determinants of an organization's marketing mix and of its success in the marketplace. Today, these elements of the four Ps must also respond to customers' greater interest in obtaining high value. After reading this chapter you will be able to reach the learning goals below.

Learning Goals

1. Identify the reasons for the shift in market control from marketer to consumer.
2. List and explain the four major goals of pricing.
3. Describe how cost, demand, and competition determine price.
4. Differentiate strategies used to price new and existing products.
5. Explain how companies use value pricing.
6. Describe the overall and specific objectives of promotion.
7. Discuss the economic and social impact of promotion.
8. List the types of advertising and describe how marketers manage advertising.
9. Identify the classes of personal sellers and list the seven steps in the personal selling process.
10. Describe the roles of direct marketing, sales promotion, and public relations in the promotional mix.
11. Relate promotional mix design to the notion of integrated communications.

Familiarity Breeds Contentment

"Mmm, it smells great in here," Carlos commented as the students joined the One Minute Manager in her office.

"That's Starbucks coffee you smell. We just started brewing it this morning and plan to have a different flavor in the office every day. I think today's flavor is hazelnut."

"Didn't we see a new Starbucks coffee store down the block?" Joanna asked.

"Yes, that's where we got the idea. Everyone has been walking down there for coffee since the store opened. By the way, have you followed the Starbucks story? It's a great illustration of good marketing in action."

"That's our cue, isn't it?" Carlos laughed. "OK, tell us about Starbucks."

"It all started when Howard Schultz visited Milan in 1983. He was struck by the fact that there were 1,700 coffee-houses in the city, even though it's no bigger than Philadelphia. They offered better fresh-roasted coffees for higher prices than we usually pay in the United States, and he realized there was a similar potential in this country. Just the year before, Schultz had joined Starbucks Corp., a small specialty seller of coffee beans in Seattle. It had been growing gradually since its founding in 1971, but Schultz realized the Starbucks product could be sold all across America—that is, if Americans could be taught what a good cup of coffee is and why they should pay more money for it. Enter pricing and promotion. Starbucks positions its product as higher in quality than other coffees, and gives it a slightly higher price to signal this difference. The price reflects the higher costs of fresh roasting and superior beans, too."

"What about promotion—what do you mean by that?" Carlos prompted.

"Well, as you know, promotion is the fourth P of the marketing mix. It is generally defined as activities designed to influence the buying decision through *communication*. And you can see that Starbucks has a big communications task if it's going to get all of America to switch from freeze-dried instant to fresh-brewed New Guinea. Anyway, Schultz bought out the 11-store Starbucks chain in 1987, and now the company operates more than 400 stores. Because he knew that the key to growth is communication with potential customers, one of the first things Schultz did to create that growth was hire an ad agency. For example, the company put up posters with the caption "Familiarity Breeds Contentment" in order to communicate why potential customers should try Starbucks coffee."[1]

"I'm already feeling content, and I've only had a smell," Carlos commented. "Do you mind if I get a cup?"

"Help yourself."

Price, Promotion, and Value

Today's consumers have embarked on an aggressive search for value, and this search pairs price and promotion at the forefront of marketing. Value is the relationship between price and performance—the quality a product offers for its price. Promotion's job is to communicate that value and convince the customer that a product is worth its price.

As the U.S. economy grew steadily through the 1980s, quality alone was enough to loosen consumers' purse strings. As economic growth slowed in the 1990s, consumers, accustomed to buying quality, shied away from buying anything else—but now quality has to come at the right price. The head of a marketing research firm explains it this way: "During the era of mad purchasing, people learned how to shop. They decide what they're going to buy—whether a TV or an industrial turbine—spec it to need, and find the specific unit they're looking for. Then they wait until the price comes down."[2] Today's tough customers buy features that add value and avoid expensive add-ons that don't. According to Barbara Feigin, executive vice president at Grey advertising, "Americans have become very purposeful shoppers. They are reengineering, just as corporate America is doing. We call it precision shopping."[3]

In addition to consumer price pressure, overproduction in some industries has created a strong downward pressure on prices and fearsome price competition. Some global companies—among them Nissan, Dow Chemical, and Siemans—have outproduced demand and created excess inventories. Worldwide overproduction of high-quality products now plagues the consumer electronics, computer, chemical, and machine tool industries. Describing this situation, Jack Welch, CEO at General Electric Corp., commented, "If you can't sell a top-quality product at the world's lowest price, you're going to be out of the game."[4]

At the same time that consumers are aggressively searching for value, they are also exercising more control over marketers' attempts to communicate with them. When we use our remotes to "channel surf" and avoid watching commercials, we are controlling advertising. The power shift from marketer to consumer shows up in other ways as well. It was brought about by four changes in the marketing environment.[5]

1. *Competition is fragmenting markets.* Until the 1990s, businesses relied on massive advertising to direct a single message at large numbers of consumers. This traditional approach is no longer effective because competing businesses have divided large markets into many smaller ones, based on people's life-styles, attitudes, and wants. "Every marketer's dream is to be able to target those little slices," an AT&T communications manager told *Business Week.*[6] One indicator of this fragmentation is the growing number of mailing lists: Currently more than 10,000 are available, and 300 new lists are added each year. Businesses now have a hard time keeping track of their markets.

2. *An empowered consumer has emerged.* These tough customers expect to make choices in their own interest. They believe they have the right not only to choose what messages they listen to but also to make themselves heard. They are well informed about products, services, and prices, and they know to shop elsewhere if they aren't kept happy.

3. *Improved technology has spawned an electronic, interactive marketplace.* Home shopping channels increasingly allow consumers to view products, price them, and buy them without ever leaving home. Soon, customers searching for a used car, for example, may be able to see available cars on their screen, call up specific information about options, and make an offer using interactive television.

1. Identify the reasons for the shift in market control from marketer to consumer.

1-800-PROFITS

As consumers increasingly control the way they shop, businesses like 1-800-FLOWERS prosper. Since the early 1980s, telemarketing companies have blossomed, reaching over half a trillion dollars in sales in 1993. No one is happier about this growth than 800-number service provider AT&T. Even rival phone company MCI uses AT&T for its 1-800-COLLECT service.

4. *Consumers have more alternatives.* Consumers have more brands to choose from, more channels to switch between, more catalogs to buy from, and more hours to shop by dialing toll-free 800 numbers. As we saw in the last chapter, the number of items stocked in a typical supermarket has skyrocketed. Bombarded by information, consumers are quite likely to change brands, channels, shops, or catalogs.

These marketplace forces are having a powerful impact on the way America does business. We begin this chapter by looking at the ways these forces influence pricing objectives, practices, and strategies. Then we examine their effects on promotion, as businesses attempt to communicate value and influence consumers to purchase their products.

Pricing Objectives

2. List and explain the four major goals of pricing.

A firm's pricing goals fall into four main categories: increasing sales, making a profit, communicating a product's image, and ensuring customer value. At the same time, many companies try to minimize the customer's focus on price by stressing nonprice features such as quality and customer service.

Increasing Sales

Recall from Chapter 1 that market share *is the proportion of total market sales captured by any single competitor.*

Pricing objectives should be tied to the organization's overall business objectives. And since a fundamental objective is growth, increased sales is a key pricing goal. Generally, sales increase when a firm reduces its price or offers a new product at a lower price than competitors. Special short-term discounts can encourage people to try a product, and, if they try it, they may buy it again. As you learn pricing strategies and methods, you will notice that many firms focus on increasing sales. Many companies price to increase sales relative to competitors' sales; these businesses measure success by changes in *market share*.

Making a Profit

A firm that doesn't make a profit is soon out of business. **Profit** is the difference between a firm's revenues and its costs:

 profit
The difference between a firm's revenues and its costs.

$$\text{Profit} = \text{Total revenue} - \text{Total costs}$$

But revenues depend both on the price of a product and on the quantity of the product sold:

$$\text{Total revenue} = \text{Price} \times \text{Quantity}$$

Of course, a product's price strongly influences its sales. A price that is too high for the perceived value of the product will reduce sales and lower profits.

Because prices influence sales and profits, *profitability* is an important goal in pricing. A business can pursue this goal in two ways. The first is *profit maximization,* or obtaining the highest possible profit. Although this seems a sound goal, it is unrealistic in practice. First, a firm can never know when it has achieved the highest possible profit. In addition, society often sees profit maximization as profiting excessively. It is considered unethical when high prices prevent consumers from buying products for which they have a strong need. For example, Medicare does not cover prescription drugs, and so most people over the age of 65 must pay for them out of their own pockets. But from 1985 to 1992, drug prices rose twice as fast as the rate of inflation. In the mid-1990s, ten companies, including Merck, Pfizer, and American Home Products, attempted to help meet the health care needs of consumers by adopting voluntary price controls to hold price increases to the rate of inflation.

An alternative to profit maximization is *target return-on-investment pricing.* Here a firm sets as its goal a profit representing a certain percentage of the money it has invested in the company. Some automobile manufacturers, for example, seek a 20 percent return on investment. The target return-on-investment approach has traditionally been used by firms with little or no competition in their industries—such as Dupont and Union Carbide. It is therefore becoming less and less common. While profit maximization and target return-on-investment pricing are difficult to use in practice, businesses do generally strive to increase company profits.

Communicating a Product's Image

A business may price a product to position it as a high-quality item in consumers' minds. *Prestige products* that symbolize high social status, such as furs, precious jewelry, and top-of-the-line automobiles, bring higher sales volumes—up to a point. But products do not have to be unusually expensive to show this kind of relationship between price and demand. They need only be higher priced within a category, especially where safety is a factor, as in baby foods or smoke detectors. When no other information about a product is known, price is especially useful as a clue to quality.[7]

Ensuring Customer Value

Now that value is such a fast-moving target, *customer value* is becoming the most important objective for pricing. Traditional pricing objectives and methods are becoming outdated as fast-paced competitors introduce new products that offer what today's consumers want—more quality for the price. A small price cut intended to boost sales will lose all effect if the competition blows by with a dramatically better product for less!

Many businesses now signal value by offering permanent discounts, or **everyday low prices (EDLP)**. The goal of retailers such as Wal-Mart, Target, and Kmart, which employ EDLP, is to keep their regular prices surprisingly low. Other organizations add value—and create a positive image—by setting prices that are socially and ethically responsible. The American Association of Retired Persons sets its annual individual membership at an affordable $8, and some hospitals offer Medicare patients discounts equivalent to their Medicare deductible.

Seeking Nonprice Competition

Of course, companies would prefer that the product's price not even be a consideration. If consumers prefer a product for reasons other than price, the company can raise its price and thereby generate more profits.[8] Adding value to basic products leads to strong preferences and less concern for price.

The most obvious way to avoid price competition is to produce superior *quality*. For instance, Goodyear Tire & Rubber Co. sold 2 million Aquatred tires in the product's first two years at a 10 percent premium over other product lines. Apparently, consumers appreciate the tire's superior traction on wet roads. But less fundamental features can also increase demand. Companies avoid price competition by positioning products on *customer service*, on *special benefits* to the consumer, or on *image*. For example, Louis Vuitton luggage and Revo sunglasses command higher than usual prices because of their status labels. In fact, some people will buy *only* if the price is excessive. Nonprice competition is difficult to use with undifferentiated, homogeneous products such as lawn fertilizers, house plants, and many services, however.

Tools and Methods for Setting Prices

3. Describe how cost, demand, and competition determine price.

Businesses set prices for their products by analyzing demand, costs, and competition. Demand sets a ceiling on how high a price can be; buyers will not pay more for a product than what they see as its value. Costs function as a floor below which price cannot fall without a loss resulting for the seller. And the prices competitors charge for similar products act as reference points against which buyers can compare prices. These three considerations form the basis for company pricing strategies. Let's take a closer look at costs: They are the most heavily relied-upon factor in determining prices.

Cost-Based Pricing

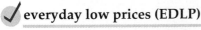
everyday low prices (EDLP)
Permanent discounts on products.

fixed costs
Costs that do not change no matter how many units of the product are produced.

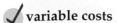
variable costs
Costs that fluctuate with the number of products produced.

Costs are primarily of two types: fixed and variable. **Fixed costs** do not change no matter how many units of the product are produced. Property taxes, plant costs, and salaries are fixed costs. **Variable costs** fluctuate with the number of products produced. Raw materials, fuel, packaging, and freight are variable charges. Fixed costs and variable costs add up to *total costs*.

In *cost-plus pricing*, the price is determined by adding a reasonable profit to the cost of each unit. As Figure 17.1 shows, Nike buys its sneakers from a supplier for $17.50 per pair; adds in its own costs of $11.67, plus a profit of $3.33 per pair; and sells the sneakers at a price of $32.50 to retailers. This approach ensures that all costs will be covered and that the desired profit of $3.33 will be achieved. However, cost-plus pricing can be dangerous, since it relies on cost estimates, and costs can change rapidly. And what if retailers refuse to buy *any* units at this price? A pricing approach like Nike's, which looks only at costs, does not consider whether the wholesale price of $32.50 is in line with retailers' perceptions of the value of the product, in this case sneakers. Similarly, competitors' prices are ignored.

However, cost-plus pricing is appropriate when the nature of the demand is known. The level of consumption of some products—bread, paper, and salt, for example—is stable and not very sensitive to changes in price.

Do you think the volume of mail increased, fell, or stayed the same when the price of first-class stamps increased in 1995 from 29 cents to 32 cents? Why?

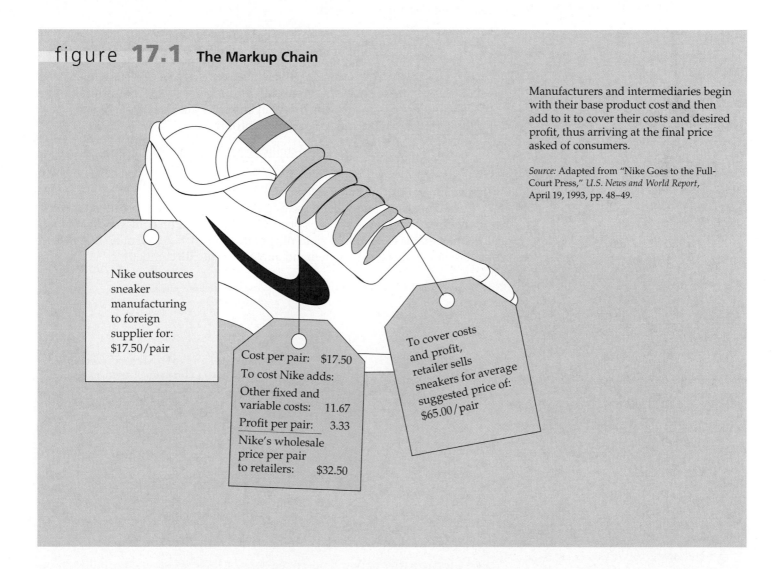

figure **17.1** **The Markup Chain**

Manufacturers and intermediaries begin with their base product cost and then add to it to cover their costs and desired profit, thus arriving at the final price asked of consumers.

Source: Adapted from "Nike Goes to the Full-Court Press," *U.S. News and World Report,* April 19, 1993, pp. 48–49.

Nike outsources sneaker manufacturing to foreign supplier for: $17.50/pair

Cost per pair: $17.50
To cost Nike adds:
Other fixed and variable costs: 11.67
Profit per pair: 3.33
Nike's wholesale price per pair to retailers: $32.50

To cover costs and profit, retailer sells sneakers for average suggested price of: $65.00/pair

Wholesalers and retailers also use a form of cost-plus pricing, called **markup pricing**, in which the intermediary's selling price is determined by adding a percentage of the product's cost to the selling price to cover the intermediary's costs plus a profit. For example, in Figure 17.1, the retailer adds $32.50 in markup to its cost of $32.50 per pair of sneakers, bringing the sales price to the consumer to $65.00. The markup amounts to 50 percent of the selling price. In many cases, the price paid by final consumers is the result of a series of markups that occur as the product moves through the distribution channel from the producer to the ultimate consumer.

 markup pricing

A form of cost-plus pricing in which the intermediary's selling price is determined by adding a percentage of the product's cost to the selling price to cover the intermediary's costs plus a profit.

✓ **break-even analysis**

A tool used by businesses to find the sales volume at which their costs are covered and their profits begin if they sell a product at a given price.

✓ **break-even point**

The point at which the units sold cover their own portion of variable costs and all fixed costs.

Break-even Analysis

Break-even analysis is a tool businesses use to find the sales volume at which their costs are covered and their profits begin if they sell a product at a given price. The **break-even point** is reached when the units sold cover their own portion of variable costs and all fixed costs. At this point, the producer breaks even, making no profit but suffering no loss. If fewer units are sold, a loss occurs because the producer's costs will not be covered. If more units are sold, the producer makes a profit. Businesses use the following formula to calculate the break-even point for a product:

$$\text{Break-even point} = \frac{\text{Total fixed costs}}{\text{Item's selling price} - \text{Item's share of variable costs}}$$

For example, consider again Nike's sneaker price of $32.50. If total fixed costs to supply these shoes add up to $45 million and Nike's only variable cost is $17.50, the price it pays the factory that supplies the sneakers, Nike must sell 3 million pairs before it makes a penny of profit:

$$\text{Break-even point} = \frac{\$45\ \text{million}}{\$32.50 - \$17.50} = \frac{\$45\ \text{million}}{\$15.00} = 3\ \text{million}$$

Figure 17.2 graphs this break-even point for Nike.

Of course, companies like Nike calculate many different break-even points as they consider various selling prices. The final price the company selects will be the one that is expected to yield the greatest profit. To determine that price, a business must also estimate demand and anticipate its competitors' actions.

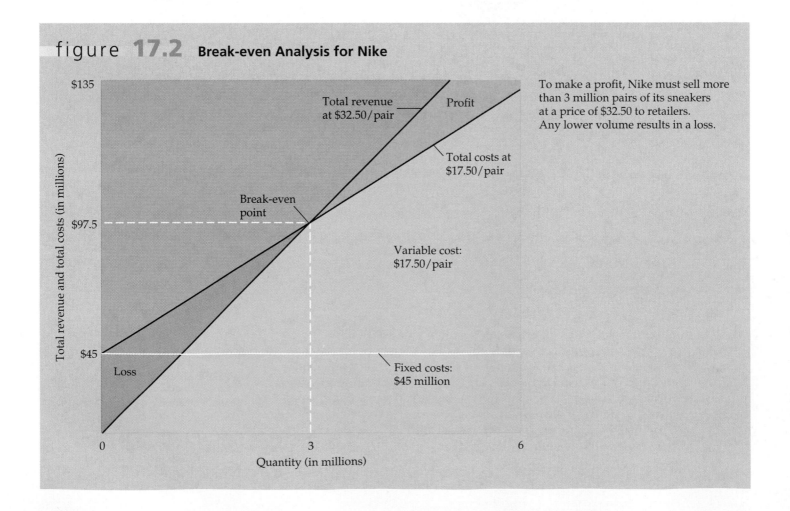

figure **17.2**   **Break-even Analysis for Nike**

To make a profit, Nike must sell more than 3 million pairs of its sneakers at a price of $32.50 to retailers. Any lower volume results in a loss.

doing business — Putting Price in the Driver's Seat

To cut costs, companies are redesigning products to reduce costly manufacturing processes, speeding products to market to cut new product development costs, and eliminating discounts and rebates. And they are finding out precisely what the customer really wants, which is resulting in less misdirected production. As an insightful industry guru told *Business Week*, "The management challenge of the 1990s is to reduce costs—and increase the perceived value of the product."

The traditional markup pricing approach is being thrown out by some businesses in favor of a demand-oriented approach. General Motors's Cadillac division, for example, first determines a target price for a new model. Then, according to a Cadillac division executive, "you say your profit is so much, and you back down into the cost. We never used to do it that way. We're backing into the [price] from the customer's perspective now."

The impact of demand-oriented pricing is felt throughout the company. For instance, if it takes the usual five to six years to develop a new car, the demand-oriented approach will not work. Consumers' price demands will have shifted by that time. A company must speed up the development process to make demand pricing work.

Compaq Computer provides another excellent example of demand-oriented pricing. New manufacturing processes slashed its costs by 60 percent in what the company calls "design to price." First a design team creates specifications for a new computer. The team then confers with marketing, production, customer service, purchasing, and others to map out a cost structure that meets a price set by marketing and a profit set by top management. To keep costs low, engineering outfits the new product with fewer parts and with parts from other products. Compaq's production processes have been streamlined to lower costs, and renegotiated supplier contracts have slashed costs further. The first products using this streamlined system hit the market in less than eight months. Typically, product development takes more than a year in the computer industry. Compaq's sales have skyrocketed 64 percent and profits have doubled as a result.

Source: Christopher Farrell and Zachary Schiller, "Stuck! How Companies Cope When They Can't Raise Prices," *Business Week*, Nov. 15, 1993, pp. 146–155.

Factoring in Demand

If costs set a "floor" for price, demand establishes its "ceiling" or upper limit. Unfortunately, demand is increasingly difficult to estimate because we consumers are constantly changing our desires and preferences.

Consider the food business, which until recently was characterized by a drive toward healthy eating. Some companies are now hitting it big by serving larger than usual portions of hot dogs, frozen dinners, English muffins, and other foods. Pizza Hut's biggest success ever was its giant Big Foot pizza, and Pillsbury's most successful product introduction was its Grands biscuits, sized 40 percent larger than others in its biscuit line. As an industry specialist told the *Wall Street Journal*, "The focus [in companies] is shifting away from price only and more to quality and size. Even if they pay more, consumers feel like they are getting a better deal when they buy a bigger sandwich."[9] This quality and size shift is consistent with the growing importance of the *value* message in price and promotion.

What price represents a fair value? It should be the top price at which the quantity demanded is still high. Noumenon Corp., a California-based software manufacturer, decided to find out what that price was. It introduced its Intuit program at $395 but found little consumer interest. It dropped the price to $50 and then raised it by $20 a week. Sales of Intuit rose steadily until the price reached $130, when sales dropped below those at any prior price. At $210, they stopped altogether. When analysis showed that the greatest number of sales occurred at $90, the company set Intuit's price at $89.95. After six months, it had sold 1,500 programs. To learn more about approaches to pricing, see the doing business box entitled "Putting Price in the Driver's Seat."

Factoring in the Competition

A company's best-laid price plans can be blown away by its competitors' actions. Most of the time, a company must focus on the prices of *direct competitors*—Federal Express versus Purolator Courier overnight mail or Nestle's Souptime versus Lipton's Cup-a-Soup. But recall from Chapter 14 that businesses also square off against *indirect competitors* that offer different products to solve the same consumer problem, overnight mail versus fax machines, for example.

Firms can set their prices at, above, or below those of the competition. In some industries, **price leaders** set the prices and competitors tend to follow their lead. For decades, computer manufacturers set their prices only after IBM announced its latest price plans. Now that it no longer dominates the market, IBM often drops its PC prices to match those of competitors.

Companies that set their prices low may do so to discourage other firms from entering a market or to drive competitors out of a market. Major carriers in the airline industry often engage in fare wars to gain market share from smaller airlines. American Airlines instituted its value pricing approach in 1992 when it did away with a vast array of prices. The result was a four-tier fare structure with only first-class, unrestricted coach, and 14- and 30-day advance-purchase tickets. The company expected this strategy to cause five of its weaker competitors to suffer over $500 million in losses. These other airlines brought a lawsuit against American for unfair competition but were unsuccessful. Generally, businesses do everything to avoid price wars. As a consumer electronics retailer told *Fortune*, "Competing on price ultimately gets you nowhere. You can say you're cheaper, but cheaper than whom, and for how long?"[10]

Pricing Strategies

A firm's pricing strategy charts the course for all its pricing decisions. It helps a firm to set prices that will enable it to reach its objectives. See the skills check entitled "Why Do CDs Cost So Much?" But pricing strategies differ as products travel through the product life cycle. And no discussion of pricing strategies would be complete without addressing today's strategy of value pricing.

Pricing New Products

Computer and electronics businesses routinely use **skimming**—a pricing strategy that initially sets a high price for a product and then lowers it. The idea is to sell the product to people who want it most. After these customers have made their purchases, the price is reduced to appeal to more price-sensitive consumers. For example, computer manufacturers set high prices on new, technologically advanced products to capture the buyers who most want the innovation at the highest price those buyers will pay. Eventually, the price is dropped to grab sales from the next lower price segment, and so on down the demand curve. Skimming maximizes sales revenues by selling to buyers at the highest price they will pay. It also creates a quality image by introducing the product at a high price. Skimming works only when competitors will *not enter the market* quickly with a similar product. Otherwise, the competitors might get to customers first.

A **penetration strategy** is the reverse of skimming: It initially sets a low price in the expectation of gaining a high volume of sales. Companies choose this approach to capture markets quickly, before their competitors can. The idea is to reach a larger portion of the market with a low price, thus generating the greatest possible demand.

---

4. Differentiate strategies used to price new and existing products.

✓ **price leaders**

Firms that set the prices that competitors tend to follow.

✓ **skimming**

A pricing strategy that initially sets a high price for a product and then lowers it.

✓ **penetration strategy**

Setting a low price in the expectation of gaining a high volume of sales.

skills check

Why Do CDs Cost So Much?

If you're a music lover, you have probably asked yourself this question. When the first CDs were produced in the early 1980s, they sold for about $25. While you can buy a new CD for $12 to $15 or less today, the price hasn't yet dropped to match the price of cassette tapes. Industry experts contend that consumers are willing to pay more for the higher sound quality and durability of CDs, however.

Manufacturing costs (pressing the CD) have dropped to less than $1 from about $3 in 1983, but costs for royalties and promotion have increased by about $1 in that time. With recording artists signing deals that would make a sports star blush and the escalating costs of promoting new albums, experts predict that CD prices are likely to stay high. But cheer up. In London, you might pay $20 for your favorite recording. And sales of used CDs that cost much less than new ones are expected to account for about 20 percent of all CD sales by 1998.

The accompanying chart breaks down the estimated costs of a CD that you buy at a retail price of $15. In this example the music store buys the CD from the recording company for $9.30, or 62 percent of the retail price. The store's costs amount to $5.70, or 38 percent of the selling price.

1. What product life cycle stage are CDs in now?
2. What would you say are the recording company's pricing objectives?
3. What pricing method do recording companies appear to use?
4. If you worked for a recording company, how would you counter the growing impact of used CD sales?

Source: David Zimmerman and Mike Snider, "Counting Up the Costs," *USA Today,* Aug. 3, 1993, p. 4D; Neil Strauss, "Pennies That Add Up to $16.98," *New York Times,* July 5, 1995, pp. C11 and C14.

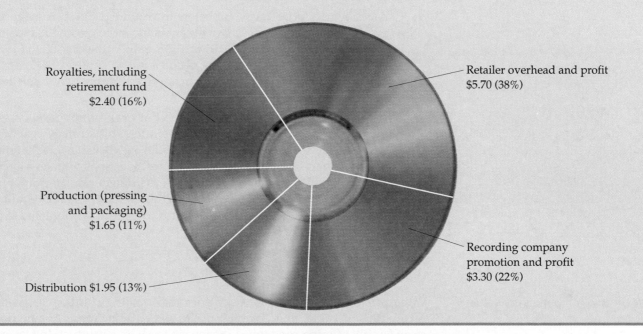

Royalties, including retirement fund $2.40 (16%)

Retailer overhead and profit $5.70 (38%)

Production (pressing and packaging) $1.65 (11%)

Recording company promotion and profit $3.30 (22%)

Distribution $1.95 (13%)

Penetration is often used when there is no "elite" market willing to pay a high price.[11] The penetration approach is generally useful when consumers are price-sensitive and when a lower price will probably produce a larger volume of sales. It is especially good for highly consumable and frequently repeated purchases such as laundry detergents or breakfast cereals. Japanese businesses used penetration pricing to enter the U.S. consumer electronics market. U.S. manufacturers held close to 100 percent of the market in the early 1950s, but only 5 percent of it by 1990. Through penetration pricing and better quality, Japanese electronics manufacturers won approximately three-fourths of the consumer electronics market in this country over a 25-year period.[12]

Pricing Existing Products

Some prices seem to have greater appeal than others, either because they are traditional or because they match some inner logic of the buyer. For example, consumers may not feel comfortable with an unrounded-out price like $18.31 for a necktie, but may find it totally acceptable to pay $3.69 for Skippy peanut butter.[13] Customary pricing uses prices that consumers are accustomed to seeing. To avoid changing the price from its customary level, the marketer may adjust the size and content of the product. Candy bars and newspapers are examples. Some other ways companies price their products are as follows:

- *Discounting* offers temporary deductions from the regular price. Discounts may be given for larger than normal purchases, for cash purchases, or for purchases made within a specific period of time; they may also be given to wholesalers or retailers. Notice that each form of discount aims to get something from the buyer in return for the lower price. For example, if a retailer buys 100 dozen golf balls from Spalding Sports Worldwide, rather than 12 dozen, Spalding saves on the cost of insuring that additional inventory of 88 dozen.

- *Price lining* is used to price a limited number of product lines. For instance, a retailer might offer women's scarves at $10, $25, and $50. These prices indicate that there are scarves for the economy-minded at $10, medium-quality scarves at $25, and top-of-the-line scarves at $50. Price lining helps to reduce consumer confusion about purchase alternatives.

- *Odd pricing* uses prices just a bit below the rounded-out dollar figure, such as $9.99. This difference of only one cent is meant to create the illusion that the price falls in the range of $0.01 to $9.99, rather than $10.00 to $19.99. Although such pricing is customary, studies fail to confirm that consumers are so easily fooled.[14] Further, products priced in this way often project a low-quality image.

- The *even-pricing* approach prices products at even numbers, such as three candy bars for $1 or $1,650 for a prestige watch. This strategy is at the heart of the surge in "single-price stores" that offer inexpensive merchandise and little atmosphere. One Price Clothing Stores, Inc., sells women's apparel at $7 per item, while at Everything's $1.00, customers can snap up anything from shoes to shampoo (well, *almost* anything!) for $1. Said a retailing consultant, "It appeals to the blatant desire to spend, without the threat of blowing your whole paycheck."[15]

Value Pricing

5. Explain how companies use value pricing.

Value pricing, a strategy that uses price and quality to influence customers' perceptions of value, first emerged in the early 1990s. Value pricing does not mean simply offering consumers the lowest price on a product. In fact, early in this decade sales of low-priced Hyundai, Daihatsu, and Isuzu cars floundered while expensive Lexus and Infiniti cars sold briskly.[16] Value pricing means giving customers what they want at a price they see as fair—*fairer than other price alternatives*. Some firms add valued features to products to enhance perceived value; others reduce prices on regular products to create value. As we saw in the doing business box "Putting Price in the Driver's Seat," new automobile models at General Motors's Cadillac division are designed to carry a set price that customers are willing to pay. Eventually costs are lowered to ensure the desired profit.

As companies seek to satisfy customers' demand for value, they emphasize *permanent* discounts through everyday low prices (EDLP). Procter & Gamble

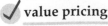

value pricing

A strategy that uses price and quality to influence customers' perceptions of value.

has priced 70 percent of its products using EDLP. This eliminates special price discounts to retailers; the brand is sold only at one standard price. For example, P&G's Dawn dishwashing liquid is pegged at $1.32, rather than selling for 99 cents one week and $1.49 the next. Shoppers are not faced with confusing price swings that encourage brand switching. And manufacturers do not have to contend with the inventory changes caused by retailers loading up during price promotion periods so they do not have to buy at full price. EDLP is one of the many responses to the growing importance of value pricing.

Recall what you learned in Chapter 16 about loading in the distribution process.

Value pricing also focuses on the performance the product will provide when it is used. Automatic teller machines (ATMs) save banks the expense of human tellers; the price banks pay for ATMs reflects these savings. This form of value pricing is particularly well suited to industrial pricing, where buyers put great emphasis on how a product will perform.[17] Boeing, for instance, uses value pricing in marketing its Boeing 777 passenger jets worldwide. It stresses the benefit of flexibility. The cabin can be reconfigured within 72 hours, the seats, galleys, and even lavatories moved to accommodate changes in the classes of service the airline needs. Although some structural changes and additional wiring and plumbing must be built, Boeing claims that the plane's flexibility does not add to its cost and hence is not reflected in the $100 million price tag.

The Objectives of Promotion

Promotion communicates. At the beginning of this chapter we defined *promotion* as any attempt by a seller to influence a buying decision. Clearly, effective promotion is crucial to successful marketing. This part of the chapter explores the objectives of promotion, discusses the promotion activities that make up the promotional mix, and explains how businesses combine the four Ps to build a sound marketing communications program.

6. Describe the overall and specific objectives of promotion.

Awareness, Interest, Desire, Action

TV shop-at-home networks know how to make the AIDA model work. Millions of loyal viewers tune in to see what's for sale—and who's selling it. Here is fitness maven Richard Simmons promoting his Deal-A-Meal Plan on QVC.

Before any exchange can take place, buyers must possess a perception of the organization and its product. Promotion shapes that perception by creating consumer *awareness*, providing information to arouse *interest*, producing favorable feelings—a *desire* for the product, and leading the buyer down the path toward *action*, the purchase. This sequence of events mirrors the consumer decision process discussed in Chapter 14. It is referred to as *AIDA*—an acronym formed from the first letter of the words awareness, interest, desire, and action. Much promotion actually reinforces buying behavior, effectively giving buyers a pat on the back for making a successful purchase. Marketers use promotion to influence the purchasing process. But purchase is the ultimate goal; to achieve it, marketers must first reach a number of specific business goals. They do this, in turn, by accomplishing several communication objectives.

The communication objectives of promotion are to inform, persuade, and remind. Job one is to *inform* potential buyers about the product. If the product is new, potential buyers need information about what it is and where they can get it. If it is not new, many potential buyers still may not realize that it exists. And when an existing product changes in any way, buyers need to be informed.

Once potential buyers know about a product, marketers must *persuade* them to buy it. This is accomplished by transmitting positive information about the product and its key features. Finally, since potential buyers are not constantly thinking about the product, marketers must continually *remind* them about it.

Whether the product is a good, a service, or an idea, these three objectives support the specific business goals of the firm: to increase sales by differentiating the product from the competition, by targeting communication at the right consumers, and by positioning the product in those consumers' minds. Promotion also serves social purposes.

The Social Impact of Promotion

7. Discuss the economic and social impact of promotion.

In any consumer economy, people seek to satisfy a huge number and variety of wants. Marketers provide a great deal of information to help people understand how certain products will satisfy those wants. By satisfying some of the information needs of consumers, promotion actually increases the volume of goods and services exchanged. In this way, promotion helps to create economic growth.

Promotion affects society in other ways as well. For instance, it can be especially valuable in informing people about social issues. The dangers of smoking, the identities of missing children, and the importance of regular medical checkups have all been the subjects of promotional campaigns. Promotion is also used aggressively in the political arena. Shortly after President Clinton took office, the Republican party used radio advertising in 20 states aimed at getting Democratic lawmakers to vote against the president's economic plan. "In the next few days, you'll be getting a package—the tax and spending package sent to you by Bill Clinton and the tax and pretend Democrats," the commercials said. "We need to send this package back to [lawmaker's name] before [he/she] votes to raise taxes again." The commercials employed background music from the movie *Jaws* and a telephone number so voters could call the targeted lawmaker and voice their objections.

Sometimes the social impact of promotion is negative. When promotion makes deceptive claims about products, it harms society. We saw in Chapter 14 how Volvo advertisements deceived the public. Also, firms sometimes emphasize promotion at the expense of product quality, using it to force inferior merchandise on the public. Finally, promotion sometimes pushes products that can harm people—cigarettes, liquor, gambling, guns.

The Activities in the Promotional Mix

From press conferences to commercials to buy one, get one free sales, businesses employ any number of promotional activities to achieve their marketing objectives. The **promotional mix** comprises the five promotional activities a business uses to communicate with its markets: advertising, personal selling, direct marketing, sales promotion, and public relations.

Advertising

Advertising is nonpersonal mass communication paid for by an identified sponsor. As a marketing activity, advertising offers both pluses and minuses. Advertising messages are reusable—they can be repeated many times. And advertising is efficient in communicating a message to a broad audience. *Reader's Digest*, for instance, reaches 37 million readers. On Super Bowl Sunday, television commercials reach more than a billion viewers worldwide. Moreover, advertising is presented in a relaxed atmosphere; there is generally little pressure on the consumer to make an immediate decision.

On the minus side, the sales impact of advertising is difficult to measure. A company can ask its salespeople about their customers' immediate response to a sales presentation, but it will have far more trouble determining customer response to a particular advertisement. Popular commercials sometimes even result in a loss. Highly visible Nuprin advertisements in which tennis's comeback kid Jimmy Connors told us to "Nupe It" were followed by a loss in market share. That cost Nuprin $5 million in sales, while sales of pain relievers as a whole were growing at 2.5 percent annually.

Effective or not, advertising is expensive. In 1994, U.S. companies and organizations spent more than $150 billion on advertising—an amount equal to 2.5 percent of the gross domestic product. The most expensive television advertising is during the Super Bowl broadcast, when a 30-second commercial costs approximately $1.2 million. A full-page, full-color ad in *Newsweek* cost $126,755 in 1995, while one in *Business Week* cost $90,300. Table 17.1 gives some examples of advertising expenditures by major U.S. companies.

Over the years, consumers have become more cynical about the claims of advertisers. This means that companies have to find alternatives to mass advertising. Businesses have, of necessity, turned to new technologies and media. In-store scanner technology allows companies to target potential buyers directly by distributing coupons right at the checkout counter. And the marketer can measure the response to these promotions. General Motors used a direct mailing of 170,000 videocassettes to promote its Cadillac Seville. Levi Strauss & Co. moved its advertising dollars from Saturday morning cartoon broadcasts to cable's MTV and Video Jukebox Networks. In 1993, businesses spent a whopping $3.7 billion sponsoring sporting events, rock concerts, social causes, and the arts. In short, advertising today is turning away from traditional approaches toward new, highly innovative promotional strategies.

ESPECIALLY Interactive television offers opportunities for further innovations in promotion. In the future, your television will be made "smart" by being part computer, part video. You will be able to play on game shows like "Jeopardy" and "The Price is Right" from your living room, "cruise the video mall" for a movie, watch a hockey game from mid-ice or behind the goal, custom build your own music video. And you will also be able to choose advertisements. You will view the resort hotel you are considering, check out its beach, and even buy an airline ticket to get there, all via your remote control. If you are in the market for a new house, you will review those for sale on your television monitor before heading out for a closer look. In short, you, the customer, will be in control of the advertising you receive.

table **17.1**

Top U.S. Advertisers by Dollars Spent

Company	Total Ad Spending in 1993 (millions of $)
Procter & Gamble	$2,397.5
Philip Morris	1,844.3
General Motors	1,539.2
Sears, Roebuck	1,310.7
Ford	958.3
AT&T	812.1
Nestle	793.7
Johnson & Johnson	762.5
McDonald's	736.6
Toyota	690.4
Eastman Kodak	624.7
Kmart	558.2
Anheuser-Busch	520.5
RJR Nabisco	499.4
Coca-Cola	341.3
Mars	337.6

Source: Advertising Age, Sept. 28, 1994, p. 4.

 promotional mix

The five promotional activities a business uses to communicate with its markets.

✔ **advertising**

Nonpersonal mass communication paid for by an identified sponsor.

8. List the types of advertising and describe how marketers manage advertising.

Institutional Advertising

Corporate campaigns such as IBM's "Solutions for a Small Planet" foster positive public perceptions and help to promote the company's entire product mix. In Dresden, Germany, IBM imaging technology helps a team of architects and artisans, including the stonemason pictured here, reconstruct the Frauenkirche, an eighteenth-century church destroyed during World War II.

Types of Advertising

Advertising can be classified in a number of ways. **Product advertising** creates awareness of and provides information about a type of product or a specific brand. "It's AT&T's True Voice" and "Just for the Taste of It, Diet Coke" are examples. In **comparative advertising**, a sponsoring company openly names its competitors and undercuts their products: "Bring Your Visa Card. Because They Don't Take American Express." Some companies use **institutional advertising**, which develops and maintains a favorable image for a particular company. In so doing, institutional advertising can promote the entire product line of an organization, as in Sears, Roebuck's "Come See the Softer Side of Sears" and IBM's "Solutions for a Small Planet." **Professional advertising** touts the benefits offered by lawyers, doctors, consultants, therapists, and other services. In the health care industry, for instance, one provider advertises "Choice Care. We Make More People Feel Better." "It's Time to Make Smoking History" is an example of **advocacy advertising**, in which a particular point of view on an issue is promoted. No matter what type of advertising is used, the business must manage the process of creating and executing the advertisement.

Advertising Management

Marketers manage advertising by choosing the message, the strategy, and the medium to deliver the message.

Frauenkirche
Dresden, Germany

IN DRESDEN, FREEDOM RISES FROM THE RUBBLE. Germany's greatest church, the Frauenkirche, was destroyed during Allied bombing in 1945. Where Bach and Wagner once performed, there now lies only broken rock. But recently, stonemason Franz Huber and a team of other artisans and architects began to painstakingly resurrect the city's symbol of harmony. Once IBM reconstructed the Baroque landmark in 3-D cyberspace, the team could begin to rebuild the ruins. Guiding them is an IBM RS/6000™ running CATIA,™ a computer-aided design tool. By 2006, the church will reach to the heavens once more, thanks to 18th-century craftsmanship and a powerful 21st-century tool. What can IBM help you build? Call 1 800 IBM-3333, ext. G102, or visit us on the World Wide Web at http://www.ibm.com

Solutions for a small planet™ IBM

The Message Behind every ad is a single, simple message, the key information the ad is supposed to convey to its target audience. It may be that the product is better or cheaper, or that the people who use the product are popular or rich or sexy. The advertisers code the message within a story or argument designed to catch your attention. Good advertisements grab the audience's attention with clever strategies such as the following:

- *Testimonials* are endorsements of a product or brand by a famous person who is viewed as an expert on the subject. Candice Bergen's witty, appealing pitch for Sprint shows how an endorser can be effective. But, as Hertz found out when O.J. Simpson was arrested, using celebrities can be risky. The company's image can become a little bit too entangled with the celebrity's image.

- *Humor* makes the audience laugh or at least smile, but this, too, is risky and may have little impact on sales.

- *Sexual appeals* tap a strong biological drive, explicitly or implicitly. Most perfume advertising employs subtle sexual overtones. But sexually oriented ads are not very effective; consumers tend to focus on the sex appeal and ignore the advertising message.

- *Slice-of-life* advertising portrays situations that are consistent with consumers' perceptions of their own life-styles. The situation usually shows how the marketer's brand can solve a particular problem. MCI's "Friends and Family" commercials are an example.

- *Infomercials* are slick, half-hour broadcasts using fictional storylines, real actors, and Hollywood-quality production. Most offer toll-free 800 numbers for convenient telephone ordering. Infomercials have become popular with marketers and with consumers. Some consumers even tape late-night infomercials for viewing at another time.

People are exposed to so much advertising that they pay much less attention to ads now than they did in the past. In 1986, 64 percent of Americans could name a television commercial viewed in the past four weeks; in 1990, those with recall slipped to 48 percent.[18] VCRs and remote controls permit viewers to avoid commercials. And, as we saw at the beginning of this chapter, today's tough consumers are smart buyers who question the advertiser's message and motive. As advertisers scramble to find something different and catchy, they often have to be careful to remember advertising's primary focus: getting the seller's message across.

The Strategy To leapfrog these barriers, advertisers are pioneering new strategies to gain the attention of the target audience. Black-and-white ads (such as those for Guess jeans, Dean Witter, and Calvin Klein underwear) encourage consumers to engage in the ad's drama without the distraction of color. Serial commercials—Taster's Choice and Duracell's pink bunny are examples—offer intriguing plots that make viewers look forward to the next installment. And accelerated movement, often computer-generated, catches the audience's eye. An example is the television commercial for Intel, in which a highly visual journey through the innards of a computer depicts the importance of the Intel chip's role in the machine.

The Medium Once message and strategy are defined, advertising managers select the proper medium to convey the message to the intended audience. **Media** are distribution channels used by companies to carry a message. Advertising media include newspapers, magazines, radio, television, on-line services, and outdoor advertising. The key media are compared in Table 17.2. Each has unique characteristics that provide both advantages and disadvantages. For in-

Think of an ad you have seen recently with a clear, powerful message. How does it appeal to its target market?

 product advertising

Advertising that creates awareness of and provides information about a type of product or a specific brand.

 comparative advertising

Advertising by a company that openly names its competitors and undercuts their products.

 institutional advertising

Advertising that develops and maintains a favorable image for a particular company.

 professional advertising

Advertising the benefits offered by lawyers, doctors, consultants, therapists, and other professional services.

 advocacy advertising

Promoting a particular point of view on an issue.

 media

Distribution channels used by companies to carry a message.

table 17.2 Comparison of Mass Media

Medium	Cost	Advantages	Disadvantages
Newspapers	Moderate to high	Easy to reach audiences; production time is short	Short message durability; low-quality reproduction
Magazines	Moderate	Quality reproduction, high message detail; customers can be segmented on the basis of reading tastes	Audience formation is slow; production time is long
Direct mail and catalogs	High, considering the costs incurred to reach each customer	Best way to target segments; messages can be tailored to audience needs with little waste	Production time is usually long for catalogs; high costs
Broadcast television	Moderate to high, depending on local or national exposure	High-quality reproduction; sight and sound makes for quick and effective communication	Long production time; short message durability; high costs
Cable television	Low to moderate	Segmentation is possible based on audience viewing tastes; quick and effective communication	Number of customers reached is not as high as broadcast television; long production time; low message durability
Radio	Low to moderate, depending on regional or national exposure	High-quality reproduction; segmentation is possible based on listening tastes	Low message durability; lower number of customers reached than television or cable; moderate message detail
Outdoor and transit	Moderate to high	Message durability is high due to repeated exposure	Low detail; high wastage of dollars spent, since the advertiser cannot effectively select the audience
Yellow Pages	Moderate to high	Message durability is high; segmentation occurs naturally; audience consists of information seekers	Low-quality reproduction; production time is long

stance, print media such as newspapers and magazines allow the reader to control the rate at which the information is received. Television and radio do not allow this kind of control. Newspapers receive the largest share of advertising dollars, with television close behind. Figure 17.3 shows where advertisers spend their money.

The media industry today is like a river after the dam has broken. Change is accelerating everywhere. Readers can choose from over 11,000 different magazines. Newspaper articles can be obtained over your computer. The surge in cable television channels, expected to hit 500 sometime soon, is further reducing viewership per commercial. Coca-Cola's advertising agency recently designed 24 different advertisements, in moods and styles to fit 20 different TV networks. Ten years ago the company used just one ad for the entire nation.

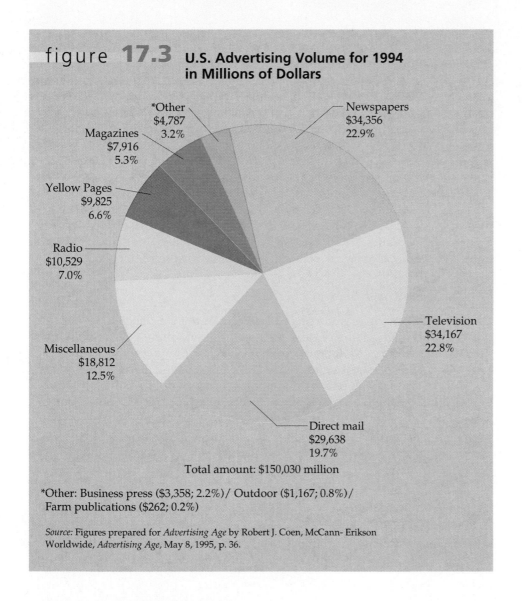

figure **17.3** U.S. Advertising Volume for 1994 in Millions of Dollars

*Other
$4,787
3.2%

Magazines
$7,916
5.3%

Yellow Pages
$9,825
6.6%

Radio
$10,529
7.0%

Miscellaneous
$18,812
12.5%

Direct mail
$29,638
19.7%

Newspapers
$34,356
22.9%

Television
$34,167
22.8%

Total amount: $150,030 million

*Other: Business press ($3,358; 2.2%) / Outdoor ($1,167; 0.8%) /
Farm publications ($262; 0.2%)

Source: Figures prepared for *Advertising Age* by Robert J. Coen, McCann-Erikson
Worldwide, *Advertising Age,* May 8, 1995, p. 36.

Global Advertising Strategies

As more businesses move into global markets, it is becoming increasingly difficult to determine the best advertising approach.[19] As we saw in Chapter 3,
some marketers believe that each national and cultural market is different and
thus deserves its own unique product and advertising campaign.[20] Other marketers claim that standardized products and advertising are appropriate because consumers are becoming similar worldwide.[21] "Eighteen-year-olds in
Paris have more in common with 18-year-olds in New York than their own parents," the director of MTV Europe told the *Wall Street Journal.*[22] Levi Strauss &
Co. is using a standardized campaign for its jeans in Europe, Latin America,
and Australia. A few other companies—Coca-Cola, McDonald's, Exxon, and
Philip Morris with its Marlboro man—are achieving great success by treating
the world as a homogeneous market.

At least for now, however, most advertisers are adopting a "think globally,
act locally" strategy. In Europe, Reebok advertises its sneakers in English, the
language of preference for youth in most countries. Ads shown in Italy, France,
Germany, and The Netherlands all contain the slogan "Planet Reebok." Yet
they also blend in some cultural differences. In France, Planet Reebok ads feature women running on the beach instead of men boxing, because the French
deplore violence.

✔ personal selling

Person-to-person communication between a seller and one or more potential buyers who provide immediate feedback through words, gestures, and facial expression.

9. Identify the classes of personal sellers and list the seven steps in the personal selling process.

Personal Selling

Personal selling is person-to-person communication between a seller and one or more potential buyers who provide immediate feedback through words, gestures, and facial expression. This enables the seller to tailor the message and obtain an immediate response. Customer communication is more precise in personal selling than in advertising, but the total number of contacts is far more limited. And the cost per contact is much higher than in advertising. Even so, because of its adaptability and personal nature, personal selling's persuasive impact is much greater than that of advertising.

Personal selling is especially appropriate when very expensive or complex products are involved. Detailed explanations or demonstrations are easily handled in this context. Personal selling is also effective when the product's benefits must be carefully matched to the customer's desires. Industrial marketers especially tend to emphasize personal selling in their promotional mixes.

Personal Selling Roles

Over 14 million people—more than 10 percent of the U.S. labor force—are employed in personal selling. Earlier we noted the enormous amount of money spent on advertising ($150 billion in 1994). That figure pales in comparison to expenditures for personal selling—over $325 billion annually! The most visible salespeople are clerks in retail stores, but most salespeople sell industrial products to other businesses. Sales jobs can be classified into three types: order getters, order takers, and support service personnel.

- *Order getters* aggressively seek out possible buyers, inform them of the firm's product, and then persuade them to purchase. Order getters must know their firm's products, understand the needs of potential customers, be familiar with the customer's possible uses of the product, and be aware of what competitors are up to.

- *Order takers* are salespeople—inside or outside the businessplace—who take orders initiated by buyers. Inside order takers receive orders over the telephone, on the sales floor, and over the counter, such as in a fast-food

Industrial Selling

Business-to-business marketing relies on personal selling, and industrial order getters work hard to nurture their accounts. This salesman is discussing delivery times and prices for high-pressure valves with a manufacturing company's hydraulics expert. To make this sale, he discovers, delivery within four weeks is more important than price. He will also check in with the company's purchasing agent on this visit to get a reading on what his competitors are offering.

restaurant. Insider order takers are salesclerks who sometimes make suggestions and assist buyers. But usually their main job is to take sales orders. Outside order takers visit customers to obtain orders. They develop regular customers and primarily focus on obtaining repeat orders. These salespeople often check inventory, deliver and stock goods, write up new orders, and service their customers. Outside order takers are most often found in the food and soft drink industries.

- *Support service personnel* provide after-sale customer service and encourage goodwill with customers. They do not actually sell products. There are two types: missionary salespeople and technical support specialists. **Missionary salespeople** are not permitted to solicit orders. They make calls to promote good feelings between seller and buyer. They also help customers (usually stores) arrange their own promotional activities, set up displays, and boost customer morale. When they receive orders, they relay them to other salespeople. *Technical support staff* provide the engineering and scientific knowledge used to design the custom details of products. They communicate directly with the customer's technical staff and often are on hand during sales calls to answer technical questions. Once the sale is made, their role is to plan and manage product development, installation, and any debugging that may be necessary.

Steps in the Selling Process

The process of personal selling takes place in seven steps. Like other promotional activities, these seven steps mirror the AIDA process. Once a prospect is located, the salesperson tries to grab the person's *attention*. An effective presentation secures *interest* and *desire* for the product. With proper handling of objections and a good closing, the desired *action*—a sale—should result. Let's look more closely at the seven steps in this personal selling process, pictured in Figure 17.4.

Step 1: Locating and Qualifying Prospects This first step involves obtaining leads on potential customers—finding and classifying potential buyers of a product. A *lead* is the name of an individual or organization that may be a potential customer, or *prospect*. Next, the leads are analyzed. They qualify as true prospects if they appear to have a need for the product, can afford to buy it, and have the authority to do so.

Good industrial salespeople can be especially creative in their search for prospects. One commercial real estate agent located manufacturing companies that might be interested in moving by looking for plants with overflowing parking lots. His reasoning was that if a firm has outgrown its parking lot, it has probably outgrown its plant.

Step 2: Preapproach Before contacting a prospect, salespeople must prepare for the contact by becoming knowledgeable about the products being sold. They also should gain some insight into the nature of the prospect. Successful, highly motivated salespeople accumulate facts that will be helpful when they approach and appeal to prospects, such as the prospect's age, position in the company, life-style, and personal interests.

Step 3: The Approach The first encounter creates a lasting impression. Clothing, automobile, grooming, business cards, brochures, and briefcase all contribute to that impression. Salespeople must pay strict attention to creating an appropriate image for the customer. To gain customer confidence, salespeople also must be professional, courteous, and concerned. They must be believable. In the initial meeting, salespeople must grab the customer's attention and interest. Many salespeople get attention by starting out by asking a question ("Aren't your information-processing needs important enough to support an

missionary salespeople
Salespeople who make calls to promote good feelings between seller and buyer.

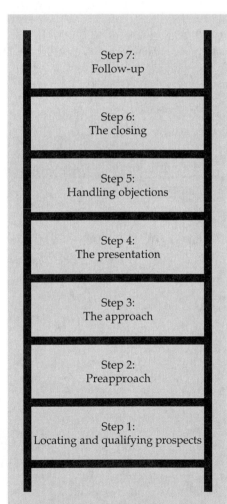

figure **17.4**

The Personal Selling Ladder to Success

Moving up the rungs, salespeople usher prospects through the stages of awareness, interest, and desire to action (purchase) at the closing.

doing business

In the World of Sales, Small Is Beautiful

In days of yore, the sales process was slow going. Salespeople used company computers mainly to mine contact lists for the best leads, prepare personalized form letters, and store marketing information on competitors. Preparing for a sales call could take days and involve people from engineering, manufacturing, and shipping, all helping to assemble internal information for prospects. Salespeople requested and then waited for recent sales literature from marketing. Finally, after placing an order, they had to check pricing, credit, and production, making dozens of calls and generating pounds of paper in the process.

Today's industrial sales representatives often come armed to the teeth with technology. Before making a call, they can fire up their laptop computer to explore previous prospect contacts, review past purchases, and identify key decision makers. The next push of a button calls up the latest price lists, engineering requirements, and status reports on previous sales. Electronic mail is accessible from any corner of the company. And when the sale is made, the sales rep can enter the order, double-check it for errors, and fire it via modem directly into the factory. Confirmations are sent to the buyer via fax, also a function on the salesperson's laptop.

The payoff is enormous. At one happy laptop-embracing company, sales that used to trigger a paper process lasting as many as 10 days can now be wrapped up in four. Price quotes take two hours, not two weeks, and orders contain 25 percent fewer errors. And all this dramatically improves the odds that the salesperson will close the sale.

As companies downsize their sales forces and their businesses, salespeople must work smarter. Information is the key that unlocks productivity. The speed, convenience, and accuracy offered by laptops translate into superior customer service, and that provides a strong competitive advantage. Said an automation manager at a division of John Deere, "We're trying to empower the salesperson with the collective intelligence of the organization."

Apparently John Deere has company. Sales force automation tools and services hit $1 billion in sales in 1993 and are expected to jump to $2.7 billion by 1997.

Source: John W. Verity, "Taking a Laptop on a Call," *Business Week*, Oct. 25, 1993, pp. 124–125.

Apple Powerbook lightning-fast laptop computer?") or stating a definite benefit ("I can save you the cost of a teller's yearly salary with this new automatic teller machine").

Step 4: The Presentation Next the salesperson delivers a presentation designed to explain to prospects how the product will meet their needs. To achieve the desired learning and avoid any misunderstanding, good salespeople use the tools of effective personal communication. Videocassettes, computer-generated presentations, slides, samples, models, and demonstrations can also be helpful in getting the point across. Some salespeople bring along laptop computers so they have access to data as they respond to customers' questions. For more on the use of laptops in business, see the doing business box entitled "In the World of Sales, Small Is Beautiful."

Step 5: Handling Objections Often a prospect will raise objections during the sales presentation. Such objections show where there's a mismatch between what is wanted and what is offered. They provide a chance for the salesperson to highlight additional product benefits or reemphasize product features that are important to the buyer. There are many ways to handle objections. The method used depends on the situation, but the most common seems to be the "Yes, but . . ." or *indirect-denial approach.* For instance, a real estate salesperson faced with the objection that his lots are too far out of town might respond, "That's what a lot of people thought about every lot we put on the market two years ago. But now all those 'far out' lots are built up and the property value has doubled. It pays to think ahead."

ethics
check

Is It OK to Train Your Customers?

Imagine you are on a new sales job, visiting store buyers with an experienced older saleswoman. She surprises you by saying that she treats all potential customers like horses. "They just need to be handled the right way to break them," she explains. "For example, a good trainer lets a new horse sniff the bridle before he tries to put it on. And you should use the same strategy to make customers comfortable with the company's order form.

"Buyers are spooked by the unfamiliar, just like horses," she continues, "so be sure to bring out the order form, handle it, and leave it in sight at the beginning of the sales call. Point to it for

information and keep handling it, so the buyer will be used to it and willing to sign it when you want him to make a purchase."

You think this sounds like a good idea, but then again, you wonder whether her tactics could trick or pressure buyers into placing orders they don't really need. Is it ethical, you wonder, to try to train your customers as if they are horses?

Source: "Order Blank Fear," The Competitive Advantage: The Newsletter for Sales and Marketing Professionals, *sample issue, 1995, p. 5.*

Step 6: The Closing The focal point of the sales presentation is the *closing*, the point where the order is actually secured. Many salespeople have difficulty closing. Afraid that the prospect will say no, they often fail to ask for an order! Among the closing techniques used are the following:

- *Closing on a minor point*: "Would you like the brush with the long bristles or the short bristles?"
- *Offering special incentives*: "If you sign a contract for home heating oil delivery today, I can give you a new-buyer reward of 250 gallons at no extra charge."
- *Asking for the order*: "Do you want to buy this now?"

Read the ethics check entitled "Is It OK to Train Your Customers?" to analyze one approach to closing with a customer.

Step 7: Follow-up Like all marketing tasks, a sale does not mean that the job of the salesperson is over. Follow-up ensures the customer's complete satisfaction. Checking back with the buyer gains goodwill for both the salesperson and the organization. Often purchases need to be adjusted—for example, when buyers forecast their needs incorrectly—and sometimes instruction in the installation or use of the product is necessary. The follow-up step also can lead to new prospects. Following up on sales helps create lasting relationships that increase the likelihood of repeat sales.

Direct Marketing

Direct marketing communicates a purchase offer designed to elicit an immediate buyer response. It generally draws from computer databases of customers to target its delivery of messages and uses a variety of promotional channels such as direct mail offers, merchandise catalogs, and telemarketing.

With *direct mail*, the effectiveness of the message in the mailed piece and the quality of the marketer's mailing list determine success. Direct mail, like other promotional activities, must grab the buyer's attention and convey information successfully to get an immediate response. Many direct mail pieces use unusual designs, prizes, and extraordinary offers to propel their messages

10. Describe the roles of direct marketing, sales promotion, and public relations in the promotional mix.

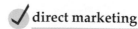 **direct marketing**

Communicates a purchase offer designed to elicit an immediate buyer response.

Direct Marketing

There's a catalog out there for everyone. It didn't take direct marketers long to target the growing numbers of Americans who are working at home. Customers can order anything from office furniture that doesn't look like office furniture to electric staplers any time of the day or night, then get right back to work.

through the clutter in our mailboxes. And with the help of better information and technology, marketers can precisely and efficiently tailor their mailings to reach people with the demographic, geographic, and even life-style characteristics of their target market.

Catalogs are pouring into our mailboxes. In 1994, catalog sales reached $57.4 billion.[23] Catalogs are very specialized and are targeted at highly segmented markets. Lands' End, Williams-Sonoma, Pottery Barn, and J. Crew are success stories because they have aimed their message and products at the convenience-valuing baby-boomers in our population. L.L. Bean offers 10 to 12 different direct-mail catalogs targeting different groups—fishermen and women, for instance. With rising postage and paper costs, catalog companies are exploring alternative methods of reaching their markets. Some catalogs are available on computer while others will soon become available on interactive television.

Telemarketing is a variation of direct marketing in which actual selling and sales support are conducted by phone. It can be very useful in prospecting and in follow-up. Most telemarketing is "outbound," in the form of unsolicited phone selling. Inbound telemarketing allows customers to call in to a toll-free 800 number or a tolled 900 number. Telemarketing is used to sell everything from the idea of donating blood in times of need, to preapproved credit cards, to aircraft. In 1983, telemarketing racked up $56 million in sales; a decade later, sales had soared to about $500 billion.[24] Five million salespeople are employed in telemarketing today, a number that is expected to double by the end of the decade. Why? Because telemarketing is very efficient. It costs less than one-third the cost of direct mail. A telemarketing call can be made for $10 per contact, compared with as much as $800 for personal selling.[25] And 80 percent of all telemarketing calls are made to businesses rather than to consumers.

Whether telemarketing is the answer to marketers' dreams remains to be seen. Consumer criticism focuses on fraudulent and annoying use of outbound telemarketing. Real estate and stock-selling scams, for example, are estimated to take $40 billion yearly from unsuspecting consumers.[26] Federal lawmakers are cracking down on these and other scams that are run through 800 and 900 phone lines. And who among us has not had dinner interrupted by a telemarketer? Some consumer groups are attempting to have telemarketing that uses computer-generated calling and recorded sales pitches prohibited. So far, the courts have found that such a ban would violate the right to free speech. In the meantime, consumers have the right to remove their names from telemarketers' databases.

Sales Promotion

Like direct marketing, sales promotion focuses on obtaining an immediate customer purchase. **Sales promotion** is the array of short-term promotional techniques that marketers use to stimulate such purchases.

Supermarkets, for example, frequently feature "buy one, get one free" promotions where the shopper makes a purchase on the spot. Sales promotion is the main promotional activity for businesses offering standardized, price-sensitive brands or products marketed through **point-of-purchase (POP) promotion**. POP promotion includes displays and demonstrations of the product at the point where it is purchased, usually retail stores. In most cases, however, sales promotion is one of several promotional tools. For example, in one of its sales promotions, Toys 'R' Us distributed coupon catalogs worth $491 in savings to 52 million households during November of 1993. This was supported by a massive advertising campaign that culminated in a Thanksgiving Day half-hour animated infomercial starring Toys 'R' Us stuffed animals. The overall goal was to stimulate Christmas sales by creating a perception of high value.

As noted earlier, mass market advertising is being deemphasized, which is greatly increasing the use of sales promotion. A number of factors have contributed to this. While advertising costs, especially for televised ads, have increased and mass market advertising has decreased, sales promotions have skyrocketed. A large number of consumer brands in the maturity stage of the product life cycle need—and can get—a quick sales boost from these promotions. When 6- to 14-year-olds were invited to enter a contest to design and name an "Outrageous" sandwich using one slice of Kraft Singles cheese, sales jumped 20 percent. And some forms of sales promotion are now better targeted than ever before, thanks to the advent of scanner technology and improvements in direct marketing.

Trade promotions are sales promotions in which manufacturers offer intermediaries trade discounts, merchandise, contests and prizes, and monetary incentives in return for sales of particular products. Trade promotion also

 telemarketing

A variation of direct marketing in which actual selling and sales support are conducted by phone.

 sales promotion

The array of short-term promotional techniques that marketers use to stimulate an immediate purchase.

 point-of-purchase (POP) promotion

Displays and demonstrations of the product at the point where it is purchased, usually retail stores.

 trade promotions

Sales promotions in which manufacturers offer intermediaries trade discounts, merchandise, contests and prizes, and monetary incentives in return for sales of particular products.

cooperative advertising

The sharing of the costs of local advertising by intermediaries and producers.

includes **cooperative advertising**, where intermediaries and producers share the costs of local advertising. Trade promotions attempt to convince new distributors to carry a manufacturer's brand and existing distributors to reorder or display specific products. Today companies are likely to use everyday low prices more frequently and trade promotions less frequently.

Consumer promotions are offered by manufacturers to ultimate consumers. Companies use a wide range of incentives to stimulate sales to both new and existing customers. Consumer promotions aid all the members of the distribution channel, since sales to ultimate consumers clear the inventory in the distribution pipeline, thereby making room for new products. Let's look at some of the more common sales promotion techniques.[27]

- Businesses employ *sampling* by distributing actual or trial-size products by mail, in stores, door to door, packed inside other products, or at high-traffic locations such as airports or shopping malls. Sampling is expensive but is the most effective means to obtain trial or use of the brand or product by potential customers. One memorable sampling promotion was the "Take the Pepsi Challenge" campaign in which consumers were asked their cola preferences in blind taste tests.

- With *couponing*, companies provide consumers with certificates entitling them to a price reduction or a cash refund. Fewer consumers redeem coupons than try free samples. Only about 3 percent of coupons distributed are ever redeemed. Couponing serves to motivate present users to buy larger sizes, discourage current users from buying competitors' products, or induce consumers to buy brand extensions. In a novel approach, several environmental groups collaborated with grocery products companies to issue coupons that tied purchases to contributions to their favorite environmental cause.

Point-of-Purchase Promotion

Catalina Marketing Corp., which has installed its electronic coupon printers in over 8,000 supermarkets in North America and Europe, offers manufacturers precise customer targeting. Say Tropicana Products wants to lure orange juice drinkers away from Minute Maid. Tropicana rents printer time from Catalina. When the checkout scanner reads a Minute Maid UPS bar code, the attached Catalina printer coughs up a coupon for Tropicana. Catalina's coupons are redeemed at a 9 percent clip, well over the rate that shoppers redeem the 285 billion coupons printed each year in newspapers.

- A *price-off* is an inducement either to try or to increase usage of the product by reducing the regular price. Refunds or rebates are price-offs, as are lower sticker prices on the product itself. Price-offs are most effective on well-known brands, since the buyer is likely to be aware of their original price. Most retailers indicate the regular price on the product along with the reduced price.

- A *premium* is a product offered free or at a lower price to induce the customer to buy. The most effective premiums are closely tied to the product or brand being sold. Marketers offer free telephone time as a premium. Send in 10 proofs of purchase for Budget Gourmet frozen dinners and Kraft Foods sends back a card worth 12 free minutes of long-distance calls.

- *Contests* award prizes in competitions that require contestants to write the best jingle or slogan.

- *Sweepstakes* offer prizes to those favored by the luck of the draw and ask, but legally cannot require, consumers who enter to purchase the product. The Publisher's Clearing House sweepstakes is perhaps the most well known program. Sweepstakes have lately been gaining while contests have been losing popularity.

- *Loyalty programs* strengthen the relationship with good customers and encourage them to buy more of the marketer's products. Airlines originated the technique with frequent flier programs. Now hotels, car rental agencies, department and grocery stores, credit card companies, and most major businesses offer similar programs. For example, Citibank Visa offers customers a range of free gifts depending on the total purchases made in one calendar year.

- *Trade shows* promote products to marketing intermediaries. Manufacturers display their products to resellers in large convention halls and hotel banquet rooms. Trade shows are common in the furniture, gift, and electronics industries, to name a few.

Public Relations and Publicity

Public relations (PR) are communications aimed at promoting goodwill and creating a favorable image of a product or a company. Every organization deals with many important groups, called *publics*: stockholders, the government, intermediaries, the community at large, employees, suppliers, the news media, and customers. Public relations activities are directed toward these publics.

PepsiCo found itself in need of PR in July of 1993, just before the height of summer soda season, when more than 50 news reports went out concerning syringes and hypodermic needles found in cans of Pepsi and Diet Pepsi. PepsiCo fought these reports with video footage of the assembly process, showing that it was impossible to put a needle into a can. Armed with the video, a carefully chosen PepsiCo executive appeared on newscasts, on "Larry King Live," and on "The MacNeil/Lehrer News Hour." The turning point for PepsiCo was the appearance of the company representative and the commissioner of the U.S. Food and Drug Administration together on ABC's "Nightline." The united front presented by PepsiCo and the impartial federal agency was enough to persuade consumers to continue buying Pepsi. Later investigations proved product tampering claims fraudulent.

Publicity is any message about an organization that is communicated through the media because of its news value. Although public relations personnel can send press releases, feature stories, and photographs to the media, organizations have much less control over publicity than they do over advertising, personal selling, direct marketing, and sales promotion. Yet audiences tend to find publicity more believable than information that comes from an identified sponsor.

Sponsorship marketing is a rapidly growing area of promotion that shares some of the features of public relations. An example is "Human Rights Now!", an Amnesty International tour of 20 cities that Reebok sponsored to the tune of $10 million. Sponsorships dispense promotional dollars to fund cultural, social,

 public relations (PR)

Communications aimed at promoting goodwill and creating a favorable image of a product or a company.

 publicity

Any message about an organization that is communicated through the media because of its news value.

Promoting Goodwill

When the product is a service, employees must be attuned to interacting with customers to heighten satisfaction. Southwest Airlines employees often use humor to break the ice with customers, from this flight attendant's antics to a contest run by gate attendants awarding a prize to the passenger with the largest hole in his or her sock. What do employee attitudes add to the promotional mix for Southwest?

athletic, or other high-interest causes or events and so achieve brand awareness, increased sales, and an enhanced company image.

Designing the Promotional Mix

11. Relate promotional mix design to the notion of integrated communications.

The objectives of promotion follow the AIDA customer decision process. *Awareness* leads to *interest*, which, in turn, fosters *desire*, which ultimately leads to *action*. Thus creating awareness is the first goal of promotion.

Each of the five promotional tools—advertising, personal selling, direct marketing, sales promotion, and public relations with its publicity component—has a different impact on the AIDA process. Because of its broad reach into the marketplace, advertising is more suited to creating awareness than is personal selling, which relies on fewer customer contacts. A strong public relations campaign can stir up great awareness when the focal issue is of concern to the public, as we saw with the Pepsi syringe scare. Finally, an especially exciting sales promotion campaign like the Publisher's Clearing House Sweepstakes can create significant awareness.

As you move from awareness and interest closer to desire for the product, personal selling and its great persuasive power become more effective, while advertising's impact slips. Direct marketing and sales promotion, with their target of immediate action, can help to heighten desire. The value of all three of these promotional tools continues to increase as the moment of action, or actual purchase, approaches. Marketers determine the promotional tools they will use depending on the stage in the customer decision process they wish to target.

You can relate the push and pull strategies used in marketing products to the push and pull processes used in producing products, as described in Chapter 10.

Companies also design the promotional mix depending on whether a pull or push strategy is appropriate. A **pull strategy** uses advertising and promotional tools to encourage consumers to request a product from retailers, who, in turn, must request it from the producers. The pull strategy works well when the product is readily differentiated, has a mass market, and carries a low price. Packaged goods companies, such as General Mills and Procter & Gamble, are typical of businesses that have motivated consumers to *pull* their products into retail outlets.

In a **push strategy**, a manufacturer encourages intermediaries to stock, promote, and aggressively sell its product. Such producers rely on trade promotions to gain the cooperation of distributors and retailers. Promotion to the consumer receives less attention. The push strategy is particularly useful for durable goods, high-priced items, and products with limited markets.

Designing an Integrated Marketing Communications Program

An emerging perspective focuses on integrating all promotional activities into a comprehensive marketing communications program.[28] As an advertising agency CEO put it, "The marketer who succeeds in the new environment will be the one who coordinates the communications mix so tightly that you can look from medium to medium, from program event to program event, and instantly see that the brand is speaking with one voice."[29]

To work, an integrated communications program requires knowledge of customers and prospects. The modern business must be able to segment and target markets. It must know consumers' buying histories, their wants and desires, their life-styles, their dreams. In short, today's companies hang all their actions on customer databases. Without sufficient information, companies will only succeed at sending out fragmented communications. Without a consumer focus, they will only be able to "send out messages when *they* want to send them, to the people *they* want to send them to, in the form *they* want to use, at the time *they* want to send them out."[30]

Integrated marketing communications programs go beyond mere promotion to encompass production, packaging, employee attitudes, in-store displays, sales brochures, even the form of the product. Even the atmosphere of the retail stores where products are sold must be managed to create a clear and unified message. Integrated programs must be directed at targeted markets. Either one person, referred to as the communications czar, or a marketing team must be responsible for coordinating the communications effort to ensure integration.

The debut of Nissan's Infiniti J30 luxury sedan offers an example. The car was designed in America, engineered and manufactured in Japan, and marketed in the United States, Canada, and Japan. Individuals from all parts of the company—marketing, advertising, public relations, distribution, research and development, manufacturing—were teamed to determine the proper positioning of the car and oversee communications. The entire integration team met monthly to ensure that all customer contact points were coordinated to offer the same message. Said a team member, "The integration team reduced duplication of effort, afforded cross-pollination and created a synergy."[31]

In the four marketing chapters we have explored the four Ps of marketing, but from one perspective, all of marketing is communication. The *product* communicates real and potential satisfaction. The package communicates the benefits of the product inside. The brand communicates the expected quality. Distribution communicates time and *place* utility. *Price* communicates value. And, of course, *promotion* communicates by its very nature. Thus, marketing communications encompasses all customer contact with the organization. Today, businesses recognize the need to coordinate all these customer contact points into an integrated marketing communications program emphasizing value. Each business activity that touches the consumer is undertaken with a common mission in mind—to create the desired perception within the marketplace.

 pull strategy

Use of advertising and promotional tools to encourage consumers to request a product from retailers.

push strategy

When a manufacturer encourages intermediaries to stock, promote, and aggressively sell its product.

Reviewing *Price and Promotion*

Price, Promotion, and Value

1. **Identify the reasons for the shift in market control from marketer to consumer.** Consumers have become knowledgeable and vocal buyers, forcing marketers to shift their emphasis from strictly profit-making to meeting consumer needs. Besides quality, consumers are demanding lower prices. Other reasons for the power shift are the fragmentation of markets by competitors, improved technology that has created an electronic, interactive marketplace, and an increase in product alternatives—not only of brands but also of product sources (catalogs, TV programs, etc.).

Pricing Objectives

2. **List and explain the four major goals of pricing.** Increasing sales or market share is a fundamental goal of any business and hence the first goal of pricing. Achieving profitability—through profit maximization, target return on investment, or another method—is also a goal of price setting: Price influences quantity, and quantity times price equals revenue, the source of profitability. Another goal of pricing is to communicate a product's image, since price tends to be a clue to quality. The final goal of pricing involves ensuring customer value through everyday low prices (EDLP). When possible, companies try to reduce price concern by adding value through quality, customer service, special benefits, or image.

Tools and Methods for Setting Prices

3. **Describe how cost, demand, and competition determine price.** In brief, cost provides the floor below which price cannot fall, demand sets the ceiling on how high price can rise, and competition provides a reference point for a company to set its price. To determine a price, a company may calculate its fixed and variable costs per unit and add a reasonable profit (cost-plus pricing). The company may conduct break-even analyses to learn what quantity must be sold at a given price to yield a profit. However, the company must also consider consumer demand for its product and its competitors' (whether direct or indirect) pricing actions as it calculates price.

4. **Differentiate strategies used to price new and existing products.** Pricing depends on the product's place in the product life cycle. New products may be priced using a skimming or a penetration strategy depending on whether the product is perceived as prestigious, as in computers, or highly consumable, as in breakfast cereals. In general, companies price existing products according to consumer comfort—they select a price either because

of tradition or because it matches some inner logic of the buyer. To increase sales, companies may use discounting, price lining, odd pricing, or even pricing.

5. **Explain how companies use value pricing.** Value pricing focuses on providing quality at a price that is perceived as fairer than other price alternatives. A "fairer" price may be a price that is discounted either temporarily or permanently. Value pricing also focuses on the performance of the product.

The Objectives of Promotion

6. **Discuss the overall and specific objectives of promotion.** Promotion's overall objectives are to create consumer *awareness*, to arouse *interest*, to produce a *desire* for the product, and to get the consumer to *act* (to buy the product), a sequential process referred to as AIDA. These objectives are met if promotion accomplishes its three communication objectives: informing potential buyers about the product, persuading them to buy it, and reminding them about it.

7. **Discuss the economic and social impact of promotion.** Economically, promotion encourages growth by convincing people to buy products, which naturally increases sales volume and improves the economy. Socially, promotion makes people aware of important issues, which may lead them to act. Promoters must be socially responsible, of course, and not mislead the public with false advertising.

The Activities in the Promotional Mix

8. **List the types of advertising and describe how marketers manage advertising.** Advertising is classified as product, comparative, institutional, professional, or advocacy, depending on the product or service and the image to be created. Advertising management involves choosing the message, the strategy, and the medium to deliver the message. A message may be a testimonial, it may make use of humor or sexuality, it may show a slice of life, or it may be an infomercial. Advertising strategy focuses on capturing the audience's attention. Advertising media include newspapers, magazines, radio, television, online services, and outdoor advertising. The increasingly global nature of business requires that companies decide whether to standardize or localize their advertising.

9. **Identify the classes of personal sellers and list the seven steps in the personal selling process.** Personal sellers may be order getters; order takers; or support service personnel, including missionary salespeople and technical support specialists. The seven steps of the process begin with (a) locating and qualifying prospects. In (b) the preap-

proach, salespeople learn about their product and about the prospect's needs, which sets the stage for (c) the approach and a solid (d) sales presentation. Salespeople must (e) handle objections and (f) close the sale but then ensure satisfaction by (g) following up.

10. **Describe the roles of direct marketing, sales promotion, and public relations in the promotional mix.** Direct marketing and sales promotion are designed to elicit an immediate response from potential buyers. Direct marketing involves the use of direct mail offers, merchandise catalogs, and telemarketing. Sales promotions for intermediaries include trade promotions and trade shows. For consumers, businesses use point-of-purchase displays and demonstrations, sampling, couponing, price-offs, premiums, contests, sweepstakes, and loyalty programs. A business's public relations activity is geared to promoting goodwill and a favorable image of the product to its publics: stockholders, the government, intermediaries, the community at large, employees, suppliers, the news media (through publicity), and customers. In some cases, companies use sponsorship marketing to promote goodwill.

11. **Relate promotional mix design to the notion of integrated communications.** Marketers design their promotional mix to accomplish their goals in terms of awareness, interest, desire, and action. The modern business perspective focuses on integrating all promotional activities into a comprehensive marketing communications program, so the product speaks clearly with one voice to a target market. Integrated communications programs must begin with a thorough understanding of the customer. All contacts with the potential market must be managed to ensure that customers form the desired perception.

 **Key Terms**

price **511**	skimming **520**	professional advertising **526**	trade promotions **535**
promotion **511**	penetration strategy **520**	advocacy advertising **526**	cooperative advertising **536**
profit **515**	value pricing **522**	media **527**	public relations (PR) **537**
everyday low prices (EDLP) **516**	promotional mix **525**	personal selling **530**	publicity **537**
fixed costs **516**	advertising **525**	missionary salespeople **531**	pull strategy **538**
variable costs **516**	product advertising **526**	direct marketing **533**	push strategy **539**
markup pricing **517**	comparative advertising **526**	telemarketing **535**	
break-even analysis **518**	institutional advertising **526**	sales promotion **535**	
break-even point **518**		point-of-purchase (POP) promotion **535**	
price leaders **520**			

● **Review Questions**

1. What four changes in the marketing environment have given consumers increased power over marketers?

2. What are the four objectives of pricing?

3. How do cost-plus pricing and break-even analysis work to set a product's price?

4. What are the differences between the skimming and penetration pricing strategies for new products?

5. What are the marketplace pricing techniques of customary pricing, discounting, price lining, odd pricing, and even pricing?

6. What is value pricing?

7. What trends are shaping the advertising industry today?

8. What are the seven steps in the personal selling process? Explain each of them.

9. What kinds of direct marketing techniques are used today?

10. What are the key sales promotion activities?

11. What is the impact of the five promotional activities on the AIDA customer decision process?

12. How do companies establish integrated marketing communications programs?

• Critical Thinking Questions

1. Zenith Radio Corp. has developed a programmable household robot that can walk, talk, hear, and lift objects weighing up to a few pounds. What suggestions would you offer Zenith about pricing its "pet"?

2. Do you believe that companies are frequently unethical in setting prices? Why or why not? How do you think firms could show greater social responsibility?

3. U.S. companies pay millions of dollars a year for celebrity endorsements of their products. Do you know anyone who has bought a product because a celebrity recommended it? Do you think such endorsements work?

4. If you worked for a firm that recruits students on your campus, how might you use the seven steps in the selling process? Be specific.

5. A U.S. company recently introduced cents-off coupons to increase sales of its food products in Chile, where coupons are rarely used. What benefits and problems would you tell the company to expect?

REVIEW CASE *Mercedes-Benz*[32]

In 1986, at the height of the roaring 1980s' consuming binge, Mercedes-Benz sold almost 100,000 cars annually in the United States. From this peak, sales slipped dramatically, until U.S. yearly sales plummeted to a low of 59,000 in 1991. While sales saw a slight recovery in 1992, they continued their fall in 1993, with the first three-quarters of the year showing a 7.6 percent decrease from the 47,645 cars sold over the same period the year before.

For the company as a whole, this slide was worsened by sales in Germany. The company's market share at home fell to 6.4 percent in 1992, from 11.6 percent in 1985. As a result, Mercedes-Benz cut back its work force by thousands to cut costs. Yet this move was not sufficient to help the company.

In 1993, competition had a field day with Mercedes-Benz. Toyota's Lexus sold 98,389 units, compared with 59,705 for Mercedes. Its German rival, BMW, sold 74,253 cars in the 1993 model year. Both Toyota and BMW seemed to reflect the sensibilities of the 1990s' consumer better than Mercedes-Benz. In response, the company made some drastic price cuts in its 1994 model-year lines to stimulate sales.

To reach the entry-level luxury car buyer, Mercedes-Benz brought out a four-cylinder C220 and a six-cylinder C280 priced from $29,900 to $34,900. These prices competed directly with the lower-priced models from Toyota Motor Corp.'s Lexus and Nissan Motor Corp.'s Infiniti divisions. At $29,900, for instance, the C220 sold for $700 less than the ES300 Lexus entry-level sedan. In 1988, Mercedes-Benz's entry-level offering was the "Baby Benz" 190. At the time, it was $11,450 more expensive than the cheapest Lexus, a $21,050 ES250. The C-Class cars replaced the 190 series and offered consumers more interior space, dual airbags, antilock brakes, and cruise control as standard.

Mercedes's new C-Class line provided a dramatic contrast to the ultra-luxurious, full-sized S-Class sedans brought out in 1991 and priced from $69,900 to $119,900. Launched in the midst of a recession, the S-Class cars were an embarrassing failure for Mercedes-Benz. This financial disaster caused the company to rethink the positioning of its products. Helmut Werner, Mercedes-Benz's chairman, decided that the company should become more customer-oriented and show more concern for the consumer than it had in the past.

1. Based on your reading of the chapter, describe the pricing strategy at Mercedes-Benz.

2. Would you have advised Mercedes-Benz to pursue this pricing approach? What are the risks associated with it?

3. Suggest to Chairman Werner how Mercedes-Benz should design its promotional mix for the C-Class cars.

CRITICAL THINKING CASE *The Church of Scientology*[33]

Founded in 1954 by L. Ron Hubbard, a science-fiction author, the Church of Scientology had 8 million members in 1993. That same year, the church was awarded tax-exempt status, which allows an organization to pay no taxes on the donations it receives. The church welcomes members of all faiths and promises them the opportunity to attain their full spiritual potential by learning how the mind works. The use of mind-altering drugs is against the teachings of the religion. In fact, the Church of Scientology has aggressively attacked the use of Eli Lily & Co.'s antidepressant, Prozac.

The motives and basic principles of the sect have been the subject of magazine and tabloid features questioning the religion's popularity and power among Hollywood celebrities. After *Time* magazine published a story entitled "Scientology: The Cult of Greed," the church filed a libel suit and ran advertisements in *USA Today* attempting to discredit the article. But the church's top executives were not satisfied. They set their sights on further polishing the church's tarnished image.

What Is Scientology?, a 590-page paperback, was published in 1993 accompanied by an advertising blitz. Priced at $19.95, the book offers what the church claims is "the story behind the headlines," describing how the organization survived 40 years of media attacks and today flourishes internationally.

To promote the book and the church itself, executives placed advertising in television and print media and conducted a national publicity tour by church officials and celebrity followers. The campaign included a half-hour "documercial" entitled "The Problem of Life" in which a couple is shown searching for life's meaning. They wonder: What's it all about? Where are we going? Wouldn't it be good to have a job that is fulfilling? After failing to get the answers from therapists and doctors, the couple find what they are looking for in Scientology. At the conclusion of the program, Jeff Pomerantz, the soap opera actor known for his role in "Dynasty," offers a direct-sales pitch for the book. The half-hour advertisement was run on national cable stations, and two-minute advertisements were aired nationally to promote the book.

1. From what you learned in the chapter, how would you describe the promotional mix used by the Church of Scientology?

2. What alternative promotional approach do you think would work better for the organization?

3. Discuss the ethical and social dimensions of religious organizations employing promotion to improve their market position.

4. How might pricing (in the broad sense of the term) play a role in the marketing of the Church of Scientology?

Critical Thinking with the ONE MINUTE MANAGER

"How much bigger can Starbucks get?" Joanna asked the One Minute Manager as they shared a coffee break in her office. "I mean, from 11 stores to 400 in under 10 years is a huge growth rate. Isn't there some limit to the number the market can support?"

"Starbucks's CEO, Howard Schultz, says he plans to have 6,000 outlets by the turn of the century, so I guess the answer is no. U.S. coffee sales total more than $5 billion a year right now, and only a quarter of that is from gourmet coffee. But gourmet coffee was almost nothing 15 years ago. If its benefits are communicated effectively, perhaps it can reach 75 percent of total sales. What Schultz worries about is the low barriers to entry for competitors. It's not very expensive to add a fancy espresso machine to an existing restaurant or convenience store, for example. So his strategy is to grow Starbucks as fast as possible, before competitors take over too many of his markets."

"Does that mean new pricing and promotion strategies?" Joanna asked.

"Starbucks is building its distribution through new outlets, and it is using promotion to attract customers to the outlets. For example, the company ran a print ad in which a photograph of a peacock carries the caption, 'How the tastebuds see Starbucks coffee.' And the company is considering TV commercials, but Schultz is worried that his educational message will not come across well in a 30-second spot."

1. Can Starbucks educate the average coffee drinker about the advantages of gourmet coffees in a 30-second spot?

2. Let's assume you said "yes." What kind of 30-second TV commercial would *you* design?

3. Let's assume you said "no." What alternatives would you suggest? Can you think of a better way to advertise Starbucks coffee on TV?

4. Let's say Starbucks decides to de-emphasize advertising. Can you think of ways to communicate its educational message using each of the *other* elements of the promotional mix?

5. If you were in charge of Starbucks's pricing strategy, would you recommend a skimming or penetration strategy for the next few years? Justify your recommendation.

6

Controlling the Business

SEARCH | TABLE of CONTENTS | HELP | SURF SITES

WHO WE ARE | AWESOME PRODUCTS | EXTREME TEC

HOW DO I BUY? | CUSTOMER SUPPORT | SERIOUS FUN

WHAT'S NEW | HEADLINES | PUBLICATIONS | EVENTS

 Our
New
Wave

 CeBIT
Intn'l
Trade Show

 WebFORCE
To Author
and to Serve

A text only version of this page is also available.

Send your comments and questions to webmaster@www.sgi.com

18 Capturing the Power of Information

Businesses view information as a strategic resource—as important to success as raw materials and labor. Successful businesses must manage information in order to meet the needs of their customers, to improve their operations, and to increase their competitiveness. Managers and employees who understand and use technology to their advantage can harness the knowledge and analytical power it provides to succeed in competitive and changing markets. After reading this chapter, you will be able to reach the learning goals below.

Learning Goals

1. Contrast data and information and name the five characteristics that make information useful to a business.
2. Describe the purpose of information systems and explain how the management information system relates to business decision making.
3. Identify and contrast the different classes of computers.
4. List and describe the basic hardware of a computer system.
5. Explain the importance of computer software and describe its applications.
6. Discuss the use and value of networking and telecommunications in business, noting the different forms of telecommunications.
7. Discuss the business impact of the Internet and on-line services.
8. Outline the five levels of information integration in a business.
9. Discuss how information management can contribute to improved processes.

Information is a Tool

*"Would you tell us how a business like yours manages information?"
Carlos asked as the students settled into chairs in the One Minute
Manager's office.*

"Business people are information *users*, Carlos, regardless of the technology or the business process. The best information *managers*, of course, see their customers' point of view. The information manager's customers are the people who work inside and outside the business to develop, produce, and market the company's products and to supply labor and materials," the One Minute Manager began. "There's an old saying in information management, 'Garbage in, garbage out.'"

Joanna and Carlos exchanged looks. "Meaning . . . ?"

"Meaning that if you just plug in lots of computers without planning the information system, you make your business dumber instead of smarter," the One Minute Manager explained. "Let me tell you how Coopers & Lybrand, a big accounting and management consulting firm, uses information. In the 1970s, C&L *integrated* computers into its auditing division. Their success with that effort made C&L highly competitive in auditing and in other key accounting and consulting services. By

mid-1995, Coopers & Lybrand was the world's fourth largest accounting firm.[1] C&L used the power of information to build a learning organization." The One Minute Manager nodded to Carlos, as though he should continue. "Meaning?" she asked finally.

"Learning organizations are businesses that develop and use knowledge in ways that help them change for the better," Carlos recited.

"Information systems and information technology can enhance organizational learning," the One Minute Manager continued. "Coopers & Lybrand's corporate mission is to help businesses use information better—to become learning organizations."

Information Systems

When James Watt patented his design for the modern steam engine in 1769, the way goods were manufactured and the means of transporting people and products changed forever.[2] As people moved from farms to cities during the Industrial Revolution, an industrial economy using mass production methods replaced the traditional agricultural economy. The invention of the electronic computer almost 200 years later is having a similar impact on our lives today.

We are now in the midst of a postindustrial Information Revolution that rivals the assembly line in its effects on the types of products and services offered by businesses, the markets in which those goods are sold, and the way people live and work. Computers fueled this change with their ability to process information accurately and efficiently. Future improvements in the collection and distribution of information will result from technological advances in communications and in the linking of computers to other electronic devices.

In business, information is power. If you can obtain information faster than your competition, and then analyze it and apply it faster, you can gain a competitive advantage in the marketplace. Why do organizations rely on information so completely? The answer is simply that information is the basis of decision making. To make good decisions, business people need good information, not just at the highest levels, but throughout the organization.

Good information alone doesn't always lead to good decisions, however. Regardless of the awe-inspiring leaps being made in technology, it is now more important than ever to keep in mind the words of President John F. Kennedy, who, more than three decades ago, brought some perspective back to a nation mesmerized by the possibilities of automation. "Man is still the most extraordinary computer of all," said Kennedy. No matter how "real" the virtual world created by computers becomes, people—not computers—will always be the most important element in business decision making. In this section, we will explain what information is and specify the qualities that make it useful. We will also describe the computing technology that streamlines information flow through organizations and distributes information to workers and managers who need it.

Taking Stock

Information systems and technology make large and small businesses more competitive. With the help of an electronic bar code reader, this clerk can reorder inventory automatically and keep store shelves well supplied so that the business never loses a sale because an item is out of stock.

Information Needs Within the Business

Although the words "data" and "information" are often used interchangeably, for our purposes, it is best to draw a clear distinction between them. **Data** are raw facts. Data become **information** when the facts are presented in a context that gives them meaning. Context and meaning are conferred on facts by analyzing them, by associating them with other facts, and by summarizing them in reports, tables, charts, and other presentation materials.

For example, consider the list of the 160,000 passengers who flew on USAir today. At the end of the day, the list resides in a computer as raw data—unanalyzed and unsummarized. By *processing the data into information*, USAir managers can quickly summarize extensive information on these 160,000 passengers. Which routes did they fly the most? How many used credit cards to purchase their tickets? Which cards did they use? How many passengers flew first class or business class versus coach? How many booked their flights through travel agents and how many booked their flights directly through the USAir reservation system?

USAir managers and workers can study this and other information obtained from passengers and use it to improve company operations to keep pace with—or beat—their competition. Decision makers can fine-tune the airline's prices to capture a specific target market. Business-class seating can be expanded on routes popular with business fliers. Users of certain credit cards can

1. Contrast data and information and name the five characteristics that make information useful to a business.

 data

Raw facts.

 **information**

Data presented in a context that gives them meaning.

Data into Information

Computerized accounting programs such as QuickBooks®, available from Intuit Software, provide users with electronic billing forms such as this invoice. By entering billing data into the on-screen invoice format, workers can also update the company's information system. In addition to printing out invoices, the data can be used to update customers' ordering and payment histories and to generate reports that track sales of products, inventory levels, and revenues. Decision makers use the information accumulated from billing data to control production levels and plan future activities.

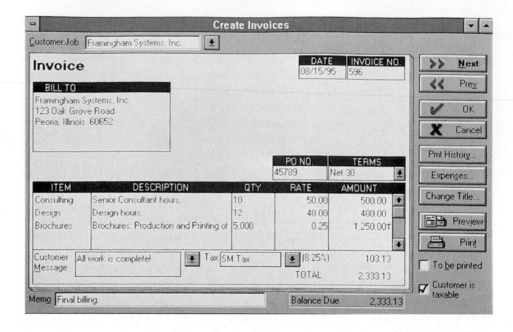

be offered incentives to book more flights with USAir. The end result is better customer service and increased sales. Without this extensive passenger information, which is available quite literally at the touch of a button, USAir management would be flying blind.

What Makes Information Useful?

USAir depends on the quick analysis of massive amounts of passenger information to make vital ticket pricing decisions. According to USAir's chief financial officer, John W. Harper, "The more you know about your consumers, the more you're able to predict what they want, and the more you're able to deliver the products that the customer wants to buy."[3] USAir uses the mountains of information that it gathers on its 160,000 daily passengers to determine the best fare for each of its routes.

For information to be useful to a decision maker, it must possess five characteristics:

Useful information is
- *Accurate*
- *Complete*
- *Relevant*
- *Focused*
- *Timely*

1. *The information must be accurate.* Good decision making relies on accurate information. Inaccurate information leads to inaccurate decisions.

2. *The information must be complete.* Incomplete information leads to poor decisions. A law firm, for example, must have a complete understanding of the costs of doing business when it sets client billing rates. If all costs are not accounted for and the billing rates are too low, the firm could lose substantial amounts of money. It could even go out of business.

3. *The information must be relevant.* Decision makers must focus only on information that is relevant. This means that all appropriate information must be sought, and that information not necessary to the decision-making process must be filtered out and ignored.

4. *The information format must be focused.* The best information is concise and focused. If you were the owner of a retailing business, it would be an incredible waste of time for you to wade through page after page of information detailing the sales performance of each and every item in your store. You would probably find it much more useful to have the information presented to you in a summary of one or two pages.

5. *The information must be timely.* Well-timed information can give an organization a substantial competitive advantage in the marketplace.

Building an Information System

An **information system** collects, processes, stores, and disseminates information in support of business decision making, control, and analysis. Providing the right information to the right managers and workers at the right time is critical to productivity, effectiveness, and competitiveness. With more information coming in from more sources than ever before, the business must establish controls, that is, regulate the flow of information.

Consider an information system set up to process bills. A clerk receives an invoice, then finds the ordering documents and checks to see that the invoice matches the services performed or the items and quantities delivered and their prices. If the information checks out, the clerk authorizes payment to the vendor. Periodically, the clerk may gather the billing information together in the form of a report to management. This may be a table or a list of similar purchases, which the managers can use in assessing costs, for instance.

In most businesses, paying bills is a computerized process. Organizations use computers for *processing*, or manipulating, data, that is, for converting data into useful information. The computer reads incoming data—the *input*, processes and stores it, and displays outgoing information, or *output*. A **computer system** is a grouping of machines—the **hardware**—that accept and process data and display the output. Sets of instructions, or *computer programs* called **software**, control the computer system's input, processing, storage, and output operations. In our billing example, the clerk inputs the figures from the invoice, and software directs the computer system to process this input and print a payment check or create a report as output (see Figure 18.1).

Finally, information systems need not be computerized. But computerized systems can help users manipulate sizable amounts of information much more accurately and efficiently than can manual systems.

information system

System that collects, processes, stores, and disseminates information in support of business decision making, control, and analysis.

computer system

A grouping of machines—the hardware—that accept and process data and display the output.

hardware

The machines that make up a computer system.

software

Sets of instructions that control a computer system's input, processing, storage, and output operations; also called *computer programs*.

2. Describe the purpose of information systems and explain how the management information system relates to business decision making.

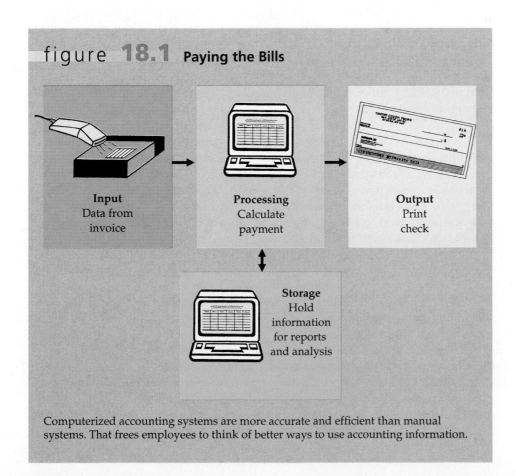

figure **18.1** Paying the Bills

Input Data from invoice → **Processing** Calculate payment → **Output** Print check

Storage Hold information for reports and analysis

Computerized accounting systems are more accurate and efficient than manual systems. That frees employees to think of better ways to use accounting information.

✓ **information technology**

The merging of computing and communications to support decision making.

✓ **management information system (MIS)**

System that supports and documents business decision making by integrating the information needs of the entire organization.

✓ **database**

A collection of computer files that can be cross-referenced or linked.

Communicating Information

Information technology, the merging of computing and communications to support business decision making, helps the business manage data and information accurately and efficiently. Where it used to take hours to update a handwritten list of revenues and expenses, for example, computers now allow businesspeople to make the same updates in minutes. And the information can then be transmitted anywhere in the world in seconds.

To get an idea of how a computerized information system can streamline a typical business process, consider the information flows required to generate an employee paycheck. As input to a noncomputerized system, an employee fills out a time card for the pay period—listing the number of hours worked and any paid time off. The payroll clerk processes this data into information by calculating the total number of hours worked times the pay rate, then subtracts any deductions for taxes, Social Security, and health insurance and arrives at a total pay amount. The clerk then issues the employee a paycheck, the output. Amounts paid, credits for earned time off, and payroll deductions for each employee are posted and tracked manually for accounting and tax purposes in separate files.

With a computerized payroll system, the payroll clerk inputs the hours worked and paid time off into the computer. The computer automatically performs all the necessary calculations and, in seconds, arrives at the total pay amount due the employee. After verification by the payroll clerk, the computer prints the paycheck and automatically adds the appropriate figures into the accounting system. Thus, the information system can be used both to pay each employee *and* to produce financial statements and annual reports.

Management Information Systems

Most firms—even the smallest—now use computerized management information systems as a planning and decision-making aid. A **management information system (MIS)** supports and documents business decision making by integrating the information needs of the entire organization. Managers and workers in all business functions, from management to human resources and from marketing to finance, access the company's management information system at one or more levels.

MIS levels
- *Transactional*
- *Reporting*
- *Decision making*

Figure 18.2 shows how MIS access works. The most basic, or *transactional* level, comprising the day-to-day operations of the business, is the foundation of the entire management information system. Workers input transactions that occur during the normal course of business into a computerized database. A **database** is a collection of computer files—such as sales, purchases, or salaries—that can be cross-referenced or linked. For example, before information systems were computerized, employee files with information such as name, address, date of birth, and Social Security number were all contained on paper files. Most businesses now store personnel information in computerized databases. At the touch of a button, a human resources manager can create a list of all employees in alphabetical order, in order of birth date, town of residence, or any other arrangement. Automated databases replace time-consuming and cumbersome manual data processing, making information much more accessible to decision makers than at any time in history.

To use the database described in Figure 18.2, sales transactions are input to the computer database. Workers and supervisory managers use these transactions to generate sales reports, which are summarized for middle managers to use in tactical analysis. Middle managers develop sales forecasts for top managers to use in strategic planning. Top management then passes the sales forecasts back to the middle managers, who will work with supervisors and workers to develop sales objectives and quotas.

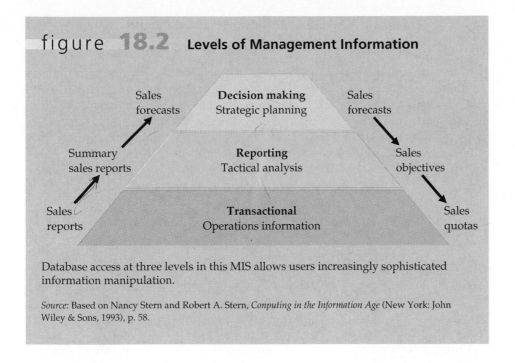

figure 18.2 Levels of Management Information

Sales forecasts

Decision making
Strategic planning

Sales forecasts

Summary sales reports

Reporting
Tactical analysis

Sales objectives

Sales reports

Transactional
Operations information

Sales quotas

Database access at three levels in this MIS allows users increasingly sophisticated information manipulation.

Source: Based on Nancy Stern and Robert A. Stern, *Computing in the Information Age* (New York: John Wiley & Sons, 1993), p. 58.

To be useful to decision makers, transactional-level data must be summarized in ways that show managers their total impact and highlight projected trends. At the next MIS level, *reporting*, managers can obtain reports that link information together to provide meaningful feedback on the operations of the business. In Figure 18.2, these reports are called summary sales reports.

At the top level of an MIS—the *decision-making* level—sophisticated analytical tools support operational and strategic decision making. In a system such as that in Figure 18.2, managers use flexible **decision support systems (DSS)** to chart the course of their sales forecasts and company's future, to analyze information, and to make decisions. For example, a decision support system allows the CEO to review sales forecasts by state or region. **Executive information systems** allow managers to develop customized solutions to broad questions beyond the scope of day-to-day business issues.

The **expert system**, a highly developed form of DSS that simulates a human expert, uses large databases, elaborate sets of rules, and artificial intelligence to develop and analyze recommendations on solutions to specific problems. **Artificial intelligence** is the computer modeling and simulation of human reasoning and learning. Expert systems are useful in every business function and process.

The implementation and maintenance of information systems is so important that at many firms a **chief information officer (CIO)** manages MIS, information technology, and human resources. It is the job of the CIO to respond to the information needs of the business by ensuring that all necessary information is immediately available to decision makers. CIOs design and implement information systems and make sure that the information is secure from hackers and viruses and backed up in case of catastrophic system failure. Although CIOs traditionally had technical backgrounds, a recent survey reports that about half of business computing departments surveyed were headed by non-technical managers. As the control and distribution of information in organizations becomes more and more dependent on computers and networks, the CIO is in a perfect position to observe a firm's most detailed and intimate workings.

 decision support systems (DSS)

Systems that allow managers to chart the course of their sales forecasts and company's future, to analyze information, and to make decisions.

 executive information systems

Systems that allow managers to develop customized solutions to broad questions beyond the scope of day-to-day business issues.

 expert system

A highly developed form of decision support system that simulates a human expert, using large databases, elaborate sets of rules, and artificial intelligence to develop and analyze recommendations on solutions to specific problems.

 artificial intelligence

The computer modeling and simulation of human reasoning and learning.

 chief information officer (CIO)

Executive who manages a firm's management information system, information technology, and human resources.

computer networks

Computing and telecommunications systems that allow users to communicate and share hardware and software resources.

 mainframe computer

System processors that are networked to multiple terminals at which many users can work simultaneously.

According to Bernard Mathaisel, director of Ernst & Young's Center for Business Innovation, "There is no better catbird seat than the information view of the organization."[4]

In the past, smaller firms were at a disadvantage in creating computerized information systems. However, as the cost of computing has declined, even small businesses can now afford to install sophisticated management information systems, sometimes bringing in outside consultants to design and install them. In response to this need, many firms have sprung up to provide customized information solutions to businesses. Computer Sciences Corp. (CSC) is one such firm. Founded in 1959, CSC has grown into one of the nation's largest providers of information technology to business and government markets. Headquartered in El Segundo, California, CSC employs approximately 30,000 people at 450 sites throughout the United States, Europe, Australia, and many other countries. In 1994, its sales reached $2.6 billion.[5]

CSC specializes in reengineering and consulting, computer systems development and integration, and technology management and systems operation. One of its clients is the California State Automobile Association (AAA), which wants to redesign the way its insurance products and other services are delivered to members. The project involves developing new management systems and work procedures, designing a new MIS, restructuring 72 field offices, and retraining 2,500 employees. Its goals are to increase the satisfaction of association members while significantly reducing the AAA's cost of doing business.

Information Technology

Information technology—computer hardware and software, cellular phones, fax machines, cable TV, and many other innovations—has a long history of improvement, from the invention of writing, ink, and paper to the invention of the movable-type printing press by Johannes Gutenberg in the mid-1400s. Handwritten books that were previously available only to the nobility and clergy were replaced by printed books. Suddenly, many more people had access to books and to the power of the printed word.

Each advance in information technology—the telegraph, the telephone, radio and television—has brought significant changes to business and to our economy. What is unique about our Information Age is the speed at which technology has been advancing. The computing power that only a couple of decades ago filled a room full of large machines is now contained in a silicon chip that can rest easily in the palm of your hand. In this section, we focus on hardware, the equipment required to build an information system, and software, the programs that enable the hardware to generate useful information. This section also introduces you to **computer networks**, computing and telecommunications systems that allow users to communicate and to share hardware and software resources. To learn about one of the downsides of the small size of computer chips, see the doing business box "These Chips Are Really Hot."

Classes of Computers

3. Identify and contrast the different classes of computers.

Computers are classified by memory size (storage) and processing speed. The largest, most powerful, and most expensive computers are *supercomputers*. Using banks of processors and incorporating tremendous amounts of data storage capability, supercomputers handle the largest databases and are used to solve complicated scientific calculations. The capability of supercomputers is measured in terms of millions of operations *per second*, and the price of a supercomputer is in the millions of dollars.

doing business

These Chips Are Really Hot

The wonder of microprocessor and memory chips is that they pack so much power into such a small package. Intel Corp's. popular and powerful Pentium chip is about the same size as a matchbook, and a typical memory chip is not much bigger than your fingernail. Of course, just because they are small doesn't mean they are inexpensive. A 4-megabyte memory chip sells for around $200, a Pentium chip for about $1,000. This combination of small size and high price has made computer chips a popular target of thieves.

One evening in 1995, Martin Wood was getting ready to close up for the night when a group of seven men armed with guns, a police scanner, and walkie-talkies charged through the door of his computer products store in Serra Mesa, California. The intruders pushed Wood to the ground and held him at gunpoint as they searched for a particularly hard-to-get memory chip. The high demand for memory chips and microprocessors has created a gray market of brokers eager to buy and sell chips with no questions asked. But why computer chips? Why not old standbys like cash, jewelry, or televisions? Wood, who survived unharmed, says, "You can fit a million dollars worth of [chips] in the back of your car. You can't do that with gold or VCRs."

Because computer chips are so small and are essentially impossible to trace, very few chip robbers are caught. Chip thieves are sophisticated. Says Michael McQuade, senior vice president of the American Electronics Association, "These guys are organized, and they know exactly what they're doing. When they break into a company, they're going in to fill an order."

Source: Elisa Williams, "Li'l Chip Rip-Offs Pay Big," (New York) *Daily News,* May 21, 1995, p. B3.

Supercomputer manufacturers such as Thinking Machines of Cambridge, Massachusetts, are adapting their products from the scientific to the commercial market. Thinking Machines computers were deployed on the set of the film *Jurassic Park.*[6] Retail giant Wal-Mart Stores, Inc., uses a supercomputer to analyze the purchasing trends of its customers. And American Express Co. uses one to perform customer marketing studies.

Mainframe computer processors are *networked*, connected to multiple terminals throughout the organization at which many users can work simultaneously. Mainframes are very efficient network and database managers. The Internal Revenue Service's national taxpayer database is stored on mainframe computers. Mainframe *servers* hold information databases for communication networks such as Compton's Electronic Encyclopedia.

CAD/CAM System

To perfect new products, engineers at Nissan's research and development facilities use powerful microcomputer workstations to integrate computer-aided design and manufacturing into their product development process.

midrange computers

Computers that incorporate networking and other features of mainframes, but are less powerful; also called *minicomputers.*

microcomputers

Computers in which all the processing power is incorporated on a single microprocessor chip.

central processing unit (CPU)

The hardware that produces information from data and controls all computer operations.

4. List and describe the basic hardware of a computer system.

Because mainframes can store huge amounts of information and process it very rapidly, and because they are very expensive, large corporations and government agencies are their primary users. Mainframe computers centralize MIS within one or more mainframe systems linked to many employee terminals. In this way, the organization provides MIS with better security and control.

Midrange computers, or *minicomputers,* incorporate many of the features of mainframes but are less powerful. Like mainframes, midrange computer systems support networks of users and perform complicated processing tasks. Originally, large corporations used minicomputers to decentralize, or "distribute," their management information systems to individual departments. The capabilities that define midrange computers change depending on the prevailing technology. For example, today's mini might have the processing power that was available a few years ago only in a mainframe.

Computers in which all the processing power is incorporated on a single microprocessor chip are called **microcomputers.** Microcomputers are designed for individual users and are the smallest and least expensive class of computer. *Workstations* are used primarily in industry for sophisticated design, drafting, and product development simulations—the *CAD, CAM,* and *CIM* processes described in Chapter 10. These powerful microcomputers rival the power of midrange systems. However, a typical microcomputer has less processing speed and storage capacity than either the mainframe or minicomputer, and many are portable.

The familiar *personal computer (PC)* that you can buy for home use is a microcomputer. *Laptop computers,* or *notebooks,* fit into a case about the same size as a 3-ring notebook. Since laptop PCs can operate on electricity or on batteries, they are truly portable. Although they are generally not as powerful as desktop PCs, they contain all of the same basic features. *Palmtop computers* are ultrasmall versions of laptops that can be held in the palm of your hand.

Computer System Hardware

Computers come in different sizes. Some are smaller than a paperback book. Others fill a small room. The smallest computers might only cost a couple of hundred dollars. The largest cost millions. Regardless of their size or price tag, all computer systems operate using the same basic hardware devices for input, output, storage, and processing.

Recall from Figure 18.1 that an *input device* is used to enter data into a computer. Keyboards, microphones, touch screens, scanners, and the mouse are all input devices. An *output device* displays information from the computer in a format understandable to its human operator. There are many different forms of output devices, including video monitors, printers, and speakers.

Storage devices hold the computer's memory. Primary memory storage includes *random access memory (RAM),* which holds data and programs as you work at the computer—as long as the power is on. When the power goes off, all RAM is wiped clean. The processor's *read-only memory (ROM)* is part of the chip. *Secondary storage devices* provide permanent memory and storage for software and data that are not being used. Tape, disks, and CD-ROMs—compact discs for computers—are all secondary storage devices. Figure 18.3 illustrates the key systems, components, and functions of basic computer hardware.

Microprocessors

The heart of any computer is the **central processing unit** or **CPU,** the hardware that produces information from data and controls all computer operations. In

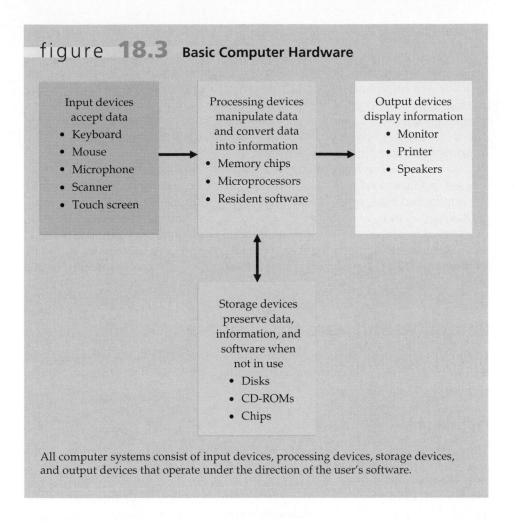

figure **18.3** **Basic Computer Hardware**

Input devices accept data
- Keyboard
- Mouse
- Microphone
- Scanner
- Touch screen

Processing devices manipulate data and convert data into information
- Memory chips
- Microprocessors
- Resident software

Output devices display information
- Monitor
- Printer
- Speakers

Storage devices preserve data, information, and software when not in use
- Disks
- CD-ROMs
- Chips

All computer systems consist of input devices, processing devices, storage devices, and output devices that operate under the direction of the user's software.

1971, a major breakthrough occurred in the development of computer processors. By successfully placing a complete CPU onto one silicon chip, Intel Corp. created the first **microprocessor**. The performance of microprocessors is ranked according to the processing speed and memory capacity of the chips. Today, microprocessor chips are 550 times more powerful than the first microprocessor, which means that they are about as fast as an IBM mainframe computer from 1986.

As the pace of improvement in microprocessors quickens—they have been *doubling* in speed and capacity every 18 months—advances in information technology will continue to be astounding.[7] At work, microprocessors operate hardware that screens and sorts telephone and computer messages and helps you plan and prioritize your workday. Microprocessors will take the scribblings on the conference room wall and produce a printed version that can be edited, transmitted electronically to co-workers, and saved in a computer for future use.

Microprocessors will also find their way into more consumer products. You won't even know that they are there. For example, microprocessors will control the lighting and climate of your home, depending on your personal preferences. Microprocessors will control all your appliances and cook your dinner. In fact, the microprocessors that powered top-of-the-line personal computers in the early 1990s have already found their way into today's televisions, microwave ovens, and automobiles.

 microprocessor
Silicon chip containing a complete central processing unit.

digital computers

Complex electronic circuits comprising simple on/off switches.

 operating system

Software that controls the internal allocation and use of hardware resources such as memory, processing time, and disk space.

 applications

Software packages for specific computing needs.

5. Explain the importance of computer software and describe its applications.

Digital Data

From supercomputers to microprocessors, all the systems we have described are **digital computers**, complex electronic circuits comprising simple on/off switches. For information to be processed by a computer, it must be digitized; that is, it must be expressed in *binary* form, as the number 0 or 1. The CPU identifies a particular electronic switch within itself as on or off and assigns to it either a 0 or a 1. Using this *code* made up of combinations of 0s and 1s, a computer can represent any unit of data.

Nowadays, everything is digital. Telephone and television cable companies are installing vast networks of fiber-optic cable to carry digital signals into our homes and businesses. Your stereo decodes the digital etchings on a compact disc and translates them into the music that plays through your loudspeakers or headphones. Your computer takes the letters, words, and sentences that you type and converts them into digital *bits* and *bytes* that can be stored in its memory or electronically transferred to another computer anywhere in the world.

Computer Software for Business

The most sophisticated computer hardware is useless without software. This section provides an overview of programming, systems software, and business applications software.

Programming

Computer software, like hardware, is constantly improving, becoming more powerful and easier to use. Software development begins with programming and problem-solving logic. When the earliest electronic digital computers were developed, the only way to program them was in binary code, the 0s and 1s of digital data just described. Succeeding generations of computer languages have become more like human languages and thus easier for computer users to understand and use. You may be familiar with computer languages such as Basic, C++, and Pascal.

Systems Software

Computer hardware and CPU operations are controlled by *systems software*. *Utility programs* are the computer's housekeepers. This software works behind the scenes, managing disk files, running performance checks when you turn on the computer, searching for computer viruses, and making computer storage more efficient.

The computer's **operating system** controls the internal allocation and use of hardware resources such as memory, processing time, and disk space. Microcomputer operating systems such as Microsoft Windows and the Macintosh System 7 make it possible for you to use software packages for specific computing needs, or **applications**.

Applications Software

Some businesses hire programmers to custom design applications software. More often, computer users buy packaged applications for word processing, communications, or other uses. Let's look at five software applications that are especially useful in business.

User-Friendly Interface
To broaden the appeal of its software for novice and even technophobic home computer users, Microsoft Corp. developed Bob, a set of eight integrated software programs that do everything from word processing to financial planning. To increase their comfort level, Bob offers users a choice from among 12 on-screen "personal guides," including the cat shown here. Bob's guides provide help at any point in any program, and users can customize the "home environment" screen to suit their personal tastes—country or city, traditional or modern.

Word Processing. *Word processing* software allows a computer user to prepare written documents such as letters, reports, and articles. The writer can enter text, correct it, delete it, and arrange it on the page before printing it out. Or the document can be stored for later use. Word processing programs also have dictionaries that allow users to check spelling, punctuation, and even grammar. *Desktop publishing* is a form of word processing that allows the user to easily manipulate text, graphics, and photographs to create newsletters, brochures, and reports. Some popular word processing programs are Microsoft Word, WordPerfect, and Lotus AmiPro.

Spreadsheets. **Spreadsheets** are tables of numbers, text, or graphics. Like word processing software, spreadsheet software allows the user to easily edit and move entries around on the page. Since the computer recalculates all amounts in an instant, the user can quickly try out different scenarios by changing key variables. Lotus 1-2-3 and Microsoft Excel are commonly used spreadsheet programs.

Database Management. Although most word processing and spreadsheet software applications also offer database capabilities, there will probably always be a market for software packages that are solely database applications. Database programs allow you to store large quantities of data—names, addresses, and phone numbers, for example—and arrange them to suit your purposes. Creating an alphabetical list of all the people in your database, or arranging them by zip code or area code, is as simple as designating the SORT range and clicking the mouse. Database market standouts include Microsoft Access and Borland Paradox.

Groupware. **Groupware** is software specifically designed to support collaboration among groups of people—both inside and outside of an organization. Group decision systems, scheduling, meeting support, and group document handling software are all forms of groupware. Available programs include Lotus Notes, Novell Groupwise, and Microsoft Exchange.

 spreadsheets

Tables of numbers, text, or graphics, and the software that manipulates them.

 groupware

Type of software specifically designed to support collaboration among groups of people—both inside and outside an organization.

Communications. Communications software allows your computer to network with other computers and performs routine tasks such as dialing phone numbers, sending and receiving files, and faxing documents. Leading communications packages include Delrina Corp.'s WinFax Pro and Datastorm Technology's ProComm Plus. The next section describes how computers communicate in networks.

Groupware

Silicon Graphics developed InPerson™ desktop conferencing software as part of its Mindshare™ collaborative environment. Using powerful workstations, team members in far-flung locations can work more productively and creatively by sharing text and graphic information, interacting with each other, and collaborating on projects via live video and audio connections.

Computer Networks, Telecommunications, and Cyberspace

6. Discuss the use and value of networking and telecommunications in business, noting the different forms of telecommunications.

Amy Arnott, an analyst at Chicago-based Morningstar Inc., was faced with a dilemma when her fiancé accepted a job in Los Alamos, New Mexico. But Arnott found a solution. She now *telecommutes* to her Chicago office each business day from the family home in New Mexico. Using a computer, a *modem* (a device that allows computers to "talk" to each other over phone lines), and a monthly CD-ROM update of Morningstar's mutual fund database, she conducts business just as if she were in Chicago. Sure, she misses out on face-to-face interactions with her colleagues, but she can still review Morningstar databases, interview portfolio managers by phone, write reports on her computer, and transmit them to Chicago. All from the comfort of her home.[8]

While some employers worry about being unable to control their at-home employees' work habits directly, telecommuting is catching on in a big way, as we learned in Chapter 12. Not only does it make for happy employees, but it can improve their productivity while helping to clear our overcrowded freeways and polluted air.[9]

Computer Networks

Computers in a network are electronically linked to share information. Networks create new ways of doing business—allowing colleagues to work together even though they may be in different states or countries and many time zones apart. Recall from earlier chapters that at VeriFone, a company that verifies credit card purchases in countries around the world, employees communicate only on-line. VeriFone employees collaborate on projects across time zones as well as national borders.

There are three major benefits to networking a business:

1. *Savings in time and money*. In a networked business, information is communicated instantaneously. Instead of memos going through interoffice mail, computer messages get the word out right away.

2. *Improved communication among departments*. Computer networks help to break down the walls that divide divisions, departments, and work groups by providing ready links among them.

3. *Improved market vision*. Communication on a network tends to be fresh and unedited. If you are on the receiving end of a customer's message, you will have a clear understanding of what the writer means to convey, and your response will be more timely and more accurate as a result.

Computer networks were originally developed on mainframe computer systems to allow several computers to share hardware—a printer, for example. Today, computers of all sizes are networked to share information and hardware peripherals. The use of *groupware*—the software that enables workers to collaborate and share ideas and information—has improved the productivity of businesses dramatically.[10]

Telecommunications

Telecommunications is the transmission of voice and digital information by cable, by telephone line, or through the airwaves.

Wireless communications systems use broadcast frequencies to transmit and receive through the air, just like radio and television. For example, the *pager* is a small radio receiver—smaller than a deck of playing cards. When the pager's telephone number is dialed, it displays the number of the caller, whose call can then be returned. More advanced (and more expensive) models can also display the caller's message or record voice messages. Since pagers receive messages but cannot transmit them, they may eventually be replaced by affordable wireless phones that incorporate paging.

The **cellular telephone** is a portable, battery-operated, wireless phone that broadcasts on a special high-frequency radio band. Although cellular phones have been commercially available only for the past decade, the industry now boasts $15 billion-plus in annual sales and more than 11 million customers in the United States alone.

The **facsimile machine**, or **fax**, is a device that digitally transmits documents such as letters, reports, and photographs to another fax machine. The receiving fax prints out a copy of the original document. The two communicating fax machines can be across the hall or halfway around the world from each other—location doesn't matter. Fax technology has also migrated to personal computers, which can now transmit and receive documents directly into storage, without being printed out first.

Everyone is familiar with telephone answering machines. Information technology took the basic idea of the answering machine and improved on it, producing *voice mail*. This is a computer-based digital system that allows telephone callers to leave messages and those on the voice mail system to manage those messages. For example, an employee can forward a phone message, along with a personal message, to another voice mail user. If the caller is also on the voice mail system, the employee can send a verbal response directly to his or her voice mailbox, and even record messages and send them to other selected mailboxes.

 wireless communications systems

Systems that use broadcast frequencies to transmit and receive communications.

 cellular telephone

A portable, battery-operated, wireless phone that broadcasts on a special high-frequency radio band.

 facsimile machine (fax)

A device that digitally transmits documents such as letters, reports, and photographs to another fax machine.

Personal Communicator

Sony Electronics' portable Magic Link communicator makes personal communications and information management a reality for business people on the move. Weighing less than 20 ounces, Magic Link integrates e-mail, fax, telephone, on-line services, and paging with information management software, *and* it recognizes handwriting.

7. Discuss the business impact of the Internet and on-line services.

 electronic mail (e-mail)

Text-driven message system similar to voice mail.

 personal digital assistants (PDAs)

Combine the features of a computer, a fax machine, a modem, wireless communications, and handwriting recognition into a small battery-operated package about the same size as a paperback book.

 Internet

Worldwide computer network.

 World Wide Web

An organizing system within the Internet that makes it easier to use.

 on-line services

Computer networks that allow users to tap into vast databases and chat live with other users worldwide.

Electronic mail, also known as **e-mail**, is similar to voice mail but is a text-driven rather than a voice-driven message system. Users on a computer network can send and receive messages and attach computer files to their e-mail messages. For example, if you are working on a draft report on product sales, you can attach a copy to an e-mail message to your boss, informing him or her of your progress to date. Your boss can then make changes to the text file and return it to you.

Personal digital assistants, or **PDAs**, combine the features of a computer, a fax machine, a modem, wireless communications, and handwriting recognition into a small battery-operated package about the same size as a paperback book. PDAs allow you to write your input on the screen using a special stylus instead of a keyboard.

Cyberspace

Using the **Internet**, the worldwide computer network, investor Remy Milad finds the most current information and financial analyses on companies that interest him. To get information on an investment, Milad dials up a site called NETworth on the **World Wide Web**, an organizing system within the Internet that makes it easier to use. Internet users can access this Web site at no charge. NETworth contains profiles on 5,000 companies, and all pay NETworth a fee to list their financial profiles. Milad can search NETworth for specific funds by name, by type, or by the Morningstar Inc. quality rating. Once he finds the listing he wants, Milad can print out the information—including graphs of company performance over several years—on his PC.[11]

By 1994, the World Wide Web held more than 10,000 sites, and the number of business addresses on the Internet had grown to 21,700 from 9,000 in 1991. Even more impressive, the total number of Internet users had mushroomed from 1 million in 1988 to an estimated 20 million users in 75 different countries worldwide.[12]

Other networks exist. CompuServe, America Online, Prodigy, and the Microsoft Network are commercial **on-line services** that allow users to tap into vast databases and chat live with other users worldwide. Each service has its own distinct personality—Prodigy, for example, features advertisements in a box at the bottom of the screen—which attracts different users depending on personal tastes or information needs. To learn more about the advances made in this new technology, read the doing business box entitled "How Surfing the Internet Got Easier."

All on-line networks offer the same basic services—e-mail, encyclopedias, weather, news, airline reservations, sports, stock prices, general-interest topics, as well as services of direct interest to business users. A sampling of topic areas on America Online includes numerous business press listings, such as *Worth* magazine on-line, *Barron's* on-line, the Microsoft small-business center, stock quotations, and information on finance and investments. Most on-line services, which generally charge a flat monthly rate along with an hourly usage fee, now offer access to the Internet.

According to Steve Case, president of America Online, "We want to make the MTV generation of the eighties the America Online generation of the nineties."[13] The major on-line services have developed some innovative new programs to attract collegiate customers:

- Prodigy, the result of a Sears/IBM partnership, offers a bulletin board for college students containing tips and advice on how to conduct a job search. Prodigy also provides listings of jobs that are available to graduating seniors.

doing business

How Surfing the Internet Got Easier

The Internet's 3 million computers are located in educational institutions, businesses, and research laboratories worldwide. Up to 20 million people use the Internet each day to exchange e-mail messages, weather maps, video clips, photographs, and any other information you can think of.

While it's unquestionably the largest computer network in the world, the Internet is not a business. Originally funded by federal research dollars, the idea behind the Internet flowered in September 1969 when a group of computer engineers at the University of California, Los Angeles, established the Arpanet, the foundation for today's Information Superhighway.

Most of the activity on the Internet is not commercial. By mid-1995, for example, less than 1 percent of Internet users bought anything on line. Technology writer Gina Smith explains that it's easy for hackers to lift information, such as credit card numbers, from Internet transactions. Beyond controlling hackers, Smith says, the challenge for businesses is making the on-line technology "compelling" to the average consumer.

One solution for business is the World Wide Web. Web users can view video clips of new films, listen to samplings of the latest compact discs, check out the latest car models and prices, search and display libraries of photographs, and send and receive e-mail. Many American companies, from AT&T and General Motors's Saturn to much smaller businesses, advertise their products at Web sites.

Gina Smith predicts that, along with easier connections to the Web, consumers will get on-line control of the information they demand. Interactivity—the lure of being able to listen, speak, and see—will make some sorts of transactions, for cars, real estate, and travel information, for example, truly compelling. Most on-line services offer trial memberships that include free time on the system and reduced monthly service rates.

Sources: "Windows 95 Set for Splash," (New York) *Daily News*, July 30, 1995, p. B4; Gina Smith, interview, *The NewsHour*, PBS, July 26, 1995; Lamar Graham, "My Wy to the I-Way," *Men's Journal*, Dec. 1994–Jan. 1995, pp. 64–65; David S. Jackson, "How the Internet Was Tamed," *Time*, Sept. 26, 1994, p. 60; James Crawley, "A Net Gain," *San Diego Union-Tribune*, Sept. 4, 1994, p. H1.

- CompuServe has inaugurated an alumni network to help graduates keep in touch with their classmates or to correspond with other graduates about job openings in their firms. Alumni can even use CompuServe to shop at the campus bookstore or buy tickets for college football games and other sporting events.
- America Online has forged a partnership with publisher Simon & Schuster that allows students using the same Simon & Schuster textbooks at different schools to share notes and exchange ideas. Students can also converse with teachers and textbook authors.

Web Browser

Mosaic NetScape software provides "both the road map and the steering wheel" for navigating the World Wide Web, according to its co-author Marc Andreessen (left), shown here with partner Jim Clark, former chairman of Silicon Graphics. Like the Internet, the original version of Mosaic was developed with government funding. "Browser" software allows computer users to access Web sites by pointing and clicking on words highlighted in blue on the screen.

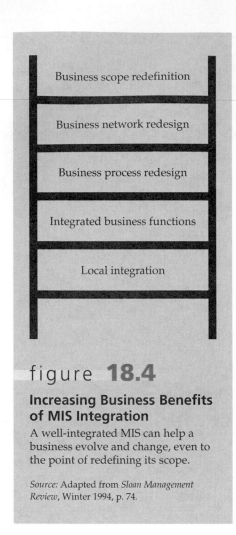

figure 18.4

Increasing Business Benefits of MIS Integration

A well-integrated MIS can help a business evolve and change, even to the point of redefining its scope.

Source: Adapted from *Sloan Management Review*, Winter 1994, p. 74.

8. Outline the five levels of information integration in a business.

We defined automation *in Chapter 10 as performing mechanical operations with little or no direct human involvement.*

knowledge workers

People whose job is to create, collect, process, distribute, and use information.

Information Management

The convergence of communications technology and information systems is creating on-line communities of users and new ways to do business. Information is an industry in its own right, spanning hardware, software, and communications. More than 60 percent of the U.S. labor force is **knowledge workers**, whose job is to create, collect, process, distribute, and use information.[14]

At companies like Bell Labs, knowledge workers are trained in strategies that enhance their productivity. The Harvard University researchers who evaluated Bell Labs training predict that in the United States and other postindustrial nations, knowledge work will drive economic performance in the future. Nations that manage brain work better will prosper economically.[15] Before we explore the impact of information management, let's examine how a business captures the power of information for its knowledge workers.

Managing Information for Competitive Advantage

Information management makes businesses more productive and competitive by getting the right information to the right managers at the right time. Ultimately, this makes businesses more responsive to changes in the marketplace, and therefore more competitive. Integrating information technology with information systems in business is an evolutionary process. In Figure 18.4, it starts at the local level with a more efficient MIS, goes on to process automation, and continues with the emergence of flexible business networks linking together different parts of the organization. As barriers to communication fall and the flow of information accelerates, each new level of integration brings increased efficiency and productivity. Higher levels of integration offer even greater benefits and may even suggest ways the business might alter its scope, for example, by entering a new market.[16]

Levels of Information Integration

One of the biggest mistakes businesses make when they automate their business functions is to do it without a comprehensive plan. When desktop PCs first became widely available, many companies simply bought hardware and software and assigned an employee to make them work together. The result was often a piecemeal system that created more inefficiencies than it cured. For business processes to be improved by information automation, managers and workers must collaborate and plan the transition.

Following, in more detail from Figure 18.4, are the steps that a business can take to integrate its information resources.

1. *Localized integration.* An example of this, the simplest level of business information integration, is the manager of records management for a large law firm who independently decides to use bar coding to track client files. This use of technology may benefit the manager's business unit, but benefits generally will not spread to other units.

2. *Internal integration.* The second level of business integration in Figure 18.4 results from building links among many information systems within a company. For example, the Frito-Lay division of PepsiCo, Inc., has successfully developed an integrated information system that provides marketing managers anywhere in the company with precise, timely, and focused information, allowing them to respond quickly to competition in regional markets.

3. *Business process redesign.* This third level of business integration applies information and technology to an existing organizational structure and *reengineers,* or redesigns, key business processes so that they are integrated as effectively as possible with the company's information systems.

4. *Business network redesign.* The fourth level extends process redesign outside, to the business's network of suppliers, customers, and stakeholders. As before, management assesses the current status of the relevant businesses and then redesigns key processes within the network to optimize the relationships among them. For example, Bose Corp., a maker of upscale audio products, invited representatives of seven key distributors to set up shop at its facilities. These empowered, in-plant representatives then could use Bose purchase orders to place orders faster and attend design engineering meetings to act as the customer's voice.

5. *Business scope redefinition.* In the fifth and most integrated information management level, the business reassesses its vision and scope: Are we competing in every viable market? How can information help our operations in new ways?

Information Management and Office Automation

As you can see, integrating information management into an organization's business functions has a wider impact as it evolves. While the first level may affect only one employee or business unit, the fifth level will have far-reaching consequences for the entire organization. Effective information management enables employees to become better knowledge workers and businesses to become more productive.

Office automation is a broad term for information systems that improve communications among knowledge workers—whether they work in the office or not. Office automation systems include the hardware, software, and communications devices described in this chapter—word processing, e-mail and voice mail, PDAs, voice and video conferencing, fax and image transmission. The goal of integrating office automation is complete communication among all business functions and processes, from the transaction-processing level to the decision support level of the MIS.

When automation first entered the business office, experts predicted that computer files would replace paper completely. But a study performed by the Lawrence Livermore Laboratory and Coopers & Lybrand in 1993 found that the so-called paperless office is actually far from paper free. In the typical office, an average of 19 copies are made of each and every original document. Approximately 7.5 percent of all paper documents are lost, and 3 percent of the remaining documents are misfiled.[17] It costs the average American business an estimated $20 in labor to file or retrieve a document and $120 to find and retrieve a misfiled document. If a document is lost, the cost to re-create it averages $250.[18]

These amounts—high as they may seem—don't even take into account the tremendous cost of organizing, storing, and maintaining the 4 trillion documents American businesses generated in 1993. As John Loewenberg, head of information services for Aetna Life and Casualty Co., says, "Paper in a service business is like cholesterol in the bloodstream."[19] Although businesses still seem reluctant to break the paper habit, they are gradually converting paper into computer files. Before you learn more about the role of office automation in service-producing industries, read the ethics check "How Private Are Your Thoughts?" on the next page.

9. Discuss how information management can contribute to improved business processes.

 office automation

Information systems that improve communications among knowledge workers.

ethics check

How Private Are Your Thoughts?

Two Nissan employees were disciplined by their supervisor a few years ago for making critical remarks about the supervisor over the company's electronic mail system. The employees, Bonita Bourke and Rhonda Hall, filed a grievance with Nissan's Los Angeles headquarters, arguing that they had a reasonable expectation of privacy on the e-mail system. They were fired. They then took the case to court and lost.

While the Fourth Amendment to the Constitution of the United States prohibits the government from unreasonable searches and seizures of citizens within the confines of their homes, nothing prohibits private employers from searching the contents of employees' desks, reading their e-mail, or listening to their voice mail messages. And though it may seem shocking, the courts have even upheld the right of employers to film employees in the company restroom and to tap their telephones.

Why would a company want to invade the privacy of its employees in this way? Employers of course have an interest in uncovering cases of employee fraud and waste or drug or alcohol abuse, and some read employees' e-mail to find evidence of

such problems. Others do it simply to check on employee loyalties. In either case, information technology has made it easier than ever for employers to learn about the private lives and thoughts of their employees. Passwords can easily be broken when the company controls the computer system. Phone calls can be recorded. Videocameras are easy to install.

What if an employer discovers something about an employee that isn't job related but that could subject the employee to harassment, discrimination, or firing? What if an employer learns that an employee has AIDS or is romantically involved with a company executive? How would you feel if you worked for a company that videotaped a co-worker in the restroom and then fired him for private remarks he made about his supervisor? As information technology becomes an even greater force in our work lives, questions about privacy will come to the forefront in the debate on employee rights.

Source: Lee Smith, "What the Boss Knows About You," *Fortune,* Aug. 9, 1993, pp. 88–93.

Interactive Shopping

Time Warner Cable's Full Service Network is part of the company's long-term vision: to evolve the existing cable TV network into a powerful, interactive medium. FSN's ShopperVision, the first interactive television supermarket (a detail is shown here) and drugstore home shopping service, features three-dimensional views of store shelves and product rotation. What a way to stock up the pantry!

Producing and Distributing Services

From Chapter 10 you know how information management contributes to factory automation. Between placement of an order and the product's delivery to the customer, many steps have to take place—in the right sequence and at the right time. As we learned in Chapters 10 and 16, automated, *JIT inventory control* allows manufacturers to fine-tune their production and distribution processes by keeping excess inventory and delays caused by shortages to a minimum.

Automating the production process is so important to a company's productivity that many companies hire information management experts to design and install their systems. To ensure that it got the best system possible for the money, Gerber Products Co. contracted with Computer Sciences Corp. (CSC) to design and develop an advanced materials management system. The end result of CSC's efforts was a system that provides Gerber management with materials requirements planning, inventory control, logistics, forecasting, and capacity planning.[20]

Advertising

Advertisers are using information technology to target their messages to their most likely potential customers. For example, interactive television systems like Time Warner's Full Service Network hold promise for advertisers. The challenge in advertising is getting the right message about a product to the right person at the right time. When a Time Warner's subscriber enters a request to view a film, the following advertisement might appear on the screen:

"Hungry? How about trying a delicious pizza from Marcello's?" Simply by pressing "yes" on the remote control, the subscriber could order the pizza and have it sent on its way.[21]

Retailing

Among retailers, America's largest drugstore chain, the Walgreen Co., has installed a vast computer network that electronically links the company's headquarters with each store via special satellite dishes. Not only can Walgreen's headquarters communicate price changes instantly to each of its 1,700 stores, it can also send background music and announcements directly to each one. The sophisticated system can even broadcast promotional information on snow brushes to stores in Minnesota at the same time that it broadcasts information on suntan lotion to its stores in Florida.[22]

Accounting and Financial Management

Information management; accounting, the topic of the next chapter; and financial management, the topic of Part 7, are closely linked business functions that affect all business processes. These upcoming chapters also explain in more detail some of the financing concepts you studied in Chapter 6.

Reviewing *Capturing the Power of Information*

Information Systems

1. **Contrast data and information and name the five characteristics that make information useful to a business.** In order for the raw data on business transactions to be useful, they must be summarized and analyzed to create information for decision making. For that information to be useful, it must be accurate, complete, relevant, timely, and focused in format.

2. **Describe the purpose of information systems and explain how the management information system relates to business decision making.** Businesses achieve their goal of profitability through the processes of decision making, control, and analysis. Information systems, such as those for payroll, provide the specific information needed. Through information technology—automated business functions—tremendous amounts of data are managed easily and efficiently. Management information systems integrate and disseminate information to the right people at the right time. Different MIS levels serve different levels of managers and workers. While the applications in most management information systems are generic, managers use decision support systems and executive information systems to customize information and gain management flexibility.

Information Technology

3. **Identify and contrast the different classes of computers.** Computers are classified in terms of memory storage size and processing speed. The most powerful computers, known as supercomputers, process the most complex data and manage the largest databases. Smaller mainframe computers are the largest computers typically used for business operations. Mainframes are networked to terminals, through which employees enter and retrieve data. Midrange computers (minicomputers) incorporate many of the advanced features of mainframes, but they are less powerful. Microcomputers are designed for individual use and are the smallest and least expensive class of computer. Today's personal computers are as capable as yesterday's mainframes.

4. **List and describe the basic hardware of a computer system.** Input devices such as keyboards, microphones, touch screens, scanners, and the mouse are used to enter data into a computer. Output devices such as printers, monitors, and speakers display information from a computer. Storage devices include random access memory (RAM), which holds data and programs as you work on them; read-only memory (ROM), which keeps the computer functioning properly; and secondary storage de-

vices such as tapes, disks, and CD-ROMs. The central processing unit (CPU) controls all computer operations. Today, a complete CPU can be placed on one silicon chip, the main feature of a *micro*processor. All processing of information on a computer is digitized.

5. **Explain the importance of computer software and describe its applications**. Without computer software the hardware would be useless. The operating system controls the basic functioning of the hardware and enables use of applications software. Depending on its needs, a business may use any number of applications programs, including word processing, spreadsheets, database management, groupware, and communications.

6. **Discuss the use and value of networking and telecommunications in business, noting the different forms of telecommunications**. Through networking, employees at different locations are able to work together. Networks save time and money and improve communications among departments. Furthermore, because networked information is current and unedited, it may improve market vision. Telecommunications has dramatically improved networking within and among businesses. Wireless communication devices include pagers and cellular telephones. Other telecommunications devices include facsimile machines (faxes), voice mail, and electronic mail (e-mail). The personal digital assistant (PDA) combines the features of a networked computer and telecommunications.

7. **Discuss the business impact of the Internet and on-line services**. The computer networks have opened a new way for businesses to communicate with one another and to advertise their products and services to a global base of 20 million users in 75 countries. Through on-line

services such as America Online and Prodigy, entrepreneurs can access vast databases of information about starting and operating small businesses, finance, business news, stock quotations, and much, much more. As a result, the business world has witnessed the globalization of computing and the ascendance of the knowledge worker.

Information Management

8. **Outline the five levels of information integration in a business**. To achieve effective and efficient computer automation, businesses begin with a plan that aims for increased efficiency and productivity. The business evolves through five levels of information integration. The first level, localized integration, involves automating a single process within a business unit. The internal integration level involves automating a process among several business units. At the third level, process redesign, the company reengineers its internal processes. The fourth level, network redesign, extends reengineering outside to the company's suppliers and customers and to its stakeholders. At the fifth level, business scope redefinition, the business reassesses its vision and scope and redefines its goals.

9. **Discuss how information management can contribute to improved business processes**. By integrating information technology with information systems, information management evolves through a more efficient, integrated MIS to process automation and network redesign to possibly redefining the scope of the business. Information management that is attuned to its internal and external customers leads to increased productivity in every business function, where knowledge workers use office automation to control their business processes.

✓ Key Terms

data **549**	decision support systems (DSS) **553**	microcomputers **556**	cellular telephone **561**
information **549**	executive information systems **553**	central processing unit (CPU) **556**	facsimile machine (fax) **561**
information system **551**			electronic mail (e-mail) **562**
computer system **551**	expert system **553**	microprocessor **557**	personal digital assistants (PDAs) **562**
hardware **551**	artificial intelligence **553**	digital computers **558**	
software **551**	chief information officer (CIO) **553**	operating system **558**	Internet **562**
information technology **552**		applications **558**	World Wide Web **562**
	computer networks **554**	spreadsheets **559**	on-line services **562**
management information system (MIS) **552**	mainframe computer **555**	groupware **559**	knowledge workers **564**
database **552**	midrange computers **556**	wireless communications systems **561**	office automation **565**

• Review Questions

1. How do data differ from information? What five characteristics must information have to be useful?

2. What role does a management information system play in business decision making? What is the database hierarchy?

3. What are the classes of computers and how do they differ?

4. What are the categories of computer hardware? Name some of the specific devices available in each category.

5. What is the relationship between software and hardware? What categories of software applications are available?

6. What is networking and how does it benefit businesses?

7. You are a salesperson for a sportswear manufacturer and you travel 40 out of 52 weeks a year. What types of telecommunications systems would you use? Why?

8. A company wants to computerize its business processes. What steps should management take to do this efficiently and effectively?

9. How does information management benefit the production, human resources, marketing, and finance functions in a business?

• Critical Thinking Questions

1. Why is the effective management of information in an organization so important to competitiveness, to profitability, and, ultimately, to success?

2. You are a team leader in the distribution department of a busy retailer. What would you do to manage the flood of information entering your office? How would you avoid information overload and focus on the most important issues?

3. Telecommuting is a volatile issue in many organizations. You submit a request to your supervisor for permission to telecommute. What organizational benefits do you cite to support your request?

4. Many large organizations have a lot of money invested in mainframe computer systems. Should these organizations consider switching over to networks of microcomputers? Why or why not?

5. Statistics show that, in terms of work force growth, the proportion of knowledge workers is quickly gaining ground on that of manufacturing workers. What are some of the opportunities you see for knowledge workers in the future? Do you see an opportunity for yourself in this rapidly growing sector of the work force? Why or why not?

REVIEW CASE *Signature Software*[23]

At 41, Steve Dente became the unlikely owner of a software development company. Years earlier, after graduating from college with a degree in geology, he had packed his bags to seek his fortune in Africa, where he soon learned the ins and outs of exporting precious gems. Upon completion of this apprenticeship, Dente returned to the United States and, with brother Eugene, started up the Serengeti Co.—a precious-stonecutting business.

In 1991, Dente bought his first computer and found that he could create original software to automate aspects of his business. "I found out that it made a lot more sense to write computer programs to fit my business, instead of trying to change my business to fit a program," Dente says. The first program he wrote was a database to keep track of sales trans-

actions. As Dente's interest in software grew, he put his mind to work, thinking up ideas that he could sell. He first developed digital business cards—computer diskettes for salespeople containing simple financial applications, as well as the salesperson's name and phone number. Dente found plenty of customers for his digital business cards, companies such as the Thomas James Associates stock brokerage and Century 21 real estate.

In 1993, Dente and his brother started up Signature Software and began developing its first commercial product for nationwide distribution. Birthday Fun Facts, a software program that prints out entertaining certificates for any birth date from January 1, 1900, to the present, is being distributed by several large national retailers including Price/Costco,

Inc., Wal-Mart Stores, Inc., Egghead, Inc., and CompUSA, Inc. One month after its release, 20,000 copies of Birthday Fun Facts had already been sold, and Dente projected first-year revenues in excess of $1 million. Signature Software has three new products in development.

1. Why would it be wise for Signature Software to consider installing a management information system even before it reached $1 million in annual sales?

2. Explain how Signature Software could apply the five levels of information integration to improve its business.

3. When Dente writes software programs on his home computer, he carries the data to his computer at the office on a diskette. What telecommunications enhancements could he use to manage his work more efficiently?

4. Dente is planning to take a computer on the road to demonstrate his products to potential customers. What type of computer should he consider buying? Why?

5. To support an e-mail system, Signature Software networked its computers. What are three benefits that the company can expect as a result?

6. Signature Software is growing rapidly. How can Dente ensure that his company keeps up with information technology?

CRITICAL THINKING CASE   *Women's Wire*[24]

While the computer users who access major on-line services such as Prodigy, America Online, and CompuServe number in the millions, only one in seven Internet users is female. Fewer than 1,000 customers subscribe to Women's Wire, an on-line service targeted specifically at women and women's issues. Despite the fact that approximately 85 percent of Internet users are men, market research indicates that women are very interested in an easy-to-use on-line service that addresses their needs.

According to Ellen Pack, who began Women's Wire in 1992 with Nancy Rhine, "All I heard was that women don't use on-line services. It was like a joke: Two shoe salesmen go to a tropical island. One calls his office and says, 'I'm coming back tomorrow—no one here wears shoes.' The other one calls his office and says, 'Don't expect me back for a month—no one here wears shoes!'" Pack and Rhine forecasted their base of subscribers to increase to 10,000 in 1995.

Women's Wire charges $2.50 per hour for use of the service. Not-for-profit organizations can solicit Women's Wire subscribers for free, but businesses pay a fee to run advertisements. With an increasing subscriber base and revenues expected to pour in from advertisers, Pack and Rhine are well on their way to making Women's Wire a successful on-line service.

1. Many of the large on-line services such as CompuServe have already devoted topic areas to women's issues. From a marketing standpoint, what advantages over the larger on-line services does Women's Wire potentially offer its subscribers?

2. Do you see a potential market for other special-interest on-line services? If you had the opportunity to start up your own specialized on-line service, what kind of service would it be and what issues would it address?

3. Once Women's Wire is well established and profitable, what other kinds of businesses could Pack and Rhine spin off from their on-line service?

Critical Thinking with the ONE MINUTE MANAGER

"Learning organizations and knowledge workers seem like a natural fit," said Carlos.

The One Minute Manager nodded in agreement. "And before it could teach others, Coopers & Lybrand had to make itself into a learning organization. One program at C&L—where they employ a manager for learning within the company—is Partner Camp, special training each year for employees who are promoted to partner at the accounting firm. At the camp, new partners learn and practice coaching, team-building, and other management strategies. Partners are linked into C&L's worldwide network. C&L also participates in real-time satellite hookups that bring hundreds of employees together with senior managers for seminars. Information systems and information technology support C&L's organizational learning goals."[25]

1. In implementing a learning organization, how did Coopers & Lybrand integrate the level of business scope redefinition?

2. How is C&L using the idea of the virtual corporation, discussed in Chapter 9, in its Partner Camp?

3. What does the saying, "Garbage in, garbage out," mean to you?

19 Accounting and Financial Controls

accounting

The process of collecting, summarizing, and reporting financial information for decision making.

People make financial decisions, just as organizations do. You keep track of the money you earn, your bills, your bank account balance, and the amount of cash you have on hand. Then you decide what you can afford to spend. Businesses do the same. At home you call it making ends met. In business, the process of collecting, summarizing, and reporting financial information for decision making is called **accounting**.

Accounting information is the basis for sound business decisions. In this chapter you will learn how—and for whom—companies collect accounting information, organize it, report it, and interpret it. You will also learn the role accounting plays in improving customer service, quality, and productivity. After reading this chapter, you will be able to reach the learning goals below.

Learning Goals

1. Discuss the role of accounting in business and describe the accounting cycle.
2. Distinguish between internal and external uses of accounting information and describe how these uses lead to different accounting specialties.
3. Identify and describe the two major categories of accountants.
4. Explain the relationship between the accounting equation and double-entry bookkeeping.
5. Identify the components of a balance sheet and explain how they relate to one another.
6. Contrast the income statement with the balance sheet and describe how specific expenses relate to revenues.
7. Describe the statement of cash flows.
8. Describe the major ratios for analyzing the financial statements.
9. Discuss the application of financial ratios by internal and external users and identify confounding factors.

The ABCs of Accounting[1]

"I wonder why she wants to meet us at the bookstore?" Joanna thought out loud as she and Carlos entered the brand-new Barnes & Noble.

"Maybe she wants to read us a story," Carlos deadpanned in reply.

"I think you're right," said Joanna. "She's sitting over there reading a book."

The One Minute Manager looked up from her reading as the students approached. "I asked you to meet me here because stores like this now dominate the bookselling industry. By the year 2000, this chain alone plans to open its 500th store.

"This store stocks over 200,000 titles, and look at all the other merchandise it carries. In just a few years, it's forced scores of mom-and-pop bookstores out of business. That's the story I want to tell you."

"I was wrong," Carlos whispered to Joanna.

"He thought you were going to *read* us a story," Joanna laughed.

The One Minute Manager laughed, too. "This is the story of a small, independent bookstore chain in Milwaukee, Wisconsin—Harry W. Schwartz Bookshops by name, founded in 1927. The Schwartz family knows almost everything about books. You name it, company president David Schwartz has seen it, and often read it. About the only books he never had a firm grasp of were the accounting ledgers and journals that told the company's financial story. And that lack of knowledge threatened the very existence of Schwartz Bookshops.

"When Schwartz and his partner Avin Domnitz visited their banker in 1986, they expected a glowing report. Their banker thought otherwise. Schwartz Bookshops was turning over its inventory far more slowly than the book industry average, its expenses for everything from health benefits to store supplies were uncontrolled, and the company was losing more money combined than before Schwartz and Domnitz had merged.

"Most alarming, thought their banker, was the encroachment of Waldenbooks, B. Dalton, and the then-emerging book superstores being opened by Barnes & Noble and Borders Bookshops. These stores, owned by large companies with great financial depth, carried a wide array of merchandise, controlled their inventory with computers, and tracked and understood their financial position. The chains were just now beginning to invade the Milwaukee market, and the banker believed Schwartz Bookshops had no plan in place to respond to the ferocious competition. He feared that the bank would lose the money it had lent the business once the chains opened stores in the region.

"So the banker told Schwartz and Domnitz that their loan was being designated for the bank's workout division, a special unit that closely monitors loans that the bank believes might go sour. And he advised the duo that unless they got serious about running the financial end of their business, they'd soon have no business to run."

The Role of Accounting

Can accounting and financial controls save Schwartz Bookshops? Probably not by themselves. As you've learned throughout this book, it's the interplay of all the business functions—management, marketing, human resources, and the rest—that makes the business process work. Control systems based on information management and accounting, however, enable owners and managers to make better decisions—to set objectives, establish and implement policies, evaluate employee performance and take action to improve it, and adjust to changes in the business environment.

Accounting tracks the financial life of the business. Businesses measure their past progress from accounting reports and financial statements, and they use those records to forecast future performance, as we will learn in this section. Just consider the following examples:

- Last year on Valentine's Day, your neighborhood florist sold $20,000 worth of roses. This year, she took in $24,000 because she ran a special offering a dozen roses for $12. Her sales rose by $4,000. But did the florist make a profit? Did she make more or less money than she did last February? Was running the special on roses worthwhile?

- Suppose your local hardware store owner wants to borrow $25,000 to open a decorating department to compete with the new Home Depot, Inc., superstore across town. How can the owner prove to the bank that he can pay back the loan needed for this expansion? How can he determine whether expanding his business will be a worthwhile investment?

The Accounting Cycle

In each case, the business owner must rely on accounting information—information collected each day, week, and month, and organized and reported annually, quarterly, monthly, or even weekly. Businesses need organized accounting information to monitor their operations, to determine whether products are generating profits for the company, and to evaluate their costs. Businesses must also report their performance to outsiders—to bankers, suppliers, stockholders, government taxation authorities, and others interested in the company.

Accounting provides the framework for business decision making through a process called the *accounting cycle*, detailed in Figure 19.1 on page 576. The accounting cycle begins by recording each transaction as it occurs and concludes with the preparation of financial statements for a specific time period. These statements are used by decision makers inside and outside the business.

As you will learn in this chapter's section on financial statements, transactions comprise revenues from selling products and two major categories of expenses: those resulting from sales of goods and services, including the amount paid for inventories, and those resulting from business operations, such as marketing, salaries, and electric bills.

As Figure 19.1 shows, the amount of revenue received or expenses paid in each transaction is entered when it occurs into a file called a journal. Next, the journal entries are classified according to the type of transaction, or *account*. Account data are then recorded in a file of accounts called a ledger, which shows all transactions for the accounting cycle by account and all account balances at the end of each cycle.

Accounting is part of the business's information systems. Information technology has streamlined the accounting cycle, improved the availability and usefulness of accounting information, and enabled decision makers inside and

1. Discuss the role of accounting in business and describe the accounting cycle.

figure **19.1**   The Accounting Cycle

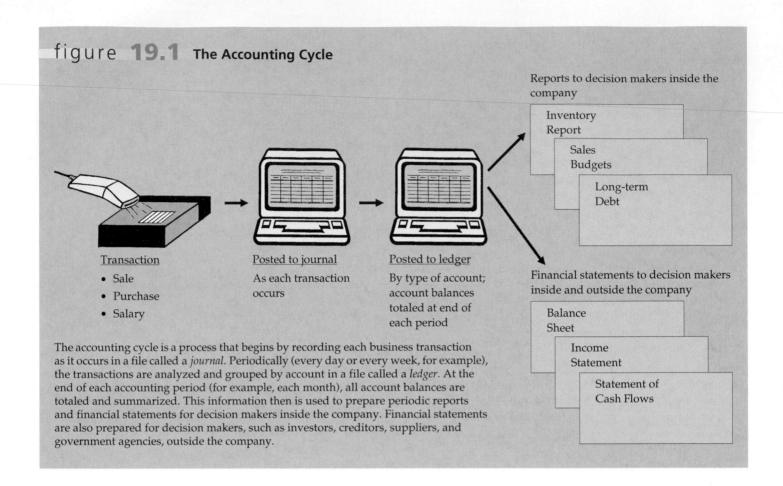

Transaction
- Sale
- Purchase
- Salary

Posted to journal
As each transaction occurs

Posted to ledger
By type of account; account balances totaled at end of each period

Reports to decision makers inside the company

Inventory Report

Sales Budgets

Long-term Debt

Financial statements to decision makers inside and outside the company

Balance Sheet

Income Statement

Statement of Cash Flows

The accounting cycle is a process that begins by recording each business transaction as it occurs in a file called a *journal*. Periodically (every day or every week, for example), the transactions are analyzed and grouped by account in a file called a *ledger*. At the end of each accounting period (for example, each month), all account balances are totaled and summarized. This information then is used to prepare periodic reports and financial statements for decision makers inside the company. Financial statements are also prepared for decision makers, such as investors, creditors, suppliers, and government agencies, outside the company.

outside the business to project future financial performance more accurately. Now let's examine some of the ways that accounting information is benefiting decision makers inside the organization today.

Internal Users of Accounting Information

2. Distinguish between internal and external uses of accounting information and describe how these uses lead to different accounting specialties.

Inside the company, managers use accounting information to plan and control business operations. *Open-book management*, discussed in Chapter 8, empowers employees to use accounting information to improve productivity and control budgets. By early 1995, according to Jay O'Connor, product manager at Intuit, Inc., about half of all small businesses were using computerized information systems. More than half a million businesses use QuickBooks, his company's business-accounting software program, and about 30 percent of the 6 million customers who own Quicken, Intuit's best-selling personal accounting software, also use it in their small businesses.[2]

Transaction data captured electronically, such as from bar codes scanned at the supermarket checkout counter, are entered directly into the supermarket's journal and posted directly to each account. Electronic data entry systems are also used by companies like Federal Express to track packages from sender to receiver, by Delta Airlines to track customer volume on certain air routes, and even by Big Sky Ski Resort in Montana to track the relative popularity of different ski trails.[3] As you learned in Chapter 16, Wal-Mart Stores, Inc., Sears, Roebuck and Co., and other retailers have direct electronic links to suppliers that provide just-in-time inventory control.

Information Sharing

The increasing use of work teams is breaking down both communication barriers and information barriers inside the firm. Business process reengineering, which encourages managers and workers to look for new and imaginative ways to do business, results in innovation.[4] A natural outcome is that more highly skilled people do more complex work. These knowledge workers need information to make decisions.

One information-sharing approach uses accounting information to quantify the **cost of quality**, that is, how much it costs to maintain an acceptable level of quality in products. For example, Sony Corp. found that televisions with a low, but acceptable, level of color density were returned more frequently for service, whereas sets with color density above acceptable levels were rarely returned. Sony reset the quality standards and greatly reduced service expenses.[5] By focusing on quality and cost, information provided by Sony's accounting system led to reduced costs, higher profitability, and greater customer satisfaction.

Benchmarking and Internal Controls

Accounting information is also proving useful in benchmarking, where firms make in-depth studies of competitors' processes or of processes comparable to theirs in an entirely different industry. A classic example is Xerox Corp.'s evaluation of L.L. Bean, Inc.'s, warehouse order picking system. By studying Bean's inventory methods, Xerox managers learned to improve their own system and thus provide customers with better, faster service.[6]

Process Accounting

Accounting information is being used to predict what the future holds for businesses. The accounting system assists decision makers by showing them the financial impact on business processes of alternative decisions.[7]

By tracing costs back to their origins, **activity-based costing (ABC)** assigns costs to specific activities rather than to departments within the company. ABC is based on the theory that every business expense has a *cost driver*, an activity that is directly or indirectly the root cause of the expense. For example, a tire

cost of quality

How much it costs to maintain an acceptable level of quality in products.

activity-based costing (ABC)

Assigning costs to root activities, or cost drivers, rather than to departments.

Accounting Information Systems

When you buy groceries, the checkout scanner captures not only the price and the item for your register receipt but also updates the supermarket's cash account and inventory. This enables your grocer to track receipts and restock shelves for optimum profitability.

purchase by Harley-Davidson, Inc., is the direct result of motorcycle assembly; in ABC, the expense will therefore be charged to that activity, rather than to inventory as it would be in a traditional system. The cost of a new factory lighting system may be traced indirectly to a joint decision by work teams and managers that better lighting will increase the productivity of the motorcycle assembly line; that expense will also be assigned to assembly in ABC.[8]

Activity-based costing can also affect consumers. After The Bell Group, a manufacturer and distributor of jewelry-making tools, equipment, and materials, instituted ABC in 1991, its accountants realized that the company was overcharging customers who ordered in volume. Bell found that it took roughly the same amount of time to fill a large order as a small one, yet it was charging far more for shipping and handling bigger orders than smaller ones. So the company devised a pricing structure that rewarded customers for placing larger orders. The new system not only built customer loyalty but also helped The Bell Group increase its sales.[9]

External Users of Accounting Information

Outside the company, suppliers, investors, creditors, and government agencies use accounting information to evaluate a firm's performance. Creditors, lenders, and suppliers use accounting information to determine whether they should do business with the company. Investors use accounting information to make investment decisions. Government agencies use accounting information to determine whether the company is meeting its tax obligations and complying with laws and regulations. And unions sometimes use accounting information to bargain with company management. For example, when the United Auto Workers union was negotiating with Chrysler Corp. for higher wages in 1993 and 1994, it pointed to the company's record profits as evidence that its workers had become more productive and thus deserved a raise.

Managerial and Financial Accounting

Managerial accounting reports financial information to internal users. Managerial accounting systems generate reports as often as internal users want them, typically at least every quarter. A company may use standard financial statements internally, or the users of such reports may develop their own. Victoria's Secret, for example, might track how well or how poorly each style of swimsuit is selling in order to decide which ones to reorder for the next selling season.

Taxation and public investment through stock ownership gave rise to **financial accounting**, which reports financial information to external users on a regular, periodic basis, usually quarterly or annually. Investors, bankers, and creditors require measures of comparison among firms in order to make business decisions regarding particular companies.

Since the information provided by financial accounting is used externally, its rules and the means of reporting it are standardized and are regulated by the federal government through the Securities and Exchange Commission (SEC). The standard accounting rules, conventions, and presentation methods used in preparing financial statements are called **generally accepted accounting principles**, or **GAAP**. An independent organization, the Financial Accounting Standards Board (FASB), monitors GAAP. FASB consists of seven representatives from public accounting firms, industry, and accounting education whose sole mission is to study and develop standard accounting rules, conventions, measurements, techniques, and presentation methods to be used in financial statements.[10]

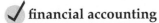 **managerial accounting**

Reports financial information to internal users.

financial accounting

Reports financial information to external users.

generally accepted accounting principles (GAAP)

Standard accounting rules, conventions, and presentation methods used in preparing financial statements.

public accountants

Professionals who sell accounting services to organizations or individuals.

audit

Independent examination of financial statements and records to determine their validity and fair presentation of information.

certified public accountant (CPA)

A licensed practitioner who has passed a qualifying examination administered by the American Institute of Certified Public Accountants (AICPA).

Remember, the major difference between managerial and financial accounting is who uses the information. Managerial accounting focuses on the information needs of people inside the firm, while financial accounting focuses on the information needs of people outside the firm.

The Accounting Profession

Managerial and financial accounting reflect the separate needs of internal and external users of accounting information. To meet those needs, two types of accountants exist: public accountants and private accountants.

3. Identify and describe the two major categories of accountants.

Public Accountants

Public accountants sell accounting services to organizations or individuals. Public accountants run their own practices or work for public accounting firms that provide services, including consulting and tax advice, to other businesses on an outsourced basis. Because public accountants are independent of their clients, external users rely on them to report financial accounting information with an unbiased, objective eye, and to be critical in their assessment of a company's financial position.

Outsourcing *is contracting with outside organizations for one or more business services.*

Accounting assessments are routinely based on an **audit**, an independent examination of financial statements and records to determine their validity and fair presentation of information. The auditing team checks to see whether the firm followed GAAP in preparing its financial statements and whether any audited information should be disclosed publicly. This would be necessary if the information could affect the firm's financial standing and thereby the decisions of those who do business with the firm or plan to invest in it.

The most well known and respected accounting professional is the **certified public accountant (CPA)**, a licensed practitioner who has passed a qualifying examination administered by the American Institute of Certified Public Accountants (AICPA). CPAs must earn a bachelor's degree in accounting, work at a public accounting firm for at least three years, and pass the AICPA's four-part, 15½ hour examination. Only about 12 percent of CPA applicants pass the exam on their first try.[11]

There are about 440,000 CPAs in the United States, and about 30,000 candidates pass the exam each year. Despite the title, CPAs may be public or private accountants; however, more CPAs work for themselves or for accounting firms than are employed by private businesses. CPAs also work for individuals, especially at income tax time. But not all tax preparers are CPAs—nor are they necessarily even accountants. At H&R Block, Inc., and other tax preparation services, CPAs are hired to supervise and train the people who prepare customers' tax returns.

Public accounting firms range in size from a single CPA in private practice to worldwide partnerships consisting of hundreds of CPAs. The largest public accounting firms in the United States, known as the Big Six, are Arthur Anderson & Co., S.C.; Coopers & Lybrand; Deloitte & Touche; Ernst & Young; KPMG Peat Marwick; and Price Waterhouse.

Competition at the top of the accounting profession is fierce. During the past decade, the Big Six firms (which used to be the Big Eight) emerged from a series of industry mergers. These are global companies, and an increasingly competitive business environment has spurred the Big Six to expand the services they offer clients. Like superstores moving into local neighborhoods, these giant firms are making survival tough for smaller accounting firms.

Consolidation in the industry also makes for less competition, higher fees, and more opportunities for unethical behavior. Business competitors that discover they are sharing the same accounting firm fear for the confidentiality of their financial information.

Accounting Goes Hollywood
On the night of the Academy Awards extravaganza, the Academy of Motion Picture Arts and Sciences relies on accountants like these from the Big Six firm of Price Waterhouse to tabulate the results of the Oscar balloting—and ensure their secrecy.

Private Accountants

Private accountants are salaried employees of a business, government agency, or not-for-profit organization. Private accountants supervise internal managerial accounting systems, ranging from day-to-day bookkeeping operations to generating internal accounting reports, preparing the organization's tax returns, and developing and interpreting its financial statements.

A private accountant may be a CPA or a **certified management accountant**, or **CMA**, a licensed specialist in managerial accounting. To be designated a CMA by the Institute of Management Accountants, a candidate must be a CPA or hold a bachelor's degree, work as a management accountant for two years or a public accountant for three years, and pass a two-day, four-part examination. CMAs review internal accounting procedures, install controls to prevent internal fraud, and develop and produce managerial accounting reports.

A private accountant who is a **certified internal auditor (CIA)** checks the company's records for accuracy, consistency, and conformity to GAAP.[12] To attain CIA certification from the Institute of Internal Auditors, the accountant must hold a bachelor's degree in any field, work for two years as an internal auditor, and pass a two-day, four-part examination.

The Financial Statements

The financial statements—the balance sheet, the income statement, and the statement of cash flows—are the end products of the accounting cycle illustrated in Figure 19.1. Business managers use these reports to make decisions, to improve processes, and to identify problems and opportunities. Investors, potential partners, and other external users also analyze financial statements in order to assess a company's performance and its quality as an investment or a business partner.

The Accounting Equation and Double-Entry Bookkeeping

Ultimately, the financial statements reveal whether or not a company has earned a profit from its efforts. The basis of financial statements is the **accounting equation**

$$\text{Assets} = \text{Liabilities} + \text{Owners' Equity}$$

where

- **Assets** are financial and economic resources owned or controlled by an organization—the oil wells owned by Texaco, Inc., or the inventory held by Foot Locker. Companies use assets to generate revenue. Assets are financed by the company's creditors, owners, or both.
- **Liabilities** are the claims of creditors against the assets of a business, representing the firm's financial obligations, or debts. For instance, your credit card balance or student loan is a liability.
- **Owners' equity** is the claims of owners against assets, representing the cash that would remain if a company sold all its assets to repay its liabilities.

The accounting equation is balanced by a system called **double-entry bookkeeping**, or recording two entries for every financial transaction. The double-entry system thus recognizes the effect each transaction has on both

private accountants
Professionals who are salaried employees of a business, government agency, or not-for-profit organization.

certified management accountant (CMA)
A licensed specialist in managerial accounting as designated by the Institute of Management Accountants.

certified internal auditor (CIA)
A private accountant who checks company records for accuracy, consistency, and conformity to GAAP, and is certified by the Institute of Internal Auditors.

accounting equation
Assets = liabilities + owners' equity.

assets
Financial and economic resources owned or controlled by an organization.

liabilities
Claims of creditors against the assets of a business.

owners' equity
Claims of owners against assets.

double-entry bookkeeping
Recording two entries for every financial transaction in order to keep the accounting equation in balance.

4. Explain the relationship between the accounting equation and double-entry bookkeeping.

sides of the accounting equation. This system was developed by a Franciscan monk, Luca Pacioli, more than 500 years ago, in 1494. The basis of double-entry bookkeeping is that every transaction is represented by a record of the expense (an increase in liabilities) and a record of the receipt of the item (an increase in assets). For instance, when the T-shirt shop at the mall receives a shipment worth $200, they record it both as an increase in assets (that is, inventory) and as an increase in liabilities (the payment due the T-shirt manufacturer). The accounting equation looks like this:

The accounting equation is sometimes abbreviated A = L + OE.

$$
\begin{array}{ccccc}
\text{Assets} & = & \text{Liabilities} & + & \text{Owners' equity} \\
\$200 & = & \$200 & + & 0 \\
\text{(shirts received} & & \text{(payment due} & & \\
\text{increases inventory)} & & \text{increases debt)} & &
\end{array}
$$

The Balance Sheet

The **balance sheet** is a statement of financial position showing an organization's assets, liabilities, and owners' equity at a specified date. The balance sheet is prepared at the end of an accounting cycle, perhaps each month, quarter, or year, and represents a snapshot of the company's financial position at that point in time.

In the sections that follow, we will refer to the financial statements for People Are Great, Inc., or PAG's, a fictitious retail clothing chain.[13] Note in Figure 19.2 (page 582) that the setup of the balance sheet reflects the three factors of the accounting equation in that assets equal liabilities plus owners' equity.

5. Identify the components of a balance sheet and explain how they relate to one another.

The balance sheet is also known as the statement of financial position.

Assets

Assets are listed on the left side or top of the balance sheet in order of their **liquidity**: the ease of converting an asset into cash. The most liquid assets are listed first; the least liquid are listed last. Thus, **current assets**, cash and any other asset that can be converted into cash within one year, are the first asset category on the balance sheet. Typical current assets include the following:

- *Cash and equivalents* are money, money market funds, marketable securities (stocks and bonds), and bank balances.

- *Accounts receivable* are money owed to the business for goods or services delivered to customers but not yet paid for. Your local Burger King, for instance, buys milk from a local dairy products distributor. The distributor bills Burger King, which then issues a check to the distributor. During the interval between billing and payment, the distributor shows that bill as an account receivable. Accounts receivable are due for payment—that is, converted into cash—within 10 to 90 days in most businesses.

- *Inventory* is the value of a firm's raw materials, supplies used in operations, work in process, and finished goods. Although inventory is necessary for manufacturing and sales, a company does not want to carry more inventory than it needs because excess inventory ties up cash. That's why the just-in-time systems you learned about in Chapters 10 and 16 are so advantageous in production and distribution operations. Service businesses such as real estate agencies and public accounting firms generally have little or no inventory, while a manufacturer or a department store might have a high inventory, especially at the start of a holiday selling season.

- *Prepaid expenses* are supplies and services paid for but not yet used. Examples include prepaid rent, prepaid insurance premiums, and prepaid taxes, all of which will reduce cash outlays over the course of the year.

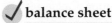

balance sheet

Statement of financial position showing an organization's assets, liabilities, and owners' equity at a specified date.

liquidity

Ease of converting an asset into cash.

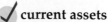

current assets

Cash and any other asset that can be converted into cash within one year.

figure **19.2** **The Balance Sheet**

PAG's, Inc.
BALANCE SHEET
at January 29, 1996

Assets

Current Assets

Cash and Equivalents	$100,000,000	
Accounts Receivable	20,000,000	
Inventory	80,000,000	
Prepaid Expenses	50,000,000	
Total Current Assets		$250,000,000

Fixed Assets

Property and Equipment	$250,000,000	
Less: Depreciation	(50,000,000)	
Net Property and Equipment	$200,000,000	
Intangible and Other Assets	50,000,000	
Total Fixed Assets		$250,000,000

Total Assets	$500,000,000

Liabilities and Owners' Equity

Current Liabilities

Accounts Payable	$ 1,400,000	
Notes Payable	83,000,000	
Accrued Expenses	15,600,000	
Total Current Liabilities		$100,000,000

Long-Term Liabilities

Long-term Debt	$ 23,000,000	
Other Long-term Liabilities	27,000,000	
Total Long-term Liabilities		$ 50,000,000

Total Liabilities	$150,000,000

Owners' Equity

Paid-in Capital	$ 80,000,000	
Retained Earnings	270,000,000	
Total Owners' Equity		$350,000,000

Total Liabilities and Owners' Equity	$500,000,000

The balance sheet provides a summary of company accounts at a particular date and is a snapshot of the firm's financial position. Note that Total Assets equal Total Liabilities plus Owners' Equity. Parentheses around a number indicate losses.

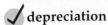

fixed assets

Capital goods with a useful life of more than one year.

depreciation

Allocating the cost of an asset over its expected useful life.

The next category in the assets portion of the balance sheet is **fixed assets**, which are capital goods with a useful life of more than one year. Fixed assets include tangible property such as a store or manufacturing plant, machinery and equipment, furniture and fixtures, leasehold improvements, and land. Fixed assets are not consumed or converted into cash in the ordinary course of business. However, fixed assets do wear out over time and lose some of their productive value. Firms account for this loss of value through **depreciation**, allocating the cost of an asset over its expected useful life.

Depreciation is an accounting concept that matches the cost of the asset to the revenue it produces so that the financial statements accurately reflect the overall financial health of a company. Consider, for example, what happens when paper manufacturer Champion International Corp. builds a new $500 million paper mill. That mill lasts for, say, 40 years. Without depreciation, Champion's balance sheet would show a $500 million asset for 40 years. Then one day, when the mill reaches the end of its useful life, that asset would suddenly disappear. In reality, however, it's been disappearing for 40 years because of wear and tear.

On a balance sheet, depreciation is subtracted from the value of the asset over its useful life. A personal computer might have a useful life of five years, so it's depreciated over that period. Note that land is neither depreciated nor is it an expense, since it is not used up or worn out over time.

The last major category of assets reported on the balance sheet is **intangible assets**, which are nonphysical resources of value such as goodwill, patents, trademarks, copyrights, and intellectual property. While these assets are the least liquid of all, they may represent a valuable resource for the firm. For example, when David Letterman moved his TV show from NBC to CBS, NBC contended that the show's title, "Late Night," as well as many of Letterman's on-air routines, such as the NBC Thrill Cam, and even the name of the show's band were the intellectual property of NBC. So at CBS, "Late Night" became "The Late Show," and Letterman was able to retain only some of his routines, such as his famous Top 10 List.

Trademarks are also intangible assets. Can you imagine that famous soft drink company without the name Coca-Cola? If Coca-Cola ever sold its name, can you even guess what the buyer might pay? That's a major problem with intangible assets: No one knows their worth until they're sold, so it's hard to accurately reflect their value on the balance sheet. Many companies don't even place their intangible assets on the balance sheet for that reason.

Liabilities

Liabilities, the financial obligations of the firm, are listed on the balance sheet in the order that they are due. **Current liabilities** are claims of creditors due to be repaid within one year from the date of the balance sheet. Typical current liability classifications shown in Figure 19.2 include the following:

- *Accounts payable* are amounts owed for goods and services bought by the company. Accounts payable are the other side of the coin of accounts receivable. When the milk distributor bills Burger King, it shows an account receivable, an asset. The Burger King restaurant shows the money it owes the milk distributor as an account payable, a liability. Accounts payable are usually due within 10 to 90 days.

- *Notes payable* are money the company owes to another business, an individual, or a financial institution that are the result of a written promise to pay a specified amount by a specified date. Only that portion of the loan that's due within one year is classified as a note payable.

- *Accrued expenses* are financial obligations incurred by the firm but not yet paid for, including such expenses as taxes due, wages due, utility bills due, and interest due on loans.

Long-term liabilities are claims of creditors payable one year or more from the date of the balance sheet. Typical long-term liabilities include maturing bonds the company has issued, mortgages, and other loans. Large firms such as AT&T Corp. may have several different types of long-term liabilities.

 intangible assets

Nonphysical resources of value such as goodwill, patents, trademarks, copyrights, and intellectual property.

 current liabilities

Claims of creditors due to be repaid within one year from the date of the balance sheet.

 long-term liabilities

Claims of creditors payable one year or more from the date of the balance sheet.

skills
check

Assembling Your Own Balance Sheet

There are more than 9 million private firms nationwide, according to the U.S. Department of Commerce, and each one regularly prepares some form of balance sheet. But businesses aren't the only ones that have assets and liabilities.

You, your classmates, your professor, and the other 260 million people in the United States are all, in their own way, businesses. We own assets—a car, a bike, clothing, perhaps even a computer or a house—and we have liabilities (though hopefully not too many). And since we do, we can all draw up our own balance sheets.

In preparing your personal balance sheet, you'll go through some of the same exercises that a company does. What is the balance in your checking and savings accounts? What is that car really worth? How much money do you owe short term on your credit card, and how much do you owe for student loans that you have to pay off in five or ten years? Finally, after subtracting liabilities from assets, do you have a positive net worth or equity?

As you prepare your balance sheet, keep in mind that you may own some intangible assets, such as the education you're receiving now. It may not seem likely at the moment, but that education will pay off down the road by helping you secure a better paying job. Can you place a value on it? Do you want to? When you're done, you'll see that it's not so easy to figure out what you're really worth. You might even end up with a negative net worth. If you do, remember that you're not really worthless—it's just that your intangible assets can't be valued at this point.

PERSONAL BALANCE SHEET

Assets

Current Assets
    Cash and Checking $ _____
    Savings Account Balance, Money Market Fund   _____
    Stocks, Bonds, Mutual Funds   _____
    Money Owed by Friends (Accounts Receivable)   _____
    Inventory (Personal Belongings)   _____
    Prepaid Expenses (Life Insurance, Pension)   _____
        Total Current Assets $ _____

Fixed Assets
    Property and Equipment (House, Land, etc.) $ _____
    Intangible Assets (Education, Reputation)   _____
        Total Fixed Assets $ _____

        Total Assets $ _____

Liabilities

Current Liabilities
    Accounts Payable (Money Due on Credit Cards, Owed Friends) $ _____
    Notes Payable (Payments Owed on Mortgage or Rent, Car Loan)   _____
    Income Taxes Payable   _____
        Total Current Liabilities $ _____

Long-term Liabilities
    Debt (Student Loan, Mortgage, Car Loan) $ _____
    Other Liabilities   _____
        Total Long-term Liabilities $ _____

        Total Liabilities $ _____

Owners' Equity

    Assets – Liabilities $ _____

        Net Worth $ _____

Owners' Equity

Owners' equity, which is listed following the liabilities on the balance sheet in Figure 19.2, represents the owners' investments in the firm or claims on its assets. It is *always* equal to assets less liabilities. There are two general categories in owners' equity: paid-in capital and retained earnings. Paid-in capital is the direct investment in the firm by its owners. When office supplies distributor Boise Cascade Corp. sold stock to the public in 1995, it counted most of the $233 million paid for the shares as paid-in capital.[14] **Retained earnings** are the portion of owners' equity held for use by the business. They are not paid out to stockholders as dividends.

It's possible to have negative owners' equity, particularly in a situation where a lot of money is borrowed to buy a business or an intangible asset. Many leveraged buyouts initially result in negative owners' equity.

To get a snapshot of your own financial position, see the skills check "Assembling Your Own Balance Sheet" on the facing page.

The Income Statement

The **income statement** is the financial statement summarizing an organization's revenues and expenses during any accounting cycle. Accountants usually prepare the income statement at the end of each quarter for external users and as often as every month or even every week for internal users. If the balance sheet is like a snapshot, then the income statement is like a motion picture, covering all the company's financial moves during that accounting cycle.

You'll note that the income statement in Figure 19.3 (page 586) covers 12 months, but not a calendar year (January 1 through December 31). That's because PAG's operates on a *fiscal year*, an accounting cycle covering any consecutive 12 months. Many companies' fiscal years are calendar years. But businesses like PAG's that are seasonal often choose a different fiscal year. The fiscal year allows these businesses to include their largest selling season in their financial reports and to record inventory at its lowest level.

Revenues

At the top of the income statement, **revenues** represent the sale of goods and services. While most revenue for a company comes from the sale of goods and services during the accounting cycle, a company such as Subway Sandwiches can generate additional revenue through franchise fees, interest received on investments, rents, commissions, and royalties.

Note in Figure 19.3 that PAG's *gross sales* were reduced by $20 million. This figure represents merchandise that customers returned for refund or store credit. The remaining $800 million is PAG's *net sales* for the period.

A company need not actually receive cash to count a sale as revenue. *Accrual basis* accounting allows a company to record a sale once it has established the right to receive revenue. This means that when you charge a $500 Kenmore washing machine on your Sears credit card, Sears records the transaction as revenue as soon as the merchandise is delivered, even though you may not pay off the entire bill for three months. An alternative method, *cash basis* accounting, recognizes transactions only when cash is actually exchanged. The IRS does not allow retail or manufacturing businesses to operate on cash basis accounting. Farmers and some service businesses can use cash basis accounting, however, so that they don't have to pay taxes on revenue that they have not yet received.

retained earnings

Portion of owners' equity held for use by the business.

income statement

Financial statement summarizing an organization's revenues and expenses during any accounting cycle.

revenues

Sale of goods and services, as well as income from franchise fees, interest, commissions, royalties, and rents.

6. Contrast the income statement with the balance sheet and describe how specific expenses relate to revenues.

The income statement is also known as the profit and loss statement, or P&L.

figure 19.3 The Income Statement

PAG's, Inc.
INCOME STATEMENT
For the Period January 30, 1995 to January 29, 1996

Revenues

Gross Sales	$820,000,000	
Less: Returns	20,000,000	
Net Sales		$800,000,000

Cost of Goods Sold

Beginning Inventory		$ 65,840,000	
Purchases	$564,400,000		
Less: Purchase Discounts	30,240,000		
Net Purchases		$534,160,000	
Cost of Goods Available for Sale		$600,000,000	
Less: Ending Inventory		80,000,000	
Cost of Goods Sold			$520,000,000

Gross Profit	$280,000,000

Operating Expenses

Total Selling Expenses	$171,000,000	
Total General Expenses	9,000,000	
Total Operating Expenses		$180,000,000
Operating Income		$100,000,000
Other Income & Expenses		
Interest Expense (Income)	$ 190,000	
Total Other Income & Expenses		190,000
Income Before Taxes		$ 99,810,000
Less: Income Taxes		39,110,000
Net Income		$ 60,700,000
Average Number of Shares		30,000,000
Earnings per Share		$2.02

The income statement provides a summary of the company's income and expenses over the course of an accounting cycle, usually twelve months.

Expenses

Expenses are costs: the resources a company uses to earn revenue. Expenses represent all the costs of doing business. These include costs that result from (1) producing products or purchasing inventory and (2) operating the business. On the income statement:

1. *Cost of goods sold* is the amount paid to suppliers for merchandise, or the cost of buying raw material and producing finished goods sold to customers. The cost of goods sold section on the income statement details the company's inventory activity for the period. For example, electric utility United Illuminating Co. paid nearly $127.5 million in 1994 for coal, oil, and other fuel to generate power, and bought another $44.8 million of electricity from other power companies. So its cost of goods sold in 1994 totaled

expenses

Costs: the resources a company uses to earn revenue.

more than $172 million.[15] In general, cost of goods sold accounts for at least 40 percent of expenses for manufacturers, retailers such as PAG's, and wholesalers. Service organizations, on the other hand, have a relatively low cost of goods sold because they sell brain or brawn, not tangible goods. As you can see in Figure 19.3, net sales revenues minus cost of goods sold equals PAG's *gross profit*.

2. *Operating expenses*, incurred for the purpose of producing revenue, are subdivided as selling expenses and general expenses. Selling expenses include marketing outlays for maintaining a sales staff, advertising and promotion, and distribution. Selling expenses also represent store rent and utilities, depreciation, maintenance, and insurance. General expenses include the administrative costs of running a business, from office supplies to tax consulting. Dividing expenses into functional areas aids financial decision makers in evaluating the efficiency of the company's operating units. A company with high general expenses compared with other firms in its industry might be seen as ripe for layoffs or other cost-cutting measures to bring expenses in line.

Net Income or Loss

In Figure 19.3, gross profit minus operating expenses equals *operating income*. Operating income is a measure used to evaluate the profitability of the firm's business operations. *Other income*, or *nonoperating expenses*, reflects expenses (and revenue) that are not directly related to the firm's primary business activities. Two major nonoperating expenses found in the last section of the income statement are interest and income taxes. Since neither produces revenue, these items are not included as operating expenses. Nonoperating revenue, such as any interest income, is listed here as well.

Subtracting other income and expenses from operating income yields *net income*, as shown in Figure 19.3. Net income is often called the company's *bottom line*. Net income represents the overall profit or loss recorded by the business for the period. Note in Figure 19.3 that PAG's provides a statistic called *earnings per share (EPS)* at the bottom of its income statement. EPS is calculated by dividing net income by the average number of shares of PAG's stock held or traded by investors during the year. Decision makers can compare PAG's EPS this year with that of previous years and with other retailers' EPS to assess the company's relative financial performance for the year. You will learn much more about this sort of financial analysis in the section coming up.

Two factors on the income statement affect the bottom line: revenues and expenses. Because the U.S. economy is growing more slowly in the 1990s than in the 1980s, revenues for most companies are growing more slowly, too. Since they can't necessarily count on increasing revenues to boost their bottom lines in the short term—even with the potential of global markets—many U.S. businesses continue to focus on stabilizing or reducing expenses in order to increase profits.

Many successful firms failed to control their expenses in the 1980s as sales soared, and early in this decade they found themselves struggling when recession caused sales to slow and profits to plummet. One of these was International Business Machines Corp. The recession led to decreased earnings, a sharply lower stock price, and the eventual ouster of company chairman John Akers. IBM brought in a new management team to turn things around, which it did by closing plants, laying off more than 100,000 employees, and reducing other expenses. By 1994, the company was again earning strong profits and even turned in record earnings for the first quarter of 1995. Jerome B. York, IBM's chief financial officer, reported that the company had trimmed $3 billion in costs in order to boost its profits.[16]

Recording Business Expenses

Intuit Software's QuickBooks® program generates business forms such as this purchase order. When a purchase is authorized and the form is processed, QuickBooks® will post the accounting data to the company's accounts payable as a liability and also add the purchase amount into an expense category, either as a cost of goods sold or an operating expense.

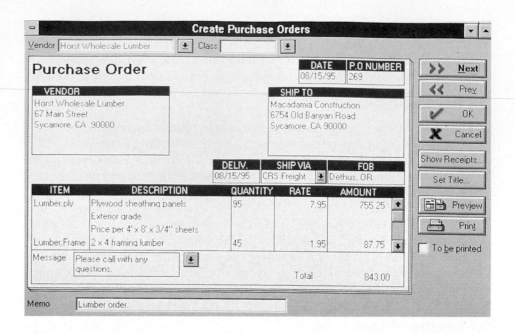

The Statement of Cash Flows

7. Describe the statement of cash flows.

Until 1987, the income statement and balance sheet were the only financial statements that companies were required to issue annually to external users of accounting information. That year, the Securities and Exchange Commission began requiring all companies whose stock is publicly traded to include a third statement. This **statement of cash flows** is a summary of the organization's sources and uses of cash for operations, investments, and financing during an accounting cycle.

- *Operating cash flows* show cash transactions related to running the business—to buying and selling its products.

- *Investing cash flows* measure cash used in or provided by the business's investment activities, such as buying stocks and bonds of other companies.

- *Financing cash flows* include cash raised by issuing new debt or equity capital, as well as expenses for repaying debt or issuing dividends to shareholders.

Recall from Chapter 6 that debt capital is funds raised by borrowing, and equity capital is funds raised by selling shares of ownership in the business.

Many private businesses also issue an annual statement of cash flows. As you will learn in Chapter 20, controlling cash flow is critical to the survival of a business. The statement of cash flows reveals how well a company generates and uses cash, and thus whether it has cash on hand to pay its bills. That may be the most important financial measure of all.

Financial Analysis

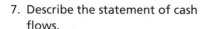

statement of cash flows

Summary of the organization's sources and uses of cash for operations, investments, and financing during an accounting cycle.

To truly comprehend how a business is performing financially, internal and external decision makers, or any other interested party, can compare a company's past and present financial statements to establish trends. Whether it focuses on trends or on a company's current performance compared with other businesses in its industry, financial analysis requires a little basic math, as we'll learn in the sections coming up.

Ratio Analysis

The primary technique used to gauge the financial health of a business is **ratio analysis**, evaluating an organization's current financial condition by calculating the relationship between two components of its financial statements, such as assets and liabilities. The decision maker then compares those ratios with the company's historical ratios and with the ratios of other businesses in the industry or to overall industry ratios. This information is available in publications put out by credit-rating firms; examples include Standard & Poor's Industry Survey Guides, Dun & Bradstreet's Key Business Ratios, and Robert Morris Associates' Statement Studies.

The four categories of financial ratios are liquidity ratios, activity ratios, debt ratios, and profitability ratios. In the following sections, we will use the information from PAG's financial statements in Figures 19.2 and 19.3 to illustrate ratios commonly used in financial analysis.

Liquidity Ratios

Liquidity ratios measure the firm's ability to pay its short-term liabilities as they come due. Liquidity measures, which include the current ratio, quick ratio, and working capital, are of special interest to firms that do business with PAG's.

- The *current ratio* shows the firm's ability to pay its current liabilities from current assets. The current ratio, one of the most commonly used financial ratios, is calculated as follows:

$$\text{Current ratio} = \frac{\text{Current assets}}{\text{Current liabilities}}$$

$$= \frac{\$250 \text{ million}}{\$100 \text{ million}}$$

$$= 2.50$$

This ratio means that PAG's has more than $2 in current assets for each dollar of current liabilities. As a rule of thumb, a current ratio of 2 or higher is considered acceptable. A lower current ratio may indicate that the firm will have trouble paying its regular bills.

- The *quick ratio* excludes inventory from the current ratio so that only the firm's more liquid assets are included in current assets. Inventory is considered the least liquid of current assets; if PAG's had to raise money in an emergency, it would have trouble selling its inventory quickly at or near full price. The quick ratio is calculated as follows:

$$\text{Quick ratio} = \frac{(\text{Current assets} - \text{Inventory})}{\text{Current liabilities}}$$

$$= \frac{(\$250 \text{ million} - \$80 \text{ million})}{\$100 \text{ million}}$$

$$= 1.70$$

Financial analysts consider a quick ratio greater than 1.0 to be a good one: Even if the company can't sell its inventory, it still has enough liquid assets to meet its current liabilities. PAG's, with a quick ratio of 1.70, can pay its bills on time, given timely collection of its accounts receivable.

8. Describe the major ratios for analyzing the financial statements.

 ratio analysis

Evaluating an organization's current financial condition by calculating the relationship between two components of its financial statements.

 liquidity ratios

Ratios measuring a firm's ability to pay its short-term liabilities as they come due.

- *Working capital* is the amount of current assets financed with long-term sources of capital. Although it is not a ratio, working capital is a measure of a firm's overall liquidity. It is calculated as follows:

  Working capital = Current assets – Current liabilities

  = $250 million – $100 million

  = $150 million

You can see right away that PAG's current assets are more than sufficient to pay off its current liabilities. Almost $150 million of its current assets are financed by long-term liabilities or owners' equity. Since working capital is a dollar figure, it can't readily be used to compare the performance of different firms in the industry. However, it is useful for internal control, and a comparison with other figures will indicate the company's financial trends.

Activity Ratios

Activity ratios measure how efficiently a firm is using its resources to generate revenue. Activity ratios such as inventory turnover and average collection period reveal how quickly the company is generating cash.

- *Inventory turnover* shows the activity—and liquidity—of a firm's inventory. The inventory turnover ratio reveals the number of times the firm's inventory was sold and replaced (turned over) during the period of the income statement. This ratio is calculated as follows:

$$\text{Inventory turnover} = \frac{\text{Cost of goods sold}}{(\text{Beginning inventory} + \text{Ending inventory})/2}$$

$$= \frac{\$520 \text{ million}}{(\$65.84 \text{ million} + \$80 \text{ million})/2}$$

$$= \frac{\$520 \text{ million}}{\$72.92 \text{ million}}$$

$$= 7.13$$

PAG's turnover ratio means that its inventory was sold and replaced more than seven times during the year—about every 51 days (365 days divided by 7.13). This ratio, by itself, is not meaningful. Decision makers would compare it with PAG's turnover ratios over time and with averages for the apparel retailers industry. Other industries differ. Supermarket retailers have relatively high turnover ratios; aircraft manufacturers have relatively low turnover ratios.

- *Average collection period* represents the average number of days it takes for a firm to collect cash after it sells a product. Generally, the shorter the time period the better, since it means that the firm is turning accounts receivable into cash quickly. The ratio is calculated as follows:

$$\text{Average collection period} = \frac{\text{Accounts receivable}}{\text{Net sales}/365 \text{ days}}$$

$$= \frac{\$20 \text{ million}}{\$800 \text{ million}/365 \text{ days}}$$

$$= \frac{\$20 \text{ million}}{\$2,191,781/\text{day}}$$

$$= 9.125 \text{ days}$$

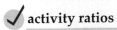 **activity ratios**

Ratios measuring how efficiently a firm is using its resources to generate revenue.

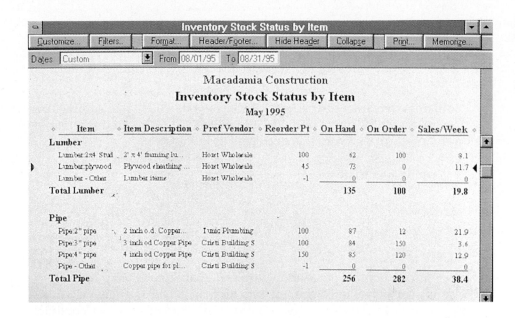

Inventory Stock Status by Item

Customize... | Filters.. | Format... | Header/Footer... | Hide Header | Collapse | Print... | Memorize...

Dates | Custom   From 08/01/95 To 08/31/95

Macadamia Construction
Inventory Stock Status by Item
May 1995

Item	Item Description	Pref Vendor	Reorder Pt	On Hand	On Order	Sales/Week
Lumber						
Lumber:2x4 Stud	2' x 4' framing lu...	Horst Wholesale	100	62	100	8.1
Lumber:plywood	Plywood sheathing...	Horst Wholesale	45	73	0	11.7
Lumber - Other	Lumber items	Horst Wholesale	-1	0	0	0
Total Lumber				135	100	19.8
Pipe						
Pipe:2" pipe	2 inch o.d. Copper...	Innic Plumbing	100	87	12	21.9
Pipe:3" pipe	3 inch od Copper Pipe	Cristi Building S	100	84	150	3.6
Pipe:4" pipe	4 inch od Copper Pipe	Cristi Building S	150	85	120	12.9
Pipe - Other	Copper pipe for pl...	Cristi Building S	-1	0	0	0
Total Pipe				256	282	38.4

Financial Analysis

Business accounting packages, such as QuickBooks® from Intuit Software, enable a business to track both the level of inventory for individual items and the rate of inventory turnover. These features assist accountants and other decision makers as they evaluate the company's liquidity and activity ratios.

Debt Ratios

Debt ratios measure the extent to which the firm uses borrowed funds to finance its operations. In this category are the debt-to-total-assets ratio and the debt-to-equity ratio.

- The *debt-to-total-assets ratio* is a measure of the percentage of assets being financed by the company's creditors. It is calculated as follows:

$$\text{Debt-to-total-assets} = \frac{\text{Long-term liabilities}}{\text{Total assets}}$$

$$= \frac{\$50 \text{ million}}{\$500 \text{ million}}$$

$$= 0.10, \text{ or } 10 \text{ percent}$$

PAG's is financing only 10 percent of its assets with debt. In other words, the company is carrying 10 cents of debt for every dollar of assets. In general, a ratio up to 50 percent of assets is acceptable, depending on the industry, the rate of inflation, and business cycle fluctuations.

- The *debt-to-equity ratio* shows the relationship between debt financing and equity financing, or how much the business relies on debt rather than owners' equity for funding. It is calculated as follows:

$$\text{Debt-to-equity ratio} = \frac{\text{Total liabilities}}{\text{Owners' equity}}$$

$$= \frac{\$150 \text{ million}}{\$350 \text{ million}}$$

$$= 0.428, \text{ or } 42.8 \text{ percent}$$

A debt-to-equity ratio of more than 1 shows that a company is relying more on debt than on equity financing and may therefore face difficulty meeting interest payments and repaying its debts. PAG's has a low debt-to-equity ratio. Debt holders can feel secure that they will receive interest payments, shareholders that they will not lose their investment, and workers that their employer is financially stable. In fact, PAG's may need to review its long-term debt management to see whether raising its debt-to-equity ratio (using more debt) would increase its profitability.

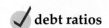 **debt ratios**

Ratios measuring the extent to which a firm uses borrowed funds to finance its operations.

profitability ratios

Ratios measuring the overall financial performance of a firm.

Profitability Ratios

Profitability ratios measure the overall financial performance of the firm. These ratios include earnings per share, return on investment, and return on sales.

- Recall from the earlier discussion of the income statement that earnings per share measures the firm's profit per share of stock. EPS is an important indicator of a firm's success. It is calculated as follows:

$$\text{Earnings per share} = \frac{\text{Net income}}{\text{Average number of shares}}$$

$$= \frac{\$60.7 \text{ million}}{30 \text{ million}}$$

$$= \$2.02$$

Earnings per share are not actually distributed to shareholders. Particularly in young companies or companies with high debt, management usually retains some or all of the earnings to finance future growth or repay creditors. The remainder may be distributed to shareholders as a dividend. Retailers often retain about 80 percent of their earnings, so PAG's might pay a dividend of about 40 cents for each share of stock and retain $1.62.

- *Return on investment* (ROI) is the ratio of income earned per dollar of owner investment. The higher the return the better. It is calculated as follows:

$$\text{Return on investment} = \frac{\text{Net income}}{\text{Owners' equity}}$$

$$= \frac{\$60.7 \text{ million}}{\$350 \text{ million}}$$

$$= 0.173, \text{ or } 17.3 \text{ percent}$$

For every dollar of investor equity, PAG's earned just over 17 cents in income after taxes.

Selling Expenses

Advertising outlays—for this "rolling billboard" developed by Transportation Displays Incorporated, for example—represent a variable cost for the business. While the precise level of revenue produced by advertising may be impossible to measure, such selling expenses may grow or shrink in relation to the firm's revenues and expenses. If you've ever ridden a bus like this one, you know that even though the exterior is completely painted, the material covering the windows allows an unobstructed view from inside the bus.

- *Return on sales* shows the ratio of sales to income before taxes—the percentage of pretax income the company has earned as profit. It is calculated as follows:

$$\text{Return on sales} = \frac{\text{Income before taxes}}{\text{Net sales}}$$

$$= \frac{\$99.81 \text{ million}}{\$800 \text{ million}}$$

$$= 0.125, \text{ or } 12.5 \text{ percent}$$

When compared with prior periods or other firms, PAG's return on sales becomes a useful measure. Return on sales varies widely from industry to industry. Manufacturing firms, for example, average a 5 percent return on sales.

The Need for Comparison

As you can see from the ratios we have calculated, the numbers that ratios represent are not useful by themselves. Is the ratio too high or too low? Is it good or bad? To answer such questions, decision makers need a standard for comparison. As noted at the beginning of this section on financial analysis, ratios are often compared with industry standards published by credit-rating firms as well as by specific industry publications. These sources allow decision makers to compare a firm's performance with the average company in its industry, as well as with the best and the worst.

Ratios can also be compared over time. Comparison of present to past performance allows the decision maker to identify positive or negative trends. Any significant variation from year to year can be investigated. Problems can be corrected and strengths reinforced. Past trends also allow the financial analyst to see whether future projections are reasonable and achievable.[17]

9. Discuss the application of financial ratios by internal and external users and identify confounding factors.

Global GAAP

Comparisons should be undertaken carefully and thoughtfully, especially when international firms are involved. Otherwise, the analyst may be comparing apples and oranges, because accounting rules and regulations vary from country to country. For example, in Switzerland, financial reporting is required only to "the extent necessary to ensure the continued prosperity of the company and to distribute as equal a dividend as possible."[18]

Not only must users of financial statements adjust for differences in accounting practices, but they must also adjust for different currency exchange rates. Whether the U.S. dollar is worth 96 or 101 Japanese yen can make a large difference on the financial statements. As changes occur, the currency exchange rate must be correctly reflected in the figures presented—from sales, cost of goods sold, and other expenses to accounts receivable and assets.

In 1973, the International Accounting Standards Committee was established to provide global consistency in financial reporting practices. With the emergence of global trading blocs represented by the European Union, the North American Free Trade Agreement (NAFTA), and the Asia-Pacific Economic Cooperation Group (APEC), the need for uniformity in international accounting is becoming stronger. As barriers among countries break down, as trade increases, and as communications improve, global trading partners will need to find a basis for uniformity in international accounting standards.

Global trading blocs are discussed in Chapter 3.

Exercising Caution in Interpreting Data

Not only do users of financial statements need to conduct ratio analysis to understand the *content* of the information, but they must also understand the *context* of the data. Because a balance sheet represents only one point in time, the information can be misleading. For example, the purchase of an expensive fixed asset for cash the day before the date on the balance sheet would result in a higher value for fixed assets and a lower value for current assets than if the purchase had been made the day after the date on the balance sheet. This, in turn, affects turnover ratios and liquidity ratios.

It is also important to recognize that the seasonality of a business can affect the financial statements. PAG's, for instance, records high sales in the three months leading into the December holiday season and in April and May when people are buying summer clothing. Its sales plummet in January when most customers are paying off their holiday bills.

General economic conditions can also affect financial analysis. As discussed in Chapter 2, in periods of rapid inflation, sales and other accounts are likely to increase rapidly. Such increases distort financial analysis over time. Inflation also causes firms with older assets to appear more efficient and profitable than firms with newer assets that were purchased at inflated prices. Just as economists adjust for nominal and real GDP, financial analysts adjust for inflation so that comparison over time is valid.

And even though firms use GAAP, they do not have to follow the same accounting treatment for all the items. GAAP allows different methods for measuring items such as depreciation and inventory. For example, the cost of inventory may be the price paid for the first item in the inventory or the last item. Because of business cycles and inflation, the cost of these items may differ, and this will affect the company's profits. The firm's top management, with guidance from its accountants, decides which inventory method is best for the company. That decision then governs the way money flows throughout the entire accounting cycle, from the time a transaction is recorded to the preparation of the financial statements. The use of these different methods can distort financial ratios, especially if the analyst is comparing two or more firms. Using audited financial statements increases the reliability of the information.

Accountants can help drive improvements by finding and applying benchmark data. In fact, they are beginning to help firms benchmark through the Continuous Improvement Center (CIC), which was launched in July 1993 by the Institute of Management Accountants. The CIC maintains a database of operations information, including such items as costs, employees, and transactions, which it then turns into industry standards. Using CIC standards is comparable to using standards in ratio analysis, except that the data are more representative of the industry as a whole and are also more dynamic. However, as you learned in ratio analysis, standards represent averages, and not necessarily good or poor performance.[19]

Careful financial analysis of all aspects of the firm's activities can aid in identifying its strong and weak points, as illustrated by the example described in the doing business box entitled "Forensic Accounting." Accountants can assist managers, creditors, and investors in making more informed and better decisions by providing more relevant, real-time information taken from management, marketing, and finance data. It is in this arena, too, that accountants can participate in the effort to improve business decision making.

Leading Change

Changes will continue in accounting and in information systems. These changes will be directed by a rapidly evolving business environment and fueled by information technology. However, the basis of external accounting re-

doing business

Forensic Accounting

Dick Tracy would be proud of Richard Lilly. Though he's not an accountant, in the summer of 1991, Lilly's sleuthing and careful analysis of the financial statements of Cascade International helped show that this women's apparel chain was a house of cards. By the end of that year, it had gone into bankruptcy and out of business.

Lilly effectively did what the best financial analysts do: He conducted an intensive analysis of Cascade's financial ratios, then attempted to verify all the information in the financial statements. All of Cascade's published data indicated that the company was growing quickly and profitably, adding scores of stores each year. What Lilly found, however, proved that Cascade was knowingly misleading investors.

Working with an analyst from Overpriced Stock Service, an investment firm, Lilly called telephone operators in every area code to verify whether Cascade had stores in that part of the country. Instead of the 181 locations claimed by the company, Lilly found only 81 stores in operation. He rightly concluded that other parts of the financial statements were also false.

Lilly's discoveries led to the eventual indictment of several of Cascade's corporate officers. Cascade shareholders also sued Coopers & Lybrand, alleging that several internal audits conducted by the accounting firm should have raised a red flag that Cascade was hiding the truth. In fact, C&L accountants had examined two money-losing subsidiaries of Cascade but had not raised serious concerns when the company's private accountants pronounced it healthy.

Lilly's findings, as well as those of financial analysts, spurred interest in *forensic accounting*, the systematic evaluation of a company's records to uncover financial misdeeds. Following the collapse of such companies as Cascade International, electronics maker Comptronix Co., and College Bound (a chain of scholastic-test coaching centers), forensic accountants reviewed all the financial records. They then passed their discoveries along to law enforcement authorities, who in some cases obtained convictions of company officials.

Sources: "CPAs, Lawyers for Cascade Defend Actions," *Miami Review*, Feb. 11, 1993, p. 1; "Fired Stock Analyst Was Never One to Compromise," *Miami Review*, Dec. 11, 1992, p. A6; "Company's Profit Data Were False," *New York Times*, Nov. 26, 1992, p. D1; "An Oasis Rich in Shady Operators," *New York Times*, Oct. 4, 1992, section 3, p. 1.

porting will still be the income statement, balance sheet, and statement of cash flows. These provide a framework for much that follows in Part 7.

As the business environment changes and evolves, the accounting information cycle will respond. The process of capturing data will change, and there will be an increasing need for real-time information. Computer systems will be an ally in this, collecting data and processing information as they do at the Big Sky Ski Resort and at Federal Express.

In the financial analysis phase, information from various business processes such as management, marketing, and finance will be integrated. Again, computers will provide information for making better-informed decisions. In the reporting phase, decision makers need to be identified and consulted about their information needs. Managers need immediate access to information when they are making critical decisions about the direction of the business. Their focus will broaden from quality decisions on manufacturing to include quality in information.

This is an exciting time to be involved in the accounting process in an organization. The traditional model of collect, summarize, and report is expanding to include more functions in each of these areas, along with the possibility of actually changing the ways in which we do business. Changing the saying that "you are what you eat" to apply to today's business, we might say that "you are what you measure." The implications are enormous. How businesses measure performance and provide information within their organizations and to decision makers outside can have a direct effect on what the organization becomes. Deciding what to measure is related to how we define the organization. Does the firm want to be driven primarily by the bottom line? Or are there broader concerns, such as customer service, quality, and productivity, by which businesses want to motivate their future success?

Reviewing *Accounting and Financial Controls*

The Role of Accounting

1. **Discuss the role of accounting in business and describe the accounting cycle.** By measuring the financial status of a company and forecasting its financial future, accounting enables owners and managers to make better decisions. This accounting information is obtained through the processes of the accounting cycle: All transactions are recorded in a journal, then classified by account and transferred to a ledger, which is summarized by account at the end of each accounting cycle.

2. **Distinguish between internal and external uses of accounting information and describe how these uses lead to different accounting specialties.** Internally, managers use accounting information—provided by managerial accounting systems—to plan and control operations. Technological advances have made the generation of this information faster and easier, and more readily available to employees at all levels. Accounting information is also useful in benchmarking and in demonstrating the financial impact of decisions on processes, through activity-based costing, for example. Externally, accounting information—provided by financial accounting systems—is used by suppliers, investors, creditors, and government agencies to evaluate a firm's performance. Because external users must be able to compare the status of different firms, financial accounting rules and reports are standardized by generally accepted accounting principles, or GAAP.

3. **Identify and describe the two major categories of accountants.** Public accountants are independent agents who provide consulting and tax advice and assess a company's financial position on the basis of an audit. The most widely known and respected accountants are licensed as CPAs. Private accountants work directly for a business, government agency, or not-for-profit organization. They supervise the preparation of the organization's internal reports, prepare its tax returns, and develop and interpret its financial statements. Depending on their specific role, they may be CPAs, certified management accountants, or certified internal auditors.

The Financial Statements

4. **Explain the relationship between the accounting equation and double-entry bookkeeping.** The accounting equation—assets = liabilities + owners' equity—is the basis of the financial statements. It shows how the assets, the company's resources, are financed, either through liabilities, the claims of creditors, or through owners' equity, the claims of owners. Double-entry bookkeeping is the system by which the accounting equation is balanced.

Every financial transaction has an effect on both sides of the equation.

5. **Identify the components of a balance sheet and explain how they relate to one another.** The balance sheet represents a picture of a company's assets, liabilities, and owners' equity at a particular point in time. Assets, in order of liquidity, include current assets (cash and equivalents, accounts receivable, inventory, and prepaid expenses), fixed assets (property, plant, and equipment, less depreciation), and intangible assets. Liabilities include current liabilities (accounts and notes payable and accrued expenses) and long-term liabilities (bonds, mortgages, and other loans). Owners' equity, which represents owners' claims on a company's assets, includes paid-in capital and retained earnings.

6. **Contrast the income statement with the balance sheet and describe how specific expenses relate to revenues.** Whereas the balance sheet shows a company's financial status at a point in time, the income statement is a more fluid statement, covering all the company's financial moves during a particular accounting cycle. Revenues, representing the sale of goods or services, may be recorded as soon as a sale is established (accrual basis accounting) or only when cash is received (cash basis accounting). Expenses, which are deducted from revenues to obtain operating income, include the cost of goods sold (expenses involved in buying raw materials and producing finished goods) and operating expenses (selling and general). Net income is derived from subtracting nonoperating expenses from (or adding nonoperating income to) operating income. Earnings per share identifies a firm's relative financial performance for the year.

7. **Describe the statement of cash flows.** The statement of cash flows summarizes a company's operating, investing, and financing cash flows. With the balance sheet and income statement, it is required by the Securities and Exchange Commission as a source of accounting information for external users. Because the statement of cash flows shows how well a company generates and uses cash, it may be the most important financial measure of all.

Financial Analysis

8. **Describe the major ratios for analyzing the financial statements.** In order to measure a company's financial performance, analysts use a variety of techniques, including liquidity, activity, debt, and profitability ratios. Important liquidity ratios, which measure a firm's ability to pay its short-term liabilities, are the current and quick ratios, as well as working capital. Activity ratios, which

measure how efficiently a firm is using its resources to generate revenue, include inventory turnover and average collection period. Debt ratios, which measure the extent to which a firm is using borrowed funds to finance its operations, include the debt-to-total-assets ratio and the debt-to-equity ratio. Profitability ratios, which measure the firm's overall financial performance, include earnings per share, return on investment (ROI), and return on sales.

9. **Discuss the application of financial ratios by internal and external users and identify confounding factors.** Ratios by

themselves are not very useful. Internal and external decision makers must be able to compare a firm's performance with industry standards, with other firms in the industry, and with earlier periods. These comparisons must be made and interpreted carefully for several reasons. For example, analysts must adjust for different accounting practices—both within the United States and throughout the world—and for different exchange rates, as well as for the context of the data, the seasonality of the business, and general economic conditions.

 ## Key Terms

accounting **573**	certified public accountant (CPA) **579**	double-entry bookkeeping **580**	income statement **585**
cost of quality **577**	private accountants **580**	balance sheet **581**	revenues **585**
activity-based costing (ABC) **577**	certified management accountant (CMA) **580**	liquidity **581**	expenses **586**
managerial accounting **578**	certified internal auditor (CIA) **580**	current assets **581**	statement of cash flows **588**
financial accounting **578**	accounting equation **580**	fixed assets **582**	ratio analysis **589**
generally accepted accounting principles (GAAP) **578**	assets **580**	depreciation **582**	liquidity ratios **589**
public accountants **579**	liabilities **580**	intangible assets **583**	activity ratios **590**
audit **579**	owners' equity **580**	current liabilities **583**	debt ratios **591**
		long-term liabilities **583**	profitability ratios **592**
		retained earnings **585**	

● Review Questions

1. You own a small stationery store. At the end of a day's business, you have $350 in the cash drawer from sales and you have issued a check to Hallmark to pay for $100 in greeting cards. Briefly, how do these transactions move through the accounting cycle?

2. Who are the internal and external users of accounting information? How are their information needs different?

3. How do public and private accountants differ?

4. One of the partners in a firm contributes $10,000; $5,000 is used to purchase inventory on credit. How does each of these two separate transactions affect the accounting equation?

5. What items are considered current assets on the balance sheet? Why?

6. How do the assets listed on a balance sheet relate to the firm's liabilities and owners' equity?

7. Rayon Manufacturing Co. buys raw materials for $20,000; writes checks for $10,000 and $5,000 for selling and general expenses, respectively; and sells $55,000 of its product, some of it on credit. How do these transactions affect the income statement?

8. How might you measure a firm's ability to pay its short-term liabilities?

9. What are three measures of profitability?

10. Given the various measures of performance that can be calculated, how would a potential investor in a firm use the ratios? What factors should be taken into account?

• Critical Thinking Questions

1. Recall from Chapter 2 that oligopoly is an industry condition in which a few firms, each large enough to influence pricing, sell similar or differentiated products. Does the public accounting industry qualify as an oligopoly?

2. In the current liabilities section of the balance sheet, notes payable include portions of long-term loans that are due within one year. How is this like the depreciation of fixed assets?

3. Retailers often use a fiscal year that differs from the calendar year in order to include revenue from their biggest selling seasons on their financial statements and to record inventory at its lowest point. Why is this good for the company's financial position?

4. Activity ratios analyze how effectively a business is using its resources to generate revenue. Consider the inventory turnover ratios of different industries. Grocery chains may have ratios over 25; aircraft manufacturers less than 4. Why is there such a difference between these industries? Within this range, where would the inventory turnover ratio of a Geo car dealership likely fall? A Hallmark card shop? A Radio Shack electronics retailer?

REVIEW CASE   *Financial Analysis of PAG's, Inc.*[20]

PAG's 1995 annual report presents information for the fiscal year ending January 29, 1996. The report follows GAAP for the financial statements and, in addition, top management relates the following information:

- PAG's, Inc., is a speciality retailer whose stores sell casual apparel for men, women, and children under three brand names: PAG, its original line; PAGpups, for children; and Il Pagliacci, fancy clothing.

- PAG stores in the United States are located in 25 states and in Puerto Rico. PAG's opened stores in Mexico and Canada in 1995.

- The success experienced this year was directly related to disappointing results last year. Clothing fashions were changing, and PAG's styles were being copied widely by the competition.

- In 1995, management aggressively addressed its problems by focusing on merchandise creativity, trying new product lines, and improving inventory control.

Using PAG's financial statements (Figures 19.2 and 19.3) and the ratio analysis presented in the chapter, answer the following questions.

1. How could PAG's use its accounting system to help in developing new product lines?

2. Would you suggest to management any changes in PAG's total liabilities?

3. What percentage of PAG's expenses is its cost of goods sold? How does this compare with the retailing industry in general?

4. How could PAG's improve its inventory turnover ratio?

5. What is PAG's return on investment after taxes?

6. What challenges and opportunities might PAG's face in conducting business in Canada and Mexico? In Europe? In Asia?

CRITICAL THINKING CASE   *Madison Square Garden*[21]

Right after it bought the group of four businesses known as Madison Square Garden as part of its $9.7 billion acquisition of Paramount Communications in 1994, Viacom, Inc., put the complex up for sale. The property consists of the world-famous Madison Square Garden arena in New York City, cable sports network MSG, the New York Knickerbockers basketball team, and the New York Rangers, the 1994 Stanley Cup–winning hockey team.

In 1993, these businesses pulled in revenues of $329 million but earned almost no profit, posting an adjusted operating cash flow of just $22.1 million. Still, that was a big improvement over 1990, when their operating cash flow was a mere $5.8 million. Even before the Viacom takeover, Paramount had expressed concerns about Madison Square Garden's operations, targeting the arena's high operating expenses and MSG Network's $486 million contract, dating from 1988, to televise New York Yankee baseball games through the year 2000. The Knicks and Rangers teams were bright spots, with the Knicks expected to boost profits from about 14 percent of revenues in 1993 to close to 17 percent in 1994. After losing $3.7 million in 1993, the Rangers's first-place showing in 1994 had helped put the team in the black.

In March 1995, a partnership of ITT Corp. and Cablevision Systems Corp., which owns Sportschannel, paid almost $1.1 billion for the Garden. Even though ITT/Cablevision's main interest was the MSG Network, which fits Cablevision's core business perfectly and has greater growth potential than the arena or the teams, ITT/Cablevision decided to retain all four businesses, at least for the time being.

1. Why is operating cash flow a better measure than profit of Madison Square Garden's financial performance?

2. For the rights to televise Knicks and Rangers games, MSG pays each team less than $4 million a year. Industry experts claim that both teams could charge the network much more if they were independent businesses. Considering that these experts also estimate that ITT/Cablevision could sell each team for $150 million, what would you advise the corporation to do—keep the sports teams or sell them? (*Hint*: Before you decide, figure out how much MSG pays each year to televise New York Yankee baseball.)

3. Operating costs at Madison Square Garden arena are high, even for a business operating in pricey midtown Manhattan. What other factors might play into the Garden's high operating expenses? What measures could managers take to lower these expenses?

Critical Thinking with the ONE MINUTE MANAGER

"What happened to Schwartz Bookshops?" asked Joanna, clearly curious.

"The company learned a lot about accounting and financial management," replied the One Minute Manager. "After the meeting with their banker, Schwartz and Domnitz called their key employees together and announced that for the first time they would impose formal financial controls."

"How many employees did they let go?" Carlos asked.

"None," said the One Minute Manager, smiling. "But both owners took 10 percent pay cuts, decreed that all employees would have to pay half of their health insurance premiums, and decided not to replace employees who resigned. They raised capital by bringing in a silent partner in 1987, and the next year they sold 25 percent of the company to an independent investor so they could pay back their creditors. You see, Schwartz was operating on virtually no working capital and had no line of credit. All its cash was tied up in its inventory of books. Because the owners were putting off their accounts payable until the last possible moment, the publishers they ordered from were refusing to fill new orders. If any extraordinary expense had popped up, the company would have been out of business."

"Did the financial controls and extra capital help? What else did they have to do?" asked Joanna.

"For one thing," said the One Minute Manager, "they gave their store managers access to the accounting records, which the group reviewed regularly, line-by-line, and they installed a computerized inventory system that improved their cash flow by limiting reorders. Before, Schwartz and Domnitz had ordered books according to which ones they had a hunch would sell and how many they thought they would need."

"And the bottom line?" asked Carlos, who wanted to know whether all these changes had worked.

The One Minute Manager smiled again. "Inventory turnover rose from less than twice yearly, which was way below the industry average, to close to four times yearly by 1989. Sales topped $5 million for the first time in 1990, and the bank took Schwartz Bookshops off its worry list. Today the company is thriving, even with a new Barnes & Noble superstore just a half mile from one of its branches."

"Good for them!" The students cheered in unison. "Now let's shop."

1. How did requiring all employees to pay for 50 percent of their health insurance help Schwartz Bookshops's cash flow?

2. Book buyers today are used to hefty discounts—up to 40 percent off the retail price for best-sellers. Schwartz Bookshops had to become experts at competitive pricing. The discount pricing strategy they created cost them 2.6 percent in gross profit in 1992, but increased their sales revenues by 35 percent. Is discounting a successful strategy for Schwartz? Why or why not?

3. Beginning in 1990, Schwartz Bookshops launched an advertising campaign with the slogan, "Milwaukee's Independent Bookseller Since 1927." The company runs promotions with the Milwaukee County Zoo and with local libraries. By 1995, their mailing list topped 27,000 customers, who receive a yearly catalog, a semiannual children's newsletter, and announcements of scheduled readings by visiting authors in the company's Writers to Readers series. How does Schwartz Bookshops account for these expenses on its income statement?

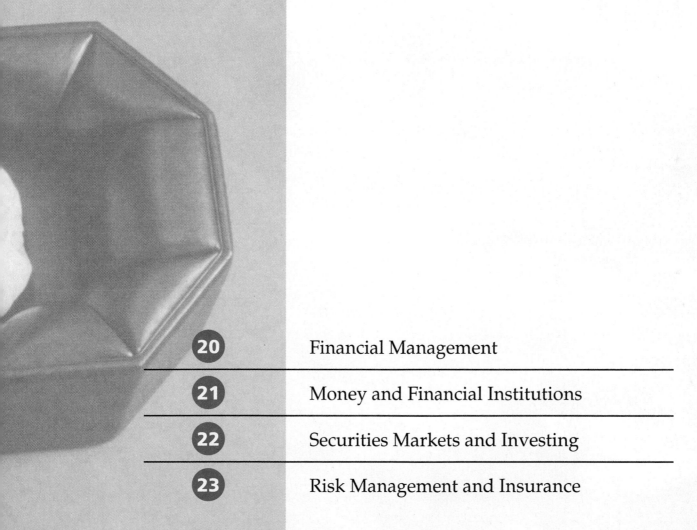

PART

7

Financing the Business

20

Financial Management

financial management

The business function of obtaining funds, managing the day-to-day flow of funds, and committing funds for long-term expenditures.

You're aware that businesses do not always generate all the cash they need from sales revenues. When necessary, they raise money either by borrowing it or by attracting new owners who buy a share of the business. This money is then used to invest in new equipment, hire more employees, or obtain other resources needed to maintain and grow the business. Of course, the money businesses earn and raise must be managed day to day as well. This chapter explains **financial management,** the business function of obtaining funds, managing the day-to-day flow of funds, and committing funds for long-term expenditures. Without sound financial management, the business will fail. After reading this chapter, you will be able to reach the learning goals below.

Learning Goals

1. Discuss the role of financial management in the business process, and identify three common reasons for business failure.
2. Discuss the influences of external factors on financial decision making.
3. Describe how forecasting is used in establishing budgets.
4. Contrast the uses of the three major types of budgets.
5. Explain the importance of risk-return analysis in capital budgeting.
6. Discuss the use of financial control in bringing actual results in line with budgets.
7. Identify and describe short-term uses of funds.
8. Explain why decisions regarding long-term investments significantly affect business profitability.
9. Identify and describe short-term sources of funds.
10. Identify and describe long-term sources of funds and note the advantages and disadvantages of each.

Bottom-Up Budgeting

Carlos and Joanna arrived at the One Minute Manager's office, only to discover that she was meeting with a group of employees in the purchasing department. As they sat down to wait, Carlos asked Joanna, "How did dinner go with your parents last night?"

"It was tense at first," Joanna confided. "They were glad that I let them know about my financial situation, but not too pleased with how I've managed my money. I guess I don't know as much about making ends meet as I thought."

Carlos could identify. "Will they help you out?"

Before Joanna could reply, in walked the One Minute Manager. "I can't wait to tell you about the financial wizards in purchasing," she beamed.

"That's funny," Joanna said, "We were just talking about budgeting and my lack of financial finesse. Maybe I should spend some time in the purchasing department."

"Good idea, Joanna. I'm sure they could tell you all about budgeting. When we began our bottom-up budgeting program, their first reaction was, 'We're clueless about budgets!' Now they provide an endless stream of ideas, which does wonders for expense control around here."

"What exactly is a bottom-up budget?" Carlos interjected.

"It's part of our open-book program," the One Minute Manager explained. "Our company's managerial accounting reports and financial statements are available to all employees so that they can construct their own budgets and make their own financial decisions for their departments."

"Isn't that rough on your financial managers—keeping track of all that information?" asked Joanna.

"Not at all. In fact, it was the finance department that suggested we adopt open-book management," said the One Minute Manager. "Since the early 1990s, more and more companies are using bottom-up budgeting. I know one company that credits the process with saving their business."

"The more we learn about financial management, the better," Carlos observed. "Please continue."

"Mid-States Technical Staffing Services is an engineering service based in Davenport, Iowa," the One Minute Manager began. "Its CEO, Steve Wilson, turned to open-book management in 1991 as a way to empower his employees to make their own operating decisions. It kept them focused on the fast-growing firm's finances rather than on the power struggles that were flaring up over sales commissions, contracts, even which projects to pursue.

"At first Wilson's plan seemed doomed. Mid-States's staff needed plenty of training seminars and workshops. Many employees were skeptical or afraid, but enough welcomed the idea to keep the plan alive. After six months of coaching and several budgeting rounds, Mid-States's employees were sold on bottom-up budgeting. By early 1995, expenses were 15 percent below 1991 figures, profits were up, and Mid-States's employees were considering the financial impact of every decision they made."[1]

"Sign me up!" cried Joanna. "Maybe I can make sense of my finances, too."

Financial Management and the Firm

The constantly changing and increasingly competitive business environment points up the importance of understanding and managing the company's funds, not only by top management but also by employees at every level. Steve Wilson, president of Mid-States Technical Staffing Services, learned that **open-book management**—a strategy that empowers employees to help control the company's finances—significantly enhances financial performance. You learned in Chapter 8 that open-book management facilitates the control function of management by training employees to understand their contribution to the company's financial status. In this chapter, we explore the role of financial management in the firm's financial planning process, the preparation of budgets, and the financial controls that ensure the firm's continued operation.

Finance managers use accounting information to evaluate the firm's past financial performance and to analyze and project the firm's current and future financial needs over the short term (one year or less) and the long term (more than a year). Finance is an oversight function that ensures that the company is effectively using revenue—from sales and investments, for example—to meet immediate obligations, such as paying bills from suppliers, salaries to workers, rent for office space, and other current liabilities. Finance managers also evaluate the company's plans for long-term activities, such as expanding operations or building new factories, and the sources of funding to achieve these plans. When necessary, finance managers obtain additional funding from sources outside the business.

1. Discuss the role of financial management in the business process, and identify three common reasons for business failure.

Recall from Chapter 19 that accounting *is the process of collecting, summarizing, and reporting information relevant to business decisions.*

The Responsibilities of the Finance Manager

In medium-size and large companies, a manager with the title chief financial officer (CFO), vice president of finance, or controller oversees financial management. In smaller companies, such as the local stationery store, the owner *is* the finance manager.

Inside the firm, the finance manager works closely with managers from different departments—marketing, production, and distribution, for example—to forecast revenues and expenses for future periods and to prepare budgets. For current activities, the various departments provide information about operating costs. For example, to estimate cash needs for a long-term project, such as the development and sale of a new product, marketing contributes an estimate of anticipated sales, production projects the cost of manufacturing the product, and distribution forecasts the cost of getting the product to consumers.

Ford Motor Co. is now redesigning its finance operations as part of its Ford 2000 restructuring plan. The plan switches finance from a centralized function to a decentralized system in which finance managers actually join product development teams, or "platforms," working with managers in design, engineering, manufacturing, and marketing. The goal is to shift finance at Ford from an after-the-fact accounting perspective to the front lines of product development. It permits earlier financial analysis and actually may boost Ford's profitability by increasing the involvement of finance in product development and production.[2] To learn more about Ford's approach to finances, see the doing business box entitled "Ford Takes Finance out of the Driver's Seat" on the next page.

Cash Flow Is Critical

The finance manager analyzes the company's **cash flows**, the pattern of actual revenues and expenditures flowing into and out of the business. A healthy cash flow enables the company to pay its bills and fund long-term projects, but idle cash is not productive. Generally, finance managers attempt to limit the

 open-book management

A strategy that empowers employees to help control the company's finances.

 cash flows

The pattern of actual revenues and expenditures flowing into or out of the business.

doing business

Ford Takes Finance out of the Driver's Seat

Henry Ford invented the assembly line and mass production. Some say that son Henry Ford II then invented centralized financial control. Finance executives call the shots at Ford Motor Co., and that has always included a centralized corporate hierarchy and tight budget controls.

Ford is also a top financial training organization. New finance managers are cross-trained intensively, spending years in manufacturing, product development, marketing, and sales, as well as in finance processes. Some remain in Ford's North American operation; more travel to the company's European, Latin American, or Asian operations for years of international experience.

For all its finance savvy, Ford trails Chrysler Corp., the number three U.S. automaker, in its profit per vehicle produced. Profit per vehicle is the auto industry's benchmark for profitability. In 1993, for example, Ford earned $323 per vehicle. Chrysler earned $828. (General Motors Corp. lost $189 per vehicle that year.) The differences are attributable in part to Chrysler's smaller size—it's half as big as Ford and nearly all its sales are in North America—and to its simpler organizational design. Yet with all its size and complexity, Ford North America still spends $200 *less* per vehicle in labor costs than Chrysler.

The Ford 2000 restructuring plan exists partly to improve profitability and other financial measures, and partly to speed up and customize product development—running "our busi-

ness the way the market looks at it," according to Murray Reichenstein, controller for Ford's worldwide automotive operations. Ford 2000 erases geographic divisions within the company by consolidating Ford's four global operations into a single unit. In financial terms, by the time its 1999 models reach dealers around the world, Ford 2000 aims to eliminate $2 billion to $3 billion in overhead yearly and to smooth out its fluctuating cash flow as avenues to increased profitability. The plan for Ford 2000 was developed by top finance executives. While some observers inside and outside the company maintain that Ford 2000 makes finance less powerful, Ford 2000 backers maintain that finance at Ford will not yield its influence and authority but rather will increase them through earlier involvement in product development and production.

Finance managers gain enormous credibility by becoming members of operating teams, according to Reichenstein. Ford 2000 promotes maximum influence from financial analysis. That translates into maximum profit. "You have all ranges of choice in the beginning," Reichenstein says, referring to basic choices about design, engineering, marketing, and cost. A year or two later, when a lot of decisions have been made, financial analysis has much less influence.

Source: Based on S. L. Mintz, "Redesigning Finance at Ford," *CFO*, March 1995, pp. 26-34.

---

amount of idle cash available, because cash in the checkbook does not earn income for the business.

Although all firms, even large, well-established businesses, may face financial problems at any time, poor financial management is a particular concern of new or small companies. When we discussed financing business start-ups in Chapter 6, we stressed the importance of securing sufficient capital to see the new business through its first critical years. In fact, failures often result for three reasons directly related to financial management: **undercapitalization**, lack of sufficient funds to meet the day-to-day expenses of a business; poor cash flow; and inadequate expense control. For example, the owner of a small wood products firm saw his company's sales double in a year and so expanded production to take advantage of a market opportunity. Unfortunately, because the owner failed to adequately forecast the amount of cash he needed to expand, he did not borrow any money to fund the expansion. Though the extra capacity helped increase sales revenue, it also drove up production and marketing expenses. The increased revenue did not cover the expansion expenses incurred months earlier. The owner realized his mistake in time and obtained a loan from his local bank that kept the company afloat.

Adequate cash flow is particularly important for seasonal businesses in which cash must be paid for inventory and supplies well before cash is received for sales. For example, a garden center in the Northeast spends the winter gearing up for the spring selling season. The owner knows that she must pay for soil, fertilizer, seeds, bulbs, and the overhead of maintaining a hothouse

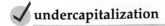

undercapitalization

Lack of sufficient funds to meet the day-to-day expenses of a business.

months before the first plants are sold. A good finance manager will plan for this variation in cash flow by obtaining a loan to see the business through the slow winter season and to be repaid during the selling season. A garden center in the Southeast, however, does not have such dramatic variations in climate or in cash flow, so its finance manager plans for a more even cash flow through the year.

If a company is to prosper, it must change as internal and external factors change. In some cases, a company will expand its operations in order to take advantage of new markets. For example, *Business Week* reports that revenues in the express shipping business topped $18 billion in 1994. Federal Express is the industry leader, with a 45 percent market share, and United Parcel Service is second, with 25 percent of the market. Both companies are expanding their operations as they compete in the overnight delivery business. To expand distribution, UPS invested $120 million in new sorting centers in Texas, Illinois, and South Carolina. And FedEx will invest $1.8 billion over five years to streamline its air fleet. To take advantage of the federal government's move to deregulate interstate trucking, both companies are expanding their truck fleets.

These expansions require long-term investment, and it is the finance manager's job to pull together all the relevant information to enable management to make appropriate and financially viable decisions. The process of weighing the costs and benefits of a new product, project, or other investment is known as **risk-return analysis**. Before IBM could decide to manufacture computer monitors in Mexico or Sears could decide to shelve its famous Big Book catalog in favor of licensing the use of its name to other catalog companies, company finance managers had to balance the cost of each decision against its estimated effect on cash inflows. Although finance managers apply basic risk-return analysis to most financial decisions, it is more formally prepared and is most significant for major long-term investments.

The Environment for Financial Decisions

Finance managers have a broad range of responsibilities that require familiarity with events outside the business, as well as with the internal operations of the business. A decision to invest excess cash in a new product may be disastrous if it is made without regard for general economic conditions, government regulations and tax policies, and global competition.

Economic Conditions

As the economic environment changes, business faces both opportunities and threats. During the late 1970s and early 1980s, inflation rates were high and the economy was headed toward recession. As a result of these financial conditions, the period beginning in the mid-1980s was characterized by the deregulation of certain industries, such as the airlines; by the assumption of high debt levels on the part of many firms; and by a wave of mergers and acquisitions. Many finance managers were able to forecast these changes and recommend strategies that would help their firms keep pace with the economy.

For example, by 1990, Sears, Roebuck and Co. was offering customers everything from socks to stocks. Through mergers and acquisitions in the 1980s, Sears had acquired the stock brokerage firm Dean Witter Reynolds, the Allstate Corp. insurance company, and the real estate brokerage firm Coldwell Banker. Sears also greatly expanded the activities of its Homart mall development unit and launched the Discover credit card. However, in the early 1990s, the company realized that it needed to refocus on its core mission of operating department stores. Beginning in 1993, Sears began selling unrelated businesses such as Dean Witter, Discover Co., and Allstate, and it even eliminated its catalog sales as part of the restructuring of its organization.

✔ **risk-return analysis**

The process of weighing the costs and benefits of a new product, project, or other investment.

---

2. Discuss the influences of external factors on financial decision making.

Government Regulations and Tax Policies

When the government enacts laws to promote the social welfare of individuals, the result is often increased business costs. Examples include laws that mandate increases in the minimum wage, family leave to workers, and restrictions on solo commuting. In analyzing operations and future projects, the finance manager must include the cost of such laws in the predicted cash flows.

For example, in Chapter 12 you learned about the Family and Medical Leave Act of 1993. This law can have an effect on the cash flow of a business, especially a small or medium-size one, because the firm must continue to provide health benefits to the employee on leave. According to the National Federation of Independent Businesses (NFIB), the cost to a firm in health insurance for a 12-week leave in 1993 was $729.[3] In addition, the company incurs the expense of training temporary personnel to replace the employee on leave or of paying overtime to other workers to carry his or her workload.

To maintain profitability the company must cut costs, increase revenues, or devise a combination of cost cuts and increased revenue to absorb the expense of the leave. The firm could offer fewer benefits or lower employees' wages or increase the prices of its products or services. All these decisions must be weighed in the context of the overall financial plan so that the company maximizes its return and minimizes the risk of a disruption in operations.

Finance managers must also stay current with the tax policies of federal, state, and local governments in order to minimize the impact of taxes on operations and eventually on profits. For example, you learned in Chapter 7 that a firm may be able to reduce expenses by locating in an *enterprise zone*, where property taxes are relatively low and companies receive abatements on income taxes as well. Enterprise zones have been established in poor, urban neighborhoods to encourage the growth of business in those areas.

Consumers also benefit from enterprise zones because state sales taxes on goods and services are generally cut in half.

Overall, however, taxes increase the cost of doing business. Companies respond to increased taxes as they do to government regulations—by cutting other costs and trying to increase revenues, often by increasing prices. One consequence of higher prices is that consumers, if they have a choice, will reduce their consumption. As a result, the number of units sold decreases, along with the profitability of the firm and the amount of taxes the government collects.

Global Competition

U.S. businesses participate increasingly in a global economy. The trend toward lower barriers to trade worldwide and the emergence of global trading blocs

Risk-Return Analysis

The decision to expand business operations into foreign markets requires detailed information about the target country's economic environment, government regulations and policies, and local competition. Before Wal-Mart and McDonald's decided to open for business in Mexico, their finance managers performed detailed risk-return analyses on the possible long-term effects of these and other factors on each company's financial performance.

such as the North American Free Trade Agreement (NAFTA) and the European Union affect not only the prices of goods and services in the United States but also the cost of financing a business. In the 1990s and into the next century, rapidly expanding telecommunications and information technology will allow businesses and individuals to invest in any country or business with relative ease. People will invest where they expect to receive the best return for the risk undertaken, and so companies will have to pay more to attract financing.

Exchange rate fluctuations can also change estimated and actual cash flows. In 1995, the value of the dollar as compared to the German deutsche mark and the Japanese yen fell drastically. This fall in value made U.S. products relatively less expensive than foreign products. As a result, profits for such companies as IBM and Coca-Cola soared. Meanwhile, Japanese automakers Honda Motor Co. and Toyota Motor Corp. suffered huge losses, in part because they had to raise the prices of their cars in the United States to compensate for exchange rate fluctuations. As a result, their sales fell.

 financial plan

The blueprint of the financial needs of a company—identifies the funds needed by the firm, estimates the timing of cash inflows and outflows, recommends investment alternatives and how to fund them, and monitors the financial performance of the company.

 forecast

A prediction of the flow of funds into and out of the business.

Financial Planning

Sound planning is the anchor of every successful business. Planning is vital to all parts of a company—from sales and marketing to production and distribution. The **financial plan** is the blueprint of the financial needs of a company. Financial planning identifies the funds needed by the firm, estimates the timing of cash inflows and outflows, recommends investment alternatives and how to fund them, and monitors the financial performance of the company.

Without finance, there is no production, no marketing, no sales. The financial planning process shown in Figure 20.1 includes preparing forecasts, developing budgets, and establishing financial controls. These activities, which are critical to the firm's profitability, assist the finance manager in accomplishing his or her overall goals for maintaining a financially sound business.

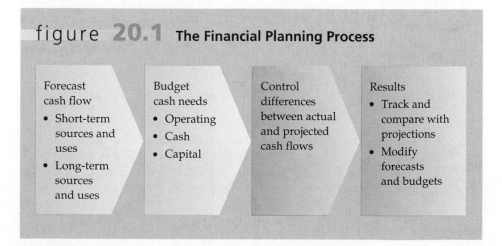

figure **20.1** **The Financial Planning Process**

Forecasting

All financial plans begin with a **forecast**, a prediction of the flow of funds into and out of the business. Using the accounting history, finance managers project revenues and expenses. As the foundation of the firm's financial plan, the forecast provides the basis for short-term and long-term investment decisions. In addition to ensuring that cash inflows are sufficient to cover expenses as they arise, the finance manager estimates the cash needed to pay for long-term expenditures such as investment in new capital goods—equipment and factories, for example.

3. Describe how forecasting is used in establishing budgets.

Short-term Forecasting

A short-term forecast predicts the flow of funds—revenues and expenses—for a period of one year or less, usually in increments of one week or one month. This forecast is particularly important for pointing out the timing of cash inflows and outflows. For example, at Ed Chow's video and computer store in Baltimore, Maryland, inventory is ordered and paid for in September and October, but strong sales tend to fall later, around the December holiday season. As shown in Figure 20.2, then, Chow will have a cash shortage (need) in September and October, and a surplus in November and December. Although by the end of December Chow will have a positive cash flow, the store won't be in business in December unless Chow finds a way to supplement the negative cash flows.[4] The forecast thus tells Chow that he should plan to borrow money to fund the purchase of inventory for sale in November and December.

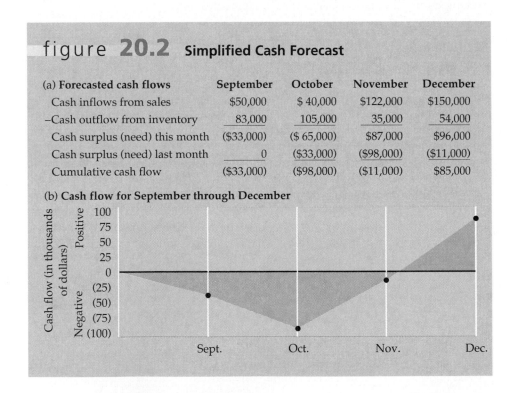

figure **20.2**   **Simplified Cash Forecast**

(a) Forecasted cash flows	September	October	November	December
Cash inflows from sales	$50,000	$ 40,000	$122,000	$150,000
−Cash outflow from inventory	83,000	105,000	35,000	54,000
Cash surplus (need) this month	($33,000)	($ 65,000)	$87,000	$96,000
Cash surplus (need) last month	0	($33,000)	($98,000)	($11,000)
Cumulative cash flow	($33,000)	($98,000)	($11,000)	$85,000

(b) **Cash flow for September through December**

The time frame of a short-term forecast depends on the business or industry. Banks, for instance, may need a weekly forecast with day-by-day cash flows specified. Manufacturing firms, on the other hand, generally prepare yearly forecasts with cash flows identified on a monthly basis.

Long-term Forecasting

Long-term forecasts estimate the flow of funds for periods of more than one year, often for three or five years or more. As you might expect, a long-term forecast is not as detailed or as exact as a short-term forecast. As we look ahead for several years, whether the cash outflow exceeds inflow in August or October is not that important. What counts is the approximate timing of cash received and paid out each year. Long-term forecasts are more difficult to prepare than short-term forecasts because the distant future is more uncertain.

Long-term forecasts must allow not only for the flow of funds from daily operations but also for the firm's long-term goals. Where does the business want to be in five years? Will it remain relatively small, servicing a narrow segment of the market, or will it expand into different markets in several locations throughout the country? Will revenues generate enough excess cash to finance new equipment that the company will need to expand production, or must the company look to outside sources of funds?

Budgeting

Finance managers use forecasts as a basis for formulating their budgets. **Budgets** allocate forecasted revenues (cash inflows) to specific costs and expenses (cash outflows). The difference between forecasts and budgets lies in the amount of detail provided. For example, a forecast may allocate $100,000 for general and administrative expenses. The budget would break this amount down into the cost of stationery, desktop computers, even staples. For example, the budget for Ed Chow's store identifies the specific inventory purchased—video equipment or computers—during each period. Similarly, the administration department's printing budget at Mid-States Technical Staffing includes graph pads, mailing labels, and envelopes.

Like forecasts, budgets allow finance managers to identify the timing of cash inflows and outflows and thus to recognize periods when additional funds may be needed. Budgets also alert the finance manager to the availability of excess funds and to the potential uses for that money. Many firms prepare forecasts and budgets simultaneously.

Because budgets cover all the expenses of a business, all departments contribute, if not a complete budget, at least detailed information about their expenses. For example, production includes the cost of labor, raw materials, work in process, and finished goods inventory during the specified period. Although most firms prepare many detailed budgets, or schedules, we will focus on the three most important—operating, cash, and capital budgets.

Operating Budget

The **operating budget** balances the business's forecasted revenues with their related expenses, generally for a period of one year or less. This master budget is the most detailed and most used budget that a firm prepares. It is made up of many other budgets, including the sales forecast and production, marketing, and administrative budgets. For example, the Mid-States administrative budget becomes what is called a *line item* on the operating budget. The major categories of a master budget form the basis for the company's income statement. The difference is that the budget is more detailed and covers projected figures, whereas the income statement reflects actual results for a period of time in the past.

The sales forecast is the most important item in the operating budget—most costs and expenses are derived from projected sales, although some income may be obtained from investments. In reviewing the operating budget, the finance manager considers many costs and expenses as a percentage of sales—from cost of goods sold to the salaries of salespeople. For example, cost of goods sold may represent 52 percent of sales. Depending on the nature of the business, the finance manager determines whether this amount warrants a review of labor and materials costs with an eye toward downsizing. Other expenses, such as rent, are fixed and are not budgeted as a percentage of sales. The bottom line of the operating budget shows whether a profit is generated—that is, whether revenues are greater than costs and expenses.

Many families operate on a budget. The family budget reflects income and the cost of running a household, from food and clothes to rent and utilities.

 budgets

Allocations of forecasted revenues (cash inflows) to specific costs and expenses (cash outflows).

 operating budget

Master budget that balances the business's forecasted revenues with their related expenses, generally for a period of one year or less.

4. Contrast the uses of the three major types of budgets.

cash budget

An estimate of anticipated cash receipts and payments (disbursements) for a period of time—usually a week, a month, or a quarter.

capital budget

Financial plan for major investments that span a period of more than one year.

Financial Planning

Computer software packages such as QuickBooks® from Intuit® feature financial planning tools that the business can use to project short- or long-term revenues and expenses. The software streamlines the financial planning process by making it easier to prepare forecasts, develop budgets, and establish financial controls.

Recall that in business, capital is defined as any form of wealth used to produce more wealth.

5. Explain the importance of risk-return analysis in capital budgeting.

Money not spent on current expenses can be considered profit and saved for use at a later time. Savings, in turn, can help finance the purchase of a new car, retirement, family vacations, or a college education.

Cash Budget

The **cash budget** is an estimate of anticipated cash receipts and payments (disbursements) for a period of time—usually a week, a month, or a quarter. Cash budgets project expected cash receipts from sales and collection of accounts receivable along with expected disbursements for materials, labor, overhead, dividends, and other normal expenses. Total disbursements plus cash to cover unexpected expenses is the amount of cash needed for the period. Subtracting this amount from the amount of cash available tells the finance manager whether excess cash is available for investment or a cash deficiency requires outside financing, perhaps through a loan.

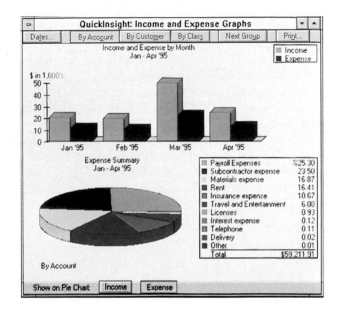

Capital Budget

When you plan a major purchase such as an automobile or a home, you must budget for the long term—a matter of years. In business, the financial plan for major investments that span a period of more than one year is called a **capital budget**. Businesses use capital budgets to plan long-term outlays for capital goods such as real estate, plant, and equipment. When a company decides to increase inventory, the decision can be reversed fairly quickly if sales do not justify the increase. But a decision to purchase a new factory cannot easily be undone: The company must live with the financial burden for years to come.

Risk-Return Analysis and the Cost of Capital In capital budgeting, managers may evaluate several long-term investments to determine which are most profitable, that is, which produce the greatest return with the least risk. For example, Ed Chow may be thinking of opening a new store in two years. To make a financially sound decision, he must balance the costs—renting the property, outfitting it with display racks and office furniture, and purchasing inventory—against expected sales revenue from the second store. If projected revenues are greater than costs, then the project is worth considering and should be part of Chow's capital budget.

How do financial managers measure *risk*, the chance of loss? A common method involves calculating the **cost of capital**, the rate of return a company must earn in order to satisfy the demands of its debt holders (those from whom the company has borrowed) and equity holders (the owners of the company). If the cost of capital is less than the projected rate of return from the investment, the project may be considered worthwhile, assuming that other factors meet company criteria.

Clearly, a well thought out risk-return analysis is vital to the financial success of a company. The risk—the cost of capital—must be less than a project can return. The cost of **debt capital**, funds raised by borrowing, depends on the nature of the business and on general economic conditions. Riskier businesses—oil well developers, for example—pay more to borrow money than more stable businesses such as utility companies. Inflation also raises the **interest rate**, the cost of borrowing money.

The interest rate a company pays is based on the **prime rate,** the interest rate charged by banks to their most creditworthy customers. Large, well-established firms with good bank relations generally pay "prime," while individuals and risky or smaller businesses pay prime plus a premium of several percentage points. In January 1981, as inflation soared and banks and the U.S. government tried to control economic growth, the prime interest rate reached 21 percent. In January 1994, by contrast, the economy was growing far more slowly and the prime rate stood at 6 percent. By mid-1995, the prime rate had climbed to a high of 9 percent. However, growth had slowed so much that the Federal Reserve then lowered interest rates in an effort to energize the economy. The variability of the prime rate clearly illustrates the difficulty of long-term financial planning.

Like debt, the cost of **equity capital**, funds raised by selling shares of ownership in a business, varies according to the risk profile of the business and according to economic conditions. A company involved in a risky venture can't sell stock for as much as a company in a safe, established business. Hence, to raise the same funding, the owners of the risk-taking company must sell a greater percentage of the company's stock to the public. What's more, when interest rates are high, the cost of equity capital is also high. A company trying to sell stock (equity) must compete for money with firms looking for loans (debt). Because those debt-seeking firms are paying high interest rates, potential investors will demand a higher return—and thus a greater share of ownership—than when interest rates are low.

Financial Control

A successful financial plan includes feedback about the performance of the company as a whole and of each project, department, and individual employee. Working closely with accounting and management information systems (MIS) managers, finance managers develop control systems that track and monitor all business activities. Then, through the process of **financial control**, they compare actual results with budgets and modify the financial plan accordingly, as shown in Figure 20.1.

As a first step, finance managers attempt to identify the size of any differences between actual and projected revenues and expenses and then to determine why they exist. Were sales forecasts wrong? Were production costs or other expenses more or less than anticipated? Only an evaluation of possible causes will provide an answer. Small differences are generally not a cause for concern, since forecasts and budgets are estimates and have some flexibility built into them. Large differences need to be explained and accounted for by finance, marketing, manufacturing, and other departments, who must then take corrective action—or keep up the good work, if they are keeping costs low.

✓ **cost of capital**

The rate of return a company must earn in order to satisfy the demands of its debt holders and equity holders.

✓ **debt capital**

Funds raised by borrowing.

✓ **interest rate**

The cost of borrowing money.

✓ **prime rate**

The interest rate charged by banks to their most creditworthy customers.

✓ **equity capital**

Funds raised by selling shares of ownership in a business.

✓ **financial control**

The business process of comparing actual results with budgets and modifying the financial plan accordingly.

Recall from Chapter 2 that the Federal Reserve is the nation's central bank. Chapter 21 discusses the Fed in detail.

6. Discuss the use of financial control in bringing actual results in line with budgets.

The Top "Hatchet Man" in America: Hero or Villain?

By his own account, Albert J. Dunlap is responsible for the biggest job cuts in modern American history. In just seven months he fired over 11,000 people, more than a third of the employees at Scott Paper Co., the 115-year-old business he runs that is headquartered in Philadelphia. His reason? To cut costs and make more money for its owners. Dunlap is variously known as "hatchet man," "chain saw," and "Rambo in pinstripes," nicknames he does not appear to mind. He says that the owners of Scott Paper have profited, and that is all that matters to him. Here is his version of the Scott Paper story, starting with his first meeting after being brought on board in late 1993:

> I looked at the . . . plans, then I looked at the managers. I listened to them talk about their priorities, their constituencies. I heard somebody talk about constituencies like the community, like employees . . . Wait a minute, I said. You have only one constituency: the shareholders. They're taking all the risk. I said to myself: This management has to go. I got rid of all of them but two.

> Nobody wants to lose his job, but I found people knew what had to be done and were looking for somebody to

step up and do it. . . . Originally, it was reported that we fired 10,500 people. The actual figure, as we sit here today, is 11,125, about 34 percent of the total corporation. . . . And that was that: the largest restructuring in corporate America today, on a pro-rata basis. Sure, IBM got rid of more people, but they only amounted to 13 percent of the corporation.

If you faced the choice of increasing profits for shareholders or saving jobs for employees, what would you do? Many managers feel that corporations have an obligation to employees, customers, the community, and society, as well as to their owners. Others agree with Dunlap that the owners come first. What do you think? (*Hint*: Examine his assumptions. Do you agree that owners take all the risk? Do you agree that cutting employees might be the best way to make a company more profitable in some circumstances? Can you think of other ways of making a company smaller? Can you think of alternatives to making it smaller?)

Source: Interview with Albert J. Dunlap in *Across the Board*, Feb. 1995, p. 17.

When the finance team compares actual results with projections and identifies excessive costs, a next step is to determine how to reduce those costs—perhaps by talking to workers involved in the operation or by learning about the methods employed by competitors. For example, in 1995, Boston's Museum of Fine Arts was faced with a $4.5 million deficit, which was increasing annually due to declining attendance, corporate contributions, and revenues from retail sales. To reduce the current deficit and prevent its further growth, Malcolm A. Rogers, the museum's director, eliminated 83 staff positions, reduced the number of management levels, and combined departments and functions. Earlier layoffs had not worked, he said, because they "were not accompanied by a restructuring of the museum's operations nor by the elimination of redundant functions and management levels."[5] For another viewpoint on downsizing, see the ethics check entitled "The Top 'Hatchet Man' in America: Hero or Villain?"

Uses of Funds

We've explored the basics of financial planning—forecasting, budgeting, and financial control of a firm's funds. In the next two sections, we investigate the uses and sources of the funds that the finance manager oversees.

The business's need for cash changes as the business cycle ebbs and flows and as the company grows. Young companies, for example, may devote more funds to inventory and marketing campaigns in order to build a reputation. More established companies often devote more resources to long-term investments such as expanding a production plant or purchasing new, more efficient equipment. Another factor that affects uses of funds is the company's selling cycle. For example, seasonal businesses such as gift merchandisers and clothing retailers sell most of their inventories in the months preceding the holiday season in December and January. Paper companies have higher sales in the spring, summer, and early fall, when catalog companies and newspapers are preparing their largest issues.

Uses of Funds

To launch its "crust-first" pizzas, Pizza Hut Corp. convinced Donald and Ivana Trump to get back together and say "cheese" for this television commercial. But the reunion wasn't cheap. The appearance cost Pizza Hut close to $1 million, which the Trumps donated to charity.

Since companies have limited funds, finance managers play a key role in applying risk-return analysis to decide which projects a firm should fund. When Towers, Perrin Inc., a New York City human resources consulting company, decided to consolidate several branch locations into a single site, it realized it was taking a risk. In order to consolidate, the company decided to abandon its high-profile, high-rent main office on Park Avenue for decidedly less glamorous rental space. Though the rent was less, the new offices were also farther away from some clients. What's more, in New York City, some believe that a Park Avenue address helps lure clients. What if Towers, Perrin suddenly started losing business to other firms that stayed on Park Avenue? After weighing all these factors, company management decided that the return, in the form of lower rent, outweighed the risk.[6]

The decision made by Towers, Perrin had an obvious effect on the short-term use of the company's funds but also made a difference in the long term. The company needed to pay for moving expenses—a short-term expense—but it saved money over the long term, freeing up funds for other uses. In general, short-term and long-term uses of funds affect each other. For ease of discussion, we'll consider several short-term uses first, working with the income statement and balance sheet items that were introduced in Chapter 19.

7. Identify and describe short-term uses of funds.

Meeting Daily Cash Needs

Operating expenses are the costs incurred by a company's day-to-day activities. Typically short-term operating expenses include *fixed costs* such as rent, utilities, and certain salaries, as well as such *variable costs* as labor and materials, reported as expenses on the income statement. Short-term operating expenses need to be paid in a timely fashion and represent an important use of funds for all firms. In fact, a firm that does not meet these daily needs will soon find itself out of business.

Recall from Chapter 17 that fixed costs *do not change no matter how many units of the product are produced.* Variable costs *fluctuate with the number of products produced.*

Besides having adequate cash available to meet expected outlays, the finance manager must have a sufficient cash reserve for unexpected expenses or unexpected investment opportunities. For example, having cash reserves enabled Patterson Dental Co., a distributor of dental products, to move quickly in October 1993 when a key competitor, Healthco, failed. The company paid $8.4 million out of its cash reserves for Healthco's Canadian unit and used almost $6 million obtained through a bank loan to help fund U.S. expansion and the purchase of merchandise.[7]

One sign of good day-to-day cash management is that payments to suppliers are delayed for as long as possible without hurting the firm's credit reputation. (In a similar fashion, individuals are advised to pay their credit card bills near the due date, not as soon as the bill is received.) On the other hand, firms should try to collect money owed to them as soon as possible. In other words, by postponing accounts payable as long as possible and collecting accounts receivable as soon as possible, the company gains maximum use of its cash to invest or to purchase an asset.

It's a dangerous balancing act. If a company delays payment of bills until creditors are knocking on its door, it loses credibility—and vendors. If it pays its bills within the 30 days most vendors require, it minimizes the risk of being cut off from its merchandise and maximizes its return by maintaining good relations with suppliers.

Small firms, which generally do not have the resources of larger firms, need to manage their cash flow more closely. In fact, more new firms fail for a lack of cash than for any other business reason. For example, in the mid-1990s, a new business, Supra Medical Co., developed several excellent products to sell to the health-care industry. However, because its initial cash supply was used to pay start-up costs and to develop products, Supra did not have the necessary cash to market and produce its products. Simply put, without cash such a firm may go out of business.[8]

Poor financial management can cause business failure through
- *Undercapitalization*
- *Poor cash flow*
- *Inadequate expense control*

Controlling Accounts Receivable

Accounts receivable represent money owed to the firm for goods or services sold to customers. Finance managers, working with the marketing department, usually determine who receives credit from the company and in what amount. Before extending credit to other businesses, finance managers examine the business customer's financial statements and often consult with credit- and financial-rating agencies such as the Dun & Bradstreet Corp., Standard & Poor's, and Moody's. In the past, these agencies focused on the financial soundness of larger firms, but today Dun & Bradstreet, for one, will evaluate companies with as few as two employees. Still, finance managers often have to rely on the word of the owner and keep a close eye on the account.

Many small retailers face increasing competition and shrinking profit margins with the spread of large, warehouse-type discount stores such as Home Depot. To remain competitive yet keep expenses low, some stores are reexamining their credit policies. For example, in an effort to reduce the cost of accounts receivable and to increase cash flow, local business owner Vincent J. Ayd of Ayd Hardware in Towson, Maryland, decided to stop accepting credit cards. Every time a customer paid by credit card, Ayd Hardware paid the credit card issuer between 3 and 6 percent of the purchase price, essentially to compensate the issuer for extending credit to the purchaser. To reduce his overall cost of doing business, Ayd decided to accept only checks. He felt safe in making this decision because many regular customers either paid in cash or had a charge account that they paid in full each month. An analysis of past purchases showed that the total dollar amount of bad checks would be less than the fee charged by the credit card issuers. The elimination of the credit card fees and the decrease in accounts receivable reduced operating costs. By lowering costs, Ayd Hardware could then lower its prices and keep pace with Home Depot and other large discount stores.[9]

Few firms are willing to follow Ayd's example, however, since every year more and more people say "Charge it." Indeed, more retailers are taking the opposite approach and becoming increasingly liberal with credit in an effort to boost sales and market share. Catalog company Lillian Vernon, for instance, offers deferred payment on purchases. As a result, more than 10 percent of its assets are invested in accounts receivable.[10]

The more liberal the credit policy, the higher the risk of nonpayment. Unless the finance manager carefully monitors credit policy, the company can easily overextend credit to increase sales and thus increase accounts receivable to a quarter or a third of the firm's total assets.

An important aspect of controlling accounts receivable is a firm's collection policies. As you'll recall, sound financial management means paying bills as late as possible within the vendor's specified time frame. At the same time, the firm must collect from its customers as soon as possible, often by offering a discount for early payment. Of course, there will always be delinquent customers. Many firms have employees who do nothing but attempt to collect receivables. When their efforts fail, the firm may hire outside collection agencies, who work for a percentage of the receivables collected.

Purchasing Inventory

In Chapters 10 and 16 you learned that JIT (just-in-time) systems help production and distribution departments determine inventory levels and order size. It is costly to have too many goods in inventory because the funds used to buy and store inventory could instead be put to other, more productive uses. The risk of outages must be balanced by the return that the funds spent on inventory could generate if put to another use—such as long-term investments.

In manufacturing and retailing companies, inventory is the primary short-term use of a company's cash because the company derives its primary profit from selling that inventory. The goal of inventory control is to fill orders as they arrive at the lowest possible cost, with minimal inventory. A seasonal business, such as Ayd Hardware, for instance, must monitor its inventory carefully, ordering snow shovels, ice melt (rock salt), and holiday items for the fall and winter and garden tools for the summer. Having on hand a good supply of snow shovels during the summer and rakes during the winter makes no sales sense. And the unneeded inventory ties up funds that might be used to purchase other items. For example, when the *Farmer's Almanac* predicted an even more severe winter for 1994 after the snows of 1993 found many stores in short supply of shovels and rock salt, many increased their inventory of snow-removal items. But when the winter turned out to be mild, they were left long on inventory but short on cash.

Funding Long-term Investments

Long-term uses of funds are represented by the fixed assets portion of the balance sheet. Recall from Chapter 19 that fixed assets include property, plant, and equipment. Manufacturing firms such as General Motors Corp. have a large

8. Explain why decisions regarding long-term investments significantly affect business profitability.

percentage of their cash tied up in fixed assets, as do firms in the transportation industry, such as Amtrak and Trans World Airlines, Inc. (TWA). As explained earlier, a risk-return analysis is particularly important for long-term investments, since the company has to live with the decision for a long time. The risk is greater not only because larger sums of money are involved but also because the difficulty of predicting cash flows far into the future increases the chance of error. Remember, the return will be based on *actual* flows, not on the estimate.

So before TWA purchases a plane, management needs to be fairly certain that the market is large enough to return the fares needed to pay for it. Obviously, the plane will not be paid for all at once, any more than you pay for a new car all at once. Rather, a minute portion of each airfare pays for the plane; the rest of the money goes to meet the airline's operating expenses. If air travel drops below projections, an airline can lose billions of dollars and be forced to surrender planes. In the early 1990s, for instance, U.S. airlines lost more than $5 billion because they improperly forecast air travel, besides failing to predict the impact of frequent-flyer mileage and the deregulation instituted in the 1970s. They also dropped several routes and, as a result, canceled the planned purchase of some planes. A few companies, such as Braniff, Eastern, and Pan Am, went out of business. An error made in the purchase of a fixed asset can have repercussions for a long time.

Because long-term uses of cash have such a major impact on a company, the decision to invest in a fixed asset is not usually made by a single finance manager or team. Rather, top management and the board of directors carefully review the recommendation and supporting materials supplied by finance before deciding whether to commit funds to long-term use.

Sources of Funds

When companies raise money, they report its sources on the income statement and the balance sheet. Sales revenues and income from other sources, such as investments, royalties, or rent, are reported on the income statement. Cash and cash equivalents, accounts receivable, and inventory represent the sources of funds reported in the asset section of the balance sheet. Debt and equity capital are reported on the balance sheet under liabilities and owners' equity.

Firms differ in the way they raise funds and in the amount of funds they need. Most businesses rely on sales revenue as their major source of funds. Cash generated by sales is readily available, and the business need not pay interest on it or give up a say in its management. Established firms may have a stockpile of earnings for use in funding investments. Chrysler Corp., for instance, was sitting on a hoard of nearly $7 billion at the end of 1994, money the company was holding to develop its next line of cars and to weather the next recession. New businesses, however, may not have adequate earnings for funding investments and may have to rely largely on outside sources of funds. In this section, we describe the sources of funds that are available to finance managers. For a review of the firm's uses of funds and a preview of its sources of funds, see Figure 20.3.

Before a business tries to obtain funds from outside sources, the finance manager evaluates the financial performance of the company to see if there are ways to generate more funds from normal operations. For example, can expenses be cut or eliminated? Can the level of inventory be reduced without decreasing sales? Reductions in expenses not only increase the cash available but also improve the profitability of the firm. As a result, the balance sheet and income statement look better to outsiders, which makes it easier to raise funds externally—at a lower cost.

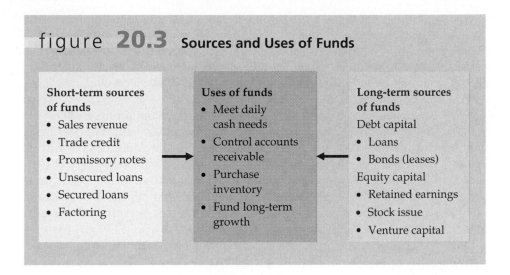

figure **20.3** **Sources and Uses of Funds**

Short-term Sources of Funds

Revenues—sales receipts and the collection of accounts receivable—provide short-term sources of funds from normal operations. They represent a recapture of funds that were originally spent on inventory plus a profit margin to cover other expenses. Investment income (for example, interest income) and cash from the sale of any of the firm's fixed assets (property, plant, or equipment) provide additional sources of funds.

In all companies—large or small, new or well established—revenues and other income are seldom enough to cover *all* expenses and investments. This is true for a variety of reasons: The company may need to increase inventory substantially to take advantage of a market opportunity; the business may be seasonal and need extra cash to carry it through the slow periods; or the company may simply be following the basic policy of paying as late as possible and collecting as soon as possible.

Finance managers obtain short-term financing—funds that must be repaid within a year—through a variety of mechanisms, including trade credit, promissory notes, and bank loans. On the balance sheet, these sources are represented as current liabilities.

Trade Credit

Credit extended by suppliers for the purchase of goods and services is called **trade credit**. Included on the balance sheet as part of accounts payable, trade credit represents the largest source of short-term financing for most companies. As is true of accounts receivable, the amount of trade credit extended and the terms of repayment depend on the type of industry and the creditworthiness of the firm. Trade credit represents a spontaneous source of financing and is critical to new firms and small businesses. Trade credit is considered spontaneous because it is the result of normal business activity and usually does not involve a formal note specifying the obligations of the firm receiving the goods or services.

In many industries, suppliers offer customers trade credit on their purchases. The invoice shows the amount of money owed and the terms of payment. For example, when a retailer buys goods from a wholesaler, the retailer might be given terms that require full payment in 30 days. Trade credit has no stated interest rate so long as the payment is made within those 30 days. How-

9. Identify and describe short-term sources of funds.

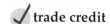 **trade credit**

Credit extended by suppliers for the purchase of goods and services.

promissory note

A written contract by which a business agrees to pay a supplier as specified on the invoice.

unsecured loan

A loan given by a bank or other financial institution and not backed by specific assets.

collateral

Specific asset pledged against a loan.

secured loan

A loan given by a bank or other financial institution and backed by collateral that the lender can sell if the borrower cannot meet the loan payments.

line of credit

A bank's commitment to lend up to a specified amount of money during a specified period (usually one year), provided the bank has the funds available.

Commercial finance companies charge higher interest rates, on average, than banks, but they may be the only resource for a new business or a risky business.

The current ratio is a measure of a company's short-term liquidity calculated by dividing current assets by current liabilities. Review Chapter 19 for the full range of financial ratios.

ever, if the wholesaler offers a discount for early payment, the credit carries an "implied" interest rate. For example, "1 in 10, net 30" on an invoice means that the money is due within 30 days but a 1 percent discount will be allowed if payment is made within 10 days. If payment is made on day 10 instead of day 30, the customer will lose the use of the money for 20 days. However, it will receive a break on the price.

The finance manager must weigh the risks of each option against the returns. In this situation, the discount is actually greater than 1 percent because it must be considered a discount over time. That is, there are about 18 periods of 20 days in a year ($^{365}/_{20} \approx 18$), so the annual discount is really 18 percent (1 percent × 18 periods = 18 percent per year). If the cost of borrowing funds on a short-term basis is less than 18 percent, the company should pay on day 10 and raise any cash needed from another short-term source. The return generally outweighs the risk of having to take on a bank loan.

Promissory Notes

Some businesses have either no credit rating or a poor credit rating. These may be new businesses with no track record or small or risky businesses with a limited or poor past history. Suppose you want to own a gift store. Before you can open your doors, you must have enough inventory to take you through your first several months in business. But you have no track record in business, and suppliers are reluctant to provide trade credit until you have proven yourself. You have three choices: Raise enough money from family and friends to purchase inventory; sell yourself well enough to convince a financial institution to lend you money (and thereby incur the additional expense of interest payments); or sign a **promissory note**, a written contract agreeing to pay the supplier as specified on the invoice. Vendors are often willing to accept promissory notes because they can be sold to a bank at a discount (the amount of the invoice less the bank's fee), ensuring that the vendor will be paid at least in part for the goods sold to you.

Short-term Loans

Loans are another major source of short-term credit for firms, as they are for individuals. Short-term loans are more formal than trade credit. Banks and commercial finance companies are the primary sources of short-term loans for small businesses and for the majority of larger companies. In applying for a loan, the finance manager needs to show the bank that the company has the resources to cover repayment. Short-term loans are broadly divided into two categories: unsecured and secured. An **unsecured loan** is a loan not backed by specific assets, or **collateral**. A **secured loan** is backed by collateral that the lender can sell if the borrower cannot meet the loan payments.

Unsecured Loans The most common type of unsecured short-term loan is a **line of credit**—a bank's commitment to lend up to a specified amount of money during a specified period (usually one year), provided the bank has the funds available. A line of credit is a formal agreement with a bank. It allows the business to access the funds without having to arrange for a loan each time money needs arise during the year.

A line of credit agreement is not a guaranteed source of funds, for the bank may place constraints on the borrower. For example, the bank may require that the firm maintain a checking account with a minimum balance, and that the line of credit have a zero balance for a certain number of days during the year. At times the bank may also limit the amount of long-term debt the firm can carry, or require that the firm maintain certain financial ratios at industry standards—for example, keep its current ratio at 2.0 or higher.

With a **revolving line of credit**, the bank *guarantees* that the company can borrow up to its credit limit whenever it wants. The cost of a guaranteed line of credit is usually a fee that covers the cost to the bank of tying up the unused funds. For example, suppose a company with a $50,000 revolving line of credit borrows $35,000. The company pays a fee of ½ of 1 percent, which covers the unused $15,000, plus 3 percent over prime on the $35,000 actually borrowed.

Credit lines are an important source of unsecured funding for seasonal and unexpected needs. We use our credit cards for seasonal shopping and vacations and for unexpected events such as a medical emergency. In fact, some new and small business owners use their personal credit cards to help finance the short-term needs of their business if they cannot arrange for a business line of credit with a bank.

Sources of Funds

Information management consultant Victoria Bondoc, shown here with clients at Hanscom Air Force Base, used "kitchen capital"—$1500 from her personal savings—to launch her company, Gemini Industries, Inc., in 1986. Within 10 years the business was earning close to $5 million in yearly revenues. With this impressive growth record, Bondoc's company may find it easier to attract outside sources of additional business financing.

Secured Loans Banks and commercial finance companies also provide the majority of *secured* short-term loans, a major source of financing for small companies. Most commonly, a secured short-term loan is backed by accounts receivable, inventory, or other assets that have been pledged as collateral. If the company defaults on payments, the bank owns the assets pledged against the loan. A car loan is an example of a secured loan; if you miss several payments, the bank can repossess its collateral—your car.

For a secured loan, the borrower signs a formal agreement that specifies the interest rate, terms of repayment, and the assets pledged as collateral. Usually the loan agreement is then filed in the local courthouse to establish the lender's security interest in the asset. For instance, car dealers and marine stores pledge their inventories of cars and boats, respectively, as collateral for inventory loans. A bank would not hesitate to lend $10,000 on a BMW 325i ($30,000 sticker price) because in the event of default it would have no problem selling the BMW for $10,000.

An inventory of finished goods that are ready for sale will generally have a higher loan value than a raw materials inventory because a consumer will pay more for the finished good. Work-in-process inventory will have the lowest value because it can't easily be used to manufacture something else. An inven-

 revolving line of credit

A guaranteed line of credit, usually involving a fee that covers the cost to the bank of tying up the unused funds.

✓ **factoring**

Selling accounts receivable at a discount to a factoring company in return for immediate cash.

✓ **leverage**

Using borrowed funds (debt capital) to finance investments.

tory loan agreement may specify a particular inventory item or inventory in general. In some cases, the firm may be required to place the inventory in a separate location. The actual agreement depends on the firm's relationship with the bank or commercial finance company, and on the characteristics of the inventory. A department store would have a general inventory loan; if it offers a store credit card, it might also pledge the accounts receivable from consumer credit. A car dealer, on the other hand, would identify each item to be pledged against the loan.

A second, more costly type of secured short-term loan involves **factoring**, whereby a firm *sells* its accounts receivable to a factoring company in return for immediate cash. Factoring is like having a fire sale—you sell items at a significant discount. Typically, when a company sells its accounts receivable to a factoring company, it receives only 60 to 90 percent of their value. The amount of cash received from the factoring company depends on the age of the accounts receivable, the type of business, the size and type of the accounts, and general economic conditions.

While factoring is very expensive, it has some advantages. The company receives cash immediately and eliminates the expense of trying to collect accounts receivable. Furthermore, new firms or firms in financial difficulty may have no other choice. New, small firms may have to rely on factoring if they have not been in business long enough to establish lines of credit with a bank. The average factoring arrangement lasts from six months to one year. If the factoring agreement runs for too long, chances are that the factoring company is making more money than the firm that factored its accounts receivable.

Financing with short-term sources requires day-to-day monitoring. Although it is relatively convenient and inexpensive, there should be a limit on short-term funding. Short-term financing should represent no more than 20 to 30 percent of the funds required by the company for operating expenses and investments. Too much short-term financing increases the riskiness of the firm—as each loan comes due, the finance manager will probably need to seek an alternative source of funds. If there is an economic downturn, or if the firm experiences even minor difficulties, the finance manager may not be able to obtain new short-term funding. Long-term sources provide a stronger foundation on which to operate the business.

Long-term Sources of Funds

10. Identify and describe long-term sources of funds and note the advantages and disadvantages of each.

Finance managers use the two major types of long-term financing, debt capital and equity capital, to purchase such items as plant and equipment and to finance any planned expansion of the firm, from a new store location to a new sales staff. While the finance manager does not have to manage long-term sources on a daily basis, the cost and use of long-term funds have a strong influence on the profitability of the firm. Long-term sources of funds generally cost more than short-term sources because the owners of the funds must be compensated for their risk. Equity capital costs more than debt capital since equity is riskier.

The cost of long-term financing depends not only on the business risk of the firm but also on the amount of debt capital the firm uses. Debt capital represents a fixed obligation; that is, interest payments must be made and principal repaid. Some companies—and some investors—use borrowed funds (debt capital) to finance investments. This practice is called **leverage**. Essentially, debt acts as a lever to raise the company's profitability. The more money a company borrows, the higher its profits can rise, so long as the company can sustain the interest payments on the debt. But like two kids on a seesaw, if the debt is too heavy, profits cannot get off the ground.

Debt Capital

Debt capital is raised in two ways: by taking out long-term loans or by issuing bonds.

Long-term Loans Banks, pension funds, insurance companies, and other financial institutions are the primary sources of long-term loans. Lenders typically grant long-term loans for periods of 5 to 20 years. The actual interest rate depends on many factors, including the length and size of the loan, general economic conditions, and the borrower's business and financial riskiness.

Beginning in the 1980s, variable interest rate loans became popular. Instead of being fixed, the loan's interest rate is pegged to the prime rate, which fluctuates depending on economic growth. Variable interest rate loans remove some of the risks faced by lenders, who are not locked into receiving, say, 5 percent interest as they watch inflation soar to, say, 10 percent. Without the variable rate, these lenders would lose money on the loan. Variable rates can also provide advantages to borrowers. When the prime rate is lowered, the interest rate on the loan is also reduced. For example, homeowners with adjustable rate mortgages (ARMs) will see their monthly payments reduced until the prime rate is increased again.

Standard provisions of a long-term debt agreement call for the borrowing firm to keep satisfactory accounting records, to pay taxes on time, and to maintain the general financial health of the firm. For financially sound firms, these debt provisions are not a burden. Small firms may find it difficult to borrow from banks or other financial institutions, however, either because they don't have a sufficient business history or because they've had a couple of unprofitable years. If they have difficulty, they may be eligible for the Small Business Administration (SBA) programs detailed in Chapter 7. The SBA is an agency of the federal government that either lends money directly to qualified small businesses and minority-owned businesses, or works with a financial institution and guarantees payment of all or part of the loan. SBA-backed loans helped fund the start-up of such companies as Apple Computer Inc.

Bonds The sale of bonds is another form of debt capital. A **bond** is a certificate issued by a business or government agency guaranteeing a specific interest rate and repayment of the principal at a specified time. The legal contract between the bond issuer and purchaser that specifies these terms is called a **bond indenture**. The indenture also indicates the rights of the bondholder (lender) and the duties of the issuing firm. Bonds typically are sold in denominations of $1,000 and mature in 10 to 30 years. Interest is paid semiannually, and at maturity the principal amount is repaid to the bondholder. The interest rate paid depends on the bond's riskiness, which is a function of economic conditions and the firm's financial rating. A low-rated company pays bondholders higher interest in order to attract investors away from other income-earning investments.

When companies issue bonds, they are selling debt to a group of institutions or individuals instead of borrowing from just one lender. Issuing bonds is relatively expensive. Only larger firms and the government sell bonds.

Leasing Instead of using debt capital to purchase a piece of equipment, a firm may lease it. A **lease** is an agreement whereby an individual or firm agrees to pay a fee (rent) for a specified period of time in return for the use of property or equipment. The lease agreement specifies the responsibilities of the lessee and any special conditions that may exist at the end of the lease—for example, whether the lessee has an option to buy the item.

Like debt financing, leases require fixed payments over a specified period of time. However, leases have several advantages. First, they are more easy to obtain than debt capital because lessors know that in the event of default, they

 bond

A certificate issued by a business or government agency guaranteeing a specific interest rate and repayment of the principal at a specified time.

 bond indenture

A legal contract between the bond issuer and purchaser specifying the terms of the bond.

 lease

An agreement whereby an individual or firm agrees to a fee (rent) for a specified period of time in return for the use of property or equipment.

skills
check

Should You Go for a New-Car Loan or a New-Car Lease?

Do you want a new car? Do you *need* a new car? Do you have enough money to make a down payment? Can you afford loan payments? Or should you lease a car?

New-car price tags are growing faster than the American family's paycheck. Three of four new-car buyers in the United States need financing. The average price of a new car in 1993 was $18,100, over two-thirds more than 1983 prices, when the average consumer spent 22 weeks' wages on a new car. In 1993 a new car required 26 weeks' wages.

Car dealers began experimenting with leases in the early 1980s, and car leasing grew from about 12 percent of new-car sales in 1986 to 25 percent in 1993—some $43 billion worth of vehicles. While the proportion of new cars leased remained at one-fourth of new-car sales through mid-1995, industry experts predict that the proportion will rise to one-half leases by 2000.

Already among car makes and models the percentage leased ranges widely. Midrange models, such as Toyota Corolla and Ford light trucks, come in around the 25 percent industry average. For luxury cars, the numbers are much different. Fully 88 percent of Jaguar XJS models were leased in 1994, along with 49 percent of Cadillac Sevilles and 46 percent of Infiniti J30s. Drivers in more affluent areas are more likely to lease, and younger drivers are more likely to lease luxury cars.

Leasing offers car makers the potential for increased brand loyalty and less seasonal fluctuation in sales. But the financial forecasts are hard to predict. For example, many vehicles coming off lease might depress used-car prices and threaten new-car sales as a result. Resale values of cars coming off lease could vary below forecast and thereby play havoc with company finances.

For the consumer, leasing offers advantages: a low down payment—or no down payment—low monthly payments, and easy exchange for a new car. Leasing's main disadvantages are that no equity builds up for the lessee, some points of lease agreements may be inflexible, and, since leasing is complex and largely unregulated, the potential exists for questionable business practices. But regulators are stepping in to improve this disadvantage of leasing. In July 1995, 20 major lessors voluntarily agreed to disclose on lease contracts the *capitalized cost*, roughly equivalent to the purchase price of the car if you were buying it, including extras. This self-regulation grew from the realization that if the customer does not know the "cap cost," the dealer can calculate the lease payments on a higher price without the customer's knowledge.

If you're in the market for a new car, ask yourself these questions to decide whether buying or leasing is better for you:

1. *Do you have the cash?* Leasing requires a lower cash outlay—for down payment, taxes, extras—than buying.

2. *How often do you want a new car?* With leasing, you're in a new car every 2 or 3 years. If you like to trade in your car every year, or if you like to drive the same car for 7 or 8 years, you should buy.

3. *How much do you drive?* Ideal candidates for a lease drive fewer than 15,000 miles a year and maintain their cars. If you drive much less, consider buying. If you drive much more (or are hard on your car) and want to lease, negotiate the cost of additional miles and maintenance up front.

4. *Do you use your car for business?* Sales representatives and other businesspeople who deduct their cars' depreciation from income taxes may be able to deduct more if they lease.

5. *Do you think of your car as an investment?* Those who do are confident of their cars' resale value and are better off buying. If the car is new, realize that its market value will be affected by the proportion of leases that expire and how much they increase the supply—and lower the price—of available used cars.

Finally, Charles J. Givens advises readers of his *Wealth Without Risk Newsletter*: "Never buy a new car. Buy the car you want after it is two years old. You'll save 50 percent."

Sources: Jane Bryant Quinn, "Look Under Hood of Car Lease," (New York) *Daily News*, July 23, 1995, p. B3; David Woodruff, "Leasing Fever," *Business Week*, Feb. 7, 1994, pp. 92-97; Douglas Lavin, "Should You Buy or Lease Your Next Car?", *SmartMoney*, Nov. 1993, pp. 143-150; "Should You Finance or Lease Your Next Car?", McGraw-Hill Employees Federal Credit Union *Dividend*, Winter 1993, pp. 1-2; James Bennet, "Detroit Pushes Leasing but May Pay Later," *New York Times*, July 27, 1993, pp. D1, D5; Charles J. Givens, "Car-Leasing Smarts," *Wealth Without Risk Newsletter*, June 1993, p. 10.

can repossess the equipment or property without having to go through bankruptcy court. Leases also require little or no down payment; their cost may be less than other sources of financing and, in many cases, the monthly payments are lower than those on loans. By leasing equipment, firms can use the money saved to pay for other assets. For these and other reasons, car leases are popular among businesses and individuals. To learn more about auto leasing, see the skills check entitled "Should You Go for a New-Car Loan or a New-Car Lease?"

Leases have some disadvantages as well. For example, the lessee must pay for any damage to the property at the end of the lease. In addition, car leases include mileage allowances. This means that any mileage above the allowance is charged at a relatively high rate—so high that salespeople who travel extensively may find the lease savings canceled out by the cost of mileage.

Equity Capital

Equity capital is raised by retaining earnings or by expanding the company's ownership base. Expanding the ownership base can be accomplished in several ways. In sole proprietorships and partnerships, the current owners, their friends, or their families can invest funds in the business; alternatively, a partner or partners can be asked to join the firm.

In corporations, partial control can be sold to venture capitalists or stock can be issued and sold in public markets. Equity capital differs from debt capital in that equity holders are owners of the firm and have a voice in its management, stock has no maturity value or date, payments to equity holders are made on the firm's after-tax income, and equity holders are paid *after* debt holders. These differences, which are summarized in Figure 20.4, mean that equity capital is a riskier investment than debt capital and that using equity capital will cost the business more.

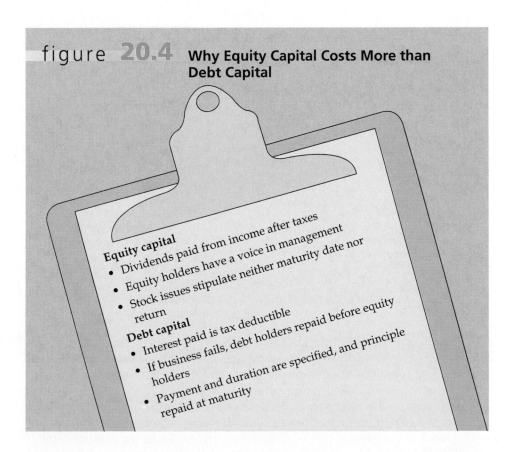

figure **20.4** **Why Equity Capital Costs More than Debt Capital**

Equity capital
- Dividends paid from income after taxes
- Equity holders have a voice in management
- Stock issues stipulate neither maturity date nor return

Debt capital
- Interest paid is tax deductible
- If business fails, debt holders repaid before equity holders
- Payment and duration are specified, and principle repaid at maturity

However, using equity as a source of financing places a minimum of constraints on the business. In return for equity ownership, investors may receive **dividends**, payments to stockholders made from a corporation's profits, as decided by the board of directors. Dividends, if paid, are usually paid quarterly. Earnings not distributed to stockholders in the form of dividends show up as part of accumulated retained earnings on the balance sheet. Retained earnings

 dividends

Payments to stockholders made from a corporation's profits.

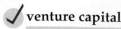

venture capital

Financing offered to high-risk ventures, usually in exchange for a substantial equity or ownership stake.

are an ideal source of funds. Finance managers recommend to the board of directors that the firm retain earnings rather than pay dividends when investment opportunities exist whose expected returns are greater than their cost. Fast-growing firms may retain all their earnings, while more slow-growing or mature firms generally pay dividends.

Venture Capital An important source of financing for business start-ups or other companies embarking on pioneering or turnaround situations is **venture capital**, financing offered to high-risk ventures, usually in exchange for a substantial equity or ownership stake. Wealthy individuals, venture capital firms, and some financial institutions provide venture capital. Finance managers exercise caution when seeking venture capital because the institution or individuals providing the funds will want some direct control or management responsibilities in the firm. As Figure 20.5 shows, however, the cost of venture capital decreases as the firm progresses toward profitability.

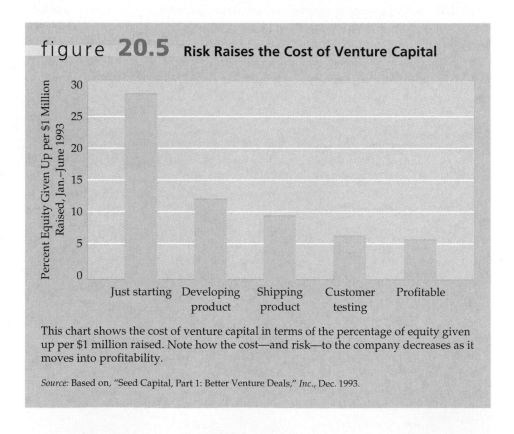

figure **20.5** **Risk Raises the Cost of Venture Capital**

This chart shows the cost of venture capital in terms of the percentage of equity given up per $1 million raised. Note how the cost—and risk—to the company decreases as it moves into profitability.

Source: Based on, "Seed Capital, Part 1: Better Venture Deals," *Inc.*, Dec. 1993.

Venture capitalists realize that some of the companies in which they invest will fail, while others will succeed. To compensate for the failures and the high risk attached to an investment, the venture capitalist expects to receive a very high rate of return—generally, more than 20 percent.

Venture capital is clearly an expensive source of funds for a firm. However, as we noted earlier, risky businesses have difficulty obtaining debt capital or selling stock to the general public. If the company succeeds, the venture capitalist will try to recover the money invested by having the company sell stock to the public. In 1994 companies backed by venture capitalists raised more than $4.1 billion by selling stock to the public.[11]

Stock Issue Stocks are bought and sold through organized exchanges such as the New York Stock Exchange, the American Stock Exchange, the over-the-counter market (NASDAQ), and several regional stock exchanges. Each year, more than 500 companies issue stock for sale to the public, and there are more than 10,000 publicly traded companies in the United States. If you look in the business section of your local newspaper, you will most likely see these exchanges listed and the names of some of the firms whose shares are traded.

The investor who buys stock expects to receive a return in the form of dividends and an increase in the market price of the stock. As owners, shareholders have voting rights in electing the board of directors of the firm. We discuss the sale of stock to institutions and individuals in detail in Chapter 22.

Reviewing *Financial Management*

Financial Management and the Firm

1. **Discuss the role of financial management in the business process, and identify three common reasons for business failure.** The success of a business depends on sound financial management, which involves obtaining funds, managing their day-to-day flow, and committing them for long-term expenditures. Finance depends on accounting for information about past financial transactions in order to project future revenues and expenses. The finance manager, who must have ongoing familiarity with events inside and outside the firm, is responsible for forecasting short- and long-term cash flows, budgeting, and financial control. Businesses fail for a variety of reasons, including undercapitalization, poor cash flow, and inadequate expense control.

2. **Discuss the influences of external factors on financial decision making.** Financial decisions are strongly influenced by the external environment. The economic growth rate and business cycle fluctuations clearly affect the availability and cost of funds, as well as the sources of funds. Government regulations and tax policies also affect financial decisions, either because they cause an increase in operating expenses or because they increase the cost of obtaining funds. The increasingly global nature of business has a major impact on financial decisions. International trade agreements, as well as rapidly expanding telecommunications and information technology, affect the prices of goods and services and the cost of financing the business. Exchange rate fluctuations affect prices and profits.

Financial Planning

3. **Describe how forecasting is used in establishing budgets.** The foundation of a firm's financial plan is its forecast of future cash flows, both short and long term. While short-term forecasts generally cover periods of less than a year, the exact time period depends on the industry. Long-term forecasts need not be as detailed or exact as short-term forecasts because cash for major expenditures is not needed on a daily basis and because these forecasts cover periods during which revenues and expenses are still uncertain. Both short- and long-term forecasts provide the basis for budgets, which are more detailed.

4. **Contrast the uses of the three major types of budgets.** Operating, cash, and capital budgets differ in the length of time covered and in their focus. Operating budgets, the most detailed and most used budgets, relate forecasted revenues to their costs and expenses and cover a year or less. Cash budgets compare projected cash receipts with projected disbursements and are prepared as often as weekly. Capital budgets deal with long-term expenditures for property, plant, and equipment. Analysis of capital budgets enables managers to select the most potentially profitable long-term projects.

5. **Explain the importance of risk-return analysis in capital budgeting.** In considering whether to undertake a project or other investment, the finance manager weighs the costs against future benefits, in the process trying to minimize risk and maximize return. The cost of capital reflects not only internal risks but also general economic factors, such as interest rates for debt funding and the risk profile of the company, which determines whether equity funding is a viable alternative.

6. **Discuss the use of financial control in bringing actual results in line with budgets.** Financial plans are projections of an uncertain future. To ensure that plans and reality are in sync, managers constantly track and monitor actual financial flows, modifying the plan as needed. Through financial control the manager determines the amount by which actual results deviate from budget and why any differences exist. Explanations for differences are provided through discussions with marketing, manufacturing, and other managers and employees. If profitability will be negatively affected, corrective action will be taken. The result may be an improvement in the company's operations and eventually in its profitability.

Uses of Funds

7. **Identify and describe short-term uses of funds.** Where funds are needed depends on the company. While established companies may emphasize long-term investments and younger companies may focus on inventory and marketing, all companies need adequate funds to meet short-term expenses—rent, utilities, salaries, and such. In addition, they should have a cash reserve in case of unexpected expenses. Equally important uses of short-

term funds involve management of accounts receivable and inventory. Although liberal credit policies may increase business, the high cost of accepting credit cards may outweigh the benefit of additional customers. Financial managers must walk the tightrope between so little inventory that they lose customers and so much inventory that they tie up funds that might be better used elsewhere in the business.

8. **Explain why decisions regarding long-term investments significantly affect business profitability.** By definition, long-term investments in the fixed assets of property, plant, and equipment use substantial funds over long periods of time. Risk-return analysis is vital for such investments. The longer the time period involved, the greater the risk and the greater the chance of error. If an investment does not generate the revenue projected for it, the result may be major financial losses, perhaps causing the company to go out of business.

Sources of Funds

9. **Identify and describe short-term sources of funds.** Short-term sources of funds include sales revenues and investment income, as reported on the income statement, and cash and cash equivalents, accounts receivable, and inventory, as reported on the balance sheet. Although companies prefer to use revenues to fund operations—

because they do not require interest payments—sometimes revenues are inadequate and the firm must turn to outside sources, which are represented as current liabilities on the balance sheet. These include trade credit; promissory notes; unsecured loans, such as a line of credit or a revolving line of credit; secured loans, backed by collateral; and factoring.

10. **Identify and describe long-term sources of funds and note the advantages and disadvantages of each.** Long-term sources of funds are broadly categorized as debt capital and equity capital. Debt capital is raised through long-term loans and the sale of bonds. Alternatively, companies may finance plant and equipment through a lease. Equity capital either exists as retained earnings or is raised by expanding the company's ownership base by selling stock, by owners contributing funds, by adding partners to the firm, or by selling partial ownership to venture capitalists, who provide a useful source for start-up or risky businesses. Debt capital has certain advantages over equity capital: It is less expensive and less risky and debt holders have no say in the firm's management. On the other hand, having retained earnings represents profitability and debt holders are paid before equity holders in the event of financial failure.

✓ Key Terms

financial management **603**	budgets **611**	equity capital **613**	revolving line of credit **621**
open-book management **605**	operating budget **611**	financial control **613**	factoring **622**
cash flows **605**	cash budget **612**	trade credit **619**	leverage **622**
undercapitalization **606**	capital budget **612**	promissory note **620**	bond **623**
risk-return analysis **607**	cost of capital **613**	unsecured loan **620**	bond indenture **623**
financial plan **609**	debt capital **613**	collateral **620**	lease **623**
forecast **609**	interest rate **613**	secured loan **620**	dividends **625**
	prime rate **613**	line of credit **620**	venture capital **626**

• Review Questions

1. Arlene is CFO of Rutherford Corp. and Jonathan is the accountant. What are their respective responsibilities?

2. What goes into a financial plan? How is it monitored?

3. You are the finance manager for a local school-bus service that is fairly profitable. If the company buys two new buses, they will provide service for 24 additional students. How will you decide whether the investment in new buses is worthwhile?

4. Action Sportswear manufactures and sells T-shirts. What are its short-term uses of funds?

5. What types of long-term uses might Action Sportswear have for its funds?

6. How might a bookstore finance its short-term operations? Mention all possible sources.

7. Exactly how do secured loans differ from unsecured loans?

8. How are debt and equity capital similar? How are they different?

9. Why would a company solicit venture capital rather than sell stock through normal channels?

10. What forces outside the finance manager's control influence financial decisions?

• Critical Thinking Questions

1. In what ways do the cross-functional responsibilities of a firm's CFO resemble the matrix organization you learned about in Chapter 9?

2. To cut costs, Federal Express introduced a service called FedEx Ship, a personal computer–based system that allows even the smallest business to order pickups, print shipping labels, and track packages without ever picking up the telephone. That saves FedEx and its clients money. FedEx Ship also cuts the costs of package pickup and sorting. In fact, most service improvements in the highly competitive express shipping business involve cutting costs. Why?

3. Times Mirror Co., a diversified media corporation that publishes magazines such as *Field & Stream* and newspapers—its flagship is the Los Angeles *Times*—decided in 1994 to sell off most of its electronic media hardware, or *delivery* systems, in order to concentrate on what it does best: providing customers with information and entertainment *content*. In other words, Times Mirror wants to sell the software—for example, interactive television programs—not own the hardware—the television stations. What basic difference in Times Mirror's cost of capital resulted from the decision to sell off its broadcast and cable television stations? Why is Times Mirror a better producer of content than of delivery systems? (*Hint*: Review the discussions of hardware and software in Chapter 18.)

4. Many Americans believe that the United States would not have accumulated a national debt of more than $4 trillion if the government were run by business managers. If a business failed to generate enough revenue to cover its expenses each year, they say, that business would fail. Based on your knowledge of financial management, it this argument sound? Why or why not? (*Hint*: Consult the section on the debt and the deficit in Chapter 2.)

REVIEW CASE *ASAP, Inc.*

ASAP, Inc., a rapidly growing four-year-old firm that provides temporary personnel services for a variety of jobs and businesses, has short-term cash flow needs. Temporary help is placed with a client, "as soon as possible," and the client is billed for the services at the end of each week. ASAP pays its temps the following week but does not receive payment from the client for 30 days, or in some cases not for several months. Mandy Fuller, president and CFO, is always facing a short-term cash flow problem.

1. How can Fuller raise cash for ASAP, Inc.?

2. How can Fuller shorten the time between billing clients and receiving payment from them?

3. How would you recommend that Fuller use short-term sources of funding? Long-term sources?

CRITICAL THINKING CASE *AES's Financial Management Strives for Wealth and Fun*[12]

At AES Corp., based in Arlington, Virginia, the chief financial officer won't discuss project financing with the company's bankers. Instead, he explains that he functions as an adviser and then gives them the phone numbers of project team members responsible for actually negotiating financing for their project.

AES, an independent power producer, is a company that has managed to "do well by doing good," a goal outlined earlier in Chapter 4 of this text. The company was founded by Dennis Bakke, the current CEO, and Roger Sant, the current chairman. Both strongly believe that businesses should incorporate values in their day-to-day operations and that departmentalization and specialization destroy trust in an organization.

As a result, AES tries to make work fulfilling and challenging, and that means allowing employees to make decisions, including financial decisions. With the exception of personnel records, all corporate data are available to all AES employees. Employee involvement is so far-reaching that the Securities and Exchange Commission (SEC) considers each employee an insider for stock-trading purposes.

AES's annual budget is prepared completely by task forces. And the job of investing $15 million of a $34 million debt reserve became a responsibility of a rotating task force at one of the company's plants. One member of that task force was a plant mechanic; another was a materials-handling technician. Company-supplied guidelines restricted the task force to money market securities, with specified ratings and maturities of 180 days or less.

The company's trust paid off, not only in its investments (which were quite successful) but also in daily operations. The plant where the $15 million investment project occurred runs at 95 percent capacity, and its accident rate is only 40 percent of the industry average.

Employees enjoy the freedom and responsibility: In a recent company survey, 58 of 67 workers cited "freedom to act" as the thing they liked best about working at AES. Workers also feel responsible for their decisions; AES's annual bonus is based on profit-sharing and given to all employees. Each employee realizes that his or her decisions will affect bottom-line figures and co-workers' well-being.

AES's mission statement stresses the firm's commitment to integrity, fairness, fun, and social responsibility. This does not mean, however, that layoffs never occur. AES laid off a substantial number of workers after buying a plant it considered overstaffed. In fact, Bakke maintains that allowing the plant to remain overstaffed would be "socially irresponsible."

Of course, AES does occasionally lose money when employees make mistakes. And some critics might question the extent of its spending on environmental causes. Roger Sant, company co-founder and chairman of the board, was very concerned about AES's contribution to global warming. As a result, he helped establish a company policy of planting trees or taking other measures to ensure that AES returns to the environment an amount of carbon dioxide equal to that used by AES plants. Sites for recent projects include Guatemala, Paraguay, and the Amazon rain forest. In another social investment, AES provided money and labor for a school in the Oklahoma town where a plant is located.

AES's investment in social responsibility is so extensive that the SEC considered it a risk that should be listed in the AES prospectus for its initial stock offering. Nevertheless, the company has shown strong, steady growth for more than a decade. Net profits were up 28 percent in 1993 and more than 35 percent in 1994. As Bakke says, "The most socially responsible thing we can do is to do a really good job of fulfilling our business mission, which is to provide clean, reliable, safe, low-cost electricity around the world."

1. As an investor, would you buy stock in AES? Explain why you would or would not invest in this company.

2. If you were a mechanic at AES, would you feel comfortable being responsible for the investment of $15 million?

3. In one case, the AES application for a start-up loan for a new plant requested $3 million for an unspecified socially responsible activity, citing activities similar to those mentioned in this case. The bank granted the loan. What might have been the reasoning used by the bank loan officer?

4. AES's plants emit about 58 percent *less* sulphur dioxide and nitrogen oxide than is permitted by law. Is AES doing its shareholders a disservice by being more responsible than the law requires it to be?

Critical Thinking with the ONE MINUTE MANAGER [13]

"I've done it!" Joanna said happily. "I've made it through a whole month without breaking my budget."

"Congratulations," Carlos replied. "Want to let me in on your secret?"

"You already know my secret, but you may not remember it. Do you recall our conversation with the One Minute Manager about bottom-up budgeting? My parents and I sat down and worked up a new budget, but this time I provided my best guess about the amount of money I would need for the items in the budget. My parents set the limits on what I could spend and gave me some pointers for unexpected spending or savings."

"What sort of pointers?" Carlos asked.

"Well, for example, I won't need as much money for food around the end of the year because I spend the holidays at home with my family. And I forgot to budget any money at all for laundry and dry cleaning. I also forgot to plan for the long weekend trip I want to take with some friends of mine. I can earn some of the trip money, but my parents told me I can keep any extra money I save by careful spending. I've managed to put aside $17 this month by shopping for specials, spending less on take-out food, and avoiding library fines."

"I couldn't help overhearing you, Joanna," said the One Minute Manager, coming out of her office. "It sounds as though you and your parents are using the same techniques Steve Wilson used to help his employees at Mid-States Technical Staffing Services learn to budget."

"Really? I was motivated by that story, but I don't see how my forgetting about laundry and travel money resembles real business spending," Joanna said, looking doubtful.

"In fact, your parents and you have a lot in common with Wilson and his employees. For example, Wilson told his employees that he would share with them any savings they were able to make on budgeted spending. They received 35 percent of the savings in the form of a bonus they shared, just as your parents let you keep the $17 you saved this month. And Wilson listened to his employees' ideas about what they thought they would need to purchase supplies for their work areas, just as your parents listened to your ideas about your budget needs."

"I wonder if Wilson's employees felt closer to him. I sure do with my parents. I guess I'm beginning to understand some of the hard choices they make when they spend their money."

"That's exactly what open-book management and bottom-up budgeting are supposed to achieve, Joanna. Looks like you've really learned a lot this month," the One Minute Manager responded, smiling.

1. Wilson tied his new budgeting plan to an employee bonus program. Do you think that's a wise decision? In your answer, consider the effects on a fast-growing company and on a company that seems to be in danger of failing.

2. If you were an employee budgeting for office supplies at Wilson's company, what would you want to know about last year's office supply budget? (*Hint:* Think about the meaning of Joanna's decreased need for food money during the holiday period.) Prepare a list of five questions you would want to have answered before preparing your budget.

3. Making predictions about spending is a difficult task, and one way to protect yourself is to pad your budget in case your predictions are wrong. If you were Wilson, what methods would you use to prevent budget padding? (*Hint:* What could you say to employees about the consequences of overspending?) What safeguard could you build into the budget itself?

21 Money and Financial Institutions

In this chapter, you will learn about the financial institutions at the center of all U.S. monetary activity and about the role of the U.S. Federal Reserve System in regulating economic conditions through the banking system. You will also become more familiar with changes that have transformed the banking industry from the heavily regulated, stable industry of the 1940s to the fast-paced banking world of mergers and acquisitions that characterize it today. First, however, you will need some background information about money—what it is and what it is not. After reading this chapter, you will be able to reach the learning goals below.

Learning Goals

1. Describe the functions and characteristics of money.
2. Identify the categories of money and describe their components.
3. Define *depository institutions* and describe the three major types of depository institutions.
4. Define *nondepository institutions*, or nonbanks, and explain their role as financial intermediaries.
5. Briefly outline the history of banking since the Great Depression.
6. Identify and describe the varied services provided by financial institutions today.
7. Discuss bank safety and outline the types of risks financial institutions face.
8. Describe the components of the Federal Reserve System.
9. Describe the three tools that the Fed uses to control the money supply.
10. Describe three important trends in the current banking environment.

Banking on Understanding

"Hi! We're on our way to the banking and finance lecture, but we hoped we could talk you into having lunch with us later today," Joanna said, smiling at the One Minute Manager.

"That's a lovely idea, Joanna, but I've got banking on my own menu for lunch today. I'm meeting with our bank's 'relationship manager,' as many loan officers now call themselves. Our company is shopping for a loan to buy a sophisticated computer system that will integrate all of our production-related information."

"Lunch seems a funny time to discuss loans with a banker," Carlos observed. "Is this person a friend of yours?"

"In a sense he is, Carlos. We believe that our bank contacts should understand our business and take an interest in it, and the person I'm meeting for lunch does that. Small businesses, which technically we are, are very important to banks right now. As you know from our earlier talks, they're a great source of jobs. But more than that, many large corporations have moved their business away from banks. Did you know that commercial banks now make only about 30 percent of all loans?"[1]

"That really surprises me," Carlos replied. "I just assumed that banks were the main source of funds for corporations. What's going on?"

"Lots of things. To begin with, some large corporations are selling bonds to finance their own needs; when they do that, they don't need bank loans. Second, there is some very serious competition going on in banking and finance today. Commercial banks and thrifts used to offer very unique products, but now a lot of other financial institutions also offer them, and sometimes their rates are lower and their service is better. To fight back, big banks are making drastic changes, and some are consolidating their resources by acquiring little banks or merging with other big banks."

"I can see that this would create a lot of confusion in the banking world, but how does it cause a 'relationship manager' to join a small-business manager over lunch?" Joanna teased.

"That's easy—Eric Rosengren, an economist from the Federal Reserve Bank of Boston, explained it to a group of us at a convention this year. His view was that as profit margins shrink on lines of business to large corporations, banks have to focus on their small-business customers.[2] Not all bankers join their clients for lunch, but those that do may find that what they've really ordered is loyalty, not soup and sandwiches."

What Is Money?

As you will soon see, the answer to that question is not as simple as it might sound. Broadly defined, **money** is anything generally accepted as a means of paying for goods and services. Without the common medium of money, people would have to rely on a barter system, in which individuals exchange items they produce for other items that they need. Barter systems sound tempting, but imagine for a moment some of the details.

Start with the assumption that you are living in Pennsylvania in the late eighteenth century. The most popular unit of barter there is the deerskin—the origin of the word *buck* as a slang term for dollar. In 1760, for example, you could purchase a longrifle for 9 pounds, 7 shillings, in state-issued Pennsylvania currency, or you could exchange 25 "bucks" for one by bartering.[3]

Let's assume that you don't have any Pennsylvania money, but you do have three bucks. Since it's planting time and you are in need of some corn, you stop at the local trading post and suggest a deal. The trader, however, has a roomful of bucks and very little corn. Who decides how much of his scarce corn equals one of your bucks? And what if you want only a little corn—two handfuls to grind for a day's bread instead of several bushels to plant your fields—how do you divide your buck to purchase just a little corn? What if you want one of those rifles that cost 25 bucks? How do you carry all those deerskins? Maybe it's worse than that—maybe you want to save all three bucks and move to a place where you don't have to make your living by shooting creatures that look like Bambi. If so, where will you store all those deerskins you've decided to save—not to mention the problem of the venison that comes with them?

As you can see, there's a lot to think about here, and it's no wonder most societies define money very carefully. Let's take a closer look at the functions of money.

The Functions of Money

Money has three functions: It is a medium of exchange, a unit of account, and a store of value. All of these functions describe to some extent the *liquidity* of money, which you may recall is the ease with which something can be used to purchase goods and services.

A Medium of Exchange

As a **medium of exchange**, money simplifies the purchase of goods and services and eliminates the need for a barter system. You can exchange money for a new shirt, a taxi ride, or corn. You needn't worry about whether you have some good or service that the other person needs. Money solves these problems through two important characteristics. It is easily *divisible*—you don't need to worry about what portion of a deerskin equals a handful of corn. Money is also *portable*—unlike deerskins, it fits easily into your pocket or a cash machine or a bank vault.

A Unit of Account

Money's second function is as a **unit of account**—it provides a common denominator for measuring the value of goods and services. Money saves a lot of negotiating—over the value of corn in relation to bucks, for example. Instead, money establishes an independent scale against which both items can be valued and compared. This is possible because of another characteristic of money—*its value is clearly established.*

 money

Anything generally accepted as a means of paying for goods and services.

 medium of exchange

A function of money that simplifies the purchase of goods and services and eliminates the need for a barter system.

 unit of account

A function of money that provides a common denominator for measuring the value of goods and services.

1. Describe the functions and characteristics of money.

A Store of Value

The third function of money is as a **store of value**—it retains its value until it is needed to purchase goods or services. This is possible because money is *durable*. Unlike deerskins and venison, money does not spoil. And money is *stable*; it does not lose its value, as deerskins might if animal-rights supporters convinced Congress to ban exchanges that use animal pelts. Because money is durable and stable, it can be saved, to be used later for special purposes like a down payment on a new home, a child's education, or a retirement nest egg. Finally, money is *not easily counterfeited*. (Nor, for that matter, are deerskins!)

The Money Supply

2. Identify the categories of money and describe their components.

Money supply is the total amount of money available to the public for buying goods and services. To make statements about money supply, the U.S. federal government has to define money in some specific way. It actually uses several definitions, but we concentrate here on the two most well known—M1 and M2.

M1—The Narrowest Definition of Money

M1 includes currency and demand deposits. **Currency** is paper money and coins. Personal or business checking accounts fall into the second category, **demand deposits**—funds that must be immediately paid out in response to a demand by the depositor or by someone who presents a check signed by the depositor—or, more simply, checking accounts. The institution holding the deposit must honor the demand as long as the funds in the account are at least equal to it. Your paycheck gives you the right to demand cash from the deposit account of your employer.

Travelers' checks, money orders, and cashier's checks are not demand deposits. Even in the restricted definition of M1, such items are, however, money—they serve as a medium of exchange and can readily be used to purchase goods and services. The difference between demand deposits and these items lies in the way they are paid out. Travelers' checks, money orders, and cashier's checks are considered equivalent to currency because they are purchased from a large institution—a bank or a post office—and their face value is then paid out of the institution's account.

Electronic Demand Deposit

More than 8 million Americans were banking by computer in 1995. Citicorp was the first bank to offer the service, and today dozens of banking companies are online. Personal computing software such as Microsoft Money, shown here, allows users to pay bills, check account balances, make transfers and deposits, and track spending with customized financial reports.

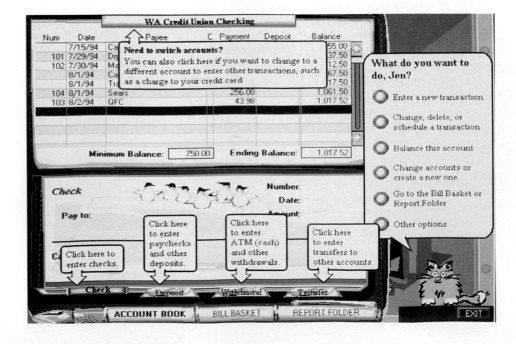

Checks are currently the most popular method of payment for individuals and businesses, mainly because checks have several advantages over currency: They are more convenient, they are safer, and they provide a record of payment. Imagine trying to send $65.83 in cash through the mail to pay an electric bill. Now multiply that image by thousands and you can see how impossible it would be for a large business to use currency for all of its transactions.

The use of checking accounts has changed during the 1980s and 1990s as automation has become an accepted part of banking processes. As you will see later in this chapter, some banks are eliminating many of the face-to-face or mail transactions traditionally associated with depositing and withdrawing money from checking accounts.

M2—"Near Money"

M2 includes everything in M1 plus savings deposits, time deposits, and other deposits on which check writing is limited or not allowed. Although less liquid than M1 funds, the funds that make up M2 are fairly easy to obtain and to use for the purchase of goods and services. For that reason, M2 is often referred to as *near money*.

You may be familiar with the standard savings account: The customer deposits funds in the account and receives a small paper passbook in which that transaction plus all future deposits, interest, and withdrawals are recorded. Interest is credited to the account at regular intervals, often monthly. Traditionally, money in a savings account had to be left in the bank's keeping for 30 days or more before it could be withdrawn. Competition from other sources has forced savings institutions to allow withdrawal on demand.

Time deposit accounts, as the name implies, require that a specified minimum amount be deposited for a specified period before any portion of the funds can be withdrawn. Time deposit accounts take several forms; two of the most common are certificates of deposit (CDs) and money market accounts. We deal with this topic in more detail later in this chapter.

Over the years, the distinction between M1 and M2 has blurred. A good rule of thumb in distinguishing the two, however, is that time deposits cannot be exchanged for goods or services, and they are therefore not considered to be part of M1. Figure 21.1 shows these two measures of the money supply.

store of value
A function of money that enables it to retain its value until it is needed to purchase goods or services.

money supply
Total amount of money available to the public for buying goods and services.

M1
A measure of the money supply that includes currency and demand deposits.

currency
Paper money and coins.

demand deposits
Checking accounts.

M2
A measure of the money supply that includes everything in M1 plus savings deposits, time deposits, and other deposits on which check writing is limited or not allowed; also known as *near money*.

time deposit accounts
Savings deposits that require a specified minimum amount to be deposited for a specified period before any portion of the funds can be withdrawn.

figure **21.1**   **M1 and M2—Two Measures of the Money Supply**

M2 (near money)
M1 plus

- Savings deposits
- Time deposits
- Other deposits on which check writing is limited or not allowed

M1
Currency plus

- Travelers' checks
- Money orders
- Cashier's checks
- Demand deposits

M1 is the most conservative measure of the money supply. It consists of currency plus demand deposits and other items that are equivalent to currency. M2, also called *near money*, contains everything in M1 plus savings deposits, time deposits, and other deposits on which check writing is limited or not allowed.

depository institutions

Banks and other financial institutions that accept deposits and make loans.

 commercial banks

Profit-making institutions that accept funds in the form of deposits (checking and savings) and provide funds as loans to individuals and businesses.

 state banks

Commercial banks chartered by the states in which they operate.

national banks

Commercial banks chartered by the federal government and regulated by the U.S. Treasury Department.

3. Define *depository institutions* and describe the three major types of depository institutions.

"Plastic Money"—Neither M1 nor M2

Credit cards are excluded from both M1 and M2. Credit cards satisfy two of the three criteria for money's functions—they are a medium of exchange and a unit of value. But credit cards are not money because they are not a store of value. Rather, they are an indication that another party—the card issuer—is willing to lend money to the card holder in an amount equal to an approved purchase. Charging the cost of an airline ticket to your credit card does not mean you are free of the cost of the ticket. You have merely transferred that debt to your loan account with the issuer of your credit card, and you must write a check on that account at the end of the month.

Nevertheless, credit cards have replaced currency as a medium of exchange in recent years. That's no surprise, considering that there are now approximately three credit cards in circulation for every person in the United States. These cards fall into two types. Well-known cards such as American Express, Visa, and MasterCard can be used at a variety of businesses and retail outlets. Private-label cards, such as those issued by your local office supply store or lumberyard, can be used only for purchases at that business. The well-known credit card companies charge businesses a small fee; for example, small restaurants pay 3.5 percent to American Express. Nevertheless, firms consider these fees a necessary cost of doing business because the cards are a convenience for their customers.

The Banking System

Financial institutions serve as intermediaries between savers, who want to earn interest, and borrowers, who are willing to pay interest in order to have the immediate use of money they need. These intermediaries fall into two main categories: depository institutions and nondepository institutions.

Depository Institutions

Depository institutions are banks and other financial institutions that accept deposits and make loans. There are three main types of depository institutions—commercial banks, thrift institutions, and credit unions. As originally established, each had a clear-cut function.

Commercial Banks

Commercial banks are profit-making institutions that accept funds in the form of deposits (checking and savings) and provide funds as loans to individuals and businesses. Most of us deposit our paychecks in checking accounts at commercial banks.

During the early 1800s, all commercial banks were chartered by the state in which they operated and, naturally enough, they were called **state banks**. These banks obtained their funds by issuing banknotes that could be exchanged for gold. (Remember those Pennsylvania pounds and shillings that could be used in place of bucks?) Unfortunately, state laws were relatively lax, and state banks were free to do as they pleased—and sometimes what pleased them was fraudulent.

In an effort to stop state-bank abuses, Congress passed the Federal Banking Act of 1863, which placed a tax on state banknotes. The act also created **national banks**, chartered by the federal government and regulated by the U.S. Treasury Department. Although this legislation did control the operation of state banks, it did not eliminate them as Congress had intended. The state banks were able to stay afloat by accepting deposits, and both state and federal banks coexist today. Although federal banks are larger and are governed by regulations slightly different from those governing their state counterparts, the two types of banks perform basically the same services.

The United States has an astonishing number of banks compared with other industrialized nations, most of which have fewer than a thousand. In the United States, 11,000 commercial banks hold almost $4 trillion in assets and almost $3 trillion in deposits. Contrast that with Great Britain, which has only 13, and Japan, which has only 150.[4] Many U.S. commercial banks are small, serving narrow local communities; more than 2,500 have assets of less than $25 million.[5] Nevertheless, as we shall see later in this chapter, the number of U.S. banks may diminish significantly in the next few years, as bank mergers create clumps of larger and more powerful institutions.

Thrift Institutions

Thrift institutions are savings banks and savings and loan associations. A **savings bank** accepts deposits in interest-bearing accounts and provides mortgage loans; it is usually state-regulated. Savings banks are sometimes known as *mutual savings banks*. A **savings and loan association (S&L)** is a federally regulated bank that accepts deposits in interest-bearing accounts and provides mortgage loans. Savings banks and S&Ls are virtually identical in terms of the services they offer. Both can be chartered by either a state or the federal government, and both may obtain deposit insurance from the FDIC.

Thrift institutions were initially established to encourage individuals to save—to be "thrifty"—and to help them achieve the American dream of owning their own home. Thrifts were allowed to offer higher interest rates on savings accounts, and they then used these deposits to make mortgage loans at current market rates.

There are now approximately 2,100 thrifts nationwide, with $1 trillion in assets and almost $750 billion in deposits. Although the number of thrifts was substantially reduced during the Depression, an even larger reduction occurred during the S&L crisis of the 1980s, as you will see later in this chapter. Indeed, some analysts project further reductions in the number of thrifts, as major commercial banks acquire and merge with other institutions.[6]

Credit Unions

Credit unions accept deposits and provide loans, but they differ from thrifts in that they are organized by and for people with a common bond. Members of a credit union may, for example, work for a particular company, government agency, or hospital. Traditionally, the primary function of credit unions was financing home construction.

The first credit union in the United States was established in November 1908 at St. Mary's Parish in Manchester, New Hampshire.[7] The earliest credit unions were organized in Germany in the 1800s to aid the poor and needy, who had to pay exorbitant interest to borrow money from commercial institutions. By banding together, they were able to pool their otherwise meager savings into a large enough amount to finance home construction. This pattern of self-help among people of limited means is found worldwide. In Northeast Africa, for example, the Amhara people of Ethiopia have long had a group savings arrangement that resembles the one found in our credit unions.[8] Credit unions are a common feature in many countries, though they now represent members with a wide range of incomes.

 thrift institutions

Savings banks and savings and loan associations.

 savings bank

Bank that accepts deposits in interest-bearing accounts and provides mortgage loans; sometimes known as a *mutual savings bank.*

 savings and loan association (S&L)

Federally regulated bank that accepts deposits in interest-bearing accounts and provides mortgage loans.

 credit union

Depository institution that accepts deposits and provides loans and that is organized by and for people with a common bond.

nondepository institutions

Financial institutions that obtain their funds from sources other than deposits, such as the premiums policyholders pay to insurance companies; also known as *nonbanks*.

 finance company

Nondepository institution that provides collateral-based, short-term loans to individuals and small businesses.

4. Define *nondepository institutions*, or nonbanks, and explain their role as financial intermediaries.

Recognizing the unique role of credit unions, the U.S. federal government has granted them nonprofit status. Although there are more than 12,000 credit unions in the United States, their assets are limited, totaling slightly more than $300 billion. Because of their limited size, most U.S. credit unions make only consumer loans and choose not to offer mortgage loans.[9]

Credit unions in some countries are much larger than their U.S. counterparts. Cosmo Shinyo Kumiai, Tokyo's largest credit union, is large enough to have made substantial loans to real estate speculators in Japan in the 1980s. When that market collapsed in 1995, officials of the credit union had to deliver vans full of cash to replenish funds as depositors began pulling out their money in fear that Cosmo Shinyo Kumiai would also collapse. In one day, depositors withdrew more than $680 million in cash, which was approximately 14 percent of the institutions's total deposits.[10]

Nondepository Institutions

At one time, almost everyone deposited their money at banks, thrifts, and credit unions and borrowed funds exclusively from them. Over time, however, a host of other important financial intermediaries have sprung up, offering similar and different services. These **nondepository institutions** or *nonbanks* obtain their funds from sources other than deposits; insurance companies, for example, obtain funds from the premiums policyholders pay to them. Nondepository institutions include finance companies, pension funds, insurance companies, and brokerage houses.

Finance Companies

Finance companies compete with commercial banks by making collateral-based, short-terms loans to individuals and small businesses. Several large U.S. corporations shelter a finance company under their umbrella; examples include General Motors Acceptance Corporation (GMAC) and GE Capital.

Finance companies charge high rates of interest because they lend to high-risk customers who often could not otherwise obtain loans. To receive a loan, borrowers must pledge collateral—property of some sort or, in the case of a business, accounts receivable.[11] Some borrowers are small firms with a higher-than-normal risk of failure or individuals with a poor credit history. Others

Microenterprise Lending

Four commercial banks rejected Wee Tai Hom's application for a $2,000 to $3,000 loan to expand AquaSource, his year-old aquaculture market and art gallery. His business was too small, too young, and too difficult to categorize. But Hom easily obtained a $1,000 loan from a microenterprise lender. These firms act as intermediaries between traditional banks and low-income entrepreneurs. While it's not profitable for most banks to make the relatively small loans that these businesses need, lending funds to a microenterprise decreases the bank's risk. Between 1990 and 1995, microenterprise sources loaned more than $44 million to small U.S. businesses. By 1995 there were about 250 microenterprise lenders operating in 45 states.

have needs that traditional banks might not feel comfortable with. Bob Kochman, a Mack/Isuzu truck dealer in Houston, Texas, turned to Associates Commercial Corp., a financing subsidiary of Ford Motor Company, after a series of unsatisfactory interactions with his commercial banker. The finance company understood the dealer's need for up-front funds to pay for the new trucks that he would later sell to customers. Kochman now has no intention of returning to traditional bankers for his financing needs.[12]

Pension Funds

Public and private **pension funds** pool contributions by employees, or by an employer on behalf of its employees, and invest these funds to provide retirement benefits. Public pension funds generate retirement benefits for U.S. federal and state government employees. Major firms such as General Motors, IBM, and MCI Communications have established private pension funds.

Because pension funds manage a large amount of money, they play an important role in channeling funds from individuals to corporations and government agencies. Pension funds normally do not provide direct loans to firms, but they do invest heavily in corporate and Treasury bonds. For that reason, pension funds are creditors to corporations and the government. And, because they also purchase common stock of corporations, they are, like all stockholders, partial owners of corporations.

Insurance Companies

Insurance companies collect premiums from selling property, casualty, health, life, and other types of insurance. They invest those funds until they must make payments to their policyholders. Like pension funds, insurance companies channel large amounts of money to other firms and to government agencies as they purchase Treasury bonds, corporate bonds, and stocks.[13]

Brokerage Houses

Brokerage houses, or securities firms, are important financial intermediaries. For example, a securities firm can serve as a broker to execute the purchase of stocks or bonds for an individual investor or one of the institutional investors mentioned earlier—perhaps a pension fund or an insurance company.[14] They also help firms obtain funds by finding investors that are willing to purchase the stocks or bonds the firms are issuing.

The Evolution of Financial Services

The traditional functions of depository and nondepository institutions began to blur during the 1980s, when the federal government removed some restrictions that determined which types of institutions could provide which services. As Ken Kaul, managing director at the New York investment banking firm Sandler O'Neill & Partners, observed, "As recently as just a few years ago it would have taken even a fairly new financial analyst about 10 seconds to review the balance sheet of a financial institution and determine whether it was that of a bank or a thrift. Nowadays, even a fairly experienced financial analyst would need to spend a few minutes in making this determination."[15]

Consider NationsBank Corp., the fourth-largest U.S. commercial bank, which is based in Charlotte, North Carolina. Twenty years ago, federal regulations would have prevented NationsBank from offering even an interest-bearing checking account. Now it provides those—plus corporate loans, brokerage services, residential mortgage loans, and international loans. In addi-

✓ pension funds

Institutions that pool contributions by employees, or by an employer on behalf of its employees, and invest the funds to provide retirement benefits.

tion, it competes with finance companies by providing loans to small firms, and it competes with brokerage houses by assisting companies in preparing new stock issues.[16]

Similarly, savings institutions such as California's Glendale Federal Bank, the seventh-largest thrift institution in the United States, now offer services that only commercial banks and finance companies could have offered two decades ago.[17] Figure 21.2 lists the traditional services provided by financial institutions. And insurance companies such as Aetna and Transamerica offer financial services, including mutual funds, for investors. Brokerage houses such as Merrill Lynch offer not only traditional brokerage services but also mutual funds and loans for firms and individuals.

In fact, the offerings by nonbanks are now so varied that one banking consultant and author, Charles Wendel, has questioned the small firm's need for traditional banks and savings institutions. "The point is that there are a lot of nonbank providers of both transaction processing and investment or borrowing services for small businesses," Wendel said.[18]

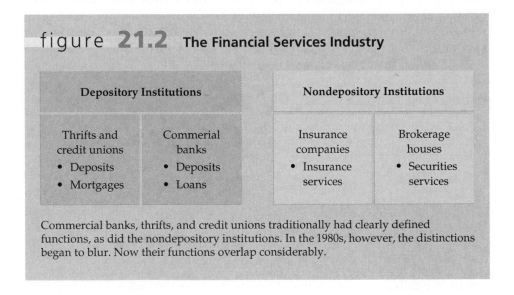

figure **21.2** **The Financial Services Industry**

Depository Institutions		Nondepository Institutions	
Thrifts and credit unions • Deposits • Mortgages	Commerial banks • Deposits • Loans	Insurance companies • Insurance services	Brokerage houses • Securities services

Commercial banks, thrifts, and credit unions traditionally had clearly defined functions, as did the nondepository institutions. In the 1980s, however, the distinctions began to blur. Now their functions overlap considerably.

The winner of the 1994 Emerging Entrepreneur of the Year award seems to agree with Wendel's views. Wayne Miller, owner of MicroVoice Applications, Inc., a software development company, transferred his business to Merrill Lynch when traditional banks were unable to pay him a satisfactory interest rate on the high cash balances in his company's checking account. (Corporations cannot own an interest-bearing checking account, according to federal regulations.) For payroll tax purposes, Miller keeps a separate checking account at a commercial bank to handle his company's payroll needs. He also admits to feeling that his corporate checking account is "small potatoes" for the large brokerage house and that he might get more attention from a traditional bank. Nevertheless, he does not doubt that he made the right choice for his needs.[19]

To understand depository institutions as they are today, we need to stop for a brief look at U.S. banking history.

Major Milestones in U.S. Banking History

The U.S. banking situation as we know it today is the end product of many social and legislative forces. We touch briefly here on only a few of the most important events that have contributed to the competition between depository and nondepository institutions.

The Great Depression and the Glass-Steagall Act

Failures of commercial banks, thrifts, and credit unions were common during the Great Depression. In 1929, there were 26,000 commercial banks and 12,000 thrifts. By 1933, those numbers were reduced to 15,000 and 8,000, respectively. As this happened, Americans lost $2.5 billion in money they had carefully set aside in 9 million savings accounts.[20] The failures resulted from a vicious cycle of depositor withdrawals, loan cancellations, loan defaults, and additional withdrawals as banks failed due to loan losses. As noted earlier in this chapter, President Franklin D. Roosevelt declared a national bank holiday on March 5, 1933, and called an emergency session of Congress to restore order.

When the banks reopened four days later, a new federal law was in place: the *Glass-Steagall Act of 1933*, designed to stabilize and regulate the banking industry. The act created the **Federal Deposit Insurance Corporation (FDIC),** a federal agency that provides insurance on bank accounts and inspects banks to ensure that they are following safe business practices. Glass-Steagall also prohibited commercial banks from paying interest on demand deposits (checking accounts) and from underwriting stocks or giving advice on stocks and bonds. These prohibitions were based on the belief that most banks that failed during the Depression had been dabbling in stock investments.

Modern research indicates that these beliefs were unfounded.[21] Nevertheless, Glass-Steagall remains in effect, even though attempts to revise it were made in 1988 and 1991. Another bill to revise Glass-Steagall is under debate in Congress at the time of this writing.

The International Debt Crisis

The provisions in Glass-Steagall and other laws that established interest-rate ceilings for deposit accounts at commercial banks and thrifts and that prohibited interest-bearing checking accounts blossomed into trouble in the late 1970s and early 1980s. During that period, inflation was high, and investors began moving funds into nonbanks, which were offering high-yield interest-bearing accounts.

As nonbanks began invading their territory and stealing away their customers, large commercial banks looked elsewhere for profits. Many of them hit upon the idea of loaning money to the governments of less-developed countries (LDCs). Regulations on loans to U.S. businesses and individuals did not apply to loans to LDCs, and banks could charge whatever the market would bear. Unfortunately, these large banks did not consider what would happen if LDCs defaulted on their loans.

By 1989, many of the large commercial banks, such as Citicorp and BankAmerica, that had provided loans to LDCs had already experienced substantial losses. As the Mexican government and several other LDC governments announced that they could not repay their loans and in fact needed additional loans to implement economic reforms, the U.S. banking industry moved to the brink of an international debt crisis. If these large banks were to fail, confidence in the banking industry would decline and depositors might begin withdrawing their money from all banks.

Congress offered some relief by passing the Brady Plan, which allowed each LDC to negotiate a settlement with the banks that made the original loans. In the case of Mexico, banks were forced either to forgive a portion of the existing loan or to provide additional loans. Agreements followed, but the Mexican economy continued to decline. In 1995, Congress passed legislation providing funds to bail out Mexico.

5. Briefly outline the history of banking since the Great Depression.

 Federal Deposit Insurance Corporation (FDIC)

Federal agency that provides insurance on bank accounts and inspects banks to ensure they are following safe business practices.

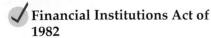

Depository Institutions Deregulation and Monetary Control Act

First step in deregulating the banking industry; also known as the *Banking Act of 1980*.

Financial Institutions Act of 1982

Legislation that further relaxed banking regulations.

Deregulation

The **Depository Institutions Deregulation and Monetary Control Act**—more commonly known as the *Banking Act of 1980*—was the first step in *deregulating the banking industry*—substantially relaxing regulations on depository institutions. Among other changes, the Banking Act of 1980:

- Eliminated ceilings on the interest rates banks can pay
- Allowed banks to offer interest-bearing checking accounts
- Expanded thrift institutions' lending powers
- Eliminated state-legislated ceilings on mortgage rates

The **Financial Institutions Act of 1982** further relaxed regulations. It authorized bank regulators to promote mergers between failing institutions and healthy institutions. It also expanded the deposit and lending powers of thrift institutions and raised the lending limits imposed on banks.

Together, these two laws enabled commercial banks and thrifts to compete more effectively with nondepository institutions. Figure 21.3 summarizes the laws' provisions. However, deregulation also opened a Pandora's box, letting loose problems that commercial banks and thrifts are still trying to solve.

figure 21.3   Deregulation Legislation: Major Provisions

Depository Institutions Deregulation and Monetary Control Act (1980)

- Eliminated ceilings on interest rates banks could pay, effective in 1986.
- Imposed uniform reserve requirements on all depository institutions.
- Made Federal Reserve services available to all depository institutions.
- Allowed NOW and other interest-paying transaction accounts.
- Raised federal deposit insurance to $100,000 per account.
- Expanded lending powers for thrift institutions.
- Eliminated state usury ceilings on mortgage loans.

Financial Institutions Act (1982)

- Authorized regulators to rescue failing banks and thrifts by promoting mergers with healthy institutions, including between states and between different types of institutions.
- Expanded deposit and lending powers of thrift institutions.
- Raised lending limits for banks to 15 percent of bank capital.
- Created federal charters for stockholder-owned savings banks.

Source: Federal Reserve Bulletin, 1981.

The Savings and Loan Crisis

Like commercial banks, thrifts were facing competition from nonbanks. In the mid-1980s, in search of higher profits, savings institutions began lending money to real estate developers to build office buildings and parks. Construction of office buildings exceeded the demand for office space, however. Some thrifts had more than 50 percent of their deposits loaned out to these developers—and when the developers defaulted on their loans, the thrifts failed.[22] The

S&L crisis was also a product of losses on investments in junk bonds (high-risk bonds issued by corporations with questionable financial backing), as well as the fraudulent behavior of management.

In 1989, the *Financial Institutions Reform, Recovery, and Enforcement Act (FIRREA)* was passed in an attempt to reduce fraud and strengthen the financial condition of savings institutions.[23] Two key provisions of the bailout bill required savings institutions to phase out their investments in junk bonds and to boost the amount of capital they hold as reserves. Current estimates set the ultimate cost to taxpayers of bailing out the failing S&Ls at between $300 billion and $500 billion by 2010. That's somewhere between $1,200 to $2,000 for each American alive in 1990.[24]

Financial Services Today

Let's now examine the broad banking functions of holding deposits and lending money, and then look at some more recent developments, particularly electronic banking and brokerage services. Table 21.1 compares depository and nondepository institutions and their sources and uses of funds.

table **21.1** Comparison of Depository and Nondepository Institutions and Services

	Depository Institutions			Nondepository Institutions			
	Commercial Banks	**Thrifts (savings and loans)**	**Credit Unions**	**Finance Companies**	**Pension Funds**	**Insurance Companies**	**Brokerage Houses**
Sources of Funds	Deposits; interest on loans (including mortgages and construction loans)	Deposits; interest on loans	Member deposits; interest on loans	Corporate and government securities; interest on loans	Employee/ employer contributions; earnings on corporate and Treasury bonds; corporate stock	Premiums paid by policyholders; investment earnings	Investment earnings
Uses of Funds	Commercial loans; individual loans (including mortgages); lines of credit	Individual loans (especially mortgages); construction loans	Short-term loans; mortgage loans	Short-term loans to individuals and small firms	Retirement funds	Treasury bonds; corporate bonds; payments to policyholders	Payments to investors
Types of Accounts	Checking accounts; NOW and Super NOW accounts; CDs; MMDAs; money market mutual funds; EFT (including ATSs)	Savings accounts; NOW and Super NOW accounts; MMDAs; ATSs	Savings accounts; share-draft accounts; MMDAs				

Holding Deposits

**negotiable order of with-
drawal (NOW) account**

Interest-bearing checking account that
requires a large minimum balance and
provides unlimited check-writing
privileges.

Super NOW account

Checking account that requires a larger
minimum balance and pays higher interest than a NOW account.

**automatic transfer from sav-
ings (ATS) accounts**

Linked checking and savings accounts
in which amounts are transferred between the accounts as needed.

share-draft account

Interest-bearing account offered by
credit unions that uses drafts—the
credit union equivalent of checks.

certificate of deposit (CD)

Time deposit that pays an annual interest rate on a fixed amount for a specified period and then repays the full
principal at the end of the period.

commercial paper

Short-term debt instrument that financial institutions and large corporations
sell to raise funds.

**money market deposit account
(MMDA)**

Combined demand and time deposit
account that allows a limited amount
of check writing per month and
requires a relatively large minimum
deposit.

money market mutual funds

Investments that are offered by banks
and independently established financial institutions and hold high-quality,
liquid assets.

All depository institutions, from commercial banks to credit unions, accept money for deposit in checking and savings or time deposit accounts. In discussing the money supply, we explained the basic form and function of checking accounts, as well as savings and time deposit accounts.

Interest-Bearing Checking Accounts Besides the standard checking account, banks now offer interest-bearing accounts. The **negotiable order of withdrawal (NOW) account** is an interest-bearing checking account that requires a large minimum balance and provides unlimited check-writing privileges. Although the interest paid on a NOW account is less than that paid on a savings account, these accounts have the advantage of being more liquid. The **Super NOW account** pays an even higher interest rate but also requires a higher minimum balance than a NOW account.

Similar to NOW accounts, **automatic transfer from savings (ATS) accounts** link checking and savings accounts. When the checking account balance reaches a certain level, a built-in mechanism moves the excess into a savings account. As checks are written and the balance falls below the specified level, the mechanism goes into reverse, moving funds from the savings account back into the checking account.

Share-draft accounts represent the credit unions' entry into the battle for depositors. Drafts, which are the credit union equivalent of checks, may be written on these interest-bearing accounts.

Time Deposits Time deposits also come in a variety of forms. A **certificate of deposit (CD)** is a time deposit in which the bank pays an annual interest rate on a fixed amount for a specified period and then repays the full principal at the end of the period. CDs were initially nonnegotiable—they could not be resold or redeemed prior to maturity. That changed in 1961, when Citibank introduced the negotiable certificate of deposit for deposits over $100,000. Most major banks now offer negotiable CDs. The total amount invested in CDs in 1994 was $350 billion.

Commercial paper is another name for a short-term debt instrument that financial institutions and large corporations sell to raise funds. Commercial paper is sold not only by banks but also by larger corporations such as AT&T. Instead of borrowing from banks to meet their short-term financial needs, large corporations raise the funds directly by selling commercial paper. Between 1970 and 1993, the amount of commercial paper in circulation increased 1500 percent, from $33 billion to $550 billion. This increase represents a trend that is becoming increasingly popular among corporations, which find that they can raise money more quickly and less expensively by issuing commercial paper than by taking out traditional commercial bank loans.[25]

A **money market deposit account (MMDA)** combines features of a demand and a time deposit account; it allows a limited amount of check writing per month and requires a relatively large minimum deposit. Account holders are allowed to write between 5 and 10 checks each month, and these checks are payable on demand, as are regular demand deposits. Nevertheless, MMDAs are considered to be primarily savings accounts and are therefore included in M2 rather than in M1.

Banks and independently established financial institutions both offer **money market mutual funds**—investments that hold high-quality, liquid assets such as Treasury bills and negotiable CDs. Fund owners may write checks on these accounts, usually in amounts of at least $500, and continue to earn market interest rates. Like MMDAs, money market mutual funds require relatively large minimum balances. Because mutual funds purchase financial instruments that are considered safe and very liquid, their popularity has grown substantially.

Types of Loans

The money banks receive as deposits does not sit idly in their vaults awaiting the return of depositors. Depository institutions pool the money they receive and lend it to individuals and to other businesses.

Business Loans As you learned in Chapter 20, much of the short-term financing needed by businesses is obtained through financial institutions. Working capital loans are useful for companies that incur costs well before they receive the related revenues. Global Market Information is a rapidly growing provider of information services for financial experts, especially stock market watchers. To keep up its rapid expansion, the New York firm borrowed more than $750,000 for working capital in 1994.[26]

Recall from Chapter 19 that working capital is the difference between current assets and current liabilities.

Financial institutions are a major source of funds not only for working capital but also for business capital investments. These long-term loans may be used to develop and construct a shopping center, office building, or other commercial real estate project; to purchase equipment to update a factory for flexible manufacturing of the type we saw in Chapter 10; or for other similar purposes.

Depository institutions that have funds available for only a very short period of time typically lend their funds to other depository institutions that need funds for a day or a week. They make these loans through the *federal funds market*. This type of lending does not put money directly into the economy, but it is a loan to a business.

You may recall from Chapter 20 that commercial banks also provide lines of credit for creditworthy customers.

Consumer Loans Banks and other financial institutions make loans to individuals as well as to other businesses. Many of you reading this chapter already have consumer loans to pay for your education; others may have installment loans to purchase automobiles and other expensive items.

In some cases, lenders have arrangements with manufacturers or retailers to make purchases easier for consumers. For example, Associates Commercial Corp., which—as we mentioned earlier—provided financing to Bob Kochman's Mack/Isuzu dealership in Houston, also offers financing to Kochman's customers on the trucks they buy. Kochman receives a portion of the interest paid to the finance company.[27] Individuals who have consumer loans must make monthly payments to the lender over a specific period, often from two to six years, to repay principal and interest.

Most financial institutions, particularly thrifts, offer mortgage loans. Individuals financing the purchase of a home repay the loan over its term, usually 15 to 30 years. Mortgages may have fixed or floating interest rates. Individuals holding adjustable-rate mortgages (ARMs) benefit during recessionary periods when interest rates are low, but they are at a disadvantage when interest rates rise.

Commercial banks and thrifts have seen a number of potential mortgage customers turn away from them recently. Big mortgage companies like Prudential and GE Capital are capturing large parts of the mortgage loan market that would have been an important source of income for banks and thrifts just a decade ago.[28]

Electronic Banking

Technology has made banking transactions more convenient for businesses, institutions, and individuals, primarily by reducing the volume of cash transactions. Many organizations rely heavily on **electronic funds transfer (EFT)**, a mechanism for transmitting funds to and from financial institutions. The federal government, for example, uses EFT to conduct large payment transactions with banks or other businesses. Such transactions include deposits of paychecks for federal employees, Social Security payments, pension payments, and even payments for the purchase of securities.

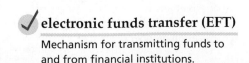

electronic funds transfer (EFT)

Mechanism for transmitting funds to and from financial institutions.

doing business

Citibank's Budapest Branch Bypasses Paper Checks

As American banks scurry to become global forces, expanding their markets worldwide, U.S. banking giant Citibank has opened offices in Budapest, where it is offering services intended to move its customers directly into the age of automated teller machines (ATMs) and electronic funds transfer. Sylvia Bornemisza-Wahr, the marketing and branch director of the Budapest offices, described the bank's plans: "We are not introducing checks. We believe Hungary will develop from cash to plastic and miss the paper phase." This will be a major revolution in a country where bank customers traditionally have had to stand in line for hours for simple transactions like depositing cash in their accounts or withdrawing it. Contrast that with Citibank's 24-hour phone service transactions and Citicard ATM transactions.

Citibank chose Budapest as a test site for the Eastern European market, where it would like to become the leading supplier of financial services. The company chose Budapest because it believes the city has a natural customer base, in terms of both income and background in technology. "These people are engineers, and some of the finest software in the world has been developed in Hungary," Bornemisza-Wahr noted.

Citibank hopes to show a profit in Budapest within three years. If its plans work out, its next move will be to introduce credit cards, which currently are used only by the elite.

Source: Based on Jane Perlez, "Citibank in Budapest: ATMs and Potted Palms," *New York Times,* June 22, 1995.

Electronic banking has become especially desirable as people seek to use their limited time more efficiently. Banks that once offered convenience by setting up branches in multiple neighborhood locations are now providing electronic money services in various locations—both in the United States and abroad. For a look at a U.S. bank's attempt to move one Eastern European country directly from currency transactions to automated transactions, see the doing business box entitled "Citibank's Budapest Branch Bypasses Paper Checks."

Automated Teller Machines (ATMs) The most familiar form of EFT is the **automated teller machine (ATM)**, which allows bank customers to withdraw funds from their account by typing in a unique personal identification number (PIN)—known only by the customer and the bank—and a withdrawal amount. A great advantage of ATMs is that they can be used at any time and in a variety of locations. One enterprising bank, Georgia-based Bank South, has even installed ATMs at eight McDonald's restaurants, believing parents will like the idea of banking while treating their children to a Happy Meal.[29]

ATMs also enable a customer to deposit funds, to check account balances, and—in some installations—to submit loan applications. Wells Fargo & Co., one of the first banks to offer 24-hour banking, has developed a highly sophisticated network of cash machines that give customers access to their IRAs, CDs, and mutual fund accounts. In addition, customers can use the machines to pay bills and can even get a printout showing their full bank statement.[30]

 automated teller machine (ATM)

Form of electronic funds transfer in which bank customers may withdraw funds at any time and in a variety of locations using a private personal identification number (PIN).

In effect, ATMs have created a new kind of banking system. NationsBank's CEO Hugh McColl described the goals he's setting for that institution: "We want you to be able to bank with us 24 hours a day, seven days a week, 365 days a year, anytime you want to, anyway you want to, from anywhere you want to."[31] According to some researchers, ATM and telephone transactions already outnumber transactions at branches of traditional large retail banks.

Because transactions involving human tellers cost 6 to 12 times as much as ATM transactions, many banks are now attempting to woo customers to use ATMs. In early 1995, First National Bank of Chicago offered several new types of checking accounts that allow free unlimited use of ATMs but only four to six free visits to human tellers each month. Customers are charged a fee, sometimes as high as $3, for each additional interaction with human tellers. If successful, such accounts would allow tellers to concentrate on selling the bank's products instead of handling routine deposit and withdrawal procedures.[32]

Debit Cards **Debit cards**, which represent the latest step toward a cashless society, are bank-issued cards that can be used directly to purchase goods and services. The card number is read and transmitted through an electronic network linked to the issuing bank; the owner's checking account balance is then reduced by the amount of the purchase. Many large supermarkets now offer debit card privileges. Some state governments have recently begun trials of debit cards for transactions formerly handled through food stamps.

Recordkeeping Banks and other businesses send billions of dollars of payment transactions daily via EFT. The computerized recordkeeping that documents the transactions can help banks tailor specialized services to customer needs. For example, Wells Fargo's system now analyzes customer credit histories to determine whether the bank should honor overdrafts. As a result, even though Wells Fargo honored twice as many overdrawn checks in 1993, customers made good on so many of them that the bank's overdraft losses fell by 10 percent.[33]

Discount Brokerage Services

Although the Glass-Steagall Act of 1933 prohibits banks from providing advice on stocks and bonds or underwriting stocks, many banks have subverted this law by providing discount brokerage services. Unlike traditional stockbrokers who offer advice about which stocks are "safe" or risky, discount brokers merely sell or purchase stocks for their clients.

Ensuring the Safety of Customers' Funds

The ability to earn interest on savings has helped convince customers to deposit more than $2 trillion in banks and credit unions. Their decisions in part reflect their confidence that the deposits are safe; they are protected by a network of insurance guarantees and by actions the institutions themselves take to reduce risk.

Protection Through Insurance

The Federal Deposit Insurance Corporation (FDIC), as mentioned earlier in this chapter, was created by the Glass-Steagall Act of 1933. The FDIC insures deposits in commercial banks up to a maximum of $100,000 per account. It provides this insurance through the Bank Insurance Fund (BIF), which accumulates its funds by charging premiums from member banks. The Savings Association Insurance Fund (SAIF), also operated by the FDIC and financed by premiums paid by member thrifts, protects money deposited in savings banks

✓ **debit card**

Bank-issued card that can be used directly to purchase goods and services.

7. Discuss bank safety and outline the types of risks financial institutions face.

and S&Ls. Credit unions carry insurance through a fund run by the National Credit Union Association (NCUA). The FDIC and the NCUA effectively stabilize the banking industry by providing insurance for depositors.

Figure 21.4, which shows bank failures between 1934 and 1993, points to the increasing difficulty faced by the FDIC in trying to protect banks from failure. One problem smaller members of the banking industry face is the FDIC policy of "too big to fail." Under this policy, the FDIC applies different rules to large and small financial institutions on the brink of failure. For example, in the 1980s, the Boston-based Bank of New England (BNE) ranked 33 among largest U.S. bank holding companies, with more than $20 billion in assets. However, almost one-third of all BNE loans were backed by commercial real estate. When the real estate market fell apart, the bank projected that its fourth-quarter losses for 1991 would be almost double its capital. Depositors panicked and withdrew $1 billion; BNE failure was imminent. At this point, the FDIC stepped in, guaranteeing all deposits, even those exceeding $100,000. This bailout cost the FDIC $2.3 billion. Smaller banks all over the country were not so lucky. The FDIC allowed many of them to fail during this same period.[34]

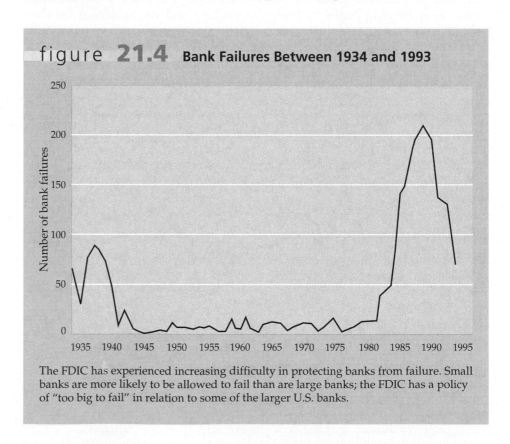

figure **21.4** **Bank Failures Between 1934 and 1993**

The FDIC has experienced increasing difficulty in protecting banks from failure. Small banks are more likely to be allowed to fail than are large banks; the FDIC has a policy of "too big to fail" in relation to some of the larger U.S. banks.

Protection Through Understanding Risks

In lending and investing the funds they receive from depositors, financial institutions must guard against three types of risk: default risk, interest-rate risk, and fraud.

Default Risk **Default risk** is simply the risk that a borrower will not repay a loan. Creditors who default fail to pay not only the interest payments but also the principal. As you saw earlier in the Bank of New England story, if defaults on loans are large and multiple, the financial institution may itself be threatened with failure.

default risk

Risk that a borrower will not repay a loan.

To minimize default risk, financial institutions carefully evaluate the credit-worthiness of borrowers. Their own credit analysts may assess the financial statements of prospective borrowers, or outside raters such as Dun & Bradstreet and TRW may perform this service for the bank or thrift. To manage risk on purchases of bonds issued by corporations, financial institutions monitor bond ratings, which are set by bond-rating agencies such as Moody's Investors Service or Standard & Poor's Corporation. Most financial institutions recognize that no matter how carefully they check on creditors, some will default; nevertheless, they do their best to minimize these cases.

Banks also attempt to limit their exposure to default risk by diversifying their credit across a wide variety of industries. For example, Florida-based Barnett Bank and Sun Bank extend credit not only to firms in the tourist industry but also to firms in many other industries as well. A slacking off in tourism will therefore affect only a small proportion of the credit they provide.

Interest-Rate Risk Many financial institutions—commercial banks, savings banks, pension funds, insurance companies, and others—hold fixed-rate mortgages and corporate bonds. Consequently, they are exposed to **interest-rate risk**, the risk that the interest they receive on loans will be less than the interest they must pay out on deposits.

Consider a bank that lent $20,000 for a 30-year, 7 percent fixed-rate mortgage in 1968. (Yes, you could buy a house for $20,000 in 1968.) Let's assume the bank obtained the funds for that loan primarily by issuing $20,000 worth of three-month certificates of deposit, on which it paid 3 percent. In 1968, that was an acceptable situation—the bank received 7 percent interest on the mortgage, paid out 3 percent to its depositors, and kept 4 percent for expenses and profit. Of course, as the CDs matured every three months, the bank had to sell new ones at competitive market rates to pay back money owed to customers whose CDs were maturing.

By 1982, banks that held these 7 percent fixed-rate mortgages were pleading with customers to refinance. Some actually sent out letters offering to reduce the principal due if mortgage holders would pay off their low-interest mortgages.[35] Why? Because interest rates had soared through the roof. The bank was still receiving 7 percent interest on the mortgages, but to be competitive, it had to pay the going market rate on new CDs—a rate that exceeded 10 percent. And that's a loss of 3 percent—or, in other words, the bank had suffered from interest-rate risk.

A similar risk exists with bonds. Banks and individuals purchasing corporate and Treasury bonds consider both the interest that the bond pays—a source of income—and the bond's ability to be resold. A bond's resale value depends on many things, as you will learn in Chapter 22, but let's keep this discussion simple by assuming nothing influences the price of our bond except rising or falling interest rates.

So let's assume further that you win $10,000 in the lottery. Being a smart person, you don't buy more lottery tickets; instead, you buy a bond that pays 9 percent interest annually. Let's also assume that two years later you decide to sell your bond to help finance a small business you are about to open. If the interest rate on new bonds is 7 percent, you should have no problem selling your bond. After all, you are offering a good deal—your bond pays 2 percent more than any new bond an investor could buy. You might even be able to ask a bit more than $10,000 for your bond because many people would be eager to have this good source of income.

But what if interest rates are now 12 percent? Remember those fixed-rate mortgages in the 1960s? Interest rates do rise, and when they do, people who want to sell their bonds have to give people a reason to buy them. So they lower their prices and settle for less than the full amount of principal. You may only be able to get $9,500 instead of the full $10,000 you invested, but if you need the money, you'll sell.

Monitoring Financial Risks

To launch its interactive Full Service Network, Time Warner Inc. formed a global, strategic partnership with US West; Toshiba Corp.; and ITOCHU Corp., the world's largest trading group. Marketwide, the annual earnings potential from new business areas such as catalog shopping, movie rentals, and video games—as well as the new distribution outlet for Time Warner entertainment products—is in the hundreds of billions of dollars. However, the potential losses are enormous as well, so the financial institutions backing the partnership closely monitor all long-term risks against default, changes in interest rates, and fraud. Shown here is the Carousel™, FSN's "navigator," from which users can access specific services. The wheel-like format allows for future expansion as new services are added to the network.

 interest-rate risk

Risk that the interest banks receive on loans will be less than the interest they must pay out on deposits.

Nondepository Institutions

Nonbanks obtain funds from sources other than deposits. For example, investment bankers such as Lamaute Capital, Inc., obtain funds from new stock issues by serving as a financial intermediary between companies that wish to issue stock and investors that wish to buy it. CEO Denise Lamaute (standing), who is also a tax attorney, finds that business development seminars like this one are an effective way to win new clients.

For just these reasons, some banks and other financial institutions attempt to limit their bond and fixed-rate mortgage holdings. Instead, they specialize in floating-rate loans or mortgages, in which they reserve the right to adjust their interest rates periodically in response to some indicator of current rates. By so doing, they reduce interest-rate risk.

Fraud Although probably less common than the other risks, fraud is the most highly publicized form of risk. For example, the S&L crisis of the 1980s was to some extent due to the fraud perpetrated by management. During that crisis, some high-ranking bank officers approved loans to friends who were not creditworthy in return for special favors, sometimes reciprocal loans at equally favorable terms. Other bank managers hung expensive art on their walls, labeling it an "investment."[36] In the end, a few went to jail, although most were allowed to retire quietly.

Banks and other financial institutions have many built-in safeguards against fraud, but staying ahead of computer-savvy criminals is an ongoing challenge.

The Federal Reserve System

8. Describe the components of the Federal Reserve System.

At the peak of all the institutions and agencies discussed in this chapter is the **Federal Reserve System (the Fed)**—a government agency, consisting of a network of 12 district banks, which regulates and monitors the banking industry. It was created by the Federal Reserve Act of 1913 as part of a centralized banking system.[37] As you will see, the power of the Fed extends well beyond the banking industry to the economy as a whole.

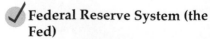 **Federal Reserve System (the Fed)**

Government agency, consisting of a network of 12 district banks, which regulates and monitors the banking industry.

Structure of the Fed

The 12 district banks that make up the network that is the Federal Reserve System are owned by member banks, which purchase stock in the district bank. Figure 21.5 shows the location of each district bank and the region it monitors.

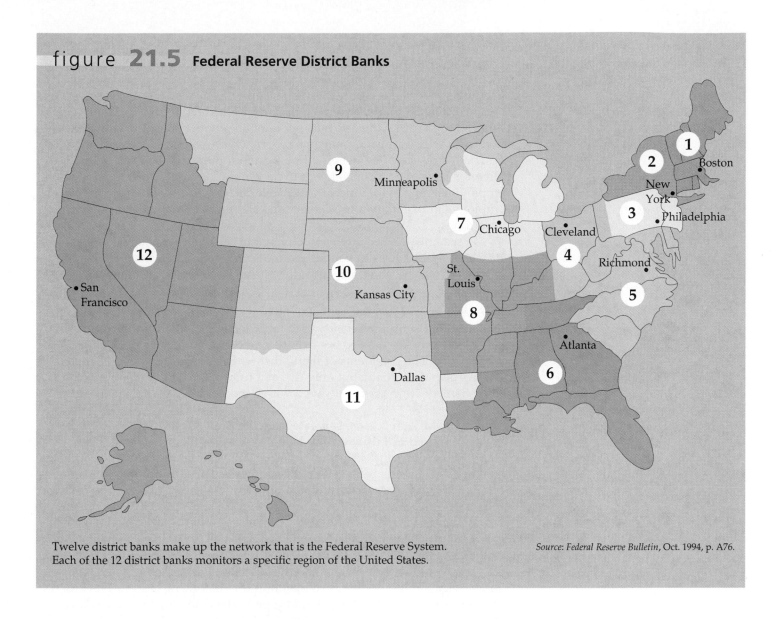

figure **21.5** **Federal Reserve District Banks**

Twelve district banks make up the network that is the Federal Reserve System.
Each of the 12 district banks monitors a specific region of the United States.

Source: Federal Reserve Bulletin, Oct. 1994, p. A76.

All national commercial banks are required to belong to the Federal Reserve System; state banks can choose to belong but are not required to do so. Approximately 4,000 commercial banks now belong to the Fed.

The Fed is headed by a seven-member board of governors; board members are appointed by the president and are confirmed by Congress. Board members serve for 14 years, and openings occur on a rotating basis, with one membership opening up every two years. The chair of the Federal Reserve System holds a powerful position, advising the president and testifying before Congress. The chair of the Fed is appointed for a four-year term.

The Functions of the Fed

The Fed establishes and implements monetary policy and negotiates economic matters between the United States and foreign governments. The 12 district banks provide a variety of services for member banks, including clearing checks, making discount loans, examining state member banks, and evaluating some merger applications. In August 1995, for example, the Fed announced it would hold hearings on a proposed megamerger in which Fleet Financial Group Inc. would acquire Shawmut National Corp.[38]

9. Describe the three tools that the Fed uses to control the money supply.

Controlling the Money Supply

You may recall from Chapter 2 that *monetary policy* involves making adjustments to the money supply aimed at influencing economic performance. The Fed increases money supply if economic growth is weak and decreases it if excessive economic growth seems to bring with it the threat of inflation. This is often a tough call. If the Fed puts into motion a policy meant to stimulate economic growth, businesses may markedly increase sales and hire new employees, but prices may rise steeply, bringing about inflation. Conversely, the Fed's attempts to slow economic growth to prevent inflation may produce rising unemployment as a by-product. The difficult decision is determining whether unemployment or inflation is a larger concern and then setting monetary policy accordingly.

To see how the Fed attempts to maintain this delicate balance, let's look at the three tools it uses to control the money supply: open market operations, changes in the discount rate, and adjustments in reserve requirements.

Open Market Operations The Federal Open Market Committee (FOMC) controls **open market operations**—the buying and selling of Treasury securities; this is the Fed's most frequently used tool for controlling the money supply. All seven governors of the Fed are members of the FOMC, which meets every six weeks or so. The presidents of the 12 district banks all attend FOMC meetings and participate in them, but only five at a time are voting members.[39] The Reserve Bank of New York is always a voting member since it holds 30 percent of the Fed's assets.

The FOMC's funds are separate from the funds flowing through the banking system used by businesses and individuals. For that reason, an FOMC purchase of government securities from a bank releases more money into the banking system. The bank selling the security receives additional funds that it can use to make loans to individuals and businesses, and they in turn increase their spending. In the end, the entire economy is stimulated by this infusion of new money.

Similarly, if the Fed sells some of its securities to banks, it siphons off part of the funds the banks have for making loans to individuals and businesses. This in turn reduces the ability of individuals and businesses to purchase goods and services, and it increases competition for customers. During this process, the risk of inflation is reduced because prices tend to remain stable or even to fall.

Changes in the Discount Rate A second tool available for adjusting the money supply is the **discount rate**, the interest rate the Fed charges on loans it makes to financial institutions. It's easy to see how lower interest rates could increase the money supply. When rates are lower, financial institutions are more willing to borrow from the Fed and to use the money they borrow to make loans to their own customers. Again, the increased spending power of individuals and businesses stimulates the economy.

If the economy threatens to grow too quickly, the Fed can raise the discount rate and put the brakes on spending. Between February 1994 and February 1995, the Fed increased the discount rate on seven occasions. By July, the economy had slowed even more than the Fed intended, so it reversed its policy and reduced the discount rate by 0.25 percent.

Adjustments in Reserve Requirements The Fed's third monetary policy tool is adjusting **reserve requirements**, or the percentage of deposits that depository institutions are required to maintain as a measure of security. By raising the requirements, the Fed effectively limits the number of loans banks can make to firms and individuals. By lowering the reserve requirements, as it did twice in the early 1990s, the Fed allows banks to lend out a larger portion of their deposited funds.

open market operations

The buying and selling of Treasury securities controlled by the Federal Open Market Committee.

discount rate

The interest rate the Fed charges on loans it makes to financial institutions.

reserve requirements

The percentage of deposits that depository institutions are required to maintain as a measure of security.

Although the Fed can use any of its three tools to increase or decrease the money supply, it typically relies on open market operations to achieve its goals. Whatever the Fed's actions, U.S. businesses monitor them closely, trying to get an advance jump on how conditions might change. Sometimes even good news can trigger major reactions in the marketplace, as when the Dow Jones industrial average dropped more than 57 points on July 19, 1995, when Fed Chairman Alan Greenspan said the outlook for the economy "on balance is encouraging."[40] Investors were spooked when they interpreted that statement as an indication that the Fed would not cut the discount rate any further.

The Current Banking Environment: Interstate Banking and "Merger Mania"

As we reach the end of the twentieth century, several trends are rippling throughout the banking world. One is the ability to operate a bank in several states. Another is the rush to create megabanks. Finally, the increasingly global nature of banking is having a profound effect on today's banking environment.

Interstate Banking

Until the mid-1980s, commercial banks were typically restricted from operating in more than one state. Seeing the advantage of interstate banking, states then began to allow banks within a specific region to expand from their home state into other states within that region.[41] The regulations were loosened further in the late 1980s and early 1990s. Beginning in 1997, barriers to interstate banking will fall completely for commercial banks.[42]

Some banks that were historically limited to their home states are already aggressively expanding into several other states.[43] Ten years ago, NationsBank, First Union Corp., and Banc One were medium-sized regional banks. When interstate banking was allowed within particular regions, they expanded across state lines, entering new markets and growing at a very fast pace.[44] Today, as Table 21.2 indicates, these three are among the 10 largest banks in the United States and rival even the large New York banks.

Bank Mergers

The 10 banks in Table 21.2 are technically bank holding companies, companies that own more than one bank. They did not simply cross state lines and create new branches; rather, they acquired existing out-of-state banks or merged with them. For example, in early 1995, Fleet Bank, a Northeast commercial bank based in Providence, Rhode Island, acquired Boston-based Shawmut National Bank, specifically because the deal gave Fleet a bigger share of the market in New England. In June 1995, First Union Corp. acquired First Fidelity Bancorp of Newark, New Jersey's largest and most prominent commercial bank. In July 1995, two major mergers were announced: PNC Bank Corp. of Pittsburgh announced plans to acquire Midlantic Corp., then New Jersey's largest bank, and the First Chicago Corporation and NBD Corporation announced plans to merge.[45] And in August 1995, Chemical Bank and Chase Manhattan announced plans to merge, a move which would make it the largest bank holding company in the United States.

Like a gathering hurricane, bank mergers are picking up speed and force. According to some banking industry analysts, the number of U.S. banks will shrink by half in the next decade.[46] Tough competition from nonbanks is part of

10. Describe three important trends in the current banking environment.

table 21.2

Top 10 U.S. Bank Holding Companies

Bank Holding Company	Assets (in billions of dollars) 7/13/95
Citicorp	$269
BankAmerica	223
Chemical Bank	185
NationsBank	184
J.P. Morgan	167
First Union Corp.	124
Chase Manhattan	121
First Chicago NBD	120
Bankers Trust New York	107
Banc One	88

Source: Stephanie Strom, "First Chicago and NBD to Merge as Banks Scurry to Grow," *New York Times*, July 13, 1995, p. D5.

doing business

Banc One's CEO Learned His Management Style at His Father's Knee

The CEO of Columbus, Ohio–based Banc One Corporation, John B. McCoy, is the third generation in his family to head Banc One, and he claims that bank management advice has been passed down from grandfather to father to son. According to McCoy, his grandfather advised his father to attend Stanford University's business school because "the future would require new thinking and . . . 'that's what they teach out there.'" McCoy repeated that advice to his son and added one more important line: that the young McCoy should remember to hire good people because "Better people will make you look better."

The advice apparently worked, for Banc One is now the tenth-largest bank holding company in the United States, with affiliates in 13 states. During the mid-1970s, Banc One was a medium-sized commercial bank with most of its operations concentrated in Ohio. After deregulation of the banking industry during the 1980s, Banc One launched an aggressive acquisitions program; in the last decade alone, the bank has acquired 112 institutions.

McCoy fills some of the key positions in acquired companies from the companies themselves and others from within the larger organization. But many other senior managers are hired from outside the banking industry because McCoy doesn't want Banc One to become inbred, as some giant corporations did in the 1970s and 1980s.

Wherever his people come from, McCoy encourages them to develop an entrepreneurial attitude and to take advantage of the experience and organization that are available company-wide. His goal is to foster both strong management and experi-

mentation in his organization, which is large, decentralized, and successful. And that requires both creativity and teamwork. McCoy tells the story of being asked to write a three-page paper in a class at Stanford. The length was the easy part; but he was required to write it with four other people: "I could rip off a 20-page paper in no time, but to be told you had to make it three pages and there had to be five people agreeing with what was said—that . . . taught you a lot about teamwork."

To maintain consistency and control in the large decentralized organization, Banc One currently uses a sophisticated integrated information system, Management Information and Control System (MICS). McCoy believes MICS is one of the reasons Banc One is a leader in its market. The system requires all member banks to account for operations in the same way, using the same format, so comparison is relatively easy. That means that problems show up quickly and that people can be referred to other branches for training.

McCoy has training programs in place for everyone from senior executives to the clerical staffers who answer customer queries by phone. Much of that training is done in-house, at Banc One College, in Columbus, Ohio. It seems that McCoy is intent not only on hiring good people, as his father taught him, but on making sure that they stay head and shoulders above the crowd.

Source: Based on Peter D. Franklin, "Number 1 at Banc One," *Stanford Business School Magazine*, Sept. 1994, pp. 14–17.

---

the reason for these mergers, for the megabanks can yield savings from lean and mean management and economies of scale in computerized service equipment and other areas. Another part is the desire to strengthen a particular kind of service offering, such as a prized credit card or mortgage business, or, as pointed out earlier, to expand a customer base into new regions of the country.

So far, most of the mergers have been friendly deals, either between equals or between a large organization and a willing small partner. As the competition for remaining banks continues, however, unfriendly takeovers may become more common, according to some observers.[47] Banc One has already tested the waters in that area in a recent bid for Bank of Boston—a bid that was withdrawn, as you will see in the Critical Thinking Case at the end of this chapter. For a closer look at the management style of Banc One's CEO, see the doing business box entitled "Banc One's CEO Learned His Management Style at His Father's Knee."

Mergers may be good news or bad news for bank customers. Although consumers will find multiple local banks replaced by a few regional banks after the mergers, they should also find more and better services. Whether those megabanks will have the same sense of loyalty toward the communities they serve remains to be seen.

The Globalization of Financial Institutions

Like every other aspect of business we have discussed in this text, U.S. banking is now a worldwide activity. Many U.S. financial institutions have expanded overseas to capitalize on global opportunities not offered in the United States. In branches established in England and Germany, for example, Citicorp and BankAmerica are able to sell stocks and bonds for corporations, a service they are prohibited from offering in the United States.

The large U.S. banks that expand overseas face intense competition from large banks based in other countries. Indeed, while American banks may seem large by our standards, they are smaller than the larger banks in other countries. The largest U.S. bank at the time of this writing is Citicorp, and its assets—$269 billion—are less than one-half the assets of the fifth-largest Japanese bank. No U.S. bank is ranked among the 20 largest banks of the world. The seven largest banks are based in Japan.

U.S. banks have also established branches in developing countries with high economic growth rates, such as Malaysia and Singapore. As corporations in those countries expand, they will need not only more funding but other financial services as well.

U.S. mutual funds, pension funds, and insurance companies are also expanding into foreign markets. Insurance companies are moving into areas where few firms and households have insurance or where economic growth is creating a need for more insurance. Mutual funds focusing completely on investments in one or more foreign countries are allowing even small investors to capitalize on global opportunities. Chapter 22 will cover the mutual funds and the securities markets in detail.

Reviewing *Money and Financial Institutions*

What Is Money?

1. **Describe the functions and characteristics of money.** Money has three functions: It serves as a medium of exchange, a unit of account, and a store of value. As such, money is anything generally accepted as a means of buying goods and services. The characteristics that allow money to perform these functions are that it is easily divisible and portable, and its value is clearly established. Furthermore, money is durable and stable, and it cannot easily be counterfeited.

2. **Identify the categories of money and describe their components.** There are several definitions of money. The most widely known are M1 and M2. M1, the narrowest definition, consists of currency and demand deposits (checking accounts). Because they are considered equivalent to currency, travelers' checks, money orders, and cashier's checks are also included in M1. M2, known as *near money,* includes everything in M1 plus savings deposits, time deposits, and other deposits on which check writing is limited or not allowed. Examples of time deposits are CDs and money market accounts. Credit cards, although not considered a form of money, are increasingly being used as a medium of exchange.

The Banking System

3. **Define** *depository institutions* **and describe the three major types of depository institutions.** Depository institutions, as their name implies, obtain funds from deposits. The three major categories of depository institutions are commercial banks, thrift institutions, and credit unions. Commercial banks, which are chartered by the federal government or by the states, accept deposits and make loans. Thrift institutions (savings banks and S&Ls) provide interest-bearing accounts and make mortgage loans; S&Ls are regulated by the federal government and savings banks are usually regulated by individual states. Credit unions also accept deposits and make loans. However, they are established by and for people with a common bond. With deregulation, the services provided by different types of depository institutions are becoming less and less distinct.

4. **Define** *nondepository institutions,* **or nonbanks, and explain their role as financial intermediaries.** Nondepository institutions, or nonbanks, obtain their funds from sources other than deposits. They include finance companies, pension funds, insurance companies, and brokerage houses. Finance companies, which obtain their funds from short-term loans to individuals and to other firms, focus on loans for these customers. They usually charge high rates of interest. Pension funds provide retirement benefits for a company's employees by investing in corporate and government bonds. Insurance companies use the funds obtained from premiums to purchase government and corporate bonds and stocks. Brokerage houses are intermediaries between stock and bond investors and sellers.

5. **Briefly outline the history of banking since the Great Depression.** Many banks failed during the Great Depression. In 1933, after passage of the Glass-Steagall Act, the banking industry was relatively stable, with financial institutions strictly limited in the types of activities they might engage in. Then in the 1970s, the emergence of nonbanks led to heavy competition among members of the financial community—depository and nondepository institutions alike. The 1980 Depository Institutions Deregulation and Monetary Control Act and the Financial Institutions Act of 1982 introduced deregulation—relaxation of controls over the services the different types of institutions could provide. Several factors—including the international debt crisis and the S&L crisis—led to renewed restrictions on bank activities.

6. **Identify and describe the varied services provided by financial institutions today.** The basic functions of financial institutions are to hold deposits and make loans. However, depository institutions now offer a variety of services, including not only the traditional checking and savings accounts, but also NOW and Super NOW accounts, ATS accounts, share-draft accounts, CDs, commercial paper (also issued by large corporations), money market deposit accounts (MMDAs), and money market mutual funds. While all time deposit accounts require minimum balances for a specified period of time, some, such as MMDAs, also provide check-writing privileges.

7. **Discuss bank safety and outline the types of risks financial institutions face.** Bank customers are protected by a network of insurance guarantees and by actions banks take to reduce risk. The Federal Deposit Insurance Corporation (FDIC), created by the Glass-Steagall Act of 1933, provides for the protection of deposits up to $100,000. The FDIC also inspects financial institutions to ensure that they are following safe business practices. Commercial banks are insured under the Bank Insurance Fund (BIF) and thrifts are insured under the Savings Association Insurance Fund (SAIF). Financial institutions must guard against three types of risk: default risk (the risk that a borrower will not repay a loan), interest-rate risk (the risk that the interest they receive on loans will be less than the interest they must pay out on deposits), and fraud.

The Federal Reserve System

8. **Describe the components of the Federal Reserve System.** The Federal Reserve System (the Fed) is the government agency responsible for regulating and monitoring the banking industry. It is a network of 12 district banks, each with its own president. All national banks are required to belong to the Fed; membership is optional for state banks. The Federal Reserve System is controlled by a seven-member board of governors, appointed by the president and confirmed by Congress for a 14-year term on a two-year rotating basis. The chair of the Fed is appointed for four years. All 12 presidents of district banks participate in meetings of the Federal Open Market Committee (FOMC), but only five can vote. The governors also are voting members of the FOMC.

9. **Describe the three tools that the Fed uses to control the money supply.** The Fed controls the money supply through open market operations—the most commonly used tool—through changing the discount rate, and through adjusting reserve requirements of member banks. Through open market operations—the buying and selling of Treasury securities held by banks—the Fed increases or decreases the money supply. This in turn stimulates or slows the economy by increasing or decreasing the amount of funds banks have available for lending. Similarly, raising or lowering the discount rate or increasing or decreasing the reserve requirement will affect the availability of funds for use as loans to businesses and individuals.

The Current Banking Environment: Interstate Banking and "Merger Mania"

10. **Describe three important trends in the current banking environment.** The following trends characterize the current banking environment. The first is interstate banking. When restrictions preventing banks from crossing state borders were relaxed, many banks took advantage of the opportunity and opened branches in other states. The second is megabanks, which are growing quickly and substantially as large banks acquire smaller banks or merge with banks from other states. The third is the globalization of banking. Although it provides vast new opportunities for U.S. banks, it has also placed these banks in an extremely competitive situation.

✓ Key Terms

money **635**
medium of exchange **635**
unit of account **635**
store of value **636**
money supply **636**
M1 **636**
currency **636**
demand deposits **636**
M2 **637**
time deposit accounts **637**
depository institutions **638**
commercial banks **638**
state banks **638**
national banks **638**
thrift institutions **639**

savings bank **639**
savings and loan associa-
   tion (S&L) **639**
credit union **639**
nondepository institutions
   640
finance company **640**
pension funds **641**
Federal Deposit Insurance
   Corporation (FDIC) **643**
Depository Institutions
   Deregulation and Mone-
   tary Control Act **644**
Financial Institutions Act
   of 1982 **644**

negotiable order of with-
   drawal (NOW) account
   646
Super NOW account **646**
automatic transfer from
   savings (ATS) accounts
   646
share-draft account **646**
certificate of deposit (CD)
   646
commercial paper **646**
money market deposit ac-
   count (MMDA) **646**
money market mutual
   funds **646**

electronic funds transfer
   (EFT) **647**
automated teller machine
   (ATM) **648**
debit card **649**
default risk **650**
interest-rate risk **651**
Federal Reserve System
   (the Fed) **652**
open market operations
   654
discount rate **654**
reserve requirements **654**

● Review Questions

1. Assuming that you owned a card shop, why would the use of money be an advantage over the barter system?

2. What is the difference between M1 and M2?

3. What are the different types of depository and nondepository institutions? Assuming that each offered only specific services, which of these would you use for each of your personal financial dealings?

4. You have just received a $5,000 bonus from your employer. You want to be able to earn interest on that money but you also want it available for use in case of unexpected expenses. In which type of checking or savings account would you consider depositing your money?

5. You have a checking account at Home National Bank, which provides EFT services. How might you take advantage of these services?

6. What role has the FDIC played in bank safety? What types of risks are a concern of financial institutions?

7. What is the Federal Reserve System? How is it structured?

8. What are the Fed's tools for controlling the money supply? How would the Fed restrict the growth of the money supply and why would it want to? How would it increase the money supply?

9. Why have financial institutions become increasingly similar in terms of the services they offer?

10. What is the relationship between interstate banking and bank mergers and acquisitions? How might recent mergers benefit consumers?

● Critical Thinking Questions

1. Is bank deregulation good for customers? Is it good for banks?

2. Should commercial banks be allowed to offer financial services such as brokerage and insurance? Should insurance companies and brokerage firms be allowed to offer banking services?

3. Is an independent monetary policy necessary, or would we be better off by allowing each administration to set its own policies?

4. Should the Federal Reserve System be independent from the U.S. president and Congress, or should the Fed merely enforce the monetary policy favored by the current administration?

5. As interstate banking continues, do you think there will eventually be only a few megabanks that control the entire market?

REVIEW CASE *A Bank Suffering from Growing Pains*[48]

United Bank of Philadelphia, a state-chartered commercial bank, is the first bank to be founded by an African-American woman since 1903. It is also Pennsylvania's only full-service, African-American-controlled bank.

Emma Chappell, the bank's founder, has a long history in banking. Her career dates back to 1960, when she began work at Philadelphia's Continental Bank as a clerk; 17 years later, she was the bank's first woman vice president. Ten years later, in 1987, she cut back to part-time work at Continental and transferred her energy to attracting African-American investors for a new bank that would, in her words, "level the playing field for all."

Chappell was successful. United Bank of Philadelphia opened its doors in March of 1992, and it turned a profit in less than two years. Its almost 4,000 shareholders are primarily (56 percent) from the community served by the bank, and they include African-American churches and businesses, as well as individual professionals, homemakers, and children. Chappell says the bank was "created to serve the African-Americans, Hispanics, and women and . . . they are the original shareholders."

In its first two years of business, United Bank grew from one office and $14.2 million in assets to seven branches and more than $95 million in assets. The branches were primarily purchases of failed banks that United bought from the federal government through the Resolution Trust Corporation, which was set up to liquidate banks that failed during the 1970s and 1980s in the savings and loan crisis. As a result of those purchases, United showed a net loss of almost $750,000 in 1994, compared with a net income of almost $870,000 in 1993.

The bank currently has about 16,000 depositors, 75 percent of them from minority groups. It has a staff of 75 (85 percent of them African Americans); 28 of those staff members were hired in 1994. Chappell's current goal is to reach $150 million in assets in the next six years and to open branches in Delaware and New Jersey within the next year.

William Michael Cunningham, an analyst who specializes in tracking and rating minority institutions, is concerned about United's rapid growth, which has reduced the bank's capital reserves to a point nearly at the limit required by regulators. Cunningham also raises the question of whether United has enough cost controls in place.

Chappell remains optimistic; she believes the downturn is temporary and that the bank will again show a good profit. The bank is currently trying to attract $2 million to $3 million in new investment capital to stabilize its position. The bank is limiting its offerings to 3,100 minority shareholders because board members want to retain United's status as a minority-owned bank, which allows it to qualify for special government programs and to continue to serve its community by providing a "level playing field."

1. Using what you have read about risk in this chapter, what recommendations would you make for ensuring that risk was minimal at United Bank of Philadelphia?

2. Using what you learned about EFT, ATMs, and computerized recordkeeping, what recommendations would you make to United Bank for using computerized systems to help contain employee costs at the seven new branches?

3. Does the danger of increased risk through further investing justify the advantages that ATMs and sophisticated information systems would offer United in your answer to question 2?

CRITICAL THINKING CASE *Battle for the Bank of Boston*

Competition to acquire smaller banks or to merge with equal-sized banks is fierce, and some players are making offers intended to prevent new major players from entering the market. One such move, by Banc One, under the leadership of John B. McCoy, brought down the CEO of Bank of Boston Corp. (For more on McCoy, see the doing business box "Banc One's CEO Learned His Management Style at His Father's Knee," on page 656.)

Bank of Boston, currently considered one of the prime targets for merger, is a 211-year-old bank that has played a major role in the history of Boston. Recently, it has supported major redevelopment projects in the city and provided financing to save the *Boston Herald* from being gobbled up by Rupert Murdoch in 1994. Now Bank of Boston may itself be gobbled up, most probably by one of the megabanks. Boston's Mayor Menino voiced the feelings of the community when he said, "I would not be real happy" if the bank is acquired by an outsider. "We don't know what the new entity would do for the community or community groups."[49]

But stockholders—65 percent of whom are mutual funds, pension funds, and other financial institutions—don't share the mayor's views. And Bank of Boston management was split about evenly between the two views. The two views were represented by two choices:

1. Acquisition of Bank of Boston by a megabank, which would pay top dollar for stock shares. Some analysts' estimates placed the price as high as $55 a share. This option favors shareholders, who want to make a profit.

2. A defensive merger with a bank of equal size, which would maintain present management in place at both banks and maintain Bank of Boston headquarters in Boston. However, the price would probably be lower than that offered by a megabank. This option favors the community, and it also favors management, which does not get downsized.

Bank of Boston's CEO, Ira Stepanian, was quietly working on a merger-of-equals deal with Philadelphia-based CoreStates Financial Corp.; the proposed agreement would give stockholders $38 per share. Stockholders were outraged by the rumored price, but community leaders were delighted.

Then came Banc One's unsolicited counteroffer: It offered $45 a share and somehow that bid was leaked to the press. Within 24 hours, the stockholders' protests over the Bank of Boston–CoreStates deal brought an end to those talks. Forty-eight hours later, Banc One withdrew its offer, and McCoy later announced that Banc One's sole purpose in making the offer was to destroy the proposed Bank of Boston–CoreStates merger. "If everyone runs around doing mergers of equals, there is nowhere for us to grow. Mergers of equals do a disservice to shareholders, and I have grown up trying to create value for my shareholders."[50]

Within another three days, the bank's board of directors met and put an end to Stepanian's 29-year career with the bank. At present, numerous rumors are circulating about which megabank will acquire Bank of Boston.

1. In considering a merger, does the management of Bank of Boston have an ethical responsibility to its community, which the bank has served for 211 years? Explain your answer in detail.

2. In considering a merger, what responsibility does the management of Bank of Boston have to its shareholders, who own the bank? Does that responsibility outweigh all others?

3. Did Banc One behave unethically in destroying the proposed merger between CoreStates and Bank of Boston? Consider both Banc One's interests and Bank of Boston stakeholders' interests in your answer. (Remember that stakeholders are all interested parties, not just shareholders.)

Critical Thinking with the ONE MINUTE MANAGER

"How's the world of banking and finance?" the One Minute Manager asked Joanna and Carlos, back in her office at the end of the day.

"I thought banking was staid and stuffy," Carlos remarked, sinking into a chair. "Instead, it looks as though it's one of the most dramatic areas of hostile takeovers in business. I sure wouldn't want to be management in a bank targeted by one of the megabanks right now."

"There is a lot going on, isn't there? Of course, there are enough banking regulations in place that megabanks have to run their proposals through a lot of people before they become final. Nevertheless, it seems there will be far fewer banks around a decade from now."

"What about you? Did you have a successful lunch with your banker? Will your company get that new computer system?" Joanna asked.

"I think so. Jim was very encouraging about our prospects for a new loan, and I was very encouraged about how much he knew about our market and our business. You know, I guess the economist from the Federal Reserve Bank of Boston was right, at least as far as our bank is concerned. I think small businesses have a good chance of being treated like valuable customers now."

1. Why are banks focusing on small businesses more than they did 10 years ago?

2. Do you think a branch of a megabank can become a part of the community it serves? Give several reasons for your answer.

3. Why would a bank holding company want to open branches in states other than the one where it is based?

American
Stock Exchange

22 Securities Markets and Investing

The securities markets are a major source of funds for businesses. As you have learned, finance managers are responsible for obtaining funds to finance their company's operations, either by borrowing from financial institutions or by issuing securities. This chapter explains the types of securities issued by companies, the concerns of investors who might purchase those securities, the markets in which securities are bought and sold, and how to track investments. After reading this chapter, you will be able to reach the learning goals below.

Learning Goals

1. Identify the types of marketable securities and the markets through which they are sold and describe the process by which companies raise funds through stock issues.

2. Differentiate between common and preferred stock.

3. Describe the characteristics of bonds and compare and contrast the different categories of bonds.

4. Explain bond yields and discuss the meaning and purpose of bond ratings.

5. Describe the purpose and types of mutual funds and derivatives.

6. Identify the categories of investors and describe five broad investment goals.

7. List and characterize the major securities markets.

8. Discuss the regulation of securities markets and securities traders.

9. Describe the process of selecting a broker and explain how to analyze securities quotations.

10. Describe the different methods of trading securities.

Go Electronic

"When you picture the securities markets, what do you see?" asked the *One Minute Manager.*

Carlos paused, then responded, "Thousands of men and women milling about the floor of the stock exchange, shouting unintelligible words and numbers, right?"

"Yes and no," replied the One Minute Manager. "Traditional markets like that are alive and well, but they are being upgraded, supplemented, and sometimes replaced by electronic markets. To survive, the securities markets, like virtually every other area of business, must step into the twentieth-century world of electronics—computers, faxes, etc. And as future businesspeople, so must you."

"But securities are traded all over the world by both small investors or huge institutions," Joanna pointed out.

"That's just the point," said the One Minute Manager. "The traditional markets are often slow and antiquated. Everything happens so fast and in so many different places, businesses need immediate, up-to-the-minute information—about the state of the economy in general or businesses and industries specifically—in order to make sound investment decisions. Only by using the latest technology can a business know whether the economy is ripe for a new stock issue, how much capital it can raise through bonds, and what these issues might cost."

Carlos interrupted: "But I recall my father calling his stockbroker—a close personal friend—and within a day he would have good, sound advice regarding his investment portfolio. With electronic transactions, you can't form such relationships—so how do you know whom you can trust, if anyone?"

The One Minute Manager smiled. "Whom would you trust more, a friend who needed 24 hours to get information for you or an acquaintance who could tell you everything you needed to know within seconds? The Charles Schwab Corp., a discount brokerage firm, can place a trade by phone, get a market update, and confirm the price of the trade within 30 seconds. And because Schwab's commissions are relatively low—the SEC removed minimal commission requirements in the 1970s—the securities markets now belong to everyone, not just large corporations or individuals with million-dollar pocketbooks."

Joanna thought for a moment. "Right, but every time I buy a stock, it goes down. I'm jinxed."

"No problem," the One Minute Manager assured her. "Many investment companies will invest your money in a variety of closely monitored securities."

"But if I want to put some money in stocks with strong growth potential and some in securities that will earn a steady income, I'll have to work with several different companies, and I just don't have the time."

"Schwab has solved that problem, too," said the One Minute Manager. "His company, and others like it (including major brokerage firms), offer a 'mutual fund marketplace'—one contact for many different funds.[1] This has all been made possible by electronics. If technology provides such benefits to individuals, imagine its value to corporations with millions of dollars of investments."

Investing in Securities: What Are the Options?

Companies and governments have an insatiable appetite for money. Whether it is capital to pay for a new Victoria's Secret store, funds to cover the research and development costs of the latest line of cars from Ford Motor Co., or cash to help purchase another company, finance managers are under constant pressure to replenish the corporate coffers.

To fund these and other ventures, finance managers can arrange for their companies to borrow money from banks or other financial institutions, as you learned in Chapter 21. Alternatively or additionally, they can issue stocks and bonds, referred to as **marketable securities**, which are bought and sold through organized markets. Recall from Chapter 19 that stocks represent ownership in a company and are included in the equity portion of the balance sheet; bonds, on the other hand, are debt instruments and are included in the liabilities section of the balance sheet.

When a company needs funds—to purchase new equipment, to build a new plant, or simply to expand operations—it can issue stock or float a bond issue. Stocks and bonds are initially issued in **primary markets**, usually intermediary institutions that bring the securities to the public. When Starbucks Corp., the fastest growing chain of coffee bars, needed to raise money to finance its expansion, the company sold an initial public offering of stock in the primary market. Once Starbucks had sold its stock in the primary market, that stock was sold to investors, who, in turn, traded it in the **secondary market**, a venue that facilitates the buying and selling of securities already owned by investors. We discuss secondary markets, such as the New York Stock Exchange, in a later section of this chapter.

Stocks

Stock, as we have said, represents ownership in a corporation, and the owners are referred to as *stockholders* or *shareholders*. People buy stock because they expect that their investment will earn a greater return than some other form of investment. Their profits come from dividends and from the sale of the stock at a price higher than the purchase price.

Stock ownership is formalized in a *stock certificate*, as shown in Figure 22.1. This certificate, which may be held by the investor or by the brokerage firm that executes the transaction, contains the stockholder's name and address, the number of shares owned, the company's registered state of incorporation, and the signatures of its officers. If the stock has a **par value**, (also called *face value*), an arbitrary amount established by the company and used as the basis for paying state corporate taxes, this is also shown on the certificate. Most companies today, however, issue stock without a par value, because par value has nothing to do with the actual market value of the stock (the price at which it is currently selling). Later in the chapter, you will learn how a person or company holding this stock certificate would check the market value of the stock.

In their formative years, most corporations are privately held—stockholders may be employees, friends, family members, or acquaintances who believe in the company's potential. As a company grows, its need for capital increases as well. To meet this growing need, the company may decide to issue stock for sale to the general public. When management decides to *go public*—to sell a stock issue—it typically employs the services of a financial institution in the primary market. The most well known and widely used of these is the **investment banker**, a firm that purchases (underwrites) the stock at a set price and sells it at a profit. The investment banker first helps to prepare a **prospectus**, a

1. Identify the types of marketable securities and the markets through which they are sold and describe the process by which companies raise funds through stock issues.

 marketable securities
Financial assets that are bought and sold through organized markets.

 primary markets
Financial markets in which new securities are issued.

 secondary markets
Financial markets that facilitate the trading of securities already owned by investors.

 par value
On bonds, an arbitrary amount set by the company and used as the basis for paying state corporate taxes (also called *face value*).

 investment banker
A firm that purchases (underwrites) a stock at a set price and sells it at a profit.

 prospectus
A detailed analysis of a company's financial history and current status, as well as a description of its officers and products or services.

figure **22.1** Stock Certificate

All stock certificates contain the same basic information as this one from General Motors Corp.: registration number, number of shares owned, company name, and type of stock. Although this certificate is for preferred stock, a share for common stock would contain the same basic information. The core of the certificate identifies the stockholder and spells out his or her ownership. In recent years, stock certificates—except those for stocks purchased before the electronic age—have become a rarity; most purchases are recorded and stored electronically.

Source: General Motors Corp.

detailed analysis of the company's financial history and current status, as well as a description of its officers and products or services. With all the necessary information in hand, the investment banker then advertises the new stock issue (the *initial public offering*, or *IPO*) in the financial press, using what is called a *tombstone* (simply an advertisement with black borders that reminds one of a tombstone). Once stock has been issued, the company is no longer involved in the sale and purchase of outstanding stock; stock trading is conducted directly between stockholders and potential stockholders in the secondary market, a process we will describe shortly.

Many companies issue two types of stock—common and preferred—which provide different rights and privileges to their owners.

Common Stock

2. Differentiate between common and preferred stock.

Common stock, the most well-known and popular form of ownership, has both advantages and disadvantages. Common stockholders have voting rights—they elect the company's board of directors and express their opinion on important issues, such as who will serve as the company's outside auditor or whether the company should merge with another. In reality, however, investors who own relatively few shares of a large corporation's common stock do not have much say in the company's operations. AT&T Corp., for example, had about 1.3 billion shares of stock outstanding in 1992 and 2.4 million stockholders.[2] You can imagine how much influence a person with 100 or even 1,000 shares has.

The major advantage of common stock is that stockholders can potentially earn a profit on their investment through dividends or through capital gains when the stock is sold. This is a risky proposition, however, for three reasons. First, a company that needs capital may decide to retain the money normally paid out in dividends in order to finance its operations. Second, if the company's performance is weak, the value of its stock generally declines, reflecting that weakness. Third, common stockholders have the smallest claim on the assets of a company that fails and is liquidated; creditors and preferred stockholders are reimbursed first.

Companies may issue different classes of common stock. For example, General Motors Corp. has several classes of stock, each one representing ownership in a different division of the company. GM is thus able to sell stock in one part of the company without diluting the ownership of its core common stock.

As companies grow, the price of their stock tends to reflect their increased profitability. However, if the price rises too high, it may discourage investors with limited funds or those who think the stock has reached its peak. To stimulate trading of their stock, companies have traditionally offered a **stock split**, which lowers the price of a share but increases the number of shares available. The total value of the stock remains the same. For example, in July 1995, Intuit Inc., producer of Quicken and other financial software products, announced plans for a two-for-one stock split on August 4. The stock was selling for $79.75 but after the split would be priced at $39.875 ($79.75 divided by 2), a per-share price much closer to that during the same period in 1994. Although the number of shares outstanding would double, the total value of the stock would be the same as before the split—and stockholders might benefit if the price of the stock rose after the split.

In the first seven months of 1995, there were only 57 splits of three shares for two. Traditionally, stocks split at $42 a share. So why were there so few splits during a period when the market was rising? Analysts suggest various reasons. Stock splits tend to lag behind stock price increases. Companies were trying to keep the number of stockholders down to avoid increased administrative costs. High prices were no longer a disincentive for all investors—successful stocks, such as those of the Washington Post Co. at $267.50, often carry a high price. The most likely reason was that companies were splitting themselves instead of their stock: ITT Corp. split into three companies, with shareholders receiving a share of each company for each share of ITT owned.[3]

Preferred Stock

Preferred stock typically provides most of its return in the form of fixed dividends, which are normally higher than those paid on common stock. For example, in 1995 Citicorp had several classes of preferred stock outstanding, paying dividends between $1.22 and $2.27 per share; its common stock paid $1.20 per share. On the other hand, dividends paid on preferred stock do not increase as the company's profits increase, as they may with common stock, and preferred stockholders generally have no voting rights, except perhaps on major decisions such as whether or not to merge with another company.

The amount of the dividend on preferred stock is guaranteed, and, when dividends are paid, preferred stockholders have priority over common stockholders. However, dividend payments to preferred stockholders may be *cumulative* or *noncumulative*. If dividends are cumulative, the firm must pay in full any dividends owed but not paid on preferred stock before it can pay dividends on common stock. Thus, for example, a company that paid no dividends

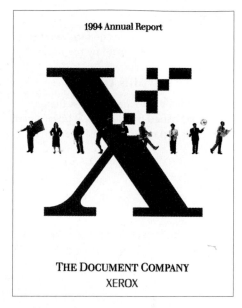

1994 Annual Report

THE DOCUMENT COMPANY
XEROX

Attracting Investors

Corporations from A to Xerox issue glossy annual reports featuring information about the company's activities and accomplishments each year—its new products or lines of business, its sales successes and failures, and its financial statements. Current and potential investors use the annual report to evaluate a company's current and potential growth, and to decide whether to buy or sell its stock.

 common stock

Corporate stock that represents equity, or ownership, in a company; common stockholders have voting rights and the opportunity to earn profits from the sale of the stock.

 stock split

An increase in the number of stock shares available, which reduces the price of each share but does not change the total value of the stock.

 preferred stock

Corporate stock that typically provides most of its return in the form of fixed dividends.

maturity date

The date on which the face value of a bond must be repaid by the issuer.

Treasury bills (T-bills)

Short-term obligations (less than a year) issued by the federal government used to pay for immediate expenses.

3. Describe the characteristics of bonds and compare and contrast the different categories of bonds.

In recent years, bond certificates have not been issued; bond purchases are electronically recorded and stored.

The federal government also issues savings bonds, which are purchased primarily by individuals.

in 1994 and 1995 would have to pay all previously owed dividends to preferred stockholders when the board of directors next voted to pay dividends—say, in 1996—before it could pay anything to common stockholders. If dividends are noncumulative, the firm is required to pay only the current year's dividends to preferred stockholders before paying common stockholders.

Historically, most companies have preferred common stock over preferred stock. This is because they want the flexibility of not having to pay dividends. In many ways, preferred stock resembles bonds, because it carries a guaranteed rate of return. As you will see shortly, however, bonds tend to be less risky for several reasons.

Bonds

Unlike stocks, which represent equity in a corporation, bonds are debt instruments, and bondholders are creditors of the corporation or government that issues them. Like stocks, bonds are first issued through investment bankers and are then bought and sold through secondary markets, as we will explain later in the chapter.

Bonds are issued, usually in units of $1,000, with a set maturity date and a par value that represents the amount to be provided to bondholders at maturity. The **maturity date**, the date on which the face value must be repaid by the issuer, is fixed at anywhere between a year or less and 30 years. In addition to the maturity date and par value, bond issues specify an interest rate—in bond terminology, the *coupon rate*—a percentage of the face value that is paid by the issuer yearly, usually in semiannual payments. Like a stock certificate, a bond certificate includes all of this information as well as the bond's registration number.

For corporations, bonds have the advantage of not diluting the value of the existing stock. For governments—which, as not-for-profit organizations, are not allowed to sell stock—bonds represent a major source of funds. For bondholders, they provide a fixed income for a fixed period of time. Bonds also are less risky than other forms of investment because, upon liquidation, a company is required to pay bondholders before it can pay dividends to stockholders.

Types of Bonds

The term *bonds* initially referred to a particular type of debt instrument; in current usage, it refers to a variety of such instruments. In this section, we discuss the more common forms, broadly categorized as government and corporate bonds. Throughout the following discussion, you may find it useful to refer to Table 22.1, which compares the characteristics of these two categories of bonds. Organizations wishing to invest excess cash in bonds must carefully consider the riskiness and the tax status of the various bonds in light of their own financial status.

Government Issues Bonds are issued both by the federal government and by state and local governments. Federal securities include bills, notes, and bonds issued by the U.S. Treasury, as well as the bonds issued by government agencies. Treasury securities, which are subject to federal taxes but not to state and local taxes, are distinguished by their maturity and their interest rate. **Treasury bills (T-bills)** are short-term obligations (less than a year) used to pay for immediate expenses. Although T-bills technically pay interest, they do not do so in the form of periodic interest payments; instead, the difference between the discounted purchase price and the price paid at maturity is considered the interest. For example, in July 1995, a three-month, $10,000 T-bill was said to have a discount rate of 5.47 percent. This means that the T-bill was selling for

table **22.1** Characteristics of Bonds

Type of bond	Par value	Maturity period	Interest and safety
Treasury bonds and notes	$1,000, $5,000, $10,000, $100,000, and $1 million	Over 10 years for bonds, 2 to 10 years for notes	Safest of all bonds, since backed by government; lower interest than other bonds
Treasury bills*	$10,000 and amounts up to $1 million	3 or 6 months or 1 year	No periodic interest; interest is difference between discounted buying price and par paid at maturity; considered risk free
Municipal bonds*	$5,000 and up	1 month to 40 years	Lower interest rate than comparable corporate bonds due to tax-exempt status
Corporate bonds*	$1,000	1 to 20 years	Riskier than government bonds, but greater potential for higher yields
Agency bonds*	$1,000 to $25,000 and up	30 days to 20 years	Marginally higher risk and higher interest than Treasury bonds

*Usually require a large minimum investment.

Source: Adapted from Kenneth M. Morris and Alan M. Siegel, *The Wall Street Guide to Understanding Money and Investing* (New York: Lightbulb Press, Inc., 1993), pp. 102–103.

$9,861.70, effectively giving it an interest rate of 5.64 percent. The discount rate on T-bills usually is the basis for adjustable-rate mortgages, which we described in Chapter 20.

Treasury notes mature in 2 to 10 years and **treasury bonds** mature in 10 or more years. Both are used to pay for federal government spending and to finance the national deficit (the excess of government expenditures over tax revenues). Every year, the federal government runs a deficit of $150 to $250 billion. In total, the U.S. government has built a total budget deficit in excess of $4 trillion. Treasury notes and treasury bonds also provide interest, usually paid semiannually when the bondholder submits a *coupon* to the relevant Treasury department. Although the interest rate is relatively low, conservative investors prefer these securities because they are backed by the federal government.

Several federal government agencies and former government agencies that have been privatized also issue bonds. (Recall from Chapter 5 that privatization is the selling of government-owned businesses to private owners.) Generally backed by pools of mortgages, the most familiar of these agency bonds are issued by the Government National Mortgage Association (commonly referred to as *Ginnie Mae*) and the Federal National Mortgage Association (*Fannie Mae*).

State and local governments issue long-term **municipal bonds**, or *munis*, to pay for general operating expenses or capital projects such as roads, bridges, and sports arenas. The two types of municipal bonds—general obligation

 Treasury notes

Debt obligation of the federal government issued for 2 to 10 years and used to pay for government spending and to finance the national deficit.

 Treasury bonds

Debt obligation of the federal government issued for 10 or more years and used to pay for government spending and to finance the national deficit.

 municipal bonds

Long-term obligations of state and local governments used to pay for general operating expenses or capital projects; also called *munis*.

ethics
check

Munis: Mixing Money and Politics

Municipal bonds (munis) were traditionally considered safe investments—and they were tax free, at least at the federal level. In recent years, though, the outlook on munis has turned from rosy to gloomy. In late 1994, Orange County, California, defaulted on $1.9 billion worth of its bonds. Why? The answer lies in part in a deadly mixture of money and politics. Robert Citron, Orange County's treasurer, was allowed to issue $600 million in taxable notes (the so-called casino bond), with which he purchased some derivative securities (see page 674) but mainly bet on interest rates, at best a highly risky investment strategy. Furthermore, Citron leveraged his investments—used a small amount of money to borrow and bet with a large amount. As interest rates declined, Citron was hailed as a hero; but then they began to rise, and by the summer of 1994 his investments had declined 7 percent in value (by approximately $2 billion). Unable to support the losses, Orange County declared bankruptcy.

Politicos in other states were similarly allowed to "do their thing," unhampered by regulatory restrictions or public oversight. For example, the husband of the governor of Kentucky received kickbacks from brokerage firms interested in handling the state's municipal bonds. And in New Jersey, the onetime chief of staff to former Governor Jim Florio "forgot" to inform his boss that his company had received kickbacks for providing First Fidelity, a major New Jersey bank, with some of the state's municipal bond business.

Municipal bonds are regulated, if at all, by the Internal Revenue Service (IRS), not the Securities and Exchange Commission (SEC). The SEC has the authority only to require that municipal bond *dealers*—not issuers—disclose all relevant information. Even the top bond-rating agencies (Moody's and Standard & Poor's), which met with Orange County officials eight times during the year, failed to see the problem. Congressional committees are currently considering measures to regulate the muni market.

1. What do you think it is that makes politics and money a "deadly mixture"?

2. Why might the IRS not be up to the task of regulating minus? (*Hint:* Consider other responsibilities of the IRS.)

3. How might full disclosure prevent such municipal fiascos?

4. How might the general public be given more of a say in local government investments?

Sources: "A Survey of Wall Street: Other People's Money," *The Economist*, April 15, 1995, pp. 19–20; Leslie Wayne, "Municipal Bond Regulation Debated at House Hearing," *New York Times*, July 27, 1995, p. D4; Terence P. Paré, "The Big Sleaze in Muni Bonds," *Fortune*, Aug. 7, 1995, pp. 113–120.

---

bonds and revenue bonds—are distinguished by their backing. **General obligation bonds** are backed by the credit and taxing ability of the state or local government that issued them and are repaid from tax receipts. **Revenue bonds**, which are issued by state or local agencies that have no taxing authority—such as the Port Authority of New York and New Jersey and the Tennessee Valley Authority—are backed by the revenue-generating project they are intended to finance. The tolls charged after a road is built, for example, are used to make payments to the bondholders. If the tolls collected are inadequate to pay the bondholders in full, the agency is not legally bound to repay the investors. Because revenue bonds are riskier and extend over longer periods than general obligation bonds, they tend to pay a somewhat higher interest rate.

In general, municipal bonds pay lower interest rates than Treasury securities. This is because they are exempt from federal taxation and from state taxation if the purchaser resides in the state of issuance. Thus, municipal bonds are quite attractive to investors in the highest tax brackets, who are always looking for a tax advantage.

In recent years, the municipal bond market has been under attack for "fast dealing, price manipulation, even bribery."[4] The highly publicized default of California's Orange County on its munis, resulting in a loss to investors of $1.9 billion,[5] clearly illustrates the types of problems cropping up all over the United States in this $1.2 trillion market.[6] For more on munis, see the ethics check entitled "Munis: Mixing Money and Politics."

✓ **general obligation bonds**

Municipal bonds backed by the credit and taxing ability of the state or local government and repaid from tax receipts.

✓ **revenue bonds**

Long-term obligations issued by state or local agencies that have no taxing authority and backed by the revenue-generating project they are intended to finance.

Corporate Bonds As mentioned in Chapter 20, corporations issue bonds when they need additional funds to expand operations, make capital investments in facilities or equipment, restructure previously incurred debt, or finance the acquisition of another company. For example, Johnson Controls, Inc., a manufacturer of plastics, car seats, and car batteries and a provider of building management services, financed plant and equipment expansion with bonds; at the end of 1994, the company had more than $52 million in bonds outstanding.[7] Furthermore, bond issues enable corporations to obtain funds without diluting their equity and without adding to the already demanding voices of current stockholders.

Corporate bonds are taxable and are backed only by the creditworthiness of the company. However, as Table 22.1 indicates, because they are riskier than government bonds, they have the potential to generate greater profits for investors.

Corporations have several options in terms of the types of bonds they can issue. **Secured bonds** are backed by specific assets that serve as *collateral*. A familiar example is the mortgage bond. As you might suspect, an unsecured bond—called a **debenture**—is not backed by collateral. Debentures are normally issued only by large corporations that are perceived to have very little risk, as well as by the government. Investors usually will not purchase bonds issued by smaller, less well-known, or riskier companies unless they are secured. One way that these firms entice investors is to issue **convertible bonds**, bonds that may be converted into shares of stock, with the number of equivalent shares of stock and the conversion date specified in the bond agreement.

Corporate bonds, whether secured or unsecured, often have a *call* feature. The corporation can elect to redeem such **callable bonds** before maturity, as specified at the time of issue. This is a valuable feature for the issuing company in times of changing interest rates, but it is not so advantageous for investors. Suppose the interest rate drops from 8 to 6 percent. If the bonds have been outstanding for the specified period of time, a corporation with an 8 percent callable bond can recall that bond and float new bonds at 6 percent. This cuts the company's expenses but reduces the profits of investors, who now have to purchase bonds at lower rates. Mortgages provide a comparable situation: If you are paying 10 percent interest and rates are now at 7 percent, you can refinance your home at the lower interest rate, substantially reducing your monthly payments.

In recent years, corporations have experimented with new types of bond issues, the most well known of which is the **zero-coupon bond**. Coupon means interest, and this is simply a bond that pays no periodic interest. Instead, investors purchase the bonds at a substantial discount and receive the full face value at maturity; the difference between the purchase price and the face value represents the accumulated interest. (T-bills, as you'll recall from an earlier discussion, are actually zero-coupon bonds.) Companies as diverse as Time Warner Inc., a multimedia producer and distributor, and Pathmark Stores, Inc., a chain of grocery stores, have issued zero-coupon bonds. Their advantage is that the issuing company can use all the money without having to keep some in reserve for interest payments, and the investor can purchase more bonds (since the price is lower) with maturity dates that provide for repayment when he or she needs the cash.

Bond Yields and Ratings

In brief, a bond's *yield* is what the investor actually earns. If the bond is purchased at issuance (in the primary market), the yield equals the annual interest divided by the bond's price—which turns out to be the same as the interest rate. If you purchase a 20-year $1,000 bond paying 5 percent interest, you will

---

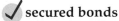 **secured bonds**

Corporate bonds backed by specific assets that serve as collateral.

✔ **debenture**

A corporate bond that is not backed by collateral.

✔ **convertible bonds**

Corporate bonds that can be converted into shares of stock, as specified in the bond agreement.

✔ **callable bonds**

Corporate bonds that can be redeemed by the issuer at any time, after a specified period, prior to maturity.

✔ **zero-coupon bond**

A bond that pays no periodic interest; purchasers receive the face value at maturity and the difference between that and the discounted purchase price represents the accumulated interest.

Recall from Chapter 20 that collateral is accounts receivable, inventory, or any asset pledged against a loan from a bank or other financial institution. For example, a house is collateral for a mortgage and a car is collateral for an automobile loan.

4. Explain bond yields and discuss the meaning and purpose of bond ratings.

earn $50 a year for 20 years. Your yield will also be 5 percent ($50 divided by $1,000). However, if you purchase the bond in the secondary market, the yield may be higher or lower than the interest rate, depending on the price you paid.

A bond's yield depends on several factors. The first and probably most important is the perceived default risk. If the company defaults on the bond, investors will not receive all the payments owed them. The greater the chance of default, the riskier the bond—and the riskier the bond, the higher the yield. Why else would investors want to purchase risky bonds?

Second, bond yields may vary because of differences in liquidity. Treasury bonds are clearly very liquid; they are easy to sell because we all feel certain (or at least relatively certain) that the U.S. government is not going to fail. Smaller companies are unknown quantities, and so they must pay a higher yield to compensate for less liquidity.

Third, you'll recall that earnings on municipal bonds are exempt from federal taxes and most state and local taxes. Treasury bonds, treasury bills, and treasury notes are exempt only from state and local taxes, and corporate and agency bonds are subject to all taxes. Clearly, then, bond issuers with tax exemptions can offer lower yields; individuals and corporations in certain tax categories willingly accept lower yields in return for tax exemption.

Fourth, callable bonds, which we described earlier, offer slightly higher yields. The companies issuing these bonds are paying for the possible inconvenience and loss of revenue to investors who must sell the bonds earlier than planned.

How do potential investors learn about the riskiness of a bond issuer? Because the finances of most companies are highly complex, several agencies provide credit ratings that rank the bonds based on the issuer's ability to repay, as shown in Table 22.2. The most popular agencies are Moody's and Standard & Poor's. Although the agencies use similar rating symbols, the symbols do differ slightly to differentiate one agency's ratings from those of other agencies. In addition, within the major categories these agencies distinguish different levels of

table **22.2**   **Bond Ratings**

Rating			
Moody's	Standard and Poor's	Descriptions	Examples of corporations with bonds outstanding in 1994
Aaa	AAA	Highest quality (lowest default risk)	General Electric, Johnson and Johnson, Wisconsin Bell
Aa	AA	High quality	McDonald's, Mobil Oil, Wal-Mart
A	A	Upper medium grade	Anheuser-Busch, Ford Motor, Xerox
Baa	BBB	Medium grade	Chrysler, General Motors, Wendy's
Ba	BB	Lower medium grade	McDonnell Douglas, RJR-Nabisco, Time-Warner
B	B	Speculative	Marriott, Revlon, Turner Broadcasting
Caa	CCC, CC	Poor (high default risk)	
Ca	C	Highly speculative	
C	D	Lowest grade	

Source: Frederic S. Mishkin, *The Economics of Money, Banking, and Financial Markets*, 4th ed. (New York: HarperCollins, 1995), p. 153.

doing business

To Russia, with Mutual Funds

Mutual funds have arrived in Russia. During the summer of 1995, Russia's version of the U.S. Securities and Exchange Commission approved rules for creating mutual funds, and President Boris Yeltsin signed a decree setting up the funds. Their goal: to attract some of the $20 billion or more believed to be stored in people's mattresses. Russian citizens were understandably cautious about putting their hard-earned cash in financial institutions, given recent substantial losses resulting from fraudulent activities involving banks and investment funds. This fear carried over to even the most staid and traditional banking institutions. Citizens feared not only losing their money but also being subjected to investigation of their finances by the authorities.

Although the Russian SEC expects it to take some time before Russians relax their stranglehold on their savings, it believes the new regulations will make them feel more secure and more willing to invest. For example, the mutual funds will have diversified investments and will be required to disclose all relevant information to shareholders.

Source: Selina Williams, "New Mutual Funds to Seek the Billions in Russian Mattresses," *New York Times*, July 29, 1995, p. 36.

riskiness. Moody's uses a numerical system, while Standard & Poor's uses a plus or a minus sign. Although the table lists only a few major corporations with bonds outstanding in 1994, you should realize that state and local governments are also rated; the federal government is considered "above rating." A major concern of corporations and governments is a *downgrade* in their rating, which reduces their ability to attract investors.

At the lowest level of the rating scale are the riskiest bonds, called **junk bonds** because there is a higher-than-average chance that the issuer will default. During the 1980s, junk bonds became a popular means of financing mergers and acquisitions. However, the economic slowdown of the late 1980s and early 1990s forced many companies that had issued junk bonds to default on their payments. Among them were two major airlines, Eastern and Pan Am. In an effort to recover their money, bondholders exchanged their debt for equity or ownership in the company—which, in turn, diluted the value of the outstanding stock. The major losses sustained by defaults on junk bonds led to the demise of the junk bond market. Today, however, with an economic recovery under way, the popularity of junk bonds seems to be on the upswing again.

Mutual Funds

In many companies, the finance manager is responsible for investing in a variety of securities that he or she hopes will earn profits for the firm. This is a time-consuming process, requiring many hours of intensive study of the markets and the performance of many different securities. For the individual investor, the task is formidable. An alternative to the direct purchase of stocks and bonds is investment in a **mutual fund**, a pool of cash collected by an investment company to purchase securities that fit the fund's investment objective. Investors buy shares in the mutual fund, the proceeds of which depend on the total performance of all the stocks and/or bonds in the fund. Because they provide diversity without effort, mutual funds are becoming increasingly popular—growing at an annual rate of 26 percent, from a single fund in 1924 to 446 funds in 1980 to over 6,700 and $1.7 trillion in investments in 1995.[8] The doing business box entitled "To Russia, with Mutual Funds" describes how mutual funds are working their way into the former Soviet Union.

5. Describe the purpose and types of mutual funds and derivatives.

 junk bond

The riskiest bond, at the lowest level of the rating scale, because there is a higher-than-average chance of the issuer defaulting.

 mutual fund

A pool of cash collected by an investment company to purchase securities that fit the fund's investment objectives.

blue chip stocks

The stocks of large, well-established companies that consistently pay dividends and show an increase in value.

growth stocks

Stocks that are riskier than blue chip stocks but represent potentially greater future gain.

derivative securities

Financial devices whose value changes in response to movement in the prices of other securities.

call option

Agreement that gives an investor the right to *purchase* a particular stock at a specific exercise, or strike, price up to a specific date.

In Chapter 21, money market mutual funds were categorized as time deposits.

When deciding on a mutual fund, investors define their goals and then select a fund that specializes in securities that will meet those goals. Mutual funds are broadly classified into bond funds, stock funds, and money market mutual funds (see Chapter 21). Bond funds are designed primarily for investors seeking periodic income from their investments. Stock funds have varied objectives. Those that focus on **blue chip stocks**—the stocks of large, well-established companies that consistently pay dividends and show an increase in value—are ideal for investors looking for a safe investment with periodic income. Other funds focus on **growth stocks**, which are somewhat riskier but represent a potentially greater future gain. Investors can select a mutual fund that is riskier than a blue chip fund but not as risky as a so-called *small-cap* fund, a fund that specializes in small companies. Still other funds offer a combination of blue chip and growth stocks for investors wishing to "hedge their bets."

Although mutual funds have in most years underperformed Standard & Poor's 500-stock index, sales of stock funds surged in 1995, with inflows of $8.2 billion in June of that year.[9] The increase was primarily in growth funds, technology funds, and small-cap funds, according to Robert Adler of AMG Data Services, of Arcata, California. Bond funds, on the other hand, showed withdrawals of $3.3 million in June, compared with inflows of $665 million in May.[10]

Mutual funds advertise their wares in a variety of business periodicals as well as in most local newspapers. As a potential investor, you simply call the number provided and ask for a prospectus, which describes the fund's objectives, its recent performance, and the riskiness of its investments. If you decide to invest, you send a check that includes a fee for processing and investing. Later in the chapter, we will describe how to track investments in mutual funds.

There are two types of mutual funds. *Open-end funds* admit any and all interested investors. These mutual funds act somewhat like savings accounts; investors can add to their accounts at any time. Some investment firms, such as Fidelity Investments, Merrill Lynch & Co., Inc., T. Rowe Price Associates, Inc., Scudder, and the Vanguard Group, sponsor 20 or more mutual funds. Their investors can usually transfer money from one fund to another. *Closed-end funds* have one offering with a fixed number of shares; no new investors are taken on after the initial sale.

Derivative Securities

We have discussed stocks, bonds, and mutual funds, the most well-known and most frequently purchased securities. Other types of securities available to investors are referred to as **derivative securities**, or *derivatives* for short. These securities are financial devices whose value changes in response to movement in the prices of other securities. Some are tied to stocks, some are tied to bonds, and still others are tied to interest rates. One of the most popular derivative securities is the stock option, which is a way of investing in securities without actually buying them.

A **call option** gives an investor the right to *purchase* a particular stock at a specific price (called an *exercise*, or *strike, price*) up to a specific date. In buying a call option, the purchaser bets that the stock's price will rise before the option expires. The purchaser pays a specified *premium* for the call option, which is substantially less than the actual purchase price of the stock. If the investor exercises the call option when the price of the underlying stock investment has risen above the strike price, he or she will earn a profit without having to lay out much cash for the investment. Alternatively, the investor may elect to let the call option expire—because the stock has decreased in value—in which case he or she loses only the amount of the premium.

Conversely, a **put option** gives the investor the right to *sell* a particular stock at a specific exercise price up to a specific date. A put option is a bet that the price of a stock will decrease. Again, the purchaser pays a premium, which is the most that can be lost if the option is not exercised. If the price of the underlying investment goes down before the option expires, the owner of the put option may sell at the exercise price, which at that point is higher than the market price.

Futures contracts, another form of derivative, are similar to options in that they involve a purchase on a specified future date at an agreed-upon price, which is established by trading in the market for that security. They differ in that they are legal agreements between buyer and seller regarding specific standardized **commodities**—raw materials or agricultural products such as wheat, silver, oil, pork bellies, and sugar. The purchaser pays a percentage of that price—buys on margin—and that amount is deducted from his or her account and is altered daily as the price of the commodity changes.

Futures contracts for commodities have been available for quite some time. In 1975, *financial futures contracts*—agreements involving financial instruments such as CDs and Treasury bonds—became available, allowing investors to *hedge* against interest-rate risk. (Recall from Chapter 21 that interest-rate risk, one of the three risks faced by financial institutions, is the chance of loss due to an increase in interest rates on deposits while the interest rate charged on loans remains the same.) In addition, investors now have the option to purchase stock market index futures, which involve several stocks within a particular category—for example, technology stocks.

Although commodities are frequently purchased as futures, producers and users—the farmer who produces wheat and the baker who buys it—often buy and sell in the *spot* (or cash) *market*, which calls for immediate delivery and cash "on the spot." Those trading in the futures market may be *hedgers* or *speculators*. Hedgers are producers and users interested in protecting themselves against price changes that will limit their profits. Hence, if they anticipate that a commodity's price will increase in the not-too-distant future, they will buy futures in that product at a lower price, which will enable them to retain their profits. Speculators, on the other hand, are simply risk takers interested in making a profit; they have no vested interest in the commodity.

Investors: Who Are They and What Are Their Goals?

We began this chapter with the observation that businesses and governments are always looking for additional capital—to increase their profits, to expand their operations, or to finance the acquisition of another company, to name just a few uses of funds. All organizations, whether for-profit or not-for-profit, revolve around the need and ability to obtain funds. Individuals also need funds—to pay for everyday expenses, to finance major purchases, or simply to increase their net worth. Therefore, when finance managers set out to obtain additional capital through the sale of stocks and bonds, they must understand the needs and desires of potential investors. Investors are broadly categorized as institutional investors and individual investors.

 put option

Agreement that gives an investor the right to *sell* a particular stock at a specific exercise price up to a specific date.

 futures contracts

Legal contracts that give investors the right to purchase a specific, standardized commodity on a specified future date at an agreed-upon price.

✓ **commodities**

Raw materials or agricultural products such as wheat, silver, oil, pork bellies, and sugar that are traded in separate markets, often as futures.

6. Identify the categories of investors and describe five broad investment goals.

Institutional and Individual Investors

Chapter 5 defined institutional investors as public and private organizations that buy stock on behalf of large institutions.

Recall from Chapter 21 that depository and nondepository financial institutions use the funds obtained from various sources to invest in securities that earn them money.

The largest group of investors, often called *institutional investors*, are organizations that use their own funds as well as those they hold in trust for others to purchase large blocks—10,000 or more shares—of securities. Institutional investors include commercial banks, pension funds, insurance companies, investment companies (including mutual funds), and not-for-profit organizations such as colleges and universities. For example, commercial banks use deposits and the interest received on loans, pension funds use employee contributions, and insurance companies use premiums from policyholders to purchase securities in pursuit of profits.

More than 50 percent of all securities trades are made by institutional investors. For this reason, any major purchases or sales by institutions can have a dramatic effect on the prices of securities. With average stock holdings of only $11,000 each, individual investors are dwarfed by the major institutions—Dreyfus Corp.'s general mutual fund, for example, has assets of more than $2.7 billion.

However, the individual investor cannot be ignored, because the activities of institutional investors actually reflect the needs and desires of millions of individual investors. Indeed, the stock market crash of October 19, 1987, caused many individuals to fear the stock market and to put their faith in professional money managers.

The Goals of Investors

People have various goals in mind when they invest their hard-earned cash in securities. Young adults who have the money are often looking to reap a high return in a short period of time, so they're willing to take some risks. Conversely, people who are retired or near retirement may want to safeguard their funds and develop a steady source of income for their "golden years."

Institutional investors also have different goals, depending on their mission. Recall that the prospectus of a mutual fund describes its goals and its performance record in meeting those goals. For example, money market mutual funds focus on returning a steady income to their participants. Others, such as the $43 billion Magellan mutual fund from Fidelity Investments, focus on stocks that can yield a high return. Investors in such funds are willing to forgo

Professional Money Managers

In the trading room at Fidelity Investments, brokers work with the company's mutual fund investors. Whether the accounts are held by individuals or institutions, the goals of all investors reflect a mix among the investment's income and/or growth potential, its liquidity, safety, and tax advantages.

dividend income in return for stocks that will appreciate in price faster than the average.

Typically, individuals and institutions look for investments that satisfy one or several of the following five goals: income, growth, liquidity, safety, and tax advantages.

Income

As we have noted, some investors rely on their investments to generate a steady income. A retired couple, for example, may rely on income from their investments to supplement their Social Security income. They would therefore invest independently, or through an institution such as a mutual fund, in bonds and stocks that consistently pay a high level of dividends. For decades, power and water utilities were known as "widows and orphans" stock companies because they provided regular, hefty dividends even as they generated steady, if unspectacular, returns. Similarly, life insurance companies commonly prefer to generate a steady stream of income with which to make continuing periodic insurance payments.

Growth

Many investors seeking to increase their wealth prefer securities that will grow in value. This means investing in smaller companies (the small-cap funds mentioned earlier) or in high-risk companies that tend to retain their earnings in order to finance business expansions that produce substantial growth. It also means being willing to take a risk, to lose everything if the company performs relatively poorly or fails.

According to the controversial *theory of efficient markets*, investing in growth stocks should not really entail any risk because the market quickly and efficiently prices securities according to the available information. Thus, stock prices should accurately reflect the value of a company. Although critics contend that the stock market crash of 1987 disproves the theory, advocates believe that it works if you take into account other factors such as market psychology. However, while semiconductor, personal computer, software, and other technology companies have grown substantially and consistently over the last 35 years, their stocks have not always reflected that growth. For example, while production of semiconductor chips increased from less than $1 billion in 1970 to more than $100 billion in 1995, the stock prices of semiconductor companies declined by 75 percent in some years during that period.[11]

Liquidity

Some investors seek securities that are liquid, that can easily be sold if and when they need their money back. To be liquid, a security should be actively traded in a secondary market. Treasury securities, for example, are issued by the federal government in huge numbers and are frequently traded in the secondary market. Although Treasury securities do not offer as high a return on investment as other securities, they are useful to investors seeking liquidity and security. This is particularly true of T-bills, which are issued for periods of less than a year.

Recall from Chapter 19 that liquidity *refers to the ease with which an asset can be converted to cash.*

Safety

Some investors prefer to invest in low-risk securities. In general, *risk* in this context refers to how much the value of a security fluctuates. Securities have different levels of riskiness. At one extreme, an investor could invest in general obligation municipal bonds or T-bills to ensure a stable value over time. In the middle are other Treasury securities and certain corporate bonds. At the other extreme, an investor could purchase junk bonds such as those of gas or oil exploration companies, whose business is highly speculative and depends on their ability to repeatedly come up with productive oil or gas wells.

The degree of safety that investors seek depends, of course, on their financial status and current needs. Young adults who are just beginning their careers and have little to lose may be willing to take some risks. Middle-aged business executives earning a six-figure income may also be willing to take certain risks in order to build a future for their families. Older adults, in contrast, are usually unwilling to risk losing their life savings; for them, safety in investing is imperative.

Tax Advantages

Investors who have high salaries tend to pay a high percentage of their income in taxes. Add to salary the income from interest on bonds or dividends from stock, and the amount of taxes paid is even higher. Such investors may therefore consider purchasing municipal bonds, which are tax-exempt at the federal level and, in some cases, at the state and local levels. They may also purchase Treasury securities, which are exempt from state and local taxes, making them less advantageous taxwise than municipal bonds but more advantageous than corporate bonds, which are taxable. Alternatively, they may buy stock in growth companies that rarely pay dividends but eventually produce capital gains. The growth in the stock's value is not taxed until the stock is sold. In addition, capital gains may be taxed at a lower rate than ordinary income or dividends. Finally, selling the stock of a young company involved in research and development has further tax advantages, depending on how long it has been held and other factors.

Portfolio Management

Most investors have more than one goal. Mr. Jones, for instance, may want income, growth, liquidity, and safety, while Ms. Smith is seeking growth and liquidity. In reality, neither may be able to achieve all of his or her goals simultaneously, but proper *portfolio management* can improve the odds. Portfolio management means selecting a variety of securities such that losses in one area will be offset by gains in another. For example, an investor who wants income, growth, and liquidity might include in his or her portfolio several blue chip stocks, such as AT&T Corp., that generate income through dividends, as well as some high-tech stock such as Microsoft Corp., which is actively traded in secondary markets and has the potential for large upward swings. The fact that more and more investors are turning to mutual funds points up the difficulty of knowing which stocks will meet which goals and when.

Securities Markets: Where Trading Takes Place

7. List and characterize the major securities markets.

As you know, when stocks and bonds are first issued, they are sold to investment bankers (the primary markets), who then sell to the public. After that, they are bought and sold—traded—in the secondary markets. Brokerage firms usually serve as financial intermediaries in these markets.

Securities are traded in the secondary markets in one of two ways: through a stock exchange where all orders to buy or sell a stock are transacted on the "floor" by a stock specialist who matches the buyer with the seller in an *auction-*

style trade, or through a dealer exchange, in which a market maker buys stock, marks up its price to cover overhead and profits, and then resells it. In this section, we discuss the largest and most well-known stock exchanges used by U.S. investors, as well as the global securities markets and the mechanisms used to regulate the securities markets. Note that bonds are also traded on the New York Stock Exchange, on the American Stock Exchange, and in some cases on regional exchanges. Options, futures, and commodities are traded in separate exchanges.

The New York Stock Exchange

The New York Stock Exchange (NYSE) dates back to 1817, when Wall Street was a stockade built to protect New Yorkers. Also known as the Big Board, the New York Stock Exchange is home to most of the oldest, largest, and best-known U.S. companies, as well as to several major foreign firms. More than 2,500 companies, with stocks worth an estimated $5 trillion, are listed on the New York Stock Exchange; the number of stocks listed, however, is much higher, since many businesses and financial institutions, such as Citicorp, have separate listings for their various classes of common and preferred stock. Table 22.3 (page 680) lists the requirements for membership on the New York Stock Exchange and on the other stock exchanges.

Still the largest national stock exchange in terms of the *dollar value* of shares traded annually, the NYSE has been surpassed in terms of the *number* of shares traded by the fast-growing, computerized NASDAQ exchange. In 1994, 73.4 billion shares of stock worth $2.5 trillion were traded on the NYSE; 74 billion shares worth $1.4 trillion were traded on NASDAQ.[12]

The American Stock Exchange and Regional Exchanges

Originally called the New York Curb Exchange because trading literally took place on the street, the American Stock Exchange (AMEX) is smaller than the New York Stock Exchange, with fewer than 900 members. Because its requirements for membership are less stringent than those for the NYSE, it attracts

The Trading Floor

Although the New York Stock Exchange has computerized many trading functions, face-to-face activity on the trading floor continues to dominate its business. The areas set aside for buying and selling specific stocks or groups of stocks are called "trading posts." No stock may be traded at more than one post. The video screen above each post reflects its activity for the day. Booths that have been rented to the stock brokerage houses ring the trading floor. These booths serve as control centers: when an order is received, the broker at the booth takes it to the trading post, where the order is executed.

table **22.3**   Requirements for Stock Market Listing

Exchange	Requirements	Type of company	Number of companies listed
New York Stock Exchange (NYSE)	Pre-tax income of $2.5 million; 1.1 million shares outstanding at a minimum market value of $18 million	Oldest, largest, and best-known companies	2,570
American Stock Exchange (AMEX)	Pre-tax income of $750,000; 500,000 shares publicly held at a minimum market value of $3 million (a second AMEX listing requires only 250,000 shares publicly held at a minimum market value of $2.5 million)	Midsized growth companies	824
NASDAQ	Pre-tax income of $750,000 or a total market value of all shares outstanding at $1 million; 400 shareholders; net assets of $4 million	Large, midsized, and small growth companies	4,902
OTC (over-the-counter)	Minimal or none	Smallest and newest companies or companies with few shares outstanding	28,000+

Sources: Kenneth M. Morris and Alan M. Siegel, *The Wall Street Guide to Understanding Money and Investing* (New York: Lightbulb Press, Inc., 1993) p. 65, and (New York) *Daily News,* July 23, 1995, Personal Finance section, pp. 1–2.

Futures, as we have noted, are traded separately from traditional securities through 11 exchanges, located in Chicago, Philadelphia, Minneapolis, New York, and Kansas City.

more midsized growth companies. Like the NYSE, AMEX is a national exchange. However, because it is smaller and less prestigious, companies often move up to the NYSE when they become larger.

Regional stock exchanges in Boston, Chicago, Cincinnati, Philadelphia, and Los Angeles (the Pacific Exchange) generally list only the most actively traded stocks from the NYSE and AMEX. These regional exchanges are linked to the NYSE and AMEX, but trading is faster and less expensive and requirements for membership are less restrictive. Furthermore, the total volume of stock traded daily on these exchanges far surpasses the volume on the AMEX.

The Over-the-Counter Market: The NASDAQ System

Both the New York Stock Exchange and the American Stock Exchange have actual trading floors, currently located in New York City. The **over-the-counter market (OTC)** is an electronic network that connects thousands of market makers—companies such as Merrill Lynch & Co., Inc., that literally create a market for a stock by quoting a *bid price,* the price at which the dealer is willing to purchase a security, and an *ask price,* the price at which the dealer is willing to sell the security. All trading in the over-the-counter market is conducted through

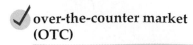

over-the-counter market (OTC)

An electronic network that connects thousands of market makers.

computers, faxes, telephones, and other electronic media. As Table 22.3 shows, 28,000 small and new companies are traded through over-the-counter markets.

A computerized system known as the *National Association of Security Dealers Automated Quotations (NASDAQ)* is the core of the over-the-counter market. A global electronic trading system—providing the largest U.S. market for foreign stocks—NASDAQ was originally established by the National Association of Securities Dealers as a means of tracking the performance of stocks on regional exchanges. It is primarily the home for high-tech, biotech, and emerging companies, many of which are now large enough to be listed on the NYSE or AMEX but prefer the format and less restrictive requirements of NASDAQ. For example, Apple Computer Inc., Microsoft Corp., and Intel Corp. all qualify for the other exchanges but are traded on the NASDAQ system. About 30 percent of the companies listed on NASDAQ, weighted according to their size, are computer-related companies and 8 percent are telecommunications companies.[13]

The basic difference between NASDAQ and the traditional markets is that NASDAQ, as an electronic market, is the wave of the future. But NASDAQ differs from the NYSE and AMEX in other ways as well. For example, traditional systems employ a single market maker for each stock; NASDAQ uses multiple market makers—an average of 12 for each stock, with a minimum of 2 and sometimes as many as 40.

NASDAQ has not been without its problems, as critics are quick to point out, but in the 20-plus years since its inception, great progress has been made. The NYSE, with its 2,500 members, has been around for 178 years while NASDAQ has grown to almost 5,000 companies since 1971 (see Figure 22.2). The

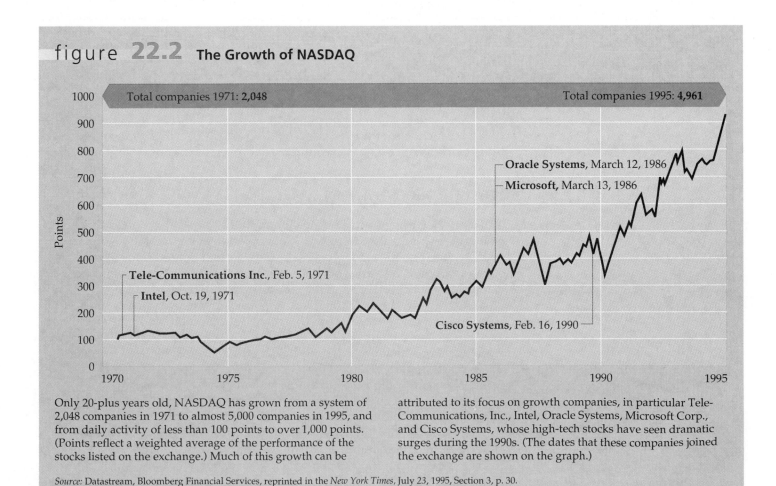

figure **22.2**   **The Growth of NASDAQ**

Only 20-plus years old, NASDAQ has grown from a system of 2,048 companies in 1971 to almost 5,000 companies in 1995, and from daily activity of less than 100 points to over 1,000 points. (Points reflect a weighted average of the performance of the stocks listed on the exchange.) Much of this growth can be attributed to its focus on growth companies, in particular Tele-Communications, Inc., Intel, Oracle Systems, Microsoft Corp., and Cisco Systems, whose high-tech stocks have seen dramatic surges during the 1990s. (The dates that these companies joined the exchange are shown on the graph.)

Source: Datastream, Bloomberg Financial Services, reprinted in the *New York Times*, July 23, 1995, Section 3, p. 30.

doing business

The NASDAQ Way

Billing itself as "the market for the next 100 years," NASDAQ differs from the traditional stock exchanges in two major ways. First, whereas the NYSE and AMEX have a trading floor, traders for NASDAQ work from thousands of computer terminals in different locations around the world. Second, while the traditional markets use single market makers for each stock, NASDAQ has multiple market makers. NASDAQ is supposed to be more efficient, less restrictive, and certainly more modern. However, this electronic market "has been plagued by probes, processing problems, and unfulfilled promise," according to Rosemary Metzler Lavan, a financial news reporter.

The most highly publicized of NASDAQ's problems was actually the result of "human error." When stock prices began plummeting on October 19, 1987, petrified dealers refused to answer the phones, inhibiting trading and perhaps aggravating the situation. Equipment problems have also created major trading problems. During the summer of 1994, the system failed three times, once supposedly because a squirrel had eaten through power lines and once because the system was simply unable to handle the high volume of trading.

Most serious of all have been the allegations of unfair business practices. For example, the SEC is investigating claims that small investors pay higher prices than institutional investors and that the system is designed to provide higher profits to large dealers. Also, NASDAQ dealers have been accused of maintaining artificially high price spreads of $.25 per share, twice the average spread on the NYSE, and of violating the 90-second rule for reporting trades.

NASDAQ has responded to these shortcomings by installing a computer network that executes trades immediately so that both small and large investors have access to the same prices. And an upgrade of NASDAQ's entire system increased its 450 million shares per day volume to 800 million. Despite its problems, NASDAQ remains the home of the major growth stocks. In July 1995, the index reached the 1,000 mark for the first time.

Sources: Rosemary Metzler Lavan, "NASDAQ: Growing Pains," (New York) *Daily News*, July 23, 1995, business section, pp. 1–2; "A Closer Look at Booming NASDAQ," *USA Today*, July 18, 1995, p. 3B.

---

doing business box entitled "The NASDAQ Way" describes some of the stumbling blocks NASDAQ has encountered and overcome.

Global Securities Markets

The use of securities to finance operations and expansion is not unique to U.S. companies. Companies in every country—even the People's Republic of China—obtain funds through the sale of stocks and bonds. Some of the 142 exchanges around the world actually predate the U.S. exchanges: London's exchange dates back to 1773 and the one in Paris to 1802.

Whereas the U.S. stock markets were once the major players internationally, those in other nations are now gaining a strong foothold in the world market. Indeed, since the mid-1980s, the value of stocks traded on the Tokyo stock exchange has sometimes exceeded that of stocks traded on the U.S. exchanges. Stock markets also exist in Toronto (Canada), Germany, Switzerland, Hong Kong, Mexico, South Korea, and India, among other countries.

Although foreign stocks are usually traded on the stock exchange of the company's base country, some are traded on U.S. stock exchanges as so-called **American depository receipts (ADRs)**. ADRs are certificates representing a specific number of shares in a particular foreign company. These certificates are held in trust by a bank, which converts dividends into U.S. dollars and performs all the necessary paperwork. Foreign stocks traded as ADRs include Volkswagen AG, Nissan Motor Co., Ltd., Sony Corp., and Toyota Motor Corp.

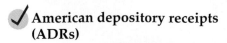 **American depository receipts (ADRs)**

Certificates representing ownership in the stock of a foreign company.

The importance of foreign stock markets is evidenced by the fact that, since 1993, Dow Jones has provided a daily report of the composite performance of foreign stock exchanges in U.S. newspapers such as the *Wall Street Journal*.

Regulating the Securities Markets

Like most things in the financial world, the securities markets were not closely regulated before the 1930s and the Great Depression. Companies could issue new securities without disclosing their financial problems, and information about companies would be made available to some people but not others. Using this *inside information*, investors in the know could "make a killing" in the stock market—selling stock before a firm reported low earnings or buying stock before it announced a major new product or a merger or acquisition bound to increase its stock's value.

The Securities Act of 1933 represented the first major step in the effort to regulate the securities industry, creating an even playing field for all investors. The act required that companies register new security issues with the federal government and disclose all financial information relevant to the securities being issued. One result of this was the prospectus we described earlier, which must be made available to all potential investors. Any investors, firms, or brokers who violated the act were penalized.

In 1934, the Securities Exchange Act established the Securities and Exchange Commission (SEC) to regulate the national stock exchanges as well as brokerage firms and others trading on those exchanges. Composed of five members appointed by the U.S. president, the commission has three overriding goals: to ensure that the public receives all relevant information regarding securities issues, to prevent fraud in securities transactions, and to prevent insider trading. Firms are required to submit an annual registration statement with the SEC, and individuals owning more than 10 percent of a firm's outstanding stock must file trading reports with the SEC.

Later amendments to the Securities Exchange Act expanded the SEC's authority to include over-the-counter and regional markets and shored up its power to penalize illegal insider trading. A 1987 study conducted by the SEC pointed out the effects of insider trading: ten days prior to a takeover announcement trading increases noticeably; three days before, trading occurs at three times the normal rate; two days before, it is five times the normal rate; and on the day of the announcement, trading increases to 20 times the normal rate. After the announcement, the takeover company's stock increases, on average, 38.5 percent. Most of this activity reflects innocent guesses and rumors, but some stems from not-so-legal activities. Ivan Boesky earned over $50 million by receiving inside information from Dennis Levine, the codirector of Drexel Burnham Lambert's mergers and acquisitions department, as well as from various bankers and lawyers. Boesky paid $100 million in fines on illegal profits and was sentenced to a total of five years in prison.[14]

Investing: How It's Done

Whether you are a finance manager investing excess cash for your company, an institution such as a mutual fund investing for thousands of shareholders, or an individual looking for some extra income, you have to understand how the investment process works and, most important, how to keep track of your investment. In this section, we describe the basic procedures and explain how to read the securities quotations published daily in newspapers such as the *Wall Street Journal*.

8. Discuss the regulation of securities markets and securities traders.

As you will learn, despite heavy regulation, the securities markets continue to be plagued by problems with insider trading, the buying and selling of a company's stock by its corporate officers or by those receiving information from them.

Monitoring the Back Room

Although employee empowerment has contributed to increased efficiency and profitability in most companies, empowerment without oversight can have disastrous results in a brokerage firm, where the stakes are high and temptation even higher.

Traditionally, at brokerage firms such as Merrill Lynch & Co., Inc., traders would buy stock and then simultaneously transmit the order orally to a clerk, who entered it into a computer, and in written form to the traders' desk. The back room would compare the written orders with the computer records and correct any errors. They would also check that each order had a customer in order to prevent the hiding of unauthorized trades.

This seemed like a reasonable system, but it had one very large loophole: Clerks were monitored by the operations department and traders were monitored by the traders' desk. At the top levels, risk managers who reported directly to the president and chairman would review all trades to ensure that investments were not too heavily weighted in one area, which could expose the company to financial disaster. All of these were independent operations, with no single group providing total oversight.

The system was particularly unsuited to monitoring brokers who were large money makers. For example, Michael Milken, head of Drexel Burnham Lambert's junk bond department, was so successful that he was allowed to move the office to Beverly Hills, California, away from the eagle eyes of the company's control people. Milken's fraudulent activities went undetected until it was too late—Drexel paid $650 million in fines and

restitution, and by 1990 was out of business. Similarly, the limited-partnership division of Prudential-Bache Securities was so successful that it was left to operate unchecked. Its misrepresentation to investors of billions of dollars of risky limited partnerships cost Prudential $1.2 billion in fines and restitution.

1. Based on what you have learned in this chapter and in the chapters on organizational design and human resources management, how might you, as a manager in a brokerage firm, have avoided such disasters?

2. What types of checks and balances could you institute to prevent fraudulent activities but retain employee empowerment?

3. Is Arthur Levitt, Jr., the chairman of the SEC, right when he says that "where you have a firm where one person or a small group of people are contributing an inordinate amount of profitability to the enterprise, then that is a warning sign that should be examined closely"?

4. Is oversight less of a problem at discount brokerage firms? Why?

5. Junk bonds are once again becoming popular investments. Will any of the changes in the operations of the major exchanges prevent a recurrence of the major financial losses of the past?

Source: Kurt Eichenwald, "Learning the Hard Way How to Monitor Traders," *New York Times*, March 9, 1995, pp. D1, D5.

Selecting a Broker

9. Describe the process of selecting a broker and explain how to analyze securities quotations.

The first and probably most important step is selecting a broker, the financial intermediary who will execute buy-and-sell transactions for you. Three basic options are available: full-service brokerage firms such as Merrill Lynch & Co., Inc., and Dean Witter, Discover & Co.; a discount brokerage firm such as the Charles Schwab Corp.; or, if you are an institution buying and selling large blocks of securities, a deep-discount broker. Recall from Chapter 21 that many commercial banks now offer discount brokerage services.

In effect, the type of service you select depends on your financial status and your confidence in your own investment decisions. Full-service brokerage firms charge a hefty commission for each transaction they perform. However, in exchange for that commission they work closely with their clients, helping them determine their goals and advising them on securities that will best meet those goals. Prior to 1975, when the SEC outlawed minimum brokerage commissions, small investors unwilling or unable to pay large commissions to full-service brokerage houses had no alternative investment source. Now there are also discount brokerage firms that provide minimal advice and charge lower commissions. The skills check entitled "Monitoring the Back Room" provides a brief description of how brokerage firms have operated in the past, noting some of the problems caused by their standard procedures.

Reading the Market

Once you have selected a broker and decided on a plan of action for purchasing stocks or bonds, you will need to know how to keep track of your investments. The following sections explain how to read the daily records of stocks (including stock mutual funds) and bonds and how to interpret securities indexes.

Analyzing Stock Quotations

The stock quotations from the *New York Times* in Figure 22.3 are typical of the listings that appear daily in most major newspapers. Readers of the *Wall Street Journal* will notice one additional bit of information: the symbol for each company listed as it would appear on the ticker tape or computer readout of the market's activities. Reflecting the results of trading on the previous day, these summaries are organized by stock exchange. Although Figure 22.3 shows stocks on the New York Stock Exchange, the format applies also to the American Stock Exchange and NASDAQ. However, NASDAQ separates its national issues from small-caps, the smallest and riskiest companies.

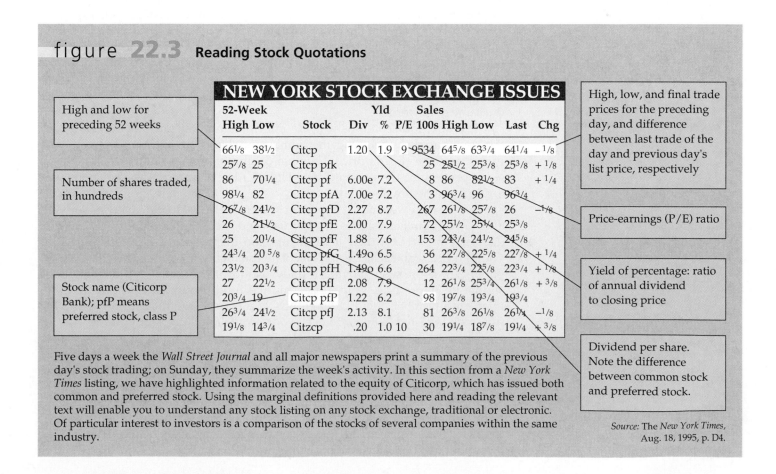

figure **22.3**   **Reading Stock Quotations**

Five days a week the *Wall Street Journal* and all major newspapers print a summary of the previous day's stock trading; on Sunday, they summarize the week's activity. In this section from a *New York Times* listing, we have highlighted information related to the equity of Citicorp, which has issued both common and preferred stock. Using the marginal definitions provided here and reading the relevant text will enable you to understand any stock listing on any stock exchange, traditional or electronic. Of particular interest to investors is a comparison of the stocks of several companies within the same industry.

Source: The *New York Times*, Aug. 18, 1995, p. D4.

Figure 22.3 explains the meaning of the information in each column. We have highlighted the figures for Citicorp Bank (CCI) to clarify how the information contained in each column provides insight into the value of a specific company. The first two columns, the high and low per-share prices for the preceding 52 weeks, show that Citicorp common stock was priced as low as $38.50 and as high as $66.13 during the year—quite a large swing in price. (Note that the fractions used for stock prices represent a portion of a dollar; for example, ¼ is $.25 an ⅝ is $.675.) Now, if you scan down the column, you will observe that the range for Citicorp's various preferred stock classes (identified as pfD, for example) is much narrower than that of its common stock. Reading across to the next-to-last column, you see that the stock is selling for $64.25, very close to its high for the year.

The third column is the name of the firm. Only if the name is followed by "pf" is the stock preferred (Citicorp has 11 classes of preferred stock); otherwise, it is common stock. An "n" beside the name refers to a new issue, and "s" indicates a stock split.

The fourth column shows the cash dividend paid by the firm on each share outstanding. Although dividends are usually paid quarterly, this amount is an estimate of dividends for the year. Citicorp pays $1.20 per share on its common stock and between $1.22 and $7.00 on one of its preferred stocks. A blank fourth column means no dividends were paid.

The fifth column, the divided yield, represents the amount of the prevailing stock price paid to investors through dividends. For Citicorp's common stock, the yield is rounded out to 1.9 percent ($1.20 divided by $64.25).

The sixth column discloses the **price-earnings (P/E) ratio**. This ratio is determined by dividing the firm's per-share stock price by its earnings per share (based on the last four quarters). Keep in mind that earnings per share (EPS) is the net income divided by the number of shares outstanding. Citicorp's P/E ratio is 9, meaning that the prevailing stock price is 9 times earnings. This ratio is useful because it enables investors to determine how well a firm is performing in relation to other firms in the industry. For example, although Citicorp's performance is within an acceptable range, it was somewhat lower than that of the Chase Manhattan Corp. or Chemical Banking Corp., whose P/E ratios on the same date were 10.

The next four columns provide information about the stock's trading on the previous day, including the number of shares traded, the high and low prices, and the closing price. The final column indicates the net change in the stock price since the previous day. Thus, Citicorp stock declined ⅛ points, or $.125, from the previous day.

Suppose, however, that you want someone else to do the investing for you, and so you purchase shares in a mutual fund. Although mutual funds provide quarterly reports on their investments, too many securities are involved for you to try to scan each one and calculate the total gain or loss each day. Newspapers therefore also provide a daily listing of the major mutual funds, as shown in Figure 22.4. Within each mutual fund group, such as Dreyfus Premier, are a number of individual funds. You would scan the column to find the fund you invested in and how well your professional investor is doing.

The first column after the fund name gives the fund's net asset value, or NAV. This is the dollar value of one share of stock in the fund. Multiplying the NAV by the number of shares owned will tell you how much your total investment is worth—whether more or less than when you purchased it.

The remaining columns show the fund's percentage return for different periods of time, from one day to five years. Because most people invest in mutual funds for the long term, the five-year return is particularly telling, especially as it compares to the returns from other funds.

✓ **price-earnings (P/E) ratio**

A firm's per-share stock price divided by its earning per share.

figure **22.4** Reading Mutual Fund Quotations

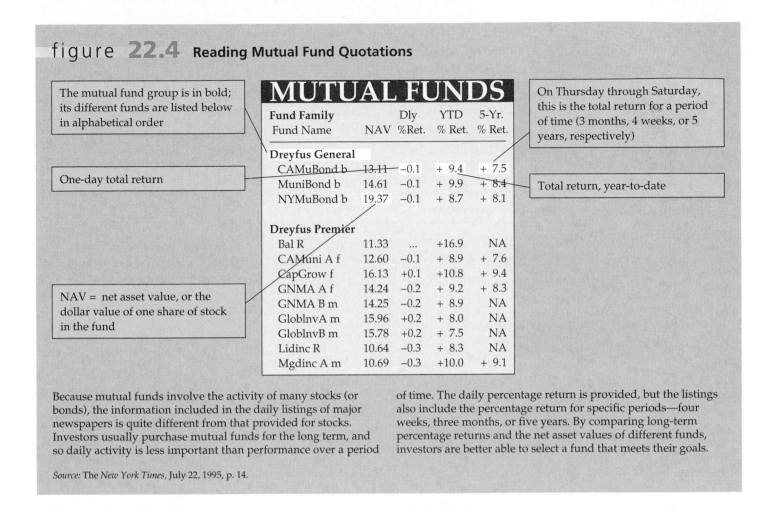

The mutual fund group is in bold; its different funds are listed below in alphabetical order

One-day total return

NAV = net asset value, or the dollar value of one share of stock in the fund

On Thursday through Saturday, this is the total return for a period of time (3 months, 4 weeks, or 5 years, respectively)

Total return, year-to-date

MUTUAL FUNDS

Fund Family Fund Name	NAV	Dly %Ret.	YTD % Ret.	5-Yr. % Ret.
Dreyfus General				
CAMuBond b	13.11	−0.1	+ 9.4	+ 7.5
MuniBond b	14.61	−0.1	+ 9.9	+ 8.4
NYMuBond b	19.37	−0.1	+ 8.7	+ 8.1
Dreyfus Premier				
Bal R	11.33	...	+16.9	NA
CAMuni A f	12.60	−0.1	+ 8.9	+ 7.6
CapGrow f	16.13	+0.1	+10.8	+ 9.4
GNMA A f	14.24	−0.2	+ 9.2	+ 8.3
GNMA B m	14.25	−0.2	+ 8.9	NA
GloblnvA m	15.96	+0.2	+ 8.0	NA
GloblnvB m	15.78	+0.2	+ 7.5	NA
Lidinc R	10.64	−0.3	+ 8.3	NA
Mgdinc A m	10.69	−0.3	+10.0	+ 9.1

Because mutual funds involve the activity of many stocks (or bonds), the information included in the daily listings of major newspapers is quite different from that provided for stocks. Investors usually purchase mutual funds for the long term, and so daily activity is less important than performance over a period of time. The daily percentage return is provided, but the listings also include the percentage return for specific periods—four weeks, three months, or five years. By comparing long-term percentage returns and the net asset values of different funds, investors are better able to select a fund that meets their goals.

Source: The *New York Times*, July 22, 1995, p. 14.

Analyzing Bond Quotations

Like stock prices, bond prices for the previous day are quoted daily in most major newspapers, but in a separate listing. Figure 22.5 (page 688) highlights the *New York Times* listing for one of Chrysler Corp.'s bonds. Much of the information—the company name, the 12-month high and low, and the previous day's performance—has the same purpose and the same basic meaning as the information provided in a stock quote. We will focus on the differences.

Following the company's name are several numbers. The first is the coupon, or interest, rate. The Chrysler bond of interest has a coupon rate of 9½, or 9.5. Depending on when they were issued, corporate bonds may carry very different coupon rates; for example, a different Chrysler bond has a coupon rate of 6½. Remember from earlier in the chapter that bond coupon rates depend on the riskiness of the company and the prevailing interest rate. The second number refers to the bond's maturity date. Chrysler's bond will mature in 1999.

The fourth column shows the current yield, 8.7 percent in Chrysler's case. This is the interest rate the investor would earn at the bond's current price. Recall that the yield will equal the coupon rate at issuance but may vary thereafter in relation to the changing price of the bond.

The fifth column shows the volume of trading on the previous day. Unlike the volume figure for stocks, which reflects the number of shares traded, the

figure **22.5**   **Reading Bond Quotations**

| Company name, interest rate, and maturity date | | | | | | | | Current yield: percentage of interest investor would earn at current bond price |

STOCK EXCHANGE BONDS

12 Mo.			Cur		Wk............... ....Chg			
HI	LO	Name	Yld	Vol	HI	LO	Cls	Chg
$103^{1/4}$	$94^{1/8}$	Chrysl $6^{1/2}9$Bj	6.5	25	$100^{3/4}$	$100^{1/8}$	$100^{1/8}$	$-\ ^{5/8}$
$113^{7/8}$	$105^{3/4}$	Chrysl 10.95s17	9.9	49	$112^{3/8}$	$110^{1/8}$	$110^{1/2}$	$-\ ^{7/8}$
$108^{7/8}$	$102^{1/2}$	Chrysl 10.40s99	9.8	262	$106^{7/8}$	106	$106^{3/8}$	$-\ ^{3/8}$
$117^{1/8}$	$105^{5/8}$	Chrysl $9^{1/2}99$	8.7	30	$108^{3/4}$	$108^{3/4}$	$108^{3/4}$	$-1^{1/4}$
101	91	Chrysl $6^{5/8}00$	6.6	3	$100^{3/8}$	$100^{3/8}$	$100^{3/8}$	$-\ ^{7/8}$

High and low for preceding 12 months

Dollar value of previous day's trading, in thousands (30 = $30,000)

High, low, and closing prices and the difference between that day's closing price and previous day's closing price

Bond quotations contain much of the same information as stock quotations—high and low prices for the year and for the preceding day, as well as the day's trading volume. However, they do have unique characteristics. The most obvious difference is the way prices are read: stocks are quoted in dollars and fractions of dollars, whereas bonds—which are issued in units of $1,000—are quoted in thousands of dollars. Bond quotations also specify the coupon rate and the maturity date, as well as the yield. The yield, as you know, equals the coupon rate on the date of issuance; bonds sold after that date may have a higher or lower yield, depending on the bond's current dollar value.

Source: The *New York Times*, July 22, 1995, p. 45.

volume for bonds is measured in thousands of dollars—in this case, the number 30 means $30,000.

The final columns, as in stock quotes, report the previous day's trading. The numbers differ in that each point represents $10 and each ⅛ is $1.25. Therefore, 108¾ means the bond is selling at $1,087.50 ([108 × $10] + $7.50).

Securities Indexes

Some investors may wish to monitor the general movement in stock or bond prices, without focusing on particular securities. The *Wall Street Journal* and most major daily newspapers provide this information in the form of an **index**, a price-weighted average of a group of securities—from various domestic indexes to the Dow Jones World Stock Index of exchanges. By themselves, these numbers are not very meaningful; as a source of comparison, they describe price patterns over time. Although the various indexes measure different categories of securities, all tend to show the same basic patterns—sometimes indicating a *bull* market, in which the prices of securities are rising, and sometimes a *bear* market, in which prices are declining.

For stocks, the most closely watched index is the Dow Jones Industrial Averages Index (DJIA), which is a composite of 30 industrial firms. Dow Jones also indexes 20 transportation firms, 15 utilities, and 65 other firms in various industries. The NYSE Composite Index averages the performance of all stocks on the Big Board, categorized into four groups—industrial, utility, transportation, and financial. Standard & Poor's 500 Index, which, like the Dow Jones, is closely monitored by investors, uses these same categories for the 500 largest companies in the United States. NASDAQ and AMEX also have their own indexes. In fact, NASDAQ stocks are separately indexed in a bank index, an insurance index, or a composite index.

✓ **index**

A price-weighted average of a group of securities.

Dow Jones provides comparable indexes for tracking bond prices. These, too, are reported in the *Wall Street Journal* and major daily newspapers. Of particular interest to many investors are the Dow Jones Bond Indexes for utility and industrial companies.

Because of the global nature of business today, and of finance in particular, investors are putting their money in companies outside the United States. The Dow Jones World Stock Index provides stock information by region—the Americas, Europe, Asia/Pacific—and by certain countries within those regions. Of great value to American investors are the columns showing the value of their investments in U.S. dollars.

Trading in the Securities Markets

The majority of stockbrokers work in the brokerage firm's offices rather than on the stock exchange floor. From the office, brokers send buy or sell orders to coworkers on the trading floor. Because timing is so important in stock trading, brokers are networked to electronic services that provide up-to-the-minute information about stock prices. At the offices of Merrill Lynch & Co., electronic ticker tapes identify the status of the major indexes and provide a running update of individual stock prices. Brokers use this information to advise clients about the best time to buy or sell a stock. They also receive current information about new stock issues that might be of interest to their clients.

Types of Securities Trades

When we think about investing, we think of calling a stockbroker, issuing an order to buy a security, and then sitting back until (hopefully) its price increases and we can sell it at a profit. In fact, trading securities is somewhat more involved than that, and you, as potential investors, finance managers, or securities dealers, should be aware of the details.

10. Describe the different methods of trading securities.

Placing an Order

When you are ready to buy stock, you do place an order with your stockbroker. If you are willing to pay the best available price or sell at the best available price, you place a **market order**, an order that has no special restrictions and that can be executed within seconds or minutes. If you are only willing to buy at a particular price, you place a **limit order**. For example, if Citicorp stock is selling at $63 but you don't want to pay that much, you place a limit order to buy, say, 100 shares at $60 per share. Alternatively, if you own 100 shares of Citicorp that you bought at $63 per share, you may place a limit order to sell these shares at $70 or above.

 market order

An order placed with a stockbroker that has no special restrictions and that can be executed within seconds or minutes.

 limit order

An order placed with a stockbroker that specifies a particular sale or purchase price.

round lot

One hundred shares of a stock to be bought or sold.

odd lot

Fewer than 100 shares of a stock to be bought or sold.

program trading

A procedure whereby computers are programmed to execute buy and sell orders under certain conditions.

margin trading

Method of using cash and borrowed funds to invest in securities.

selling short

Selling shares borrowed from a broker in order to buy them later at a lower price, thereby earning a profit.

In our example, we were planning to buy or sell 100 shares of stock, in stock parlance, a **round lot**. An amount below 100 is considered an **odd lot**, and brokers, although they will handle such small transactions (for a larger commission), will do so only when they have gathered enough odd lots to make a round lot.

With the advent of computers, investors have tried to simplify and speed up the trading process. A relatively new and controversial process, called **program trading**, takes advantage of the fact that computers can be programmed to automatically execute orders under certain conditions. Program trading is controversial because it is considered to be partially responsible for the stock market crash of 1987. Computers had been programmed to sell certain stocks when they reached specific prices, and as prices began to fall on that fateful Monday, the computers executed their orders and so triggered further declines. To offset the problem of program trading, the stock exchanges have "fail-safe" switches that shut trading down for a time if the Dow Jones averages fall by 250 points. This solution works well if the problem is simply a technical one, but if other, uncontrollable factors are involved, nothing can stop a downslide.

Buying on Margin

When placing an order to purchase stock, investors must specify whether they plan to pay the entire amount up front. An alternative is to buy on margin. **Margin trading** involves the use of cash along with funds borrowed from the brokerage firm. For example, an investor purchasing $10,000 in stocks may give cash for 60 percent of the purchase and borrow the remaining 40 percent from the brokerage firm.

Margin trading has several advantages. Investors who do not have sufficient cash on hand will not lose the opportunity to make a strongly desired investment. In addition, investors can purchase more and different stocks with the same amount of money they would otherwise have had to pay to purchase a single stock. Margin trading does not affect the size of any capital gain, but when a smaller amount of cash is used, that gain represents a higher percentage of the amount of cash put up by the investor.

On the other hand, if the stock's price declines over time, margin trading is a definite disadvantage. Because the investor must repay the borrowed money, the dollar amount lost represents a higher percentage of the investor's cash investment. Furthermore, the investor must endure the loss on the stock bought with his or her own money.

Selling Short

Like margin trading, **selling short** is a form of trading in which, in a sense, you use your broker as a bank. Selling short, however, involves borrowing stock shares, not funds, and it requires a keen sense of the market. Selling short works this way. You borrow shares of stock from your broker, say, 100 shares. You sell those shares for $10 each. Then, when the stock's price goes down, say, to $8, you use that money to buy 100 shares. You return the shares to your broker and you have earned $200, that is, [100 shares × $10 = $1,000] − [100 shares × $8 = 800] = $200.

If stock prices decline in a short time, selling short is a good way to earn fast money. If prices don't decline for a while, you begin to lose money because you are paying interest to your broker for the borrowed shares. And, if prices rise, your losses increase substantially because your purchase price will be higher than your sales price.

Reviewing *Securities Markets and Investing*

Investing in Securities: What Are the Options?

1. **Identify the types of marketable securities and the markets through which they are sold and describe the process by which companies raise funds through stock issues.** Marketable securities include stocks and bonds that are bought and sold through organized markets. Primary markets are the markets in which stocks and bonds are initially issued (investment bankers, for example), whereas secondary markets are the markets in which stocks and bonds already owned by investors are bought and sold. When a company decides to go public—to sell its stock to the general public—management employs an investment banker, who helps it prepare a prospectus and facilitates sale of the company's IPO by advertising in the financial press.

2. **Differentiate between common and preferred stock.** Both types of stock represent equity, or ownership, in a corporation; both may be issued with a par, or face, value but are more likely to be offered with no par value. Common stock provides voting rights and a better chance to earn a profit by selling the stock at a price higher than the purchase price. Common stockholders may also benefit from a stock split. Preferred stock provides for fixed dividends, which are normally higher than those paid on common stock. In addition, if dividends were not paid in the previous year, holders of cumulative preferred stock receive those dividends before common stockholders receive the current year's dividends.

3. **Describe the characteristics of bonds and compare and contrast the different categories of bonds.** Bonds are debt instruments, making bondholders creditors of the corporation. They are issued, usually in units of $1,000, with a set maturity date, a par (or face) value, and a coupon (or interest) rate specified on the bond indenture. The two broad categories of bonds are government issues and corporate bonds. Government issues include Treasury bills, notes, and bonds, which are distinguished by their maturity, as well as agency bonds and municipal bonds. Municipal bonds may be general obligation or revenue bonds, depending on whether the issuer has taxing authority. Corporate bonds may be secured or unsecured (debentures), or they may be convertible to stock. Some corporate bonds have a call feature, allowing the company to reduce its expenses. Recently, corporations have begun issuing zero-coupon bonds, which allow them to use all the money until the bond matures.

4. **Explain bond yields and discuss the meaning and purpose of bond ratings.** Bond yields represent actual earnings on a bond. At issuance, yield equals the coupon rate; after issuance, yield depends on the bond's default risk, liquidity, and tax status, and on whether the bond has a callable feature. Bonds are rated by several agencies, particularly Moody's and Standard & Poor's. Ratings basically define the riskiness of a bond for investors. At the top of the ratings are Treasury securities; at the bottom are junk bonds.

5. **Describe the purpose and types of mutual funds and derivatives.** Mutual funds provide an investment source for investors wishing to rely on professionals to select a diversified portfolio for them. There are stock, bond, and money market mutual funds, which represent different investment goals. Investors select a fund that they think will meet their goals—for periodic income through bond funds or blue chip stock funds, or for growth, for example. Open-end mutual funds accept new investors, while closed-end funds are limited to a fixed number of shares. Derivatives are simply financial devices whose value changes in response to movement in the prices of other securities. The most well-known derivatives are put and call options and futures contracts. Commodities, which may be bought and sold on the spot market, are more frequently traded as futures.

Investors: Who Are They and What Are Their Goals?

6. **Identify the categories of investors and describe five broad investment goals.** Investors belong to one of two broad categories: institutional investors and individual investors. Institutional investors include commercial banks, pension funds, insurance companies, investment companies, and not-for-profit organizations. Institutional investors have a major effect on the prices of securities, since they buy and sell large blocks at a time. All investors, institutional or individual, may have one or more of five investment goals: income, growth, liquidity, safety, and tax advantage. The ideal portfolio contains a diverse selection of securities.

Securities Markets: Where Trading Takes Place

7. **List and characterize the major securities markets.** Securities are traded by stock specialists in an auction-style trade or through a dealer exchange. The major exchanges are the New York Stock Exchange (NYSE), the American Stock Exchange (AMEX), and the regional exchanges that are linked to the NYSE and AMEX. Equally important in this electronic age are the over-the-counter markets with NASDAQ at their core. Although the NYSE is the oldest and largest exchange, NASDAQ, only 20-plus years old, lists twice as many members as the NYSE. Besides differing from traditional exchanges in its use of

electronics, NASDAQ also differs in employing multiple market makers for each stock. Although these exchanges are important to U.S. companies, in this time of increasingly global business, investors cannot ignore the activities of the large exchanges around the world, some of which have outperformed U.S. exchanges in recent years. Investors also trade in foreign stocks, either directly or as ADRs.

8. **Discuss the regulation of securities markets and securities traders**. The Security Act of 1933 and the Securities Exchange Act of 1934, which created the Securities and Exchange Commission (SEC), were responses to fraudulent activities prior to the Great Depression. In an effort to regulate the national securities markets and those who traded in these markets, these acts required the registration of all new securities and the disclosure of all relevant information. Today, the SEC has the authority to regulate over-the-counter and regional markets as well. Its goals are threefold: to ensure that the public receives all relevant information, to prevent fraud in securities transactions, and to prevent insider trading.

Investing: How It's Done

9. **Describe the process of selecting a broker and explain how to analyze securities quotations**. Depending on your investment needs and abilities, you may select a full-service broker, a discount broker, or a deep-discount broker; these differ primarily in the amount of advice they provide and the fees, or commissions, they charge. Once you have selected a broker and decided on a portfolio of securities for investment, you can track the progress of your investments by reading daily price quotations for stocks, bonds, and mutual funds—in effect, for any type of security you can think of. All major daily newspapers contain these quotations, accompanied by an explanation of the abbreviations used in the listings, so that you can see how your investments are doing, individually or in comparison to other securities. The various indexes, particularly the Dow Jones Industrial Averages and Standard & Poor's 500, indicate patterns of activity for specific categories of securities.

10. **Describe the different methods of trading securities**. Beyond the straightforward buying and selling of stock by issuing a market order, investors have several options for trading in the securities markets. Program trading is a controversial process because it relies on programmed instructions to a computer to execute certain transactions. Margin trading and selling short are two techniques used to purchase more stock for less money. The risks involved in these types of trading are heavy, however.

 Key Terms

marketable securities **665**	Treasury bonds **669**	mutual fund **673**	price-earnings (P/E) ratio
primary markets **665**	municipal bonds (munis)	blue chip stocks **674**	**686**
secondary markets **665**	**669**	growth stocks **674**	index **688**
par value (face value) **665**	general obligation bonds	derivative securities **674**	market order **689**
investment banker **665**	**670**	call option **674**	limit order **689**
prospectus **665**	revenue bonds **670**	put option **675**	round lot **690**
common stock **666**	secured bonds **671**	futures contracts **675**	odd lot **690**
stock split **667**	debenture **671**	commodities **675**	program trading **690**
preferred stock **667**	convertible bonds **671**	over-the-counter market	margin trading **690**
maturity date **668**	callable bonds **671**	(OTC) **680**	selling short **690**
Treasury bills (T-bills) **668**	zero-coupon bond **671**	American depository	
Treasury notes **669**	junk bond **673**	receipts (ADRs) **682**	

● **Review Questions**

1. As financial manager of LaLa Company, you decide to raise capital by issuing stock. How do you proceed?

2. If you decided to purchase a company's stock with the goal of earning a profit from an increase in the stock's price, would you buy common or preferred stock? Why?

3. How do bonds differ from stocks?

4. How do Treasury securities and municipal bonds differ?

5. What are the possible characteristics of a corporate bond?

6. You decide to purchase shares in a mutual fund. What types of mutual funds are available? What are their different goals?

7. You have several thousand dollars that you want to invest for a quick profit. What types of derivatives might you select from? How do they differ?

8. How do the five investor goals and portfolio management work together?

9. How do the traditional securities markets differ from the electronic markets?

10. What does it mean to buy on margin and sell short?

● Critical Thinking Questions

1. Why do you think stocks that pay high dividends have low growth?

2. Suppose that you are compiling a portfolio of stocks and bonds. What factors should you consider, and why?

3. Why would you be willing to buy a debenture or junk bonds?

4. Why would you consider purchasing mutual funds rather than stocks?

5. If buying stocks on margin can magnify returns, why don't all investors buy their stocks on margin?

REVIEW CASE   *Splitting Teddies from Dresses*[15]

Teddies and toiletries have been a great business for The Limited, Inc. In roughly a decade, The Limited built a $2 billion-plus business selling lingerie, intimate apparel, perfume, soaps, and other women's items through its Victoria's Secret retail and catalog business and its Bath & Body Works chain of personal care product stores. Between 1991 and 1995, the combined sales of these divisions more than doubled, with profits soaring from $93 million to $200 million. Considering that Victoria's Secret had less than $50 million in sales in 1982 and that Bath & Body Works was first created by The Limited in 1990, $2 billion is an impressive number.

One would expect such a financial bonanza to attract flocks of investors. Not so. Despite the strong performance of Victoria's Secret and Bath & Body Works, The Limited's stock price declined from 1991 to 1995 because sales at the company's women's clothing chains—Express, The Limited, Lerner New York, and Bryant—weren't nearly as good and in some cases had declined.

Company chairman and CEO Leslie Wexner was troubled by the sluggish stock price for several reasons. First, he had a legal responsibility to shareholders to maximize their investment in the firm. Second, it hurt his pride, particularly since some stockholders were openly questioning the company's operating strategy. Third, he personally was losing money. Even after The Limited went public in the 1980s, Wexner had retained a large percentage of the company's stock. To appease investors and rebuild some of his own wealth, Wexner knew he had to do something to increase the price of The Limited's stock.

In May 1995, he made plans to split off Victoria's Secret, Bath & Body Works, and several smaller divisions into a separate company called Intibrands and to sell 15 percent of the new company's equity to the public. The money received from this initial public offering would be used to pay off $250 million in debt and allay investors' fears. It would also provide Intibrands with working capital to open more stores, mail out more catalogs, and perhaps even establish new businesses. Most important to investors, the offering would place a value on the lingerie and personal products businesses.

1. Why would investors be concerned about the performance of a few divisions when the performance of Victoria's Secret and Bath & Body Works was so spectacular?

2. What were Wexner's goals in establishing Intibrands as a separate company?

3. In light of the chapter's discussion of bonds, what else might Wexner have done to reduce The Limited's $250 million debt?

4. Which of the five goals would potential investors in The Limited probably be seeking?

5. The Limited is listed on the New York Stock Exchange. What does this mean in terms of its size and its assets?

6. Referring to the text discussion of new stock issues, how do you think the price of Intibrand stock reacted before, during, and after the issue of Wexner's IPO?

7. The Limited clearly had a substantial debt obligation. Why would Wexner prefer to split off his most successful divisions into a separate company with a new stock offering rather than increase The Limited's number of shares outstanding?

8. What might Wexner's rationale have been in splitting off his most successful divisions but letting The Limited retain 85 percent ownership in Intibrands?

CRITICAL THINKING CASE *Securing Funds with Securities*

You have been employed as chief accountant for Pandora Corp., a manufacturer of decorative boxes used for display or to hold small items such as pins or buttons. Pandora is a large company, established in 1911, and its stock—with 500,000 shares of common stock outstanding—is traded on the New York Stock Exchange. Recently, the stock has been selling for $47.85, up 3½ points from the preceding quarter. Last year, the company retired its last outstanding bond obligation.

The chief financial officer (CFO) was recently promoted to chief executive officer (CEO) and has asked that you take her old job. She has already sketched out a basic forecast for the next quarter, including projected revenues and expenses for daily operations. You agree to take the job and soon begin reviewing the CFO's forecast and meeting with department managers to discuss their plans and needs for the year. After talking with marketing and production, you learn that a new box with an unusual shape is scheduled for release within the next year and is expected to sell very well. Production explains, however, that keeping up with the demand for the new box plus all the old items will require that the operating facility be expanded. This, of course, will take a large capital outlay, clearly exceeding the revenues available from normal operations. Furthermore, the company does not want to invest operating capital in a long-term project. You calculate that the company will need approximately $10 million to cover the expansion.

It is now your responsibility to plan for this capital expenditure and to recommend to management the best sources of funds. You narrow the choices down to issuing new stock or floating a bond issue.

1. What facts about the company's outstanding equity and its debt obligations must you consider in making your decision?

2. What characteristics of stocks and bonds in general should you consider in recommending the issuance of one or the other type of financing?

3. What steps would you take in preparing a stock issue?

4. If you recommend floating a bond, what bond features should Pandora include?

5. After you have considered all the factors, would you recommend a new stock issue or a bond? Why?

Critical Thinking with the ONE MINUTE MANAGER

"We began by focusing on the value of information technology to individual investors. You should realize by now, however, that all we've been saying about the importance of efficiency and speed applies as well, if not more so, to business decision making," concluded the One Minute Manager. "To succeed, all businesses—whether they are issuing securities, making investments, or acting as enablers in the securities markets—must change and grow to meet the changing environment. And, as you learned during earlier discussions, the people on the front lines, the ones doing the work, are in the best position to know what is needed. Charles Schwab, drawing on his own needs and interests and recognizing an opportunity, brought the securities markets to the general public and did so at a handsome profit for himself. Indeed, technological innovations such as TeleBroker—a 24-hour transaction service—have made it easier for investors and reduced the company's operating expenses. A more recent innovation, in which clients can use a single account for investing and for electronic banking, will also benefit both the public and Charles Schwab."

Joanna wondered aloud: "If the electronic market is so efficient, why do the traditional markets continue with many of the same old methods?"

"Well, nothing changes overnight," the One Minute manager answered carefully. "These markets are changing, albeit slowly, with many more functions now being performed via computers. It's likely that 20 years from now, all the securities markets will consist of hundreds of thousands of individual computers across the nation and the world, all telecommunicating without any face-to-face connections."

1. The electronics age is not without problems, as you have seen. What advantages might the old systems have? Can you think of a way to combine the advantages of the old and the new?

2. Although the new securities markets are electronic, people remain an integral and important factor. Why is this so? How might the use of teams, as discussed in Chapter 9, be applied to the securities markets in terms of issuing companies, investors, and stockbrokers?

23 Risk Management and Insurance

Tornadoes, earthquakes, floods—businesses always face the chance of loss from disasters like these. In fact, the 10 costliest natural disasters in U.S. history occurred between the mid-1980s and the mid-1990s, causing a total of more than $40 billion in damage.[1] In addition, businesses engage in *speculative risk*, the possibility of either loss or gain. Financial managers and investors take speculative risks when investing, hoping that they will gain, but realizing that they may lose. In general, businesses can exert some control over speculative risk, but they have limited control, if any, over **pure risk**, the threat of loss without the possibility of gain. You are about to learn how businesses manage pure risk and how they protect themselves and their employees with insurance coverage. After reading this chapter, you will be able to reach the learning goals below.

 pure risk

The threat of loss without the possibility of gain.

Learning Goals

1. Identify and describe the four basic strategies of risk management.
2. Explain why self-insurance has become increasingly popular.
3. Differentiate between insurable and uninsurable risks and explain the law of large numbers.
4. Explain how the law of adverse selection reflects current problems of insurers.
5. Identify and describe several different forms of public insurance and discuss some problems that make their future uncertain.
6. Distinguish between stock and mutual insurance companies in their role as private insurers.
7. Identify and describe the types of commercial liability insurance.
8. Describe the various forms of property/casualty and income insurance.
9. Discuss reasons for new forms of health insurance.
10. Identify and describe the categories of personal insurance.

By All Means, Plan Your Disasters[2]

The One Minute Manager gave a wave when Carlos and Joanna appeared at her door. "I'll be right with you," she said. The students stepped into the outer office to wait.

Carlos looked back. "That meeting looks important. Maybe she doesn't have time to see us today."

"If she were too busy, she'd say so," Joanna said. "Did you hear about the big warehouse fire last night?"

"The sirens woke me up," Carlos replied. "It must have been two or three in the morning."

Before Joanna could speak, a group of familiar faces filed out of the office, followed by the One Minute Manager. "Come in," she said. "We were just reviewing our disaster plan. That fire last night made my CFO edgy. He wants to make sure nothing like that ever happens here."

Carlos was puzzled. "I don't understand. How can you plan for disaster?"

"How can you not? These past few years U.S. businesses have coped with what seems like an unending string of disasters—major storms, floods, earthquakes, riots, terrorism. Catastrophe can strike anywhere. That's why we review our plan every year."

The One Minute Manager pointed to a large display board mounted on the wall. It was divided into four columns labeled Potential Risks, Prevention, Control, and Opportunity. "Our CFO got the idea for this from reading about CDA Management Consulting, a firm based in Ohio," she continued. "They advise business owners to develop damage control strategies by setting aside time each year to brainstorm about protecting their businesses in the event of a disaster. If you want to stay in business, you have to manage the risks you face."

Now Joanna looked puzzled. "How do you *manage* risk? I thought businesses *took* risks. How can you manage something you can't control?"

"You can't, but like a good scout, you can be prepared. And that brings me back to our disaster strategy."

The One Minute Manager continued: "In the Potential Risks column we try to list every situation we're vulnerable to, and it includes a lot more than natural disasters."

Joanna read down the list. "Why is your name there?" she asked. "If you look further, you'll see that the names of other key staff are there as well, in case there comes a time when we're *not* here," the One Minute Manager replied. "We have to plan what to do if we lose key staff, just as we have to have a plan if we lose our largest supplier, if our customers are slow in paying their bills, or if interest rates go up."

"You mean there are ways to head off all those risks?" Carlos asked.

"Look at the Prevention column and you'll see our latest ideas," said the One Minute Manager. "In the Control column are our action plans—things we can do now to prepare for the situations we might face. Finally, in the Opportunity column, we look for ways to turn risk into reward—that is, to think about the good that might eventually result from a disaster."

"And the best time to do that is when your head is clear," Carlos offered, "not in the middle of a crisis."

Risky Business

Risk is a fact of life. Take, for instance, an automobile dealership that spends thousands of dollars on both newspaper advertising and direct mail to promote a one-day sale. The dealer is taking a speculative risk that the extra money spent on advertising will generate publicity and sales. The promotion also involves pure risks that the dealer faces every day—the danger of, say, a flash flood that would carry away the cars on the lot and tear the showroom apart.

Risk Management

Just because the dealer has no control over pure risk doesn't mean that he or she can't prepare for a flood or any other calamity by developing disaster control strategies like the ones you read about in the One Minute Manager example. Part of that process involves a concerted strategy of **risk management**, the process of analyzing risks and choosing ways to minimize loss from those risks.[3] There are four basic strategies in risk management:

1. Avoid the risk
2. Reduce the risk
3. Assume the risk
4. Shift the risk

Avoid the Risk

Fundamentally, risk avoidance is simple. Don't put yourself in a position of risk, and you won't incur a loss. There's only one small problem with taking risk avoidance to such an extreme: no risk, no reward. Instead, most companies engage in a modified form of risk avoidance, knowingly taking on some risks and avoiding others.

A.O. Smith Electrical Products of Tipp City, Ohio, for instance, is trying to do more business overseas. However, the $300 million company is wary of selling goods to companies in politically unstable countries. So it tries to get insurance to cover the risks associated with international trade and to shift the risk of loss to the insurer. In recent years, though, such insurance has gotten harder to come by. When A.O. Smith tried to obtain coverage in March 1993 for a $250,000 shipment to Iran, one U.S. insurance company agreed to provide it at a cost of $50,000—and that would only cover half the value of the order. Such a charge would have severely reduced the company's potential profit. On top of that, there was still the risk that it would not get paid for the goods even if it shipped them. Instead, A.O. Smith simply avoided the risk and let the deal die because it couldn't get the necessary insurance at the right price.[4]

Reduce the Risk

For most businesses avoidance is the least popular risk strategy. After all, no company wants to turn away customers willing to buy. Instead, many businesses turn to a risk reduction strategy. Every day, each of us tries to reduce risk in some way—by driving within the speed limit, crossing the street with the light, coming to class to avoid flunking. Risk reduction in business is the same.

The airline industry has an entire set of procedures designed specifically to reduce risk. For instance, pilots can fly only a certain number of hours per day, per week, and per month. Similarly, planes must be inspected for wear and tear after a certain number of takeoffs and landings, and whenever a pilot reports a possible problem.

1. Identify and describe the four basic strategies of risk management.

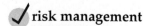 **risk management**

The process of analyzing risks and choosing ways to minimize loss from those risks.

Risk Reduction Strategy

Accidents and injuries on the job can threaten the financial health of a business, both by boosting insurance expenses and draining productivity because of lost labor time. Putting the emphasis on workplace safety is a fundamental risk reduction strategy. At office-furniture manufacturer Trendway Corp., all 300 employees take five minutes of exercise at the beginning of the work day to increase upper-body flexibility and decrease the risk of injury. And one employee in 10 participates in Trendway's employee-directed safety program.

Risk reduction often involves swapping a pure risk for a speculative risk. Apple Computer, Inc., for example, sells a computer keyboard that alleviates stress on hands, wrists, and the rest of the arm. Companies are buying this keyboard for their employees to reduce the risk of computer users incurring repetitive stress injuries such as carpal tunnel syndrome. Injuries on the job reduce employee productivity and potentially expose the business to liability—lawsuits, for example, brought by employees claiming that it provided an unsafe working environment. The keyboard also reduces Apple's exposure to liability for selling a defective product. The company is taking a speculative risk that its investment in product development will pay off by reducing its pure risk.

Occasionally, a company turns to risk reduction after it incurs a loss. In 1991, a storm sewer overflowed in Brentwood, Missouri, flooding the basement of Colt Safety, Inc., a distributor of protective equipment. Merchandise worth $500,000 was destroyed. The extent of the damage might have been reduced, however, if the boxes of merchandise had not been stacked from floor to ceiling. Under three feet of water, the bottom boxes had crumbled, sending those on top cascading into the water. Since then, the company has purchased special shelving that keeps its merchandise at least 36 inches off the ground.[5]

The government plays an active role in risk reduction in the workplace. As discussed in Chapter 4, the Occupational Safety and Health Administration (OSHA) is a federal agency that develops regulations to ensure American workers a safe workplace. Some of its rules are as simple as requiring companies to label hazardous materials. Others, such as banning smoking in the workplace, are more controversial.

Assume the Risk

When risk can be neither avoided nor completely reduced, it must be taken on, or assumed. Think for a minute about your decision to take this class, or even to enroll in college in the first place. You're assuming a risk: the money you spend on tuition and the time you spend in class, against the chance of being well prepared for a successful career. You could have decided not to go to college, which would have protected you from some of the risks. But what about your career?

Every day, on a basic level, companies assume risk simply by opening their doors for business. Entrepreneurs and small-business owners, in particular, assume greater risks than larger companies because they often have their own money at stake.

There are a couple of ways for a firm to assume risk. Perhaps the most dangerous involves **going naked**, that is, having no protection of any kind against loss. Such a business tactic, however, is foolhardy at best and dangerous at worst. Without insurance, a simple fall by a customer could end up costing an owner his or her business.

A more common and increasingly popular form of risk assumption is **self-insurance**, setting money aside in a special company-run fund to guard against future losses. Consider the case of Trendway Corp., a Holland, Michigan, office furniture manufacturer. The company self-insures for **workers' compensation**, insurance that pays the wages and medical bills of employees who are injured on the job. Instead of setting aside money every month to pay an insurance company for workers' compensation coverage, the company pays claims out of its own self-insurance fund.

In addition to saving Trendway the up-front money it would have to pay to buy insurance, self-insurance gives the company and its employees an additional motivation to prevent workplace injuries—larger distributions from its profit-sharing program. In essence, by keeping the workplace safe, employees make more money, and so does the company. From 1988 through 1994, Trendway's 300 employees suffered just one injury that resulted in lost work time.[6]

Self-insurance is nothing new. For hundreds of years, until the appearance of modern insurance companies, it was the only insurance most companies had. Even when commercial insurance policies became widespread, big companies still self-insured against health and other forms of risk. Until the last two decades, however, self-insurance was not a viable option for many small companies, which could not afford to put themselves at risk for a single large loss.

The federal Risk Retention Act of 1981 changed all that. It made self-insurance a viable option for small companies by allowing them to band together as self-insurers. As a result, self-insurance has become part of the risk management strategy of many small companies. Assuming risk is increasing in popularity for two reasons: availability and cost savings.

Right now, about 28 percent of all businesses nationwide cannot afford workers' compensation insurance coverage; others cannot obtain it because insurance firms are unwilling to take on companies that operate in high-risk industries.[7] If, like Trendway, such companies self-insure, coverage is always available, and often it is cheaper, as well.

These benefits have caused a large increase in the self-insurance market. According to a study by Johnson & Higgins, a New York insurance research firm, 30 percent of all the money spent in 1992 on workers' compensation insurance was paid into individual company and group self-insurance funds. By contrast, in 1986, 20 percent of workers' compensation money came from self-insurance funds.[8]

Self-insurance has one major drawback. Just like going naked, it exposes a company to exorbitant losses. From 1991 to 1993, E.I. du Pont de Nemours and Co. paid out more than $800 million to settle lawsuits brought by scores of farmers over damage to their farmland allegedly caused by the company's Benlate DF fertilizer. That money came out of reserves the company had set aside as part of its corporate self-insurance plan.[9]

Shift the Risk

Even companies that self-insure do not want to expose themselves to unlimited risk. So they look to shift the risk to others. The main means of doing this is well known to all of us: insurance.

2. Explain why self-insurance has become increasingly popular.

 going naked

Assuming risk with no protection of any kind against loss.

 self-insurance

Setting money aside in a special company-run fund to guard against future losses.

 workers' compensation

Insurance that pays the wages and medical bills of employees who are injured on the job.

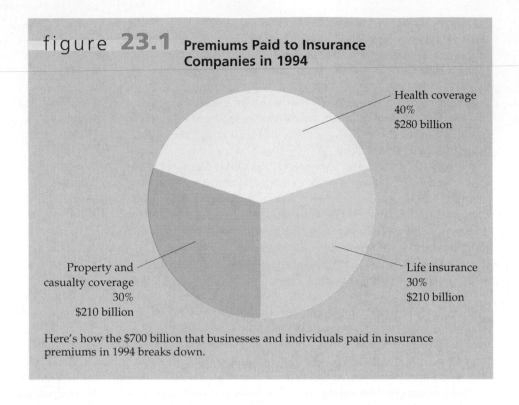

figure **23.1**   **Premiums Paid to Insurance Companies in 1994**

Health coverage
40%
$280 billion

Life insurance
30%
$210 billion

Property and
casualty coverage
30%
$210 billion

Here's how the $700 billion that businesses and individuals paid in insurance premiums in 1994 breaks down.

insurance

A system that makes financial loss more affordable by transferring it from individuals to large groups.

premium

The amount an insurance company charges for an insurance policy.

deductible

A set amount paid by the policyholder to absorb a certain percentage of the loss.

coinsurance clause

(1) In property insurance, requires the policyholder to carry insurance equal to a specified percentage of the value of the property in order to receive full coverage on a loss; (2) in health insurance, requires the insured individual to pay a percentage of his or her medical expenses above and beyond the deductible.

Insurance is a system that makes financial loss more affordable by transferring it from individuals to large groups. In 1994 alone, individuals and companies in the United States paid more than $700 billion to insure their lives, health, and property. Health insurance accounted for about 40 percent of all paid **premiums**, the amount an insurance company charges for an insurance policy. As shown in Figure 23.1, the remaining premiums were divided almost evenly between life and property/casualty coverage.[10]

Insurance gives companies, particularly small ones, the peace of mind that comes from knowing that one catastrophic loss will not destroy them or cause them to lose an investment. When actor John Candy died in March 1994 of heart failure, he was in the middle of filming the movie *Wagons East*. But the film production company had taken out an insurance policy on Candy and was paid $14.5 million by the Fireman's Fund to cover the costs associated with replacing Candy and reshooting the scenes in which he appeared.[11]

Most businesses shift risk in another way: They require employees to pay part of the cost of their insurance. Most insurance policies, whether for businesses or individuals, require the policyholder to pay a set amount called a **deductible** to absorb a certain percentage of the loss before the insurer is forced to pay. Automobile insurance policies, for instance, typically carry a deductible of $200 or more for collision damage. If you have an accident, you have to pay the first $200 of the amount it costs to repair the car. Health insurance is similar. Over the course of a year, companies require employees to pay up to a certain deductible before the insurance policy takes over.

Over the last decade, companies have found a way to shift more of their health insurance costs to employees. To remain covered, employees *coinsure*, or "copay," a percentage of each medical expense above and beyond the deductible, most commonly 20 percent, up to a preset limit. **Coinsurance clauses** are used in both health insurance and property insurance policies. In property coverage, the coinsurance clause requires the policyholder to carry insurance equal to a specified percentage of the value of the property in order to receive full coverage on a loss. In health policies, a coinsurance clause requires the insured individual to pay a percentage of his or her medical expenses above and beyond the deductible.

In the debate on national health care, the growing use by businesses of deductibles and coinsurance to shift a portion of losses to policyholders is referred to as **cost shifting**. Deductibles and coinsurance are also two of the primary ways that insurance companies shift and reduce their risk. Deductibles benefit insurers by forcing individuals and companies to absorb the cost of small losses. They also enable insurance companies to avoid the cost of handling a large number of claims for such losses. Deductibles benefit individuals and business firms because they reduce the insurer's cost of doing business; this, in turn, allows the insurer to lower its premiums. Coinsurance limits an insurer's exposure to loss, that is, the amount it has to pay out in claims.

Insurance companies have yet a third way to shift risk. They buy **reinsurance** policies, which shift some of their risk to another insurer in return for a percentage of the premium. That is, reinsurers assume part of a risk that an insurance company takes on in return for part of the premium that the insurer receives from the policyholder. Lloyd's of London is perhaps the best-known reinsurer, but hundreds of other companies, such as General Re and Swiss Reinsurance, annually provide reinsurance worth more than $14 billion in the United States.[12]

cost shifting

The use by businesses of deductibles and coinsurance to shift a portion of losses to policyholders.

reinsurance

A policy bought by an insurance company that shifts some of its risk to another insurer in return for a percentage of the premium.

Insurance companies shift risk through
- *Deductibles*
- *Coinsurance*
- *Reinsurance*

Bedrock of the Insurance Market

After more than 300 years, the ship's bell at Lloyd's of London continues to herald both good news (with two rings) and bad (one ring). Lloyd's is the largest insurance exchange in the world, underwriting 40 percent of the world's marine cargo and more than half of all private-sector political risk insurance. But between 1988 and 1993, Lloyd's also paid out a fair percentage of the record $77 billion in insured losses that resulted both from natural and human-caused disasters around the world—everything from hurricanes to terrorist bombings. As a result, Lloyd's lost about a quarter of its capital base (In fact, many insurers were forced to discontinue traditional lines of coverage altogether). To survive, Lloyd's is adopting new business strategies to attract a fresh supply of capital from outside investors.

The Insurance Market

Perhaps the most famous of all insurance outfits, Lloyd's of London, got its start in 1688 when a group of shipowners met at Lloyd's coffeehouse in London and agreed to cover each other against the risk associated with sending cargo all around the world. Over the next two centuries, individuals and companies formed thousands of mutual aid or benevolent societies, typically run by one of the members. Some still exist today. The dues collected by these societies were disbursed when members ran into emergencies, such as a flood, a building fire, or a death. Benevolent societies evolved into modern-day insurance companies, which operate with professional management and often serve customers around the globe.

How Insurance Works

Lloyd's of London, benevolent societies, and insurance companies all operate under the same principles. They generate income through the premiums they charge customers and through investments. To make a profit, insurers must more than offset the money they pay out to policyholders who incur losses, and they must cover their own business expenses.

Insurers will write a policy for anyone with an **insurable interest**, that is, with a direct stake, financial or otherwise, in the person, place, or thing being insured. For example, a company that owns property in Miami can buy an insurance policy that reimburses it for any loss sustained from a hurricane. As a shareholder in the company, however, you cannot obtain your own policy on that same property, since your direct stake is in the shares of the company, not in the property itself.

Realistically, however, just because you have an insurable interest doesn't mean you can actually obtain insurance. Over the years, insurers have divided risks into two basic categories: uninsurable and insurable.

Insurable and Uninsurable Risks

3. Differentiate between insurable and uninsurable risks and explain the law of large numbers.

No insurance company will cover an **uninsurable risk** because the probability of loss that such a risk carries cannot be determined. In general, speculative risks are also uninsurable risks. For instance, Coca-Cola cannot buy an insurance policy to guard against possible losses if a new soft drink fails, because no insurer can determine the probability of the product's success or failure.

Some risks that were once insurable have now become uninsurable. During the 1950s and 1960s, insurers routinely provided health and property/casualty insurance for shipbuilders, automobile brake manufacturers, and other companies that handled or produced asbestos. But with the revelation in the 1970s that even small amounts of asbestos have the potential to cause cancer in humans, the health risk associated with working in such businesses became uninsurable.

Labor disputes are also typically uninsurable. When baseball players went out on strike in 1994, owners were forced to refund millions of dollars in unused tickets and to forgo income from concessions and other sources. Nor could the teams or the league turn to their insurers for compensation. After private insurers had to pay team owners $44 million following the 1981 baseball strike,[13] they decided that the threat of a baseball strike was an uninsurable risk.

 **insurable interest**

A direct stake, financial or otherwise, in the person, place, or thing being insured.

Some risks have become uninsurable because the premiums are simply too high to justify the insurance. For instance, developers of new medical devices and prescription drugs often must self-insure, that is, set money aside in a special corporate-run fund to guard against future losses.

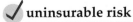 **uninsurable risk**

A risk no insurance company will cover because the probability of loss that it carries cannot be determined.

Conversely, some risks that were once uninsurable have become insurable. An **insurable risk** is one that a company will cover because the probability of loss that it carries can be determined. For instance, in the early days of automobile travel, car insurance was unobtainable because no insurer could calculate the risk of an individual's having an accident. Similarly, at the dawn of the Information Age, few could have imagined that one day insurance policies would

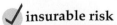 **insurable risk**

A risk an insurance company will cover because the probability of loss that it carries can be determined.

table **23.1**	An Insurance Company's List of Insurable and Uninsurable Risks	
Insurable	**Uninsurable**	
In general, pure risk	In general, speculative risk	
Liability	Business competition	
Property	Labor disputes	
Health	Political change	
Life	Unemployment	
Business interruption	Gambling	
Malpractice	Floods	

exist for computer malfunctions. But nowadays, standard commercial insurance policies cover this and other risks that come with modern technology.

Table 23.1 lists general categories of risks that insurance companies consider to be either insurable or uninsurable. As a rule, insurance companies find that insurable risks must have five characteristics:

1. *The person or company taking out the policy must have an insurable interest,* or a direct stake in the person or thing being insured.

2. *The insurer must be able to calculate the odds of loss.* Odds calculation is the heart of the insurance business. Without knowing the odds, the insurer will not know how often it will have to pay a claim and thus will not be able to figure out how much it should charge for a policy. Insurers rely on **actuaries**, statisticians who calculate the potential for an insurance company's future loss based on historical loss data. The more information actuaries have about past losses, the better they can predict an insurance company's future losses. Life insurers know with a high degree of certainty, for example, that the 130 million women in the United States will live to an average age of 78. This enables insurance companies to easily calculate how much to charge a 30-year-old woman every year so that her survivors receive, say, $100,000 upon her death.

3. *The insurer must be able to measure the loss.* A policy generally has a *cap,* or upper limit, on the amount that can be paid out. When you buy automobile insurance, for instance, the policy typically contains a cap on the amount you can receive in hospital benefits. Insurers also limit collision coverage to the value of the car, which protects them from having to pay out more than they take in. More and more, health insurance policies also carry a lifetime cap, typically $1 million, on benefits payable. The cap allows the insurer to measure its maximum possible loss.

4. *The loss must not be intentional.* Insurance is designed to cover the unexpected. Arson and embezzlement on the part of the policyholder, however, are not accidental. They are, in fact, speculative risks from which the policyholder stands to benefit, unless he or she gets caught.

5. *The risk of loss must be spread over a wide group.* Geographic or demographic diversity is critical. Otherwise, a natural disaster such as a flood in Missouri could wipe out an insurance company that provides homeowner's coverage only in that state.

The largest insurance companies use supercomputers to calculate risks based on many decades of claims data.

 actuary

A statistician who calculates the potential for an insurance company's future loss based on historical loss data.

✓ **law of large numbers**

The larger the number of people or objects in a pool, the smaller the variation between actual and predictable losses.

✓ **law of adverse selection**

Individuals who are risk-prone are more likely to obtain or continue coverage than people who are less likely to have a claim.

The Law of Large Numbers

These five conditions for insurable risk govern virtually every policy an insurance company writes. Together they constitute the basis for the **law of large numbers**, which holds that the larger the number of people or objects in a pool, the smaller the variation between actual and predictable losses.[14] Worldwide Weather of Great Neck, New York, uses the law of large numbers to develop rates for the specialized weather insurance policies it underwrites. For instance, when Gingras Jewelers and Gemologists of Hartford, Connecticut, ran a holiday season promotion promising customers free jewelry if it snowed on New Year's Eve, it turned to Worldwide Weather for a special policy protecting it against a loss in the event of snowfall. Worldwide studied global weather patterns and historical snowfall data before charging a premium of about 5 percent of sales.[15]

The Law of Adverse Selection

Just because a risk meets all five criteria, however, does not make it automatically insurable. Take, for example, bad drivers who get into a $1,000 accident every 5,000 miles or so. Because they are so accident-prone, their premiums would be sky high. What's more, insurers would refuse to insure them because of the high cost of administering the policies.

Such drivers are victims not only of their own poor judgment but also of insurers' keen awareness of the **law of adverse selection**, which holds that individuals who are risk-prone are more likely to obtain or continue coverage than those who are less likely to have a claim.[16] Such behavior by consumers concentrates risk rather than spreading it out, driving up insurance company losses—and premiums—in the process.

The 1994 Los Angeles earthquake is an excellent example of the law of adverse selection at work. While most homeowners in the United States don't give a second thought to earthquake insurance, millions of Californians take out extra policies that cover earthquake damage. For 20th Century Industries, the ninth largest insurer of California homes, with a heavy concentration of policies in southern California, that customer tendency produced a near crisis. The insurer paid out $815 million to the 150,000 L.A.-area homeowners it insured, raising concerns among government regulators that the company might fail. As a result, 20th Century decided to withdraw completely from the California homeowners' insurance market.[17]

The law of adverse selection plays a larger role today than ever before in the debate over national health care reform. According to the 1990 census, more than 35 million Americans are not covered by health insurance. Many in this group are unemployed or otherwise unable to afford individual private health insurance. Millions more cannot obtain coverage because of adverse selection: Their health conditions make them a high risk for any insurer to cover. And additional millions are reluctant to switch jobs, fearing that a new employer's insurer would not cover so-called preexisting conditions, such as diabetes or a heart ailment. From the insurer's viewpoint, the odds are high that such a preexisting condition will lead to significant claims or losses, or that it will greatly increase paperwork and other costs of doing business.

4. Explain how the law of adverse selection reflects current problems of insurers.

Insurance Providers

The early discussion of national health care reform focused on a proposal to create a federal agency to oversee health insurance. The debate crystallized a fact that many of us already knew: We get our insurance from both public, government-run sources and from private sources.

Public Insurers

The single largest public insurer is one that many people don't even consider a provider—the Social Security Administration. Also known as Old-Age, Survivors and Disability Insurance, Social Security provides a pension (retirement income) for roughly 90 percent of current and future retirees, as well as financial support for some physically and emotionally disabled individuals. Social Security, which grew out of the failure of many private pension funds in the 1930s during the Great Depression, now takes in more than $300 billion in premiums every year through the FICA tax on income. In 1995, every employee contributed 6.2 percent of wages or salary up to $60,600 to the Social Security fund; employers paid an equal amount. The government puts that money into a trust fund from which our retirement income is drawn.

Some critics warn that the Social Security fund will go broke sometime after 2020 because it is ignoring the third precept of the law of large numbers. They claim that the administration has failed to recognize that Americans are living longer than ever and are thus receiving more benefits than anticipated. As a result, these critics allege, the government is paying out too much now and is not building up enough reserves to cover the large number of baby-boomers who will begin retiring after 2010.

5. Identify and describe several different forms of public insurance and discuss some problems that make their future uncertain.

Self-employed workers pay the full 12.4 percent FICA tax, plus a 2.9 percent Medicare contribution

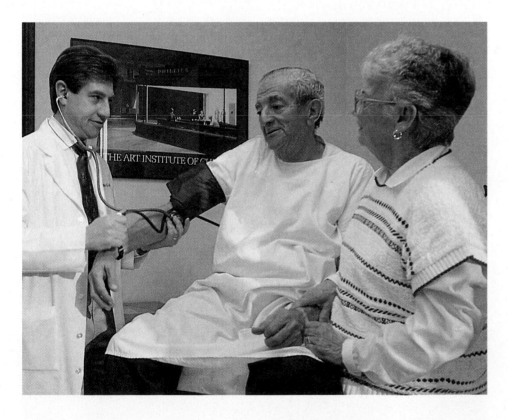

Public Health Insurance

Through Medicare, U.S. taxpayers underwrite the cost of this man's medical exam. Without serious financial reforms, public programs such as Medicare and Medicaid will fold, leaving many of the nation's most vulnerable citizens without health insurance. The public debate on health care reform centers on the government's role in the lives of Americans and on our national priorities.

A second major public insurance program, unemployment insurance, faces other challenges. This government program, also an outgrowth of the Great Depression, requires an employer to contribute to a state-run insurance fund from which employees can collect if they're laid off the job. During the recessions of the late 1980s and early 1990s, however, many state unemployment insurance funds ran dry, and businesses and federal and state governments had to come up with additional money to cover benefits.

The federal government also runs several other insurance programs. Medicaid and Medicare provide health insurance for the elderly, the infirm, and the indigent; every employee pays 1.45 percent of his or her wages or salary into Medicare, an amount matched by the employer. Crop insurance is also available in some areas. After floods wracked the Midwest in 1993, farmers received $1.6 billion to pay for crop damage. Unfortunately, each of these programs has been plagued at one time or another by fraud, which has renewed calls from some politicians to do away with them.[18]

All these public insurance programs have one major common characteristic: They are designed to provide a social benefit to the entire nation. By developing and running programs that safeguard people against loss, the government is able to relieve retirees of the burden of worrying about pension and health benefits and farmers about the threat of losing their livelihood because of crop failure. The public policy decisions to take on these burdens are one role of government. A for-profit business would not undertake such programs because the outcome runs counter to the law of large numbers. Since there's no cap on loss, a private business could not assume the risk these programs involve.

Recall the discussions in Chapter 2 regarding public goods, externalities, and the role of government in a market economy.

Of course, the government is aware of the risk, which is why contributions to many of these programs, such as Social Security and unemployment insurance, are compulsory. That way, money goes back into the programs even as other money is paid out. Figure 23.2 shows the dramatic rise in health care benefits paid out by the federal government between 1984 and 1994.

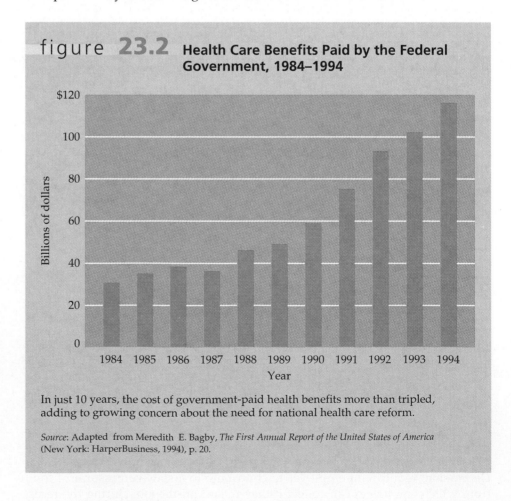

figure **23.2** **Health Care Benefits Paid by the Federal Government, 1984–1994**

In just 10 years, the cost of government-paid health benefits more than tripled, adding to growing concern about the need for national health care reform.

Source: Adapted from Meredith E. Bagby, *The First Annual Report of the United States of America* (New York: HarperBusiness, 1994), p. 20.

Private Insurers

6. Distinguish between stock and mutual insurance companies in their role as private insurers.

In contrast, private insurance, with a few exceptions, is totally voluntary and operates in a market economy. Private insurance companies issue a wide variety of policies covering everything from liability and property to health and life. Private insurers break down into two categories: stock insurance companies and mutual insurance companies.

A **stock insurance company** is shareholder-owned, and it attempts to maximize profits for its owners. Aetna Life, Government Employees Insurance Company (GEICO), and Prudential are all stock insurance companies. A **mutual insurance company** is owned by its policyholders, and it attempts to minimize losses and thus rebate excess income to policyholders either as dividends or as lower future premiums. As their names indicate, Mutual of Omaha and Mass Mutual Insurance are owned by their policyholders. Mutual insurance companies tend to serve consumers more than businesses, and many specialize in life insurance.

Industry Watchdogs

Forty years ago, mutual insurance companies made up more than 20 percent of all life insurers in the United States. But since 1954, the proportion of mutual life insurance companies has fallen to just over 14 percent.[19] Meanwhile, stock companies have grown increasingly dominant as providers of life and other forms of insurance. This is in large part because, over the last 30 years, many state governments have required insurers to set aside more money to protect policyholders in case of unexpectedly high claims. Stock companies can sell stock to the public and quickly build up this cash reserve. Mutual companies can build up funds only by reducing their losses or expenses, a slower and more difficult way to accumulate reserves.

The growth in stock insurance companies masks an important point. Stock companies are supposed to be owned and run by private citizens. In reality, however, state governments have a large say in the way such insurance companies operate. Each state has its own set of insurance laws that may govern everything from premiums to benefits to consumer rights. Typically, a state insurance commissioner, heading up an insurance department, enforces these laws. New York State insurance regulators, for instance, fined National Benefit Life Insurance $500,000 in November 1994 for submitting false information about the training of its agents.[20]

State regulators often take a more active role than simple law enforcement. In many states, such as California, the commissioner serves as an *ombudsman*, a person to whom consumers can turn to help mediate disputes. Consumers with complaints about their insurance can call the commissioner's office for help in getting their problems resolved. In a few states—Massachusetts, for example—the insurance commissioner, in conjunction with business and consumer groups, decides how much an insurance company can charge for automobile and some other types of policies. In other cases, the state agency decides how much a worker injured on the job should receive as an insurance settlement. Though laws vary from state to state, the National Association of Insurance Commissioners attempts to create some uniformity across the nation to ease the paperwork and regulatory burden both on local insurers and on insurance companies that operate in numerous states.[21]

Insurance Products

It should be obvious by now that insurance plays a major part in most companies' risk management strategies. The same can be said about the role insurance plays in an individual's life. But just what types of insurance are out there, and what purpose does each type serve?

Insurance products break down into two categories: commercial lines and personal lines. **Commercial product lines** are insurance products that are de-

 stock insurance company

A shareholder-owned company that attempts to maximize profits for its owners.

 mutual insurance company

A policyholder-owned company that attempts to minimize losses and thus rebate excess income to policyholders either as dividends or as lower future premiums.

 commercial product lines

Insurance products that are designed for and bought by businesses.

doing business

The Minibusiness Policy

Imagine that you've decided to join the ranks of the estimated 12 million owners of home businesses nationwide. How do you choose your business insurance? Until recently you would have had just two options: an endorsement, or added provision, to your homeowner's or renter's policy or a separate small-business policy. The homeowner's endorsement is all right for some small businesses, but it doesn't offer sufficient coverage for the business you're about to open. The commercial policy offers too much coverage. It's designed for a business that is run in a separate location outside the home. It's too complex, and you can't afford the premiums.

Insurers, realizing that there are a lot of entrepreneurial souls like you who are searching for a middle ground in business insurance coverage, have designed a new product to meet the needs of this market segment. It's called a "minibusiness" policy. These policies don't cover all types of businesses. For example, it's hard to find coverage when large amounts of inventory are kept at home because insurers see a high risk of theft or fraud.

Both the Firemen's Insurance Co. in Washington, D.C., and RLI Insurance in Peoria, Illinois, have introduced full-fledged minibusiness coverage. Continental Insurance, Aetna Life and Casualty Co., and State Farm Mutual Insurance Co. offer endorsements to their homeowner's policies for qualified customers.

RLI's In-Home Business Insurance Program, available in every state but Texas and Maine, offers policies for 62 types of low-risk, home-based businesses. Coverage choices include the following:

- $5,000 to $50,000 worth of at-home business equipment, plus coverage for equipment located off the premises

- $300,000 to $1 million in liability coverage
- 12 months' business interruption coverage
- Optional coverages, such as for the loss of up to $10,000 in petty cash

The Firemen's Insurance Home Enterprise Policy is similar, but available only in Maryland, Virginia, Delaware, North Carolina, and the District of Columbia. In addition to coverages comparable to those offered by RLI's In-Home Business program, the Home Enterprise Policy covers the loss of business documents up to $5,000 and will reimburse you, up to $10,000, for bills that cannot be collected because of damage to your records. Both companies' policies carry yearly premiums of under $200.

Continental Insurance offers HomeWork, an endorsement available to qualifying customers of the company's LinkPlus combined homeowner's and auto policies. The home business must be unincorporated and employ only family members. HomeWork is available in 31 states and features up to one year of lost business income if damage to your home causes you to close down your business. Coverage for theft, forgery, and loss of valuable business documents is also available, along with liability protection for personal injury, defective products, and advertising errors. Cost is comparable to the Fireman's Insurance and RLI policies. Aetna Life and Casualty has experimented in Connecticut, Illinois, Maryland, and Ohio with similar endorsements to homeowner's policies, priced at about half the cost of comparable coverage by a separate small-business policy.

Source: Based on Jane Bryant Quinn, "You and Your Money: Biz Insurance at Home," (New York) *Daily News*, Jan. 8, 1995, p. B3.

signed for and bought by businesses, and **personal product lines** are designed for and bought by individuals. Product liability, malpractice, equipment breakdown, and workers' compensation are all commercial lines, while automobile, private property, and life insurance are generally considered to be personal lines. Health insurance actually is a hybrid of both commercial and personal lines. The doing business box entitled "The Minibusiness Policy" looks at some of the insurance options open to home-based businesses.

Insuring the Business

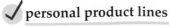

personal product lines

Insurance products that are designed for and bought by individuals.

Business, or commercial, product lines generally fall into three categories—liability, property, and income insurance. You could almost think of these as insurance for what might be, for what is, and for what could have been.

Liability Insurance

Liability insurance protects the policyholder against losses resulting from injury to other persons or damage to other people's property caused by the insured. At one time, most businesses got by with a product called *commercial general liability insurance*, a broad policy covering liability for poorly designed or defective products, for injuries occurring on the policyholder's property, and for other instances of injury or property damage.

Over the years, however, insurers have developed more specialized liability insurance products with coverage for special situations. For instance, the management and directors of many public and private companies carry **directors and officers (D&O) insurance**, which covers them for negligent acts or misleading statements that expose a company to loss. For example, when shareholders successfully sue a company for misleading statements made by a company officer, they typically collect from the D&O insurer. However, according to a survey conducted by insurance consultants Wyatt & Co., only 80 to 90 percent of all publicly traded companies actually have D&O policies, exposing both the corporations and their officers to high risk.[22]

Malpractice insurance, also known as *professional liability* or *errors and omissions insurance*, covers specialists for negligence and/or errors and omissions that injure their clients.[23] We usually think of doctors, dentists, and lawyers when malpractice comes up, but its use is also growing in other professions. The number of mortgage brokers applying for malpractice insurance increased 50 percent from 1993 to 1994. Similarly, real estate appraisers are now taking out malpractice insurance because of several recent multimillion-dollar lawsuits.[24]

Such major lawsuits as those just described have made product liability insurance a subject of debate in both state and federal legislatures. Many manufacturers contend that jury verdicts are requiring them to pay millions of dollars in punitive damages even when their products meet all government standards for safety. Punitive damages are awards in excess of normal compensation to a plaintiff (the alleged victim) to punish a defendant (the company) for a serious wrong. For example, ladder manufacturers claim that they must charge 20 percent more for their merchandise because of the cost of product liability insurance. A 1988 survey of 500 chief executive officers conducted by The Conference Board, a highly respected organization of business leaders, found that 36 percent had stopped making a product because of actual or threatened product liability lawsuits. Another 15 percent had laid off workers, while 8 percent had gone so far as to close a plant. What's more, the U.S. Chamber of Commerce estimates that product liability insurance costs are 20 times higher in the United States than in Europe and 15 times higher than in Japan, stifling international competitiveness.

All these problems are spurring calls for a reform of state product liability laws. At the federal level, Congress has considered several pieces of legislation over the past decade that would establish uniform product liability standards. Other bills that have come under consideration would limit a plaintiff's ability to collect damages from a company, effectively doing away with the huge lawsuits that drive many companies out of business.[25]

Product liability is not the only form of liability insurance that is the subject of much debate. Insurance reformers are also targeting workers' compensation, intent on slowing the runaway growth in insurance premiums. As we noted earlier, workers' compensation is a state-run program that pays the wages and medical bills of employees injured on the job. It's considered a form of liability insurance because the business is liable for the injuries of the worker.

Workers' compensation has great potential for fraud simply because it is compulsory, and the worker who benefits from it picks up none of the tab. It is

7. Identify and describe the types of commercial liability insurance.

The customer base for malpractice insurance is broadening to include, in addition to lawyers, medical doctors, and dentists:

- *Therapists*
- *Company directors*
- *Stockbrokers*
- *Mortgage brokers*
- *Real estate appraisers*

 liability insurance

Protects the policyholder against losses resulting from injury to other persons or damage to other people's property caused by the insured.

 directors and officers (D&O) insurance

Covers directors and officers of public or private companies for negligent acts or misleading statements that expose a company to loss.

 malpractice insurance

Covers specialists for negligence and/or errors and omissions that injure their clients; also called *professional liability* or *errors and omissions insurance*.

property/casualty insurance

Protects a company and its property against loss from perils such as fire, wind, hail, riot, and smoke.

 fidelity bond

Protects a company against a loss of property caused by the dishonest acts of an employee or other individual associated with the firm.

✓ **surety bond**

Protects one party against another party's failure to fulfill a contract or to otherwise perform as agreed.

8. Describe the various forms of property/casualty and income insurance.

also hard to control because the cost of medical procedures is rising faster than inflation, and the types of injuries covered by workers' compensation have greatly expanded.

Workers' compensation originated in Wisconsin in 1911 as a regulatory response by the state government to companies that simply fired workers injured on the job with no compensation. It is now mandatory for businesses in 47 states and voluntary in New Jersey, South Carolina, and Texas. Originally, workers' compensation did not cover stress-related workplace disabilities; now, such injuries are covered in virtually every state. As a result, employers currently pay an average of 2.3 percent of their payroll costs in workers' compensation, up from 1 percent in 1970.[26]

Product liability reform has yet to take hold, but workers' compensation reform is beginning to have an effect on costs. A number of states have passed laws that mete out stiffer penalties for fraudulent claims. Many states are also giving employers more power to monitor and manage the care their injured employees receive and are helping them to improve the safety inside their factories and offices. In Oregon, for instance, a series of reforms helped to cut claim costs by 40 percent in just four years, from 1990 to 1994.[27]

Property/Casualty Insurance

While liability insurance protects a company from claims that it has injured others, **property/casualty insurance** protects the company and its property against loss from perils such as fire, wind, hail, riot, and smoke. Of the $15.5 billion paid out by insurers in the wake of Hurricane Andrew, which devastated southern Florida in 1992, almost $4 billion went to businesses to cover wind damage to their property. *Boiler and machinery insurance*, which covers the breakdown of boilers, air conditioning, heating, computer, and other systems, is a common form of property insurance.

A different form of insurance, called a **fidelity bond**, protects a company against a loss of property caused by the dishonest acts of an employee or other individual associated with the firm. Bank tellers or jewelry store employees might be covered by a fidelity bond because of the large sums of money they handle, as might an accountant, treasurer, or other individual with access to a company's funds.

Still a third type of property insurance covers nonperformance. A **surety bond** protects one party against another party's failure to fulfill a contract or to

Business Interruption Claim

At the height of the 1993 Mississippi River flooding, the water level inside these offices topped out above four feet, and the business was losing between $6,000 and $7,000 in sales each day. Multiply those losses by thousands of small and midsized businesses, and you get an idea of the scope of the disaster. A business cannot prevent all disasters, but it can plan ahead and thereby maximize the speed with which it recovers from a disaster.

otherwise perform as agreed. Surety bonds are most commonly required for public works projects. If you look at the legal notices in almost any newspaper, you'll see government projects listed requiring all bidders to post a surety bond. That way, if the bidder that gets the contract defaults on its obligation, the government can turn to the insurer to pay off the bond or find someone else to finish the project. Many private firms also require surety bonds for construction companies, importers, and people seeking to replace lost stock certificates.

Commercial property insurance typically comes with a coinsurance clause. As noted earlier in the chapter, this requires a policyholder to carry insurance equal to a specified percentage of the value of the property in order to receive full coverage on a loss. Most coinsurance clauses require a business to carry property insurance for at least 80 percent of the value of the property in order to collect in full. For example, imagine you own an office building worth $2 million, but you only carry $1.2 million in property insurance. One sweltry August evening, the building is hit by a tornado that causes $1.2 million in damage. Without a coinsurance clause, you'd collect the full amount of the policy even though you still owned a building worth at least $800,000. Essentially, the insurer would have been forced to take all the risk, and you'd have taken none. With coinsurance, however, you'd collect only $960,000.

Income Insurance

The third main type of commercial insurance provides companies with a way to recover sales and income that they lose because of a loss of property. **Business interruption insurance** reimburses an owner for lost profits and continuing expenses during the time a business must stay closed following a flood, hurricane, or other disaster. When a fire struck the offices of certified public accountant William J. Withrow on April 9, 1994, just six days before the deadline for filing personal income taxes, his business interruption insurer covered some of his expenses while he set up a new office.[28]

Businesses often take out special **key person insurance** to protect themselves and their stockholders or owners against the loss of a key executive. Recall that this was one of the risks outlined in the chapter's One Minute Manager example. Mecklermedia Corp., a publisher of magazines and books and an organizer of trade shows relating to information technology, carries $1 million of key person insurance on the company's founder and chairman, Alan M. Meckler. The company believes that the loss of Meckler would have an adverse effect on its current and prospective business, and it wants to have a cushion in the event of his death or incapacitation.[29]

Business insurance is big business. In 1992, companies paid $118.6 billion for commercial insurance to protect their operations.[30] That's above and beyond what they paid for health insurance, which protects employees rather than the companies themselves.

Health Insurance

Of all insurance products, health coverage is the most popular—and the one that comes under the most fire. Health insurance covers medical treatment and expenses and includes **disability insurance**, which replaces income lost when the policyholder is unable to work because of an accident, injury, or illness. Health insurance is not limited to the employee benefits described in Chapter 12. Auto insurance and workers' compensation insurance policies include provisions that pay for medical expenses, as do several government programs such as Medicare, Medicaid, and veterans' benefits.

For a long time, insurers offered only one choice in health insurance, the "plain vanilla" indemnity plan. **Indemnity insurance** reimburses the insured for "reasonable and customary" fees, that is, for those charges that are consis-

business interruption insurance

Reimburses an owner for lost profits and continuing expenses during the time a business must stay closed following a flood, hurricane, or other disaster.

key person insurance

Protects a business and its stockholders or owners against the loss of a key executive.

disability insurance

Replaces income lost when the policyholder is unable to work because of an accident, injury, or illness.

indemnity insurance

Reimburses the insured for "reasonable and customary" fees.

9. Discuss reasons for new forms of health insurance.

tent with what other health care providers in the same area are charging. These plans generally cover at least 80 percent of a medical expense, subject to certain limitations. Larger, older companies and those that are heavily unionized, such as General Motors, General Electric, and even the federal government, are more likely to provide indemnity insurance than are smaller, entrepreneurial firms.

But indemnity insurance is quickly falling out of favor even among large companies. According to a survey conducted by benefit consultant A. Foster Higgins & Co., 47 percent of all employees were enrolled in traditional indemnity plans in 1993, down from 53 percent in 1992. Why a 6 percent drop in one year? Indemnity insurance costs a lot. The average yearly cost per employee rose from $3,268 in 1992 to $3,500 in 1993—a jump of almost $250 per employee.[31]

Those figures don't even tell the entire story. The U.S. Department of Commerce estimates that Americans spent $1.061 *trillion* on health care in 1994, a 12.5 percent jump from 1993. Health care expenditures account for about 15 percent of gross national product, or $1 of every $7 spent. What's more, the government estimates that health care costs will continue to increase by 12 to 15 percent a year through the end of the century, unless "significant changes occur in the health-care system."[32]

A number of factors are driving up health care costs:

- Advances in medical technology that prolong life but are extremely expensive

- An aging population that uses more medical services

- The growth in the number of cases of AIDS

- More defensive medicine performed by doctors fearing lawsuits

- Increasing numbers of uninsured and underinsured people seeking care only in emergency rooms, where medical costs are highest

These factors are leading companies and individuals to look for new ways to control insurance costs. Many are settling on a risk management strategy called **managed care**: Employers and insurers arrange with health care providers to furnish health care services to members of the insured group. The goal of managed care is to cut costs by ensuring appropriate, quality health care.

Managed care groups usually employ a team of doctors or nurses to manage their cases and review treatments for medical appropriateness. There are two established types of managed care groups—health maintenance organizations (HMOs) and preferred provider organizations (PPOs). A third group that is growing in popularity is point-of-service (POS) plans.

Health Maintenance Organizations   HMOs provide services to groups of individuals for a fixed, prepaid, per capita fee. According to the Foster Higgins study, HMOs had an average cost per employee of $3,276 in 1993—about the 1992 level for indemnity coverage. The ability to save money has pushed businesses to enroll about 25 percent of their workers in HMOs. Some companies, such as American Express, are even lowering the deductible and coinsurance for workers who enroll in health maintenance organizations and are trimming the amount employees must contribute to the plan by 20 percent or more.

Many people believe they are getting better service from health care providers who work for HMOs than from those who accept only traditional indemnity insurance. A survey of the members of U.S. Healthcare, Inc., an HMO based in Pennsylvania, showed that 94 percent were satisfied or highly satisfied with their treatment.[33]

Preferred Provider Organizations   PPOs differ slightly from HMOs in that health care providers are paid on a fee-for-service basis similar to traditional indemnity plans but on a negotiated, discounted fee schedule. This cost control

✓ managed care

A risk management strategy in which employers and insurers arrange with health care providers to furnish health care services to members of the insured group.

Big Business

As the signs at this medical center in San Antonio, Texas, testify, health care is a major U.S. industry, claiming $1 in each $7 spent by Americans. At the same time, one American in seven is not covered by any health insurance plan. So while the United States leads the world in medical research and quality medical care, our health insurance system fosters a lack of incentive to use these abundant services wisely. As a result, health care costs continue to rise much faster than inflation.

measure helped employers contain the average cost per employee for PPO insurance to $3,317 in 1993.

Point-of-Service Plans POS plans combine attributes of indemnity plans and PPOs. POS plan members pay one fee if they visit a physician who has negotiated a discounted rate with the insurer; they pay another, higher fee if they visit an out-of-network physician. About 7 percent of all U.S. employees were enrolled in POS plans in 1993.

Insuring Households

Companies are obviously not the only groups that need to protect themselves against loss. You, your classmates, your professor, all of us also face risks, such as property damage, lawsuits, medical illness, and death. To combat these risks, insurers have developed personal product lines. Generally, these policies fall into three categories: personal property/casualty policies, including automobile and homeowner's insurance, which safeguard us against loss of property and from liability in the event of accident; health insurance, as covered in the preceding section, which covers the cost of medical treatment; and life insurance, which provides our survivors with income after we die.

10. Identify and describe the categories of personal insurance.

Personal Property/Casualty Insurance

Automobile insurance is the most common form of property insurance taken out by individuals. It provides protection against loss for the owner of a car. In 1992, individuals took out $88.4 billion worth of auto insurance policies. Car owners in 41 states and the District of Columbia are required to carry auto insurance. In the other nine states, car owners who do not wish to purchase auto insurance must prove that they have the ability to pay for losses if they are found liable for causing property damage or personal injury. This requirement effectively forces most people to take out auto insurance.[34] Auto insurance covers a wide variety of risks. Although not every policy covers every possibility, the insurance breaks down into two broad categories: property, also known as collision and comprehensive, and liability.

Collision and Comprehensive Coverage Collision insurance pays for damage to the policyholder's car caused by a collision or accident. The coverage is optional in all states and is capped at the current book value of the car. Older cars, with the exception of antiques, are usually worth less than newer models, and many car owners drop their collision insurance on cars that are seven or more years old.

Comprehensive insurance protects the car owner from loss due to theft or damage not resulting from a collision. The policies cover damage caused by fire, vandalism, hail, windstorm, and collision with animals or falling objects. Car owners can also purchase an *endorsement* that alters a policy's coverage, terms, or conditions in order to gain protection for glass breakage. Most collision and comprehensive insurance carries a deductible that requires the insured individual to pay the first $200 or so of damage per claim. The higher the deductible, the lower the cost of coverage.

Liability Coverage Mandatory automobile liability insurance covers a hodgepodge of situations. Among the types offered are property damage insurance, which pays benefits if your car damages or destroys another person's property; medical insurance, which pays for your medical treatment and that of family members and others riding in your car; bodily injury insurance, which covers the medical care of others injured by your car; uninsured and underinsured motorist insurance, which covers you and your passengers if your car is hit by someone who is either uninsured or insufficiently insured; and disability insurance, which pays benefits if you or your passengers are totally disabled because of an auto accident.

Homeowner's Insurance Homeowner's insurance, like auto insurance, protects the policyholder against both property loss and personal liability. These two types of coverage generally come in a single comprehensive policy. About two-thirds of all Americans own their own homes, condominiums, or cooperative apartments, and virtually all of them carry homeowner's insurance. In fact, banks require a homeowner taking out a mortgage to purchase insurance for the property. Insurers took in more than $20 billion in homeowner's insurance premiums in 1992.[35] A form of homeowner's insurance is available for renters. A renter's insurance policy covers the contents of an apartment but not the actual building.

Homeowner's insurance comes in two flavors: replacement-cost and actual-value. In the former, the insurer pays the homeowner the cost of replacing the home, up to the limit of the policy. In actual-value coverage, the insurer reimburses the homeowner for the current value of the property, which includes the depreciation caused by wear and tear and age. Premiums for homeowner's insurance vary widely, depending on the location of the property. In parts of Florida, North Carolina, and other states along the Atlantic Coast, premiums have increased by more than 20 percent following a series of hurricanes and floods that caused billions of dollars in damage.[36]

Life Insurance

While automobile and homeowner's insurance protect you against loss during your lifetime, life insurance protects your family or other designated parties by paying them money in the event of your death. In 1993, insurers collected $298.9 billion in life insurance premiums, or more than $1,000 for every man, woman, and child in the United States. Life insurers have assets of approximately $1.79 trillion dollars, many of them purchased with money collected in premiums. This allows insurers to set aside funds out of which beneficiaries are paid when a policyholder dies.[37] For a glimpse at how life insurance can also help the policyholder, see the ethics check entitled "Living Benefits Versus Viatical Settlements."

There are two basic types of life insurance: term and cash-value coverage. **Term life insurance**, as the name implies, pays a benefit in the event of the insured's death, but only during the term of the policy. If the policy expires before

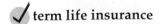

term life insurance

Pays a benefit in the event of the insured's death, but only during the term of the policy.

ethics check

Living Benefits Versus Viatical Settlements

Facing a terminal illness is the ultimate adversity. And as financial resources dwindle, coping with the prospect of death is often complicated by coping with the prospect of living: how to pay the bills, maintain medical care, and provide for the family. Until the late 1980s, the terminally ill basically had no options. Today there are at least two, one offered by the insurance industry and one by the investment industry.

Since 1988, increasing numbers of terminally ill people have turned to viatical settlement companies to raise immediate cash. These investment companies buy the life insurance policies of the terminally ill for up to 80 cents on the dollar, and their investors take over the premium payments. When the policyholder dies, the insurance proceeds are distributed to investors.

The transaction comes from the Latin word *viaticum*, the provisions given a traveler before a risky journey in Roman times. In the Christian religion, the viatica are last rites given a person near death. Most policy sellers to date are people with AIDS, but viatical companies also buy the policies of cancer and heart-disease patients with terminal conditions. With a growth rate of 25 percent per year, the policies funded by viatical companies reached an estimated $350 million in 1994 compared to about $50 million in 1991. By mid-1995, viatical companies remained unregulated.

In response to the growth of viatical settlements, insurance companies began offering "living benefits," or accelerated death benefits (ADB), as provisions of life insurance plans. ADBs provide for early payment of up to 50 percent of policy value. The payment decreases the value of the life insurance policy in proportion (a $50,000 policy becomes a $25,000 policy, for example), with premiums, cash value, and loan provisions lowered to reflect the new amount. But unlike viatical settlements, the policyholder retains possession of the policy, and his or her beneficiaries remain eligible to collect death benefits. Hewitt Associates, a consulting firm, estimated that as many as one-quarter of U.S. employers offered an ADB provision in their company-sponsored life insurance plans in 1995.

1. Viatical investments are also called "death futures." The sooner the seller dies, the fewer premium payments the investor makes and the larger the profit. Do you see viatical settlements as an ethical or unethical business? Do you think that insurance companies would have created living benefit provisions if viaticals did not exist?

2. Insurance companies contend that viatical settlements are too costly because the seller gets a one-time payment but beneficiaries must sign away the rights to any death benefit. Viatical companies respond that until they came into existence, insurance companies profited from life insurance policies that formerly were allowed to lapse without a payout. What are the pros and cons of each group's position?

3. Should the government regulate viatical settlement companies? How?

Sources: Gracian Mack, "Insurance for the Living," *Black Enterprise*, July 1995, pp. 11-14; "Ask a Benefit Manager: 'Living Benefits' Can Offer Flexibility and Security," *Business Insurance*, May 22, 1995, p. 23; Cecile Gutscher, "Viatical Settlements: Cashing in on Death," *San Francisco Examiner*, April 21, 1995, p. B2; Bill Henson, "Viatical Settlements a Growing Business," *Columbus Dispatch*, March 24, 1995, p. 1G; Dan Harrie, "Leavitt Faces Decision on Veto of Viaticals," *Salt Lake City Tribune*, March 14, 1994, p. C1.

the person dies, the beneficiaries collect nothing. When a company buys a group life insurance policy to provide financial security to the families of its employees, it typically buys term insurance.

The second type, **cash-value life insurance**, combines a death benefit with a savings feature. Cash-value coverage is more expensive than term insurance because it allows the insured to build up savings even as it provides beneficiaries with protection against the insured's death. *Whole life* is the best-known type of cash-value life insurance. In the initial years of such a policy, its actual cash value is quite low. Over time, however, its cash value can come to exceed the amount of money an individual might put aside into conventional savings vehicles such as stocks and bonds.

An alternative form of whole life insurance, called *variable life insurance*, became popular in the early 1980s. It allows individuals to control how the cash value of their premiums is invested and so offset the loss in real economic value of their policies. The insured person can use the cash value of the policy to buy stocks or bonds or to make other investments that historically have grown faster than the rate of inflation. These policies can be risky for the novice investor, however, because if he or she invests poorly, the death benefit and cash value of the policy can actually be less than a standard whole life policy.

 cash-value life insurance

Combines a death benefit with a savings feature.

Reviewing *Risk Management and Insurance*

Risky Business

1. **Identify and describe the four basic strategies of risk management.** Although businesses cannot protect themselves against speculative risks, they can manage pure risks by avoiding, reducing, assuming, or shifting them. Risk avoidance is the least viable technique because it also inhibits profitability. Risk reduction is accomplished by identifying potential problems and setting up procedures to limit them or by swapping a pure risk for a speculative risk. Through OSHA, the government attempts to reduce risks in the workplace. Assuming risk is most commonly accomplished through self-insurance. Even companies that self-insure need to shift some of the risk—which is where insurance companies come in. In addition, companies shift risk by requiring employees to pay part of the cost or by reinsurance.

2. **Explain why self-insurance has become increasingly popular.** Self-insurance is less expensive than monthly payments to an outside insurer. Furthermore, in profit-sharing firms it provides an incentive for the company and its employees to keep the workplace safe (the less money needed to pay claims, the more there is for distribution). Self-insurance is now more available to small businesses, which can band together as self-insurers.

The Insurance Market

3. **Differentiate between insurable and uninsurable risks and explain the law of large numbers.** Risks are identified as insurable or uninsurable according to whether the probability of loss can be determined. Speculative risks are uninsurable, as are labor disputes and products deemed unsafe or so risky that they would require exorbitant premiums. Insurable risks range from health, life, and automobile travel to computer operations. For a risk to be insurable, it must adhere to the law of large numbers. This means that the policyholder must have a direct stake in the item being insured, the insurer must be able to calculate the odds of loss, the loss must be measurable and cannot be intentional, and the risk of loss must be spread over a wide group.

4. **Explain how the law of adverse selection reflects current problems of insurers.** In recognition of the law of adverse selection, insurers set high premiums for or reject potential policyholders who are risk-prone. For example, accident-prone people have to pay high premiums, as do people who have preexisting medical conditions or who live in disaster-prone areas—if they can even find an insurer willing to accept them as clients. Recent natural disasters have caused some insurers to withdraw certain types of policies because these concentrated risks violate the law of large numbers. The law of adverse selection also plays a role in the debate over health care reform.

5. **Identify and describe several different forms of public insurance and discuss some problems that make their future uncertain.** Public, or government-run, insurance includes Social Security for current and future retirees and for the emotionally and physically disabled; unemployment insurance; Medicare and Medicaid for the elderly, infirm, and indigent; and crop insurance for farmers. These insurance programs provide protection in areas that private insurers are unable or unwilling to cover because the chance of loss is too great or cannot be measured. Unfortunately, although the government is assured of funding through compulsory contributions, even it is having funding problems due to the increasing needs and aging of the population and losses from fraud.

6. **Distinguish between stock and mutual insurance companies in their role as private insurers.** Unlike public insurers, private insurers are voluntary. Both stock and mutual insurance companies provide a wide variety of policies, although mutual companies focus on consumers and on life insurance. Stock companies are owned by shareholders, whereas mutual companies are owned by their policyholders. Stock companies are becoming increasingly popular because they have the flexibility to raise additional capital to set aside in case they need to satisfy large claims. Mutual companies, however, can increase funds only by reducing losses and expenses. To protect consumers, state governments enforce laws related to premiums, benefits, and consumer rights, as well as provide ombudsmen to mediate consumer disputes with insurers.

Insurance Products

7. **Identify and describe the types of commercial liability insurance.** In the past, commercial general liability insurance covered most payments to injured persons or damage to property caused by the insured. Today, more specific types of liability insurance are needed, including directors and officers (D&O), malpractice, and product insurance, and workers' compensation. Liability insurance has recently been subject to much debate due to the large lawsuits instituted against major firms. D&O protects the company against loss stemming from negligent acts or misleading statements by a company official. Malpractice insurance is carried by doctors, lawyers, and mortgage and real estate brokers, to name a few. Product liability is particularly problematic because of the size of the lawsuits. Workers' compensation has more potential for fraud than other insurance because it is compulsory, and workers pay none of the cost.

8. **Describe the various forms of property/casualty and income insurance.** Besides providing the usual protection against natural disasters, property/casualty can protect against dishonest acts by employees (through fidelity

bonds) and against nonperformance (through surety bonds). Property insurance usually includes a coinsurance clause. Income insurance provides reimbursement for loss due to business peril and for loss of a key executive.

9. **Discuss reasons for new forms of health insurance.** Health which includes disability, insurance, is the most popular and the most controversial type of commercial and personal insurance. Because of the constantly increasing cost of health care, many companies are replacing indemnity insurance with managed care through health maintenance organizations (HMOs), preferred provider organizations (PPOs), or the newer point-of-service (POS) plans. HMOs apply a fixed, prepaid, per capita fee; PPOs are paid on a fee-for-service basis; and POS plans combine attributes of indemnity plans and PPOs. Health care is also insured in specific ways through auto insurance, workers' compensation, Medicare, Medicaid, and veterans' benefits.

10. **Identify and describe the categories of personal insurance.** Like businesses, individuals need protection against losses. Most personal insurance falls into three categories: property/casualty, life, and health. Property/casualty includes automobile and homeowner's insurance. The latter offers repayment at replacement cost or actual value. Life insurance may be term or cash-value (either as a whole life or a variable life policy). Health insurance is of several types as discussed in number 9.

✔ Key Terms

pure risk **697**	insurable interest **704**	commercial product lines **709**	business interruption insurance **713**
risk management **699**	uninsurable risk **704**	personal product lines **710**	key person insurance **713**
going naked **701**	insurable risk **704**	liability insurance **711**	disability insurance **713**
self-insurance **701**	actuaries **705**	directors and officers (D& O) insurance **711**	indemnity insurance **713**
workers' compensation **701**	law of large numbers **706**	malpractice insurance **711**	managed care **714**
insurance **702**	law of adverse selection **706**	property/casualty insurance **712**	term life insurance **716**
premium **702**	stock insurance company **709**	fidelity bond **712**	cash-value life insurance **717**
deductible **702**	mutual insurance company **709**	surety bond **712**	
coinsurance clauses **702**			
cost shifting **703**			
reinsurance **703**			

• Review Questions

1. What four strategies can a business use to protect itself against risk? Which is the least useful?

2. You own and operate a small brush manufacturing company with 10 employees. How would you shift the risk of loss from property damage, employee illness, and product liability?

3. Tomaso's Soup Co. decides to market a line of salad dressings. Would the risk be insurable? Why or why not?

4. What are the two laws that insurers follow when deciding whether a risk is insurable?

5. What role does government play in providing insurance, and why?

6. Why do stock insurance companies dominate mutual insurance companies in the private insurance market?

7. What types of liability insurance could a business or professional obtain from a private insurer?

8. The management of the firm National Jewelers Corporation knows it needs more than liability insurance to protect itself against losses resulting from internal or external events. What other types of insurance might this producer of solid gold jewelry purchase?

9. What types of insurance coverage would be appropriate for people who own a car and either rent an apartment or own a home?

10. What are the two main types of personal life insurance? Is one preferable to the other? Which one? Why?

• Critical Thinking Questions

1. What sorts of risks do companies that self-insure face?

2. How does the federal government reduce exposure to risk in its insurance programs? How could the government improve its risk management strategies?

3. What types of insurance would you buy if you were starting a new exporting business?

4. According to experts, 80 to 90 percent of corporations buy directors and officers insurance. Why would a corporation decide not to carry a D&O policy?

5. What can companies do to rein in the runaway cost of health insurance?

REVIEW CASE *Weathering the Storm*[38]

To house his catalog business, Bernd Nagy had long wanted to erect a building resembling the Bavarian chalets in his native Germany. He thought the architecture would be fitting for his company, Tyrol International, which sells German and Austrian steins and other gift items. Finally, after more than 20 years in the catalog business, Nagy's wish came true. In early 1993, the $15 million company moved into its new $1.7 million, 40,000 square foot office and distribution facility in the hamlet of Cleveland, Georgia.

But Nagy's crowning achievement quickly turned to disaster. On March 27, 1994, the last Sunday of the month, a trio of tornadoes descended on Cleveland. Funneled by the surrounding mountains, the tornadoes converged on Tyrol's building. Thanks to a warning phone call from Nagy, the two order takers on duty scurried into the basement and escaped with only cuts and bruises. The building and the business were not so lucky. In less than a minute, Nagy's dream was reduced to splintered wood, twisted steel, and broken cement blocks. Envelopes containing customer orders and checks were blown as far away as Virginia. The storms destroyed more than $400,000 worth of merchandise inventory.

But the story had a happy ending. Tyrol's computer system, the lifeblood of a catalog company, escaped intact. Though computer tapes containing information about customers were damaged, the company had backup tapes holding virtually all the same information.

What's more, thanks to careful planning and risk management, Nagy had the right insurance coverage. His policy, which carried a deductible of $1,000, covered the replacement of the building, the interruption in business, and the inventory of merchandise. For this coverage, Tyrol paid its insurers about $2,000 a month. The policy protected Tyrol in the event of a tornado, hurricane, or other storm. For $2 more a month, Nagy even had the company covered in the event of earthquake, an unlikely occurrence in Georgia.

1. What was Nagy's primary risk management strategy?

2. Using the information provided in the case, name the specific commercial insurance products that Tyrol International purchased to protect it from disaster.

3. What other specific policies might the company also carry?

CRITICAL THINKING CASE *From Worst to First in Oregon*[39]

In 1990, business owners in Oregon were skeptical about newly enacted reforms to the state's workers' compensation program. The insurance premiums paid by Oregon businesses were among the highest in the nation, yet injured workers received among the lowest benefits. Today, Oregon business owners are believers. Benefits to injured workers have doubled while businesses have saved $200 million in premiums, and Oregon's workers' compensation program ranks among the best in the United States. Reforms have saved the state system about $2 billion. Now states across the nation are calling on Oregon for advice in reforming their own programs.

Here's what happened. Oregon's Occupational Safety and Health Division, which administers the state's OSHA programs, enacted the following reforms in 1990:

• Created Associated Oregon Industries (AOI) to administer an insurance plan called Compwise, which pools diverse small businesses for the purpose of buying insurance, and offered it free safety and management training programs

• Required all businesses employing more than 10 workers to set up joint labor-management safety and health committees

- Assigned 30 additional OSHA staff members to voluntary consultations with business rather than to enforcement of OSHA regulations

The reforms led to four straight years of declining workers' compensation claims. Between 1989 and 1992, while the state's work force increased by nearly 62,000 employees, disability claims dropped by nearly 8,400, from more than 39,000 in 1989 to fewer than 31,000 in 1992. Work-related deaths in the four-year period decreased from 75 to 63 per year. As a result, the premiums businesses pay for workers' compensation coverage declined by more than 10 percent in each year.

The key to the turnaround, according to Gary K. Weeks, director of the Oregon Department of Insurance and Finance, is a joint emphasis on voluntary consultation and employer education in conjunction with OSHA. Educational seminars are free, and enforcement inspectors are informed only when consultants find that employees are in immediate danger and the employer refuses to take action.

But it took some doing for companies to trust the intent of the reforms and arrange for voluntary safety checkups by OSHA consultants. Once businesses were satisfied that the state was working in their best interests, however, requests for consultations nearly quadrupled. By mid-1993, more than 800 companies were on the agency's waiting list for consultations.

In 1992, more than 11,000 businesses attended OSHA's free conferences and workshops on safety and health. The state's smallest employers are praising AOI Compwise, which offers them affordable insurance premiums. Most of the participating firms have only two or three employees.

1. AOI Compwise has found that most workers' compensation claims are filed in the first year of employment. What are the likely reasons for these claims?

2. Businesses were slow to accept OSHA's offers of voluntary consultations, since the new law tripled the fines for safety violations. How did OSHA overcome the suspicion that their consultants were really just whistle blowers for enforcement inspectors?

3. AOI Compwise was created by the Oregon legislature after its state-run Accident and Insurance Fund announced that it would cancel coverage for 10,000 small businesses whose claims costs far exceeded their premiums. What alternative risk management strategies might these employers have pursued without AOI Compwise?

4. What human resources issues do you suppose the AOI small-business seminars and the larger employers' labor-management committees stress? (*Hint*: Think about the management and empowerment strategies you studied in Chapters 8 through 13.)

Critical Thinking with the ONE MINUTE MANAGER

"To show you that good things can come from a disaster," said the One Minute Manager, "let me tell you about Adorno & Zeder, a law firm based in Miami. When Hurricane Andrew swept through Florida in 1992, most of the southern part of the state lost all power. After the storm passed, Adorno & Zeder employees used flashlights to climb 15 flights up blacked-out stairwells to salvage computers and files. Then the firm struggled to continue operating in temporary offices.

"A year later, Adorno & Zeder had a disaster plan in place, complete with a disaster manual. The manual has information about what to do in any crisis—hurricane, fire, crime, power failure, downed phone lines, medical emergency—just about any situation you can think of. Since the law firm's files are so important, they also have a special plan to protect their computer systems."[40]

"So by planning before disaster strikes, you're making sure that if your company ever faces a catastrophe, you can keep the business running," Joanna offered.

"That's right." The One Minute Manager looked as serious as the students had ever seen her. "Too many people inside and outside this company depend on it—our employees, their families, our suppliers and customers. No one likes to think about disaster striking, but you can't run a business without planning for everything and taking the time to make sure you are managing your risk."

1. CDA Management Consultants recommend that business owners and managers begin developing a disaster strategy by filling in a chart with four columns headed Potential Risks, Prevention, Control, and Opportunity. Draw up such a chart and fill in the columns as you think the One Minute Manager did for her electronics company. (*Hint*: Don't limit the risks in column 1 to natural disasters. Remember that the One Minute Manager's name also appeared on her list.)

2. What sort of risk management strategy would you implement for each of the risks listed on your chart?

Planning Your Career

Your presence in this course suggests that you already have some ideas about the kind of career you want to pursue. As we've explained in several places in this text, *planning* is the first step in managing—managing a project, managing a company, or managing a career. Whether you are an entry-level student or a nontraditional student returning to school, your career is now in a planning phase. In this appendix, we give you some pointers to consider as you outline your next steps. We present them in four parts:

1. Some tips on sorting out your skills and interests and polishing those that will help you launch a successful career.

2. A "how-to" section on preparing a resumé, including some sample resumés.

3. Some hints on what to expect when you are called for an interview.

4. A sampling of jobs to be found in the diverse areas of business described in the seven parts of this text.

Analyzing Your Skills and Interests

Are you a logical person who enjoys solving problems? A social person who likes a lot of interaction with others? A studious person who prefers working in solitude? A hands-on type who can't resist fixing broken things—or relationships? These and a number of other questions can give you some hints about your strengths and weaknesses in relation to specific kinds of employment. And that's the first step in planning your career—analyzing your abilities and interests so that you can understand yourself better and, as a result, set clear goals. After all, you must know your product before you can market it to prospective employers—especially when that important product is you.

A number of books can help you focus on your skills and interests. Here are just a few of them:

- Richard Nelson Bolles, *What Color Is Your Parachute?* (Berkeley, Calif.: Ten Speed Press, 1995). *Note:* A new edition of this book is published annually.

- David C. Borchard, *Your Career: Choices, Chances, and Changes*, 6th. ed. (Dubuque, Iowa: Kendall/Hunt, 1994).

- Barry Gale and Linda Gale, *Discover What You're Best At* (New York: Fireside, 1990).
- Robert B. Nelson, *The Job Hunt* (Berkeley, Calif.: Ten Speed Press, 1986).
- Edgar H. Schein, *Career Anchors* (New York: DBM Publishing, 1990).

As your image of your strengths and weaknesses emerges more clearly, remember what you learned in this text about the current business climate. Employers are relying more and more on employee teams who can manage a large part of their work operations and goals themselves; a person who works well in a group can expect to have an edge over a temperamental lone wolf. But you should also cultivate a spirit of independence so that you won't be afraid to make decisions, whether on your own as an independent entrepreneur or in combination with others as a team member. A willingness to cooperate with co-workers and an ability to communicate clearly is also essential, no matter where you work.

As we noted in Chapter 12, you should also be prepared to be a fast and flexible learner, willing to adapt your skills and talents to the needs of an employer rather than expecting the employer to create your ideal job. That means taking advantage of opportunities that allow you to add skills and contacts. If your school sponsors internships—whether paid or not—apply for one of the openings. Internships are opportunities to build your experience and skills in a real business environment. Also take advantage of temporary job and volunteer opportunities; you will walk away from them better trained and with a wider network of business contacts.

Throughout this text, we have tried to include discussions and exercises that would help you get a better view into the world you will work in. You may want to review some of the text sections and features related to career development, such as those listed in Table A.1.

Sources of Information About Job Openings

When you have identified your career goals, you are ready to find a niche in which to accomplish them. That niche may occur with a private company or with a temporary employment agency, which will place you in a temporary spot within another company. In either case, you will need to do some research to locate an opening. You already know that you are applying for a job in a tight market. Only about 14 million jobs are anticipated for the approximately 18 million graduates who are entering the work force between 1992 and 2005.[1] That does not mean you will not find a job; it does mean you will have to plan your search and be more resourceful than some of the other graduates.

You may recall that Chapter 12 described a number of places where employers list job openings. As a job applicant, you can use that information in your job hunt. Sources for possible openings of interest include the following:

- College recruitment offices: Does your school hold a job fair in the spring or fall?
- Local newspapers: If you are committed to staying in your local area, check the listings in the help-wanted section regularly. You should know, however, that many openings never make it to these sections because they are filled through other sources, often through networking.
- National newspapers: Are you willing to relocate? If so, expand your area of search by checking national listings.

table **A.1** **Text Sections and Features Related to Career Development**

Chapter	Section	Feature
1	The Changing Job Market (pp. 25–27)	Skills Check: The Problem-Solving Process (p. 19)
		Critical Thinking Case: What Are They Doing to Your Career? (p. 30)
4		Skills Check: Job Seeker's Ethics Screen (p. 129)
6	Networking: Building Business Contacts (pp. 176–178)	Skills Check: Evaluating Your Readiness for Entrepreneurship (p. 171)
7	Finding a Job in Small Business (pp. 217–219)	Skills Check: Finding "Immortal" Employers (p. 219)
8		Skills Check: Evaluating Your Management Skills (p. 252)
9		Skills Check: Honing Your Skills for New Career Paths (p. 282)
10		Skills Check: Can You Identify Waste? (p. 306)
11		Skills Check: Putting It All Together (p. 343)
12	Preparing to Be a Flexible Employee (p. 378)	Skills Check: Careful What You Say—Your Job May Depend on It (p. 360)
17	Steps in the Selling Process (pp. 531–533)	
18		Ethics Check: How Private Are Your Thoughts? (p. 566)

- Private employment agencies: Most charge a fee, but you may not mind paying it if the job is a special one. Just be sure you understand your responsibilities for paying the agency and their power to restrict your search. *Read the contract before signing it.*

- Federal or state employment agencies: These agencies do not charge a fee. They list private company openings as well as some government openings. Many also have job lines.

- Company job lines: Do some data gathering; a morning spent making informational calls can yield a list of job-line phone numbers you can check on a regular basis.

- Networking: Do you have a friend or relative working at a company you especially respect? Check with them frequently and ask them to let you know if they hear of an opening, either at their company or at similar companies.

It's good to be ambitious and to search for the most interesting and high-paying job you can find, but don't overlook unglamorous entry-level jobs if they allow you to get started in your field of interest. Career paths don't start at the top of the company; as we mentioned in Chapter 12, Lee Iacocca, who retired a few years ago as president and chief executive officer of Chrysler Corporation, began his career path as a Ford Motor Company engineering trainee after he graduated from college. Many companies expect employees to assume positions of greater responsibility and pay as they learn to handle increasingly complex tasks. Even if your first employer does not readily promote from entry-level positions, your increased knowledge of your field will give you valuable experience and will position you on a higher rung of the ladder when you apply for your next job.

Preparing Your Resumé

Employers interview only a small fraction of the people who apply for an opening. The rest of the applicants are rejected on the basis of their *resumé*, a brief summary of their relevant experience, ideally one or two pages in length. Kim Marino, who saw a need and an opportunity for a resumé-writing service, describes the resumé as a "custom-designed, self-marketing tool tailored to your career objectives."[2]

Remember that the purpose of a resumé is to get you an interview, not a job. People reading it will form their first impression of you. Since it is your only chance to make that first impression, take time to prepare your resumé carefully, stating your personal, educational, and occupational skills and accomplishments. Remember that time is scarce in our fast-paced society, and you must therefore make your points quickly and succinctly, preferably on one page, giving just enough information to pique your potential employer's interest. If you know someone who works for the company that has the opening, talk with that person about special skills, traits, or backgrounds that the company especially values. Then be sure to stress those points in your resumé—to the extent that you can legitimately claim them as your own. Nothing will end your career more quickly than fabricating the information on your resumé.

Appearance counts, and your resumé should be as neat and attractive as possible. If you don't have an ink-jet or a laser printer, consider paying someone to help you turn out a high-quality resumé. Many small companies offer this service for a moderate fee. There is no "right" organizational form for a resumé, but the two most common types are chronological and functional. Although both contain the same information, they organize it in different ways.

Chronological Resumés

Chronological resumés are organized by month and year, showing the history of your education and work-related experience, beginning with the most recent. They are especially effective when your most recent experience is directly related to the job you are applying for. Chronological resumés can effectively demonstrate that your education and work experience have refined your skills and talents to lead directly to your current career objective. You may want to highlight these skills by presenting them in a summary paragraph like the one in Figure A.1, which shows a typical chronological resumé from a graduate of a community college who completed a two-year associate's degree and worked

figure **A.1** **Sample Chronological Resumé**

Ginetta Alvarez
12192 Saint Paul Drive
Pittsburgh, Pennsylvania 15230
Phone: 412-555-1212

PROFESSIONAL GOAL
Paralegal position including research and writing on cases in corporate and international law.

SUMMARY OF SKILLS
Experienced in library and online research and day-to-day law office routines; able to work independently, prioritize tasks, pay attention to details, and meet deadlines; fluent in Spanish; proficient in WordPerfect and Word for Windows.

WORK EXPERIENCE

1992-1995
(full time)
Law Offices of Kelly, Cohen, and Stone.
Senior administrative assistant in firm specializing in class-action lawsuits. Prepared and proofed papers and correspondence for senior partner. Scheduled meetings and appointments. Supervised receptionist and data entry clerk.

1990-1992
(part time)
Seton Community College Library.
Began as circulation clerk: maintained files, assisted users with access to on-line catalog, processed interlibrary loans. Promoted to library assistant in 1991: supervised two work-study clerks; opened and closed library on Sundays.

1990-1992
(summers)
Wilson Park Memorial.
Tour guide in mansion donated to the city by Wilson Park, philanthropist and factory owner during the Gilded Age in Pittsburgh. Greeted visitors, gave tour of grounds, described architecture and furnishings, sold souvenirs in gift shop.

1990-1992
(volunteer)
Seton Community College Friends Around the World Program.
English language tutor and cultural resource for students from Spanish-speaking countries.

EDUCATION

1995-
present
Enrolled in classes leading to a paralegal study certificate, Western Pittsburgh University, Pittsburgh, Pennsylvania.

1992
Associate's degree, business studies, Seton Community College, Pittsburgh, Pennsylvania. Dean's Honor List (GPA 3.75), President's Key Award for Community Service.

PERSONAL INTERESTS
Travel, photography, Latino Community Literacy Program, classical guitar, cross-country skiing.

REFERENCES: On request.

for three years before resuming classes. Note that this resumé lists relevant experience first, followed by educational credits. A recent graduate of a four-year college might choose to list educational credits first, followed by relevant summer or term-time job experience. In listing your experience, be sure to include volunteer work; many people learn valuable business skills while working as volunteers.

figure A.2 Sample Functional Resumé

Alexander Schmidt
10 Allen Place
Allston, Massachusetts 02134
617-555-1234

OBJECTIVE

Obtaining a challenging entry-level management position, preferably in marketing division of software development company emphasizing teaming and total quality control.

EXPERIENCE

Planning and Organizing: Proposed and supervised introduction of self-management team concept for Virtual Reality Games hot-line staff. Planned and organized activities for 25 inner-city children as part of summer program for Boston Parks Department.

Problem Solving: Assisted customers in detecting and resolving problems in their games software or system hardware. Helped summer campers resolve conflicts and cooperate for mutual benefit. Represented student body during three years on student senate.

Team Coaching: Recruited student workers for hot-line support; formed teams in which 15 students shared responsibility for round-the-clock staffing of user hot line; formed mutual support group; trained staff in procedures and functioned as resource person.

Communication: Four years' experience instructing students and customers in use of personal computers, packaged software, and networks. Helped produce user handbook for Westlake Personal Computer Center. Developed self-confidence about speaking and performing in front of a group during community theater work.

Technology: Working knowledge of DOS- and Windows-based environments; strong personal computer skills.

JOB HISTORY

1993–1995 Supervisor, customer support staff, evenings and weekends, Virtual Reality Games.
1992–1993 Customer support staff, evenings and weekends, Virtual Reality Games.
1991–1992 Student support-staff aide, Westlake University Personal Computer Center.
1991–1993 Camp counselor, Boston Parks Department Summer Program.

EDUCATION

1995   Bachelor of science, Westlake University.
            Combined major, computer science and business administration. GPA 3.5, honors.
            Student senate, 1992–1995.

PERSONAL INTERESTS

Community theater, hiking, tennis, volunteer firefighter.

REFERENCES: On request.

Functional Resumés

A functional resumé highlights various categories of skills and experiences you can offer to an employer, like those in Figure A.2. Organizing a resumé by function is a good way to stress that you have a wide variety of skills and that you have applied them successfully in several different work environments.

Cover Letters

Resumés are incomplete without a cover letter. Cover letters are always more effective when addressed to a real person, which means that you should try to

figure **A.3** **Standard Cover Letter**

12192 Saint Paul Drive
Pittsburgh, Pennsylvania 15230

February 21, 1996

Ms. Sara Dicara
Jones, Griffin, and DiCara
1298 Bigelow Boulevard
Pittsburgh, Pennsylvania 15219

Dear Ms. Dicara:

George Schlemm, who was employed with your firm until his recent return to California, suggested that I write to you about your expected June opening for a corporate paralegal. I will receive my paralegal certificate in May of this year from Western Pittsburgh University, just in time to begin work in June. I am very excited about the possibility of working with you because my goal is to work for a firm that has a broad base of corporate clients with international offices.

I believe that my strengths correspond with your goals of serving the global business community. I have three years' experience working as an administrative assistant in a law office. I am fluent in Spanish, and my ongoing involvement in the Latino community has given me a multicultural perspective. During my courses and library jobs I received rigorous training in research techniques and the use of on-line technology. My enclosed resumé gives more information about my work experience, educational background, and personal interests.

I will phone your office on February 28 to see if you are interested in meeting and discussing your opening. If you require any further evidence of my qualifications, please contact me and I will get back to you immediately.

Sincerely,

Ginetta Alvarez
Phone: 412-555-1212

enclosure: resumé

get the name of a person in authority—someone in the human resource department, if not the manager who is actually doing the hiring. After addressing your letter to that person, briefly indicate your strong interest in the job and in the company. Show that you are enthusiastic about the chance to work for the organization. You might, for example, give some specific reason why your own work philosophy, experience, or skills correspond to the company's reputation and strengths. Also note that you will follow up in a week or so by phone; this will give you a chance to check that your letter and resumé were received and that you are being considered for the opening. A typical cover letter appears in Figure A.3.

Show That You Are Computer-Savvy

Your future employer is probably actively participating in the electronic workplace, and you should be prepared to show you are willing to do the same. Employers may even require applicants to fax their resumés or to transmit them via electronic mail. It's a quick and easy way of finding out if applicants are up to speed in using computers and networks.

Another way computers are affecting the job-search process is through the job-listing services appearing on many of the on-line services' bulletin boards, such as Prodigy's Careers Bulletin Board and America Online's Careers Board. Would-be applicants and employers swap information on these bulletin boards, which cover many categories of jobs. Currently, the boards are not yet a fully developed source of job leads equal to newspaper or agency listings, though they may be a convenient place to share feelings about the job-search process.[3]

Some employers—and some independent employment agencies and databanks—are scanning high-quality resumés directly into electronic databases for future matching with job openings.[4] Employers who maintain these databases are rarely willing to re-key resumés that are not picked up by the scanner.[5] To be sure you aren't eliminated on that kind of technicality, keep in mind the following:

- Black type on white paper will produce clean, crisp copy; colored papers may not scan properly.
- The page should be free of creases and folds; scanners interpret these as characters and they can lead to gibberish.
- Information should appear in a single-column format; double columns may produce gibberish.
- Multiple type faces, tiny type, and elaborate graphics will not scan well and the information conveyed by them will be lost.

Also be aware that your resumé may be filed under key words that will be used to match your skills against job openings. Be sure you have listed the important terms that fairly represent your technical skills.[6]

Preparing for an Interview

If your resumé has piqued the interest of the firm's owner or human resource department, you will be invited to come in for an interview. This is a hopeful sign, but you probably will not come away from the first interview with a job offer. It's more likely that the first round of interviews will be another sorting process to narrow the field of candidates to a few of the most qualified. A member of the human resource department will assess your overall potential and ability to work within the company's organizational culture. You will be asked to fill out the company's own application form. If all goes well, the human resource interviewer will recommend you to the supervisor or manager directly responsible for the department in which you would be employed—the person who will decide your employment fate.

To make it into the group of finalists, you will want to prepare carefully for your first interview. Hopefully, your preparations began when you decided you were interested in the job opening and wrote your cover letter. If so, you already have accumulated a reasonable amount of background information on the company, its industry, its competition, and the way this job opportunity would fit into your own career objectives. If the company is a public corporation, you can get a copy of its prospectus or annual report from your school or public library. (All public corporations are required by law to file such reports; see Chapter 22.) If you are applying to a small or midsize privately held company, you might check with local businesses or friends who may know something about the company. Alternatively, your school's placement service may have some information. If you cannot obtain the information you seek, prepare a list of tactful questions to ask during the interview. Interviewers are impressed by applicants who display a sincere interest in the business.

You will, of course, want to look your best—well groomed and professional but not overdressed in terms of that company's organizational culture. Beyond that, however, be aware that interviewers are particularly watchful for good communication skills and an air of confidence. Express yourself clearly; ask specific, relevant questions and don't talk too much. If the interviewer's eyes begin to glaze over, you know you've gone on too long. Remember that your resumé has already provided basic information about your education and experience, so your goal during the interview is to fill in some gaps, to explain why you want this particular job, and to find out more about the company and the extent to which it fits your career objectives. If you have done your homework and you know your own abilities, you will exude the type of confidence that will earn the interviewer's respect and interest. Let the interviewer know that you know you can do the job and that you have a goal beyond a weekly paycheck. Chapter 12's skills check, "Careful What You Say—Your Job May Depend on It," lists some statements and questions that interviewers often ask applicants. Here are some questions you can ask the interviewer to gather more information about whether the company is right for you:[7]

- How would you describe the organizational culture of your company?
- What criteria will be used to judge my performance if I'm chosen for this job? Who evaluates job performance, and how often?
- Does the company have a mission statement? How are company values manifested in relationships with employees, customers, and suppliers?
- How would you describe the company's management style and the philosophy of top management?
- What commitment does the company have to the career development and training of its employees? How will the company help me achieve my maximum potential?

Follow up your first interview with a thank-you note for the interviewer's time and attention. State that you are still interested in the job and, if you feel that there were gaps in the information you supplied earlier, send it along with the note.

If all goes well, you will be invited back for a second round of interviews of final candidates and, possibly, a series of employment-related tests. At that time you will go through another round of face-to-face meetings, perhaps with different and more varied people. In team-based organizations, potential coworkers often participate in second interviews; managers who are too busy to see all applicants often sit in on the second round. You probably will have some questions that remained unanswered after the first interview; now is the time to raise them. If you don't already know the terms for salary range, work hours, starting date, work locations, travel requirements, dress code, and relocation prospects, now is the time to find out. Don't assume too much, however. You've made it to the short list, but you probably are not the only one on it. Concentrate on making a good impression and on being yourself. After all, if the potential employer is not comfortable with you as you are, you probably won't be happy working there.

Career Options: A Sampler

In spite of all the trends we have described in this text, the U.S. economy continues to churn out new jobs—7.5 million net new jobs, to be exact, from January 1990 through June 1995. Can you guess which business is showing the greatest growth? Even if you didn't guess, the answer probably won't surprise you: temporary and full-time employment agencies, the busy hubs of activity that produce so many of the country's contingent work force.[8] There also appears to be good growth in what Nuala Beck, an author and economic researcher and consultant, labels "knowledge workers."[9] These are employees who require professional training or technical expertise to do their jobs. That's good news because those jobs pay well, unlike many of the fast-food and other service jobs that have recently replaced higher-paying manufacturing and management jobs. Other booming job categories are in the areas of health care and information technology, according to *Money* magazine's annual career survey, which found that 4 of the top 50 fastest-growing jobs were related to computers and 16 were related to health care.[10] But that still accounts for only 20 of 50 categories; if you aren't attracted by those, keep doing your research. Jobs—jobs that pay well—are available, and three out of four graduates will enter the work force, according to the U.S. Labor Department statistics quoted earlier.

Table A.2 offers a sampler of occupations that correspond to the general topics explored in the seven parts of this text. Remember that for each job described in that table, there are a number of other related jobs requiring similar skills and paying similar salaries. For example, although we list only management consultant, consulting work is available in many other areas, such as information systems and human resources. Furthermore, there are many options for some occupations: An accountant may work on staff at a large firm or in his or her own business serving small firms. A bank loan officer might specialize in mortgages, automobiles, or commercial loans. In short, you must take control of your career and do some research to find the occupation that best fits your skills and interests.

Before you narrow your choices, you might want to consult the *Occupational Outlook Handbook*, published by the U.S. Department of Labor. It is a rich source of job information, with descriptions of 250 occupations, including job requirements, experience needed, and salaries. (Contact the Superintendent of Documents, P.O. Box 371954, Pittsburgh, Pennsylvania 15250-7954.) The Department of Labor also publishes a two-volume *Dictionary of Occupational Titles*, in which it describes 13,000 jobs in nine general categories and many specific occupational groups. (The fourth edition, published by VGM Career Horizons, Lincolnwood, Illinois, was revised in 1991 and reprinted in 1994.)

table A.2 Sampling of Occupations in Fields Discussed

PART 1 The World of Business

Occupation	Job Description	Requirements and Career Path	Salary	Growth Prospects (Number of Jobs)
Statistician	Designs, implements, compiles, and interprets results of surveys and experiments.	Bachelor's degree with major in statistics or mathematics. Promotion opportunities are best for those with advanced degrees.	Average annual salary for statisticians in federal government was $51,893 in 1993.	Slower than average.
Economist	Studies the ways a society uses land, labor, raw materials, machinery, and other scarce resources to produce goods and services.	Bachelor's degree with a major in economics or marketing for entry-level research, administrative, management trainee, or sales jobs. Beginning workers do considerable clerical work. A Ph.D. is necessary for top positions.	In 1993, the average starting salary was $25,200. Median base salary for business economists was $65,000 in 1992.	Average, due to increasingly complex and competitive global economy and increased reliance on quantitative methods of analyzing business trends, forecasting sales, and planning.
Inspector/ Compliance Officer	Enforces adherence to laws, regulations, policies, and procedures for health, safety, food, immigration, licensing, interstate commerce, and international trade.	Combination of education, experience, and often a passing grade on a written examination. Employers generally prefer applicants with college training, including courses related to the job.	Varied substantially in 1993—from $24,800 to $59,300 —depending on the nature of the inspection or compliance activity.	Faster than average, due to increased expansion of government regulatory and compliance programs.
Social Scientist/ Urban Planner	Studies various aspects of human society—from the distribution of goods and services to the beliefs of newly formed religious groups to modern mass transportation systems.	Bachelor's degree for limited opportunities such as entry-level research assistant, administrative aide, or management trainee. M.A. or Ph.D. for jobs with greater responsibility.	In 1992, the median salary for all social scientists was about $36,700.	Faster than average due to rising concern over issues such as the environment, crime, communicable diseases, mental illness, and the growing elderly and homeless populations.
*Interpreter	Translates spoken words from one language to another.	Bachelor's degree preferred but not required except in scientific, technical, or professional fields. Top positions found within public and government organizations and with large international business companies.	Senior interpreters with the U.S. government start at $55,000; self-employed freelance interpreters can earn $350–$500 per day.	Tempered by extreme competition for top jobs. Experienced practitioners fill most vacancies.

(cont.)

PART 1   **The World of Business** (cont.)

Occupation	Job Description	Requirements and Career Path	Salary	Growth Prospects (Number of Jobs)
**International Law Specialist	A lawyer who specializes in negotiating legal contracts for organizations that comply with the laws of different countries.	Beyond traditional legal profession requirements, familiarity with U.S. trade laws and tariffs is necessary. May be permanent counsel with firms specializing in world trade or work in private practice hired on a single contract basis.	No specific salary information on this specialty is available. However, the average for most experienced lawyers in private industry is $120,000.	Faster than average employment growth is expected in the legal profession as a whole.
**Foreign Exchange Position Clerk	Specializes in information about foreign monetary systems. Manages data involving a bank's foreign investment and currency holdings.	College degree preferred but high school graduates with business skills considered for entry-level positions. Foreign language may be required.	Average annual earnings for bank clerical workers range from $8,550–$12,040.	Average growth expected for bank clerks and related workers.

*Joyce Jakubiak, ed. *Specialty Occupational Outlook: Professions* (Detroit: Gale Research, 1995), pp. 180–181.
**William E. Hopke, ed. *The Encyclopedia of Careers and Vocational Guidance,* 9th ed. (Chicago: J.G. Ferguson, 1994), pp. 200, 284–285, 654–657.

PART 2   **Launching the Business**

Occupation	Job Description	Requirements and Career Path	Salary	Growth Prospects (Number of Jobs)
Corporate Attorney	Advises company about legal questions connected with its business activities.	Four years of undergraduate study followed by three years of law school. Most beginning lawyers start as research assistants to more experienced lawyers. Some use their legal training in administrative or managerial positions.	Varies widely depending on type, size, and location of employer. In private industry in 1992, annual salaries of beginning lawyers averaged $36,000; salaries of most experienced lawyers averaged $134,000.	Faster than average in response to growth in population and business activity.

(cont.)

Occupation	Job Description	Requirements and Career Path	Salary	Growth Prospects (Number of Jobs)
Paralegal	Paralegals who work for corporations help attorneys with such matters as employee contracts, shareholder agreements, stock option plans, and employee benefit plans.	Formal paralegal training. Most are two-year programs; some involve four years. Advancement opportunities include promotion to managerial or other law-related positions within the firm.	Varies greatly depending on education; training and experience; type and size of the employer; and geographic location. Average annual salary was $28,300 in 1993.	Much faster than average as law firms and other employers of legal workers restructure tasks to make greater use of paralegals.
†Temporary Employment Service Owner	Secures contracts with local companies for temporary workers; tests, assigns, and handles payroll for work force.	Owners recruit temporary work force and sell services to local employers. Some agencies specialize in certain fields, such as word processing or computer programming. Franchise opportunities are also available.	Minimum start-up costs range from $15,000 to $50,000. Annual net profits before taxes vary widely, from $12,000 to $500,000, with an average of $45,000.	Three times that of all other service industries combined, with a projected growth rate of 5 to 10% per year through the year 2000.
†Information Broker	Fulfills requests to research, gather, and deliver targeted information for individuals and organizations.	Most new brokers start out of their homes with a computer, printer, and modem, subscribing to on-line information resources. Finding clients is the most challenging aspect for start-ups; targeting specific fields—such as financial or medical—yields best results.	Start-up costs estimated at $3,000 to $9,000. Average annual income potential after three years of breaking even, $50,000 to $60,000.	Demand for information from business, financial, medical, government, and private endowment sectors has been escalating annually.
Medical Claims Processing Service	Expedites insurance payments for doctors and patients by preparing medical claim forms.	New claims processors usually begin out of their homes—some may rent office space near medical offices. Establishing a strong client base through a careful marketing strategy is essential.	Start-up costs estimated at $5,000 to $10,000 plus reserve capital. Average annual profit before taxes is $25,000.	An aging population, coupled with a large number of claims and complex forms, should keep demand steady.

†Suzanne M. Bourgoin, ed. *Small Business Profiles,* vol. 1 (Detroit: Gale Research, 1994), pp. 167–168, 184–185, 247–249.

PART 3 Managing the Business

Occupation	Job Description	Requirements and Career Path	Salary	Growth Prospects (Number of Jobs)
Hotel Manager	Responsible for the efficient and profitable operation of the establishments.	Postsecondary education preferred. Graduates of hotel or restaurant administration programs usually start as assistant manager trainees.	Varies, depending on responsibilities and the size of hotel. In 1993, assistant managers averaged $32,500; general managers averaged $59,100.	Generally, average, with growth in business and vacation travel and foreign tourism.
Health Services Manager	Plans, organizes, coordinates, and supervises the delivery of health care for a facility.	Bachelor's degree in health administration. Entry level is as administrative assistant or assistant department head in larger hospitals, or department head or assistant administrator in small health care facility.	Varies by type and size of the facility and level of responsibility. Assistant administrators average $35,000; small group administrators average $46,000; very large group administrators average $166,700.	Much faster than average as the health care industry expands and diversifies. Most new jobs will be in hospitals, M.D.'s offices and clinics, nursing facilities, and home-health care.
Blue-Collar Worker/First-Line Supervisor	Ensures that workers, equipment, and materials are used properly and efficiently to maximize production.	Many supervisors still rise through the ranks, but many employers now require technical degrees. A business or engineering master's degree or in-house training is needed to advance to department head or production manager.	In 1992, the median annual income for blue-collar worker supervisors was about $30,700.	Slower than average, with slight decline in manufacturing.
Administrative Assistant	Responsible for a wide variety of administrative and clerical duties necessary to run and maintain organizations efficiently.	High school degree with basic office skills. Knowledge of word processing, spreadsheet, and database management often required. Qualified people who broaden their skills may be promoted to positions of executive assistant or office manager.	Varies, depending on skill, responsibilities, and experience. In 1992, the average annual salary was $26,700.	Slower than average as increases in the amount of office work available are tempered by office automation gains.

(cont.)

Occupation	Job Description	Requirements and Career Path	Salary	Growth Prospects (Number of Jobs)
Management Analyst/ Consultant	Collects, reviews, and analyzes company or industry information; makes recommendations; possibly assists in the implementation of proposals.	Master's degree in business administration or a discipline related to the firm's area of specialization preferred. Individuals with only a bachelor's degree and no experience are likely to work as research associates or junior consultants.	Varies widely by experience, education, and employer. Average salary for management consultants was $40,300 in 1992; average salary for research associates was $31,300 in 1991.	Much faster than average because of the growing tendency for businesses to rely on outside experts for many functions previously carried out internally.
Industrial Production Manager	Coordinates activities related to the production of goods and directs the work of first-line supervisors.	Some companies hire college graduates as blue-collar worker supervisors and then promote them; others hire business administration or industrial engineering graduates and train them.	Varies significantly by industry and plant size. Average salary was $60,000 in 1992.	Little change expected as the trend toward team self-management and automated production limits demand.
General Manager or Top Executive	Formulates policies and directs the operations of an organization.	Depends on areas of responsibility. Most general manager and top executive positions are filled by promoting experienced lower-level managers.	General managers and top executives are among the highest paid U.S. workers. Salary levels vary widely, depending on the level of managerial responsibility; length of service; and type, size, and location of firm.	Slower than average as companies restructure managerial hierarchies to cut costs.

PART 4   Empowering the Employee

Occupation	Job Description	Requirements and Career Path	Salary	Growth Prospects (Number of Jobs)
††Labor Relations Specialist	Ensures employer's compliance with local, state, and federal antidiscrimination laws. Investigates and resolves employee grievances, monitors corporate policies, compiles and submits statistical reports.	Bachelor's degree in personnel administration, industrial relations, psychology, sociology, counseling, or education. Master's degree in labor relations or human resources preferred. Entry-level workers often enter formal or on-the-job training programs. Exceptional employees may be promoted to management and executive positions.	In 1991, the average annual salary was $40,091.	Faster than average as legislation and court rulings increase demand for experts.
††Corporate Personnel Trainer	Develops skills in new and experienced employees. Assesses needs, then plans and conducts training programs to improve skills.	Bachelor's degree in liberal arts or business recommended with emphasis in personnel, human resources, or labor relations. After working for larger corporations, many trainers go into business for themselves.	In 1991, corporate personnel trainers averaged $30,870.	Faster than average due to growing need for training new workers in basic skills and experienced workers in new skills.
Employment Interviewer	Acts as a broker between employers and employees, putting together the best combination of applicant and job.	Four-year degree preferred but not always required. Interviewers of highly trained individuals generally have some training or experience in a specialized field. Advancement to supervisory positions in the public sector is highly competitive.	Earnings vary. In 1991, the average annual salary for employment interviewers ranged from $17,000 to $25,000.	Average except in temporary help or personnel supply firms, which will produce new jobs. Little growth expected in state job service offices.
*Employee Assistance Program Counselor	Maintains a company's productivity by providing confidential counseling and referral services for employees.	Bachelor's or master's degree preferred. Some states require certification. Capable counselors may find advancement within larger organizations or in different types of counseling.	Varies according to education, experience, and size and type of employer. Average annual salaries range from $15,000 to $60,000.	Faster than average.

(cont.)

Occupation	Job Description	Requirements and Career Path	Salary	Growth Prospects (Number of Jobs)
*Employment Counselor	Counsels job seekers in evaluating their current skill levels using standardized tests and helps clients find employment.	Master's degree in counseling, education, psychology, or sociology preferred. State licensing may be required. Advancement to management or supervisory positions possible in public sector; promotion and self-employment possible in private.	In 1992, the median annual salary for vocational counselors was $30,000.	Due to government budgeting constraints, most new employment growth will occur in the private sector.
Industrial/ Organizational Psychologist	Applies psychological techniques to personnel administration, management, and marketing problems.	Ph.D. is generally required. Holders of an M.A. can administer tests as psychological assistants. Holders of a B.A. can assist psychologists and other professionals in health care, vocational, and correctional programs or work as research assistants, administrative assistants, or trainees in government or business.	In 1991, the median annual salary of industrial/ organizational psychologists was $76,000.	Much faster than average due to increasing public concern for the development of human resources.
Human Resource Specialist or Manager	Recruits and interviews employees and advises on hiring decisions in accordance with policies and requirements established in conjunction with top management.	Bachelor's degree in human resources, personnel administration, or industrial and labor relations for entry-level openings. Previous experience required for many specialized jobs in this field, especially managerial positions.	In 1992, human resource specialists averaged $32,000, with very experienced specialists averaging $76,900; human resource managers averaged $37,000, with very experienced managers averaging $105,000.	Faster than average as greater resources are devoted to job-specific training, an aging work force, and compliance with new government standards.

††Carol Kleiman, *The 100 Best Jobs for the 1990's and Beyond* (Chicago: Dearborn Financial, 1992), pp. 246–247, 251–253.
*Jakubiak, *Specialty Occupational Outlook: Professions*, pp. 121–124.

PART 5 Pleasing the Customer

Occupation	Job Description	Requirements and Career Path	Salary	Growth Prospects (Number of Jobs)
Public Relations Specialist	Compiles information to keep the general public, interest groups, and stockholders aware of an organization's policies, activities, and accomplishments.	Four-year degree with public relations experience—usually gained through an internship—is excellent preparation. Larger organizations may offer formal training for new employees.	Average starting salary for entry-level public relations account executives was almost $21,000 in 1992; median annual salary for full-time public relations specialists was $32,000.	Average. Organizations of all sizes will need good public relations in an increasingly competitive business environment.
Manufacturer/ Wholesale Trade Sales Representative	Markets products to manufacturers, wholesale and retail establishments, government agencies, and other institutions.	Four-year degree preferred but not required. Many companies have formal training programs that last up to two years. Promotion often means assignment to a larger account or territory where commissions are likely to be greater. May advance to sales supervisor or district manager.	Compensation methods vary. In 1992, median annual salary of full-time representatives was $32,000.	Slower than average as more firms rely on new sales technologies and as more large companies negotiate directly with suppliers.
Buyer/ Purchaser	Determines which commodities or services are best, selects suppliers, negotiates contracts, and ensures that conditions are met.	Large stores and distributors accept applicants with associate's or bachelor's degrees from any field of study. Manufacturing firms place greater emphasis on more formal training. Both require extended training in employer's specific business. New hires usually begin as trainees, purchasing clerks, expediters, or junior or assistant buyers.	Median annual earnings for buyers and purchasers was $33,067 in 1992.	Slower than average due to consolidation resulting from mergers, changes in the way purchases are made, and increased use of automated systems.

(cont.)

Occupation	Job Description	Requirements and Career Path	Salary	Growth Prospects (Number of Jobs)
Restaurant/ Food-Service Manager	Sets menu and prices; directs use of food and supplies; oversees food preparation and service; recruits, trains, and supervises employees; handles administrative aspects of the business.	Two- or four-year degree, preferably in restaurant and food-service management. New management hires receive 6 to 12 months of rigorous training before their first permanent assignment as an assistant manager.	In 1993, manager trainees had median base earnings of $21,200 to $30,900. Assistant managers had earnings of $24,400 to $35,700. Managers had earnings of $29,900 to $53,000. Fast-food restaurants averaged $19,800 for assistants and $24,900 for managers.	Much faster than average due to population growth, rising personal incomes, and increased leisure time, which should produce growth in the number of eating and drinking establishments.
Retail Manager	Coordinates and directs all aspects of retail trade including ordering, inspecting, pricing, and inventorying of goods. Develops merchandising plan, coordinates marketing, and maintains customer relations. Interviews, hires, trains, and supervises employees.	Most managers begin as clerks, cashiers, or customer service workers and are promoted to assistant or department manager positions. Though not required, two- or four-year degrees are increasingly important for promotion to more responsible positions.	In 1992, assistant store managers' median salary ranged from $13,100 to $14,300. For store managers, the range was $18,400 to $23,700.	About average as increases in retail establishments are balanced by computerized registers, labor-savings, and inventory control systems.
Marketing/ Advertising/ Public Relations Manager	Directs the sale of products and services offered by the firm and the communication of information about the firm's activities.	Many employers prefer a broad liberal arts background. Most positions are filled by promotions from within the company.	Average salary for marketing, advertising, and PR managers was $41,000 in 1992.	Faster than average resulting from intense domestic and global competition.
*Advertising Account Executive	Serves as a direct liaison between advertising agencies and their clients by becoming familiar with the clients' needs.	Bachelor's degree in marketing, advertising, business journalism, or business administration preferred. Training programs are available for entry-level positions. Advancement is usually an assignment to larger accounts. Promotion to management and supervisory positions possible.	In 1990, the average annual salary for nonsupervisory advertising personnel was $28,000.	Higher than average.

*Jakubiak, *Specialty Occupational Outlook: Professions*, pp. 1–2.

PART 6 Controlling the Business

Occupation	Job Description	Requirements and Career Path	Salary	Growth Prospects (Number of Jobs)
Operations Research Analyst	Helps organizations coordinate and operate efficiently through the application of scientific methods and mathematical principles.	Master's degree in operations research or management science and a high level of computer skills. Beginning analysts usually do routine work under the supervision of experienced analysts before being assigned to more complex and independent tasks.	In 1992, starting salaries averaged $30,000 to $35,000. Experienced analysts averaged about $50,000.	Much faster than average. Quantitative analysis in decision making and computing resources are used with increasing frequency.
Systems Analyst	Defines business, scientific, or engineering problems and designs solutions via computers.	Bachelor's degree in computer science, information science, computer information systems, or data processing. Background in business management. Systems analysts can advance to positions of manager of information systems or chief information officer if they have appropriate social skills.	Median annual earnings in 1992 were about $42,100.	Much faster than average as organizations demand technological advances, update systems, and install computer networks for sharing information.
Budget Analyst	Searches for new ways to improve efficiency and increase profits. Advises and assists in the preparation of annual budgets.	Bachelor's degree. Entry-level analysts may receive some formal training and usually work under close supervision. Promotion to intermediate, senior, and supervisory positions is possible within a few years.	In 1992, the median annual salary of experienced budget analysts was $39,700.	Strong demand will be tempered by productivity gains from downsizing and automation.
Accountant	Prepares, analyzes, and verifies financial reports and taxes and monitors information systems that furnish this information.	Bachelor's degree in accounting or related field. Beginners may start as cost accountants, junior internal auditors, or trainees. Career path may include accounting manager, chief cost accountant, budget director, manager of internal auditing, controller, treasurer, financial vice president, chief financial officer, or corporation president.	In 1992, certified management accountants had an average annual salary of $58,700.	Faster than average due to increases in the complexity of financial information and the number of automated systems.

(cont.)

Occupation	Job Description	Requirements and Career Path	Salary	Growth Prospects (Number of Jobs)
Computer Programmer	Writes, updates, and maintains the programs or software that enable computer systems to perform their functions.	Most programmers hold four-year degrees in computer science or information systems, but many find employment with two-year degrees or certificates. Beginning programmers initially work under close supervision. Programmers with general business experience may become systems analysts or be promoted to managerial positions.	In 1992, the median salary was $35,600.	Faster than average as organizations specify new applications for computers and improvements to their software.
††Database Manager	Supervises the collection, storage, and retrieval of company data.	Bachelor's degree in computer science required, master's degree preferred by larger firms. Opportunity for advancement to managerial positions.	Average annual salary was $38,587 in 1991.	Expected growth as more and more manufacturing plants are automated.

††Kleiman, *The 100 Best Jobs for the 1990's and Beyond,* pp. 185–186.

PART 7   Financing the Business

Occupation	Job Description	Requirements and Career Path	Salary	Growth Prospects (Number of Jobs)
Securities Sales Representative	Buys and sells securities for investors. May offer financial counseling and advice on the purchase or sale of securities.	Four-year degree, usually including courses in business administration, economics, and finance. Securities sales representatives must meet state licensing requirements. Most employers provide on-the-job training to help new employees meet requirements. Advancement is usually an increase in number and size of accounts.	In 1992, the average annual salary of beginning representatives was $28,000. Experienced reps serving individual clients averaged $78,000; those serving institutional accounts averaged $156,000.	Faster than average due to increases resulting from economic growth, rising personal incomes, and greater inherited wealth.

(cont.)

PART 7 Financing the Business (cont.)

Occupation	Job Description	Requirements and Career Path	Salary	Growth Prospects (Number of Jobs)
Financial Manager	Prepares financial reports, oversees cash flow, analyzes investments, and develops information to assess the financial status of the organization.	Four-year degree in accounting, finance, or business administration (with emphasis on accounting or finance). Many firms fill this position by promoting experienced accountants, budget analysts, credit analysts, insurance analysts, loan officers, or security analysts.	1992 average salary was $39,700.	Average. Downsizing will balance increased need for skilled financial management resulting from global trade, proliferation of complex financial instruments, and changing laws and regulations.
Loan Officer/ Counselor	Prepares, analyzes, and verifies loan applications; determines whether credit extensions are justifiable; and helps borrowers complete loan applications.	Bachelor's degree in finance, economics, or a related field. Many loan officers have several years experience in various other occupations, such as teller or customer service representative. May advance to larger branches of the firm or to a managerial position.	In 1993, real estate mortgage loan officers averaged $25,000 to $45,000; consumer loan officers averaged $27,000 to $44,000; loan counselors averaged $15,000 to $35,000.	Faster than average as growth in population and economy produce increased numbers of applications for commercial, consumer, and mortgage loans.
Actuary	Assembles and analyzes statistics to calculate the probabilities of death, sickness, injury, disability, unemployment, retirement, and property loss.	Four-year degree, usually in mathematics or a business-related discipline. Advancement to more responsible work as assistant, associate, and chief actuary depends on job performance and number of actuarial exams passed.	In 1992, starting salaries averaged $31,800; associates averaged $46,000; fellows averaged $65,500.	Faster than average growth, especially for consulting actuaries, but the absolute number of job openings will remain low.
Underwriter	Decides whether an insurance applicant is an acceptable risk. Analyzes applications, loss-control consultant reports, medical reports, and actuarial studies.	Business administration or finance degree preferred, and basic computer skills are also required. Underwriter trainee or assistant underwriter is typical entry-level position. Experienced underwriter may advance to chief underwriter or underwriting manager.	In 1991, the median salary ranged from an entry level of $25,000 to $40,600 for senior level. Median salary for underwriting managers was $61,000.	About average. Demand for more life, property, and casualty insurance should rise as 40- to 60-year-old group increases in size.

(cont.)

Occupation	Job Description	Requirements and Career Path	Salary	Growth Prospects (Number of Jobs)
Insurance Agent/Broker	Sells insurance policies that protect businesses and individuals against loss. Specialists in group policies may help employers provide employees with the opportunity to buy insurance through payroll deductions.	Insurance companies prefer college graduates—especially those who have majored in business or economics. All insurance agents and brokers must obtain a license in the states where they plan to sell insurance. New agents usually receive company training to prepare for examinations. Capable agents and brokers can advance to managerial and executive positions or establish independent agencies or brokerage firms.	In 1992, the median annual salary for salaried insurance sales workers was $30,100. Most independent agents are paid on a commission-only basis.	Average job growth is expected as increasing productivity moderates rising sales of insurance and other financial products.
Insurance Adjustor	Plans and schedules the work required to process an insurance claim. Investigates and determines the extent of the insurance company's liability.	Most companies prefer to hire college graduates, though persons without college training may be hired if they have specialized knowledge. Most large companies provide on-the-job training and preparation for state licensing requirements. Beginning adjustors work on small claims under the supervision of an experienced worker. With experience, they are assigned larger, more complex claims. Capable adjustors can progress to supervisory and managerial positions.	Earnings vary significantly for adjustors. In 1992, the median weekly earnings for adjustors averaged about $400.	Job growth is expected to be about as fast as average due to increases in the population, the economy, and the volume of insurance sales.

Glossary

A

absolute advantage   When a country can produce a good or service far more efficiently than its trading partner.

accountability   Being answerable for the actions taken to complete a task.

accounting   The process of collecting, summarizing, and reporting financial information for decision making.

accounting equation   Assets = liabilities + owners' equity.

acquisition   The outright purchase of one corporation by another corporation, either in whole or in part.

activity ratios   Ratios measuring how efficiently a firm is using its resources to generate revenue.

activity-based costing (ABC)   Assigning costs to root activities, or cost drivers, rather than to departments.

actuary   A statistician who calculates the potential for an insurance company's future loss based on historical loss data.

administrative law   Rules and regulations created by administrative authority.

advertising   Nonpersonal mass communication paid for by an identified sponsor.

advocacy advertising   Promoting a particular point of view on an issue.

AFL-CIO   National federation of craft and industrial unions formed from the merger in 1955 of the AFL and CIO.

agency shop   Workplace that requires all members of a bargaining unit—union and nonunion—to pay union dues if they receive benefits from union-negotiated contracts.

agents   People who bring buyers and sellers together and assist in making the exchange but never own the product.

American depository receipts (ADRs)   Certificates representing ownership in the stock of a foreign company.

American Federation of Labor (AFL)   National organization comprising individual craft unions focused on the economic well-being of members.

analytic process   Production process that breaks down incoming materials into separate products.

applications   Software packages for specific computing needs.

arbitration   Intervention by a neutral third party whose decision is legally binding.

articles of incorporation   Document describing the organization and naming it.

artificial intelligence   The computer modeling and simulation of human reasoning and learning.

assembly line   Work layout in which the product flows through a sequence of workstations where employees perform specialized tasks.

assets   Financial and economic resources owned or controlled by an organization.

attrition   Policy of reducing an organization's work force through normal turnover and voluntary terminations.

audit   Independent examination of financial statements and records to determine their validity and fair presentation of information.

authority   The power to take the actions and make the decisions necessary to fulfill one's responsibility.

autocratic leader   A leader who adopts a style based largely on the use of authority.

automated teller machine (ATM)   Form of electronic funds transfer in which bank customers may withdraw funds at any time and in a variety of locations using a private personal identification number (PIN).

automatic transfer from savings (ATS) accounts   Linked checking and savings accounts in which amounts are transferred between the accounts as needed.

automation   Performing mechanical operations with little or no direct human involvement.

B

balance of payments   The total flow of money into and out of a country during a specified period of time.

balance of trade   The relationship between a country's imports and its exports.

balance sheet   Statement of financial position showing an organization's assets, liabilities, and owners' equity at a specified date.

benchmarking   Adapting better approaches from other businesses.

benefit segmentation   Dividing the market by focusing on the primary benefit that the consumer is seeking.

benefits   Noncash compensation, such as health insurance, paid vacations, or retirement plans, which employees select or receive by virtue of being members of the organization.

bid rigging   Collusion between one bidder and the buyer in order to gain a contract.

bill of materials   List of all parts and materials that are to be made or purchased.

blue chip stocks   The stocks of large, well-established companies that consistently pay dividends and show an increase in value.

board of directors   Elected governing body of a corporation that protects the stockholders' interests by setting policy and selecting top management.

bond   A certificate issued by a business or government agency guaranteeing a specific interest rate and repayment of the principal at a specified time.

bond indenture   A legal contract between the bond issuer and purchaser specifying the terms of the bond.

bonus   A cash payment that rewards employees for achieving an organizational goal.

boycott   An organized refusal to buy, sell, or use targeted goods or services.

brainstorming   Thinking out loud to try to list as many ideas as possible without criticizing any of them.

brand   A name, term, symbol, or design (or a combination of these) that identifies a firm's goods or services and differentiates them from those of competitors.

brand extension strategy   Taking the brand name from one product category and using it in another.

brand name   The words, letters, or numbers that identify a brand.

break-even analysis   A tool used by businesses to find the sales volume at which their costs are covered and their profits begin if they sell a product at a given price.

break-even point   The point at which the units sold cover their own portion of variable costs and all fixed costs.

budget deficit   The difference between the amount the government spends on purchases and transfer payments and the amount it receives from taxation in a given time period.

budgets   Allocations of forecasted revenues (cash inflows) to specific costs and expenses (cash outflows).

business   Any organization that maintains itself by taking in resources and increasing their value for customers.

business cycle   Pattern of overall, up-and-down fluctuations in economic growth over time.

business ethics   The application of moral principles to business decision making.

business incubator   Facility that provides entrepreneurs and small businesses with low-cost access to office space and equipment, legal and accounting advice, and training in how to run a business.

business interruption insurance   Reimburses an owner for lost profits and continuing expenses during the time a business must stay closed following a flood, hurricane, or other disaster.

business law   Laws that set enforceable standards of business conduct.

business network   Linked businesses that cooperate to achieve a common purpose.

business plan   A written document that analyzes and describes all the important issues involved in the start-up and ongoing operations of a business.

C

call option   Agreement that gives an investor the right to *purchase* a particular stock at a specific exercise, or strike, price up to a specific date.

callable bonds   Corporate bonds that can be redeemed by the issuer at any time, after a specified period, prior to maturity.

capacity   The quantity of goods or services a business can produce under normal working conditions.

capital   Any form of wealth used to produce more wealth.

capital budget   Financial plan for major investments that span a period of more than one year.

capital goods   Expensive, durable items used in the production of finished goods.

capitalism   A political system that encourages free markets and private ownership of money, land, equipment, and other resources businesses need.

career development   The process of planning and coordinating the progress of employees through positions of increasing responsibility within an organization.

career path   A succession of jobs that employees hold as they move upward through an organization to positions of increasing responsibility and pay.

cash budget   An estimate of anticipated cash receipts and payments (disbursements) for a period of time—usually a week, a month, or a quarter.

cash flows   The pattern of actual revenues and expenditures flowing into or out of the business.

cash-value life insurance   Combines a death benefit with a savings feature.

cause-effect (CE) diagram   An illustration of causes, effects, and their relationships.

cell layout   Work layout in which small teams of workers make entire components, functioning as a subprocess in a larger production process.

cellular telephone   A portable, battery-operated, wireless phone that broadcasts on a special high-frequency radio band.

central processing unit (CPU)   The hardware that produces information from data and controls all computer operations.

centralization   Concentration of decision making in one primary location.

certificate of deposit (CD)   Time deposit that pays an annual interest rate on a fixed amount for a specified period and then repays the full principal at the end of the period.

certification   A union's right, obtained by majority vote, to act as the exclusive bargaining agent for employees for one year.

certified internal auditor (CIA)   A private accountant who checks company records for accuracy, consistency, and conformity to GAAP, and is certified by the Institute of Internal Auditors.

certified management accountant (CMA)   A licensed specialist in managerial accounting as designated by the Institute of Management Accountants.

certified public accountant (CPA)   A licensed practitioner who has passed a qualifying examination administered by the American Institute of Certified Public Accountants (AICPA).

chain of command   The line of reporting relationships that describes the flow of responsibility, authority, and accountability from the top of an organization to the bottom.

channel captain   The distribution channel member with the power to influence the behavior of others.

chief executive officer (CEO)   The person hired by the board of directors who is responsible for all of a company's operations and management decisions.

chief information officer (CIO)   Executive who manages a firm's management information system, information technology, and human resources.

circular flow   The constant interactions among buyers and sellers in an economy.

Clayton Antitrust Act   Passed in 1914; along with the Norris-LaGuardia Anti-Injunction Act, prevents court intervention in most labor disputes.

closed shop   Workplace that requires membership in a union as a condition of gaining employment.

coinsurance clause   (1) In property insurance, requires the policy holder to carry insurance equal to a specified percentage of the value of the property in order to receive full coverage on a loss; (2) in health insurance, requires the insured individual to pay a percentage of his or her medical expenses above and beyond the deductible.

collateral   Specific asset pledged against a loan.

collective bargaining   The process by which representatives of management and labor determine wages and working conditions for employees.

command economy   An economic system whereby the government determines both prices and quantities to be produced.

command-and-control management   Management exercised through a chain of command.

commercial banks   Profit-making institutions that accept funds in the form of deposits (checking and savings) and provide funds as loans to individuals and businesses.

commercial paper   Short-term debt instrument that financial institutions and large corporations sell to raise funds.

commercial product lines   Insurance products that are designed for and bought by businesses.

commission   Pay based on a percentage of the money an employee brings into a business.

committee   A group to which decision-making power is delegated for specific purposes.

commodities   Raw materials or agricultural products such as wheat, silver, oil, pork bellies, and sugar that are traded in separate markets, often as futures.

common law   Legal interpretations of the law based on past court decisions.

common market   A form of economic cooperation among several nations, such as is found in the European Union.

common stock   Corporate stock that represents equity, or ownership, in a company; common stockholders have voting rights and the opportunity to earn profits from the sale of the stock.

communism   A political system in which almost all resources needed for business are owned by the state.

comparable worth   The payment of equal compensation to women and men in different positions that require similar levels of education, training, and skill.

comparative advertising   Advertising by a company that openly names its competitors and undercuts their products.

compensation   The payment—pay and benefits—that employees receive for their work.

computer system   A grouping of machines—the hardware—that accept and process data and display the output.

computer-aided design (CAD)   The use of computers to help people design better products.

computer-aided manufacturing (CAM)   The use of computers to control machines that produce goods.

computer-integrated manufacturing (CIM)   System that uses a central computer to drive robots and control and coordinate the flow of materials and supplies in a production process.

conceptual skills   The ability to perform complex, abstract thinking tasks.

Congress of Industrial Organizations (CIO)   Organization resulting from a split within the AFL and formed as a federation of industrial unions.

consumer markets   Markets that contain the more than 260 million Americans who ultimately use the goods and services produced in our economy.

consumer price index (CPI)   A measure of inflation calculated by comparing how the cost of a typical basket of goods that a household might buy changes from month to month or year to year.

consumerism   The promotion of buyers' interests.

containerization   Packing smaller packages into large, standardized, easy-to-handle containers for shipping.

contingency planning   The process of preparing alternatives in case of a change in the situation or a problem with the plans.

contingent work force   Part-time, temporary, and self-employed workers who do not conform to the traditional model of the 9-to-5, full-time employee.

continuous process   Production process with high setup costs and long start times that make it most efficient when run constantly.

contract administration   Interpretation and implementation of a contract in particular situations.

contract law   The body of laws that defines the rights and obligations of parties engaged in business relationships.

controlling   The process of monitoring and evaluating activities to ensure that objectives are being achieved.

convenience products   Inexpensive goods and services that consumers purchase frequently and want to buy with the least possible effort.

convenience stores   Retail establishments located near the residences or workplaces of their target customers; they carry a wide assortment of products and emphasize location, parking, easy movement within the store, long hours, and quick checkout service.

convertible bonds   Corporate bonds that can be converted into shares of stock, as specified in the bond agreement.

cooperative Business owned by a group of individuals working toward some common economic goal.

cooperative advertising The sharing of the costs of local advertising by intermediaries and producers.

copyrights Rights to written work, art, or software.

corporate by-laws Document defining the procedures for distributing ownership, appointing directors, and running the company.

corporation A business that has legal rights, privileges, and liabilities separate from those of its owners, the shareholders.

cost of capital The rate of return a company must earn in order to satisfy the demands of its debt holders and equity holders.

cost of quality Sum of costs incurred as a result of defects and errors in a process.

cost shifting The use by businesses of deductibles and coinsurance to shift a portion of losses to policyholders.

countertrade The exchange of one good for another without using money. Also known as *barter*.

craft union Small, local organization limited to skilled handworkers in specific trades.

credit union Depository institution that accepts deposits and provides loans and that is organized by and for people with a common bond.

critical path method (CPM) Scheduling technique that highlights the sequence of tasks that will determine the minimum time in which a project can be completed.

cross-functional teams Teams that draw together personnel from different functional areas of an organization to improve operations and communication.

currency Paper money and coins.

current assets Cash and any other asset that can be converted into cash within one year.

current liabilities Claims of creditors due to be repaid within one year from the date of the balance sheet.

customer service Paying attention to every detail in the process of delivering satisfaction.

customers The people or organizations that consume what businesses produce.

cycle time The time required to complete a process once.

cyclical unemployment Joblessness due to business cycle fluctuations.

D

database A collection of computer files that can be cross-referenced or linked.

debenture A corporate bond that is not backed by collateral.

debit card Bank-issued card that can be used directly to purchase goods and services.

debt capital Funds raised by borrowing.

debt ratios Ratios measuring the extent to which a firm uses borrowed funds to finance its operations.

decentralization Dispersal of decision making throughout an organization.

decertification Withdrawal, by majority vote, of a union's right to represent employees.

decision support systems (DSS) Systems that allow managers to chart the course of their sales forecasts and company's future, to analyze information, and to make decisions.

deductible A set amount paid by the policyholder to absorb a certain percentage of the loss.

default risk Risk that a borrower will not repay a loan.

delegation The assignment of a manager's responsibility and authority for a task to employees.

demand The willingness to buy a good or service.

demand curve The entire range of quantities consumers will demand at different prices.

demand deposits Checking accounts.

demarketing Marketing that is used to discourage people from buying a product.

democratic leader A leader whose style is based on empowerment and employee participation.

demographics The statistical study of the characteristics of a population, such as age, gender, marital status, income, and education.

demotion Movement of an employee to a position of lesser responsibility, usually as a result of poor performance in a higher-level position.

department stores Retail stores that carry a wide variety of product lines divided into departments to facilitate merchandising.

departmentalization The organization of work groups or activities into subunits within a company.

depository institutions Banks and other financial institutions that accept deposits and make loans.

Depository Institutions Deregulation and Monetary Control Act First step in deregulating the banking industry; also known as the *Banking Act of 1980*.

depreciation Allocating the cost of an asset over its expected useful life.

deregulation The process of removing restrictions on business competition.

derivative securities Financial devices whose value changes in response to movement in the prices of other securities.

devaluation Occurs when a government actually lowers the rate of exchange for its currency relative to foreign currencies.

developed countries The 34 countries in which per capita GDP is relatively high, over $10,000 per year.

developing countries The 175 countries in which per capita GDP is relatively low, less than $10,000 per year and typically below $5,000.

digital computers Complex electronic circuits comprising simple on/off switches.

direct export   A form of exporting used by companies that have grown sufficiently large, in which the company creates its own export department or division to conduct business directly with foreign buyers.

direct marketing   Communicates a purchase offer designed to elicit an immediate buyer response.

directors and officers (D&O) insurance   Covers directors and officers of public or private companies for negligent acts or misleading statements that expose a company to loss.

disability insurance   Replaces income lost when the policyholder is unable to work because of an accident, injury, or illness.

discount rate   The interest rate the Fed charges on loans it makes to financial institutions.

discount stores   Self-service general merchandise stores that combine low price with high volume.

discrimination   The unequal treatment of an individual based on group affiliation.

dispatching   Sending people, materials, and equipment to where they are needed.

distribution centers   Streamlined storage facilities geared to turning orders into quickly delivered products.

distribution channel   A chain of organizations that moves products from producers to consumers and industrial users; includes all the marketing intermediaries that move raw materials into factories and finished goods into the hands of the ultimate consumers.

diversity training   Training in awareness of and respect for individual, social, and cultural differences among co-workers and customers.

divestiture   The process of selling a subsidiary or other unit.

dividends   Payments made to stockholders from a corporation's profits.

division of labor   Dividing large, complex tasks into smaller, distinct tasks that are assigned to specialized workers.

double-entry bookkeeping   Recording two entries for every financial transaction in order to keep the accounting equation in balance.

downsizing   Eliminating jobs to cut costs and make the business smaller.

draw   Distribution of business earnings to an owner.

dual distribution   When businesses use more than one distribution channel.

dumping   Occurs when a company sells goods abroad below cost or at a lower price than it charges in its protected home market.

E

economics   The study of how scarce resources are allocated among competing uses.

electronic funds transfer (EFT)   Mechanism for transmitting funds to and from financial institutions.

electronic mail (e-mail)   Text-driven message system similar to voice mail.

embargo   A total ban on imports in designated categories.

employee leasing   Purchasing the long-term services of a worker from another company.

employee orientation   Training that brings new employees up to speed on how the business and its industry work.

employee referral   A current employee's recommendation of friends or acquaintances.

employee stock option plan   Program that attempts to motivate employees to maintain high levels of performance by allowing them to buy company stock at discounted prices.

employment at will   An employer-employee relationship in which either party may, in the absence of a contract, terminate the arrangement at any time and for any reason.

empowerment   The transfer to employees of authority and responsibility for a task, along with the necessary resources and power to excel at the task.

enterprise zone   A district, typically in an economically depressed area, in which state or local government-sponsored incentives are offered to businesses that locate there.

entrepreneurship   Risk-taking behavior associated with the start-up and growth of a business.

environmental scanning   The term marketers use to describe their efforts to monitor the marketing environment and to forecast changes within it.

equilibrium price   The one price at which the quantity supplied and the quantity demanded are exactly equal.

equity capital   Funds raised by selling shares of ownership in a business.

ethical management   A strong commitment to aligning the interests of a business with those of its stakeholders.

ethics screen   An evaluation of a business by potential employees, customers, communities, or other stakeholders to make sure it meets ethical criteria.

ethics statement   A written outline of the ethical principles of a business.

everyday low prices (EDLP)   Permanent discounts on products.

exchange   A process in which buyers and sellers each benefit by trading things they value in order to satisfy their wants and needs.

exchange rate   The price of one currency in terms of another currency.

exclusive distribution   A strategy in which only one retailer has the right to represent the manufacturer in each geographic territory.

executive information systems   Systems that allow managers to develop customized solutions to broad questions beyond the scope of day-to-day business issues.

expenses Costs: the resources a company uses to earn revenue.

expert system A highly developed form of decision support system that simulates a human expert, using large databases, elaborate sets of rules, and artificial intelligence to develop and analyze recommendations on solutions to specific problems.

exporting Selling resources, goods, and services to buyers in foreign countries.

exports The opposite of imports—goods or services produced in one country and sent to customers in other countries.

express warranty A formal written promise of performance.

externalities Actions by individuals or businesses that either impose costs or confer benefits on society at large.

extrinsic motivation Motivation that derives its power from forces outside the individual.

F

facsimile machine (fax) A device that digitally transmits documents such as letters, reports, and photographs to another fax machine.

factoring Selling accounts receivable at a discount to a factoring company in return for immediate cash.

factors of production The four classes of limited resources: land, capital, labor, and entrepreneurship.

Family and Medical Leave Act Federal law requiring firms with 50 or more employees to grant up to 12 weeks of unpaid leave following the birth or adoption of a child or the placement of a foster child, or during the serious illness of the employee or a member of his or her family.

family brand strategy Using the same brand name for all of a company's products.

Federal Deposit Insurance Corporation (FDIC) Federal agency that provides insurance on bank accounts and inspects banks to ensure they are following safe business practices.

Federal Reserve System (the Fed) Government agency, consisting of a network of 12 district banks, which regulates and monitors the banking industry.

fidelity bond Protects a company against a loss of property caused by the dishonest acts of an employee or other individual associated with the firm.

finance company Nondepository institution that provides collateral-based, short-term loans to individuals and small businesses.

financial accounting Reports financial information to external users.

financial control The business process of comparing actual results with budgets and modifying the financial plan accordingly.

Financial Institutions Act of 1982 Legislation that further relaxed banking regulations.

financial management The business function of obtaining funds, managing the day-to-day flow of funds, and committing funds for long-term expenditures.

financial plan The blueprint of the financial needs of a company—identifies the funds needed by the firm, estimates the timing of cash inflows and outflows, recommends investment alternatives and how to fund them, and monitors the financial performance of the company.

fiscal policy The taxing and spending decisions of government.

fixed assets Capital goods with a useful life of more than one year.

fixed benefits Benefits that all employees receive by virtue of being a member of the organization.

fixed costs Costs that do not change no matter how many units of the product are produced.

fixed layout Work layout in which all equipment and workers are brought together at one stationary location.

flat organizations Organizations with few layers of management and wide spans of control; also known as *horizontal organizations*.

flexible benefits Benefits that employees choose according to their wants and needs. Also called *cafeteria benefits*.

flexible manufacturing systems (FMS) Automated systems designed to be easily modified to produce varied quantities of multiple products; also called *soft manufacturing* or *agile production*.

flextime Program that allows employees to work during hours of their choices as long as they work their required number of hours and are present during prescribed core periods.

floating exchange rate system A system of exchange in which the values of all currencies are determined by the forces of supply and demand.

flow diagram A process portrayed in symbols and words that map the steps and sequence of activities.

follow-up Activities by managers or employees to compare actual work performed with plans and schedules for that work.

forecast A prediction of the flow of funds into and out of the business.

Foreign Corrupt Practices Act A law that forbids American companies from paying bribes to foreign officials, political candidates, or government parties.

foreign (free trade) zones A form of trading agreement in which a foreign company is allowed to import goods free of tax if it creates domestic jobs in the import zone.

form utility The satisfaction buyers receive from a product's tangible (physical) characteristics—its shape, function, or style.

formal organization The official structure of reporting relationships developed by management to achieve the organization's goals.

four Ps The four elements of marketing—product, price, place, and promotion.

franchisee An individual who buys a license to operate a franchise.

franchising An agreement in which one business grants another business the right to distribute its products or services.

franchisor   A company that grants others a license to use its knowledge and identity.

free trade   An open situation in which no barriers to trade exist and countries can trade freely.

frictional unemployment   Joblessness related to the normal workings of the labor market.

full-line strategy   Employed by companies offering a large number and wide assortment of product lines.

futures contracts   Legal contracts that give investors the right to purchase a specific, standardized commodity on a specified future date at an agreed-upon price.

G

gain sharing   The granting of periodic (quarterly, semiannual, or annual) bonuses to employees based on organizational performance, not individual performance.

Gantt chart   Bar chart that shows both *when* tasks take place and *how long* they should take.

gazelle   A fast-growing business that consistently increases its sales by 15 percent or more a year.

General Agreement on Tariffs and Trade (GATT)   The trade pact that binds 124 of the world's trading nations to mutual agreements that set limits on both tariff and nontariff barriers.

general obligation bonds   Municipal bonds backed by the credit and taxing ability of the state or local government and repaid from tax receipts.

general partnership   A business partnership in which co-owners are jointly and separately liable for everything the business does.

generally accepted accounting principles (GAAP)   Standard accounting rules, conventions, and presentation methods used in preparing financial statements.

generic name   The name for an entire product category.

givebacks   Union concessions to management to save jobs and help the company remain competitive.

glass ceiling   The limit on the job level to which a woman will be promoted.

global strategy   "Selling the same product, the same way, everywhere"; based on the assumption that consumers around the world are growing more and more similar.

going naked   Assuming risk with no protection of any kind against loss.

going public   Process of offering shares to the public.

good faith   A set of assumptions about the mutual duties and responsibilities of both a business and its stakeholders.

good-faith bargaining   Management's and labor's willingness to consider alternative proposals and to compromise in order to reach a mutually acceptable agreement.

government-owned corporation   Organization owned and usually operated by a government for the benefit of society.

grapevine   An unofficial and informal communication network that exists in virtually all organizations.

grievance procedures   The process for handling disputes over the interpretation of some component of the collective bargaining contract.

gross domestic product (GDP)   The dollar value of all the goods and services a country produces within a given time period.

groupware   Type of software specifically designed to support collaboration among groups of people—both inside and outside an organization.

growth business   A small business that is managed for rapid growth and that may take high risks to achieve that growth.

growth stocks   Stocks that are riskier than blue chip stocks but represent potentially greater future gain.

H

hardware   The machines that make up a computer system.

Hawthorne effect   Increases in employees' productivity when special attention makes them believe that their work is considered important.

holding company   A company that owns most or all of a subsidiary's stock but takes no part in its management.

human relations skills   The ability to communicate with, motivate, and work together with others.

human resource management   Ensuring that a business has an adequate supply of skilled, trained, and motivated employees to meet the organization's objectives.

I

implied warranty   The expectation that products are fit for normal use even if no written guarantee is provided.

importing   Purchasing resources, finished goods, and services from a foreign country.

imports   Goods or services brought into a country for purchase from another country.

income statement   Financial statement summarizing an organization's revenues and expenses during any accounting cycle.

incongruities   Surprising events that clash with assumptions about a business and its environment.

indemnity insurance   Reimburses the insured for "reasonable and customary" fees.

index   A price-weighted average of a group of securities.

indirect export   The most common form of exporting among companies entering international markets; the company contracts with host country nationals who provide various services plus international selling expertise.

individual brand   A name applied to only one product

industrial marketing   Marketing that involves exchanges between the manufacturers that produce the goods and services that are sold to other firms for use in making finished products, which are then sold to the ultimate consumers.

industrial unions   Organization of workers in many different crafts, all working within the same industry.

inflation Increase in the overall price level.

informal organization An unofficial network of personal relationships and interactions among employees.

information Data presented in a context that gives them meaning.

information system System that collects, processes, stores, and disseminates information in support of business decision making, control, and analysis.

information technology The merging of computing and communications to support decision making.

information utility The satisfaction derived from the flow of information between customers and the business.

injunction Court order forbidding workers to perform certain acts, like striking or boycotting.

innovation A creative change in products or processes.

institutional advertising Advertising that develops and maintains a favorable image for a particular company.

institutional investors Public and private organizations that buy stock on behalf of large institutions.

insurable interest A direct stake, financial or otherwise, in the person, place, or thing being insured.

insurable risk A risk an insurance company will cover, because the probability of loss that it carries can be determined.

insurance A system that makes financial loss more affordable by transferring it from individuals to large groups.

intangible assets Nonphysical resources of value such as goodwill, patents, trademarks, copyrights, and intellectual property.

intellectual property Intangible personal property such as ideas, patents, brand names, trademarks, and copyrights.

intensive distribution A strategy used to achieve wide market coverage, giving products the greatest exposure.

interest rate The cost of borrowing money.

interest-rate risk Risk that the interest banks receive on loans will be less than the interest they must pay out on deposits.

interlocking directorate A situation in which the same people sit on the boards of directors of two competing firms.

intermittent process Production process with low setup costs and short start times that allow it to be shut down and restarted often and run efficiently for short periods of time.

internal customer A person or group within your business who uses the work you produce.

International Monetary Fund (IMF) Western governments created this fund both to administer short-term loans to help countries establish international trade and to oversee the orderly exchange of currencies.

Internet Worldwide computer network.

intrapreneurship Behavior associated with the start-up and growth of new products, systems, and processes within an existing business.

intrinsic motivation Motivation arising from forces within the individual.

inventories Stores of raw materials, partially made products, or finished products.

inventory control (1) Maintaining an adequate assortment of products to meet customer demand. (2) System for determining the amount of inventory a business will have on hand and for tracking and maintaining that inventory.

investment banker A firm that purchases (underwrites) a stock at a set price and sells it at a profit.

investors People or organizations that exchange money for a share in the future income of a business.

J

job analysis A general overview of all aspects of a particular job.

job description A statement of the tasks and responsibilities of a particular job.

job enrichment The addition of such motivators as responsibility, scope, and challenge.

job guarantees Assurance that workers will not be laid off.

job posting A notice advertising available positions within an organization.

job requisition A request for hiring submitted to the human resource department.

job rotation The practice of moving employees through a series of jobs for set periods of time to give them an understanding of a variety of business functions.

job sharing Arrangement in which two employees share a full-time job, each working part time.

job specification A statement of the qualifications, skills, and previous experience a person needs to perform a given job.

joint ventures Arrangements in which domestic and foreign companies join together in a partnership in which they share ownership, control, and risk.

junk bond The riskiest bond, at the lowest level of the rating scale, because there is a higher-than-average chance of the issuer defaulting.

just-in-time (JIT) system Method of inventory control that ensures parts are delivered or assembled only as they are needed.

K

key person insurance Protects a business and its stockholders or owners against the loss of a key executive.

kitchen capital Personal savings used to finance a start-up business.

Knights of Labor Late-nineteenth-century industrial union that focused on political issues and action.

knowledge workers People whose job is to create, collect, process, distribute, and use information.

L

labeling   Some means—packaging or a tag—for providing information about a product.

labor   The time and effort expended by individuals to produce goods and services.

labor federation   A labor organization made up of a variety of individual unaffiliated local and national unions.

labor force   Everyone who is either employed or unemployed.

labor unions   Organizations of workers with shared concerns, such as wages, working hours, benefits, and workplace conditions.

land   All nonhuman natural resources.

law of adverse selection   Individuals who are risk-prone are more likely to obtain or continue coverage than people who are less likely to have a claim.

law of large numbers   The larger the number of people or objects in a pool, the smaller the variation between actual and predictable losses.

layoff   Dismissal of an employee because of financial constraints on the firm.

leadership   The ability to inspire others to achieve exceptional performance.

leading   The process that involves both directing and motivating employees to accomplish tasks.

learning cycle   The constant improvement of products and processes to offer more value to customers.

learning organizations   Businesses that are good at developing and using knowledge in ways that help them change for the better.

lease   An agreement whereby an individual or firm agrees to a fee (rent) for a specified period of time in return for the use of property or equipment.

leave   Time away from the job, with or without pay.

leverage   Using borrowed funds (debt capital) to finance investments.

liabilities   Claims of creditors against the assets of a business.

liability insurance   Protects the policyholder against losses resulting from injury to other persons or damage to other people's property caused by the insured.

licensing   An arrangement that allows the partner in the host country (the licensee) to produce some good or service by bearing the costs of production and paying some fee or royalty to the business granting the license.

life-style business   A small business that supports its owners and tends to be stable in size.

limit order   An order placed with a stockbroker that specifies a particular sale or purchase price.

limited liability corporation (LLC)   A privately owned for-profit that combines lower C corporation tax rates with the simple structure of an S corporation.

limited liability   Limitation of owners' legal responsibility to the value of the stock they hold.

limited-line strategy   Employed by companies offering a limited set of products.

limited partnership   A business in which each partner's liability is limited to his or her share in the partnership.

limited-service wholesaler   A wholesaler who performs a limited number of services for the businesses it serves.

line employees   Employees who perform activities directly related to the goals of the business.

line extensions   New variations on growing or mature products.

line of credit   A bank's commitment to lend up to a specified amount of money during a specified period (usually one year), provided the bank has the funds available.

line organization   An organization in which responsibility, authority, and accountability flow in a direct line from the highest person to the lowest.

line-and-staff organization   An organization that combines the direct reporting relationships of line employees with the advisory relationships of staff employees.

liquidity   Ease of converting an asset into cash.

liquidity ratios   Ratios measuring a firm's ability to pay its short-term liabilities as they come due.

loan guarantee   Another party's promise of full repayment of a loan if the borrower defaults.

local union   Small union—often a subunit of a national union—that represents workers in a limited area.

lockout   Management pressure tactic of closing company doors to union members and not permitting them to work.

long-term liabilities   Claims of creditors payable one year or more from the date of the balance sheet.

M

M1   A measure of the money supply that includes currency and demand deposits.

M2   A measure of the money supply that includes everything in M1 plus savings deposits, time deposits, and other deposits on which check writing is limited or not allowed; also known as *near money*.

macroeconomics   Study of the workings of an economy as a whole.

mainframe computer   System processors that are networked to multiple terminals at which many users can work simultaneously.

maintenance factors   Characteristics of a work environment that, when deficient, cause employee dissatisfaction.

malpractice insurance   Covers specialists for negligence and/or errors and omissions that injure their clients; also called *professional liability* or *errors and omissions insurance*.

managed care   A risk management strategy in which employers and insurers arrange with health care providers to furnish health care services to members of the insured group.

management   Accomplishing organizational goals through people and other resources.

management by objectives (MBO)   Method for motivating employees through participation in goal setting, notification of factors that will be used in evaluating performance, and notification of when periodic reviews of progress toward the goals will occur.

management by walking around   A technique for promoting accessibility in which managers make themselves available where the work gets done and keep the lines of communication open to employees and customers.

management information system (MIS)   System that supports and documents business decision making by integrating the information needs of the entire organization.

management rights clause   Clause in union contracts itemizing the rights and responsibilities of management alone.

managerial accounting   Reports financial information to internal users.

manufacturer's agent   An independent sales representative who works for several manufacturers of related but noncompeting product lines.

manufacturing resource planning (MRP II)   Computerized system that integrates information from all aspects of the company and its production processes to provide a clear picture of materials flow into and through the production process.

maquiladora   A form of free trade zone that allows U.S. companies to ship their raw materials and parts from the United States to Mexico for processing by low-wage Mexican workers.

margin trading   Method of using cash and borrowed funds to invest in securities.

market   A group of people or businesses that has an interest in buying products and has the ability to pay for them.

market economy   An economic system in which individuals and businesses make their own decisions about what to produce and consume, and the market determines how much is sold at what price.

market order   An order placed with a stockbroker that has no special restrictions and that can be executed within seconds or minutes.

market segmentation   Dividing markets into smaller segments whose members share characteristics that make their desires similar.

market share   The proportion of total market sales captured by any single competitor.

marketable securities   Financial assets that are bought and sold through organized markets.

marketing   The process of creating, pricing, promoting, and distributing ideas, goods, and services to create exchanges that satisfy the customer and the business.

marketing concept   A philosophy that views the consumer as the focal point of the business and views profits as the result of satisfying customers through high-quality goods and services.

marketing intermediaries   Businesses that help move products from producers to consumers; sometimes called *middlemen*.

marketing mix   The planned use of the four Ps: product, price, place, and promotion.

marketing research   Formal research methods that produce useful and accurate information about consumers and the marketing environment.

markets   Groups of customers who want a good or service and have the ability to pay for it.

markup pricing   A form of cost-plus pricing in which the intermediary's selling price is determined by adding a percentage of the product's cost to the selling price to cover the intermediary's costs plus a profit.

mass production   Manufacturing large quantities of identical products by using standardized parts, an assembly-line layout, and the repetition of specialized tasks; also called *hard manufacturing*.

master limited partnership (MLP)   An arrangement in which one business controls another business from a distance through contractual obligation, not ownership.

material requirements planning (MRP)   System that uses computerized records based on bills of materials to keep track of what is bought and where it is delivered.

materials handling   All the activities involved in a company's warehouses and distribution centers.

materials management   The planning and organization of the flow of materials needed to support the production process.

matrix organization   A hybrid structure in which line and staff employees work together as a team on specific projects.

maturity date   The date on which the face value of a bond must be repaid by the issuer.

media   Distribution channels used by companies to carry a message.

mediation   The use of neutral or third-party individuals to help resolve a bargaining impasse.

medium of exchange   A function of money that simplifies the purchase of goods and services and eliminates the need for a barter system.

mentoring   An informal relationship in which a more experienced employee guides and sponsors a less experienced employee in a similar work role.

merchant wholesalers   Intermediaries who take ownership to the products they sell and account for 60 percent of wholesaling sales.

merger   The combining of two corporations into one company.

micro-loan   A direct loan from the SBA, limited to $25,000 or less, made to women, minority, and low-income entrepreneurs in economically distressed areas.

microcomputers   Computers in which all the processing power is incorporated on a single microprocessor chip.

microeconomics   Study of the economic activity of individual buyers and sellers.

microprocessor   Silicon chip containing a complete central processing unit.

middle management   The managers who report directly to top management and are responsible for the organization's short-term goals.

midrange computers   Computers that incorporate networking and other features of mainframes, but are less powerful. Also called *minicomputers*.

Minority Business Development Agency (MBDA)   U.S. Department of Commerce agency responsible for developing legislation and programs that assist the development of minority-owned businesses.

Minority Small Business and Capital Ownership Development Program—the 8(a) Program   A contracting set-aside program for minority-owned small businesses.

mission statement   A written description of the goals the business should accomplish through its planning and management.

missionary salespeople   Salespersons who make calls to promote good feelings between seller and buyer.

mixed corporation   Corporation that is established and regulated by a government but that sells stock to private investors.

mixed economy   An economic system in which there is a blend of government and private ownership of resources.

monetary policy   Adjustments to the money supply aimed at influencing economic performance.

money   Anything generally accepted as a means of paying for goods and services.

money market deposit account (MMDA)   Combined demand and time deposit account that allows a limited amount of check writing per month and requires a relatively large minimum deposit.

money market mutual funds   Investments that are offered by banks and independently established financial institutions and hold high-quality, liquid assets.

money supply   Total amount of money available to the public for buying goods and services.

monopolistic competition   An industry condition in which sellers differentiate their products on the basis of price and quality and so have some influence over price.

monopoly   An industry condition in which one firm sells a unique product and there is no competition.

moral muteness   The reluctance to discuss ethical questions with others.

motivation   Inspiring people to work.

motivators   Characteristics of work that make individuals try to excel.

multinational corporation (MNC)   A corporation based in one country (called the parent country) that produces goods and/or services in one or more host countries.

multiple franchising   An arrangement whereby a franchisee combines several franchises to reduce risk.

municipal bonds   Long-term obligations of state and local governments used to pay for general operating expenses or capital projects; also called *munis*.

mutual fund   A pool of cash collected by an investment company to purchase securities that fit the fund's investment objective.

mutual insurance company   A policyholder-owned company that attempts to minimize losses and thus rebate excess income to policyholders either as dividends or as lower future premiums.

N

national banks   Commercial banks chartered by the federal government and regulated by the U.S. Treasury Department.

national brand   A brand owned and marketed by its manufacturer; also called a manufacturer's brand.

national debt   The total of all budget deficits added together.

National Labor Relations Act (NLRA)   Passed in 1935; protects the rights of workers to unionize and bargain collectively. Also called the *Wagner Act*.

National Labor Relations Board (NLRB)   Administrative and enforcement agency established by the NLRA that supervises union elections and prohibits unfair management practices.

national union   Countrywide union organized by craft or industry.

need   A feeling that something necessary to one's well-being is lacking.

negative feedback   A response that discourages an unwanted behavior.

negotiable order of withdrawal (NOW) account   Interest-bearing checking account that requires a large minimum balance and provides unlimited check-writing privileges.

negotiations   Collective bargaining stage in which labor and management explore each other's positions, offer counterproposals, and bargain toward a mutually acceptable agreement.

networking   The informal process in which people who share an interest provide advice, information, and resources to one another.

networks   Computing and telecommunications systems that allow users to communicate and share hardware and software resources.

new product development   Determining what customers want and developing a product to satisfy that want.

newly industrializing countries (NICs)   Developing countries that are undergoing rapid economic growth.

niche marketing   Cutting up markets into smaller segments and targeting those that are least competitive.

nominal GDP   GDP measured in today's dollars, unadjusted for inflation.

nondepository institutions   Financial institutions that obtain their funds from sources other than deposits, such as the premiums policyholders pay to insurance companies; also known as *nonbanks*.

Norris-LaGuardia Anti-Injunction Act   Passed in 1932; along with the Clayton Antitrust Act, prevents court intervention in most labor disputes.

North American Free Trade Agreement (NAFTA)   A 1993 agreement that extended the U.S.–Canadian treaty to include Mexico, creating a market of 366 million people.

not-for-profit corporation   Private organization with a public interest rather than a profit-making goal.

O

odd lot   Fewer than 100 shares of a stock to be bought or sold.

office automation   Information systems that improve communications among knowledge workers.

oligopoly   An industry condition in which a few firms, each large enough to influence pricing, sell similar or differentiated products.

on-line services   Computer networks that allow users to tap into vast databases and chat live with other users worldwide.

on-the-job training   Training in which employees learn by doing a job or by receiving one-on-one instruction—usually from a manager or co-worker—in how to do a job.

open market operations   The buying and selling of Treasury securities controlled by the Federal Open Market Committee.

open shop   Workplace where employees cannot be forced to join a union or to pay union dues as a condition of getting or holding a job.

open-book management   A strategy that empowers employees to help control the company's finances.

operating budget   Master budget that balances the business's forecasted revenues with their related expenses, generally for a period of one year or less.

operating system   Software that controls the internal allocation and use of hardware resources such as memory, processing time, and disk space.

operational plans   Plans that give the details needed to carry out strategic plans in daily work.

opportunity cost   The value of sacrificed possibilities.

order processing   All the procedures that enable orders to be received and shipped.

organization chart   A diagram of an organization's formal structure and reporting relationships.

organizational culture   The shared customs, beliefs, values, and attitudes that give a company its identity and sense of community.

organizational design   The process of organizing employees and their work.

organizing   The process of arranging employees and material resources to carry out plans.

organizing by customer   Forming subunits focused on customers who share particular characteristics.

organizing by function   Grouping employees by the specialized, related tasks they perform.

organizing by geography   Forming subunits focused on regional offices and facilities.

organizing by process   Grouping employees by the logical flow of work.

organizing by product   Grouping work tasks around specific products or product lines.

outsourcing   Contracting with outside organizations for one or more business services.

over-the-counter market (OTC)   An electronic network that connects thousands of market makers.

owners' equity   Claims of owners against assets.

ownership utility   The satisfaction derived from possessing the legal right to use a product.

P

packaging   All the activities related to designing and producing a product's container or wrapper.

par value   On bonds, an arbitrary amount set by the company and used as the basis for paying state corporate taxes, (also called *face value*).

parent company   A company that holds most or all of a subsidiary's stock and also takes a direct role in managing the subsidiary.

Pareto diagram   Bar chart ordering causes from most to least common.

partnership   A business owned by two or more people under the terms of a written partnership agreement.

partnership agreement   Legal document setting out the nature of the business and each partner's rights, duties, and responsibilities.

patents   Exclusive rights to make, use, and sell new inventions for 17 years.

pay   Cash compensation in the form of wages, salary, or incentive bonuses.

pay for performance   Linking pay increases directly to an employee's level of performance.

penetration   Setting a low price in the expectation of gaining a high volume of sales.

pension funds   Institutions that pool contributions by employees, or by an employer on behalf of its employees, and invest the funds to provide retirement benefits.

perfect competition   An industry condition in which there are many sellers, the products are virtually identical, individual sellers have no influence on price, and firms can freely enter into and exit from the industry.

performance appraisal   A periodic written evaluation of an employee's performance compared with specific goals, which are often stated in a performance plan.

performance standards   Formal descriptions of expected levels of performance.

personal digital assistants (PDAs)   Combine the features of a computer, a fax machine, a modem, wireless communications, and handwriting recognition into a small battery-operated package about the same size as a paperback book.

personal product lines   Insurance products that are designed for and bought by individuals.

personal selling   Person-to-person communication between a seller and one or more potential buyers who provide immediate feedback through words, gestures, and facial expression.

PERT (program evaluation and review technique)   Scheduling technique that arrives at a statistical average time for each task in a production process.

physical distribution   The activities that serve to transport and store products during their journey through a distribution channel.

physiological needs   Needs stemming from the biological requirement for such essentials as food and water.

piggyback service   Transportation service in which loaded trucks are taken directly onto railroad flatcars.

piracy   The unauthorized use or reproduction of copyrighted or patented material.

place utility   The satisfaction buyers receive from being able to purchase a product in a convenient place.

place   The process of making the product available when and where the consumers want it. Also called *distribution.*

planned obsolescence   Intentionally forcing a product to become outdated in an attempt to increase replacement sales.

planning   The process of defining goals and the strategies and tactics for reaching them.

point-of-purchase (POP) promotion   Displays and demonstrations of the product at the point where it is purchased, usually retail stores.

positioning   Using the marketing mix to create a unique image of a product or brand in the consumer's mind.

positive feedback   A response that encourages a desired behavior.

precipitating event   A change in the environment that spurs an individual to take action.

preferred stock   Corporate stock that typically provides most of its return in the form of fixed dividends.

premium   The amount an insurance company charges for an insurance policy.

price   What the buyer must give up—usually money—to receive the product.

price fixing   Any effort to set high prices by collaborating with other sellers.

price leaders   Firms that set the prices that competitors tend to follow.

price-earnings (P/E) ratio   A firm's per-share stock price divided by its earning per share.

primary data   Original information collected by a market researcher for a specific purpose.

primary markets   Financial markets in which new securities are issued.

prime rate   The interest rate charged by banks to their most creditworthy customers.

private accountants   Professionals who are salaried employees of a business, government agency, or not-for-profit organization.

private brand   Brands created and owned by dealers—wholesalers or retailers.

private corporation   Corporation owned by private individuals or other private corporations.

private warehouses   Storage facilities owned and controlled exclusively by the manufacturers and intermediaries that use them.

privatization   Selling government-owned businesses to private owners.

probation period   An initial trial period, often of three to six months, in which newly hired employees may be terminated if their job performance is unsatisfactory.

process improvement teams   Teams of employees who redesign their own processes to save time and money; also called *quality circles.*

process need   A weakness or bottleneck that exists in a business system and that may present an opportunity for innovation.

product   A good, service, or idea that is designed, produced, and offered for sale.

product advertising   Advertising that creates awareness of and provides information about a type of product or a specific brand.

product differentiation   Creating the perception of product superiority in the minds of consumers.

product life cycle   A four-stage process that begins with new product development and ends with the removal of the product from the market.

product lines   Groups of products within the product mix that are similar in terms of use or characteristics.

product mix   The selection of products that a company offers to consumers.

production   The transformation of resources into goods and services that have value to customers.

production and operations management   The coordination of an organization's resources and activities to produce finished goods or services.

production contracting   An agreement with a local producer in a foreign country to make a product.

production control   Five-step subprocess of planning, routing, scheduling, dispatching, and follow-up.

production planning   Estimating materials and resources that will be needed and stating where and when they will be used.

productivity   The total value of output per hour of labor.

professional advertising   Advertising the benefits offered by lawyers, doctors, consultants, therapists, and other "professional" services.

profit   The difference between a firm's revenues and its costs.

profit sharing   An incentive system that gives some or all employees a percentage of the profits earned by a business.

profitability ratios   Ratios measuring the overall financial performance of a firm.

program trading   A procedure whereby computers are programmed to execute buy and sell orders under certain conditions.

project team A group, usually temporary, formed to deal with a specific product, project, problem, issue, or task; also known as a *task force*.

promissory note A written contract by which a business agrees to pay a supplier as specified on the invoice.

promotion (1) Advancement to a position of greater responsibility and higher compensation. (2) All the forms of communication organizations use to inform and persuade consumers.

promotional mix The five promotional activities a business uses to communicate with its markets.

property/casualty insurance Protects a company and its property against loss from perils such as fire, wind, hail, riot, and smoke.

prospectus A detailed analysis of a company's financial history and current status, as well as a description of its officers and products or services.

protectionism The attempt to protect domestic industries from foreign competition through the erection of legal barriers to trade.

psychographic segments Division of the market based on consumers' activities, values, attitudes, and interests.

public accountants Professionals who sell accounting services to organizations or individuals.

public goods Goods or services that benefit everyone in society.

public relations (PR) Communications aimed at promoting goodwill and creating a favorable image of a product or a company.

public warehouses Storage facilities owned by private companies that rent space to others as needed.

public-service partnerships Collaborations between a business and a not-for-profit organization that help each party achieve its goals.

publicity Any message about an organization that is communicated through the media because of its news value.

publicly traded companies Companies whose stock is traded on the open market.

pull process Production process that produces goods and services only when a company receives a customer's order.

pull strategy Use of advertising and promotional tools to encourage consumers to request a product from retailers.

pure risk The threat of loss without the possibility of gain.

push process Production process that produces goods in quantities estimated in management plans.

push strategy When a manufacturer encourages intermediaries to stock, promote, and aggressively sell its product.

put option Agreement that gives an investor the right to *sell* a particular stock at a specific exercise price up to a specific date.

Q

quota A specific limit on the number of items of a particular kind that may be imported.

R

rack jobbers Full-service wholesalers that assume complete responsibility for a particular section of a retail store.

ratification A vote by a majority of union members to accept a contract.

ratio analysis Evaluating an organization's current financial condition by calculating the relationship between two components of its financial statements.

real GDP Inflation-adjusted GDP.

recessions Prolonged downturns in economic activity.

reengineering The clean-slate redesign of a process that cuts costs by simplifying business processes.

reinsurance A policy bought by an insurance company that shifts some of its risk to another insurer in return for a percentage of the premium.

relationship marketing A personalized approach to customer retention.

repositioning strategy Attempting to change the perception of a brand or product through advertising or promotional campaigns.

representation election Election to determine whether a union will become the official representative of workers in negotiations with management.

reserve requirements The percentage of deposits that depository institutions are required to maintain as a measure of security.

resources The inputs used to produce goods and services.

responsibility An employee's obligation to perform an assigned task.

resumé A brief summary of an applicant's relevant experience, ideally one or two pages in length.

retailers Businesses that sell products directly to consumers.

retained earnings Portion of owners' equity held for use by the business.

retirement An employee's voluntary departure from a job on reaching a certain age.

revenue bonds Long-term obligations issued by state or local agencies that have no taxing authority and backed by the revenue-generating project they are intended to finance.

revenues Sale of goods and services, as well as income from franchise fees, interest, commissions, royalties, and rents.

reverse channels Channels in which intermediaries such as soft drink distributors and redemption centers move products back through the channel.

revolving line of credit A guaranteed line of credit, usually involving a fee that covers the cost to the bank of tying up the unused funds.

right-to-work laws State laws granting employees within the state's boundaries the right to get and hold a job without belonging to a union.

risk management The process of analyzing risks and choosing ways to minimize loss from those risks.

risk-return analysis   The process of weighing the costs and benefits of a new product, project, or other investment.

robotics   The use of computer-controlled machines to perform repetitive production tasks.

root cause   Something that explains some or all of the variation in a particular outcome of a process.

round lot   One hundred shares of a stock to be bought or sold.

routing   Deciding what value-adding activities should take place, where, and when.

S

S corporation   Special type of corporation that enables owners to pay taxes like partners but to have limited liability like shareholders.

safety needs   The need for such things as shelter, protection, and job security.

salary   Pay provided to professional employees in weekly, monthly, or yearly amounts.

sales promotion   The array of short-term promotional techniques that marketers use to stimulate an immediate purchase.

savings and loan association (S&L)   Federally regulated bank that accepts deposits in interest-bearing accounts and provides mortgage loans.

savings bank   Bank that accepts deposits in interest-bearing accounts and provides mortgage loans; also known as a *mutual savings bank*.

scheduling   Preparing a detailed timetable for labor, materials, and production activities.

scientific management   A management approach that involves developing and enforcing prescribed methods of working to increase efficiency.

scrambled merchandising   A strategy of carrying a nontraditional mix of product lines.

secondary data   Data used in marketing research that have already been collected for a purpose other than the one at hand.

secondary markets   Financial markets that facilitate the trading of securities already owned by investors.

secured bonds   Corporate bonds backed by specific assets that serve as collateral.

secured loan   A loan given by a bank or other financial institution and backed by collateral that the lender can sell if the borrower cannot meet the loan payments.

selective distribution   A strategy that gives a limited set of retailers the right to sell a product in a given geographic area.

self-actualization needs   Needs that stem from our desire for a sense of purpose.

self-directed work teams   Groups of employees responsible for managing their own activities.

self-esteem needs   The need for such things as feeling important and feeling that one's contributions are valuable.

self-insurance   Setting money aside in a special company-run fund to guard against future losses.

selling short   selling shares borrowed from a broker in order to buy them later at a lower price, thereby earning a profit.

separation   The severing of an employee's relationship with an employer through layoff, termination, or retirement.

Service Corps of Retired Executives (SCORE)   Volunteer organization staffed by active and retired business executives who provide counseling, training, and workshops.

setup costs   The time and money invested in setting up a production process to make a specific product.

sex discrimination   The unequal treatment of individuals because of their gender.

sexual harassment   Repeated, inappropriate sexual advances that create a hostile environment or harmful stress.

share-draft account   Interest-bearing account offered by credit unions that uses drafts—the credit union equivalent of checks.

shop steward   A company employee and union member who represents co-workers within large companies.

shopping products   Goods and services that consumers purchase after carefully comparing price, quality, and service.

situational leadership   An approach that varies the level of direction and support to suit the follower's developmental level.

skimming   A pricing strategy that initially sets a high price for a product and then lowers it.

skunk works   Independent intrapreneurial unit that develops new products within an existing business.

small business   A business that is independently owned and operated, is not dominant in its field of operation, and meets SBA standards for number of employees and income.

Small Business Administration (SBA)   Agency established under the Small Business Act of 1953 to foster the development of small businesses.

Small Business Development Centers (SBDCs)   One-stop centers where entrepreneurs can receive written information, counseling, and business training classes and workshops at a reasonable cost.

Small Business Institutes (SBIs)   School-based programs that provide specialized help to small businesses in the areas of accounting, marketing, and business plan preparation.

small-group incentives (SGIs)   Incentives that link pay to accomplishment of an independent work group's objectives.

SMART goals   Goals that are specific, motivational, attainable, relevant, and trackable.

social audit   Critical analysis of a business's impact on society.

social environment   All the people who affect the performance of a business or are affected by it.

social needs   The need for such things as belonging to a group and being well-regarded by co-workers.

social responsibility   The balance a business strikes among its commitments to its own goals, to its stakeholders, and to society at large.

socialism   A political system that encourages government planning and ownership of vital industries along with private ownership of other businesses.

software   Sets of instructions that control a computer system's input, processing, storage, and output operations. Also called *computer programs*.

sole proprietorship   A business with only one owner, who bears full responsibility for its legal obligations and its compliance with the law.

span of control   The number of people one manager supervises directly; also known as *span of management*.

specialty products   Goods or services for which there are no acceptable substitutes in the consumer's mind.

specialty stores   Full-service stores offering variety in a single merchandise category.

spreadsheets   Tables of numbers, text, or graphics, and the software that manipulates them.

staff employees   Employees who advise and support line employees but have no authority to assign tasks to them or to direct them.

staffing   The hiring, development, and assignment of people to activities and positions.

stakeholders   All the people affected by an action of a business.

start-up financing   Funds to develop a product and conduct beginning marketing efforts.

state bank   Commercial banks chartered by the states in which they operate.

statement of cash flows   Summary of the organization's sources and uses of cash for operations, investments, and financing during an accounting cycle.

statutory law   Laws created by a legislative body.

stock insurance company   A shareholder-owned company that attempts to maximize profits for its owners.

stock split   An increase in the number of stock shares available, which reduces the price of each share but does not change the total value of the stock.

store of value   A function of money that enables it to retain its value until it is needed to purchase goods or services.

strategic alliances   Agreements between organizations that may or may not involve ownership.

strategic plans   Plans that describe broad objectives and general methods for achieving them.

strike   A refusal by employees to perform their job duties until their demands have been met.

strikebreakers   Replacement workers legally hired by employers faced with a strike. Also known as *scabs*.

structural unemployment   Joblessness that results from the permanent displacement of workers due to changes in technology or long-term shifts in demand for certain products.

subsidiary company   A company whose stock is wholly or partly owned by another corporation.

succession planning   A formal evaluation to determine which individuals within an organization are capable of future moves into key positions.

Super NOW account   Checking account that requires a larger minimum balance and pays higher interest than a NOW account.

supermarkets   Large self-service stores that carry a full line of food products and some non-food products.

supervisory management   The managers who give daily direction and assistance to nonmanagement employees; also known as *first-line management*.

supply   The willingness to sell a good or service.

supply curve   The entire range of quantities sellers will supply at different prices.

surety bond   Protects one party against another party's failure to fulfill a contract or to otherwise perform as agreed.

sweat equity   Uncompensated labor that increases the value of a business.

synthetic process   Production process that combines materials into a single product.

T

tactics   Detailed descriptions of the actions employees will need to take to carry out strategic plans.

Taft-Hartley Act   Passed in 1947, it amends the NLRA and limits the power of unions by outlawing specified practices. Also called the *Labor-Management Relations Act*.

tall organizations   Steep, pyramid-shaped organizations with many layers of management and narrow spans of control; also known as *vertical organizations*.

target marketing   Marketing that is directed toward the market segments with the greatest potential for profit.

tariff   A tax on imported goods.

task clarity   The strength, speed, and accuracy of feedback on one's work.

technical skills   The ability to understand and use the specialized aspects of a job or function.

technological environment   The body of scientific and practical knowledge available for product and process development.

telecommuting   A form of work-at-home program in which employees communicate with the office by computer or fax machine.

telemarketing   A variation of direct marketing in which actual selling and sales support are conducted by phone.

term life insurance   Pays a benefit in the event of the insured's death, but only during the term of the policy.

termination   A voluntary or involuntary permanent departure from a job.

Theory X   Managerial assumption that people don't like to work, work only because they must, and need constant supervision and persuasion.

Theory Y   Managerial assumption that people like to work and will excel if given the right opportunity.

Theory Z   Managerial emphasis on employee involvement in all aspects of the job, including decision making.

theory of comparative advantage   A country's productivity increases when its businesses specialize in the products they can make most efficiently.

thrift institutions   Savings banks and savings and loan associations.

time deposit accounts   Savings deposits that require a specified minimum amount to be deposited for a specified period before any portion of the funds can be withdrawn.

time utility   The satisfaction buyers receive from being able to purchase a product when they want it.

top management   The employees who have the most power and responsibility in the organization.

tort law   The body of laws governing civil wrongs arising from causes other than a breach of contract.

total quality management (TQM)   The continuous improvement of a business and its processes by its employees and for its customers.

trade credit   Credit extended by suppliers for the purchase of goods and services.

trade deficit   When a country imports more than it exports; a negative balance of trade.

trade promotions   Sales promotions in which manufacturers offer intermediaries trade discounts, merchandise, contests and prizes, and monetary incentives in return for sales of particular products.

trade secrets   Information that a business wants to keep secret but that is not protected by intellectual property laws.

trade surplus   When a country exports more than it imports.

trademark   A brand that is legally protected for exclusive use by its owner for as long as the owner uses the brand.

trademarks   Words, symbols, and designs that identify a product or business.

trading blocs   Countries that band together as one market of regional trading partners and that apply the same rules and regulations to trade among themselves as to trade with nations outside the bloc.

transaction   An exchange of values by two or more parties.

transactional leaders   Leaders who define what employees must do to achieve work goals and then help them do it.

transfer   A lateral, or sideways, move from one job to another with a similar level of authority and compensation.

transfer payments   Cash payments made by the government directly to individuals.

transformational leaders   Leaders who inspire employees to change in pursuit of a compelling vision of the future.

Treasury bills (T-bills)   Short-term obligations (less than a year) issued by the federal government used to pay for immediate expenses.

Treasury bonds   Debt obligation of the federal government issued for 10 or more years and used to pay for government spending and to finance the national deficit.

Treasury notes   Debt obligation of the federal government issued for 2 to 10 years and used to pay for government spending and to finance the national deficit.

two-tiered wages   Provision of one wage schedule for current employees and a lower schedule for new hires.

tying contracts   A business practice that forces buyers to purchase unwanted products in order to purchase the products they do desire.

U

undercapitalization   Lack of sufficient funds to meet the day-to-day expenses of a business.

unemployment insurance   Program that pays workers who have lost their jobs a basic level of compensation for a limited time while they look for new work.

unemployment rate   Percentage of the labor force that is unemployed.

uninsurable risk   A risk no insurance company will cover, because the probability of loss that it carries cannot be determined.

union shop   Workplace that requires union membership after some minimum probationary period.

unit of account   A function of money that provides a common denominator for measuring the value of goods and services.

unlimited liability   Personal responsibility for the debts and actions of a business.

unsecured loan   A loan given by a bank or other financial institution and not backed by specific assets.

unsought products   Goods and services, such as new products, that consumers do not know they want or need.

usury laws   Laws regulating the maximum rate of interest on loans.

V

value pricing   A strategy that uses price and quality to influence customers' perceptions of value.

values   Deep-seated beliefs that are important to the survival and future direction of a business.

variable cost   Costs that fluctuate with the number of products produced.

venture capital   Financing offered to high-risk ventures, usually in exchange for a substantial equity or ownership stake.

vertical marketing system (VMS)   Planned partnerships between businesses and their suppliers to build mutually beneficial, cooperative relationships with their customers.

virtual company   Company that contracts with other businesses to perform such core functions as manufacturing and marketing.

W

wage concessions   Union agreement to accept lower wages for some job categories.

wages   Pay provided to hourly employees.

want   A need that has been given a form and a definition by your experience, surroundings, and personality.

warranty   A legal guarantee that a manufacturer's product will serve the purpose for which it is intended.

wheel of retailing   A cycle in which new forms of retailers replace established retailers that have become high-cost competitors.

wholesalers   Businesses that sell products to retailers, to manufacturers, to the government, and to large institutions that purchase in quantity.

wireless communications systems   Systems that use radio frequencies to transmit and receive communications.

work rules   Specific regulations that govern workers on the job.

work slowdowns   Union pressure tactic of performing the minimum amount of work required by job descriptions or company procedures; also called *working to rule*.

work teams   Project-oriented groups of employees.

work-at-home programs   Benefit that allows employees to work all or some of their working hours at home.

Worker Adjustment and Retraining Notification Act   Requires employers to give employees 60-day notice of their intent to close a facility or lay off a large number of workers.

workers' compensation   Insurance that pays the wages and medical bills of employees who are injured on the job.

workplace diversity   Ethnic and cultural differences among workers.

World Bank   An entity created by Western governments to administer long-term loans to countries for economic development.

World Wide Web   An organizing system within the Internet that makes it easier to use.

Z

zero-coupon bond   A bond that pays no periodic interest; purchasers receive the face value at maturity and the difference between that and the discounted purchase price represents the accumulated interest.

zero-sum game   A situation in which there can be only one winner because what one wins another loses.

Notes

CHAPTER 1

1 David Walters, "Goya Grows, Seeks New Markets,"*Christian Science Monitor*, May 27, 1993, p. 8.

2 Walters, "Goya Grows."

3 Adele Hast, *International Directory of Company Histories* (Detroit: St. James Press, 1991), p. 259.

4 Seth Godin, ed., *The 1994 Information Please Business Almanac & Desk Reference* (Boston: Houghton Mifflin, 1993), p. 485.

5 Blayne Cutler, "North American Demographics," *American Demographics*, March 1992, p. 42.

6 Kathleen Murray, "The Unfortunate Side Effects of 'Diversity Training,'" *New York Times*, Aug. 1, 1993. p. F5.

7 K. Eichenwald, "He Told. He Suffered. Now He's a Hero," *New York Times*, May 29, 1994, Section 3.

8 Telephone interviews with representatives of Rollerblade, Inc. and the National Sports Marketing Assoc., March 1995.

9 Walter Nicholson, *Microeconomic Theory*, 6th ed. (Orlando, Fla: Dryden Press, 1995).

10 Lester Thurow, *Head to Head: The Coming Economic Battle Among Japan, Europe, and America* (New York: William Morrow, 1991), p. 17; *Economic Report of the President*, 1994, GDP tables.

11 "A Global Game of Monopoly?" *The Economist*, March 27, 1993, p. 17.

12 William G. Ouchi, *The M-Form Society: How American Teamwork Can Recapture the Competitive Edge* (New York: Addison-Wesley, 1984).

13 "America's Little Fellows Surge Ahead," *The Economist*, July 3, 1993, p. 59.

14 H. Ansoff and P. Sullivan, "Empirical Proof of a Paradigmic Theory of Strategic Success Behaviors of Environment-Serving Organizations," *International Review of Strategic Management*, Vol. 4 (1995).

15 From a survey of 429 British managers conducted by Digital Equipment Corp. and cited in "Corporate Values, British Style," *Training*, May 1993, p. 91.

16 Estimates by Cognetics, Inc., Cambridge, Mass. Cited in John A. Byrne, "Enterprise," *Business Week/Enterprise 1992*, p. 12; Juliet Schor, "Trendicators," *Working Woman*, Nov. 1994, p. 16.

17 Darrell Nordeen, telephone interview with authors, Jan. 1995.

18 Byrne, "Enterprise."

19 Transcription of a speech, *Conference Board Report Number 1021* (1993), p. 14.

20 Thomas J. Peters and Robert H. Waterman, Jr., *In Search of Excellence: Lessons from America's Best-Run Companies* (New York: Warner Books), 1982, p. 201.

21 Philip D. Olson, "Choices for Innovation-Minded Corporations," *Journal of Business Strategy*, Jan./Feb. 1990, p. 43.

22 Paul A. Allaire, speech delivered at the Conference Board, New York City, Oct. 1, 1991. Transcript provided by Xerox Corp.

23 Xerox Corp., *1992 Annual Report*, p. 2.

24 Dirk Dusharme, "Statistical Process Control Enables Operators to Control the Quality of Their Processes," *Quality Digest*, July 1993, p. 24.

25 Norman S. Nopper, "Reinventing the Factory with Lifelong Learning." *Training*, May 1993, p. 55.

26 Johnna Howell and Rose Cohan, "Career-Long Learning: A Shared Commitment," *Technical & Skills Training*, Nov./Dec. 1991, p. 7.

27 Numerous definitions of the learning organization exist in the recent literature. Our definition is based on the one we think is best: "an organization skilled at creating, acquiring, and transferring knowledge, and at modifying its behavior to reflect new knowledge and insights." In David A. Garvin, "Building a Learning Organization," *Harvard Business Review*, July-August 1993, p. 80.

28 Garvin, "Building a Learning Organization," p. 81.

29 From remarks made at a Goal/QPC conference, Boston, Mass., Nov. 12, 1991. Cited in Alexander Hiam, *Closing the Quality Gap: Lessons from America's Leading Companies* (Englewood Cliffs, N.J.: Prentice Hall, 1992), p. 105.

30 Judith H. Dobrzynski, "Rethinking IBM," *Business Week*, Oct. 4, 1993, p. 89.

31 *Total Quality Performance*, Report No. 909 (New York: Conference Board), pp. 80–81.

32 Ken Blanchard and Sheldon Bowles, *Raving Fans: A Revolutionary Approach to Customer Service* (New York: William Morrow, 1993).

33 Thomas H. Davenport, Robert G. Eccles, and Laurence Prusak, "Information Politics," *Sloan Management Review*, Fall 1992, p. 53.

34 From "Quest for Excellence," a speech given at Georgia Institute of Technology, Atlanta, April 10, 1990. Provided courtesy of Terry May, public affairs director, Milliken & Co.

35 "Malcolm Baldrige National Quality Award 1989 Winner: Milliken & Company," U.S. Department of Commerce information sheet, 1993.

36 Thomas A. Stewart, "Reengineering: The Hot New Managing Tool," *Fortune*, August 23, 1993, p. 41.

37 Bob Filipczak, "Unions in the '90s: Cooperation of Capitulation?" *Training*, May 1993, p. 25.

38 Arlene A. Johnson and Fabian Linden, *Availability of a Quality Work Force*, Report No. 1010 (New York: Conference Board, 1992), p. 17; "The New World of Work," *Business Week*, Oct. 17, 1994, p. 80.

39 Joseph F. Duffy, "How Defense Cuts Affect Quality," *Quality Digest*, April 1992, p. 36.

40 David Pauly, "P & G Will Cut 13,000 Positions," *Boston Globe*, July 16, 1993, p. 57.

41 "When to Take on the Giants," *Fortune*, May 30, 1994, p. 111.

42 "Leaders of Corporate Change," *Fortune*, Dec. 14, 1992, p. 106.

43 "CEOs to Workers: Help Not Wanted," *Fortune*, July 12, 1993, p. 42.

44 Karen Kaplan, "Roller Derby," *Los Angeles Times*, August 20, 1994; Alexander Hiam and Charles Schewe, *The Portable MBA in Marketing* (New York: John Wiley & Sons, 1992), pp. 268–69.

CHAPTER 2

1 Michael Riedel, "Designing Brothers," (New York) *Daily News*, April 9, 1995, p. 24.

2 Andrea Gerlin and Scott McCartney, "Regal Comeback: King Cotton Reigns Once Again in South as Production Surges," *Wall Street Journal*, May 2, 1995, pp. A1, 8.

3 "One Microsoft, Indivisible," *New York Times*, April 30, 1995, p. B3.

4 Based on *Economic Report of the President*, 1993, Table B-2.

5 John W. Verity, "Introduction to 'The Information Revolution,'" *Business Week* special edition, 1994, p. 12.

6 James Sterngold, "Facing the Next Recession Without Fear," *New York Times*, May 9, 1995, pp. D1, 5.

7 "Americans Are Saving More," (New York) *Daily News*, May 14, 1995, p. B3.

8 Meredith E. Bagby, *The First Annual Report of the United States of America* (New York: HarperCollins, 1995), p. 30.

9 Bradley T. Gale, "Customer Satisfaction—Relative to Competitors Is Where It's At!" Keynote presentation, Conference Board's Sixth Annual Quality Conference, New York, March 16, 1993.

10 Bagby, *First Annual Report*, p. 28.

11 "No Airplanes, No Revenues, No Jobs," *Fortune*, Sept. 6, 1993, p. 40.

12 Gerlin and McCartney, "Regal Comeback," p. A8.

CHAPTER 3

1 Kenichi Ohmae, *The Borderless World* (New York: Doubleday, 1990), p. 235.

2 John D. Daniels and Lee H. Radebaugh, *International Dimensions of Contemporary Business* (Boston: PWS-Kent, 1992), p. 1.

3 John D. Daniels and Lee H. Radebaugh, *International Dimensions of Contemporary Business* (Boston: PWS-Kent, 1993), pp. 4–8.

4 Alan Farnham, "Global—Or Just Globaloney?" *Fortune*, June 27, 1994, p. 98.

5 Valerie Reitman, "Global Money Trends Rattle Shop Windows in Heartland America," *Wall Street Journal*, Nov. 26, 1993, p. A4.

6 Douglas Harbrecht, "The Secret Weapon That Won't Start a Trade War," *Business Week*, March 7, 1994, p. 45.

7 "Happy Ever NAFTA?" *The Economist*, Dec. 10, 1994, pp. 23, 24.

8 "Northern Rumblings," *The Economist*, Jan. 14, 1995, pp. 26–27.

9 Bob Ortega, "Some Mexicans Charge North in NAFTA's Wake," *Wall Street Journal*, Feb. 22, 1994, p. B1.

10 Geri Smith, "Why Wait for NAFTA?" *Business Week*, Dec. 5, 1994, p. 53.

11 Philip R. Cateora, *International Marketing*, 8th ed. (Homewood, Ill.: Irwin, 1993), p. 183.

12 Marcus W. Brauchli, "Chinese Flagrantly Copy Trademarks of Foreigners," *Wall Street Journal*, June 20, 1994, p. B2.

13 Michael Litka, *International Dimensions of the Legal Environment of Business* (Boston: PWS-Kent, 1988), pp. 22–23.

14 Gary Bonvillian and William A. Nowlin, "Cultural Awareness: An Essential Element of Doing Business Abroad," *Business Horizons* (Nov.-Dec. 1994), pp. 44–50.

15 Edward T. Hall, "The Silent Language of Overseas Business," *Harvard Business Review*, Vol. 38, No. 3 (May-June 1960), pp. 87–96.

16 Vern Terpstra and Kenneth Davis, *The Cultural Environment of International Business*, 3rd ed. (Cincinnati, Ohio: South-Western Publishing Co. 1991).

17 Rahul Jacob, "The Big Rise," *Fortune*, May 30, 1994, p. 75.

18 Jacob, "The Big Rise," p. 78.

19 J. J. Boddewyn, Robin Soehl, and Jacques Picard, "Standardization in International Marketing: Is Ted Levitt In Fact Right?" *Business Horizons*, Vol. 29, No. 6 (Nov.-Dec. 1986), pp. 69–75; W. Chan Kim and R. A. Mauborgne, "Cross-Cultural Strategies," *Journal of Business Strategy*, Vol. 7, No. 1 (Spring 1987), pp. 28–35; "The Issue Globalists Don't Talk About," *International Management*, Vol. 42, No. 9 (Sept. 1987), pp. 37–42; James F. Bolt, "Global Competitors: Some Criteria for Success," *Business Horizons*, Vol. 30, No. 1 (Jan.-Feb. 1988), pp. 34–41; David M. Szymanski, Sundar G. Bharadwaj, and P. Rajan Varadarajan, "Standardization Versus Adaptation of International Marketing Strategy: An Empirical Investigation," *Journal of Marketing*, Vol. 57, No. 4 (Oct. 1993), pp. 1–17; Imad B. Baalbaki and Naresh K. Malhotra, "Marketing Management Bases for International Market Segmentation: An Alternate Look at the Standardization/Customization Debate," *International Marketing Review*, Vol. 10, No. 1 (1993), pp. 19–44.

20 Theodore Levitt, "The Globalization of Markets," *Harvard Business Review*, Vol. 61, No. 3 (May-June 1983), pp. 92–102.

21 Pete Engardio, "Murdoch in Asia: Think Globally, Broadcast Locally," *Business Week*, June 6, 1994, p. 29.

22 Calvin Sims, "Walt Disney Reinventing Itself," *New York Times*, April 28, 1994, pp. D1, D9; Kevin Fedarko, "Mirror, Mirror on the Wall . . .," *Time*, August 1, 1994, pp. 44–45.

23 Amy Feldman, "A Second Generation on the Hot Spot," *Forbes*, Aug. 1, 1994, pp. 88–89.

CHAPTER 4

1 K. Blanchard and N. V. Peale, *The Power of Ethical Management* (New York: William Morrow, 1988), p. 11–13.

2 Interview with Paul Fineman, *Business Ethics*, May/June 1994, p. 18.

3 *Wall Street Journal*, April 27, 1993.

4 Frank Edward Allen, "Western Farmers Love Sludge," *Wall Street Journal*, Nov. 24, 1992, p. B1.

5 "Burger King Spots on Staying in School," *New York Times*, May 29, 1990, p. D15.

6 Russell Mitchell with Michael Oneal and Bureau reports, "Managing by Values," *Business Week*, Aug. 1, 1994, p. 46.

7 Paul Duke and Lawrence Ingrassia, "Laker Airways Suit Is Settled for $48 Million," *Wall Street Journal*, July 15, 1985, p. 4.

8 Roger LeRoy Miller and Gaylord Jentz, *Fundamentals of Business Law* (Minneapolis, Minn.: West Publishing, 1993), p. 291.

9 "Baby Formula Counterfeited: Man Arrested," *New York Times*, Feb. 12, 1995, p. 29.

10 K. H. Blanchard, "Ethics in American Business," in *New Traditions in Business: Spirit and Leadership in the 21st Century*, edited by J. Renesch (San Francisco: Berrett-Koehler, 1992), p. 228.

11 Kari Huus, "Look Out, Chinese Love Solution," *Advertising Age International*, Sept. 28, 1992, p. I6.

12 A. M. Freedman, "Peddling Dreams: A Market Giant Uses Its Sales Prowess to Profit on Poverty," *Wall Street Journal*, Sept. 22, 1993, p. A1, 10.

13 Howard Kohn, "Service with a Sneer," *New York Times Magazine*, Nov. 6, 1994, pp. 43–47.

14 Miller and Jentz, *Fundamentals of Business Law*, p. 109.

15 Miller and Jentz, *Fundamentals of Business Law*, p. 155.

16 Blanchard, "Ethics in American Business."

17 Brian O'Reilly, "J&J Is on a Roll," *Fortune*, Dec. 26, 1994, p. 178–192, (photo, p. 190).

18 Martha Burk and Josh Feltman, "How to Get Paid and More—Really," *Executive Female*, Jan.–Feb. 1995, p. 47.

19 E.J. Wagner, *Sexual Harassment in the Workplace: How to Prevent, Investigate, and Resolve Problems in Your Organization* (New York: AMACOM, 1992), p. 5–6.

20 J. W. Russell, "A Borderline Case: Sweatshops Cross the Rio Grande," *Essentials of Business Ethics*, edited by P. Madsen and J. M. Shafritz (New York: Merden, 1990), pp. 400–407.

21 R. Barnet and J. Cavanagh, "Just Undo It: Nike's Exploited Workers," *New York Times*, Feb. 13, 1994, p. F11.

22 Miller and Jentz, *Fundamentals of Business Law*, p. 602.

23 Blanchard and Peale, *The Power of Ethical Management*, p. 14–15.

24 Christopher Palmeri, "Dumpster Diving," *Forbes*, Sept. 26, 1994, p. 94.

25 Mitchell Zuckoff, "Taking Profit, and Inflicting a Cost," *Boston Sunday Globe*, July 10, 1994, p. 18.

26 Blanchard and Peale, *The Power of Ethical Management*.

27 Blanchard and Peale, *The Power of Ethical Management*, pp. 20–24.

28 Robert D. Haas, "Ethics in the Trenches," *Across the Board*, May 1994, p. 12; Shannon Peters, "Levi Strauss Promotes Employee Health," *Personnel Journal*, May 1994, p. 23; G. Pascal Zachary, "Exporting Rights: Levi Tries to Make Sure Contract Plants in Asia Treat Workers Well; Inspector in Malaysia Checks Safety, Labor Practices Despite Local Wariness; Heeding Customer Concerns," *Wall Street Journal*, July 28, 1994, p. A1; Russell Mitchell, "Managing by Values: Is Levi Strauss' Approach Visionary—or Flaky?" *Business Week*, Aug. 1, 1994, p. 46.

29 L. Nash, "Johnson & Johnson's Credo," in *Corporate Ethics: A Prime Business Asset* (The Business Round-Table, 1988), p. 77–104.

30 O. F. Williams and P. E. Murphy, "The Ethics of Virtue: A Moral Theory for Marketing," *Journal of Macromarketing*, Spring 1990, pp. 19–29.

31 F. B. Bird, and J. A. Walters, "The Moral Muteness of Managers," *California Management Review*, Fall 1988, pp. 73–88.

32 M. G. Velasquez, "Corporate Ethics: Losing It, Having It, Getting It," in *Essentials of Business Ethics*, edited by P. Madsen and J. M. Shafritz (New York: Meridian, 1990), pp. 228–44.

33 Velasquez, "Corporate Ethics."

34 Bird and Walters, "The Moral Muteness of Managers."

35 Velasquez, "Corporate Ethics."

36 Velasquez, "Corporate Ethics."

37 John Schermerhorn, *Management Productivity* (New York: John Wiley & Sons, 1993), p. 85.

38 Velasquez, "Corporate Ethics."

39 Velasquez, "Corporate Ethics."

40 Zuckoff, "Taking Profit," pp. 1, 18.

41 "Managing by Values," *Business Week*, Aug. 1, 1994, p. 46.

42 R. Steckel and R. Simons, *Doing Best by Doing Good: How to Use Public-Purpose Partnerships to Boost Corporate Profits and Benefit Your Community* (New York: Dutton, 1992).

43 Steckel and Simons, *Doing Best by Doing Good*.

44 K. Eichenwald, "He Told. He Suffered. Now He's a Hero," *New York Times*, May 29, 1994, section 3.

CHAPTER **5**

1 Karen Avenaso, "Education Inc.," (New York) *Daily News*, Jan. 15, 1995.

2 Edmund Andrews, "Bell Atlantic's (Mild) Interest in Public Broadcasting Stake," *New York Times*, Jan. 24, 1995, p. D1.

3 Jay Gallagher, "Small Business Gets Limited Liability," *Press and Sun Bulletin*, August 2, 1994.

4 Gallagher, "Small Business Gets Limited Liability."

5 Ripley Hatch, "A Liability Shield for Entrepreneurs," *Nation's Business*, August 1994, p. 36.

6 "What Are Corporate Boards Worried About?" *Journal of Accountancy*, July 1993, p. 22.

7 The Section of Business Law, the Section of Litigation, and the Division for Professional Education, the American Bar Association, "The New Dynamics of Industrial Control V" (Dec. 5–6, 1991), The Plaza Hotel, New York.

8 J.K. Lasser Tax Institute, *How to Run a Small Business* (New York: McGraw-Hill, 1989), pp. 39–53.

9 "Where the Gazelles Roam," *Biz Magazine*, March 1994, p. 19.

10 Jim Manzi, "Computer Keiretsu: Japanese Idea, U.S. Style," *New York Times*, Feb. 6, 1994, p. F15.

11 Robert Cox, telephone interview with authors, Feb. 1994.

12 Dawnyielle Peeples, "Workers Use a Buyout to Buy In," *Black Enterprise*, Jan. 1994, p. 19.

13 Peeples, "Workers Use a Buyout."

14 *Amherst Bulletin*, July 9, 1990.

15 Clyde Farnsworth, "Experiment in Worker Ownership Shows a Profit," *New York Times*, August 14, 1993, p. 13, 33.

16 The Conference Board, "Privatization," in *Global Business White Paper* (June 1992), pp. 5–6.

17 Alexander Hiam, *The Portable Seminar on Change Management*, (Cincinatti: Thomson Executive Press, in press, 1995).

18 Hiam, *The Portable Seminar*.

19 Hiam, *The Portable Seminar*.

CHAPTER **6**

1 Rosabeth Moss Kanter, "Championing Change: An Interview with Bell Atlantic's CEO Raymond Smith," *Harvard Business Review*, Jan.–Feb. 1991, pp. 119–130.

2 San Diego Small Business Development Center, *Small Business Resource Guide* (1994).

3 "Nationwide Study Finds 77 Percent of Entrepreneurs Remain in Business After the First Three Years," American Express Travel Related Services Co. news release, Oct. 1989.

4 Jeffrey Hornsby, Douglas Naffziger, Donald Kuratko, and Ray Montagno, "An Interactive Model of the Corporate Entrepreneurship Process," *Entrepreneurship Theory and Practice*, Winter 1993.

5 Patricia Wright, "The Candle Man Can," *Massachusetts*, 6, Winter 1995, p. 24.

6 Andrew Serwer, "America's 100 Fastest Growers," *Fortune*, August 1993, pp. 40–56.

7 Alan Webber, "Japanese-Style Entrepreneurship: An Interview with Softbank's CEO, Masayoshi Son," *Harvard Business Review*, Jan.–Feb. 1992, pp. 93–103.

8 Webber, "Japanese-Style Entrepreneurship," pp. 93–103.

9 "This Is the Body Shop," Body Shop brochure, Spring 1994.

10 Peter F. Drucker, *Innovation and Entrepreneurship: Practice and Principles* (New York: Harper & Row, 1985), p. 35.

11 Alexander Hiam and Karen Olander, *The Prentice Hall Handbook of Entrepreneurship and Small Business Management* (Englewood Cliffs, N.J.: Prentice Hall, in press).

12 Webber, "Japanese-Style Entrepreneurship," p. 99.

13 Andrea Larson and Jennifer Starr, "A Network Model of Organization Formation," *Entrepreneurship Theory and Practice*, Winter 1993.

14 Bradford McKee, "Outside Directors Can Help Obtain Capital for Growth," *Nation's Business*, Feb. 1993, p. 8.

15 Charles Schwenk and Charles Shrader, "Effects of Formal Strategic Planning on Financial Performance in Small Firms: A Meta-Analysis," *Entrepreneurship Theory and Practice*, Spring 1993.

16 "Nationwide Study Finds 77 Percent of Entrepreneurs Remain in Business After the First Three Years."

17 San Diego Small Business Development Center, *Small Business Resource Guide*.

18 David E. Gumpert, "Creating a Successful Business Plan," Chapter 5 in *The Portable MBA in Entrepreneurship*, edited by William Bygrave (New York: John Wiley & Sons, 1994), pp. 113–139.

19 J. Tol Broome, "How to Write a Business Plan," *Nation's Business*, Feb. 1993, p. 29.

20 Bygrave, *The Portable MBA in Entrepreneurship*.

21 "Venture Firms' Roles in Financing Grow," *New York Times*.

22 This account of the rise of the Saint Louis Bread Co. and quotations from Ken Rosenthal are from Leslie Brokaw, "Minding the Store," *Inc.*, Nov. 1993. More recent data are from a telephone interview with Lisa Thuelkeld, Saint Louis Bread Co., June 20, 1995.

23 The skunk-works concept has been championed by Tom Peters since he reported its success in *In Search of Excellence*. See also Tom Peters, *The Tom Peters Seminar: Crazy Times Call for Crazy Organizations* (New York: Vintage Books, 1994), p. 187.

24 Hornsby et al., "An Interactive Model of the Corporate Entrepreneurship Process."

25 Based on Cheryl Jarvis, "Prescribing Good Manners," *Nation's Business*, May 1994, p. 18.

CHAPTER **7**

1 Quotes from Joan Szabo, "Offering Careers, Not Just Jobs," *Nation's Business*, June 1994, p. 56.

2 Margaret Simms, *Black Enterprise*, Sept. 1993.

3 *The Adams Job Almanac* (1994), p. 238.

4 William Bygrave, *The Portable MBA in Entrepreneurship* (New York: John Wiley and Sons, 1994).

5 David Hale, "Small Business Tax Plan's Victim," *Wall Street Journal*, July 1993, p. A8.

6 "Flying Hundred, These 100 Companies Grew 14 Times as Fast as the Forbes Sales 500," *Hispanic Business*, August 1993.

7 SBA (Small Business Association) On-line (June 1994).

8 Alexander Hiam, "Total Quality Marketing," working paper, University of Massachusetts School of Management, Amherst, Mass., 1995.

9 Thomas J. Peters and Robert H. Waterman, Jr., *In Search of Excellence: Lessons from America's Best-Run Companies* (New York: Warner Books), 1982, p. 201.

10 John Naisbitt, *Megatrends: Ten New Directions Transforming Our Lives* (New York: Warner Books, 1984).

11 Troy Segal, "Don't Mess with Stress," *Entrepreneur*, Oct. 1994, p. 146.

12 John Ward and Craig Aronoff, "Managing Family-Business Conflict," *Nation's Business*, Nov. 1994, p. 54.

13 *Economic Report of the President* (Washington, D.C.: Government Printing Office, 1994), p. 378; U.S. Department of Commerce statistics, 1995.

14 Alexander Hiam and Karen Olander, *The Prentice Hall Handbook of Entrepreneurship and Small Business Management* (Englewood Cliffs, N.J.: Prentice Hall, in press).

15 SBA On-line (June 1994).

16 Tom Ehrenfeld, "The Demise of Mom and Pop?" *Inc.*, Jan. 1995, p. 46.

17 SBA On-line (June 1994).

18 SBA On-line (June 1994).

19 Carol Steinberg, "Grow or Die, Success," June/August 1994.

20 *Statistical Abstract of the United States: 1993* (Washington, D.C.: Bureau of the Census, 1993).

21 SBA On-line (June 1994).

22 *Statistical Abstract of the United States: 1993*.

23 Jeanne Saddler, "Young Risk-Takers Push the Business Envelope," *Wall Street Journal*, May 1994.

24 Saddler, "Young Risk-Takers."

25 SBA On-line (June 1994).

26 Margaret Simms, "Minority Business Looks to Clinton," *Black Enterprise*, Sept. 1993.

27 Michael Selz, "Business Giants Hope to Score Big by Looking Small," *Wall Street Journal*, Sept. 1993.

28 Bygrave, *The Portable MBA in Entrepreneurship*.

29 Bygrave, *The Portable MBA in Entrepreneurship*.

30 Bygrave, *The Portable MBA in Entrepreneurship*.

31 Bygrave, *The Portable MBA in Entrepreneurship*.

32 Otto Johnson, *The 1994 Information Please Almanac* (New York: 1994).

33 John DeMott, "Recasting Enterprise Zones," *Nation's Business*, Feb. 1993, p. 16.

34 Deborah Miller, "First Class to Graduate from Innovative San Diego Housing Commission Program," *News Release*, June 1994.

35 Sharon Nelton, "Blue Chip Performances," *Nation's Business*, Sept. 1993, p. 44.

36 Kevin Thompson, "Forging a Perfect Partnership," *Black Enterprise*, Sept. 1993, p. 66.

37 Otis Port et al., "Quality: Small and Midsize Companies Seize the Challenge Not a Moment Too Soon," *Business Week*, Nov. 30, 1992, p. 66.

38 Port et al., "Quality."

39 *The World Almanac and Book of Facts 1994* (Funk and Wagnalls, 1993).

40 Laurel Touby, "The Big Squeeze on Small Businesses," *Business Week*, July 19, 1993, p. 66.

41 Debra Phillips, "Wish List," *Entrepreneur*, Jan. 1995, p. 92.

42 Lisa Moore, "The Flight to Franchising," *U.S. News & World Report*, June 10, 1991, pp. 68–71.

43 Janean Huber, "Changing Times," *Entrepreneur*, Jan. 1995, pp. 122–128.

44 Seth Godin, ed., *1995 Information Please Business Almanac* (Boston: Houghton Mifflin, 1994), p. 542.

45 Karen Sulteis, "O Pioneers!," *Entrepreneur*, Sept. 1994, pp. 139–40.

46 Godin, ed., *1995 Information Please Business Almanac*.

47 Ross Tyler, International Franchise Association, telephone interview, March 3, 1995.

48 "Sixteenth Annual Franchise 500," *Entrepreneur*, Jan. 1995, pp. 140–231.

49 Steven Spinelli, "Franchising," in *The Portable MBA in Entrepreneurship*, edited by William Bygrave, pp. 356–69.

50 Shante Morgan, "Good for the Hood," *San Diego Union-Tribune*, July 1994.

51 "Creating Gold," *Success*, Nov. 1993.

52 Jeffrey Tannenbaum, "For Every Niche, There's a Franchiser Wanting to Fill It," *Wall Street Journal*, April 26, 1993, p. B2.

53 Robert J. Cooke, "Famous Last Words: 24 Quick and Easy Ways to Kill Your Business," *Entrepreneur*, June 1994, pp. 84–90.

54 *Prentice Hall Small Business Survival Guide: A Blueprint for Success* (Englewood Cliffs, N.J.: Prentice Hall, 1993).

55 Jeanne Saddler, "Young Risk-Takers Push the Business Envelope," *Wall Street Journal*, May 12, 1994, pp. B1, 2.

56 Susan Greco, "Looking for Mr. Right," *Inc.*, May 1994, pp. 41–45.

CHAPTER **8**

1 Arnold Cooper and F. Javier Gimeno Cásón, "Entrepreneurs, Processes of Funding, and New-Firm Performance," in *The State of the Art of Entrepreneurship*, edited by Donald Sexton and John Kasarda (Boston: PWS Kent Publishing, 1992), p. 308.

2 Noel Tichy and Ram Charan, "Speed, Simplicity, Self-Confidence: An Interview with Jack Welch," *Harvard Business Review*, Sept.–Oct. 1989, pp. 112–120.

3 Lena Williams, "Profile; A Silk Blouse on the Assembly Line? (Yes, the Boss's)," *New York Times*, Feb. 5, 1995, Sec. 3, p. 7.

4 John P. Schermerhorn, Jr., *Management for Productivity*, 4th ed., (New York: John Wiley & Sons, 1993), p. 123.

5 Nadirah Sabir, "Keeping the Lines of Communication Open," *Black Enterprise*, May 1995, p. 54.

6 Henri Fayol, *Industrial and General Administration* (Paris: Dunod, 1916).

7 Sabir, "Keeping the Lines of Communication Open," p. 54.

8 Thomas J. Peters and Robert H. Waterman, Jr., *In Search of Excellence* (New York: Warner Books, 1982), p. 20; Thomas J. Peters, *Thriving on Chaos* (New York: Harper & Row, 1987), p. 3.

9 Brian Dumaine, "Creating a New Company Culture," *Fortune*, Jan. 15, 1990, p. 127.

10 Alexander Hiam, *Quality Profile: Hoechst Celanese Corporation* (New York: Conference Board's Total Quality Management Center, 1995), p. 3.

11 Quoted in Alexander Hiam, *Closing the Quality Gap* (Englewood Cliffs, N.J.: Prentice Hall, 1992), p. 59.

12 Hiam, *Closing the Quality Gap*.

13 Hiam, *Quality Profile*, p. 4.

14 Robert H. Waterman, Jr., *Adhocracy* (New York: W.W. Norton & Co., 1990); Ruth Tearle, *The Versatile Organization* (San Diego, Calif.: Pfeiffer & Co., 1994).

15 Daniel M. Duncan, "A Bad Structure Can Be Fatal," in *The Change Management Handbook*, edited by Lance Berger and Martin Sikora (New York: Irwin, 1994), p. 167.

16 Williams, "Profile; A Silk Blouse on the Assembly Line? (Yes, the Boss's)"; *The National Directory of Addresses and Telephone Numbers*, 1995 ed. (Detroit: Omnigraphics, Inc., 1995), p. 268.

17 *Top Executive Compensation*, 1994 Ed. (New York: Conference Board) p. 22; Dept. of Labor, Bureau of Labor Statistics, *Economic Report of the President*, Feb. 1994, Table B–45, p. 320.

18 Rachel Jacob, "The Struggle to Create an Organization for the 21st Century," *Fortune*, April 13, 1995, p. 94.

19 Ricardo Semler, *Maverick* (New York: Warner Books, 1993), p. 332.

20 Bernard M. Bass, "Leadership: Good, Better, Best," *Organizational Dynamics*, Vol. 13, No. 3 (Winter 1985), pp. 27–28, 31.

21 Kathleen Teltsch, "Sanitation Department Honored for Innovation," *New York Times*, Sept. 23, 1992, p. B4.

22 Richard L. Daft, *Understanding Management* (Fort Worth, Texas: Dryden Press, 1995), p. 177.

23 Ken Blanchard and Spencer Johnson, *The One Minute Manager* (New York: Morrow, 1982), p. 34.

24 Noel Tichy and Ram Charan, "The CEO as Coach," *Harvard Business Review*, March–April 1995, p. 16. This distinction was originally drawn by J. McGregor Burns, in *Leadership* (New York: HarperCollins, 1978).

25 Tichy and Charan, "The CEO as Coach," p. 70.

26 Robert Tannenbaum and Warren H. Schmidt, "How to Choose a Leadership Pattern," *Harvard Business Review*, March–April, 1958.

27 Richard W. Hallstein, *Memoirs of a Recovering Autocrat* (San Francisco: Barrett-Koehler Publishers, 1992), pp. x, 1.

28 Sherry Suib Cohen, "Beyond Macho: The Power of Womanly Management," *Working Woman*, Feb. 1989, p. 82.

29 Jody Rosener, "Ways Women Lead," *Harvard Business Review*, Nov.–Dec. 1990, p. 120.

30 Don Shula and Ken Blanchard, *Everyone's a Coach* (New York: Harper Business, 1995).

31 Kenneth Blanchard and Drea Zigarmi, *Leadership and the One Minute Manager* (New York: Morrow, 1985), pp. 28–58.

32 Vijay Sathe, "The Controller's Role in Management," *Organizational Dynamics*, Vol. II, No. 3 (Winter 1983), pp. 31–48.

33 Stephanie Gruner, "The Employee-Run Budget Work Sheet," *Inc.*, Feb. 1995, p. 81.

34 Williams, "Profile; A Silk Blouse on the Assembly Line? (Yes, the Boss's)," p. D2.

35 Robert L. Katz, "Skills of an Effective Administrator," *Harvard Business Review*, Sept.–Oct. 1974, pp. 90–102.

36 John Huey, "Where Managers Will Go," *Fortune*, Jan. 27, 1992, p. 51.

37 Peter Senge et al., *The Fifth Discipline Fieldbook: Strategies and Tools for Building a Learning Organization* (New York: Doubleday, 1994), p. 14.

38 Williams, "Profile; A Silk Blouse on the Assembly Line? (Yes, the Boss's)."

39 In Barret L. Bergen and William V. Haney, *Organizational Relations and Management Action* (New York: McGraw-Hill, 1966), p. 3.

40 Barbara Presley Noble, "Dissecting the '90s Workplace," *New York Times*, Sept. 19, 1993, Sec. 3, p. 21.

41 Blanchard and Johnson, *The One Minute Manager*, p. 19.

42 Sabir, "Keeping the Lines of Communication Open," p. 54.

43 Semler, *Maverick*, p. 40.

44 Angela Sheard, "Learning to Improve Performance," *Personnel Management*, Vol. 24, No. 11, 1992.

45 Robert H. Waterman, Jr., *What America Does Right* (New York: W.W. Norton, 1994), p. 70.

46 Marianne T. Ilawd, Girl Scouts spokesperson, telephone interview with authors, March 25, 1995.

47 Ray Stata, "Organizational Learning—The Key to Management Innovation," *Sloan Management Review*, Spring 1989, p. 64.

48 Walter Kiechel III, "The Organization that Learns," *Fortune*, March 12, 1990, p. 136.

49 Thomas A. Stewart "The Search for the Organization of the Future," *Fortune*, May 18, 1992, p. 96.

50 Carol Hymowitz "When Firms Cut Out Middle Managers, Those at Top and Bottom Often Suffer," *Wall Street Journal*, April 5, 1990, pp. B1–3.

51 This case is based on ideas generated in an article by Anna Sobkowski, "How to Manage with a Skeleton Staff," *Executive Female*, Nov.–Dec. 1992, p. 9. None of the details provided here refer to real companies or individuals described in that article.

52 Tichy and Charan, "Speed, Simplicity, Self-Confidence."

CHAPTER **9**

1 Tom Peters, *Liberation Management* (Fawcett Columbine, 1992), p. 380.

2 *Hoover's Handbook Database* (Austin, Texas: The Reference Press, Inc., 1994) on-line.

3 Jeanne Sather, "It's Tea Time Again for Starbucks," *Puget Sound Business Journal*, Dec. 16, 1994, p. 1.

4 Interview with Starbucks assistant manager Mark Johnson, Pacific Beach, California, May 6, 1995.

5 Robert Nelson, *Empowering Employees Through Delegation* (Chicago: Richard D. Irwin, 1994), p. 16.

6 Thomas A. Stewart, "New Ways to Exercise Power," *Fortune*, Nov. 6, 1989, p. 64.

7 James A.F. Stoner, R. Edward Freeman, and Daniel R. Gilbert, Jr., *Management* (Englewood Cliffs, N.J.: Prentice Hall, 1995), pp. 96–97.

8 "Ed Artzt, The Prince of Darkness," *Advertising Age,* Sept. 27, 1993, p. 18.

9 Peters, *Liberation Management*, pp. 87–92.

10 Peters, *Liberation Management*.

11 Peters, *Liberation Management*.

12 U.S. West, Inc., executive organizational chart, Jan. 30, 1994.

13 Sumantra Ghoshal and Christopher A. Bartlett, "Changing the Role of Top Management: Beyond Structure to Processes," *Harvard Business Review*, Jan.–Feb. 1995, p. 93.

14 Ghoshal and Bartlett, "Changing the Role of Top Management."

15 Peter Block, *Stewardship* (San Francisco: Berrett-Koehler, 1993).

16 Leslie Brokaw, "Thinking Flat," *Inc.*, Oct. 1993, p. 88.

17 Tom Peters, *The Tom Peters Seminar* (New York: Vintage Books, 1994), pp. 33–34.

18 Peters, *Liberation Management*.

19 Thomas A. Stewart, "Welcome to the Revolution," *Fortune*, Dec. 13, 1993, p. 72.

20 Peters, *Liberation Management*.

21 Thomas A. Stewart, "The Search for the Organization of Tomorrow," *Fortune*, May 18, 1992, p. 93.

22 John Huey, "The New Post-Heroic Leadership," *Fortune*, Feb. 21, 1994, p. 44–45.

23 Huey, "The New Post-Heroic Leadership."

24 Stewart, "The Search for the Organization of Tomorrow," p. 94.

25 Tracy Benson Kirker, "Edy's Grand Ice Cream," *Industry Week*, Oct. 18, 1993, p. 29.

26 Toni Mack, "Energizing a Bureaucracy," *Forbes*, Sept. 17, 1990, pp. 76, 80.

27 Ghoshal and Bartlett, "Changing the Role of Top Management," p. 92.

28 Daniel Simpson, "The Planning Process and the Role of the Planner," *Planning Review*, Jan.–Feb. 1995, p. 20.

29 Stoner, Freeman, and Gilbert, *Management*, p. 173.

30 George C. Homans, *The Human Group* (New York: Harcourt, Brace & World, 1950).

31 Tom Harbison, "Seize the Customer Day," *Computerworld*, Nov. 30, 1992, pp. 77–78.

32 Shawn Tully, "The Modular Corporation," *Fortune*, Feb. 8, 1993, p. 106.

33 Edward Gargan, "'Virtual' Companies Leave the Manufacturing to Others," *New York Times*, July 17, 1994, p. F5.

34 Jeffrey Hudson, quoted in Gargan "'Virtual' Companies Leave the Manufacturing to Others."

35 Stewart, "The Search for the Organization of Tomorrow," p. 98.

36 Dale D. Buss, "Hitching Your Wagon to a Retailing Star," *Nation's Business*, Nov. 1994, p. 33.

37 Stewart, "The Search for the Organization of Tomorrow."

38 All quotes from Charlene Marmer Solomon, "Behind the Wheel at Saturn," *Personnel Journal*, June 1991, pp. 72–74.

39 Michael Rothschild, "Coming Soon: Internal Markets," *Forbes*, June 7, 1993, p. 19.

40 Brian Dumaine, "The Bureaucracy Busters," *Fortune*, June 17, 1991, p. 38.

41 Brian Dumaine, "The Bureaucracy Busters," p. 42.

42 Michael Rothschild, "Coming Soon: Internal Markets," *Forbes*, June 7, 1993, p. 19; Brian Dumaine, "The Bureaucracy Busters," p. 42.

43 "Xerox Corporation," *Hoover's Handbook Database* (Austin, Texas: The Reference Press, Inc., 1995) on-line.

CHAPTER **10**

1 Lance Davidson, *The Ultimate Reference Book: The Wit's Thesaurus* (New York: Avon Books, 1994), p. 316.

2 Michel Perigord, *Achieving Total Quality Management: A Program for Action* (Cambridge: Productivity Press, 1990), p. 204.

3 Jerry Ackerman, "What Price Good Jobs?" *Boston Globe*, April 2, 1995, pp. 75–76.

4 From Patagonia press kit, 1995.

5 Laurel Shaper Walters, "A Factory That Workers Helped Design," *Christian Science Monitor*, March 15, 1995, p. 11.

6 Manufacturers Survey of 1,042 Factories, December 1994, cited in "The Calling Out of America," *The Economist*, December 17, 1994, p. 63.

7 "The Calling Out of America," p. 63.

8 Calculated from statistics in *Economic Report of the President, 1993* (Washington, D.C.: Government Printing Office, 1993), pp. 348 and 408.

9 Alex Pham, "Nypro Plastics Finds It Can Prosper in Massachusetts," *Boston Globe*, April 23, 1995, p. A82.

10 John Holusha, "Industry Is Learning to Love Agility," *New York Times*, April 25, 1994, p. D1.

11 Robert W. Hall, "The Challenges of the Three-Day Car," in James Cortada and John Woods, eds, *The Quality Yearbook* (New York: McGraw-Hill, Inc., 1994), pp. 65–66.

12 Hall, "The Challenge of the Three-Day Car," pp. 65–66.

13 Holusha, "Industry Is Learning to Love Agility," p. D5.

14 Jack Campanella, ed., *Principles of Quality Costs*, 2nd ed. (Milwaukee: ASQC Quality Press, 1990) p. 6.

15 Peter Baker, "Simple Problem Leads Professor to Discover Flaw in Pentium Chip," *Boston Globe*, December 18, 1994, p. A17.

16 Alex Hiam, *Closing the Quality Gap: Lessons from America's Leading Companies* (Englewood Cliffs, N.J.: Prentice Hall, 1992).

17 Kathryn Troy, *Change Management: An Overview of Current Initiatives* (New York: Conference Board, 1994), p. 18.

18 Theodore Kinni, "A Reengineering Primer," *Quality Digest*, January 1994, p. 26.

19 Hans-Dieter Wiedig, quoted in Richard Stevenson, "Europe, Inc. Has a Novel Idea: Cut Costs," *Wall Street Journal*, July 17, 1994, p. F1.

20 Glenn Mangurian and Allan Cohen, "Reengineering's Stress Points: Dealing with the Inevitable," *Insights Quarterly* (Winter 1993), pp. 4–17.

21 Based on Karen Bemowski, "Dictionary of TQM," *Quality Progress*. February 1992, and Alex Hiam, *Does Quality Work? A Review of Relevant Studies* (New York: Conference Board, 1993), p. 7.

22 Masao Nemoto, *Total Quality Control for Management: Strategies and Techniques from Toyota and Toyota Gosei* (Englewood Cliffs, N.J.: Prentice Hall, 1987), p. 9.

23 Lee Iacocca, *Talking Straight* (New York: Bantam Books, 1988), p. 255.

24 "Interview with James Champy," *Industry Week*, Feb. 7, 1994, p. 14.

25 Robert L. Reid, "Taking Training, Staying Skilled," *Technical & Skills Training* (Aug./Sept. 1994), pp. 14–15.

26 J. Stephen Sarazen, *Using Quality Improvement Tools to Build Customer Satisfaction* (Boston: American Management Association, 1992), p. 19.

27 Hiam, *Closing the Quality Gap*, p. 326.

28 Hiam, *Closing the Quality Gap*, Figure 14.4, p. 330.

29 M. Barrier, "Adversity Brings Opportunity," *Nation's Business*, April 1993, pp. 31–34.

30 Hubert Herring, "Aquafuture, Inc.," *New York Times*, Nov. 6, 1994, p. 10.

31 "Granite Rock Co.," *Business America*, Nov. 2, 1992, p. 15.

CHAPTER **11**

1 Annetta Miller, "Are We Really that Lazy?" *Newsweek*, Feb. 17, 1992, pp. 42–43.

2 "What Price Freedom?" *Entrepreneur*, 1991.

3 Abraham H. Maslow, *Motivation and Personality*, 2nd ed. (New York: Harper & Row, 1970), pp. 38–58.

4 Kevin G. Salwen, "Incentive Plans Keep Spreading Beyond Executive Suites. But Do They Work?" *Wall Street Journal*, Nov. 6, 1990, p. A1.

5 Joan E. Rigdon, "Managing," *Wall Street Journal*, Nov. 2, 1992, p. B1.

6 Frederick Herzberg, "One More Time: How Do You Motivate Employees?" *Harvard Business Review*, Sept.–Oct. 1987, p. 114.

7 James S. Hirsch, "Now Hotels Provide More Than Keys," *Wall Street Journal*, March 5, 1993, pp. B1, 6.

8 Paige Berson-Besthoff and Charles Peck, *Small Group Incentives: Goal-Based Pay*, Report No. 1006 (New York: Conference Board, 1992).

9 Thane S. Pittman, Jolee Emery, and Ann K. Boggiano, "Intrinsic and Extrinsic Motivational Orientations: Reward-Induced Changes in Preference for Complexity," *Journal of Personality and Social Psychology*, May 1982, pp. 789–797.

10 Katherine Shaver, "No, There Won't Be Any Contest to See Who's the Best Tip Grabber," *Wall Street Journal*, July 24, 1991, p. B1.

11 Benson P. Shapiro and Stephen X. Doyle, "What Counts Most in Motivating Your Sales Force," *Harvard Business Review*, May–June 1980, p. 133; "Make the Sales Task Clear," *Harvard Business Review*, Nov.–Dec. 1983, pp. 72–76.

12 Kenneth Blanchard and Spencer Johnson, M.D., *The One Minute Manager* (New York: Morrow, 1982), pp. 25–60.

13 Frederick Taylor, *Scientific Management* (New York: Harper & Row, 1947), pp. 39–73.

14 Jerry Ackerman, "For Foxboro Co., 'Teams' Work," *Boston Globe*, April 23, 1995, p. A81.

15 "United Parcel Service Gets Deliveries Done by Driving Its Workers," *Wall Street Journal*, April 22, 1986, pp. 1, 23.

16 Zandy Leibowitz, Charles Schultz, H. Daniel Lea, and Stephen E. Ferrer, "Shape Up and Ship Out," *Training & Development*, Vol. 48, No. 8 (Aug. 1994), pp. 38–42.

17 Elton Mayo, *The Human Problems of an Industrial Civilization* (New York: Macmillan, 1933).

18 Ralph Stayer, "How I Learned to Let My Workers Lead," *Harvard Business Review*, Nov.–Dec. 1990, p. 66.

19 "American Automakers Need Major Overhaul to Match the Japanese," *Wall Street Journal*, Jan. 10, 1992, pp. A1, 6.

20 Steve Paloncy, "Team Approach Cuts Costs," *HR Magazine*, Nov. 1990, pp. 61–62.

21 Willie E. Hopkins, Karen Sterkel-Powell, and Shirley A. Hopkins, "Training Priorities for a Diverse Work Force," *Public Personnel Management*, Vol. 2, No. 3 (Fall 1994), p. 429–435.

22 Meredith E. Bagby, *The First Annual Report of the United States of America* (New York: HarperBusiness, 1995), p. 8; Peter A. Morrison, "Congress and the Year 2000: Peering into the Demographic Future," *Business Horizons*, Vol. 36, No. 6 (Nov.–Dec. 1993), pp. 55–63.

23 Morrison, "Congress and the Year 2000."

24 Suneel Ratan, "Generational Tension in the Office: Why Busters Hate Boomers," *Fortune*, Oct. 4, 1993, pp. 56–70; Kevin Doyle, "Young and Restless," *Incentive*, June 1993, pp. 76–78, 83; Claire Raines, *Twenty-Something*: *Managing and Motivating Today's New Workforce* (New York: MasterMedia, 1992).

25 Advertisement placed by EDS, "Do Businesses Owned by Minorities and Women Really Have Equal Opportunity?", *Black Enterprise*, Sept. 1993, pp. 38–39.

26 Robin McClain, "New Surveys Show Benefits of Family Programs," *Business & Incentive Strategies*, Aug. 1993, p. 6.

27 Allan Halcrow, "For Your Information," *Personnel Journal*, Feb. 1986, pp. 12–13.

28 "Good Samaritan Hospital: When Workers Care," *Incentive*, March 1990, pp. 40–41.

29 Handson, "Tailor-Made Rewards," *Inc.*, Feb. 1991, p. 76.

30 Ellen Kolton, "Paddling for Profits," *Inc.*, March 1985, pp. 137–38.

31 Halcrow, "For Your Information."

32 Charlene Marmer Solomon, "How Does Disney Do It?" *Personnel Journal*, Dec. 1989, pp. 50–57.

33 Dr. Jane Templeton, "Carving Out True Recognition," *Sales and Marketing Management*, June 1986, pp. 108–09.

34 McClain, "New Surveys Show Benefits of Family Programs."

35 Robert Levering and Milton Moskowitz, *The 100 Best Companies to Work for in America* (New York: Currency Doubleday, 1993) p. 211.

36 Levering and Moskowitz, *The 100 Best Companies to Work for in America*; Bob Nelson, *1001 Ways to Reward Employees* (New York: Workman Publishing, 1994), pp. 26–27.

37 Nelson, *1001 Ways to Reward Employees*, pp. 38–39.

CHAPTER **12**

1 Jaclyn Fierman, "The Contingency Work Force," *Fortune*, Jan. 24, 1994, p. 31.

2 Fierman, "The Contingency Work Force," p. 3.

3 Vicki Elliot and Anna Orgera, "Competing for and with Workforce 2000," *HR Focus*, June 1993, p. 3.

4 Data from the National Association of Manufacturers and the Hudson Institute; William B. Johnston and Arnold E. Packer, "Workforce 2000; Work and Workers for the 21st Century (Indianapolis, Ind.: Hudson Institute, 1987), pp. xiii–xxvii.

5 1992 AMA Survey on Basic Skills Testing and Training (New York: American Management Association), p. 3.

6 Lynn Franey, "Failure Stalks the Halls in L.A.," *San Diego Union-Tribune*, Dec. 12, 1993, pp. A33, 42.

7 Sharon Nelton, "Nurturing Diversity," *Nation's Business*, June 1995, p. 25.

8 Perri Capell, "'Young Turks' at Work," *National Business Employment Weekly*, Nov. 26–Dec. 2, 1993, p. 15.

9 "Automatic Data Processing, Inc.," *Hoover's Handbook Database* (Austin, Texas: The Reference Press, 1995), on-line.

10 Personal communication with authors, Blanchard Training and Development, Inc., 1995.

11 Albert R. Karr, "Labor Letter: Lease, Don't Hire," *Wall Street Journal*, March 16, 1993, p. A1.

12 Charles Stein, "The Stingy Boss Syndrome," *Boston Sunday Globe*, May 21, 1995, p. 106.

13 Laura M. Litvan, "Casting a Wider Employment Net," *Nation's Business*, Dec. 1994, p. 49.

14 William B. Johnston, "Global Work Force 2000: The New World Labor Market," *Harvard Business Review*, March–April 1991, p. 115.

15 *The 1994 Information Please Almanac*, (New York: McGraw-Hill, 1993).

16 Litvan, "Casting a Wider Employment Net."

17 Nelton, "Nurturing Diversity," p. 25.

18 James P. Womack, Daniel T. Jones, and Daniel Ross, *The Machine That Changed the World*: *The Story of Lean Production* (New York: HarperPerennial, 1990), pp. 198–99.

19 Litvan, "Casting a Wider Employment Net."

20 Litvan, "Casting a Wider Employment Net."

21 Kathy Rebello and Evan I. Schwartz, "How Microsoft Makes Offers People Can't Refuse," *Business Week*, Feb. 24, 1992, p. 65.

22 Litvan, "Casting a Wider Employment Net."

23 Hal Rosenbluth and Diane McFerrin Peters, "The Customer Comes Second," *Audio-Tech Business Book Summaries, Inc.*, July 1993, p. 5.

24 Paul Burnham Finney, "A Temp(t)ing Solution," *Newsweek*, Dec. 20, 1993, p. 4.

25 Finney, "A Temp(t)ing Solution," p. 1.

26 Linda Grant, "A School for Success; Motorola's Ambitious Job-Training Program Generates Smart Profits," *U.S. News & World Report*, May 22, 1995, p. 53.

27 Ronald Henkoff, "Companies That Train Best," *Fortune*, March 22, 1993, pp. 62, 64.

28 Michael L. Dertouzos, Richard K. Lester, and Robert M. Solow, *Made in America: Regaining the Productive Edge* (New York: Harper-Perennial, 1989), pp. 82, 88.

29 Grant, "A School for Success; Motorola's Ambitious Job-Training Program Generates Smart Profits."

30 William Wiggenhorn, "Motorola U: When Training Becomes an Education," *Harvard Business Review*, July–Aug. 1990, p. 71.

31 Cherrington, *Personnel Management*, 3rd ed., 1990, p. 239; George T. Milkovich and William F. Glueck, *Personnel and Human Resource Management*, 4th ed. (Plano, Texas: Business Publications, 1985), p. 348.

32 "Kelly Services, Inc.," *Hoover's Handbook Database* (Austin, Texas: The Reference Press, 1995), on-line.

33 Grant, "A School For Success: Motorola's Ambitious Job-Training Program Generates Smart Profits."

34 Robert Levering and Milton Moskowitz, *The 100 Best Companies to Work for in America*, rev. ed. (New York: Currency Doubleday, 1993), p. 164.

35 Catherine Romano, "Fear of Feedback," *Management Review*, Dec. 1993, p. 38.

36 Federal Express leadership survey, 1993, quoted by Federal Express executive in interview with author.

37 Joan E. Rigdon, "Sideways Moves Grow Increasingly Common," *Wall Street Journal*, Jan. 27, 1992, p. B1.

38 "Iacocca, Lee," *Microsoft Encarta*, 1993, on-line.

39 Dertouzos, Lester, and Solow, *Made in America: Regaining the Productive Edge.*

40 Womack, Jones, and Roos, *The Machine That Changed the World: The Story of Lean Production*; S.L. Mintz, "Redesigning Finance at Ford," *CFO*, March 1995, pp. 26–34.

41 Linda Grant, "GE: The Envelope, Please," *Fortune*, June 26, 1995, p. 89.

42 Alexander Hiam, *Closing the Quality Gap: Lessons from America's Leading Companies* (Englewood Cliffs, N.J.: Prentice Hall, 1992), p. 237.

43 Shawn Tully, "Your Paycheck Gets Exciting," *Fortune*, Nov. 1, 1993, p. 95.

44 Tully, "Your Paycheck Gets Exciting."

45 Charles Stein, "The Stingy Boss Syndrome," *Boston Sunday Globe*, May 21, 1995, pp. 105–106.

46 Joan E. Rigdon, "Three Decades After the Equal Pay Act, Women's Wages Remain Far from Parity," *Wall Street Journal*, June 9, 1993, pp. B1, 8.

47 Alex Taylor III, "Now Hear This, Jack Welch!" *Fortune*, April 6, 1992, p. 94.

48 W. Keith McLeod, "Survey Shows What Benefits Banks Offer," *ABA Banking Journal*, Oct. 1993, p. 47.

49 Jill Andresky Fraser, "'Tis Better to Give and Receive," *Inc.*, Feb. 1995, p. 84.

50 Christine Woolsey, "Not All Firms Want to Offer a Health Plan, Study Finds," *Business Insurance*, July 4, 1994, p. 58.

51 Julie Amparano Lopez, "Undivided Attention: How PepsiCo Gets Work Out of People," *Wall Street Journal*, April 1, 1993, pp. A1, 9.

52 Sue Shellenbarger, "GE Unit Sees Advantage in More Family Benefits," *Wall Street Journal*, Feb. 12, 1992, p. B1.

53 "Active Savers," *Boston Globe*, Business Section, June 25, 1995, p. 1.

54 Jaclyn Fierman, "Are Companies Less Family-Friendly?" *Fortune*, March 21, 1994, p. 65.

55 Fierman, "Are Companies Less Family-Friendly?"

56 Fierman, "Are Companies Less Family-Friendly?"

57 Sue Shellenbarger, "Some Thrive, but Many Wilt Working at Home," *Wall Street Journal*, Dec. 14, 1993, p. B1.

58 Sue Shellenbarger, "Work-Family Plans Cut Absenteeism, Stress," *Wall Street Journal*, Jan. 20, 1992, p. B1.

59 Sue Shellenbarger, "Allowing Fast Trackers to Stay in One Place," *Wall Street Journal*, Jan. 7, 1992, p. B1.

60 John A. Byrne, "The Pain of Downsizing," *Business Week*, May 9, 1994, p. 61.

61 Ellyn E. Spragins, "Eliminating Layoffs," *Inc.*, Sept. 1992, p. 31.

62 "Musical Chairs," *The Economist*, July 17, 1993, p. 67.

63 Norman R. Deets and Timothy D. Tyler, "How Xerox Improved Its Performance Appraisals," *Personnel Journal*, April 1986, pp. 50–52.

64 Womack, Jones, and Roos, *The Machine That Changed the World: The Story of Lean Production.*

CHAPTER **13**

1 "What's Ahead for Unions?" *Financial World*, June 23, 1992, p. 72.

2 Alex Pham, "Still Making It in Massachusetts, New Labor Tactic: Cooperation," *Boston Sunday Globe*, April 23, 1995, p. A83.

3 Ben Webb, "Striking Contrasts," *New Statesman and Society*, Sept. 2, 1994, p. S6.

4 Bob Filipczak, "Unions in the '90s: Cooperation or Capitulation?" *Training*, May 1993, pp. 25–34.

5 Barbara Ettorre, "Will Unions Survive?" *Management Review*, Aug. 1993, pp. 9–15.

6 Dana Milbank and Joan E. Rigdon, "Union Organizers Fall on Harder Times," *Wall Street Journal*, Jan. 29, 1991, p. 1.

7 "What's Ahead for Unions?" p. 73.

8 "What's Ahead for Unions?"

9 Barry Bluestone and Irving Bluestone, *Negotiating the Future: A Labor Perspective on American Business* (New York: Basic Books, 1992).

10 Sam F. Parigi, Frank J. Cavaliere, and Joel L. Allen, "Improving Labor Relations in an Era of Declining Union Power," *Review of Business*, Winter 1992, pp. 33–34.

11 Walter P. Reuther, "Trade Unions in the United States," *Microsoft Encarta*, 1993.

12 "Knights of Labor," *The Concise Columbia Encyclopedia* (New York: Columbia University Press, 1991) on-line.

13 "Knights of Labor."

14 Frank Swoboda, "Kirkland Faces Union Revolt. Labor's Future at Issue in AFL-CIO Chief's Election Fight," *Washington Post*, May 10, 1995, p. A1.

15 Louis Uchitelle, "A New Labor Design at Levi Strauss," *New York Times*, Oct. 13, 1994, p. D1.

16 "National Labor Relations Act," *Microsoft Encarta*, 1993, on-line.

17 Shari Caudron, "The Changing Union Agenda," *Personnel Journal*, March 1995, p. 42.

18 Uchitelle, "A New Labor Design at Levi Strauss," p. D1.

19 Uchitelle, "A New Labor Design at Levi Strauss," p. D1.

20 Jacob M. Schlesinger, "Job-Guarantee Contracts Are Becoming More Common," *Wall Street Journal*, June 29, 1987, p. 6.

21 James A.F. Stoner, R. Edward Freeman, and Daniel R. Gilbert, Jr., *Management* (Englewood Cliffs, N.J.: Prentice Hall, 1995), pp. 544–45.

22 Caudron, "The Changing Union Agenda."

23 Peter Nulty, "Look What the Unions Want Now," *Fortune*, Feb. 8, 1993, p. 129.

24 Reuther, "Trade Unions in the United States."

25 Amal Nag, "Auto Makers Discover 'Factory of the Future' Is Headache Just Now," *Wall Street Journal*, May 13, 1986, pp. 1, 10.

26 J. Ernest Beazley, "USX Workers Win Jobless Pay in Pennsylvania," *Wall Street Journal*, Aug. 22, 1986, p. 4.

27 David Kirkpatrick, "What Give-Backs Can Get for You," *Fortune*, Nov. 24, 1986, p. 64.

28 Shawn Tully, "Comeback Ahead for Railroads," *Fortune*, June 17, 1991, p. 108.

29 Uchitelle, "A New Labor Design at Levi Strauss," p. D6.

30 Juliette Shor, "The Overworked Americans," *Occupational Hazards*, April 1992, p. 25.

31 C. Pascal Zachary and Bob Ortega, "Workplace Revolution Boosts Productivity at Cost of Job Security," *Wall Street Journal*, March 10, 1993, p. A1.

32 "Big Strikes, Lockouts at U.S. Companies Hit 45-Year Low in '92," *Wall Street Journal*, Feb. 4, 1993, p. A2.

33 John B. Judis, "Can Labor Come Back?" *The New Republic*, May 23, 1994, p. 25.

34 "Union Members in 1994," U.S. Department of Labor report, Bureau of Labor Statistics, Feb. 8, 1995.

35 Judis, "Can Labor Come Back?"

36 *Wall Street Journal*, Dec. 17, 1993, p. A1.

37 "Adapt or Die," *The Economist*, July 1, 1995, p. 54.

38 "Unions for the Poor," *The Economist*, July 1, 1995, p. 54.

39 Judis, "Can Labor Come Back?"

40 Judis, "Can Labor Come Back?"

41 Ralph Whitehead, Jr., "New Collars . . . Bright Collars," *Psychology Today*, Oct. 1988, pp. 44–49.

42 Jonathon Tasini, "Big Labor Tries the Soft Sell," *Business Week*, Oct. 13, 1986, p. 126.

43 Zachary Schiller, "Bridgestone Is Nearing Some Hairpin Curves," *Business Week*, Apr. 22, 1991, pp. 32–33.

44 Aaron Bernstein, "Busting Unions Can Backfire on the Bottom Line," *Business Week*, March 18, 1991, p. 108.

45 Daniel Machalaba, "At East Coast Ports, Labor Relations Often Determine Prosperity," *Wall Street Journal*, Dec. 3, 1990, p. A1.

46 Kevin G. Salwen, "Unions Believe Expansion of Employees Power Outweighs Dismissals," *Wall Street Journal*, Sept. 8, 1993, pp. A2, A4.

47 Charlene Marmer Solomon, "Behind the Wheel at Saturn," *Personnel Journal*, June 1991, pp. 72–74.

48 Peggy Stuart, "Labor Unions Become Business Partners," *Personnel Journal*, Aug. 1993, pp. 54–63.

49 Doron P. Levin, "Back to School for Honda Workers," *New York Times*, March 29, 1993, p. D1.

50 Michael Kinsman, "Labor Speaks; Will Business Listen?" *San Diego Union*, Feb. 25, 1994, p. C1.

51 "The Future of Unions," *The Economist*, July 1, 1995, p. 15.

52 Michael J. Ybarra, "Janitors' Union Uses Pressure and Theatrics to Expand Its Ranks," *Wall Street Journal*, March 21, 1994, pp. A1, 8.

53 Nulty, "Look What the Unions Want Now," p. 132.

54 Uchitelle, "A New Labor Design at Levi Strauss," p. D1.

CHAPTER 14

1 Clive Burrow, "More Charity for the Homeless," *New York Times*, September 27, 1992, p. F13.

2 Lawrence Ingrassia, "Gillette Holds Its Edge by Endlessly Searching for a Better Shave," *Wall Street Journal*, December 10, 1992, p. A8.

3 Franklin S. Houston, "The Marketing Concept: What It Is and What It Is Not," *Journal of Marketing*, Vol. 33, No. 2, April 1986, pp. 81–87.

4 Philip Kotler, "A Generic Concept of Marketing," *Journal of Marketing*, Vol. 36, No. 2, April 1972, pp. 46–54; Philip Kotler and Sidney J. Levy, "Broadening the Concept of Marketing," *Journal of Marketing*, Vol. 33, No. 1, January 1969, pp. 10–15.

5 Valerie Reitman, "Down-to-Earth Ads Are Aimed at Those Thinking of Heaven," *Wall Street Journal*, August 13, 1993, p. A1.

6 Philip Kotler and Sidney J. Levy, "Demarketing, Yes, Demarketing," *Harvard Business Review*, Vol. 59, No. 6 (November–December 1971), pp. 74–80.

7 Robert L. Desatnick, *Keep the Customer* (Boston: Houghton Mifflin, 1990); Charles Sewell, *Customers for Life: How to Turn the One-Time Buyer into a Lifetime Customer* (New York: Pocket Books, 1990); William H. Davidow and Bro Uttal, *Total Customer Service: The Ultimate Weapon* (New York: Harper & Row Publishers, 1989).

8 Raymond Zimmerman, *Retail Business Review* (September 1992), p. 4.

9 Frederick E. Webster, Jr., *Market-Driven Management: Using the New Marketing Concept to Create a Customer Driven Company* (New York: John Wiley & Sons, 1994).

10 "Customers Must be Pleased, Not Just Satisfied," *Business Week*, August 3, 1992, p. 52.

11 Theodore Levitt, "Marketing Myopia," *Harvard Business Review*, Vol. 48, No. 4, July–August, 1960, pp. 45–56.

12 Kathleen Deveny, "Marketscan," *Wall Street Journal*, Dec. 17, 1992, p. B1.

13 "The Real Thing Is Thundering Eastward," *Business Week*, April 13, 1992, p. 96.

14 For some interesting ways to learn about customers, see Francis Gouillart and Frederick D. Sturdivant, "Spend a Day in the Life of Your Customers," *Harvard Business Review*, Vol. 82, No. 1, January–February 1994, pp. 116–27.

15 "The Real P & G Story," *Advertising Age*, July 26, 1993, p. 12; Jennifer Lawrence, "Don't Look for P & G to Pare Detergents," *Advertising Age*, May 31, 1993, pp. 3, 42.

16 Itamar Simonson, "Get Closer to Your Customers by Understanding How They Make Choices," *California Management Review*, Vol. 35, No. 4, Summer 1993, pp. 68–85.

17 William O. Beardon and Michael J. Etzel, "Reference Group Influence on Product and Brand Purchase Decisions," *Journal of Consumer Research*, Vol. 9, No. 2, September 1982, pp. 183–94.

18 Wendell R. Smith, "Product Differentiation and Market Segmentation as Alternative Marketing Strategies," *Journal of Marketing*, Vol. 20, No. 3, July 1956, pp. 3–8.

19 "The Real P & G Story," p. 12; Lawrence, "Don't Look for P & G to Pare Detergents," pp. 3, 42 (quote from p. 42).

20 Lawrence, "Don't Look for P & G to Pare Detergents," p. 42.

21 U.S. Department of Commerce, *Statistical Abstract of the United States*, 110th ed., 1990.

22 George S. Day, *Market Driven Strategy Processes for Creating Value* (New York: Free Press, 1990).

23 Kathleen Deveny and Peter K. Francese, "Shrinking Markets: Finding a Niche May Be the Key to Survival," *Wall Street Journal*, March 9, 1990, p. B2.

24 Robert E. Linneman and John L. Stanton, Jr., "Mining for Niches," *Business Horizons*, Vol. 35, No. 3, May–June 1992, pp. 43–52; David Shani and Sujang Chalasani, "Exploiting Niches Using Relationship Marketing," *Journal of Consumer Marketing*, Vol. 9, No. 3, Summer 1992, pp. 33–43.

25 Laura Zinn, "This Bud's for You. No, Not You—Her," *Business Week*, November 4, 1991, p. 86.

26 Al Ries and Jack Trout, *Positioning: The Battle for Your Mind*, rev. ed. (New York: Warner Books, 1986).

27 James R. Norman, "With or Without Ketchup?" *Forbes*, March 14, 1994, p. 107.

28 The article used as the source for this case (including the direct quotes in the opener) is Clive Burrow, "Squeezed by Recession and Weather," *New York Times*, September 13, 1992, p. F10.

CHAPTER **15**

1 Theodore Levitt, "Marketing Intangible Products and Product Intangibles," *Harvard Business Review*, Vol. 59, No. 3, May–June 1981, pp. 94–102.

2 Leonard L. Berry, "Services Marketing is Different," *Business: The Magazine of Managerial Thought and Action*, Vol. 40, No. 4, May–June 1980, p. 24.

3 Damon Darlin, "Shoe Biz as Show Biz," *Forbes*, June 7, 1993, p. 59.

4 Faye Rice, "The New Rules of Superlative Service," *Fortune*, Autumn/Winter 1993, p. 53.

5 Edwin McDowell, "Ritz-Carlton's Keys to Good Service," *New York Times*, March 31, 1993, p. D5.

6 Jim Impoco, "Ely Callaway Hits the Green," *U.S. News & World Report*, April 11, 1994, p. 47.

7 Lois Therrien, "Brands on the Run," *Business Week*, April 19, 1994, p. 27.

8 Frederick F. Reichheld and W. Earl Sasser, Jr., "Zero Defections: Quality Comes to Services," *Harvard Business Review*, Vol. 68, No. 5, September–October 1990, pp. 301–07.

9 Richard Gibson, "Label Law Stirs Up Food Competition," *Wall Street Journal*, June 2, 1993, p. B1.

10 Mark Maremont, "The Hottest Thing Since the Flash Bulb," *Business Week*, September 7, 1992, p. 72.

11 Philip Kotler, *Marketing Management*, 8th ed. (Englewood Cliffs, N.J.: Prentice Hall, 1994), pp. 436–39.

12 Ronald Henkoff, "Keeping Motorola on a Roll," *Fortune*, April 18, 1994, p. 72.

13 Larry A. Constantineau, "The Twenty Toughest Questions for New Product Management," *Journal of Consumer Marketing*, Vol. 9, No. 2, Spring 1992, pp. 51–53.

14 Michael Treacy and Fred Wiersema, "Customer Intimacy and Other Value Disciplines," *Harvard Business Review*, Vol. 71, No. 1, Jan.–Feb. 1993, pp. 84–93; George Stalk, Philip Evans, and Lawrence E. Shulman, "Competing on Capabilities: The New Rules of Corporate Strategy," *Harvard Business Review*, Vol. 70, No. 2, March–April 1992, pp. 57–69.

15 Donald Gerwin, "Integrating Manufacturing into the Strategic Phases of New Product Development," *California Management Review*, Vol. 35, No. 4, Summer 1993, pp. 121–35.

16 B. Joseph Pine II, Bart Victor, and Andrew C. Boynton, "Making Mass Customization Work," *Harvard Business Review*, Vol. 71, No. 5, September–October 1993, pp. 108–19.

17 Bruce Nussbaum, "Hot Products: Smart Design Is the Common Thread," *Business Week*, June 7, 1993, p. 55.

18 Christopher Power, "Flops," *Business Week*, August 16, 1993, p. 77.

19 C. Merle Crawford, *New Products Management*, 4th ed. (Homewood, Ill.: Richard D. Irwin, 1994), p. 6.

20 Kathleen Kerwin, "GM's Aurora," *Business Week*, March 21, 1994, p. 95.

21 Chester R. Wasson, *Dynamic Competitive Strategy and Product Life Cycles* (Austin, Texas: Austin Press, 1978).

22 Laura Zinn, "Does Pepsi Have Too Many Products?" *Business Week*, February 14, 1994, p. 65.

23 Byron M. Sharp, "Managing Brand Extension," *Journal of Consumer Marketing*, Vol. 10, No. 3, Summer 1993, pp. 11–18.

24 Joe Dodson, "Strategic Repositioning Through the Customer Connection," *Journal of Business Strategy*, Vol. 12, No. 3, May–June 1991, pp. 4–8.

25 Elaine Underwood, "Carnival Caught a Wave, Positioned Cruising as Fun," *Brandweek*, October 11, 1993, pp. 22–24.

26 Bill Saporito, "Beyond the Tumult at P & G," *Fortune*, March 7, 1994, pp. 74–82.

27 "Ritz-Carlton Wins Mexico's National Quality Award," *The Quality Observer*, January 1995, p. 16; Company publicity materials from Ritz-Carlton Hotel Co.; Rik Fairlie, "Ritz-Carlton Lowers Rates for Guests Using Amexco Card," *Travel Weekly*, April 28, 1994, p. 11.

CHAPTER **16**

1 Michael Treacy and Fred Wiersema, "Customer Intimacy and Other Value Disciplines," *Harvard Business Review*, Vol. 71, No. 1, Jan.–Feb. 1993, p. 87.

2 U.S. Industrial Outlook 1994, *Retailing* (Lanham, MD: Department of Commerce), Chapter 39, p. 1.

3 Frank G. Bingham, Jr., and Barney T. Raffield, *Business to Business Marketing Management* (Homewood, Ill.: Richard D. Irwin, 1990), p. 335.

4 Faye Rice, "The New Rules of Superlative Service," *Fortune*, Special ed., Autumn/Winter 1993, p. 52.

5 Emily Thorton, "Revolution in Japanese Retailing," *Fortune*, Feb. 7, 1994, pp. 143–46.

6 Wendy Zeller, "Clout," *Business Week*, Dec. 21, 1992, p. 67.

7 U.S. Industrial Outlook 1994, *Retailing*, pp. 39–42; Lorraine C. Scarpa, "Fast, Flexible, Computerized, That's Today's Analytic World," *Brandweek*, Nov. 15, 1993, p. 32.

8 Patricia Sellers, "The Dumbest Marketing Ploy," *Fortune*, Oct. 5, 1992, p. 88.

9 Sellers, "The Dumbest Marketing Ploy," p. 89.

10 Rashi Glazer, "Marketing in an Information-Intensive Environment: Strategic Implications of Knowledge as an Asset," *Journal of Marketing*, Vol. 55, No. 4, Oct. 1991, pp. 1–19.

11 George Stalk, Philip Evans, and Lawrence E. Shulman, "Competing on Capabilities: The New Rules of Corporate Strategy," *Harvard Business Review*, Vol. 92, March–April 1992, pp. 57–69.

12 Frederick E. Webster, Jr., "The Changing Role of Marketing in the Corporation," *Journal of Marketing*, Vol. 56, No. 4, Oct. 1992, pp. 1–17.

13 Myron Magnet, "The New Golden Rule of Business," *Fortune*, Feb. 21, 1994, p. 60.

14 U.S. Bureau of Economic Analysis, Survey of Current Business, Nov. 1993, pp. 442, 773.

15 Ronald Henkoff, "Delivering the Goods," *Fortune*, Nov. 28, 1994, p. 66.

16 Philip Kotler and Paul J. Stonich, "Turbo Marketing Through Time Compression," *Journal of Business Strategy*, Sept./Oct. 1991, p. 27.

17 Michael Jenkins, "Gaining a Financial Foothold Through Public Warehousing," *Journal of Business Strategy*, Vol. 13, No. 3, May–June 1992, pp. 53–58.

18 Ira P. Krepchin, "Efficiency Up 25% With Automated Item Picking," *Modern Materials Handling*, Dec. 1991, p. 48.

19 U.S. Department of Commerce, *Statistical Abstract of the United States* 1992, p. 600.

20 Barnaby J. Feder, "Winners as Well as Losers in the Great Flood of '93," *New York Times*, Aug. 15, 1993, p. F5.

21 U.S. Industrial Outlook 1994, *Wholesaling* (Lanham, MD: Department of Commerce), Chapter 38, p. 1.

22 U.S. Industrial Outlook 1994, *Wholesaling*, Chapter 38, p. 1.

23 Richard S. Teitelbaum, "Companies on a Roll," *Fortune*, special issue, Autumn/Winter 1993, p. 32.

24 Carla Rapoport and Justin Martin, "Retailers Go Global," *Fortune*, Feb. 20, 1995, p. 103.

25 Larry R. Katzen, "Retailing: The Global Mandate," *Retailing Issues Letter*, Vol. 5, No. 5, Sept. 1993, p. 2.

26 James M. Clash, "Micro-Brewmeisters," *Forbes*, Sept. 13, 1993, pp. 172, 176.

27 Ann Imse, "Across From Lenin's Tomb, a Monument to Capitalism," *New York Times*, Sept. 19, 1993, p. F5.

CHAPTER **17**

1 Alice Z. Cuneo, "Starbucks' Word-of-Mouth Wonder," *Advertising Age*, March 7, 1994, p. 12.

2 Stratford Sherman, "How to Prosper in the Value Decade," *Fortune*, Nov. 30, 1992, p. 91.

3 "Beyond Quality & Value," *Fortune*, special issue, Autumn/Winter 1993, p. 8.

4 Sherman, "How to Prosper."

5 Don E. Schultz, *Integrated Marketing Communications: Pulling It Together & Making it Work* (Lincolnwood, Ill.: NTC Business Books, 1993).

6 Jonathan Berry, "Database Marketing," *Business Week*, Sept. 5, 1994, p. 61.

7 Kent B. Monroe, "Buyers' Subjective Perceptions of Price," *Journal of Marketing Research*, Vol. 1, No. 1, Feb. 1973, pp. 70–80.

8 Kent B. Monroe, *Pricing: Making Profitable Decisions*, 2d ed. (New York: McGraw-Hill, 1990), p. 292.

9 Eben Shapiro, "Portions and Packages Grow Bigger," *Wall Street Journal*, Oct. 12, 1993, p. B1.

10 Andrew Serwer, "How to Escape a Price War," *Fortune*, June 13, 1994, p. 85.

11 Monroe, *Pricing*, p. 293.

12 Michael L. Dertouzos, Richard K. Lester, Robert M. Solow, and the MIT Commission on Industrial Competitiveness, *Made in America: Regaining the Competitive Edge* (New York: HarperPerennial, 1990), p. 217.

13 Thomas T. Nagle, *The Strategy and Tactics of Pricing: A Guide to Profitable Decision Making* (Englewood Cliffs, N.J.: Prentice Hall, 1987); Gerard J. Tellis, "Beyond the Many Faces of Price: An Integration of Pricing Strategies," *Journal of Marketing*, Vol. 50, No. 4, Oct. 1986, pp. 146–60.

14 Zarrell V. Lambert, "Perceived Price as Related to Odd and Even Price Endings," *Journal of Retailing*, Vol. 51, No. 3 (Fall 1975), pp. 13–22.

15 Christina Duff, "Single-Price Stores' Formula for Success: Cheap Merchandise and a Lot of Clutter," *Wall Street Journal*, June 30, 1992, p. B1.

16 Sherman, "How to Prosper," p. 94.

17 Michael H. Morris and Donald A. Fuller, "Pricing an Industrial Service," *Industrial Marketing Management*, Vol. 18, 1989, pp. 139–46.

18 Mark Landler, "What Happened to Advertising?" *Business Week*, Sept. 22, 1991, p. 68.

19 James Wills, A. Coskun Samli, and Lawrence Jacobs, "Developing Global Products and Marketing Strategies: A Construct and Research Agenda," *Journal of the Academy of Marketing Science*, Vol. 19, Winter 1991, pp. 1–10.

20 Yoram Wind, "The Myth of Globalization," *Journal of Consumer Marketing*, Vol. 3, No. 2, Spring 1986, pp. 23–26.

21 Theodore Levitt, "The Globalization of Markets," *Harvard Business Review*, Vol. 61, No. 3, May–June 1983, pp. 92–102.

22 Ken Wells, "Global Ad Campaigns, After Many Missteps, Finally Pay Dividends," *Wall Street Journal*, August 27, 1992, p. A1.

23 Susan Chandler, "Strategies for the New Mail Order," *Business Week*, Dec. 19, 1994, p. 82.

24 Jon Hamilton, "Telemarketers Say Legislation Would Affect Sales Call Quality," *Advertising Age*, Oct. 25, 1993, p. S-15.

25 John Greenwald, "Sorry, Right Number," *Time*, Sept. 13, 1993, p. 66.

26 Greenwald, "Sorry, Right Number."

27 Terence A. Shimp, *Promotion Management & Marketing Communications* (Orlando, Fla.: Harcourt Brace Jovanovich, 1993), Chapter 17.

28 Schultz, *Integrated Marketing Communications*.

29 Laurie Petersen, "Pursuing Results in the Age of Accountability," *Adweek's Marketing Week*, Nov. 19, 1990, p. 21.

30 Don E. Schultz, "Maybe We Should Start All Over with an IMC Organization," *Marketing News*, Oct. 25, 1993, p. 8. Italics added.

31 Deborah Hauss, "Global Communications Come of Age," *Public Relations Journal*, Vol. 49, No. 1 (August 1993), p. 26.

32 Oscar Suris, "Mercedes-Benz Tries to Compete on Value," *Wall Street Journal*, Oct. 20, 1993, p. B.1; Raymond Serafin, "Mercedes-Benz of '90s Includes Price in Its Pitch," *Advertising Age*, Nov. 1, 1993, pp. 1, 55.

33 Laura Bird, "Church of Scientology to Launch Campaign to Improve Its Image," *Wall Street Journal*, Oct. 20, 1993, p. B5.

CHAPTER **18**

1 Judith Rosenblum and Reed A. Keller, "Building a Learning Organization at Coopers & Lybrand," *Planning Review*, Sept./Oct. 1994, p. 44; "Coopers & Lybrand L.L.P.," Hoover's *Handbook* Database (Austin, Texas: Reference Press, 1995), America Online, 6/27/95.

2 Compton's Encyclopedia, America Online, Nov. 8, 1994.

3 Ira Sager, "The Great Equalizer," *Business Week*, special issue, May 18, 1994, p. 102.

4 James B. Treece, "The New Catbird Seat," *Business Week*, special issue, May 18, 1994, p. 114.

5 Computer Sciences Corp., factsheet, July 1994.

6 "Crunched," *The Economist*, Aug. 6, 1994, p. 55.

7 John Verity, "The Information Revolution," *Business Week*, special issue, May 18, 1994, pp. 10–18.

8 Catherine Arnst, "Tackling Technophobia," *Business Week*, special issue, May 18, 1994, pp. 144–150.

9 Peggy Wallace, "Are You Ready to Support Telecommuters?" *Infoworld*, Sept. 5, 1994, pp. 57 and 60.

10 David Kirkpatrick, "Here Comes the Payoff from PCs," *Fortune*, March 23, 1992, pp. 93–102.

11 Anthony Effinger, "Mutual 'Net' Gains: Wealth of Data, Choices Bloom in Cyberland," (New York) *Daily News*, May 21, 1995, p. B4.

12 John Verity and Robert Hof, "The Internet. How It Will Change the Way You Do Business," *Business Week*, Nov. 14, 1994, pp. 80–88.

13 Louis Richman, "Interactive U.," *Fortune*, Sept. 19, 1995, p. 18.

14 Jeffrey L. Whitten, Lonnie D. Bentley, and Victor M. Barlow, *Systems Analysis & Design Methods*, 3d ed. (Burr Ridge, Illinois: Richard D. Irwin, 1994), p. 40.

15 Robert Kelley and Janet Caplan, "How Bell Labs Creates Star Performers," *Harvard Business Review*, July–Aug. 1993, p. 131.

16 N. Venkatramaan, "IT-Enabled Business Transformation: From Automation to Business Scope Redefinition," *Sloan Management Review*, Winter 1994, pp. 73–87.

17 R.A.M., "The Optical Disk: Big Files on Small Budgets," *Inc.*, May 1993, p. 48.

18 R.A.M., "The Optical Disk: Big Files on Small Budgets."

19 William Bulkeley, "Advances in Networking and Software Push Firms Closer to Paperless Office," *Wall Street Journal*, Aug. 5, 1993, p. B1.

20 Computer Sciences Corp., factsheet.

21 Ken Auletta, "The Magic Box," *The New Yorker*, April 11, 1994, pp. 41–42.

22 Gene Walden and Edmund O. Lawler, *Marketing Masters* (New York: HarperBusiness, 1993), pp. 58–59.

23 Review Case based on Steve Dente, interview with the authors, Aug. 25, 1994.

24 Stephanie Losee, "*Fortune* Checks Out 25 Cool Companies for Products, Ideas, and Investments," *Fortune*, July 11, 1994, pp. 118–120; Gina Smith, interview, *The News Hour*, PBS, July 26, 1995.

25 Judith Rosenblum and Reed A. Keller, "Building a Learning Organization at Coopers & Lybrand," *Planning Review*, Sept./Oct. 1994, p. 44; "Coopers & Lybrand L.L.P.," Hoover's *Handbook* Database (Austin, Texas: Reference Press, 1995), America Online, June 27, 1995.

CHAPTER **19**

1 Based on Tom Ehrenfeld, "The New and Improved American Small Business," *Inc.*, Jan. 1995, pp. 34–45.

2 Tom Ehrenfeld, "Before and After: The Five Attributes That Set Professionalized Small Businesses Apart," *Inc.*, Jan. 1995, p. 44.

3 Personal communication with Taylor Middleton, director of marketing, Big Sky Ski and Summer Resort.

4 Louis Vlasbo, "Improving Management Accounting," *New Account*, Oct. 1993, pp. 22–23.

5 Thomas L. Albright and Harold P. Roth, "Managing Quality Through the Quality Loss Function," *Journal of Cost Accounting*, Winter 1994, pp. 20–28.

6 William F. Hester, "True Quality Cost with Activity Based Costing," *The Quality Management Forum*, pp. 4–5.

7 Thomas G. Greenwood and James M. Reeve, "Process Cost Management," *Cost Management*, Winter 1994, pp. 4–19.

8 David E. Keys, "Tracing Costs in the Three Stages of Activity Based Management," *Journal of Cost Management*, Winter 1994, pp. 30–37.

9 *Catalog Age*, Sept. 1994, p. 75.

10 Robert H. Mundheim and Noyes E. Leech, eds., *The SEC and Accounting: The First 50 Years*, Arthur Young Professors' Roundtable (Amsterdam: North–Holland, 1986); *HBJ Miller Comprehensive Governmental GAAP Guide* (San Diego, Calif.: Harcourt Brace Jovanovich, 1993).

11, J. Peder Zane, "Immigrant's Search for Logic Leads Him to Top of C.P.A. Class," *New York Times*, April 30, 1995, p. F13.

12 *Standards for the Professional Practice of Internal Auditing* (Miami, Florida: Institute of Internal Auditors, 1993).

13 Balance sheet and income statement categories in this chapter are based on The Gap, Inc., 1993 Annual Report and Form 10K. All dollar entries are significantly altered for purposes of this example and for ease of computation.

14 Boise Cascade Corp., prospectus, 1995.

15 United Illuminating Co. Annual Report, 1994, p. 28.

16 "IBM Expense Cuts," *Dow Jones News Service*, April 21, 1994; Margaret O. Kirk, "When Surviving Just Isn't Enough," *New York Times*, June 25, 1995, p. 11.

17 *Corporate Cashflow Magazine*, Oct. 1992, p. 46.

18 Nancy Anderson, "The Globalization of GAAP," *Management Accounting*, Aug. 1993, pp. 52–54.

19 Vlasbo, "Improving Management Accounting."

20 Information based on The Gap, Inc., 1993 Annual Report and Form 10K.

21 Geraldine Fabrikant, "Where Fame Exceeds Fortune," *New York Times*, July 28, 1994, pp. D1, 18; "Viacom, Inc., Completes Sale of Madison Square Garden," *Business Wire Release*, March 11, 1995.

22 Based on Ehrenfeld, "The New and Improved American Small Business."

CHAPTER 20

1 Stephanie Gruner, "The Employee-Run-Budget Work Sheet," *Inc.*, Feb. 1995, p. 81.

2 S.L. Mintz, "Redesigning Finance at Ford," *CFO*, March 1995, pp. 26–34.

3 Jeanne Saddler, "Small Firms Try to Curb Impact of Leave Law," *Wall Street Journal*, Aug. 5, 1993, p. 1.

4 Personal communication with Edward Chow. Figures have been substantially modified.

5 William Grimes, "Financial Restructuring at Boston Arts Museum," *New York Times*, Feb. 17, 1995, p. C3.

6 "Real Estate Briefs," *New York Times*, May 17, 1995, p. D1.

7 Patterson Dental Co. Annual Report, 1994, pp. 5, 19, 21.

8 Personal communication with Richard J. Reinhart, former CEO of Supra Medical Co.

9 Personal communication with Vincent J. Ayd.

10 Lillian Vernon Annual Report, 1995.

11 David T. Gleba, "IPO Market '94 Winners," *Upside*, March 1995, p. 82.

12 Bill Birchard, "Power to the People," *CFO*, March 1995, pp. 38–43.

13 Gruner, "The Employee-Run-Budget Work Sheet," pp. 81–83.

CHAPTER 21

1 Linda Grant, "Here Comes Hugh," *Fortune*, Aug. 21, 1995, p. 45.

2 Alessandra Bianchi, "Learning to Live with (or Without) Your Banker," *Inc.*, March 1995, p. 34.

3 Richard F. Rosenberger and Charles Kaufmann, *The Longrifles of Western Pennsylvania* (Pittsburgh: University of Pittsburgh Press, 1993), p. xx.

4 "America's Latest Financial Fling," *The Economist*, June 24, 1995, p. 67.

5 "America's Latest Financial Fling," p. 67.

6 FDIC Quarterly Banking Profits, Fourth Quarter 1994.

7 Connecticut Credit Union League, *A Common Bond, Connecticut's Credit Unions, 1935–1985* (Connecticut: Connecticut Credit Union League, 1985), p. 6.

8 Personal communication, Harold C. Fleming, professor emeritus, Anthropology Department, Boston University, Boston.

9 Personal communication, Rita Sarff, Office of Public Affairs, National Credit Union Administration, March 24, 1995.

10 Sheryl WuDunn, "Japanese Regulators Suspend a Credit Union," *New York Times*, Aug. 1, 1995, p. D2.

11 Carol J. Loomis, "Victims of the Real Estate Crash," *Fortune*, May 18, 1992, pp. 70–83.

12 Bianchi, "Learning to Live with (or Without) Your Banker," p. 42.

13 "Why Insurers Aren't the S&Ls of the 1990s," *Business Week*, Dec. 5, 1994, pp. 51–53.

14 Russell Mitchell, "The Schwab Revolution," *Business Week*, Dec. 19, 1994, pp. 88–98.

15 Quoted in Ken Kaul, "Joint Stand Needed on Insurance Funds," *American Banker*, April 28, 1995, p. 30.

16 Matt Walsh, "Two Bankers, Same Strategy," *Forbes*, Dec. 5, 1994, pp. 51–53; Emory Thomas, Jr., "NationsBank Wins Approval to Merge Branch Networks Across a State Line," *Wall Street Journal*, Feb. 7, 1994, p. A2.

17 Gordon Matthews, "Glendale Federal Rises in Lively Trading After Paine Webber Upgrade," *American Banker*, April 28, 1995, p. 32.

18 Quoted in Bianchi, "Learning to Live with (or Without) Your Banker," p. 34.

19 Bianchi, "Learning to Live with (or Without) Your Banker," pp. 35–36.

20 Mary Beth Norton et al., *A People and a Nation* (Boston: Houghton Mifflin, 1986), p. 716.

21 "Break Glass-Steagall," *The Economist*, July 1, 1995, p. 25.

22 Loomis, "Victims of the Real Estate Crash," pp. 70–83.

23 Catherine Yang, "The Thrift Mop-Up Is Already a Mess," *Business Week*, Feb. 5, 1990, p. 70; Kathleen Kerwin, "California's Ailing S&Ls: The Pulse Grows Fainter," *Business Week*, March 19, 1990, pp. 98–99.

24 Kevin Phillips, *Boiling Point* (New York: HarperPerennial, 1994), p. 187.

25 Grant, "Here Comes Hugh," p. 43.

26 Global Market Information Prospectus, July 14, 1994, p. 33.

27 Bianchi, "Learning to Live with (or Without) Your Banker," p. 42.

28 Grant, "Here Comes Hugh," p. 43; Juliana Ratner, "Being Midsize Doesn't Cut It in Mortgage Servicing World," *American Banker*, April 28, 1995, p. 1.

29 "Eight Bank South ATMs at Georgia McDonalds," *American Banker*, April 28, 1995, p. 19.

30 Russell Mitchell, "The Banking Industry's Best-Kept Secret," *Business Week*, Aug. 8, 1994.

31 Quoted in Grant, "Here Comes Hugh," p. 49.

32 James C. Allen, "First Chicago Sets Premium Fees for Transactions Using Tellers," *American Banker*, April 28, 1995, p. 5.

33 Mitchell, "The Banking Industry's Best-Kept Secret."

34 John Sheehan, "A Shock to the System: How Far Will Banking's Crisis of Confidence Spread?" *Business Week*, Jan. 21, 1991, p. 26.

35 Author's personal experience.

36 Phillips, *Boiling Point*, p. 187.

37 Norton et al., *A People and a Nation*, p. 612.

38 Chris Reidy, "Fed to Hold Meetings on Fleet Deal," *Boston Globe*, July 28, 1995, p. 65.

39 *The Federal Reserve System* (Washington, D.C.: Board of Governors of the Federal Reserve System).

40 Charles Stein, "Stock Market on White-Knuckle Ride," *Boston Globe*, July 20, 1995, p. 35.

41 Mike McNamee, "Are Fewer Banks Better?" *Business Week*, Aug. 17, 1992, pp. 92–93.

42 Robyn Meredith, "14 National Banks Leapfrogging the Official Startup of Interstate," *American Banker*, Feb. 24, 1995, p. 3.

43 "Interstate Banking Given Boost by U.S.," *Wall Street Journal*, Jan. 11, 1994.

44 Thomas, "NationsBank Wins Approval to Merge Branch Networks Across a State Line," *Wall Street Journal*, Feb. 7, 1994, p. A2.

45 *American Banker*, Feb. 22, 1995, p. 24; Don Stancavish, "PNC Acquiring Midlantic," *The Bergen Record*, July 11, 1995, p. B-1; Stephanie Strom, "First Chicago and NBD to Merge as Banks Scurry to Grow," *New York Times*, July 13, 1995, p. D1.

46 Grant, "Here Comes Hugh," p. 43.

47 Steven Bailey, "Hostile Bank Takeovers Seen Likely to Rise," *Boston Globe*, July 27, 1995, p. 37.

48 Quoted in Maria Shao, "Battle Lines Drawn over Merger," *Boston Globe*, July 26, 1995, p. 29.

49 Quoted in Saul Hansell, "Spurned Bank Says It's Not Up for Sale," *New York Times*, July 25, 1995, p. D1.

50 Case, including all quotes, is based on Shelley Donald Coolidge, "Black Woman Founds a Bank 'To Help Level the Playing Field,'" *Christian Science Monitor*, June 13, 1995. p. 9.

CHAPTER **22**

1 Eric Tyson, "Everybody's Broker," *Stanford Business School Magazine*, June 1995, pp. 17–18.

2 Kenneth M. Morris and Alan M. Siegel, *The Wall Street Journal Guide to Understanding Money & Investing* (New York: Lightbulb Press, 1993), p. 35.

3 Nick Ravo, "Why the Stocks Aren't Splitting," *New York Times*, July 23, 1995, section 3, p. 5.

4 Terence P. Paré, "The Big Sleaze in Muni Bonds," *Fortune*, Aug. 7, 1995, pp. 113–120.

5 Leslie Wayne, "Municipal Bond Regulation Debated at House Hearing," *New York Times*, July 27, 1995, p. D4.

6 Paré, "The Big Sleaze in Muni Bonds," pp. 113–120.

7 Johnson Controls, Inc., 1994 Annual Report, note 5, p. 33.

8 Walter L. Updegrave, "Why Funds Don't Do Better," *Money*, Aug. 1995, pp. 60–61.

9 Updegrave, "Why Funds Don't Do Better," p. 58.

10 Sara Calian, "Stock Funds Still Popular Despite Tumble in Market," *Wall Street Journal*, July 27, 1995, p. C16.

11 World Semiconductor Trade Statistics, Robertson, Stephenson & Co. estimates. The Pacific Stock Exchange, as graphed in Edward Wyatt, "Beware the Rosy Reasoning of Tech Bulls," *New York Times*, July 23, 1995, section 3, p. 3.

12 Rosemary Metzler Laran, "NASDAQ: Growing Pains," (New York) *Daily News*, July 23, 1995, pp. 1–2.

13 "A Closer Look at Booming NASDAQ," *USA Today*, July 18, 1995, p. 3B.

14 Gary Smith, *Financial Assets, Markets, and Institutions* (Lexington, Mass.: D.C. Heath, 1993), p. 278.

15 Intibrands Inc., prospectus, May 23, 1995.

CHAPTER **23**

1 "Largest Insured Catastrophe Losses," *Property Insurance Report*, Sept. 5, 1994, p. 9.

2 Based on Sharon Nelton, "Prepare for the Worst," *Nation's Business*, Sept. 1993, p. 22.

3 *Handbook for Reporters* (New York: Insurance Information Institute, 1994), p. 93.

4 Lori Ioannou, "Running from Cover," *International Business*, July 1993, pp. 46–52.

5 Sharon Nelton, "Prepare for the Worst," *Nation's Business*, Sept. 1993, pp. 20–22.

6 Roger Thompson, "Taking Charge of Workers' Comp," *Nation's Business*, Oct. 1993, pp. 18–23.

7 Thompson, "Taking Charge of Workers' Comp."

8 Thompson, "Taking Charge of Workers' Comp."

9 "Briefly Noted," *Business Insurance*, Oct. 3, 1994, p. 48.

10 *U.S. Industrial Outlook 1994* (Washington, D.C.: U.S. Department of Commerce, 1994), chapter 48; "Property/Casualty Insurance Facts," *The Fact Book 1994* (New York: Insurance Information Institute, 1994), p. 5.

11 "Live Fast, Die Young—Pay Up," *Worth*, Oct. 1994, p. 21.

12 *U.S. Industrial Outlook 1994*.

13 Murray Chass, "Strike Over, Baseball Resumes Aug. 9," *New York Times*, Aug. 1, 1981, p. 1.

14 Siegel et al., *Directory of Personal Finance* (New York: Macmillan Publishing Co., 1992), p. 171.

15 John S. DeMott, "Special Coverage for Special Risks," *Nation's Business*, June 1994, pp. 33–37.

16 *Handbook for Reporters*, p. 5.

17 Nanette Byrne, "California Insurers Keep Feeling Aftershocks," *Business Week*, Sept. 26, 1994, p. 110.

18 Douglas Frantz, "Reports Describe Widespread Abuse in Farm Program," *New York Times*, Oct. 3, 1994, p. 1.

19 *1993 Life Insurance Fact Book* (New York: Insurance Information Institute, 1993), p. 58.

20 "Travelers Inc.," *Wall Street Journal*, Nov. 3, 1994, p. 4.

21 Jane Bryant Quinn, "The Regulator's Boogie," *Newsweek*, Oct. 3, 1994, p. 54.

22 Janet A. Knight, "Obsolete Coverage Prompts New D&O Endorsements," *Corporate Cashflow*, May 1994, p. 19.

23 *Handbook for Reporters*, p. 20.

24 Raymond Wahl, "As Professionals Fret, D&O Gains in Popularity," *Best's Review*, property-casualty insurance edition, July 1994, p. 54.

25 Ruth Gastel, ed., "Product Liability Tort Reform," *Insurance Information Institute Reports*, Aug. 1994.

26 Thompson, "Taking Charge of Workers' Comp," p. 19.

27 Thompson, "Taking Charge of Workers' Comp"; Ruth Gastel, ed., "Workers' Compensation," *Insurance Information Institute Reports*, Oct. 1994.

28 Bruce Chase, William J. Withrow, and Gwen L. Withrow, "A Sole Practitioner's Tough Lesson in Disaster Planning," *Journal of Accountancy*, Aug. 1994, p. 4.

29 Mecklermedia Corp., prospectus, Feb. 11, 1994.

30 *The 1994 Fact Book of Property/Casualty Insurance Facts* (New York: Insurance Information Institute, 1994).

31 Jerry Geisel, "Health Plan Inflation Held to 8% in 1993," *Business Insurance*, Feb. 14, 1994, p. 1.

32 Ruth Gastel, ed., "Controlling Medical Care Costs in Property/Casualty Insurance," *Insurance Information Institute Reports*, Nov. 1994.

33 "Will the Cost Cutting in Health Care Kill You?" *Fortune*, Oct. 31, 1994, p. 221.

34 *The 1994 Fact Book of Property/Casualty Insurance Facts.*

35 *The 1994 Fact Book of Property/Casualty Insurance Facts.*

36 "Home Insurance That Won't Let You Down," *Kiplinger's Personal Finance Magazine*, Aug. 1994, p. 42.

37 *U.S. Industrial Outlook 1994.*

38 Harry Chevan, "Suppliers Get Tyrol Back in Business," *Catalog Age*, July 1994, p. 66.

39 Thompson, "Taking Charge of Workers' Comp," p. 22; Gastel, ed., "Workers' Compensation."

40 Nelton, "Prepare for the Worst," pp. 22, 26.

A P P E N D I X

1 Kristina J. Shelley, "More Job Openings—Even More New Entrants: The Outlook for College Graduates, 1992–2005," *Occupational Outlook Quarterly*, Summer 1994, p. 9.

2 Kim Marino, *The College Student's Resume Guide* (Berkeley, Calif.: Ten Speed Press, 1992).

3 Amy Saltzman, "An Electronic Job Hunt," *U.S. News & World Report*, March 28, 1994, p. 73.

4 Margaret Mannix, "Writing a Computer-Friendly Resumé," *U.S. News & World Report*, Oct. 26, 1992, p. 90.

5 Mannix, "Writing a Computer-Friendly Resumé," p. 90.

6 Mannix, "Writing a Computer-Friendly Resumé," p. 93.

7 Victor R. Lindquist, *The Northwestern Lindquist-Endicott Report*, *1994* (Evanston, Ill.: The Placement Center of Northwestern University, 1993), p. 13.

8 James Aley, "Where the Jobs Are," *Fortune*, Sept. 18, 1995, p. 53.

9 Reported in Aley, "Where the Jobs Are," p. 53.

10 Leslie M. Marable, "The Fifty Hottest Jobs in America," *Money*, pp. 114–115.

Illustration Credits

CHAPTER **13**

p. 384 Mark C. Burnett/Stock, Boston   p. 389 Rob Crandall/The Image Works   p. 393 Library of Congress   p. 395 Michael A. Schwartz/The Image Works   p. 403 Duane Burleson/Sygma   p. 407 Charlie Westerman/Gamma Liaison Network   p. 410 Tom Campbell/Gamma Liaison Network

PART **5**

p. 416 Randy Taylor/Sygma

CHAPTER **14**

p. 418 Bob Daemmrich/Stock, Boston   p. 421 Chris Corsmeier   p. 425 Michael Schwartz/Gamma Liaison Network   p. 427 Courtesy Mattel, Inc. BARBIE is a trademark of Mattel, Inc. © 1959 Mattel, Inc. All rights reserved.   p. 432 Robert Fried/Stock, Boston   p. 439 Reprinted with permission of The Source   p. 441 Courtesy The Keds Corporation

CHAPTER **15**

p. 448 Courtesy Boston Market™   p. 452 Joel Gordon   p. 453 Rob Crandall/The Image Works   p. 458 Courtesy Ferolito, Vultaggio and Sons   p. 461 MADD, Minnesota State Office and Clarity Coverdale Rueff, Minneapolis   p. 464 Courtesy Phone Card Express™   p. 473 Courtesy S.C. Johnson and Son, Inc.

CHAPTER **16**

p. 478 Ron McMillan/Gamma Liaison Network   p. 486 Fujiphotos/The Image Works   p. 498 Bill Gallery/Stock, Boston   p. 500 Gottlieb/Monkmeyer Press   p. 501 Mimi Forsyth/Monkmeyer Press   p. 502 Courtesy Shop Inc.

CHAPTER **17**

p. 512 Photography by Ken Davies, model Tim Lee, photo courtesy Sprint Communications Company L.P.   p. 514 Andrew Garn   Figure 17.1 "Nike Goes to the Full-Court Press," *U.S. News and World Report,* April 19, 1993, pp. 48–49.   p. 523 Yvonne Hemsey/Gamma Liaison Network   p. 526 Courtesy IBM Corporation   p. 530 Nubar Alexanian   p. 536 Courtesy Catalina Marketing Corp.   p. 538 Louis Psihoyos/Matrix

PART **6**

p. 544 Spencer Grant/Photo Researchers, Inc.

CHAPTER **18**

p. 546 Courtesy Silicon Graphics, Inc.   p. 549 Charles Gupton/Stock, Boston   p. 550 Courtesy Quickbooks® from Intuit®   p. 555 Peter

Yates/Zuma Images   p. 559 Courtesy Microsoft Corporation   p. 560 Courtesy Silicon Graphics, Inc.   p. 562 Courtesy Sony Electronics, Inc.   p. 563 Andy Freeberg/Time Magazine © Time Warner, Inc.   p. 566 Courtesy Time Warner Cable Full Service Network

CHAPTER **19**

p. 572 Charlie Westerman/Gamma Liaison Network   p. 577 John Blaustein/Gamma Liaison Network   p. 579 Scott Downie/Celebrity Photo Agency   p. 588 and p. 591 Courtesy Quickbooks® from Intuit®   p. 592 Courtesy TDI

PART **7**

p. 600 Andrew Sacks/Tony Stone Images

CHAPTER **20**

p. 602 Ron Coppock/Gamma Liaison Network   p. 608 Sergio Dorantes/Sygma   p. 612 Courtesy Quickbooks® from Intuit®   p. 615 AP/Wide World Photos   p. 621 Rick Friedman/Black Star

CHAPTER **21**

p. 632 Richard Lord/The Image Works   p. 636 Courtesy Microsoft Corporation   p. 640 Edward Santalone   p. 651 Courtesy Time Warner Cable Full Service Network   p. 652 Voldi Tanner

CHAPTER **22**

p. 662 Edward Santalone   p. 666 Joel Gordon   p. 667 Courtesy Xerox Corporation   Table 22.1 Adapted from Morris/Siegel, *Wall Street Guide to Understanding Money and Investing*® 1995, pp. 102–103. Reprinted by permission of Prentice-Hall Inc., Upper Saddle River, NJ.   Table 22.2 From *The Economics of Money, Banking, and Financial Markets,* 4th ed. by Frederic S. Mishkin. Copyright © 1995 by HarperCollins College Publishers, Inc. Reprinted by permission.   p. 676 Frank Siteman/Stock, Boston   p. 679 Andrew Popper/Zuma Images   p. 689 Nubar Alexanian/Stock, Boston

CHAPTER **23**

p. 696 Gilles Mingasson/Gamma Liaison Network   p. 700 Brian Masck   p. 703 Janet Gill/Tony Stone Images   p. 707 Ed Kashi   Figure 23.2 Adapted from *The First Annual Report of the United States of America* by Meredith E. Bagby. Copyright © 1994 by HarperBusiness, a division of HarperCollins Publishers, Inc.   p. 712 David Sutton/Zuma Images   p. 715 Bob Daemmrich/The Image Works

Name and Company Index

Subject Index